Special Edition Using Lotus Notes and Domino R5

Randy Tamura, et al.

201 West 103rd Street,
Indianapolis, Indiana 46290

Contents

1. Introducing Lotus Notes and Domino 11
2. What's New in Release 5.0 of Notes and Domino? 27

II Using the Lotus Notes R5 Client

3. Installing and Customizing the Notes Client 45
4. The Notes User Interface and the Standard Databases 69
5. Using Electronic Mail 101
6. Working with Text and Documents 123
7. Contact Management with the Personal and Public Directories 151
8. Getting Organized with the Calendaring and Scheduling Features 167
9. Using Sametime Collaboration 189
10. Using Mobile Features from Home or on the Road 205
11. Using the Notes Client on the Internet 231

III Introducing Domino Designer R5

12. Creating and Accessing Domino Databases 255
13. The Integrated Development Environment (IDE) 281
14. Designing Pages, Forms, and Subforms 299
15. Developing Views and Folders 341
16. Using Outlines, Framesets, and Navigators 383
17. Access Control Lists (ACLs) and Application Security 413
18. Working with Formulas, Functions, and Commands 431

IV Using LotusScript, Java, and JavaScript

19. Using the IDE with LotusScript, Java, and JavaScript 451
20. Object-Oriented Programming and the Domino Object Model 475
21. LotusScript Variables and Objects 495
22. LotusScript Subroutines, Functions, and Event Handlers 519
23. Creating and Using Java Applets and Agents 543
24. Using the Lotus eSuite DevPack 581
25. The Session and Front-End Classes 609
26. Database, View, and Document Classes in LotusScript and Java 631
27. Using Fields and Items in LotusScript and Java 661

V Developing Internet Sites with Domino

28. Building Your Own Web Site with Domino 679
29. Using External HTML Tools with Domino 701
30. Moving to Electronic Commerce on Your Domino Site 719
31. Integrating Domino with Legacy Systems 729

continues

VI Installing and Configuring the Domino Servers

32 The Domino Family of Servers 745
33 Initial Planning and Installation 757
34 Upgrading from Domino R4.x to R5 777
35 Initial Configuration of Servers with the Domino Directories 807
36 Domino Security Overview 845
37 Firewalls, Virtual Private Networks (VPNs), and Internet Security 871

VII Administering the Domino Servers

38 Administering Users, Groups, and Certification 895
39 Administering Electronic Mail 923
40 Replication and Its Administration 947
41 Administering Files and Databases 975
42 Managing Your Domino Server Configuration 1005
43 Troubleshooting and Monitoring Domino 1037

VIII Advanced Domino Administration

44 Performance, Scalability, and Capacity Planning for Domino Servers 1071
45 Upgrading from cc:Mail, Microsoft Mail, and Exchange to Domino 1091
46 Using the Enterprise Domino Server with a Large Domino Network 1115
47 Integrating Domino with Phone, Fax, and Imaging Systems 1141
48 Using Lotus NotesPump/Lotus Enterprise Integrator 1157
   Epilogue 1179

Appendixes

A Notes/Domino Class Reference 1183
B @Function and @Command Listings 1213
   Index 1229

Special Edition Using Lotus Notes and Domino R5

Copyright© 1999 by Que

All rights reserved. No part of this book shall be reproduced, stored in a retrieval system, or transmitted by any means, electronic, mechanical, photocopying, recording, or otherwise, without written permission from the publisher. No patent liability is assumed with respect to the use of the information contained herein. Although every precaution has been taken in the preparation of this book, the publisher and author assume no responsibility for errors or omissions. Neither is any liability assumed for damages resulting from the use of the information contained herein.

International Standard Book Number: 0-7897-1814-6

Library of Congress Catalog Card Number: 98-86477

Printed in the United States of America

First Printing: August 1999

01 00 99   4 3 2 1

Trademarks

All terms mentioned in this book that are known to be trademarks or service marks have been appropriately capitalized. Que cannot attest to the accuracy of this information. Use of a term in this book should not be regarded as affecting the validity of any trademark or service mark.

Warning and Disclaimer

Every effort has been made to make this book as complete and as accurate as possible, but no warranty or fitness is implied. The information provided is on an "as is" basis. The authors and the publisher shall have neither liability or responsibility to any person or entity with respect to any loss or damages arising from the information contained in this book or from the use of the CD or programs accompanying it.

Acquisitions Editor
Tracy Williams

Development Editor
Sean Dixon

Managing Editor
Lisa Wilson

Project Editor
Natalie Harris

Copy Editor
Nancy Albright

Indexer
Sandra Henselmeier
Kevin Kent
Greg Peterson

Proofreader
Benjamin Berg

Technical Editor
Karen Fishwich
Victor Mascari

Software Development Specialist
Aaron Price

Interior Design
Dan Armstrong
Ruth Lewis

Cover Design
Maureen McCarty

Layout Technicians
Brian Borders
Susan Geiselman
Mark Walchle

Contents

Who Should Read This Book   2

How This Book Is Organized   3

Conventions Used in This Book   7

I Presenting Notes and Domino Release 5

1 Introducing Lotus Notes and Domino   11

Lotus Notes, Domino, and the Internet   13

Knowledge Management   18

The Domino Designer   19

Database/Web Design   20

Programming Tools for Notes and Domino   21

The Domino Object Model   21

Domino Administration Client   22

From Here…   25

2 What's New in Release 5.0 of Notes and Domino?   27

Notes Client   28

The Domino Designer Client   32

The Domino Administration Client and Domino Server   37

From Here…   40

II Using the Lotus Notes R5 Client

3 Installing and Customizing the Notes Client   45

Steps to Install the Notes Client   46

Logging on to the Notes Client   51

Exploring Lotus Notes   52

Task Buttons   60

Bookmarks   61

ID Files and Changing Your Password   62

Setting Up a Printer   66

Summary   67

From Here…   68

4 The Notes User Interface and the Standard Databases   69

The Welcome Page   70

Standard Databases   73

Your Personal Address Book Database   74

Your Mail and Calendar Database   77

Reviewing the Public Directory   80

The Personal Web Navigator Database   82

Bookmarks   83

Subscriptions   86

Changing Your User Preferences   88

Summary   99

From Here...   100

5 Using Electronic Mail   101

A Tour of the Notes Mail Application   102

Defining Mail Preferences   110

Other Email Forms   113

Creating and Using Stationery   115

Archiving   117

Using Mail Tools   118

Rules for Handling Mail   119

Using Other Mail Packages with Notes   121

Mail and Messaging Standards   121

Using POP3 Internet Protocol Mail   122

From Here...   122

6 Working with Text and Documents   123

Notes Documents Defined   124

Working with Text   125

Working with Rich Text   127

Working with Tables   137

Working with Graphics in Rich-text Fields   139

Working with Attachments   141

Working with Documents in Views   141

From Here...   149

7 Contact Management with the Personal and Public Directories   151

Contact Management with the Personal Address Book   152

Sending a Message to a Contact   158

Scheduling a Meeting with a Contact   160

Visiting Web Pages   161

Making Group Functions Easier by Creating Groups   162

Contact Management with the Public Directory   164

From Here...   165

8 Getting Organized with the Calendaring and Scheduling Features   167

An Overview of Scheduling in Notes   168

Setting Up Calendar Preferences   169

Creating a Calendar Entry   172

Managing a To Do List on Your Calendar   182

Working with the Calendar Views   183

Working with Multiple Calendars   184

Calendaring and Scheduling While Traveling   185

Using the Resource Reservations Database   186

Using Calendaring and Scheduling with Other Software   187

From Here...   188

9 Using Sametime Collaboration 189

Understanding Sametime 190

Using Sametime in a Collaborative Learning Environment 192

Exploring the Workspace 193

Sametime Quizzes 201

Sharing Applications 202

Beyond the Classroom—Sametime Support for Meetings and Shared Viewing 203

From Here... 204

10 Using Mobile Features from Home or on the Road 205

Setting Up a Workstation for Mobile Computing 207

Setting Up Ports 208

Setting Up a Modem 211

Setting Up Location Documents 213

Setting Up Passthru Servers 220

Selecting Databases for Replication 222

Using Mobile Notes After It Is Set Up 227

From Here... 229

11 Using the Notes Client on the Internet 231

Setting Up and Using TCP/IP Protocol 232

Working with Notes and a TCP/IP Connection 237

Looking at the Integrated Notes Client 237

A Web Tour Using Notes 5.0 248

From Here... 252

III Introducing Domino Designer R5

12 Creating and Accessing Domino Databases 255

What Is a Domino Database? 256

How Can You Create a Domino Database? 258

Using Database Templates 259

Creating a Database from a Template 260

Creating a Copy of a Database 264

Creating a Replica of a Database 266

Database Access Control 267

Database Design Elements 269

Updating the Database Documentation 270

Database Properties 272

Replacing and Refreshing Designs 277

From Here... 279

13 The Integrated Development Environment (IDE) 281

Starting the Domino Designer 282

The Domino Designer Window 283

The Design Elements 285

From Here... 297

14 Designing Pages, Forms, and Subforms 299

Using the Page Editor   300

Basic Hypertext Markup Language (HTML)   305

Enhancing Your Page   309

Creating Tables   309

Embedding Pictures   321

Organizing Data with Rules, Sections, and Page Breaks   323

Designing Forms   324

Creating a New Form   326

Working with Fields   326

Creating Form Actions   333

Using Layout Regions   335

Using Subforms   337

Using Sections on Forms   338

Summary   340

From Here...   340

15 Developing Views and Folders 341

Organizing Documents Within Your Database   342

Creating and Opening a View   342

Types of Views   346

Creating Folders   348

View Column Properties   348

Sorting a View Column   354

Sorting by a Hidden Column   356

Using Icons in View Columns   356

View Properties   362

Programmer's Pane View Properties   372

View Actions   373

Embedded Views   374

Single Category Embedded Views   379

From Here...   381

16 Using Outlines, Framesets, and Navigators 383

What Are Outlines?   384

Using the Outline Editor   384

Outline Entries   385

Using Frames and Framesets   389

Creating Framesets with Domino Designer   392

Enhancing an Existing Frameset   394

Specifying Frame Contents   395

Designing Navigators   399

Using Hotspots With and Without Navigators   403

Using Embedded Elements on a Page or Form   409

Putting It All Together: Outlines, Views, Framesets, Navigators, and Beyond   410

From Here...   411

17 Access Control Lists (ACLs) and Application Security 413

ACL Basics   414

Assigning ACL Levels   415

Defining and Using Roles   421

Monitoring Changes to the ACL   423

Setting Advanced Options for the ACL   423

The Role of ACLs in Replication   428

Summary   429

From Here…   430

18 Working With Formulas, Functions, and Commands   431

Where and Why Should I Use Formulas?   432

Special Formulas   440

@functions   441

Selected Text and Conversion Functions   442

Selected List, Date, and Time Functions   443

Selected User Interface Functions   443

Selected Name and Access Functions   444

@DbLookup and @DbColumn   444

@Commands   446

From Here…   447

IV Using LotusScript, Java, and JavaScript

19 Using the IDE with LotusScript, Java, and JavaScript   451

Scripting Languages, Notes, and Domino   452

Scripts, Applets, Servlets, and Agents   453

Choosing a Language   455

Using LotusScript   455

Using the Integrated Development Environment   456

Getting Help   462

Accessing the Domino Object Model   464

Event-Driven Programming   465

Hello Again, and Again, and Again   466

Getting an Opinion: Requesting Input   469

Putting in Your Two Cents: Inputting Numbers Rather than Text   471

From Here…   472

20 Object-Oriented Programming and the Domino Object Model   475

A Bit of Object-Oriented Programming History   476

What Is Object-Oriented Programming?   477

Traditional Programming Versus Object-Oriented Programming   477

Objects—Tangible Items   478

Classes—Describing Groups of Objects   479

Class Containment   481

Collection Classes   481

Class Inheritance   482

Object Models   483

Domino Object Model Architecture   484

Front-End and Back-End Classes   485

Events   487

The LotusScript:Data Object   491

Differences Between Java and LotusScript Implementations   492

Domino Object Model (DOM) Objects   493

Summary   493

From Here...   494

21   LotusScript Variables and Objects   495

Identifiers   496

Identifier Scope   496

Variables and Constants   498

Classes and Objects   504

Naming Conventions   507

LotusScript Statements   509

Comments   509

Structured Programming   510

Sequential Flow Control   510

Selection Flow Control   510

Repetition Flow Control   512

Summary   516

From Here...   517

22   LotusScript Subroutines, Functions, and Event Handlers   519

The Purpose of Procedures   520

Different Types of Procedures   521

Error Handling   529

GoSub and Return   530

String Handling   530

File Input/Output   534

Reusing LotusScript Programs and Calling DLLs   538

Summary   540

From Here...   541

23   Creating and Using Java Applets and Agents   543

Setting Up the Java Environment   544

The Java Language   547

The Session Class   562

Java Agents, Applets, Applications, and Servlets   563

CORBA and IIOP for the Acronym-Impaired   573

Debugging Your Java Code   575

Summary   579

From Here...   579

24   Using the Lotus eSuite DevPack   581

The eSuite Workplace   582

eSuite DevPack Overview   586

The eSuite Data Presentation Applets   589

The eSuite Data Access Applets   598

The eSuite Utility Applets   600

Combining eSuite with Domino   604

Summary   607

From Here...   608

25 The Session and Front-End Classes 609

The NotesSession, Session, and AgentContext Classes 610

NotesSession Properties 613

Where Do New DOM Class Objects Come From? 613

Time Out for Dates and Times 618

The NotesUIWorkspace Class 619

The NotesUIDatabase Class 624

The NotesUIView Class 625

The NotesUIDocument Class 627

Summary 628

From Here... 629

26 Database, View, and Document Classes in LotusScript and Java 631

The NotesDatabase LotusScript Class and the Java Database Classes 632

Database Security 636

Accessing Documents Within a Database 638

The NotesDocumentCollection LotusScript and the Java DocumentCollection Classes 642

The NotesForm LotusScript and the Form Java Classes 644

The NotesDocument LotusScript and Document Java Classes 645

Summary 658

From Here... 659

27 Using Fields and Items in LotusScript and Java 661

Fields, Forms, Items, and Documents 662

Rich Text Items 666

The NotesTimer Class 671

The NotesName, NotesACL, and NotesACLEntry Classes 674

From Here... 675

V Developing Internet Sites with Domino

28 Building Your Own Web Site with Domino 679

Background 681

Web Browsers Versus Notes Client 682

Philosophy 683

Challenges 697

Resources 698

Summary 699

29 Using External HTML Tools with Domino 701

Why Use an HTML Tool? 703

Using the HTML Tools with Domino 706

Installing the Domino Design Components on Your Local Machine and Server 708

Other Tools: BeanMachine, Authoring Server, eSuite 716

Summary 718

30 Moving to Electronic Commerce on Your Domino Site 719

Chrysler SCORE—Commerce but Not Product Sales 722

Selling Online 723

Summary 727

31 Integrating Domino with Legacy Systems 729

What Do We Mean by Legacy Systems? 730

Third-Party Tools 732

Tools from Lotus 737

Summary 740

From Here... 741

VI Installing and Configuring the Domino Servers

32 The Domino Family of Servers 745

Members of the Family of Domino Servers 746

From Here... 756

33 Initial Planning and Installation 757

An Overview of Domino System Planning 758

Technical Planning for Your Domino Deployment 759

Domino Domains 759

Naming Conventions 760

Initial Setup of the Installation Files 763

Installing Your First Domino Server 767

Creating a Certification Log 770

Creating Organizational Unit (OU) Certifiers 771

Installing Additional Domino Servers 772

From Here... 776

34 Upgrading from Domino R4.x to R5 777

An Overview of the General R4-to-R5 Upgrade Process 778

The Five Stages of Your Domino/Notes Upgrade 780

Upgrading Your Domino Servers 783

Upgrading to the R5 clients 797

Upgrading Databases and Applications 800

Conclusion 804

35 Initial Configuration of Servers with the Domino Directories 807

The Importance of the Domino Directory 808

The Server Document 810

The Connection Document 834

Domain Documents 839

New Server Configuration Documents 842

Other Important Server Configuration Documents 842

Summary 843

From Here... 843

36 Domino Security Overview 845

Keeping Your Password Secure 846

An Overview of Notes Security 846

The Role of Notes IDs in Security 849

LDAP Authentication on the Web 852

Cross-Certification 852

Securing the Server Console with a Password 857

People Responsible for Notes Security 858

Encryption in Lotus Notes 861

Added Security Features for the Internet 866

From Here... 870

37 Firewalls, Virtual Private Networks (VPNs), and Internet Security 871

Firewalls 872

Virtual Private Networks 880

Internet Security 883

From Here... 891

VII Administering the Domino Servers

38 Administering Users, Groups, and Certification 895

Introducing the Domino Administrator 896

Administering Users Within the Domino Directory 899

Integrating User Account Administration with Windows NT 916

Administering Groups Within the Domino Domain 917

Administering Certification 920

Summary 920

From Here... 920

39 Administering Electronic Mail 923

Administering Electronic Mail Within the Domino Administrator 925

Administering the Domino Mail Server 927

Administering Shared Mail 939

Administering the Domino POP3 Server 942

Administering the Domino IMAP Server 944

Summary 944

From Here... 945

40 Replication and Its Administration 947

Understanding Replication 948

Creating Database Replicas 953

Enabling Selective Replication of Database Components 954

Setting Up and Initiating Replication 957

Customizing Replication 961

Monitoring Replication and Maintaining Replica Databases 968

Summary 973

From Here... 973

41 Administering Files and Databases 975

Managing General Disk Information 977

Managing Files and Directories   977

Managing and Maintaining Databases   981

Updating Database Designs   1000

Rolling Out Databases   1000

Summary   1002

From Here...   1002

42 Managing Your Domino Server Configuration   1005

Administering Domino Servers   1006

Maintaining Server Configuration Documents and Running Server Tasks   1012

Modifying Networks and Domains   1029

Analyzing and Monitoring Server Performance   1032

Summary   1034

From Here...   1035

43 Troubleshooting and Monitoring Domino   1037

Monitoring Servers with the Domino Administrator   1038

Troubleshooting Domino   1049

From Here...   1068

VIII Advanced Domino Administration

44 Performance, Scalability, and Capacity Planning for Domino Servers   1071

R5 Performance   1072

Scalability   1078

Capacity Planning   1085

Summary   1089

From Here...   1090

45 Upgrading from cc:Mail, Microsoft Mail, and Exchange to Domino   1091

Upgrading to Notes and Domino R5   1092

Upgrading from Previous Releases of Notes and Domino   1095

Migrating Users to Notes and Domino R5: An Overview   1099

Upgrading from cc:Mail to Notes and Domino   1101

Upgrading from Microsoft Mail and Exchange to Domino   1107

Importing from an LDAP Directory   1111

Summary   1113

From Here...   1114

46 Using The Enterprise Domino Server with a Large Domino Network   1115

Forming a Game Plan   1116

Summary   1138

From Here...   1138

47 Integrating Domino with Phone, Fax, and Imaging Systems 1141

Unified Messaging 1142

Voice Mail Systems 1143

Interactive Voice Response Applications (IVR) 1146

Paging 1146

Less Paper: Moving Toward a Paperless Office 1146

Integrating Fax with Domino 1147

Integrating Imaging Technology 1152

From Here… 1155

48 Using Lotus NotesPump/Lotus Enterprise Integrator 1157

What Is the Lotus NotesPump/Lotus Enterprise Integrator? 1158

NotesPump/LEI Activities 1161

All the Tools You Need 1163

Case Study: InterFusion Energy 1164

Other Information Resources to Check Out 1177

From Here… 1178

Epilogue 1179

Appendixes

A Notes/Domino Class Reference 1183

Lotus Notes Front-End Classes 1185

Lotus Notes Back-End Classes 1189

ODBC Data Access Classes 1209

B @Function and @Command Listings 1213

@Function Listing 1214

@Command Listing 1220

About the Lead Author

Randall A. Tamura is president of the Graphware Corporation, a consulting company specializing in Lotus Notes and Domino development. He has more than 25 years of experience in the computer field, and before founding Graphware, he was the general manager of Engineering Systems Development in the Application Solutions Division at IBM. Tamura is a Lotus Business Partner and has worked with Notes and Domino for several years.

Tamura has experience in helping both small and large companies with software development and strategies. Working with Notes as well as other technologies, he has helped his clients plan, implement, and deploy applications. He has helped a variety of companies in the financial, insurance, manufacturing, and high-tech industries.

Tamura is a graduate of the University of California at Berkeley and has a masters degree in computer science from Princeton University. You can contact him through Internet email at RandTamura@gwcorp.com, visit the Graphware Corporation web site at www.gwcorp.com, or contact him by phone at (310) 649-0310. Randy wrote Chapters 1-2, 4, 12-16, 18-27, and 33.

About the Contributing Authors

Don Child is a senior technical writer with DataHouse, a Lotus Premium Business Partner in Honolulu. He is a certified Domino R5 Application Developer and a Certified 4.6 Domino Administrator. He has worked as a Lotus instructor and has written end-user documentation for numerous Notes applications. Child is a senior member and current president of the Aloha Chapter of the Society for Technical Communications (STC). He authored *Sams Teach Yourself Lotus Notes 4.5 in 14 Days* and contributed to three Lotus Notes books in the Sams Publishing Unleashed series. Child can be reached at don_child@datahouse.com. Don wrote Chapters 3, 5-11, 17, 32, and 33.

Kenneth Adams is CEO of InterFusion (http://interfusion.com), a Lotus Premier Business Partner focused exclusively on Domino and Notes software development and consulting, located in Merchantville, NJ. InterFusion was founded in December of 1994 and has focused on the Internet and groupware since then, making it one of the more experienced consulting firms working with Lotus Internet technology.

Ken's background is in both software development and in building and managing networks. Ken has more than 15 years of experience in the computer networking field. He has deployed and managed large networks, developed application software, managed support, and developed and conducted training. He has experience in many technologies including NetWare, DOS, Windows, NT, OS/2, Lotus Domino/Notes, Internet, LAN and WAN design, database systems, network management systems, host integration, email systems, and application integration. Ken has been working with Lotus Domino and Notes technology for almost seven years. Ken founded InterFusion, which introduced the industry's first InterNotes Web hosting service in 1995, and put the first Domino Web server on the Internet (other then Lotus) in June 1996.

Ken has had a very active and highly visible role in the industry. Including his role as a volunteer and board member for several nonprofit professional associations. He holds two R5 Principal Certified Lotus Professional (CLP) designations, Master CNE designation from Novell and a Certified Computing Professional (CCP) designation from the Institute for Certification of Computer Professionals (ICCP). Kenneth wrote Chapters 47 and 48.

Soman Dutta is a director at netConnections Ltd., in London, UK. He began playing with Lotus Notes in 1989 in Boston, MA. After moving to NY City in 1991, Soman has been working as a Lotus Notes consultant to companies that include Bankers Trust, Chase Manhattan Bank, Nynex, Citibank, IBM, General Reinsurance, Monsanto, KPMG, and Energis Communications. In 1996, he launched in London a specialist quarterly publication titled universal net.connect, which contains features, news, product reviews, and programming tips around the world of Lotus Notes, Domino, and Designer. Since 1997, he has been responsible for the creation and marketing of netConnections product suite. These products are modular, integrated, Web enabled set of business applications powered by the Domino server and used through a Web browser or Notes client. For more information, go to www.netconnections.co.uk or contact Soman at sdutta@netconnections.co.uk. Soman wrote Chapter 34.

Christopher B. Lavagnino, a Principal Lotus Notes Professional, has an extensive software development background in Open Systems Interconnection (OSI) and Internet standard messaging, directory, and managment technologies. He currently leads a research and development team within Computer Associates International focusing on building administrative and management applications for the Lotus Notes Domino and Internet/ITU-T messaging and directory infrastructures. He was formerly the director of Engineering and Product Development at QXCOM, which was acquired by Computer Associates in August, 1998; the director of Server Products at ISOCOR; and research and development manager of Messaging and Directory Services at Retix. He is a member of the Association Computing Machinery (ACM), the Computer Society, and the IEEE. Christopher wrote Chapters 38-42 and 45.

Rocky Oliver is the senior architect at Synergistics, Inc. He is a co-author of *Teach Yourself LotusScript for Notes/Domino 4.6* (MIS Press; 1997), articles on LotusScript for Domino Advisor, and has been developing LotusScript since its introduction. Rocky is also an "ex-Loti", having worked for Lotus Word Processing Division. Rocky spends his free time entertaining his five children and wife. Rocky wrote Chapters 35, 43, and 46.

Ralph Perrine is a senior management consultant with DataHouse Inc. of Honolulu, and an experienced webmaster and developer. He co-authored DataHouse's Internet Enterprise Methodology, which provides a proven framework for planning, developing, implementing and operating all of the components of an Internet Enterprise including network infrastructure, messaging, Web applications, workstations, rollout, training and user support. This methodology is based on project experience and includes complete coverage of Internet governance, organizational dynamics, operations, and user support. In addition, Ralph developed the Knowledge Flow model which guides DataHouse's Knowledge Management

Practice and is used to diagnose technology, process and organizational problems that impact the flow of knowledge through an organization. Ralph and his wife Dina currently live in Honolulu. Ralph is also the creator of Cyber Reef (http://www.cyberreef.com). Ralph wrote Chapters 37 and 44.

Ken Schweda is a Chicago-based Notes professional, and has worked with Notes for the past seven years. He's been involved with all aspects of Notes including support, design and development, architecture planning, standards development, and project management. He is the contributing editor for *The Lotus Notes & Domino Advisor*, responsible for the Tips, Tricks, and Traps column. He has published articles in *Advisor*, *Solutions Now!*, *Domino Update*, and speaks at Advisor and Lotus sponsored Developer Conferences. Contact Ken at kenschweda@yahoo.com. Ken wrote Chapter 31.

Rob Wunderlich is a groupware consultant for NuTechs, a Lotus Premier Business Partner in Bloomfield Hills, Michigan. He's an R5 CLP, Application Development and System Administration, as well as an R5 CLI—Certified Lotus Instructor. In addition to doing consulting and development work with Notes and Domino, Wunderlich is NuTechs' webmaster and employs Domino technology at his firm's web site at http://www.nutechs.com. He has conducted seminars and written numerous articles on groupware in general and Lotus Notes in particular. He was a contributing author for *Lotus Notes 4.6 Unleashed*, *Domino Administrator's Survival Guide*, and *Complete Guide to Using Lotus Notes 4.6*. He founded the Detroit Notes Professionals Association (DNP), the Lotus Notes user group in Detroit, and serves on the board of the Detroit Area Network User Group (DANUG). A volunteer webmaster for Ronald McDonald House of Detroit (http://ww.rmhdet.org), Wunderlich lives in suburban Detroit, Michigan, with his wife and two daughters, and can be reached at rwunder@nutechs.com. Rob wrote Chapters 28-30.

Dedication

I'd like to dedicate this book to my life's companion, best friend, and wife Mari as well as my buddy and son, Eric. They have both given me the space and support to complete this book.

Acknowledgments

I'd like to thank all of my family and friends for their support while I wrote this book. It has been an especially long journey that began over a year ago. Release 5 was initially scheduled to come out at the beginning of 1998. While the resulting code from Lotus was worth the wait, multiple betas and changing user interfaces are especially difficult for authors because each change means another rewrite.

I want to thank my wife Mari for her support not only during this effort, but all the time. I'm proud of my son, Eric, who is not only doing great in school, but well on his way to becoming an Eagle Scout.

The co-authors of this book have also put in a lot of time and effort toward the success of this book and it is evident throughout. I'd like to thank them for all of their contributions because without them, this book would not be possible.

Sean Dixon was the development editor for this project, and although he joined the project after it had already started, he did a good job in keeping everything moving. Karen Fishwich, the technical editor, did an outstanding job of improving the accuracy of the book. Although I will take responsibility for all errors remaining in the book, Karen was a great help in finding inconsistencies and helping to debug the book.

Finally, thanks to you, the reader for the investment you have made in this book. I hope you find it useful and I hope it helps you to achieve your goals.

Tell Us What You Think!

As the reader of this book, *you* are our most important critic and commentator. We value your opinion and want to know what we're doing right, what we could do better, what areas you'd like to see us publish in, and any other words of wisdom you're willing to pass our way.

As a publisher for Que, I welcome your comments. You can fax, email, or write me directly to let me know what you did or didn't like about this book—as well as what we can do to make our books stronger.

Please note that I cannot help you with technical problems related to the topic of this book, and that due to the high volume of mail I receive, I might not be able to reply to every message.

When you write, please be sure to include this book's title and author as well as your name and phone or fax number. I will carefully review your comments and share them with the author and editors who worked on the book.

Fax: 317.581.4666

Email: opsys@mcp.com

Mail: Publisher
Que Corporation
201 West 103rd Street
Indianapolis, IN 46290 USA

INTRODUCTION

Super.human.software. This is the moniker that Lotus has placed on Notes and Domino R5. There is no doubt that Lotus has succeeded in making its product, already the best-selling messaging and groupware product, even better. It has been quite a wait for those of us who have been anticipating it for over a year, but the wait has been well worth it.

The new software is able to provide email to tall buildings with a single server, is more powerful than a locomotive, and it runs faster than a speeding bullet. It provides these services and more while remaining unaffected even by kryptonite.

As we near the threshold of the 21st century, Notes and Domino R5 are ready to carry us forward. They provide a great leap ahead with powerful Web serving functions, workflow and groupware capabilities, email, replication, integration with legacy systems, and more.

If you are currently deciding whether to consider Domino for your enterprise, the answer is simple. You should. There are so many applications and capabilities of the system that you may be able to use it to replace and consolidate older systems you may be using. If you already use Notes and Domino and are considering upgrading to the latest release, the answer is simple. You should. You already know about the huge return on investment the system provides, and the capabilities of R5 make your gains even larger.

Who Should Read This Book

This book is designed to give you comprehensive coverage of Notes and Domino. It is intended to provide you with the information you need to install, deploy, develop applications with, and use Notes and Domino R5 to their fullest.

This book gives you a look at R5 from three major perspectives: the Notes user, the Domino application developer, and the Domino administrator. For example, you may be one of the following types of readers:

- **A Notes user**   Whether you are a new user of Notes or an experienced Notes release 4 user, you should read this book to find out about the new features of release 5. You'll learn about email, calendaring and scheduling, Sametime features, and using Notes remotely.

- **A Domino application developer**   As a developer, you should be familiar with the new features of Notes release 5 and how to best take advantage of them for your users. The approach of this book is much more Internet- and Web-centric than previous Notes and Domino books. In addition to core Domino topics, this book includes information on HTML, Java, JavaScript, pages, and framesets, as well as details on LotusScript and building Web sites.

- **A Lotus Business Partner**   This book was written almost completely by Lotus Business Partners. As such, the authors know the kind of information you're interested in, including advice on many third-party integration tools. It includes advanced topics, such as legacy system integration, performance, capacity planning, and upgrading from

cc:Mail or Exchange. The CD-ROM that accompanies this book includes many actual demos of third-party tools.
- A Domino administrator   I have included useful information on configuring your system and upgrading from release 4 to release 5 of Notes, and advanced information about troubleshooting and security concerns when connecting to other companies. This book also tells you about firewalls, Virtual Private Networks (VPNs) and other security issues. I'll cover the new Domino Administrator interface in detail, as well as tips for troubleshooting and monitoring Domino.

If you're using Domino now, or are trying to decide whether Domino is the right product for your company, this book is for you. It describes why you should consider Notes and Domino, how to use them, how to develop applications, and how to administer your Domino network.

How This Book Is Organized

This book is organized into eight parts, each part consisting of several chapters. Part I, "Presenting Notes and Domino Release 5," is a general introduction to Notes and Domino. It is designed to help you understand the product and why you should consider it for your company.

Part II, "Using the Lotus Notes R5 Client," describes how to get started with Notes and how to use some of its more important features. Part III, "Introducing Domino Designer R5," and Part IV, "Using LotusScript, Java, and JavaScript," provide you with information about creating Notes release 5 applications.

Part V, "Developing Internet Sites with Domino," is devoted to topics relating to the Internet and Web development. Part VI, "Installing and Configuring the Domino Servers," provides you with some core information on Domino Server installation. Part VII, "Administering the Domino Servers," covers ongoing administration of your system. It includes topics such as adding and deleting users, handling email, and replication. Part VIII, "Advanced Domino Administration," covers specialty or advanced topics. Items such as performance, upgrading email, large Domino networks, and other topics are covered.

Part I "Presenting Notes and Domino Release 5"

Part I covers some basic concepts and information about Notes and the groupware category of software. Chapter 1, "Introducing Lotus Notes and Domino," describes Notes and Domino and gives you an overview of the system's capabilities.

Chapter 2, "What's New in Release 5.0 of Notes and Domino," highlights new features of Notes release 5. Release 5 is a major upgrade of Notes and Domino. This chapter gives you a taste of the new features for end users, developers, and administrators.

PART II "USING THE LOTUS NOTES R5 CLIENT"

Part II provides you with information about using the Notes release 5 client. Whether you are just using Notes, developing applications for Notes, or administering a Notes system, you should read this part.

Chapter 3, "Installing and Customizing the Notes Client," begins at the beginning, showing you how to install and customize the Notes client. Chapter 4, "The Notes User Interface and the Standard Databases," examines the new user interface and the standard databases supplied by Lotus. Chapter 5, "Using Electronic Mail," covers the use of email and general applications. Email is now a critical part of business, and with release 5, Lotus has enhanced the email interface so that it is even more user friendly than before.

Chapter 6, "Working with Text and Documents," shows you the key features of documents in Notes that are used in all databases. Chapter 7, "Contact Management with the Personal and Public Directories," illustrates these two key databases. In R4.x, these directories were called Name and Address Books, but in R5, Lotus is now using the terminology of Directory. Chapter 8, "Getting Organized with the Calendaring and Scheduling Features," explains how to make appointments and meetings. R5 makes you even more productive than before.

Chapter 9, "Using Sametime Collaboration," describes the new Sametime product that works with Notes and Domino. If you are familiar with AOL "buddy lists," this exciting new product provides a similar capability and more. The capability of using Notes on a mobile computer or from a remote computer, such as an office at home, is a great benefit. Chapter 10, "Using Mobile Features from Home or on the Road," covers the topics you need to know to set up replication and usage for your mobile or remote Notes environment. Chapter 11, "Using the Notes Client on the Internet," highlights features and capabilities that Web cruisers find useful.

PART III "INTRODUCING DOMINO DESIGNER R5"

Part III, Part IV, and Part V of this book are devoted to application development issues. Part III begins with Chapter 12, "Creating and Accessing Domino Databases," which is a description of Domino databases and an introduction to the Lotus templates and the various methods of creating and using Domino databases. Chapter 13, "The Integrated Development Environment (IDE)," shows you how to use the new user interface for Domino development.

Chapter 14, "Designing Pages, Forms, and Subforms," and Chapter 15, "Developing Views and Folders," cover both the traditional Domino design elements and some of the new elements as well. Chapter 16, "Using Outlines, Framesets, and Navigators," completes the trio of design element chapters, which show you how to use the design elements in both Web and Notes client environments.

Chapter 17, "Access Control Lists (ACLs) and Application Security," gives you information on securing your applications. Chapter 18, "Working with Formulas, Functions, and

Commands," completes Part III and covers important functions you need to develop Domino applications.

Part IV "Using LotusScript, Java, and JavaScript"

In Part IV, I cover programmability of Notes and Domino. Chapter 19, "Using the IDE with LotusScript, Java, and JavaScript," begins Part IV by describing the development environment within the Domino Designer. Chapter 20, "Object-Oriented Programming and the Domino Object Model," provides you with the knowledge required to effectively use either LotusScript or Java. Chapter 21, "LotusScript Variables and Objects," is a tour of LotusScript, the BASIC scripting language for Notes, and many of the other Lotus products. Chapter 21 covers both the fundamental language elements and the data types used within the language. Chapter 22, "LotusScript Subroutines, Functions, and Event Handlers," describes how to modularize your program and provides information on the built-in functions of LotusScript.

In Chapter 23, "Creating and Using Java Applets and Agents," you learn about both the Java language and how to create applets and agents for Domino. Chapter 24, "Using the Lotus eSuite DevPack," describes version 1.5 of the eSuite DevPack, a group of Java applets that you can use to make your application development easier.

Chapter 25, "The Session and Front-End Classes," Chapter 26, "Database, View, and Document Classes in LotusScript and Java," and Chapter 27, "Using Fields and Items in LotusScript and Java," describe the Domino Object Model (DOM) classes. These chapters cover the model, using both LotusScript and Java examples to ease your learning experience. If you are familiar with one language, it should make it much easier to learn the other. Meanwhile, you will become familiar with the DOM classes in the process.

Part V "Developing Internet Sites with Domino"

Part V provides you with information about an important topic: creating Web sites with Domino. Chapter 28, "Building Your Own Web Site with Domino," describes some approaches you can use to building your Web site with Domino. Chapter 29, "Using External HTML Tools with Domino," illustrates how Domino can be used with other HTML tools to ease your transition to Domino or as a means of providing additional capabilities for your Web site. Chapter 30, "Moving to Electronic Commerce on Your Domino Site," discusses points you need to know when using Domino as your electronic commerce Web server. Chapter 31, "Integrating Domino with Legacy Systems" provide a brief overview of the various products and tools for making Domino work with legacy systems.

Part VI "Installing and Configuring the Domino Servers"

Part VI covers the initial installation and configuration of your Domino server. Chapter 32, "The Domino Family of Servers," begins Part VI and discusses the different servers and their capabilities. Chapter 33, "Initial Planning and Installation," tells you what you should consider before you actually install the system. You'll learn about certification, domains, and the initial setup of a server. Chapter 34, "Upgrading from Domino R4.x to R5," is an important chapter for anyone considering upgrading from R4.x to R5 of Domino. You'll find the information you need to make the upgrade here. Chapter 35, "Initial Configuration of Servers with the Domino Directories," discusses the Domino Directory, which was formerly called the Name and Address Book. Key configuration parameters are described. Providing security for your Domino system is the topic of Chapter 36, "Domino Security Overview." The security discussion continues in Chapter 37, "Firewalls, Virtual Private Networks (VPNs), and Internet Security."

Part VII "Administering the Domino Servers"

Whereas Part VI covers the initial installation and configuration of Domino, Part VII focuses more on the ongoing administration of your Domino system after you have installed and configured it. Chapter 38, "Administering Users, Groups, and Certification," covers the main points you need to know about administering users and groups in Domino. You'll learn about adding and deleting users, creating groups, and more. Electronic mail is one of the most important applications of Domino today. Chapter 39, "Administering Electronic Mail," provides the keys to a successful implementation in your business.

Chapter 40, "Replication and Its Administration," discusses replication, one of the core features of Domino. You'll learn when a database is a replica of another database, how to schedule replication, and some points regarding replication of mail databases. Chapter 41, "Administering Files and Databases," shows you some of the great new features of R5 that you can use to manage the databases in your system. Chapter 42, "Managing Your Domino Server Configuration," describes some of the topics not described elsewhere that are contained in the Domino server record in the Domino Public Directory (Name and Address Book). Chapter 43, "Troubleshooting and Monitoring Domino," rounds out Part VII with important tips and hints to get you out of trouble and keep your system running smoothly.

Part VIII "Advanced Domino Administration"

The last part of the book, Part VIII, discusses some advanced administration topics. Chapter 44, "Performance, Scalability, and Capacity Planning for Domino Servers," describes key points to consider when deciding what kind of server(s) you require for your network. Upgrading email is covered in Chapter 45, "Upgrading from cc:Mail, Microsoft Mail, and Exchange to Domino." Chapter 46, "Using the Enterprise Domino Server with a Large Domino Network," examines some of the unique features of this version of the Domino server and provides hints and tips for managing a large Domino network. Chapter 47, "Integrating Domino with Phone, Fax, and Image," keeps you on the leading edge of technology. It examines the latest ways to obtain even greater value from Domino when it is used with these other technologies. Chapter 48, "Using NotesPump and Domino Enhanced Search," covers these additional tools to integrate Domino with other parts of your business. The ability to obtain data from other sources, and to search it, is vital to managing the knowledge in your company. Appendixes A and B provide a class reference and function and command listings, respectively.

—Randall Tamura

Conventions Used in This Book

This book uses the following conventions:

- Menu names are separated from menu options by a comma. For example, "File, Open" means "Select the File menu and choose the Open option."
- New terms appear in *italic*.
- Words that you type appear in regular text in `monospace`.
- Placeholders (words that stand for what you actually type) in regular text appear in *`italic monospace`*.
- All code appears in `monospace`.
- Placeholders in code appear in *`italic monospace`*.
- When a line of code is too long to fit on only one line of this book, it is broken at a convenient place and continued to the next line. The continuation of the line is preceded by a code-continuation character (➥). You should type a line of code that has this character as one long line without breaking it.
- An ellipsis (…) indicates that the remaining or intervening code required to complete a statement or code structure has been omitted for the sake of brevity.

PART I

Presenting Notes and Domino Release 5

1 Introducing Lotus Notes and Domino

2 What's New in Release 5.0 of Notes and Domino?

CHAPTER 1

INTRODUCING LOTUS NOTES AND DOMINO

Welcome to the world of Lotus Notes, Domino, and the Internet. We live in a world where information and knowledge translate into power. Notes and Domino are tools to help you use, find, organize, and manage your information and knowledge. In this book you'll learn how you can use the information stored in Notes and Domino and how to provide some of that information to your customers, employees, clients, vendors, and other business partners. You'll also learn how you can use the Internet with Domino as a strategic tool for obtaining information, providing information, and performing transactions with others. Notes, Domino, and the Internet have made huge advances in just the last few years. Let's briefly roll the clock back to see how far we've come.

In the early days of Lotus Notes, the product was labeled with the term *proprietary*. This negative label was attached by competitors to indicate that the system was not an open system. In many ways, however, the label was accurate because there was a lot of proprietary technology within Lotus Notes. The reason, of course, was that there were no standards, no off-the-shelf components, and no technology readily available to implement the concepts in Notes. Lotus simply had to invent this technology, which of course made it proprietary.

In the early 1990s, Lotus had to do a lot of evangelizing to explain the concepts in Notes, to explain groupware, and to show how using networks, document databases, and communication could improve productivity within companies. At that time, most people used the file system of the operating system to store their documents and they didn't understand the value or importance of storing documents in a database.

If we advance the clock to the present day, we find that the computing landscape has changed dramatically since those early days of Lotus Notes. In fact, with the advent of the Internet, many of the early, proprietary, and innovative concepts in Notes have now become commonplace on the Internet. As the computing environment has changed, so has Notes.

First, in release 4.5 Lotus divided Notes into two separate programs, one still called Notes, the other Domino. Simplistically, this gives separate names to the client and server components in a client/server architecture. In reality, Lotus is building a separate identity and brand for the Domino server. In release 5.0, the Domino Designer and Administrator clients have been substantially improved and are also obtaining their own identities. Each product continues to evolve and improve.

Second, the major force changing not only the computing community, but the world as we know it, is the Internet. In 1996, many were saying that Lotus Notes was in serious danger of becoming obsolete, insignificant, or extinct because of the Internet. As it turns out, those pundits have been proven wrong because the Internet has shown people the power of the applications that Notes and Domino can provide. By combining the strength of the Domino database with Web serving capabilities, Lotus has transformed Domino into almost superhuman software. Notes and Domino licenses recently have grown geometrically, nearly doubling in each of the last several years.

In Notes R5, this transition continues. You see more features and functions to integrate the Internet and Web with Notes and Domino. You see more standards-based implementations, open architecture, and a powerful and dynamic product with many significant improvements.

Lotus Notes, Domino, and the Internet

If you're new to Notes and Domino, you might be interested in a short description of what they are and what they do. If you've been using Notes for a while, you've developed your own view, but read on because there are a lot of changes in release 5. I'll try to provide here a short description of Notes and Domino for those of you new to these programs.

Notes and Domino have a common ancestry. They share a lot of common program code, and so sometimes features available in one are available in the other. For your purposes now, you can consider Notes as the name of the client portion and Domino as the server portion of the system. Originally, a Notes client had to work with a Domino server. As time progresses, however, they are becoming increasingly independent and a Notes client now works with many different servers while a Domino server can work with non-Notes clients. For example, the Notes client can act as a Web browser and can be used independently of the Domino server. Domino can act as a Web server and interact with Web browsers such as Netscape Navigator or Microsoft's Internet Explorer.

The Notes client is not an application, it is an application platform. By this I mean that it is different from typical applications such as word processors and spreadsheets. As a platform, I mean that Notes provides many powerful features and tools that developers can use to create customized applications for their users. Just as Microsoft Windows is a platform, so is Notes. Just as UNIX is a platform, so is Domino. Developers can use the Notes and Domino platforms as the basis, the foundation for creating customized applications.

You can think of the Notes and Domino platforms as a hierarchical layer on top of the operating system level. One of the primary advantages provided by Notes and Domino is operating system independence. Although the Microsoft Windows operating system is a platform, you cannot typically use applications built for Windows on UNIX, OS/2, OS/390, OS/400, or other operating systems. Notes and Domino, however, provide you with a layer of operating system independence so that you can choose your hardware and OS independently from your applications. You can even use one operating system, such as UNIX, for your server operating system and a different operating system, such as Windows, for your client. Applications built for the Notes and Domino platforms provide this fundamental operating system and hardware independence which, in the end, gives you the power to choose the operating systems and hardware that best suits your environment. In order to be useful, Lotus recognizes that applications must be available, so it bundles several applications with Notes and Domino. Some of the applications that are included with Notes client are email, group calendaring, Web browsing, discussion databases, contact management, and directory services. These applications can be used out-of-the-box, without any customization. Server applications for Domino include email, Web serving, database replication, and directory services and synchronization.

In addition to these standard applications, Lotus provides *templates* for use in creating your own custom applications with little or no programming required. These templates have been developed by Lotus and can be instantiated on your Domino system with a very minimal amount of work.

Notes and Domino also provide a set of tools for you to write your own applications. A major part of this book is devoted to these tools to show you how you can use them and get the most out of them. The applications you build can use Domino services so you can provide them on your World Wide Web site or on your intranet.

In addition to all the tools and services provided by Notes and Domino, the Lotus Business Partner community has invested a great deal of time and effort to provide customizable solutions for you as well. There are over 20,000 Lotus Business Partners today and by using their software products and services, you can usually find a Notes/Domino-based product to solve your business problem.

So, recapping Lotus Notes and Domino, they provide an operating system–neutral platform and tools for applications. The Notes client can be used with the Domino server or the two parts can be used independently. Lotus ships several important applications, such as email, that are ready to use and provides templates for you to easily create many other applications as well. Notes and Domino provide a very rich set of tools for you to create custom applications that you can use internally or on the World Wide Web. Finally, Business Partners provide a wealth of applications to solve most common business problems.

The First Look at the Notes Client

There are actually three different Notes clients. In addition to the regular Notes user client, there is the Domino Designer client and the Domino Administrator client. In this section I'll show you the user client and in subsequent sections I'll show you the Designer and Administrator clients.

The Notes client is probably the first component you'll use, so I'll start the discussion there. In Figure 1.1 you'll see an example of the Notes welcome page. A welcome page is also sometimes called a headline page. This new feature of Notes 5.0 greets you when you first start the Notes client.

The welcome page is where you start your session and can be considered your base of operations. You can customize your welcome page with information that is important to you.

At Lotusphere 1999, Lotus announced an agreement with America Online (AOL) to provide content for Lotus. The welcome page can be customized to include news. See Figure 1.2 for an example of the welcome page configured with email, the daily calendar, and the news of the day.

You can see by contrasting Figures 1.1 and 1.2 that the welcome page is very flexible. You can include information from your own company databases or you can include information that comes directly from the World Wide Web. In addition, your company system administration staff can customize the welcome page to provide you with companywide information or important notifications.

LOTUS NOTES, DOMINO, AND THE INTERNET | 15

Figure 1.1
The default Notes welcome page provides basic options.

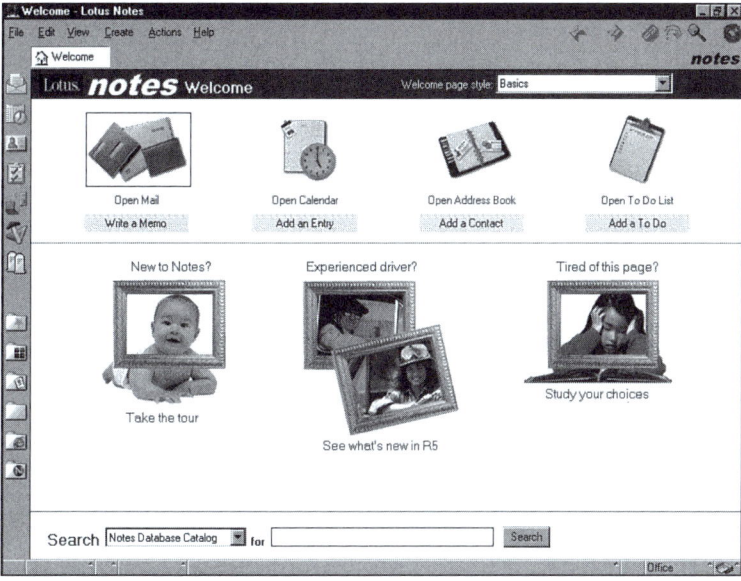

Figure 1.2
The My News welcome page provides email, a calendar, and news.

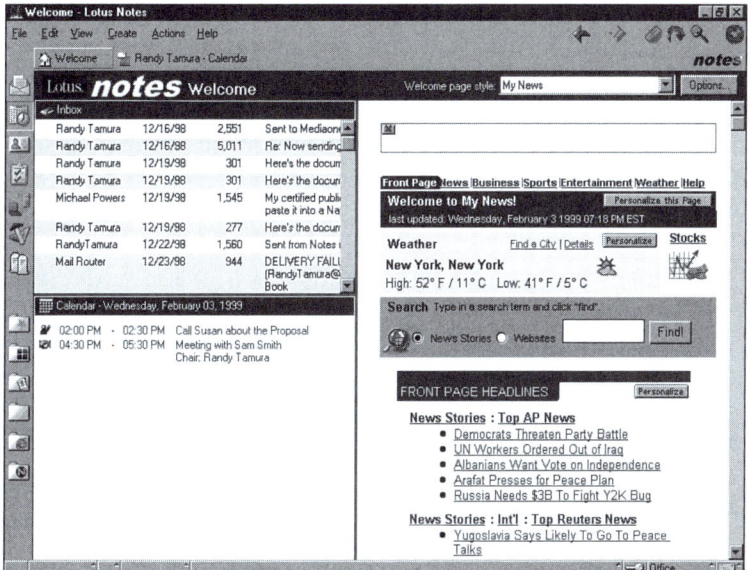

ELECTRONIC MAIL (EMAIL)

Electronic mail is one of the primary strengths of Lotus Notes and Domino. It has been an integral part of these products for many years and has had a chance to mature in capabilities and reliability. With the ubiquitous nature of email these days, it is important to have a reliable and stable system for sending email.

Some email systems such as cc:Mail and Microsoft Mail use file servers as the primary mechanism for sharing email data. They use code running on separate clients to access a shared mail file. The file server prevents two clients from updating the file at the same time. This mechanism works fairly well for small groups; however, as the number of clients increases, say to 500, 1000, or 10,000 users, the system has problems scaling up.

The Domino email server works differently. By having a Domino program that manages multiple mail databases, Domino can scale to hundreds of thousands of users because of its client/server model. The server can communicate with other servers, send and receive mail, and communicate with the clients as well.

How does Domino compare with its most frequently cited competitor, Microsoft Exchange? Well, both of these systems fundamentally deliver mail. However, comparing them is a little like comparing, say, a BMW engine with a Mercedes car. They both have good, fundamental engines, but comparing an engine to a car is a bit like the famous apples and oranges comparison.

Domino has a much more comprehensive list of features and capabilities. This is not to say that Microsoft doesn't have products that it can integrate with Exchange, it is just that you have to do it yourself. To get the functionality of Domino, you might have to integrate 5 to 10 different Microsoft products. Table 1.1 is a summary of some important similarities and differences.

TABLE 1.1   COMPARISON BETWEEN DOMINO AND EXCHANGE FEATURES

Lotus Notes and Domino	Microsoft Exchange
Operating Systems: NT 4.0, Windows 95, OS/2, OS/390, OS/400, Sun Solaris, IBM AIX, HP UX (and Linux later in 1999)	NT 4.0
Standards-based protocols: SSL, POP3, IMAP, LDAP, NNTP, SMTP, HTTP	SSL, POP3, IMAP, LDAP, NNTP, SMTP, and HTTP require Microsoft IIS.
Mobile features: Selective replication, field-level updates, offline Web browsing	Partial support and Web browsing require Internet Explorer.
Mobile directory with 100KB+ user capacity	Not available
Group Calendaring and Scheduling: Built-in	Available in Outlook client
Document Management, versioning	Not available
Integrated workflow applications	Partial support for workflow
Directory Services integrated	NT Directory for user authentication, Exchange directory for messaging
Tools and templates available for easy Web application development	Separate package with Internet Information Server and Visual InterDev
Cross platform, Web based, and offline administration	Windows NT administration only
Graphical, drag and drop UI for ease of administration	Not available

Figure 1.3 shows you the user interface for mail in the Lotus Notes client. The Notes client also allows you to use POP3 and SMTP for email services so you don't necessarily have to use Domino as your email server. These are Internet standard protocols for email, and most Internet service providers (ISPs) use these protocols. What this means for you is that you can use your existing email account with an ISP and use the Notes client as your email repository.

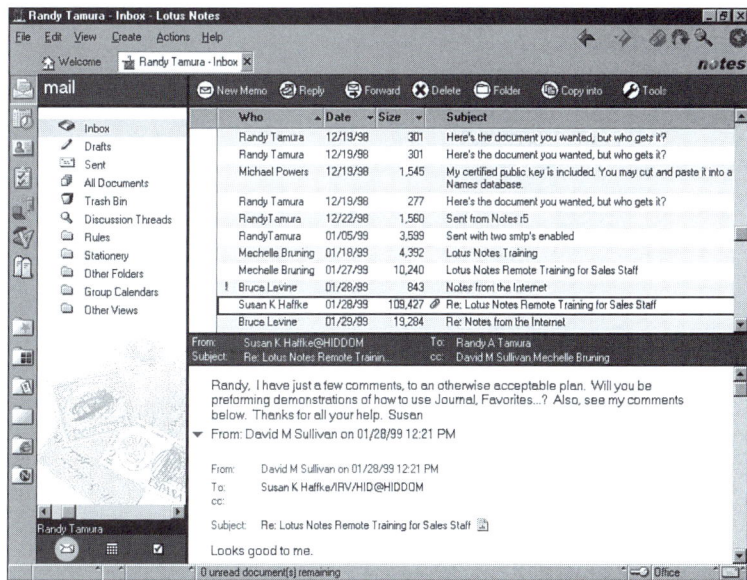

Figure 1.3
A look at the Lotus Notes R5 mail interface.

With this feature, you can use a single database to access company mail that might use a Domino server and a personal email account from an ISP. You no longer have to look on two different email systems; you can access them both from a single inbox.

WEB BROWSING

Browsing the World Wide Web has become both a pastime and an important business tool. At this writing the browser wars between Netscape Navigator/Communicator and Microsoft Internet Explorer are still being waged, but mainly in the courtroom. Lotus has taken a middle-of-the-road approach to Web browsing by trying to accommodate both Netscape and Microsoft as well as its own Web navigator product. With Notes, you can specify the Notes browser, Netscape Navigator or Communicator, or Microsoft Internet Explorer (MSIE).

With MSIE you can also specify that you would like the browser embedded within the Notes client. In this mode, Notes uses MSIE as a customized component. Notes provides the main user interface but calls on MSIE to perform the actual retrieval and rendering of the Web pages inside the window, as shown in Figure 1.4.

Figure 1.4
Lotus Notes client can browse the Web.

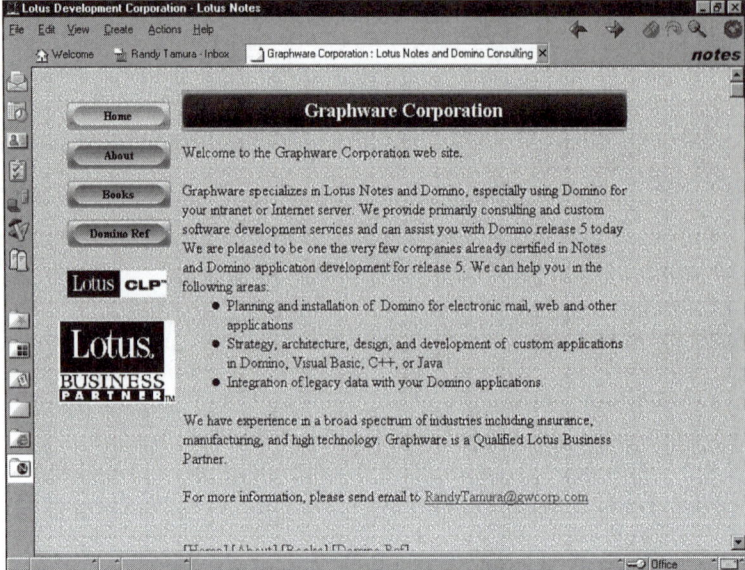

The Notes client can also read bookmarks from both the Netscape and Microsoft browsers. If you switch back and forth between several Web browsers, with Notes you always have the most recent set of bookmarks from your other browser.

KNOWLEDGE MANAGEMENT

Knowledge management (KM) seems to be a buzzword these days. What exactly is knowledge management? In a nutshell, it is what Lotus Notes has been doing for years. Knowledge management is providing a repository for unstructured information within your corporation and the ability to be able to search and use that information when you need it.

Whereas relational databases are good for storing data such as names, address, and financial figures, they are not very suited for storing free-form, unstructured data. Relational databases are very efficient tools for retrieval of structured data. You should use a relational database whenever you need fast retrieval of traditional, tabular information.

Knowledge, however, is usually not well suited for rows and columns. Knowledge is usually stored, if at all, in the filing cabinets, letters, memos, and reports that are in your office. Typically these reports and memos are each individually written in a word processor and the files are stored one-at-a-time in the file system on your computer. Although most of the documents you originate are captured in a machine-readable format, they are not really managed. Of course, you probably know where to find all your own documents. But if you wanted to find all the reports and memos for your whole department, organization, or company that have been written on a particular topic, could you do it?

If you could, great, but if your company is like most, the files are scattered across a network, on individual computer hard disks and stored in paper form in filing cabinets. No, it would probably take a lot of manual effort to retrieve all the information about a particular topic within your complete organization.

Lotus Notes knowledge management really means converting all those individual documents into documents that are stored in Domino databases on your server. When these documents are stored on a Domino server, they are accessible for searching, sorting, and sifting. In other words, your documents are managed and you will actually be able to find something.

Management of your knowledge involves storing your documents in databases, not word-processing files. It involves the ability to categorize and retrieve information that other people have written. To be able to share the collective knowledge of the organization is what can give you a competitive advantage.

THE DOMINO DESIGNER

The Domino Designer client is the second type of Notes client. It has a slightly different user interface and different licensing requirements from the regular Notes client. With the Domino Designer, you can create your own Domino applications that can be used with Notes clients or with Web browsers (see Figure 1.5).

Figure 1.5
The Domino Designer contains a rich set of tools for application design.

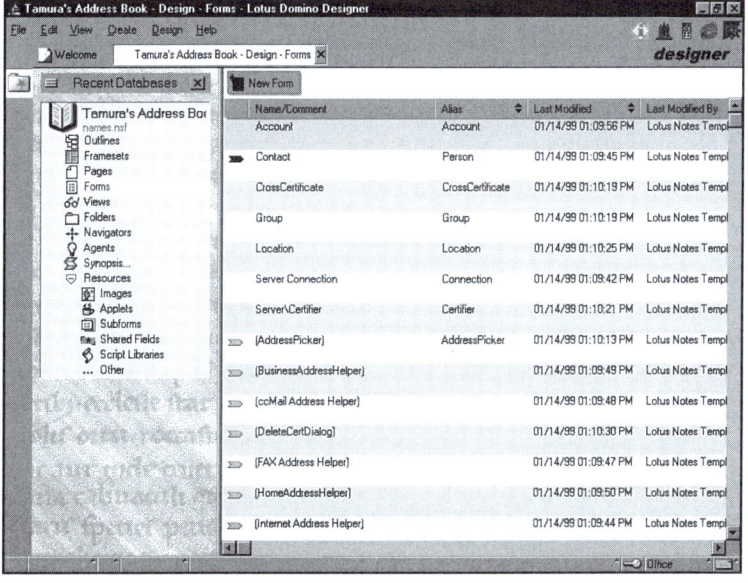

If you have designed applications with a previous release of Notes, you will recognize forms, views, folders, navigators, and subforms as a few of the familiar design elements. These elements were central to the design of Lotus Notes applications in prior releases of Notes. All the design elements from these previous releases are still available with release 5 of Domino, but there are several new elements as well. You can now see design elements such as outlines, framesets, and pages, which provide you with a rich set of features for Web development. I will cover these and other additional elements in detail in later chapters.

The Domino Designer Integrated Development Environment (IDE) has been greatly enhanced to provide the additional features to make it a great development environment. New language support for Java and JavaScript is included and many of the IDE features are designed to make Web development easier.

Database/Web Design

The release 5 Domino Designer is a powerful tool that you can use to create compelling Web sites. With the Designer, you can create Notes databases that can be used with either Notes clients or with Web browsers. In addition, because Notes and Domino have an open architecture, you can use other third-party tools with Notes and Domino. For example, Domino uses standardized formats for text and graphics. You can use HTML for text and you can create it or import it from another tool. You can also use GIF or JPEG formats for graphics. Although previous releases would do graphic conversions on GIF or JPEG, release 5 stores, serves, and displays the formats natively which dramatically improves performance. All these formats are standardized and commonly available with other tools.

The power of using the Notes/Domino combination is not just in the Web page and design tools, however. The real power of using Notes as a development platform comes when you leverage its other strengths in groupware. For example, you can use Notes workflow capabilities to route Web pages for approval before they are published to the Web. You could use the Domino replication feature to do Web page development in multiple, separate geographical locations.

Domino replication allows you to have multiple copies of a database located on different servers. Frequently these servers are geographically dispersed. Domino replication automatically synchronizes the contents of these separate databases.

With Domino replication, you could have Japanese language Web pages designed in Japan for their local market, French pages designed in France, and English language pages designed in multiple sites in the United States. All these different locations could work on a common company Web site database or set of databases. These databases could be replicated so everyone has access to the same information. You could also use this feature to provide mirror sites and Web site backup.

With a typical Web server, the Web pages are organized by directories within the file system on a single server. It is easy to see how storing your Web site in databases and being able to replicate these databases gives Domino a powerful advantage over other approaches. It is important not only to quickly get your Web site operational, but to manage the site by managing the processes involved. You can manage not only the creation process, but the ongoing update and maintenance process as well.

Programming Tools for Notes and Domino

Notes and Domino have many programmability tools. These tools consist of several levels:

- Pages, forms, buttons, and other user interface elements can be programmed to handle user events. These events can be handled with the Lotus formula language, LotusScript, JavaScript, or Java.
- Web pages can use JavaScript and Java for Applets.
- Agents, which are small programs, can be written in formula language, LotusScript, or Java. They can be triggered automatically when certain events occur or they can be run under user control.
- You can use script libraries, which are libraries of program code written in either LotusScript or Java.
- You can use LotusScript Extensions (LSXs) to enhance LotusScript. Lotus and other third parties have written LSXs and they typically provide specialized functions such as database access.
- There are APIs in C, C++, and Java to write your own customized code to access Domino databases. Your applications can run within the Notes environment or as standalone applications. You can also use the APIs to write your own LSXs.

You can choose any or all of these techniques to program your application. The tools range in complexity and power so that simple tasks can be performed by nonprogrammers, while complex data access programs can be written by programming experts. There is usually a tool to fit your need.

The Domino Object Model

The Domino Object Model is both a conceptual model and a set of programs. The conceptual model provides the framework for database access from programming languages such as LotusScript, Java, and C++. The conceptual model is the same for each programming language, but the syntax for using it is somewhat different for each environment.

At its core, the Lotus programs to manipulate the database are the same for all the programming languages. Lotus provides a set of interfaces, one for each language, that allows the language to access the core functions. For example, although LotusScript and Java provide two very different programming languages, the Domino functionality is provided by common code. The access to the common code is unique to each language.

In release 5, Lotus has also added support for Common Object Request Broker Architecture (CORBA) and Internet Inter-ORB Protocol (IIOP) . Although the first sounds like a snake and the second something out of Star Trek, they are actually pretty important. Before your eyes glaze over from the acronyms, I'll try to explain them in a couple of sentences. CORBA is simply an industry standard architecture for communication between client programs and server programs. IIOP is a specific implementation for communication that can be used over the Internet or TCP/IP.

Stated even more simply, this support allows you to write an application that will run on a Web browser and access Domino databases. You might think this should be easy, but remember, Web browsers typically don't know anything about Notes or Domino, so being able to access Domino databases from the Web browser in a client machine requires quite a bit of elegance and class (I couldn't resist an object-oriented reference).

Domino Administration Client

Prior to release 5, Domino administration was mainly achieved by editing documents in the Domino Public Address Book. With release 5, Lotus has enhanced the administration with an easy-to-use interface.

There are really several generic kinds of tasks involved with system administration, as listed in the following:

- Initial installation and configuration of the Domino software.
- Ongoing management of server hardware. Adding and changing communication lines, memory, disks, and connectivity parameters.
- Ongoing management of users. Adding, deleting, and changing user IDs.
- Ongoing management of databases. Making sure that access control lists (ACLs) are correct and database security is maintained.
- Real-time monitoring of server status. Making sure that the various Domino services such as Web serving, email routing, and database replication are up and running.

Of course, if you are a system administrator, you know that there are many more parts of your job. With Domino release 5, the administration user interface has been greatly enhanced to make many parts of your job easier. For example, to manage people, groups, and mail-in databases, the user interface looks a lot like the Microsoft Explorer, as shown in Figure 1.6.

In addition to managing users, you can now access the Domino directories (previously known as address books) to manage databases. You can even set the access control lists for multiple databases at once, all through an easy interface shown in Figure 1.7.

The Server section of the administration client allows you to see real-time status of your servers and to monitor and review server statistics. You can see who is logged on, send broadcast messages, and perform a variety of other useful functions, as shown in Figure 1.8.

Domino Administration Client | 23

Figure 1.6
You can now manage people and groups with an Explorer-like interface.

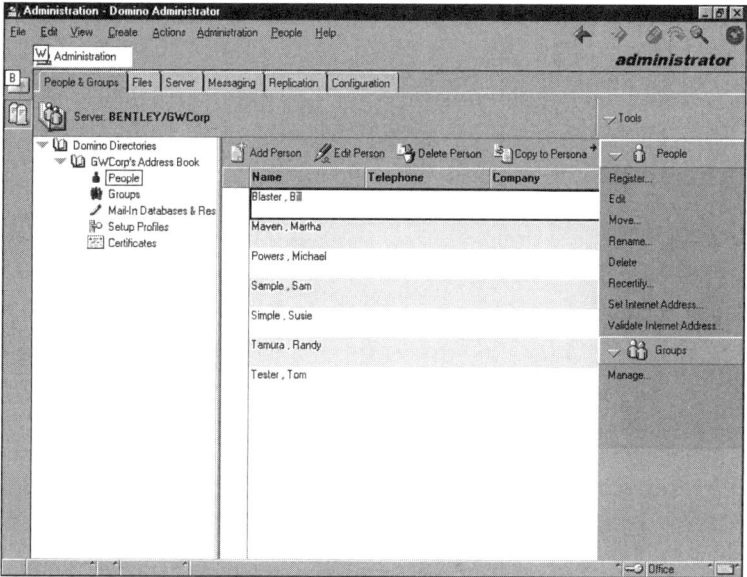

Figure 1.7
You can now change the ACLs for several databases at once.

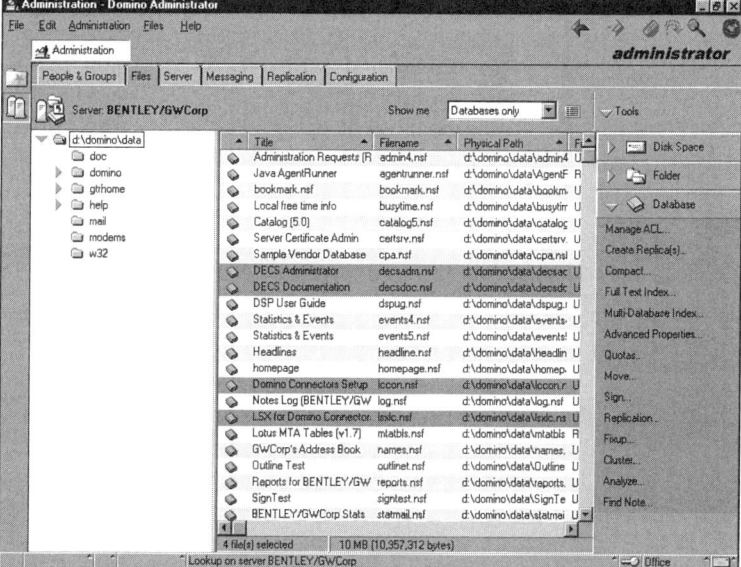

Figure 1.8
You can now monitor your servers in real-time from the administration client.

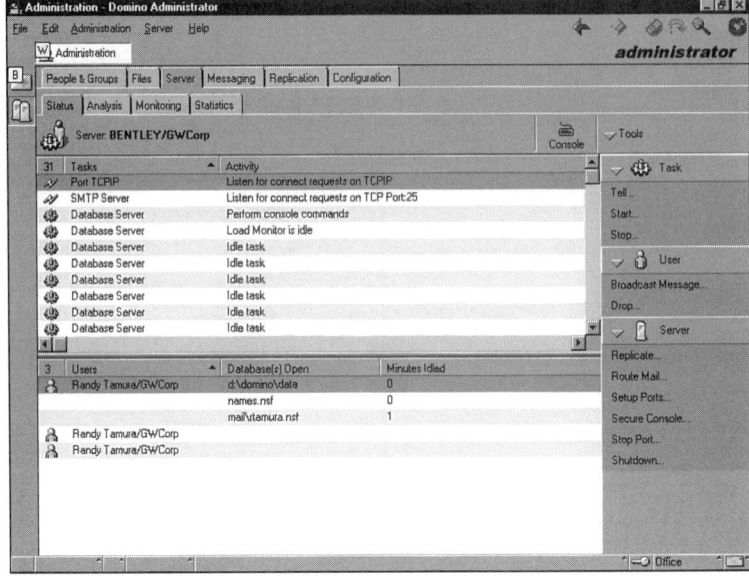

The Messaging and Replication tabs provide a variety of new features that will be covered in depth in Chapters 39, "Administering Electronic Mail," and 40, "Replication and Its Administration."

The configuration section allows easy access to the information for each server. The server document now consists of multiple tabs, making it easier to find specific settings. See Figure 1.9 for an example of just one aspect of the configuration.

Figure 1.9
All configuration information is centrally located and easily accessible.

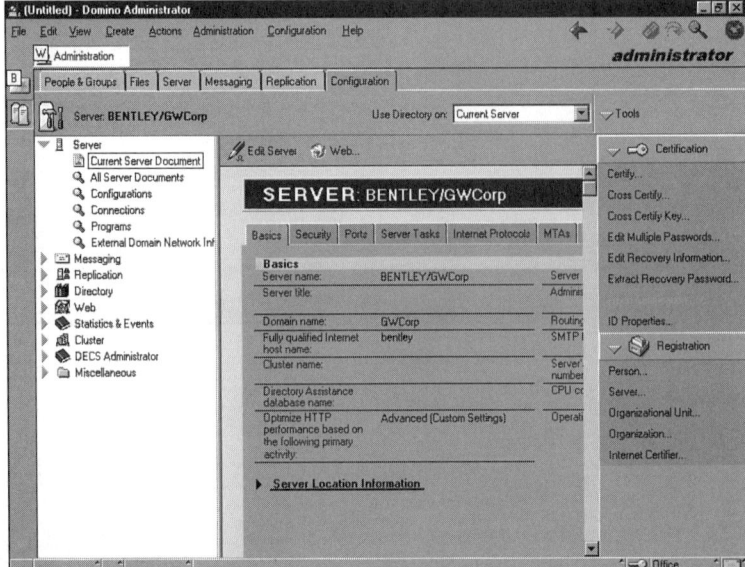

From Here...

In this chapter, I have provided an overview of what Notes and Domino can do for you. You can learn more about specific topics in the following chapters and parts:

- Chapter 2, "What's New in Release 5.0 of Notes and Domino," covers the new features in the Notes client as well as the Domino server. This will be interesting if you are upgrading from a previous release of Notes and Domino.

- Part II, "Using the Lotus Notes R5 Client," provides you with fundamental information on using Notes R5. This part covers important topics such as the new user interface, email, working with the Domino Directories (formerly Name and Address Books), Calendaring and Scheduling, Sametime collaboration, and using Mobile features of Notes.

- Part III, "Introducing Domino Designer R5," provides you the basics for developing Notes and Domino applications.

- Part IV, "Using LotusScript, Java, and JavaScript," gives you detailed programming language information. It covers object-oriented programming and how to use the Domino Object Model with LotusScript, Java, and JavaScript.

- Part V, "Developing Internet Sites with Domino," shows you how to build your own Web site using Domino and covers some of the tools you can use to integrate Domino with your legacy systems.

- Part VI, "Installing and Configuring the Domino Servers," covers the initial installation and configuration of your Domino server as well as information about Domino and Internet security.

- Part VII, "Administering the Domino Servers," covers ongoing administration topics for Domino. It includes information on setting up users, groups, email, databases, and more.

- Part VIII, "Advanced Domino Administration," gives you specialized information about topics such as performance and capacity planning, upgrading from other email systems, and integration with phones, fax, and image.

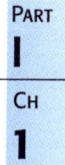

CHAPTER 2

WHAT'S NEW IN RELEASE 5.0 OF NOTES AND DOMINO?

Lotus executives have claimed that release 5.0 of Notes and Domino is the most important release since 1.0. It is hard sometimes to distinguish hype and hyperbole from the real situation though. What makes release 5 so important and are there really a lot of changes? In short, the answer is that Lotus is changing Notes and Domino to become more and more Internet savvy, to make it more powerful, more user-friendly, and to endow it with superhuman strength. Okay, so there was a little hyperbole there. But yes, there are a lot of changes.

The changes in release 5 permeate the product and include new features in the Notes client, the Domino Designer client, the Domino Administrator client, and the Domino server itself. I'll cover highlights in each of these areas in this chapter.

In this chapter I'll assume you are at least familiar with Notes and Domino terminology, because I don't describe concepts such as forms, documents, views, and so forth here. If you're not familiar with these terms, don't worry because they are covered elsewhere in this book. This chapter is mainly meant for users familiar with a current version of Notes and Domino and summarizes the enhancements of release 5.

Notes Client

From a high-level perspective, probably the most important, fundamental change in the Notes client is that Lotus is moving toward a model that separates the client from the Domino server. Beginning with release 5, you can actually purchase and use the Notes client without a Domino server. In addition, the Domino server can be used with Web browsers and you don't need to purchase the Notes client at all.

Lotus achieves this goal because it uses standards-based protocols for all of its communication and infrastructure. Whereas before Notes relied on the proprietary RPC (remote procedure call) mechanism, the current release supports HTTP, IIOP, NNTP, and other Internet protocols, as well as Java and CORBA. If you don't understand all the terms and abbreviations at this point, don't worry. I'll cover what you need to know elsewhere in this book. The point is, because of Lotus's standards-based approach, it is becoming feasible to separate the Notes client and the Domino server.

The Welcome Page

Probably the most visible change in Notes R5 is the client user interface. Lotus has provided a new, Web-based model for its client. It is both familiar and new at the same time. You can customize the new user interface, providing you with the set of tools you find the most useful in your own work. You can even revert the interface to the old, familiar release 4 workspace layout if you prefer. In Figure 2.1 you can see the AOL Headlines welcome page. This page contains customizable news and information, downloaded from the Internet. It can contain news stories, sports and entertainment information, stock quotes, and business news, along with the local weather. This information is made possible by the collaboration of AOL and Lotus.

Notes Client

Figure 2.1
The My News welcome page provides email, a calendar, and news.

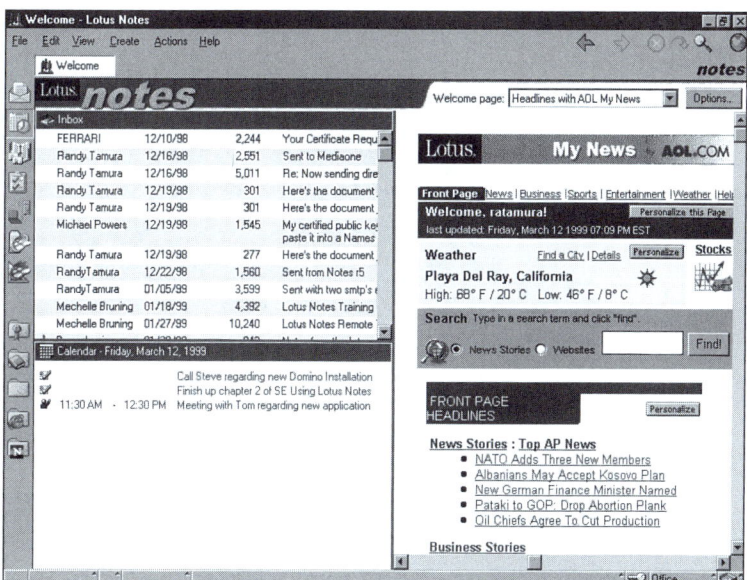

The welcome page serves as your new home base when you use the release 5 interface. You can customize it to include several panes of information. Within each page you can include Web pages, your email, your calendar, and specific Domino databases that you use every day. The ability to customize your welcome page gives you the freedom to improve your productivity.

In Figure 2.2 you can see the familiar workspace with a second window showing you the Domino directory, formerly known as the Public Name and Address Book.

Administrators with large user populations might want to provide defaults using the old workspace instead of the new Web interface. This allows an easy transition to release 5 and allows training to occur over a longer period of time. After users have been trained, they can use all the features that the new client interface provides.

By default, the client opens up each new document or view in a separate window, and adds a task button in the area just below the SmartIcons. You can easily navigate to one of these windows by clicking on its task button. You can also close the window by clicking the "X" that appears to the right of the window name when you move your mouse to the task button.

Email, Calendaring, Contacts, and Todo list

The main four application areas of email, calendaring, contact list, and todo list are now always easily accessible on the bookmarks bar at the left side of the screen. The first four icons on this bar immediately access these applications, as shown in Figure 2.3.

Figure 2.2
With R5, you can still access the familiar workspace and open multiple windows.

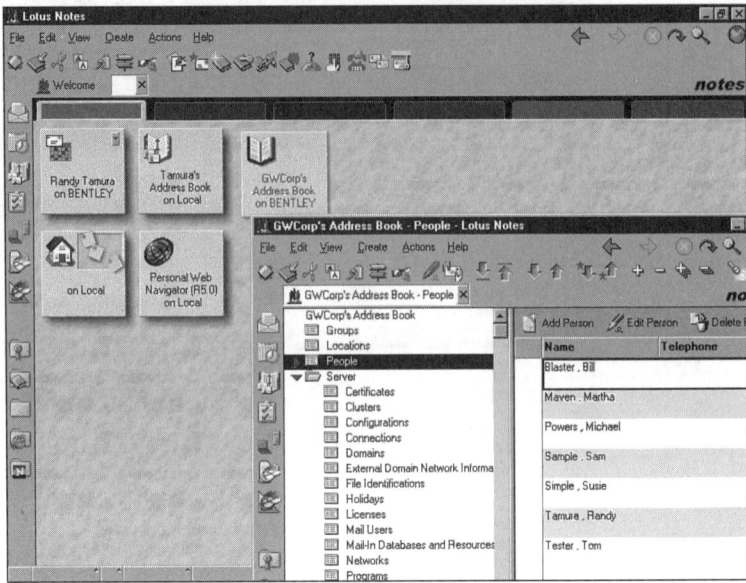

Figure 2.3
With the new R5 client you can have drop-down actions.

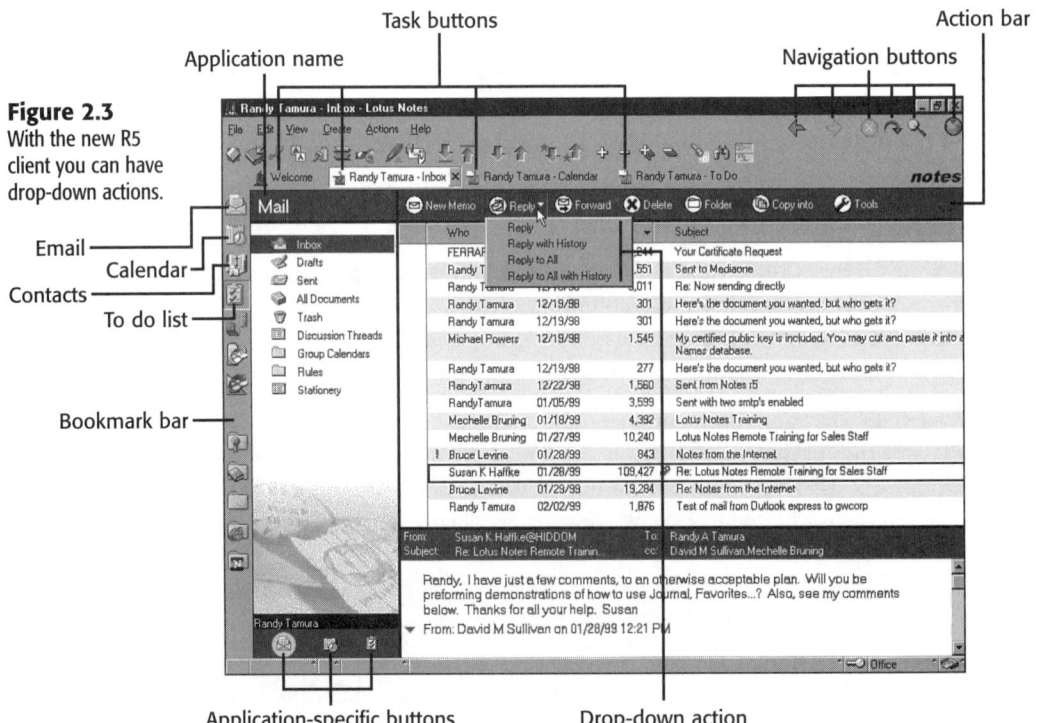

As you can see from Figure 2.3, the email client is familiar, but has been improved in many small ways. Now, all the templates for the Lotus applications have a common look and feel. The action bar line typically has a background color that spans across the window. The upper-left corner displays the application name and the window typically consists of several panes, with the left pane used for navigation. At the lower-left there might be optional, extra buttons for navigation within the application.

Drop-down actions are a new feature with release 5. You can now specify extra options for your actions and group related actions under a single action button rather than using several action buttons for related activities.

Although it is not a new feature, the ability to use non-Domino servers for email has been enhanced. You can now specify multiple accounts and use the Notes client to access your Internet mail using POP3 or IMAP. The same inbox can be used to access your Domino server, so you can have multiple email sources accessible via a single inbox.

Bookmarks

Bookmarks allow you to organize your data and return to frequently used databases, views, documents, or URLs. By using bookmarks, you can save your place so you can return later. The Notes concept of bookmarks is similar to bookmarks within Web browsers. They are also sometimes called favorites.

In Figure 2.4 you can see one of my groups of bookmarks. You can drag and drop bookmarks to be saved. Bookmarks take the place of the Notes workspace in previous releases of Notes and Domino but are more powerful. You can only store databases in your workspace, but with bookmarks you can save views, documents, URLs, or databases. This gives you the flexibility to return directly to the information you want to work with.

The bookmarks area can expand (as shown in Figure 2.4), or automatically contract to take up less space on your screen. If you prefer to leave the bookmarks pane open all the time, you can do that, too.

In addition to the ability to create your own bookmarks, the Notes client will also import both your Netscape Navigator bookmarks and Internet Explorer favorites. This allows you to easily access these links as well.

32 CHAPTER 2 WHAT'S NEW IN RELEASE 5.0 OF NOTES AND DOMINO?

Figure 2.4
Bookmarks can store Web pages, views, documents, or databases.

Replicator
Administrator
Designer
Internet Explorer Favorites

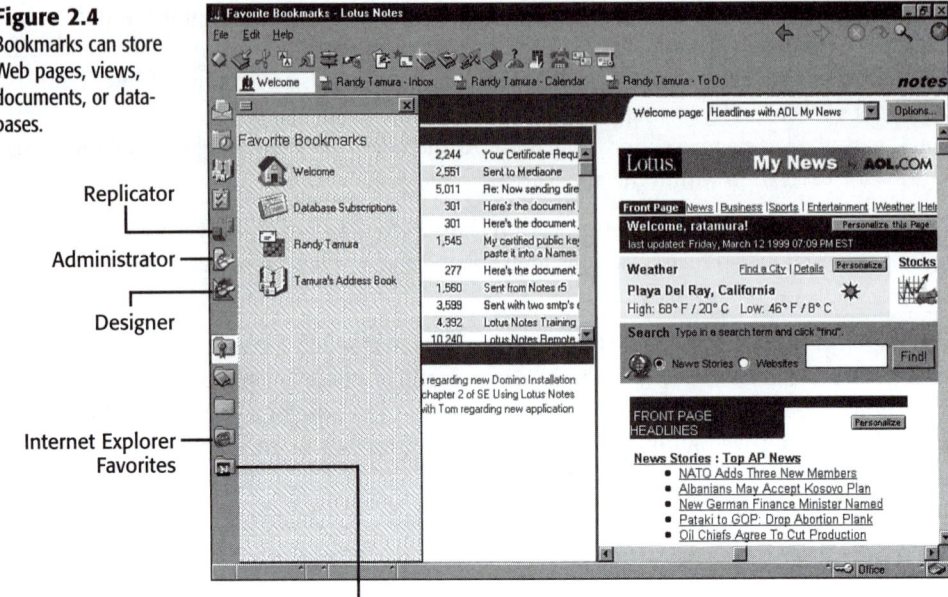

Netscape Navigator Bookmarks

THE DOMINO DESIGNER CLIENT

While the Notes client now presents a much prettier face, the Domino Designer client provides the brains to make it work. The Designer client has now been completely split from the Notes client and now provides a different user interface that has been optimized for designers rather than everyday Notes users.

There are two types of enhancements provided by release 5. The first is the Designer client itself with its new features, and the second is the impressive array of new design elements that are available to you as a designer. In the second category, there are outlines, pages, framesets, image libraries, and JavaScript and Java support, among many other features. In Figure 2.5 you can see an example of the new Designer client.

OUTLINES, PAGES, AND FRAMESETS

Outlines are a new type of navigational element. When outlines are embedded on a form or page, a user can click one of the entries and link to another document, view, database, or URL. In a typical Web page, you see this type of navigational element along the left side, top, or bottom of the page.

THE DOMINO DESIGNER CLIENT | 33

Figure 2.5
There are many new design elements and features in the new Domino Designer.

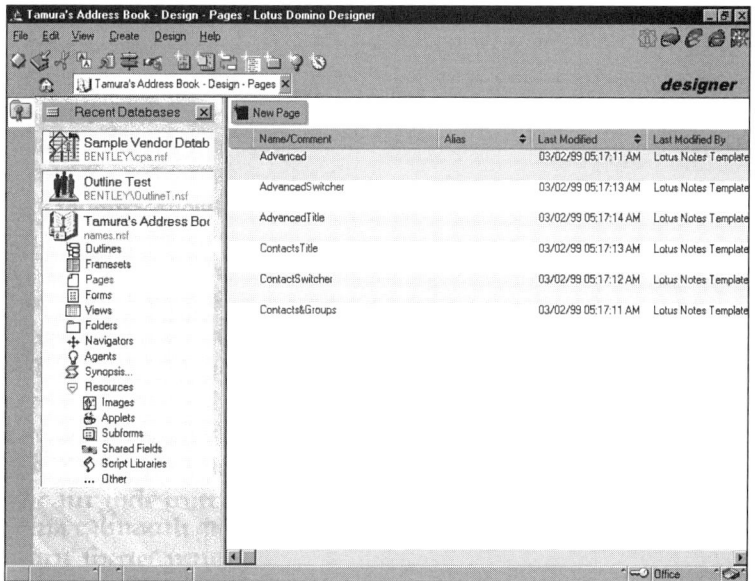

With outlines, you specify the logical linkage of your Web site. You can include more than one outline on a page or form, and in fact you can include the same outline twice. You might want to do this, for example, if you want to render the outline once horizontally, and once vertically.

In Figure 2.6 you can see the outline designer.

Figure 2.6
With the outline editor you can design your Web site navigation.

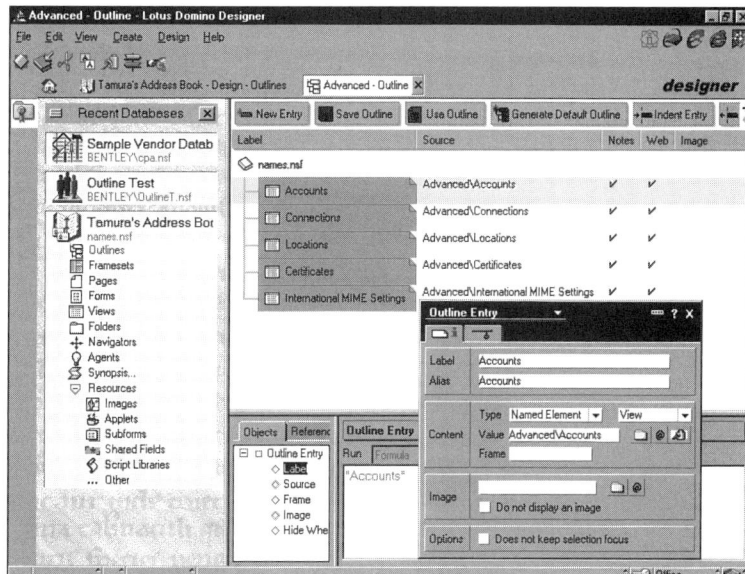

Each outline entry has many attributes to control its content and linkage. Outline entries can link to other named elements within the database or externally via URLs.

Pages are another new design element in release 5 of Notes and Domino. They are actually a kind of cross between a Domino form and a document. Like a document, a page typically contains unique content. In other words, in a Web page context, each page is separate and distinct from other pages. For unique content page, you create a separate Domino page.

Like forms, pages can contain other design elements such as graphics and text. A big difference from forms, however, is that pages cannot contain Domino fields. Pages work well when you need more-or-less static content. For example, in Figure 2.7 you can see the home page for Boy Scout Troop 764. As you can tell, this page really does not need input fields. The page contains hotspots that can be clicked by a user.

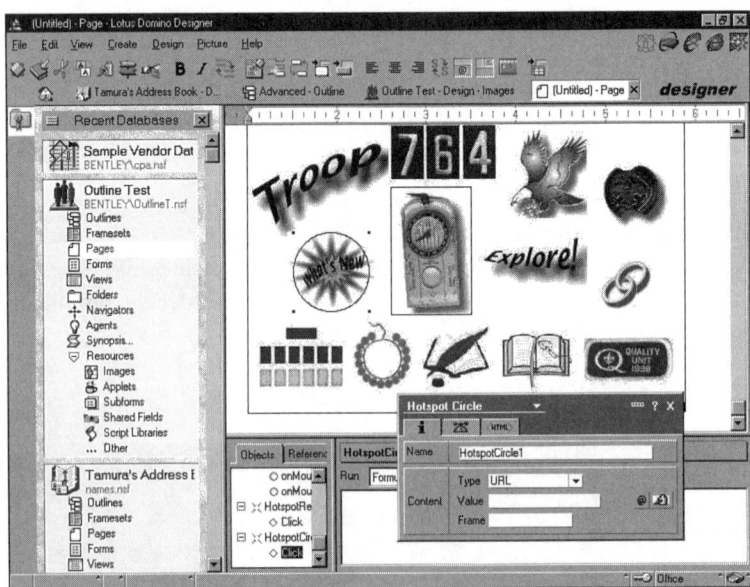

Figure 2.7
A home page might be a typical use for a page design element.

Note that pages are not full-text indexed, so if you have content that should be indexed, you should use the traditional Domino forms and documents.

Pages are very useful with both outlines and framesets. Framesets allow you to divide a user's window into multiple panes, with different content in each pane. Typically, you have at least one navigational pane and at least one content pane. Separating the navigation from the content improves the user experience because the entire context of the screen is not changing with each change of page.

In Figure 2.8 you see the frameset designer and an example of a three-pane frameset. In the main frame is the home page that that I showed you previously.

The Domino Designer Client   35

Figure 2.8
A frameset allows you to separate navigation from content.

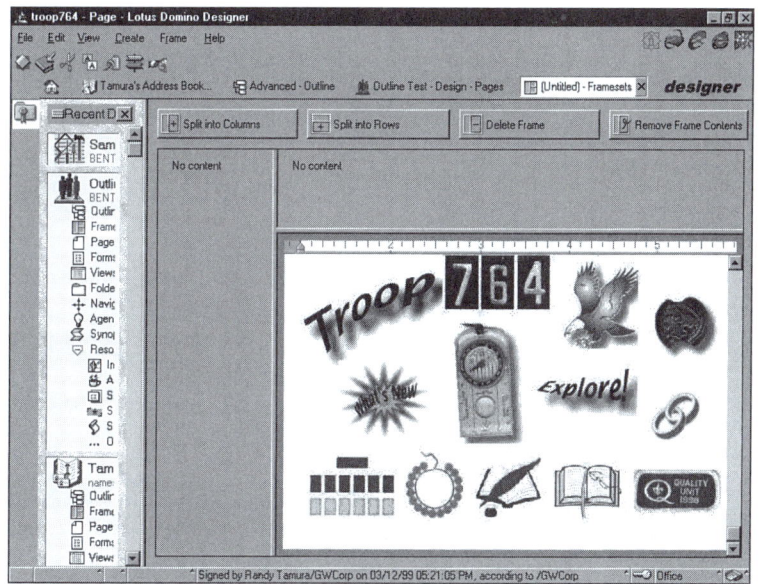

Support for Java, JavaScript, and HTML 4.0

Release 5 greatly improves the support for both Java and JavaScript. Java can now be used for both applets and agents. If you use the CORBA support, you can even access Domino databases via Java applets running in a Web browser. This feature is described in more detail in in the section titled "CORBA and IIOP for the Acronym Impaired" in Chapter 23, "Creating and Using Java Applets and Agents."

As you might know, the JavaScript language is not really related to Java, other than the similarity of its name. JavaScript is a language that can be used to automate or script the actions of a Web browser. With release 5 of Notes and Domino, JavaScript is supported in the Notes client and you can use JavaScript support in the Domino Designer as well.

In Figure 2.9 you can see the list of new JavaScript events, which are the ones with a small circle to the left of the name. JavaScript events begin with on and have names such as onMouseOver or onMouseOut. You can click one of these names and add code to the event in the programmer's pane on the right.

One really cool new feature of the IDE is that when there is code contained in an event handler, the icon to the left of the name becomes filled in. Thus, you can immediately see, without opening them, which events contain code and which ones do not. Notice in Figure 2.9 that the circle to the left of the onClick event is filled in.

Color-coding is now supported within the Integrated Development Environment (IDE) for all languages, including the formula language. The formula language also now displays more descriptive error messages to aid in debugging.

36 Chapter 2 What's New in Release 5.0 of Notes and Domino?

Figure 2.9
JavaScript events are the ones with small circles.

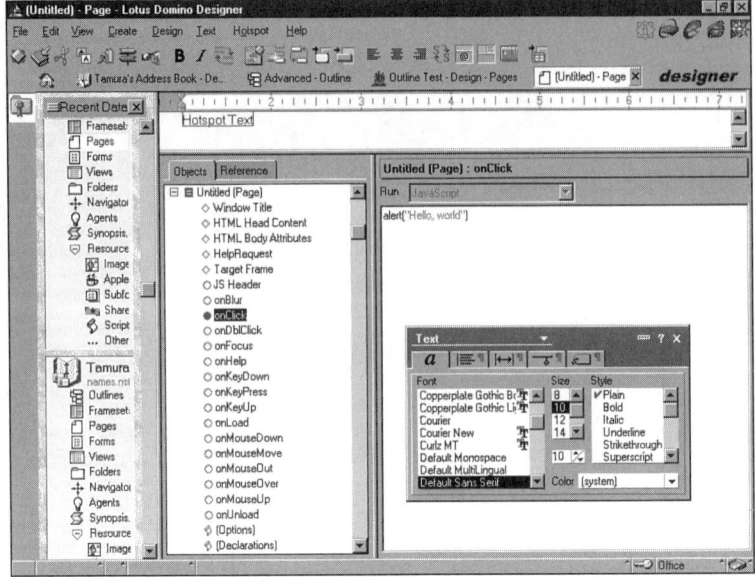

In Figure 2.10 you can see Java within the IDE. You can use the IDE to create Java agents that run on either the Domino Server or Notes client. Although you cannot use the Notes IDE to create Java applets, you can use any other Java IDE such as Symantec Visual Café, IBM Visual Age for Java, or Inprise JBuilder to create your Java applet and import the applet class files into your Domino database.

Figure 2.10
You can create Java agents directly in the Designer IDE.

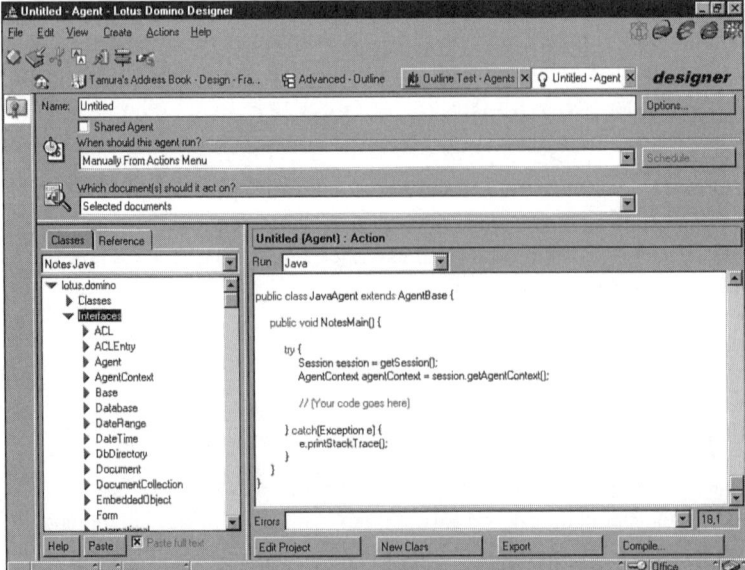

With Notes and Domino R5, you can now create and store HTML directly in documents, pages, and forms in your database. This means that you can create the HTML from within Domino, save it, and have Domino serve the pages just as if they were stored in the file system.

You can also use your favorite HTML authoring tool, save the pages, and import them into Domino. Alternatively, you can save the Web pages to a file directory on your Domino server and have Domino serve them from the file system. Best of all, you can use a combination of all these techniques to leverage other tools and existing systems to gain the most benefit. The HTML support gives you a variety of options to use in the way you like to work.

The Domino Administration Client and Domino Server

The Notes client and Domino Designer are not the only areas that have been greatly enhanced with release 5. The Domino server contains many new features and the administration client gives you the power to manage your resources much more effectively.

Domino Server Architecture

To begin with, the Domino database format has been revised for release 5. It has been redesigned to provide better performance, increased capacities, and more robustness while at the same time providing compatibility with prior releases.

The R5 database now supports transaction logging. Transaction logging has long been a staple of relational database systems. As a matter of fact, Lotus enlisted the help of some of the leading database authorities at IBM to help redesign the Domino database. By using transaction logging, you can write sequentially to a file rather than needing to update various parts of the database randomly. This sequential access greatly improves performance.

The addition of transaction logging support allows features such as online database backup. In the past, file locking sometimes prevented a database to be backed up while Domino was running. By using the logs, you can do incremental backup. Robustness is improved because the logs can be used to quickly restore transactions to a database after a system failure.

The internal format of the database has been improved to reduce the number of times that the system must perform I/O on the disk. Also, there are now additional advanced options that a database designer can employ to further improve database performance. There have been many internal performance improvements in areas including compression, paging, disk I/O, and memory utilization.

Whereas in Domino 4.x you could have databases up to 4GB, with release 5 there is no specific theoretical limit to the database size. There are, of course, always practical limits and Lotus has certified databases up to 64GB. Most companies really won't have a need for databases that large, but it's nice to know that you have that capacity if you need it.

For mission critical applications, Lotus has improved cluster support, which allows several Domino machines to act in concert. This feature can do load balancing as well as failover, which improves reliability. In addition, you can use the Internet Cluster Manager (ICM) for clustering of Web (HTTP) requests. The ICM routes Web requests among the servers for high availability and load balancing.

For messaging, Domino R5 now uses Simple Mail Transfer Protocol (SMTP) —one of the major Internet standards—as its native protocol. This means that there is no protocol conversion required to communicate within your intranet or externally via the Internet.

Domino Server Administration

Figure 2.11 shows a snapshot of the administration client. The screen is broken up into three parts. The left frame is used to select the main area of interest. The middle frame displays information that has been selected. On the right is a tools frame that contains additional useful tools.

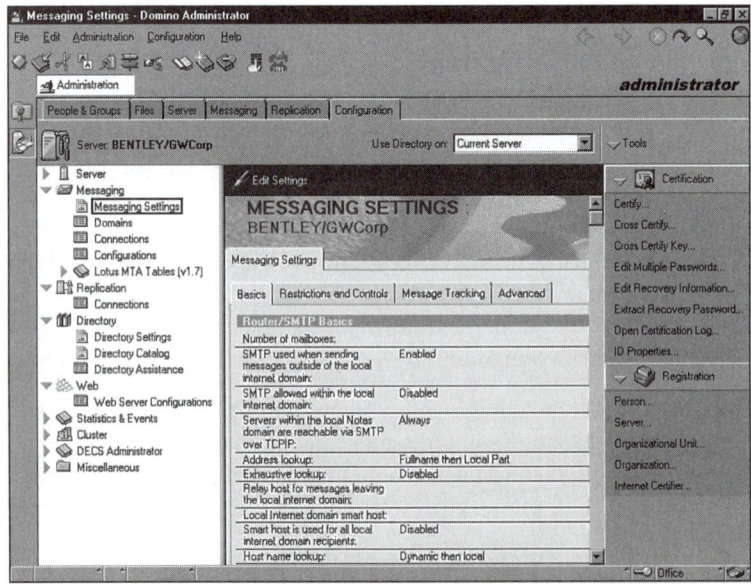

Figure 2.11
The administration client makes configuration easy.

There are six major tabs in the administration client. These tabs allow you to configure your server, add and delete users, and manipulate databases. In addition, the administration client now allows you to monitor the status of a server. See Figure 2.12.

The Domino Administration Client and Domino Server   39

Figure 2.12
Monitor the status of server tasks and easily tell them what to do.

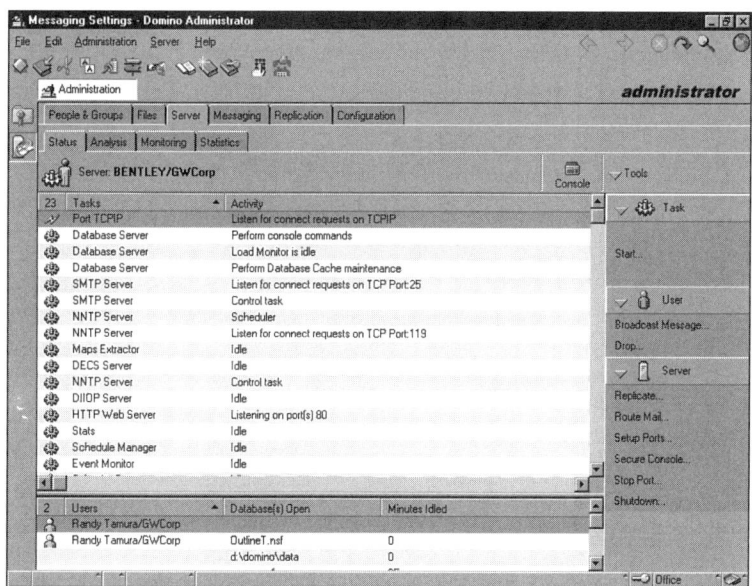

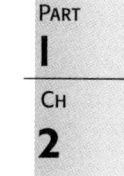

The server also keeps statistics on its various operating parameters. With the administration client you can see statistics for agents, databases, calendaring, disk and memory utilization, and much more. See Figure 2.13.

Figure 2.13
Domino keeps statistics that you can query.

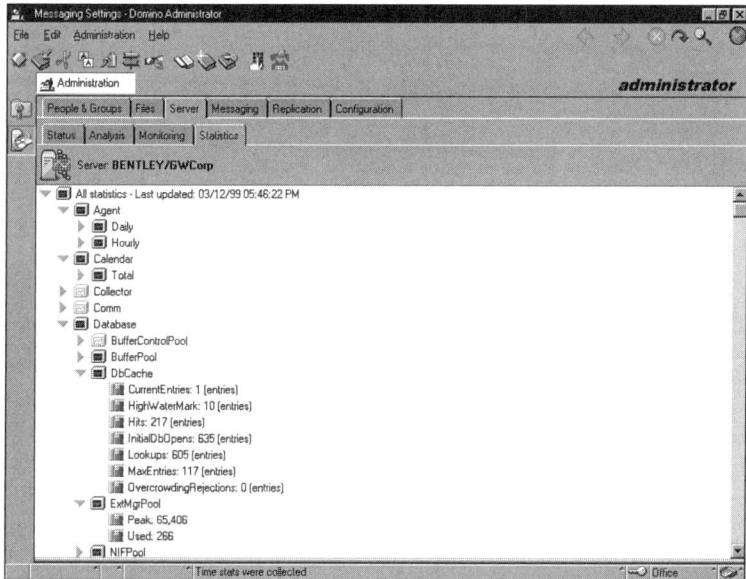

One of the main tasks a Domino administrator must perform is managing mail. Within the messaging tab, you can monitor messaging (see Figure 2.14), examine your mail routing topology, review reports, and even track mail messages that have already been sent.

Figure 2.14
Monitor the number of dead and waiting messages.

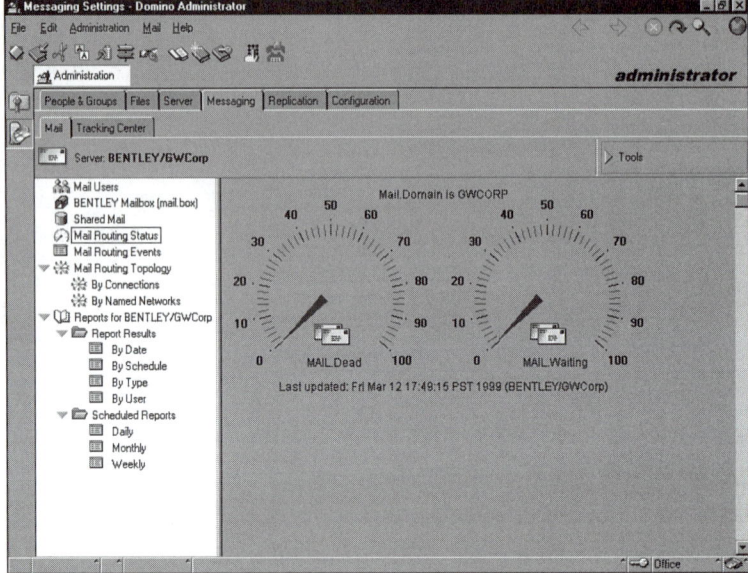

As you can tell, the figures I have shown you touch on only a small portion of the new enhancements within the Domino administrator client. In addition you can manage the ACLs for multiple databases at once, drag-and-drop databases to request replication, and much, much more.

The new Domino administrator client is a quantum leap in ease of use and functionality for administrators. As you work with the release 5 administrator client, you will wonder how you were able to get along before without all the features that are now available.

FROM HERE...

In this chapter, I have provided you an overview of the new features of Notes and Domino. You can learn more about specific topics in the following parts:

- Part II, "Using the Lotus Notes R5 Client," provides you with fundamental information on using Notes R5. This part covers important topics such as the new user interface, electronic mail (email), Domino Directories (formerly Name and Address Books), Calendaring and Scheduling, Sametime collaboration, and the Mobile features of Notes.

- Part III, "Introducing Domino Designer R5," provides you the basics for developing Notes and Domino applications. It focuses on the new design elements of R5.
- Part IV, "Using LotusScript, Java, and JavaScript," gives you detailed programming language information. It covers object-oriented programming and how to use the Domino Object Model with LotusScript, Java, and JavaScript.
- Part V, "Developing Internet Sites with Domino," shows you how to build your own Web site using Domino and covers some of the tools you can use to integrate Domino with your legacy systems.
- Part VI, "Installing and Configuring the Domino Servers," covers the initial installation and configuration of your Domino server as well as information about Domino and Internet security.
- Part VII, "Administering the Domino Servers," covers ongoing administration topics for Domino. It includes information on setting up users, groups, email, databases, and more.
- Part VIII, "Advanced Domino Administration," gives you specialized information about topics such as performance and capacity planning; upgrading from other email systems; and integration with phones, fax, and image.

PART II

Using the Lotus Notes R5 Client

- **3** Installing and Customizing the Notes Client
- **4** The Notes User Interface and the Standard Databases
- **5** Using Electronic Mail
- **6** Working with Text and Documents
- **7** Contact Management with the Personal and Public Directories
- **8** Getting Organized with the Calendaring and Scheduling Features
- **9** Using Sametime Collaboration
- **10** Using Mobile Features from Home or on the Road
- **11** Using the Notes Client on the Internet

CHAPTER 3

INSTALLING AND CUSTOMIZING THE NOTES CLIENT

You must install one of the Notes clients before you can use it. There are three types of clients you can install: the standard Notes client, the Domino Designer client, and the Domino Administrator client. As a user, you can fulfill one or more of these roles for your organization. You can install a single client or all three at once.

Steps to Install the Notes Client

The following installation procedure assumes that your user ID has already been set up by the Domino server administrator. It is much easier to install the software on your computer if your user ID has already been added to your Domino server. The process of adding a user to the Domino system is described in Chapter 38, "Administering Users, Groups, and Certification." When the administrator sets up your user ID, an ID file is created. That ID file is either stored in the Domino public directory for your use in the steps that follow, or given to you on a floppy disk. You need to know how to access your ID file, your user ID, and your password, so make sure you know which method your organization uses before you embark on the following steps. Otherwise, you'll get halfway through these steps and get stuck. Finally, before you start you must also know the fully distinguished name of your Domino server. If you don't know it, ask your system administrator. It will be a name such as Server1/LA/Acme.

When you know how you'll access your ID file, perform the following steps:

1. Invoke `Setup.exe` from the CD-ROM or from your network. The setup program for Notes release 5 (on Win32—Windows 95, 98, or NT) uses InstallShield.
2. You then see the Welcome dialog box. Click Next.
3. You then see the license agreement box. Make sure to read the license agreement. Assuming you agree with it, click Yes.
4. The Name and Company Name box then appears. Fill in the dialog box with your name and company name. You should normally leave the Shared Installation check box empty. This option allows system administrators to install a single copy of the program files on a network server that will be shared by multiple users. Click Next.
5. A dialog box to enter directories (Folders) for program and data will then appear. See Figure 3.1. To change either of the directories, click browse and find the directory or type it in. Normally you should keep the program and data directories separate. Doing this makes subsequent maintenance easier. Click OK after you have changed the directory. When finished specifying the directories, click Next.
6. Select client type (see Figure 3.2).

Figure 3.1
The Destination Folder dialog box allows you to choose where the client programs and data are installed.

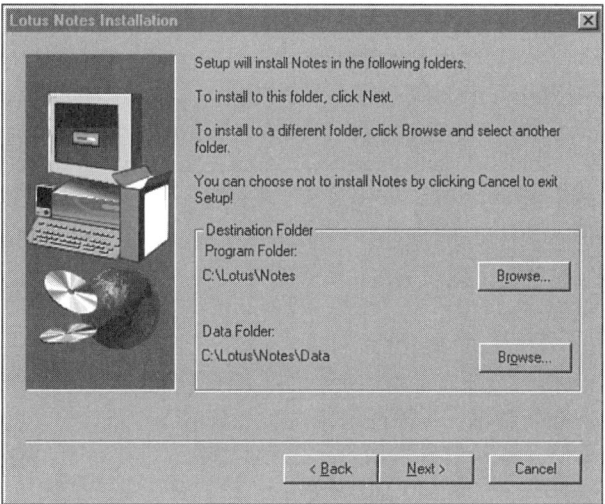

Figure 3.2
The client type selection dialog box allows you to choose the type of client to be installed.

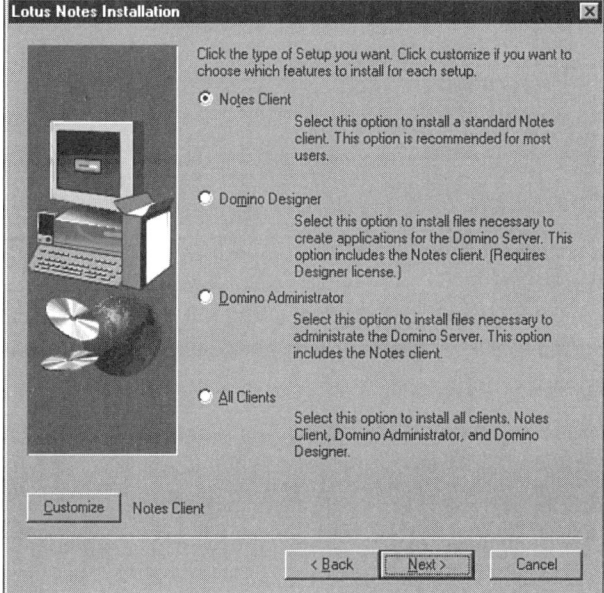

The following is a list of the available types:

- Notes Client—Recommended for most users. Installation with the most common options.
- Domino Designer—Allows design of Domino applications and databases.

- Domino Administrator—Allows remote administration of the Domino server.
- All Clients—Installs the standard Notes client, Domino Designer, and Domino Administrator.
- Customize—Click this button to select custom installation options. You can selectively include or exclude optional features. Figure 3.3 shows the top-level dialog box for customization. Several of the options shown can be further customized. Select the item you want to customize and click the Change button. You will be shown a separate dialog box you can use to choose suboptions within the component you selected.

Figure 3.3
The Lotus Notes Installation dialog box can be used to customize the components you install.

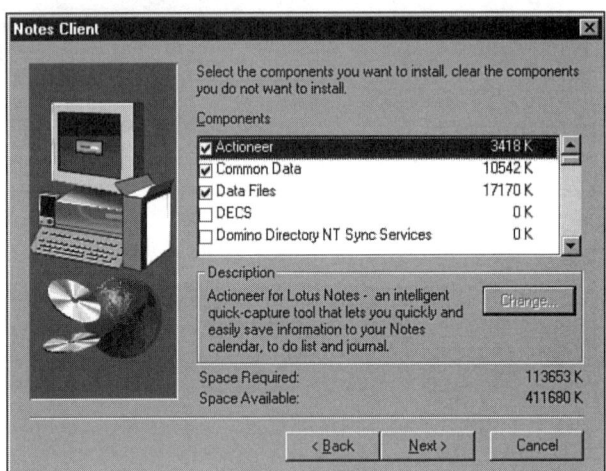

7. Choose a folder for the client program icons. You can use the default folder, pick another existing folder, or type a new name to create a new program folder.
8. Click Next when you are ready to start copying.
9. After the install program has copied the Notes program files, you are requested to register your program. Fill out the forms and submit your registration.
10. Click Finish to finish the first part of the installation.
11. Select the Notes client from your operating system and run it. In Win32 (Windows 95, 98, NT), you can do this by clicking the Start button, then select Programs and the folder you chose previously (the default is Lotus Applications), and finally choose the Lotus Notes client item.
12. You see a splash screen and then the Lotus Notes Client Configuration wizard this first time you run the client. See Figure 3.4. Remember I told you to find out this information before you started. Well, here is where you need to know how you are accessing your server.

Figure 3.4
The Notes Client Configuration Wizard leads you through the installation process.

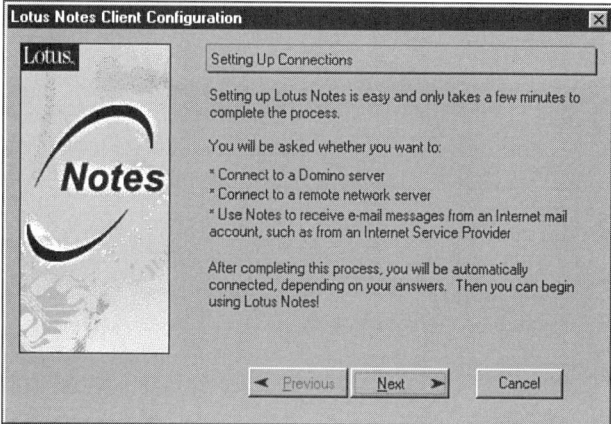

13. The first question you must answer is whether you want to connect to a Domino server. Normally you will be connecting to a Domino server. Answer the question and click Next.

14. Assuming you have indicated that you will connect to a Domino server, the next question asks you how you want to connect to the server. See Figure 3.5.

Figure 3.5
You can connect to the Domino server either locally (LAN) or remotely via a phone.

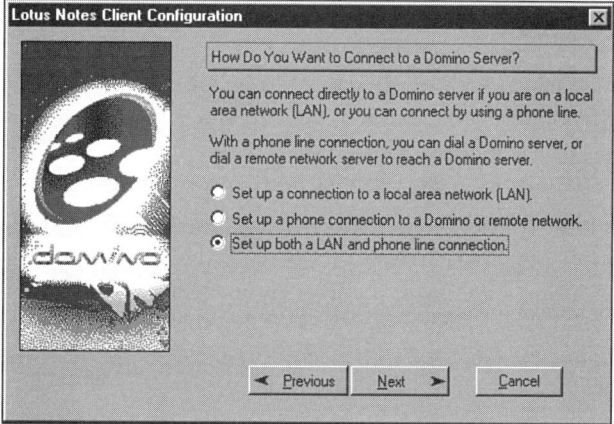

Choose one of the options:

- Set Up a Connection to a Local Area Network (LAN)—This is the most common option for office environments. Choose this option if you are connected to an office local area network.

- **Set Up a Phone Connection to a Domino or Remote Network**—Use this option for two different cases:
  - Use this if your Domino server has modems attached and you will dial via phone directly from a remote location to the Domino Server. This is one possible option for laptop computers. This option is easy and relatively inexpensive to implement, but it can incur expensive phone charges.
  - Use this if you have a modem but you will not be dialing directly to your Domino server. You typically choose this option if you are dialing into an Internet service provider (ISP). In this case, your Domino server must be attached to the Internet and you will access Domino via the ISP and the Internet. This is more costly to set up and maintain, but it can significantly save on phone expenses if you need frequent long-distance calls. Typically this method allows remote users to dial a local phone number to gain Internet access.
- Set up both a LAN and phone line connection. Use this option to set up LAN and phone connections.

15. You are now asked for your Domino server name. Enter a fully distinguished name such as Server1/LA/Acme.
16. You now need to identify yourself. Enter either the filename of your user ID file, or your name. If you supplied a user ID file, you must enter the password.
17. Your LAN setup is now complete. If you requested both a LAN and remote (phone) connection, you are now asked whether you want to directly dial a Domino server or dial a remote network server. Typically you will use the remote network server option if you will use an ISP. You can also set up both types. For dialing a Domino server, you must supply phone number information. For a remote network connection, you must supply a Windows remote phonebook entry, along with your user ID and password. You can also set up or modify this feature after Notes has been installed.
18. After your remote phone access is complete, you can optionally set up an Internet mail account. You would use this if you have an Internet mail account with an ISP. In order to set this up, you must know your SMTP (outbound) server name, your POP or IMAP (inbound) server name, your account name, and your password. You can also set up or modify this feature after Notes is installed.
19. Click Finish to complete the installation. The Notes installation process then creates several databases on your machine.

Congratulations. You have installed the Notes client. Your screen should now resemble Figure 3.6.

You are now ready to start using Notes. However, before you start, you might want to customize your new Notes environment with your personal preferences. In later sections, I'll cover some of the ways you can customize the environment.

Figure 3.6
The Lotus Notes default welcome page greets you after installation.

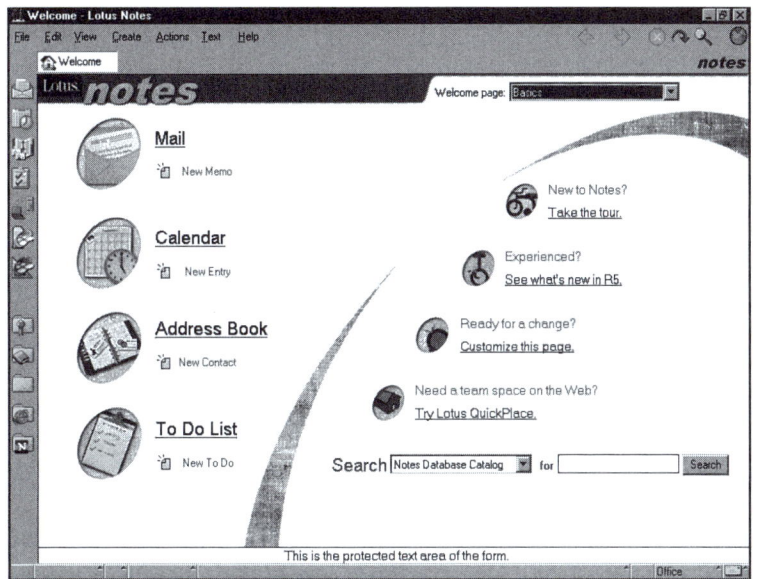

LOGGING ON TO THE NOTES CLIENT

Most computer networking systems today require you to log on in order to be able to access network resources. Typically when you log on you supply a user ID and a password, which are then checked by a server. If you supply a password for the user ID, you are allowed to access whatever resources have been authorized for your use. Although Notes authentication appears similar to the user, it works quite differently.

In Notes, when you supply your password, your identity is authenticated with an ID file. This file can be (and typically is) located on your local computer, not the server. By typing the correct password for an ID file, you are granted rights associated with the ID file. Most users have only a single ID file, but some users (such as administrators) can have several. Each ID file can have different rights associated with it and if you know the correct password, you can use databases and other resources associated with that ID. I'll explain ID files in more detail later in this chapter.

In Figure 3.7 you see the Enter Password dialog box. As you type your password into the dialog box, a random number of *X*s appear in the box. This prevents someone looking over your shoulder from knowing which characters you are typing or even how many characters are in your password. Knowing how many characters are in your password might compromise its security.

Passwords are case sensitive, so if you have trouble logging on, check the Caps Lock key on your keyboard. If the Caps Lock key is inadvertently left on, your capitalized password will not match your real password.

Figure 3.7
A random number of Xs prevents casual observers from knowing how many characters are in your password.

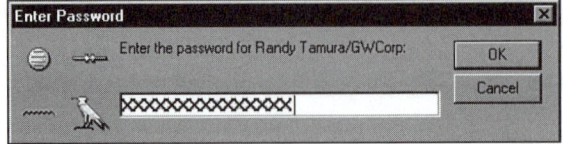

You'll also notice that there are four Egyptian hieroglyphics displayed to the left of input field. Starting with the fifth character you type, these hieroglyphics change with each character. You might be wondering what the heck hieroglyphics has to do with passwords. Do you have to be able to read the Rosetta stone to be able to use Notes?

Well no, the answer, as you might imagine, has to do with security. And, for this particular security measure to work, you need to know what it is for and why it is important. The hieroglyphics are shown on the password screen to prevent spoofing. Spoofing is a technique that a hacker might use to fool you into giving him or her your password. The way it works is that the hacker writes a program that looks and behaves like some other, valid program. In this case, the hacker might try to write a program that resembles the Enter Password dialog box of Notes.

When you come in to the office the one morning, you power up your machine, see a password dialog box, and type your password, and it goes right into the hacker's program. When you have typed your password into the hacker's program it typically saves the password, sends it over the Internet, or does something else that is undesirable.

How can Notes prevent spoofing? You need to know that when you type your password into the password dialog box that it is actually Notes asking for it, not some hacker's program. Here come the hieroglyphics. When you type your password, Notes uses a special algorithm to compute the hieroglyphics that are shown. Every time you type your correct password, the hieroglyphics change each time, with the same sequence of symbols and, in particular, they end with the same four symbols also.

It would be nearly impossible for a hacker to write a program that showed you the same symbols as you typed them in. So, the next time you type your password, watch the hieroglyphics carefully. If you ever find that the symbols are not what you expect or that there are none (probably very unlikely), you might be dealing with a spoofing program. You now know the secret of the Rosetta stone.

Exploring Lotus Notes

When you work with Notes, you typically work with many different databases. In addition, you can also work with the Internet and its millions of Web pages of information. The Notes window allows you to organize all this information so that it makes your work easier. You can see the parts of the Notes window in Figure 3.8.

EXPLORING LOTUS NOTES | 53

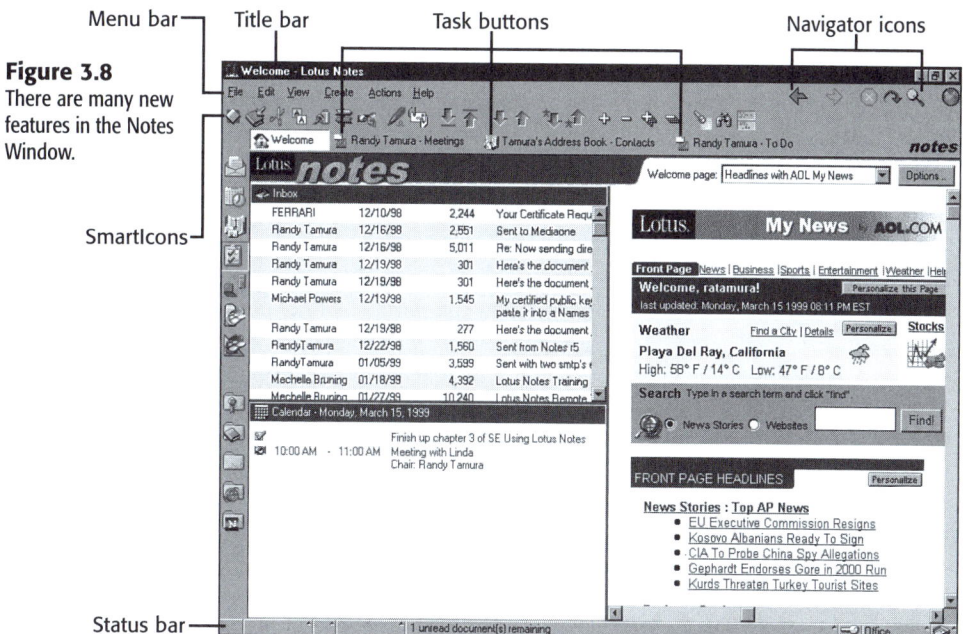

Figure 3.8
There are many new features in the Notes Window.

PART
II

CH
3

THE MENU BAR

In Figure 3.8 you can see the various parts of the Notes window. I've actually shown you an alternative welcome screen. The very top line of the screen contains the Windows title bar. The contents of the title bar change depending on your context. Directly below the title bar are the Windows menu items in the menu bar. You can issue many general-purpose commands from the menus. The menus are context sensitive and also change depending on what you are viewing at the time.

You see the following menu items while you are in the welcome screen (in other contexts the menus are different):

- File—This menu item allows you to open and manipulate databases. It allows you to attach, import, and export files and also contains the Print menu item and Tools item. The Tools menu item contains several useful tools that you will use in Notes. From the File menu you can also find out about a document's attributes by issuing Document Properties.

- Edit—The Edit menu contains the traditional Cut, Copy, Paste, and Undo menu items. You can clear (delete) an object or find its properties. From this menu you can select or deselect all objects within a given context. You can search and replace text or check the spelling of your document. Finally, you can control links and unread marks from this menu.

- View—The View menu allows you to refresh the screen to obtain new information, show the horizontal scrollbar, and control document previewing.

- Create—The Create menu allows you to create mail messages, and (in the Domino Designer) use certain database design elements such as an Agent, Folder, or View.
- Actions—The Actions menu is context sensitive. The actions allowed here depend on the database being viewed. Some typical actions are editing documents, forwarding mail, moving documents to folders, and other kinds of document manipulation.
- Help—The Help menu allows you to get additional help about the Notes client. You can also access the Internet (if your machine has been properly configured). Two special documents are normally contained in each database: the About document and the Using document. The About document describes the purpose of the database, who should use it, and what the database does. The Using document describes how to use the database. The database designer must create these documents, but if they have been created, they are available via the Help menu.

THE NAVIGATION ICONS

The navigation icons are shown in the upper-right corner of the screen. Here are the navigation icons:

- Back—The Back navigation button works similarly to the Back button found in any Web browser. Just to the right of the Back button is an area where you can click to get a drop-down list of previous locations.
- Forward—The Forward button behaves like a Forward button in any Web browser. Just to the right of the Forward button is an area where you can click to get a drop-down list of locations.
- Cancel or Stop—The Cancel button works similarly to the Stop button found in a Web browser. It cancels the current operation. Note that some operations cannot be cancelled in the middle and complete before stopping automatically.
- Refresh—The Refresh button works like a Refresh button in a Web browser. If you are a Notes user, this icon is similar in function to the Refresh button that appears in Views when new documents are available in a view.
- Search—The Search button can be used to search for documents or Web pages containing certain text. You can also use the Search button to look for people on the Web and databases, and to access many of the common Web search engines. There is an area directly to the right of the icon you can click to get a drop-down list of your various search options.
- Open URL—The Open URL icon allows you to type a URL address. When you click this icon, an input area opens up on the line immediately below the icon. A thumbtack also appears which allows you to indicate you would like to keep the URL entry field visible on the screen all the time.

Using SmartIcons

SmartIcons are buttons that can streamline your work and allow you to work faster. Immediately after you install Notes, they are turned off by default. You can easily turn them on or off. They appear just under the Windows menu items and are shortcuts to commonly used operations. Better yet, depending on what kind of work you do, you can customize the icons to show you the operations you perform most frequently. SmartIcon buttons can perform operations that correspond to menu selections or you can supply a custom formula to be executed when the button is clicked.

You can see what a particular SmartIcon will do by moving your mouse cursor over the button without clicking it. You will see a ToolTip description as shown in Figure 3.9.

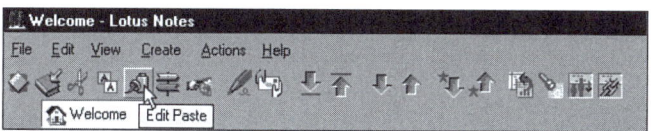

Figure 3.9
The SmartIcons ToolTips shows you the menu command equivalent.

Notes provides about 170 predefined SmartIcons that are associated with common tasks within Notes. Some of these icons work only within a particular context. For example, one SmartIcon changes the currently selected text to Bold. If you are not editing text and do not have text currently highlighted, the SmartIcon does not work.

The SmartIcon bar is divided into two sections. The section on the left by default displays a set of SmartIcons called the Universal set. As its name implies, this set of icons is available in all contexts. You can change the icons that are displayed in the Universal set or you can create your own SmartIcon sets and give them separate names.

The set on the right is the context-sensitive set. This set is managed and displayed automatically by Notes. You cannot change the icons that are displayed in the context-sensitive set. However, you can turn the display of context icons off.

In addition to the predefined icons, you can define a formula macro that executes when you click a custom SmartIcon. With this capability, you have quite a bit of flexibility because your formula macro has virtually the entire power of Notes. With it, you can manipulate text, send messages, and even create new databases.

Customizing a Set of SmartIcons

You can customize the Universal set of SmartIcons, or you can create and customize your own sets. The process is pretty much the same for doing either. To customize a set of SmartIcons, do the following:

1. From the menus, select File, Preferences, SmartIcon Settings to open up the SmartIcons dialog box. See Figure 3.10.

Figure 3.10
The SmartIcon dialog box allows you to customize your SmartIcons.

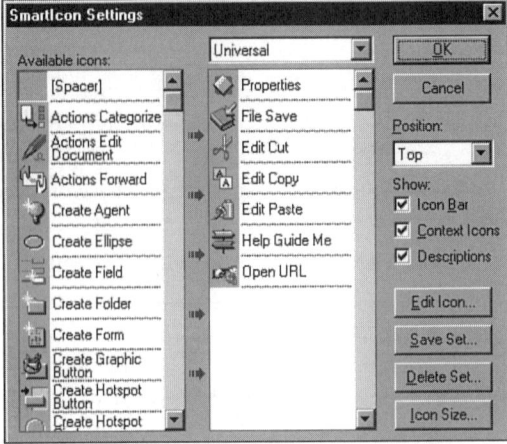

2. The icons on the right comprise the current set of SmartIcons. This name of this set appears directly above the icons. Initially, if you click the drop-down box containing the name Universal, you will see that there are no other SmartIcon sets defined. If you want to modify the Universal set, proceed with the following step. If you want to define your own set, click Save Set. See Figure 3.11. Enter the new name for your set and a filename with the extension SMI. When you have finished, click OK.

Figure 3.11
You can give names to your saved SmartIcons sets.

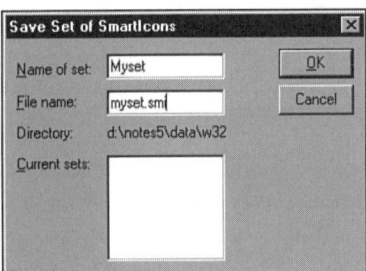

3. If you created your own set, you see the name appear at the top of the SmartIcons to the right, otherwise it says Universal. See Figure 3.10 for the following operations.
    - To add a SmartIcon to the set, scroll the set of icons on the left until you find the one you want and drag it to the right window. Drop it within the icon set at the point you would like it to appear.
    - To delete a SmartIcon from the set, click the icon within the right window, drag it, and drop it outside the window anywhere. It is removed from the set.
    - To reorder the icons, click the icon you would like to move within the right window, drag it to the location you would like it to appear, and drop it.
    - You can add, delete, and move spacers by clicking the Spacer icon on the left and treating it like one of the other icons.

4. There are a few other options within the SmartIcon dialog box:
   - The Position drop-down box allows you to position the SmartIcon set along any of the edges of the window or to display it as a floating palette.
   - The Icon Bar check box allows you to turn the SmartIcons off completely.
   - The Context Icons check box gives you the option to display the context-sensitive set of icons. You cannot customize the set of context icons, but you can simulate it by developing several named sets of icons depending on the work you do.
   - The Descriptions check box allows you turn off the display of the ToolTips for the SmartIcons. I really can't think of any particularly good reason why you might want to turn this help off.
   - The Save Set button allows you to save a new, named set of SmartIcons. You supply a name for the set as well as the filename and your set is saved. The Delete Set button allows you to delete a previously saved set.
   - The Icon Size button allows you to change the size of your SmartIcons. You can specify either Small or Large. The default display size is small. Normally this is desirable because you can then use many more icons than if you specify large.
5. To finish your customization, click the OK button.

> **Tip**
>
> One useful icon that you might consider for your Universal set is the File Print icon. If you put this icon on your Universal set, you'll be able to print from virtually any part of the Notes client.
>
> If you plan to use several SmartIcon sets, another useful icon is the File-Tools-SmartIcons icon. You should place this icon on every one of your SmartIcon sets in the same place. By putting this icon on each of your sets in the same place, you make it very easy to switch from one set to another. Click the button, drop down the list of icons to pick your new set, and click OK. It is important to put it in the same place in each set so that you'll easily know where to find it no matter which SmartIcon set you are using.
>
> Note that you can also change the icon color scheme. The icon color scheme affects both the SmartIcons and the bookmark icons, so it is located in the User Preferences. To access the user preferences, issue File, Preferences, User Preferences.

Editing a Custom SmartIcon

Occasionally you might find it useful to create your own SmartIcon that performs a task that you cannot execute with a Notes menu command. Suppose, for example, that you would like to invoke a program from within Notes. I'll show you how to do this with the Windows Paint program within Windows 95/98, but you can use any program. Also, you are not restricted to executing programs; you can use the formula language to write any custom formula. See Chapter 18, "Working with Formulas, Functions, and Commands," for more details on the Formula language.

To create your own SmartIcon to execute the Paint program, do the following:

1. From the menus, select File, Preferences, SmartIcon Settings to open up the SmartIcons dialog box.
2. If you would like to add your custom icon to a set other than the current set, select the icon set from the drop-down list.
3. Click the Edit Icon Button to display the Edit SmartIcons dialog box. See Figure 3.12.

Figure 3.12
You can attach your own Formula macro to one of the custom icons.

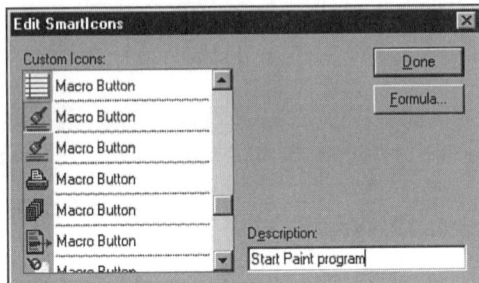

4. Scroll the icon list and select one of the macro buttons. Click the Formula button. See Figure 3.13.

Figure 3.13
The SmartIcons Formula dialog box enables you to use the full power of Notes.

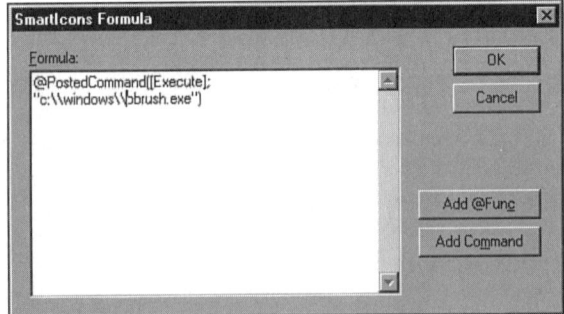

5. Enter your formula in the SmartIcons Formula dialog box. To try the Paint sample, enter the following formula:
   `@PostedCommand([Execute];"c:\\windows\\pbrush.exe")`
6. You can also click the Add @Func or Add Command button to see the list of @Functions and Commands. When you are finished, click OK.
7. You should now enter a description for your new custom icon in the description field. The description you enter will be displayed in the ToolTip for your new custom icon. Click Done after you have entered your description.
8. Now add the custom icon to your SmartIcon set by dragging the icon from the list on the left into the SmartIcon set on the right.

9. Close the SmartIcons dialog box by clicking OK.

You can test your SmartIcon by clicking it and making sure that it behaves as you expect.

THE STATUS BAR

The status bar is located at the bottom of your screen. It appears in all contexts, gives you useful information about various aspects of your Notes session, and also allows you to change certain settings. See Figure 3.14.

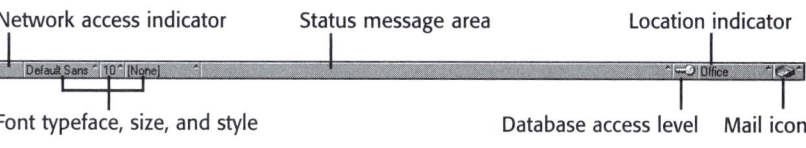

Figure 3.14
The status bar allows you to view and change important information about your session.

The status bar is divided into eight sections. Here are descriptions of these sections:

- Network Access Indicator—The network access indicator shows a lightning bolt when Notes is accessing the network. If you are using a mobile connection, a modem with flashing lights appears.

- Font Typeface Indicator—Shows the current font typeface when you are editing a document. If you click this indicator, you can change the current typeface by selecting one of the fonts that shows in the pop-up list.

- Font Size Indicator—The font size indicator works like the font typeface indicator. You can view the current size and change it by clicking it and selecting from the list.

- Font Style Indicator—The style indicator shows you the current style, if there is one, and allows you to change the style by clicking the indicator. This indicator, as with the font typeface and size indicators, appears only when you are editing a document.

- Status Message Area—The fourth section is the status message area. Notes displays status messages here and you can find a recent history of messages by clicking this indicator.

- Database Access Level Icon—This icon visibly shows your access level for the currently selected database. If you click this icon, you will get more detailed access level information.

- Location Indicator—The location indicator shows you the name of the current location document. If you click this indicator, you will see a complete list of all your locations and you can select a new location from the list or edit your current location document.

- Mail Icon—The mail icon displays an inbox when you have new mail. Otherwise, this icon shows an envelope. If you click this icon, you can send and receive mail, open your mail database, and create a new email message.

TASK BUTTONS

The Notes release 5 user interface has changed quite a bit from release 4. One of the new features is the availability of task buttons. In release 4, when multiple windows were open, they could be displayed randomly overlapped on the screen. In release 5, windows all occupy the same area and you can switch easily between the windows by clicking the task buttons. This maximizes the information you can see in each window while still allowing you to switch easily from one window to another.

> **Tip**
> You can still open up multiple windows with the Notes client. You do this when you open a database. From the bookmark bar, right-click the database and select Open In New Window. This opens a second window, complete with its own set of task buttons. You might want to use this feature to compare two different versions of the same database in two windows side-by-side, for example.

The window currently being viewed has a white task button and the windows not displayed have a gray task button. When you view a document window with the default setup, the task buttons appear below the SmartIcon bar, if you have turned them on. To switch from one window to another, click the task button of the window you want to view. See Figure 3.15.

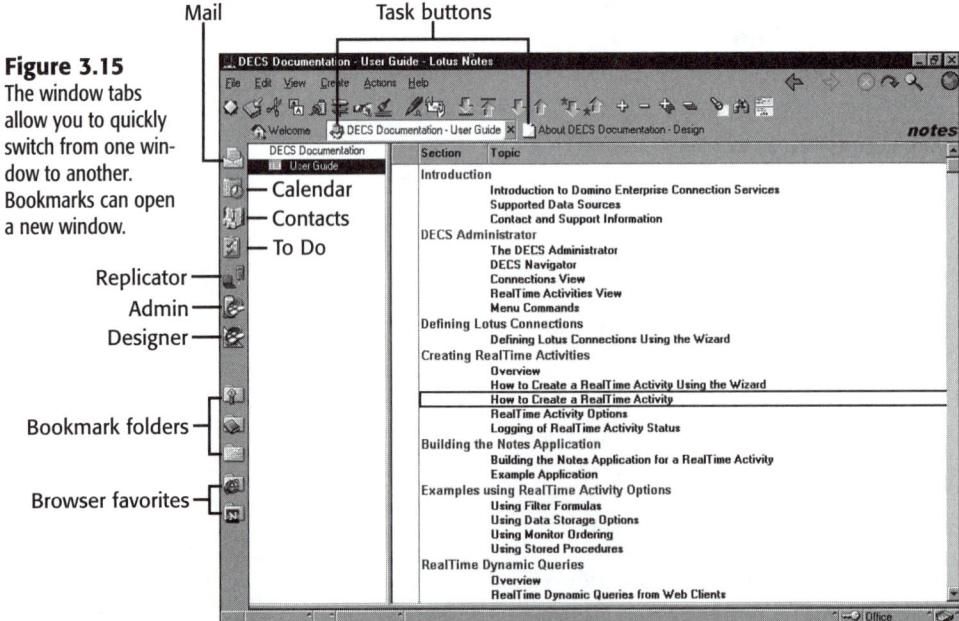

Figure 3.15
The window tabs allow you to quickly switch from one window to another. Bookmarks can open a new window.

Notice that on the right side of the active task button there is an X. If you move your mouse over an inactive task button, an X will also appear. This X can be used to close the window without actually viewing it. Previously, you would have to switch to a window in order to close it. Now you can close the current window or any other active window very easily.

BOOKMARKS

The icons at the left edge of your screen are used to store bookmarks. See Figure 3.15. The bookmarks in Notes behave similarly to bookmarks in Web browsers. They are used to store the location of Web pages, Notes documents, or views that you use frequently to do your job.

When you initially start Notes, the top four bookmark icons are used for your four basic operations: Mail, Calendar, Contacts, and To do. Under these four is the Replicator icon, which is similar to the Replicator tab of release 4.x of Notes.

Under the Replicator icon are two optional icons. The first launches the Domino Administrator and the second launches the Domino Designer. These icons appear only if these clients are installed on your machine.

After a little space on the bar, you see up to five folders that you can use to store your bookmarks. The first three are standard: Favorite bookmarks, Databases, and More bookmarks. Underneath these three are folders for Internet Explorer Links and Netscape Navigator Links. These last two folders appear only if you have the corresponding Web browser installed on your machine.

You can add bookmarks to the bookmark bar or to the folders. Each folder can hold multiple bookmarks. A bookmark can be a link to a document, view, or folder within a Notes database. You can also link to Web pages or Web sites. Add a bookmark by clicking the item you want to save and dragging it to the bookmark tab where you would like the bookmark to appear.

When you click one of the folders, a window frame pops out from the left. This frame shows you the objects within the folder. See Figure 3.16.

This bookmark frame can be sized by clicking and dragging its right edge. You can leave this area permanently open by clicking the rectangular icon in the upper left corner and enabling the option Pin Bookmarks Window.

By right-clicking a bookmark in the bookmark bar, you can open it, create a new folder, remove the folder, rename the folder, or change its icon.

Figure 3.16
Bookmark folders can be left permanently open.

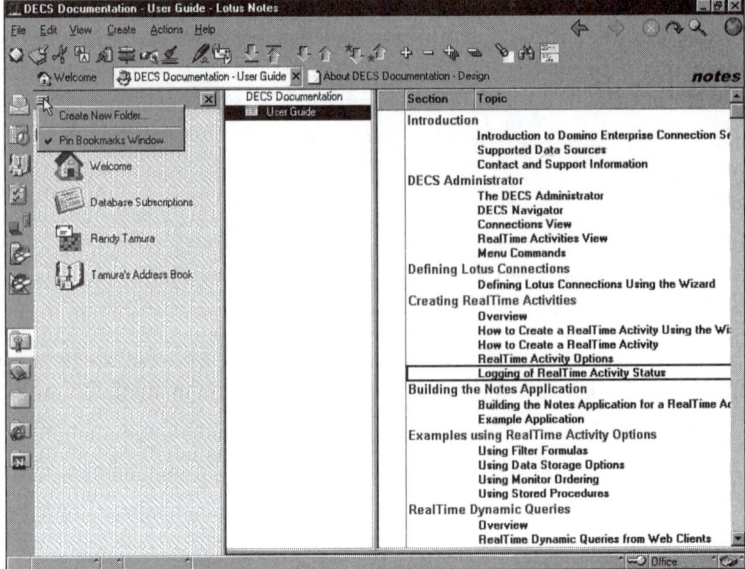

ID Files and Changing Your Password

When you log on to most systems these days, you are required to have a user ID and a password. The Notes client requires these items as well. In addition, however, Notes uses one extra element of security, the ID file. This is actually a file that is stored on a floppy disk or on your local hard drive. These ID files are an important part of the Notes security system.

In the most basic sense, security is based on one of two characteristics: What you have, or what you know. For example, a padlock can use a key (what you have) or a combination lock (what you know). When you log on to most computer systems, they are usually based on a password (what you know). If you work for a large company, you might have a cardkey security system to let you in your building or parking lot. This cardkey system is based on what you have.

The most secure systems, however, are based on a combination of what you have and what you know. For example, if you use an ATM card at your bank or the local grocery store, you must both have the card, and also know the personal identification number (PIN). This system means that if someone has your card, but does not know your PIN, the card is useless. The user must have something and know something.

The Notes ID file is a physical file that you must possess in conjunction with your user ID and password. In other words, even if someone knows your password, unless they also have your ID file, they cannot log on with your user ID. This mechanism is much stronger than systems with only a user ID and password. If you keep your ID on a floppy disk, for example, and store it locked away in your desk, no one can log on with your ID unless they can also get the floppy from your desk.

The most common cause of security breaches, however, is the careless handling of passwords. One bank, for example, was rigorous about changing passwords daily. The bank thought changing a password daily would surely foil anyone trying to electronically rob them. However, because the tellers would forget passwords that changed daily, they posted the password on the wall. Guess what? Of course when they investigated how millions of dollars were stolen, it was traced back to this rather careless handling of the password itself.

The moral, of course, is not only to change your password, but be careful on how you handle the passwords themselves. Don't post them next to your computer, leave them where someone else can find them, or share them. These are common-sense rules, but sometimes you violate them when you are in a hurry to get the job done.

Passwords

Passwords in Notes can be up to 63 characters long and can consist of letters, numbers, spaces, or other keyboard characters. The first character of your password must be an alphanumeric character.

Passwords are case sensitive. The following passwords are *not* identical: HomeRun, homerun, and HOMERUN. They are considered different because of the capitalization. To make your password more secure, you can use the following techniques:

- Make your password at least eight characters long.
- Use a combination of upper- and lowercase.
- Use one or more numbers or special characters.
- Do not use your name, your birthday, or other common information a hacker might guess.
- For the strongest passwords, use a random combination of letters and numbers, not regular words. This has the drawback that these passwords are easier to forget, however, so weigh the pros and cons.

Changing Your Password

Here is the process to change your password:

> **Note**
>
> If you use the Windows NT client and you have specified that you want Single Password Logon, you must keep your passwords for Notes and Windows NT synchronized. If you change your Notes password, you need to change your Windows NT password to continue to use the Single Password Logon feature. Notes prompts you if you change one but not the other.

1. From the menu, select File, Tools, User ID and you are prompted for your current password. See Figure 3.17. This first password prompt is to allow you to review information contained in your ID file.

Figure 3.17
You must first enter your old password before you can access the User ID dialog box.

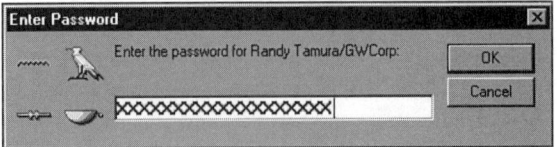

2. After you type your current password, you see a box similar to Figure 3.18.

Figure 3.18
The User ID dialog box allows you to examine many aspects of your ID file.

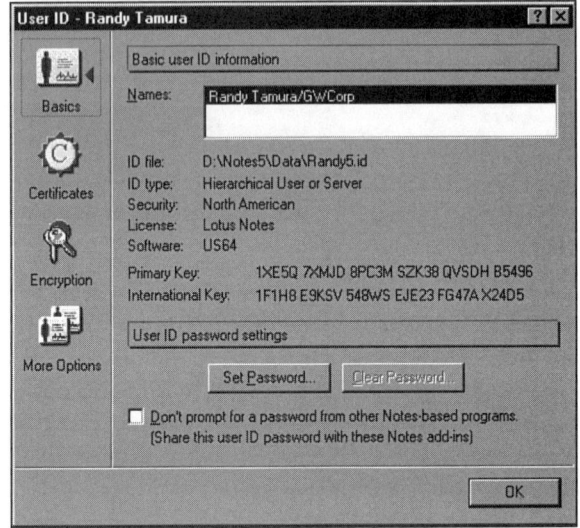

3. To change your password, click the Set Password button or press Alt+P. You are again prompted to enter your current password. After you type your password, you see the Set Password dialog box as shown in Figure 3.19.

Figure 3.19
Your new password is case sensitive.

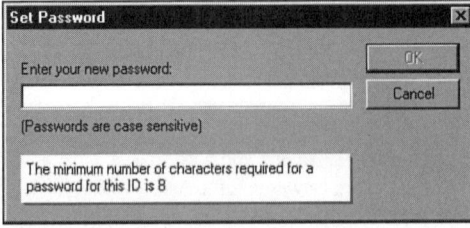

4. In the Set Password dialog box, enter your new password. Passwords are case sensitive. Mixed-case passwords, as well as passwords containing both letters and numbers, are the most secure, but the easiest to forget. The system administrator sets up a minimum length for your new password.

5. When you have entered your password, you are prompted to type it again. This ensures that you have typed it correctly because you cannot see the characters as you are typing them. When you have finished, click Done at the User ID dialog box to exit.

Before you move on to the next topic, let me briefly summarize the other items contained in the User ID dialog box. Besides the Basics tab, which allows you to change your password, the Certificates tab allows you to view certificates that are contained within your ID file. See Figure 3.20.

Figure 3.20
Certificates are authorizations that allow you to access servers.

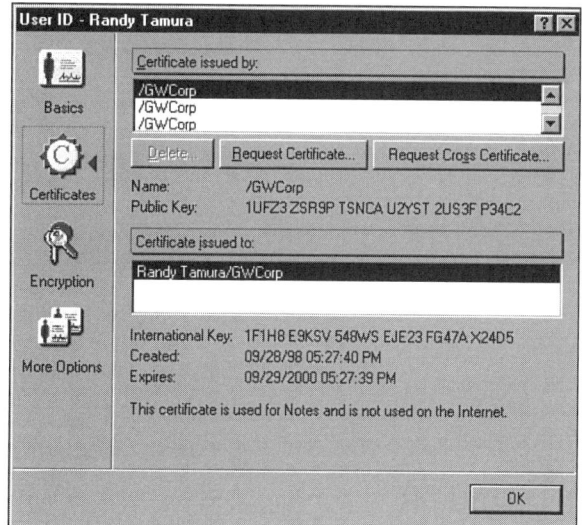

You must have a certificate to access a Domino server. When your user ID is created, a certificate is issued and placed in your ID file. Normally, certificates are organized via a hierarchical organization which is defined by your system administrator. You can think of a certificate as an authorization for access. If you do not have this authorization, you are not allowed to access your organization's servers.

You do not typically need to do much with certificates, but if your organization has a complex hierarchy, or if you deal with several domains or external companies, you might need to request certificates or cross-certificates (allowing cross-domain access). Certificates are covered in more detail in Chapter 36, "Domino Security Overview."

The Encryption tab in the User ID dialog box can be used to create encryption keys. See Figure 3.21. These keys are stored in your ID file and can encrypt fields within documents. If a document is encrypted with a key, only users who have the key contained in their ID file can read the encrypted fields of the document. When you have created a key, you can mail the key to others. Note also that the designer of the form must enable encryption on fields to be encrypted. Encryption on fields is not enabled by default.

Figure 3.21
Encryption keys allow you to encrypt fields within documents.

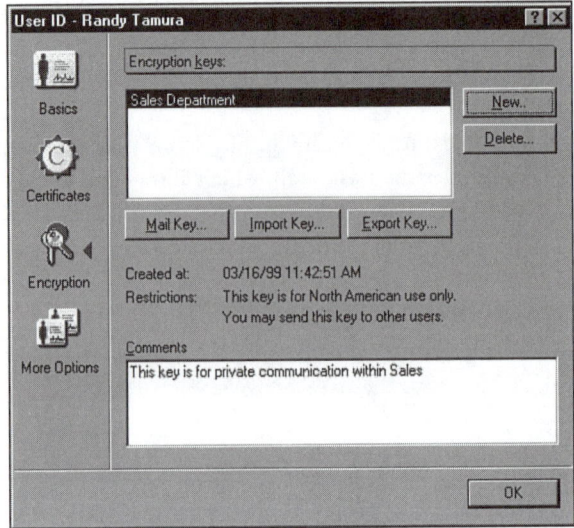

You can access other ID management options in the More Options tab in the User ID dialog box. In this tab you can request a name change, obtain a new public key, and create a safe copy of your ID which can be used by an administrator of another domain to cross-certify your ID.

Setting Up a Printer

Typically when you install your operating system the printer is configured at the same time. If you are on a network, you can have several printers on which you can print. If your printer is not yet set up with the operating system, you must first do that before you do any Notes customization.

For Windows 95/98, issue the following:

1. Click the Start button to get the Windows 95/98 menu.
2. From the menu, select Settings, Printers to get the printers icon display. If the printer you want is already there, you have nothing to do. If it is not yet shown, double-click the Add Printer icon.
3. Follow the instructions from Windows 95/98 to set up your printer. You should print a test page to make sure your printer is working with Windows.

For other operating systems, follow the instructions in your operating systems reference. When your printer has been set up with the operating system, you should be able to print.

To test printing within a database, open up a database, such as a discussion database and issue the following from the menu:

1. Select File, Print or press Ctrl+P to open the Print dialog box. See Figure 3.22.

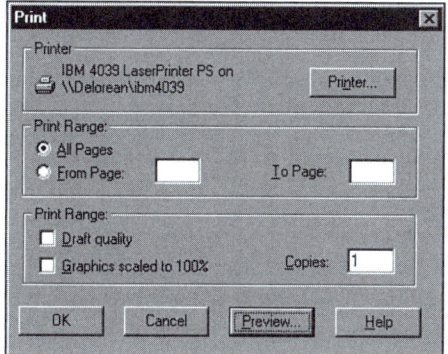

Figure 3.22
The Print dialog box specifies what you want to print.

2. In the dialog box, you can specify the printer to use, whether you want the view printed or you want to print each of the selected documents within the view, and the page ranges. You can also specify the print quality, graphics scaling, and number of copies.

3. If you want to preview your document prior to printing, click the Preview button.

4. To set up the printer before printing, click the Printer button.

   - You are then given a choice of printers. Select the printer you want to customize.
   - Click Setup to set up the selected printer. The next dialog box you receive depends on the type of printer you have. Typical options include the layout (1 up, 2 up, or 4 up), whether you want portrait or landscape orientation, and the paper source.
   - Select the options you want and click OK.

5. When you are satisfied with the options you have selected, click the OK button to send your output to the printer.

Summary

In this chapter, I have shown you how to install the Notes client. I showed you the various parts of your workspace such as menus, navigation icons, SmartIcons, window tabs, bookmarks, and the status bar. Bookmarks can be used to quickly access databases, views, Web pages, or other information. You can save the bookmarks by dragging and dropping the item onto your bookmark bar or one of its folders.

Task buttons allow you to quickly navigate among your open Notes windows. Click the task button of the window you want to see. You will move directly to that window. You can use the back button at the top right of the screen to move backwards through windows you have visited, similar to the way in which the Back button works in Web browsers.

Your user ID file contains your keys and certifications. This is an important file and you can't log on to Notes without it. Don't lose this file. You can put additional encryption keys into your ID file so that you can encrypt documents stored within shared databases. Other users need to have a copy of the encryption key you use in order to be able to read the encrypted fields.

Setting up your printer is a fairly easy task, but you might also need to use some features of your operating system in order to connect properly to your printer.

From Here...

In this chapter, I showed you how to install and configure your Notes client. You can learn more details about specific topics in the following chapters:

- Chapter 4, "The Notes User Interface and the Standard Databases," provides you with more information about the new user interface as well as a quick tour of the standard databases.
- Chapter 5, "Using Electronic Mail," gives you detailed information on using the new email features of Notes and Domino.
- Chapter 7, "Contact Management with the Personal and Public Directories," gives you information on how to keep track of the people you work with, both inside and outside your company.
- Chapter 8, "Getting Organized with the Calendaring and Scheduling Features," covers information you need to know about using the Notes calendaring features effectively.

CHAPTER 4

THE NOTES USER INTERFACE AND THE STANDARD DATABASES

70 | Chapter 4 The Notes User Interface and the Standard Databases

Previous releases of Lotus Notes used a concept called the workspace. This workspace contained big, square button icons that represented databases. Although the workspace is still available, mainly to ease transition and training, Notes release 5 has introduced a Web browser–type user interface. I won't be discussing the workspace user interface much here because users upgrading from prior releases are already familiar with it, and users new to Notes with release 5 don't really need to learn it.

In the new interface, the square icons are gone and bookmarks now replace their functionality. In addition to the bookmarks, the welcome page now greets you when you first start Notes. The welcome page is fully customizable and can bring you news and information relevant to your job.

The Welcome Page

In Figure 4.1 you see the default welcome page, also sometimes called a headline page.

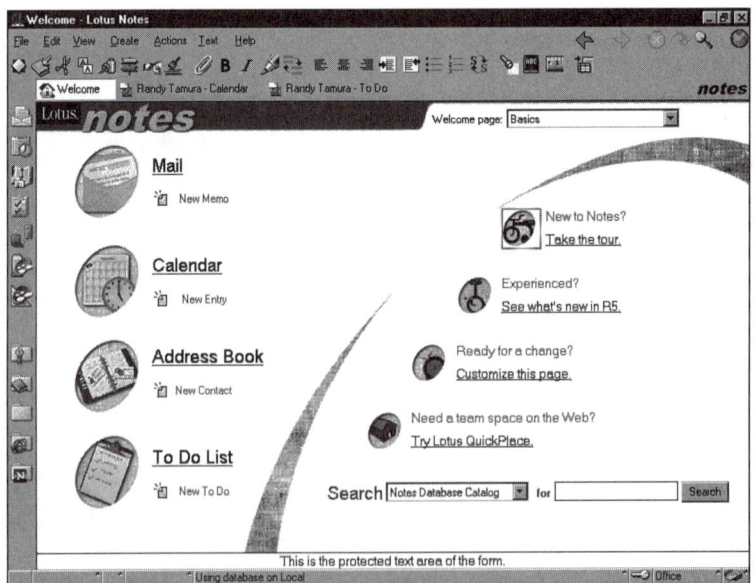

Figure 4.1
The default welcome page allows you to quickly access common applications.

The Default Welcome Page

On the left side of the screen you see the four common applications of mail, calendar, address book, and to do list. I'll give you an overview of each of these topics within this chapter, but each is covered in detail in a subsequent chapter. Mail is covered in Chapter 5, "Using Electronic Mail". The calendar and the to do list are covered in Chapter 8, "Getting Organized with the Calendaring and Scheduling Features". The address book is discussed in Chapter 7, "Contact Management with the Personal and Public Directories."

On the right side of the screen you see icons for additional help. This information is especially useful for first time users of Lotus Notes. You can take a guided tour of Notes if you are new or you can see what is new in R5 if you are experienced. The third icon gives you information about changing the welcome page and the fourth icon takes you to the Web to find out information about QuickPlace at http://www.quickplace.com/notes.

Customizing the Welcome Page

I've shown you several different welcome pages, but I have not yet shown you how to change or create your own page. You can choose a style from the built-in welcome styles or you can create your own welcome page style.

To change your welcome page style, click the drop-down box next to the Welcome Page prompt in the upper-right corner of your screen. You will see the built-in options. If you choose Headlines with AOL My News, for example, you will see a three pane welcome page containing your mail, calendar, and an AOL news page. See Figure 4.2.

Figure 4.2
You can show your email, calendar, and news on your welcome page.

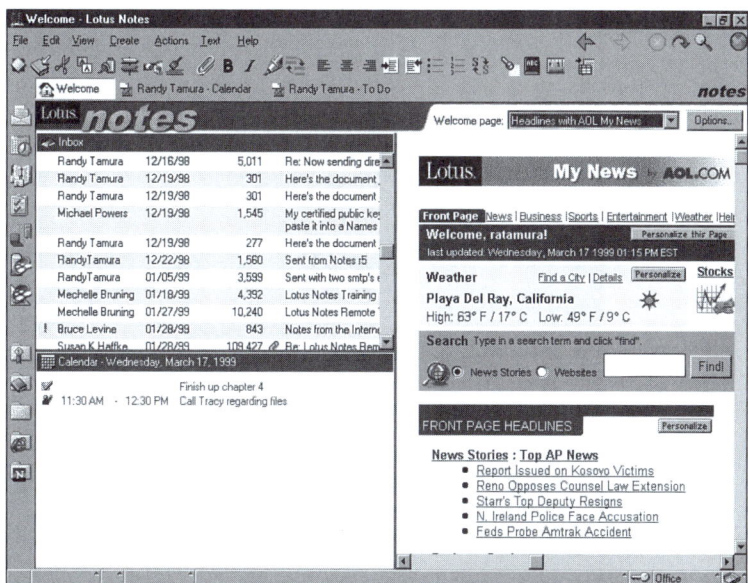

Figure 4.2 shows you a three pane welcome page containing useful information. Suppose you want different information? No problem. Here is what you do:

1. Click the Welcome Page drop-down menu.
2. Select Create New Page Style.
3. You will see a dialog box like Figure 4.3.

Figure 4.3
You can choose from several different custom layouts.

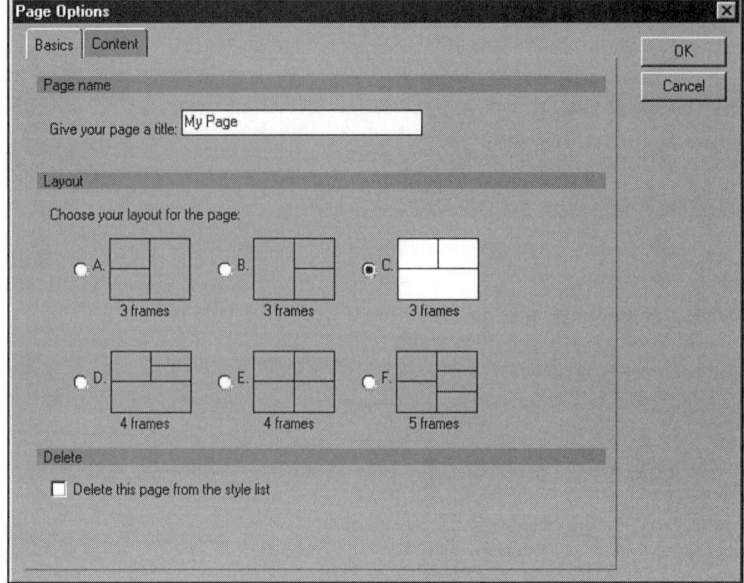

4. Give your welcome page a name and select the number of frames and layout you want.
5. Click the Content tab. You will see a dialog box similar to Figure 4.4.

Figure 4.4
You can choose custom content for each frame.

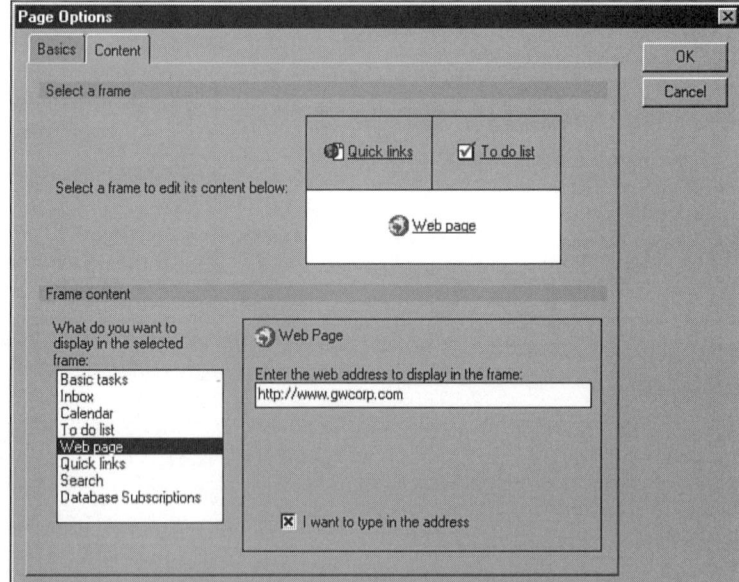

6. Choose a frame in the upper part of the dialog box and then choose its content from the lower section. You can choose from the built-in contents, or you can type the URL of a Web site. Figure 4.5 shows the result of customizing the welcome page.

Figure 4.5
A sample welcome page.

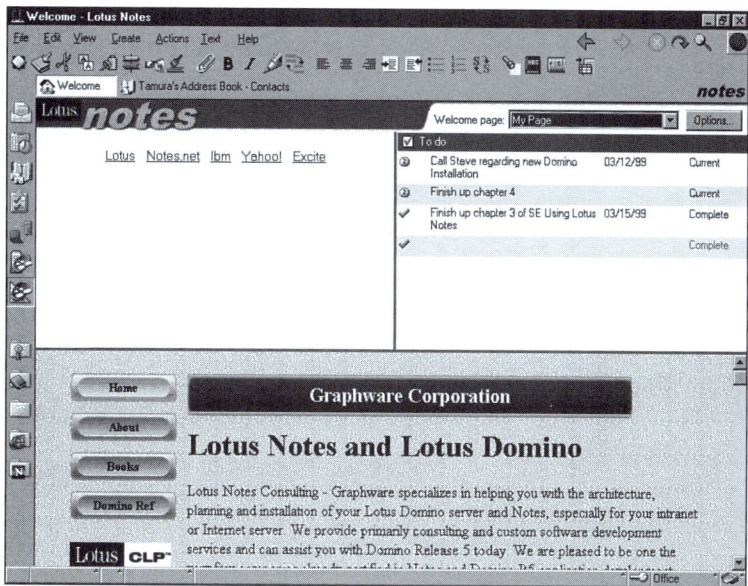

After you create your custom welcome page, it appears in the list of welcome pages. You can have several welcome pages, so if you are working on several different projects, you can conveniently switch back and forth among the various different welcome pages you set up.

Standard Databases

The standard Notes client installation creates several databases and makes them available to you. I'll introduce four of these databases—your personal address book, your email database, the public directory, and your personal Web navigator—in this chapter. In addition, your system administrator might have customized your company's version of Notes and Domino so that you have company-specific databases on your desktop as well. You need to refer to your company's documentation to find out how to use these custom databases.

I'll begin the tour with the personal address book, which stores information about your personal contacts. After that, I'll give you an overview of your email database, which you can use to send and receive email. The public directory is typically stored on your Domino server, and contains information about all the users of your Domino system as well as information used by your system administration staff. The personal Web navigator database is used when you browse the World Wide Web.

Your Personal Address Book Database

Your personal address book database is where you store information about your personal contacts and information on how to access servers from your local machine. You can see the list of your contacts in the address book in alphabetical order. In addition, you can use the letters to the left of the names to rapidly access names. See Figure 4.6.

Figure 4.6
You can see the list of your contacts in the Address book.

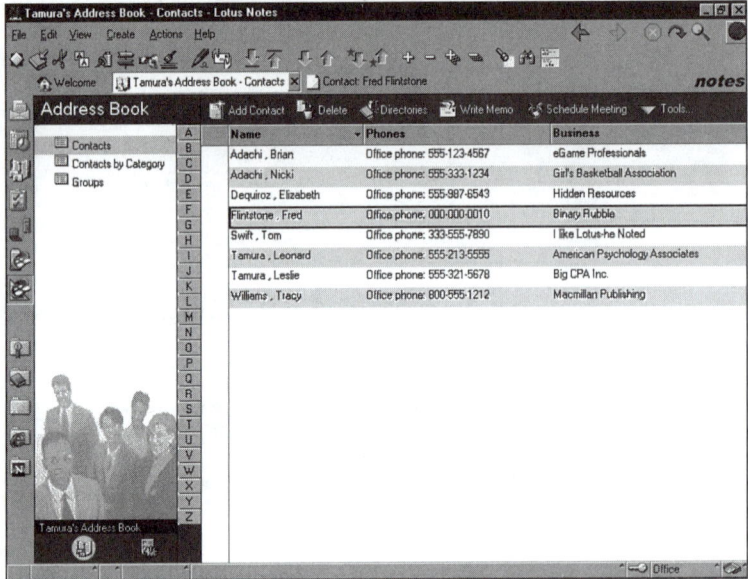

For each contact you can fill in information such as name, company, address, phone numbers, and email addresses. See Figure 4.7.

For each contact, in addition to the name and address information you can also store comments. Click the Comments tab and you have plenty of room to save information about the contact.

You can organize your contacts into groups and you can assign categories for each contact on the Advanced tab. After you assign the categories, you can view the contacts by the categories you choose. In Figure 4.8, notice that you can have many categories and that a particular contact can be in more than one category. You create the categories yourself and then organize the contacts within these categories. There is only one contact record, but by using categories, Notes allows you to flexibly organize your data.

YOUR PERSONAL ADDRESS BOOK DATABASE | 75

Figure 4.7
You can store names, phone numbers, addresses, and comments for each contact.

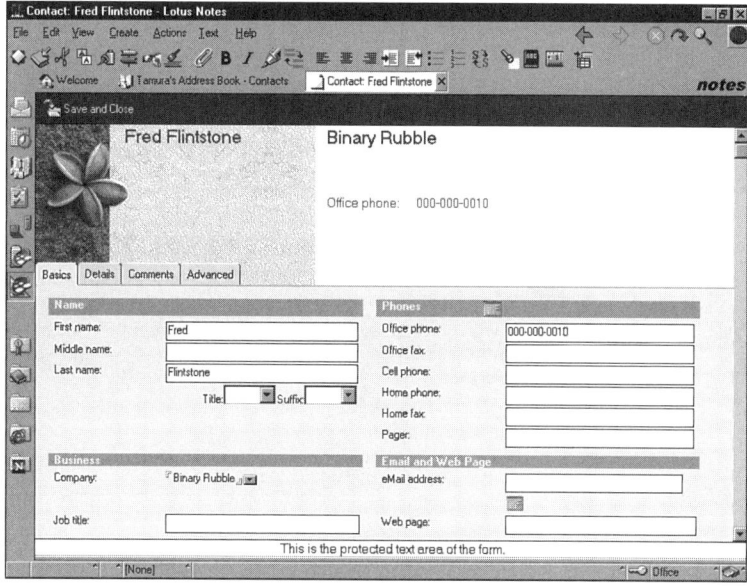

Figure 4.8
Contacts can be in more than one category.

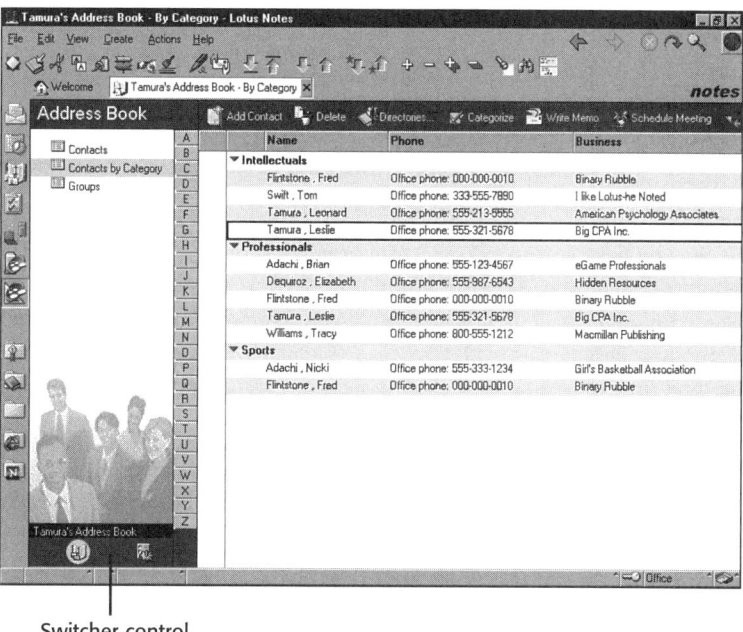

Switcher control

PART
II
CH
4

The switcher control, which you can see in the lower left corner of Figure 4.8, allows you to switch between information about your contacts and the connectivity settings for your workstation. The left icon is for your contacts and the right icon switches you to the settings view.

In Figure 4.9, you can see the Accounts view within the Personal address book. The Accounts view allows you set up different accounts for email, newsgroups, and directory services on the Internet. You can use IMAP, POP, or SMTP for email; NNTP for newsgroups; and LDAP for directories. By configuring your accounts, you will be able to access non-Domino servers from your Notes client. This is where you can configure your account to download mail from an Internet service provider (ISP).

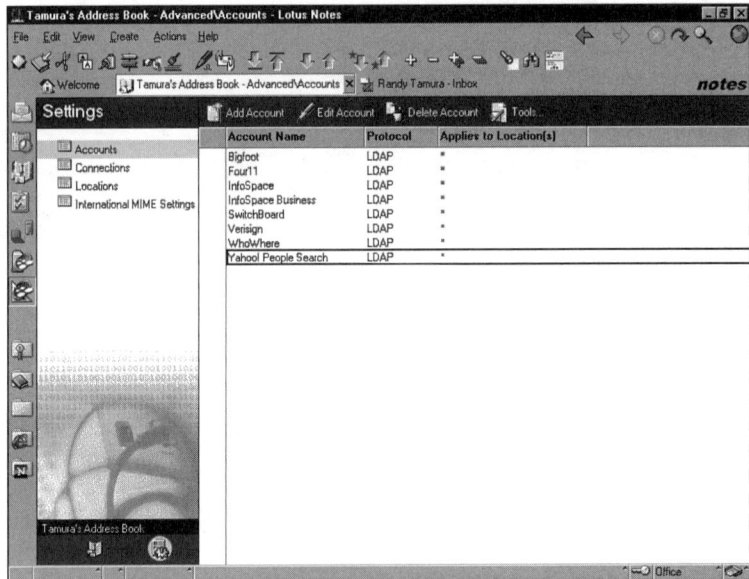

Figure 4.9
The Accounts Settings view allows you to set up ISP email accounts.

Connection documents specify communication protocols—such as TCP/IP, SPX/IPX, or Modem—and a specific destination. A connection document is used when you try to connect from your machine to a server. Notes selects the appropriate connection document depending on your user ID, the location you are connecting from, and the communication method protocol you are using. Connection documents also allow you to limit the users that can use the connection and the locations from which they can initiate the communication.

As shown in Figure 4.10, the location document can be used if you have a mobile computer or a home office computer and you access your office server remotely. You can configure settings such as the type of connection (Local Area Network, Notes Direct Dialup, Network Dialup, Custom, or No Connection). You can also indicate your preferences for Internet browser, replication, mail, and other parameters that might vary when you are in one location or another. Notice that in the lower-right corner of the status bar on the bottom of the window you can change your current location. In Figure 4.10, you see the location Office. By clicking it, a window pops up so you can choose the location document you want to use.

Figure 4.10
The location document specifies where you are and how you are connected.

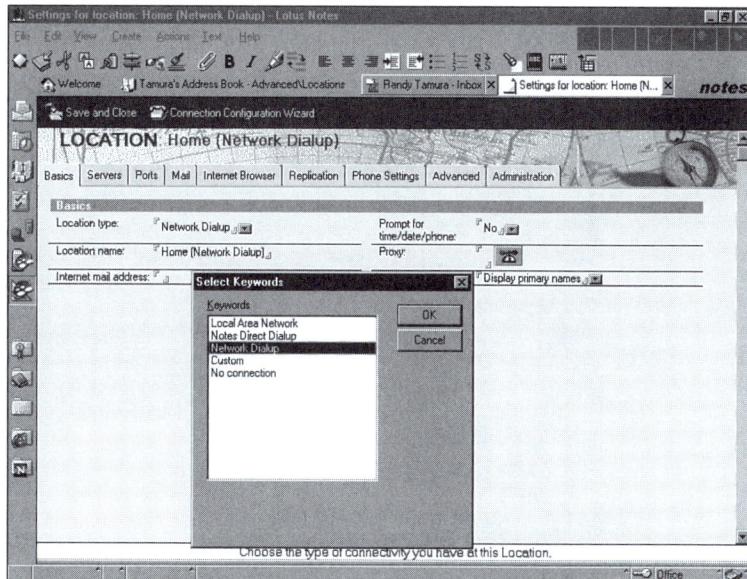

Your Mail and Calendar Database

Your mail database is one of the most important databases on your desktop. Your mail database includes not only your mail, but also your calendar, meeting manager, and to do list. By keeping all this information in a single place, in a single database, you can easily organize your day. Another important reason for keeping this information together is that you can use Domino replication features to replicate this database to your laptop so you can handle your email and calendar tasks offline.

You can view your calendar with a one, two, seven, or fourteen day view or a monthly view. See Figure 4.11. Click the number of days you want to view in the upper-right of the calendar window. When you view the monthly format, you can also double-click a date's header line to zoom to see the contents of that day in two-day format. If you double-click a calendar entry, you see a zoomed view of that entry.

There are several kinds of user preferences you can set in your mail and calendar database. To access the preference settings

1. Open the mail database by clicking on its bookmark icon.
2. From the menu bar select Actions, Tools, Preferences. A dialog box opens, allowing you to set Mail, Calendar, and Delegation Preferences.

Figure 4.11
If you hold your mouse over a calendar entry that is truncated, you see a longer display.

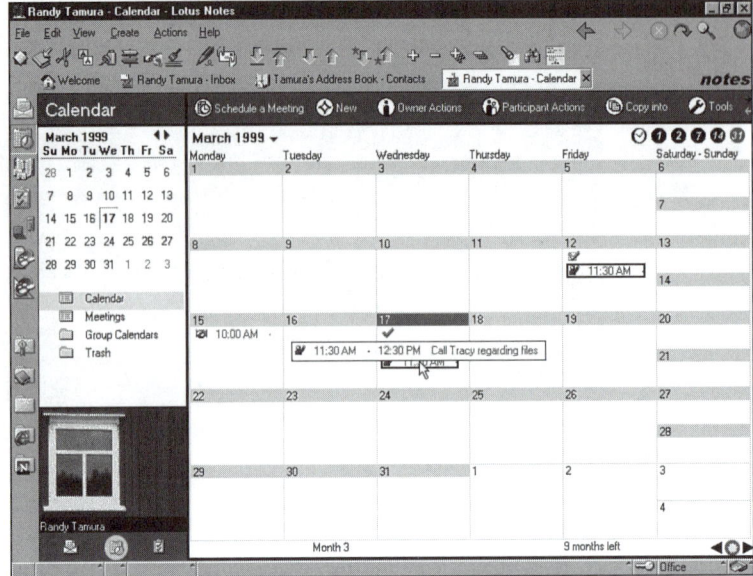

Mail User Preferences

Open the mail preferences as described above. Mail preferences consist of

- Basics—This tab allows you to specify the owner of the mail database and whether you want an automatic spelling check of outgoing mail.
- Letterhead—This tab allows you to indicate the graphic letterhead to use when sending email. There are many styles to choose from.
- Signature—The Signature tab allows you to specify a signature in either text or image format. This signature is appended at the bottom of your outgoing email if you enable the check box within the Option tab.

Calendar Preferences

Calendar preferences allow you to set default time lengths for appointments and meetings. You can also indicate the default you would like when you double-click a time slot in the calendar. See Figure 4.12.

In the calendar preferences section you can also define your normal work day so that the Free Time search programs know when you are normally available. The Alarms tab can be used to enable and disable calendar alarms. The Display tab allows you to change the starting and stopping times in the calendar view.

In the Autoprocess tab you can set up automatic processing of meeting invitations. You can process invitations from all users or a specified set of users and you can delegate meeting invitations.

Figure 4.12
There are many calendar preference settings to make your work easier.

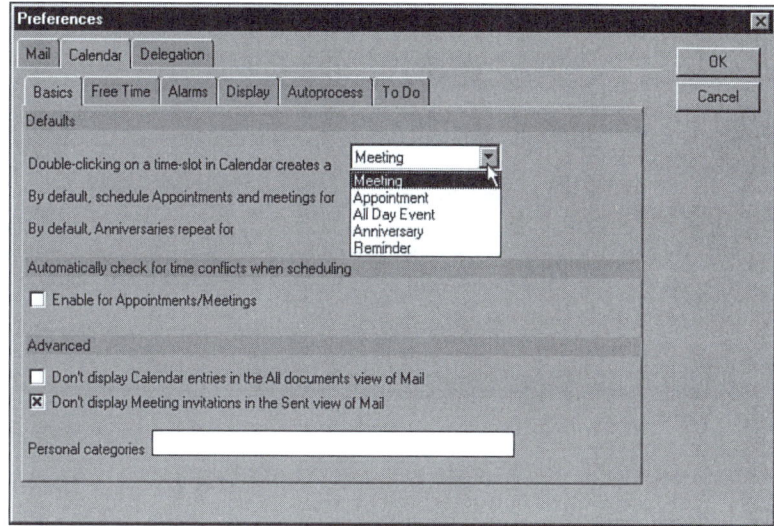

The To Do tab allows you to enable or disable the viewing of to do items on today's calendar.

Delegation

You can set up delegation in your mail database so that your secretary or co-workers can read or modify your calendar on your behalf. You can also set up delegation to email so that people you designate can read or answer mail on your behalf. Those who have email capability can also access your calendar. To set up your mail delegation and calendar delegation, click the Delegation tab.

You'll see the Delegation options as shown in Figure 4.13. From here, you can allow others to read your calendar and email. Think carefully about the security aspects of letting others access your mail database before enabling these options.

There is a lot more you can do with your calendar. Please refer to Chapter 8.

80 Chapter 4 The Notes User Interface and the Standard Databases

Figure 4.13
The Delegation Preferences in your mail database shows who you have allowed to access your email and calendar.

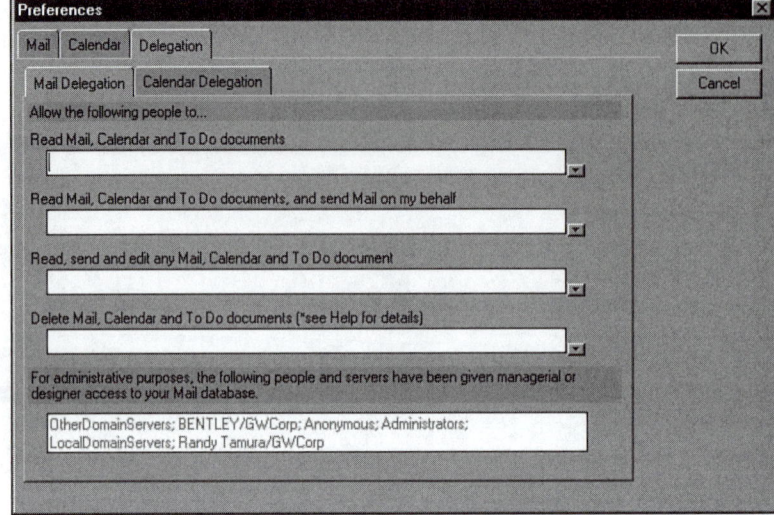

Reviewing the Public Directory

Now take a look at the public directory. This section assumes that you set up your Notes client with a connection to a server. If you set it up as a standalone client with no server connection, you will not have a Domino Public directory. For most people, however, the Public directory is available and contains information about other people and servers in your company.

Most likely, you will not need to make any modifications to the Public directory located on your server. In fact, it's pretty likely that you don't have the authority to make any changes to it anyway. If you try to change something, unless you are an administrator, you will receive a message indicating that your action is not allowed.

Although you won't make any changes, let me give you a quick look at the structure of the Public directory, so you'll know what information is available. To open your public directory

1. From the menus, select File, Database, Open, or click Ctrl-O.
2. You will see the Open Database dialog box. In the Server field, click the drop-down box and select your server from the list.
3. Scroll down the list and find an entry for your company's name with the phrase "Address Book." The filename for this database is typically `names.nsf`. See Figure 4.14.
4. Click the Open button. Your screen should resemble Figure 4.15.

REVIEWING THE PUBLIC DIRECTORY | 81

Figure 4.14
Open your company's address book, also called the Public directory.

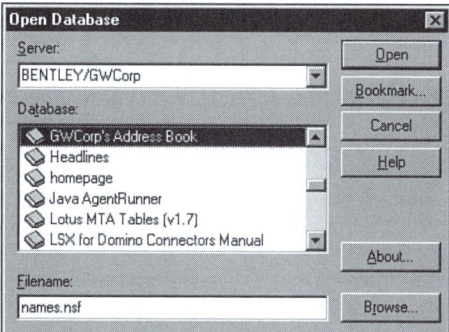

Figure 4.15
The Public directory contains information about all the people and servers in your domain, and much more.

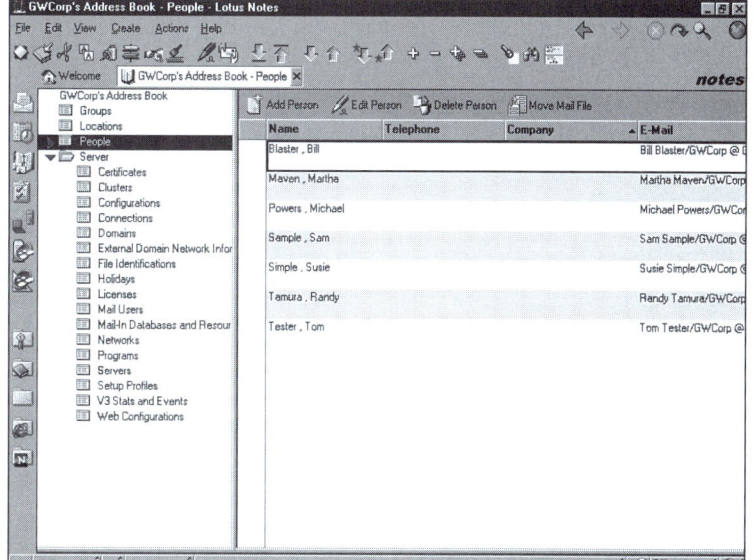

Note

The Domino Public directory has been called the Public Address Book almost since the beginning of time. Lotus, however, is changing its terminology to become more consistent with the industry. In the industry, when you have lists of users, computers, and resources, this list is called a directory. Novell, for example, has Novell Directory Services (NDS) and Microsoft has something called an Active Directory. So the Public Name and Address Book is now the Public directory. However, as you have seen, you will occasionally still see the Address Book terminology in various places in the product. As time goes on, this dual terminology will move more towards the Directory terminology.

The People section of the Public directory is probably the most useful section for you. You can use this section as a phone book for other people within your company. The Groups section contains information your administrator has set up to manage groupings by function

PART
II
CH
4

(engineering, marketing, finance), by departments within these functions, by location, managerial authority, or other criteria.

Location documents describe connection parameters. The connection parameters indicate ports to use, servers to access, mail databases, phone numbers, and other items you many want to configure. The administrator can set up location documents that can be then used or copied to personal address books by users.

There is a lot of information contained under the Server section of the Public directory. This information is configured by the administrator and includes Certificates (security authorizations), Connections (how and when servers connect to each other), Domains (logical groupings of servers and users), Holidays (days you wish you had more of), and other parameters that administrators can tweak.

If you are a current administrator of a Notes/Domino system, the Public directory corresponds to the Public Name and Address Book of previous releases. You can continue to edit this database; however, in release 5 there is a brand-new, powerful user interface for administrators. Read Parts VI, "Installing and Configuring the Domino Servers," and VII, "Administering the Domino Servers," for much more information about Domino servers.

THE PERSONAL WEB NAVIGATOR DATABASE

The Personal Web Navigator database is used when you browse the Web. It is used as a page and resource cache, so that when you access the same page multiple times, your response time is improved. Normally, if all you do is browse the Web, you don't really need to open the Personal Web Navigator database. The database does have a few useful features, however, if you would like to do offline Web browsing, if there are Web sites you would like to monitor, or if you want to control page caching.

The Personal Web Navigator database keeps recently accessed pages and sometimes it is interesting to review the pages. See Figure 4.16.

There are also some additional features in this database to make your Web browsing more productive. Here are some features of the Personal Web Navigator database:

- Offline browsing—Because the database caches pages, you can download Web pages for offline viewing. This is great for use on a disconnected laptop.
- Page caching—As mentioned, caching improves performance.
- Web Ahead—This is related to page caching. Web Ahead is an agent that runs in the background on the Notes client. It checks the links that are located on a particular page and downloads them so you can read them later. You can indicate how many levels of pages you want the agent to retrieve. To use Web Ahead, click its name in the navigator pane and double-click the instructions line that will appear in the view.

Figure 4.16
The Personal Web Navigator database stores previously viewed pages.

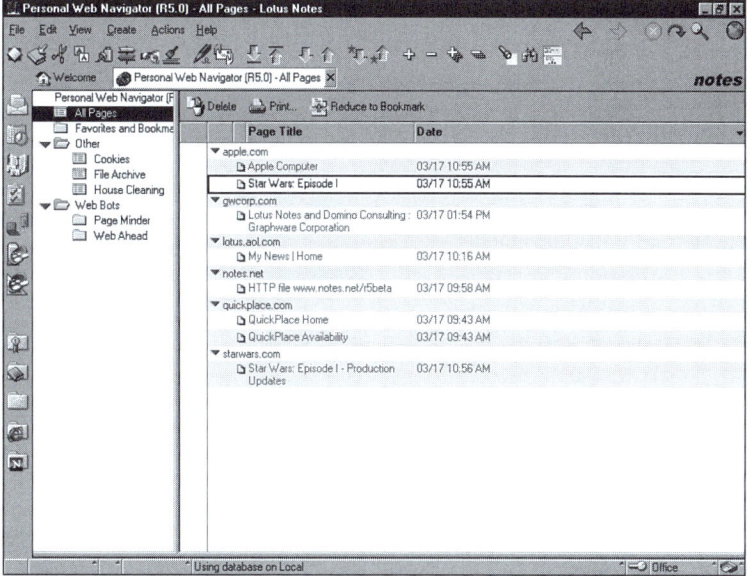

- Page Minder—This is a scheduled background agent that runs on the Notes client. You can specify the frequency from one hour to a day or week. The agent checks Web pages you specify to see whether they have changed. If so, it can notify you via email. To use Page Minder, click its name in the navigator pane and double-click the instructions line that appears in the view.

BOOKMARKS

In Chapter 3, "Installing and Customizing the Notes Client", I explained what bookmarks are, and how you can use them to launch your Domino database applications. At this point I'd like to show you a little more detail on how you can use the bookmarks bar to organize your databases. If you are familiar with release 4.x of Notes, this functionality is similar to organizing the databases on your workspace.

Notes comes with several built-in folders and applications. You can also create your own folders. The folders you create either can be at the top level on the bookmark bar or can be embedded within other existing folders. After you create a folder, you can also change its icon, rename it, or delete it if you want to reorganize.

To create a bookmark folder

1. Right-click the bookmark bar.
2. Select Create New Folder. A Create Folder dialog box appears. See Figure 4.17.
3. Give the folder a name in the Folder name field. Leave the folder type set to Shared.

Chapter 4 The Notes User Interface and the Standard Databases

4. In the bottom area, navigate to the parent folder where you would like your new folder to appear. If you want your new folder to appear on the bookmark bar, highlight the top line titled -Folders-.

5. Click OK.

Figure 4.17
You can create your own bookmark folders.

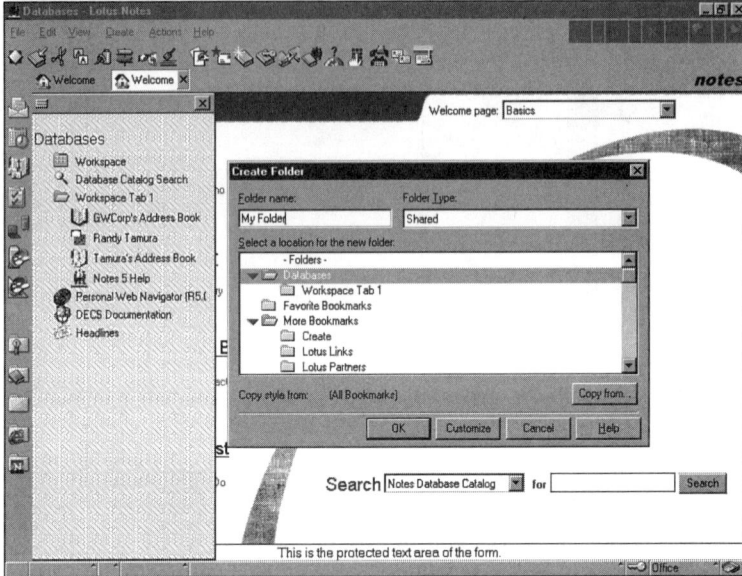

To remove a bookmark folder, right-click it and select Remove Folder. To rename the folder, right-click it and select Rename. You can also drag and drop bookmarks from one folder to another folder.

In the Databases folder you will also find a special bookmark called Workspace. If you click this bookmark, Notes will open the familiar 4.x workspace. See Figure 4.18.

As you can see in Figure 4.18, there is also a bookmark folder called Workspace Tab 1 that has been automatically created. This can give you the false impression that bookmarks are somehow synchronized with the Workspace. They are not closely synchronized. When you create new bookmarks, they are not automatically placed on your workspace, and when you create new icons in your workspace, they are not automatically placed in a related bookmark folder. The Workspace Tab 1 folder is created when you first set up your workstation, but after that you can customize its contents.

Another small, but important difference between the Workspace and bookmarks is that you must double-click a workspace icon to open the database. You single-click a bookmark to open it.

Figure 4.18
The Notes 4.x Workspace is still available.

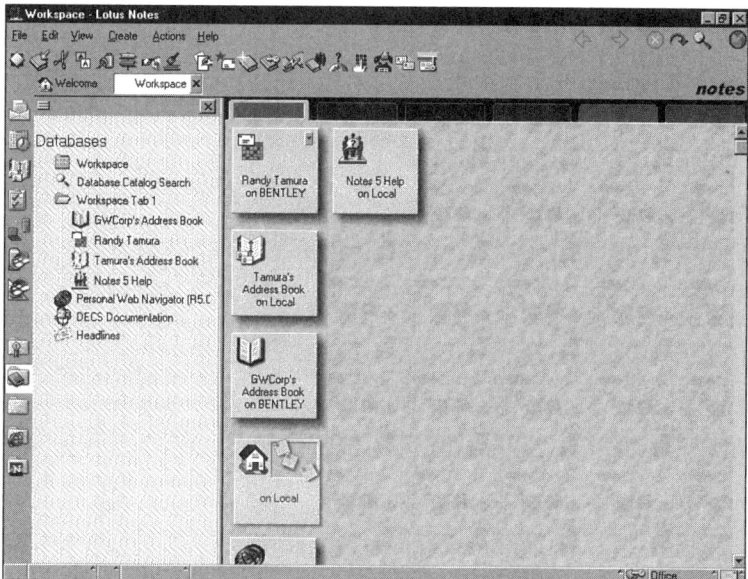

In the Notes workspace, a handy little down-arrow indicator can appear in the upper-right corner of the database icon. See Figure 4.18. This down-arrow indicates that there are multiple replica databases represented in the workspace. Clicking this arrow shows you a list of the replicas.

Bookmarks lack the immediately visible replica indicator, but you can still conveniently find this information by right-clicking on the database name. When the menu list appears, select Open Replica. A menu list appears, showing you the available replicas for the database. In addition, there is a new feature called Manage List. If you select Manage List, you will see a dialog box similar to Figure 4.19.

Figure 4.19
You can now manage the list of Replica servers for a database.

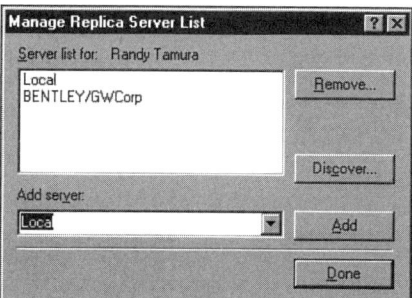

From the dialog box, you can remove, add, or discover new replica servers for the specified database.

SUBSCRIPTIONS

Subscriptions are a new feature of release 5 of Notes. Essentially, subscriptions allow you to monitor databases that you choose, and you will be notified when the contents of the database change. You are notified of the changes not via an active notification such as email, but by a passive notification. By this I mean that the changes are stored in your Subscription results database and you can view what's new whenever you like.

You can also include the Subscription results on your welcome page, so you will immediately know what's new as soon as you log on. The important feature here is that you have control over which databases to monitor, and you can look at the updates at your leisure.

The essence of the process to create a subscription is that you open the database to be monitored. From the menus select Create, Subscription, then give the subscription a name, and give some options on what you want monitored. Now look at an example.

Suppose you are a friendly person. Or perhaps you are curious, or maybe you like to gossip. In any of these cases, suppose you wanted to know whenever a new employee joined your company. In this case, assume that the addition of a person to the Domino directory (Name and Address Book) signifies the addition of a new employee. How can you set up a subscription to give you this information?

To set up a sample subscription to monitor for new or changed employees

1. Open your company's Domino directory.
2. From the menus, select Create, Subscription. A dialog box appears. See Figure 4.20.

Figure 4.20
You can add a subscription to monitor databases.

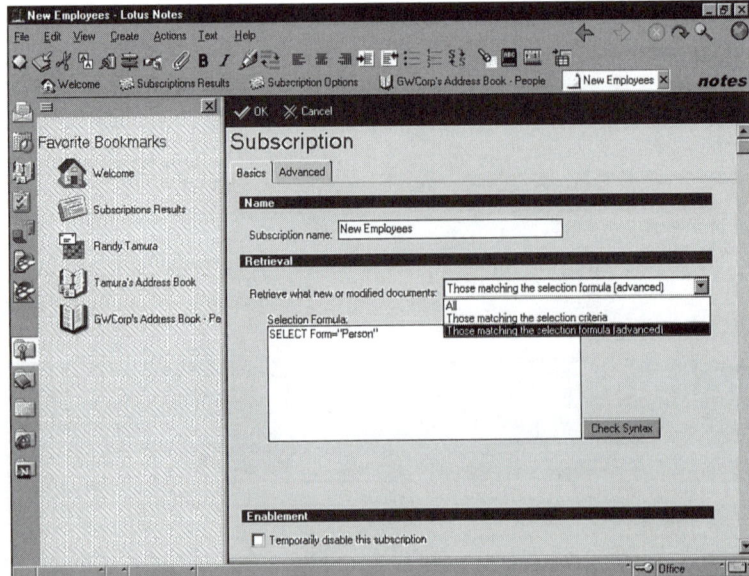

3. In the dialog box, enter New Employees as the subscription name.
4. Under Retrieval, choose Those Matching the Selection Formula (Advanced).
5. For the selection formula, enter SELECT Form="Person".
6. Click the OK button.

That's it. You now have a subscription to tell you when new employees arrive. Actually, it also tells you whenever any person's record changes, as well. Now take a look at how you can monitor the results. Open your Favorite Bookmarks folder. Click Subscription Results. Your subscriptions should appear as in Figure 4.21.

Figure 4.21
Your subscription results can be found in the Favorite Bookmarks folder.

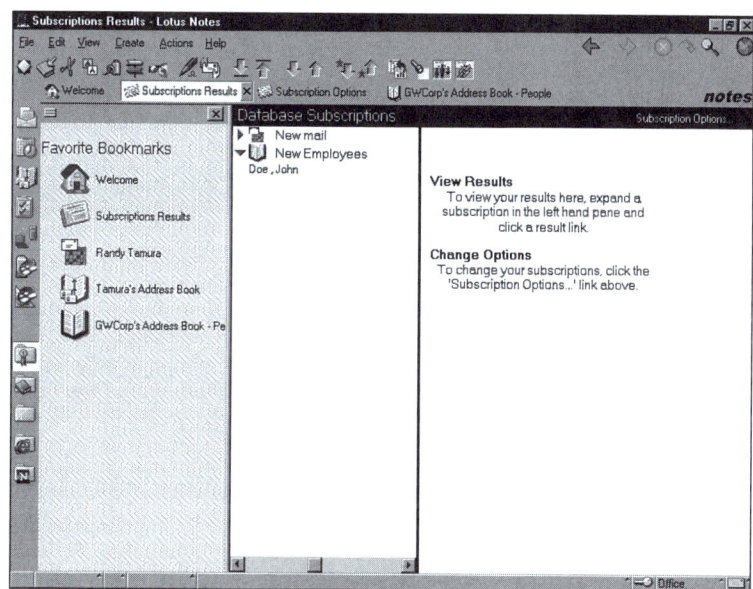

As you can see from Figure 4.21, a new employee, John Doe, has joined the company.

By clicking the Subscription Options hotspot in the upper-right corner of the screen, you can see a list of all your subscriptions, you can selectively enable and disable, and edit your subscriptions.

> **Note**
> Note that subscriptions are actually stored in a database called Headline.nsf. Don't confuse this database with the welcome pages that are sometimes called headline pages. Welcome pages are actually stored with bookmarks in Bookmark.nsf.

Changing Your User Preferences

You can control and customize many settings within Notes. Although some settings are stored within individual databases, such as the mail database, global settings can be changed via the User Preferences dialog box. To change these preferences, follow this procedure:

1. From the menus, select File, Preferences, User Preferences to open the User Preferences dialog box. See Figure 4.22.

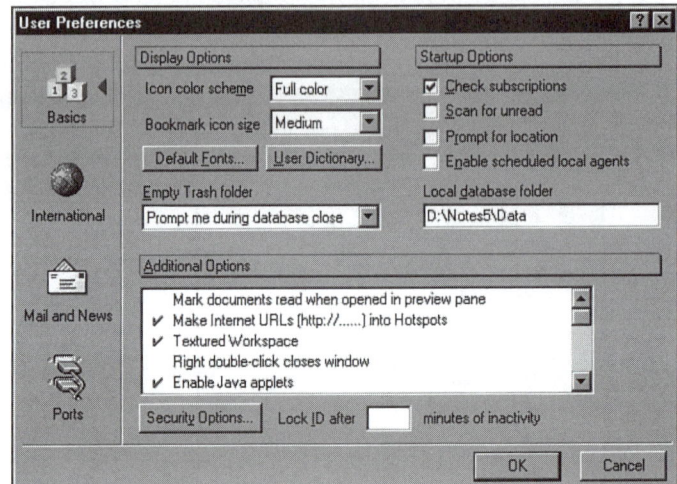

Figure 4.22
The User Preferences dialog box allows you to customize your workspace, international language settings, mail, and ports.

2. When the dialog box appears, you can change many options. The options are divided into four categories.
    - Basics—Allows you to change startup options and the local database folder and allows you to lock your workstation (requiring a password to reactivate). You can also set several many options regarding the operation of your workspace.
    - International—Allows you to change collating sequences, character sets, international dictionaries, and the starting day of the week.
    - Mail and News—Changes the mail options such as message format, frequency of checking for new mail, and which local address books should be used for name lookup.
    - Ports—Enables or disables communication protocols and set protocol options. You can also perform communication diagnostics with the Trace feature. This tab is for advanced users and you should use it only when initially setting up your machine or if you are having problems.

3. After you have changed your options, click the OK button to close the User Preferences dialog box.

Basic User Preferences

When you issue File, Preferences, User Preferences, the Basic user preferences are shown as in Figure 4.22. You can specify startup options.

Icon Color Scheme

Use the Icon Color Scheme setting to control the appearance of both the SmartIcon icons as well as the bookmark icons. Options include Full Color, Gray Color, System Color, and Pale Color.

Bookmark Icon Size

You can control the bookmark icon size. The settings are Small, Medium, and Large. When you change the setting, it does not take effect until you exit Notes and restart it.

Default Fonts

You can click the Default Fonts button to set the fonts that Notes uses by default. You change the settings for four fonts: Default Serif Font, Default Sans Serif Font, Default Monospace Font, and Default Multilingual Font. If you set fonts for your own use, you can change each of these to a font that you find appealing. If you design databases for others, be careful because the end user might or might not have the same fonts available that you do.

User Dictionary

The User Dictionary button within the User Preferences dialog box is used to add, update, or delete words from your local user spelling dictionary. You can add words such as names or places that you frequently use to your local dictionary.

Check Subscriptions

If you enable the Check Subscriptions options, your subscription database is searched for the subscriptions you have created. In essence you enable a background agent that will go and query each database subscription for new data. If you use subscriptions, you should enable this option.

Scan for Unread

The Scan for Unread option allows you to have Notes scan your preferred databases for unread documents when you start Notes. You specify your preferred databases by issuing Edit, Unread Marks, Scan Preferred from the menus. If you select this option, it takes Notes longer to start up depending on the size and number of your preferred databases.

Prompt for Location

If you travel frequently and use your computer in several different locations, it might be convenient to have Notes prompt you for the location each time you start Notes. If you select this option, Notes shows you a dialog box of all the location documents that are contained in your personal Domino directory database.

Enable Scheduled Local Agents

When you select Enable Scheduled Local Agents, the agent manager and Notes Web retriever programs are started when you start the Notes client. Both of these programs are separate processes that run in the background while Notes is running. The agent manager manages when agents are initiated and run. The Web Retriever program manages retrieval of Web pages in the background while Notes runs.

Empty Trash Folder

You can specify how you want your Trash folder handled as you exit your databases. You can have your Trash folder emptied every time you exit your database, you can be prompted to delete the items (the default), or you can indicate you want to delete your trash manually. If you specify manual deletion, you will need to issue from the menus Actions, Empty Trash. When you issue this menu command the trash is emptied.

Local Database Folder

The Local Database Folder is the root directory for all of your Notes databases. This directory is set when you install Notes, but you can change it from the User Preferences. In addition to the databases, Notes relies on this directory for system information, icons, and so forth. You should not change this directory unless you make sure that Notes will still be able to access its system information.

Additional Options

The Additional Options are a set of options that can be on or off. Each option controls an aspect of your environment. Some options deal with the display, others deal with user interface actions, and some deal with security.

Mark Documents Read When Opened in Preview Pane

If you normally work in a three-pane view when handling your mail, you might want to set this option. Mark Documents Read means that the unread marker (the star) disappears from the inbox folder if you view a document in the preview pane. If you want to use the preview pane in a true preview mode, you might want to leave this option off. The unread mark will only be turned off if you open the document (or you turn the mark off manually via Edit, Unread Marks, Mark Selected Read).

Make Internet URLs (http://…) into Hotspots

When you review documents, it is convenient to have all references to Web pages turned into hotspot links. If you turn this option on, you will easily be able to link to a Web page that is referenced in material you are reading. Without this option on, you would have to manually type the URL into your Web browser to access the page. Normally you should leave this option on unless you do a lot of work with Web addresses and you don't want them turned into links.

Textured Workspace

The textured workspace is a more visually appealing 3D look than the single color workspace background, which appears flat. The workspace is available in the Databases folder and the user interface is the same as in release 4.x of Notes. In order to view the textured workspace, your display adapter must be set to handle at least 256 colors. By turning this option on, it is a little easier to see when a database is selected and the workspace looks more interesting. Normally you should leave this option on.

Right Double-Click Closes Window

The right double-click option to close a window has been a part of Notes for a long time. If you are accustomed to this feature (or even if you are not) you might want to enable this option. It is a convenient feature of Notes and allows you to close a window by double-clicking with the right mouse button when the cursor is placed on or in the window. There is not too much danger in leaving this option on because right double-clicking is not really used in too many other programs, so you are unlikely to do it by mistake.

Enable Java Applets

By now you've certainly heard of Java. It is a language that can be used by Web page developers to enhance their Web pages and is triggered on Web pages via the <APPLET> tag. This option and several others control the operation of the Notes Web Navigator (the Web browser embedded within Notes). Note that if you use the setting Notes with Internet Explorer in the location document in your Personal directory database, you might also need to change some settings in Internet Explorer also. There are several locations in Notes and Domino that affect Java security and access.

In addition to enabling Java applets within the User Preferences, you must also review and enable the Java Applet Security section within Advanced tab in the location document in your personal address book database. In the Java Applet security section of the location document you can allow Java programs to connect to other network resources.

Normally Notes does not allow Java programs to access your local resources such as files, but in the Execution Control List security option, you can enable file access. See the section "Security Options," later in this chapter.

Finally, if you will use Java agents on the server, you must review and enable the Run (Un)restricted LotusScript/Java Agents entry in the Domino directory (Name and Address Book) for your company.

Enable JavaScript

The Enable JavaScript option enables JavaScript within the Notes browser. JavaScript is the scripting language used to control browser functions. Several functions in Domino can generate JavaScript so normally you should consider leaving this option enabled. On the other hand, enabling JavaScript does allow programming that potentially comes from an untrusted server to run on your client. If this is a major concern, you can disable this option.

Enable Java Access from JavaScript

Java and JavaScript are two distinct programming languages. Java is a compiled language and can operate in many contexts, including browser applets, Java Notes client agents, Domino server agents, and Domino server servlets. JavaScript generally runs only in Web browsers. By enabling this option, you allow JavaScript programs to invoke Java applets in the Notes Web browser.

Enable Plugins in Notes Browser

Whereas Java programs are typically created by Web page designers and apply usually to a small number of Web pages, plug-ins are useful programs that augment the Web browser itself. Plug-ins are available to all Web pages viewed by the browser and support various enhancements such as video, multimedia, enhanced sound, and so forth. Plug-ins are triggered on a Web page with the <EMBED> tag.

If you use the Notes Web Navigator, you enable plug-ins by checking this option within the User Preferences dialog box.

Enable ActiveX in Notes Browser

ActiveX programs are similar to plug-ins. Plug-ins is a Netscape technology, whereas ActiveX controls were developed by Microsoft. The Notes browser supports both kinds of technology. You can enable ActiveX controls via this option.

Accept Cookies

Cookies in a Web browser are inedible. They are containers that can store information between browser sessions. This enables the browser and server to retain persistent information. Normally, cookies provide convenience features, such as eliminating the need to constantly reenter data to a Web site. On the other hand, you might not want a Web site to be able to store and access information without your knowledge. You can enable or disable cookies with this option.

Retain View Column Sorting

One of the big raging debates (well, okay maybe not so big), is whether or not the mail stored in the mail database should be sorted most recent or most ancient first. I feel that it should be sorted with the most recent first because then when I open the database, I don't have to scroll down through pages of my inbox to see the newest email. Others, I'm not sure why, feel that they would rather see the same old email when they open their mail.

Well, now everyone can all have their preferences with the Retain View column sorting setting. By enabling this option, you can sort your email with the most recent mail first, and the next time you open the view it will retain its previous sort setting.

Dither Images

Dithering is not something politicians do. It is a process to improve the appearance of a graphic image. When you have a display adapter that can only show 256 colors, but you want to view an image with, say, several thousand colors (such as a photograph), you have a problem. A dithered image approximates the original colors by using a combination of adjacent pixels with available colors to match the missing colors.

You should turn on dithering if

- You do a lot of image work. If you're not using lots of colors, dithering slows you down. If you view a lot of Web pages with pictures, you might benefit from this option.
- You have a display adapter with 256 colors. If you have more colors available, dithering is unnecessary; if you have fewer than 256, dithering is turned on automatically.

If you don't meet the above criteria, you should probably leave dithering off.

MAKE NOTES THE DEFAULT WEB BROWSER ON MY SYSTEM

If you make Notes your default Web browser, when you link to the Internet from other applications, such as word processors or other programs, Notes is launched automatically. If you now use Microsoft Internet Explorer or Netscape Navigator/Communicator, you might find that one of these browsers is installed as your default browser. Checking this option replaces that browser with the Notes Web browser.

ENABLE MS OFFICE 97 SENDTO TO NOTES

If you use Microsoft Office 97, you might have noticed that if you issue the File command in say, Microsoft Word, there is an option called Send To. This option enables you to send the current document as an attachment via email to a recipient that you specify.

Enabling this option allows you to use Notes as your email system rather than a Microsoft product to deliver the email. After enabling the option, you must exit Notes for the option before the option becomes effective.

After it is effective, you can open a Microsoft Office product, issue File, Send To, Mail Recipient from the Office menu bar. At that point, the Notes program launches and sends your document as an email attachment.

USE WEB PALETTE

Now that just about everyone is using the World Wide Web, some conventions have developed. Because everyone browsing the Web might be using different browsers, operating systems, and hardware, the set of colors used by browsers might easily be chaotic. Lotus has its own color palette for use within Notes. In addition, it supports a platform-independent 256 color palette called the Web palette.

If you are developing for Notes only, you can use either palette. However, if your applications will be used on the Web, you should enable the Use Web Palette option. Using this option provides better graphics fidelity with Web browsers.

SHOW EXTENDED ACCELERATORS

Extended accelerators allow you to access Task buttons and bookmark icons in the Notes workspace via the keyboard. Normally if you have a mouse, you can click these buttons, but if you want to access the buttons from the keyboard you can do it via the extended accelerators. The accelerators work with or without the Show Extended Accelerators option checked, but if the option is turned on, you will see prompts on your screen.

To use the extended accelerators, hold down the Alt key and press either W or B. To access the Task buttons, press the W key, and to access the bookmarks, press the B key. If the Show Extended Accelerators option is on, you are then prompted with a number. Each number corresponds to a different button. Press the number that corresponds to the window or bookmark you want to access.

ENABLE UNICODE DISPLAY

The Enable Unicode Display option should normally always be on. If this option is off, Notes uses native-language fonts. If you get mail in Unicode format but don't have the fonts, Notes automatically displays the information using the available fonts, so there is no harm in leaving this option on. This option is mainly available to disable usage of Unicode fonts that are corrupted.

LAUNCH THE CORBA (DIIOP) SERVER ON PREVIEW IN WEB BROWSER

CORBA is the technology that Lotus uses to allow Web browsers to implement remote procedure calls. Essentially this is a sophisticated form of client/server computing using Web browsers as the client to communicate with the Domino server.

When you design using a local database, however, you might not use a Domino server. This option launches the server portion locally so you can test CORBA development without a Domino server. This option is for advanced developer use only.

SECURITY OPTIONS

The Notes workstation security options are accessed from the User Preferences screen by clicking the Security Options button. You see a dialog box similar to Figure 4.23.

> **Note**
> Your system administrator might have created an Execution Control List for the entire organization and disabled your ability to modify it. If so, you will not be able to see or use the Workstation Security dialog box.

You control programs based on whether the program is signed or who has signed the document or mail message. Regular workstation security allows you to control

- Access to file system
- Access to current database
- Access to environment variables

- Access to non-Notes databases
- Access to external code
- Access to external programs
- Ability to send mail
- Ability to read other databases
- Ability to modify other databases
- Ability to export data
- Access to Workstation Security ECL

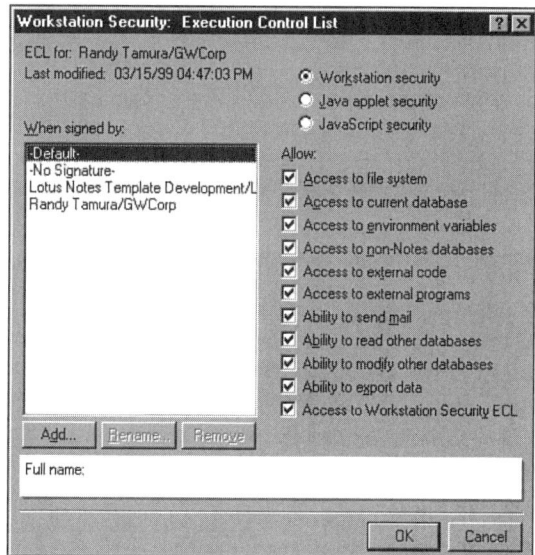

Figure 4.23
The Workstation Security dialog box gives you fine-grained control over programs that execute on your workstation.

The Java Applet Security ECL can be seen in Figure 4.24.

Java applets run within a Web browser on your workstation, but they are created by some unknown Web page designer. So you are running someone else's program on your machine. For this reason, you typically do not want to allow Java applets to access your file system. I recommend that you enable this option only for specific groups or individuals, not for default access.

Access to the Notes Java classes allows a Java applet to access data stored within a Notes database that might reside on your local machine. The same caution applies. You will be running someone else's Java program and it can access data within your local databases. I would recommend that you enable this option only for trusted groups or users.

Figure 4.24
Normally Java applets cannot access the file system.

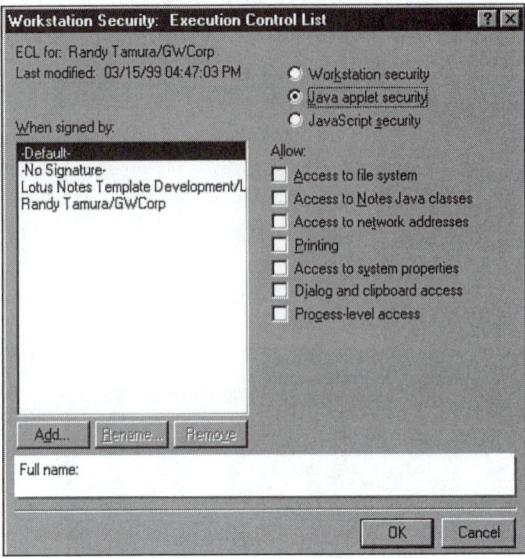

> **Note** Java applet security is controlled in three places. First, in the User Preferences Advanced options. You must enable Java applets. Second, here within the Execution control list you can control whether Java applets can access your file system or the Notes Java classes. Third, within the current Location document in the Advanced tab there is a Java Applet Security tab. Review all these places if you suspect Java security is giving you a problem. Finally, Java agents running on a Domino server are enabled in the Domino directory (Name and Address Book).

The JavaScript security controls can be seen in Figure 4.25.

The JavaScript ECL controls reading and writing data access. In addition, you can enable or disable the opening of URLs.

LOCK ID AFTER INACTIVITY

Notes allows you to lock your workstation if you have not had any keyboard or mouse activity within a specified amount of time. This feature protects your system in case you happen to leave your desk. If the time expires you need to reenter your password before you can access the Domino server again.

INTERNATIONAL PREFERENCES

To change your international preferences, click the International icon within the User Preferences dialog box. The international preferences dialog box can be seen in Figure 4.26. In this dialog box you can change the collation order (which is used for sorting), units of measurement (imperial or metric), and character sets.

CHANGING YOUR USER PREFERENCES | 97

Figure 4.25
JavaScript security ECL controls reading, writing, and URL open access.

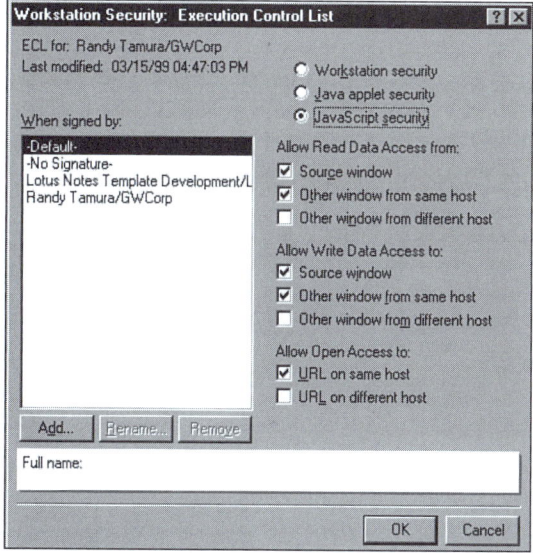

Figure 4.26
The International preferences control collation (sort order) as well as the calendar view starting day.

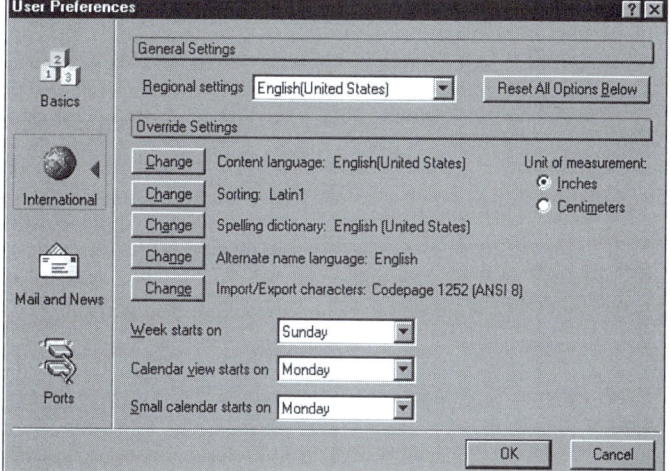

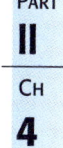

PART
II
CH
4

This dialog box also controls the starting day of the week and starting calendar view day. These are not strictly international options, so if you use Notes within the United States, do not ignore the International preferences box.

MAIL AND NEWS PREFERENCES

Click the Mail and News icon within the User Preferences dialog box to access the Notes Mail and News options. See Figure 4.27.

Within the Mail and News preferences box you can turn off Notes mail completely with the Mail Program option. You can choose an alternative mail editor, such as Microsoft Word or Lotus WordPro. You can also control the Internet mail and news formats and specify HTML or plain text.

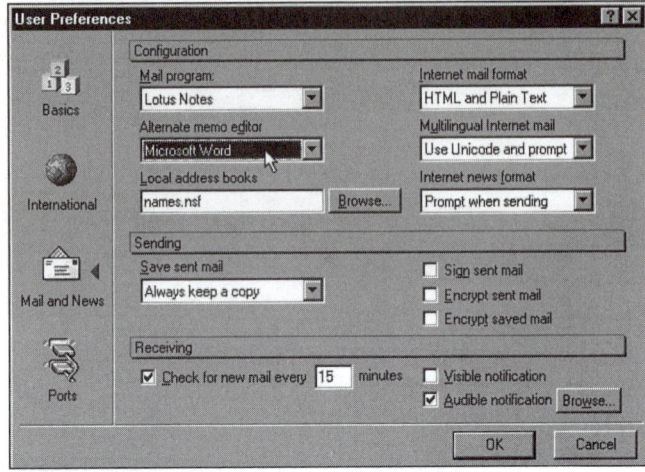

Figure 4.27
You can control which editor to use for email memo documents.

The Local Address Books field allows you to indicate the filename for your personal address book and local replica copies of other company address books (Domino directories).

When sending mail you can choose to keep copies of email you send as well as automatically signing or encrypting email you send. You can also choose to encrypt saved mail.

The receiving options allow you to control how frequently your Notes mail client checks with the server to see whether there is new mail. You can also control whether you will be notified and whether you would like visible or audible notification.

PORTS PREFERENCES

The Ports preferences contain only advanced options. If you don't know the difference between TCP/IP and SPX you typically do not need to worry about the options in this area. The only exception might be if you need to enable your modem for remote access. In this case, you might need to enable one of your COM ports.

You can see the Ports preferences dialog box in Figure 4.28.

You can enable or disable any of your ports by highlighting the port in the list and clicking in the Port Enabled check box. For each different port you can also click the Options button to obtain specialized options for that port. You can reorder the ports so that they will be searched in a different order, show the status of a port, and trace a port.

Tracing a port is an important diagnostic tool if you have communications problems. If you get a message indicating that Notes is unable to access the server, open the Ports User Preferences, and click the Trace button. You will see a dialog box similar to Figure 4.29.

Summary

Figure 4.28
You enable, disable, and trace ports using the Ports User Preferences.

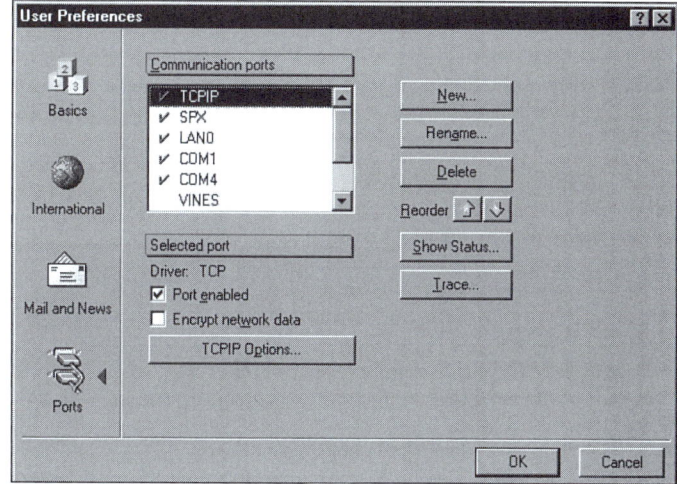

Figure 4.29
You can trace the connection to a server with Ports User Preferences.

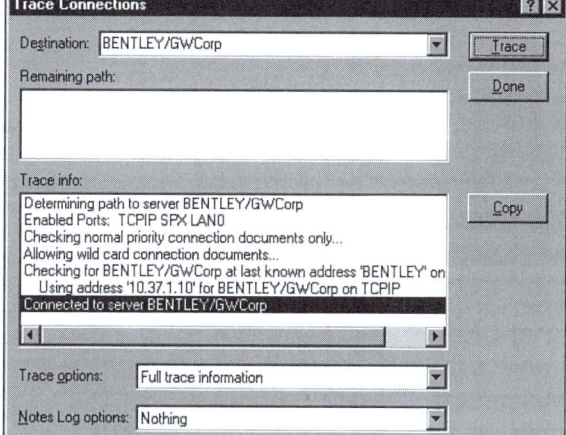

To trace the connection to a destination server

1. Select the server from the Destination drop down list.
2. Click Trace. You will see the trace in the window. This is usually very helpful information in diagnosing any connection problems with your ports.

Summary

I have introduced several of the important pages and databases you need to use with Notes. First is the welcome page. You can use one of the built-in welcome pages or you can create your own customized welcome page. Your Personal Address book database contains information about the people you work with. It is a contact database and contains names, company information, addresses, email addresses, and other commonly used information. I introduced your mail database, which contains your email, calendar, and to do list.

The Public directory contains information about people, groups, and servers within your organization. Normally you will not edit this database, but you might find it useful for looking up contact information for other people in your company.

Finally, I showed you how to use the User Preferences settings to customize Notes to the way you work. There are four major sections in the User Preferences dialog box: Basics, International, Mail and News, and Ports.

From Here...

Although I've introduced all the major databases you'll be likely to use, there is still much more to learn about each one. You can find more information in the following chapters:

- Chapter 5, "Using Electronic Mail," goes into much more depth on the features of electronic mail.
- Chapter 6, "Working with Text and Documents," covers information about working with documents of all kinds. No matter what kind of document you edit, you need to know how Notes handles editing and formatting of documents.
- Chapter 7, "Contact Management with the Personal and Public Directories," provides you with in-depth knowledge of these address books. If you are an administrator, administration aspects of the Domino Public directory will be covered in much more detail in Parts VI, "Installing and Configuring the Domino Servers," and VII, "Administering the Domino Servers."
- Chapter 8, "Getting Organized with the Calendaring and Scheduling Features" shows you how to create and use calendar entries to organize your day.
- Chapter 10, "Using Mobile Features from Home or on the Road" contains information on how to use Notes and Domino remotely. This can apply to you whether you work from home or from a hotel room.

CHAPTER 5

Using Electronic Mail

CHAPTER 5 USING ELECTRONIC MAIL

Lotus Notes 5.0's email application follows a store-forward paradigm. That means that email is stored in a central repository on the Domino server until it can be routed to the recipient's mail database.

On a local area network, that usually means that mail is delivered instantaneously. On a dial-in workstation, mail is stored in a local outgoing mailbox until a connection is made to the Domino server. The mail is then sent to the server and routed from there. If a recipient's mail database is in another domain, the server routes the mail to that domain, and that other domain handles the task of delivering the mail.

The process is actually similar to sending mail via the post office. You address the letter and it gets picked up by the mail carrier who takes it to a substation. From there, it is routed to the appropriate zip code and handed to another carrier who delivers it to the addressee. In the case of Notes mail, the Domino server's Router service handles the delivery, using the Domino directory to determine the correct location for an addressee's mail database.

A TOUR OF THE NOTES MAIL APPLICATION

To help you get oriented, take a quick tour of the Notes Mail application. When you first open your Notes Mail (usually on the first Bookmark page), you see your mail application. It is typically contained in a file named with your first initial and up to the first seven letters of your last name, to make up an eight-character filename. For example, a mail database for Don Child would be named DCHILD.NSF. The default Inbox view of the mail database is shown in Figure 5.1.

Figure 5.1
The Inbox view is displayed when you first open your Notes 5.0 mail application.

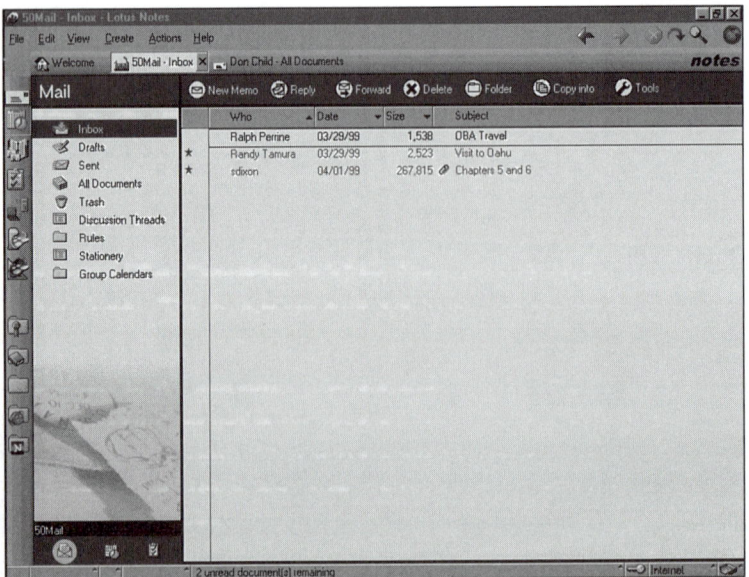

As with any Notes application, you can open a preview pane at the bottom of the screen so you can see the contents of a document before you open it. You can open the preview pane by clicking on the View Show/Hide Preview Pane SmartIcon.

VIEWS IN THE MAIL APPLICATION

The left pane lists the different views and folders in the mail application. The views include the following:

- Inbox—This folder holds incoming mail until you decide what to do with it.
- Drafts—This view holds various types of mail documents that you created and saved, but have not yet sent.
- Sent —This view holds various types of mail documents that you have sent to others. Saving sent documents is optional.
- All documents—This view is a collection of all documents in the various views and folders.
- Trash —This folder holds documents that have been marked for deletion and provides a single location for checking on documents before they are irretrievably deleted.
- Discussion Threads—This view organizes documents so that Reply documents are grouped with the memo documents to which they are responding. This makes it easier to follow threads when you have a complex exchange of documents discussing a topic.
- Stationery —This view holds documents that have been saved as stationery templates. When you open a stationery document and edit then send it, a copy of the stationery document is used, and the original stationery document remains intact in the stationery view.
- Folders —There are a couple of default folders, Rules and Group Calendars, and a variety of personal folders that you can create and use to group documents that you want to refer to at a later date.

SENDING A BASIC MESSAGE

Sending a basic email message is what most people think of when talking about email. In Notes, the basic email message uses the Memo form.

If your mail application is set up correctly—as a local application when you are working remotely, or on the Domino server when you are working on a LAN—you can create a memo from anywhere within Notes. Here are several ways you can start the process of creating a memo:

- Select Create Memo from the mail icon on the status bar (in the lower-right corner of the screen).
- Select Create, Mail, Memo from the menu bar. If you have the Mail application open, the menu option is Create, Memo.
- Press Ctrl+M from anywhere within Notes.
- Click the New Memo button on the Action bar in the Mail application.

After you initiate a memo, a form similar to the one in Figure 5.2 is displayed.

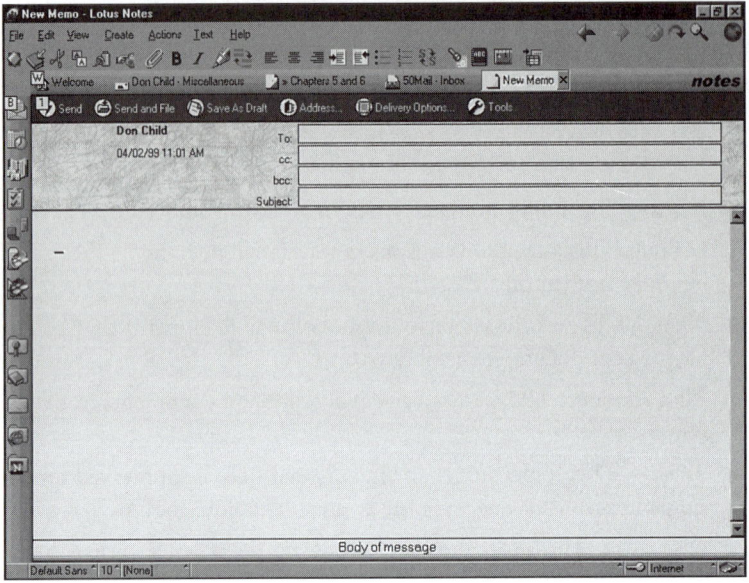

Figure 5.2
Use the basic Memo form to create a new email message.

This basic form has only five fields. The first three fields are used to address the memo to one or more individuals or groups of individuals. These three fields are for the primary addressees, carbon copies, and blind carbon copies. The Subject field provides the subject of the memo, which appears in the views so the receiver will know what to expect when she opens the message. The final field is a rich-text field in which you create the body of your message, including attachments, tables, section, graphics...anything you can place in a rich-text field.

ADDRESSING AN EMAIL MEMO

In each of the addressee fields, names have to be entered in a way that Notes recognizes them. This is made simple through directory lookups. As you type, Notes looks up names in Domino directories or in your Personal Address Book. Notes types ahead, displaying the name as soon as it is recognized. Usually, all you have to do is type enough of a person's (or group's) name until Notes can recognize it as unique. Typeahead works for first names and/or last names. The name you enter can be a common name or even a nickname, as long as the Domino server can resolve the name in the Domino Directory. For example, you could address a memo to Fiona and the chances are good that you would have only one user named Fiona. The server would resolve the name, and Fiona Chang would get the memo you addressed to her. You can also look names up in the Domino directories by clicking on the Address button. It is a good way to ensure that you enter names correctly.

If you want to send a memo to someone who is not listed in any of the directories, you have to enter an explicit address; for example, if Fiona Chang were a user in another domain, you could address her as fiona_chang@xanadu.com. The Domino server would attempt to deliver the message to the Internet domain, provided that appropriate connections are in place to allow mail routing.

Completing Your Memo

Complete the memo by entering a subject in the Subject field, and entering the body of your memo in the rich-text field below the address portion of the memo form. A completed memo is shown in Figure 5.3.

Figure 5.3
This completed email memo is ready to be sent.

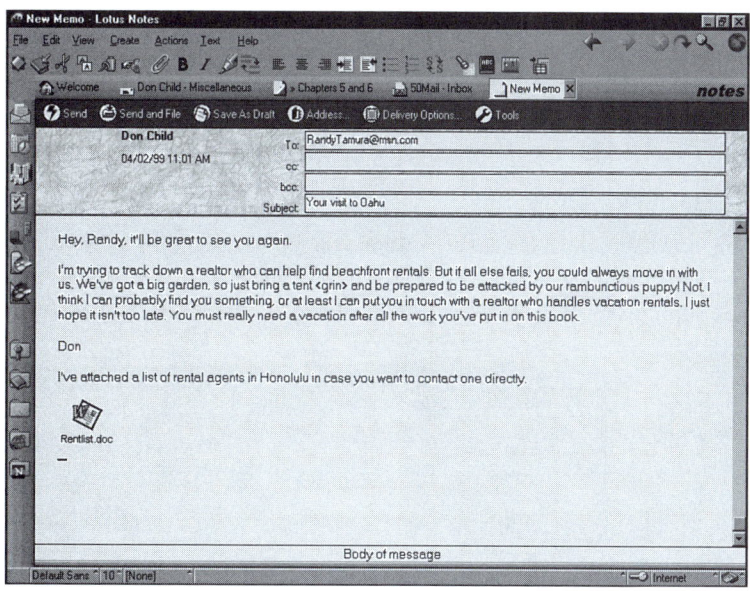

The attached file in Figure 5.3 was added to the memo by selecting File, Attach and selecting the file to be attached. It could be any type of file, but in this case, it is a Domino application.

Sending the Memo

From the Action bar, you can click a button for any of the following three send options. The button you click determines, to some extent, what happens to your sent mail:

- Send—When you click Send, the memo is sent immediately. The memo is saved in your mail database unless you have elected not to save sent mail (an option under File, Preferences, User Preferences).

- Send and File—When you select this option, the memo is sent immediately. A dialog box is displayed that lets you select which folder the memo should be saved to. When saving to a folder, you might want to add a new folder if there isn't one that is appropriate. You can add a new folder from within the dialog box shown in Figure 5.4.

CHAPTER 5 USING ELECTRONIC MAIL

Figure 5.4
Save outgoing mail in the folder of your choice.

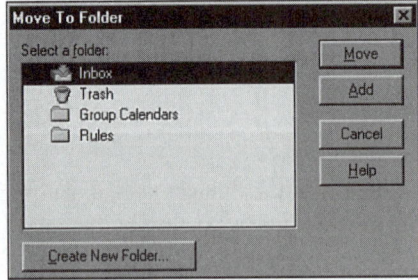

- Save as Draft—When you select this option, the memo is saved in the Drafts folder in your mail database. The memo is not sent. You can open the draft memo later, edit it, and send it by selecting either of the send options described previously.

SPECIAL DELIVERY OPTIONS

Sometimes, the default delivery options might not be enough for you. You can customize delivery options by clicking on the Delivery Options button on the Action bar. You can then select options in the Delivery Options dialog box shown in Figure 5.5.

Figure 5.5
Set special delivery options for your outgoing memos.

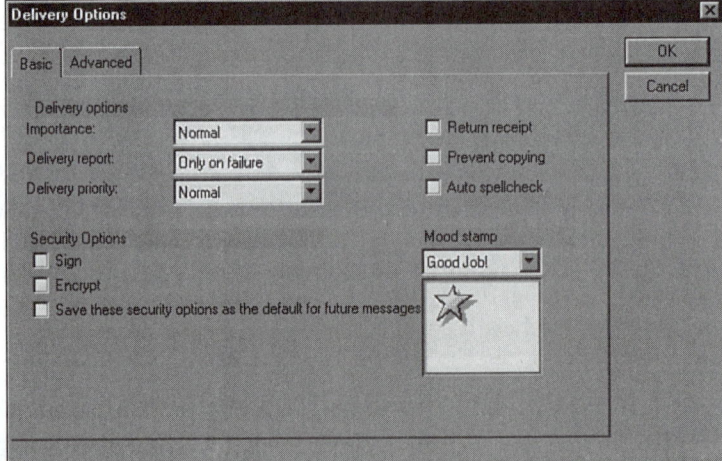

The Basic tab of the Delivery Options dialog box provides you with the following options:

- Importance—You can set an importance marker to indicate whether a memo is of high, normal, or low importance. High priority memos have a red exclamation point displayed beside them in the user's mail database.
- Delivery Report—The Delivery Report lets you select what type of notification you receive when your memo is successfully delivered to the recipient.

- Delivery Priority—High priority mail is always delivered immediately. Normal priority mail is delivered immediately within your own Domino Named Network, but if destined for a server in another Named Network, it is delivered on a schedule determined by the Domino administrator. Low priority mail is delivered during off-peak hours: usually during the middle of the night, again at the discretion of the administrator.

- Return Receipt—If you select this option, Notes generates a memo to you at the moment the addressee opens your memo using a Notes client. That way, you know that the user not only received but actually opened your memo to read it.

- Prevent Copying—When you select this option, the recipient cannot copy the data in the memo electronically, nor can they print it from a Notes client. This feature also prevents the recipient from forwarding the memo or replying with history.

- Auto Spellcheck—If you do not have spell checking turned on as a workstation preference, you can select it for this one document.

- Sign—If you select this option, Notes attaches your digital signature to the message. This digital signature provides proof that you, or at least someone using your Notes user ID, created the memo.

- Encrypt—If you elect to encrypt this memo, the only person who can read it is the person to whom it is addressed. The memo is scrambled during transit to prevent unauthorized reading.

- Save these security options as the default for future messages—If you select this, all subsequent memos will have the same delivery options.

- Mood stamp—This displays an icon on your memo when it is opened by someone with Notes mail. Examples of icons include FYI, Confidential, Personal, and Joke.

- On the Advanced Delivery Options page, you can stamp the message with a "Please Reply by" date to indicate time sensitivity; you can define an expiration date for the memo; you can provide an alternative address to which replies should be sent, for example so that replies can be collected in a mail-in database; and you can define the display format for Internet messages.

> **Caution**
> Most of the delivery options increase the size of the memo and the amount of processing needed. Use the options judiciously.

Reading Your Mail Messages

There are several ways to open your email. You can locate it on the Favorites bookmark page or locate the Mail bookmark. You can follow a link from your Welcome page. And from anywhere in Notes, you can click the mail icon in the lower-right corner of the workspace and select Open Mail.

When you open your mail, the Inbox view is displayed. Locate a document you want to read. Open the document by double-clicking it, or by selecting it and pressing Enter. An example of the Inbox with a preview pane opened at the bottom of the screen is shown in Figure 5.6.

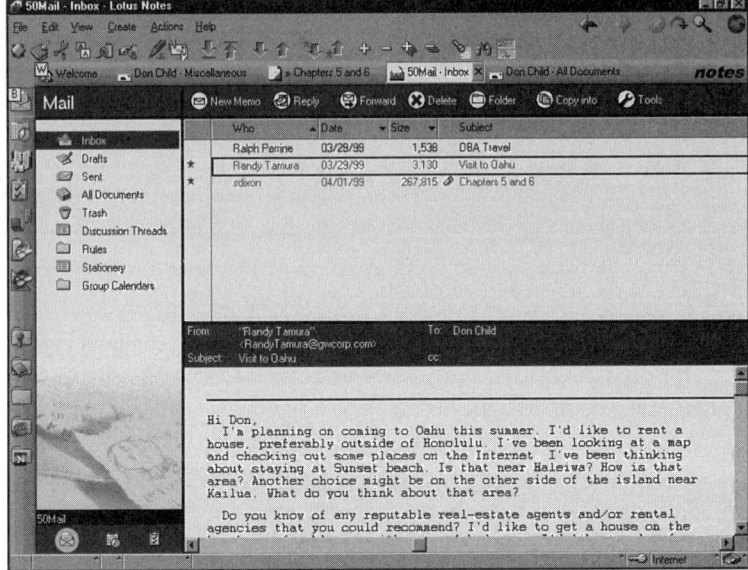

Figure 5.6
Open and read a document from the Inbox in the Notes mail application.

You can close a document by clicking the × beside the document name on the taskbar at the top of the workspace. You can also close the document by pressing the Esc key, or by selecting File, Close (Ctrl+W). Notice in Figure 5.6 that some of the documents are preceded by an asterisk and are displayed in a different color. The asterisk indicates that the document is *unread*. An unread document is one that has not yet been opened. You can manipulate the list of unread documents by selecting a document and selecting Edit, Unread Marks. You can then mark a document read or you can mark it unread so you can locate it later.

When you are reading documents in a view, it is easy to move from one document to the next. If a document is opened for reading, you can navigate to other documents as follows:

1. Press Enter to close the current document and open the next document in the view.
2. Press Backspace to see the previous document in the view.
3. Press Tab to view the next document that is marked as *unread*.
4. Press Shift+Tab to view the previous unread document.
5. Press up and down arrow SmartIcons to view Next, Previous, Next Unread (*), and Previous Unread (*) documents.

A TOUR OF THE NOTES MAIL APPLICATION | 109

OTHER BASIC MAIL FUNCTIONS

There are a couple of other basic email functions that you would rightly expect any good email application to handle. When using Notes 5.0 email, it is easy to delete documents, and it is easy to reply and forward documents to others.

DELETING DOCUMENTS

To delete a document, press the Delete key while the document is selected in a view or is opened for reading. When you press Delete, a small delete icon is displayed beside the document. You can unmark it for deletion by selecting the document and pressing the Delete key again. Documents that are marked for deletion are not actually removed from the application until you refresh the view or actually close all documents and views in the application. When the application is fully closed, you are given the option of deleting the marked documents or exiting the application without deleting the marked documents.

You can also delete documents by dragging them to the Trash folder. You can then go to the Trash folder and refresh the view (select View, Refresh or press the F9 key) or select Empty Trash. You will see all the documents slated for deletion. The Trash folder is shown in Figure 5.7.

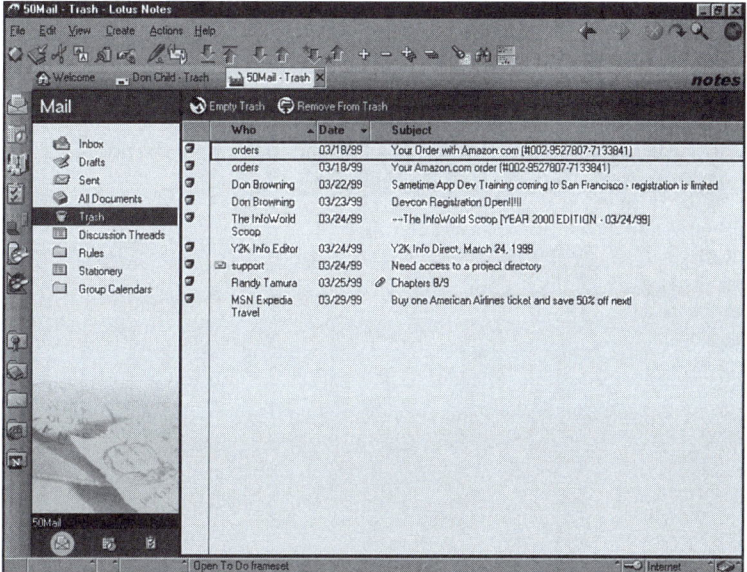

Figure 5.7
Use the Trash folder to work with documents that are due to be deleted.

You can then easily change your mind and unmark any documents you want to keep by selecting them and pressing the Delete key again. If you refresh the view, you will have the option of deleting the documents or canceling the deletion.

> **Note**
> You can also use the Empty Trash and Remove from Trash buttons to manage the documents in your Trash folder.

REPLYING TO A MESSAGE

To reply to a message, open the message for reading or select it in a view. Click the Reply button on the Action bar and select one of the following options:

- Reply—This creates a new memo to the person who sent the original memo.
- Reply with History—Reply with History creates a reply that includes a copy of the original memo.
- Reply to All—Reply to All is just like a Reply, only it is also addressed to everyone who was listed in the To: or the cc: field in the original message.
- Reply with History to All—Reply with History to All is like a Reply with History, only it is addressed to everyone who was listed in the To: or the cc: field on the original memo.

You will learn how to tailor your message defaults in the next section.

DEFINING MAIL PREFERENCES

You can define all your mail preferences in a Mail Preferences dialog box that is new to Notes 5.0. To open this dialog box, click the Tools button and select Preferences. The first page of the Preferences InfoBox is shown in Figure 5.8.

Figure 5.8
Define spell checking and owner options on the first page of the Preferences InfoBox.

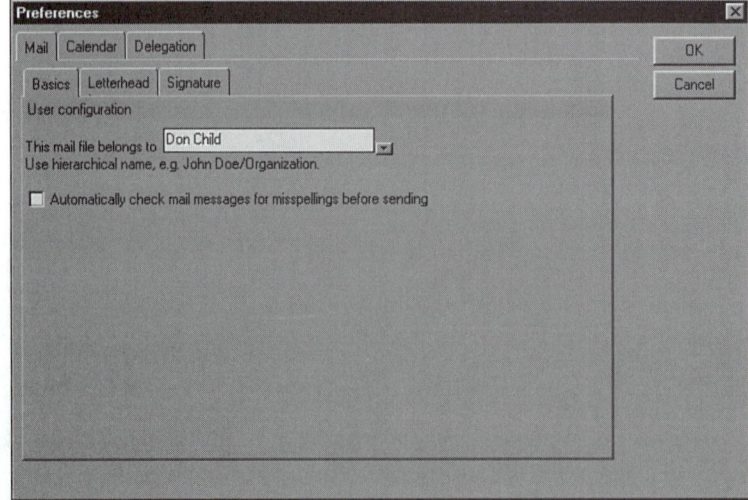

By default, you are the owner of your own mailbox. However, you can assign ownership to someone else by selecting his or her name from a Domino directory using the helper button beside the Owner field. You might want to do this with a corporate Info@YourCompany mail application, for example, when responsibility for answering incoming mail is passed to someone new.

The other option on the first page is automatic spell checking. You can turn automatic spell checking on or off. If it is turned on, all outgoing mail will be checked for misspelled words automatically before being sent.

DEFINING A LETTERHEAD

You can select from one of the numerous letterheads that come with Notes 5.0, or you can design your own. The letterhead styles are stored as subforms. You can copy and rename a subform you like and insert your own graphics. Figure 5.9 shows some of the available letterhead templates that are available on the second page of the Preferences InfoBox.

Figure 5.9
Select a new letterhead from this list of predefined styles or create your own.

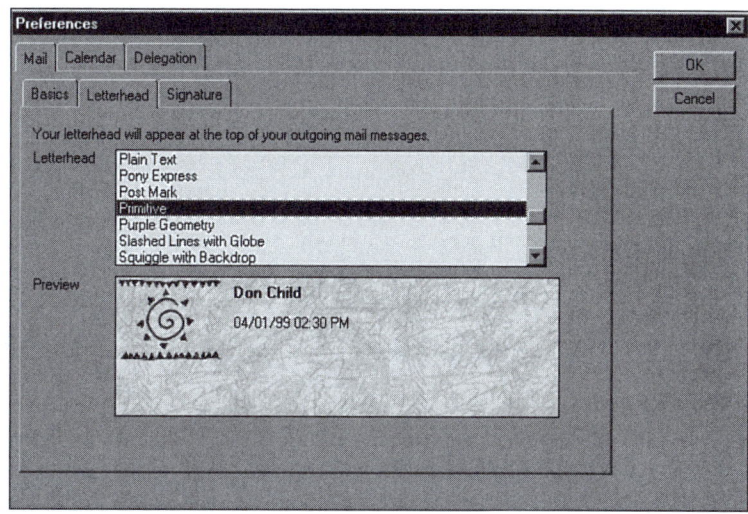

APPENDING A SIGNATURE TO YOUR MEMOS

You've probably seen email messages that have a quote, or someone's business address, a bit of humor, or maybe even a copy of their actual signature at the bottom of the message. Well you can do that too!

On the Signature page of the Preferences InfoBox, you have the choice of typing a message of your own choosing, or referencing a Sig file, an HTML file, or a graphics file. A Sig file is a text file that can be automatically imported and appended at the end of your messages. Some people even use message generators so that a new random quote is generated every time a message gets sent. The Signature page is shown in Figure 5.10.

112 CHAPTER 5 USING ELECTRONIC MAIL

Figure 5.10
Automatically append a signature or quote at the bottom of all your memos.

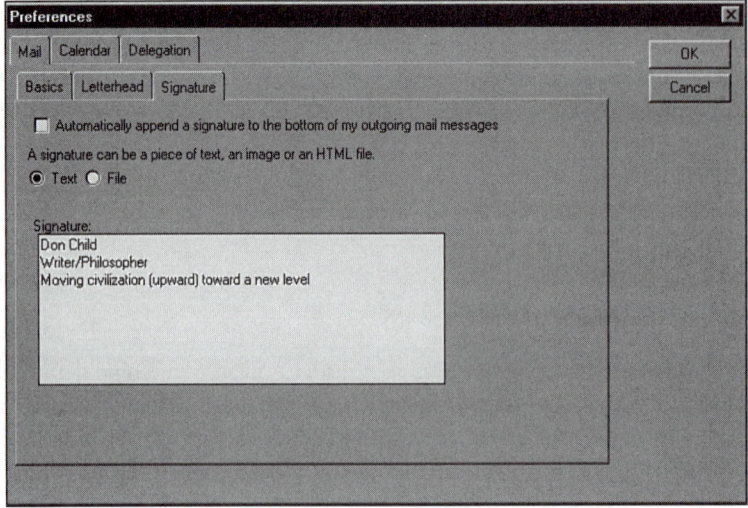

DELEGATE FUNCTIONS IN YOUR MAIL APPLICATION

The Delegation page of the Preferences InfoBox lets you delegate authority to perform certain functions in your mail application, including mail and calendar delegations. For example, you might have an executive secretary who screens your email for you. Before you ever see the mail, the junk mail has been weeded out, and misdirected messages have been forwarded to the appropriate person within your organization. You can delegate functions in your mail application using the page shown in Figure 5.11.

Figure 5.11
Give others the ability to access your mail for certain functions.

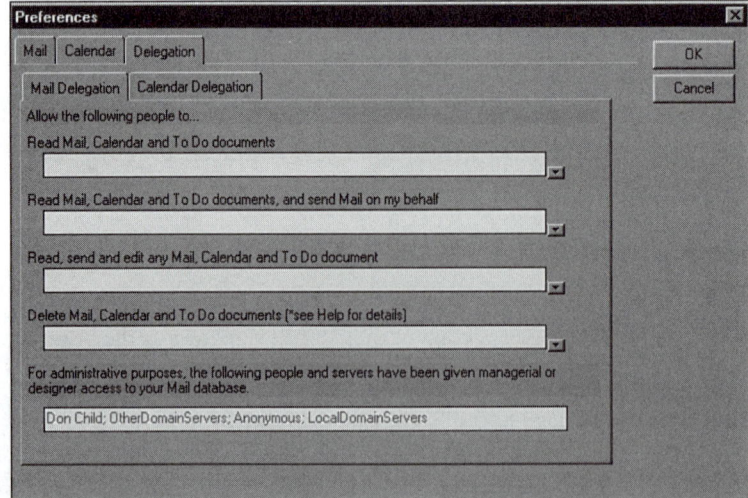

You will notice, when you learn about Access Control Lists in Chapter 17 "Access Control Lists (ACLs) and Application Security," that the delegation options closely parallel application security options. You can give specific people or groups the ability to read your mail; read your mail and create new messages using your mail application (that is, under your signature); read, create and edit messages; and read, create, edit, and delete messages.

When you finish selecting preferences, click OK. Your preferences take effect for all subsequent memos.

OTHER EMAIL FORMS

Notes Mail is considerably more than just email. For example, there are the Calendaring and Scheduling functions described in Chapter 8, "Getting Organized with the Calendaring and Scheduling Features." There are to do forms, and the special message forms described later in this chapter. Some are located under the Create, Special menu, and others are directly under the Create menu.

CREATING LINK MESSAGES

If you want to refer a colleague to a particular document, you can create a Link Message and mail it to them. It is quite simple.

1. Open a document or select the document in a view. Make sure the document is in a Domino application to which others (the recipient, in particular) have access.
2. Select Create, Special, Link Message.
3. Address the Link Message to one or more people.
4. Select any special delivery options.
5. Send the Link Message.

An example of a Link Message is shown in Figure 5.12.

When recipients receive a Link Message, they can open the linked document by clicking on the DocLink, which looks like a small document icon. There are a couple of other ways you can handle links, even if you don't want to use the Link Message documents. In any richtext field, you can create a DocLink to a Notes document or a hyperlink to a Web page. To create a DocLink to a Notes document

1. Open the document to which you want to create a link, or select the document in a view.
2. Select Edit, Copy as Link and select the type of link you want to create. The link will be copied into the clipboard.
3. Switch to the document where you want to place the link.
4. Position the cursor where you want the link placed.
5. Select Edit, Paste (Ctrl+V). You can also select text or a graphic, and select Create, Hotspot, Link Hotspot to create a customized hotspot instead of a simple DocLink icon.

Figure 5.12
Create and send a link to a document using the Link Message form.

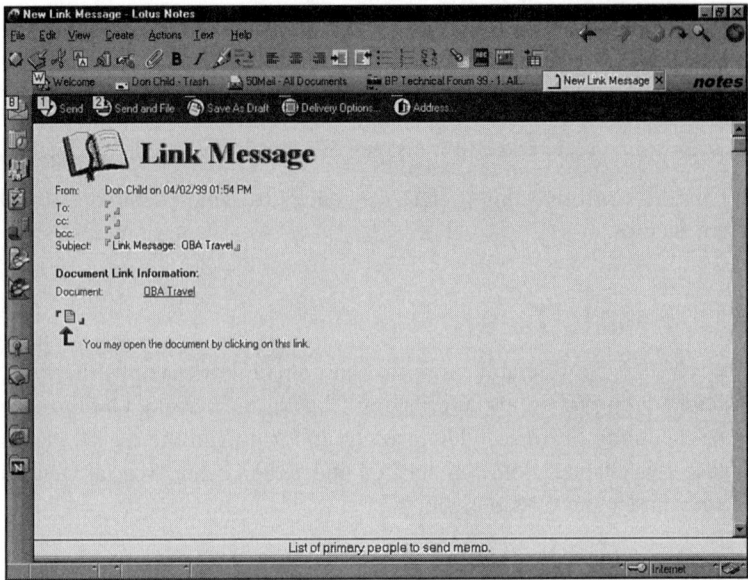

The types of DocLink you can create include the following:

- Document link
- View link—A View link takes whoever clicks on the link to a View rather than to a specific document.
- Database link—A Database link takes the user to the default view of a Domino application, rather than taking them to a specific view or document.
- Anchor Link—An anchor link takes the user to specific location within a document, including a specific location within the document that is currently open.

Links will work when accessed with a Notes client or from a Web browser. If you want to create a link to a Web page, there are a couple of approaches that will work, depending on your circumstances:

- You can open the Web page and copy the URL into memory. Then return to Notes, select text, and select Create, Hotspot, Link Hotspot.
- You can create a Personal Web Navigator application on a Domino Server, and create a DocLink to a document in that application. In the Personal Web Navigator, Web pages are saved as Notes documents so they can be read offline.

When you have created a link hotspot of any sort, you can use the Link Properties InfoBox to modify the appearance of the link.

CREATING AND USING STATIONERY | 115

PHONE MESSAGES

Phone messages can be taken and routed with a simple form designed specifically for the purpose of tracking phone calls. The phone message form is shown in Figure 5.13.

Figure 5.13
Save paper by creating an email version of a phone message.

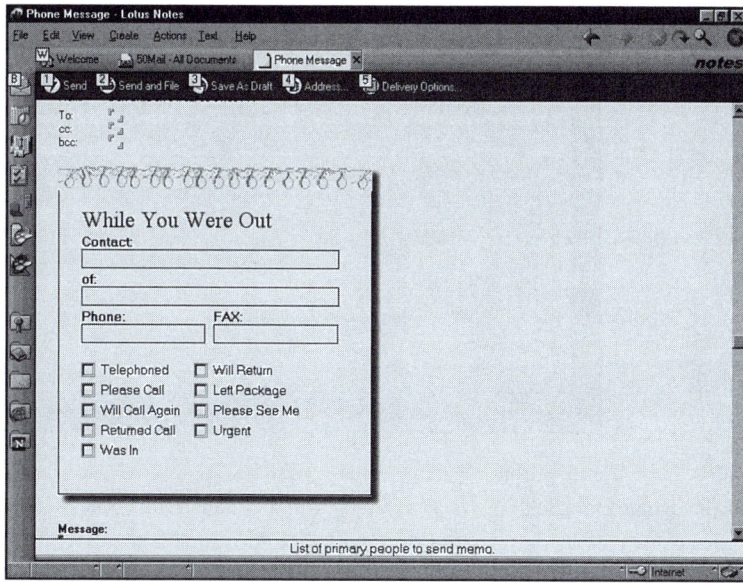

Not visible on the Phone Message form in Figure 5.13, but visible if you scroll down, is a rich-text field in which you can enter a detailed message.

CREATING AND USING STATIONERY

In Notes terms, stationery is an email template that you want to reuse. For example, in your office, you might get a reminder notice every two weeks telling you that your timesheets have to be turned in before you can get paid. The only thing that changes from one pay period to the next is the deadline for turning in timesheets.

It is an ideal application for stationery. To create stationery, do the following:

1. Switch to the Stationery view.
2. Click New Stationery.
3. Select Memo or Personal.
4. Create a memo that you want to be able to reuse.
5. Click Save.
6. Enter a name for your stationery, as shown in Figure 5.14.

Chapter 5 Using Electronic Mail

Figure 5.14
Create a memo and save it as Memo Stationery.

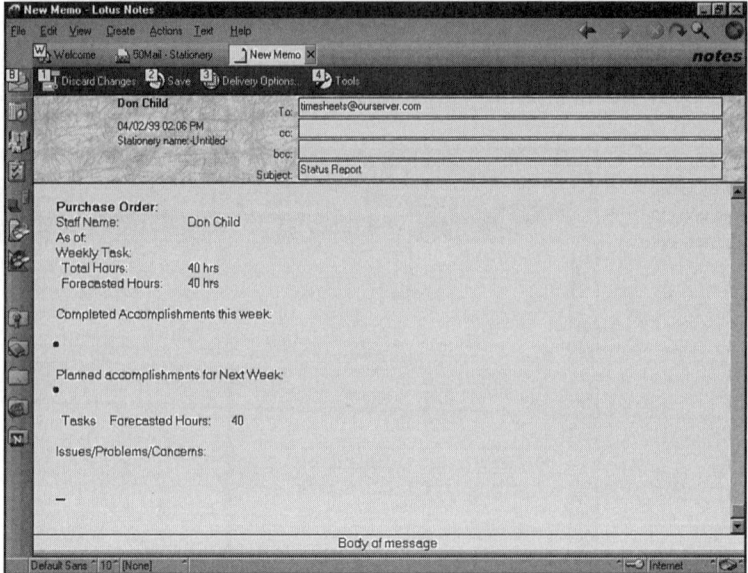

The stationery is saved in the Stationery folder under the Memo Stationery category. If you don't like any of the letterheads provided with Notes, you also have the option of creating your own Personal Stationery. From within the Stationery folder, click the Create Stationery button and select Personal. The Personal Stationery template has two extra rich-text fields that can be used for inserting your own graphics and text, as shown in Figure 5.15.

Figure 5.15
Create Personal Stationery, which has two extra rich-text fields for inserting text and graphics of your choice.

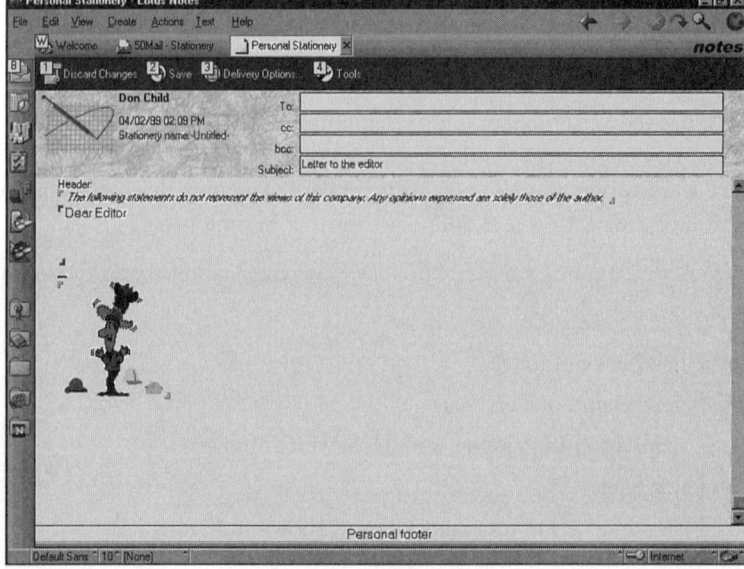

After you have created your stationery, you can use it at any time. To create a new memo using your stationery, do the following:

1. Open the Stationery folder.
2. Click the New Memo button.
3. Select New Memo - Using Stationery. A selection dialog box is displayed. Alternatively, you can select Actions, Tools, New Memo - Using Stationery.
4. Select the stationery you want to use in your new memo. A new memo is displayed using your stationery template.
5. Modify any information you want, and send the memo just like a normal memo.

ARCHIVING

You can set up archiving for the Mail application just as you can with any other Notes application. Archiving copies documents to an archive database and deletes the documents from the original application.

Archiving is automatic, based on the criteria you define in your archiving profile. To set up an archiving profile, open the Database Properties InfoBox for your Mail application. On the Basics page, click the Archive Settings button. The Archive Profile is displayed. The profile is shown in Figure 5.16.

Figure 5.16
Use the Archive Profile to define how documents are archived.

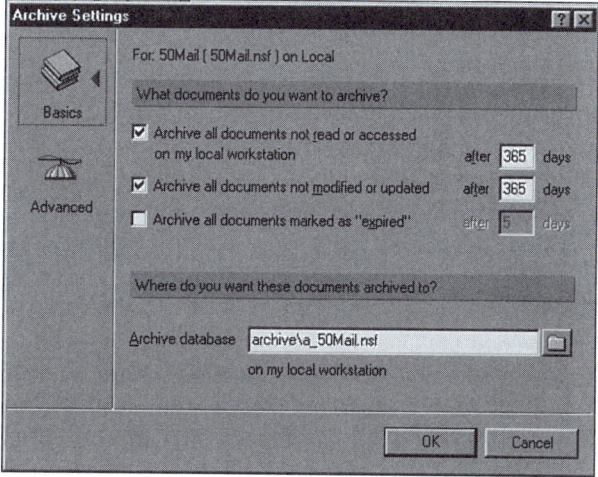

The options in the Archive Profile include when to archive documents, where to archive them, whether to archive locally or on a server, and how to handle archived documents.

Using Mail Tools

If you check under the Actions menu, there are special mail tools. Some are found directly under the Actions menu, while others are found under the submenu called Tools. The options are simply various tools that you can use to make it easier to use your email. In this section, I will describe these tools.

Add Recipients

When you receive an email that is addressed to a group of users, sometimes you might want to add those users to your Personal Address Book or to a group calendar. For example, I am helping to plan a conference. I received an email addressed to everyone on the planning committee. To add all the committee members to a single group in my address book, all I have to do is select Actions, Add Recipients, to New Group in Address Book. The individuals are added to the address book, and a new group is created. All I have to do is name the group. For example, I could name it *Conference*, then I could mail to everyone on the committee by addressing my memo to Conference.

Add Sender to Personal Address Book

This is a corollary to adding recipients to the Personal Address Book. When you receive email from someone you want to add to your Personal Address Book, select Actions, Tools, Add Sender to Personal Address Book. The person's name and email address will be added to your address book automatically. You can later return to your address book to enter additional information about the individual.

Out of Office

Wouldn't it be nice to take a vacation and not come back to the office to face dozens of unanswered email messages? You can set up an Out of Office agent that automatically informs people that you are not in the office. If people know that you are not answering your email, your mailbox will be a lot less full when you return.

To create an Out of Office profile, select Actions, Tools, Out of Office. The InfoBox in Figure 5.17 is displayed.

Here is what you can do in the Out of Office profile. Enter the dates you will be out of the office; book busytime in your calendar during those dates; create a message that is sent to people the first time they email you while you are out of the office; create a special message for specific individuals; and identify people who should not be sent your out-of-office message.

The Out of Office profile does not take effect until you enable it. You can toggle between enabled and disabled by clicking on the Enable/Disable button. When the profile is enabled and you are out of the office, messages that come into your mailbox on your home server are answered automatically based on the parameters in your Out of Office profile.

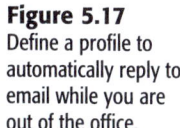

Figure 5.17
Define a profile to automatically reply to email while you are out of the office.

Send Memo to Database Manager

This option creates a new memo addressed to anyone who is listed as Manager in the Access Control List (ACL) for the currently open database. The To: field is the only one filled in. You are responsible for filling in the body of the message.

Because you are the Manager for your own mail database, it wouldn't make much sense to use this option while you have your mail open. However, when you have another database open and are having access problems, you don't always know who to ask for help. This option ensures that your memo goes to the correct person.

Rules for Handling Mail

Notes 5.0 allows you to set up rules for handling incoming email. Rules are similar to Actions, or macros that perform certain actions based on the rules that you define. When you select the Rules view, you see a list of all your current rules. You can change the order in which the rules are applied by moving them farther up the list, so they are applied before other rules, or down the list. To create a new rule, select the Rules folder and click the New Rule button to display the New Rule screen shown in Figure 5.18.

Specifying Conditions

You can build the conditions for a Rule using the helper buttons on the New Rule screen. First, you have to specify the part of an email message to examine. The choices include any of the following:

   Sender

   Subject

Body

Importance

Delivery Priority

To

CC

BCC

To or BCC

Body or Subject

Internet Domain

Size (in Kbytes)

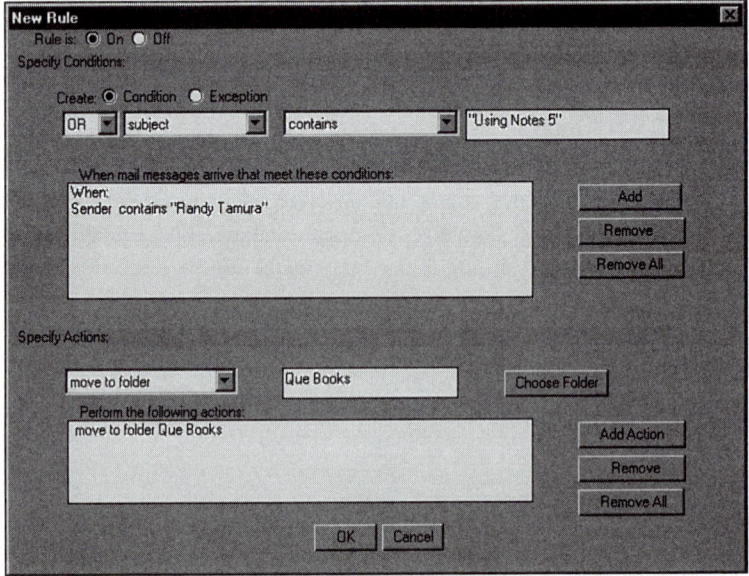

Figure 5.18
Define rules for handling email messages on the New Rule screen.

Next, you have to specify whether you want to test the field to see if it contains, does not contain, is, or is not a specified value. You then enter the value you are looking for, and click Add to add the condition to the list of conditions.

Subsequent conditions allow you to specify whether the action uses AND logic or OR logic. You can delete a condition by highlighting that line and clicking on the Remove button or you can remove all conditions and start over from scratch.

Specifying Actions

You specify actions in a similar manner to how you specify conditions. You can specify a folder to which you want to move or copy the message, you can promote or demote the importance of the document, or you can have the message automatically deleted.

Before you click OK to save the Rule, notice at the top of the New Rule page that you can click a button to turn the rule on or off.

Using Other Mail Packages with Notes

Although you are using Lotus Notes mail, you do have the option to use alternative document editors, and you can access a Notes mail database using another mail program such as Microsoft Exchange. To use an alternative editor, select File, Preferences, User Preferences. Navigate to the Mail and News page and select an alternative mail editor from a list of compatible word processors installed on your workstation.

To use Microsoft Exchange to access a Notes mail database, the Domino administrator has to create a profile that lets you use Notes Service Providers for the Messaging Application Programming Interface (MAPI). This is done during setup of the Domino server.

After you are set up for MAPI mail, you can send mail as usual, selecting the profile for the Notes Service Provider. Addressing is done using the address book you specified in your Notes Service Provider profile. You can use the Exchange interface to access the Notes Mail database. You can actually use the Exchange commands to create, send, and read mail, and you can address mail using an Exchange address book, but it must be resolved using a Domino Directory, and you use the Notes mail database to store your mail. You're able to do virtually anything you can in Notes except that you cannot verify the signature on encrypted data.

You must use the Notes mail template when accessing Notes from a MAPI application. You cannot change the design of this template.

Mail and Messaging Standards

Notes is a standards-based mail platform, with a universal mail client. The Notes Mail applications previously described take place entirely within the Notes environment, but Lotus has other mail clients that are already available, including a Java Mail client, and the POP3/SMTP mail client described later in this chapter.

The Domino Server includes an integrated SMTP Message Transfer Agent (MTA). In addition, the server includes the following:

- IMAP protocol support lets users with an IMAP client program such as Netscape Navigator read Notes mail databases that are stored on a Domino server.
- LDAP V2 Protocol RFC1777 is supported for searching. A subset of LDAP Object classes is supported for searching, including Person Organizational Person, GroupOfNames, Organization, and OrganizationalUnit.
- MIME support is available for Internet mail. The SMTP/MIME MTA stores incoming Internet mail messages as attachments, a technique which ensures that message integrity is maintained. This functionality is optional. Appended messages are also stored as attachments.

- News and NNTP support are provided as add-ins for reading Internet news with clients that use the NNTP protocol. You can also replicate news feeds from server to server by using Internet standard news servers such as USENET News servers.

Using POP3 Internet Protocol Mail

You have the option of using Internet mail as your default mail database. You can use Internet mail even if you are running the Notes client without a Domino server. You pick up your Internet mail from your ISP or from your own POP3 mail server and can share the same mail database with your Notes mail. Outgoing mail goes through an SMTP server or through the SMTP MTA which is included in the Domino server.

To set up POP3 mail, you create or modify a Location document in your Personal Address Book that defines the database in which incoming mail is stored. This database appears on the Replicator page and gathers mail from your ISP when you select Send and Receive Mail from the Replicator page or connect using a replication schedule. You can also collect your mail using a menu command. Outgoing mail is sent through the SMTP MTA if you are connected to the Internet when the mail is created. Otherwise, the outgoing mail is held in an outgoing mailbox (`SMTP.BOX`, based on the `MAILBOX.NTF` template) until you connect to the Internet again.

The Notes mail client supports multipurpose Internet mail extensions (MIME) for both outgoing and incoming mail from the Internet. That means that you and Internet mail recipients will both see mail with full fidelity. Notes also supports S/MIME for sending and receiving encrypted mail.

From Here…

The Notes mail application also includes Calendaring and Scheduling functions. You can read more about these functions and explore other aspects of Notes Mail in the following chapters:

- Chapter 6, "Working with Text and Documents," describes many of the text editing functions that can be used when creating mail messages.
- Chapter 8, "Getting Organized with the Calendaring and Scheduling Features," describes the calendar that is associated with the Notes mail application.
- Chapter 10, "Using Mobile Features from Home or on the Road," describes how to use Notes Mail when you are not connected to a local area network.
- Chapter 11, "Using the Notes Client on the Internet," describes how to use many of the built-in Internet capabilities of Notes 5.0.

CHAPTER 6

WORKING WITH TEXT AND DOCUMENTS

If release 5.0 of Lotus Notes and the Domino server is your first introduction to the world of Notes, there are a few important concepts to understand before getting down to brass tacks. For starters, every document, along with every Domino design object, can be called a *note* if you want.

NOTES DOCUMENTS DEFINED

Notes is a document-centric system. All data is stored in documents. When you create a new document, it is given a unique identity the instant you save it.

Part of the data stored in a document includes the name of the form that should be used to display and format the document the next time it is opened. The form may or may not be the same one that was used to guide you in creating the document. If the original form was designed with a field named form (usually a hidden field), the form identified in that field will be used to display the document when it is next opened.

Documents are created using a variety of forms within Lotus Notes. *Forms* consist of one or more *fields* that define what type of data the form can contain and how it should be displayed. There are a number of data types that an application designer can assign to a field. Examples of data types include text, rich text, time, and numeric. The form usually also contains a variety of design elements, such as graphics, static text, buttons and hotspots, and hidden header fields that also can contain vital data that can determine how the document is processed. Every application has its own forms.

Forms include everything from email forms and simple discussion forms to complex workflow forms that change dynamically as you enter data, and route your completed document to others for approval or for further action. There are hundreds of forms. Some come from standard Notes templates, and some are custom-built.

ANATOMY OF A DOCUMENT

A form gives underlying structure to every document in a Domino database. As already mentioned, the form is a template through which data is displayed. By changing the form used to display Domino data, you can change the appearance and organization of documents. In other words, the raw information is the important component. The form is used to format the information. The information is organized into documents as a convenient way to package and deliver information to the person using the data.

An example of a Discussion document is shown in Figure 6.1. Note the graphical element at the top of the form and the field labels that are static parts of the form. The text entered into editable fields is the data that has been entered into this form.

The data within a document can come from practically anywhere. It can be retrieved from an enterprise system running on a mainframe computer or an AS/400, for example. It can be downloaded from the Internet, or it can be picked up from another Domino database. It can be inherited from another document, and, of course, it can be entered directly into the form when you create a new document.

Notes Documents Defined | 125

Graphical design elements   Static text

Figure 6.1
A document is raw data entered into and displayed via a form.

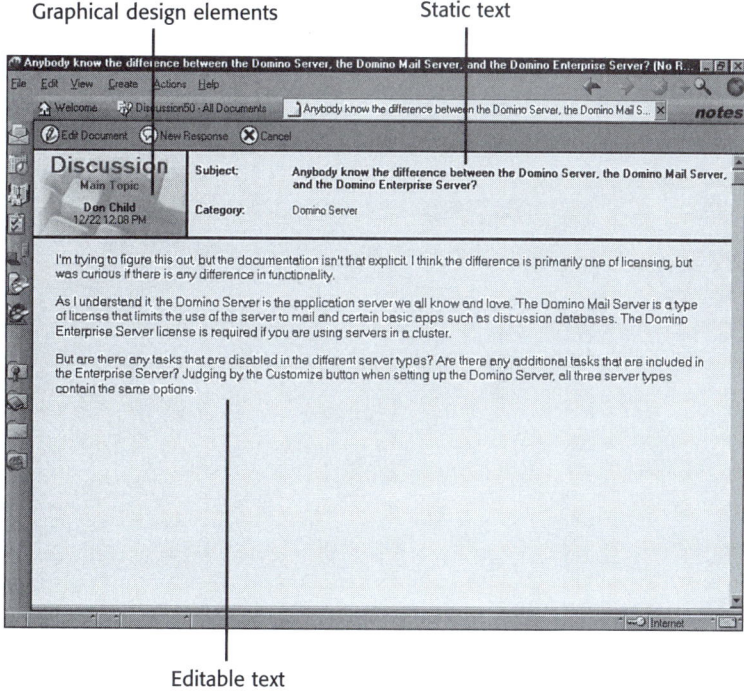

Editable text

Working with Text

Virtually any data other than graphics that is stored in a Domino database can be considered "text" in one form or another. The designer of an application determines how information is displayed. The designer defines which form is used and the appearance and data type of all fields on the form. By defining the data type for each field, the application designer determines whether the text in a particular field will be formatted and stored as a date—for example, a username, simple alphanumeric text, rich text, or even HTML. In this chapter, we are concerned mostly with plain text and rich text.

Static Text Versus Document-Specific Text

When you look at a form before any data has been entered into it, you will see two things in addition to any design elements such as graphics and tables. You will see *static text*, which provides a context for users and guides them to the parts of the form where they need to enter data, and *fields*, the predefined areas on the form where users can enter data. The static text is part of the form, and any document created and displayed with the same form will have the same static text.

Data is input and displayed using the form. When you create a new document, some fields may already be filled in by inheriting data from a parent document or by formula. Other fields will be empty, awaiting your input.

PART
II
CH
6

With Notes 5.0, the location of input fields may not always be apparent. For some types of fields, you may see only a cursor to indicate where data should be entered. Other fields may be displayed as rectangular input areas, as bracketed fields (as with earlier versions of Notes) or with various selection-type fields, such as radio buttons, check boxes, or list boxes. Examples of input fields are illustrated on the screen in Figure 6.2.

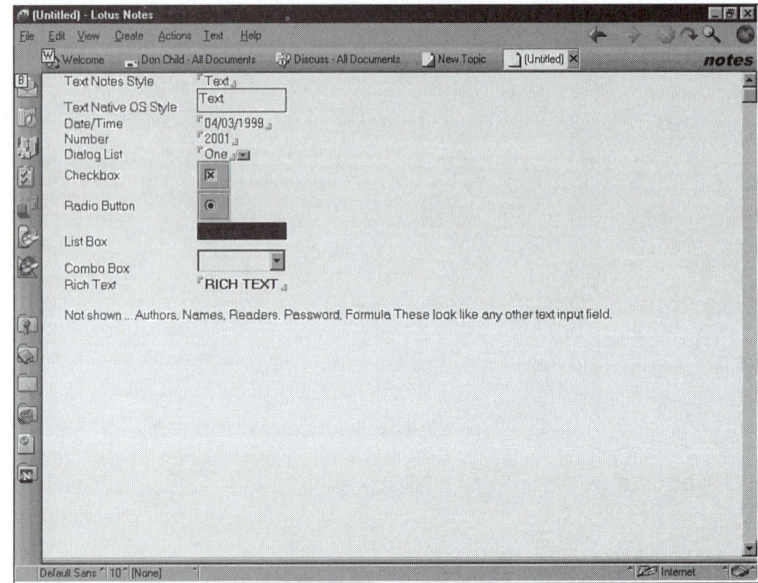

Figure 6.2
The appearance of the input field depends on how the form was designed.

FIELD DATA TYPES

Most data can be displayed on the computer screen as text. When you input data, it will be displayed on the screen as you type. But the type of data allowed in a field depends on how the field was defined by the application designer. The data types include the following:

- Text
- Date/time
- Number
- Dialog list
- Check box
- Radio button
- List box
- Combo box
- Rich text
- Authors

- Names
- Readers
- Passwords
- Formulas

With the exception of rich text, an end user has no control over how information is displayed. The application designer defines the layout and appearance of the information in a field.

> **Tip**
> Some fields remain hidden from users, even though they may hold information such as that used in calculations or information that provides identifying information unique to a document. For example, reader or author fields and password fields are usually hidden. Other fields are hidden in certain circumstances. Some information may be hidden when a document is printed on the Web, for example, although it is not hidden when seen through Notes.

Editing Text Versus Viewing Text

When you view a document, the text cannot be edited unless you are in the *edit mode*. Some text that is visible while editing or creating a document may be hidden when the document is being viewed, and vice versa. When you create a new document, it is automatically in edit mode. When you open a document that has previously been created and saved, it usually is in read mode. If you have document editing privileges (defined in the Access Control List), you can put the document into the edit mode by pressing Ctrl+E or by double-clicking anywhere in the document. Another popular way to put the document into edit mode is to click on the Actions, Edit Document SmartIcon. Sometimes, there is an Edit action button that can be clicked.

Working with Rich Text

Rich text is essentially a free-form field. You can add and delete text just as you can with a regular text field. However, you can also format the text; change the font, size, and color of the text; format paragraphs; apply styles; add links; insert or embed graphics and objects, such as spreadsheets; create tables; and attach files. In short, you can let your imagination loose and create the same sort of pages you would with a word processor or page layout program.

There are three simple signals that tell you when you are in a rich-text field. First, you can expand the drop-down Text menu and you will see that the options on the menu are not grayed out. Second, you can look at the status bar at the bottom of the workspace. If you see the name of the font, the size of the font, and the name of the current style near the left edge of the status bar, you are currently in a rich-text field. Third, you can right-click anywhere in the field and you will see a floating menu that offers Text Properties as the first option. The first page of the Text Properties InfoBox is shown in Figure 6.3.

Figure 6.3
The Text Properties InfoBox is used to define the appearance of text.

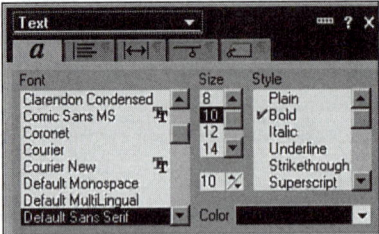

To learn about the text-editing features, we will go through the different pages in the Text Properties InfoBox.

> **Tip**
>
> At the top on the right side of the InfoBox, there is a small icon representing a button bar. You can click on this icon, and the InfoBox will be collapsed but will leave you with shorthand access to font properties from any page in the InfoBox.

Working with Fonts

In the Text Properties InfoBox, you can see that the default font for Lotus Notes is 10-point Default Sans Serif, which is designed for easy online reading. You can change to another font of another point size by scrolling through the font and size windows in the InfoBox. Directly beneath the Size box is a control that lists the current font size. Clicking on the down or up arrows next to the current size decreases or increases the font size a single step at a time. As with most word processors, when you change to a new font attribute, the attribute is effective from that point forward. However, if you have text selected, only the selected text is changed to the new attributes. You can change the font style to include a variety of attributes, as shown in Figure 6.3.

> **Tip**
>
> Some of the common font attributes are also available from the drop-down Text menu and from the floating menu (right-click). You can also select bold, italic, and underline attributes using keyboard shortcuts (for example, Ctrl+B to select bold).

You can select a new color by clicking on the color control. A panel is displayed so you can select from up to 256 colors, including 16 primary colors that can also be picked from the drop-down Text menu. Red and blue can also be picked from the floating Text menu.

Working with Rich Text | 129

Using the Permanent Pen

After you define unique font attributes on the first page of the Text Properties InfoBox, you can select Text, Permanent Pen, Set Permanent Pen Style to set a Permanent Pen style. The attributes you currently have selected become your new Permanent Pen font.

The Permanent Pen enables you to type anywhere within a document in a unique font. For example, suppose you want to annotate a document, as shown in Figure 6.4, and then forward the document with your annotations. You want to make sure your annotations are in a unique font, so you select Permanent Pen and begin typing. Everything you type from then on will be in your Permanent Pen font—for example, red italics in a larger point size. Move the cursor to a new location, and you will still be in your Permanent Pen font. It is like picking up a red pen, for example, and editing a document.

Figure 6.4
The Permanent Pen types your selected font wherever you start typing.

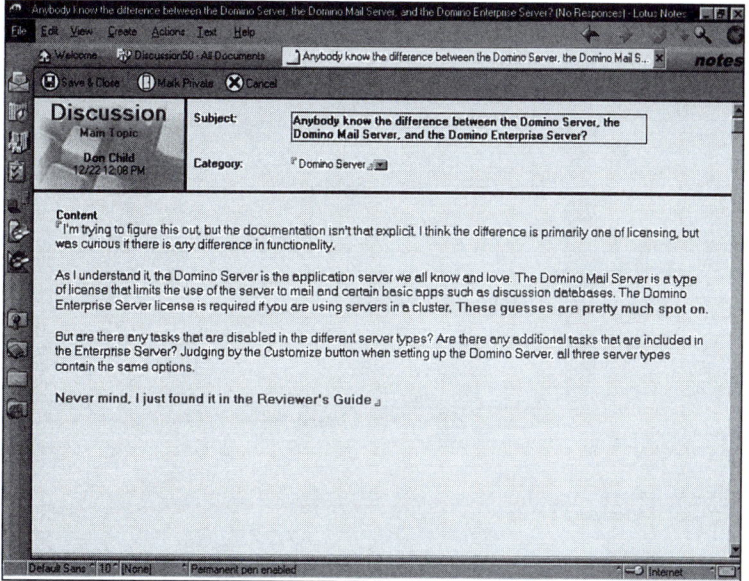

If a document is being routed to several members of a workgroup, each can use a unique Permanent Pen font so everyone can see who inserted which text into the document. If you do not have Permanent Pen selected, Notes picks up whatever the font is at the cursor position.

> **Tip**
> You can toggle the Permanent Pen on by clicking on the Permanent Pen SmartIcon. You can toggle the Permanent Pen on or off by selecting Permanent Pen from the Text drop-down menu.

Part II
Ch
6

USING THE HIGHLIGHTER

Somewhat similar to the Permanent Pen is the Highlighter function. The highlighter is not available from the Text Properties InfoBox. It is available from the Text menu (select Text, Highlighter) only when a document is in the edit mode. With the highlighter activated, you can hold down the left mouse button and drag the cursor over text to highlight it in yellow, pink, or blue, just as you would when highlighting text using a highlighter pen. This is illustrated in Figure 6.5.

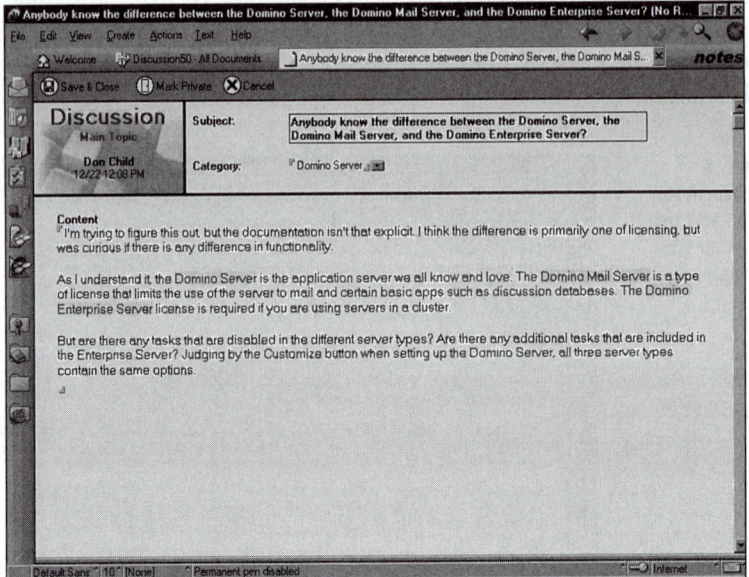

Figure 6.5
Use the Highlighter to mark text as you would with a highlighter pen.

PARAGRAPH FORMATTING

The second page of the Text Properties InfoBox enables you to control paragraph formatting. This page is shown in Figure 6.6.

On the first line, you can set the paragraph alignment to flush left, centered, flush right, or fully justified. You can also turn justification off. Normally, when you type using the Domino editor, text wraps automatically to the width of the screen. This is true no matter what type of justification you set. Full justification wraps at three inches if you have your editing window set to three inches in size (by using the minimize button in the top-right corner of the workspace), and it wraps at seven inches if your screen has seven inches of workspace.

With fully justified text, the Domino editor pads word spacing so that both ends of the line to the edge of the editing window remain justified. When you turn justification off, there is no line wrapping until you get to the maximum line length.

Working with Rich Text 131

Figure 6.6
The second page of the Text Properties InfoBox is used to format paragraphs.

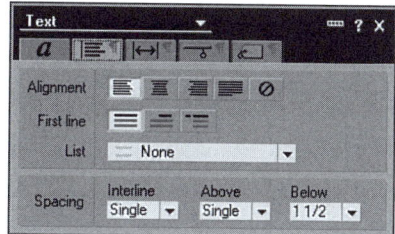

The second item on the paragraph-formatting page of the Text Properties InfoBox controls the indentation of the first line of text in paragraphs. If the cursor is in a paragraph, or if any portion of the paragraph is selected, the indent rules are applied to that paragraph.

You can set your paragraphs so they have no indent, so they are indented to the first tab (.5 inches by default), or so the paragraph has a hanging indent (that is, the first line hangs out to the left of the remainder of the paragraph). To change the indent, simply place the cursor in a paragraph and click on the icon representing the type of indentation you want.

The third line of icons is used to control the appearance of *lists*. Lists can include a variety of characters, such as numbered text, bulleted text with solid bullets, circles, solid squares, check boxes for To Do lists, and upper- or lowercase alpha characters. You can also turn bullets off by clicking on a SmartIcon.

You can also create a list within a list within a list within a list. For example, you can start a numbered list, and then click the text indent SmartIcon to indent a line. A new numbering series will be restarted on the indented line, or you can change the line to bullets. You can restart the previous numbering sequence by clicking on the text outdent SmartIcon.

The next paragraph setting on the second page of the Text Properties InfoBox is used to set line and paragraph spacing. You can set interline spacing so that a paragraph is single-spaced, spaced at 1 1/2 lines, or double-spaced. You can also offset the paragraph from the one above by 1, 1 1/2, or 2 lines. You can also set a paragraph apart from the one following it by the same increments.

Interparagraph spacing is especially useful if you want to set off bulleted text from the main body of your typing. For example, you can have the regular paragraph spacing set to double, but the bulleted text can be set off by one-and-a-half spaces from the text above and below. For certain international settings, you can also define the reading order of text—left to right or right to left.

Pagination

The third page of the Text Properties InfoBox is used to set pagination and tabs. With pagination, you can define whether a paragraph should start on a new page; whether it should be kept on a single page without breaking, if possible; and whether it should be kept on the same page as the next paragraph. Pagination relates to text only when it is printed, because there are no pages in a scrolling document.

Setting Tabs in the Text Properties InfoBox

The third page of the Text Properties InfoBox is also used to set tabs. If you have the Tab stops selector on Individually Set (as shown in Figure 6.7), you can set specific tab locations. Tabs are left tabs by default, but you can specify C, R, or D for centered, right, or decimal, plus the number of inches from the left margin. You should separate multiple settings with semicolons. For example, a setting of 1;C3;R5 gives you a left tab at one inch, a center tab at 3 inches, and right tab at 5 inches. When you type the settings into the Text Properties InfoBox, double quotes (") are automatically inserted to represent inches as soon as you click outside the InfoBox.

Figure 6.7
Inserting tabs using the Text Properties InfoBox.

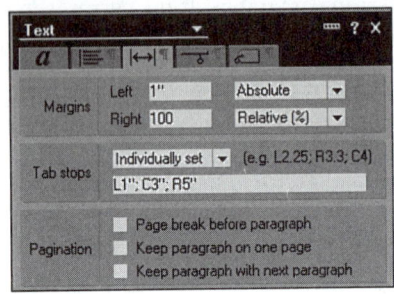

If you select Evenly Spaced, you can enter the number of inches or decimal fractions of inches between tabs.

Setting Tabs with the Ruler Bar

You can do more customizing of margins and tab settings using the ruler bar. To display the ruler bar, select View, Ruler, or click on the Ruler SmartIcon.

The left side of the ruler represents the left margin. You can drag the top triangle to set the first line of a paragraph to a new location. You can drag the bottom triangle to set the location of all other lines in the paragraph. You can drag both the top and bottom triangles by dragging them from the small rectangle beneath the two triangles.

You can set tabs by clicking on the ruler at the location where you want a tab. The tab setting applies to the paragraph where the cursor is located, and any paragraphs that are at least partly selected, by holding and dragging the mouse over them.

You can remove tabs by clicking directly on them. You can move tabs by holding down the mouse button while pointing at the tab. Slide the tab to its new position, and then release the mouse button. An example of the ruler bar is shown in Figure 6.8.

By default, there is a tab every half-inch, although they do not show on the ruler bar. If you set any tabs, the default half-inch tabs begin to the right of the last tab that you set. When you click on the ruler bar using the left mouse button, a left tab is set at the spot. With a left tab, your typing will be left-justified from the tab setting. If you click on the ruler with the right mouse button, a floating menu appears from which you can select a left tab, a right tab, a centered tab, or a decimal tab. A right tab causes text to be right-justified from the tab setting. Text is centered with a center tab. With a decimal tab, text is justified on a decimal—for example, when you are typing a column of prices.

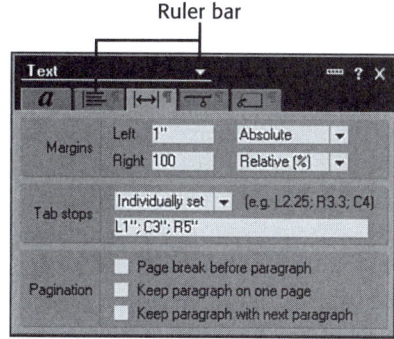

Figure 6.8
Set margins and tabs using the ruler bar.

> **Tip**
>
> You can also set margins using the margin setting page of the Text Properties InfoBox. You can set absolute margins from the left edge of the page, such as 1" and 7". You can also set relative margins as a percentage of the page width. For example, the default left margin is 13%, and the right margin is 100%.

Hiding Paragraphs

As mentioned earlier, text is hidden under certain circumstances. Text may be hidden under any of the following conditions, using the window-shade tab in the Text Properties InfoBox:

- **Hide from Notes 4.6 clients or later** If you are using advanced functionality, such as embedded Java or programs that depend on newer LotusScript functions, you can hide that portion of your document. Or you may have instructions for workarounds that are explicit to users of earlier versions of Notes. This function is commonly used to hide parts of the document from Notes clients when functionality is put in especially for Web clients.

- **Hide from Web browsers** You may have information that is intended for Notes users, but not for people who access the same page using a Web browser. By highlighting the paragraph and clicking Web Browsers, the paragraph will not be visible when the document is viewed from the Web.

- **Hide when document is previewed for reading** You can adjust a Notes view so that you can preview documents without opening them. To make the preview more meaningful, you may want to hide unessential design elements so that the previewer can quickly have a meaningful idea about the content of your document.

- **Hide when opened for reading** You can use this to hide text that is intended only as annotation or instructions while the document is being edited or created. If text is hidden when opened for reading, it is automatically hidden when printed, as well.

- **Hide when printed** This option can be used to prevent information from being printed. For example, you may have information intended to be read only when a document is accessed online, so you can hide it when the document is printed.

- **Hide when previewed for editing** You can do limited editing when accessing a document through the Preview Pane. Hiding text with this option is the way to limit what can be edited from the Preview Pane.

- **Hide when opened for editing** With this option, you can have information that is visible to someone reading the document, but the information is hidden from anyone who is editing the document. For example, you may have a standard template where only certain paragraphs are edited. The remainder of the template can be hidden to avoid confusion on the part of editors.

> **Tip**
>
> As a document creator or editor, you cannot hide an entire field when the document is being edited. The first and last paragraphs in the field must remain unhidden. You can make these lines blank as a workaround if you want to hide the entire contents of a rich-text field.

- **Hide when copied to the clipboard** This option enables you to be sure that somebody does not copy confidential text and paste it into another document in an unsecured database. If you check this and Hide when printed, the only way data can be copied from the document is to do a screen print or gain Editor access to the document.

- **Hide paragraph if formula is true** You can create a formula that tests for the presence or absence of a certain value and hides the paragraph when the formula's criteria are met. Notes formulas are described in Chapter 18, "Working with Formulas, Functions, and Commands."

How to Hide Text

You can hide text using the Text Properties InfoBox. Most of the hide-when options are displayed as simple check boxes. The hide-when page can be recognized by the window-shade icon on the tab.

Place the cursor anywhere in the paragraph that you want to hide. Click on the appropriate check box. The text will be hidden under the checked conditions the next time the document is opened after it has been saved. Hide-when is used extensively by designers to show certain parts of the form under certain conditions, but is not likely to be used much by end users when working with documents.

Using Text Styles

It has taken a lot of work to get this far. Imagine what it would be like if you had to go through every step in the Text Properties InfoBox for every paragraph in every document! It would hardly be worth it. Well, I have some good news for you. When you get a paragraph so it works just the way you want it, you can save the text attributes as a style. The style can then be applied to other paragraphs within the same document. You even have the option of using the same style for other documents in the same Domino database, or in other databases on the same workstation.

Creating a Text Style

To create a new style, you first format a paragraph that has all the attributes you want in your style. You then highlight the paragraph and save it as style. When saved, the style can be applied to other paragraphs. To save a new style, complete the following steps:

1. Select the text whose attributes you want to save as a style. All you have to do is place the cursor anywhere in the paragraph you want to make into a style.
2. On the Style Tag page of the Text Properties InfoBox, click Create Style.

   The Create Paragraph Style dialog box will be displayed. This is shown in Figure 6.9.

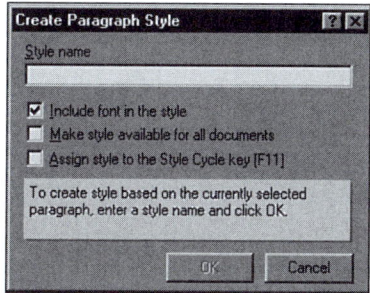

Figure 6.9
Define your new style in the Create Paragraph Style dialog box.

3. Enter a name for your style.
4. Indicate whether you want to include the font in the named style (default), whether to make the style available to all documents in the Domino database, and whether to include the style in the Style Cycle key (see the next section, "Applying Styles to Text," for a discussion of the Cycle key).
5. When you are done, click OK to save the style.

Applying Styles to Text

There are three ways you can apply a named style to a paragraph:

- From the drop-down Text menu, select Named Style and select the style you want to apply.

- Click on the Cycle SmartIcon to cycle through any styles that have been assigned to the Text Style Cycle key, or press F11 to cycle through the styles.
- Select the style from the Style indicator near the left side of the status bar, near the font and size indicators.

If you decide later that you want to assign or remove a style from the Text Style Cycle key, you can do so with the following steps:

1. Open the Text Properties InfoBox.
2. Click on the Assign to Keyboard button on the Style Tags page.
3. Select or deselect styles from the list.
4. Click on OK to save your changes.

The Assign Style to Keyboard dialog box is shown in Figure 6.10.

Figure 6.10
Place a check beside styles you want to assign to the Cycle key.

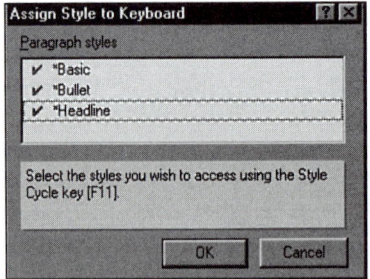

If you want to redefine a style, select a paragraph to which the style has been assigned. Edit the text attributes to what you want, and then click on the Redefine Styles button. The new attributes will be applied to all paragraphs defined with that style.

USING LINKS IN RICH-TEXT FIELDS

In a rich-text field, you can insert hypertext links to Web pages, Notes documents, Notes views, and Domino databases, and you can insert anchor links to text within the same document. With Notes 5.0, you can move with fluidity between HTML documents and Notes documents or other Notes elements, and the links are one of the tools that makes that navigation transparent. Click on the link and you go to the target of the link. If the target is a Web document, the link has an HTTP format. If the link is to a Notes document or view, or a Domino database, the link is in the same format, only it points to C:\Notes or wherever the element happens to be located. The Notes client moves seamlessly between the Web and Notes.

Creating any type of link from a Notes document or from a Web page opened through the Personal Web Navigator involves the same basic process:

1. Go to the location to which you want to link.
2. Select Edit, Copy as Link, and select Anchor Link (not available for Web pages), Document Link, View Link, or Database Link.
3. Return to the Notes document where you want to place the link.
4. Select the text (or a graphic) that you want to turn into a link.
5. Select Create, HotSpot, Link HotSpot.
6. The HotSpot Resource Link Infobox is displayed, as shown in Figure 6.11. You can modify the link appearance and properties.

To create a URL Link to a Web page opened outside Notes (for example, a page opened in Internet Explorer), copy the URL for the page while in your Web browser. Return to Notes, highlight the text you want as a hotspot, and select Create, HotSpot, Link HotSpot, as you did previously.

You can tailor a link using the HotSpot Resource Link InfoBox, shown in Figure 6.11.

Figure 6.11
Set attributes for a link in the HotSpot Resource Link InfoBox.

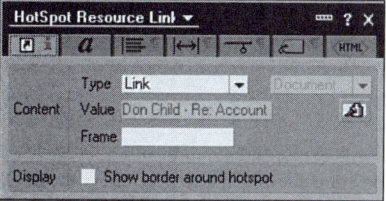

The link can be a Notes link, a URL link, or a Named Element link (that is, a page, a form, a frameset, or a view). The Value field holds the name of the link, whether it is a URL or doclink, a formula, or the name of a named element. The Frame field identifies in which frame the linked document or element should be displayed.

On the second page of the HotSpot Resource Link Infobox, you can define HTML tags to control the appearance and behavior of the link when it is viewed using a Web browser. The other pages enable you to define the text attributes of the linked text, just as you would define the attributes of any other text. To remove a link, put the document into edit mode and place the cursor on the link. Select HotSpot, Remove HotSpot.

Working with Tables

If you are familiar with tables in earlier versions of Notes, you are in for a treat with the tables in Notes 5.0. Among the features added are alignment of tables, collapsible and tabbed tables, gradient colors, drop shadows, backgrounds, and auto resizing of columns based on the text included in the cells. Figure 6.12 illustrates some of the features of tables in Notes 5.0.

Figure 6.12
Notes 5.0 offers a rich variety of graphical features.

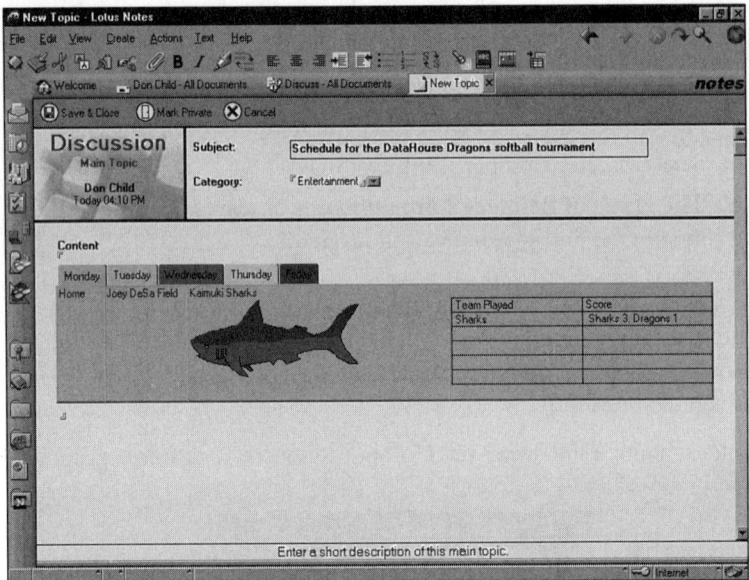

You can create a table in a rich-text field by clicking on the Create Table SmartIcon, or by selecting Create, Table from the drop-down menu. Select the number of rows and columns for your table in the Create Table dialog box; you can also select the type of table. You can select a basic table, a tabbed table, an animated table that displays rows one at a time on a timed basis, or a programmed table that displays rows based on the value in a field. After the table is created, you can add colors, change the width of columns, stack rows, insert graphics, embed other tables, and so forth.

Opening InfoBoxes
By now, you should realize that there are InfoBoxes available for anything that you can assign attributes to in Notes. To open any Property InfoBox, do one of the following: Select the item and click on the Properties SmartIcon, right-click on the item and select Properties from the floating menu, or select Properties from the drop-down menu for the selected item.

To modify the attributes of a table, you use the Table Properties InfoBox. Moving from page to page in the InfoBox, you can do any of the following with a table:

- Define the size of the table, the rows, and the cells within the table. Experiment with a variety of sizing options on the first page of the InfoBox.

- Define the borders of the cells. Borders can be colored; they can be made solid, ridged, or grooved; or they can be made selectively invisible by making the cell border the same color as the cell background. This is done on the second page of the InfoBox.

- Define color cells, rows, or the entire table. You can add color gradients and you can add a drop shadow. These are done on the third page of the InfoBox.

- Define table borders similarly to the way you defined borders for individual cells. This is done on the fourth page of the InfoBox.

- Set absolute margins from the edges of the page, as you can with text, on the fifth page of the InfoBox.

- Set the row attributes, including height, and define whether rows are fixed or expandable (for example, Don't Wrap) and where in the row text is displayed on the sixth page of the InfoBox.

- On the last page, define HTML tags for the entire table, for individual rows, or for cells to give you more control over how the table is displayed on the Web.

You have a lot of control over the table. For example, depending on the type of table you create, you can collapse the table, if you want. With a collapsible table, you have a number of options. You can show a single row and have the next row appear when the user clicks on the table. You can set the table so that it starts automatically, with a timer that is set in milliseconds. You can have the table cycle through each row once when the document is first loaded, or when the table is first clicked on. With any of the cycle options, you can also set a number of transition effects. You can also select Tabs, as shown previously in Figure 6.12, or you can name the different rows and have different rows displayed based on the contents of a field.

> **Tip**
> Table attributes can be used in a number of ways. Just to start you thinking, here are a few of my ideas. You can create banner ads, a stock ticker, or a display of inspirational thoughts. You can create an effect such as an animated gif, you can display credits, or you can display information that reinforces company policies.

Working with Graphics in Rich-text Fields

You can insert graphics into rich-text fields, and you can then manipulate those graphics using the Picture Properties InfoBox. You can do the following to a picture:

- Change the size of the graphic.
- Set the position of the graphic so that text wraps around it (float left) or so that it spans multiple lines of text.
- Create alternative text for displaying through a Web browser, and define the alternative text as a caption.

The capability of wrapping text around graphics is new in Notes 5.0. The technique for floating a picture is illustrated in Figure 6.13.

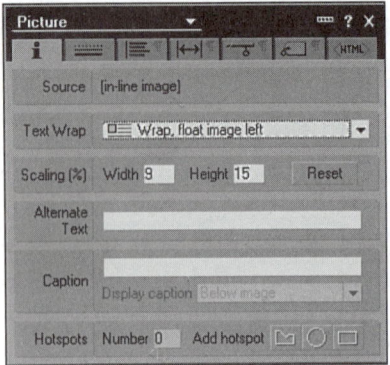

Figure 6.13
Float a picture to display text to the left or right of it.

To work with a graphic, select Create, Picture; or you can import a graphic using File, Import. Click on the picture and open the Picture Properties InfoBox.

> **Tip**
> You will get better results if you insert rather than import a picture. Importing can distort the color palette, giving you unpredictable results. If you will be using pictures on the Web, you may want to select Use Web Palette from the Advanced Options portion of the Notes Preferences dialog box (File, Preferences, User Preferences) to ensure that graphics are optimized for the Web.

Most of the options in the InfoBox are the same as text options, except for the first page of the InfoBox (refer to Figure 6.13). On this page, you have the following options:

- **Text Wrap** You can set the position of a picture as left, right, or center using text alignment. But you can also align or wrap text. The alignment options include top, center, baseline, and bottom, which describe the position of a single line of text beside the picture. If you choose float image left or float image right, the picture will be on the left or right side of the picture, with text wrapped around it. You can also place text to the side of the picture by selecting Span Lines.

- **Scaling** Scaling is used to change the size and proportions of the picture. You can grab a corner of the picture and drag it, but you will get better results if you change the height and width by the same percentage.

- **Alternate Text** You can type alternative text to appear when a graphic is loading in a browser, and to appear as a caption with the picture. You cannot select Display text as caption until after the text has been typed and saved by clicking on a check mark that will be displayed beside it.

- Caption   You can add a caption to your picture.
- HotSpots   You can transform a graphic into a hotspot (a link or an action defined by a formula).

Working with Attachments

You can attach files in the rich-text field of any document. When someone reads the document with an attached file, it may be possible to view the attachment (for over 100 different file formats) or launch the attachment if you have a local application capable of opening the attached file; or the user can copy the file to a local drive.

Don't be confused by the terminology. You are given the option to "Detach" the file. Actually, you don't detach the file; you make a copy of it. The terminology can be confusing. After you detach a file, it is still stored in the Notes document for the next person who reads the document.

To create an attachment:

1. Place the cursor where you want the attachment to be located.
2. Select File, Attach.
3. Select the name of the file you want to attach.
4. Click on the Create button.

The attachment is inserted. An icon represents the attachment. If you have the application that was used to create the file, the icon for the application will be displayed. If you don't have the application on your system, a generic document icon will represent the attachment.

Working with Documents in Views

You can work with documents in a Notes view, from links on the Headline Page or from links within other documents. After a document is opened, you can use navigation icons to move backward and forward, to cancel loading, to refresh a page or view, or to search for documents. But first, you have to locate documents. That is usually done in a Notes view.

A Notes view is a list of documents that meet predefined selection criteria. For example, a view might contain all documents created using a form named Product. You can create views that select documents based on unique values in any field except rich-text fields. In a typical view, you use the left pane to navigate to other views. You use an optional bottom pane for previewing documents. The remainder of the screen contains a list of documents that are available for reading, editing, printing, or performing other actions on, such as copying or deleting. A typical view is shown in Figure 6.14.

PART
II

CH
6

142 CHAPTER 6 WORKING WITH TEXT AND DOCUMENTS

Figure 6.14
A typical Notes Discussion database view.

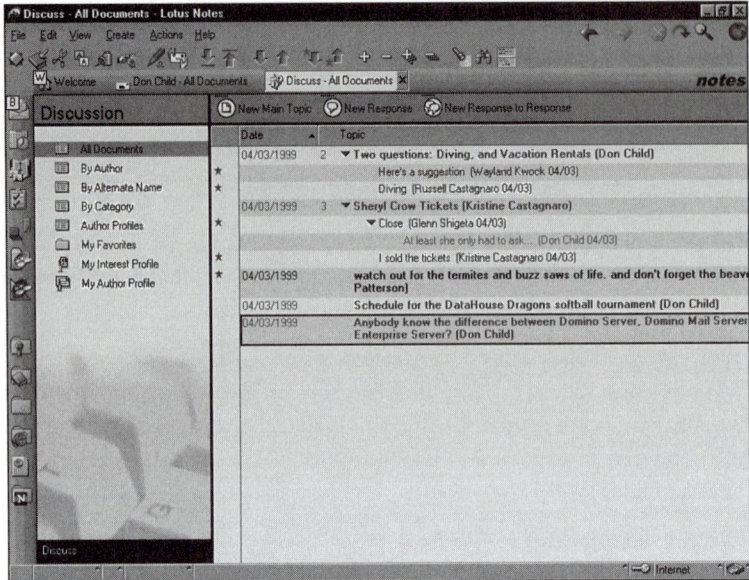

In Notes 5.0, documents may reside in a Domino database, but don't necessarily have to. Documents can also be stored on the Internet as Web pages or documents that contain data that resides in various types of databases. Traditionally, however, documents are stored in a Domino database. For the sake of clarity, Figure 6.14 shows a typical view in a Domino database so you can more easily understand the different elements.

Some views contain all documents in a database. But the strength of views is their capability of filtering out documents, showing you only what you need. For example, suppose you have a database that you use to track sales. You probably have a view that displays active invoices. You have another view with orders sorted by salesperson. The documents in each view are from the same database, but they are selected because they contain specific criteria—an invoice form with a status of Active, and an order form that is categorized based on the Sales Person field.

The documents that you see in the view are those that meet the selection criteria and are in the database at the moment the view is opened. If a document is added to the database after the view is opened, you have to refresh the view before you can see the new document.

To refresh a view, press F9 or select View, Refresh from the drop-down menu. You can also click on the browser Reload button. The view is automatically refreshed if you close and reopen a view.

ELEMENTS OF A VIEW

The view has numerous elements that can guide a user, making the view more useful. Figure 6.15 shows a Mail database view and identifies some of these elements.

WORKING WITH DOCUMENTS IN VIEWS   143

Figure 6.15
The key elements of a view.

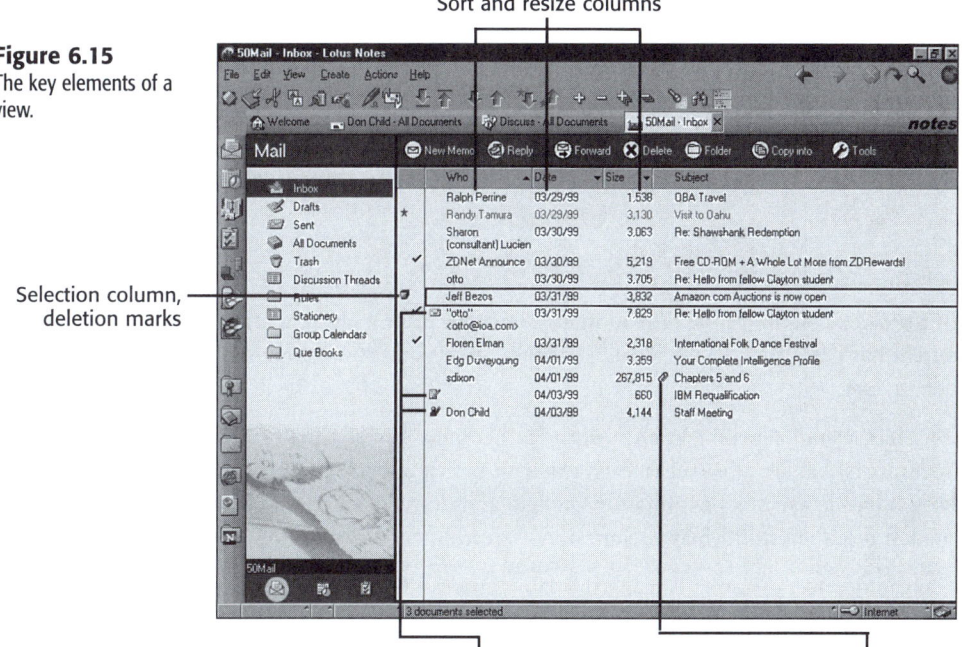

USING UNREAD MARKS

The column to the left of the list of documents contains "unread" marks. These are displayed at the discretion of the application developer. Sometimes there will be an asterisk beside a document—and in some instances, a different line color—to indicate that document has not been opened for reading. The list of unread documents is maintained for each individual as part of his or her Notes desktop. The unread marks disappear when a document is opened.

Unread marks are a real help in views that hold a large number of documents—for example, a view in a research database. You can toggle a document between read and unread by selecting Edit, Unread Marks and selecting the appropriate entry. I sometimes mark a document as unread so that I can find it more easily the next time I open the view.

DELETING DOCUMENTS FROM A VIEW

To delete a document from a view, select the document and press the Delete key. A deletion icon will be displayed beside the document in the same column as the unread marks. If you change your mind, select the document and press the Delete key again to turn it off. The document is deleted when you exit the database or when you refresh the view.

> **Caution**
>
> When a document has been deleted, it cannot be easily recovered. There are a couple ways to restore a document, though, depending on how Notes is used in your organization. If there is a copy of the document in a replica database, you can edit and save the document in the replica, and then replicate the document to the replica copy of the database you normally access. You can also restore a backup copy of the database. However, you will lose any changes that have been made in the database since the backup was made.

SELECTING DOCUMENTS FOR BATCH PROCESSES

In the same column as the unread marks, you can place a check mark to indicate that a document has been selected for a batch process, such as printing, copying, or deleting multiple documents.

To select a single document, click in the left column beside the document. To select multiple documents that are adjacent to each other in the view, click and hold down the left mouse button beside the first document in the list, and drag the mouse up or down the list. Release the left mouse button when you are done selecting documents.

You can deselect documents using the same process. Click on a check mark and it will disappear. Hold down the left mouse button while pointing to a check mark, and drag the mouse up or down the column to deselect other documents. Release the mouse button when you are done.

After you have selected the documents you want, you can copy them, mark them for deletion, or print them as you would a single document.

WORKING WITH VIEW COLUMNS

Rows in a view represent documents (and in some view designs, a single document may span multiple rows). The columns display the values held in specific fields within a document, or they contain values computed based on the value in view column formulas. Each view column has a header at the top of the view, and some of these headers are dynamic. If a column header has a small triangle, the column can be resorted by clicking on the header. For example, in the Mail database, the default view shows unread incoming messages in the order that they are received. But you can click on the first column header to display documents sorted by author. You can click on the header for the second column to show the documents by date, with the most recent documents at the top. You can also change the width of some columns by clicking and dragging the edge of the column in the header.

WHAT ARE DOCUMENT AND ATTACHMENT ICONS?

Many views use visual clues to tell you something about the contents of a document. In the view shown in Figure 6.15, one column contains small envelope icons, exclamation points, and a handshake icon, for example. The envelope icons indicate that I, the owner of the mail database, sent the documents. The exclamation point indicates that the sender marked the document as high priority. The handshake represents a meeting invitation, and the string around a finger represents a reminder. The icon selection is based on the results of a formula provided by the view's designer.

The Attachment icon, which looks like a paperclip, is in another column in Figure 6.15. This indicates to users that the document contains an attached file. This visual clue helps them decide what they want to do with the document.

Categorized Documents

In a categorized view, the first column of the view displays a category. When the category is expanded, you can see the documents within the category. Figure 6.16 illustrates a categorized view from the Discussion database used earlier. Some categories are expanded, and other categories are collapsed. Note that some individual documents have responses, and they can be expanded or collapsed, as well, to show/hide the responses.

Figure 6.16
A view showing documents contained in categories.

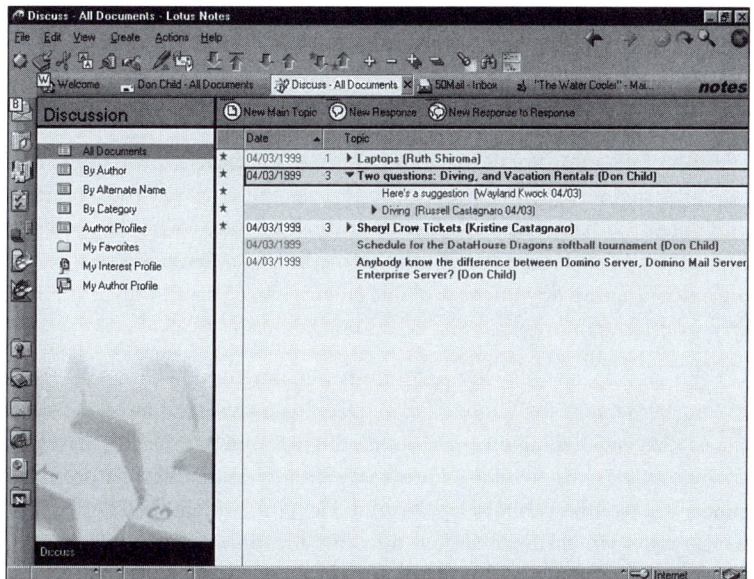

The small arrowhead to the left of the first sorted and categorized column in a row is commonly referred to as a *twistie*. A twistie pointing to the right indicates that the row is a category and that it includes one or more documents. To see the documents, you have to expand the category by clicking on the twistie.

If the twistie points downward, the category is already expanded and you can see any documents (or other categories) contained within the category.

You can expand or collapse categories by clicking on the twistie. You can also press the +, *, and - keys on the numeric keypad; or you can select View, Expand/Collapse, and then select

Expand Selected Level, Expand Selected & Children, or Collapse Selected Level. If a document has been categorized under multiple categories, it will be listed in the view under each of its categories.

OPENING DOCUMENTS FOR READING OR EDITING

If you want to read one of the documents in the view, you can double-click on it to open it for reading. Another option is to select the document and press the Enter key.

When the document is open for reading, you have a number of means to get to the next or previous document in the view. You can do any of the following:

- Press the Enter key to see the next document in the view.
- Press the Backspace key to see the previous document in the view.
- Click on the Next Document or Previous Document SmartIcon to see the next or previous document in the view.
- Press Tab to see the next unread document in the view.
- Click on the Next Unread or Previous Unread SmartIcon to see the next or previous unread document in the view.

You can open a document for editing only if you have Editor rights for that document. You can open the document in edit mode by pressing Ctrl+E (from the view, or with the document open), or you can double-click on the document when it is open in the read mode. Another popular method of getting into edit mode is to choose the Actions Edit Document SmartIcon. Some documents are designed so that you can open them for editing by clicking on an Action edit button.

When you are done viewing or editing a document, you can close it by pressing the Esc key, or you can select File, Close (Ctrl+W from the keyboard). You can close any document from the taskbar by clicking on the x beside the document name. If changes were made to the document, you are given the option of saving your changes before the document is closed. If you select Yes, the changes are saved. Closing the document returns you to the view from which you opened the document or to the locationof the link from which you opened the document.

COPYING A DOCUMENT

To copy a document, highlight the document in a view. Select Edit, Copy or press Ctrl+C. Then select Edit, Paste or press Ctrl+V to paste a copy of the document.

You can paste a document into any view in any Domino database as long as you have document creation privileges. However, the document will be displayed only in views for which it matches the selection criteria.

> **Caution**
>
> You can paste a document into another database. However, the data and the form are stored separately, and you may not have the right form for viewing the data in the new database.

PRINTING A DOCUMENT

The basics of printing a document are simple. With the document selected in a view or opened for reading, select File, Print or click on the Print SmartIcon (if you have added the SmartIcon to your SmartIcon bar). The document is sent to your default printer from the dialog box shown in Figure 6.17.

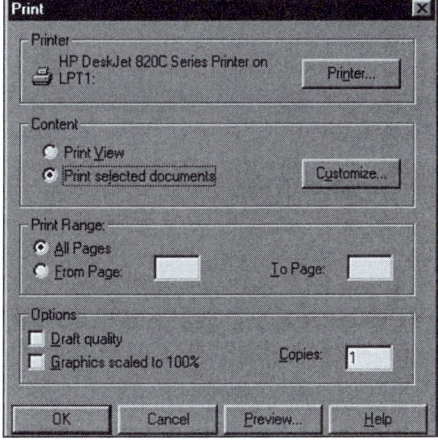

Figure 6.17
Select printing options from the Print dialog box.

You have the option of printing the view or selected documents. If you print the view, you get a list of all the documents in the view, not just those shown as selected on the screen.

If you print a document, you have the option of limiting printing to a range of pages. You can also elect draft mode, and you can scale graphics to 100%.

When you are done selecting options, you can preview the printed document online by clicking on the Preview button at the bottom of the Print dialog box. As you preview your print options, remember that most documents were designed for online display. They might not look good when printed. You have a couple options to improve the appearance of documents: headers and footers, and using alternate forms.

CREATING HEADERS AND FOOTERS FOR PRINTING

You can tailor your document printing by creating headers and footers for a single document or for an entire database. If you have a header/footer setting for a single document, this setting will override any settings you have for the database as a whole.

To create headers and footers for your printed documents, display the Document Properties InfoBox (display the Database Properties InfoBox if you want to apply headers and footers to the entire database). Click on the Printer tab of the InfoBox. The printer page is shown in Figure 6.18.

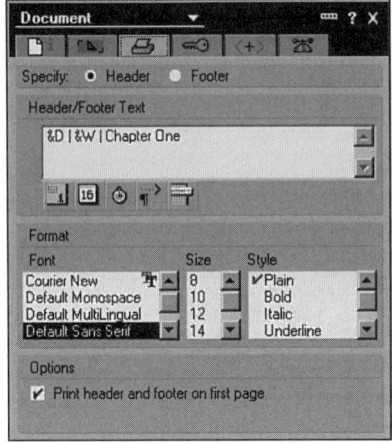

Figure 6.18
Create a header and footer using the Printer tab in the Database Properties InfoBox.

Do the following to create a header:

1. With the Header button selected, position the cursor inside the header field.
2. Select the calendar icon to insert the system date (given the notation &D), the clock icon to insert the current time (&T), the page icon to insert the page number (&P), or the title icon to insert the document title (&W); or type your own text to appear in the header.

   Whatever you insert will be positioned on the left side of the header.
3. Click on the paragraph indent icon to insert a vertical marker (|). The vertical marker is used to separate the left, center, and right sides of the page.
4. Insert another item (page, text, date, time, or title). Anything placed immediately to the right of the first vertical bar will be centered at the top of the page.
5. Click on the paragraph indent icon again to insert another vertical marker.
6. Insert another item. Whatever you insert after the second vertical bar will be right-justified at the top of the page.
7. Select the font for your header (footer).
8. Click on the check box if you want the header/footer to appear on the first page of your print job.

Here is an example of a header:

&D | &W | Chapter One

The header will have the date on the left, the document title in the center, and the text Chapter One on the right. If you want your entire header to be right-justified, you enter two vertical bars before entering a code or some text:

¦¦Knowledge Base.

The process for creating a footer is the same. Click the Footer radio button and then create your footer.

Using an Alternative Form for Printing

Another strategy for printing good-looking documents is to use a form that is formatted especially for printing. I won't teach you how to design that form in this chapter, but I will show you how to select an alternative form.

Go back and look at Figure 6.17. If you elect to print selected documents, the Customize button next to the Print Selected Documents radio button is activated. Click on the Customize button to display the dialog box shown in Figure 6.19.

Figure 6.19
Select an alternate form for printing documents.

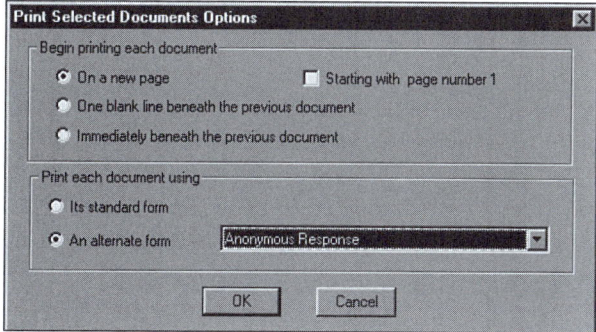

At the bottom of the Customize dialog box, click on the Alternate form radio button and select the name of the alternative form to be used. A list of all forms in the database is displayed for your selection.

Caution
The alternative form used for printing must have matching field names for any fields on the original the form that are to be printed.

From Here...

You have now learned how to work with simple documents that are primarily text. There are many complex documents with specific functions that you will be learning about that will build on the knowledge you have gained here.

The following chapters go into detail about working with specific types of documents:

- Chapter 5, "Using Electronic Mail," provides information about creating and working with email messages.
- Chapter 8, "Getting Organized with the Calendaring and Scheduling Features," provides information about the document types in the calendaring and scheduling functions of Lotus Notes 5.0.
- Chapter 9, "Using Sametime Collaboration," provides information about communicating through Notes without having to create and save documents.
- Chapter 11, "Using the Notes Client on the Internet," provides information on how you can use some of the document editing functions on the Internet without having to leave the Notes user interface.
- Chapter 14, "Designing Pages, Forms, and Subforms," provides information about how to go about designing an alternative form for printing.

CHAPTER 7

CONTACT MANAGEMENT WITH THE PERSONAL AND PUBLIC DIRECTORIES

Lotus Notes and the Domino Server are designed to run in a networked environment where everyone uses Notes or a Web browser. Businesses implement Notes as a communication tool within their organization, but many also use Notes as an indispensable tool for communicating with contacts outside the organization, as well. To stay in contact with a number of people, you might find that you need a contact manager—software that helps you keep track of your contacts.

There are some very good contact management applications that can be purchased. Many of these even run in a Lotus Notes environment. But before looking at a dedicated contact management system, you might want to look at what you already have on your desktop. The Notes Personal Directory and the Domino Public Directory include many of the contact management functions included in dedicated packages. You might find that the built-in functions are perfectly adequate for your needs.

Contact Management with the Personal Address Book

The Personal Address Book is used to keep track of your workstation's connections to the world of Domino servers. It is also used to keep track of the people you communicate with frequently, whether they are inside or outside your organization. To describe to you how to use the contact management features of the Personal Address Book, I will begin by assuming you are opening your address book for the first time.

Setting Up Your Personal Preferences

When you open your Notes 5.0 Personal Address Book for the first time, you can define the appearance and some of the functionality of the Address Book by defining preferences. The Preferences page, accessible from the Tools button or the Actions menu, is shown in Figure 7.1.

Selecting an Address Book Owner

The first field on the Preferences page is the Address Book owner. The owner is the person or group who is allowed to use the Address Book for lookups when sending email. By default, you are the owner of the address book, although you can assign ownership to someone else. Your Notes user ID identifies you to Notes, which can then determine whether you are the owner of the Personal Address Book or a member of an owner group.

When you click the helper button next to the Address Book owner field, a Names dialog box is displayed. In this dialog box, you can select an address book or directory, and then look up a username or group from the selected address book. The selected name or group is inserted as the owner of the address book.

Contact Management with the Personal Address Book | 153

Figure 7.1
The Personal Address Book Profile is used to define your personal preferences for your address book.

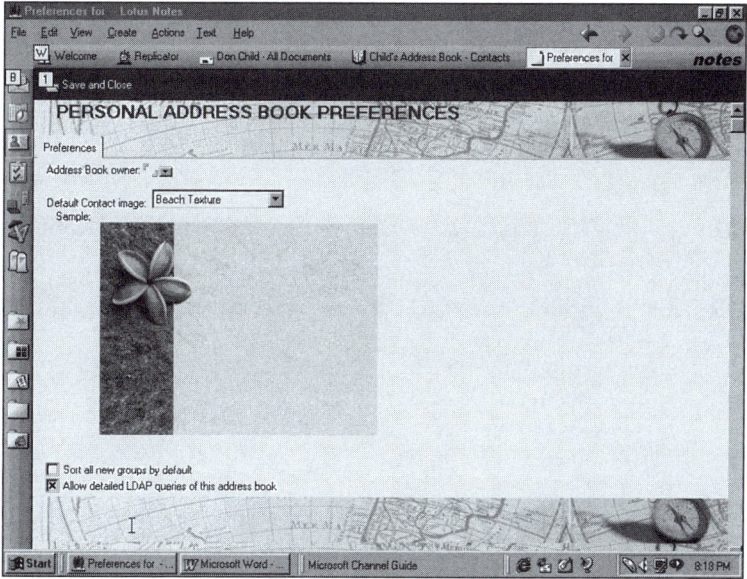

Automatic Group Sorting and Allowing LDAP Queries

There are two check boxes you can select by clicking on them:

- Sort all new groups by default
- Allow detailed LDAP queries of this address book

If you choose to sort all new groups, groups are displayed in alphabetical order. If you turn this option off, groups are displayed in the order in which they are created.

If you allow detailed LDAP queries of your address book, any user who sends mail from your workstation will be able to look up addressees from your Personal Address Book, even though the user is not the owner of the address book.

Selecting a Default Background Image

You can choose from five default background images to give your contact form a business card–like appearance. To select a different image, click the helper button next to the Default Contact image field to display a list of backgrounds. When you select an image, it is immediately displayed so you can see whether you like it.

At the bottom of the Preferences form, you can select how your contacts are listed on the Contact form and in the Contact view.

Adding a Contact to Your Address Book

When you want to put a new person into your address book, you add a Contact document. This can be done automatically when you receive mail from someone (Actions, Tools, Add

Part II
Ch
7

Sender to Address Book), or it can be done manually from either the Contacts view or the Categories view. You can also add a card by selecting Create, Contact from the menu.

When you add a card, the first page of the Contact form is displayed. Enter the name of the person. If you want to be able to send email to the person, an email address is also required. This is illustrated in Figure 7.2.

Figure 7.2
Enter a person's name and email address to create a Contact document.

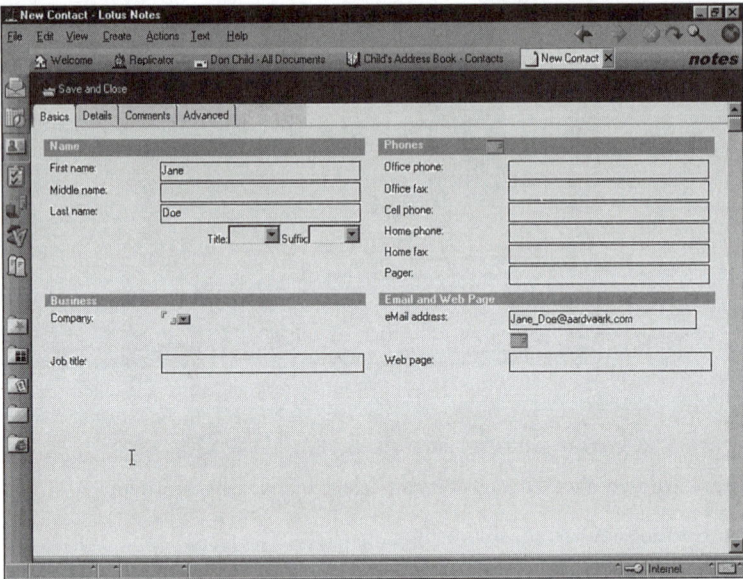

Under the Business section of the first page of the Contact form, you can add the name of the company the person works for. If you already have other Contacts within your address book who work for the same company, you can look up the name of the company using the helper button beside the Company field. If this is the first person, enter the name of his company, and her job title. You can enter additional information about the company on the second page of the Contact form.

Under the Phones section, enter any phone numbers that you have available or that you are likely to use. You can add an office phone number, an office fax, a cell phone number, a home phone number, a home fax, and a pager number.

GETTING HELP WHILE ADDING A CONTACT

On some field labels (those that display a pointing hand when you hold the cursor on them) you can point to the label and hold down the left mouse button to display a brief help message. The message remains in view as long as you hold down the left mouse button. When adding or editing a Contact, you can get help for the eMail Address and Web Page fields in this way.

There are also wizards available for more difficult fields. For example, when you click the helper button below the eMail Address field, a Mail Address Assistant guides you as you enter the email address. In the Mail Address Assistant, you have a choice of the following types of addresses:

- Fax
- Internet Mail
- Lotus cc:Mail
- Lotus Notes
- Other
- X.400 Mail

An assistant is displayed after you make your selection and click OK. The assistant helps you fill in any required information for that type of address.

If you select Other, you can enter the name of another mail system not included in the list. You also have to specify a Notes gateway domain used to get to that mail system.

Additional Information on the Contact Form

Continue to add information to the Contact. As you go from page to page, here is what you encounter:

- Details   On the Details page, you can add the business address and details about the person's position within the company. This includes both the physical location/department, and the names of her manager and assistant. You can also add her home address, the names of her spouse and children, and her birthday.

- Comments   The Comments page of the Contact form is a rich-text field. If you read the previous chapter on working with text and documents, you know that you can do practically anything you want in this field. Want to add a picture of the contact? This is the place to do it. Want to attach a sound file with her voice? Place the cursor on the Comments page, select File, Attach, and locate the file that has her voice. Refer to Chapter 6, "Working with Text and Documents," for details on using a rich-text field.

- Advanced   Use the Advanced page for more advanced options, for example, if you need to set up secure communications with the person you are creating a Contact for. On this page, you add the person's full username and the short name you want to use to address her. The full username is her hierarchical Notes name, for example, Fiona Chang/Accounting/Absalom. You can add other names in the full username field, and you can then address email to the person using any of the variants in this field or in the short name field. Enter her email domain, which is the domain portion of her email address.

    If you need to share encrypted mail with the person and do not have access to her Domino Directory or public address book, paste in her certified public key after she sends it to you, or enter her Flat name key if the user does not use hierarchical names. When you have the correct key, you can decrypt documents she sends to you.

You can also specify personal categories by which you can group your contacts; you can specify the background texture for this Contact document, overriding the default background; you can enter a phonetic name to assist you with locating the person using a name picker dialog box if you have other contacts with similar names; and you can override the default firstname/lastname order for displaying this person's name.

ADDING A NEW CARD FROM NOTES MAIL

You can add a person to your Personal Address Book from within Notes mail. Open a message from the person. Select Actions, Tools, Add Sender to Address Book to see the dialog box shown in Figure 7.3.

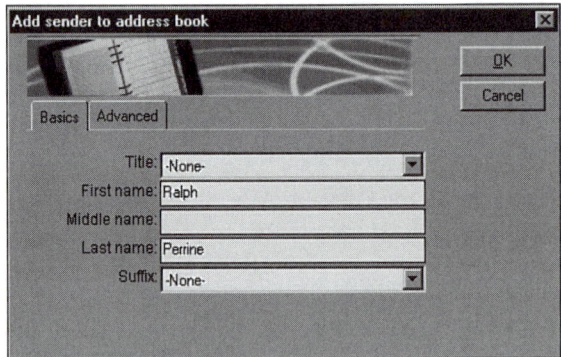

Figure 7.3
Add a person to your Personal Address Book from within Notes Mail.

The person is added to your address book automatically. Later, you can open that person's Contact document, put it into edit mode, and enter additional information about the person. But you can use that Contact for addressing email immediately.

If you have Create privileges in the Domino Directory (the public address book), you can also open the directory and create Person entries that are accessible to everyone in your Notes network. Usually only Notes administrators have this privilege. Even though a person is listed in the Domino Directory, he cannot access the Domino server using Notes without a valid Notes user ID.

CATEGORIZING YOUR CONTACTS

The primary purpose of any contact management application is to make it easy to keep in touch with people. When you use the Personal Address Book, I'm assuming you will also use Notes email to keep track of the contacts you make. The basics of using Notes as an email client were covered in Chapter 5, "Using Electronic Mail."

CONTACT MANAGEMENT WITH THE PERSONAL ADDRESS BOOK | 157

In the Personal Address Book, there are two views that can be used to simplify the task of contacting someone listed on a Contact document. You can use the default Contacts view itself, or you can use the Contacts By Category view shown in Figure 7.4.

Figure 7.4
Use the Contacts By Category view to communicate easily with your contacts.

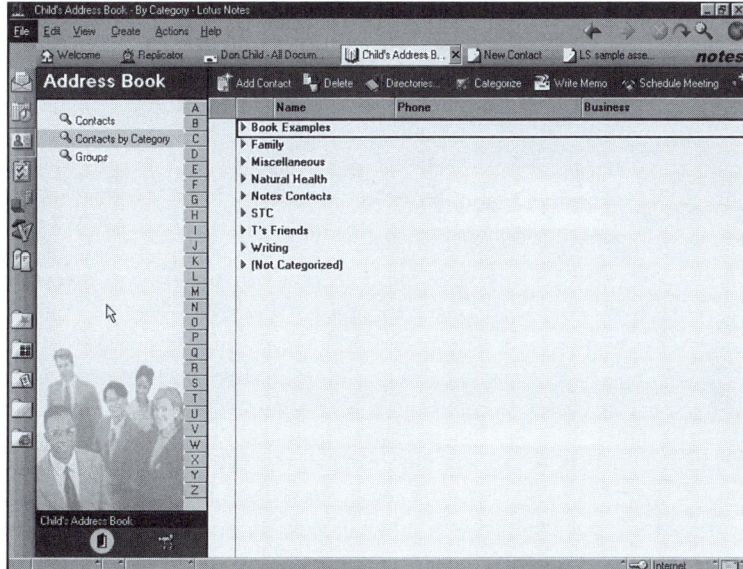

The only difference between the Contacts view and the By Category view, aside from the way documents are sorted and categorized, is that the Categorize button is displayed on the Contacts By Category view.

> **Tip**
> The Contacts By Category view helps prevent confusion between people with similar names. It also provides a context for locating a person quickly when you are unsure of the spelling of his or her name. You can quickly move the focus to the vicinity of a particular category by using the alphabet tabs to navigate.

Adding a Contact to a Category

When you create a Contact, you can categorize the individual by filling in the Categories field on the Advanced page. But if you are like me, you end up with people in the wrong category, or you change your mind and want to rename some of your categories. You can do either of those using the Categorize button.

You can categorize multiple Contacts at a single time by selecting the documents with a checkmark. For example, in Figure 7.5, I have selected the Contact documents of two people for categorizing. I then clicked on the Categorize button to display the dialog box.

PART
II
CH
7

Figure 7.5
Select an existing category or create a new one for one or more contacts.

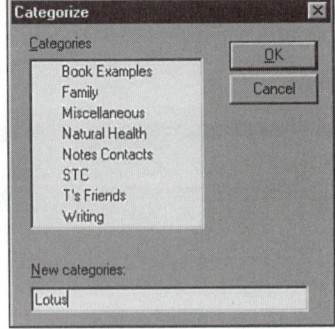

In the Categorize dialog box, you can assign a contact to an existing category by clicking on the category so that a checkmark appears next to it. Clicking on it again turns the category off. You can also create a new category by typing the name of the category at the bottom of the dialog box. When you click OK to indicate that you are finished, the new category is created and the document is placed into that category.

A single document can appear in more than one category. Documents that are not assigned to any categories are listed under the generic Not Categorized heading. If you add people to your address book from an email memo, this is where you will find them listed. You can expand the Not Categorized category and assign them to an existing category so they will be easier to find next time.

Sending a Message to a Contact

When you want to communicate with someone, you can always do it the old-fashioned way—look up their Contact document, dial them on the telephone, or send them a letter. But if the person has an email address on their Contact document, you can email them by clicking on a button. The Personal Address Book makes the process pretty much automatic.

To send an email message to a contact, do the following:

1. Highlight the name of the contact in either the Contacts view or the By Category view.
2. Click the Write Memo button.

   An email is created in your default mail client. The memo is automatically addressed to the client whose name was selected.

3. Fill in the Subject and the body of the memo.
4. Send or Send and File the memo.

If you want to send the same message to multiple people, place a checkmark beside the names you want, and click the Write Memo button. All selected names will be included in the To field of your memo.

Keeping Track of Sent Messages

If you want to keep track of all the times you contact with a client, it will take a little bit of discipline, because the process is not totally automatic. After all, you probably don't have your computer logging all your phone calls. But you can make the process as automatic as possible.

You can automate the process first by creating folders in your mail database. Then when you send a memo to one of your contacts, you can file a copy of the memo in the appropriate folder.

Creating a Folder

Although folders were discussed in Chapter 5, I will walk you through the basics of setting up and using the folders in the context of contact management. Here is how to create a folder:

1. With your mail database open to any view that contains mail messages, select Create, Folder. You can also select Create Folder from the Folder button at the top of views in the Mail database.
2. Give the folder a name that matches one of the categories in your contact list. For example, I have a category called Book Examples. I could create a folder with that same name.
3. Select a location for your folder. The folder can be at the top level, or you can place it within another folder. The folder you click is the one under which your new folder will appear. You might want to embed folders, for example, putting all your contact folders under a top-level folder called Contact Management.
4. Click OK to create the folder.

Adding Sent Messages to a Folder

When your folders are created, you can send memos and save copies in your new folders. When you send a memo, click the Send and File button to initiate the transfer of the mail. The Folder dialog box is displayed as shown in Figure 7.6.

Figure 7.6
When you send an email message, you can decide which folder to store a copy in.

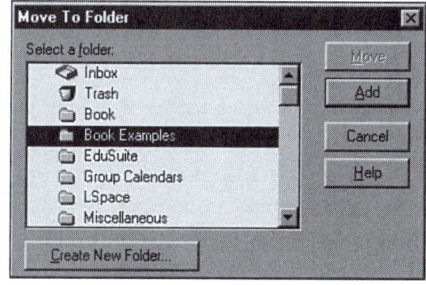

Click the name of the folder where you want the memo stored. Click Add to send and save the memo. In the example shown earlier, the message to Fiona Chang will be mailed and saved in the Book Examples folder. That will make it easy for me to retrieve my copy of the message if I need to refer to it at a later date.

Removing Messages from Folders

If you put a message in the wrong folder or for any reason want to remove it, you can do any one of the following:

- Drag the document and drop it on another folder.
- Select the document and click Move to Folder. Select another folder to move the document to.
- Move the document to the inbox if you want it to be an uncategorized document.
- Select Actions, Folder, Remove from folder from the menu bar.

> **Caution**
> Do not delete a document from a folder thinking you are just moving out of the folder. Deleting a document while it is in a folder also deletes it from any other views in the mail database.

Scheduling a Meeting with a Contact

When you want to schedule a meeting with a contact, you can use the scheduling functions of the Notes mail client. It is similar to what you did when sending a memo to the client, only in this instance, you are using the calendaring and scheduling functions, which are described in detail in Chapter 8, "Getting Organized with the Calendaring and Scheduling Features." You will get a quick taste of one of those features here.

To schedule a meeting, here is what you do:

1. Select the people you want to invite to the meeting.
2. Click the Schedule Meeting button.

   The Calendar Entry form is displayed. The names you selected are listed in the Invite field. Selecting names and clicking on the Schedule Meeting button is illustrated in Figure 7.7.

3. Fill out the Calendar Entry form, described in Chapter 8. When you are scheduling a meeting with someone inside your organization, you can tell whether the person is available by looking up his or her free time. You don't have this option when you are dealing with people outside your organization. In addition to not having access to free time, you might not have locations set up for making room reservations for outside sites. You still have to do a bit of work to set up a meeting location and find a time that is mutually agreeable. But you can be assured that the process is as automatic as possible on your end.

VISITING WEB PAGES | 161

Figure 7.7
Select multiple people and then schedule a meeting that is automatically addressed to them.

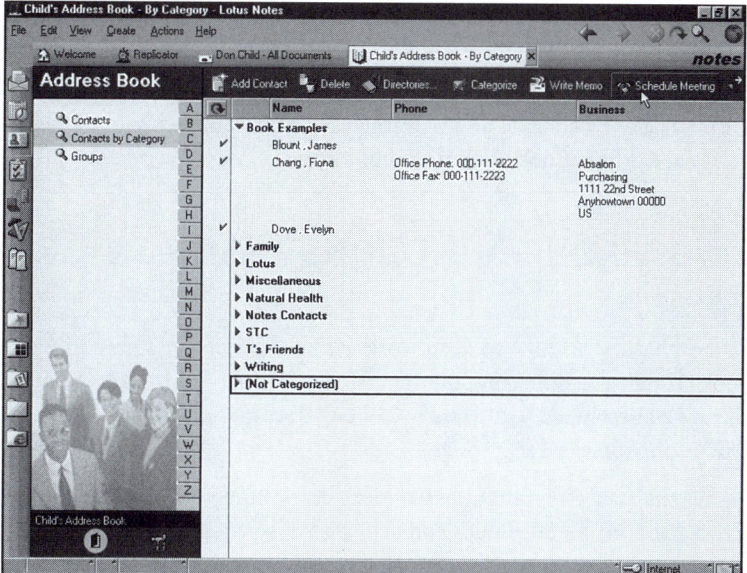

VISITING WEB PAGES

If any of the Contacts in your Personal Address Book lists a Web page, you can link directly to that person's Web page. You do not have to leave Notes. You can visit a Web page or a Notes document with equal ease. Notes automatically uses its built-in Web browser if a link leads to a document stored on the Internet.

When you use the Personal Address Book for contact management, visiting a person's Web page is a simple two-step process:

1. Highlight the name of the person whose Web page you want to visit.
2. Select Actions, Tools, Visit Web Page.

Setting up Web integration can involve a number of variables, but there are two essential steps for the integration to work within Notes using the Personal Address Book and the built-in Web browser.

- You need to enter a person's Web page URL on the Contact.
- You have to set the Location document for the your current location to use Notes with Internet Explorer as your Internet browser.

> **Note**
> This assumes that you have Internet access and are connected to the Internet through either a LAN connection or a dial-up PPP connection, or you can dial-up automatically to a RAS connection.

PART
II
CH
7

Setting up Location documents is covered in detail in Chapter 10, "Using Mobile Features from Home or on the Road."

When you have Notes and your browser correctly configured, you can open a Web page automatically by clicking a link. In the case of the contact management functions in the Personal Address Book, the link is built into the View Web Page button.

Making Group Functions Easier by Creating Groups

So far, you've seen how you can work with people one at a time using your Personal Address Book. When scheduling appointments, you learned how to select more than one person by placing a checkmark next to their Contact document. But what if you frequently work with groups of people?

Rather than selecting multiple Contacts every time you want to deal multiple people, you can create a group document and deal with the group as a single unit. When you address something to that group—for example, a mail memo or an invitation to a scheduled meeting—all you have to do is address the group. Each individual in the group automatically receives a copy of the same memo or invitation.

To create a group, do the following:

1. In the Personal Address Book, select the Groups view.
2. Click either the Add Group or the Add Mailing List button.

> **Note**
> A mailing list is simply a group that can be used only for email-related functions. For contact management, a mailing list is the only type of group you need.

Notes displays the Group (or Mailing List) form shown in Figure 7.8.

3. Enter a Group name and a description of the group.
4. Make the Group Type Mail Only if you are creating a Mailing list. Otherwise select a group type such as multi-purpose, ACL, servers, deny access, and so on.
5. Enter the names of the people to include in the group. The names can be selected from your list of Contacts in your Personal Address Book by clicking on the helper button beside the Members field. The Names dialog box is displayed as shown in Figure 7.9.
6. In the left panel, click to add a checkmark beside the names you want to add to your group. Click Add to copy the names to the right panel. When the right panel contains all the names you want to add, click the OK button to add them to the group.
7. Click Save and Exit when you are finished creating or editing the group.

MAKING GROUP FUNCTIONS EASIER BY CREATING GROUPS | 163

Figure 7.8
Use the Group form to define a group of users who can be addressed as a unit.

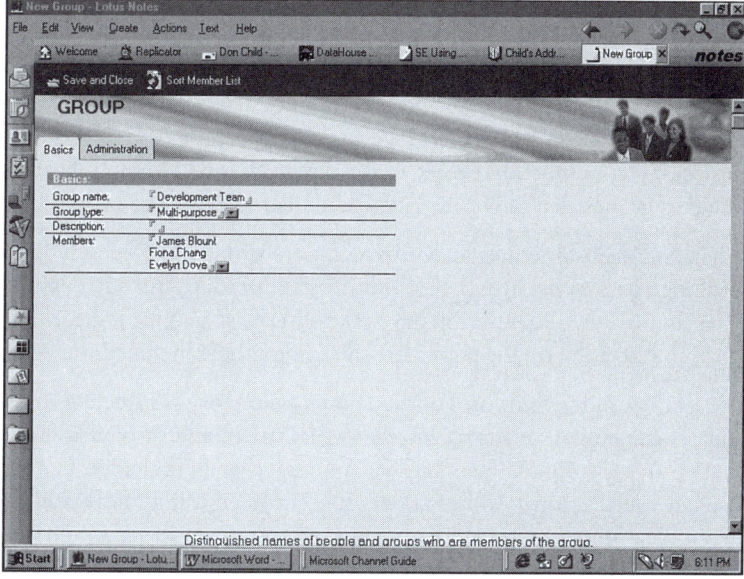

Figure 7.9
Use the Names dialog box to select names to add to a group.

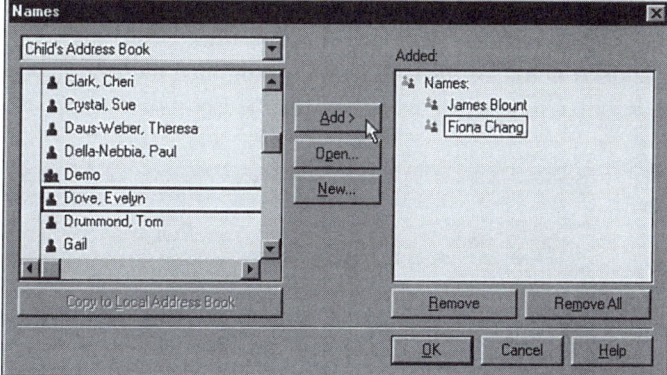

When a group has been added, you can create a mail memo to your group from anywhere in Notes. The keyboard combination Ctrl+M displays a new mail message form. Enter the name of the group in the To field—for example, "Demo"—and the message is sent to everyone you have added to your Demo group in your local Personal Address Book.

Note

You can also add names to a group from other directories, for example, from the public Domino directory. Select the name of the directory from the Names dialog box, and add the names to your local group. When mail is sent, Notes expands the names in the group into valid email addresses.

PART
II
CH
7

Contact Management with the Public Directory

The public Domino directory is used for contact management, but there are some distinct differences as to what you, an end user, can do. The Domino directory holds the names of people registered as Notes or HTTP users within your organization, but for all intents and purposes, you cannot add people to the directory. The Domino directory also contains the names of groups, but only the system administrator can add people and groups.

When you mail something to a group of users within the Domino directory, the mail goes to all members of the group, just as it does with groups in your Personal Address Book. But other users in the organization have access to the same group record. The groups in the Domino directory are for public use (meaning others in your Notes organization).

One of the primary purposes of the Domino directory is to define to the router how to route documents to others within the organization, and through gateways to people outside of your organization. When you send a message or an invitation to a meeting for someone listed in your Personal Address Book, it gets routed using information stored in the Domino directory. Without access to the Domino directory, messages would not be able to find a route to an Internet domain, for example.

You have some control over how much the Domino directory gets used when you are addressing and sending mail. For example, in the Location document for your current location, you can define whether type-ahead lookups work using only your local directory (the Personal Address Book), or the local directory and then the Domino directory. Figure 7.10 shows the information that can be adjusted in the Location document.

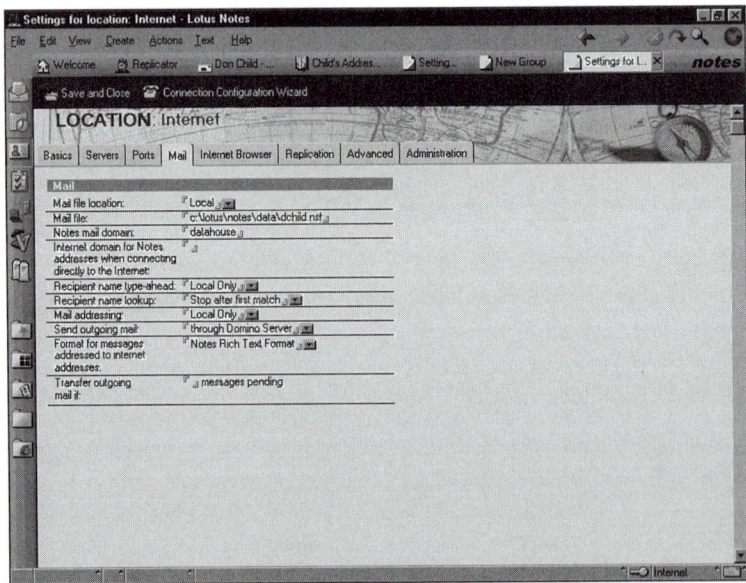

Figure 7.10
Use the Mail page in the Location document to define how local and public directories are used.

The important information for contact management includes the following:

- Recipient name type-ahead
- Recipient name look-up
- Mail addressing
- Send outgoing mail

From Here...

Contact management involves setup issues that are common to email and system administration, as well as calendaring and scheduling, and mobile computing. These issues have been covered briefly here, but they are covered in-depth elsewhere in the book.

The following chapters provide more detailed information on issues related to contact management.

- Chapter 5, "Using Electronic Mail," describes in greater detail how mail is routed.
- Chapter 8, "Getting Organized with the Calendaring and Scheduling Features," describes in greater detail some of the options you have available when scheduling appointments.
- Chapter 10, "Using Mobile Features from Home or on the Road," helps you understand what you have to do to use messaging features from different locations.

CHAPTER 8

GETTING ORGANIZED WITH THE CALENDARING AND SCHEDULING FEATURES

In today's hectic business environment, time management is an important part of your daily work. You have to keep track of appointments, events, and anniversaries, and you have to schedule meetings with other people. Many times, your schedule changes, and you can't contact everyone attending to determine a new time to meet.

In the past, several applications, including Lotus Organizer, have had strong group scheduling features. Lotus Notes 5.0 takes those features a step further, integrating group scheduling and group calendars with workflow and information databases.

With Notes, you can easily schedule a meeting by checking other people's schedules for free times and finding a room that is available when you want to meet. Notes will send invitations to the attendees and will automatically reserve the room for you.

The calendaring and scheduling features in Notes 5.0 enable the mobile user to create appointments and meetings while disconnected from the network. The Free Time database can be replicated to your local machine to enable you to easily schedule meetings while you are traveling.

AN OVERVIEW OF SCHEDULING IN NOTES

The calendaring and scheduling features of Notes are integrated into your personal mail database. You use the calendar features by creating appointment, meeting invitation, anniversary, reminder, or event documents in your mail databases and viewing your schedule using the new Calendar view, shown in Figure 8.1.

Figure 8.1
You can view your appointments using the Calendar view in your Mail application.

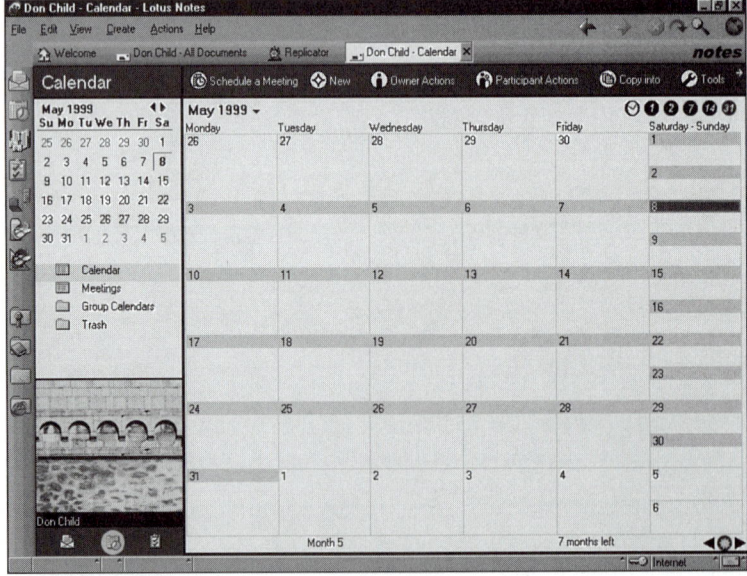

The elements of the calendar include the following:

- Calendar view, which enables you to view appointments and events using hourly, One Day, Two Days, One Week, Two Weeks, and One Month formats.
- Calendar Entry forms, which are used to create personal appointments, meeting invitations, all-day events, reminders, and anniversaries.
- A Meetings view that enables you to work with calendar entries as Notes documents in a view.
- Group Calendars, which enable you to view the calendars of multiple users.
- A Trash view, which enable you to view all Calendar entries that are marked for deletion.

You also have the option of viewing To Do tasks on your Calendar. This option can be selected when you create a task.

You manage your schedule by creating appointments, inviting others to meetings, and responding to invitations to meetings. If you invite other people to a meeting, Notes mails the invitation to the attendees who, in turn, can choose to accept or decline the meeting. Notes can also automatically reserve a room and resources, such as an overhead projector.

Setting Up Calendar Preferences

Before you start using calendaring features, you should fill out a Calendar Preferences document to define the details of how your calendar functions. The Calendar Preferences screen enables you to define default information that is used when you schedule meetings and events. Examples of settings in the calendar preferences include the following:

- Set when your valid free time occurs.
- Define default appointment durations.
- Enable alarms for appointments, events, and anniversaries.
- Restrict access for other users to see your free time.

The Calendar Preferences screen is in the same screen used to define your mail preferences. To view the Calendar Preferences, select Actions, Tools, Preferences or select Preferences from the Tools button. Figure 8.2 shows the first page of the calendar profile.

The pages in the Calendar Preferences include the following:

- Basics

   The Defaults section is used to define the default type of Calendar Entry and the default duration. You can also define how many years into the future an anniversary should be marked in your calendar, and you can prevent calendar entries from being displayed in your mail database's All Documents view and sent invitations from being displayed in your Sent view.

In the conflict checking section, you can define the types of events that are flagged when a conflicting event is scheduled.

In the Advanced Section, you can define whether Calendar entries should be displayed in Mail views, and you can define Personal categories of events that can be selected from a drop-down list of event types.

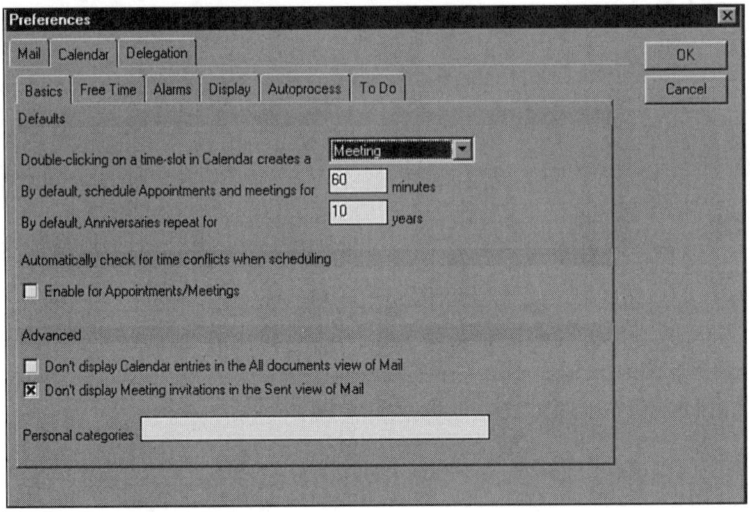

Figure 8.2
Complete a Calendar Preferences screen before using the scheduling features.

- Free Time

    On this page, you define the times during which you are available for appointments. In other words, you define your work hours during the week so that others will know when you are available for meetings.

- Alarms

    You can enable alarms for various types of calendar entries. If alarms are enabled, a visual notice is displayed on the screen a set interval before the calendar event begins. You can also select a sound file to be played at the time of the alarm.

- Display

    On the Display page, you can define the range of hours and the default intervalstart shown on daily calendars.

- Autoprocess

    On the Autoprocess page, youcan automate how invitations are handled when they are sent to you. If you want meeting invitations processed automatically, you can elect to have all invitations processed, or only those from a set list of individuals. You can also have your meeting requests forwarded to another individual, for example, if someone is handling your duties for a period of time. Autoprocessing automatically adds meetings to your calendar if your free time allows it.

- To Do

    On the To Do page, you can define whether tasks that you or others have assigned to you should be displayed on your calendar until they are completed.

- Delegation

    The Delegation page is common to Notes Mail, To Do lists, and the Calendar. You can use the Delegation page to allow other users to read and edit your email, your To Do documents, and your Calendar. This access is in addition to the ability to view your free time. Figure 8.3 shows the Delegation page of the Calendar Preferences dialog box.

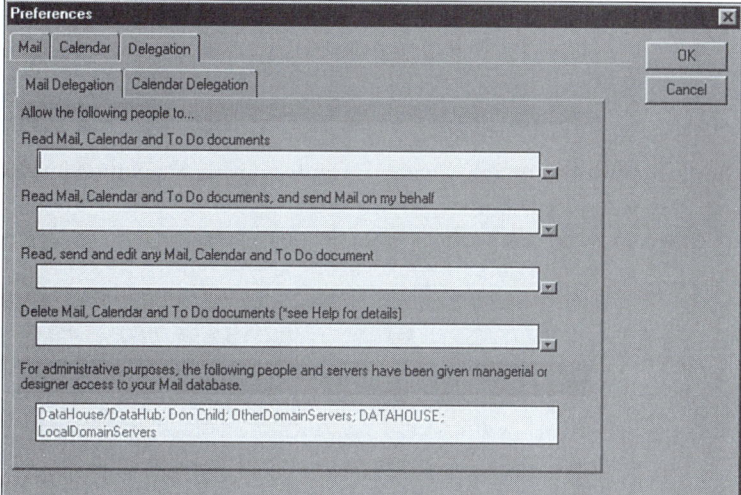

Figure 8.3
You can delegate to others the right to read or edit your calendar.

You can choose to allow everyone to read or manage your calendar, or you can specify individual people or groups who should have that access. If someone is granted read access to your calendar, he or she will be able to open your mail database and read your appointments and meetings. This feature is useful if someone needs to find you, but does not know where you are at a given time. A person with editor delegation can create, modify, and delete start entries from your calendar. For example, an administrative assistant who needs to maintain a manager's schedule might be delegated as an editor.

> **Note**
> Users with reader or manager access to your calendar will not be able to read or edit your personal mail or any start calendar entries that are marked Private.

CREATING A CALENDAR ENTRY

After you havestart completed a calendar profile, you are ready to start creating your calendar entries. For all of the entries, you do the any one of the following:

- Open your mail database and choose Create, Calendar Entry. The default Calendar Entry type will be displayed. In the Navigation pane, click on the type of entry you want to create—for example, Appointment.
- Click on the Calendar icon at the bottom of the Mail Navigator. Click on the New button and select the type of entry you want to create.
- Choose Create, Mail, Calendar Entry from within any other Notes application. When the default Calendar Entry form is displayed, click on the type of entry you want to create.
- Double-click on your calendar on the day you want to create an appointment. When the default Calendar Entry form is displayed, click on the type of entry you want to create.

SCHEDULING AN APPOINTMENT

The Appointment form (a Calendar Entry form with Appointment selected as the entry type) is used to block off personal free time on your calendar. Figure 8.4 shows the Appointment form.

Figure 8.4
Fill in the Appointment form to create a new appointment on your calendar.

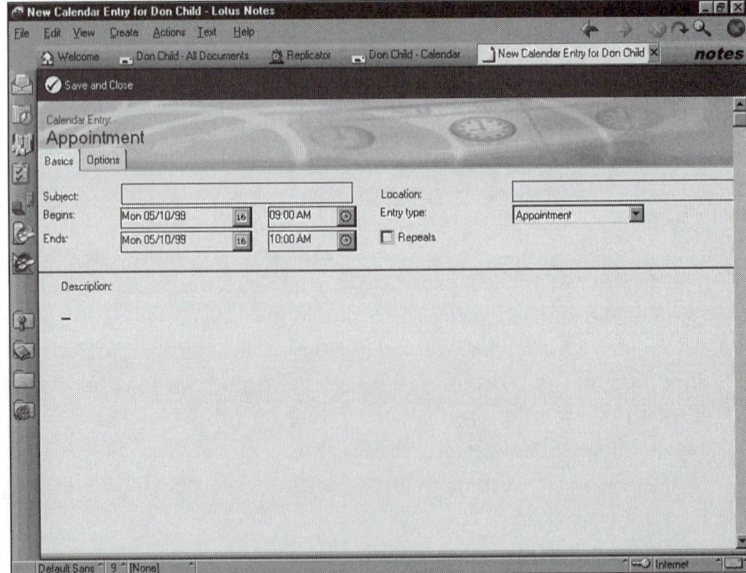

On the Appointment form, fill in the following information:

- Subject

  Enter a brief description of the appointment. The description will be visible when you rest the mouse pointer on the appointment in the Calendar view.

- Begins and Ends dates

  Enter the begin and end dates of the appointment. The default date is today's date. You can pick a date from a calendar by clicking on the calendar helper button. A pop-up calendar will be displayed, as shown in Figure 8.5.

Figure 8.5
Select a date using the pop-up calendar.

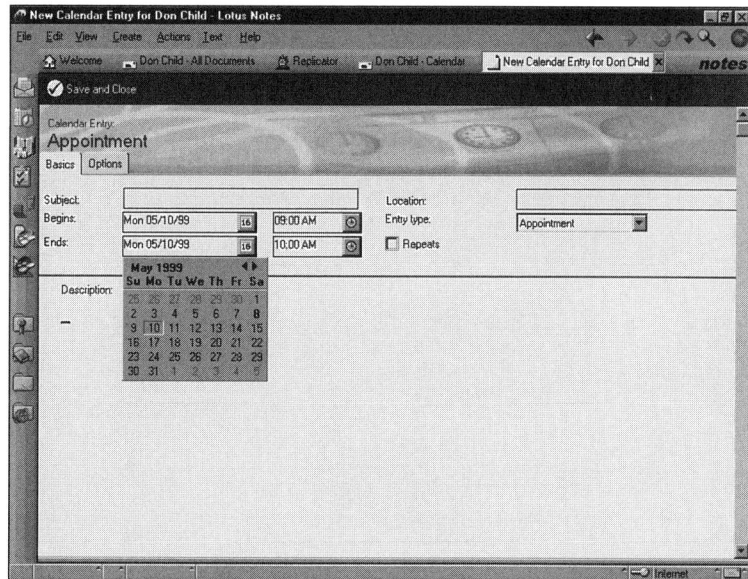

- Time

  Select a begin time and an end time for the appointment. If you type just a number—for example 7—the time will default to 7:00 a.m. If you type 7 pm, the system will display 7:00 p.m. You can also click on the Clock helper button to display a slider bar. Slide the bar to the desired start time (or end time) for the appointment. The end time will automatically be set to the default interval after the start time, but you can adjust the end time. The slider bar is illustrated in Figure 8.6.

- Repeats

  If you click on the Repeats checkbox, a Repeat Options dialog box is displayed so you can select rules for the repeating appointment. For example, you may have a meeting that repeats on the third Thursday of every month for the next two years, or every second day for 2 weeks. This is set up in the dialog box shown in Figure 8.7.

174 CHAPTER 8 GETTING ORGANIZED WITH THE CALENDARING AND SCHEDULING FEATURES

Figure 8.6
Use the Clock slider bar to set the begin or end time.

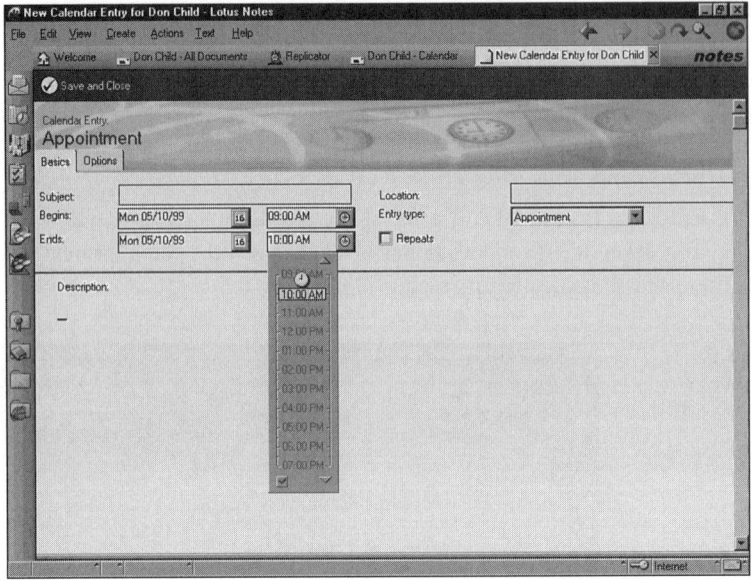

Figure 8.7
Define the repeat interval for repeating appointments.

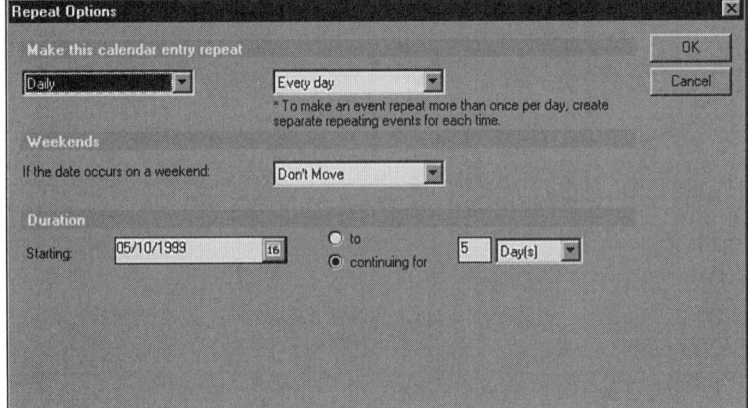

When you save a repeating appointment, Notes automatically creates calendar entries for all occurrences of the appointment for the time period you specified. Later, if you need to move or delete a single occurrence of the appointment, Notes asks whether you want to apply the change to all the repeating appointments, update all future or all past occurrences, or change only a single occurrence.

- Location

  Because the appointment is for you alone, you do not need to reserve a location, but you may want to enter the location of the appointment as a reminder to yourself.

- Options

    Options are set on a separate tabbed page. Click Pencil in to make the appointment without blocking off any free time. For example, you may want to pencil in a tentative appointment, and then change it later. If the appointment is penciled in, you can still schedule another activity at the same time without creating a scheduling conflict.

    Click Mark Private if you do not want the appointment viewed by people to whom you have delegated read or edit access to your calendar. Others will still see that your free time has been blocked during the time of the appointment.

    Click Notify me to enable alarms (visual and audio) for the appointment. If you select Alarms, a dialog box is displayed so that you can set the alarm options. The dialog box is shown in Figure 8.8.

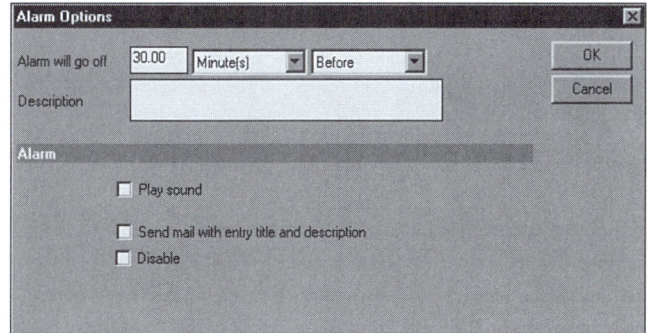

Figure 8.8
Select alarm options for your appointment.

    Categorize your appointment with categories such as Holiday. Select a category for your appointment from the Categorize list. Note that you can add new categories to the drop-down list by entering them in the Categories field on your Calendar Preferences document.

- Description

    The Description field is a rich text field, so you can enter details regarding the appointment.

INVITING OTHER PEOPLE TO A MEETING

Use theMeeting Calendar Entry type to create a meeting and invite people to it. The first page of the form is virtually identical to the Appointment form, but there are several meeting-specific features on a second page labeled Meeting Invitations & Reservations (see Figure 8.9).

Figure 8.9
Invite others to a meeting using the Meeting Invitations & Reservations form.

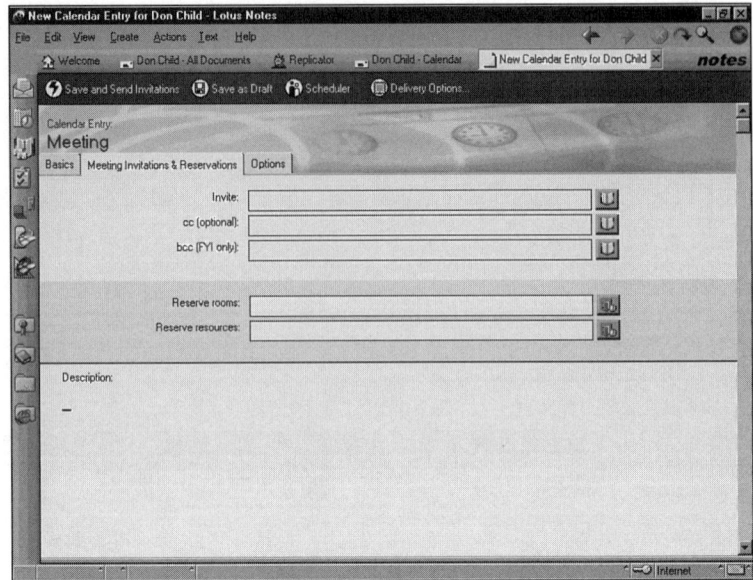

You will still have to enter a subject and a begin and end date and time on the first page. You can set the invitation up for a repeating meeting. You can enter a description of the meeting location. You can also enter calendar display options and enter a category. But the fields on the Meeting Invitations & Reservations page are specific to a meeting invitation. On that page, you enter the following information:

- Invite

    Enter the names of invitees, including those whose attendance is required, those who are optional attendees, and those who should receive an informational notification. As you type names, Notes does a lookup in your Personal Address Book or the Domino Directory, as it would if you were addressing an email. Click on the helper button beside a field if you want to look up names in an address book.

- Reserve Rooms and Reserve Resources

    You can reserve a room, and you can reserve other resources. Rooms and resources are defined by the Domino Administrator in the Domino Directory, and they are maintained in a separate view in the Domino Directory. You can do a lookup in the Domino Directory by clicking on the helper button beside a field.

- Check Schedules

    When you click on the Scheduler button and select Check All Schedules, you will see aFree Time dialog box. You can move the time slider around and change dates until you find a time when everyone is free. Figure 8.10 shows the Free Time dialog box.

Figure 8.10
Click on Check All Schedules to view free time for invitees so you can find a good meeting time.

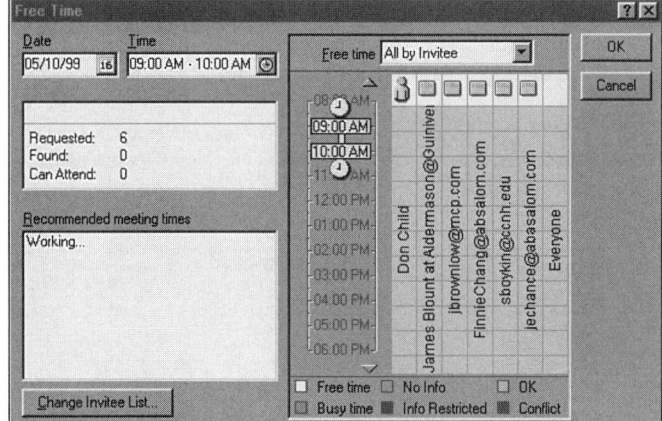

You can look at the free-time schedules for those who have to attend the meeting, and then pick a time. Alternatively, you can view the list of suitable times that Notes finds for you and select one of those free times.

- Find Rooms

   The Find Rooms function on the Scheduler button is similar to the free-time scheduler, but you are looking for free time in one of the meeting facilities defined in the Resource Reservations view of the Domino Directory. You enter the time and size of your meeting and specify the Domino Directory where your resources are kept.

- Resource Scheduler

   The Find Resource(s) function on the Scheduler button is like the Find Rooms function. Resources, such as rooms, are defined in the Domino Directory. Examples of resources include items such as audio-visual equipment, refreshments, or even an outside instructor or facilitator for your meeting. It's up to you how you define resources.

- Delivery Options

   Click on the Delivery Options button to define how your meeting invitation will be handled. You can tell the system that you don't want responses from invitees—for example, you might invite people to attend a free lunchtime seminar on the company's 401(k) plan. It's up to them if they want to attend, and you don't need an RSVP. You can sign and/or encrypt the invitation. You can prevent people from proposing an alternative meeting time. You can also prevent them from delegating the meeting to someone on their staff. The dialog box for defining these options is shown in Figure 8.11.

> **Tip**
>
> You can schedule a meeting any time, even if one of the attendees is busy during the meeting. The busy attendee will still receive an invitation and can decide to modify his or her schedule to accommodate your meeting, decline your meeting, or accept the meeting as a time conflict. Notes can display time conflicts in the new Calendar view so the attendee will know when he or she is scheduled for concurrent appointments.

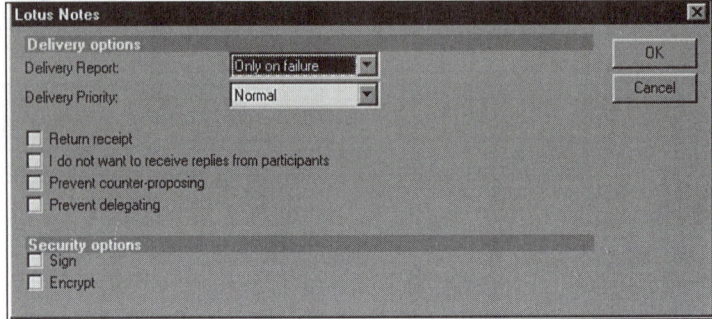

Figure 8.11
Define how your invitation is handled by the system in the Delivery options dialog box.

TRACKING A MEETING INVITATION

When you send out an invitation, the invitees who receive the invitation have different ways they can respond. They can accept the invitation. They can decline. They can delegate someone else to attend the meeting in their stead. They can propose an alternative meeting time. This is all handled in the invitation itself.

Shown in Figure 8.12 is an invitation I have just received from Fiona Chang. She wants me to meet her for a status meeting.

By clicking on the Respond with Comments button, you have several options:

- Accept

  If you want to accept the invitation with comments, a mail memo is displayed. The memo is addressed to the convener, the person who sent out the original invitation.

- Decline

  If you want to decline the invitation, a dialog box is displayed that gives you the option of keeping updated if there is any further correspondence related to the invitation. Your message is sent automatically to the convener.

- Delegate

  If you choose to delegate the meeting to someone else, a dialog box is displayed in which you can specify the person you delegate. There is an address book lookup for delegating. You also have the option of receiving any further correspondence regarding the invitation. Your message is sent automatically to the convener.

Figure 8.12
You have several options when responding to a meeting invitation.

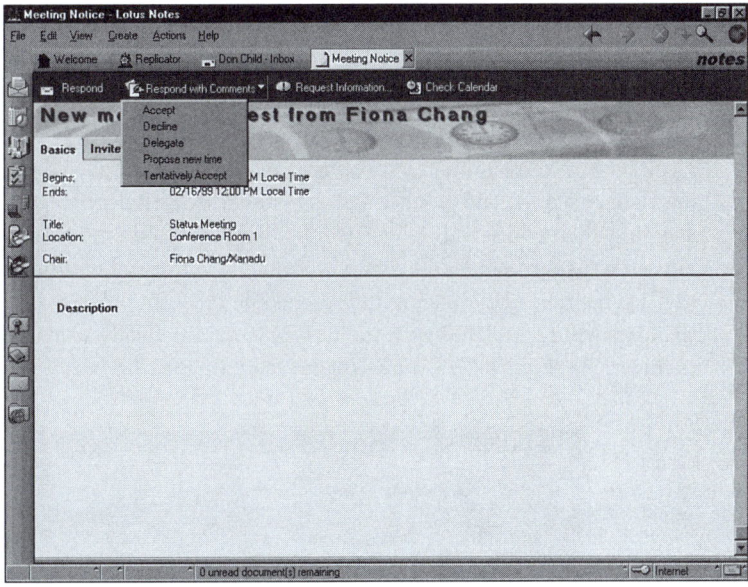

- Propose new time

   If you want to propose a new time, a dialog box is displayed in which the new time is proposed. This is sent automatically to the convener.

- Tentatively Accept

   If you want to tentatively accept the invitation, a memo is addressed to the convener with a Comments field.

If you simply want to accept the invitation without comments, you can click on the Respond button. If you change any information relating to the meeting, the information on your calendar will be updated automatically.

If you need additional information about the meeting, you can send an email to the sender of the invitation by clicking on the Request Information button.

If you need to check your own calendar before accepting the invitation, you can click on the Check Calendar button.

ACTIONS YOU CAN TAKE AS CHAIR

If you sent out the original invitation, you can also take various actions, such as changing or canceling a meeting, or sending out additional information to attendees prior to the meeting.

Open the saved invitation by double-clicking on the entry in a Calendar view or locating the document among your saved email. Click on the Actions button (not the Actions option on the menu bar) to display a drop-down list with the following options:

- Reschedule

    If you have to reschedule the meeting, a dialog box is displayed that enables you to set a new date and time, check schedules, and add a written note to go along with the time change. When you save the Reschedule dialog box, a memo form is displayed on which you can write a message. The memo is already addressed to all meeting participants, with a subject line referencing the rescheduled meeting. After it is submitted, invitees' calendars will be updated with the new time automatically when people acknowledge the new time. Figure 8.13 shows the rescheduling dialog box.

Figure 8.13
The rescheduling dialog box.

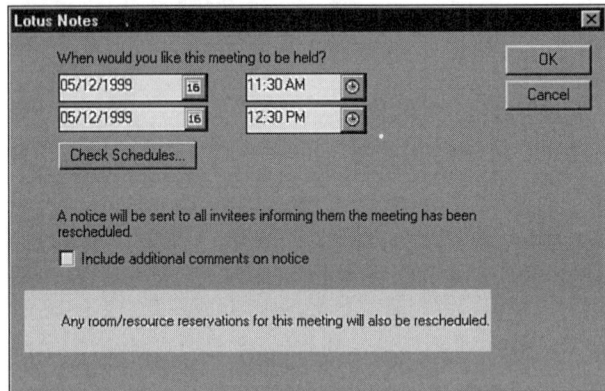

- Cancel

    When you cancel a meeting, a dialog box is displayed that enables you to select options to clean up calendar notices and resource reservations for the meeting, and to create a message to meeting participants. The dialog box is shown in Figure 8.14.

- Confirm

    If you select Confirm, a confirmation is sent to all participants. You also have the option of including a message with the confirmation notice.

- View Participant Status

    When you select View Participant Status, a status box is displayed, as shown in Figure 8.15. You can scroll through a list of all invited participants, see whether their attendance is required or optional, and see whether they have accepted, declined, proposed a new time, and so forth. You can sort the Participant Status list by clicking on the arrow above one of the boxes. You can sort the list alphabetically by name, by required versus optional attendance, or by response status.

Figure 8.14
Canceling a meeting optionally deletes all entries and reservations associated with the meeting.

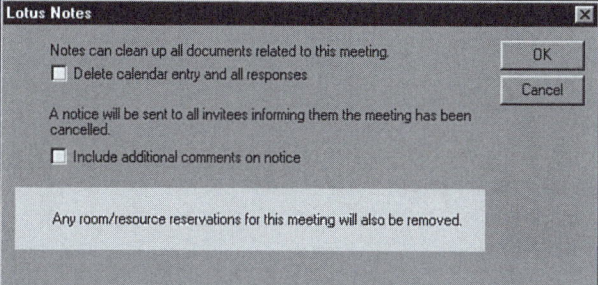

Figure 8.15
You can get a quick overview of the responses to your invitation.

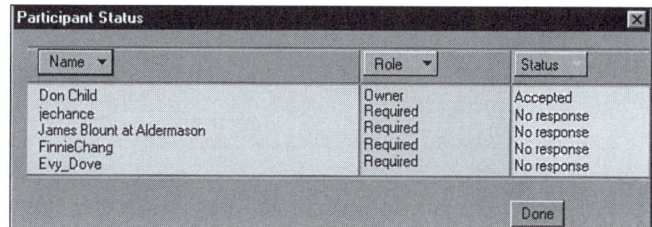

- Send Memo to Participants

    This option addresses a memo to all participants. You can use this to send out a meeting agenda, background information, last minute instructions, and so forth. The meeting participants become a de facto mailing group until after the meeting.

Creating an Anniversary on Your Calendar

An anniversary is just what it says: a once-a-year date to remember. Somebody's birthday. Your first day on the job. A wedding anniversary. Or if you like, you can set once-a-month anniversaries. A meeting of your professional organization, for example.

There is ordinarily no set time of day for an anniversary, as there is with an appointment or a meeting. To create an anniversary, you merely fill in the subject, the date, the location (if relevant), display options, and details. These fields are all used exactly as they are on the Appointment form described earlier.

Anniversaries repeat on the same date each year. You can use the Calendar Preferences dialog box to define how many years you want your anniversaries to extend into the future.

In addition to setting up your own anniversaries, you can import anniversaries into the calendar. For example, you might want to import all the religious holidays for your religious affiliation, plus all the national and state holidays. You find the Import Holidays function under Tools on the Actions menu, or from the Tools button on the Calendar view. National holidays are included in a special view in the Domino Directory. If you want

Creating a Calendar Event

other holidays downloaded, you work with the Domino Administrator to put them into the Domino Directory for importing.

An Event entry on your calendar is another variation on a theme. An event is considered a one- or multiple-day occurrence, such as a trade fair or a conference you will be attending. You could even book your vacation as an event, because it is a block of days during which you won't have any free time.

I won't show you a copy of the form, because there is nothing new to show. You enter a subject, a begin and end date, a location, options, and a description. You can also set up repeat intervals if it is a recurring event.

Creating a Reminder

A Reminder is another variation on the same theme. With a reminder, you have a begin date and time, but there is no end date or time. For example, you might want to set an alarm to remind you that you have to submit a status report every Monday morning, or that taxes are due anytime after January 31. If you really need someone to nag you to get the taxes done, you can even set the reminder for every day.

Managing a To Do List on Your Calendar

You can manage your personal tasks or assign tasks to others using the To Do list feature of Notes. The To Do forms look very much like the other calendar forms, but they include a priority and status field to help you keep track of tasks until they have been completed. You can navigate to your To Do list by clicking on the check mark icon at the bottom of the mail navigator. Create a To Do by clicking on the New To Do Item button, or by selecting To Do from the Create menu when you are in your Mail database.

There are two To Do types. The first type is for a personal To Do list. The other type is similar to a meeting invitation. You can assign a task to one or more people and can track the response of the assignees as well as tracking the status of the task. With both types of To Do lists, you can set alarms to remind you to keep after the task until it has been completed. Figure 8.16 shows the Group To Do form.

You can assign a start date and a due date. You can assign a priority. On the Participants page, you can assign the task to one or more individuals, entering their names into an address field just as you did with a meeting invitation.

The handling of a task is pretty similar to the way you handle a meeting invitation. Invitees must respond by accepting or declining a task or by proposing a new timeline for the task. You, as the task originator, can cancel the task, change the dates, or send additional information, just as you did with an invitation.

The Personal To Do is similar to a Group To Do, but it is addressed to you alone.

Figure 8.16
Define a task and assign it to others using the Group To Do form.

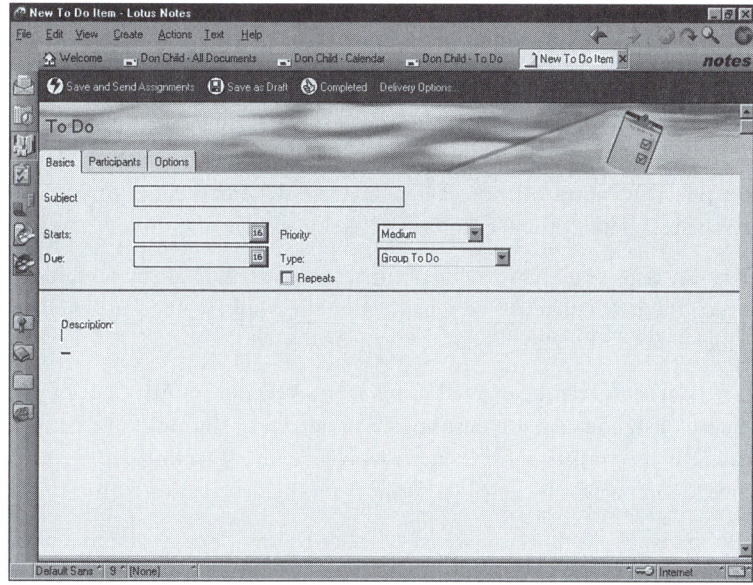

Working with the Calendar Views

Notes 5.0 has a number of different ways of looking at your calendar. You can look at your schedule using five calendar types: One Day, Two Days, One Week, Two Weeks, and One Month. The Calendar views are similar to the interface of Lotus Organizer or your notebook planner. Figure 8.17 shows the Calendar view using the One Week display.

Figure 8.17
The Calendar views enable you to see appointments using a standard calendar format.

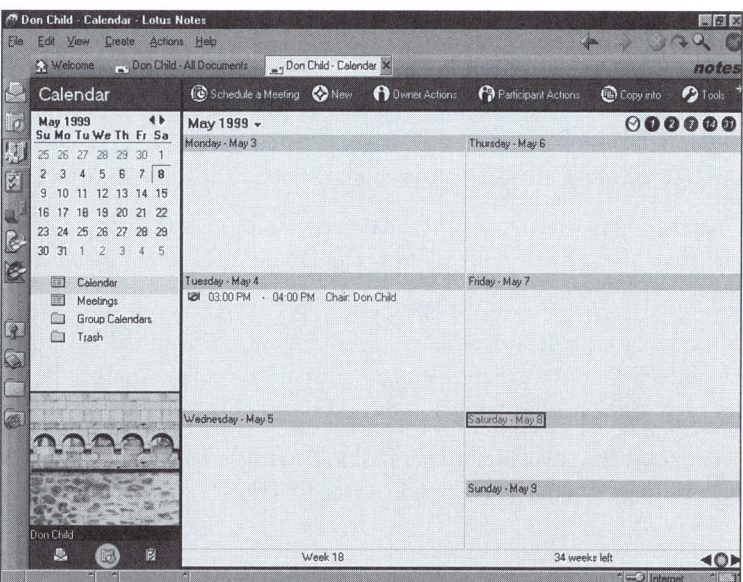

You can choose which view type you want to see by selecting it from the buttons on the view action bar (1, 2, 7, 14, or 31 days). You can display timeslots by clicking on the clock icon next to the view-type icons.

The Calendar view enables you to easily change your schedule using drag-and-drop. If you want to move an appointment, simply click on the entry in the Calendar view and drag it to the new day. Notes will automatically move the entry, check for time conflicts, and send reschedule notices to meeting attendees if necessary.

You can also create new calendar entries in your calendar by double-clicking on the day in which the new entry will be scheduled. Notes will display a new Calendar Entry form on which you can type the details of your new entry.

Calendar views can be printed using a day, week, or month view, or you can print the calendar as a list. You can also customize the calendar printing. For example, you can set up the calendar so it prints only certain hours of the day. Printing can be initiated using the Print SmartIcon or by selecting File, Print from the drop-down menu.

Alternatively, for more advanced calendar printing needs, you may want to access your calendar using Lotus Organizer to access the calendar file on the server, and then print using the various formats provided by Organizer.

Working with Multiple Calendars

New to Notes 5.0 is the capability of creating a group calendar. On a group calendar, you can select any number of individuals from the Domino Directory and display their free time.

You can define multiple group calendars for different project teams. You might have one calendar for in-house sales staff. When a new client enters your office, you can look at the group calendar and immediately see who is available. You could have another calendar for executives so you can see who is available for a quick brainstorming session. A third calendar might list everyone in the company so you can project a time for scheduling a staff meeting.

To set up a group calendar, select Group Calendars from the calendar navigator. Click on the New Group Calendar button to display the dialog box shown in Figure 8.18.

Give the group calendar a title and enter the names of the people whose calendars you want included. You can select names from the Domino Directory by clicking on the helper button beside the Members field.

After the group calendar is defined, you can open it from the Group Calendars view. Double-click on the group calendar you want to display. You will be able to see the free time for each of the people defined in the calendar. This is illustrated in Figure 8.19.

You can use the small arrow keys to flip forward or back one week at a time. You can schedule meetings by double-clicking in a free timeslot.

Figure 8.18
Name a new group calendar and list the people who should be included in the calendar.

Figure 8.19
The group calendar displays free time for multiple users.

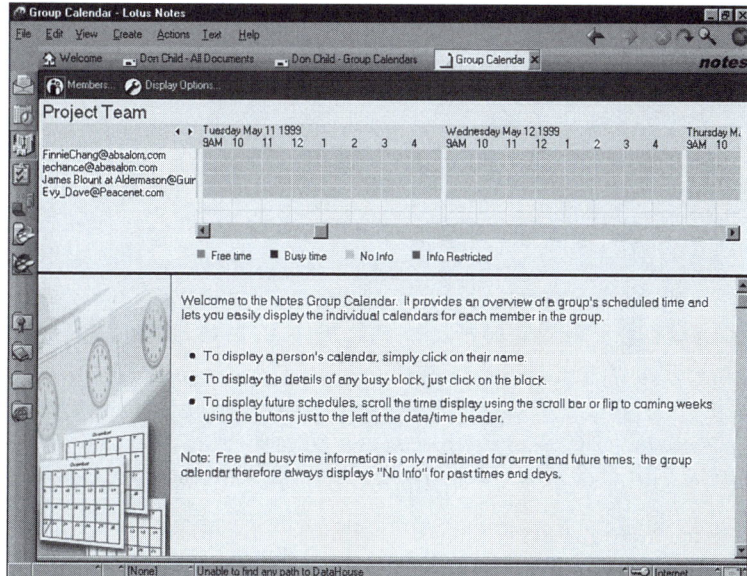

Calendaring and Scheduling While Traveling

The calendaring and scheduling features can be used even when you are disconnected from the network. You can create new calendar entries, including invitations, while traveling. The invitations will be stored in the outgoing mailbox and be routed to the attendees when you perform your normal mail replication. Your schedule will also be updated in the Notes server Free Time database during replication.

One unique feature of Notes calendaring and scheduling is the capability of checking other people's free time while disconnected. You can create a replica of the Free Time database on your local computer that will be used when displaying the Free Time dialog box. The information reflects the other user's free time at the time you last replicated with the server.

You can edit the free-time replication options to set which user's free time is reflected in your local Free Time database, the amount of free-time information that is stored, and how often the local free time is updated. Click on the arrow next to Local free time info on the replication page to select whose free time you replicate. The selective free-time replication options dialog box is shown in Figure 8.20.

Figure 8.20
Select the users for which you want to replicate free time.

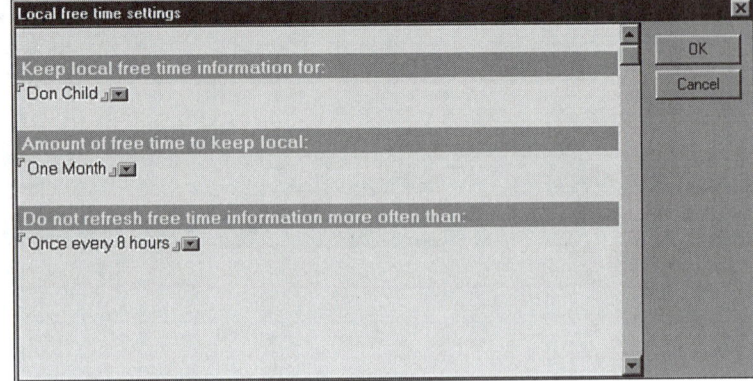

USING THE RESOURCE RESERVATIONS DATABASE

Lotus Notes automatically tracks room and resources using the Resource Reservations database. The Notes administrator creates this database on the server using the RESRC50.NTF database template. This database is used to create site, room, and resource documents, and can be used to directly enter a reservation without using the standard invitation process.

Before using the Resource Reservations database, the system administrator should choose Create, Site Profile to compose a site profile document. This document contains information about your office and domain.

The administrator must then create new rooms and resources in the database. The room and resource documents include the time ranges when the room is available for reservations. Notes will automatically create a request for the administration process (adminp) to enter a resource document in the Name and Address Book.

Notes uses resource categories when multiple resources are available. For instance, you might have three overhead projectors available. The person reserving a projector does not care which projector he or she uses, only that one is available. Notes will randomly reserve a projector out of all of the projectors available to balance the resource usage.

Rooms and resources are normally reserved as part of creating a meeting invitation in your mail database. If you need to reserve a room or resource without creating a meeting, you can use the Resource Reservations database directly. Choose Create, Reservation to compose a new reservation form directly in the Resource Reservations database. Notes will guide you through the reservation process, asking you to choose a resource type and then requesting more details after you click the Continue button.

Using Calendaring and Scheduling with Other Software

The Lotus Calendar Connector for OfficeVision, LCCOV, enables calendar users of Time and Place/2, OV/VM, OV/MVS, and OV/400 to share free-time information with Lotus Domino servers and to translate and deliver meeting notices to and from Lotus Notes users. You set this up by creating a Foreign Domain document in your Domino Directory. Choose Create, Server, Domain to compose a new domain document. Using the domain form, select Foreign Domain for the domain type and enter a domain name and description. Enter the name for the server and the calendar system that will process the scheduling requests for the other scheduling application. If a Notes mail user is using a different scheduling application, enter the name of the foreign domain in the Calendar Domain field of the user's person document in the Name and Address Book. Notes will automatically route invitations and free-time requests to the server defined in the foreign domain document.

Lotus Organizer 97 GS offers built-in support for the calendaring and scheduling features of Lotus Notes. Organizer can store its calendar data on a Domino server, enabling free-time and calendar read access to both Notes and Organizer users. In addition, Organizer users can replicate a local copy of their calendar data and free-time data for other users for offline scheduling. Note, however, that the Millennium edition of Lotus Organizer offers less integration. It is a PIM (personal information manager), and offers no support for integrated calendaring and scheduling the way earlier versions did.

Calendaring Server Tasks

Two server tasks support the calendaring and scheduling process. The first of these, the Schedule Manager, automatically creates the Free Time database (BUSYTIME.NSF) and updates the database as users create new calendar entries. When a user requests to view free time, the Schedule Manager references the Free Time database to populate the Free Time dialog box. The Free Time database is a special database that can be accessed only by the Schedule Manager task.

The second task, the Calendar Connector, is used when a server receives a free-time request for a person whose mail is located on another server. The Calendar Connector automatically communicates with the other server in real-time to retrieve the free-time information and display it to the current user.

Using Calendaring and Scheduling in Other Notes Databases

All the calendaring features in your mail file are available to you while you're designing new Domino applications. You can create special calendar entry forms, check free time, and display your Notes documents using the Calendar views.

There are many potential uses of these features in Notes design. For example, a customer service application could display customer orders by order date or ship date using the new

Calendar view. Managers and production staff would be able to easily see which orders needed to be shipped in the next day or week.

The date and time controls make any time-based application more user-friendly. Your Notes users will no longer need to waste time figuring out which day of the week the 15th of next month falls on; they can simply click on the date using the new calendar control.

From Here...

In this chapter, you learned about the calendaring and scheduling features in Notes. You can learn more about specific topics in the following chapters:

- Chapter 10, "Using Mobile Features from Home or on the Road," expands on what you need to do to set up your computer for mobile computing, which includes how to set up for replication.
- Chapter 14, "Designing Pages, Forms, and Subforms," provides insight into how you can use the date and time controls in the Domino applications you create.
- Chapter 31, "Integrating Domino with Legacy Systems," discusses other ways besides calendaring in which you can share data with legacy systems.
- Chapter 45, "Upgrading from cc:Mail, Microsoft Mail, and Exchange to Domino," provides details on how to migrate data to Notes from other applications.

CHAPTER 9

USING SAMETIME COLLABORATION

Sametime is a major new initiative that will lift collaboration using Lotus Notes to new levels. Lotus/IBM is already the leader in collaboration computing. But that communication was built on giving people access to information from anywhere, at any time of day or night. Sametime adds to that model the capability of collaborating directly in real-time.

Imagine working on a document—an important proposal, for example—and as you are working, you can see that somebody else just opened the document and started making his or her own edits. With Sametime, you can initiate a real-time conversation with that person. Launch a Chat applet, use an audio connection, or even share an application with the other person. Then imagine expanding that conversation into a full-fledged online meeting with several of your colleagues. That is what Sametime is all about.

In this chapter, you learn about the Sametime tools that work in tandem with Notes to achieve a richer collaborative environment. The tools are demonstrated as they are implemented using the Sametime server, which is a major part of the Sametime technology.

Understanding Sametime

If you are at all familiar with the World Wide Web, you may be familiar with some of the components of Sametime. Sametime enables you to collaborate with other users in real-time. It extends the groupware concept from "anyplace, anytime," to "now." In other words, Sametime provides Notes with a real-time business collaboration solution.

Sametime is newly integrated into Notes and is also available to Web clients. Because it is new, there are a few technical standards that you might not be familiar with. I'll look at those standards first before taking you on a tour of Sametime.

The Technical Components of Sametime

Sametime is actually a family of tools that follow emerging standards and enable you to share conversations and objects in real-time. Sametime conferencing applications support T.120 International Telecommunications Union (ITU) standards and can work with any other client that supports the T.120 standard, such as Microsoft NetMeeting. Audio and video conferencing with Sametime supports the H.323 standard. Lotus is participating in the Internet Engineering Task Force (IETF) to set standards for online presence and awareness.

Because it is standards-based, Sametime applications will be able to work with a variety of networking and audio products that are just starting to appear in the telecommunications and telephony arenas.

Sametime clients include Lotus Notes 5.0, which provides what is called *awareness* information on active databases and documents, along with real-time conferencing, which enables Notes users to share documents in real-time with anybody who has a T.120-based conferencing client. The client also includes Java and ActiveX components that enable Notes clients to collaborate in real-time with users who have Web browsers.

Sametime server functionality is also included in the Domino server. Server functionality closely parallels client functionality with awareness, instant messaging, application sharing, collaborative browsing, whiteboarding, and other real-time services for Notes clients, Web browsers, and Microsoft NetMeeting and other T.120- or H.323-based clients.

For those who are not familiar with real-time collaboration, here are a few key terms:

- Awareness   Awareness is knowing who is connected to the network at any one time. You may be familiar with other terms, such as *buddy lists*, where a friend can tell when you are online so he or she can get in touch with you. This is a version of awareness.
- Conversation tools   Conversation tools are tools that enable you to communicate with others in synchronous, or real-time, mode. Conversation tools can be used for chat, telephone, and video conferencing, for example.
- Shared objects   Shared objects are the objects or documents that you share with others in a business transaction. For example, you might share a graph or chart, a proposal, a graphic, a spreadsheet, and so forth. Although Notes has always enabled people to share these objects, Sametime enables synchronous (real-time) sharing of these objects.
- Instant messaging   This is the simplest form of real-time communication found in text-based chat rooms.
- Buddy lists   Buddy lists are groups of users that you want to communicate with. With the buddy list, your computer can be aware when anyone from the list is available on the network.

Synchronous Collaboration

What is *synchronous collaboration*, besides two big words? It means two or more people working together on something at the same time. Notes has always been famous as a tool for asynchronous collaboration. Adding synchronicity makes it an even more powerful tool for collaboration.

For example, imagine working on a difficult proposal. Someone is helping you and he or she lives somewhere across the country from you—or in my case, across the ocean. I live in Hawaii, and I am working on a proposal with Tom, who lives in Washington, and Jim, who lives in Los Angeles. Some tasks we can complete as individuals, but there comes a time when we have to work together. I could put my thoughts into a document in a database that gets replicated. Tom and Jim could comment on or edit my document when they receive it. That is the traditional way to do it in Notes. But here is the synchronous scenario.

I am working on the proposal. On the side of my Sametime screen are my buddy lists. When I first look, I see that neither Tom nor Jim are on the network, so I continue working. As I'm about to save my document, I see the red awareness button next to Tom's name turn green. He has just logged on.

I send a chat message in real-time. `Hey, Tom. Can you take a look at this document? I'll pass control over to you, and you can edit the details about the client's offices in the northwest.`

A couple of clicks, and Tom now has control of the document. I watch the changes Tom is making. Meanwhile, I notice that Jim has logged on. I invite him into the collaboration. As the originator of the session, I can control who is "speaking," who is editing in the shared application, and who else is allowed to join the collaboration.

Jim has an idea. He brings up a whiteboard and draws a flowchart to illustrate his point. Tom and I can see his drawing on the screen as Jim creates it.

By the time we drop the Sametime session, we have accomplished more in half an hour than we could have in two hours of asynchronous communication. We have had a brainstorming session within a Lotus Notes discussion database, in real-time. One of us was in Hawaii, one in the Pacific northwest, one in southern California.

That is what Sametime makes possible—sharing information in real-time. Add telephony and other multimedia tools, and every Notes workstation is potentially a teleconferencing port.

Using Sametime in a Collaborative Learning Environment

To give you a flavor of what Sametime is all about, I want to walk you through a recent learning experience I had. It shows one way that Sametime can be implemented. The Sametime server runs on a separate machine from the Domino server, but it takes advantage of many of the Domino and Notes tools to elevate the possibilities of groupware computing. I went through a session using Sametime, so I will give you a taste of what Sametime collaboration is all about.

I signed up for a seminar on how to use the DataBeam server. Lotus acquired DataBeam, and the server is now known as the Sametime server. The session was to be held at 1:00 p.m. EST, which is 7:00 a.m. in Hawaii, where I live.

Prior to the session, I had to try out my server and browser to be sure they were compatible. Because the Sametime client consists of a number of Java applets, I had to have a Java-capable browser (for example, IE4). I also had to sign up for the seminar. Enrolling students or guests is an activity that Lotus Notes lends itself to. In fact, you can use a registration feature, such as the one used by LearningSpace, and then work with an environment that is a mix of asynchronous and synchronous communications.

In Sametime, you can set up a buddy list using the Sametime Connector, which ties in to AOL's Instant Messenger. The server will maintain a state of awareness, listening for the members of your workgroup so that you know when they are online. However, for the session demonstrated in this chapter, it was up to me to log in to the Sametime Learning server at the correct time. I logged in through the screen shown in Figure 9.1.

In the session I joined, I also had to place a conference call on a separate telephone line. The audio capability of the Sametime server is not as good as a phone line, and not everyone has a multimedia workstation. However, you will soon be able to listen to full audio and watch streaming video as easily as you can make a conference call. In fact, Lotus recently announced a new partnership with RealNetworks, which will provide the streaming audio and video within Sametime.

Figure 9.1
Log on to a scheduled session. Later, you can wait until someone on your buddy list connects to the server.

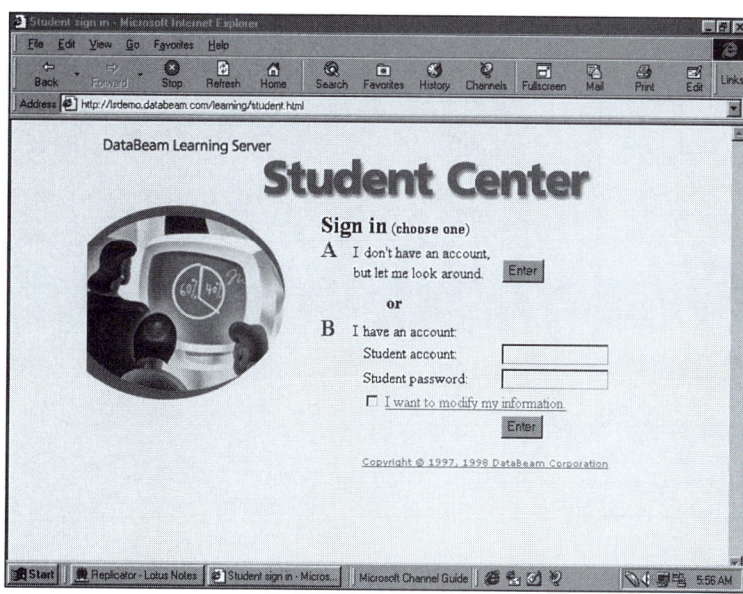

Exploring the Workspace

When I got logged on to the Sametime seminar, I was greeted with the Sametime workspace, shown in Figure 9.2.

The entire application is actually a series of Java applets. All the applets are docked into set frames. However, you can free applets from their homes in the framework. Notice the Float button in the upper-right corner of various frames. Click on a Float button and that particular frame becomes a floating window. When it is floating, you can grab the applet frame and drag it to wherever you want. You can minimize a floating applet. You can toggle different applets using Alt+Tab. You can bring an applet to the foreground quickly and easily by clicking on the control button (for example, the Chat button). You can redock an applet in the framework by clicking on the X in the corner of the applet window. The floating window will close and the applet will be reapplied to its standard place within the frame.

Figure 9.2
A "student" can navigate around the workspace using the buttons at the top of the screen.

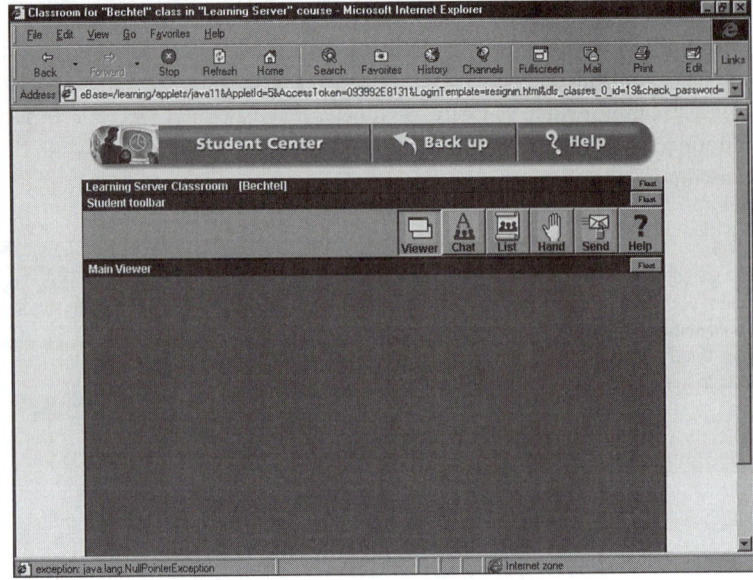

Navigation Buttons

The six large buttons near the top of the screen launch the six Java applets that make up the Sametime student workspace. The following briefly describes these applets:

- Viewer

    The FarSite Viewer displaces the screen area where the instructor can display information to students, share applications with them, or pass control to the students so they can contribute to collaborations.

- Chat

    The Chat application enables students to chat with one another while a class session is taking place.

- List

    The List applet displays a list of all registered students who are currently participating in the session.

- Hand

    One of the ground rules when using the Sametime server in a real-time session is that the instructor has control over who speaks. The Hand icon enables students to "raise" their hands until they are recognized by the instructor.

- Send

    Send enables you to compose private messages to the instructor.

- Help

    The Help button displays online help specific to the student applet.

THE VIEWER

The main portion of the workspace is the Viewer, where the instructor shares applications and where everyone in the classroom can collaborate on the Presentation Whiteboard. It is where the instructor can present a slideshow. In short, the Viewer is the area where most of the work of the virtual classroom takes place.

In the example shown in Figure 9.3, the instructor is displaying a slide she prepared before the session. In this case, the information being presented is moving in a single direction, from the instructor to the students. You get a taste of the application-sharing capabilities in this section. As you look at the figures in this chapter, notice the background and how it is used to reinforce various aspects of the seminar that is taking place during the entire session.

Figure 9.3
Among other functions, the Viewer can be used to communicate using prepared slides.

Look at the bottom of the window. Every applet has a status bar at the bottom of the screen. You can see how many students there are. You can tell who has control of the screen, and who has the microphone if you are using the audio. You can also tell when someone new raises a hand, lowers a hand, leaves the classroom, and so forth. The status bar can give a quick overview of the current situation in the classroom.

The Presentation Whiteboard (the whiteboard) can be used to present information. If desired, you can also use the whiteboard to collaborate with others. The use of the whiteboard begins with the instructor, but the students can also play a role, as described in the following sections.

THE INSTRUCTOR'S ROLE IN PREPARING A WHITEBOARD PRESENTATION

Presentations have to be prepared in advance of a classroom session. You can prepare a presentation using any software you like—Freelance Graphics, Powerpoint, PageMaker, even Lotus Notes.

After a presentation has been prepared, you print the presentation using the SametimeServer Print Capture. This utility is available by downloading the DataBeam Learning Server Utilities from http://www.databeam.com, or from Lotus. The presentation is "printed" to a FarSite file, which has an .fst extension. The instructor can then select this or any other FST file to display on the whiteboard.

THE INSTRUCTOR'S ROLE IN SHOWING THE PRESENTATION

When the classroom session begins, the instructor can show the pages of the presentation. They are held in what is called a *workbook*. The pages of the workbook can be displayed one at a time, as easily as showing the pages of any presentation. But the instructor has more tools available.

A palette of drawing tools can be used to highlight items on the screen, adding emphasis to the classroom lecture. For example, Figure 9.4 illustrates how the instructor has given emphasis to parts of her presentation by using drawing tools.

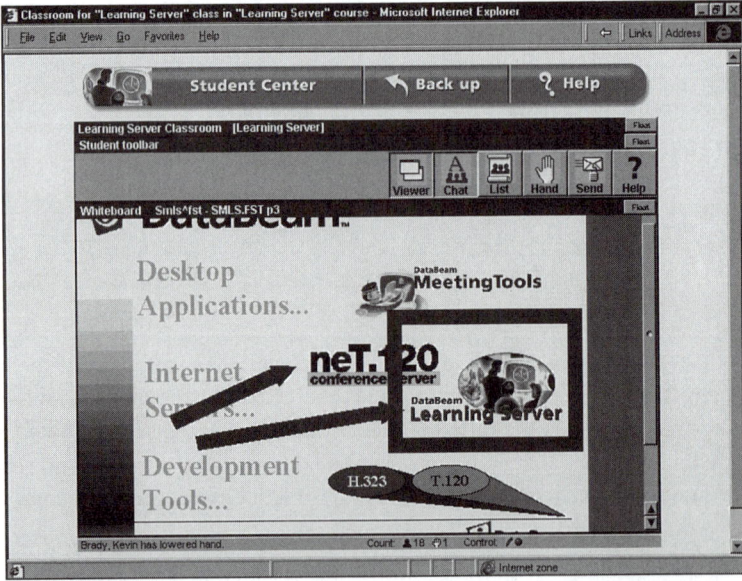

Figure 9.4
The instructor can use drawing tools to add emphasis to a presentation.

The instructor has default control over the whiteboard, but can pass control to one or more of the students. The instructor has an expanded button bar that enables him or her to control much of what happens during the session.

THE STUDENTS' ROLE IN WHITEBOARD PRESENTATIONS

While the instructor has control of the whiteboard session, the students can participate only via voice or using the chat. When the teacher temporarily passes control to the students, they can use the whiteboard using a set of drawing tools similar to those found in any drawing application. In Figure 9.5, the instructor has passed control to the students, who are experimenting with the drawing tools.

Figure 9.5
When control is passed to you, a toolbox of drawing tools is at your fingertips.

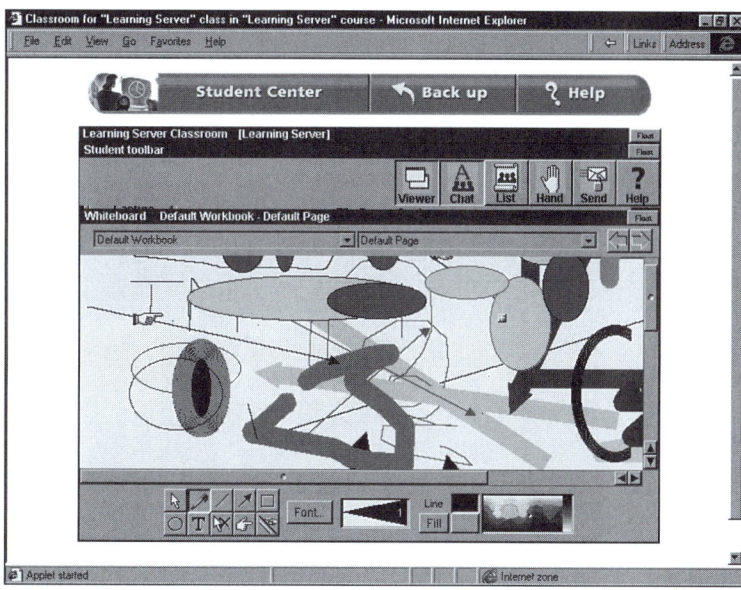

Using the drawing tools, you can draw lines, shapes, arrows, and text. You can change colors and line/text size. You can paint with a freehand tool, or you can pick the color you want to use as a fill. You cannot cut and paste, nor can you drag and drop on the whiteboard. However, you can select objects and delete them.

Incidentally, as you work on the whiteboard, other students can instantly see what you are doing. If you are working in *controlled* mode, only you can mark up the whiteboard, but only while you have control. If more than one person has control (*uncontrolled* mode), you can quickly get a chaotic situation. That's what happened on the whiteboard shown in Figure 9.5. When the instructor is ready, he or she can revoke the controls, regaining virtual control over what can be an unruly classroom.

Remember that the whiteboard is an area for collaborating, for brainstorming. You cannot save the images on the whiteboard. You can't cut and paste them. If you want to save an image, you have to use a screen capture utility or a screen print utility, such as the FarSite screen capture program used to create the Presentation Whiteboard files in the first place.

Discovering Who Else Is Online

When you step into any classroom for the first time, there is usually a period of introductions. The instructor gives his or her name and then asks the students to provide a bit of background about themselves. This is also true in a virtual classroom.

I attended two sessions of the seminar on using the Sametime Learning server. Periodically throughout the session, I clicked on the List button to see who else was in the classroom. I saw a screen like the one shown in Figure 9.6.

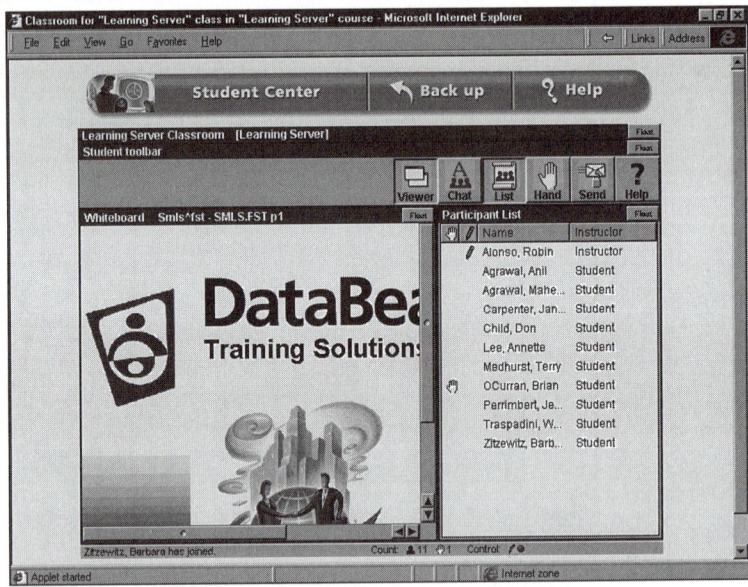

Figure 9.6
You can view a list of everyone who is logged in to the Sametime session at any moment.

On the list, the person with a pencil next to his or her name is the person who is currently controlling the session. In this case, the instructor has control, but she can temporarily pass control of the whiteboard to any of the students in the session.

The list of students changes as students enter or leave the virtual classroom. During the two sessions I attended, there was a student from Croatia, at least two students from France, one from Italy, and up to 24 others at a time attending the class from various locations around the world.

The list of students is similar to a buddy list, which you might use if you are on America Online or if you use tools such as ICQ. When using the SameTime application in Notes, a similar buddy list will be available. The buddy list displays the names of predefined users, with a small light beside the user's name. If the light icon is red, your buddy is not currently online. If the icon is green, it means that your buddy is logged on the server, and is therefore available for chatting or application sharing if you choose to initiate a session.

On the Sametime server, you can hide the list of students and instructors at any time by clicking on the List button again. Every time you click on it, the list is toggled on or off. You can also float the List applet and minimize it or move it to a different part of your screen, if you want.

CHATTING WITH YOUR FELLOW STUDENTS

Anyone attending the online session can join in an online chat with others who are in the classroom at the time. To launch the Chat applet, click on the Chat button. Floating the Chat applet enables you to chat while watching everything else going on in the classroom at the same time.

Chat rooms can be public—for example, any student can join the chat session—or they can be restricted to predefined workgroups. If you are working on a proposal using Sametime, for example, you want to restrict chat sessions to those who are actively involved in the proposal process. You can set up private team rooms, just as you can in the asynchronous classrooms in Lotus LearningSpace. If you have a chance to work with Sametime, explore this feature on your own.

The chat client is a Java applet that displays the most recent messages, but enables you to scroll to messages earlier in the session. Each message clearly identifies the sending party. If you want to participate in the chat, you can type your own message.

Press Enter to post your message so others can see it. If you click on the Send button, the message is also posted to the instructor's private message applet. Figure 9.7 shows a chat session.

Figure 9.7
Use the Chat applet to communicate directly with fellow students while class is in session.

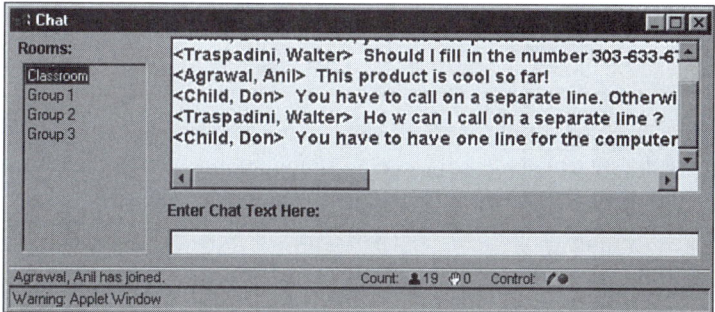

RAISING YOUR HAND TO ASK A QUESTION

You can get the instructor's attention by "raising your hand," as if you were sitting in a regular classroom. To raise your hand, click on the Hand icon. A small hand will appear next to your name in the list of students. You can see an example of this by referring to Figure 9.6. There also is a message at the bottom of the screen saying, for example, `Don has raised his hand`.

When your hand is raised, the instructor can call on you to answer your question via the microphone if you have an online voice setup, via phone line if you are on a conference call, or via the Chat applet.

After your question has been answered, you can put your hand down by clicking on the Hand icon a second time to toggle it off. Because the instructor is in charge of the session, he or she can also clear a raised hand from that screen at any time.

Sending Private Messages to the Instructor

The Send button (on the Button bar) is used to send private messages to the instructor during a session. The instructor has a private message box in addition to the regular Chat applet. When you click on Send, the Private Message applet is displayed, as shown in Figure 9.8.

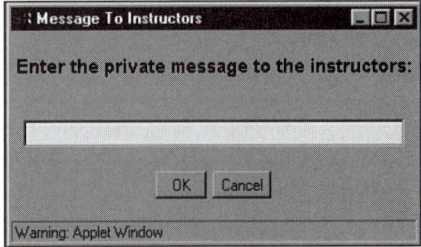

Figure 9.8
Create a private message that only the instructor can see.

Type a message and click on OK. The message is immediately visible to anyone defined as an instructor. It provides one more level of communication within the open framework of the Sametime server.

Getting Help

The final applet available on the student button bar is the Help applet. It provides online help for the student applets. The help system provides comprehensive coverage of both student and instructor functions on the Sametime server. Figure 9.9 illustrates the help system.

Figure 9.9
A complete online help system is available within the application.

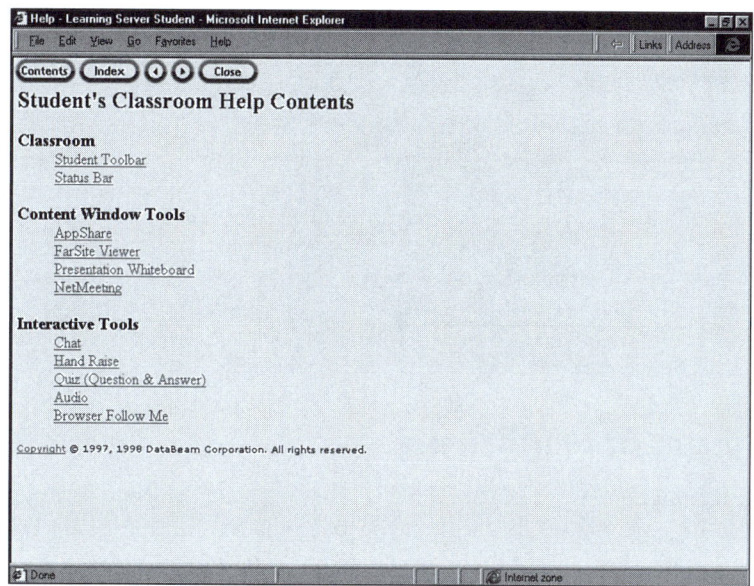

SAMETIME QUIZZES

The instructor can give a short quiz or survey to the students, and he or she can then provide immediate results. There are five types of questions that can be sent by the instructor:

- Multiple-choice questions
- Multiple-choice with multiple answers
- True/False
- Yes/No
- Text entry

When the question is submitted to the students, they see a question box. The students select their answers and then click on the Submit button to return their answer to the instructor. An example of a question is shown in Figure 9.10.

Quiz responses can be seen only by the instructor. If you want to relate the response of everyone to the students, it has to be done via voice. The instructor also has the option of inviting responses via the Chat applet, and then students can see each other's responses.

Figure 9.10
A multiple-choice, multiple-answer quiz box gathers information from students.

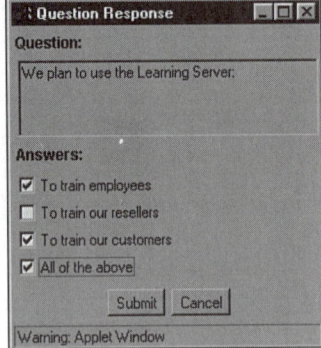

Sharing Applications

Using the AppShare Content Window, the instructor can copy part of the screen and share it in a transparent window with the Share Frame feature. The Share Frame window can be moved anywhere on the desktop by the instructor. For example, during one session, the instructor can copy the Instructor Toolbar and display it in the whiteboard.

The Share Frame feature is much more versatile than that, however. The instructor can define an area of the desktop and share any application on his or her computer. When the instructor wants to share an application, he or she can select the application using a Host Control Panel. The Host Control Panel can also be used to allow students to "drive" the application. Figure 9.11 shows a shared application that is illustrated in the Sametime help application.

Figure 9.11
Students can "drive" an application hosted on the instructor's computer.

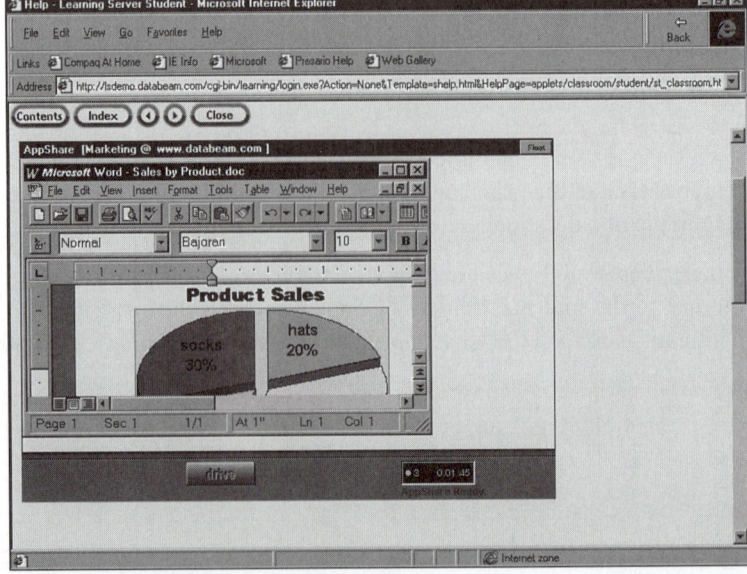

When control is given to the students, it is all or nothing. In other words, if you allow student control of a hosted application, anyone can drive the application by clicking on the Drive button at the bottom of the application window.

The instructor needs to maintain tight control when the students have control of the application. The Drive button is available to all students. They can steal control from each other, in which case nothing gets accomplished. Through discipline, you can have a single person drive the application. When that person is done, another student can become the driver by clicking on the Drive button.

What does it mean to drive the application? It means that you have access to all functions within the application. In a word processor, you can add, modify, or delete documents and format the document. In a spreadsheet, you can add data, change formulas, and display graphs. You can save documents. You can even click in the corner and close the application.

One thing you cannot do with a Host application is print the document on your local printer. If you try to print the document, it will be printed on the Host computer's printer, not on your own.

The instructor has the ability to revoke control. This is vitally important, because when a student has control of an application, he or she has access to the instructor's entire system. The student can go to a File menu and copy documents from anywhere on the computer or can delete files. There has to be a level of trust, but the person hosting the application has to be able to revoke control.

> **Note**
>
> Another tool you should be aware of is the browser Follow tool. The instructor can ask students to follow him or her to another Web site during a session. The second Web site opens in a second browser session so that no students are lost along the way. This provides one more way in which you can extend application sharing so that you are sharing Web applications as well as applications that reside on the instructor's computer. When the instructor is done sharing the Follow Me Web site, students can close the second browser window and they will be right back in the classroom.

BEYOND THE CLASSROOM—SAMETIME SUPPORT FOR MEETINGS AND SHARED VIEWING

You have now seen most of the tools that go into the Sametime implementation in Lotus Notes. The Sametime server used in this chapter's tour is a specific use of those tools. When integrated with Lotus Notes, those same tools provide new opportunities.

The Lotus vision for Sametime is to take the best asynchronous messaging system, Lotus Notes and Domino, and marry it to the best synchronous tools available. Here is what that marriage will look like eventually.

Today, Notes tracks who has edited each document in a Domino application. When and if Sametime is fully integrated into Notes, you will be able to tell who else is editing the document right then, and you will have the option of initiating a conversation—through chat, online audio, or telephone—if you need to discuss the document.

In Web documents, hyperlinks to individuals become *aware*. Instead of sending email to someone, you can invite them to chat. For example, if you are visiting a help desk application, you can search for information, but if you cannot find it, you can launch a Chat applet or a private message to the person staffing the help desk. You can even share your application on the screen so the help desk knows exactly what you are looking at. If you give the editor access to your document, he or she will be able to make changes online rather than describe the changes that you will have to make.

Visitor awareness includes both Notes documents and specific Web pages. When people are looking at a page, you know it, and you can selectively invite one or more people to join you in some type of real-time collaboration.

The individual sharing of conversations and documents is a real boon to collaborative communication, but it extends beyond creating a virtual community. You can still schedule virtual meetings using all the same tools highlighted in the tour of the Sametime server.

In summary, you can use Sametime to move collaboration to a new level. With Notes, you already have new and unread document flags, access logs, email, bulletin boards and discussion databases, document archiving, attachments for sharing documents, and hyperlinks. But with Sametime, you add real-time collaboration tools.

Sametime is the next generation of collaboration. Sametime currently runs on a separate box from the Domino server, but Lotus is exploring the possibility of running Sametime as a task on the Domino server. There are security issues that need to be resolved, however. For example, the Sametime server requires full-time bidirectional lines of communication and requires that you have Java applets enabled. Such exposure to the outside world is an unacceptable security risk for most servers.

FROM HERE...

Sametime extends many of the features available in the asynchronous mode of replicated Domino applications. Some of the related features are described in the following chapters:

- Chapter 5, "Using Electronic Mail," describes how to hold a conversation in asynchronous mode using Lotus Notes.
- Chapter 7, "Contact Management with the Personal and Public Directories," describes how to maintain lists of people that you communicate with using Lotus Notes.
- Chapter 11, "Using the Notes Client on the Internet," gives you a taste of the integration between Notes and the Internet. Sametime extends that integration to a new level.
- Chapter 23, "Creating and Using Java Applets and Agents," describes how to integrate Java applets into a Notes and Domino environment. Learning about Java applets in Notes should give you insight into some of the thinking behind Sametime.

CHAPTER 10

USING MOBILE FEATURES FROM HOME OR ON THE ROAD

When you think about it, the Notes workgroup exists in virtual space. The members of your team might all work in the same office and might be constantly connected to the same local area network, at least from 8 a.m. until 5 p.m. But then again, they might be scattered around the globe. Connections between team members might take place once a day or once a week. Users might be replicating at noon in Bangalore, India; at midnight in Paris; or at 8 a.m. in Boston.

Notes users might well say that they carry their office desk with them on their laptop computer. For example, imagine a busy sales representative, Janet Aubrey, who travels to visit several sales areas and occasionally visits a regional office. At the company headquarters in San Diego, she is connected to the local area network (LAN). She reads her Notes mail, which is stored on the Notes server, and works with several of the corporate databases on a daily basis.

We will follow her on one of her sales trips. On the morning before she is scheduled to leave, she updates a local replica copy of her mail database. She also updates a few other vital databases, such as her company's customer-tracking database, an online sales brochure, and a travel planner that lists good places to eat in the cities she will be visiting. If she made full replicas of all the databases she used in the office, her laptop computer would quickly run out of storage space, so she uses a replication formula that collects only those documents that might be relevant to her during her travels. Then she leaves with her entire desktop stored on her laptop computer.

The first hop of her journey is a short one to Los Angeles, where she has a connecting flight to Honolulu. She visits the Los Angeles office for a meeting before continuing. She connects to the office LAN and selects LA OFFICE as a location. She has already defined the parameters for that location. She doesn't have to define the protocol she is using. She doesn't have to tell the computer that her home/mail Notes server is in San Diego.

Soon, she heads to the airport. Just as she is going toward the departure gate, her beeper goes off. An urgent email is waiting for her. She finds a pay phone, connects a phone line to the laptop, and changes the location setting to LA MOBILE. She goes to the Replicator page and selects Send & Receive Mail. As soon as Notes is finished picking up her mail, Janet puts her laptop in her briefcase and heads for the plane.

The call from the airport didn't dial directly to her home/mail server. Instead, the LA MOBILE Location document in her Personal Address Book dialed the LA branch office. There, she had defined a Passthru server that put her through to San Diego. Because her company uses the Passthru-Server feature, she was able to connect to her personal-mail file directly. She used a local call even though her home server was in San Diego.

Soon, she is airborne somewhere high above the Pacific Ocean. She opens her laptop and reads her email. She creates responses to mail when necessary. She selects Send and File as soon as she is done creating a memo. The outgoing mail is held in an outgoing mailbox right on her laptop computer, ready for transfer to the server the next time she connects. She sends another memo to co-worker Wally Takayama, who sent a spreadsheet she will need in Honolulu. The spreadsheet was sent as an attachment in a message. She addresses a memo simply to `Wally`, knowing that Notes will look up the correct address in her Personal Address Book.

The urgent message she picked up in LA mentions a new client who can see her for only 15 minutes in the airport, because he is catching an outgoing flight. No problem. The client is in the Client Tracking database on her laptop. She opens the client's profile to brush up on his background. She examines her proposal, and works on a Freelance presentation for her 15-minute meeting. When she meets the client, she will be able to launch the application from within the proposal in Notes.

She continues to read and respond to her email, takes time out for lunch, browses the latest updates to the Lotus Web pages (offline, of course) and then has a nap. After all, this will be a 27-hour day when the time zones are factored in.

When she lands in Honolulu, she meets the client as soon as she gets off the plane. She shows him her proposal. He likes it. As soon as he boards his flight, she hooks up her laptop to a phone line in the airport and changes the location to Travel, another location she has predefined. From the Replicator page, she selects Send outgoing mail. Notes dials an Internet account with a local number set up through a Location document that has her ISP's local phone number. The proposal is routed through her home server in San Diego along with all the other mail in her outgoing mailbox. By the time she gathers her luggage and picks up a rental car, the proposal is sitting in the client's mail box. The result is another sale. The elapsed time—half an hour on the ground.

When she finally reaches her hotel, she hooks up her modem line to the hotel telephone and switches to a location named Hotel. She clicks on Start from the Replicator page. Notes prompts her for the telephone number to call. She selects the phone number for the Internet provider, and the modem dials 9 before dialing out. By the time she sits down to dinner, she has current data on her laptop computer, an order from her newest client has already been sent to the fulfillment clerk, and she is ready to enjoy a stroll down Waikiki beach.

Notes 5.0 deserves a lot of the credit. It made her work effortless because of the mobile features.

Setting Up a Workstation for Mobile Computing

There are several necessary steps to set up for all the events in the scenario described. You need Notes 5.0 and a valid Notes user ID. You need a Notes-compatible modem set up to use with your workstation. You need the phone numbers of the Domino servers you want to contact, or alternatively, the phone number for an Internet provider and the IP address of the Domino server. You need an analog phone line to connect to, plus a phone cord, extra batteries, a power adapter, and so on.

Within Notes itself, there are four items that need to be set up properly before you can take full advantage of Lotus Notes on the road:

- You need to set up and define ports.
- You need to set up and define locations.
- You need to make local replica copies of databases.
- You need to set up and define replication schedules if you will be replicating on a scheduled basis.
- The Domino Administrator needs to set up Passthru Servers, if necessary, and you need to create server connection documents to identify the Passthru server and any other servers you will be using.

Many of the mobile options can be initiated from the File, Mobile menu option. The options on this menu include the following:

- Choose Current Location displays a list of available locations from which you can select. The same list is available from the Locations section of the status bar, found near the bottom-right corner of the Notes workspace.
- Edit Current Location displays the location record for the currently selected location. You can also edit the location record from the Locations section of the status bar.
- Edit Current Time/Phone displays a dialog box so you can enter specific dialing information for the current location, including the current time, the number to dial to get an outside line, and the country and area codes.
- Advanced, Locations displays the Locations view in the Personal Address Book; from here, you can select Location documents for editing or create new locations.
- Server Phone Numbers displays the Advanced, Connections view in the Personal Address Book so you can edit existing server connection records or create new records. The server connection documents hold the phone number to call for a specific server.
- Call Server enables you to select a server from a list of those servers for which a connection document exists, and initiate the call so you can directly access databases on the server (assuming you are authorized to do so).
- Hang Up disconnects your modem from the server.

Setting Up Ports

Any discussion about Notes 5.0 as a mobile computing platform depends on your ability to establish communications between your workstation and the Domino server with which you are communicating. That means either configuring a network connection or a connection via a modem.

You can set up multiple ports. You can then choose which port to use for a specific location depending on the type of connection that is available. Each port uses a specific communications protocol, which must match one of the protocols being used by the Domino server that you are communicating with.

COMMUNICATIONS PROTOCOLS

All connections between a Notes client and a Domino server are classified as either a network connection or a dial-in connection, regardless of whether the connection is made locally or from a mobile computer. Although we usually think of network connections as being local, physical connections to a network, a network connection also includes a wide area network (WAN), with a link to the server through a bridge or router and a connection over the Internet via TCP/IP. Notes provides several communications drivers (in other words, protocols), including the following:

- AppleTalk is used to communicate with Macintosh clients or with other Notes servers using AppleTalk.
- Banyan VINES is used for communication over a Banyan VINES network.
- DECnet Pathworks uses a NetBIOS driver to communicate.
- Lotus Notes Connect for SNA is used to communicate across IBM SNA networks using either the OS/2 Communications Manager or DCA Communications software for the server or workstation and the associated hardware. Both the server and workstation must use Lotus Notes Connect for SNA, which is available as an add-on product.
- NetBIOS is used to communicate over any network that uses NetBIOS. There is a separate NetBIOS driver for IBM Extended Edition LAN Requestor.
- NetWare SPX is used to communicate over a Novell network using native SPX protocol rather than NetBIOS.
- TCP/IP is used to communicate between client and server and between Notes servers across all supported Notes hardware platforms. Because of its cross-platform capabilities, TCP/IP is widely used. TCP/IP is, of course, also the protocol used on the Internet. This means that you can connect to a Notes server via the Internet as if you were making a local call to an ISP, no matter what your location.

> **Tip**
> Although one of the banner applications in Notes 5.0 is the integrated browser, you do not need to use TCP/IP on your workstation to navigate on the Web. You can also have the Domino server handle all Web retrievals, while you connect to the server over an internal network using a protocol other than TCP/IP. In such a setup, you would read Web pages as Notes documents. Browsing the Web while on the road is discussed in greater detail near the end of this chapter.

- XPC is built into every Notes client and server, and is used to communicate over dial-up or null-modem connections when no other communication drivers are available. You can also use the XPC driver's asynchronous communication scripts to dial in to an X.25 Packet Assembler Disassembler (PAD). This gives you the ability to issue commands to communicate with any X.25 address.

- Lotus Notes Connect for X.25 is an add-on product so that Notes can communicate directly with X.25 private or public networks. The Lotus Notes Connect for X.25 driver can be used to communicate over X.25 leased lines using Eicon hardware and software, although the Eicon Technology components are not included with Notes. They must be obtained from Eicon. If a server supports X.25, PAD-connected users do not need Lotus Notes Connect for X.25 to communicate.

Defining a New Port

You can define more than one port. Each port you define is associated with a particular communications protocol.

Communications protocols are set on the User Preferences screen, displayed by selecting File, Preferences, User Preferences, and clicking on the Ports icon on the left of the dialog box. The User Preferences screen is shown in Figure 10.1.

Figure 10.1
Set up ports using the User Preferences dialog box.

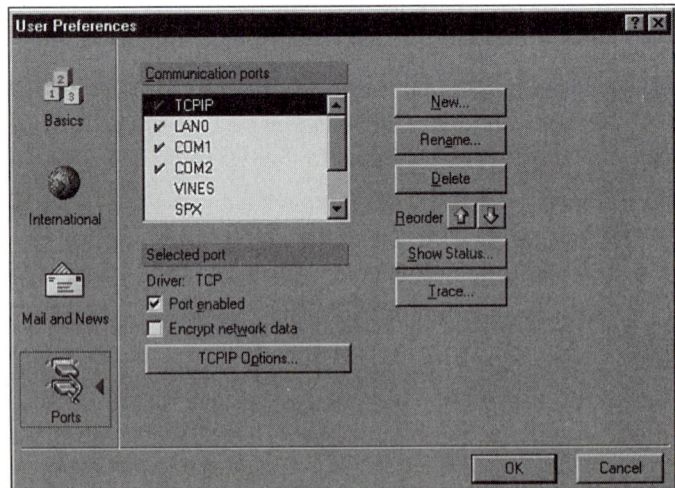

Click on the New button to display a dialog box where you type the name of the new port (for instance, COM5), select the protocol, and specify at which locations you will use this protocol.

Each port name is associated with a single communications protocol. You can rename or delete a port, but you cannot change the protocol assigned to that port. If you want the port to have a different protocol, you must delete the port, and then create a new port by the same name using the new protocol.

After you name the port, select a protocol, and identify locations where the port will be used, you can define additional optional information by clicking on the Options button under the protocol name, as listed here:

- TCP/IP   You can define the duration of a connection-attempt timeout.
- NetBIOS   You can choose between automatic or manual setup. If you choose manual setup, you can specify the NetBIOS unit/LANa number.
- IPX/SPX   You can choose between automatic or advanced configuration for NetWare Services. The advanced configuration enables you to choose between NetWare Directory and Bindery Services, NetWare Directory Services (NDS), or Bindery Services. You can also define a Fallback Name Server for the workstation.
- VINES   There are no additional options when you set up the VINES protocol.
- XPC   For all COM ports, the default protocol is XPC, which depends on having a modem connected to the COM port (either internally or externally), or a null modem that connects one computer to another directly via a null modem cable.

Setting Up a Modem

Because we are talking about the mobile use of Notes, you need a modem and a phone connection in order to communicate with the Domino server. Setting up a modem is done when you select the XPC protocol. In fact, if you select XPC, you have to define the type of modem you are using before you can finish defining the port.

Because we created a new port named COM5, the User Preferences dialog box will display a button labeled COM5 Options. Click on this button to display the Additional Setup dialog box, shown in Figure 10.2.

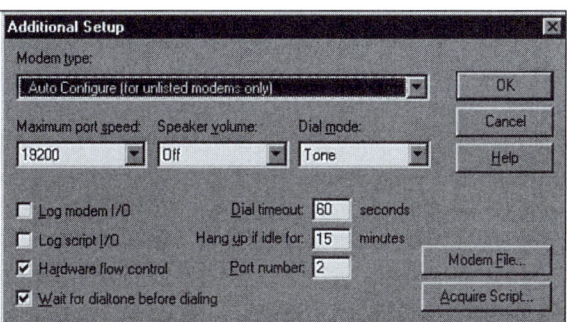

Figure 10.2
The Additional Setup dialog box is used to define modem communications for a COM port.

In this dialog box, you select a modem type from among the nearly 150 modem files that ship with Notes. If you cannot find a file that matches your modem, there are some utility generic modem files available. If you cannot find your modem, you can select Auto Configure near the bottom of the list of modems, and Notes will select the file that most closely matches your particular modem. The modem files are placed in a Modems directory in Notes' default data directory on installation, so if you have moved the modem files to another location, Notes might have a hard time locating the files.

After you select a modem type, you can select the following options for the modem:

- **Maximum port speed**   Select the first speed above the highest-rated speed for your modem, because Notes will use the lesser of the Maximum port speed and your modem's maximum speed. For example, if your modem is rated at a port speed of 14400, select 19200 as your Maximum port speed, and your modem can then operate at its highest-rated speed. If you are having problems with a noisy phone line, try dropping back to a lower speed.

> **Caution**
>
> Some modems might not connect if the Notes speed is set too high. You might have to experiment if you are having trouble connecting with your modem.

- **Speaker volume**   Set the speaker volume on your modem to Off, Low, Medium, or High.
- **Dial mode**   The dial mode can be Tone or Pulse, depending on the type of phone system you have. Normally, this should be left on Tone.
- **Log modem I/O**   If you select this option, modem-control strings and responses will be recorded in the Miscellaneous Events view of your local Notes log database. Keep this selected only if you are troubleshooting suspected modem problems. Otherwise, leave it deselected; the logging adds a lot of extra information to the log files.
- **Log script I/O**   If you select this, asynchronous script-file responses get recorded in the Miscellaneous Events view of your local Notes log database. Keep this selected only if you are troubleshooting suspected problems with a script file. Otherwise, keep it deselected, because this also adds a lot of extra information to your Notes log.
- **Hardware flow control**   This controls the flow of data between your computer and the modem. Select this for most modems. You want to deselect this only if your modem doesn't support flow control, or if you are using certain null-modem connections or some types of add-in equipment, such as older versions of DigiBoard. If a modem doesn't support flow control, set the maximum speed for the computer and the modem to the same lower-speed settings to reduce CRC errors.
- **Wait for dial tone before dialing**   This makes sure that you have a dial tone before the modem starts attempting to make a connection.
- **Dial timeout**   This is used to tell the modem to pause for a set length of time before trying again, if a connection cannot be made with the server. It keeps the modem from

dialing constantly, and it gives the server a better chance of being available on the next try. You might want to increase the timeout to 120 or 180 seconds to minimize the number of retries.

- Hang up if idle for   This setting tells the modem to hang up if there is no activity on the phone line for a set length of time. If the phone line is idle for too long, the connection is broken and the modem hangs up the phone. This will greatly reduce the cost of long distance calls if you are away from the computer when your call is finished.
- Port number   This is the COM port that is being used by the modem.
- Modem File   This button displays the modem text file for the selected modem. If you are familiar with modem drivers, you can edit and customize the modem file.
- Acquire Script   This button opens up a box that lists available acquire scripts. An acquire script is a text file used to acquire a communication device, such as an ISDN modem, before the modem script is run. For example, you might need an acquire script to connect to one of the modems or connect to a PAD device. The acquire script is stored in the modem directory and has a filename extension of .SCR. When you select an acquire script, it is permanently associated with that COM port. To disconnect from the script, edit the port, select the Acquire Script button again, and select NONE as the script that you want to associate with the port. If you need to create or edit a script file, you should refer to the Administrator's Guide that comes with Notes. The guide provides sample files and definitions of script file keywords and script command lines.

    Lotus Notes Connect for Integrated Services Digital Network (ISDN) connects Domino Servers and Notes workstations to ISDN directly or via a Passthru server.

When you are done selecting advanced options, click on OK to save your changes.

Back on the first page of the port selection dialog box, there is one other selection you should be aware of—the Encrypt Network Data check box. If you select this option, all communication through the port will be encrypted, no matter whether it is implemented on the workstation end or on the Notes server end. If you elect to encrypt data through the port, the other end will also be forced to encrypt the data. This will slow down the transmission of data slightly.

To activate the port, highlight the port name and click on the Port Enabled check box.

Setting Up Location Documents

Workstation setup automatically creates a Personal Address Book. Some of the commonly used locations in the Personal Address Book include

- Office (Network Dialup), which you use when you are directly connected to the Notes network in your office
- Home (Notes Direct Dialup), which uses a modem to dial in to a Notes server

- Island (Disconnected), which enables you to work as an isolated workstation with no connection to a Notes network
- Travel (Notes Direct Dialup), which enables you to define how to connect to the Notes server when you are on the road
- Internet, which enables you to connect over the Internet using TCP/IP as if you were on the Local Area Network

You can edit the definitions for each of the locations, and you can create additional Location documents. For example, you might want to define a Hotel Location document that automatically enters your phone card number when you dial.

A Location document defines where to find your mail file, how to make a connection to your home server (the one that holds your mail file), and other specifications for the location.

The Location Document

To view a Location document, select Advanced, Locations in the Personal Address Book. Click on an existing Location document or click on Add Location to add a new location. You can also select File, Mobile, Locations to open the Locations view.

Each type of location from which you want to use Notes has its own Location document, as shown in Figure 10.3. The document is divided into several information areas. The Location document is context-sensitive, so the actual content varies, depending on the type of location you are creating. The information areas include basic information, server information, ports, mail information, Internet browser information, and replication information. Dial-up locations have a tab for phone settings. Two additional tabs provide access to advanced and administrative functions.

The pages of the Location document are described in the following sections.

Basics

The information on the Basics page includes the name of the Location document. Select the type of connection from among the following:

- Local Area Network (including Internet connection to a Domino server)
- Notes Direct Dial-up (modem connection to a Domino server)
- Network Dial-up (modem connection to a network)
- Custom
- No Connection (Notes on a standalone workstation)

Depending on the type of location, you will be prompted for other information. For example, with a dial-up connection, you can elect to have Notes prompt you for the time, date, and phone number every time you connect. This might be necessary if you travel a lot and don't want a separate Location document for each time zone. At a minimum, you must enter the name of the location, and you can enter an Internet address, whether to prompt for date, time and phone number, and whether to display your primary name or alternate name from the Domino Directory.

Figure 10.3
Name your Location and define the type of connection on the first page of the Location document.

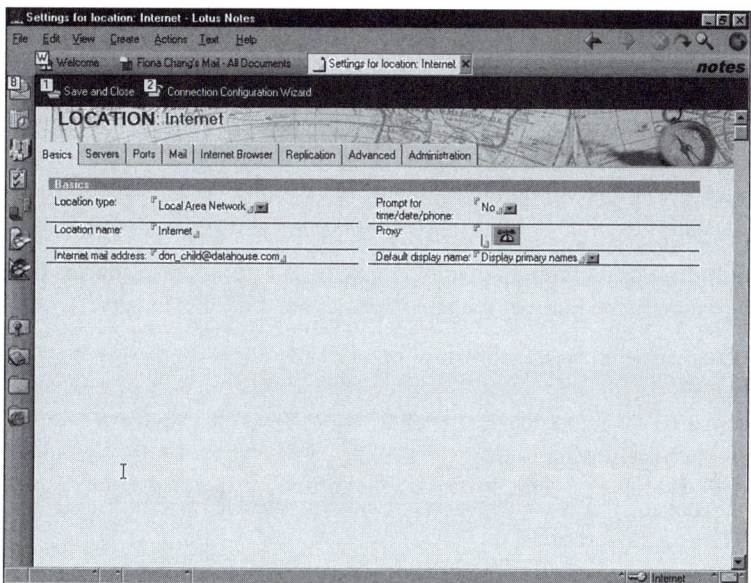

Servers

You can define four different servers for a location;

- The home/mail server is the Notes server on which your mail database is stored.
- The Passthru Server is your default Notes Passthru server, if you have one defined. The Passthru server enables you to dial one Notes server, and from that single connection, get passed through to other Notes servers, thus enabling you to make a single phone call and replicate all your databases, even if they reside on different servers. Refer to "Verifying the Passthru Server in the Location Document," later in this chapter, for details.
- The Catalog/domain search server is the server on which you want to perform domain-wide searches for information using the Search icon on the toolbar.
- The Domino Directory server is the server where Notes should look for the Domino Directory when doing name lookups.

Ports

Select one or more ports for use at this location. You will see a list of all ports you have set up and enabled. If a connection cannot be made from the first enabled port, Notes tries the next one until a successful connection is made.

Mail Options

For each location, you can specify details about your mail. For Notes mail, you specify where your mail database is located—on the Domino server or on your workstation. If you have server-based mail selected, you have to connect to the server either remotely or via a LAN in order to access your mail. If you have workstation-based mail selected, you can perform functions such as composing mail or forwarding documents without having to connect to the server. The difference between the two types of mail is that, with server-based mail, documents are immediately routed to the user's mail file on the Notes server. With workstation-based mail, documents are held locally in an outgoing mailbox (with the filename `mail.box`) and are transferred later, when a connection is made to the home-server. Enter the path to your mail file from the Notes data directory.

If you are using Internet mail, you specify an Internet mail address on the Basics page. You also specify the Internet domain (that is, your ISP's POP3 server).

The mail setup page is shown in Figure 10.4.

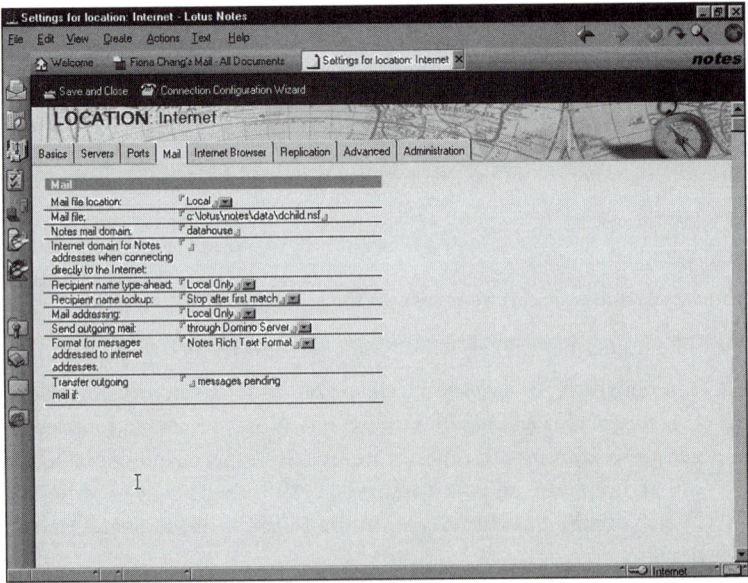

Figure 10.4
Enter mail information on the Mail page of the Locations dialog box.

Other fields on the mail setup page include the following:

- **Recipient name type-ahead** This enables you to address mail memos using type-ahead, with Notes looking in either your Personal Address Book or the Domino Directory on your mail server to find a name and display it as soon as you type enough letters to uniquely identify the addressee.

- **Recipient name lookup** You can limit the type-ahead feature so that it looks only in your Personal Address Book if you want, or you can have it look in your local directory, then on the server.
- **Mail adressing** You can have your mail do lookups in your Local Address Book, or locally and on the server.
- **Send outgoing mail** With Notes mail, the mail goes through the Domino server, where it is routed to the Internet. If you are using an alternative form of mail, you can opt to send it directly to the Internet.
- **Format for messages addressed to internet addresses** You can specify Notes Rich Text Format or MIME for mail going to the Internet.
- **Transfer outgoing mail if** The final field in the Mail section of the Location document has to do with mail routing. If you have set up a location with the mail file defined as local then you can have your workstation dial the server automatically when a certain number of outgoing messages are waiting. As soon as the minimum threshold is reached, your workstation automatically calls the home server and transfers outgoing mail.

INTERNET BROWSER

The Internet Browser section is used to define which browser you want to use from this location.

If you select Notes as your browser, you can define whether to retrieve Web pages from the local workstation (that is, directly from the Internet) or from the InterNotes Server (the shared Web browser database on the Domino server), or whether no retrieval is allowed.

Otherwise, you have a choice of using Notes with Internet Explorer (IE), Internet Explorer by itself, Netscape, or another browser whose EXE file you can identify. For a fully integrated browser in the Notes client, you should select Notes with Internet Explorer. Notes uses the Notes browser interface, but uses the IE engine and executables to retrieve pages, so you can move between Notes and the Web seamlessly. You do not have to have IE4 installed on your computer to use this option.

REPLICATION

The process of replication is described in detail in Chapter 40, "Replication and Its Administration." Basically, it is the process of synchronizing databases that have a single, identical ID, but that reside on different systems. Replication takes place between two servers or between a workstation and a server. There is, however, no peer-to-peer replication between workstations.

The replication that is initiated from the Location document is workstation-to-server replication. You can enable a schedule, and when the scheduled replication time arrives, the workstation will automatically call the server and replicate. The process takes place in the background so you can continue working without interruption. On Windows workstations, you have to run the program SHARE.EXE before Windows is started. Otherwise, the background program cannot run. Running in the background means that you can continue doing other work while replication is taking place.

The Replication section on the Location document gives you the option of enabling or disabling a schedule.

You can set up a schedule that includes a range of times during which scheduled replication will take place, or you can set specific times for replication. Multiple times are separated by commas. If you define a range of times, you can also enter a repeat interval. A repeat interval of 360 minutes, for example, means that the workstation will dial the server 6 hours after the last successful replication completed.

Normally, you will want to set up scheduled replication only for time-sensitive databases. You can then select a repeat interval that is appropriate for your situation. Note that you can also set the schedule up so it works only on specified days of the week. You may want to set up scheduled replication if you are working from home on certain days of the week and use manual replication when you are on the road away from your office or home, when your connection times to the Domino server are likely to be of shorter duration.

There is also a check box so you can enable high-priority replication. Replication priority is set using the Replication Settings button in the Database properties dialog box. If a database is defined as a high-priority database, it shows up on the Replicator page with a red exclamation mark beside it. You can save time on the road and replicate just high-priority databases using a scheduled replication or selecting Replicate High Priority Databases from the Other Actions button on the Replicator page.

PHONE SETTINGS

The Phone Settings section defines how phone calls will be made from a location, assuming that a dial-up modem connection is defined. You can enter the prefix for getting an outside line at the location (such as 9). If necessary, enter the country code for the location as well as the area code.

If you want to use a calling card to charge all your dial-up modem calls from a particular location, enter the calling card access number (the number you dial before a phone number to indicate that you want to use a calling card). Then, in the calling card number field, enter the calling card number to use. You can use an alternative phone number for a server by clicking on the Dialing Rules button and selecting the server, and then entering a different prefix, phone number, and/or suffix for the server.

SETTING UP LOCATION DOCUMENTS | 219

> **Tip**
>
> Commas can be entered into a phone number or dialing prefix to force a delay, if necessary. Each comma forces a two-second delay.

Enter commas to force the modem to pause while dialing. For example, consider the following number:

9,0,8082345678,,,,,480834565678789

This will dial 9 to get an outside line, pause, dial 0 to get the long distance carrier, pause, dial the phone number, pause long enough for the number to dial and for the carrier to request your telephone credit card number, and then dial your credit card number. The order in which you enter various numbers will depend on the requirements of your carrier. For example, you may have to enter your card number before entering the phone number.

ADVANCED OPTIONS

The Advanced Options section has a number of fields used to refine how Notes work with data. The Advanced Basics page for a direct dial-up connection is shown in Figure 10.5.

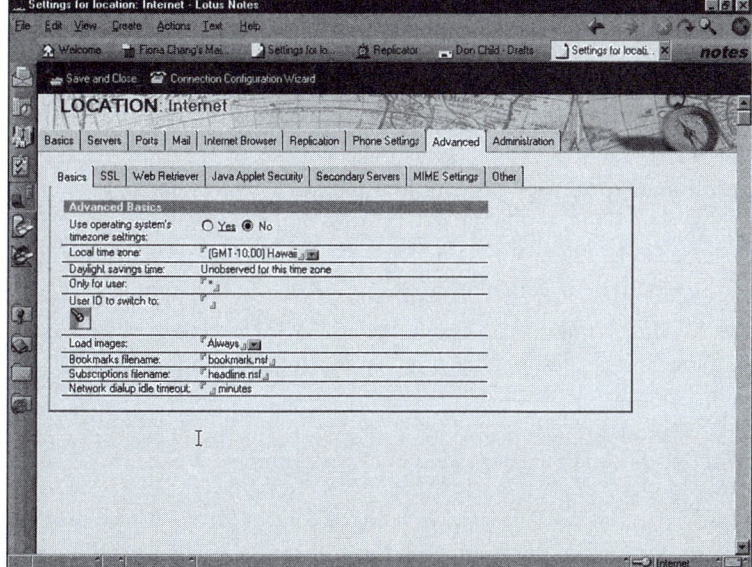

Figure 10.5
Define advanced location options by moving between tabs on the Advanced page in the Locations document.

All Location documents enable you to specify whether daylight savings time is observed at the location so Notes can coordinate differences in time between the server and the mobile workstation.

If a workstation is being used by more than one user, you can specify which user or users are authorized to use a particular Location document in the Only for user field. You can also specify which user ID should be used from the location. This is useful only if you have multiple user IDs and/or multiple users on the workstation.

You can specify whether to download images immediately or on request.

You can specify the name of your Bookmarks file. The Bookmarks file determines which Domino applications are available from the bookmark buttons. You can also specify which database to use for your Headlines page. Using these two databases, you can set up a workstation so that it can be customized for different users by switching between locations.

The last option on the Advanced Basics page lets you set the length of idle time after which a dial-up connection should automatically disconnect.

Other Advanced option pages include

- **SSL** You can determine whether your computer will accept SSL site certificates and expired SSL certificates. You can also define which SSL protocol version you want to use.
- **Web Retriever** You can use this page to define options for your integrated Web browser, including the name of your Personal Web Browser database, how many concurrent retrievers you can have open (up to 25), what level of activity logging you want for your Web retriever, and how often to update the cached Web pages.
- **Java Applet Security** Use this to define location-specific security settings for Java applets.
- **Secondary Servers** If your location is a LAN connection, you can set up secondary servers. If you set up TCP/IP as the communications protocol, for example, you can use a secondary Domain Name Server when the first server is not available. When TCP/IP is used as your communications protocol, the Location is set up as a LAN connection.
- **MIME Settings** You can define how MIME conversions are handled—for example, on attachments destined for use on a Macintosh computer.

Setting Up Passthru Servers

Passthru servers provide a single point of contact for users who may want to contact multiple servers. Instead of calling each server separately to work with one or two databases, you can call a single Passthru server, and it will forward-link you through itself and possibly through other intermediate Passthru servers until you are in contact with the destination server.

Passthru provides a couple of advantages. First, the Passthru server can act as a conduit for all requests to a number of servers in an organization. All the external communication comes through a communications hub server, which passes users through to the server they want to contact. The Passthru server does not need to hold replica copies of the databases users want to access. Instead, it has to provide only the connection to the destination server. Second, the Passthru server can handle multiple protocols, thus enabling connection from a variety of users. The destination servers need only a single protocol, one that can communicate with the Passthru server, and the users need only a single protocol that can communicate with the Passthru server. The server provides the connection between the different protocols. This simplifies setup by minimizing the number of multiple-protocol servers needed in the organization.

The Mobile Notes user at the beginning of this chapter was able to call a local Passthru server in Los Angeles. The server passed her through to her home server in San Diego. In this way, all the communication costs were incurred through the corporate WAN, which is a fixed cost to the corporation, rather than through a long-distance telephone call at much higher rates.

Setting up the Passthru server is an administrative function and requires the correct documents in four locations:

> A Passthru Connection document has to be created for each server in the Domino Directory.
>
> The Passthru Restrictions for each Server document must be properly filled in. This is done in the server document itself, not in the Passthru Connection document.
>
> Users must verify that they have the correct information in a Passthru Server Connection document in their Personal Address Book.
>
> The Default Passthru Server field in the Location document must correctly identify the Passthru server that will be used from that location.

The first two steps are for the system administrator. The second two steps are done on your local machine and are described in the next sections.

Mobile-User, Passthru Connection Documents

Mobile users also have to set up a Connection document for the Passthru server in their Personal Address Books. To do this, open the Personal Address Book and add a Passthru Server Connection document, shown in Figure 10.6.

Select Passthru Server as the connection type. Enter the name of the destination server and the name of the Passthru server that will be used to connect to the destination server.

In the Advanced section of the Connection document, you can specify which locations can use this Passthru server connection. For example, suppose you have a laptop that you take to client sites and a docking station with a modem at home. You can define two Location documents (such as Home and Client) to use the same Passthru server. But if you are staying in a hotel in another city, it might be more economical to dial the destination server directly. You can restrict the use of this Connection document so that it is valid only for certain locations.

Figure 10.6
Add a Passthru server document in your Personal Address Book.

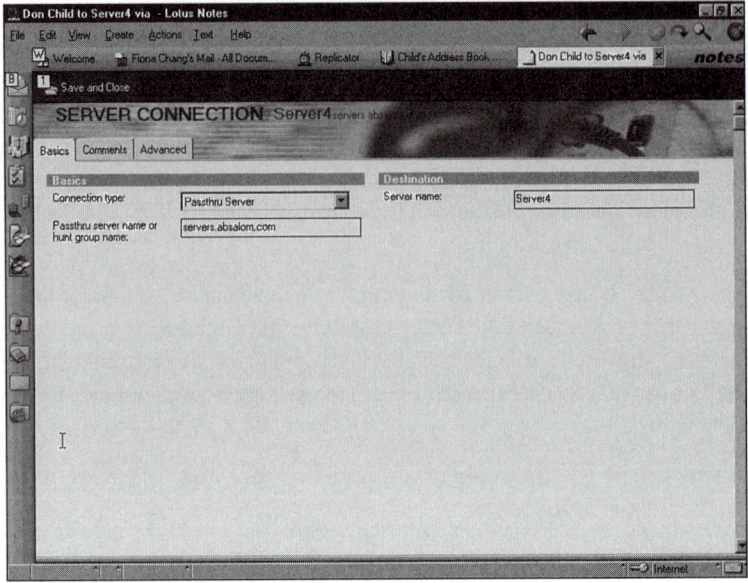

VERIFYING THE PASSTHRU SERVER IN THE LOCATION DOCUMENT

On each Location document in the your Personal Address Book, there are four server fields, described earlier: the Home/Mail server, the Passthru server, the Search server, and the Domino Directory server. You should verify that the correct server is named in the Passthru Server field, and that the server name is spelled correctly. Use the fully distinguished name of the Passthru server—for example, `Server1/Sales/Acme`.

The end result of setting up a Passthru server is that the process of connecting is automated as much as possible. You select a replica of a database that is on the destination server, and then you replicate with it. Assuming that you are hooked up to a telephone at some mobile site, Notes does everything without having to prompt you for information. Notes automatically calls the server. The Passthru server authenticates your user ID. The Passthru server then calls the destination server, authenticates with the server, then passes you through to your destination. Authentication takes place at every step of the way, so you cannot use the Passthru to gain unauthorized access to another Notes server.

SELECTING DATABASES FOR REPLICATION

The primary tool that gives you access to remote data is replication. As a mobile user, there are a couple of things you should consider: which databases you will need to have available locally, and which documents within those databases you will need.

A corollary to those two considerations is to determine when you should replicate. As a rule, you will want to make an initial replication before you leave. The initial replication is much quicker over the LAN, and you don't have to tie up the telephone lines as you would if you decided later to replicate from somewhere on the road.

For a database to replicate, there have to be at least two replica copies of the database: one on your workstation, and one on the Domino server. You create the replica on your workstation by opening the server application and selecting File, Replication, New Replica. Make selections in the dialog box that is displayed to create the new replica on your local workstation. Replication is discussed in detail in Chapter 40.

If you are using a Notes desktop instead of bookmarks, you can stack the icons for different replicas by selecting View, Stack Replica Icons. You will then have only one icon showing on the desktop at a time. You can switch from one replica to another by clicking on the small arrowhead in the corner of a stacked icon and selecting the replica you want. Whichever icon is on top is the currently selected version of the database. So, if the top icon is the server-based replica of the database, when you select it, Notes will attempt to contact the server. If it is a local replica, Notes will open the replica that is on your workstation. The stacked icons are location-sensitive, so if you have a mobile location selected, local replicas of databases should be on the top of the stack.

Notes determines which databases are replicas of each other by comparing each database's replica ID to see whether they are the same. The replica ID can be seen on the information page of the database Properties box, shown in Figure 10.7.

Figure 10.7
Identical replica IDs mean that two databases are replicas of each other.

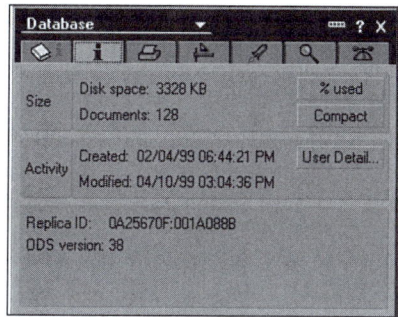

If the replica IDs are the same on two databases, they are replicas of each other, even though you might have renamed one of the databases. The databases might even contain a different subset of documents as the result of selective replication. You can also tell whether they are replicas by switching to the workspace from the bookmarks and stacking replica database icons on your workspace. If they are stacked on top of each other, they are replicas. If they are not stacked, they are not replicas.

INITIATING REPLICATION

To replicate a local database from a mobile location, the database must have a replica on the server you call, or on another server that can be reached using a Passthru server.

There are several ways to initiate a replication from a mobile workstation:

With the application open, select File, Replication, Replicate.

From the workspace, you can click on the small arrow on a stacked icon, ensure that you have the local replica selected, and click on Replicate.

Set up scheduled replication on the Location document.

Use the Replicator page to manually initiate replication. You can open the Replicator page by clicking on the Replicator icon on the bookmark bar. The icon illustrates a laptop communicating with a server.

The Replicator page consolidates all the replication options in a single location. (See Figure 10.8.) This page holds entries for all the databases that you want to replicate. You can select specific databases for replication by clicking in the check box to indicate that those databases should be replicated during the next replication with the server. Note that you can select replicas that are on different servers if you are using a Passthru server for replication.

Figure 10.8
You can control replication from the Replicator page.

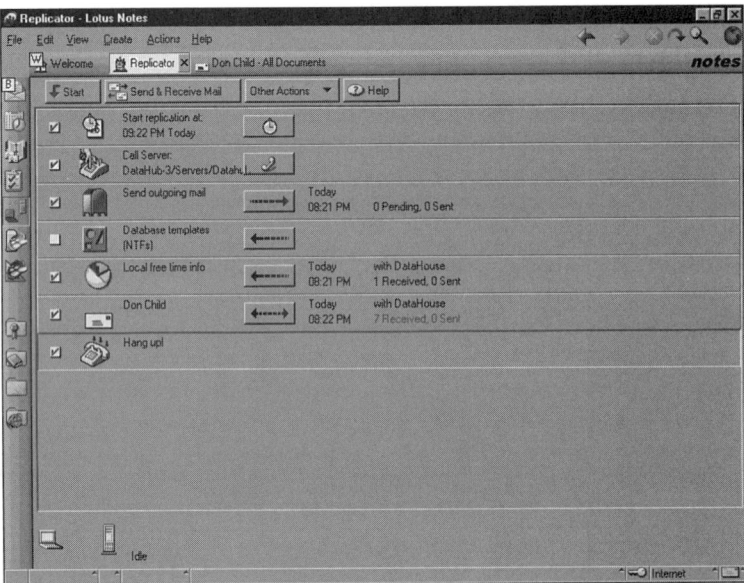

Each row on the Replicator page has a check box beside it. If an item is checked, it will be replicated during the next replication session. If it is not checked, it will not replicate during the next replication session:

- If you check Start replication at, any replication schedules you have enabled will cause replication to occur in the background.

- If you check Call Server, Notes will call the selected server even if the replica is not on that server. You could specify a Passthru server to call. Call Server is created only for

Selecting Databases for Replication 225

replication through dial-up connections. You can add this to your Replicator page by selecting Create, Call Entry from the menu. It can be paired with a Hang Up entry to complete the call when you are done replicating.

- If you check Send outgoing mail, Notes will check your store/forward mailbox and send any outgoing mail messages at the same time it replicates.
- If you check Database templates, template files will be replicated.
- If you check any databases, those databases will be replicated.

    Notes automatically puts databases on the Replicator page when the replica is first created. If you want to remove an icon from the Replicator page, you can select the icon and press the Delete key. If you want to put the icon back onto the Replicator page, you can select File, Database, Open from the Replicator page or initiate replication from the File menu. Note that you can set replication settings for an individual database by selecting File, Replication, Settings. This enables you to specify which documents will get replicated before replication actually takes place.

- If you check Hang Up, Notes will hang up as soon as the replication is completed. If the Hang Up icon is not checked, Notes will remain in communication with the server after the replication is completed.

You can manually initiate replication from the Replicator page by selecting the Start action button. You can manually initiate sending and receiving mail without replication by selecting the Send and Receive Mail action button. You can replicate high-priority databases or just send mail from the Other Actions action button.

Finally, for each row on the Replicator page, except the Hang Up row, you can click on the button to the right of the descriptive text to change settings for the action or database. For example, you could change a database's replication settings to send documents but not receive any new documents.

> **Note**
>
> Replication is discussed here in the context of the mobile user. However, there are instances where a user might use replication over a local area network. For example, a designer might want to make design changes on a replica of a database, rather than making modifications directly on a production database. When the design changes are completed, they can be replicated back to the production database.

Replicating over a Dial-up Connection

There are a couple of ways you can connect over a modem, depending on the type of work you are going to be doing. If you are always working with a particular subset of documents that you carry around with you on your laptop, you will want to connect to the server to replicate those databases, either on a regularly scheduled basis, or on an as-needed basis. On the other hand, if you are looking something up in a large database that you do not need to access routinely, you can stay connected to the Notes server for a few minutes, open the database to find the information you want, and then disconnect from the server.

Part II
Ch
10

To replicate a single database, you can do the following:

1. Open the local replica of the database you want to replicate.
2. Select File, Replication, Replicate, and then go to step 3

   or

   Locate the database icon on the Replicator page and make sure it is the only database with a checkmark beside it. Then click on the Start button to start background replication immediately.
3. Notes will display a dialog box that enables you to decide between background replication or replication with options for this one-time replication. Options include which server to replicate with; whether to send documents; whether to receive documents; and whether to receive whole documents, summary information plus 40KB of rich text, or summary information only.
4. Click on OK to begin replication. When replication is done, Notes will disconnect from the server connection automatically if you have the Hang Up icon checked.

To replicate multiple databases, display the Replicator page, make sure the databases you want to replicate are checked, and click on the Start button. Databases will replicate one at a time, with a pointing hand indicating which database is currently being replicated. You can also edit the Location document to enable automatic replication, as described earlier in this chapter.

You also have a couple of options if you want to connect to the server so that you can work with databases online, or so that you can add new databases to your desktop:

Open the database using File, Database, Open and select the name of the server. Notes will display a dialog box to verify that you want to make a dial-up connection, and then call the server and open the database. You will remain connected to the server when you are done working with the database, so remember to hang up (described later) when finished.

Select File, Mobile, Call Server. A list of phone numbers that can be called to connect to the server will be displayed. Select or type the number you want to call and click Auto-Dial. Notes will call the server. You can then work with any databases to which you have access on the server. When you are done, remember to hang up.

Click on the File Mobile Call Server SmartIcon (the finger pressing a button on a phone dialer). Everything else is the same as calling the server from the drop-down menu.

To hang up when done connecting to a server, select File, Mobile, Hang Up or click on the File Mobile Hang Up SmartIcon (a hand placing a handset back onto a phone). Notes will display a list of COM ports. Select the port that is currently connected and click on Hang Up.

Using Mobile Notes After It Is Set Up

So far, the focus of this chapter has been how to get set up as a mobile user. Now let's assume that everything is set up correctly, and you are ready to work on the road. There is no single correct way to work with Notes. How you manage your databases and your connections to the Notes server depends on the type of data you are using and the type of organization you are working with. The options described in the following sections are, therefore, just some of the ways you can work with Mobile Notes.

Establishing a Telephone or Direct Connection

Depending on the type of communications you have set up, you need to connect to a telephone outlet, or to some sort of device that provides a connection to the server via a WAN. If you are on the road, take along a phone cord that you can use to connect your computer's modem to a phone jack—either on the bottom or back of a telephone—or a wall jack. You can then communicate with your server via the telephone line.

Selecting a Location

As a mobile user, you select a location to work from by selecting the appropriate Location document. You can do this in either of two different places:

> Select File, Mobile, Choose Current Location and then select the location you want from a list.

> Click on the Location button (located near the right side of the status bar at the bottom of the Notes workspace) and select the current location from a list.

The Location document contains relevant information for each location, such as what type of connection you have to the server (if any), whether your outgoing mailbox is local or on your home server, and which databases should be replicated on what sort of schedule. You can edit the current Location document so replication and mail parameters suit your particular needs. After it is set up the way you want it, all you have to do is select the location, and Notes takes care of everything else. Notes knows whether to dial the server directly or use a Passthru server, which databases should be replicated, which phone numbers to dial, and so on—all based on the Location document for that location.

Connecting over the Internet

To connect to a Domino server over the Internet, you have to have your server set up with a direct connection to the Internet, the server has to be running TCP/IP, and it must have its own IP address.

If you already have an account with an Internet service provider (ISP) for browsing the Web, and your Domino Server is connected to the Internet using TCP/IP, you are all set—as long as you know your server's Internet IP address.

After everything is set up, you have to do the following:

- Establish either a direct or dial-up Internet connection. You can use either a Serial Line Internet Protocol (SLIP) or a Point-to-Point Protocol (PPP). This gives your workstation the equivalent of TCP/IP functionality.
- After you have an Internet connection, start Notes and make sure you are using a Location document that uses a TCP/IP port—for example, the Internet location. You are then seen by the server as a node on the local Notes network, and you can open databases or replicate databases from the server, just as you would if you were in the office working over the local area network.

According to Lotus Notes Internet Cookbook (available from Lotus at http://www.lotus.com), these are the acceptable SLIP/PPP protocol stacks you can use with Notes. Check for the latest information if you have any questions:

- IBM TCP provides SLIP (for OS/2)
- Windows 95 Dial-Up Networking
- LAN Workplace for Windows 4.2 (for Windows 16)
- FTP Software (for DOS, Windows 16, and OS/2)
- NetManage Chameleon (Windows 16 and Windows 32)
- Trumpet Winsock shareware (for Windows 16)

To set up SLIP/PPP on your Notes server, follow the instructions provided with the SLIP/PPP protocol stack that you choose.

The Internet Cookbook should answer most of your questions regarding how to connect to a Domino server via the Internet.

Sending Mail as a Mobile User

To send mail, create a memo just as you would if you were directly connected to the office LAN. When you are disconnected as a mobile user, however, you are creating a memo using your local replica copy of your mail file. Notes can look up names for addressing in any address books you have defined under File, Preferences, User Preferences, Mail. You must have a local replica of the Address Book or Domino Directory in order to do a lookup while disconnected.

Outgoing mail is placed into your outgoing mailbox. The mail is sent to the server's mailbox by the router when you replicate. This assumes you have Send outgoing mail checked on the Replicator page. Otherwise, you can send mail without replicating other databases by clicking on the Send & Receive Mail button on the Replicator page. You can also send and receive mail from the mail icon in the right corner of the status bar at the bottom of the screen.

You can replicate your mail database with your mail database on your home server, just as with any other database.

Database Security for Mobile Notes

The one problem with using Notes on the road has always been the fact that a laptop computer can be lost or stolen. That means that databases on the laptop can also be stolen, and those databases might contain valuable information that you don't want to fall into the wrong hands. Notes 5.0 provides two security features for databases that the mobile user should be aware of:

- Local enforcement of the Access Control List   The Database Manager can elect to enforce a consistent Access Control List across all replicas of a database. With this feature turned on, replica databases on your laptop cannot be accessed unless the user has a valid ID (and a password that lets them use that ID).
- Encryption of local databases   You can elect to encrypt local databases, thereby making the database unusable to anyone unless he or she has the proper user ID and its associated password(s). This is set up by clicking on the Encryption button on the first page of the Database properties box and selecting the options you want.

From Here...

After you get set up, using Notes on the road is very similar to using Notes in the office. There are a couple of features that you are likely to use more on the road than in the office: The Personal Web Navigator and replication. To learn more, refer to the following chapters:

- Chapter 11, "Using the Notes Client on the Internet," describes in greater detail the setup needed for a TCP/IP connection. It also describes how to use the Personal Web Navigator database.
- Chapter 40, "Replication Its Administration," describes in greater detail how to set up and manage replication in Notes 5.0.

CHAPTER 11

USING THE NOTES CLIENT ON THE INTERNET

Lotus Notes has evolved quickly along with the Internet. Today, your data can be sitting on a computer practically anywhere in the world, and you can still access it over your local area network. You have to be using TCP/IP protocol, and you need an Internet connection. The rest of the puzzle depends on how the data is stored.

Setting Up and Using TCP/IP Protocol

If data is on a Domino server, you can gain access to the data using a Notes client. If the data is being served to the World Wide Web, you can use any Web browser to access it.

Because a Web browser is an integral part of the Notes environment, you can open Web pages from within Notes. If the document is available via Notes, the Notes client will be used to access the document. If the document is a Web page, the Web browser will be used to open the document. You can bookmark either page, and you can use Web browser controls such as Previous and Next buttons to go to either type of document.

In order to take full advantage of the integrated Notes client on the Internet, you must use TCP/IP as a communications protocol. You also need either a direct connection to the Internet, or you need to have access to a Domino server that is connected to the Internet. If you have a direct TCP/IP connection to a LAN in a corporate environment, all you have to do is define which Web browser you want to use. If you use a dial-up connection to the Internet through an Internet service provider (ISP) , you need to go through all the steps in this section.

When you have an Internet connection through an ISP, you can access Domino applications directly using a LAN connection, even if the application is on a Domino server on the far side of the world. You can open documents or Web pages with equal ease. You can browse the Web using the built-in browser within Notes. You can communicate directly in real-time with others using Sametime features.

To set up TCP/IP, you need to do one of the following:

- Have a TCP/IP port defined
- Have a Location document that has TCP/IP as its communication protocol
- Have a Connection document to access a Domino server that has access to the Internet
- Have a direct connection to the Internet through an ISP

Defining a TCP/IP Port

You have to set up a port to use TCP/IP. In the previous chapter, there was an overview of setting up ports. Here, we look specifically at TCP/IP, the protocol used for communicating over the Internet. Note that before you can use TCP/IP, it must be configured to run with your operating system. The following information assumes you have already set up TCP/IP to run with your operating system.

To set up a TCP/IP port, do the following:

1. Select File, Preferences, User Preferences.
2. Click on the Ports icon to display the Ports page.
3. Click on TCPIP in the Communications Ports list box.
4. Click on Port enabled to enable TCP/IP. This is illustrated in Figure 11.1.

Figure 11.1
Enable the TCP/IP port in the User Preferences dialog box.

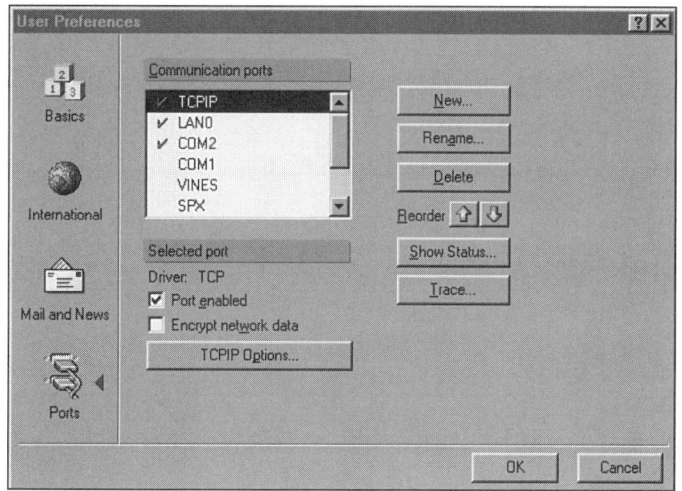

5. Click on the TCP/IP Options button to select the timeout period before a reconnection is attempted. This is done using the dialog box shown in Figure 11.2.

Figure 11.2
Set the default time-out interval for your TCP/IP connection.

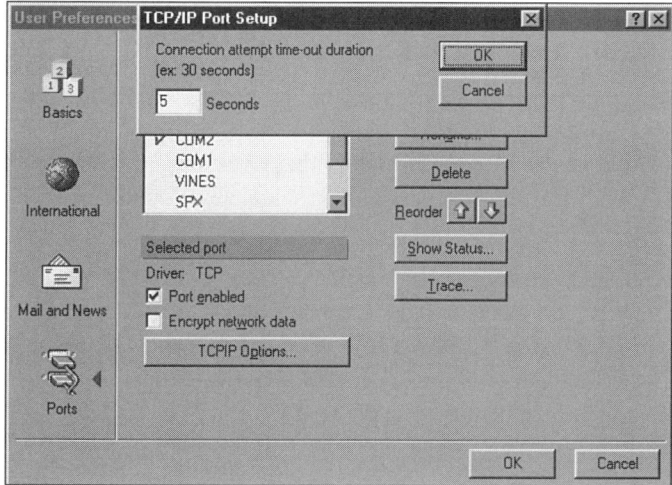

6. Click on Show Status if you want to verify the driver that is being used for your TCP/IP port.

7. Click on Trace if you want to trace the connection to a particular server. Enter the server name or TCP/IP address in the dialog box shown in Figure 11.3, and click on Trace to view all the logged messages as your workstation attempts to reach the designated server. (Note: you must have an active Internet connection before you send a trace.) You can also copy these messages and paste them into another application, or you can have them logged automatically to help you troubleshoot communication problems.

Figure 11.3
Trace TCP/IP connections to a server if you are having communication problems.

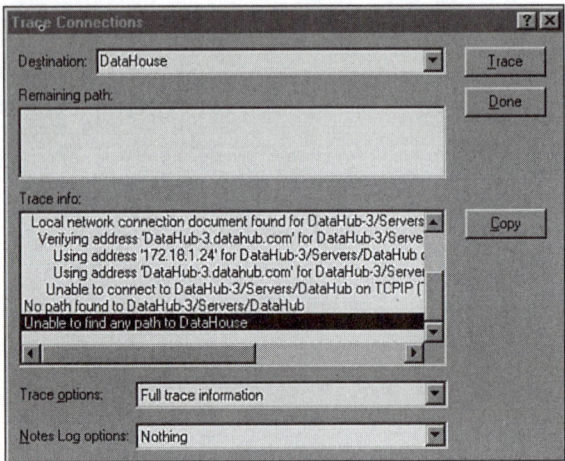

After the TCP/IP port is set up, click on OK to accept your changes. You can then make TCP/IP available from any Location document.

SETTING UP AN INTERNET LOCATION DOCUMENT

You can easily switch to a TCP/IP location by defining a Location document that uses your TCP/IP port for communications. When you want to use Notes using TCP/IP on the corporate LAN or on the Internet, switch to that Location document and connect to the Internet through an ISP if you do not have a full-time connection, and you are up and running.

In the Location document, you set up the ability to browse Web pages from within Notes. That means that you can view fully featured Web pages from within Notes while you are connected to the Internet. You can later review those pages offline from within a Notes database or share them as Notes documents with other users. Links to documents can lead to either a Notes document or to a Web page.

There are fields on the Location document used specifically to define your Internet setup. To ensure that you set up Personal Web Navigator correctly, we'll begin there as we look at the Location document. You can view Location documents in your Personal Address Book;

by selecting File, Mobile, Locations; or by clicking on the name of the current location on the status bar in the lower-right corner of the screen.

The Internet Browser page of the Notes 5.0 Location document is shown in Figure 11.4. The location is set up using a TCP/IP connection so that you can connect directly to the Internet.

Figure 11.4
Set up a Web browser on the Location document so you can access the Internet directly from within Notes.

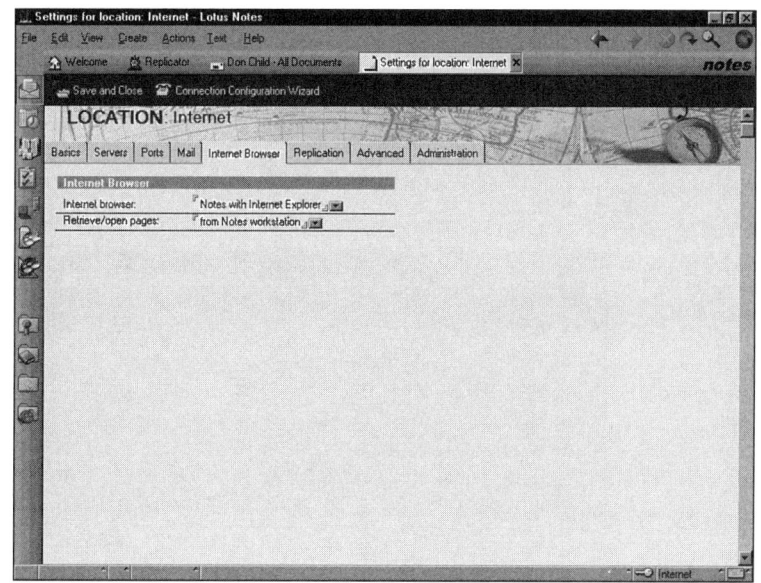

On the Internet Browser page, you have a choice of how to connect to the World Wide Web from within Notes. You can select one of the following:

- Notes

    You can elect to use the Personal Web Navigator to view Web pages directly using a built-in Notes browser. You can retrieve Web pages from an InterNotes server. Or you can choose not to retrieve Web pages, even though you have a TCP/IP connection.

- Notes with Internet Explorer

    Notes has the Internet Explorer browser built into it through a licensing agreement with Microsoft. You can use the built-in browser (it has a different interface than the regular Internet Explorer, but it is the same engine in the background). Or you can choose not to retrieve Web pages. You can still use Notes with Internet Explorer to view pages that you have stored locally in your Personal Web Navigator application. You do not need Internet Explorer on your workstation in addition to Notes, if you select this option.

- Netscape Navigator

    If you select this option, Netscape Navigator will be launched if it is not already running, and it will be used to view any links to Web pages.

- Microsoft Internet Explorer

  You can use the full version of Microsoft Internet Explorer rather than the built-in Internet Explorer. The full version of Microsoft Internet Explorer will be launched if it is not already running to view any links to Web pages.

- Other

  If you have another browser that you prefer, you can search for the EXE file for that browser, and Notes will launch it when you want to link to a Web page.

If you are using a proxy Web server rather than connecting directly through an ISP or over a corporate LAN, enter the proxy setup information in the Web Proxy field. This is found on the first page of the Location document. Figure 11.5 shows how to define proxies after clicking on the propeller beanie.

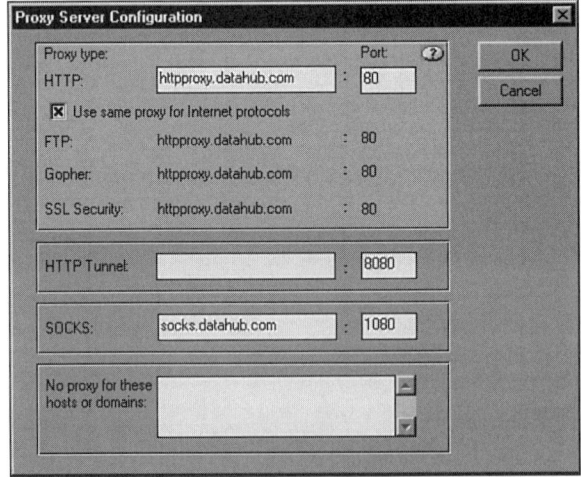

Figure 11.5
The Proxy Server Configuration dialog box is used to set up a proxy server for use with your integrated Web browser.

You can enter separate proxies for different application services, including FTP, Gopher, and SSL security, or you can use the same proxy for all Internet protocols. Separate proxies provide additional security by limiting what can be done through any one proxy. You can also set up a Notes RPC proxy, which is used for all Notes-to-Notes communications, such as replication over the Internet.

You can enter a SOCKS proxy as well. This is a proxy server for IP hosts behind firewalls. In other words, it intercepts and reissues requests to an Internet provider when you use a dial-up connection from your server. If you use a SOCKS proxy, it overrides an HTTP proxy, but it does not override a Notes RPC or SSL Security proxy.

A proxy server provides an extra layer between you and the Internet. When you request a Web page by clicking on a link or typing a URL, that request is intercepted and reissued by the proxy server. Because there is no direct connection between you and the Web, external users can't use a Web connection to piggyback into the corporate network to steal data. The proxy server is one form of *firewall*. The Domino server is not a proxy server. If you want to set up a firewall using a proxy server, refer to any of the popular books on firewalls.

WORKING WITH NOTES AND A TCP/IP CONNECTION

After you have a TCP/IP connection set up correctly, you have a choice of how to work:

- You can open a database directly on the Domino server. The connection is the same as if you were working over a LAN. If you are using TCP/IP on your local LAN, in fact, the connection will be virtually instantaneous and you won't need a connection document. However, if the connection is through the Internet via an ISP, the connection is apt to be somewhat slower if you are using a dial-up connection.

- You can create replicas on your workstation and replicate the databases that you use most frequently. See Chapter 10, "Using Mobile Features from Home or on the Road," and Chapter 40, "Replication and Its Administration," for details on replication.

The first time you open a new database, you may need to enter the name of the server on which it resides. After you have opened and bookmarked a database from a server, it will show up in the search list in the future.

LOOKING AT THE INTEGRATED NOTES CLIENT

Consider how you have used the Internet in the past. Usually, you had to start the Web browser and leave it running in the background. If you wanted to visit a Web page, you had to toggle to your browser. More recently, you clicked on a hyperlink and your system toggled to the browser automatically.

The other option, available in earlier versions of Notes, was the InterNotes Web Browser. The browser could connect directly to the Web, or it could open Web pages through the InterNotes Web Server, which ran on the Domino server.

Both alternatives had their strengths. Many people preferred the freedom of a direct connection to the Internet afforded by a standalone product. Others preferred the InterNotes browser, which enables you to handle Web pages with Notes tools such as full-text searching and workflow processing. With the InterNotes Web Browser, you could also easily browse Web pages offline and share your favorite Web pages with others in your workgroup.

With the integrated Lotus Notes 5.0 client, you have the best of both worlds. You still have the Personal Notes Navigator application, which enables you to store Web pages and work with them as Notes documents. But you also have an integrated Web browser. It is no longer necessary to have another browser running in the background.

THE BROWSER INTERFACE

The Notes browser interface is never further away than the top-right corner of your Notes workspace. Browser controls are always available, whether you are working with Notes documents or Internet Web pages. The controls are used whenever you access Notes documents or access Web pages using Notes with Internet Explorer as your preferred browser. The buttons can be seen in Figure 11.6.

Figure 11.6
The browser controls near the upper-right corner of the screen are always available when you are in Notes.

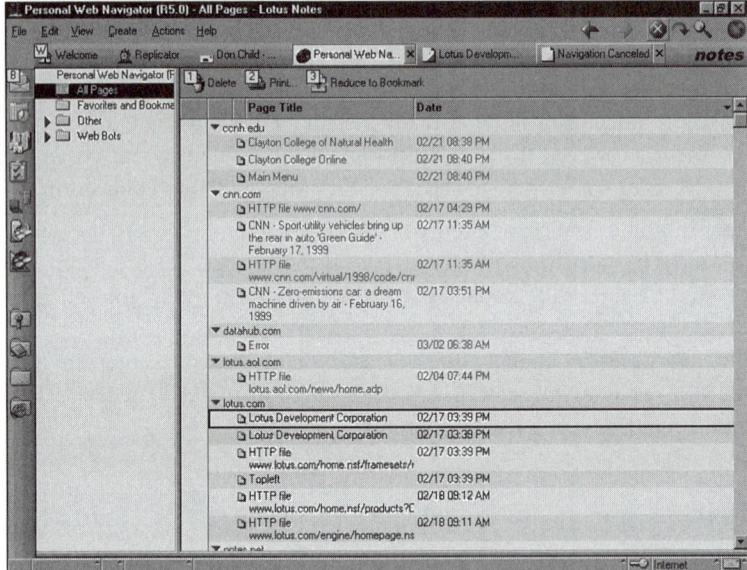

The browser controls, from left to right, are

- Go Back

    This takes you to the previously opened document. You can navigate quickly to any document you have had open by right-clicking on the Go Back button, and then selecting the document you want to view. If the document is a Notes document, the Notes client will be used to view it. If the document is a Web page, the built-in Internet Explorer browser client will be used to view it.

- Go Forward

    The Go Forward control functions like the Next button on a Web browser. You can go to the next document, or you can right-click to view a list of documents that are available. If the document is a Notes document, the Notes client is used to view it. If the document is a Web page, the built-in Internet Explorer browser client is used to view it.

- Stop

    The Stop control halts the current download process. You can stop a Web page or a Notes document from downloading. Clicking on this control is the same as pressing Ctrl+Break in the Notes client.

- Refresh

    The Refresh control causes the current page to be reloaded. On a Web page, you may want to do this to display the latest data rather than looking at a cached Web page. On a Notes document, clicking the Refresh control (or pressing F9) causes all fields to be recalculated. If you are displaying a view, any documents added to the view since you opened the page are displayed in the refreshed view.

- Search

    The Search control is context-sensitive. You can search the current Web page, search the current Notes document, or search the current Notes view. You can also select a Domino Domain search, or you can select a popular Internet search engine such as Yahoo or Excite.

- Open URL

    Open URL looks like a globe, signaling that a field will be displayed in which you can enter Internet URLs. When you click on the Open URL control or press Ctrl+L, the right side of the Notes button bar turns into a field for entering a URL. Enter the URL and press Enter to retrieve the document or Web page. If a URL points to a Web page, the Web browser is used to retrieve the page. If the URL points to a Notes document, the Notes client is used to retrieve the document.

    You can expand the URL bar so it spans the entire page by clicking on the pushpin icon in the URL field. It will then stay in place as you navigate the Web. Otherwise, it will collapse as soon as you retrieve a page.

In addition to the control buttons, you can launch Web pages by clicking on links within Notes documents and links on Web pages.

THE PERSONAL WEB NAVIGATOR

The Personal Web Navigator is a Domino application that stores Web pages as Notes documents. The documents can then be accessed using full-text searching. They can be shared with other users. They can be read when you are offline.

With the Personal Web Navigator on your desktop, you click on a link within a Web page stored as a Notes document. You can click on a SmartIcon or select a URL dialog box from a menu and then type a URL. You can transform the search bar (used for full-text searching) into a URL launching pad. Or you can browse through a list of Web pages that are stored as Web pages in the Personal Web Navigator database and open them as Notes documents.

You can have Notes automatically refresh selected Web pages that are stored as Notes documents. An agent handles this task, scanning the Web for changes to the databases that you want to keep refreshed. The agent will even notify you when a page has been changed. Another agent will automatically load all links on a Web page for you. For example, if you have enough disk space available, you can point to

`http://www.cnn.com`

and tell the computer to load links three pages deep. You now have your own electronic newspaper fully loaded, and all you had to do was point to a single page on the Web to do it. This can be particularly handy if you are getting ready to unplug your computer to take on the road with you and you want to browse a favorite Web site while on the airplane. This is described in Chapter 10, "Using Mobile Features from Home or on the Road."

Consider how you can use the Web as a workgroup! When you locate a new document you want to share, you can use NotesMail to forward the entire document (or you can forward a URL link) to others on your work team. You can have Notes automatically forward documents to a shared Web database, such as the InterNotes Web Browser (which is now called the Server Web Browser to distinguish it from the Personal Web Browser). You also can create Web Tours, which are links that record an entire navigation session on the Web so it can be replayed at a later time. You can edit the session and move links around to create the Web Tour you want to recall.

If you think that a tool with this much versatility must have a lot of options, you're right. Follow along and learn how to customize the Personal Notes Navigator for your work environment as well as for your needs.

Setting Up the Personal Web Navigator

As you set up the Personal Notes Navigator, you'll have occasion to touch the following screens:

- The Location document in your Personal Address Book
- The Internet Options document in your Personal Web Navigator database
- The Properties box for your Personal Web Navigator database
- The User Preferences screen under File, Tools

Opening the Personal Web Navigator

To put the Personal Web Navigator database on your desktop if it isn't already there, select Open URL from the File menu on your Notes desktop. In the Open URL dialog box, type the URL of one of your favorite Web sites. For example, type the following:

`http://www.notes.net`

In addition to opening the Web site, Notes will create and open a Personal Web Navigator database using `PERWEB50.NTF` and save a copy of the Web page as a Notes document for offline viewing. The Personal Web Navigator database is shown in Figure 11.7.

LOOKING AT THE INTEGRATED NOTES CLIENT   241

Figure 11.7
The Personal Web Navigator has a View pane, a Navigation pane, and a document preview screen like any other Notes database.

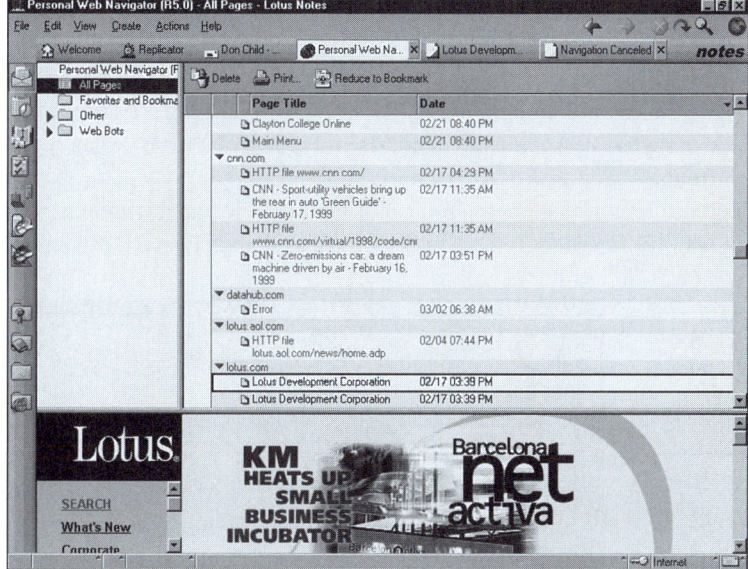

VIEWS AND FOLDERS IN THE PERSONAL WEB NAVIGATOR DATABASE

You can navigate through the Personal Web Navigator database just as you would with any other Notes database. Click on a view or folder in the Navigation pane to display a list of documents (that is, Web pages) in that view or folder.

The views and folders available in the database include the following:

- All Pages view   This view contains all the Web pages that have been retrieved using the Notes Web browser interface.

- Favorites and Bookmarks folder   This folder holds links directly to Web pages, rather than stored Web pages. If you click on a link, you open the live Web page, not a Web page stored as a Notes document.

- Other/Cookies view   This view holds all your cookies. Cookies hold information about a Web site, such as the URL, and tell the site that you have visited before.

- Other/File Archive view   This view displays all Web pages that contain attachments.

- Other/House Cleaning view   This view displays Web pages sorted by size. You can choose which ones you want to delete or reduce to URLs.

- Web Bots/Page Minder folder   You can drag Web pages into this folder to be notified when they are updated. The Page Minder is set up on the Internet Options page, which can be accessed by selecting Actions, Internet Options from within the Personal Web Navigator.

- Web Bots/Web Ahead folder   You can drag Web pages into this folder to start an agent that will retrieve all linked pages, as defined on the Internet Options page.

PART
II
CH
11

Many of these views and folders will be revisited in the next section, as I show you how to customize your Personal Web Navigator.

THE INTERNET OPTIONS SCREEN: CUSTOMIZING YOUR SETUP

Now that you know your way around the Personal Notes Navigator screen, it is time to customize the screen with your personal preferences. Your navigator is customized using the Internet Options document. You can display this document, shown in Figure 11.8, by selecting Actions, Internet Options in the Personal Web Navigator database.

Figure 11.8
The Internet Options document is used to customize your Personal Web Navigator application.

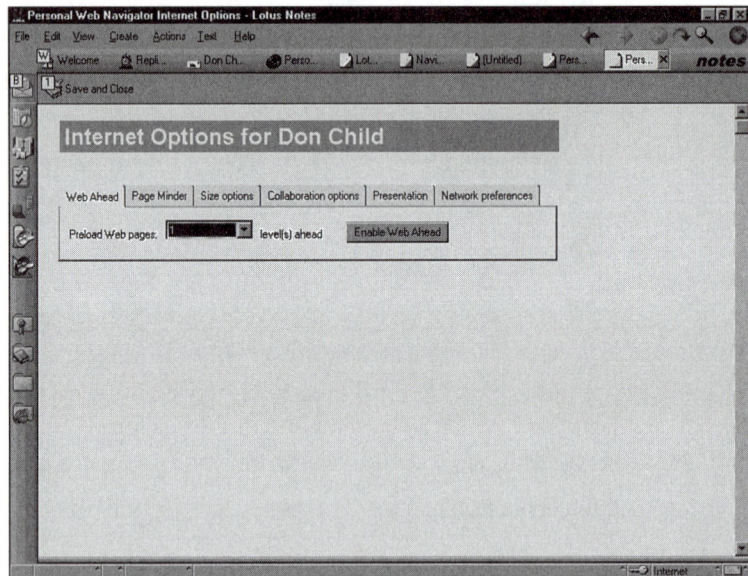

The Internet Options screen is divided into six tabbed pages with the following functions:

- Web Ahead

    Notes preloads Web page links up to four layers deep if you activate this option. Enter the number of pages you want to preload and then click on the Enable Web Ahead button. To preload pages for a site, drag and drop the Web page into the Web Ahead folder. While you are reading the first page, Notes will be busy in the background loading additional pages that are linked from that page. You can then access those linked pages more quickly, or you can read them offline at a later time.

    The Web Ahead feature runs an agent on your local workstation or on a Domino server that you designate. You must have permission to execute agents on the server you designate.

- Page Minder

    If you enable Page Minder, Notes automatically searches Web pages that have been dragged and dropped into the Page Minder folder. If a page has changed on the

Internet, you or the person you designate will be mailed a summary of the page or a copy of the full page, depending on the options you select. You can have the Page Minder run once an hour, once every four hours, once a day, or once a week.

The Page Minder feature, like the Web Ahead feature, runs an agent on your workstation or on the Domino server that you designate. You must have permission to execute agents on the server you designate.

- Size options

   You can specify that documents are automatically deleted or reduced to links if they have not been read in 15, 30, 60, or 90 days. You have to enable Housekeeping for Notes to automatically delete documents or reduce them to links. You can also have Notes warn you when the Personal Web Navigator reaches 5, 10, 25, or 50MB in size. You can then go to the House Cleaning view and delete pages that you no longer want to save.

   The Housekeeping feature, like the Web Ahead and Page Minder features, runs an agent on your workstation or on the Domino server that you designate. You must have permission to execute agents on the server you designate

- Collaboration options

   You can specify a server and a shared Web Navigator database where Web pages and your personal ratings are sent when you select Actions, Share.

- Presentation

   You can specify how the Personal Web Navigator displays rich text that is defined using different HTML tags, such as body text, address text, and anchor text (that is, links). You can also specify that you want to save rich text and HTML if you want to have access to the code used to create the page, or you can save pages as MIME only.

- Network preferences

   Network preferences are set up on the Locations document. There is a button within the Internet Preferences dialog box that takes you directly to the Internet Location document.

User Preferences

In the Additional Options list box, found at the bottom of the Basics page of the User Preferences dialog box (File, Preferences, User Preferences), there are several options you can check that control some aspects of the Personal Web Navigator when it is used with the Notes browser. You can check the following options to turn them on:

- Make Internet URLs (http://....) into Hotspots
- Enable Java applets
- Enable JavaScript
- Enable Java access from JavaScript
- Enable Plugins in Notes Browser

- Enable ActiveX in Notes Browser
- Accept Cookies
- Make Notes the default Web browser on my system
- User Web Palette
- Enable MIME save warning
- Launch the CORBA (DIIOP) server on Preview in Web browser

ADVANCED SETUP OPTIONS

The Advanced section of the Location document provides further control over the Personal Web Navigator. On the Network Options page of the Internet Preferences document, there is a link to the Location document, or you can open the Location document from the status bar at the bottom of the screen. You can also open the Location document from within your Personal Address Book.

There are five types of Internet parameters that can be set up in the Advanced section of the Location document:

- SSL Configuration
- Web Retriever Configuration
- Java Applet Security
- Secondary Servers
- Mime Settings

SSL CONFIGURATION   SSL is a Secure Socket Layer, a type of secure data transfer that is used on the Internet. By way of contrast, Notes has RSA security built in. RSA security uses a public key in the Public Address Book and a private key (part of the Notes User or Server ID) to solve mathematical algorithms to ensure that communications are authentic.

However, when navigating the Web, you'll encounter secure Web sites that require a certificate (such as a public key) from a Certificate Authority (CA) other than RSA in order to authenticate communications:

- **Accept SSL site certificates**   Indicate whether you want to accept SSL site certificates. Sites that require these certificates can be handled in one of two ways.

    The first method of handling certificates from SSL sites, which negates the security afforded by certificates, is to say Yes in the Accept SSL site certificates field in the Location document. This basically tells Notes that you don't want to take advantage of certificates, so just go ahead and accept all certificates without authenticating.

    The second, more secure method entails adding a new certificate from a CA before accessing a secure Web site using that CA's certificates. To get a certificate, open the SSL Certificate database (`SSLCERT.NSF`) from the Home/Notes/Net server. From the Certificates, Internet Certifiers view, select the certificate you want and then paste it into the Server, Certificates view in your Personal Address Book. After you have the certificate in your Personal Address Book, you can access any secure Web site as long as you share a certificate. When you select this option, you do not have to open your workstation to all certificates, as you do with the first option.

> **Tip**
>
> You can get to the Home/Notes/Net server by selecting File, Database, Open Special and then selecting Notes NIC Welcome.

- **Accept expired SSL certificates**   You can choose to accept expired SSL certificates, or you can decline certificates that have expired.
- **SSL protocol version**   You can select which version of SSL protocol you use, including V2.0 only, V3.0 handshake, V3.0 only, V3.0 with V2.0 handshake, or negotiated. Negotiated is the default value.

WEB RETRIEVER CONFIGURATION   The Web Retriever Configuration section of the Advanced options in the Location document enables you to work with how the Personal Web Navigator is configured on your system. The Web Retriever is the process that retrieves Web pages so that you can view them with the Notes Web browser. The Web Retriever information is shown in Figure 11.9.

Figure 11.9
Set up your Web Retriever on the Advanced, Web Retriever page of the Location document.

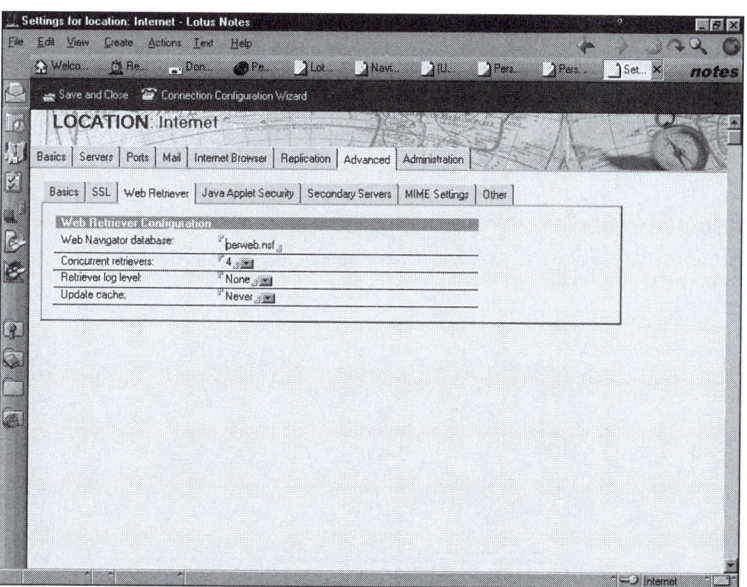

The fields that you can set include the following:

- **Web Navigator database**   This field holds the name of the Web Navigator database. The default name is `PERWEB.NSF`, but you can change the name of this file at the OS level, or you may have multiple Web Navigator databases for different purposes.

Chapter 11 Using the Notes Client on the Internet

- **Concurrent retrievers**   You can set up to 25 concurrent retrievers and then open multiple documents and select them in your Navigator. In other words, you can have up to 25 Web pages open at one time.

- **Retriever log level**   You can determine how Web Retriever events are recorded in your LOG.NSF file. Options include None, Terse, and Verbose. LOG.NSF is created automatically during Notes setup. It provides a log for tracking the various communications that take place on the Notes workstation.

- **Update cache**   When you open a Web page that is already stored in your Personal Web Navigator database, you can determine how often Notes refreshes the stored document from the Internet. Options include the following:

    Never   Notes opens the locally stored version.

    Once per session   Notes reloads pages only once during a session.

    Every time   Notes always downloads pages from the Web, even if they are already stored in the Personal Web Navigator database.

JAVA APPLET SECURITY   With Notes 5.0, you can run Java applets using either the Web or the Notes client. Security for Java applets is set up on the Advanced page in the Location document. Figure 11.10 shows the Java Applet Security page.

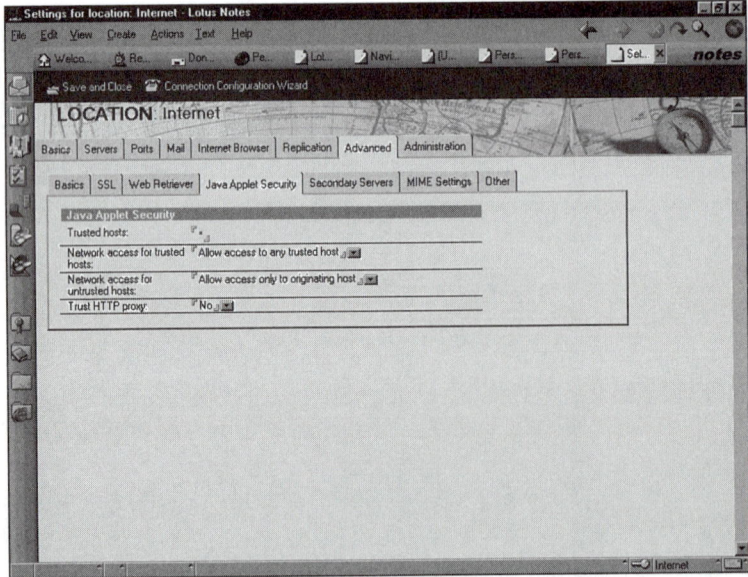

Figure 11.10
In the Location document, define how Java applet security is handled.

The options on this page include

- **Trusted hosts**   Enter the names of specific Java hosts that you trust, or use a wildcard to indicate that all hosts are trusted.

- **Network access for trusted hosts** You can disable Java, allow no Java access, allow access only to the originating host, allow access to any trusted host, or allow access to any host.
- **Network access for untrusted hosts** You can disable Java for untrusted hosts, allow no Java access at all, or allow access only for the originating host.
- **Trust HTTP proxy** You can choose to trust or not trust the HTTP proxy.

If you need help understanding hosts and proxies, talk to your network administrator or refer to almost any publication on Internet setup.

SECONDARY SERVERS   Secondary servers are servers that Notes turns to when the primary home server is not available for some reason. Defining a secondary server is not required, but it helps to ensure uninterrupted Internet availability:

- **Secondary TCP/IP Notes name server** Enter the name of the Domino server that is to be contacted for Domino Directory information in the event your home server is not available on the TCP/IP network.
- **Secondary TCP/IP host name or address** Enter the fully qualified host name or IP address to be contacted for Address Book information in the event that your home server is not available on the TCP/IP network.

Secondary NDS Notes name server and Secondary NDS name server address are used for identifying a secondary Domino server on an IPX/SPX network, and a secondary NetBIOS Notes name server identifies a secondary NetBIOS Domino server. These types of network connection can be used for Internet access only if the Domino server provides the access, and you open up Web pages as Notes documents from the Web Navigator database on the server.

MIME CONVERSION   The Mime Conversion section on the Advanced page of the Location document is used to define how attachments are encoded for those who cannot read them. Attachments can be encoded as Base64 (the default value) or Quoted-Printable. For outbound Macintosh attachment conversion, you can try AppleDouble (Base64 only) or BinHex 4.0.

A SUMMARY OF THE PERSONAL WEB NAVIGATOR SETUP

To use the Personal Web Navigator, you need to be connected to the Internet. This connection can be over a network or via a dial-up connection. The connection also can be direct to the Internet, or it can be through an HTTP proxy server.

You need to set up your location to recognize the HTTP proxy server if that is how you are connecting, and you have to define Notes as the Internet Browser. You also have to define Web retrieval as being from the Notes workstation as opposed to retrieving Web pages from the server. In effect, this says that you want to connect directly to the Internet instead of sharing a Web Navigator database with others in your organization.

In the Location document, you also can configure advanced options, such as logging and how to handle SSL certificates, and Java options if you are running Notes under Windows 95, Windows NT/Intel, Sun Solaris (SPARC and x86), HP-UX, and AIX platforms. Java applets must also be enabled in the advanced options on the User Preferences page.

Finally, you can determine how the Personal Notes Navigator displays and handles documents using the Internet Options page, opened from the Actions menu when you are in the Personal Notes Navigator database.

A Web Tour Using Notes 5.0

You are ready to feel the power of the integrated Web browser in Notes if you have the Notes browser or Notes with Internet Explorer selected as your Web browser, TCP/IP as your communications protocol, and a connection to the Internet.

To help you understand how the Notes client works with the Internet, I will take you on a tour.

Opening a Web Page from the Notes Desktop

We begin the tour by calling up the Lotus home page:

1. Click on the Globe icon near the upper-right corner of the Notes workspace.
2. Click on the pushpin icon to make the URL field stay in place.
3. Enter the URL for the Lotus Web page:
   http://www.lotus.com.

   Note that you do not need to type http:// because this is the default protocol for Web pages.
4. Press Enter to display the Web page, as shown in Figure 11.11.

When you open a page using either the Notes Web browser or Notes with Internet Explorer, the opened page is saved in your Personal Web Navigator database. When using Notes with Internet Explorer, you will notice that the performance is very comparable to the performance of Internet Explorer on its own. For pure Web browsing, the Notes browser interface could well become your browser of choice.

You can access your recent history using forward and back browser arrows, or you can click on the down arrow beside the URL field (displayed by clicking on the globe icon) to jump to any of your bookmarked favorites. You can also place bookmarks to Web pages on the IE4 or Netscape folders on your Bookmarks bar on the left side of the screen.

Opening a Web Page from the Personal Web Navigator

Now that you have seen how to open a Web page from anywhere in the Notes 5.0 workspace, it is time to explore the Web from within the Personal Web Navigator database. Open the Personal Web Navigator. The system will display in the Preview pane which page was last selected in the Navigator pane, as shown in Figure 11.12.

Figure 11.11
Retrieve a Web page directly into the Notes workspace using the integrated browser.

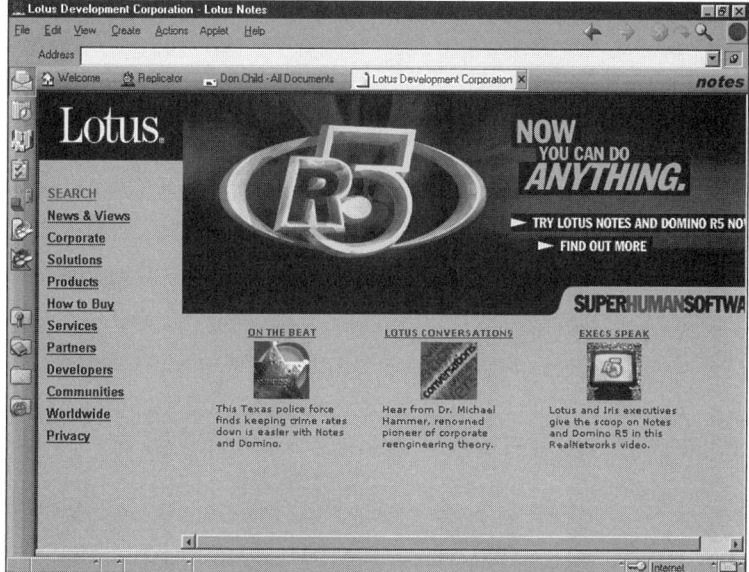

Figure 11.12
The Personal Web Navigator shows a Web page rendered by Notes in the Preview pane.

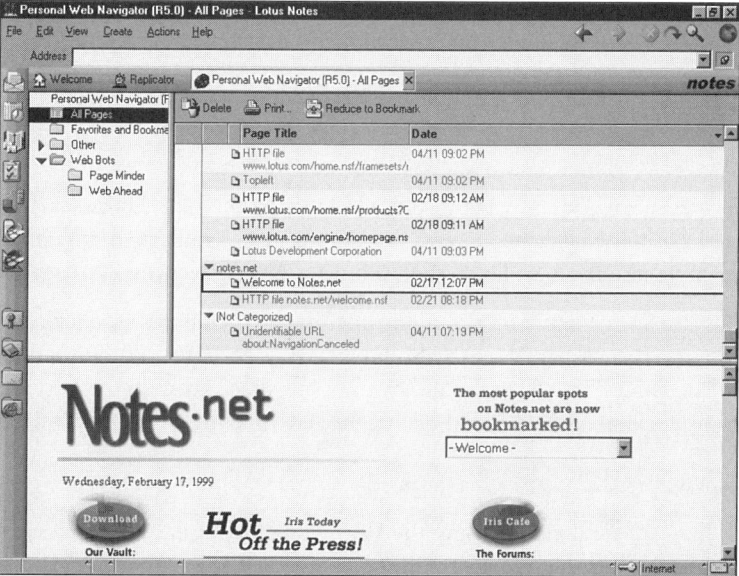

You can retrieve a page directly from the Web by entering a URL, or you can retrieve a Web page that is stored as a document in the database. Select a view or folder that contains the page you want and double-click on it to load it as a Web page rendered by the Notes browser. Notes can determine the difference between a Notes document and a Web page, using the appropriate client to display each type of document. For example, in Figure 11.13, the Notes.net home page was opened from within the Personal Web Navigator, and it is rendered as a Web page.

Figure 11.13
Open a Web page rendered by Notes as an HTML page from within the Personal Web Navigator.

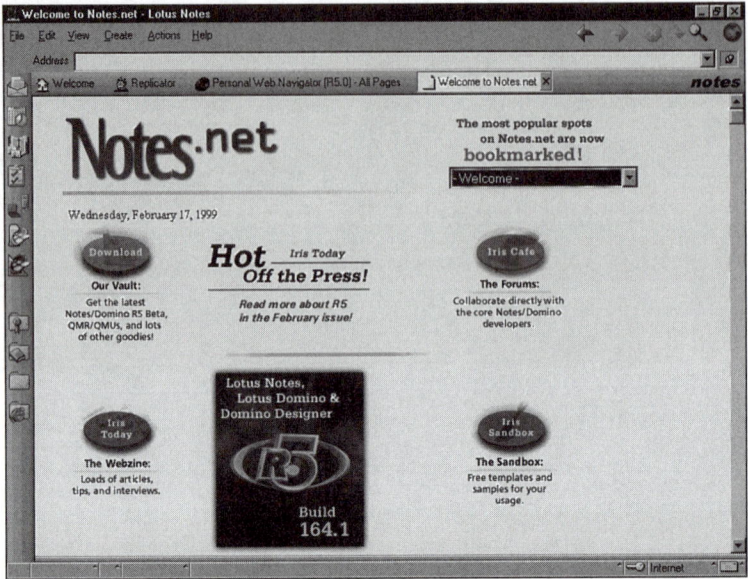

The actual Web page address for this page is

www.notes.net.

However, the page is being displayed locally by the Notes browser. Despite being displayed in the Notes client, the links on the Web page are still active. If you click on a link—for example, the Iris Café link—the Web browser retrieves the live page from the Internet.

You can switch between Notes documents and Web pages by clicking on the document titles on the taskbar. You can also bookmark Web pages and Notes documents by dragging the document title from the taskbar to a bookmark icon on the left of the screen, or by right-clicking on the opened document and selecting Bookmark from the context menu.

Sharing Web Pages with Others

When you are done browsing the Web, you have all the Web pages saved in a Domino database. Now the power of Notes comes into play.

Using Notes, you can copy the database to a laptop computer, generate a full-text index, and then perform powerful searches on the Web pages, even when you are disconnected from the network.

You can open a Web page from the Personal Web Navigator and then forward it to a work colleague by selecting Forward from the Actions menu. This includes the Web page in a Notes email memo or a bookmark to the Web page. A dialog box enables you to select whether you want to forward the page or a bookmark.

You also can maintain a public Server Web Navigator on the Domino server. You can share a Web page in the Server Web Navigator without having to forward copies of the pages to individuals.

There is a real advantage to sharing the full Web page on the Domino server. The Web page is still a Notes document. People can open the document even if they don't have a Web connection. They can even open Web pages using IPX/SPX or another non-Internet protocol. They can also copy the Web page to their own local version of the Personal Web Navigator so they can browse it offline when they go on the road.

Here are a few things you can do with your Personal Web Navigator much more efficiently than you can with a Web page on the Internet:

- You can create a full-text index for searching.
- You can replicate the Web page over a dial-up connection to your Domino server.
- You can email the Web page to someone.

If you are familiar with Notes workflow applications, you'll recognize how easily Notes could be set up using features such as Page Minder and full-text searching agents to automate the process of distributing new information from the Web. You are not restricted to the Forward and Share buttons when it comes to sharing information with others. The workflow capabilities of Notes demonstrate a new paradigm for using the Internet as a business tool.

Links—One More Way to Open a Web Page

Every page opened in Notes is represented by a button on the taskbar at the top of the screen. Whether a task involves an open Notes document or a Web page, it can be accessed immediately from the taskbar. You can move quickly between previously opened Notes documents and Web pages using the Previous and Next Web navigation buttons, or by clicking on the task buttons.

You can create a link to any Web page or Notes document by dragging the task button onto one of the Bookmark icons on the left side of the screen. The page or document will then be saved as a link. You can launch the Web page or document again by locating and clicking on the link.

From Here...

The location of documents is transparent to the end user. A document can be stored within Notes, or it can be stored on the Internet as a Web page. Notes will select the correct client software to open the document. You can learn more about working in an extended environment in the following chapters:

- Chapter 28, "Building Your Own Web Site with Domino," describes how to publish a Web site using Notes documents.
- Chapter 31, "Integrating Domino with Legacy Systems," describes how Notes and Domino work in an extended environment, which can include a combination of Notes documents, Web pages, and data stored in legacy systems.
- Chapter 37, "Firewalls, Virtual Private Networks (VPNs), and Internet Security," describes some of the ins and outs of security when working with Notes and Domino on the Internet.

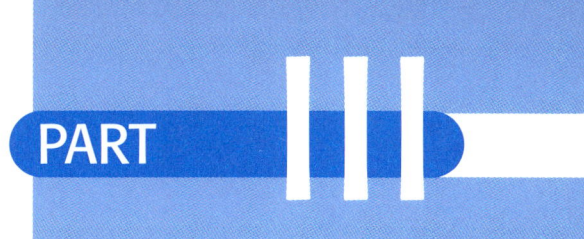

Introducing Domino Designer R5

12   Creating and Accessing Domino Databases

13   The Integrated Development Environment (IDE)

14   Designing Pages, Forms, and Subforms

15   Developing Views and Folders

16   Using Outlines, Framesets, and Navigators

17   Access Control Lists (ACLs) and Application Security

18   Working with Formulas, Functions, and Commands

CHAPTER 12

CREATING AND ACCESSING DOMINO DATABASES

You've seen and used Domino databases in many of the previous chapters. In this chapter, you investigate databases in a little more detail. I'll show you how to create new databases, which is the first step in Domino application development. After you create a new database, you can begin to customize, enhance, and tailor the database to your business requirements.

WHAT IS A DOMINO DATABASE?

A Domino *database* is a repository primarily for documents. In addition, it contains design and programming elements. The database is typically stored on your Domino server, but it can also reside on your laptop or desktop machine. Domino databases can exist on any of the server platforms supported by Domino, which means anything from Intel *x*86 and Pentium to UNIX, AS/400, and S/390 mainframes. In addition to multiple platform support, Domino databases also support multiple national languages. This means that the content of your databases can be in English, French, German, Spanish, or any of the other—over 40—supported languages.

DOMINO DOCUMENTS

You may already be familiar with another database system, such as Oracle, DB2, or some other relational database system. Domino databases are *not* relational. By this I mean that the fundamental data stored within the database is not organized in the typical rows and columns of a relational database.

> **Note** With NotesSQL, a Domino database can be accessed via SQL statements and can be made to appear relational, but this does not really make the database relational.

Perhaps one of the greatest strengths of Domino databases is precisely the fact that the databases are not relational. In typical relational databases, data is stored in tables made up of rows and columns. Each row is similar in format to the other rows in the same table. On one hand, this homogeneity makes access to rows of the table very fast because each row has the same format. On the other hand, this same homogeneity makes the tables rather inflexible. The rows of a table are not allowed to vary.

The counterpart to a row within a relational database is called a *document* in Domino. This is obviously a very specialized use of the word document and somewhat different from our everyday usage. A Domino document typically contains several *items* of data. Each of the items corresponds to a field. Each field has a name.

For example, suppose you had a document describing names and addresses of your friends. This document might contain fields with the following names: FirstName, LastName, Address, HomePhone, WorkPhone. Each of these fields could contain information about a friend. If you have several friends, you may have several documents in the database, each containing the same fields. So far, this is similar to how you might organize this data within a relational database.

In Domino, however, we do not have the restriction that each document contains the same fields. Some documents may have additional fields, and some of the documents may omit some fields. In our example, some documents may not have a HomePhone field. Other documents may not have a WorkPhone field, and some documents may have additional fields containing birthdays or children's names.

Notice that the Domino scheme is different from a relational database system, which requires an identical set of fields, but allows NULL values in some fields. In Domino, the entire field might be absent. Other documents may have additional fields.

I'll cover documents and fields in more detail later on, but for now it is sufficient to realize that in Domino, documents are where your data reside. Each Domino database can have many, many documents, and the fields in the documents can vary from one document to another.

Database Programs

In addition to being a repository for documents, a Domino database can also be considered an application, or perhaps part of an application. By this I mean that in operating systems such as Windows or UNIX, an application is typically equated with an executable file. In Notes and Domino, an application is typically associated with a database instead of an executable file.

How can this be? Isn't a database just a repository for data? Well, yes and no. In Notes and Domino, databases contain programs as well as data. In particular, there are typically many LotusScript, Java, or JavaScript programs and formulas associated with the database. Each of the programs is associated with a part of the database and can be triggered by user actions.

For example, you can trigger programs to run when a user opens a database, when the user opens up a particular document, or when a document is saved. You can trigger programs to run when a user clicks a button or enters data within a particular field. Each of these occasions and scores of others can cause programs to run within the database.

Taken together, these programs within the database actually constitute an application. The application might be to support a help desk, or as an ISO9000 repository, or to control your expense accounts, or as a manufacturing database. The list, of course, is endless and only up to your imagination. With Domino Web support, you can also create databases that can implement an e-Commerce application. Some applications may even span more than one database, and they can be linked together automatically via programming.

Domino Release 5 Database Highlights

Before we move on, I'd also like to highlight some of the new features of release 5 of Domino databases. The most important change is the fact that the On-Disk Structure (ODS) has changed for release 5. The ODS is the binary format for the data within a Domino database. There is good news and bad news with this change. The bad news is that after you create a database with R5, you will not be able to directly read that database with a previous version of Notes or Domino. In other words, the older programs do not understand the newer format. The good news is that

- Domino R5 can read previous versions of databases directly.
- If you use a Domino R5 server, you can access the server (and hence databases) from an R3 or R4 client. This gives effective access to previous release clients, but they are not directly reading the database. Of course, older clients cannot use newer R5 database features, but they can access the data.
- The new database format was created to improve performance and robustness within Domino.
- There is a much larger capacity with the new database format.
- The new database format allows transaction (rollback) processing as well as incremental, online backup.

One dramatic change involves the Domino Lightweight Directory, also known as the *directory catalog*. The Directory previously had limitations that made it unwieldy when it contained tens of thousands of entries. With the new directory structure, the Lightweight Directory will be able to hold up to a million entries, even on a laptop machine.

Changing the format of a database from the old format to the new format works similarly to previous releases. When you compact the database, it is automatically upgraded to the new release 5 format. If you wish to leave the database in the release 4 format, you can name the database with an `.NS4` extension instead of `.NSF`.

How Can You Create a Domino Database?

There are several ways to create a database within Notes and Domino. In this chapter, I cover the Notes and Designer user interfaces. The administrator user interface is covered later in this book. The administrator interface is quite different from the Notes and Designer interface and is used by system administration personnel to add new users, monitor performance, manage security, perform database maintenance, and for many other tasks.

Although you can access Domino databases from a Web browser, you cannot create a new Domino database from a browser. You can administer databases via the Web browser interface. You must use a Notes or Designer client to create a new database. Databases can be created in one of the following ways:

- Use a database template.
- Start with a completely blank database.
- Copy an existing database.
- Create a replica of an existing database.

We'll now take a look at these methods in more detail.

Using Database Templates

A database *template* is really just a special type of Domino database. It typically contains a design template, but no data. There are many design templates that are shipped with the standard Lotus product, and you can create your own templates as well.

The reason you might want to start with a design template is that the design has already been done for you. If you start with a template, the hard work of designing forms, views, pages, framesets, and so forth has already been done by a designer. You can just pick up the design and either use it as-is, or slightly customize it to suit your application. This method will clearly result in a working database much more quickly than starting from scratch.

In release 5, there are over 50 templates supplied with the Domino server, of which approximately 30 are also supplied with the Notes client (including Designer and Administrator). Most of the extra templates supplied with Domino, but not the Notes client, deal with the operation and administration of Domino itself. The templates are divided into the standard templates and the advanced templates. The templates are used for a variety of purposes. Some of the templates are useful for common applications and will be used by many sites and users. Other templates are much more specialized and may be used only by administrators or users that need special features. Table 12.1 lists some of the more useful templates.

TABLE 12.1 Useful Templates Shipped with Domino R5

Template Name	Description
DiscussionNotes and Web (R5.0)	This is a general-purpose discussion database and will be suitable for many applications. It can be used from Notes or the Web.
Doc Library—Notes and Web (R5.0)	This is a general purpose document library database that can be used to store reference information on any topic. Documents can also undergo a review cycle. It can be used from Notes or the Web.
Microsoft Office Library (R5.0)	This database can be used as a repository for Microsoft Office documents. It activates the documents in place so that the data appears within a Notes window.
Personal Address Book	A personal address book is automatically created for you when you install the Notes client. It contains contact information and information on how to access servers. You can use it as a personal information manager.
Personal Journal (R4)	The personal journal template can be used to store personal notes. After the notes are stored, you can categorize them.
Personal Web Navigator (R5.0)	This database caches information about Web sites that you have visited and is the basis of the Notes Web browser. This database is created automatically for you, so you will normally not need to create another one.

continues

TABLE 12.1 CONTINUED

Template Name	Description
Team Room (5.0)	A team room database is similar to a discussion database, but it has many more features for facilitating team interaction. You can use this database from the Notes client or a Web browser. This template is located on the Domino server, not the Notes client.

CREATING A DATABASE FROM A TEMPLATE

To create a database from a template, perform the following steps:

1. First, you should know which template you will use. Choose from one of the templates listed in Table 12.1, one of the others shipped by Lotus, a template from a third party, or one that has been developed by your company. You need to know the name of your template in the following steps.

2. From the client desktop, select File, Database, New or press Ctrl+N. The New Database dialog box is shown. See Figure 12.1.

Figure 12.1
The New Database dialog box enables you to select from over 50 predefined templates.

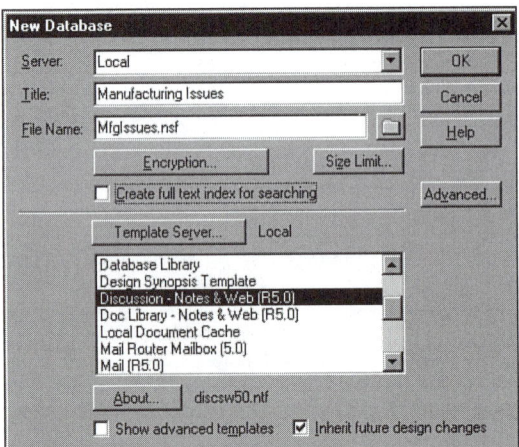

3. Select the server where you would like the new database to reside. Local indicates your local desktop machine. If you want to create a new database on a server other than your desktop, you need to be authorized in the Domino Directory for the server.

> **Tip**
>
> Typically, you will not want to initially create a database on your server, because you need to customize the database before it is ready to use. You should create the database on your local workstation. After you have created the database locally and customized it for use, you can replicate it to your server. This ensures that by the time it gets to your server, it will be complete and coherent.

4. Enter a title for the new database in the Title field of the dialog box. This title will be shown in the database icon of the desktop. It can contain spaces and may be up to 32 characters. The title is important, because users will use this information to decide whether the information in the database is relevant to them. Choose the title carefully.

> **Note**
>
> Lotus Notes and Domino now support over 40 national languages, including (new with R5) Arabic and Hebrew. This new support is notable because these languages are bidirectional, with text sometimes reading from right to left. Localization features enable database titles to be stored in DBCS (double-byte character sets) to allow characters such as Chinese and Japanese Kanji.

5. The File Name field is used to specify the filename that is used by the operating system. If you are using multiple operating systems (such as a UNIX server and Windows clients), you should pay careful attention to the naming of files. Each operating system has its own rules for whether files are case sensitive, the valid character set, and so forth. To be safe, use 8 characters or less for the filename portion before the extension. Even if you do not use multiple operating systems, it is a good idea to establish file-naming conventions for your company so that when you have hundreds (or thousands) of databases, they will be easier to manage. If you use the default .NSF extension, the release 5 On-Disk Structure format will be used for the database. Note that release 5 and release 4 use different formats on disk and that a release 4.x server will not be able to directly read a release 5 database. Release 4.x servers can replicate databases, however, with release 5 servers. You can create a database with the release 4.x format by using the extension .NS4 instead of .NSF.

6. You may choose to encrypt your database at the time you create it by using the Encryption button. You can also decide later to encrypt an existing database, so you are not forced to make the decision when you create the database. Encryption is useful, because there may be opportunities for other people to access data stored in a Domino database. In particular, if you have a laptop that might be used or stolen, if someone other than you has access to a desktop machine, or if other people in your organization might have access to your disk files through the network, you might want to consider encryption. In any situation where someone might copy files via the operating system and not via Domino, there is a threat that the person may use tools other than Domino or Notes to access the data. If you encrypt the database, other tools, such as text editors, cannot be used to compromise database security. A person will need to go through Notes or Domino security to access the data. When you choose encryption, you can use Simple, Medium, or Strong encryption. Generally, the stronger the encryption, the longer it will take to encrypt and decrypt information in the database. See Chapter 36, "Domino Security Overview," for more information about Domino Security.

7. Use the Size Limit button to change the maximum size of a database with an .NS4 extension or that has not yet been upgraded to the R5 format. Release 5 has removed the absolute size limitation for databases. This was one of the benefits of the new On-Disk Structure (ODS) used for R5. Although Domino databases no longer have an

absolute size limitation, databases have been certified by Lotus to be as large as 64GB (depending upon your operating system capabilities). However, it is not necessarily a good idea, because databases this large will generally not perform as well as smaller databases. Carefully consider whether you can break up a large database into smaller, more topical databases.

8. The Create full text index for searching check box can be used to create a full text index. You can also create an index after the database has been created, so you don't have to decide on this issue when you create the database.

9. The Advanced button is new in release 5 of Notes. It enables you to specify several advanced options about the database. These options are primarily optimizations that will improve performance of the database. Here are the options:

   - Don't maintain unread marks   Maintaining unread marks takes CPU time. If you do not need them, you can improve performance by checking this box.

   - Document Table bitmap optimization   This optimization is to speed the rebuilding and updating of views. Domino stores tables internally to determine whether documents appear in a view. This optimization enables tables to be associated with forms. This enables Domino to search only documents associated with forms that appear in a view, which improves performance. This optimization works only if you use `Form=` as part of your view selection formula. You must compact the database before this optimization becomes effective.

   - Don't overwrite Free space   Normally, Domino overwrites deleted documents with a bit pattern on disk. This is a security feature to prevent unauthorized access to deleted data. This overwriting causes disk I/O and uses CPU time. However, in some databases security is not an issue, such as in a Help database. You can improve performance, at the expense of slightly decreased security, by checking this box.

   - Maintain LastAccessed Property   The Document properties box maintains information about the last time and date a document was modified. The LastAccessed property can also keep track of the last time a document was accessed for a read. Doing so, however, causes extra disk activity to log this information back to the database. By default, the LastAccessed property does not keep track of reads. If you enable this check box, this extra information will be kept. If you disable the check box, performance will be improved but you will not know when the last read access occurred. You should enable this check box if you have enabled document deletion based on days of inactivity.

   - Disable transaction Logging   Transaction logging is a new feature of R5. It greatly enhances reliability, because if there is a power failure or some other type of server problem requiring a restart, the log can be used by Domino to reconstruct your database. The logging also facilitates online backup of databases while the server is running. Transaction logging must be first enabled on the Domino server. After enabled on the server, all R5 databases automatically use transaction logging. This check box enables you to selectively disable transaction logging for

- **Allow soft deletions** Enabling soft deletions allows you to create a database where, for a limited amount of time, a user can easily recover documents that have been deleted. You can create a special view, similar to a trash folder, that users can use to recover deleted documents. See the $Undelete expire time option at the end of this list.

- **Don't Support specialized response hierarchy** In order to support the two @functions @AllChildren and @Descendants, documents must keep track of their parent and/or response documents. This tracking consumes disk space and CPU time. If you are not using either of these functions, you can enable this check box to improve performance. Remember, however, that if you change your mind after the database has been operational for a while, your documents may not contain the information you need. Make sure that you have carefully planned your database before you enable this option.

- **Don't Allow headline monitoring** Users can enable their headline database, also known as the subscription database, to search other databases. If this is used extensively, this can cause Domino performance to suffer. You can disable headline monitoring and searching of the current database by enabling this option.

- **Limit entries in $UpdatedBy fields** Documents maintain an audit trail of the people that have updated them in the $UpdatedBy field. If a document undergoes a significant number of updates, this field can get very large. You can improve performance by limiting the number of entries in the $UpdatedBy field. If the limit is reached, the oldest entry will be discarded when a new entry is added.

- **Limit entries in $Revisions fields** The $Revisions fields are used to manage replication and store up to 500 entries by default. Setting a lower limit can improve performance; however, setting the value too low can cause documents to replicate incorrectly. Consider setting this value lower if your database has no replicas or replicates frequently, thus requiring less history to be maintained. Also consider enabling this option if your database contains a large number of documents and you need to conserve space.

- **$Undelete Expire Time (in hours)** This option sets the time window during which a deleted document can be undeleted. This option is effective only if you have enabled soft deletions (see previous discussion).

10. The template server is the server where the template resides. Note that the template server can be different from the server where you want your new database to be stored after it is created. You may not have all the templates loaded on your desktop machine (that is, Local), so if you cannot find the template you are looking for, make sure to check your company's server.

11. The Show advanced templates check box can be used to show additional templates. Most of the advanced templates supplied by Lotus relate to systems administration, so

you will not normally be concerned with them. As a database designer, you can specify whether you want your databases to show up in the normal template list or in the advanced list.

12. Pick the template you would like to use from the list by clicking on it with your mouse or by using your keyboard. The special list item called "Blank" is used to create an empty database. Using the "Blank" template essentially is similar to using no template at all.

13. The Inherit future design changes check box is used to specify the relationship between your newly created database and the template you are using as a base. You may be using the template in one of two scenarios. Normally, most databases will follow the first scenario, which is that you are using the template just as a basis to get a quick start on developing a custom database. In this case, you would want to disable (uncheck) the Inherit future design changes check box. Any future changes to the template will not affect your database.

The second scenario is that you have developed a template, such as a company application or library, that will have several instantiations. In this case, you enable the inheritance check box. If inheritance is enabled, you can use the template as a single source of your design changes for the application, and all versions of the database will be updated when the template itself changes. As an example, suppose you want to create several document libraries, each with a different topic, but you would like all the libraries to share a common look and feel. You then enable inheritance on all these library databases when you create them. To make any changes, you update the template, and the design changes will propagate automatically to the individual databases. This inheritance saves you from manually changing the design of each database individually.

Note
Even if you disable the Inherit future design changes check box, you can manually update the design of a database from a template. This operation is called *refreshing* (that is, installing a newer version of the existing template) or *replacing* (removing the old and replacing it with a completely new template).

You can find out whether a database has an associated template by opening the Database Properties box and then clicking on the Design tab. You can also change the inherit option here if you later change your mind about inheriting future design changes.

14. After you have selected all your options, click the OK button. Your database will be created and an icon will be placed on the workspace page you selected. If the database has an About document, it is displayed. You can safely close this document.

Congratulations! You have successfully created a new database from a template.

CREATING A COPY OF A DATABASE

Besides creating a database from a template, you can create a new database by making a copy of an existing database. This method is similar to using a template, because design elements from an existing source are copied into your new database and you do not have to create them from scratch. A copy of a database differs from using a template, however, because you do not have the option of inheriting design changes. In addition, when you make the copy, you can optionally copy database documents as well as the design elements. After you have made a copy of the original database, the copy starts to live a life of its own, and changes made to either database do not affect the other database.

It is important to note that a copy of a database is not a replica copy. In other words, when you use the following procedure to copy a database, it does not replicate the original database. To make a replica copy that replicates the original database, skip to the next section, "Creating a Replica of a Database."

You will typically use the next copy procedure as a shortcut to simplify your design of a new database or perhaps to make a backup copy of an existing database. This is similar to the use of templates, but with the copy procedure, you can start with any existing database, not just templates.

To make a copy of a database, perform the following steps:

1. Open the bookmarks section on the left of the screen and right-click on the source database you would like to copy. From the menu, select Database, New Copy. See Figure 12.2.

Figure 12.2
The New Copy menu item enables you to copy an existing database with or without its documents.

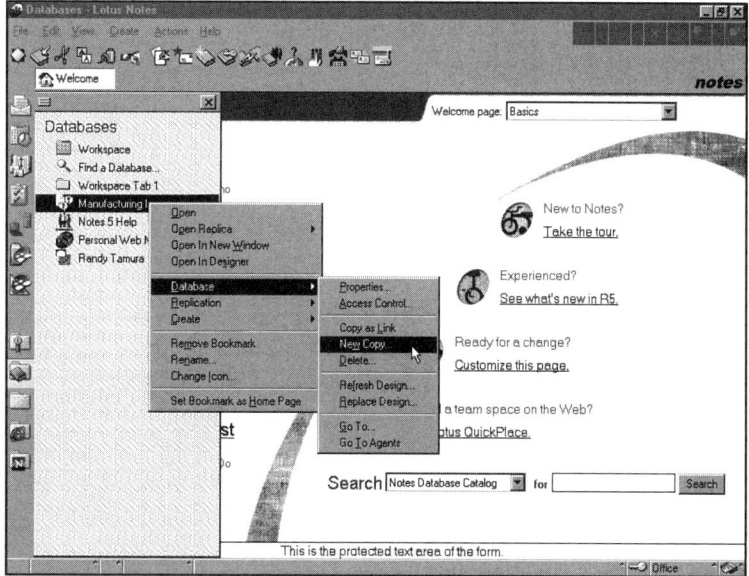

2. The Copy Database dialog box will open. Select the Server where you would like the new database to reside. Local indicates your local desktop machine.

266 CHAPTER 12 CREATING AND ACCESSING DOMINO DATABASES

3. Fill in the Title and File Name fields. They are initialized with the information from the source. Even though this is a copy of an existing database, be sure to give the new database a different title. This allows users to distinguish between the two databases. You also need to give the database a new filename.

4. Encryption and Size Limit are set just as in creating a new database from a template. They specify whether you want the new copy encrypted and the size of the new database.

5. In the Copy section at the bottom of the dialog box, you can choose to copy both the design and existing documents or just the design to the new database. See Figure 12.3.

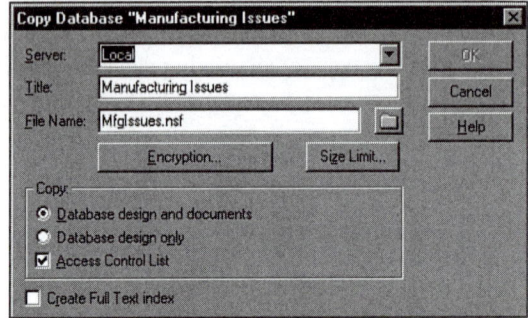

Figure 12.3
The Copy Database dialog box enables you to copy designs, documents, and ACLs, and to create a full text index.

6. You can also choose to copy the Access Control List (ACL) from the existing database, or you can start by creating a new ACL for the new database.

7. The Create Full Text index check box enables you to create a full text index at the time you create the database. You can also create a full text index at a later time.

8. Click OK when you have completed choosing your options. A new database will be created for you with your selected options.

CREATING A REPLICA OF A DATABASE

You typically create replica copies of databases on different servers. The power of Domino is to find replica databases on different servers and automatically synchronize them through replication. As an example, you typically have your mail database stored on your Domino server. You may want to replicate your mail database to your laptop so you can read and answer your mail while you are traveling. In this scenario, you would make a replica of your mail database on your laptop. Do not make a copy (as in the previous section) of your mail database, because the database will not replicate.

To make a replica of a database, perform the following steps:

1. Open the bookmarks section on the left of the screen and right-click on the source database you would like to replicate. From the menu, select Replication, New Replica. You will see a dialog box similar to Figure 12.4.

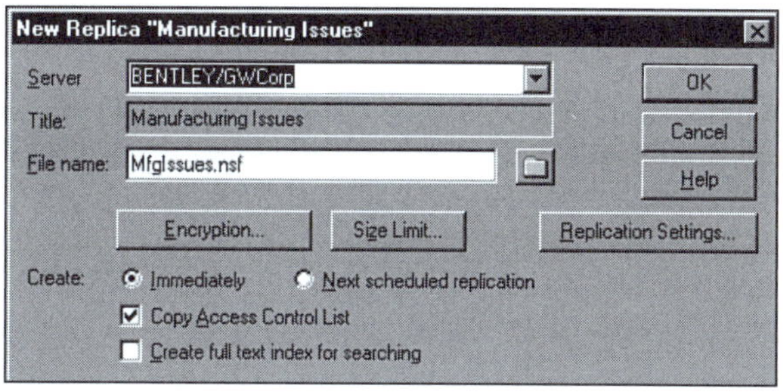

Figure 12.4
The New Replica dialog box enables you to create a replica of an existing database.

2. Select the Server where you would like the new replica database to reside. Local indicates your local desktop machine. Typically, the server will be different from the source because you want the databases to replicate. Another usage for replication is for backup purposes. Consider this as you make a replica on the same or a different server.
3. Fill in the File Name field. You cannot change the title of the database. The title must be the same as the source. It is usually a good idea to make the filename the same as the source also (assuming that the replica is on a different server than the source).
4. Encryption and Size Limit are set just as in creating a new database from a template. They specify whether you want the new copy encrypted and the size of the new database.
5. The Replication Settings button is enabled if you are creating a replica on a different server from the source. These settings enable you to control space-saving parameters, priority of replication, and whether only a subset of the information should be replicated. The replication settings are described in more detail in Chapter 40, "Replication and Its Administration."
6. You can control whether the replication should occur immediately or at the next scheduled replication.
7. You can also choose to copy the Access Control List from the existing database, or you can start by creating a new ACL for the new database.
8. The Create Full Text index check box enables you to create a full text index at the time you create the database. You can also create a full text index at a later time.
9. Click OK when you have completed choosing your options. A new replica database will be created for you with your selected options.

DATABASE ACCESS CONTROL

After you create a database, one of the first items of consideration should be who will be allowed to access the database and what operations will be allowed. The core mechanism for database security is the Access Control List (ACL) for the database. Each database can have a separate ACL. Because security is so important, Chapter 17, "Access Control Lists (ACLs) and Application Security," is entirely devoted to the subject. In this section, I give you a quick overview of the access levels provided by ACLs.

There are seven access levels that can be associated with a database. A particular user's access for a database will resolve to one of these seven levels. A given user may have different access levels for different databases. There are no automatic superuser type user IDs, such as administrator. If the administrator is not granted access via the ACL, he or she will not be able to access the database.

Here are the seven access levels, in increasing order of control over the database:

- No Access   This is pretty clear. Access is not allowed.
- Depositor   A depositor has write-only access. Useful for surveys and possibly for e-Commerce order entry.
- Reader   A reader can read database documents.
- Author   An author can read documents, and create and edit documents only he or she has created.
- Editor   An editor can read and write anyone's database documents.
- Designer   A designer can edit documents and also change the database (that is, application) design elements.
- Manager   A manager can edit, change design elements, and change the database ACL.

EDITING ACL ENTRIES

You can add ACL entries for users, servers, or groups. The most common method for specifying ACLs is to make one or more groups for users and assign access levels via the groups. You should use specific user IDs sparingly and only for exceptions, because you may frequently have personnel changes—new people arriving and existing employees leaving. If each person were individually listed in each database, it would create an administrative nightmare. By using groups for access, you can simply add or delete people from the group, and the person will automatically have all the privileges of the group. The group definitions are stored in the Domino Directory and are usually maintained by an administrator.

Groups can contain arbitrary combinations of people, but most companies group people by department or job function. Remember that a person can also be a member of several groups, so don't try to organize into completely nonoverlapping groups. Use groups to make your job of administering the databases easier. A user will not usually be in two groups for the same database, but might be in different groups for different databases.

If a user is listed in two groups for the same database, the user will generally be given the higher access level. If, however, a user is specified by a user ID, the specific entry takes precedence over the group entry, even if it lowers authorization.

When you first create a database, a default ACL is created for you. This default ACL contains five entries: Default, Anonymous, LocalDomainServers, OtherDomainServers, and the username of the person that creates the database. See Figure 12.5.

Figure 12.5
The Access Control List dialog box enables you to control who has access to a database.

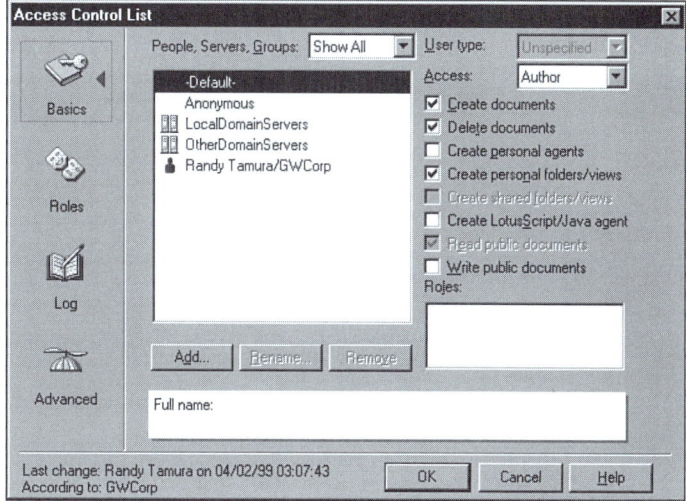

The Default entry is used for Notes clients accessing this database that are not otherwise specified in the ACL. Normally, you should set this level to one of the lowest levels, such as No Access, Reader, or Author. This low level should be used because you normally will create groups that allow access to the users you designate.

The Anonymous entry is used for anonymous Web access to the database. Again, unless the database is specifically designed for Web access, you should set this level to No Access or, at most, Reader. If a database is specifically designed for use with Web browsers, you can set this level higher, as appropriate.

LocalDomainServers and OtherDomainServers are groups in the Domino Directory. Usually, you give Designer or Manager access to LocalDomainServers because it will be required for database replication. OtherDomainServers is typically not given a high access level.

Finally, the user that creates the database is given Manager access by default. Notes requires that at least one user has Manager access. Manager is the only level that can change the ACL. If a database does not have at least one user with Manager access, the ACL can no longer be changed.

For more details on ACLs, see Chapter 17.

DATABASE DESIGN ELEMENTS

Within a Domino database, in addition to user documents, application information is stored in design elements. These design elements make up the structure, design, and display of the application in the database. The design elements control how the application stores data and how the application appears to the user, and they contain application logic.

The design elements are created using the Domino Designer and typically come from a design template or are created by the Designer. The design elements are described in more detail in subsequent chapters, but here is a listing of the kinds of elements that are stored in a Domino Database:

- **Outlines** Used as a tool by the user to navigate through the database.
- **Framesets** A configuration of frames that can be used to show multiple pages or documents.
- **Pages** Used to store Web pages.
- **Forms** Predefined formats used to view documents.
- **Views** A tabular display of a set of documents selected by a formula from a database.
- **Folders** Similar to a view, but documents selected by a user.
- **Navigators** A graphics-based database navigational tool.
- **Agents** A program that can be automatically triggered within a database.
- **Images** A library of image resources that may be used throughout the database. The images can be in a number of standardized graphic formats, such as GIF, BMP, or JPEG.
- **Applets** A library of Java applets that can be used in Web browsers or the Notes client.
- **Subforms** Reusable subparts of forms that can be used for consistency among forms.
- **Shared Fields** Field definitions that can be reused on many forms to enforce consistency of user interface and to provide a single element for design changes.
- **Script Libraries** A library of LotusScript routines within a database.
- **Other** The database icon, descriptive documents, database script, and database shared actions.
- **Synopsis** This is not really a design element, although it appears in the Design pane. If clicked, you can obtain a summary of the database design elements in either printed or database format.

The database design elements are described in more detail in subsequent chapters.

Updating the Database Documentation

Each database is capable of storing two special documents called the About Database document and the Using Database document. The About Database document is intended to be a summary of the purpose of the database. The Using Database document should describe information for a user of the database and should explain how to use the database's features.

Information contained in the About Database document will typically be viewed by every user of your database. If you create a database from a template supplied by Lotus, a default

About document is included. This document contains very general information about the database. Before you put your database into production, you should be sure to update this document with more specific information, explaining the purpose of the database, who should use it, and when it should be used. To update the About document, perform the following steps:

1. Open the design for the database by selecting View, Design from the menu.
2. Select the tool marked Other in the Navigation pane. See Figure 12.6.

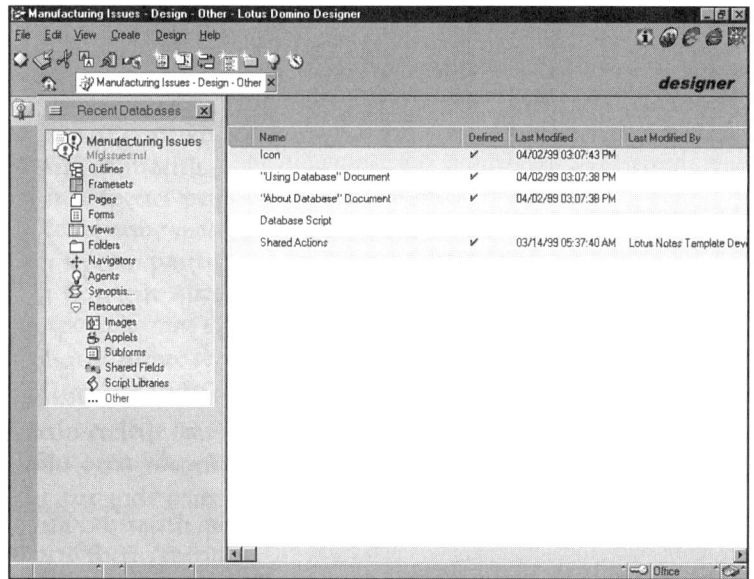

Figure 12.6
The Other section of the design elements contains the About Database document, Using Database document, and the database icon.

3. Double-click on the About Database document in the pane on the right. After you open the About document, you should customize it and add content relevant to your database.
4. After you have updated the document, close it by clicking the X in the upper-right corner of the document tab, by selecting File, Close from the menu, or by pressing Ctrl+W.

You can update the Using Database document in a similar manner. The Using Database document should contain information on how to use the database. For Lotus-supplied templates, a Using document is created for you by default. If you customize the operation of the database, be sure to update the Using document with any instructions that are unique to your database.

To change the database icon, you can double-click on the word Icon within the Other section. An icon editor will appear, and you can use it to modify the icon. See Figure 12.7.

Figure 12.7
The Design Icon dialog box enables you to edit the database icon.

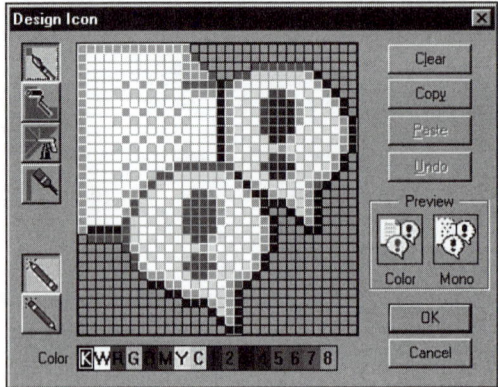

With the database icon editor, you can modify individual pixels of the icon, fill entire areas (with the paint roller), and perform several other operations. You can also use the Clipboard to copy and paste icons from other sources as a starting point. The best way to learn about the icon editor is to try it.

DATABASE PROPERTIES

Domino databases have many properties associated with them. Many of these properties can be specified when you create the database, and some properties can be set or changed after the database has been created. You can change the database properties with the following steps:

1. First open the database, and then click File, Database, Properties from the menu.
2. The Database Properties dialog box appears. See Figure 12.8.

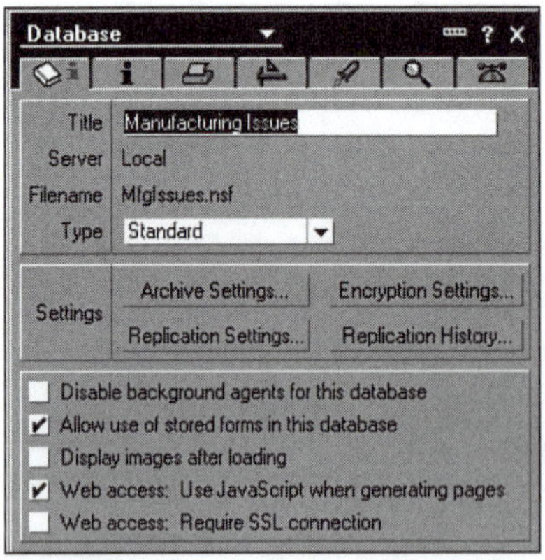

Figure 12.8
The Database Properties dialog box enables you to change database attributes.

3. There are seven tabs within the properties box. These are Basics, Information, Printing, Design, Launch, Full Text, and Advanced. Select the appropriate tab and change the desired properties.

DATABASE BASICS

The Basics tab enables you to change several key database attributes. As you can see in Figure 12.8, you can change the database title, its type, archive settings, encryption settings, and replication settings, and you can view the replication history. Typically, you will not modify the database type. You will almost always use a standard database type. Other types are usually associated with a special-purpose database type, such as a library or directory.

New in release 5 is the capability to controll archiving documents for any database. In previous releases of Notes, you could archive your mail file, but there was no built-in support for archiving an arbitrary database. When you archive documents, they are copied to the archive database and they are deleted from the original database. Within the database properties box, you can now control which documents you want to archive, based upon the time and date they were last accessed or modified.

> **Note**
> If you enable archiving for a database, you should enable the Maintain LastAccessed property advanced database option. Enabling this property will enable Domino to keep track of read access to documents as well as write access.

You can also control the name and location of the archive database. By default, the database will be in the archive subdirectory of your Notes data directory. The filename will be the prefix a_ plus the first six characters of the original database. See Figure 12.9.

Figure 12.9
The Archive Settings dialog box enables you to control archiving parameters.

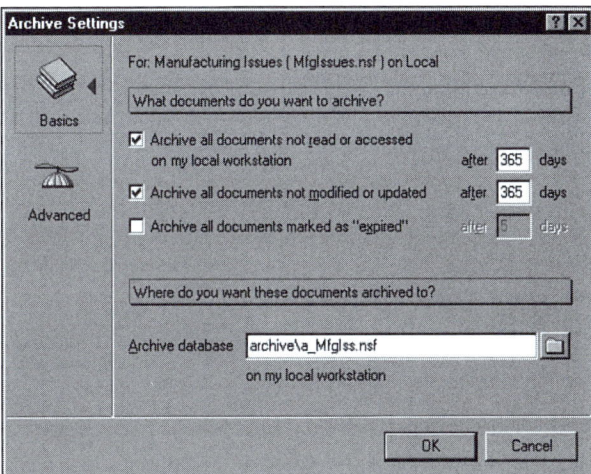

Advanced archiving options enable you to archive to a server and to control logging, deletion of documents that have responses, and whether documents should be deleted without archiving them.

In the database properties Basics tab, the check boxes enable you to specify other attributes. The Disable background agents for this database check box will disable the running of agents in this database that otherwise would be triggered by external events, such as new documents or scheduled tasks.

Documents within a database can be stored with or without the forms used to create them. Normally, forms are not stored with the documents because there is a single copy kept in the database. When you move a document from one database to another, however, the form may not be available in the destination database. The check box for Allow use of stored forms in this database solves this problem.

Display images after loading causes graphic images to be displayed after the text of the document. This enhances performance when documents are displayed over slow communication lines. If this box is not checked, the document will display the elements in the order in which they are encountered. You should probably check this box if you are creating a database for Web use.

The Web access: Use JavaScript when generating pages option is a performance and functional enhancement option. If this box is checked, certain options of the Web page are not evaluated until the user uses them on the page. If it is not checked, Domino will evaluate these options at the time the page is displayed and some @functions are not available. Another restriction is that only one submit button is allowed if the option is not checked, whereas multiple buttons are allowed if JavaScript is enabled. Normally, you should enable this option for Web applications.

The Web access: Require SSL connection option causes Secure Socket Layer (SSL) protocol to be required to access this database. This option enhances security for Web applications and should be used for Web transaction databases. If you check this option, you also need to ensure that SSL is configured and enabled on your Domino server.

Database Information

The database Information (Info) tab displays key information about the database. It tells you the size of the database, the number of documents, and the percentage of the space within the database that is used. You can also compact the database and specify archiving parameters from the Information tab. See Figure 12.10.

The creation date and last modified date are shown in the Activity section. You can click the User Detail button to get more information.

The replica ID is a hex value that is used for replication. Each originally created database has a unique replica ID. If a database is created as a replica copy of another database, the two databases will have identical replica IDs. When you use a database copy, all elements of the database are copied to the new database, but the new database will have a different, unique replica ID.

Figure 12.10
The Information tab shows you the size, dates, and replica ID of a database.

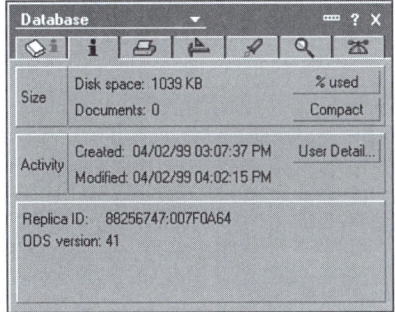

The ODS (On-Disk Structure) version tells you the format of the database on disk. In general, each release of Notes and Domino can read prior database versions, but they cannot read future versions. In other words, release 5 can read release 5–and–prior databases. Release 4 of Notes cannot read a release 5 database. The ODS version is an incremental counter and is not the same as the external release number.

DATABASE PRINTING AND DESIGN

The Printing tab can be used to specify headers and footers as well as fonts to be used for printing this database. You can specify dates, times, and formatting information.

The first line of the Design tab tells you whether the design for the database is hidden. The vast majority of databases you work with will not have a hidden design. This feature is mostly for third-party vendors or corporate developers that want to ensure that the design of the database cannot be modified after it's deployed. If you choose to hide the entire database design, you will not be able to modify the design to fix bugs or for any other reason. Therefore, you'd better keep an extra copy of the database without the design hidden. I show you how to hide the database design in the section called "Replacing and Refreshing Designs," later in the chapter. Note that you can also hide some design elements without hiding the entire database design. See Figure 12.11 for an example of the Design tab.

The first two check boxes within the Design tab enable you to control whether this database inherits design information from other databases and whether this database can be used as a template for other databases. Normally, if you make a database a template, you should use the .NTF extension and remove all user data from the database. The .NTF extension is not required to make a database a template (the only requirement is to check the Database is a template check box). However, you should follow the NTF naming convention so that when you deal with the databases from the operating system, you will know which databases are templates and which are not. You can make a template appear only in the advanced template list by checking the List as advanced template in New Database dialog check box.

The List in Database Catalog option enables you to control whether this database is listed in the catalog accessible to users. This makes it easier for users to find information about this database. The Show in Open Database dialog is another option to make it easier for users to find the database. While you are developing the database and before it is ready for production, you should leave this option unchecked. This will ensure that users don't accidentally open the database before you are ready. When it becomes ready for production, check this box and users will be able to see the database in the Open Database dialog box.

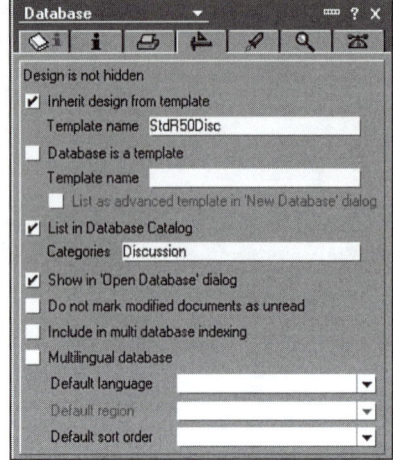

Figure 12.11
The Design tab shows you template, catalog, indexing, and language options for a database.

Do not mark modified documents as unread enables you to control unread marks for this database. Include in multi database indexing is an important option. You need to enable this option if you are using the multidatabase index template. In that template, you list the databases you want to appear in the multidatabase index. However, if this check box is not enabled, the database will not be indexed. It can be very confusing to set up the multiple database index and find that the databases you specified are not being indexed.

Domino R5 enables you to have multiple national languages associated with a database. The final options on the Design tab enable you to indicate a multilingual database and the default language.

Database Launch

The database Launch tab controls what the user sees when the database is opened. Normally, you want to display the About document the first time the database is opened. This gives the user a summary of the purpose and usage of the database. On subsequent opens, you can set it up to restore the last view of the user, or to always open to a particular frameset or navigator.

For Web usage, you can use the same options as for Notes, or you can specify the launching of a doclink contained in the About document. You have quite a bit of control over the initial page or frameset of the user.

Database Full Text Indexing

A user can search a database whether or not it is full text–indexed. However, if the database does contain a full text index the search will be much, much quicker. This is a traditional trade-off between the additional resources required versus a performance improvement for searching. If you create a full text index, additional disk space is used, and additional CPU time is required to keep the index up to date.

Databases are not full text–indexed by default. Good candidates for indexing are databases that are frequently used, are frequently searched, or do not change much. In fact, the Domino Help databases fit this category. You might consider indexing the Help databases, especially if they are frequently used within your organization.

When you index a database, you can specify whether you want case sensitivity (normally you do not), whether you want to index attachments or encrypted fields (this is up to you), or whether to exclude words in the Stop Word file (normally, you do want this). The Stop Word file is a listing of common words, (such as *a*, *the*, *and*, and so forth) that should not be indexed.

Database Advanced Properties

The advanced database properties are primarily performance improvements. You can control whether you want Domino to maintain unread marks or the LastAccessed property. You can also specify whether you want free space to be overwritten within the database, and you can disable transaction logging.

The advanced options are essentially the same as the options available in the advanced button when you are first creating a database. See the section titled "Creating a Database from a Template," earlier in this chapter, for details on each of the options.

Replacing and Refreshing Designs

After you have created and designed your database, how do you manage changes and updates to the design? You can use either the replacement or refreshing of designs. Refreshing is the easier concept because it involves updating a database design from the template that was used to create it. You first make and test the changes, update the template, and then refresh the design from the updated template. To refresh the design, select Database, Refresh Design from the menus.

> **Note**
>
> In addition to the capability of manually refreshing the database design, Domino has the capability of automatically refreshing designs. A task called `Design` runs on the Domino server during the night and will automatically refresh databases with designs from associated templates that have been updated. Only databases located on the server will be updated.

In order to understand design replacement, remember that there are basically two kinds of information in a Domino database: design elements and user documents. Replacing the design essentially means leaving the user documents, but replacing the entire set of design elements with a new set. Why would you do this? A common example might be to update or upgrade the mail database template. In this case, you want to leave all the mail messages, but add additional functionality to the mail database.

To replace a database design, perform the following steps:

1. First, right-click on the database in the bookmark area. From the menu, select Database, Replace Design. You will see a dialog box similar to Figure 12.12.

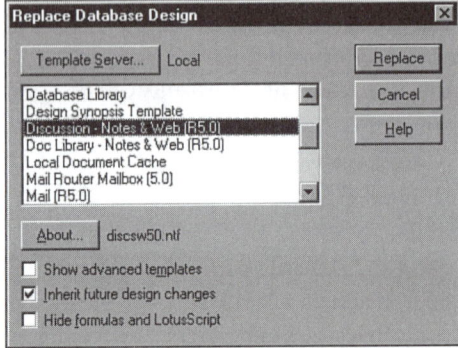

Figure 12.12
The Replace Database Design dialog box enables you to replace all design elements and hide the design.

Click the Template Server button and select the server where the new template resides. Select the Show Advanced templates check box if you want an advanced template.

The Inherit future design changes check box will cause future design changes in the template to propagate to the current database. See the previous section entitled "Creating a Database from a Template" for more information on this option.

3. If you want to completely hide the design in the target database so that it can never be edited again, select the Hide formulas and LotusScript check box.

> **Caution**
>
> If you select the Hide formulas and LotusScript check box, the target database design can no longer be edited. This option is normally used only by third-party developers or if strict security of the database design is required. If you use this option, it is very important to keep an unhidden design version also. The best way to use this feature is to have two templates, one unhidden and one hidden. You modify and update the unhidden template and then replace the design of the hidden template (with this check box set); then you refresh the hidden design into the real databases with data.
>
> You should also be aware that after a database has a hidden design, you can no longer update the server specification within agents. If you need to update the agent server at runtime, you need to write formula or LotusScript code.

4. Click the Replace button.

From Here...

In this chapter, I told you about Domino databases. I covered the ways you can create them, the kind of information they hold, how to control access to them, and information about database properties. Domino databases hold documents, design elements, and programs. In many ways, a Domino database can be viewed as an application, not just a database.

The easiest way to create a Domino database is to use a template. This copies design elements into your new database so you don't have to create them from scratch. You also can make a copy of a database or a replica copy, which enables replication. Starting from a blank database gives you the most freedom to create a new database masterpiece, but involves the most work.

After you create your database, you can modify many of the database properties for security or performance reasons. When you have changes to make to a database, you can update the database directly, or you can update a template and propagate the changes to several databases at once.

You can learn more details about specific topics in the following chapters:

- Chapter 13, "The Integrated Development Environment (IDE)," provides you with an introduction to developing your own databases. Learning how to use the IDE is the first step.

- Chapter 14, "Designing Pages, Forms, and Subforms," continues the discussion of database development. It shows you how to use these important design elements to provide a user interface for your application.

- Chapter 15, "Developing Views and Folders," shows you how to create document lists called views and folders that can act as a summary for the documents in your database.

- Chapter 17, "Access Control Lists (ACLs) and Application Security," goes into much greater depth on database security. You'll learn how to use ACLs to secure your database to let the good guys in and keep the bad guys out.

CHAPTER 13

THE INTEGRATED DEVELOPMENT ENVIRONMENT (IDE)

If you are familiar with a previous release of Notes and Domino, you will immediately see that the Domino Designer IDE has been updated significantly. The main objective of the newly designed environment is that it can be used by two distinct user groups: designers familiar with the original Notes designer interface and designers familiar with existing third-party Web development tools.

The new designer interface makes it easy to develop Web pages using native HTML or by using traditional Notes and Domino design elements. People familiar with tools such as NetObjects Fusion or Microsoft FrontPage should be able to learn quickly and begin to develop pages using the Domino Designer.

This chapter is meant to be an overview of the Domino Designer. It will provide you with an introduction to the various parts of the Designer and how to use them. I'll cover the various different types of design elements you can use. Later chapters in this part will cover each of the major design element types in more detail.

STARTING THE DOMINO DESIGNER

In previous releases of Notes, the Domino Designer was a part of the client user interface. Starting with release 5, the Domino Designer is a separate executable program. You can start the Designer directly from your operating system. For example, in Windows, you can select the program from your Start button, or by clicking an icon if you have placed one on your desktop.

You can also start the Designer by clicking the Domino Designer icon in the regular Notes client. The Domino Designer icon is one of the new navigation icons located in the bookmarks section of the regular Notes client. See Figure 13.1.

Figure 13.1
The Domino Designer icon appears in the regular Notes client.

Note that if you do not have the Domino Designer client installed, the icon will not appear. After you launch the Designer client, you will notice that it appears in a window that is separate from the Notes client. You can have both windows open at once, and if you also have the administration client installed, it is even possible to have all three client windows opened at once.

Another way to open the Designer is to open a database in the regular Notes client, and then select View, Design from the menus. At this point, the Designer client will be launched if it is not already running. If you have previously developed Notes and Domino applications, this method is already familiar to you. It seems a little strange at first when a menu option launches a completely separate application, but this enables you to immediately start working with the new designer. You launch it in a way that is very familiar, and you can later start to launch it as a separate application if you choose.

THE DOMINO DESIGNER WINDOW

After the Designer client is launched, you see the welcome screen for the Designer. From this window, you can either create a new database or you can open an existing database. Creating a database was covered in Chapter 12, "Creating and Accessing Domino Databases." If you open a new database, you will see a display similar to Figure 13.2.

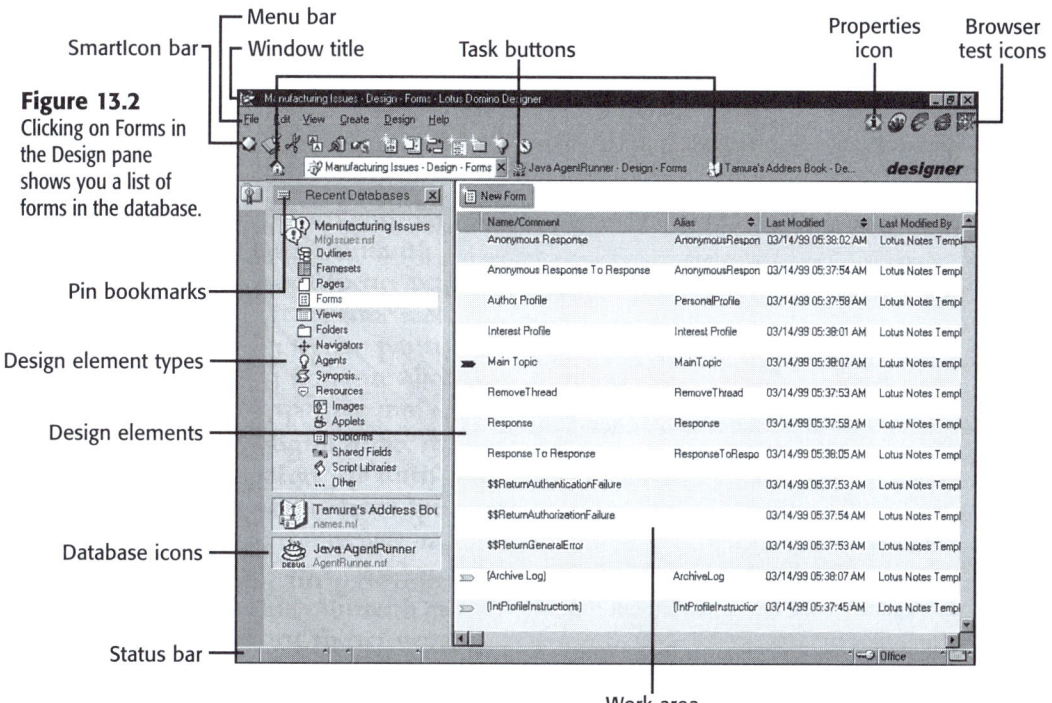

Figure 13.2
Clicking on Forms in the Design pane shows you a list of forms in the database.

Notice that you can have several databases open at once in the Designer. Domino Designer keeps track of the most recently used databases and makes them easily available to you.

In Figure 13.2, you can see the various parts of the Domino designer window. This window is similar in many respects to the Notes client, but there are some subtle differences.

The top line contains the window title, just as in the Notes client. As you change your context by clicking on the various design elements in the Design pane, you see the window title change. It includes the name of the database and the design element type you are viewing.

The menu bar appears just below the window title. The menu bar is context-sensitive, so as you change from one design element type to another, the menus will change. Most of the elements will contain the following menu items: File, Edit, View, Create, Design, and Help. To the right of the menu bar, you see icons that are useful for testing your database. These icons are different than the ones that appear in the regular Notes client. In the regular Notes client, this area contains the Universal Navigation icons. In the Domino Designer, this area contains the Properties icon followed by icons for previewing your design. You will normally see at least the Properties, Notes Preview, and Domino Preview icons. Following these three, you may optionally see the Microsoft Internet Explorer Preview icon and/or the Netscape Navigator Preview icon. In Figure 13.2, both the IE and Navigator icons are shown.

Also in Figure 13.2, you see the SmartIcon bar below the menu bar. By default, the SmartIcon bar is turned off, but I have turned it on to illustrate the parts of the screen. The left side of this bar contains the Universal SmartIcons, and the right side is context-sensitive and contains SmartIcons useful for design tasks. For example, there are icons for creating forms and views. To turn the SmartIcons on or off and to modify the icons on the left side of the bar, you can select File, Preferences, SmartIcons from the menu.

Below the SmartIcon bar, you see the task buttons. These buttons enable you to switch from one open window to another. Each time you open a new design element, a new task button appears. You can easily switch from one element to another by clicking its task button. You can even design within several databases at the same time. This is a very useful feature, because it is now much easier to review and copy design elements from one database to another. You just open the design element of the first database, copy it to the Clipboard, click on the second database, and then paste. To close a window, click on the X that appears to the right of the name.

At the far left is a column of bookmarks. In Figure 13.2, there is only one icon in the bookmarks column. The Design pane is immediately to the right of the bookmarks. The regular Notes client does not contain a Design pane. When the Design pane is open, it displays the most recently used databases and all the different types of design elements within each one. If you prefer to leave the Design pane open while you work, you can click on the small rectangular icon in the upper-left corner of the Design pane, then check the Pin Bookmarks On Screen option. This leaves the Design pane open. With this option enabled, when you close and reopen the Design pane, it stays open. If you disable this option after each use of the Design pane, it automatically closes again.

At the bottom of the screen is the status bar, which gives you current information about the status of your session. This is the same status bar that appears in the Notes client.

The large main area on the right of the screen is called the Work pane. The contents of this pane change as your context changes. It can contain a list of design elements, or it can contain the work area for a particular element that you are editing.

THE DESIGN ELEMENTS

The Design pane of Figure 13.2 shows you the types of design elements that are available to you. Many of these design elements may be familiar to you from previous releases of Notes and Domino. There are also some new design elements, such as outlines, framesets, pages, images, and applets. The purpose of these new design elements is to make it easier for you to develop applications for your intranet or your Internet Web site.

When you click on a design element type in the Design pane on the left, the Work pane on the right shows you a view containing the actual elements of that type stored in your database. For example, in Figure 13.2, Forms has been chosen on the left, and on the right is the list of forms in the database. Notice that the format of the right pane is very similar to a regular Notes view. In this case, you can see the name of the design element with an optional comment, an optional alias, and information about the time of last modification, with the name of the user who last modified the element.

If you double-click on the name of an actual design element in the Work pane on the right, the selected design element is placed in edit mode. Here is the list of design elements you can use.

- **Outlines** Outlines are a new design element in release 5. Outlines are essentially high-level navigation tools. In Web site design terminology, an outline is similar to a site map or the navigational elements that frequently appear at the left of a Web page. In Notes/Domino terminology, you can think of an outline as a way to program the traditional Navigation pane. This is the pane that normally lists all the views of a database.

- **Framesets** Frames are the Web terminology for panes in Notes. Although in previous releases of Notes, the end user could manipulate the panes to a small degree, the database designer could not easily create panes or frames to control the user experience. Framesets are layouts that are used to control the display of multiple frames to the user.

- **Pages** Pages are very familiar to Web designers. Pages contain the main information to be displayed to the end user. Of course, pages can be very complex if they include sophisticated HTML or JavaScript or invoke Java applets. If you have a Domino background, pages are similar to a Domino form. The main difference is that pages cannot contain Domino fields. They can contain HTML INPUT fields.

- **Forms** Forms are a part of the traditional Notes/Domino system. A form is a visual template through which you view a document. This template typically contains static information as well as field definitions. Information from a document is extracted and displayed in the field locations on the form and then rendered to the display.

- **Views** Views enable you to see a tabular summary of information from many documents at once. With a formula, you can select the documents you want to see in the view. The view columns typically extract information from the documents in the database.
- **Folders** Folders are very similar to views. They present data in a tabular format. The major difference is that in a view the documents are selected by a formula, whereas in a folder the documents can be any arbitrary collection. Folders are typically used by an end user to organize documents in a database.
- **Navigators** Navigators were introduced in release 4 of Notes and Domino to provide users with a graphical method for navigating through a database. If the Designer includes a navigator with various links to a database, the user can just click on an area of the navigator. The major function of a navigator can now also be accomplished with an outline or page design element.
- **Agents** Agents are small programs that are associated with a database and can be run automatically or under user control. They can be written in LotusScript, Java, or formula language, and they can be run on either the Domino server or the Notes client.

Below the Agents design element, you can see the word Synopsis. This is not actually a design element. By clicking on this word, you can obtain a synopsis, or summary, of all the design elements used within your database. So, it is actually a command rather than a design element. The reason it is located within the list of design element types is so that it is readily accessible, no matter what editing task you are performing.

The following design elements can be found within the Resources twistie with the other design elements. These resources represent items that can be shared within the database.

- **Images** Image Resources are a new feature of release 5 and enable you to store images once and reuse them throughout your database. You give each image a name and can then reference the image from other design elements, such as pages, forms, and subforms. Domino supports industry standard formats, such as GIF, BMP, and JPEG.
- **Applets** Java applets are small programs written in Java that execute within the browser environment, including the Notes client. The shared applets feature of the Domino Designer enables you to save a Java applet in a central location in the database, give the applet a name, and then reuse it throughout the database. In release 5, with Java and CORBA support, there are now mechanisms to enable Java applets in Web browsers to access the Domino Object Model on the server.
- **Subforms** Subforms are similar to forms in almost all major respects. The difference is that a subform may be reused by incorporating it on several different forms. A subform may not be used by itself. Typical uses for subforms include headers and other information that you would like to reuse for consistency across multiple forms. You can also conditionally include different subforms within a form, depending upon context.
- **Shared Fields** Shared fields are field definitions with attributes such as font, size, data type, and formulas that can be shared across multiple Domino forms. By using shared

fields, you can implement consistency in visual design and formula programming across several forms.

- Script Libraries   You can use Script libraries to share common LotusScript or Java code. Code that is stored within a Script library can be used throughout a database.
- Shared Actions (within the Other section)   Actions are small programs that are typically used in forms and views. Actions can be invoked by the user by clicking an action button or from the menus. Either or both of these options are enabled by the Designer. I'll now provide you a summary of the various design elements of Domino Designer release 5. Each of these elements is covered in more detail in later chapters, but this chapter gives you an overview of the various elements.

OUTLINES

If you double-click on the name of a design element in the Work pane on the right, you enter edit mode on the element (see Figure 13.3).

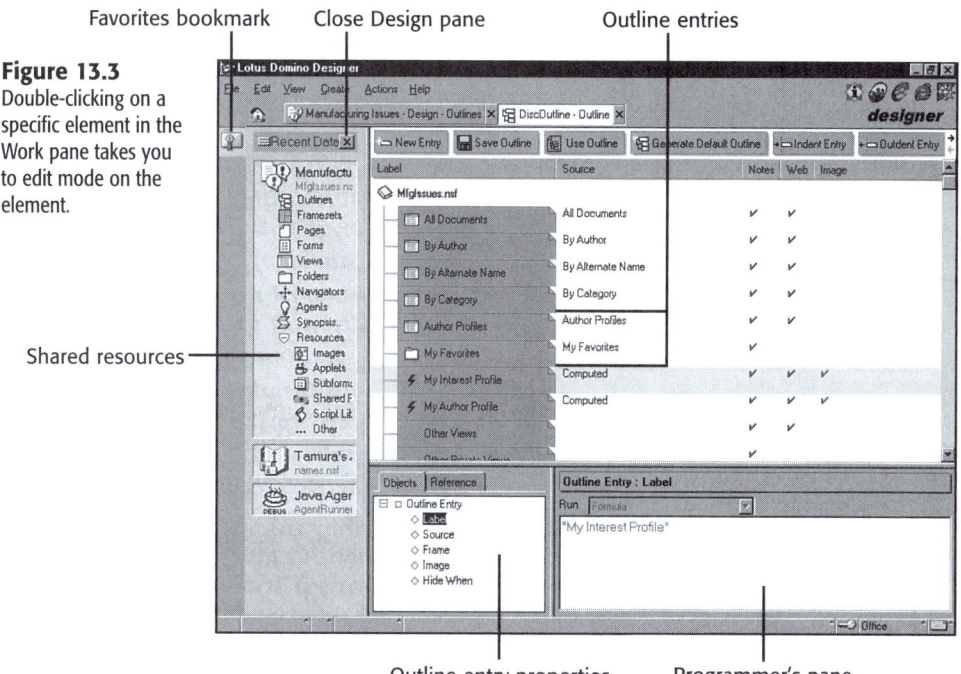

Figure 13.3
Double-clicking on a specific element in the Work pane takes you to edit mode on the element.

In Figure 13.3, you see the design environment for outlines. The screen layout in the Work pane of each of the different design elements (such as outlines, framesets, pages, forms, and so forth) is different, but the outline layout is fairly typical.

To the right of the Design pane, the window layout is a three-pane view. The work area for outlines is in the top pane. The bottom pane is called the Programmer's pane and includes two parts. On the left is typically an area where you can see your object list and reference material. In the right of the Programmer's pane, you can usually enter information that affects the design element.

The action buttons, just below the task buttons, show you the actions you can take with the current design element type. For outlines, you can create new entries, save the outline, use (embed) an outline on a page, generate a default outline, and control indentation of the outline entries. In Figure 13.3, you can see there are several outline entries. They begin with the following: All Documents, By Author, By Alternate Name, and By Category.

For each outline entry, you can determine whether the entry applies to the Notes client, a Web client, or both by looking at the check marks to the right of each outline entry. You can also supply a small image to replace the little icon that appears next to the outline entry label.

In the InfoList pane in the left half of the Programmer's pane, you can see all the properties and methods of the object. For example, in Figure 13.3, you can see all the properties of an outline entry. In this case, there are five properties of an outline entry: Label, Source, Frame, Image, and Hide When.

To modify a property for an entry, first select the entry in the upper pane, and then select the property on the left in the Programmer's pane. On the right, you can enter a definition for the property.

I cover outlines in more detail in Chapter 16, "Using Outlines, Framesets, and Navigators."

FRAMESETS

Framesets are a new feature of release 5 of Notes and Domino. Figure 13.4 shows the frameset designer. I have hidden the Design pane in this case, because when you are designing frames, it is usually easier to work if you have as much screen real estate as possible.

Notice that with the frameset designer, you can add and delete frames, move frame borders, and change the contents of each frame. In Figure 13.4, there are actually four frames defined, three on the left and one on the right. The middle frame on the left is highlighted. You can see in the properties box that the contents of this middle frame on the left is a page called MasterDiscOutline. This page contains an outline control, and when the user selects one of the items from the outline on the page, the default target is the right frame. The right frame is called NotesView, and the target is specified at the bottom of the properties box.

I cover framesets in more detail in Chapter 16.

THE DESIGN ELEMENTS | 289

Figure 13.4
You can design the layout of your frames with the frameset designer.

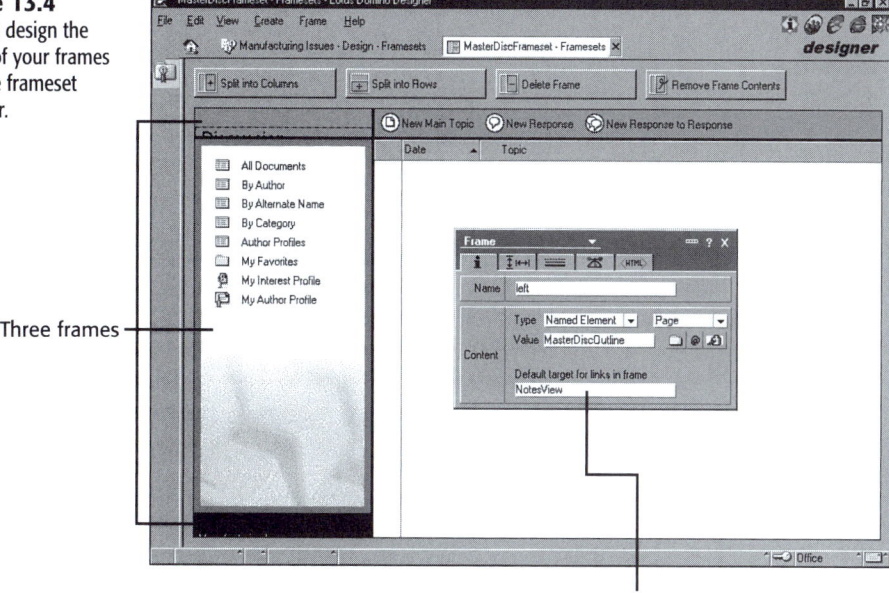

Three frames

NotesView frame

PAGES

Pages in Domino Designer are a new design element (see Figure 13.5). If you are familiar with other Web design tools, pages are easy to understand. If you are coming from a Notes/Domino background, pages seem a little bit like a simplified form. First, like a form, you can use certain design elements. For example, you can insert horizontal rules, sections, hotspots, tables, pictures, navigators, and several other elements. However, you cannot add fields to a page. A page can be useful as a container for an embedded view. Remember, however, that you do not create documents via pages, and pages will not appear in any view. Also, any content that you place on a page will not be full text–indexed or searched because it is a design element, not a document.

Figure 13.5 shows you a page from a Help file. Normally, you want to use standard documents and forms, but with the page capability, you can perform special processing on a single page if you need it. Remember that pages are not full text–indexed. In this case, the Help database uses a page for the welcome page, which typically is not needed in a search. When you define a page, you can use the Domino Designer rich text editor to edit the page in a WYSIWYG manner. You can change fonts and make text bold. In addition, you can also edit the page as if it were HTML text. By opening the page properties box and checking the Treat page contents as HTML box, you can add HTML markup directly to the page. As you can see from Figure 13.5, Domino also supports JavaScript, and you can define JavaScript processing with the Designer.

PART
III
CH
13

290 Chapter 13 The Integrated Development Environment (IDE)

Figure 13.5
You can define rich text and hotspots on pages.

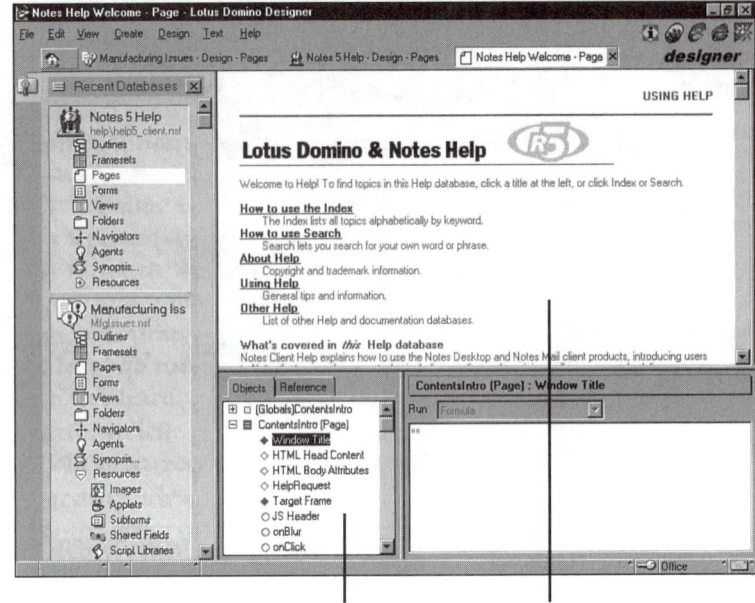

JavaScript events   Page being edited

> **Tip**
> You should be careful when using both fonts and colors. When your page is displayed on the Web by a user's Web browser, you have no control over the level of software, the fonts installed on the user's machine, or the capabilities of the user's display adapter. You should try not to use fancy fonts or extreme colors. One trick you can use to allow the display of an arbitrary font is to render the font into a bitmap. Then you can display the bitmap image. By implementing fonts this way, the user does not have to have any particular fonts loaded.

I cover pages and how to use them in more detail in Chapter 14, "Designing Pages, Forms, and Subforms."

Forms and Subforms

Forms are like visual templates that can be used to display documents. Documents in Notes and Domino are the fundamental data structure. Nearly all data in Notes and Domino is stored in a document within a database. Even design elements are stored in special documents within the database.

A document stores information by name in items. Each item can hold one or more values, but usually each item stores a single value. The values can be text or numeric. Each item within a document has a name, so you can retrieve the value by name.

In Figure 13.6, you can see a Domino form being edited in the middle of the screen. In the form, you can see that there are several fields, each with a box surrounding the field name.

This form displays documents by associating field names in the form with item names in the document. Whenever there is an item in the document with the same name as the field, the value of the item is displayed.

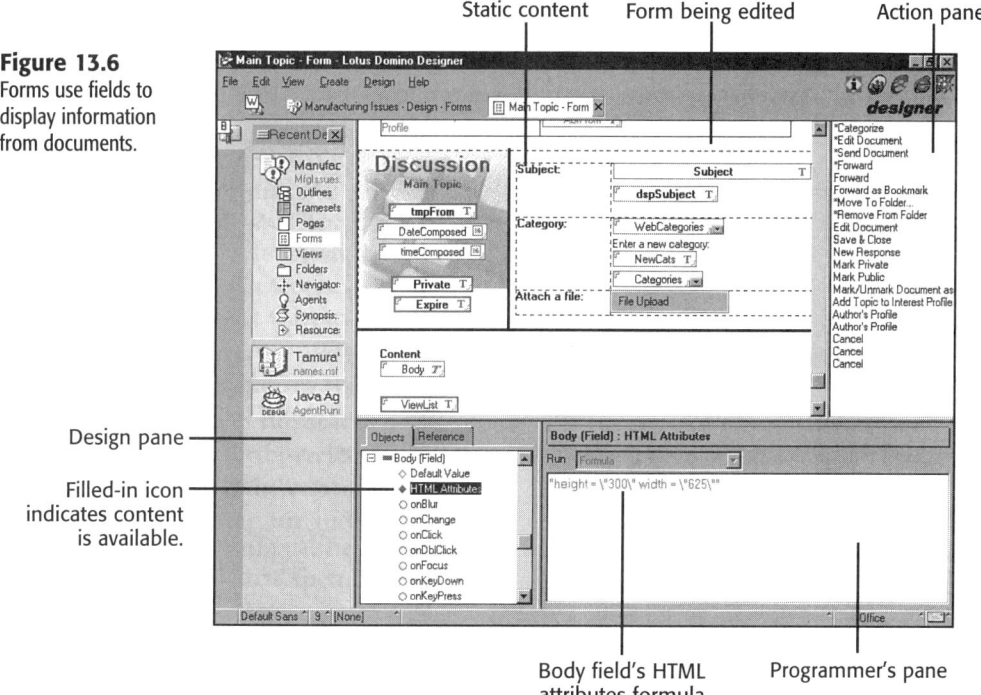

Figure 13.6
Forms use fields to display information from documents.

While you are editing the form, you can see static information and the various fields that have been defined for the form. For example, in Figure 13.6, you see the static text Subject: and Category:. Note that there is also a field called Subject. You can tell the difference because field names are those with a box surrounding them, such as DateComposed, WebCategories, and NewCats. The icon to the right of the name signifies the type of the data field. For example, the little 16 within a calendar means that it is a date field, so DateComposed will display a date. WebCategories has a little down arrow, which indicates that it is a drop-down list. NewCats as well as the Subject field both have a *T*, which indicates that they are text fields. A rich text field is symbolized by an italic *T*. As you work with the Designer, you will learn the symbols, which are very useful. I would like to point out a few aspects of the Designer windows in Figure 13.6. You'll notice that on the right side of the form an extra pane is shown. This pane is called the Action pane and contains a list of the actions that have been defined for this form. Actions can be displayed either as action buttons or in the Action menu, or both. When you highlight an action in the Action pane, it is selected in the object window of the Design pane at the bottom of the screen. You can supply a program that will execute when a user activates an action.

The left side of the Programmer's pane at the bottom displays the objects available within the form. There is a global object, the form object, field objects, embedded objects, and actions within the form. Each object typically has methods and properties. You can see in Figure 13.6 that the Body field has extra HTML attributes defined. These attributes are displayed in the right half of the Programmer's pane and will be used with an HTML client.

> **Tip**
>
> One great new feature the Programmer's pane offers is the capability of seeing whether a property or method contains a definition. In previous versions of Notes and Domino, you had to pull down a list box and then open an element to find out whether there was anything defined. Usually, there wasn't anything defined and it caused wasted effort. Now, the icon for a property is filled in when there is a definition. You can see at a glance the properties and methods that have a definition, and you can go directly to them to find out what they do.

You edit Subforms just as you edit forms. The major difference between forms and subforms is that subforms may be referenced from several different forms in the database. The subforms design element type is found within the resources area in the Design pane. I cover both forms and subforms in more detail in Chapter 14.

Views and Folders

Views are used to display summary information from documents (see Figure 13.7). Just as a form displays a single document to the user, a view displays information from a set of documents. Typically, each row of a view is information extracted from a single document, so if there are 20 rows displayed, they represent 20 different documents.

In Figure 13.7, you can see the Designer panes for editing views. The main Work pane shows the view itself, and just to the right you can see the Action pane. The Action pane shows the view actions available and is similar to the form Action pane. The Programmer pane at the bottom shows the objects on the left and the definitions on the right. In Figure 13.7, you can see that the value to be displayed in the Topic column is calculated using a formula. You can use simple functions, document fields, or formulas for displaying information in views. You can find more information about using formulas in Chapter 18, "Working with Formulas, Functions, and Commands."

In Figure 13.7, in the left side of the Programmer's pane, you can see that there is a second tab next to the Objects tab. This tab is for reference information. If you click the Reference tab, you can find the names of all of the fields stored in the database, along with reference information for @formulas and @commands. I cover views and folders in more detail in Chapter 15, "Developing Views and Folders."

The Design Elements

Figure 13.7
You can control many aspects about the design of your views.

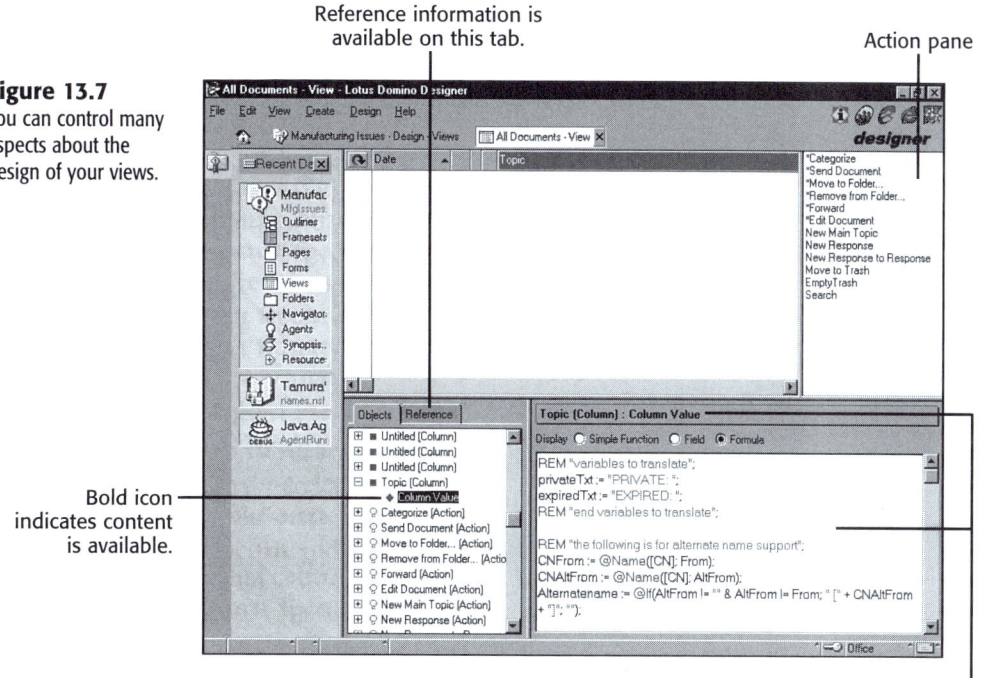

Navigators

Navigators were introduced in release 4 of Notes and Domino. In some ways, they were a precursor to the current Page concept. You can add graphic elements to navigators, provide links to multiple different locations, and use them to provide an attractive user interface. There are several reasons why you might want to use navigators.

First, you may already have navigators within your database, so they are provided in release 5 for compatibility with release 4.x. Second, navigators provide you an opportunity to use a simple set of graphic editing tools, which a page element does not provide. If you want to create graphic elements with associated hotspot links, navigators are a good choice. Third, you may now embed a navigator within a page, so you can get the best of both worlds. You can use page editing as well as navigators on the same page, but remember that the page will be accessible only to the Notes client.

I cover navigators in more detail in Chapter 16.

Agents

An agent is a program that is contained in a Domino database (see Figure 13.8). It can be written in LotusScript, Java, formula language, or it can be a simple action entered from a dialog box. An agent can be triggered to run in several ways. It can be triggered to run when certain events occur, at specific time intervals, or manually by a user.

294 | Chapter 13 The Integrated Development Environment (IDE)

Figure 13.8
Agents can be written in Java (shown here), LotusScript, formula language, or in simple actions.

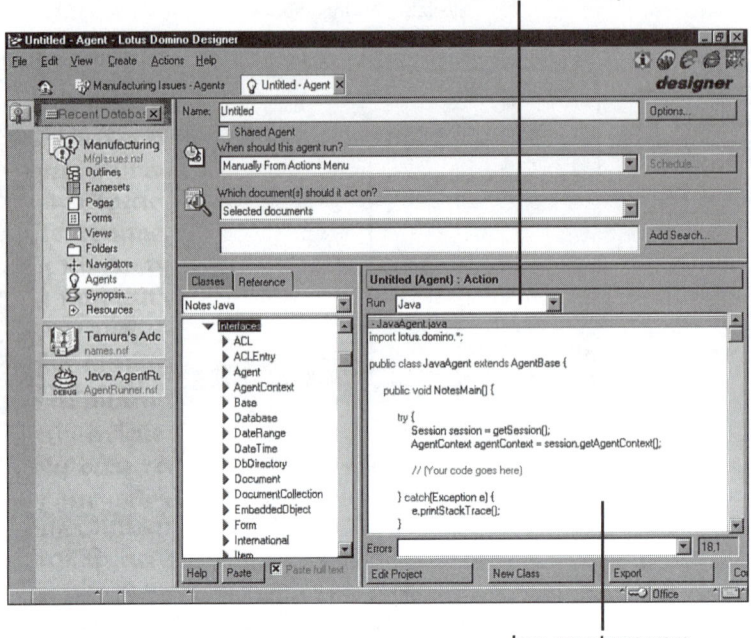

In Figure 13.8, you can see the Domino Designer panes for agents. At the top half of the work area window you see the name of the agent and whether the agent is shared or private. You also specify the triggering mechanism for this agent, which can be a time interval or an event, such as a new document being created within the database.

When the agent is run, it can access a set of documents that are applicable. For example, if the agent is triggered when a new document is pasted, the pasted document is available. If the agent is run on a schedule, such as hourly, the documents can either be the new and modified documents or the complete set of all documents in the database. You can even add more complex search criteria, if needed by your agent.

The Programmer's pane below includes two parts. In the right part, you can now write your agents in Java, as shown. Reference information can be shown on the left. In this section for Java, you find information for both the Domino Object Model (DOM) classes as well as the core Java classes (such as `java.awt`, `java.lang`, and so forth). If you explore the reference material and you find a method you want to use, you can double-click on it and it will be transferred into the Design pane programming area. I cover Java programming in more detail in Chapter 23, "Creating and Using Java Applets and Agents."

Resources

There are five major types of resources within the Resources twistie and five additional types of resources contained in the Other category. The five major types are Images,

Applets, Subforms, Shared Fields, and Script Libraries. Of these five types, Images and Applets are new shared resources in release 5 of Domino. I've already discussed subforms, so in the next few sections, I cover Images, Applets, Shared Fields, and Script Libraries.

IMAGES

Image resources enable you to import an image that will be used in several places on your Web site and store them only once in your database. You can give your resources a name, as shown in Figure 13.9, and then reference the image name from other parts of your database.

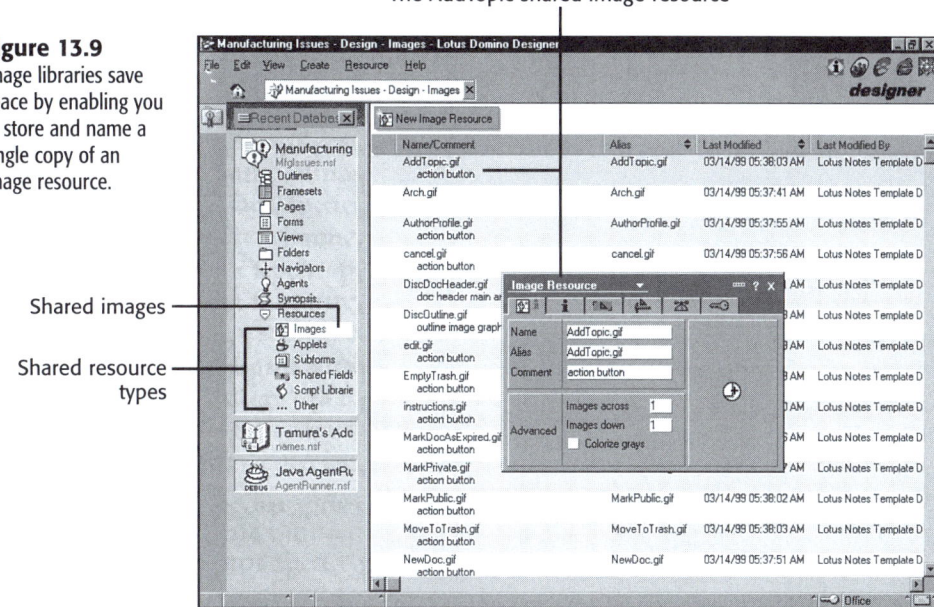

Figure 13.9
Image libraries save space by enabling you to store and name a single copy of an image resource.

Image resources are valuable for storing logos, headers, or other graphics that you want to display on several pages throughout your site. In addition, you store multiple images within one image resource. This saves additional overhead if you have a group of related images.

APPLETS

Applets are Java programs that are downloaded from a server and executed within a Web browser. Here are the typical steps in applet development and execution:

1. The applet is developed in the Java language within a Java development environment, such as IBM Visual Age for Java, Borland JBuilder, NetObjects Bean Builder, Symantec Visual Café, or Microsoft Visual J++.

> **Note**
> If you use Microsoft Visual J++, you may have some difficulties, depending upon the version you use. Prior to a court decree, Microsoft was using some nonstandard calling conventions for Java. Microsoft has recently released a version of Visual J++ that complies with Sun Microsystems' Java Native Interface (JNI) definition. If you use Visual J++, be sure to carefully test your Java applets for compatibility.

2. The applet is compiled in the development environment to create a set of class files. Class files are similar to compiler object code. They are binary files that define machine operations. The class files, however, are machine-independent. They are read and operate within a virtual machine called the Java Virtual Machine or JVM. All the major Web browsers include a JVM. The JVM is the component that enforces security by disallowing the Java program from accessing system resources, such as the file system.
3. Class files are grouped in an archive file that can be of type ZIP, JAR, or CAB. These formats store a collection of files in a compressed format.
4. The archive files are stored in a directory or within a Domino database in a location where the Web server can find them.
5. A Web page is developed that references the applet via special HTML tags. The tags specify the applet name and any parameters required by the applet.
6. When a user is viewing the Web page that references the Java applet, the applet class files are sent from the server to the Web client and are loaded into the Web browser's JVM for execution.
7. The applet runs either continuously or to completion within the JVM.

Notice the difference between agents and applets. Domino Agents may be written in any of several languages, including Java, LotusScript, formula language, or simple actions. Applets may be written only in Java. Agents can be triggered on a scheduled basis or when documents arrive in a database. Agents can run on either the Notes client or the server, but cannot run in a non-Notes Web browser. Applets are triggered via HTML tags and run only on the client. Applets can run in either a Web browser or the Notes client, but not on the server.

You can develop agents in Java within the Domino Designer, but the Designer does not contain facilities for developing applets. You must use another third-party tool to develop applets. After they have been created, you can import the Java applet class files into your database. I cover applets in more detail in Chapter 23, "Creating and Using Java Applets and Agents."

SHARED FIELDS

A Domino field is defined in the context of a form. Pages cannot contain fields. Fields are used for data input and display. They may contain formatting information, such as the font, size, whether it is bold, formula definitions, and so forth.

Normally, each form contains the definition of the fields it contains. However, you may have an application where certain fields are displayed on several separate forms within an application. Some common examples might be a Name, document creation date, or other user information.

Shared fields enable you to define common attributes of a field and then share the definitions across multiple forms. For example, suppose you want to define a Name field that uses an Arial, Bold, 14-point font. You want this field definition to be used on all forms that display the Name. You can create a shared field, and then just refer to this field on all of your forms. Another example is if you have a field that has complex input validation requirements. You can program the validation formula once, share the field, and then any time the field is used, the validation formula will always be the same.

Script Libraries

Script libraries enable you to store subroutines that are used throughout your database. You can create either LotusScript or JavaScript libraries, but you cannot mix LotusScript and Java types within the library. You may, however, have two or more separate script libraries, so you can have one or more of each type. You give each script library a separate name.

After you create a script library, you can add subroutines to the library and then reference them from other locations in your database.

From Here...

In this chapter, I showed you how to invoke the Domino Designer. This program is now separate from the Notes client. You can either invoke the executable module directly from your desktop or from within the Notes client.

After you start the Designer, there are many different types of design elements available for your use. Some of the new elements in release 5 include outlines, framesets, and pages. You can use these elements to create a Web site without even using the original Domino design elements. Of course, if you are familiar with Notes and Domino, you are still free to use the traditional forms and views.

Release 5 enables you to use many different types of shared resources within a database. This cuts down on the amount of storage needed to house a Web site. In addition, by storing all the design elements within a database rather than in the operating system file structure, the elements are more easily managed.

In following chapters, I show you more detail on how to use the design elements to create applications that can be Web-enabled.

In this chapter, I gave you information about how to use the IDE. In addition, I gave you an introduction to some of the major Domino design elements. You can learn more details about the design elements in the following chapters:

- Chapter 14, "Designing Pages, Forms, and Subforms," provides you with detailed information about these major elements, as well as an introduction to HTML, and the usage of tables, fields, layout regions, sections, and much more.

- Chapter 15, "Developing Views and Folders," gives you detailed information on creating views and folders, adding and formatting view columns, sorting and using hidden columns, showing icons in columns, and using views on the Web.

- Chapter 16, "Using Outlines, Framesets, and Navigators," shows you how to use outlines, framesets, and navigators to provide end-user navigational features to your Domino database or Web site. You'll learn about graphic backgrounds and hotspots, and how to link from one page to another.

- Chapter 17, "Access Control Lists (ACLs) and Application Security," shows you how to secure your application with the database ACL. It describes the different levels of access and their capabilities.

- Chapter 18, "Working with Formulas, Functions, and Commands," describes some of the more important @functions and @commands. You use @formulas and @commands to program certain events and elements of your database. It describes some of the more important @functions, such as the text-handling functions, Time and Date functions, and `@DBLookup` and `@DBColumn`, which can be used to look up information to be shown to the user.

- Chapter 19, "Using the IDE with LotusScript, Java, and JavaScript," describes how and when you can program agents, applets, and other programmable elements of your database. The rest of Part IV covers LotusScript, Java, and JavaScript in greater detail.

CHAPTER 14

Designing Pages, Forms, and Subforms

300 | CHAPTER 14 DESIGNING PAGES, FORMS, AND SUBFORMS

In previous releases of Notes and Domino, the major user interface element was the form. A Domino form enables you to place static text and graphic elements together with fields as a template for display to a user. The form is then combined with different document data items, and it is displayed to the end user.

Release 5 of Notes and Domino introduces a new Web development paradigm, the page. Well, not new really. This paradigm is exactly the one used by other Web page development tools and is now available for use within the Domino Designer. Now Domino provides the best of previous releases of Domino with the best of the other Web development tools, and you can mix and match their capabilities.

USING THE PAGE EDITOR

And now, here's something completely different. If you are already familiar with Notes and Domino design, but relatively new to Web design, let me show you how different page development can be from previous releases. To illustrate, first I'll create a new, blank database called Page Design. You can follow along by selecting File, Database, New, and then typing Page Design for the title and filename. You can leave the server Local and the template name "Blank."

CREATING YOUR FIRST PAGE

Open the database you want to use for your page in the Domino Designer and click the Pages design element within the database. Your screen should resemble Figure 14.1.

Figure 14.1
The Domino Designer with the Pages design element selected.

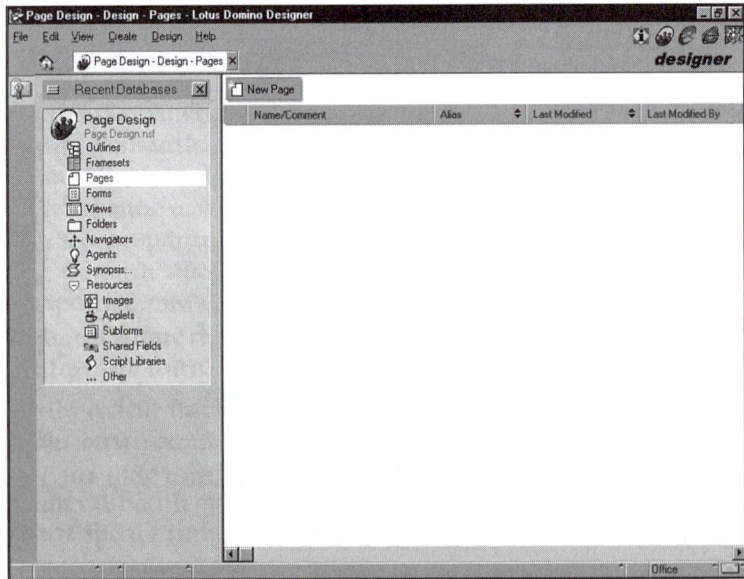

To create a new page:

1. Open the database you want to use for your page.
2. Select the Pages icon in the Bookmarks window.
3. Click the New Page action button. Your new page will appear.

Here is where things get interesting. To follow along with this example, perform the following steps:

1. Open a properties box by clicking the Properties icon in the upper-right area of your screen or by selecting Text, Text Properties. Use the default font (Default Sans Serif) and change the size to 24 points and the style to Bold.
2. Enter Some text on the first line of the page.
3. Skip one line and then select Text, Pass-Thru HTML.
4. Type the following on the page:
   `<h1>This is a Header 1</h1>`

This line uses Hypertext Markup Language (HTML) tags. HTML tags normally have a beginning tag and a matching end tag. In this case, `<h1>` begins the header text and `</h1>` ends it. When you read HTML, a tag preceded by a slash means that it is the closing tag of a pair. Notice that the HTML text has a gray background so that you can differentiate HTML from text entered directly on your page. At this point, your screen should look like Figure 14.2.

Figure 14.2
You can enter some text directly on your page along with some HTML.

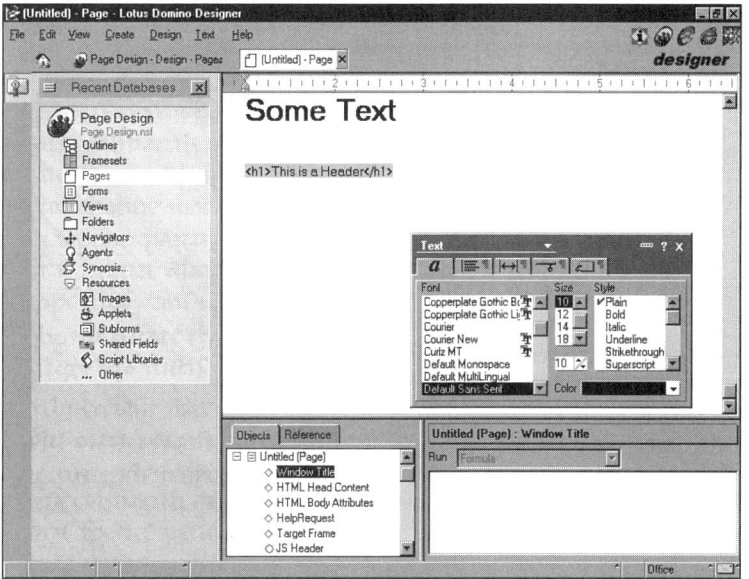

Notice that when you enabled the Pass-Thru HTML, the font automatically changed back to 10-point plain text. This is a good point to test our Web page. The icons in the upper-right part of your screen can be used to invoke a Web browser. If you have Internet Explorer or Netscape Navigator installed (or both) you will see their respective icons. To preview your test page, do the following:

1. Click one of the browser icons to test your Web page. If you prefer, you can also select Design, Preview in Web Browser. At this point, you see a listing of Web browser choices. Choose the Web browser you want to use.

2. You will be prompted for a name for your page. You can name your page anything. I chose PageTest.

3. Click OK and your Web browser should appear. The browser selected by Domino Designer will be whichever browser you have chosen. Look at Figure 14.3.

Figure 14.3
You can preview your page with Internet Explorer (shown) or Netscape Navigator.

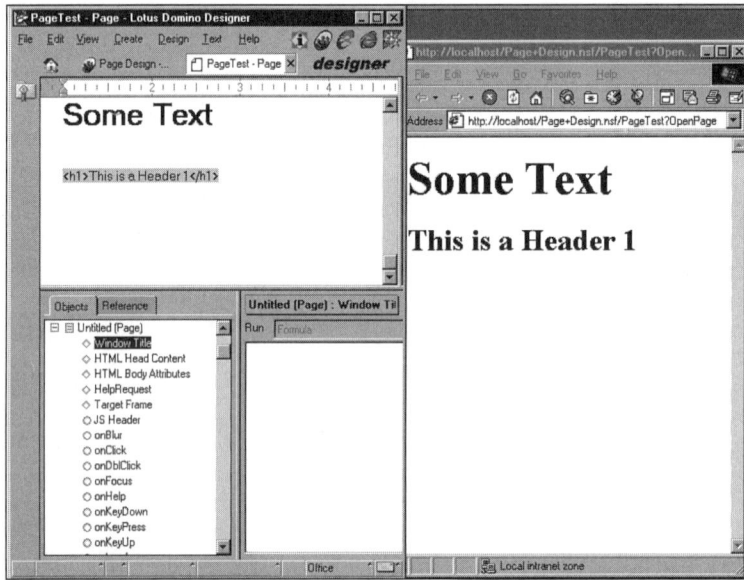

Here are several points to notice about our first Web page:

- The font for `Some Text` doesn't seem right, and the size is large, but slightly different than the source.

- The size for `This is a Header 1` is larger than the input, and the font is also different. Also, the beginning and ending tags are gone.

- You'll notice that the uniform resource locator (URL) address in the browser window includes `localhost`, the database name, the page name, and the command to open the page.

I wanted to show you immediately the importance and convenience of testing your Web page designs with the browser buttons in the upper-right corner of your screen. Now here are some explanations of why our Web page looks different than you might think it should:

- The first line does not appear in the browser as it does in the Designer because fonts in the Designer are not necessarily available to the browser when your page is displayed. Because of this, standard Web fonts have been defined. Because we used the default font (Default Sans Serif), no font information was sent to the Web browser, and the text displays in the default font for the browser, which is Times Roman. Sizes are also standardized, and by default, are not available with fine granularity, so the browser uses an approximation to the size.
- A size is associated by default with the h1 tag, and it is used for the text. There are other heading tags—h2, h3, and so forth—that are defined and use different styles. The font is also associated with the h1 tag, and the default browser font is used again for the h1 tag.

I should note here that with HTML you can control many different aspects of the presentation with cascading style sheets (CSS). This facility of HTML is beyond the scope of this book, however, and if you're interested, you should consult an HTML reference.

As an alternative to using the Pass-Thru HTML text property, you can enclose text within square brackets ([ ]), and it will be treated as Pass-Thru HTML. This makes it very easy and convenient to mix HTML source directly in your page without resorting to menu items all the time. In our example, if we used the bracket syntax, here is how it would look:

```
[<h1>This is a Header 1</h1>]
```

Page Properties

The Basics tab of the Page properties box is shown in Figure 14.4.

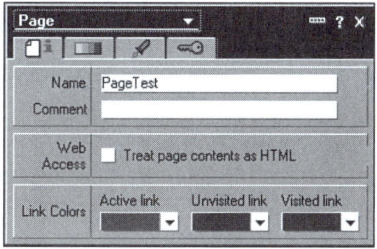

Figure 14.4
You can treat an entire page as HTML.

Notice that you can treat an entire page as HTML. To do so, just check the box titled Treat page contents as HTML. If you check this box, you don't have to include the square brackets because your entire page will be treated as HTML automatically. This is an extremely useful setting if you are new to Domino but you are already familiar with HTML, or if you want to use a separate HTML editing tool and just import your HTML.

I have now shown you three different ways to specify HTML in your page:

- Create text on the page, and then highlight the text and give it the Pass-Thru HTML attribute. You do this on the Text menu. You can mix and match HTML and non-HTML with this method.
- Place square brackets ([ ]) around any text on the page that you want to be considered HTML. You do not have to use the menus. You can mix and match HTML and non-HTML with this method.
- Go to the Page properties box and check the box labeled Treat page contents as HTML. This will treat the entire page contents as HTML. This makes it easier to import text directly from another HTML authoring tool.

In the Page properties dialog box you can also set the colors for the Active link, Unvisited link, and Visited link. Normally, you should just leave these set at the default values.

Pasting and Importing Graphic Backgrounds

To change the graphic background, do the following:

1. Open the Page properties box for the page.
2. Click the Background tab. See Figure 14.5. You can select a background color by opening the drop-down box.
3. Use one of the following methods to obtain a graphic background:
   - You can use another graphics editing program and copy the graphic to the Clipboard. After you have copied the graphic to the Clipboard, go to the Page properties dialog box and click the Paste button.
   - If you want to load an image from a file, click the Import button. You will be prompted and can locate your file.
   - If you have saved your graphic image as an image resource, type in the name or click the folder icon on the Image Resource line. You can specify a formula by clicking the @ symbol.

Figure 14.5
You can set the background color and image with the Page properties box.

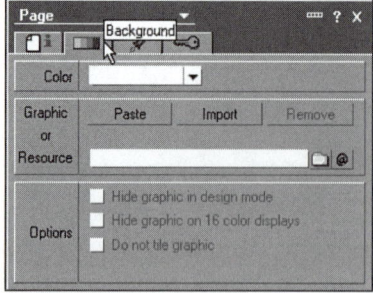

4. (Optional) You can specify that you want to hide the image during design or for 16-color displays. Turning off the image during design makes it easier to edit your page. On 16-color displays, sometimes 256-color (or higher) photos or graphics look more like modern art than an attractive background. This can be distracting to users, so you can turn off the background.

5. (Optional) You can specify that you want to turn off tiling of the graphic background. Normally, by default, graphic backgrounds are tiled.

Basic Hypertext Markup Language (HTML)

There are complete books covering HTML, so there is no way to cover it completely here. However, I'd like to give you a simple introduction on HTML so you can see the syntax and a few features of the language. This should get you started, and you can consult an HTML reference for more detailed information.

Let's start by defining a new test page in your Page Design database. To follow along with this example, perform the following steps:

1. Open your database, click Pages in the Design Pane, and then click the New Page action button.

2. Select File, Document Properties.

3. When the Page properties box appears, enable the Treat page contents as HTML check box and give the page the name `HTMLtest`.

4. In the main page Editing Pane, enter the following:

```
<FORM name="MyForm">
<H1>HTML Test page</H1>
<P>Here is an input field</P>

<INPUT type="text" value="MyDefault" name="MyField">
<A href="http://www.lotus.com">and a link to Lotus</A>
<BR>

<INPUT type="button" value="Hot Button" OnClick="alert('You pushed my hotbutton')">

</FORM>
```

In Figure 14.6, you can see this sample input and the results in both Netscape Navigator and Internet Explorer.

Figure 14.6
HTML input and two browsers showing the output.

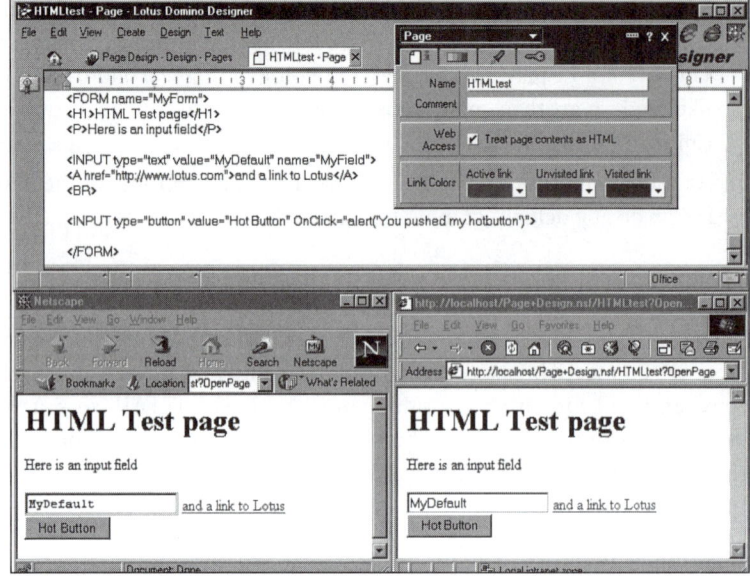

Basic HTML Syntax

HTML is a language that is used to "mark up" text. That is, to add tags around content to define the meaning of the text associated with the tag. The syntax for HTML tags is very simple. In its basic form the syntax is

`<start-tag> element contents </end-tag>`

You can see this simple syntax with the Header 1 `<H1></H1>` pair and the paragraph `<P></P>` pair. Between the start and end tags are the contents of the element. A more complex tag sometimes has attributes. For example, notice the `<FORM>` tag. The syntax using attributes is

`<start-tag attr1="value1" attr2="value2" ... attrn="valuen"> element contents </end-tag>`

In the previous example, the `<FORM>` tag follows this convention by having the name as a parameter. The `<INPUT>` tag also has several attributes associated with it, as shown in the example. In this case, notice that there is no need for a closing `</INPUT>`, although you can include one if you want. Capitalization in the tag names and attribute names is ignored and you can enter them in lower- or uppercase, although by convention, tags and attributes are usually shown in uppercase.

In general, HTML syntax and most browsers are fairly forgiving. By this, I mean that if you make mistakes in your HTML, most of the time you won't get an error message—although you may not get the result you expect, either. In fact, the HTML that I showed you left off some official tags, such as `<HTML>`, `<HEAD>`, and `<BODY>`. Here is the official form for an HTML document:

```
<HTML>
    <HEAD>
        Optional HEAD section tags, such as <TITLE>
    </HEAD>
    <BODY>
        Main body of document
    </BODY>
</HTML>
```

The `<HTML>` tag introduces the following text as being written in HTML. The `<HEAD>` tag is grouped around text that defines the header for the document. This section includes the `<TITLE>` tag, if there is one. As usual, the format for the `<TITLE>` tag is

`<TITLE>Your title here</TITLE>`

The `<BODY>` tag surrounds the main section of HTML. If you are using framesets, the `<FRAMESET>` tag is used instead of the `<BODY>` tag.

As you have seen, both browsers enable you to completely leave off the `<HTML>`, `<HEAD>`, and `<BODY>` tags. I don't necessarily recommend that you use this type of shortcut in HTML. If you don't follow the official rules in HTML, your output may work in some but not other browsers. I showed you this example to explain that browsers in general are pretty forgiving, but you should use careful judgment in assuming anything, and you should test your HTML with several browsers.

HTML automatically formats your document, so it is not really a WYSIWYG environment. You'll probably realize this when you think about what happens when you change the size of your browser window. Typically, text reflows within the window. This means that the display of text is dependent upon how large the browser window is at the time it is displayed to the user. A tall, narrow window will look different from a short, wide window.

The implication of this formatting is that any blank lines of text you include in your document will automatically be ignored. To force line breaks, you must use the `<P>` and `<BR>` tags, which are described in the next section.

A Few Common HTML Tags

Although there are quite a few HTML tags, I'll cover a few of the most common ones here so you'll have a head start in being able to read HTML. We've already covered the main document structure; Table 14.1 lists a few tags that are frequently included in the `<BODY>` section.

TABLE 14.1   SOME COMMON HTML TAGS

`<A></A>`	Anchor. This is used to make a link. The HREF attribute specifies the URL destination address.
`<B></B>`	Bold. Make included text bold.
`<I></I>`	Italic. Make included text italic.

continues

Table 14.1	Continued
`<S></S>`	Strikethrough. Make included text strikethrough.
`<U></U>`	Underline. Make included text underlined.
` `	Line Break. This causes a line break, and the next line of text will start on the line below. No lines are skipped.
`<P></P>`	Paragraph. This breaks the current line, does an additional line break (that is, skips a line), and starts a new paragraph. The end paragraph tag is frequently omitted.
`<INPUT>`	Input. This defines several different types of user input field, depending upon the `TYPE` attribute. The type can be
	TEXT—Text box input.
	PASSWORD—Text box with characters hidden when input.
	CHECKBOX—Selection check box.
	RADIO—Radio button selection.
	BUTTON—Pushbutton.
	SUBMIT—Submit button. This special button causes the form to be submitted to the server.
	RESET—Reset button. This special button causes all input fields to be reset.
	IMAGE—This creates a graphical submit button.
	FILE—Enables users to select files to be submitted with a form.
	HIDDEN—A value that cannot be seen by the user, but may be used for storing values by the program and transmitting to the server.
`<TEXTAREA></TEXTAREA>`	This creates a multiline input field. You can specify the number of rows and columns via attributes. Text supplied between the tags becomes the initial value of the text area.
`<SELECT>` and `<OPTION>`	Used for creating list boxes.
`<IMG>`	Used to display an image. Common formats are GIF, JPEG, and PNG. You use the `SRC` attribute to specify the URL of the source image.
`<OL></OL>`	Ordered list. Automatically numbers items (`<LI>` tagged items) within the list.
`<UL></UL>`	Unordered list. Places bullets in front of items (`<LI>` tagged items) within the list.
`<LI>`	List item. Used to tag items within either an ordered or unordered list. You don't need to include an end tag.

Looking back at the HTML on our page in Figure 14.6, you'll notice that there are three kinds of elements: a paragraph with static text, an input field, and a button. The static paragraph text is self-explanatory. The input field as shown is not much use, because the value entered by the user is not processed in any way by the form. With JavaScript, you can access the input control fields and process the values. Information stored in the fields can also be sent back to the host for processing.

The `button` object shows you an elementary JavaScript program of one line. The `OnClick` attribute of the button tells the browser what to do if the button is clicked. In this case, the `alert` routine of JavaScript is called, and a message box will be displayed. You can also define much more complicated JavaScript programs and invoke them when someone clicks a button or on other events such as mouse movement.

One final HTML tag that deserves mention here is the Anchor tag, also known as a Link tag. The simplified format for this tag is

```
<A href="url-address">link display text</A>
```

For example, you can enter:

```
<A href="http://www.lotus.com">Lotus Web Site</A>
```

In this case, `Lotus Web Site` is the text that will appear in the form, but if clicked, the browser will go to http://www.lotus.com. This is similar to a document link within Notes and Domino. You can also use an image in place of the `link display` text. If you do this, the user can click on the image to follow a link. To specify an image, you typically use the `<IMG>` tag.

Enhancing Your Page

With our whirlwind tour of HTML, you might think that you have to code in HTML to use pages in Domino. You really don't. If you are familiar with HTML, you can use all of its power, but if not, you can use the Domino page editor to edit your page directly. You can use Domino features, and Domino will actually generate the HTML for you. This is what Domino has always done for Notes forms and documents. You can also import HTML from an HTML editor or another product that generates HTML for you.

The real beauty of Domino is that you can use the power of HTML if desired, but you don't have to. Probably the most powerful attribute is that you can combine Domino formulas, LotusScript, JavaScript, and Java with HTML to produce compelling Web sites.

Let's look at a few more features you can use within the page editor to enhance your pages.

Creating Tables

Remember that HTML automatically does formatting for you. So, if you carefully line up your input text into columns, the browser will cheerfully ignore the columns you set up. What can you do to format your text so that you get the artistic look you want from your page?

You can use tables. In fact, using tables is an important technique because tables can be used as formatting tools in addition to their traditional purpose as a means to display text and numbers. HTML 4 has additional formatting capabilities and styles to accomplish positioning, but many users are not yet using the latest browsers, so learning how to use tables is still valuable.

With release 5 of Domino Designer, you can create several different styles of tables, including a tabbed interface, a timed interface, and a table that will display different rows depending upon the contents of a field (in a form). To format different elements of a page, however, all you need is the basic type of table. I'll show you the other types later.

To create a basic table, do the following:

1. Place the cursor on the page (or form) where you want your table to appear.
2. Select Create, Table. You will see a dialog box, as in Figure 14.7. We are interested in creating a basic table, which uses the first icon button. You can leave the default number of rows and columns or enter the number of rows and columns you want to use for your table. Your table can fit the window width or be a fixed-width table. If you want your table to have a fixed width, click the Fixed width radio button.

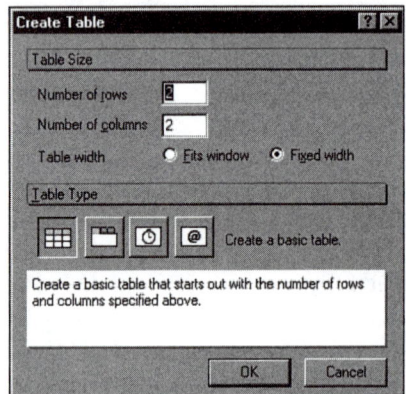

Figure 14.7
When creating a table, you can enter its size, the table width type, and the type of table.

3. Click OK to create your table.

By default, tables are created with borders displayed and will extend to the full width of your page.

Adding Rows and Columns

After you have created your table, you may want to add rows or columns. There are several ways to add rows and columns, depending on where and how many you want to add. Click your mouse cursor inside the table and then click the Table menu. See Figure 14.8.

If you want to add rows to the end of your table, you can select the Append Row option. The row will be added to the bottom of your table. To add a column to your table, select the Append Column menu option. The column will be appended on the right side of your table.

To insert a row or column at the beginning or middle of your table, select the Insert Row or Insert Column menu option. The row or column will be inserted prior to the selected row or column.

Figure 14.8
There are several ways to add and delete rows and columns of your table.

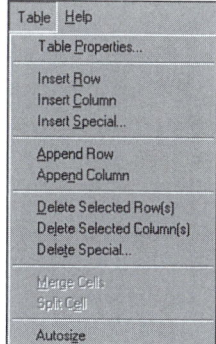

The Insert Special menu option is used when you want to insert or append more than one row or column. The Insert Row/Column dialog box will appear. See Figure 14.9.

Figure 14.9
Use Insert Special to insert more than one row or column to your table.

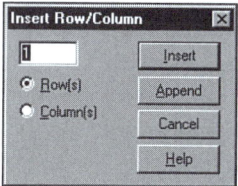

Enter the number of rows or columns you want to add, and then select Insert to insert prior to the currently selected row or column and use Append to append the desired items to the end of the table.

DELETING ROWS AND COLUMNS

Deleting rows and columns operates similarly to inserting. To delete rows or columns:

1. Select a cell—either the topmost cell in a set of rows or the leftmost cell in a set of columns—that you want to delete.
2. Drag the mouse to select cells in the rest of the rows or columns. If you are deleting rows, you must have at least one cell selected in each row you are about to delete. If you are deleting columns, make sure to select at least one cell in each column to be deleted.
3. After you select the cells, select Table, Delete Selected Row(s) to delete rows, and Table, Delete Selected Columns to delete columns.

> **Note**
> Delete Special can be used as a shortcut to delete a contiguous set of rows or columns. First, select the topmost or leftmost cell (as in step 1 in the previous instructions). Then, select Delete Special. You will be prompted for the number of rows or columns to delete.

TABLE PROPERTIES

You can view the table properties by clicking the Properties icon, by issuing Edit, Properties, or by clicking Alt+Enter on the keyboard. You can also click inside any cell of a table, and then select Table, Table Properties. When the properties box appears, if Table is not listed on the top line of the dialog box, you can click the drop-down box and select Table. See Figure 14.10.

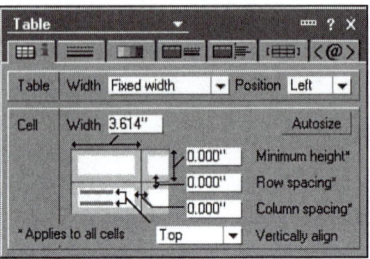

Figure 14.10
The Table properties box enables you to change column widths and spacing.

The Table Layout tab (the first tab) of the properties box enables you to change the type of width to use (Fixed, Fit to window, or Fit with margins), the position of the table (Left, Right, or Center), and the fixed spacing between columns and rows. Note that the amount you enter into the columns and rows fields applies to all columns and rows. Also, the sizes you enter apply to each side of the cell. For example, if you enter a column space of `0.5"`, you will get 0.5 inch on both the left and right side of the column. This means that you will get a full inch between columns. Note that column spacing, row spacing, and minimum height are not supported in Web applications. Some of these values may affect the width of a cell, however, which is supported.

CHANGING TABLE BORDERS AND MARGINS

The Cell Borders tab is shown in Figure 14.11. This tab affects cell borders, not the border for the entire table. The Border tab controls the border for the entire table.

Figure 14.11
The Cell Borders tab enables you to change the cell border style, color, and thickness.

You can specify the style of the table as Solid, Ridge, or Groove. Clicking the color drop-down enables you to select a color for the borders. If you click the Set All To 0 button, you will get no borders because all the border thicknesses will be zero. If you set all the borders

Creating Tables

to 1, you will get the default thickness. Note that the style options Ridge and Groove, as well as individual cell coloring, are not supported for Web browsers. You can set the border color for a table, but all cells will be the same color.

Setting all borders to zero, along with setting the widths of columns enables you to specify text formatting on your page. By using tables, you can place elements relatively easily. Just by changing the table column widths, you can specify spacing between separate items for viewing. This is especially useful if your target audience will be Web browsers.

If you are familiar with layout regions in Notes, you should be aware that they cannot be rendered to Web browsers. Typically, in previous releases of Notes and Domino, you might have used a layout region for precise positioning. You should become familiar with tables as another means to accomplish formatting, because you can use tables with zero thickness to manipulate positions, and this will work fine with either browsers or Notes clients.

The Table Border tab is used to change settings that affect the whole table rather than specific cells. In Figure 14.12, you can see the Table Border tab.

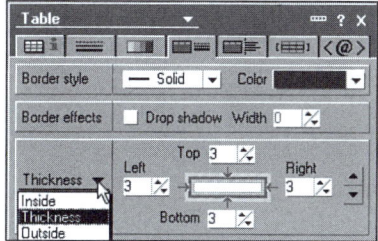

Figure 14.12
The Table Border tab enables you to change the table border style, color, thickness, and spacing.

In the Table Border tab, you can set the style of the table border to None or one of eight predefined styles, such as Solid, Double, or Dotted. This is the line style used for the border surrounding the table. The cells each have their own border, but you can have an extra border around the entire table. You can set the thickness of the table border as well as its color. You can change the spacing between the table and its border. This spacing is called the Inside spacing. The Outside setting is the space outside the table border that separates the table from its surroundings. To set Thickness, Inside spacing, and Outside spacing, first select which one you want by the drop-down box, and then adjust the Top, Bottom, Left, and Right numbers. Refer to Figure 14.12. Each of the three parameters can have four different numbers. Finally, you can add a shadow effect by checking the Drop shadow check box. If a shadow is enabled, you can control its width.

The Table Margins tab appears immediately to the right of the Table Border tab and can be used to specify the left and right margins for the table. You can specify each margin as either an offset measurement or a percentage of the window.

Implementing Newspaper Style Columns

With release 5, you can format columns within your table in newspaper style, with text flowing from one column of a table to the next column. See Figure 14.13.

314 | Chapter 14 Designing Pages, Forms, and Subforms

Figure 14.13
The Table Margins tab enables you to create newspaper style flowing from one column to another.

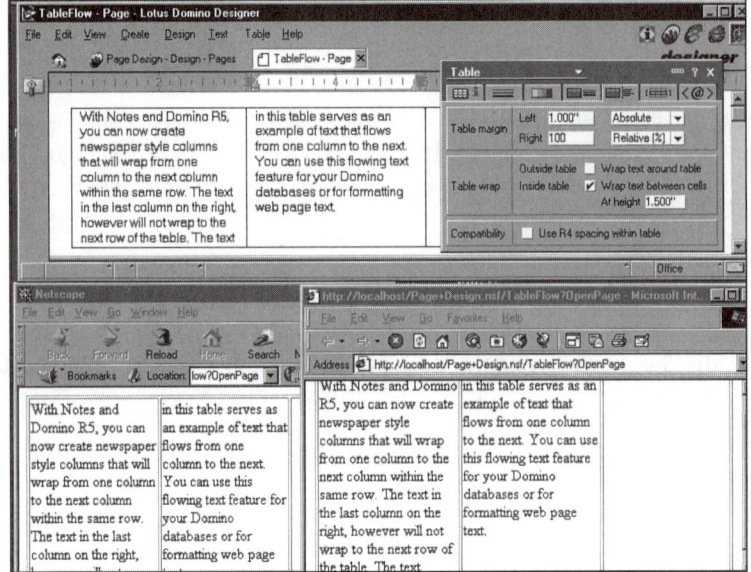

In Figure 14.13, you can see the table within the Domino Designer as well as within Web browsers. The newspaper-style flowing is obtained by checking the Inside table wrap between cells. When you enable this feature, you must specify the column height in the At height input field.

Text will flow between cells within the same row. Text will not wrap from the last cell on the right to the next table row. If you enter more text in the rightmost column than the column height setting, the table row height will just expand to accommodate the larger height.

Setting Table/Cell Backgrounds

In release 5, there are many new options for setting background colors and/or images in tables. The Table/Cell Background tab is the third tab in the Table properties box. See Figure 14.14.

In the properties box, you can set a table color style. This will give colors to the entire table at once. There are two colors involved; one called Color, and the other called Body. You can change these colors with the drop down-boxes in the dialog box. By default, two shades of gray are used with the Body color: dark gray and the highlight color light gray. In the Table Style drop-down list, you can select from one of the following styles:

- Solid   No automatic row or column header highlighting.
- Alternating rows   Alternate rows are different colors. By default, two shades of gray are used.
- Alternating columns   Alternate columns are different colors. By default, two shades of gray are used.

- Left and Top   The top row and the left column are highlighted. I have changed the colors so that the header color is dark and the Body color is light gray. This is a table that an accountant or spreadsheet guru would love. See Figure 14.14.
- Left   the left column is highlighted with the color you specify.
- Right and Top   The top row and the right column are highlighted. This is a bit unusual. Perhaps left-handed accounts might like this one or you could use it to highlight row totals on the right.
- Right   The right column is highlighted with your color.
- Top   The top row is highlighted.

Figure 14.14
The Colors tab enables you to set cell backgrounds, headers, and gradients.

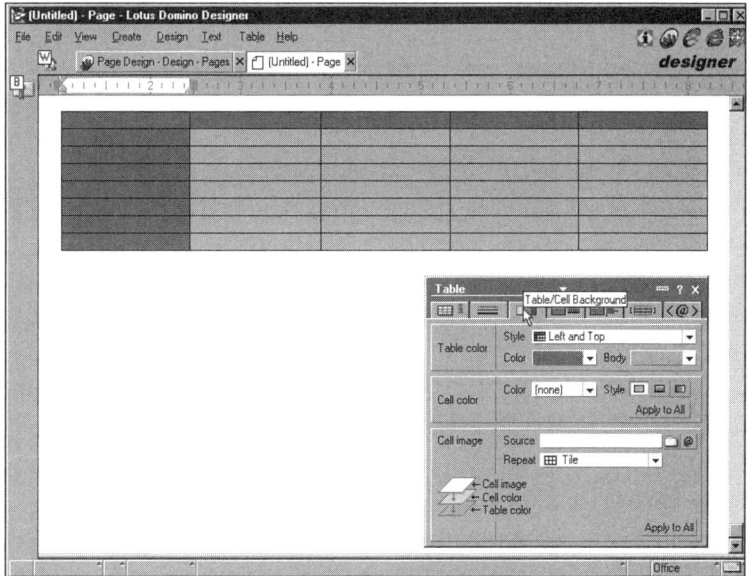

You can override any of the default styles by highlighting one or more cells, and then clicking the cell color drop-down to select a color. If you select a color, it overlays the default color of the style. To make the style color show through again, you can click the (none) button, which appears in the top row of the color drop-down.

You can make gradients (gradual color shifts) within a cell. You do this by using three selections. The background color will be the starting color, the cell color will be the ending color, and the direction can be set to either Top to Bottom or Left to Right. You specify the direction by clicking one of the Style buttons. Gradients will display only if you are using a Notes client. Internet Explorer and Netscape Navigator will both display a solid background color.

The final option on the Table/Cell Background tab is to set the Cell image. With this option, you can include an image within a table cell. Using this feature, you can format an attractive page. See Figure 14.15.

Figure 14.15
You can include a background image within a table cell.

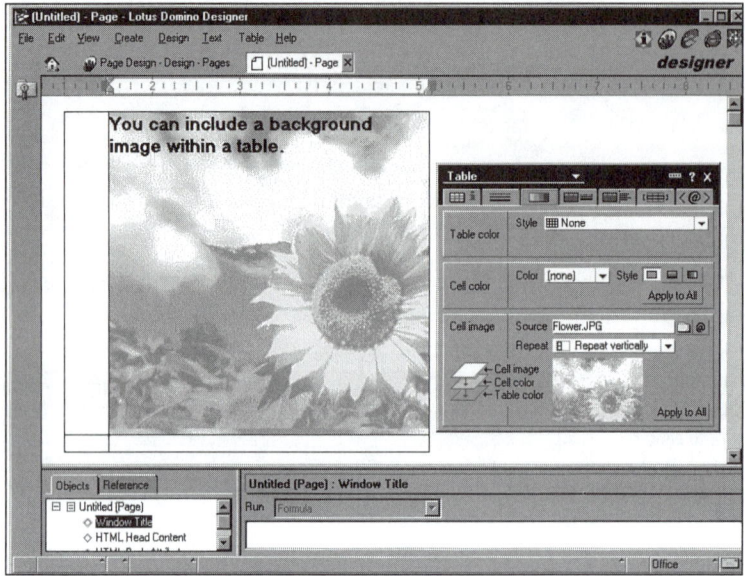

You can include an image by name, via a formula, or from your image library. Images from your image library are resources and will replicate along with your database.

The major constraint on using images within tables is the fact that the height of all rows within a table must be the same. The height of a table row is set on the Table layout (first) tab.

MERGING AND SPLITTING CELLS

In Figure 14.16, I used another table technique known as cell merging. In this case, I merged all the cells in the top row to become a single cell. After that, I used a gradient that stretches across the entire width of the title, and I centered the text within the long cell.

To merge several cells into one cell:

1. Select the cells within the table that you want to merge.
2. Select Table, Merge Cells. This option is valid in the menu only if you have more than one table cell selected. You can select cells in rowwise direction or columnwise direction. You can also select cells that have already been merged previously.
3. Your cells are now merged.

To split cells that have been previously merged:

1. Select a cell that was previously merged within the table.
2. Select Table, Split Cell. This option is valid in the menu only if you have selected a cell that was previously merged. Your cells are now split back into their original, elementary state prior to being merged. If you merged cells more than once, the previous state is not kept. Your cells will split back into their original, single state.

Figure 14.16
You can merge cells to get a continuous gradient and centered text.

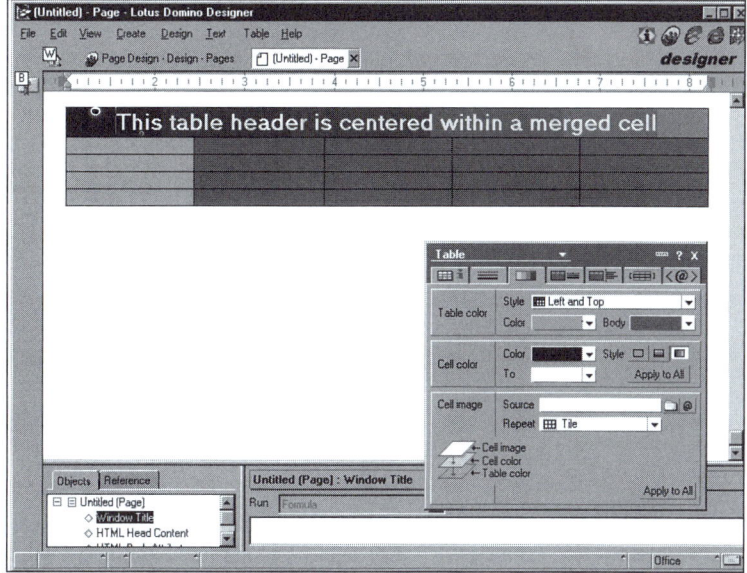

Advanced Fun with Tables

There are several special effects that you can create with tables. They all revolve around a concept called the collapsible table, which you can create either initially or on the Advanced tab of the Table properties box. The one factor that these tables have in common is that only a single row of the table is shown at a time. Various methods are used to determine which row to show. There are three types of special tables:

- Tabbed tables   Each row of the table will correspond to one tab of the tabbed table. Only the row containing the selected tab will be shown.

- Timed tables   Each row of the table will appear for a specified amount of time. The default is two seconds. You can use these tables to display animation.

- Programmatic control   In addition to the table, you must supply a field. The name of the field is the same as the table name with a $ prefix. The contents of the field determines which row to display. You can programmatically update the field, which can then be used to select the row.

You can create a table of any of these three types or the standard table type initially and later convert it to any of the other types. You control the type of table on the Table Rows tab of the Table properties box. This is sixth tab in the properties box.

Let's look at the example in Figure 14.17.

I created a tabbed table with five rows and four columns. You can create a tabbed table on the table creation dialog box by clicking on the Tabbed Table icon (the second icon), entering the number of rows and columns, and then clicking OK.

Figure 14.17
Tabbed Table with five rows and four columns.

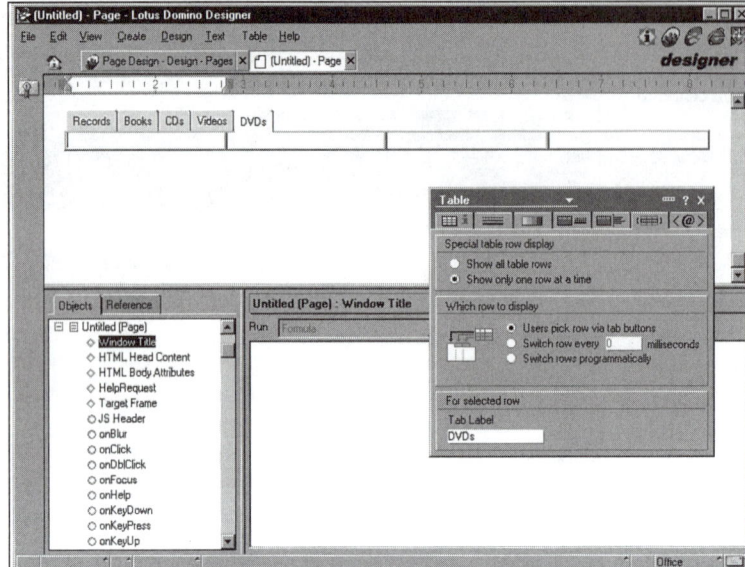

After you create the table, you can add information to each of the table rows. In Figure 14.17, you see that I have added tab labels for each row. You enter a tab label in the bottom of the Table Rows tab of the properties box. Because there are five rows in this example, there are five tabs. One common use might be to use only a single column with several rows. In this way, you could create a tabbed interface similar to a dialog box.

Another option for tables is to use the timed table option. This will show each row for a fixed amount of time. The default is two seconds, but you can adjust this time. In Figure 14.17, you see that you can set the second radio button option in the middle of the properties box. The timed display can be used for creating an animated appearance to the user.

To use this option, create a table with several rows and one column. Each row should contain a graphic file—from your image library, for example. Set the timer for the amount of time you want to show each graphic. You can specify a transition effect such as left-to-right, dissolve, or explode, among several others. You can also specify that you want to cycle through the graphics continually or when clicked by the user.

> **Tip**
>
> New with release 5 of Domino, you can include nested tables, or tables within tables. This is particularly useful with tabbed tables. You can include a tabbed table within a tabbed table. This technique is used in the Domino Public Directory database.

PROGRAMMATIC CONTROL OF TABLES

The final type of single-row table gives you programmatic control over the table to be displayed to the user. Normally, this table type should be used with a form, because fields are not allowed in a page. I'll describe fields and forms in much greater detail later in this chapter.

Let's examine programmatic control of tables. In Figure 14.18, you can see the Table dialog box. Notice that the option Switch rows programmatically has been checked. You can optionally show the tabs when you use the programmatic selection method.

Figure 14.18
You can programmatically show rows of a table.

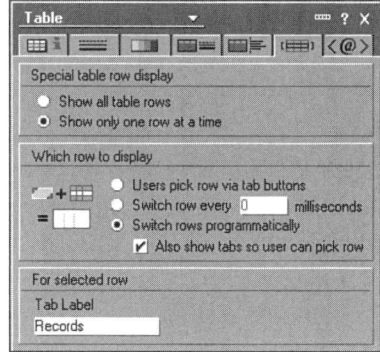

At the bottom of the dialog box, I can give the tab a label. This label is used for display only and not for the selection of the row. In Figure 14.19, you can see the dialog box for the HTML header.

Figure 14.19
Name the table and its rows within the Table Programming tab.

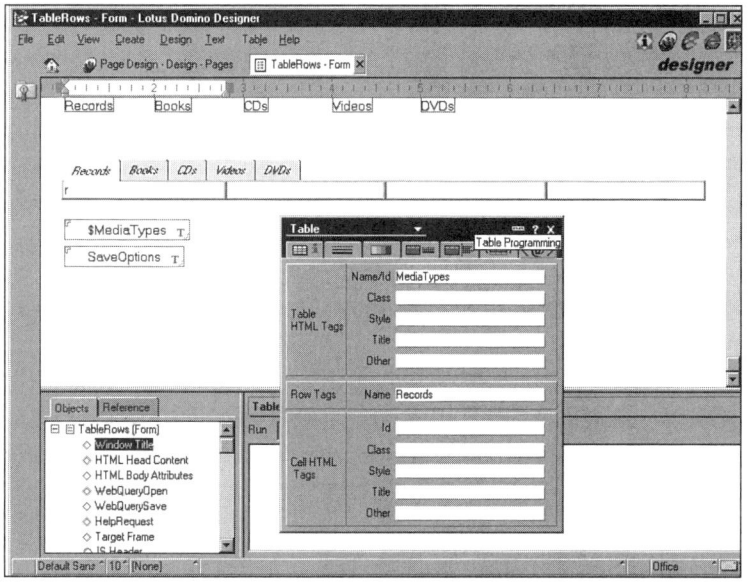

In the Table Programming tab, you give the table its name, and you also give a name to each row. You can pick the row to display either by its name or by its 0-origin numeric row index. In this example, I named the table MediaTypes. The name of the row shown is Records, which is the first row.

> **Note**
>
> The row names are case sensitive. Be careful to specify the exact string when using programmatic row selection. Also note that the row's name is not necessarily the same as its label. In this example, I used the word Records for both the row label and its name to avoid confusion. If they are different, remember the name is used for selection, not the label.

In the form in Figure 14.19, there are five action hotspots across the top of the screen. These hotspots are Records, Books, CDs, Videos, and DVDs. Each hotspot of Figure 14.19 has a Click formula similar to one of the following:

```
FIELD $MediaTypes:=0;
@Command([RefreshHideFormulas])
```

OR

```
FIELD $MediaTypes:="Books";
@Command([RefreshHideFormulas])
```

The first case uses the 0-origin index, and the second case uses the row name. Normally, you use only one type or the other, but I'm showing you both just for the sake of example. The $MediaTypes field is the special field that controls which row will be displayed. The $MediaTypes field name is constructed by prefixing the table name with a $. I use a computed field to control the table. The two formula statements set the field and then refresh the display. The value you put into the $MediaTypes field is the name of the row (not its label).

Finally, notice in Figure 14.19 that I have a SaveOptions field. This field is also a specially named field. This field is also a computed field with a value of 0. If this specially named field contains a 0, the document created with this form is not saved to the database. This is very useful if you do not want the document saved and you do not want the user to be prompted. In this example, if you do not include the SaveOptions field, the user will be prompted to save the document when it is closed. You can hide both the $MediaTypes and the SaveOptions fields from the user. The user will not normally need to see these fields.

In Figure 14.20, you see the same table as before, but I have included it in a page instead of a form. Although normally you need to have a field to control the table row selection, you can use an action hotspot formula to create the necessary field. As you can see in the figure, the contents of one of the action hotspots is

```
FIELD $MediaTypes:="Books";
FIELD SaveOptions:="0";
@Command([RefreshHideFormulas])
```

Notice that we are creating both the table selection field and the SaveOptions field in the hotspot formula. The operation of the table is essentially the same as with the form.

EMBEDDING PICTURES | 321

Figure 14.20
You can use programmatic tables in pages.

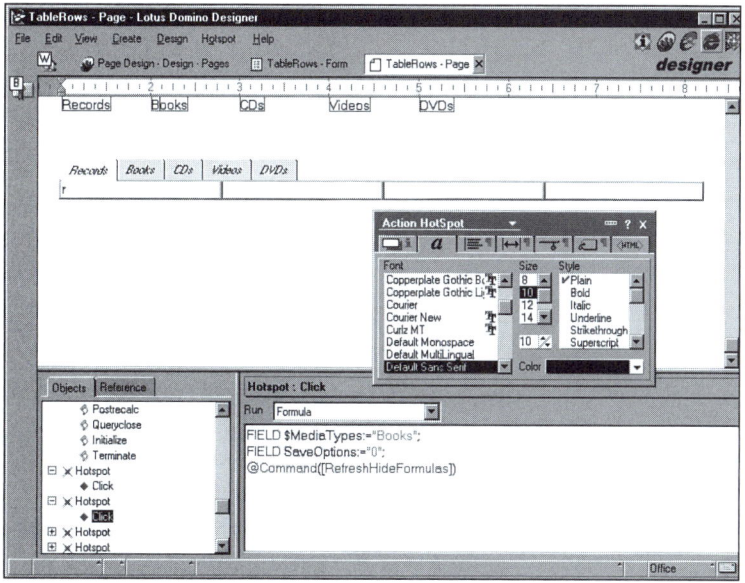

> **Caution**
> If you do not include the `SaveOptions:="0"` statement in the formula, the Notes client will prompt the user to see whether he or she wants to save the document when the page is closed. This is unusual, because normally a page does not contain fields and cannot be saved by the user. If the user says OK to save, a document will be created. The form field will be set to the page name. This document will then potentially show up in views. If there is a form with the same name as your page, the form will be used to show the document. If there is no form with the same name and there is no default form, the user will not be able to view the document. After the document is saved, there is no way to use the page to view the saved document.

EMBEDDING PICTURES

Earlier in this chapter, I showed you how to change the background color and set an image as your page background. In this section, I cover the embedding of smaller graphics, such as buttons, on your page. There are several methods for using graphics on your page, depending upon how you want to use the graphic.

IMPORTING GRAPHIC FILES

One way you can use a graphic image is to embed it directly on your page. To embed a graphic picture on your page, perform the following steps:

1. Create or open the page you want to use for your graphic.
2. Move your cursor to the location where you want to place your picture and select Create, Picture. You will see a dialog box similar to Figure 14.21.

PART
III
CH
14

Figure 14.21
The Import dialog box for Create Picture used to import graphics.

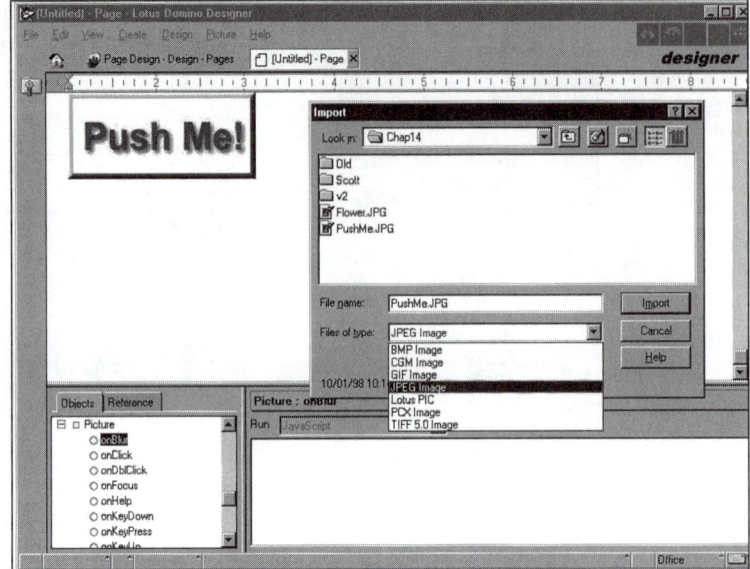

3. Notice that you can choose among a variety of graphics file formats. The most common Web formats are GIF and JPEG formats. BMP is a native Windows format. Several of the other graphics formats are popular as well. Select the format you want to use.

4. After you select your format, the files of that type will appear in the dialog box. In this case, you can see a PushMe.JPG file.

5. You can double-click on the file you want to import, or you can single-click on the file you want to import, and then click the Import button. Your graphic will then appear on your page.

Using Image Resources

An important new feature of release 5 is the ability to store graphic images in an image resource library. You can then reference the images from other locations in your database. In previous releases of Domino, shared images were not as important, because the forms and subforms and their contents are already shared resources. With the advent of pages, however, it is important to have shared images; otherwise, the identical images will be duplicated on each page and will take up unnecessary space.

To save a new image in your image resource library:

1. Open the Resources twistie and select Images in the Design Pane.
2. Click the New Image Resource action button. An Open dialog box will appear.
3. Select the type of image you want to store in your image resource library. Note that only GIF, JPEG, and BMP type images are supported. This is more restrictive than the types available for direct import to a page.

4. Double-click on the file you want to put into your library. You can also single-click on the file and click Open. The image will be stored in your image resource library.

5. (Optional) You can add an alias to the image resource by opening the properties box for the image and entering an alias into the box. If you refer to this image via an alias, you will be free to change the image later without changing any programs that refer to the image in the library.

After you have stored the image resource in your library, you can use it on your page. To use the image resource on your page:

1. Create or open the page you want to use for your graphic.

2. Move your cursor to the location where you want to place your picture and select Create, Image Resource. You will be prompted for an image name and an image type, and you will see a list of the available images.

3. If you click on an image name, you will see a preview of the image on the right side of the dialog box. After you have found the image you want to include, select its name and click OK.

4. Your image will be displayed on your page.

Organizing Data with Rules, Sections, and Page Breaks

To make your page look better and provide more organization, you can use horizontal rules and sections. A horizontal rule is just a line that goes across the page. With the rule properties, however, you can modify the width and height of the rule. The width can be expressed as a percentage, or you can specify an exact measurement, such as inches.

Rules can also include color gradients, which start in one color and gradually change to another color. The gradients change colors from top to bottom. To create a horizontal rule, move your cursor to the location on the page or form where you want your rule to appear. Then, select Create, Horizontal Rule. After your rule has been created, you can change its properties via the properties box. You can see an example of a rule with a gradient in Figure 14.22.

Creating sections is easy and fun. To create a section, here is what you do:

1. Move the cursor to where you want to create your section. Type all the text that you want included in the section.

2. After the text has been entered on the page, select the text you want to make into the section with the keyboard or the mouse.

3. Select Create, Section to create your section. The first line of the text that you selected will become the section title and will display if the section is closed.

4. (Optional) After the section has been created, you can change the title with the Section properties box. You can also change the rules that are used to automatically expand and collapse the section. See Figure 14.22.

Figure 14.22
The Section properties box can be used to control the expand/collapse rules.

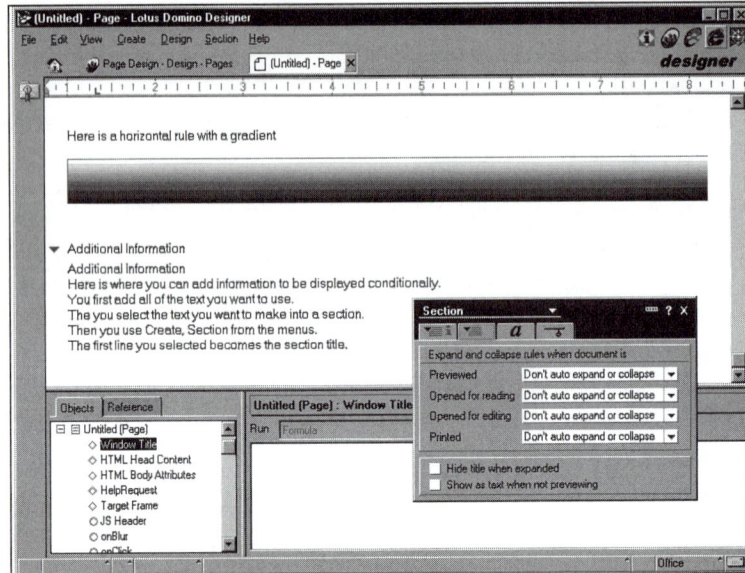

You can control printer page breaks by inserting a page break. To insert a page break, first move the cursor to the location where you want your page to break, and then choose Create, Page Break. Note that the page break will not affect formatting for display in either the Notes client or Web browsers. It is strictly an aid to formatting your printed output.

DESIGNING FORMS

I have covered most of the basics of page creation and use, so let's move on to forms. Forms have always been a fundamental part of Notes and Domino, so if you're familiar with previous releases, you probably already know a lot about forms. If you have not used previous releases of Notes or Domino, you get an introduction to how forms and documents work in the next sections. Then I'll move on to a comparison of these design elements with pages.

FORMS AND DOCUMENTS

In Domino, the *document* is the fundamental unit of storage for information. Documents contain named items to store information. The item has a data type, such as numeric or text, and if the item contains multiple values, they are all the same type. A typical item within a document might contain, for example, a name, address, or phone number. Sometimes these document items are also called fields.

You may have hundreds or thousands (or more) of documents in a database. The documents do not all have to have the same item names. For example, one document might contain the items Name and Address, and another document might contain TotalAmount and DueDate.

Not all of the data contained within documents is necessarily visible to a user. Documents contain data, but they are typically used with user interface elements, such as forms and views. Forms and views are the means to present information stored within documents to the user. Views present summary information from many documents, and forms enable you to see detailed information from one document.

A *form* is like a visual template. By this, I mean that the form in Domino is much like a blank paper form. Think for a moment about the form you fill out in the dentist's office with your name, address, and medical history. This form indicates the information desired and leaves several blank areas for you to fill in.

With Domino forms, the blank areas are called fields. Each field within a form has a field name so you can reference it and obtain the information you need. A form contains both static information and field information. It is a visual object, much like the page that I previously showed you.

Suppose Domino is showing an empty form to a user. When the user fills the empty fields of the form, the information is stored in a document. Domino separates the user interface (form) from the field data stored within the document. This way, you can view the same fields with different forms, and you can change the look and feel of your application without changing the underlying data stored in the document fields.

What happens if the names in the document don't match the names in the form? Actually, this happens quite often and is normal. If the document contains items that have names that do not appear on the form, the values are not displayed to the user. If the form contains field names that don't appear in the document, when the user enters a value, it automatically creates a corresponding item value in the document.

So to recap, forms are used for visual display to a user, and documents are used to store data within the database. The correspondence of names in forms and documents enables Domino to display fields filled in with the values from a document. For display to a Web browser, Domino first merges the form definition with the document values and then converts the result to HTML, which is then sent to the browser.

How Do Forms and Documents Compare to Pages?

We have now talked about pages, forms, and documents. How are these all used and how do they compare? In Table 14.2, an *X* indicates that the feature is available. There may be minor exceptions, but I've tried to show you the major differences so you can contrast the database elements.

TABLE 14.2 COMPARISON OF PAGES, FORMS, AND DOCUMENTS

	Pages	Forms	Documents
Visual User Interface	X	X	
Can be viewed in a Web browser	X	X (with a document)	
Stores field data values			X
Can contain Domino field definitions		X	
Can contain HTML formatting and INPUT items (HTML-type fields).	X	X	
Is a design element	X	X	
Full Text searched			X
Data can be shown in views			X
Single element can be used with multiple documents		X	

CREATING A NEW FORM

To create a new form in your database, follow these steps:

1. In the Domino Designer, open the database where you want your form to appear.
2. Click on Forms in the Design Pane.
3. Click the New Form action button. Your new form will appear.

The form editor is very similar to the Page editor. You have a large area at the top to lay out your form and the Programmer's Pane on the bottom to manipulate details of the elements within the form.

WORKING WITH FIELDS

I have explained that fields can be placed on forms (but not pages). They represent the blank areas of a paper form. In the United States, we fill out forms to pay our taxes to the Internal Revenue Service (IRS). If you are outside the U.S., you probably pay taxes to your own government. (If not, let me know where you live.) On those forms for taxes, the blank boxes where you enter your numbers are fields. The good news is that working with fields in Domino is much less painful than filling in the fields on tax forms.

Adding Fields to a Form

To create a new field on your form, do the following:

1. Open the form on which you want to add the field.
2. Select Create, Field. Your new field will be created with the name Untitled. See Figure 14.23.

Figure 14.23
You can change the name and type of fields in the properties box.

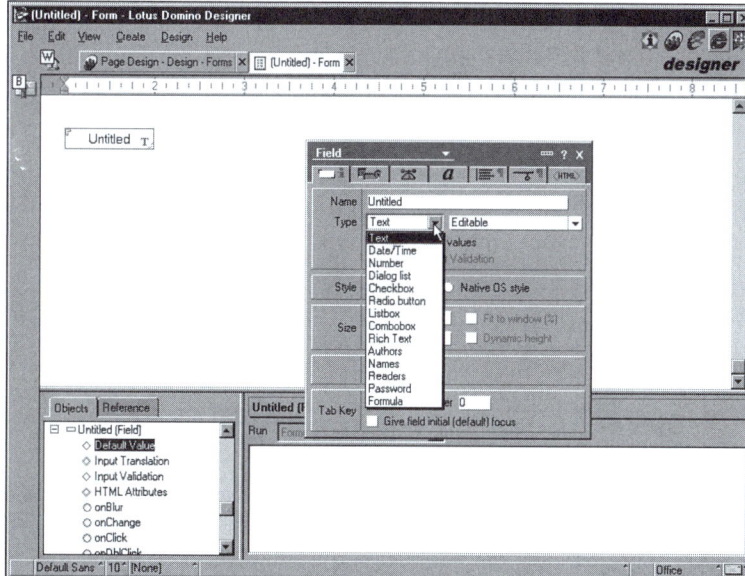

Each field on the form must have a unique name, so if you enter a name that already exists, the Domino Designer will automatically append a numeric suffix. For example, the second unnamed field will be Untitled2.

One of your first tasks should be to change the field name. A set of fields called Untitled, Untitled2, and Untitled3 would be pretty boring, not to mention rather hard to debug. An important part of application design is to have naming conventions for the various design elements.

Naming Conventions

When you create field names, you have great flexibility. You can call your fields just about anything you want, and they won't complain back at you. You can call one field Input, another Output, and a third one TextField. The main characteristic of all three of these names is that they are terrible field names. They are valid and Domino won't complain, but they represent poor programming practice.

Officially, field names must begin with a letter, or $, or _. Following the initial letter, names may use letters, numbers, $, and _. Names cannot contain spaces and may be up to 32 bytes. For single-byte character languages, this is the same as 32 characters. For multibyte languages, you can use only half as many characters.

Your field names should be meaningful in their context. For example, the field names LastName, FirstName, and PhoneNumber are much better names because you can almost immediately tell just from their variable names how these fields will be used. The field PhoneNumber is a little ambiguous, however. Is that field a numeric field or a character field? Well, the answer is it might be either. Normally, phone numbers are stored as text strings, but with the field name PhoneNumber it becomes a little more ambiguous. What can we do?

Another convention that is becoming widespread is to add a prefix on to the variable name and to use capitalization to help make the name easier to read. The prefix represents the data type of the variable, and then the rest of the variable name follows. Here are some sample prefixes:

txt	Text Field
n	Numeric Field
rt	Rich Text
dt	Date/Time

Using these prefixes, the field names would become txtLastName, txtFirstName, and txtPhoneNumber. Some people use c for character. This is shorter, so if you prefer, it could be cLastName, cFirstName, and cPhoneNumber. Notice that by using cPhoneNumber and nPhoneNumber, you can immediately see which field is a character field and which field is a numeric field.

It does not really matter which conventions you use, but you should definitely find a naming convention for your entire organization, and then standardize on this convention. By using one style of naming variables, you will promote easier maintenance for your entire group. It will become much easier for one person to read another person's code.

Naming conventions are also a simple, easy way to improve your productivity, because you will spend less time trying to remember the data types of each of your variables. You really appreciate these conventions the most when you must maintain code someone else has written.

FIELD DATA TYPES

I've alluded to the fact that there are several different types of data that can be stored in documents. The basic data types include text, rich text, date/time, and number values, but most data is stored as text. There are several kinds of user interface elements (called field types) that can be used to display and obtain information from users. In Figure 14.24, you see the various types of fields that can be used on a form. An icon on the right side of the field shows its type.

Several field types can be used to display lists of information. User interface types for lists include Dialog list, Checkbox, Radio button, Listbox, and Combobox. These field types typically store text information. Table 14.3 describes the various field types.

Figure 14.24
There are many different types of fields you can use on a form.

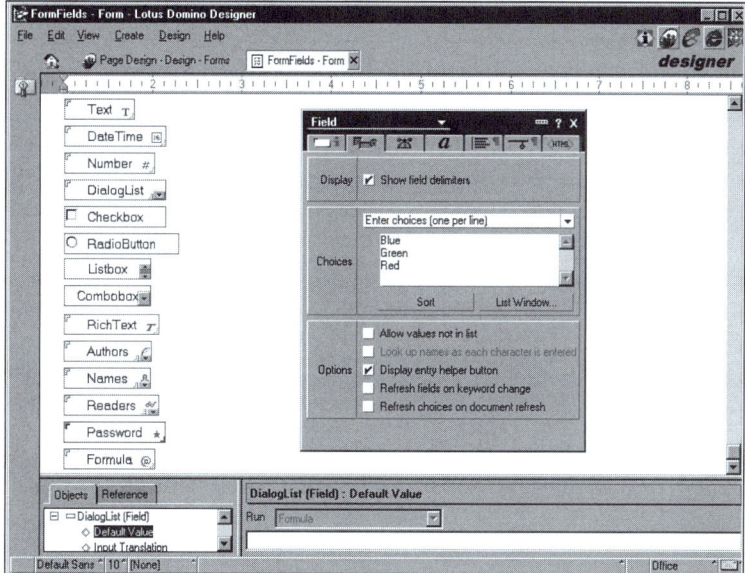

TABLE 14.3   FIELD DATA TYPES

Data Type	Description
Text	A text field can hold letters, numbers, and special characters. A designer can assign formatting attributes, such as bold or italic, to regular text fields, but after set, the end user cannot change the formatting.
Date/Time	Date/time fields store date and/or time information. They can be displayed in a variety of formats, including date-only or time-only.
Number	Use number fields for storing numeric information that will be used in calculations.
Dialog list	A dialog list field displays a list of choices. It can optionally have a helper button so the user can choose one of a set of predefined values. You can specify the choices by formula or by typing them directly, or you can allow the user to add a choice not in the list.
Checkbox	You use a check box when you have a set of options and you want to allow the user to select zero, one, or more of the available options.
Radio button	Radio buttons are used with a set of selections where only one of the choices is allowed from the set.

continues

TABLE 14.3	CONTINUED
Data Type	**Description**
Listbox	A list box shows a scrollable list of choices. The list can contain predefined values or values specified by a formula, or you can allow the user to add a value that is not in the list.
Combobox	A combo box is similar to a list box, but takes up less screen space. It is shown as a single line with a drop-down button. The user can click on the button to reveal a list of choices. As with the other list options, you can predefine values, enter a formula, or allow the user to add values that are not in the list.
Rich Text	Rich text fields allow the user to add formatting information such as bold and italic. These fields can also hold extra information, such as attachments, hotspots, doclinks, and tables. Rich text fields cannot be displayed in views.
Authors	Authors fields basically affect users with Author-level ACL access. If a document contains an authors field, and the user's name is stored in it, the user is allowed to edit the document, even if he or she did not originally create it. This type of field can be used by a designer to overcome the normal ACL restrictions for Author-level access.
Names	Names fields are used to store names when you don't need to associate rights such as Authors or Readers. You can use a names type field when you want to display the Notes name in a particular format.
Readers	The Readers field is used to control reading rights to users that otherwise would be able to read a document. If a readers field exists and contains usernames, only users found within the field can read the document. Even if a user has Manager ACL privilege, if that user is not listed in the Readers field for the document, he or she cannot read it. This field refines ACL privileges.
Password	A password field is used to show asterisks on the screen for data entry.
Formula	A formula field is used to store the text value of a selection formula.

EDITABLE AND COMPUTED FIELDS

In addition to the data type of the field, each field has an attribute of being editable or computed. Here are the types and what they mean:

Data Entry	**Description**
Editable	In editable fields, the user can enter data directly into the field. This is the most common type of field.
Computed	The value of a computed field is determined by a formula. A user cannot enter data into the field;, it is for output only. A computed field is reevaluated whenever the form is created, refreshed, or saved. The computed value is saved in the document.

Data Entry	Description
Computed When Composed	A Computed When Composed field is also specified by a formula. The formula is evaluated at the time the document is created, but it is not ever reevaluated. The value is saved in the document.
Computed for Display	The value of a Computed for Display field is evaluated at the time the document is created or opened. It is reevaluated whenever the document is saved or refreshed. Although the value is reevaluated when the document is saved, the value of a Computed for Display field is *not* stored in the document. Another implication of this is that Computed for Display fields may not be used in views because there is no value stored in the document.

OTHER FIELD ATTRIBUTES

When you create fields, you can specify many other attributes with the Field properties box. You can specify several attributes dealing with the display of the field:

- **Allow multiple values**   This enables the field to accept multiple values. The values are stored internally as a list. This check box is particularly valuable with any of the list and name type fields.

- **Compute After Validation**   This check box applies only to computed fields. This is useful when a field is dependent upon other fields. If checked, the field will be computed only after the validation occurs on other fields. Note that this option is not supported for Web browsers.

- **Style: Notes style/Native OS style**   Notes style is the standard style for controls. There are certain controls, such as the date/time controls that are supported only in the Notes client when the Native OS style box is checked. Native OS style controls are not supported by Web browsers.

- **Show field delimiters**   This normally enabled option causes the brackets that surround editable fields to be shown. If you disable this option, make sure that you provide prompts for the user because there will be no visible marking within the window to tell the user there is a field that accepts user input.

In addition to the basic properties just mentioned, the properties box enables you to change the following attributes for fields:

- **Date/Time formatting (in Control)**   There are several options that enable you to specify the style of date formats. You can, for example, specify that you always want four-digit years, four-digit years for 21st century only, or to show year only when it is not this year. You can specify the order of day of week, day, month and year. When you show times, you can show hours, minutes, and seconds, and perform time zone adjustments. You can also require the user to enter four-digit years.

- **Date/Time formatting (in Layout Region)** Within a layout region, a date/time field has a calendar control that enables a user to pick dates visually. This is not available in a regular form date control.
- **Number Format (in Control)** This enables you to specify numbers as decimal, percent, scientific, or currency. You can control the number of decimal digits displayed, use parentheses when negative, and use punctuation at thousands.
- **Help Description (in Advanced)** This <enables you to specify a help text message for the field.
- **Multi-Value Options (in Advanced)** This <enables you to specify the separators that can be used by a user when entering multiple values. The choices are space, comma, semicolon, new line, and blank line. This section also enables you to choose the separator used for display between multiple values in a multivalue field.
- **Security Options (in Advanced)** This enables you to sign the field, enable encryption, or require at least Editor access to use a field.
- **Font (in Font)** This enables you to specify a typeface, point size, and style for the field.
- **Alignment (in Paragraph Alignment)** This enables you to specify whether the field will be left-aligned, right-aligned, centered, or justified. It also enables you to specify first-line indentation style, list styling (numbered, bulleted, and so forth), and paragraph spacing (single, one-and-a-half, double). Paragraph type can also be specified for right-to-left languages.
- **Hide Paragraph (in Paragraph Hide When)** This enables you to control hiding the paragraph from Notes clients or Web browsers. You also can control hiding when the document is previewed and opened for reading or editing. You can specify a formula that controls the hiding.
- **HTML (in Field Extra HTML)** This enables you to add an Id, Class, Style, Title, or other extra HTML attributes. Some particularly useful attributes are SIZE and MAXLENGTH. When Domino converts the field to HTML, it converts it to an HTML <INPUT> field. The HTML SIZE parameter on an <INPUT> field specifies the width on the screen. The MAXLENGTH parameter specifies how many characters can be input into the field.

Field Formulas: Default Value, Input Translation, and Input Validation

Domino fields can have three special formulas associated with them called the Default Value, Input Translation, and Input Validation formulas. All three of these formulas are optional. The Default Value formula provides an initial, default value for the field. This enables the user to leave a field blank, and the Designer can specify the initial value.

The Input Translation and Input Validation formulas are run whenever a document is refreshed or saved. The Translation formula enables you to do processing that will put the data in a canonical format. In other words, you can capitalize words, you can trim leading and trailing blanks, and you can replace user input with codes you look up.

After input translation is performed, the Input Validation formula is run. This formula evaluates to Success or Failure. If successful, the field passes validation. If it fails, the user is prompted with an error message you provide and must edit the field to correct the problem.

SINGLE USE AND SHARED FIELDS

The most common type of field is called a single-use field, whose definition is included with the form on which it is created. Sometimes, however, you may want to define a field that will be used on several forms. In this case, you can create a shared field, which is a shared resource. Remember that here we are talking about the field definition itself, not any data that is stored within any documents. You do not need to use a shared field to share data within documents.

Shared field definitions enable you to define attributes of the field, such as its font, style, and—importantly—its formula definitions. For example, suppose you want to create a field to be used for part numbers. You want to perform an input translation and/or validation on the part numbers, so you specify formulas associated with the field. By making this field a shared field, you can use the part number entry field throughout your database, and the formulas will be shared.

You can easily create a shared field by creating a regular, single-use field and then converting it to a shared field. To convert a single-use field into a shared field, select the field, and then select Design, Share This Field.

To convert a shared field back into a single-use field, select the field, and then use Edit, Cut followed by Edit Paste.

After you have created a shared field, you can use it on a form by doing the following:

1. Open the form you want to use for your shared field.
2. Move the cursor to the location where you want your shared field to appear.
3. Select Create, Insert Shared Field. A dialog box will open displaying the names of the available shared fields.
4. Select the desired shared field and click OK. Your shared field will be inserted into the form.

CREATING FORM ACTIONS

Actions are programs that can be implemented using predefined simple actions; or you can write your own custom actions in LotusScript, JavaScript, or formula language. Simple actions include modifying a field, copying a document to a database or folder, running an agent, or sending a mail message.

Actions can be invoked by clicking an action button in a form or view. They can also be displayed in the Action menu. The Action Bar, if displayed, appears just above the document or view window. Because the action buttons do not appear inside the window, they are independent of any scrolling of the document window itself.

You can associate actions with individual forms or views, or you can create Shared Actions. Shared Actions are useful whenever you need to provide functions that may be common across several forms or views. Shared Actions are found in the Design Pane under Resources, Other, Shared Actions.

There are six predefined actions that are shown with an asterisk in the Action Pane. If these actions are shown on a form, the action will apply to the currently viewed document. If the action appears on a view, the user can select one or more documents and apply the action to the selected documents. The predefined actions are

- Categorize   This pops open a dialog box that enables a user to add and remove categories from a document being viewed or listed in a view. In order to use this feature, the form must have a keyword field named `Categories`.
- Edit Document   This enables editing of a document currently being viewed or listed in a view. This does not enable a user to override the ACL; it just provides a convenient method to put the document into edit mode.
- Send Document   This sends the document to a user or mail-in database. The form must contain a SendTo field, and the value within the field supplies the destination.
- Forward   This forwards the document in an email message.
- Move To Folder   This moves the selected document(s) to a folder.
- Remove from Folder   This removes the selected document(s) from a folder.

Figure 14.25
When you can define your own actions, you can see them in the Action Pane.

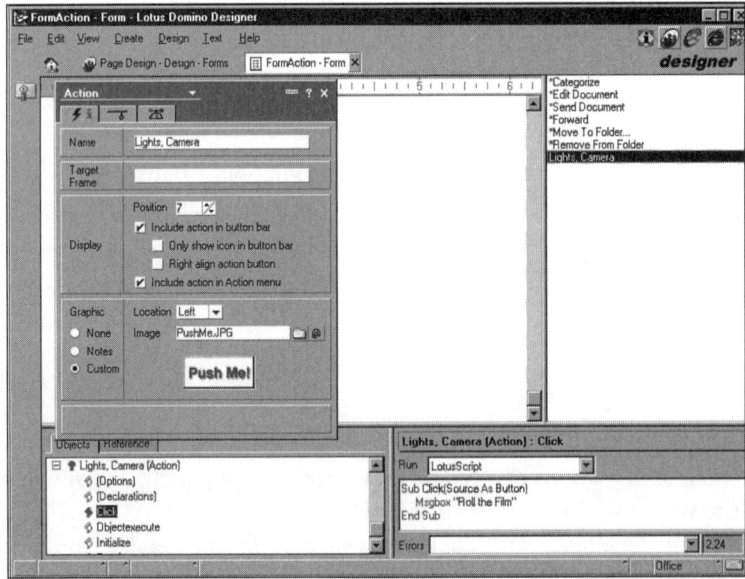

In addition to the built-in actions, you can define your own actions. Programmer-defined actions can appear in the Action Bar and/or the Action menu. In Figure 14.25, I have defined the Lights, Camera action. You can specify the action to take with a formula,

Simple Action, LotusScript, or JavaScript program. The example uses LotusScript, and when the action button is clicked, a message box will appear. In Figure 14.25, I have specified a custom graphic to be used instead of one of the standard Domino graphics. You can also specify a graphic button to appear in the action button by selecting one of the Notes graphics in the Action properties box.

The complete list of action graphics that can be used is shown in Figure 14.26. Release 5 has added 24 new graphics that can be used for a total of 156 pictures.

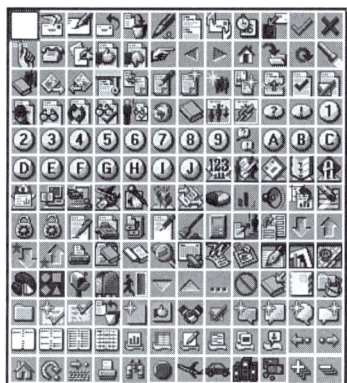

Figure 14.26
You can choose from 156 different Notes graphics for actions.

Using Layout Regions

Layout regions provide you with a means to more precisely specify the layout of controls. When you use pages or forms, much of the layout of design elements is left up to the display program. In some ways this is good, because you can view the form from Notes clients and a variety of different Web browsers. Unfortunately, this does not give the form designer fine control over the presentation. Fields, for example, may move left or right or they may expand and cause other fields to move.

Layout regions provide control so that input fields will not change in size and you can finely tune the appearance of your form. Layout regions have one major disadvantage, however. Layout regions cannot be shown in Web browsers, so anything you place in a layout region will be visible only to Notes clients. If you are developing for both Notes clients and Web browsers, you should avoid layout regions. If you will be using only Notes clients, you can use layout regions.

To create a layout region in your form, perform the following:

1. Open the form you want to use with your layout region.
2. Move your cursor to the location where you want your layout region to appear.
3. Select Create, Layout Region, New Layout Region. Your new layout region will appear. See Figure 14.27.

Figure 14.27
You can change the size and location of a layout region with the properties box.

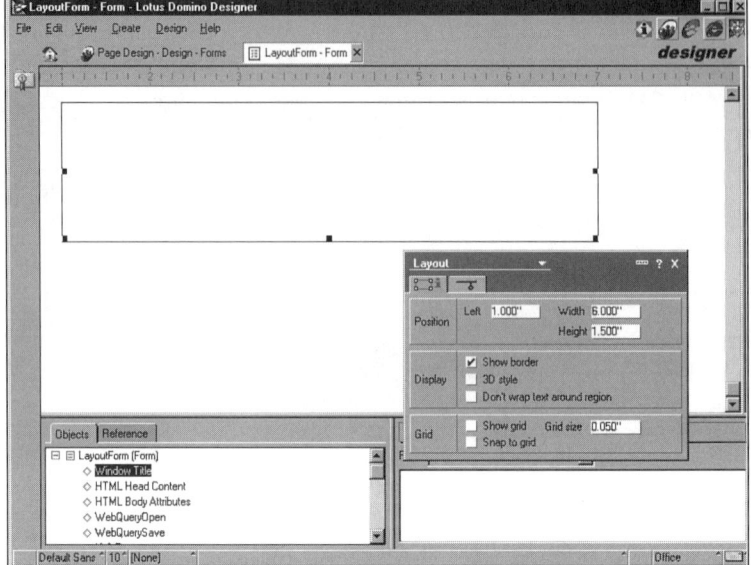

4. You can change the size and move the layout region with the properties box. The Left field enables you to adjust the left margin. The Width and Height properties enable you to change the size.

5. You can optionally show the border and change to 3D style. 3D style uses a gray background instead of a white one. You can also display a grid to make it easier to align controls. The Snap to grid option automates some alignment tasks.

After you create the layout region, you can add elements. For all these elements, you must first highlight the layout region. The following are elements you can add to the region:

- Static text   You create static text by selecting Create, Layout Region, Text.
- Graphic   You can create a graphic image within a layout region. To do this, first copy the bitmap you want to use to the Clipboard. Then select Create, Layout Region, Graphic.
- Graphic Button   You create a graphic button in a manner similar to a regular graphic. You must first copy the bitmap to the Clipboard and then select Create, Layout Region, Graphic Button. The main difference between a graphic button and a regular graphic is that the graphic button is considered a hotspot and has a `click` event, and a regular graphic object does not. You can program the graphic button with a simple action, formula, LotusScript, or JavaScript. A graphic can overlay a graphic button, or vice versa within a layout region.

> **Note:** Remember that layout regions do not work in Web browsers, so even if you create a graphic button with JavaScript, your program will still work only in the Notes client, not in Web browsers.

- **Picture** A picture is really nothing more than another name for a graphic or graphic button. If you select Create, Picture, you can import a graphic from the file system. Using this method, you do not have to use cut and paste. After you issue Create, Picture, you will be prompted whether you want to paste your image as a graphic or a graphic button. Make your selection and click OK.
- **Field** You create a field within a layout region by issuing Create, Field (with the layout region highlighted).

Using Subforms

Subforms enable you to create a reusable component that can be embedded in several different forms. One typical application for a subform might be when you want to have common information (such as name and address) on a form, but also want to have additional information (such as policy information) that varies depending upon the customer. In this case, the common information can be stored directly on the form, and variable information can be stored in a set of subforms. Domino can dynamically select the appropriate subform to use for the variable information. You can also use subforms for various adornments, such as headers or footers. The letterhead feature of your mail database is implemented using subforms.

On a subform, you can include any of the design elements that would normally be allowed in a form. The subform can be included in the form at the time you design the form, or the selection of the subform can be deferred until a document using the form is created. When the document is created, you can programmatically include the desired subform (as in your mail database), or you can ask the user to select a subform from a list that you provide.

To open or create a subform:

1. Open the Design Pane in the database in which you want to create your subform.
2. Click on the Resources twistie in the Design Pane.
3. Click on Subforms. A view showing you the existing subforms will appear in the work area on the right.
4. If you are opening an existing subform, double-click on its name in the Work Pane. If you are creating a new subform, click on the New Subform action button.
5. When your subform is open, you can use all the editing tools that were described for forms.

When you insert a subform based on a formula, it is called a computed subform. The formula is called the insert subform formula. This formula is computed when the form is opened and will not be recomputed if the document is updated and refreshed. The formula must evaluate to a subform name. If the subform name does not exist, no error message will be displayed. The subform will simply not appear.

Using Sections on Forms

In the section describing pages earlier in this chapter, I told you how you could use sections to organize the data on the page. Standard sections are also available on forms. You create a standard section on a form with the following steps:

1. Open the form to include your section.
2. Add the text and fields to be included in your section.
3. Highlight all the text and fields to be included.
4. Select Create, Section, Standard. Your section will appear. The first line of your text will appear as the default title of your section. You can modify the title by using the Section properties box.

Access-Controlled Sections

Forms also have an additional type of section called the access-controlled section. Access-controlled sections are typically used in workflow applications where a form may be routed, but only particular individuals are allowed to approve the form. By controlling the access to these sections, and by implementing signed fields (in the Field properties Options tab), you can ensure that only authorized individuals can approve the form. An access-controlled section controls the editing, not the reading of the information within it.

To create an access-controlled section:

1. Open the form to include your access-controlled section.
2. Add the text and fields to be included in your section.
3. Highlight all the text and fields to be included.
4. Select Create, Section, Controlled Access. Your section will appear. The first line of your text will appear as the default title of your section. You can modify the title by using the Form Section properties box. Notice that the Form properties box has additional tabs. In the Formula tab, you supply an access formula. There are also tabs for editors and noneditors to control whether the section is expanded or not.

In access-controlled sections, you can define the access list as editable, which will allow the document creator to specify who can edit the section. If you want to specify ahead of time who will be able to edit the section, you can supply an access formula. The formula can be made up of user, group, or role names, or you could use an @formula, such as @DBColumn to populate the list.

Using Sections on Forms | 339

Here is an example of the use of a controlled-access section. Suppose that you have an expense account workflow application. An employee enters information about the expenses and then submits it for approval by a manager. You want to ensure that only a manager can approve the form, so you include the approval within a controlled-access section. See Figure 14.28.

Figure 14.28
Access-controlled sections can be used for approval.

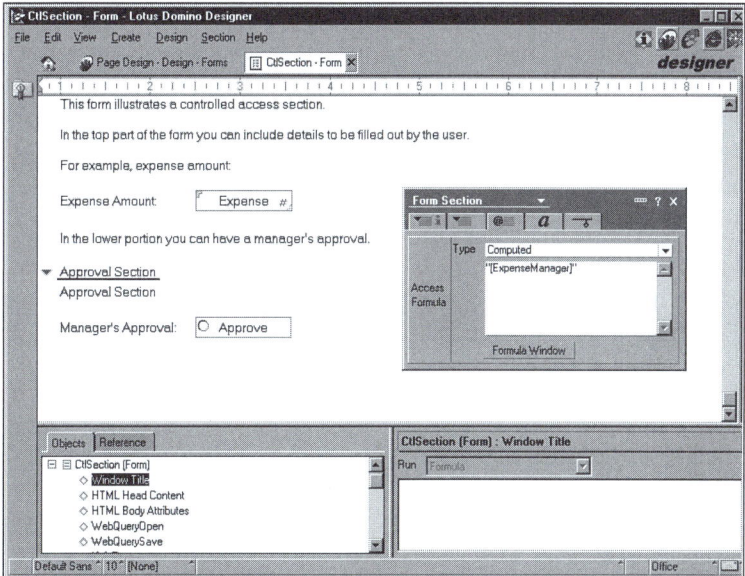

In Figure 14.28, I have shown the access formula as a computed value with the role name of ExpenseManager. You can tell this is a role name because it is enclosed in square brackets. This value for the access formula means that only users with the role ExpenseManager in the ACL will be able to access the Approval section in edit mode.

> **Note**
> Be careful with your use of access-controlled sections. Note that anyone with read access can read the contents of access-controlled sections. The access control applies only to the ability to edit the section. Also note that the access-control applies only to databases on a Domino server unless you have specified the Enforce a consistent ACL across all replicas of this database option in the database ACL. If this option is not selected in the ACL, anyone will be able to edit the section on a local replica of the database.

You can also specify the access formula via a `@DBColumn` lookup or via group names.

If you require two or more separate approvals for a form, you must use a separate section for each one. A single access-controlled section can have only one list of approvers.

Summary

In this chapter, I showed you how to create pages and forms, and we explored the major design elements for pages and forms. There are many similarities, but here are the fundamental differences. Pages are self-contained elements that typically will hold HTML formatting. They can contain graphics, tables, hotspots, text, and several other objects. You can create the HTML with another editor and import the HTML into Domino Designer.

Forms are used in conjunction with documents. Documents store data, and forms contain user interface elements called fields. This enables the user interface to be defined separately from the data. When you view a form and document combination, you are actually viewing the data items from the document filling in the fields on the form. If you enter information into the fields, they will be stored back into the document.

Forms have several design elements that cannot be used on pages. Fields, subforms, layout regions, and controlled access sections are the most important design elements that cannot be used on pages. Layout regions will not display in Web browsers, so use them only if you do not plan to access your databases via Web browsers on your intranet or the Internet.

From Here...

For further information on additional topics, check these chapters:

- Chapter 15, "Developing Views and Folders," continues the discussion on application development, showing you how to create summary views of information for your users.
- Chapter 16, "Using Outlines, Framesets, and Navigators," brings together these user navigational design elements. It shows you how to create applications that are organized and easy for your users to navigate.
- Chapter 17, "Access Control Lists (ACLs) and Application Security," tells you how to secure your applications so that only authorized users will be able to use the features you specify.
- Additional programming topics are covered in Part IV, "Using LotusScript, Java, and JavaScript." The chapters in this part cover the details of programming Notes and Domino.

CHAPTER 15

DEVELOPING VIEWS AND FOLDERS

Views and Folders are a fundamental part of Notes and Domino. They enable both the designer and user to organize documents within a Domino database. In essence, a view or folder provides a tabular display of selected fields from documents contained in a Domino database. In this chapter, I show you how to create and use views and folders in your Domino application.

ORGANIZING DOCUMENTS WITHIN YOUR DATABASE

You often see views and folders discussed at the same time because they are very similar. The major difference between views and folders is the criteria used to select documents to be shown.

Views use a formula, so the selection of documents is automatic. The formula is typically written by a designer and is generally used to filter the documents. Designers frequently use several different views in a database, each with a different formula. This enables the user to see various collections of documents, grouped and sorted in meaningful ways.

Folders don't use formulas for their selection. The documents in folders are typically moved to the folder by an end user. In the mail database, for example, a user can create and use folders to organize email. The user can decide the documents to put into each folder.

Because of the similarities in view and folder design, in this chapter I describe view design, but folder design is essentially equivalent. The difference between folders and views is mainly the method used to select documents, not differences in how they are designed.

CREATING AND OPENING A VIEW

A view is a tabular display of data extracted from a set of documents. Each row of the table represents one document, and the values in each column can be field data or can be based on a formula. Column formulas can combine data from multiple fields or use @functions to compute their result. The process of creating a view is initially creating the view itself, and then defining the data that should be included in each column.

For the purposes of this example, I'm going to create a new database from the Blank template. If you want to follow along, create a new Domino database on your local machine called View Design. Alternatively, you can find a copy of the database on the CD-ROM that reflects the final database contents.

After you create your database, click on the Views line in the Design pane on the left. Your screen should be similar to Figure 15.1.

This is very interesting. Although you created a blank database, you already have a view defined in your database. Domino always requires at least one view in your database, and so even when you create a blank database, an initial view is created for you. You cannot open a database that does not have at least one view. As you can see, the name of this view is `untitled`. This is pretty boring, and as you might imagine, the content of this initial view is pretty boring also. Let's see what Domino Designer has created for us by default.

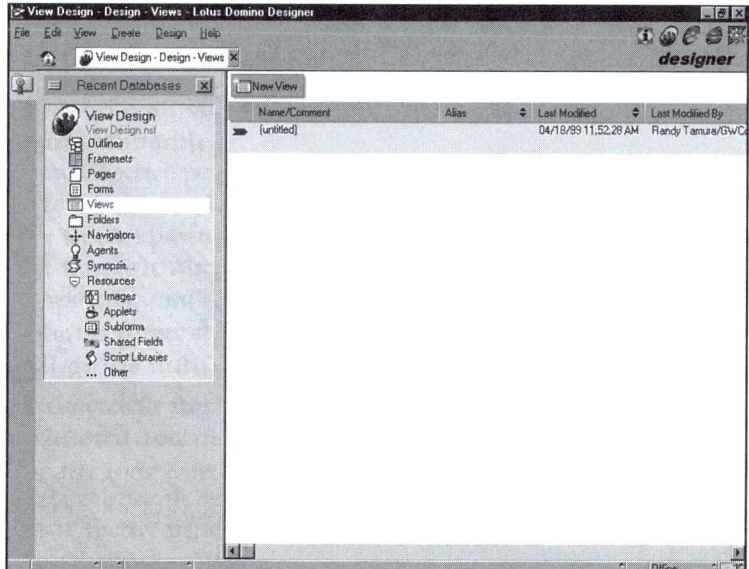

Figure 15.1
The Domino Designer with the Views design element selected.

To open or create a view for editing:

1. Open the database that contains your view and highlight Views in the Design pane on the left.

2. To create a new view, click the New View action button. To open an existing view, double-click on the line containing the view.

3. If you double-click on the untitled line, you will see the definition of your default view. See Figure 15.2.

The default view, called `untitled`, contains only a single column. The column appears with the number sign (#) in the column header.

SELECTING DOCUMENTS TO INCLUDE IN A VIEW

In Figure 15.2, notice that the words View Selection appear just above the drop-down box in the Programmer's pane at the bottom of your screen. The View Selection is used to enter the formula for selecting documents that will be shown in the view. On the right half of the Programmer's pane, there is a drop-down list, and you can select either Easy or Formula. If you select Easy and then click the Add Condition button, you will see the Search Builder dialog box. See Figure 15.3.

Figure 15.2
The untitled view as initially created by Domino Designer.

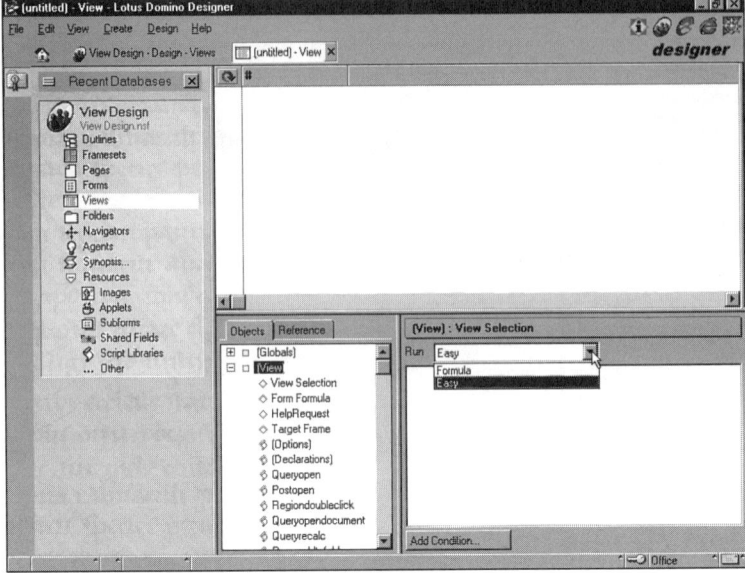

Figure 15.3
The Search Builder dialog box appears if you choose Easy for View Selection.

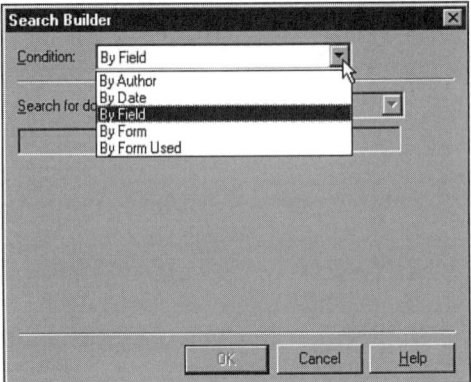

The Condition drop-down box shows the option By Field. With this option, you can choose to include documents in the view if a particular field of the document contains a specified value. For example, you could choose the field Color, and the contents could be Red. This specification shows documents in the view only if Red is contained in the Color field. You can include more than one condition, so if there were a Car field, you could include a specification for the contents Ferrari. Your view selection would then show only documents with Red for Color and Ferrari for Car. This view would clearly have good taste in cars.

> **Note**
>
> The Search Builder will display only field names that exist on forms within your database. If you have not yet defined any forms (and thus no fields), you will not be able to use the Search Builder with the By Field option. To follow with this example, you need to create a form called `Car` with two fields: `Car` and `Color`. If you do this, they will show up in the Search Builder. Normally, in your design process, you will design and build your forms prior to building your views.

You can choose documents by the following keywords in the Search Builder:

- **By Author** — The author of the document. The author name for the document must contain text that you supply.
- **By Date** — You can specify the date the document was created or last modified. You can choose a specific date, older or newer than a particular date, or within or outside a date range.
- **By Field** — As in the example, you can enter specific text. The text must be contained in the field you name. A string comparison is made, so the field should be a text field.
- **By Form** — A shorthand for multiple By Field specifications. When you select this option, a data entry field shows for all fields contained on the form. You can enter data for all the fields or some subset of them all at once.
- **By Form Used** — You can select documents based on the form used to compose the document.

As you create your view selection, it will appear in the right side of the Programmer's pane. Each of the conditions will appear as a small button within the pane. To edit a condition you have already entered, you can double-click on the button. See Figure 15.4.

Figure 15.4
Each of the conditions built by the Search Builder has a separate small button in the Programmer's pane.

Click these buttons to edit.

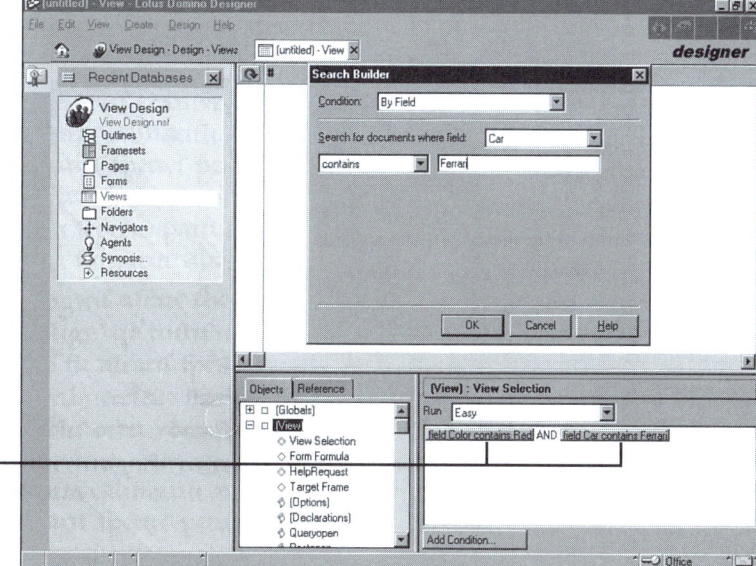

To select documents by formula, select Formula in the Run drop-down box. If you do not modify the formula, you can also switch from Easy to Formula to see the formula that Domino Designer has created for you.

If you become proficient with the @formula language, you may prefer to use formulas because they are much more powerful than the Search Builder functions. The formula language is covered in more detail in Chapter 18, "Working with Formulas, Functions, and Commands."

TYPES OF VIEWS

As mentioned previously, to create a view, first select Views in the Design pane, then click the New View action button. You will see the Create View dialog box. See Figure 15.5.

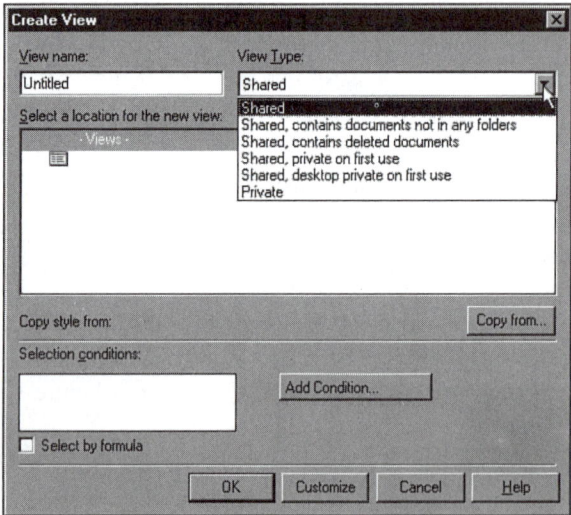

Figure 15.5
There are several types of shared and private views.

When you first create a view, in addition to the view name you must specify the view type. You cannot change the type after the view has been created. Views are generally categorized into shared views and private views. Multiple people can use shared views, but private views are restricted to a single user. Within these categories, however, there are several possibilities. Here are the view types:

- **Shared**   Shared views are the most common type of view. Shared views are available to users with at least Reader access to the database. Editor-level users with the privilege Create shared folders/views enabled in the ACL can create shared views. Otherwise, you must have Designer- or Manager-level access to create a shared view.

- **Shared, private on first use**   These views provide an opportunity for a designer to deliver customized views to end users. For example, you could use the @UserName function in the view selection so that only a single user's data appears in the view. Each user will see different data, and after a user has used the view, it will become private. A disadvantage of this setting is that after a view becomes private, users will no longer see updates made in the shared version. If you add or delete columns or change formulas in the shared version, the user will not see the changes if the view already became private. This type of view will be stored in the database unless the Create personal folders/views ACL setting for the user is disabled. In this case, the view is stored in DESKTOP.DSK.

- Shared, desktop private on first use   This type of view is the same as private on first use except that the view is stored in the user's DESKTOP.DSK file. The reason for storing the view in DESKTOP.DSK is that if you have a lot of users, the database could become very large if each user's private view is stored in the common database.

- Private   Users, not designers, create private views. Private views can be used to sort and organize data in a personal way without affecting the operation of the database for other users. In release 4.x of Notes and Domino, private views were called personal views. You may see some documentation refer to personal views, but private views and personal views are just two names for the same thing.

> **Note**
>
> There is a setting in the Access Control List (ACL) for a database that is called Create personal folders/views. This setting can be either enabled or disabled. If you disable this setting, it does *not* mean that the user is prevented from creating private (personal) folders and views. A user of Reader level and above can always create a private view or folder. The ACL setting enables or disables the user from creating the private view within the database. If the setting is disabled, the private views and folders are stored in the user's DESKTOP.DSK file on the local machine.
>
> Also note that Web browsers cannot view private views, whether they are created initially as private or they are initially shared and become private. If you want to make a customized view (similar to a shared-to-private view) accessible to Web browsers, you may be able to use a new release 5 feature called a Single Category embedded view. This feature is described later in this chapter.

The following two view types are new to release 5 of Domino. These types are available for views, but not for folders. Implicit in their type is a view selection formula, so they do not have a selection formula:

- Shared, contains documents not in any folders   A view of this type shows all the documents that have not been placed by a user in a folder. You can use this type of view for an inbox-type application where you want the document to disappear from the inbox if the user moves it to a folder. After it appears in a folder, it will automatically disappear from the inbox.

- Shared, contains deleted documents   This type of view is used to support the new soft deletions. Soft deletions enable you to implement a "Trash" type of folder where documents can temporarily be stored, but later recovered if desired. To use this type of folder, you must also enable soft deletions in the database properties Advanced (beanie hat) box.

348 CHAPTER 15 DEVELOPING VIEWS AND FOLDERS

> **Note**
> Soft deletions are a feature available only beginning with the release 5 database structure. If you are using the Domino Designer on a release 4.x database, you will not be able to select the deleted document type of view because it is not supported in the database. You can find the version of the database by looking at the Info tab of the database properties box. The ODS version should be 36 or greater to be a release 5 database.

CREATING FOLDERS

You create folders almost identically to the way you create views. Here's how:

1. Click on the Folders design element on the left; then in the right pane, click the New Folder button.
2. Give the folder a name in the dialog box that appears. Select the type of folder. The folder types are the same as the first four types of views. The new nonfolder type and soft deletion type of view cannot be specified for folders.
3. Select a location for your folder within the folder hierarchy. Do this by selecting the parent of where you want your folder to appear.
4. A default set of columns will be copied from the view/folder shown as Copy style from. If you want to choose a different folder or view, or start from a blank view, click the Copy from button. You will then see a dialog box, and you can choose your template.
5. You can click OK and your folder will be created, or you can click Customize. If you click Customize, your folder will be created, and you will be placed in edit mode on your newly created folder.
6. Customize your folder and save it.

VIEW COLUMN PROPERTIES

After you specify the documents you want selected in your view (via the View Selection formula), you must define the fields and information you want to show in your view. Each row of your view represents one document of the database, and the values in the columns are information extracted from those documents. Frequently, a column will hold the value from a single field. There are, however, other types of information that you can include. Let's go back and look at the default view of the View Design Database.

VIEW COLUMN BASICS

Each view column has several attributes besides the definition of the data to be shown. Figure 15.6 shows the default view formula and properties box for the default view column.

As you can see, the title of the column is found in the Properties box and is a simple number sign (#). In the Programmer's pane at the bottom of the window, you see that the Column Value of the # column is highlighted in the left half of the pane, and a simple function appears in the right half of the pane.

VIEW COLUMN PROPERTIES 349

PART
III
CH
15

Figure 15.6
A column can be defined by a simple Function, Field, or Formula.

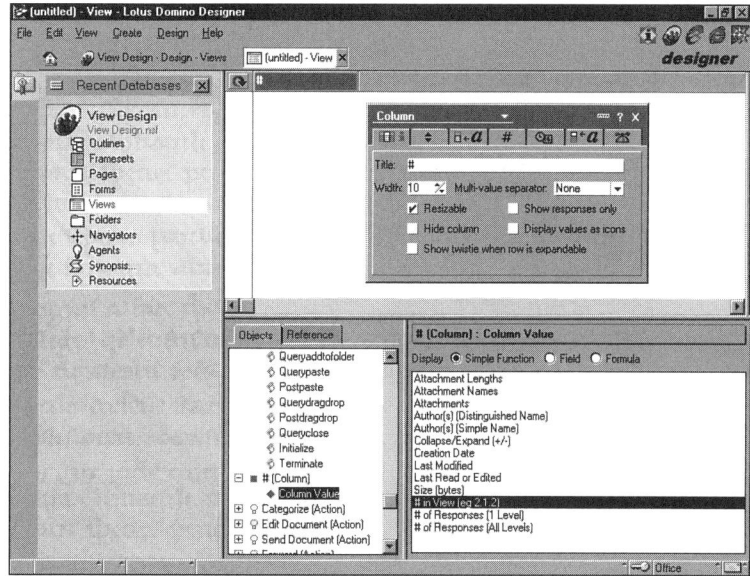

You can define a column's contents with a simple function. The functions can be information, such as attachment lengths or names, authors, creation or modification dates, or document numbers within the view. To specify a simple function:

1. Open the view containing the column you want to modify.
2. Click on the column object's Column Value in the left half of the Programmer's pane at the bottom of the window. Alternatively, you can double-click on the column header of the column you want to modify in the View pane at the top of the window.
3. In the right half of the Programmer's pane, select Simple Function in the Display radio button group. If you had previously selected a different option, a warning may be displayed that your prior definition will be lost.
4. In the list box below, select the simple function you want to use.

As an alternative to a simple function, you can define a column to contain a field value from a document. To use a document field as a column value:

1. Open the view containing the column you want to modify.
2. Click on the column object's Column Value in the left half of the Programmer's pane at the bottom of the window. Alternatively, you can double-click on the column header of the column you want to modify in the View pane at the top of the window.
3. In the right half of the Programmer's pane, select Field in the Display radio button group. If you had previously selected a different option, a warning may be displayed that your prior definition will be lost.
4. In the list box below, select the field name you want to use.

Finally, you can use a formula as the definition for what to display in a column. To use a formula, follow the steps for simple function or field, but click the formula radio button instead. Type the formula in the area below the radio buttons.

To modify properties other than the value, you use the Column properties box. You can specify the width of the column by typing a value into the width box, by clicking the up or down arrows next to the width value, or by dragging the column separator in the view header on the right side of the column you want to modify.

Adding and Removing View Columns

Adding and removing columns is pretty easy within the Domino Designer. To append a column at the right side of your view, you can select Create, Append New Column. Alternatively, you can double-click on the column header to the right of the last column. This creates a new column and brings up the Properties box for the newly created column.

To insert a new column in the middle of the view, select the column to the right of the location you want the new column, and then select Create, Insert New Column. You can use this technique to insert a new column as the first column.

To delete a column, click on the header of the column and click the Del key. Alternatively, you can click on the header of the column, and then select Edit, Clear. Either technique will prompt you with a warning that you are about to permanently delete a column. You can select multiple columns for deletion by clicking on the header of the first, and then holding down the Ctrl key and selecting the other columns. Click the Del key or use the menus after you have selected all the columns you want to delete.

Document Types and Hierarchies

When I introduced forms and documents in the previous chapter, I did not discuss the different types of documents, because they are a bit hard to understand until you understand the concept of views. Well, here we are in the midst of views, so let's retrace our steps a bit and talk about the different kinds of documents and how they can be displayed in views.

There are three kinds of documents you can create with a form:

- **Document** A normal, regular, ordinary document. It can contain text fields and all the other goodies I have showed you. This is also sometimes called a *main document*.
- **Response** A special kind of document that is a response to a main document. It is differentiated because within a view, a response document can be shown indented under its parent main document.
- **Response to Response** This is a special kind of response. It can be either a response to a main document or a response to a response.

When you create a form, you specify the type of document you want associated with the form. You make your selection in the Form properties box. See Figure 15.7.

Figure 15.7
You select the document type in the Form properties box.

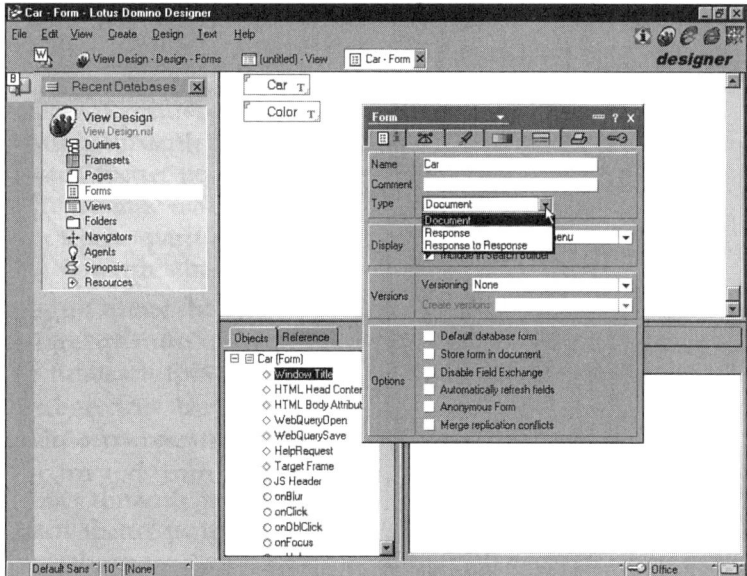

When a response document is created, you can have the response document inherit values from its parent document. Typically, the parent document and the response document will both have some fields in common. By inheriting the values from the parent document at the time the response document is created, the user's job will be easier, because some fields will automatically be filled in.

To enable inheritance of fields on response documents from the parent documents, you use the Form properties box on the Defaults tab. See Figure 15.8. After you enable inheritance on the response document, you must also create a formula on each field that you want to be inherited from the parent document. Thus, you can control inheritance for selected fields only.

To illustrate these concepts, I have created a view called CarView and three forms. The forms are for a main car document (the Car form), a response (the CarResponse form), and a response to response (the CarRtoR form).

In the sample CarView view, I have defined three columns. The view is shown in Figure 15.9.

In the view, I have defined the Car column and the Color column to display fields directly from the document. In the figure, only the first line in the view and the last line in the view are main documents. The second and fourth lines are response documents and the middle line is a response to response document.

I said there were three columns, but it appears that there are only two columns, the Car and Color columns. The other column is actually the very first column of the view. The Column properties dialog box shows you the properties for this first column. Lines 2, 3, and 4 are actually shown using this column as you can see from the formula definition in the Programmer's pane. You can tell the formula is used because the lines begin with the text string Resp.

Figure 15.8
You can enable inheritance by selecting an option in the Response document's form properties.

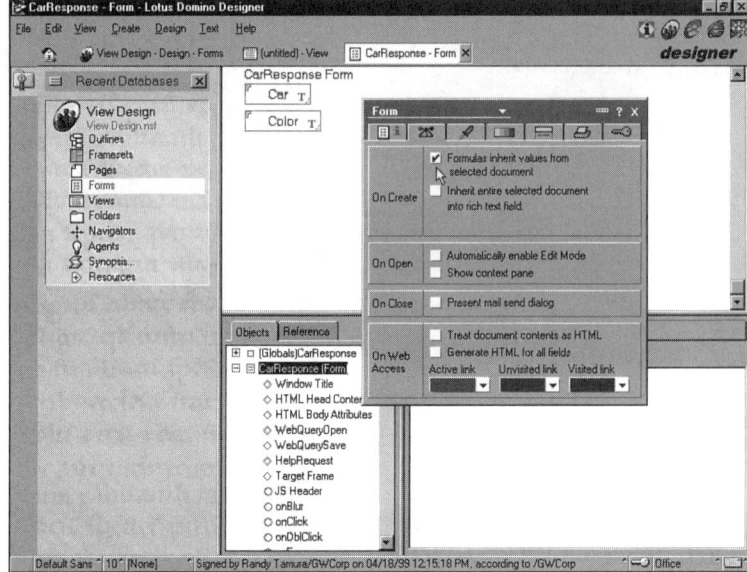

Figure 15.9
Views can show response documents below their parent document.

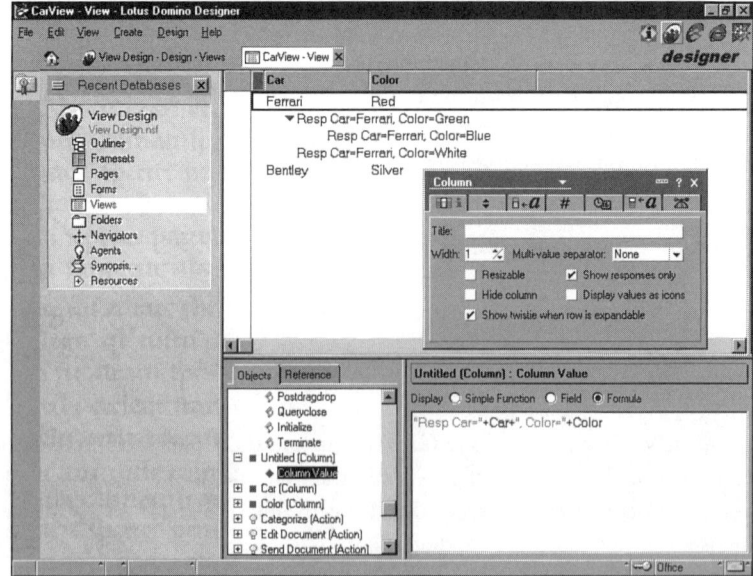

A response document displays differently from main documents because it is typically formatted via a formula contained within a single column. This is what I have shown in the example, although you would probably use a more interesting formula for your application. In order to display the responses as shown, you should

- Define a column (typically only width 1) to the left of your first data column. In this case, I made it the first column of the view. This column does not need to have a title. Typically, it doesn't because there is no need to show anything in the title line.
- Enable the Show responses only check box for this column. When this check box is enabled, the other column definitions will not apply for this row, so you need to define your output for the line via a formula. The output can extend to the width of the entire view. Typically, you'll want to include summary information, such as the document author, the date, and perhaps a title field.
- Enable the Show twistie when row is expandable check box. This will enable the user to expand and collapse the rows of the view.

You might be wondering about the difference between regular response documents and response to response documents. Here is a little more detail. At the time you create a response document of either type, the outcome depends upon two things: what type of document is selected (main or response) and the type of form used to create the new response document. If the row selected is a main document then if you create either type of response, the result is a document that shows up immediately below the selected main document. Line 2 of the view in Figure 15.8 is a response document, and it shows directly under the main document.

If the selected document is any type of response and you create a new response, you get two different results depending upon the type of document you create. If you create a response to response, your new document will be shown directly underneath your selected document (line 3 of the view), pretty much as you would expect.

If the selected document is any type of response and you create a regular response document, it will appear immediately below the corresponding main document, not indented from the selected document. Line 4 of the view was created by highlighting line 3 (the Ferrari-Blue line) and creating a response document.

Finally, to give you an example of this rather hard to describe phenomenon, look back at Figure 15.8. In Table 15.1, I show you what happens if you have a certain document highlighted and you create a new document.

TABLE 15.1 RESPONSE AND RESPONSE TO RESPONSE

Line Selected upon Create	Type of Document Created	Shows Up as Line
Red	Response	Green or White
Red	Response to response	Green or White
Green	Response	White
Green	Response to response	Blue
Blue	Response	White
Blue	Response to response	New under Blue

As a designer, you sure don't want to have to explain that table to your users. In summary, if you want your response documents to keep on indenting regardless of level, you need to use response to response forms. If you want all your responses to stay only one level below the main, then you need to use regular response forms. You probably won't need to use both kinds of response documents in your database. If you do, it will be pretty confusing for the users. Pick one type and just stay with it.

SORTING A VIEW COLUMN

After you define the contents of your view, you may want to sort the documents based on certain columns. Although not absolutely required, I would recommend that if you sort, you use your leftmost columns. These are the columns that people will see first, and if they are ordered, it will be more obvious. There are also certain @functions, such as @DBColumn, that work based on the first sorted column, and if you keep them to the left, it will be easier to remember and maintain these functions.

Figure 15.10
You can sort and total by column.

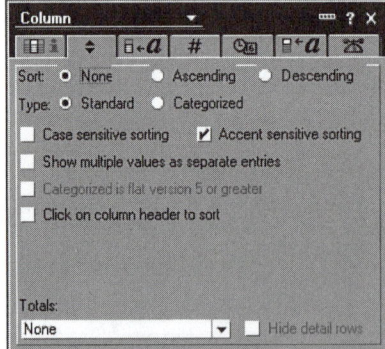

In Figure 15.10, you see the sorting options. The first option is the direction of sort, either Ascending or Descending. If you sort multiple columns, they can be in different directions, the leftmost column will have the highest precedence, and the columns are sorted from left to right.

A Categorized column enables the documents to be sorted by a special field contained in the document named Categories. This field should be defined as a text field (or one of the list fields, such as a Dialog list or Combobox), and you may also want to enable multiple values. When a user enters a category in this field, it is used to group the documents for display.

For example, if several documents contain the value Sales in a field called Categories, these documents will be shown together if the sort column is categorized.

A user can enter two or more values into the Categories field. The user typically does this by checking multiple items in a Dialog List box. For example, suppose a user enters Sales, Contests as the two values. If the Show multiple values as separate entries check box is enabled, the document will show up twice within the view: once under the category Sales, and a second time under the category Contests.

When you make a Categorized view, a special category line is created automatically for each category. The documents within the category are shown underneath the appropriate category line. The Categories field itself is not shown within the document line. Sometimes, however, you want the category to appear as a regular field within the document line instead of a separate line. New with release 5, you can check the Categorized is flat version 5 or greater option. This will show the Categories field as a regular field within the document line, even if the Show twistie when row is expandable option is enabled.

If you enable Case sensitive sorting, capital letters are sorted before lowercase letters. Accent sensitive sorting is an option for languages other than English. Sorting will be dependent upon the current language being used on the workstation.

When you enable the Click on column header to sort option (see Figure 15.11), additional options become available in the properties box. You can choose Ascending, Descending, Both, or Change to View.

Figure 15.11
You can enable the user to choose the sort method.

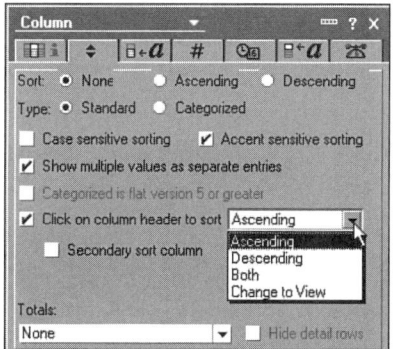

If you choose Ascending, Descending, or Both, little triangles appear on the column header when the user uses the view. The Ascending sort is signified by a triangle pointing up. If the user clicks on this triangle, the documents will be sorted in ascending order by the values in the column. A Descending sort works similarly, and when Both is specified, the user can choose either Ascending or Descending sorting.

The Secondary sort column option enables you to choose another column for secondary sorting. The current column will be sorted first, and then within each identical value of the primary column, the documents will be sorted by the value contained in the secondary column.

The Change to View option implements a hyperlink to another view if the column header is clicked. For example, suppose the primary view is a summary view showing high-level information. Occasionally, users may want to see details for a particular document. Columns could contain the Change to View option, and each column could go to a different detailed view. When the user clicks a particular column heading, the view will change and the new view will show the same document (but with different fields displayed) that was selected in the primary view. This enables you to extract different, perhaps more detailed, information from the same document.

Sorting by a Hidden Column

Sometimes you want to display information sorted by a field that you don't want to show. For example, suppose you have a view column that contains days of the week: Sunday, Monday, Tuesday, and so forth. The typical sort for this would be in order of the days of the week, but with regular sorting, you get this list in alphabetical order, which is not particularly useful.

To sort the days of the week in their weekday order, you can use a hidden column. Within the hidden column, you can put a formula. See Figure 15.12.

In the figure, you can see the value of the column as it is calculated by the formula. The formula is specified in the Programmer's pane at the bottom-right side of the window. It basically converts a day of the week into a number. You then specify the sorting for the hidden column and leave sorting unspecified in the actual day column. After you hide the column, the user will only see the view starting with the day column, which is sorted in the proper order by day of week.

Using Icons in View Columns

Many times, applications use icons to display status. In Figure 15.13, you see the standard mail database inbox. Notice that the highlighted line contains a paper clip. This is a fairly standard way to denote a file attachment. One of the other lines contains an exclamation point to indicate an important message.

USING ICONS IN VIEW COLUMNS 357

Figure 15.12
A formula and hidden column can change the sort order.

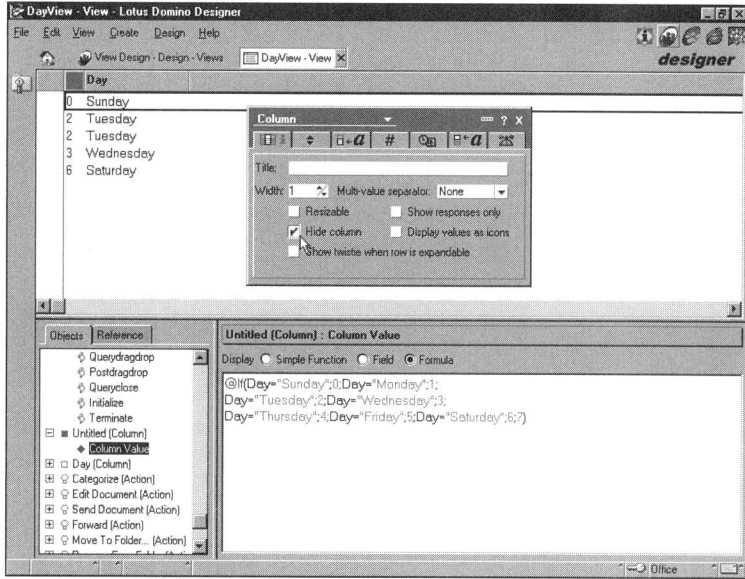

Figure 15.13
Column icons can display status information very compactly.

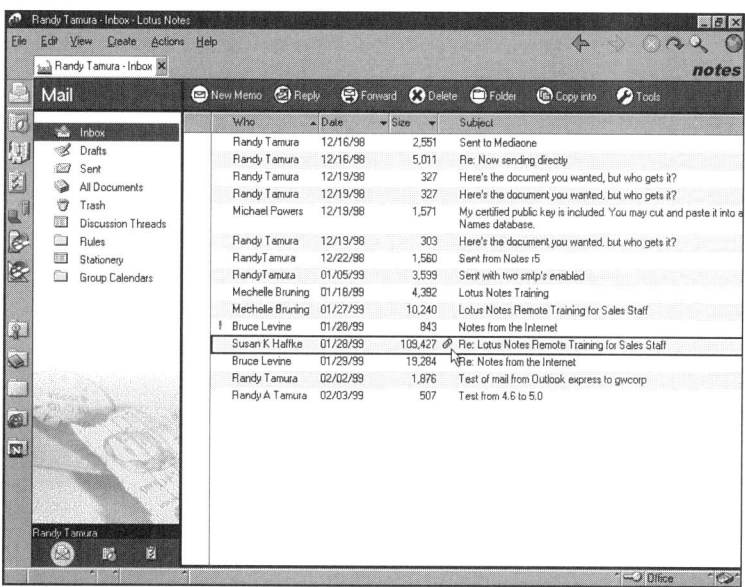

What if you could incorporate your own paper clips, exclamation points, and other icons into your own views? Wouldn't that be great? Well, it would, and I'll show you how to do it. (Okay, you don't have to get overexcited about it.)

To use an icon in a column, here's all you have to do:

1. Open the view you want to contain the icon.
2. Select the column you want to contain the icon and open the Column properties box. You can do this with the properties SmartIcon or by selecting Design, Column Properties.
3. In the Column properties box, adjust the width of the column. A width of 1 to 3 characters is probably appropriate.
4. Select the Display values as icons check mark.
5. As the column value, use a field or formula that evaluates to a number. You can use a number from 0 to 176. Zero will display no icon.

There are 176 valid icons in Domino release 5. You can see a table of the icons in Figure 15.14.

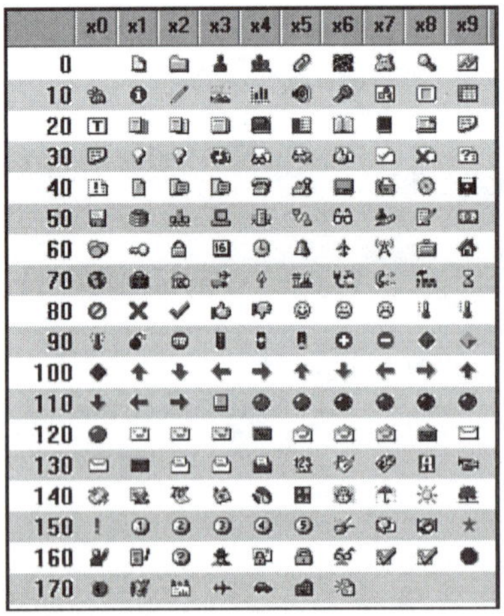

Figure 15.14
There are 176 valid icons in Notes/Domino release 5.

Here's how to read the table. The first row consists of the icons numbered 0 to 9. Actually, you use 0 for a blank space with no icon. The second row contains icons numbered 10 to 19. Look through the table to find the icon you want to use, then look to the left and to the top. Add the two numbers. For example, to use the smiley face, look to the left and you see 80. Look at the top of the column and you see it is x5, so the value to use is 85.

As an added bonus, on the CD-ROM in the View Design database, there is one form, one agent, and one view that I used to create Figure 15.14. The form is called Icon, the agent is called Make Icons, and the view is called Icons.

FORMATTING FONTS IN A VIEW COLUMN

When you create and edit view columns, you have a lot of control over the formatting of the column. First, you have control over the fonts used within the column itself. See Figure 15.15.

Figure 15.15
You can control the font face, size, and style used within view columns.

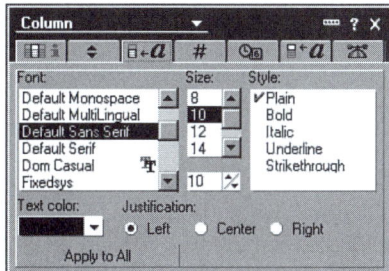

Within the Font (the third) tab, you control the fonts for the column, and within the Title (next-to-last) tab, you can control the fonts for the title line.

As with most windowing programs, you can control the font face (name), its size, and the style (plain, bold, italic, and so forth). You can also choose the justification within the column as left, center, or right. If you click the Apply to All button at the bottom of the dialog box, your change will apply to all the view's columns. Before you choose a wild font, however, take into consideration whether your application will be used on the Web by Web browsers. If so, you should probably choose from the generic font families that you can use with Domino. These three are Default Serif, Default Sans Serif, and Default Monospace. These translate into commonly used fonts, such as Times Roman (Times), Helvetica, and Courier. One of the most vexing problems in Web development today is the use of fonts.

When HTML was originally conceived, its purpose was to mark up the content of the Web page with the semantic meaning of the page. In other words, it was to inform the browser about titles, headers, links, and so forth. The formatting of these elements was up to the browser and the user. That's right, the user was—and is—able to control the appearance of the Web page. After the HTML author identified certain text as a heading level 1, the user could format these elements with Serif fonts or Sans serif fonts, and make them purple if so desired.

Well, you can imagine the clash that developed because Web site developers also wanted to control the look and feel of their Web site. The ongoing debate is still not totally resolved yet, although the major way for Web developers to gain back some control is with cascading style sheets (CSS). It's too far afield for me to explain this technology here, but if you are interested, pick up a current book about HTML and read about them.

Of course, if the views you developed will be used just by Notes clients, you can use fonts as you please, as long as you make sure that the fonts are available on the client machines.

Formatting Numbers in a View Column

In Figure 15.16, you see the numeric formatting tab in the view Column properties box.

Figure 15.16
You can control the formatting of numbers with the view Column properties box.

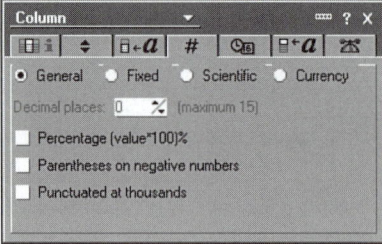

For numeric formatting, if you use general formatting, the display of numbers will vary depending upon how the value was input. Leading zeros will be suppressed. If you use fixed formatting, each number will be formatted with a fixed number of decimal places that you can specify. With scientific formatting, numbers will be displayed in scientific notation. Currency will display the currency symbol and two digits after the decimal.

You can also show values as percentages, which will display a value that is 100 times the numeric value. You can add parentheses on negative values by checking that box, and you can punctuate at thousands.

The punctuation for the currency symbol, decimal character, and the punctuation at thousands varies, depending upon the international language used.

FORMATTING DATES IN A VIEW COLUMN

In Figure 15.17, you see the options for date formatting.

Figure 15.17
You can format date/time values to show both date and time or just one without the other.

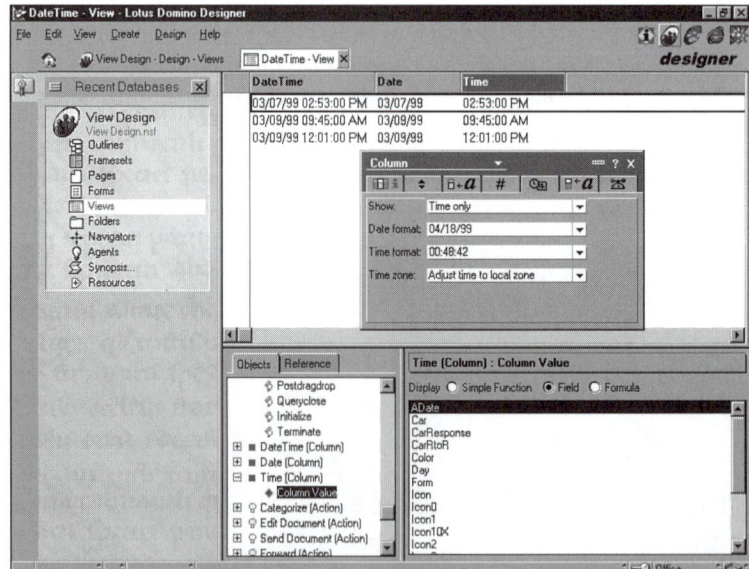

In the Show option, you can choose to show both date and time, as shown in column 1 of the view, just dates (column 2), or just times (column 3). The date format itself can be month/day, month/year, month/day/year, or month/4-digit year.

Time values can be hours:minutes or hours:minutes:seconds. Time zones can automatically be adjusted to the local time zone and can show the time zone in the display.

Programmatic Column Name

In the Advanced tab of the View Columns property box, you see a section titled Programmatic Use. See Figure 15.18. In this section, you can specify a name for the column. If the column contains a field, the default value for the column name is the field name. If the view column contains an expression, the name will automatically be constructed by Notes to be of the format $n. For example, you might see names such as $0, $1, or $2.

Figure 15.18
The View Column properties box enables you to change the column name and specify links.

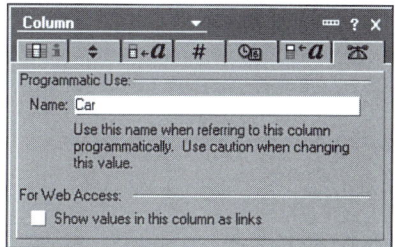

Although you can change the name for the column, you will rarely need to do so. The name you specify can be obtained in LotusScript via the ItemName property of the NotesViewColumn class. In Java, you can access the name via the getItemName method of the ViewColumn class.

The dialog box that enables you to change the name says you should use caution when changing the column name, because if the column contains a field, it would be rare that you would want another name for the column. Also, if the column contains a formula, the formula is compiled, stored internally within Domino, and may be internally referenced. Thus, the names such as $0 and $1 may be used within the database, and changing them may have unpredictable results.

Showing Values as Links

When Domino displays a view in HTML to a browser, it will normally highlight the first column with tags to link to the document. Sometimes, however, you may want to highlight a column other than the first column as your link column. You can do this on the Advanced tab of the View Columns properties box.

To enable this feature, first highlight the column you want to use for linking, then in the advanced (beanie hat) tab, enable the option: For Web Access: Show values in this column as links. You can enable more than one column, in which case all of the columns you specify will be highlighted, but they will all open the same document.

Note that this feature is not supported with the Java view applet, which will be described later in this chapter.

VIEW PROPERTIES

In addition to the properties that can be adjusted for each column, the view itself has properties. In Figure 15.19, you can see the View Basics tab.

Figure 15.19
The View Basics tab enables you to give an alias and a comment for a view.

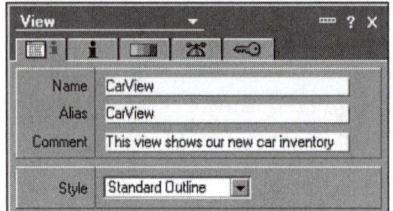

Besides the view name, you see that the view has an alias. The alias is an important part of the view, and you should probably include one with every view you make. One thing you may find as you develop applications for Notes and Domino is that they always need to be changed and updated. As a result of these changes, the names you give to design elements may also change. When you make changes to view and form names, however, you don't want to have to go back and change all references to the new names.

Aliases enable you to assign a name to a view or form that can remain constant for the life of a database. You can assign the alias when the view is initially created. Typically, you use the original form or view name as the initial alias name. You make all internal references to the alias name. You can change the external name as frequently as you like, and you will not have to change any references to your view.

If you enclose the view name (not the alias) in parentheses, the view becomes hidden. You can use it for `@DBColumn` and `@DBLookup` formulas, but it will not be shown to the user.

The Comment field of the View Basics tab is used to enter a comment for the view. This comment will appear just below the name of the view when you are reviewing all your views.

The view style can either be Standard Outline or a Calendar view. All the views we have seen so far in this chapter are Standard Outline views. A Calendar view enables you to display a calendar, and documents that are displayed in the view can be placed on the calendar in a manner similar to the calendar found in your mail database.

Calendar views are fairly restricted in their format. They typically have from two to five columns. The first two columns are mandatory, and the next three are recommended. Here is the layout you should have:

View Column	Contents
1	Date/Time, Hidden, Sorted. This contains the Start Date.
2	Numeric, Hidden. Duration of calendar entry, in minutes.
3	Time value, not hidden. This displays the start time of the calendar entry.
4	Integer numeric, Icon, not hidden. This displays an icon in the calendar. It is typically used to signify the type of calendar entry.
5	Text, not hidden. This is the text to display in the calendar entry.

If you create a Calendar view with these types of columns, you can display it with the Calendar view style. You may find this useful in certain applications where you want to display dates, times, and durations.

View Options

There are several view options that can be enabled on the Options tab for the view properties. See Figure 15.20.

Figure 15.20
The View Options tab allows you to enable various options for the view.

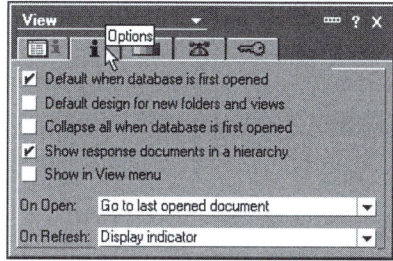

Here are the options:

- **Default when database is first opened**   This option makes the current view the default view. In the view list, a solid arrow will indicate that this view is the default. You can have only one default view for the database. If you enable the option for one view, it will disable any previous selection on a different view.

- **Default design for new folders and views**   When a new view is created, the current view will serve as a model for the newly created view. The newly created view will start out with the same column definitions. If you will have several similar views in a database, you can create one, set this option, and then create the others. This will save you some time in the view creation process.

- **Collapse all when database is first opened**   This option will collapse any twisties that group a set of documents. By setting this option, the initial view will be more compact and perhaps easier to work with for the user.

- **Show response documents in a hierarchy** You previously saw how to create hierarchical response documents. In order for this feature to work, you must enable this option. If you do not enable the option, each column will show its own data rather than use the formula specified in the response column.
- **Show in View menu** This option .displays the name of the view in the View menu for users. If you enable this option, it will give your users another way to navigate to the view. Normal navigation is via the Navigator pane, but if you are using a graphic navigator, you may want to also enable the View menu option.

At the bottom of the dialog box there are two options, On Open and On Refresh. Here are the choices for these two options:

- **On Open** The choices are go to last opened document, go to top row, and go to bottom row. When the view is first opened, the view will be positioned to the document you specify here.
- **On Refresh** The choices are Display indicator, Refresh display, Refresh display from top row, and Refresh display from bottom row. This option controls the action taken when new documents are available for the view. These options apply only to the Notes client because Web browsers do not have an indicator.

VIEW STYLE PROPERTIES

The View Style properties are found on the third tab of the view properties. See Figure 15.21.

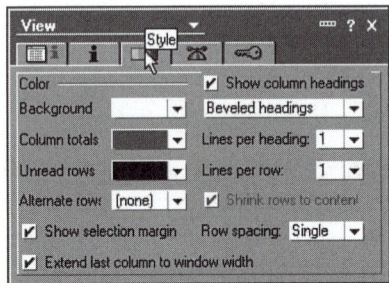

Figure 15.21
The View style tab enables you to control visual aspects of the view.

There are four color options on the left of the dialog box. These are the options:

- **Background color** This is the overall background color for the view. You can choose from the 256-color palette or select from the custom color palette, and the color choice works for both Notes client and Web browsers. As usual, you should be careful in choosing a color other than one found in the Web palette if your view will be displayed in Web browsers. You should generally choose white or another light color unless you have an overall color scheme that you are using for your Web site.

- **Column totals** You can choose from the 16-color palette for this option. Gray is the default color, and you typically will want to choose a color that will highlight the column total.

- **Unread rows** In the mail database, the unread documents are red. The default color for normal views is black. If you are using unread rows as a design feature of your database, you may want to choose a color that dramatically highlights them. You can choose from the 16-color palette for this option.

- **Alternate rows** This option enables you to specify a second color for alternating rows. You can choose to have no alternate row colors, colors from the 256-color palette, or a custom color. If you have already chosen a color and want to go back to no alternating color, you must select the leftmost icon in the top row of the color picker. This is pretty obscure, so see Figure 15.22. The middle icon enables you to choose a color from the 256-color palette, and the rightmost color circle icon enables you to select a custom color.

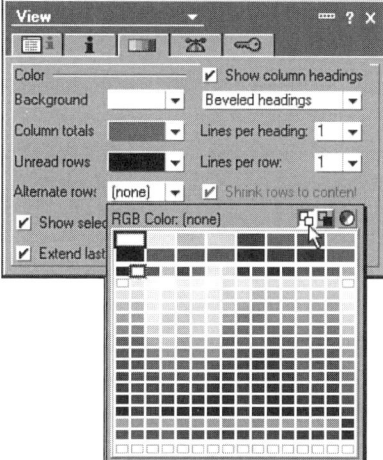

Figure 15.22
To select (none) for the alternating color, choose the leftmost icon in the top row.

- **Show selection margin** (Refer to Figure 15.21.) This option affects only the Notes client and Web browsers when using the Java view applet (described shortly). If you use a Web browser without the Java view applet, the option is ignored. This option enables a column for icons to the left of your view. This column displays unread marks (star), user selection (check mark), replication or save conflicts (diamond), and deleted marks (trashcans). Normally, you should leave this option enabled.

- **Extend last column to window width** Enabling this option allows the contents of the rightmost column of a view to extend past the column bounds. If not enabled, the rightmost column contents will be truncated at the column bound, even if there is more room in the window.

- **Show column headings** Checking this option causes the column titles to be displayed. This option works both in the Notes client and browsers.

- **Beveled or simple headings** This option changes the format of the displayed headings. It applies only to Notes clients and is ignored for Web browsers. Beveled headings have a gray color (and are the default); simple headings adopt the background color of the view.
- **Lines per heading** This is the number of lines that the headings should use. This is useful if you have long headings or a lot of columns. When you have a lot of columns, you can use multiple line headers and thereby possibly make the columns narrower. You can specify up to five lines for the header.
- **Lines per row** You can use up to nine lines for view content rows. This option would be useful if you have a lot of content to display.
- **Shrink rows to content** If you use multiple content lines per row, I would recommend enabling this option. It allows each row to contain only the number of lines necessary to display its content. The number of lines is calculated separately for each row. If you use multiple lines without enabling this option, you will probably see many blank lines.
- **Row spacing** This option can be Single, 1 1/4, 1 1/2, 1 3/4 or double. Normally, you would leave this option set for single spacing unless you want to allow extra spacing per row.

View Advanced Properties

The View Advanced tab (with the beanie hat) enables you to change the view index settings, the handling of unread marks, the view's form formula, and ODBC and Web access options. The first two options deal with a view's index. Refer to Figure 15.23 for the next few sections.

Figure 15.23
To Advanced tab enables you to modify some important options, such as applet usage.

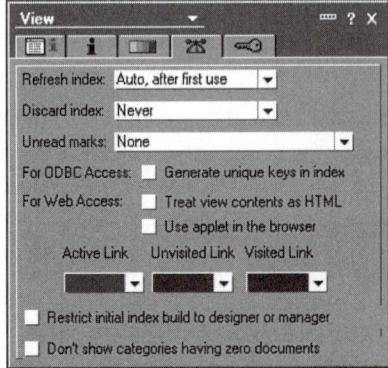

The View Index

Each view has an associated index, which is used for displaying the view. This index is different from a full text index. The view index options you set in the properties dialog box control when this index is created and when it is deleted. The view index has important performance and usability considerations. These considerations are

- If the view index is out-of-date with respect to the documents it displays, the user will see out-of-date information.
- The view index can take considerable time to build, especially for large databases, so if it is built frequently, users may have to wait a long time for it to be built before they can see the view.
- The view index takes significant space in the database, so if you build it but it is not used, you may be requiring too much space in your database for data that is not needed.

Because of these important considerations, it is not possible for Domino to guess what type of refresh strategy to use for all views in all databases. This job must be left to the designer and should be based on the usage pattern of the database and the type and frequency of change of the data shown in the view.

Note that each view can have separate settings, so in some databases you may have different strategies for different views. Here are your choices:

- **Auto, after first use**   In this case, no view is built until the view is used at least once. Thereafter, it is updated automatically as in the Automatic setting listed next. When you use this option, users may notice a delay when the view is first used due to the creation of the index. Use this option for databases that may be used in cycles. For example, it may be used frequently for some time, but then not used for some time. While it is being used, the index will be updated automatically, but when it isn't being used, the automatic deletion will discard the index and it won't appear until the view is used again.
- **Automatic**   This option always keeps the view updated. As documents are added, the view index is incrementally updated. This option updates the index even if there are no users using the database. Because the index is always up-to-date, users will not notice a delay to build the index when the view is first used. Use this option for views that will be frequently used.
- **Manual**   This option will not update the view until the user requests it. It is most useful for views containing a large number of documents that do not change frequently.
- **Auto, at most every *n* hours**   With this option, you must also specify a time limit in hours. This option limits the frequency of view index updates. If you use the default—12 hours, for example—the view is updated no more frequently than 12 hours since the last update. Use this option for databases where changes are slow. Suppose, for example, you had only one document change every 3 hours. By limiting the view index update to once every 12 hours, you can group the 4 changes into one view index update. Remember that users can also manually update the view at any time if they desire.

The Discard index options control when the view index is deleted. This is a trade-off of space for time. The space taken by the view index is considered against the time the user must wait while the index is constructed. The discarding is actually done on the Domino server, by default at 2 a.m. by the server task UPDALL. The discard index options are

- **Never** The index is permanently kept. Because this option will reserve space on the server for the index, you should use this option for views that are frequently used. If you can afford the space, you might also consider this option if the view is very large, because for large views your users may have to wait a very long time for the view index to be reconstructed. By keeping the view index permanently, users will not have to wait as long when the view is first opened.
- **After each use** This option will flag the view as eligible to be discarded as soon as it is closed. It will not actually be discarded until the next time the UPDALL server task runs. Use this option for infrequently used databases.
- **If inactive for *n* days**. This option is a compromise between the never and always options just described. You can specify a time limit, and if the view has not been used during that time, the view index will be discarded the next time UPDALL runs.

UNREAD MARKS IN THE VIEW

Unread marks are an aid to the user of a database so that he or she knows what information is new. The unread marks are calculated separately for each user so that if two people are viewing the same database, they will see different sets of unread marks. As you can imagine, keeping track of the unread marks does cause a performance penalty, so there are several options that you, as a designer, can control.

> **Note**
>
> A new option in R5 is a database property called Don't maintain unread marks. This enables you to completely disable unread marks for the entire database. It can be found in the Advanced (beanie hat) tab within the database properties box. To improve performance, check this box. You typically set this option when you create a database, as described in Chapter 12, "Creating and Accessing Domino Databases."
>
> Note that the database property should provide much more of a performance improvement than the view options because the unread marks are not maintained. The view options control only the display of unread marks, and all the time to maintain the marks within the database is still done.

The following unread marks options control how a view displays unread marks. These options do not affect whether the unread marks information is stored, only how it is displayed. For example, you could choose two different options in different views, and the unread marks would display differently. Here are the options:

- **None** This option causes the view to display faster because the unread marks are not displayed.
- **Unread Documents Only** This displays unread marks only on top-level documents. It does not display unread marks for collapsed groups of documents in a view.
- **Standard (compute in hierarchy)** This displays unread marks on top-level documents or on collapsed groups of documents where one of the lower-level documents is unread.

ODBC Access

The next option in the Advanced tab is for ODBC Access. It says Generate unique keys in index. This is one of the most mysterious options for a view. First of all, this option is not for accessing ODBC databases, as it may appear. Tools that access the current Domino database via ODBC use this option.

Lotus has a product called NotesSQL that enables a Notes/Domino database to be accessed as if it were a relational database via ODBC. Other products, such as Visual Basic, Delphi, or other third-party tools, can use the NotesSQL interface. If you check the option Generate unique keys in index, NotesSQL will make the view appear to other programs as if the sorted columns of the view comprise a unique key.

This option requires careful use, however. Just because you check the box does not mean that you have defined the view selection and column definitions to meet the criteria that the other program is expecting. In order to avoid problems, you should follow these rules if you enable this check box:

- Do not enable this check box for more than one view per form. The external system may try to update the document through more than one path, and you may get inconsistent data in your document.
- The sorted columns within the view are very important. Make sure that the column definitions for the sorted columns
    - Are defined by fields only, not formulas or expressions.
    - Taken as a group, uniquely identify a document within the database. In database terminology, this is called a *composite key*.

You should normally enable this option only if you are using NotesSQL. If so, you should refer to the NotesSQL documentation for more information.

Web Access

The section for Web access contains two options. These options are used when a Web browser accesses the view. The options are

- Treat view contents as HTML   This is a great option. It enables you to specify HTML in the view column definitions. This HTML will be served to the browser. In effect, each document line of the view can contain HTML formatting that you define. I'll show you an example of this when I discuss embedded views.
- Use applet in the browser   Originally, the first implementation of Domino converted views to HTML and then served them to browsers. This method is still the default and works well. However, because the view is calculated on the server each time it needs to be updated, there can be a lot of round trips from the client to the server when the user is navigating the view. For example, just opening a twistie on the view causes a round trip to the server for redisplay. New with release 5 is the capability of downloading a

Java applet to the browser to take over some of the view functionality. If you enable this check box, the view will format slightly differently and will have more functionality. See Figures 15.24 and 15.25.

Figure 15.24
Without the view applet, a view in the browser is relatively static.

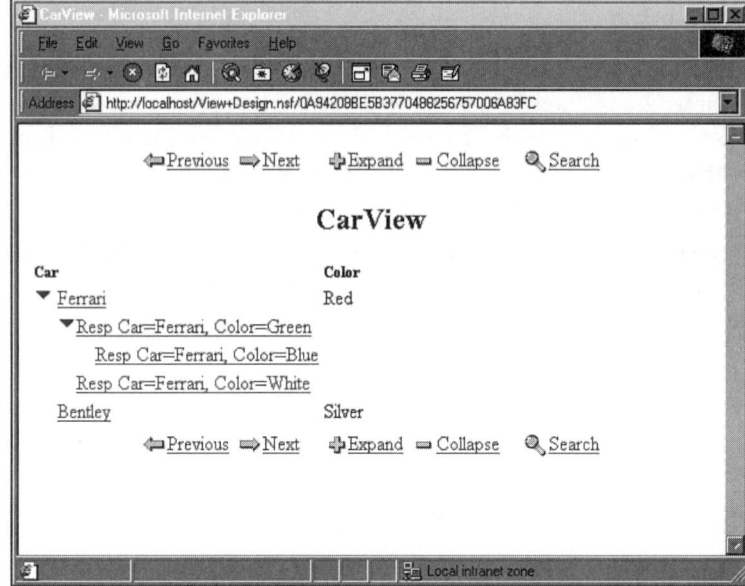

Figure 15.25
With the view applet, you can interact locally, select documents, and open and close twisties.

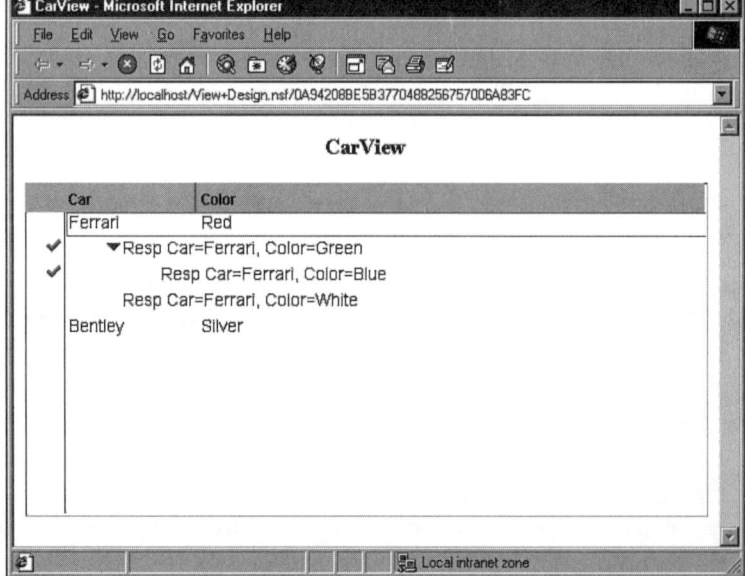

You can also change the colors for active links, unvisited links, and visited links in the view. To change one of these colors, click on the drop-down box and select the color within the color picker.

OTHER ADVANCED VIEW PROPERTIES

The remaining two advanced view properties are

- Restrict initial index build to designer or manager   This option will most likely be used with the Auto after first usage refresh option. By selecting the restriction, you can control when the database will go into automatic index building mode.
- Don't show categories having zero documents   This feature enables you to suppress the display of categories when no documents are included. By enabling this option, users will not have to waste time exploring and navigating extraneous view categories.

VIEW SECURITY PROPERTIES

You can see the Security tab (key icon) in Figure 15.26. This tab may be used to control who has access to the view.

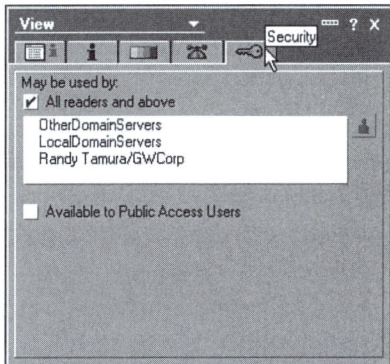

Figure 15.26
With the view Security tab, you can control who can use the view.

The default is that the view can be used by all readers and above. You can enable this check box so you don't have to specifically list the users. If you disable the check box, you can specify exactly the list of users you want to be able to use the view. This list is called the view access list. This list does not override the Access Control List (ACL) for the database; it can only refine the access.

Note that the view access list is not really a security feature, only a usability feature. Although you can restrict people from using the views you create, a user could conceivably create a private view containing exactly the same columns and fields as your view. The user would then be able to view all the data in the documents. To secure the data in the documents, you should use security at the form level. You can enable form access lists, reader and author fields, and use encryption to provide security for your documents.

If you create a view access list, make sure to include servers either directly or via a group. If you do not include servers, your views may not replicate correctly.

You can enable public access by checking the Available to Public Access Users check box. Enabling this check box will allow users with No Access or Depositor access to view public documents. In addition to enabling the view for public access, you will also need to enable one or more form(s) for public access and create documents with a field called $PublicAccess with a value of 1. Any document with this field set to 1 will be available for viewing in a public access view.

Programmer's Pane View Properties

There are several view properties that are not located in the view properties dialog box. These properties are set in the Programmer's pane at the bottom of your screen. The first option, View Selection, I have already discussed briefly, but here are some additional details.

View Selection

The View selection property enables you to specify a formula that is used to select documents to display in the view. The default is to select all documents in the database. If you specify a formula, the formula is evaluated for each document in the database to determine whether to show the document in the view. As you might imagine, this is potentially a time-consuming task.

There is a new performance enhancement option for release 5 to speed the display of views. The option is found in the Advanced tab of the database properties box, and you can also specify it when you create the database. The option is called Document table bitmap optimization. Now, although it is fairly clear that the option optimizes something, it is not clear what, why, or how this optimization works.

Because selecting documents for a view potentially means going through every document in the database, Domino stores some (bitmap) tables to speed the process. Essentially, these tables link documents, forms, and views. The tables enable Domino to tell whether a form is used in a view. Then, by knowing whether a document uses the form, Domino can quickly determine whether a document is a candidate for a view. This optimization will work only if your view selection formula has one or more Form= conditions. If you use Form= in your view, which is fairly common, you can enable this option to improve your database performance.

When would you not want to use this optimization? Well, if you don't use Form= in your view, there is extra computing and storage required, and you will not gain any benefit. The default is for this option to be turned off. You should definitely consider using it where appropriate, though, because for large databases, you may be able to improve your view performance dramatically.

The Form Formula

The form formula is a formula associated with a view that enables you to control the form that is used to display a document opened from within the view. The form formula is one option in the selection process Domino uses to select the form to use to display a document. Here is the sequence Domino uses:

1. If there is a form stored with the document, it is used to display the document. This option is selected in the Defaults tab of the Form properties dialog box. Use this option to enable sending a document to another database where the associated form may not exist. For example, if you are mailing a document to another person that may not have the associated form, you should enable storing the form with the document. In general, you should use this option sparingly because it uses up significantly more space in the database.

2. If no form is stored with the document, the form formula associated with the view is evaluated. The formula must evaluate to the name of a form that is available in the database. You can create or edit the form formula by highlighting the Form Formula property in the Programmer's pane under the view. You can then enter your formula in the right half of the Programmer's pane. One possible use of this option might be to select different forms based on the state of the document: (New versus Existing), (Viewing versus Editing), (Inquiry versus New Order), and so forth.

3. If there is no form formula in the view, the document will be displayed using the form name contained in a field called Form within the document. This field is automatically filled in with the synonym of the form name (or form name if no synonym exists) of the form used to create the document. Unless this field is changed, the document will be displayed using the form used to create the document. This option is the default for most documents.

4. If there is no field called Form within the document or the form cannot be found, the default form for the database is used. You can specify the database default form in the Defaults tab of the Form properties dialog box.

5. Finally, if there is no default form, you will get an error and the document will not be displayed.

View Actions

View actions enable you to make commonly used actions available for users via the action button bar. There are six built-in view actions: Categorize, Edit Document, Send Document, Forward, Move To Folder, and Remove From Folder. In addition, you can create your own custom actions.

The action can be activated by the user by clicking the action button or via the menus as a choice of the Actions menu. As a designer, you can choose to enable either menu access or button access, or both.

You have four language options for programming the action. You can use the formula language, create a simple action, use LotusScript, or use JavaScript. The details of programming are covered in other chapters in this book.

If you create a view action, it is unique to the particular view, and you need to have separate copies for each view if you want identical function. Another option would be to create a Shared Action. Shared Actions are new with release 5 of Domino. A Shared Action can be used in multiple views or forms. This is another great way to implement code once, and then use it from multiple locations within your database.

To create a Shared Action, click on Resources in the Design pane of your database, then Click on Other. In the work area, you can double-click on Shared Actions. An action will be created for you. You can name it, provide the code, and then save it.

Embedded Views

With Domino release 5, you can embed many elements on a page or form. On both pages and forms, you can embed outlines, a view, navigators, date pickers, or a Folder pane. On forms, you can embed a group scheduler or file Upload control as well.

In this section, I describe how you can embed a view on a form for display in a Web browser. This capability gives you a lot of flexibility in the formatting of the view rows through the use of HTML. In addition, through the use of Single Category embedded views, you can create views that present customized lists to users.

Let's see how all this is accomplished. This example will be comprised of one form for data entry, a view, and a second form that embeds the view. I've tried to distill this example to its simplest components for the purposes of explaining how to make Domino forms and views work well with the Web.

Here is the scenario. You have an online shop that sells games over the Web. There are several categories for the games, and some games can fall into more than one category. The first form you can create is the form that enables someone in your company to enter new games on your Web site. See Figure 15.27.

This form is very simple; there are only two fields. When you develop your form, you'll want to include more fields and make it more attractive for data entry. Notice that there is a field called Categories. This special field name identifies the field as one to use when a view is categorized. I've also enabled the field to have multiple values on the Basics tab. This form is simple enough.

The next design element we'll create is a view. This view will eventually be embedded in a form, and I'm going to illustrate how you can use HTML to add some spice to your view and form. See Figure 15.28.

Figure 15.27
The sample game definition form is used to add a game and its categories.

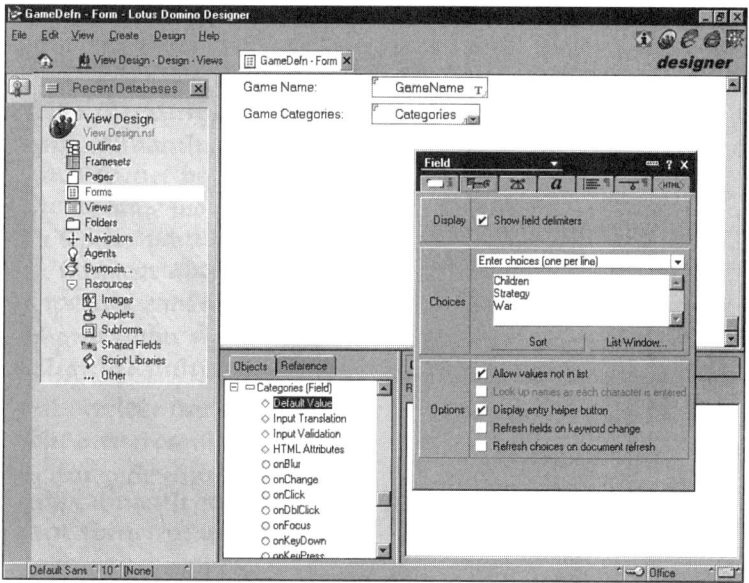

Figure 15.28
The sample GameList view has enabled Treat view contents as HTML.

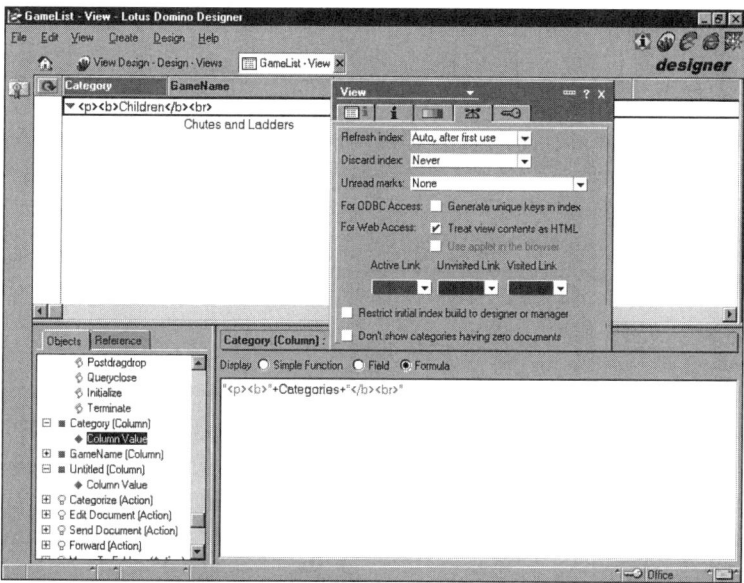

The GameList view I've created has three columns. The first column is for the category, the second is for the game name and the third will be for an icon that will display any time we have recently listed a new game. Many Web sites use a starburst New. With Domino, we can automatically add these icons via programming.

The first column is sorted in ascending order and categorized. The contents of the column can be seen in Figure 15.28. Notice that I have included a paragraph tag, a bold tag, the Categories field, end bold, and a line-break tag. The effect of these HTML tags will be to space prior to the new category, and then show the category name in bold, followed by a line break so the next text will follow on the next line.

The second column of the view just contains the field GameName. I have not included any special formatting, although you could use the HTML tags to add features such as document linking, bold, or other characteristics.

The third column formula can be seen in Figure 15.29. Here it is:

```
@if(@Now> @Adjust(@Created;0;0;7;0;0;0);"<br>";
"<IMG SRC=\'/"+@ReplaceSubstring(@Text(@Subset(@DbName;-1));" ";"+")+
"/actn124.gif\'><br>"
```

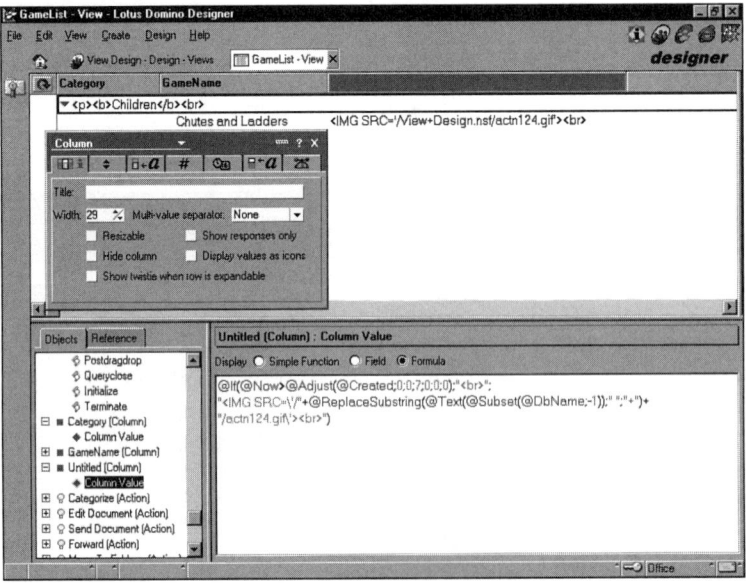

Figure 15.29
The formula conditionally generates an icon using HTML.

In Figure 15.29, you can see both the column value formula in the Programmer's pane and an example of the generated HTML in the view window. In essence, I am generating a reference to a GIF file that has been stored within the image library of the database. You can extract and show the image by using a URL, as shown. Using this technique is much better than having graphics stored in the file system. All the related graphics can be stored within the Domino database and will replicate automatically with the application.

The formula I've used will create conditional HTML. That is, there are two versions of HTML that will be generated, depending upon the outcome of the if statement. The first version of HTML will just generate a <br>, which means to break to a new line. The second version of HTML will generate a reference to an icon (GIF file) in the image library.

> **Note**
>
> In the URL that refers to the image file, I issue a @ReplaceString that substitutes a plus sign (+) instead of a blank space. You may not use embedded blanks within a URL string. Plus signs are used to indicate an embedded blank. This substitution is performed in case (as it is here) the database name has an embedded blank. In Figure 15.29 you can see that the embedded blank between View and Design has been changed to a plus sign.

The essence of the formula is that an icon reference will be generated if the creation date of the document is within the last seven days. The @Adjust function takes the document creation date and adds seven days. It then compares the adjusted date to the current time. If the current time is later than the adjusted date, the document is old and we just generate a line break. If it isn't, the document's date is within the last seven days and we generate the HTML for an image with the IMG tag. In this case, I have loaded the image resource into the image library of the database, so I do not need to enter a path. If you keep the image resources within the database, they will automatically replicate with the database, and the database will be self-contained. Do you think this is cool yet?

Now we are ready to create the last design element of our example. We are now going to create the form that will embed the view that we just made. When we create an embedded view, Domino will not automatically include the navigation bars that are shown when Domino natively shows a view. With embedded views, we have more control over the appearance shown to the user. See Figure 15.30.

Figure 15.30
Create an embedded view to control the view's appearance.

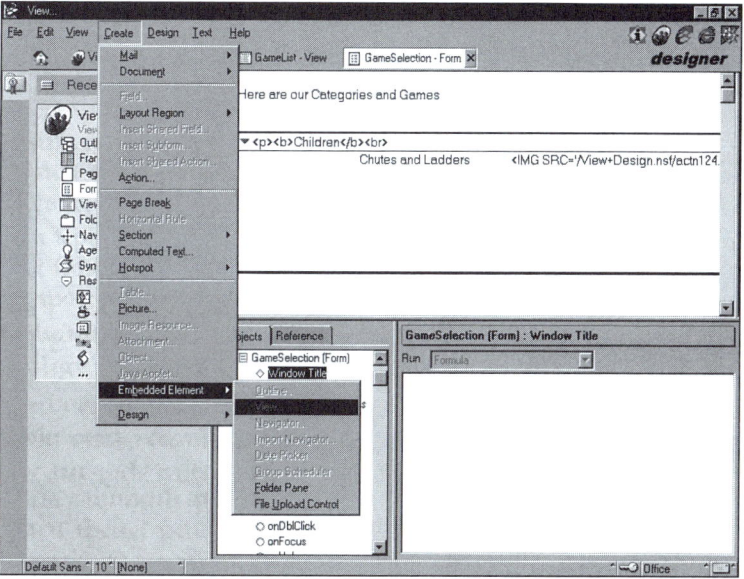

To create an embedded view:

1. First create your form. Call it GameSelection.

2. Select Create, Embedded Element, View. Note that you can include only one embedded view per form.

3. From the dialog box that appears, choose a particular view or check the box that says Choose a View based on formula. For our example, we will select the GameList view. Click OK.

4. If you selected the formula option, you must enter the formula in the Programmer's pane. The formula you enter must evaluate to the name of a view.

5. Open the properties for the embedded view by clicking the Properties Icon or selecting Edit, Properties. For our example, we cannot use the view applet because it will not properly handle the formulas and dynamically generated HTML we are creating. In our example, in the Basics tab, we choose Using HTML under the Web Access Display option.

> **Note**
>
> The view applet is written in Java and is downloaded to the browser. This code executes in the client environment and does not use HTML to render the view. For this reason, pass-through HTML does not work with the view applet. View applets are great for improving user interactivity and response time for standard views, but if you need to combine HTML with the view, you must use the HTML (Domino server–generated) version of views.

Figure 15.31
In the Display tab, you can control the height and width of an embedded view.

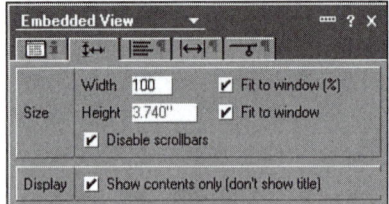

6. In the Display tab (the second tab) for our example, we enable Fit to window Width, Fit to window Height, Disable scrollbars, and Show contents only (don't show title). See Figure 15.31. In your form, you may choose to use different options.

Well, we're now ready to test our form and embedded view. You can click one of the browser icons in the upper-right corner of your screen. See Figure 15.32 for our sample output.

In the figure, you can see the dynamically generated icons. The ability to generate these icons programmatically is one of the features that makes Domino such a powerful Web server. In other systems, the Webmaster must add the icons manually. In Domino, you can just add documents, specify the rules you want to use for how long documents stay "new," and then the icons will appear and disappear automatically as they age.

I didn't include other powerful Domino features, such as document and URL linking in this example, but I think you get the idea.

Figure 15.32
In the new document, icons are dynamically generated.

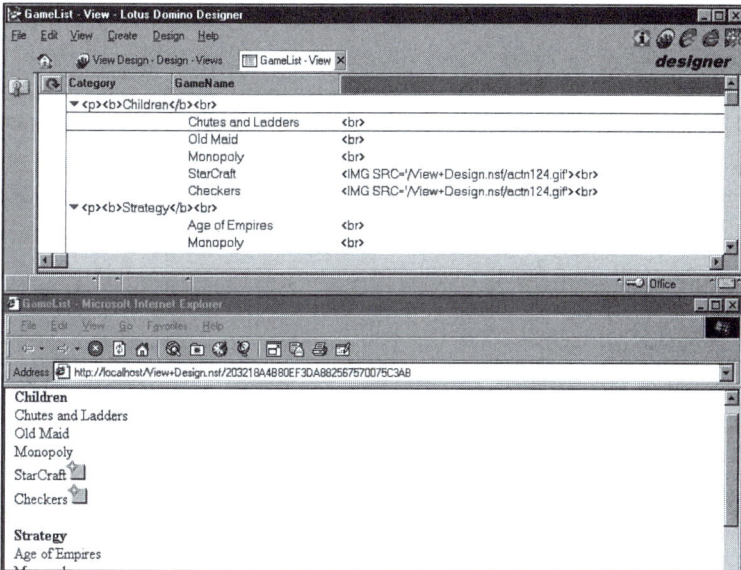

SINGLE CATEGORY EMBEDDED VIEWS

Single Category embedded views are a neat new feature of release 5. They enable you to create customized views, similar to a shared-private on first use view. The nice thing about Single Category embedded views is that they work well on the Web.

You can use a Single Category view to provide custom information to a particular user. The way it works is simple. You first create a categorized view and use as the category the value some data which will distinguish one user from another. For example, you could use the user's name as the categorization value. Other sample applications are the game categories of the previous example, categories for user preferences, or just about any kind of grouping where you want to select a group of documents to customize the user's experience.

To illustrate Single Category embedded views, I am going to modify the previous games example. I will create one additional view (the Single Category view) and one form, which will contain the embedded view. First, let's do the view.

Create an additional view that is the same as the GameList view. You can do this by cutting and pasting the view within the view list. Rename the new view `GameSingle`. The only change we will make to this new view is to the column formula for the first column, the Categories column. In GameList the formula is

```
"<p><b>"+Categories+"</b><br>"
```

Change this for the GameSingle view to

```
Categories
```

That is, we just want to make it the regular contents of the Categories field with no HTML formatting. Save and close the GameSingle view.

Now, create a new form and call it `GameSingle` also. There is no restriction on a form and view having the same name. Create a radio button field called `Cat`. See Figure 15.33.

Figure 15.33
Create a Radio button in the GameSingle form with the Refresh fields on keyword change option.

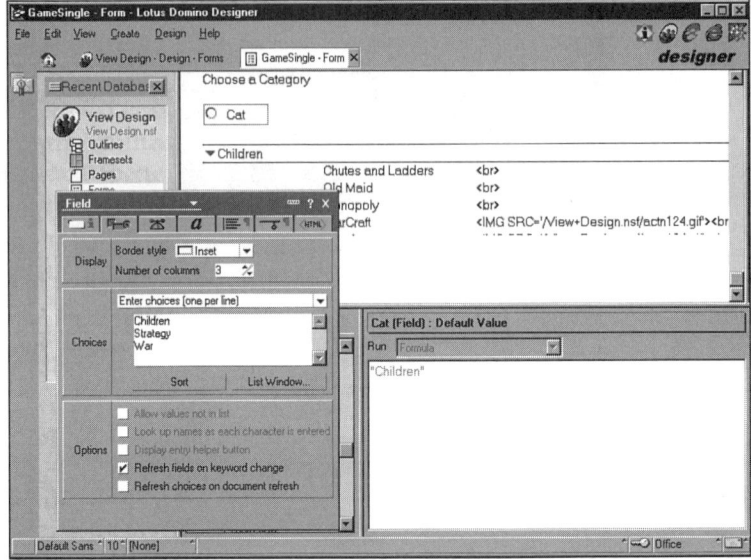

On the Control tab, enter the three options: `Children`, `Strategy`, and `War`. Also be sure to check the Refresh fields on keyword change option. This will force a reevaluation of our Single Category view. The default value for the Cat field is Children.

Now you can embed the GameSingle view as we did in the previous example. Do this by selecting Create, Embedded Element, View. After the view is embedded within your form, choose the Show single category property in the Programmer's pane. Enter `Cat` in the formula area within the Programmer's pane. See Figure 15.34.

By specifying Cat in the formula area, we are essentially telling Domino to use the Cat field as the criterion for the Single Category. We force the option to be one of the three that we know are valid by using a radio button. After the user selects one of the radio button options, the Refresh fields on keyword change option will cause the view to recalculate and display the Single Category specified in the Cat field. See Figure 15.35 for an example.

In this example, when the user selects each of the different radio button options, the games shown will change. Each time, the "new" icon will appear automatically as before.

Figure 15.34
The Single Category specification can be a field name or formula.

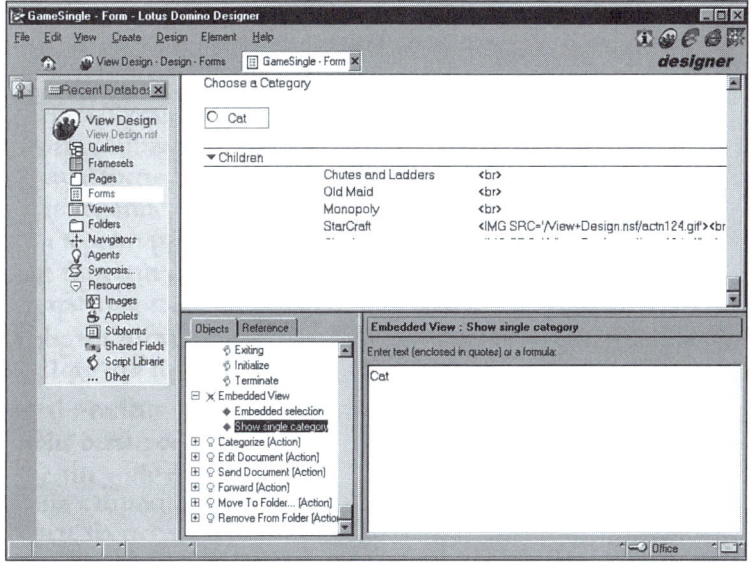

Figure 15.35
Selecting a radio button option changes the games shown.

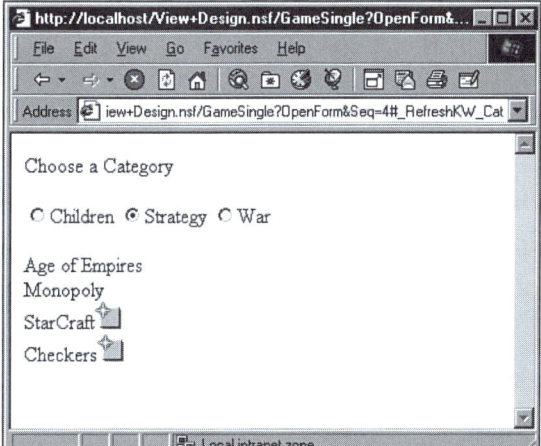

FROM HERE...

In this chapter, I covered the fundamentals of views and folders. I showed you how to create a view or folder, how to specify its type, and how to select documents for inclusion in a view. There are two new types of views in release 5: one showing documents not in folders, and the other showing deleted documents. The deleted document feature uses the new soft deletion support of release 5 databases.

View columns display your data. You can use formulas to specify the data to be displayed, so values can be straight from a field or computed from several fields. You can sort and categorize view columns. View columns can also be hidden or used to show icons.

You can add styling to a view by modifying colors and using multiple lines for the headers or contents. New with release 5 is the capability of downloading the view applet to a Web browser. The user can then interact with the view applet, expand and collapse sections, and select documents.

I showed you an example of combining the power of Domino forms and views with HTML. You can use Domino programming to programmatically alter what is displayed. In the example, I showed you how you can include a "new" icon for documents that have been recently modified. By using this technique, all new documents will be flagged automatically, and the flags will be removed automatically when the time period expires.

Single Category embedded views is a new feature of release 5 that allows you to provide personalized information to a user. You can use a formula to compute a personalization criterion, such as a name, and then use the name to select one category within a view. This Single Category will then display only those records that have the name as the category.

Here are some additional chapters you can read for more information on developing your own applications:

- Chapter 16, "Using Outlines, Framesets, and Navigators," shows you how to take advantage of elements that an end user can use to navigate through your application.
- Chapter 17, "Access Control Lists (ACLs) and Application Security," delves into the details of securing your intranet and Internet applications. ACLs provide a powerful mechanism for security.
- Chapter 18, "Working with Formulas, Functions, and Commands," shows you how to use formulas in a variety of contexts, such as computation, view selection, input translation, and more.

CHAPTER 16

Using Outlines, Framesets, and Navigators

Domino provides several capabilities for organizing information and enabling users to navigate through your Web pages. This chapter gives you information about some of the navigation tools available in Domino release 5. Outlines are one mechanism you can use to enable navigation functions for your users. Framesets enable you to create several panes or frames within your window. You can control the initial number and placement of the frames. After the frameset is displayed, the user will typically have the ability to move the borders between the frames. Navigators are a feature from release 4 of Notes and Domino that are still available in release 5. Let's take a look at these features in more detail.

What Are Outlines?

An outline is a tool to enable you to control user navigation. Outlines can be styled vertically or horizontally, and roughly correspond to a list of destinations. Typically on a home page, you see these kinds of navigation tools on the left side of the page, along the top or on the bottom of the page. In Notes release 4.*x*, the View Navigation pane in the upper-left corner is a kind of outline. It gives a list of the available views in the database, and by clicking on a view name, you can see the view in the upper-right pane. Outlines can perform a similar function.

You must embed an outline in either a page or form to be used. You can create as many outlines as you like, and you can embed more than one outline on a single page. The formatting of the outline is done via the Embedded Outline properties box, which I'll show you later. Normally, you use outlines within pages in framesets, because they can reside in one frame but control the contents of another frame. I'll cover this in the section about frames and framesets.

Note that there are two separate kinds of information about outlines. The first is the navigational information. You specify this information when you create and program the outline entries. The second kind of information is the display formatting for the outline. The same outline can be used in two different pages, with different formatting styles in each. Although the outline looks different on each page, the navigation for each respective entry in the outline will be the same.

Using the Outline Editor

If you want to follow along, you can create a new, blank, local database called Outline Design. You can open the outline editor in the Domino Designer by clicking on Outlines in the Design pane. By default, there are no outlines created for you within a database. You can easily have the Designer create one for you by following these steps:

1. Open the outline editor by clicking on Outlines in the Design pane.
2. Click on the New Outline action bar button. You will see a new set of action bar buttons.
3. Click on the Generate Default Outline action button. Your new default outline will be generated for you. See Figure 16.1.

Outline Entries 385

Figure 16.1
The default outline as initially created by Domino Designer.

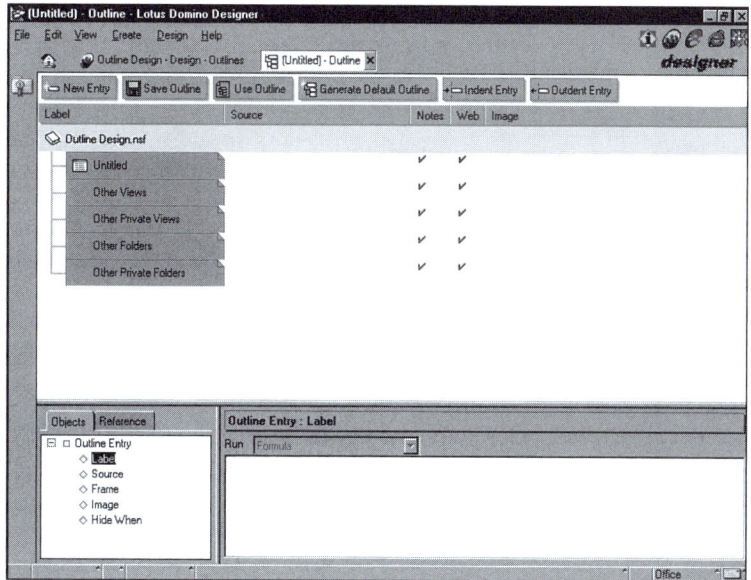

You can see from Figure 16.1 that Domino Designer will automatically create five outline entries for you: Untitled (the default view), Other Views, Other Folders, Other Private Views, and Other Private Folders. The first outline entry represents the single view of your database. If you had generated this outline after creating several views and folders, they would be included in the default outline as well.

The four additional outline entries that are created for you automatically have suggested names, but you do not have to use all these entries. You can delete some of the entries if they do not apply to your application.

If you prefer to create your entire outline from scratch, first create the outline, and then begin adding outline entries as described in the following section.

OUTLINE ENTRIES

In Figure 16.1, you can see five outline entries, each represented by a rectangular gray box. When the application executes, the user will see a text or graphic item for each of the outline entries. By clicking on one of these entries, the user will be able to navigate through your application.

You can add, delete, move, and rename the outline entries.

To add a new entry, follow these steps:

1. Create a new outline or open an existing outline.

2. Click on the existing outline entry where you want to locate your new entry. The new entry will go below the one you select. If you want your entry to be the new first entry, click on the database line. For our example, click on the database line to create a new first entry.
3. Click on the New Entry action button. A new entry will be created for you under the existing entry you selected.
4. In the Outline Entry properties dialog box, enter a label for the new entry. The text you enter will be displayed to the end user. In our example, you can use the word Home for the name.
5. You can optionally add an alias for the outline entry. If you add an alias, you can refer to the outline entry by the alias name even if you change the name of the outline. This allows you to change the user interface without reprogramming your application. I recommend adding an alias. In our example, you can use the word Home for the alias.
6. The Content section describes what will happen if the user clicks on this outline entry. There are four types: Action, Link, Named Element, and URL. See Figure 16.2. These options are described in the next section.

Figure 16.2
There are four types of content for an outline entry.

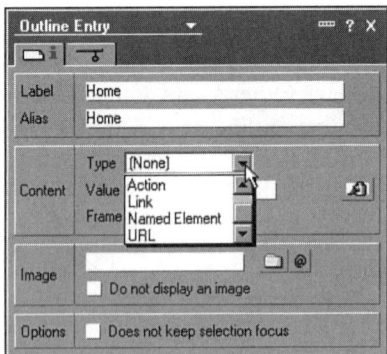

7. You can optionally enter the name for an image. You can enter the name of an image within your image library, or you can specify a formula that will result in the name of an image. The image itself will be displayed as a small icon next to the label you specified previously. Note that you cannot use the image field to display a large graphic for the outline entry.
8. An outline entry has a status that is either selected (that is, has the focus) or not selected. When you click on an outline entry, the action you have specified will occur, and the focus normally changes to the clicked outline entry. You can specify that you do not want the outline entry to retain the focus by enabling the Does not keep selection focus option. Even if this option is enabled, the outline entry's action will still work.
9. After you have entered all the fields, you can close the properties box or click on another outline entry and enter its information.

OUTLINE ENTRY CONTENTS

As stated previously, the action for an outline entry can be one of four types: Action, Link, Named Element, and URL. Here is what happens with each of these types:

- If you specify Action, you can supply a @formula to be executed when the outline entry is clicked. You specify the formula by clicking on the @ character at the right of the Value line. You will then see a dialog box where you can enter your formula.
- If you specify Link, the outline entry can be a link to a database, view, document, or anchor. To utilize this type of link, you must
    - Go to the Notes client and open the desired database, view, or document and select Edit, Copy As Link, followed by the type of link you desire: Anchor Link, Document Link, View Link, or Database Link.
    - In Designer, open the properties box for the outline entry.
    - Set the type field to Link.
    - Click on the Paste icon. Your link will be pasted into the outline entry. For confirmation, the type of link will be displayed next to the type field. Note that the value line will contain a reference to your link, but that it will not be editable. Figure 16.3 shows you the result of a document link that has been pasted into the outline entry.

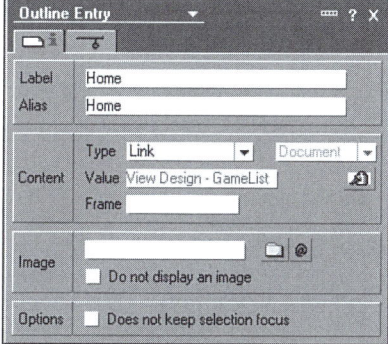

Figure 16.3
The outline entry property box after a document link has been pasted.

- If you specify Named Element for the outline entry type, you can provide linkage to a page, form, frameset, or view. To use this type of outline entry:
    - Open the properties box for the outline entry you want to change.
    - Set the type field to Named Element.
    - To the right of the Named Element field, select the type of element you want to use. You can select Page, Form, Frameset, or View.
    - After you select the type of named element you want to use, you can specify the actual element by selecting it directly or by supplying a formula that will evaluate to the name of the element. If you click on the folder icon, you can directly select

the element, and if you click on the @ icon, you can supply a formula. Figure 16.4 shows you the result of clicking on the folder icon. You will see a second dialog box that enables you to again choose the type of object, and then select a specific object from a drop-down list.

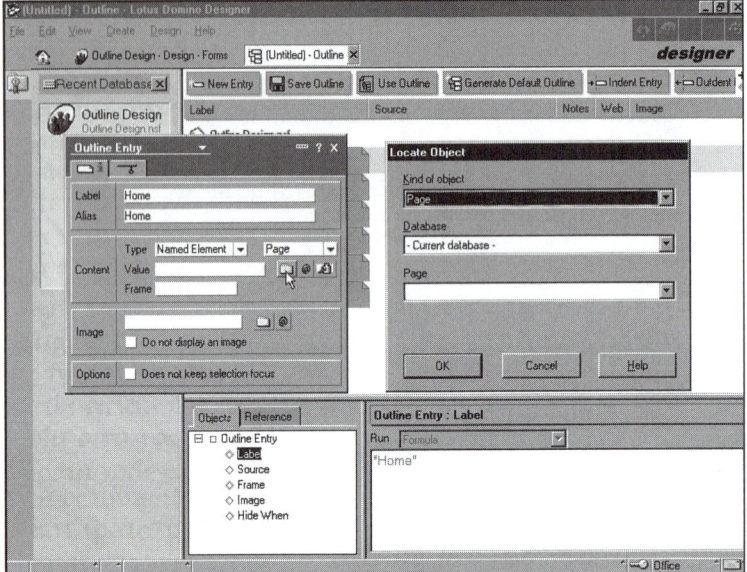

Figure 16.4
The outline entry showing Named Element selection.

- If you specify URL for the outline entry type, you can specify a URL in the value field. Be sure to specify the complete URL, including the `http:` at the beginning of the string.

HIDING OUTLINE ENTRIES

You can optionally hide outline entries by using the Entry Hide When tab of the Outline Entry properties box. See Figure 16.5.

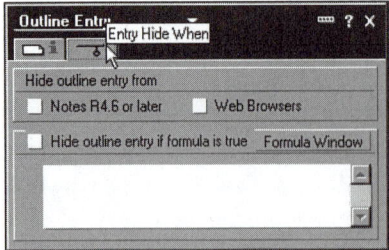

Figure 16.5
The Entry Hide When tab of the Outline Entry properties box.

You can hide the entry from Notes 4.6 or later, or you can hide the entry from Web browsers. These options enable you to create conditionally displayed outline entries that display depending upon the viewing capabilities of the user.

In addition, you can supply a formula for hiding the outline entry. This type of Hide When formula is useful if you want to supply or restrict application capability based upon user ID, roles, groups, or other criteria. The outline entry linkage is displayed only under the conditions you specify.

Moving Outline Entries

Moving an outline entry within the hierarchy is very simple. You just click on the entry and drag it to its new location. You can move entries up or down.

You can also indent entries so that they appear as a subsidiary to another outline entry. To indent an entry, click on it and click the Indent Entry action button on the top of the window. Clicking the Outdent Entry action button can outdent an entry that has already been indented.

Using Frames and Framesets

What are framesets, exactly? To answer that question, I'm going to give you some background by describing the HTML definitions of pages, framesets, and frames. You actually don't need all this detail to use the Domino Designer Frameset designer, but I think it will be useful for you to know what Domino is doing behind the scenes for you. After we have covered the background material, I'll return to the Domino Designer interface and show you how to use it.

HTML Background for Framesets

To describe framesets, let's first start with the definition of a regular HTML page without frames. To display a regular HTML page, you must specify a document with the following framework:

```
<HTML>
<HEAD>
</HEAD>
<BODY>
     ... Main contents of page here ...
</BODY>
</HTML>
```

With this structure, a single page will be displayed, showing the contents contained within the `<BODY>` and `</BODY>` tags.

One of the early observations about Web pages was that frequently they contained two types of information: navigation information and content. The navigation elements are typically on the borders of the screen: left, top, bottom, or sometimes on the right. The content is typically in the middle of the window.

The two types of information have different characteristics: The page content varies from page to page, and the navigation elements are frequently similar or stay constant while the user navigates around the site. It is desirable to have the navigation elements always available, in much the same way as the top menu line of the typical Windows application is always available. From any point within the Web site, you can navigate directly to another place.

Frames and framesets were developed to combine the relatively static navigational elements and the relatively dynamic content. Framesets enable you to define separate frames, such as panes, within a window where one frame can remain visible and unchanged while the contents of the other frame changes. Here is the structure for a frameset-enabled HTML file:

```
<HTML>
<HEAD>
</HEAD>
<FRAMESET>
    ... Frame definitions here ...
</FRAMESET>
</HTML>
```

Notice that the main difference between a regular HTML page and one with frames is that we replace the <BODY> tags with <FRAMESET> tags. You cannot use both the <BODY> tag and the <FRAMESET> tag in the same document. If you do include both, the browser will display the first and ignore the second.

In addition to the simple format I've shown, you can optionally include a <NOFRAMES> section for browsers that don't support frames. You can also have *nested framesets*. That is, you can have framesets within framesets. The frameset tag itself is used to allocate space in the window for the various frames, but without specifying the content of the frame, which will be in the <FRAME> tag.

You specify the frame layout and the orientation of a frameset by using either the ROWS or COLS attributes within the frameset. Although you can specify both parameters, it is typically not done. Typically, you will specify only one of the keywords for a given frameset. It is common, however, to have a column-oriented frameset within a row-oriented frameset and vice versa. Here is an example:

```
<FRAMESET ROWS="100,*,10%">
    ... Frame definitions here ...
</FRAMESET>
```

In this example, I specify three rows, which means that there will be three frames in the frameset. In this case, all the frames will take the entire width of the window because they are row-oriented. There are three separate height specifications. The first means 100 pixels, the last element means that the frame will take 10% of the remaining window height, and the middle element (the asterisk) will take whatever space remains.

Here is a more complex example:

```
<FRAMESET ROWS="100,*,10%">
   <FRAME>
```

```
<FRAMESET COLS="200,*">
    <FRAME>
    <FRAME>
</FRAMESET>
<FRAME>
</FRAMESET>
```

I have enhanced the previous example by nesting one frameset within another. You can see the result of this frameset nesting in Figure 16.6.

Figure 16.6
Nested frameset definitions.

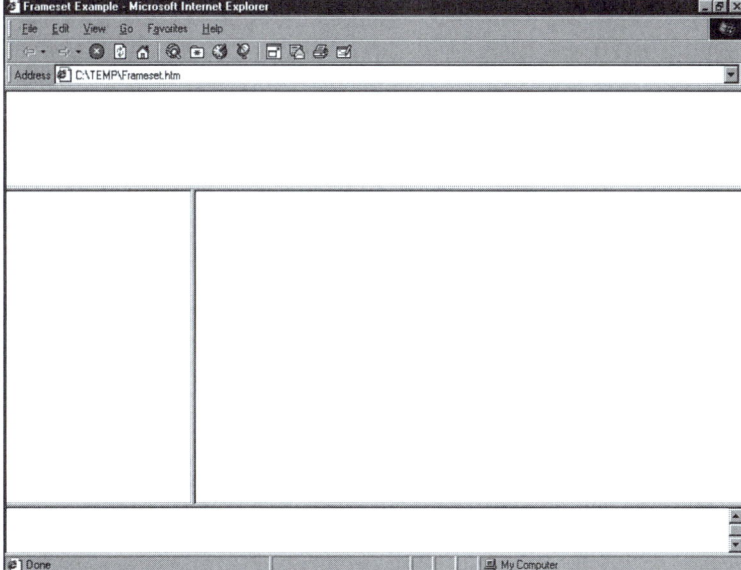

In this case, the major orientation is rowwise with three rows. Within the middle row, however, I have defined another frameset with two columns. This type of layout, perhaps with different frame proportions, is very common on the Web. In fact, in the Domino Designer, if you indicate you want four frames, this configuration is the default configuration of the four frames.

So to summarize, framesets define the layout and orientation of frames, such as panes, within a window. The content of each frame is defined with HTML like a page. In the next section, I show you how you define the frame itself.

HTML BACKGROUND FOR FRAMES

After you define the structure of your Web page with the <FRAMESET> tags, you can define the contents of the individual frames with the <FRAME> tag. If you are using regular HTML, the simplified syntax for the <FRAME> tag is

```
<FRAME SRC="url">
```

Notice that you specify the content via a URL. In particular, the implication is that the content of a framed page is stored separately from the frame and frameset definitions. This contrasts with a regular page where the content and structure are stored together. You cannot supply the contents of a frame "inline" with the definition of the <FRAMESET>.

Additional attribute parameters on the <FRAME> tag are NAME, MARGINWIDTH, MARGINHEIGHT, SCROLLING, and NORESIZE. These attributes enable you to refer to the frame and give additional information about the visible display of the frame. The NAME attribute, for example, is required when you want to use one frame as the target of a different frame because you refer to the target by name.

SUPPORTING BROWSERS WITHOUT FRAME CAPABILITY

Frames and framesets were not originally part of the HTML specification. During the time period of the version 3 browsers (Netscape Navigator 3 and Internet Explorer 3), it was very important to test whether a browser was capable of displaying frames. These days, almost all browsers support frames, but to be safe, you still may want to code defensively and test whether the user viewing your Web site can utilize frames.

To code defensively in HTML, you use the <NOFRAMES> tag. The contents of this tag enable you to specify separate HTML for browsers that do not support frames:

```
<HTML>
<HEAD>
</HEAD>
<FRAMESET>
    ... Frame definitions here ...
</FRAMESET>
<NOFRAMES>
    ... HTML for browsers that do not support frames.
</NOFRAMES>
</HTML>
```

In Domino, you can use an @function called @BrowserInfo to determine whether the browser has frame capability. To use it within one of your formulas, you use @BrowserInfo("Frames"). This formula returns true if the browser supports frames, and false otherwise.

CREATING FRAMESETS WITH DOMINO DESIGNER

In HTML, the content of a frame within a frameset is specified by a URL. The URL points to a file that can contain HTML or perhaps a graphics file, such as a GIF or JPEG file. With Domino, you have many more options because in addition to specifying a simple URL, you can also specify Domino design elements, such as views or documents.

Now that you are familiar with some of the HTML theory behind framesets, let's see how you can use the Domino Designer to create your own framesets, without having to drop down to the HTML level.

In Domino Designer, to create a frameset:

1. Click on the word Framesets in the Design pane of the Domino Designer. The Work pane will show you a list of existing framesets, if you have any.
2. To create a new frameset, click on the action bar button titled New Frameset. The Create New Frameset dialog box will appear. See Figure 16.7.
3. From the dialog box, first select the number of frames you want to use. You can enter 2, 3, or 4. This is just an initial setting. In the unusual case that you want to use more than four frames, you can modify the initial configuration by adding and deleting frames. You should be aware, however, that most good graphic designs will not require much more than four frames. Start simply and add complexity later if needed.
4. After you select the number of frames, select the desired layout by clicking on one of the pictures across the top of the dialog box. See Figure 16.7 for a frameset using three frames.

Figure 16.7
The Create New Frameset dialog box with three frames selected.

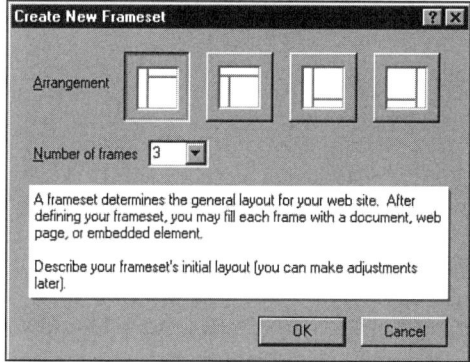

5. After you select the layout, click OK. Your frameset will be created. See Figure 16.8.

Just for comparison to our previous HTML introduction, here is the relevant HTML that Domino Designer will generate for the frameset:

```
<FRAMESET COLS="20%,80%">
   <FRAME>
   <FRAMESET ROWS="20%,80%">
      <FRAME>
      <FRAME>
   </FRAMESET>
</FRAMESET>
```

Although Domino will not indent the HTML code, I have done it for clarity. Notice the similarity to the hand-written HTML code you would otherwise have to write. The HTML source generated by Domino will vary by browser and by release, so your code may be slightly different. Also, note that although you create a single Domino frameset with three frames, Domino will actually generate two nested HTML framesets to get the desired layout.

Figure 16.8
A newly created frameset with three frames.

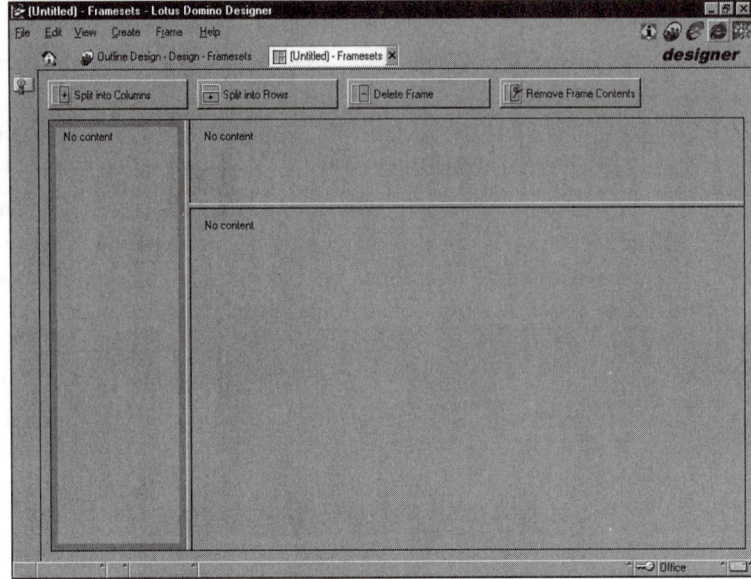

ENHANCING AN EXISTING FRAMESET

After you create your frameset, you can edit the layout by adding or deleting frames. The result of these actions is to change the number of nested framesets and their contents. In Figure 16.8, you see that there are four action bar buttons within the frameset editor. You can use these buttons to change the layout of the frameset.

To create a new frame, you must split one of the existing frames. You can split the frame into either two columns or two rows. The first two action bar buttons accomplish these tasks. By clicking either button, you end up with one additional frame.

To add a frame to an existing frameset:

1. Edit the frameset by double-clicking on the frameset's name within the list of names in the Work pane.
2. After the frameset is open, click within the frame you want to split. A dark gray highlight will show you which frame is currently selected.
3. Click either the Split into Columns or Split into Rows action button. The highlighted frame will turn into two frames, either by columns or by rows. Your new frame has been added.
4. You can change the split percentage by highlighting one of the borders between the frames and moving it.

To delete a frame of an existing frameset:

1. Edit the frameset by double-clicking on the frameset's name within the list of names in the Work pane.
2. After the frameset is open, click within the frame you want to delete. A dark gray highlight will show you which frame is currently selected.
3. Click the Delete Frame action button. The highlighted frame will be deleted and merged with one of its neighbors.

SPECIFYING FRAME CONTENTS

As mentioned, in the Domino Designer you have several options for specifying a frame's contents. This gives you a much easier, high-level design paradigm than working directly with HTML. You may wish to have some frames store relatively static information and other frames dynamic content that will vary from page to page. In addition, frames within a frameset can be linked. That is, a click on items in one frame can cause the contents of a different frame to change. This is the essence of many common frame layouts.

On the Web, you will frequently see the frame on the left contain graphic menu items, and clicking on them causes the main frame on the right to change. In Domino, the left frame can contain an outline as you saw earlier in this chapter, and each outline element can cause a different page to display on the right.

When I was covering outlines earlier in the chapter, I did not discuss the linkage between frames, because we had not yet covered framesets. Now that you know about both concepts, let's put them together.

USING AN EMBEDDED OUTLINE IN A PAGE

In order to use an outline, it must be embedded in a page or a form. If you haven't yet read Chapter 14, "Designing Pages, Forms, and Subforms," you may want to go back and read that chapter.

Most of the time, you will use an outline in conjunction with a frameset, and if so, you will normally want to embed the outline in a page. You will normally use a page rather than a form, because the contents of the page containing the outline are usually static. Navigation frames containing outlines do not typically need to have the dynamic content that a form allows.

Creating an outline and then inserting a page is really easy. Here is all you have to do:

1. Create the desired outline with the outline editor. You can use the New Entry action button to add outline entries. See Figure 16.9 for an example.

Figure 16.9
An outline with four outline entries.

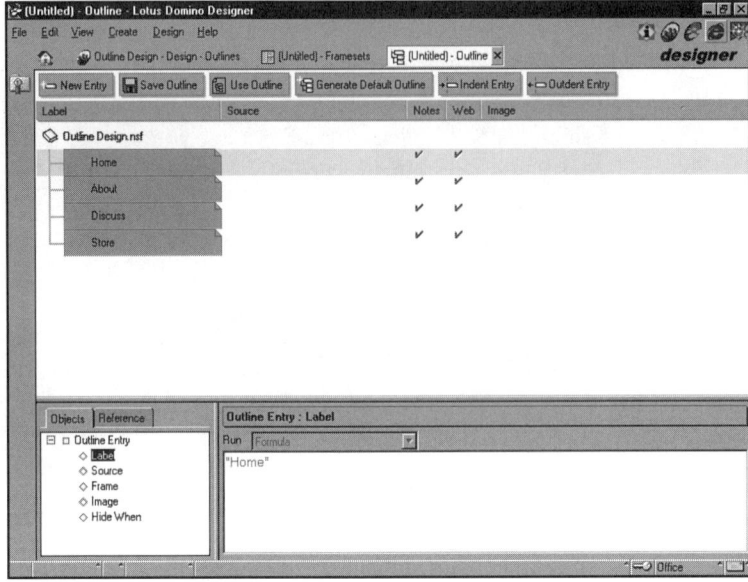

2. After your outline is created, just click the Use Outline action button. A new page will be created for you with the outline already embedded. See Figure 16.10 for the resulting page from the outline.

Figure 16.10
The page with embedded outline with four outline entries.

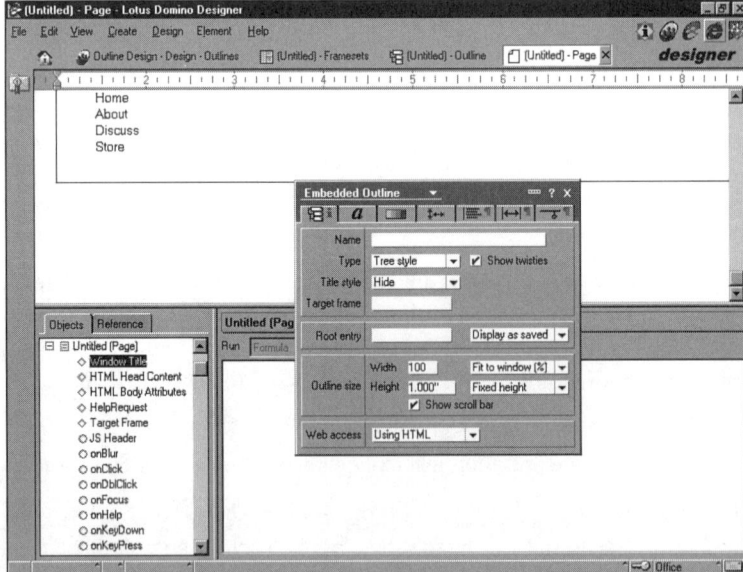

That's it. All you have to do is click one button: A new page is created for you and the embedded outline is automatically added to this new page. Cool, eh?

After the page is created, you can edit it normally. You also need to set the properties for your embedded outline. As you can see from the figure, there are many properties that you can adjust for the embedded outline.

On the Info page of the properties box, you should specify the name for the embedded outline control and also its type. The type can be either Tree style or Flat. When you use Tree style, you see the familiar indented folders. Flat means that when you drill down one level in the outline, the new level replaces the original level in the display.

You can check the Show Twisties box to show triangles to the left of outline entries that can be expanded. The Title style enables you to either hide or show the database title above the outline.

The Target frame entry is one place where you can specify how you want to link your frames. If your outline is going to appear in the left frame and the contents in the right frame, within the properties box you can indicate that you want the target frame to be the right frame.

Actually, there are several places where you can specify the target frame. In addition to the Embedded Outline dialog box, you can also define the target frame within the Outline Entry properties dialog box and in the Frame properties dialog box. How does Domino reconcile these multiple definitions?

The general rule is that the smallest design element will have priority. In other words, an Outline Entry's definition will override the Embedded Outline definition, which will in turn override the definition found in the Frame properties. This makes sense because you may have several links within a frame, and each one may use a different target frame.

Normally, as I've mentioned, you should start simply with just a few frames and use a consistent design. In this way, you won't really have to worry about conflicting definitions. You can, for example, just define the target frame at the frame level and not use the definition of the embedded outline at all.

Using a Page in a Frameset

After you generate your outline page, you can edit it normally as you would edit any other page. You can add other items or move the outline around on the page. After you edit the page and like the way it looks, you can then include it in your frameset. The outline page will be used to navigate and will cause the contents of linked pages to change.

Here is what you do to include your page within your frameset:

1. Click on Framesets in the Design pane to see a list of your framesets.
2. Double-click on the frameset name in the list in the work area to open the desired frameset.

3. Select the frame you want to use for your page by clicking within the frame. In our example, we use the left frame.

> **Tip**
>
> You should have a naming convention for your frames so you can keep track of their contents. A very simple naming convention is to use the frame's position as its name. In my examples, I use the name `left` for the left frame, `top` for the top-right frame, and `right` for the bottom-right (main) frame. You can, of course, use different conventions, but naming the frames with some indication of their location allows you to easily remember when you see that something is going to appear in the `left` or `right` frame.

4. After you select the frame, change the content type to named element and page.
5. Click on the folder icon. This brings up a dialog box, and you can choose your page from the list. Click OK. Change the default target to be the right frame. See Figure 16.11.

Figure 16.11
An outline page set as content for the left frame with the target in the right frame.

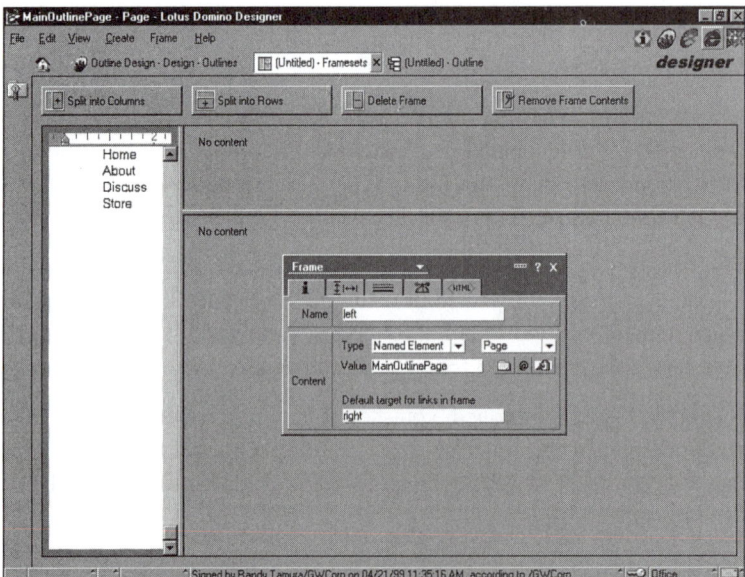

Now we have created a frameset with three frames. We use the left frame for navigation. In the left frame, we included a page, that in turn includes an outline. When a user clicks on the outline entries in the left pane, the outline will control what will be displayed in the target (right) frame.

It seems a little complicated at first because you have to be familiar with outlines, pages, and framesets, but when you put them together, you can easily create framesets that work wonderfully.

Designing Navigators

Domino navigators have been around since release 4, so they should be familiar to developers that have worked with that release. If you have a Web development background, you can think of navigators as imagemaps. A typical navigator contains a background image with hotspots, and you can program the hotspots to perform various actions. There are several built-in Simple Actions you can use or you can program more complex actions by using either the @formula language or LotusScript. Note that JavaScript and Java are not available for use with navigators.

Here is a list of the built-in Simple Actions you can associate with a navigator hotspot:

- Open another navigator
- Open a view or folder
- Alias a folder
- Open a link (document, view, or database)
- Open a URL

As mentioned, you can also use the @formula language or LotusScript to program custom actions.

To create a new navigator, follow these steps:

1. Click on Navigators in the Design pane. The work area will contain a list of the existing navigators, if any.
2. Click on the New Navigator action bar button. Your new navigator is created.
3. You will then be placed in edit mode within the navigator graphical editor. In the navigator properties box, you should ensure that the check box Web browser compatible is enabled (this is the default). This property ensures that Web browsers will be able to view your navigator.

Graphic Backgrounds: Are They for You?

Before drawing any objects onto your new navigator, decide whether you wish to use a Graphic Background. Use a Graphic Background if you have at your disposal an image that contains areas that the user would immediately identify as discrete objects that may be selected to initiate an action.

For example, the image of a bookcase may be used as a Graphic Background. Each shelf, or book, on the Graphic Background may be used as a link for a particular view in the database. Another obvious example of a Graphic Background is a map, where particular regions may be used to initiate actions.

> **Tip:** To remove a Graphic Background, select Design, Remove Graphic Background.

Drawing Navigator Objects

After you choose to insert a Graphic Background (or decide to skip this step), navigator objects may be inserted.

Navigator objects include the following:

- Standard shapes, including rectangles, rounded rectangles, ellipses, lines (referred to as polylines) and polygons. All of these shapes, with the exception of lines, are automatically filled with a user-defined color.
- Hotspots, in the form of rectangles, circles, or polygons. A *hotspot* is simply an outline that may be used to identify a particular region of a Graphic Background. Because hotspots are only outlines, they are never filled with a color. Hotspots may be used, for example, to outline geographical regions, such as cities, on a state map.
- Text boxes, enabling text to be displayed anywhere on a navigator. Font, size, and color area all configurable.
- Two varieties of buttons: graphic buttons, which are essentially rectangular Clipboard objects (such as a bitmap pasted to the Clipboard); and hotspot buttons, which are standard buttons that contain a single line of text.

Objects may be created using either the Create menu or the second set of SmartIcons that represent various objects that may be created. The easiest way to create an object is through the use of these SmartIcons. To enable SmartIcons, select from the menu: File, Preferences, SmartIcon Settings. Enable the Icon Bar option and click OK. See Figure 16.12 for a sample navigator.

The first click of a particular object on the SmartIcon bar enables object-creation mode, represented by a crosshair cursor when the mouse pointer is over the navigator Design pane. The second click of the same SmartIcon object turns off creation mode and enables object-manipulation mode. In this mode, you may manipulate objects that have been drawn; they may be moved, resized, or deleted.

After an object has been selected, drawing it is fairly straightforward—especially to those already familiar with other drawing programs. Here are some quick drawing tips:

- To draw an ellipse, rectangle, rounded rectangle, hotspot rectangle, or hotspot circle, move the cursor to the anchor point in the navigator, and then click and hold down the mouse button. With the mouse button depressed, move the mouse pointer to size the object. Release the mouse button to complete your drawing.

Figure 16.12
A sample navigator with a rectangle and an ellipse.

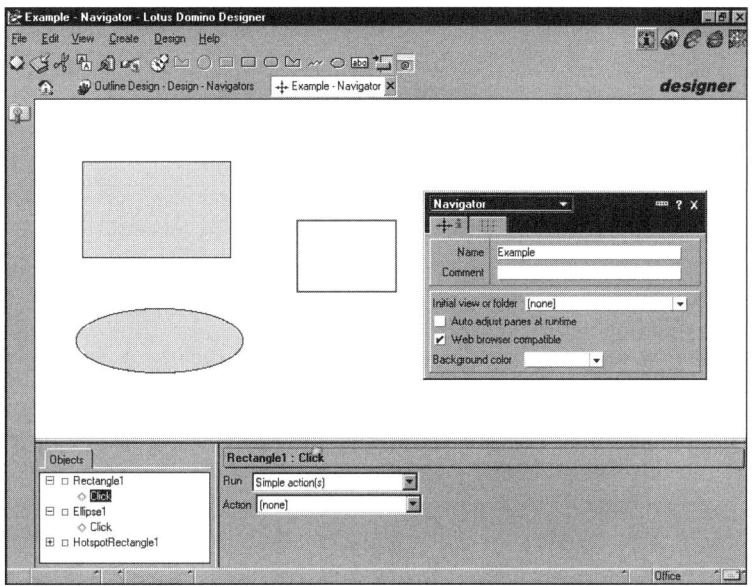

- To draw a polygon, hotspot polygon, or polyline, move the cursor to the first point, and then click once on the mouse button to begin your drawing. Each subsequent, single, mouse-button click adds a new point to your polygon. To complete drawing a polygon-type object, double-click the mouse button. For polygons, a double-click automatically draws a line from the last point to the first point, closing the bounds of the object.
- To move several objects simultaneously, hold down the Shift key and click once on each object that must be moved. When the last object is selected, continue holding the Shift key, click the left mouse button, and move the mouse to relocate all selected objects. Release the mouse button when the new positions are satisfactory.
- To draw a circle or a square, hold down the Shift key, and then begin drawing an ellipse or rectangle. The Shift key acts to constrain the object to a symmetric pattern rather than a freely sized shape. This trick also works after an object is drawn, when one of these objects is resized.

After an object has been drawn, properties for each object may be modified via the properties dialog box. To make the properties box visible, click with the right mouse button over any object, and then select Object Properties.

Each object will have different properties that pertain to it. For example, a text object will enable the selection of a font and point size. However, the HiLite tab applies to all navigator objects. See Figure 16.13.

Figure 16.13
The Hotspot Rectangle properties box.

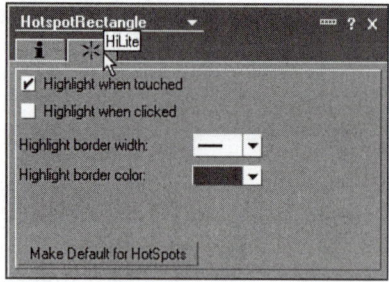

For objects that will trigger events, one or both of the options presented in this screen should be selected:

- **Highlight when touched**   Enabling this option draws the border for the object, as specified by the Highlight Outline Width and Highlight Outline Color settings, when the user moves the mouse over the navigator object. This option should typically be selected for hotspot polygons, hotspot circles, or hotspot rectangles.

- **Highlight when clicked**   Enabling this option flashes the border for the object, as specified by the Highlight Outline Width and Highlight Outline Color settings, when the user clicks on the navigator object.

> **Tip**
>
> See a navigator in another database that you want to use in your database? No problem! Navigators may be "cut" and "pasted" to and from databases just like forms and views. Simply highlight the source navigator in Design Mode and select Edit, Copy (Ctrl+C). Next, open the destination database, select Navigator from the Design folder (from Design Mode), and then select Edit, Paste (Ctrl+V).

Acting upon Clicks

After you have drawn navigator objects, you must determine how an object will react to a Click, the one and only runtime event for navigator objects.

When the user clicks on a navigator object, one of the following may occur:

- A Simple Action may be initiated, enabling common navigator functions, such as opening a new view, to be developed with no programming effort.
- A Formula may execute, for those that are comfortable with Notes Formulas.
- Script may execute, enabling simple or complex LotusScript statements to be executed.
- Nothing. Objects do not necessarily have to initiate one of the previous actions. They can be included in the navigator for artistic reasons alone.

To designate an appropriate action for navigator objects, first select the object whose action(s) need to be defined. Next, in the Programmer's pane, select the programming method that you want to use for this object (Simple Action, Formula, or Script).

In many cases, Simple Actions are the most appropriate way to deal with navigator events. The five Simple Actions available for each object include the following:

- **Open another Navigator**   Use this choice to link one navigator to another. When selected, a combo box will appear containing a list of available navigators.
- **Open a View or Folder**   This option is used to display a new view or folder in the View pane. When selected, a combo box will appear containing a list of available views.
- **Alias a folder**   This particularly useful option does two things. First, it switches the View pane to the folder specified. Second, it enables objects from other views and folders to be dragged and dropped into the navigator object itself. When selected, a combo box will appear containing a list of available folders.
- **Open a link**   This choice enables a document, view, or database link to be opened. When selected, a button will appear that will enable a link to be pasted. First, however, you must switch to a database, document, or view; then choose Edit, Copy as Link for the appropriate object. After a link is copied to the Clipboard, switch back to the navigator designer and click on the Paste Link button.
- **Open URL**   This choice links to an arbitrary URL on the World Wide Web. When you select this option, an additional button appears: Enter URL. Click this button and enter the URL that you want to link to the navigator.

Using Hotspots With and Without Navigators

You don't have to use a navigator to use hotspots. In fact, you can create hotspots on pages and forms as well as navigators. Hotspots created on pages and forms have slightly different capabilities than hotspots created on navigators. Here is a summary of the differences.

Navigator Hotspots

- Can open another navigator, view, or folder
- Can alias a folder (not available on Web)
- Can open a document, view, or database link
- Can open an arbitrary URL
- Can execute a @formula or LotusScript program
- Can use only a frame's target specification

Hotspots on pages or forms

- Can open document, view, database, or anchor links
- Can open named elements: pages, forms, framesets, or views
- Can open an arbitrary URL
- Can specify a particular frame to use as a target
- Can be used for text pop-ups

- Can be displayed and used as buttons
- Can be used as formula pop-ups
- Can be used as an action hotspot, which can utilize @formulas, LotusScript, JavaScript, or simple actions

As you can see from the two lists, hotspots directly on pages or forms are just as powerful—or perhaps more so—than hotspots that are created on navigators.

Another difference between navigators and page elements is that navigators are separate design elements. Therefore, navigators can be embedded on more than one page or form. If your design requires the same navigator-like structure in several places, you should consider a navigator rather than page elements.

Prior to release 5 of Notes and Domino, there were no pages, and some items could not be placed directly on a form, so navigators were very important. With the advent of release 5, however, it might be easier to create your navigational images directly on a page or form. This will simplify your design and reduce the number of different design elements you need to use.

You can use hotspots directly on pages and forms in Domino Designer. When you use a hotspot directly on a page or form, it is associated with text. You can also directly create an image on a page or form, and then create hotspots on the image. Let's first investigate the various forms of text hotspots.

LINK HOTSPOTS

As mentioned previously, there are several different types of hotspots you can use on a page or form. The first type of hotspot is the link hotspot. This type of hotspot enables you to specify a document, view, database, or anchor. To create a link hotspot:

1. First, open the target of your link. For example, open the specific document, view, or database you want as the destination in the Notes client. From the menu, select Edit, Copy As Link, and then Anchor Link, Document Link, View Link, or Database Link depending upon your preference. This copies the link to the Clipboard. Alternatively, you could open a design element in the Domino Designer. You can use either a Named Element or Database link from within the designer. Again, from the menu, select Edit, Copy As Link, followed by your choice.
2. Return to the page or form that you want to contain the hotspot. Highlight the text you want to serve as your link.
3. From the menu, select Create, Hotspot, Link Hotspot.
4. The Hotspot Resource Link properties box should appear. See Figure 16.14.
5. If you copied a document link, the link may automatically appear. If you copied a design element, you may need to click the Paste icon, which you can do in any case. The link from the Clipboard will be pasted, and the type of your link should change to the type of link you copied to the Clipboard. Your link is complete.

Figure 16.14
The Hotspot Resource Link properties box.

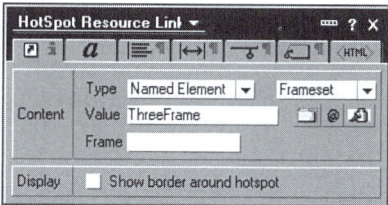

You can also change some of the link properties directly from the properties box. For example, you can specify a URL rather than a document link as the hotspot destination. In this case, manually change the type of link to URL, and then type the URL into the Value field of the dialog box.

Finally, you can specify a frame where you want the result of the hotspot to appear. If you don't specify a frame, the link will appear within the same frame as the hotspot, unless a frameset target frame overrides it.

Hotspot Text Pop-ups

Hotspot text pop-ups are very useful for supplying help information. You can arrange it so that helpful text will appear either when the user's mouse hovers over the hotspot or when the user clicks on the hotspot. See Figure 16.15.

Figure 16.15
The Hotspot Pop-up properties box.

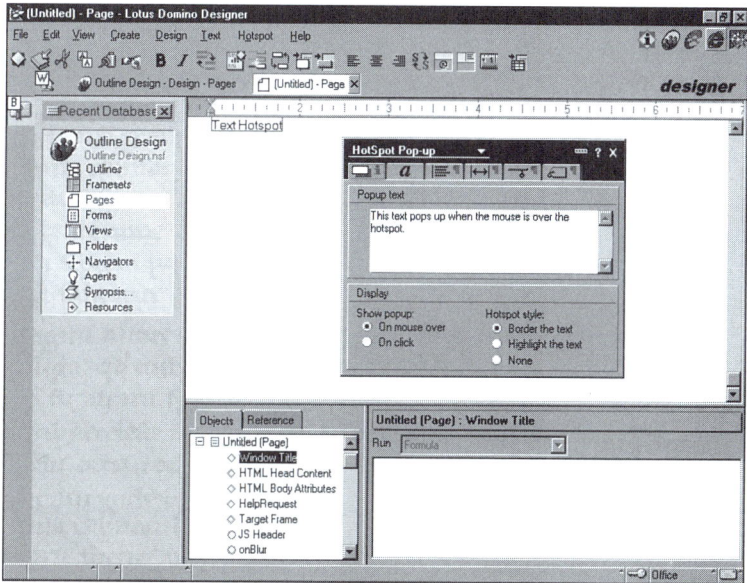

To create a hotspot text pop-up:

1. Add the document text to a page or form.

2. Highlight the text that will be used to trigger the hotspot.
3. Select Create, Hotspot, Text Pop-up.
4. The Hotspot Pop-up properties box will appear. Enter the pop-up text. Choose whether the text should appear on a user Mouse Over or on a click by selecting the appropriate radio button.
5. Show a border around the hotspot or use a highlight color by checking the appropriate box.

> **Note** Hotspot text pop-ups do not work in Web browsers, only in the Notes client.

Hotspot Buttons

Buttons that are displayed on a page or form are called *hotspot buttons*. You can program the action of the button using one of four different methods. You can use a Simple Action, an @formula, a LotusScript program or a JavaScript program. Simple Actions enable you to assign values to fields, copy documents, send or reply to email, and many other common preprogrammed actions. If you use one of the other methods, you have the full power of the programming language at your disposal.

To create a hotspot button:

1. Move the cursor on the page or form to the location where you want your button to appear.
2. Select Create, Hotspot, Button.
3. The Button properties box will appear. Enter the label that you want to appear on the button in the Button label field.
4. In the Programmer's pane, select the language you want to use. The default is formula language, but you can choose Simple Action, LotusScript, or JavaScript also.
5. After you choose your language, you can use the Programmer's pane to enter your action.

Formula Pop-up Hotspots

A formula pop-up hotspot has some characteristics of a text hotspot and a hotspot button. Formula pop-up hotspots must be associated with text on the form or page. When the user clicks on the hotspot, the formula is executed. Note that the Mouse Over option is not available for formula hotspots.

To create a formula hotspot:

1. Move the cursor on the page or form to the location where you want your formula hotspot to appear. Highlight the text you want to use to trigger the formula.
2. Select Create, Hotspot, Formula Pop-up.

3. The Hotspot Pop-up properties box will appear. You can change attributes of the text, such as the font or color.

4. In the Programmer's pane, the formula language is automatically selected for you. You cannot use LotusScript or JavaScript for a formula hotspot.

5. In the Programmer's pane, enter the formula that you want to execute if the user clicks on the hotspot text.

> **Note**: Formula pop-ups do not work in Web browsers, only in the Notes client. Use an action hotspot instead.

Action Hotspots

An action hotspot is much more powerful than a formula pop-up hotspot and also has the advantage that it works in browsers. With an action hotspot, you can specify your action with one of four different languages: Simple Action, Formula language, LotusScript, or JavaScript. When the user clicks on the hotspot, the action you supply is executed. Note that the Mouse Over option is not available for action hotspots, but if you use JavaScript, you can specify a JavaScript program for the onMouseOver event.

To create an action hotspot:

1. Move the cursor on the page or form to the location where you want your formula hotspot to appear. Highlight the text you want to use to trigger the formula.

2. Select Create, Hotspot, Action Hotspot.

3. The Action Hotspot properties box will appear. You can change attributes of the text, such as the font or color, and you can specify a frame for the target if required.

4. In the Programmer's pane, select the language you want to use. The default is formula language, but you can choose Simple Action, LotusScript, or JavaScript also.

5. In the Programmer's pane, enter the formula or other program that you want to execute if the user clicks on the hotspot text. If you choose JavaScript, there are several mouse actions that you can program.

Hotspots on Imagemaps

You can define hotspots on imagemaps in a manner similar to the way you work with hotspots on navigators. Imagemaps, also known as pictures, can be placed on a page in one of two ways. You can import an image file from the file system or you can use a shared image, which is an image that is already stored within a database in the shared image library. The terms *image*, *picture*, and *imagemap* are used almost synonymously. The only slight difference in meaning is that an image is typically called an imagemap after it has one or more hotspots on it. So you can call it either an image with hotspots or an imagemap.

To import an image from the file system:

1. Open the page or form you want to use. Move the cursor to the location where you want your image to appear.
2. Select Create, Picture. A dialog box showing the file system will appear.
3. You can navigate through the file system looking for the image to import. You can import the following types of files: BMP, CGM, GIF, JPEG, Lotus PIC, PCX, and TIFF 5.0.
4. Find the file you want to import, and click the Import button. Your image will be imported.

To use an image that is already within your shared image resources:

1. Open the page or form you want to use. Move the cursor to the location where you want your image to appear.
2. Select Create, Image Resource. A dialog box will appear showing you all the images that are in your shared image library.
3. Select the desired image from the list of images, and click OK. Your image will be shown on your page or form.

After you create an image on your page or form through either of the methods, you can add a hotspot to the image. Hotspots on an image can be one of three shapes: polygon, circle, or rectangle. To create a hotspot on an image:

1. First place the image on the page or form using one of the techniques described previously.
2. Open the Picture Info properties box. See Figure 16.16.
3. Click on one of the pictures in the bottom row for polygon, circle, or rectangle.
4. Move your cursor into the image area. It should now appear as a cross.
5. Click on one corner of the area where you want the hotspot to be located and drag the mouse to the other corner. You will see a rubber-band shape of the hotspot area. You can adjust the location and size of the hotspot area by clicking and dragging on the handles for the shape, which look like dots. To move the hotspot shape, click and drag it.
6. After you place the hotspot on the image, you can specify an action to be taken when the user clicks on the hotspot. You can choose a Link, a Named Element link, or a URL. A Link can be a document, view, database, or anchor link. A Named Element will link to a design element, such as a Page, Form, Frameset, or View. You specify the type within the Hotspot properties box.
7. You can optionally also specify an action to take in the `Click` event for the hotspot. The `Click` event can be programmed as a Simple Action, Formula, LotusScript, or JavaScript program.

USING EMBEDDED ELEMENTS ON A PAGE OR FORM | 409

Figure 16.16
The Picture Info properties box and an imagemap with three hotspots.

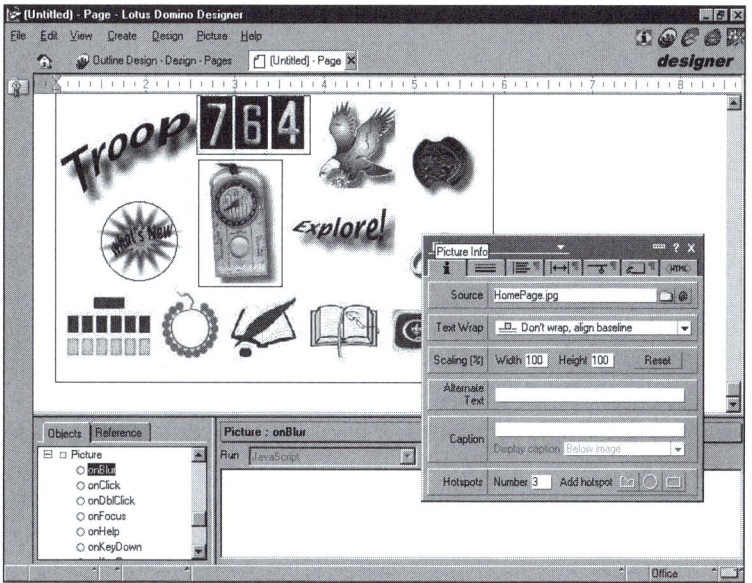

Using Embedded Elements on a Page or Form

In defining a page, you can embed several different types of elements. In addition to outlines, which I discussed in a previous section, you can embed navigators, views, Folder panes, and a date picker in pages. On forms, you can embed all those elements as well as a group scheduler and file upload control. To embed one of the following design elements, select Create, Embedded Element, and then choose one of the embedded element types. Here is a synopsis of these embedded elements:

- **Embedded Outlines** These enable you to specify navigation elements for your Web site or database. Use the outline editor to edit the outline entries. Each outline entry can serve as a link to a page, form, or URL within a database. Embedded outlines are especially useful when used with framesets.

- **Embedded Views** You can embed a view on a page. You embed a view so you can control the formatting of the view display. When a view is embedded on a page or form, the user will not see the standard view navigation elements. One of the important properties of an embedded view is the capability of specifying the use of a Java applet for Web browsers. Do this in the embedded view properties box.

- **Embedded Navigator** When you embed a navigator, the page or form refers to the navigator design element. Navigators can include graphics and hotspot definitions. If you change a navigator, all references to the navigator will get the changed graphics.

- **Embedded Import Navigator** When you choose Import Navigator, the graphical design elements of the navigator are imported into the page. After the design elements have been imported, you can edit them directly on the page. Note that after you have imported the navigator, it is no longer linked to the original navigator definition.

- **Embedded Folder pane** The embedded folder pane enables you to have a Folder pane embedded within a page or form of your own design. The Folder pane is the pane that appears in the upper-left pane when you are looking at a view or folder. It contains a hierarchical listing of the views and folders of the database. Embedding this pane in your own page or form allows the user to navigate to one of the existing views or folders easily.
- **Date Picker** The Date Picker works only on the Notes client; it will not work in a Web browser. If you choose this item, it will display a calendar. This object works in conjunction with a Calendar view in another frame within the same frameset. If you insert a date picker in one frame and a Calendar view in another, they will be linked automatically. The user can choose a date on the date picker, and the Calendar view will move to that date automatically.
- **Group Scheduler** The group scheduler can be embedded only on forms, not on pages. One reason is that the refresh for the group scheduler can be controlled by a reserved field named `$GroupScheduleRefreshMode`. Pages cannot have fields, so this option is not available. The refresh mode enables you to control what happens when the user clicks the refresh (F9) key. Because there may be many users and many databases to search for updates, you can control how much detail Domino will search upon refresh.
- **File Upload control** The file upload control enables Web users to attach files to documents. To use it, you embed the control on a form. When the form is displayed to a user, a text field and a browse button appear, and the user can enter a filename or browse for a file to be uploaded. Note that for this control to work, the Domino server administrator must define a temp directory. If a temp directory is not defined, the attachment will not be uploaded. Also, the file upload control will work only in a Web browser, not the Notes client.

PUTTING IT ALL TOGETHER: OUTLINES, VIEWS, FRAMESETS, NAVIGATORS, AND BEYOND

Notes release 5 provides you with a rich set of tools for presenting applications to users in both the Notes client and Web browsers. It is easy to become confused about which design element to choose, so I'll try to bring all these concepts together in this section.

When you present an interface to the user, there are several important considerations. The first is content, the second is layout, and the third is navigation. These are not separate concepts; in fact they should join seamlessly to form the user interface.

You provide basic content to the user on pages or forms. If you want to have users provide feedback, you must use a form. A page is a read-only design element that the user can view, but in which the user cannot enter any input (unless you manually code HTML and JavaScript). Pages are suitable if you have a small number to be displayed to the user. Forms are useful if you want to have more of a database-driven design with potentially hundreds or thousands of documents shown to the user within the form. Pages and forms are also containers that can house embedded elements, such as views, navigators, outlines, and so forth. Pages are typically used when you want to solely include outlines or navigators. You can provide basic layout within a page by just editing the content of a page and placing the elements where you want them to appear.

More complex layouts are achieved by using framesets. Frames within a frameset can contain documents, URLs, pages, forms, views, or other framesets. For most good designs, you won't need more than four or five frames, and you should typically start your frameset design simply. The content in one frame can cause changes in another frame. It is very common to have navigational elements (such as an outline in a page) in one frame, and have the navigation change the content of a separate frame (the target).

The last type of design element is the navigational element. In this category are outlines, views, imagemaps, and navigators. A view is the traditional Notes navigational element, and it enables the user to navigate among documents within a database. Each outline entry within an outline performs a similar purpose, but is much more powerful. With outline entries, you can navigate to URLs, pages, and forms as well as documents. A navigator is a design element that enables you to draw graphical items and create hotspots. It is a standalone design element, and to be used, it must be included in a page or form. Thus, it can be created once and used in multiple locations if desired. An imagemap is created and directly associated with a specific page or form. It is similar to a navigator, but is not an independent design element. You can create hotspots on imagemaps and link them to pages, forms, or URLs.

From Here...

In this chapter, I showed you the important navigational elements of outlines, framesets, and navigators. Here are some additional chapters you can read to complete your understanding of the Notes and Domino design elements:

- Chapter 17, "Access Control Lists (ACLs) and Application Security," shows you how to secure your applications to prevent unauthorized access.
- Chapter 18, "Working with Formulas, Functions, and Commands," tells you about these important programming features of Notes and Domino. You will frequently need to use formulas, functions, and/or commands to automate your application.
- Part IV, "Using LotusScript, Java, and JavaScript," includes nine chapters covering these three languages in detail. You'll learn not only about the programming languages and their syntax, but the Domino Object Model as well.

CHAPTER 17

Access Control Lists (ACLs) and Application Security

Every Domino application is protected by a unique Access Control List (ACL). The ACL defines who can make which changes to an application and restricts where those changes can be made from. The ACL works in tandem with Notes usernames taken from ID files and from Web logins. If a username matches a name in the ACL, the user is granted the level of access defined for his or her name.

Every Domino application has its own ACL. If the application is accessed through a Domino server, the ACL is always enforced—even when an anonymous user opens the application from the Web.

The application manager can also set an application parameter so that the ACL is enforced even when the application is opened on a local hard drive.

As Notes matured as a groupware product, so did the ACL. It has become more and more granular, letting you define right down to the finest level what can and cannot be done by an individual within an application. In this chapter, the layers of the ACL will be peeled back to reveal the heart of Notes and Domino security.

ACL Basics

When you first access the Domino server or open a local replica of an application on which the ACL is locally enforced, you are prompted for your Notes user ID and your password. The same Notes ID remains valid throughout the Notes session, or until you clear the user ID (for example by pressing F5).

Every time you open a Domino application for which the ACL is enforced, the username on your ID file is compared against names in the ACL to determine what type of access you have. You may be listed in the ACL with your username, or you may be included in the ACL as a member of one or more groups. If, as a result of multiple listings, you have more than one level of access to a database, you will automatically be given the highest authorized level. In other words, if you are listed explicitly with Author access, but you are a member of group that has Editor access, you will have Editor access.

The ACL contains seven major categories of access, ranging from the most restrictive to the most inclusive:

- **No Access**   Those with no access cannot access the application…period.
- **Depositor**   A Depositor can create documents, but after documents have been saved and closed, a Depositor cannot view the documents or any other documents in the application.
- **Reader**   A Reader can only read documents in the application.
- **Author**   An Author can edit documents for which that Author is listed in an Authors field, and optionally can create, edit, and/or delete documents for which that Author is listed in an Authors field.

- **Editor** An Editor can create, read, modify, and may be able to delete, any document in the application. An Editor also can run agents.
- **Designer** A Designer can create or modify design elements in the application; can create and run agents; and can create, read, modify, and optionally delete documents within the application. Delete privileges can be allowed or disallowed.
- **Manager** An application Manager can perform all the functions of other application users. In addition, a Manager can make changes to the application ACL. The Manager is also the only one with the authority to delete an application.

These basic levels of the ACL can be restricted in various ways. The restrictions allow the application manager to define specialized functions for individuals within the boundaries of those basic ACL levels.

Assigning ACL Levels

Examine the Basics page of the ACL dialog box shown in Figure 17.1.

Figure 17.1
People and groups are assigned a level of access on the Basics page of the Access Control List.

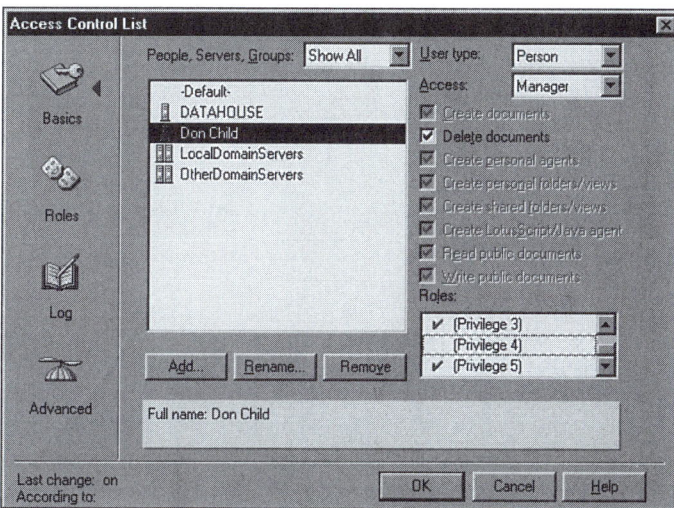

The People, Servers, Groups drop-down list at the top of the dialog box enables you to decide what will be displayed in the ACL. You can display only people in the ACL, only groups, or only servers. You also can leave the default selection to show all entries in the ACL for the application.

In Figure 17.1, all people, servers, and groups who have been assigned to the ACL are listed.

A Closer Look at What Gets Listed in the ACL

To ensure that you are not confused, I'll outline in greater detail what I mean by people, groups, and servers.

People in the ACL

People includes individual users. If a user is in the Domino directory, you can use his or her common name in the ACL. But if a user from another domain is to be listed in the ACL, that person has to be listed using the full hierarchical name so the name in the ACL can be compared with the name on the Notes user ID—for example, Fiona Chang/West/Acme.

For tighter control over security, you might want to add full hierarchical names for those in the local domain. For example, if you have `John Smith` listed in the ACL, any user with the name John Smith can access the application. But if the name is `John Smith/Sales/ABC`, the ACL is far more restrictive.

If the application will be exposed to the Web via the Domino server, an http name and password (listed in the Domino directory) allow access to the application for those who are listed individually or as members of a group.

New to Notes 5.0, names listed in a Directory Assistance application can also be authenticated and can be allowed access to Domino applications. The Directory Assistance application has to be defined so that the names in it are trusted for authentication. Group names can be expanded only from the Domino directory and one LDAP directory, but there is no practical limit on individual names.

The person who created the application is automatically inserted into the ACL as a Manager.

Groups in the ACL

Groups can be created in the Domino directory and then listed in the ACL. If a group of people needs similar access to data in your organization, you can put everyone who shares similar interests into a single group. You can then grant the entire group the same level of access in an application's ACL. If a new employee shares the interests of the group, that employee can be added to the group in the Domino directory's group document. With that single entry, the new employee has access to any applications that have the group name in the ACL. It is much easier than trying to manage individual names in dozens of applications.

To illustrate how easy it is to use groups, assume that someone is leaving your accounting team and going into the sales department. You have to remove that person's name from all the ACL in all the accounting applications, and add it to the sales applications. It takes only two simple steps. Delete the name from the accounting group. Add it to the sales group. Assuming that you have not put the name into any of the accounting ACLs as an individual, you are done. The person is now a member of the sales group and has access to all the sales applications.

If you use hierarchical names in your organization, you can also use wildcards in the ACL. For example, `*/Sales/ABC` allows the entire sales unit to access the application as a de facto group.

If your server allows Anonymous access, you can include a user named Anonymous in your ACL to define which level of access Anonymous users have. Anonymous is a group that includes anyone who gains Anonymous access to the application through the Web.

> **Note**
> If a user has access to the application as a member of a group and as an individual, the highest access level prevails. For example, if you give a person Reader access but he or she also belongs to a group that has Editor access, the individual will be able to edit documents.

SERVERS IN THE ACL

Servers are listed in the ACL as members of one of two groups—LocalDomainServers and OtherDomainServers. LocalDomainServers are those within your Notes domain—that is, those that are registered in your Domino directory. OtherDomainServers are those that are listed in other Domino directories within your Notes organization. These two groups should contain only servers within your organization, because you can then give them a higher level of access than any servers outside your organization.

By putting all your local domain servers into a single server group, you make it easy to grant access to all the servers at once. Documents and design elements can be created or modified on any server in the organization, and then replicated to other servers within the domain. You may want to limit servers from other domains to making changes to documents. In other words, you can assign LocalDomainServers to Manager access and OtherDomainServers to Editor or Designer access.

If you want to give access to a server from outside your organization, you will probably want to create a separate group or add the server individually with its full hierarchical name. If servers are not included in the ACL via a group record or explicitly, they will have only the default level of access for the application.

> **Note**
> You can also include applications individually in the ACL. This is important when you are using the application for lookups from other applications. Include the Replica ID for any application that has to access the application in order to run agents using `@DbColumn` or `@DbLookup` to retrieve data.

ADDING A USER TO THE ACL

To add a user to the ACL, click on the Add button in the ACL dialog box. The Add User dialog box in Figure 17.2 is then displayed.

Figure 17.2
Type a name or click on the Person icon to select a person, group, or server from an Address Book.

It is important that you enter names into the ACL accurately. A simple misspelling in the ACL will keep a user from being able to access an application. To prevent this problem, you should develop the habit of selecting names from the Domino directory. You can select names from the Domino directory as follows:

1. Click on the Person icon in the Add User dialog box. A Names dialog box is displayed, as shown in Figure 17.3.

Figure 17.3
Select names from a Domino directory or Personal Address Book to ensure accuracy.

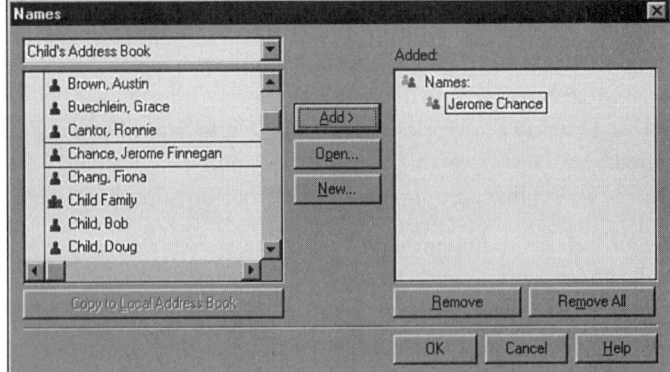

2. Select the directory or Address Book you want to use.
3. Click on the person, group, or server you want to add to the ACL.
4. Click on the Add button to add the name to the right side of the dialog box.

   If you have to remove a name from the right side, highlight the name and click on Remove, or click on Remove All to empty all names from the right side so that you can start over.

5. When the name or names you want are listed on the right side, click on OK to add the names to the ACL.

The names you add are given the same level of access as the name you highlighted in the ACL dialog box before you started to add names. After you add a name, however, you are free to change the access level in the Access list of the ACL dialog box.

In the ACL dialog box, under User type, you can also select which type of user the name represents—a person, a group, or a server. This user type determines, in part, what you can do with a user ID. For example, if you identify a name as a server, that server ID cannot be used to access the application with a Notes client to edit documents. If you leave an ACL entry as the default Unspecified, there are no restrictions on the user type, and the entry could be any type of Notes ID.

Refining Access Levels

After you select a level of access, you can refine the level of access by allowing or disallowing access to certain specific functions, even though those functions would normally be allowed, based on the user's access level.

To the right of the list of names in the ACL are several check boxes defining specific functions that can be performed by members of a specific access level.

For example, in a Domino directory application, you might be granted Author access so you can edit your own Person document, but you may not be allowed to add or delete documents. With Author access, you can only view documents, or edit sections of documents where you are listed specifically as an authorized Author.

To refine the ACL privileges for an individual, you can click on certain check boxes to turn them on or off. Refer to Figure 17.1 to see the check boxes used to restrict access. Table 17.1 indicates which privileges are automatically available (X), optional (O), or not available (blank) for the different levels of access. The optional privileges can be turned on or off.

TABLE 17.1 PRIVILEGES (X) AND OPTIONAL PRIVILEGES (O) FOR DIFFERENT LEVELS OF ACCESS

Privilege No Access	Manager	Designer	Editor	Author	Reader	Depositor
Create documents	X	X	X	O		X
Delete documents	O	O	O	O		
Create personal agents	X	X	O	O	O	
Create personal folders/views	X	X	O	O	O	
Create shared folders/views	X	X	X	O		
Create LotusScript/ Java agents	X	O	O	O	O	
Read public documents	X	X	X	X	X	O
Write public documents	X	X	X	O	O	O

Here is what each privilege means:

- **Create documents** Only users with Create documents access can add new documents to an application. You can turn off this option for Authors if you want, and they still will be able to edit documents for which they are listed in an Authors field. There is an exception, in which users can create public documents but cannot otherwise create documents in the application. See Write public documents, later in this list.

- **Delete documents** If a user does not have Delete documents privileges, he or she cannot delete any documents, including those that he or she created. An archive application or a tracking application are examples of where this option might be used. By default, nobody can delete documents, so you have to set this option if you want to allow Managers, Designers, Editors, or Authors to delete documents.

- **Create personal agents** Anyone with Reader access or higher can theoretically create agents on a server-based application. However, this does take up system resources, so the ability to create personal agents can be restricted for anyone below an application manager. Also, the system administrator can restrict anyone from running personal agents on the server. This is done in the Server document in the Domino Directory.

- **Create personal folders/views** Anybody with Reader access or higher can create personal folders and views on a server-based application, unless they are restricted from doing so. Managers and Designers always have this ability. A server-based folder or view can be replicated so that it will be available on multiple servers, but it does take up disk space. If this option is deselected, users can still create local personal folders and views.

- **Create shared folders/views** Designers and Editors can be given the ability to create shared folders and views if desired, or you can restrict this access to save disk space on server-based applications. The Manager is always able to create shared folders and views.

- **Create LotusScript/Java agents** You can grant anyone with Reader access or higher the ability to create LotusScript or Java agents. However, these agents can hog the server processing time, so you might want to restrict this ability so that only the Manager can create these agents.

- **Read public documents** You can enable those who come into the application with No Access to see certain public documents. This option is used primarily to allow access to calendar functions so that, for example, people can see a listing of scheduled functions without having access to any other information in an application. You can use it with any form that has the property Available to public access users set.

- **Write public documents** This option is also used for individuals who otherwise have no access to an application but need to have limited access to calendaring and scheduling or other functions.

Defining and Using Roles

Roles provide another means of controlling access to specific functions within an application. Roles can be used in any of the following places within a Domino application to control access:

- Author fields that determine who can edit specific documents
- Reader fields that determine who can read specific documents
- View or folder properties that determine who can access specific views or folders (set these on the last page of the View Properties InfoBox)
- Form properties that determine who can see documents created with a specific form
- Form properties that determine who can create documents using a specific form
- Controlled Access Sections that can be edited only by specific individuals or specific roles

Note that roles can be used for reasons other than controlling access. The previous list illustrates only places where roles are used for access.

To assign roles to users, you must do the following:

1. Create the role in the ACL.
2. Assign the role to entries in the ACL.
3. Enter the role name in fields used to restrict access within the application.

You must complete all three steps for roles to work. The steps are described in greater detail later in this chapter.

If you are limiting access to a function based on roles, enter the name of the role into the field used to limit access. For example, enter [SectionReader] in the appropriate Readers field on a form to restrict Reader access to people who have been assigned to the SectionReader role.

Although you can put individual names, server names, or group names into access fields on forms, views, sections, and so forth, using roles enables you to be more granular in defining who can do what in the application. For example, in a Sales application, you can have all the members of your sales force able to place their own orders as Authors, but you want to give team leaders the exclusive right to create new client records. You can do this using a ClientCreator role on the Client form and assigning team leaders to that role.

Adding a New Role

To create a new role, follow these steps:

1. Open the Roles page of the ACL dialog box.
2. Click on the Add button to display the Add Role dialog box, shown in Figure 17.4. You can have up to 75 Roles per application.

Figure 17.4
Enter a new Role Name in the Add Role dialog box.

3. Type the name of the role in the Role Name text box. Role names can contain up to 15 characters, including spaces. When the name is saved, it will be displayed in square brackets.

Assigning a User to a Role

After a role is defined, you assign a user to that role on the Basics page of the ACL dialog box. The Basics page, with roles available for assignment, is shown in Figure 17.5.

Figure 17.5
Highlight a user and click on a role to assign a user to the role.

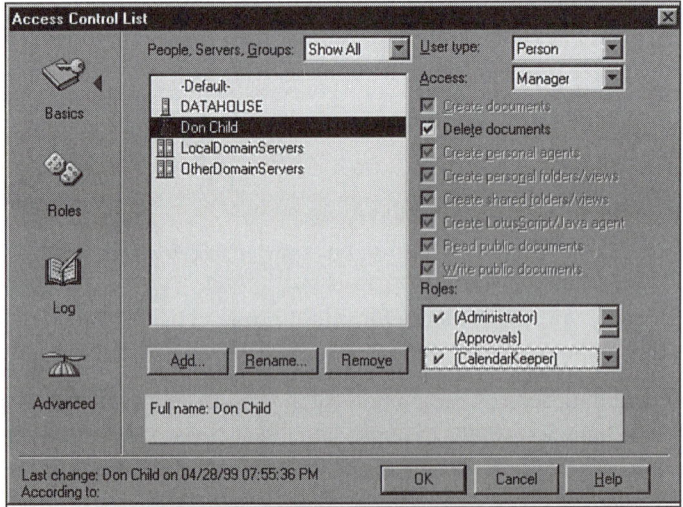

To assign a person to a role, do the following:

1. Click on the name of the person, server, or group that you want to assign to the role.
2. Click on the role name in the lower-right corner of the ACL dialog box.

The user then is assigned to the role and will have any privileges that go along with the role.

You should assign the LocalDomainServers and OtherDomainServers groups to all roles to ensure that servers have access to all elements in the application so that the elements can be replicated.

Monitoring Changes to the ACL

Changes to the ACL are tracked automatically. To view a log of changes to the ACL for an application, click on the Log icon. The past 20 changes to the application ACL are displayed, with the most recent changes shown at the top of the list. An example of the log is shown in Figure 17.6.

Figure 17.6
A log of changes and updates to the application ACL is maintained in the ACL dialog box.

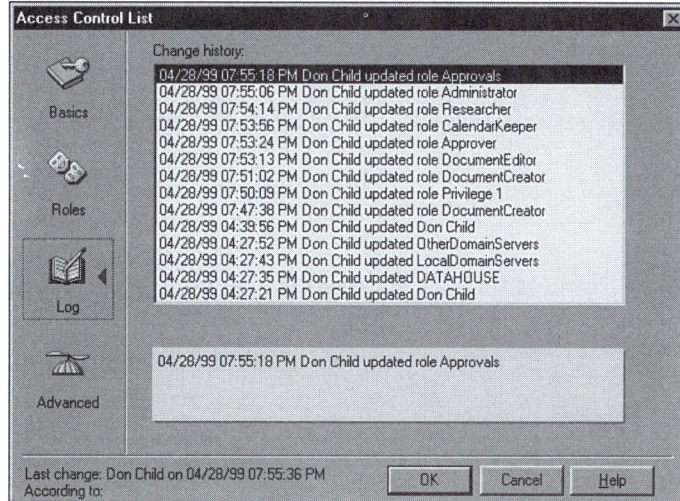

Other ways to monitor the ACL changes include having the Notes administrator set up an ACL Monitor document from the Server Administration panel, or having users check their own level of access by clicking on the Access icon on the status bar.

You can always tell from the status bar what level of access you have to an application. Click on the Access Level icon and you can see a list of which groups you are in that have access to the ACL, which roles you are assigned to, and which Notes user ID you are using to access the application.

Setting Advanced Options for the ACL

The overall concept of the ACL is fairly simple and straightforward. There are logical barriers beyond which certain users cannot pass. When you have just one application and a few users, it is easy to figure out who should be able to do what. But when you increase the number of Domino applications to the hundreds found in some organizations, and open them up to a user community that numbers in the thousands, it is easy to lose track of who has access to which applications. If someone leaves the organization or changes his or her name, it can be nearly impossible to track all instances of the person. The person might be in groups, in Reader fields, in Author fields, in roles in obscure applications, or in other places.

There is an Administration Process that can make global changes to ACLs within a Notes organization, but you need to set up the ACL to accept changes from the Administration Process.

Additional complexity arises when users are accessing applications through Web browsers, or when they are carrying around replicas on laptop computers that can be stolen or misplaced.

The Advanced page in the ACL dialog box holds the tools for handling these complexities.

ALLOWING THE ADMINISTRATION PROCESS TO UPDATE THE ACL

By default, applications are not touched by the Administration Process (ADMINP task on the Domino server), which can make systemwide changes when there are changes in the Public Address Book. You have to intentionally give permission for ADMINP to work on an application. This is done on the Advanced page of the ACL dialog box, shown in Figure 17.7.

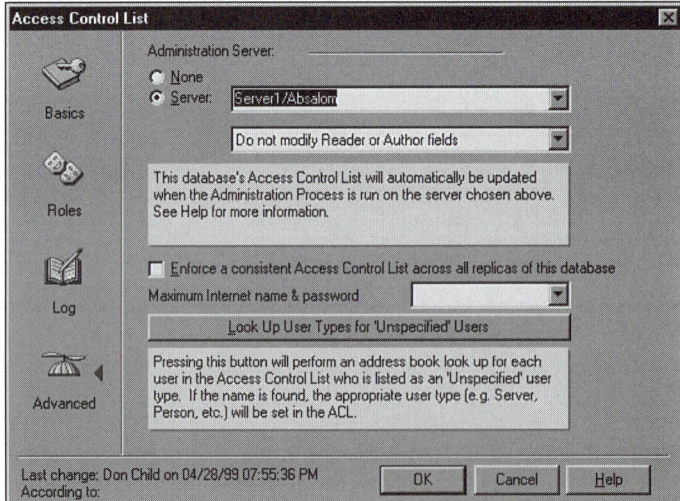

Figure 17.7
Define an Administration Server on the Advanced page of the ACL dialog box.

At the top of the page, the default setting for the Administration Server is None. To define an Administration Server—the server on which the ADMINP process will update the ACL for this application—click on the Server button. You can then click on the helper button beside the Server field and select the name of the server on which you want the ADMINP process to run.

After the Administration Server is defined, you can also define whether you want the ADMINP process to update Reader and Author fields as well. These fields will not be updated unless you specify that they should be modified. The system displays messages recommending how to handle changes to the application if you do change the settings.

Defining the Administration Server for Multiple Applications

The scenario previously described assumed that you were setting up the Administration Server for a single application. If you need to set up the Administration Server for multiple applications at one time, here is how you do it:

1. Select File, Tools, Server Administration from the drop-down menu. If you installed the Administration client, it will be displayed.
2. Click on the Files tab if it is not already selected.
3. Select Databases only from the Show Me drop-down list.
4. Click on the Tools button and select Database Tools.
5. In the bottom half of the screen, select the databases that you want to work with. You can select multiple database files (that is, Domino applications) by holding down the Ctrl key while you click on the files you want to work with.
6. Click on Manage ACL (on the lower-right side of the screen) to display the Multi ACL Management dialog box. Select the Advanced page. This is shown in Figure 17.8.

Figure 17.8
Use the Administration client to select the databases on which the Administration Process will run.

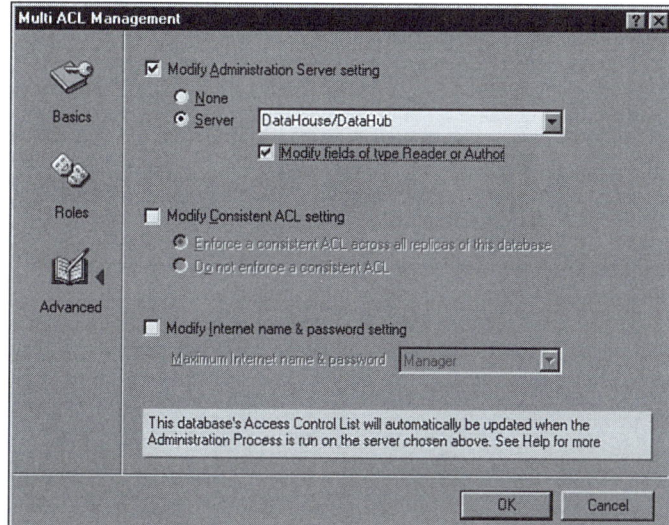

7. Click on OK to complete the selection of the Administration Server for your applications.

As you can see from Figure 17.8, the same Administration client is used to apply various administrative settings for applications.

Enforcing the ACL on Local (and other) Replicas

When you access a Domino application on your local drive, you have Manager access by default. That means that you can change the design of the application. You can edit documents. You can also delete the application from your local drive. However, just because you have Manager access doesn't mean that you can replicate those changes to a Domino server. The only changes that get replicated to the Domino server are those allowed by the ACL on the server-based replica.

I mention this only for the sake of discussion. As far as the applications on the Notes network are concerned, a local ACL is not important. The ACL on the server determines what changes can be replicated. But the local ACL can be important for another reason.

Applications, by definition, contain data. Data can be confidential for any number of reasons. The ACL is designed to protect that data and to protect that confidentiality. So what happens when somebody opens a local replica of a confidential application on the laptop computer you accidentally lost? That person has Manager access to your applications and data. The thief can quickly and easily steal all the confidential data.

To prevent that scenario, you can enforce the ACL on all replicas of an application, regardless of whether they are local or on a server.

Use the check box in the center of the Advanced page of the ACL dialog box for enforcing the ACL on local copies of a database. See Figure 17.9.

Figure 17.9
Enforce a consistent ACL on all replicas of a database from the Advanced page of the ACL dialog box.

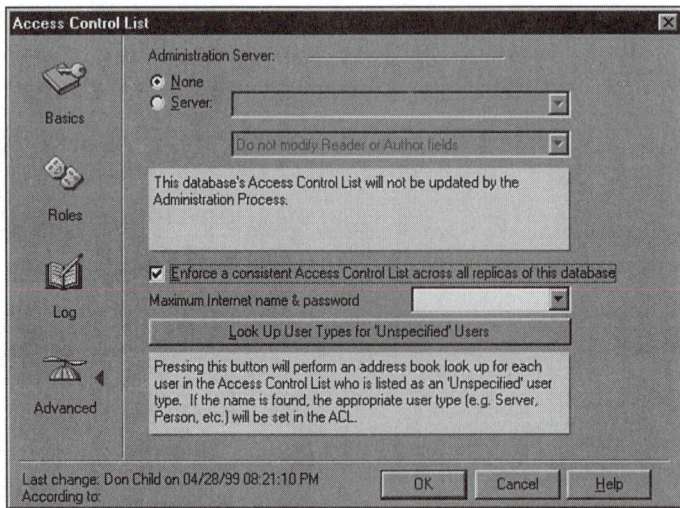

Use the simple check box to enforce a consistent ACL across all replicas of the application. Then people cannot access the database, even on a local workstation, unless they have user IDs and their names are listed in the ACL.

> **Note**
> You can enforce a consistent ACL on multiple databases at one time using the Administrative client. The process is similar to the process described previously, where you assigned multiple applications to the Administration Process.

Enforcing a consistent ACL is not as secure as encrypting a database, but it will keep your data safe from a casual intruder. And in Notes 5.0, the locally enforced ACL has been made more secure by closing a loophole that allowed people to gain access to hidden data by creating private views.

SETTING THE MAXIMUM INTERNET BROWSER ACCESS

If Web browsers from the Internet access the Domino server, you can use a variety of tools to protect the data in applications on the server. You can use a firewall to segregate public from private data, for example. But what happens if you have to access your private data over the Web? How do you protect your data?

With an *extranet* application, for example, you may want to let your customers access your corporate network to view product catalogs and submit online order forms. They can do this using any Web browser. But by the same token, you do not want customers to be able to return to that order and change it after it has already been submitted. You can limit all Web browser access for authenticated users by using the Maximum Internet name & password setting shown in Figure 17.9.

The Maximum Internet name & password setting enables you to limit what someone with a Web browser can do in your application. You can limit Web access, even though a user may have a higher level of access if he or she is using a Lotus Notes client. To set the maximum level of Internet browser access, use the helper button to display a list of access levels. Select the maximum level of access you want to allow for Web browsers.

Many administrative functions, including changing the ACL, can be performed from a Web browser. If you want all changes to be made from a Notes client, you can set the maximum browser access to a level lower than Manager.

As another example, consider someone with Editor access trying to access an application from the Web. If the Editor has to edit documents using his or her Web browser, you have to set the maximum browser access to at least Author so documents can be edited.

LOOKING UP USER TYPES

When you add individual names to your ACL, you have to manually define each one as a person, a server, or a group. Groups may contain people, other groups, and servers. Sometimes, it can be tricky trying to figure out whether you want to assign a name to a person group, a server group, or a mixed group. Well, don't worry. Let Notes do the work for you.

In Figure 17.9, there is a button that says Look Up User Types for 'Unspecified' Users. Unspecified users are any names that have not been assigned as a person, a group, or a server. Unspecified users will be looked up in the Domino directory to determine which type of user they are. This is done automatically from the Advanced page of the ACL dialog box.

Near the beginning of this chapter, you learned how to select which type of users you wanted to display in the ACL. A restricted list of users is easier to work with when you are dealing with a complex application.

The Role of ACLs in Replication

Although it is easy to think of the ACL simply in terms of user access, the ACL has more far-reaching impact. For example, when a user runs an agent, the agent cannot do anything unless the user is authorized to do so. In other words, a person with Reader access to an application cannot run an agent that modifies documents.

In a similar vein, the Domino server is subject to the restrictions in an ACL. Replication involves servers reading documents and database designs and ACLs that have been added or modified on another replica of an application. Therefore, a server has to be listed in the ACL so that it can make those changes to the application on other servers. As a rule of thumb, give the server at least as high a level as a user needs to make the same changes. If you want the server to replicate edits to all documents, give it at least Editor access. If you want the server to replicate design changes, give it Designer access. And of course, if you want the server to be able to replicate changes to the ACL, the server must have Manager access in the ACL.

Assigning servers an access level is easy because of the two default server groups in the Domino directory. When a new server is created using any of the organization's certifier IDs, the server name is automatically added to the LocalDomainServers group in the Domino directory. When a developer creates a new application, the LocalDomainServers group is automatically added to the ACL, and it is given Manager access. The OtherDomainServers group is given Designer access by default. Therefore, all you have to worry about are the exceptions. What level of access do you want to grant to servers from outside organizations? Do you want to prevent changes from getting replicated? If so, set a lower level of access.

You also have to include servers in all roles and in all Reader and Author fields (if the server has Author access) and Controlled Access Sections. Otherwise, the server will be prevented from making certain changes to documents.

Here are some of the things that you should consider when assigning access to servers:

- Manager access lets a server modify the ACL on applications. You might want to limit Manager access to a single server so that you can control updates to the ACLs of replicated applications. This is a common practice for servers that are set up in a hub-and-spoke configuration. You can also determine whether the server should have the capability of deleting documents in the application. If you want the server to have deletion privileges, you have to explicitly highlight the server or server group on the Basics page of the ACL and check the deletion function.

- Designer access lets an application receive design changes from the server. Design changes can include forms and views, agents, application icons, About and Using application documents, and replication formulas, for example. If a server has Designer access, it cannot make changes to the ACL of the application. Deletions are accepted only if you specifically mark the check box to allow deletions.

- Editor access for a server lets an application receive new documents and modifications to documents from the server, as well as document deletions if that option is explicitly selected. ACL and design changes are not allowed.

- Author access for a server lets an application receive new documents and modifications from the server, as well as deletions if that option is selected. However, updates and new documents from other users who have Author access are not replicated to the server. If you want to replicate updates from users with Author access, give the server at least Editor access to your application.

- Reader access lets the server pull changes from other replicas, but the replicas on other servers will not accept changes sent by the server.

- Depositor access does not apply to servers.

- No Access prevents the server from accessing the application.

If a server is not listed in the ACL, it may still be able to access an application using the default level of access, if the ACL default is set to allow at least Reader access.

As mentioned earlier, as a rule of thumb, you should give servers an access level at least as high as the highest level required by users. This technique ensures that the users can perform their duties using a replica of the application and have their changes replicate to other servers within the organization.

SUMMARY

The Access Control List is handled on an application-by-application level, defining what different types of users are able to do within the application. You can assign users (individuals, groups, or servers) to one of seven levels of access in an application. Within each of those seven levels, you can refine the ACL so that users are restricted to only certain functions. The ACL is always enforced on server-based Domino applications, and there is an option to enforce the ACL on local applications.

You can specialize the users of an application by placing them into roles, and then defining—within the design of the application—which roles can read or modify certain forms or sections of documents, and which roles are allowed to use certain views.

Notes also has tools for working with multiple applications, such as defining which applications can be updated by the Administration Process from a particular server, and identifying which applications should have the ACL enforced across all application replicas. The application tools are accessed through the ACL dialog box or the Administration client.

In a complex environment, you have to consider not only what level of access Notes users have in an application ACL, but also what type of access users have when they visit the application using a Web browser. Finally, you must consider what level of access servers have to the application, because this setting determines what does and does not get replicated.

If you have trouble accessing an application or performing certain editing functions, you will inevitably find that you are running into some sort of ACL restriction, either in the ACL itself or in one of the roles used within the application.

From Here...

You have now learned about one of the key security features within a Domino application. There are many other security features that you will encounter as you read through the remainder of this book.

Specifically, you should look at the following chapters to learn more about Domino and Notes security:

- All chapters in Part III, "Introducing Domino Designer R5." This chapter is part of that section.
- All chapters in Part VI, "Installing and Configuring the Domino Servers." In particular, look at Chapter 36, "Domino Security Overview," and Chapter 37, "Firewalls, Virtual Private Networks (VPNs), and Internet Security."

CHAPTER 18

Working With Formulas, Functions, and Commands

The Lotus Notes formula language has been part of the Notes client since its very early releases. Now with LotusScript, Java, and JavaScript, there are many tools with which you can program Notes. In some ways, the formula language is a primitive tool. It was originally conceived when Lotus 1-2-3 was just about the only spreadsheet in town, and the Notes language was similar to that found in 1-2-3. Although somewhat archaic, there are several places in Notes where the formula language comes in very handy because sometimes it is more succinct than LotusScript. There are other places where you must use formulas because it is the only language allowed.

Where and Why Should I Use Formulas?

Formulas are used in several different contexts within the Notes client and Domino server. They are used for default values, view selection, input translation, and several other purposes. Basically, a formula is an expression that is evaluated and results in a value. The usage of the resultant value depends upon the formula context. In view selection, for example, the formula is evaluated for each document and if the formula results in a `true` value, the document is selected to be shown in the view; otherwise, it is skipped. In other contexts, formulas are used to test the validity of an input value or choose documents for replication.

Formula Basics

Formulas are attached to objects within Notes. Depending upon the context of the object, the formula can be used to specify

- Values or an action to take when triggered
- Titles for windows, sections, or column contents
- Access and hiding of information
- Selection of forms, subforms, or documents

Here are the objects and contexts where formulas can be used:

Object	Purpose
	Values and Actions
Button	Button action to take
Hotspot	Hotspot action to take
Hotspot pop-up	Evaluates to a text string to be shown when a user clicks on the hotspot
Action	Formula evaluated for action to take
Event	Action(s) to take if event occurs
Agent	Selects documents to be processed and actions to take on them
SmartIcon	Action(s) to take if SmartIcon invoked
Field	Default value

Object	Purpose
	Values and Actions
	Input translation
	Input validation
	Field value
	Keyword field for choices
	Ttitles and Display
Section title	Evaluates for section title
Window title	Evaluates for window title
Column formula	Determines what to show within a column of a view or folder
	Access and Hiding
Section access	Determines whether user is allowed edit access to section
Hide paragraph	If true, paragraph is hidden
Hide action	If true, action is hidden
	Selection
Insert subform	Evaluates to determine subform to insert
Agent	Selects documents to be processed and actions to take on them
Replication	Determines documents to be replicated
Form formula	Determines form to use to view and edit a document
Selection formula	Determines which documents show in view or folder

Syntax

Now that I've told you where formulas can be used and what they are used for, let me give you some of the details of their syntax. Formulas in Notes are made up of expressions. If you are familiar with any traditional programming language, Notes formulas will seem similar in many respects. The most basic formula is a single expression:

```
RegularPrice * 0.20
```

In this example, the value in the price variable is multiplied by `0.20`. You can take the result of an expression and save it in a variable:

```
Discount := RegularPrice * 0.20
```

Notice that the assignment operator is :=, rather than just an equal sign. In a single formula, you can have several expressions, each terminated by a semicolon (;):

```
Discount := RegularPrice * 0.20;
DiscountPrice := RegularPrice - Discount;
SalesTax := DiscountPrice * 0.08;
TotalPrice := DiscountPrice + SalesTax;
```

When a formula has multiple expressions, the value of the last expression is the value of the formula. In this example, we don't actually need to assign the `TotalPrice` variable; we need only to specify the expression. However, by including the variable, we make the intent of the formula explicitly clear to anyone reading the formula.

Formulas can be made from the following elements:

- Constants (such as `0.274` or `"Hello"`)   There are three types of constants: text, numbers, and time/date values. The format for these constants is given in the next section.
- Variables (such as `Discount` or `SalesTax`)
- Operators (such as +, -, *, or /)
- @functions (such as `@Prompt`)
- Keywords (such as `FIELD` or `REM`)

One major source of confusion is the difference between temporary variables and fields. *Temporary variables* are used only within the scope of a formula, whereas *fields* are used to permanently store information within Notes documents. All the assignment statements shown in the previous examples are temporary variables. Temporary variables are very useful for making longer formulas easier to code and understand. You can compute and save intermediate values and then use them later within the formula. To assign a value and save it permanently in a field, you must use the `FIELD` keyword. I will show you an example of this in the section describing keywords later.

Data Types

There are five types of values you can use within formulas:

- Text values (such as `"White House"` or `"politics"`)   These values are probably the most frequently used type in Notes and Domino. There are many built-in functions to manipulate text values. Text constants are enclosed in double–quotation marks. To use a double-quote within the string, you must precede it with a backslash (\). You must use two backslashes to represent a single backslash within a string. Here is an example:
`"Enter \"Exit\" to leave the program."`
- Numeric values (such as `37`, `-2.87`, or `7.2E3`)   Numeric values are usually used for calculations of amounts, but can be used for any purpose, such as counters, numeric identifiers, or quantities. A numeric constant can be a signed integer, it can include a decimal point, or it can be expressed in scientific notation. If you use scientific notation, you enter the number, enter an E, and then supply a positive or negative exponent for a power of 10. For example, `7.2E3` represents 7200, and `7.2E-2` represents 0.072.
- Time/date values (such as `[9/23/1998 9:25 AM]`, `[9/24]`, or `[16:30]`)   Time/date values can be used to store dates, times, or a combination time/date. You can use them in time/date calculations and for storing time stamps within documents. Time constants are expressed within square brackets. You can supply a date, a time, or both.

- **Logical values (true and false)** These values are used within formulas and are used to test whether a particular situation exists. If so (true) you can take one action, and if not (false) you can take another, different action.
- **List values (`"CA":"NY":"CT"`)** List values are expressed by using colons between the elements. You can use lists to process several elements at once with the same formula.

Expression Evaluation

Using the various data types, you can put constants, variables, and operators together to make simple expressions. I've shown you simple examples of adding and subtracting, but suppose you have a more complicated expression involving several different operators. How do you determine which operation will be performed first?

Each operator has a precedence level. There are six levels of precedence. Operators with the highest precedence are performed first. When there are several operators at a given precedence level, they are performed from left to right. For example, suppose you have the following two expressions:

```
BaseAmount + Taxable * 0.06
Taxable * 0.06 + BaseAmount
```

Looking carefully at these expressions, it seems pretty clear that you want them both to yield the same answer. If they don't, our basic understanding of mathematics will not be followed. This can be achieved by giving the multiplication a higher precedence than the addition so it will always be performed prior to the addition, whether it is on the left or on the right. Here is the table of operator precedence. In this table, precedence level 1 is the highest, and 6 is the lowest:

TABLE 18.1 OPERATOR PRECEDENCE

Operator	Operation	Precedence
:=	Assignment (for fields, you must also use the `FIELD` keyword)	NA
:	List concatenation	1
+	Unary positive	2
-	Unary negative (change sign)	2
*	Multiplication	3
**	Permuted multiplication (lists only)	3
/	Division	3
*/	Permuted division (lists only)	3
+	Addition (numeric values)	4
+	Concatenation (text values)	4

Table 18.1 Continued

Operator	Operation	Precedence
*+	Permuted addition (numeric lists only)	4
*+	Permuted concatenation (text lists only)	4
-	Subtraction	4
*-	Permuted subtraction (lists only)	4
=	Equal	5
*=	Permuted equal (lists only)	5
!=	Not equal	5
=!	Not equal	5
<>	Not equal	5
><	Not equal	5
*!=	Permuted not equal (lists only)	5
*=!	Permuted not equal (lists only)	5
*<>	Permuted not equal (lists only)	5
*><	Permuted not equal (lists only)	5
<	Less than	5
*<	Permuted less than (lists only)	5
>	Greater than	5
*>	Permuted greater than (lists only)	5
<=	Less than or equal	5
*<=	Permuted less than or equal (lists only)	5
>=	Greater than or equal	5
*>=	Permuted greater than or equal (lists only)	5
!	Unary logical NOT	6
&	Logical AND	6
¦	Logical OR	6

You can override the normal precedence by using parentheses. Anything within the parentheses will be calculated first. For example, in the following expression, the addition is performed before the multiplication:

`(BaseAmount + Taxable) * 0.06`

If you have multiple sets of parentheses, they are evaluated from the inside out and from the left to the right. In the following expression, A+B is evaluated first, then C+D, then the multiplication by E, and finally the multiplication of the two subexpressions:

`(A + B) * ( (C + D) * E)`

Text Concatenation

One operation you may use frequently is text concatenation. Concatenation of two text strings means to append a second string on the end of the first string. To concatenate text, use the plus (+) sign operator:

```
Name := "Mary ";
"Mary had " + "a little lamb";
Name + "ate " + "a big pie";
Name + "saw " + "a big wolf, " + "a little pig, " + "and a dinosaur.";
```

Lists and List Operators

Lists are a special kind of data type within Notes. Lists enable you to store multiple values within a single variable or Notes field. The values within the list must all be of the same type. For example, you may use

```
EastStates := "NY" : "CT" : "NJ";
WestStates := "CA" : "OR" : "WA";
SomeStates := WestStates : EastStates;
```

The colon (:) is the list concatenation operator and can be used to append two lists together in a manner similar to string concatenation. In addition to combining lists, you can perform operations on the list elements in either a *pair-wise* or *permuted* manner:

- Pair-wise operations take two lists and operate on an element-by-element basis. If one list is shorter, it is extended to the length of the longer one by using the last element repeatedly.

- Permuted operators take two lists and perform the operation for every combination of the elements of the lists. It takes the first element of the first list and operates with each element of the second list. Then, it goes back and takes the second element of the first list and operates with every element of the second list. This pattern is followed until every element of the first list has been used.

Here is an example of pair-wise operations:

```
InvoiceAmounts := 27.92 : 82.47 : 37.41 : 14.95;
SalesTax := InvoiceAmounts * 0.06;
TotalAmounts := InvoiceAmounts + SalesTax;
```

Note in the example that when the multiplication occurs on the second line, the single value of 0.06 is extended to have the same number of elements as the first list. Normally in your program, you won't be assigning constants to the first variable, but you can see the usefulness of the list expressions by being able to process multiple values at once.

If you looked at the table of operator precedence carefully, you noticed that some operators had an asterisk (*) in front of them and were called permuted operators. Here is an example of permuted string concatenation:

```
CodeBases := "HW" : "SW" : "SVC";
Categories:= "01" : "02" : "03" : "04";
AllCodes := CodeBases *+ Categories;
```

After executing these assignment statements, the `AllCodes` variable will contain

HW01:HW02:HW03:HW04:SW01:SW02:SW03:SW04:SVC01:SVC02:SVC03:SVC04

This enables you to quickly create a list of all of the possible combinations of codes.

When using logical values in a pair-wise manner, all pairs are evaluated; then if any of the pairs result in a true value, the expression result is true. Otherwise, it is false. Here are some examples:

Type	Expression	Value
Pair-wise	1 : 2 : 3 = 5 : 5 : 5	0 (false)
Pair-wise	1 : 2 : 3 = 5 : 5 : 3	1 (true)
Pair-wise	1 : 2 : 3 = 5 : 3	1 (the 3 on right is extended)
Permuted	WestStates = "WA" : "OR" : "CA"; "CA" : "NY" *= WestStates;	1 (at least one is in the list)

KEYWORDS IN FORMULAS

There are five keywords that perform special functions within Notes: DEFAULT, ENVIRONMENT, FIELD, REM, and SELECT. Notice that keywords are normally shown in all-capital letters. Also, keywords, if used, must appear at the beginning of the statement. They cannot be used in the middle of a statement.

DEFAULT

The DEFAULT keyword specifies a default value for a document field. If the field does not exist within the document, the default value is used. If the field does exist within the document, the default value in the statement is ignored. You use the DEFAULT keyword as follows:

DEFAULT *fieldname* := *value*;

For example:

DEFAULT CompanyName := "ACME, Inc.";

ENVIRONMENT

The ENVIRONMENT keyword is used to set an environment variable in the operating system environment. For Windows, OS/2, and UNIX, the value is stored in the NOTES.INI file. The value must be a text string. You cannot retrieve the value with this keyword. You may want to use the @functions @Environment and @SetEnvironment to retrieve and set environment variables instead of using this keyword.

You normally use environment variables when you need the following characteristics:

- The values are stored persistently between sessions.
- The values may differ from one database user to another.

The syntax for the ENVIRONMENT keyword is

```
ENVIRONMENT varname := value;
```

Note that environment variables also pose a few problems. First, because they are stored on the workstation outside the Notes environment, if a single user has both a laptop and desktop machine, the environment variables may become different. Second, if two users use the same physical workstation, the environment variables may contain inconsistent values. Third, because they are stored on the workstation, they will not be accessible from a Web browser. Finally, because environment variables are stored in a local, easily accessible file instead of a Notes database, there is a potential security risk.

You may want to consider *profile documents* as an alternative to environment variables. They are stored within a database and can be used to store information that varies from one user to another. Within the formula language, you can use @GetProfileField and @SetProfileField. Because profile fields are stored within a database, they can be replicated. Environment variables cannot be replicated.

FIELD

You use the FIELD keyword to specify that you want to store a value in a field within a document. If you leave this keyword off an assignment statement, the value will be stored only in a temporary variable, not within the document.

The syntax for the FIELD keyword is

```
FIELD fieldname := value;
FIELD fieldname := @DeleteField;
```

The value may be any type that is valid for the specified field. If the field does not exist prior to the statement, it will be created in the document. If it does exist, the value will be replaced.

@DeleteField has a special meaning. If you use the second format, the value of the field will be deleted from the document.

REM

The REM keyword stands for the word *remark*. This keyword is used to add comments to a formula. If you've had any programming background, you probably already know the reasons why you should write comments in your code. You also know you should probably write more comments than you actually do write. I won't sermonize on that, but as the shoe commercial says, "Just do it."

Here's how:

```
REM "your comment here";
```

SELECT

The `SELECT` keyword is used for selection of documents. There are three contexts in which formulas are used to select documents:

- View selection formula
- Replication formula
- Agent document selection

In each case, the formula is evaluated for each document within the context. If the formula result is true, the document is selected for inclusion; if false, the document is skipped. To use the `SELECT` keyword, use the following syntax:

`SELECT expression;`

In a view, a view selection formula is used to determine the set of documents that are displayed in the view. If you want to include all documents within the database, you can use

`SELECT @All;`

Agent formulas are rather unique, because an Agent formula must include both a `SELECT` keyword statement, which selects the documents to be processed, and additional statements, which actually process the documents.

> **Note** The `SELECT` keyword in Notes and Domino is quite different from the `SELECT` statement of SQL. You may not use the SQL syntax where Notes/Domino expects its own `SELECT` statement. Although they have a similar purpose, the Notes/Domino `SELECT` statement roughly corresponds to the SQL WHERE clause. Again, however, don't confuse the two completely different statements.

Special Formulas

As mentioned previously, formulas are used in a variety of contexts within Notes, but they generally fall into the following categories:

- Values and actions to perform
- Titles and display
- Access and hiding
- Selection

There are some specific locations in Notes where formulas can be used. Most of the uses of formulas are clear and calculate simple results, but some formulas have specific conventions. Here are some of the special formulas:

- **Form formulas** These formulas are used to determine which form will be used to display and/or edit a particular document. This type of formula must result in the name of a form. Form formulas are optional, and if present, are associated with a view, not a form. Here is an example: Suppose you have two expense approval forms, one used for amounts less than $1,000 and another used for amounts greater than $1,000. You could display all expense documents within one view, but show alternative forms, depending upon the approval amount. In this example, the two form names are `"ApproveLow"` and `"ApproveHigh"`. The form formula in the view would be something like this:

```
@if(amount <= 1000; "ApproveLow"; "ApproveHigh")
```

- **Input validation formulas**   An input validation formula can be associated with each field within a form. It is invoked for a document whenever it is saved, recalculated, or refreshed. The purpose is to determine whether a field has a valid value. You return a result of either `@Success` or `@Failure`. If you return `@Failure`, you also specify an error message to be displayed to the user. Suppose you want to limit a field's data values to less than $1,000. You could supply a validation formula:

   ```
   @if(amount <= 1000; @Success; @Failure("You must supply a value less than or
   equal to $1,000"))
   ```

- **Input Translation formulas**   An input translation formula can be associated with each editable field within a form. It is invoked for a document whenever it is saved, recalculated, or refreshed. The purpose of the input translation formula is to convert data that has been entered by the user into a standard format. For example, you can add (or remove) capitalization, extra blank spaces, and so forth. Suppose you have a field for a city. You could supply this formula:

   ```
   @ProperCase(@Trim(City))
   ```

- **Window title formula**   This formula is evaluated to determine what to show on the title line of the window that displays the document. You can use this formula to vary the title to correspond to data that is within the document. Here is an example that displays `"New Document"` for newly created documents; otherwise, it displays a title showing the name contained in the document:

   ```
   @If(@IsNewDoc; "New Document"; "Document for " + Name)
   ```

@FUNCTIONS

There are nearly 200 @functions in Lotus Notes release 5. These functions are available to help you automate the processing of your documents. The @functions include mathematical functions, string handling, date-time manipulation, list handling, database, security, and many other functions. The syntax for calling functions is as follows:

```
@function(argument1; argument2; ... argumentn);
```

You can combine @functions by using them in a nested fashion. For example, you could specify the following:

```
@ProperCase( @Trim(UserNameField) )
```

In this case, after you accept the user input, you first trim off any leading or trailing blanks, and then change the name to initial capitalization.

Because there are so many @functions, it is not possible to describe them all in detail in this book. I will cover a few of the important @functions. A complete listing of the @functions can be found in Appendix B. Further details on the @functions can be found in the Domino Designer help file.

Conditional Execution

The `@if` function is really the only control flow mechanism that exists within the formula language. Therefore, you are almost guaranteed to use this function at one time or another. The syntax of the `@if` function is

```
@if(condition1; action1 [; condition2; action2; ... [; condition99; action99;]] else_action )
```

In its simplest form, you could specify

```
@if(condition1; action1; else_action)
```

Here is an example:

```
@if(@Left(ZipCode;1) = "9"; "West Coast"; "Somewhere Else");
@if(@Left(ZipCode;1) = "9"; "West Coast"; @Left(ZipCode;1) = "0"; "East Coast"; "Middle Stuff");
```

Notice that you can specify only one action per condition. If you need to specify a more complicated set of actions, you can use the `@Do` function, which groups a sequence of expressions into a single expression:

```
@if(@Left(ZipCode;1) = "9"; @Do(@if(@Left(ZipCode;3) = "900"; "Los Angeles"; "West Coast")); @Left(ZipCode;1) = "0"; "East Coast"; "Middle Stuff");
```

Selected Text and Conversion Functions

Text string handling and conversion functions are probably the most frequently used functions in the formula language. Here are some important text handling and conversion functions:

- `@Left(string; n)` or `@Left(string; substring)` Returns the leftmost *n* characters or all the characters left of the *substring*. Examples: `@Left("sample";3) = "sam"` and `@Left("simple simon"; " ") = "simple"`.

- `@Right(string; n)` or `@Right(string; substring)` Returns the rightmost *n* characters or all the characters to the right of the *substring*. Examples: `@Right("sample";3) = "ple"` and `@Right("simple simon"; " ") = "simon"`.

- `@LowerCase(string)`, `@UpperCase(string)`, and `@ProperCase(string)` Converts a string to all lowercase, uppercase, or proper case. *Proper case* means that each word has an initial capital, but the rest of the word is lowercase.

- `@Trim(string)` This function removes leading, trailing, and duplicate internal spaces from a string. Example: `@Trim("  This   is a sample  ") = "This is a sample"`.

Selected List, Date, and Time Functions

Lists are aggregate data structures. They typically contain multiple data values. There are functions to convert lists to strings, and vice versa, as well as extract list items. Date and time functions are used to access and manipulate date and time values. Here are some selected list, date, and time functions:

- @Explode(*string* ; [*separators* ; [*includeempties*]])   This converts a string into a list of multiple values. Each time it finds a value in the *separators* list, it creates a new text value in the output list. The default value for *separators* is ,; (blank, comma, semicolon), which means that any of these delimiters will cause a new entry in the output list. *Includeempties* is a Boolean value, and if true, the list will be allowed to contain "" values. Example: @Explode("Mon,Tue,Wed") = "Mon":"Tue":"Wed".

- @Implode(*textlist* ; [*separator*])   This function converts a list of text values into a single text string. If you supply a *separator* string, it will be used between each value. The default separator is a blank. Examples: @Implode("sis":"boom"; " bah ") = "sis boom bah". @Implode("Jan":"Feb":"Mar") = "Jan Feb Mar".

- @Subset(*list* ; *number*)   The @Subset function returns a subset of the values of a list. If you supply a positive number, the values are taken from the front of the list; if you supply a negative number, the values are the end of the list. Example: @Subset("red":"green":"blue":"white"; 2) = "red":"green".

- @Created, @Modified, and @Accessed   @Created returns the date and time the current document was first created. @Modified returns the date and time the current document was last modified. @Accessed returns the date that the document was last accessed, whether for read or write. The @Accessed value is accurate only to a day, not to a time. In order for the @Accessed function to work, you must enable the advanced database option "Maintain LastAccessed property". This option is off by default to improve performance.

- @Adjust(*DateToAdjust* ; *years* ; *months* ; *days* ; *hours* ; *minutes* ; *seconds* ; [*dst*])   This function adds to the *DateToAdjust* value by the number of *years*, *months*, *days*, *hours*, *minutes*, and *seconds* supplied. If a negative value is supplied for one of the parameters, it will be subtracted from the *DateToAdjust*. *Dst* is optional and can be either [InLocalTime] or [InGMT]. Example: @Adjust([3/25/1999]; 0 ; 1 ; -1; 0 ; 0 ; 0) = [4/24/1999].

Selected User Interface Functions

The user interface functions enable you to control aspects of the user interface by prompting and requesting information. Here are some of the user interface functions:

- @Prompt([*style*] : [NoSort]; *title* ; *prompt* ; [*defaultchoice* ; *choicelist* ; *filetype*])   There are several types of styles for the @Prompt dialog box. You can select from OK, YesNo, YesNoCancel, OkCancelEdit, OkCancelList, OkCancelCombo,

`OkCancelEditCombo`, `OkCancelListMult`, `LocalBrowse`, and `Password`. The optional `NoSort` keyword enables you to display the choices in the order you specify. If you leave it off, the choices are shown alphabetically. *Title* is the dialog box title. *Prompt* is the prompt text to be shown. The other parameters are optional and are used depending upon the type of box you specify. See the Domino Designer online help for more information. Example: `@Prompt([OK] ; "Worldly Comment" ; "Hello world!")`.

- `@DialogBox(form ; flags ; title )`   This function enables you to create a form in your database, and then use it as a template for the dialog box. The *flags* enables you to specify additional options. The *title* is the dialog box title. See the Domino Designer online help for more information.

- `@PickList([Custom] : [Single] ; server : file ; view ; title ; prompt ; column ; categoryname )`   In addition to the syntax shown for `@PickList`, there are seven other variations. With the syntax shown, you can display a view in a dialog box. It will return information from the column you specify. New with release 5 is the option to show a single category specified by *categoryname*. See the Domino Designer online help for the seven other variations and more details.

Selected Name and Access Functions

Some functions enable you to inquire about database usernames and privileges. Here are some of the important functions in these categories:

- `@DbName`   Returns a list of two elements: the server name and the filename of the database. Example: If the server name is `"SERVER1"` and the database name is `"PARTS.NSF"`, `@DbName` will return `"SERVER1":"PARTS.NSF"`. You can extract the full path of the database with `@Subset(@DbName; -1)`, which returns the last element of the list.

- `@UserAccess(server : file)`   Returns three values. The first is the access level for the current user, the second is a Boolean indicating whether the user can create documents, the third is a Boolean indicating whether the user can delete documents. The access level has these values: 1 (Depositor), 2 (Reader), 3 (Author), 4 (Editor), 5 (Designer), 6 (Manager). Example: `@UserAccess("REPORTS.NSF")` might return `"5":"1":"1"` if the user is a Designer and can create and delete documents.

- `@UserNamesList` and `@UserRoles`   `@UserNamesList` returns a list of the current username, any groups or roles that apply to the current user. `@UserRoles` returns a subset of the `@UserNamesList`, which consists just of the roles of the current user.

@DbLookup and @DbColumn

The `@DbLookup` function is used in Notes databases to find a set of documents in a view or folder. You supply a key, and the function looks for the value in the first sorted column of the view. After the documents are found, you can have the function return either a field from the documents, or the contents from a particular column of the view. You can also use `@DbLookup` with ODBC to access other relational database systems.

Here is the syntax for `@DbLookup` with Notes:

```
@DbLookup(class : "NoCache" ; server : database ; view ; key ; fieldname |
columnNumber )
```

The `class` parameter may be either `""` or `"Notes"`. The `"NoCache"` is optional and, if specified, tells Domino not to cache the results of the search. If you leave this parameter off, the results will be cached, which improves performance at the possible expense of retrieving slightly out-of-date information.

The `server : database` parameter specifies the server and database filename. If the `server` is specified as `""`, it is assumed to be local. If the `database` parameter is `""`, it is assumed to be the current database. The `view` parameter is the name of the view to be used. The `key` parameter is the value to be searched for. The final parameter indicates the type of response you want. If you supply a text string, it will be interpreted as a field name. If you supply a number, it is assumed to be a column number within the view. Here is an example:

```
@DbLookup("" : "" ; "Server1" : "Customer.nsf" ;
"ByName" ; "IBM" ; "ContactName" )
```

In this example, the `"Customer.nsf"` database on `"Server1"` will be searched. The first sorted column of the `"ByName"` view will be inspected for the value `"IBM"`. When the record is found, the value of the `"ContactName"` field will be returned. If more than one document is found, the result will be a list. If no documents are found, a null value is returned. If the view does not contain a sorted column, an error message is generated.

> **Tip**
> You can return the contents of any fields in the documents that are found, even from fields not displayed in the view. This type of retrieval, however, is much slower. If you retrieve by field name, it is faster to include the field within the view. Retrieval by column number is very efficient, but is prone to error because column numbers may change as you modify the view.

`@DbLookup` with ODBC uses a more complicated syntax:

```
@DbLookup("ODBC" : "NoCache" ; datasource ; userid1 : userid2 ; password1 :
password2 ; table ; column : null_handling ; key_column ; key ;
"Distinct" : sort )
```

The `"ODBC"` parameter indicates it is an ODBC version of `@DbLookup` rather than a Notes version. `"NoCache"` indicates that results are not to be cached. `datasource` is the ODBC data source name. `userid1` and `userid2` may be required by the database system. `password1` and `password2` may also be required by the database system. `table` is the name of the table to be searched, and `column` is the column name for the column from which the result will be returned. The `null_handling` parameter can be one of three values: `"Fail"` reports an error, and the function will not return any values. `"Discard"` discards null values and returns a shorter list, and `"replacement value"` returns a replacement value for null values found.

`key_column` is the name of the column to be searched within the table, and `key` is the value to be searched for. The database system may treat the `key_column` name as case sensitive.

"Distinct" causes the database system to remove duplicate entries. The *sort* parameter may be specified as either "Ascending" or "Decending".

@DbColumn is another search function. You specify a particular column number of a view or folder, and the function returns all the values contained within the column. One useful application for @DbColumn is to supply values for keyword type fields, such as dialog lists, list boxes, and combo boxes. Here is the syntax for @DbColumn:

@DbColumn(*class* : "NoCache" ; *server* : *database* ; *view* ; *columnNumber*)

The *class* parameter may be specified as either "" or "Notes". The *server* and *database* parameters specify the database to use. If the *server* is specified as "", it is assumed to be local. If the *database* parameter is "", it is assumed to be the current database. The *view* parameter is the name of the view to use. *columnNumber* is the column number of the column values to be returned. Here is an example:

@DbColumn("" : "" ; "" : "" ; "Keywords" ; 2)

This looks up, in the current database, the "Keywords" view and returns the second column.

You can also use @DbLookup with ODBC. Here is the syntax for use with ODBC:

@DbColumn("ODBC" : "NoCache" ; *datasource* ; *userid1* : *userid2* ; *password1* : *password2* ; *table* ; *column* : *null_handling* ; "Distinct" : *sort*)

The fields in the @DbColumn function are used just as they are within @DbLookup. The only difference is that no key or key column is supplied, because the function returns the contents of the entire column.

@Commands

There are two special @functions called @Command and @PostedCommand. The syntax for an @Command is similar to an @function:

@Command([*CommandName*]; *argument1*; *argument2*; ... *argumentn*);

@PostedCommand([*CommandName*]; *argument1*; *argument2*; ... *argumentn*);

The command names that are used for the first parameter are enclosed in square brackets. In the syntax example, the square brackets do not mean that the CommandName is optional. As a matter of fact, it is the only required parameter. Here are some examples:

@Command([CreateView]);

@Command([OpenView]; "MyView");

There can be zero or more arguments when you invoke a command. The difference between @Command and @PostedCommand is the timing in which they are executed. @Command functions are executed in order as they are encountered in the formula. @PostedCommands are executed *after* all other expressions within the formula, but in the order they were encountered.

Most `@Commands` correspond to a menu item within the Notes client. You can sometimes tell by the command name the menu correspondence. For example, `EditCut`, `EditCopy`, and `EditPaste` correspond to those three menu items. However, some of the `@Commands` date back to earlier versions of Notes, so the correspondence with the current menu items may not be obvious. In Notes release 3, for instance, the `Compose` command was used to create a new document. This menu item disappeared in release 4 and hasn't been seen since. We still use the `Compose` `@Command`, however, to create a new document.

A complete list of the `@Commands` can be found in Appendix B.

From Here...

In this chapter, I told you about formulas, @functions, and `@Commands`. Formulas are used in many different contexts within Notes and Domino. They are used for values and actions, titles, hiding values, and for selection.

@functions are built-in functions that you can use to assist you in constructing formulas. There are almost 200 @functions that can manipulate lists, text strings, and numbers.

`@Commands` roughly correspond to menu actions within the Notes client. You can use them to perform menu type commands within your formula. Here is where you can find additional information:

- Appendix B, "@Function and @Command Listings," provides you with a complete listing of all the @functions and @commands, grouped by their functional areas.
- Chapter 19, "Using the IDE with LotusScript, Java, and JavaScript," gives you a further introduction into programming Notes and Domino. You'll find out how to use these other programming languages. The rest of Part IV goes into depth on these topics.

PART IV

Using LotusScript, Java, and JavaScript

19 Using the IDE with LotusScript, Java, and JavaScript

20 Object-Oriented Programming and the Domino Object Model

21 LotusScript Variables and Objects

22 LotusScript Subroutines, Functions, and Event Handlers

23 Creating and Using Java Applets and Agents

24 Using the Lotus eSuite DevPack

25 The Session and Front-End Classes

26 Database, View, and Document Classes in LotusScript and Java

27 Using Fields and Items in LotusScript and Java

CHAPTER 19

USING THE IDE WITH LOTUSSCRIPT, JAVA, AND JAVASCRIPT

LotusScript, as you probably know by now, was the primary scripting language used within Notes and Domino to automate many tasks prior to release 5. New with release 5, JavaScript can now also be used for scripting Notes and Domino. The Java language can be used in applets and agents with Domino. In this and subsequent chapters, I'll cover these languages, explain their similarities and differences, and show you how to use them in your applications.

Scripting Languages, Notes, and Domino

What exactly is a *scripting* language, and what makes it different from other kinds of programming languages? Actually, a scripting language is a programming language, but it is designed for a specialized use. Scripting languages are normally used to control other programs.

In the case of LotusScript, it can be used to control or automate Notes or Domino. Lotus also uses LotusScript to automate tasks in its office products, such as Lotus 1-2-3. Java was created by Sun Microsystems and has become very popular for writing applets that work in conjunction with Web pages. Java is a full-featured language that can also be used to write applications. JavaScript was created by Netscape and is a different language from Java. It is primarily used within Web pages for scripting purposes, such as automating button pushes, opening windows, and processing fields.

Originally, scripting languages, which are sometimes called *macro languages*, were part of the application they were controlling. For example, in Lotus Notes, the original "formula" language, which uses @formulas, was built into Notes. Lotus 1-2-3 had a similar formula language, and Microsoft Excel had a language that used = instead of @. The disadvantage of a proprietary language built into a system is that it makes users learn the specifics of not only the system, but the programming language as well. When a scripting language is separated from the underlying system it controls, the language can be used in several systems, and it can be more generic, easier to learn, and more useful in various situations.

In addition to LotusScript and JavaScript, what are some other examples of scripting languages? One well-known example is Visual Basic for Applications (VBA), a cousin of LotusScript. Both Visual Basic for Applications and LotusScript are variants of the BASIC language. Each has added features, but the two remain very similar in both function and syntax. Microsoft's version of JavaScript is called Jscript; the name is similar but different enough to add to the confusion. Finally, another example of a scripting language is Rexx, the scripting language for many IBM systems, including VM and OS/2.

LotusScript, VBA, and JavaScript (among others) have one thing in common: They can easily control other applications. In addition, because of their dynamic nature, scripting languages are frequently implemented as interpretive languages rather than compiled languages. *Compiled languages* translate a program into the raw machine codes of the underlying hardware. This makes them very efficient. *Interpretive languages* are usually processed in a higher-level format, which makes them more flexible and dynamic. Interpreters can generally make decisions while the program is running, but compilers must usually make most decisions about the program before it starts execution.

SCRIPTS, APPLETS, SERVLETS, AND AGENTS

Now that I've described the primary languages, let me tell you a little more about where you can use the various languages. Although it would be nice to use any language anywhere, you cannot. In addition to LotusScript, Java, and JavaScript, you can program with the @formula language and simple actions. With all these choices, sometimes it has not made sense for Lotus to greatly enhance some of the older technologies. Lotus has, however, added capabilities to the @formula language in each release to enable the existing Notes and Domino users to access new features as they become available.

Scripts are program routines that are associated with objects. Simple objects include buttons and fields, and more complex objects include pages, forms, and views. Each of these different object types can have scripts associated with them. Scripts are associated with different events that can occur within the object. For example, in a button, there is a `Click` event; a form has many events, including the `QueryOpen` and `QuerySave` LotusScript events and the `onLoad` JavaScript event. Depending upon the object, you can use LotusScript, JavaScript, formula language, or simple actions to program scripts. You cannot use Java, which is currently available only for applets and agents. JavaScript scripts will work with Web browsers (or the Notes client), but LotusScript will not.

Applets are routines that are used primarily on Web pages. They can provide animation and local processing within the Web browser. Applets run in the client browser or Notes browser, not on the server. Applets may be written only in Java. With release 5 of Domino, using the CORBA and IIOP support, you can now access the Domino back-end classes, running on the server from an applet running in a Web browser.

Servlets are programs similar to applets, but as the name implies, run on the server instead of the Web browser. With Domino, there are other options you can use for server programming including the C/C++ API and CGI; however, I will not be covering these options here.

Agents have been a part of Notes and Domino since release 4. Agents can run on either a Notes client or a Domino server. They can be scheduled to run at specified intervals, or they can be triggered by certain events, such as new documents, arriving in a database. Agents can be written in any of the following: LotusScript, Java, formula language, or simple actions.

Table 19.1 summarizes the availability of the various languages.

TABLE 19.1   AVAILABILITY OF PROGRAMMING LANGUAGES

Object Situation	LotusScript	JavaScript	Java	Formula Language	Simple Actions
Object scripting	X	X		X	X
Notes client agent	X		X	X	X
Applet			X		
Web browser		X	X		
Notes client browser	X	X	X	X	X
Domino server agent	X		X	X	X
Domino server servlet			X		
Standalone application			X		

Here are some additional comments to clarify some questions you may have. *Object scripting* means associating event-handling programs with user interface elements, such as buttons, forms, pages, and views. Every language may not be available for every object, but I've added an *X* where the language is available for at least some objects.

An agent, as I'll show you shortly, is a program that can be triggered automatically or by the user and is not necessarily tied to a specific object. It must run in the context of either the Notes client or Domino server. An agent cannot run in a Web browser.

An applet may run in either a Web browser or the Notes client.

The Web browser line and the Notes client browser line have an additional capability, which is to interpret and display HTML. Because they can interpret and display HTML, they can run JavaScript.

A Domino server servlet is different from a server agent. The servlet interface has been defined by Sun Microsystems and enables the server to run Java programs. Running a servlet requires additional configuration on the server and is not as automatic as running a Domino agent. Servlets and applets can be written to run on multiple different platforms and servers. They are not limited to the Domino server, whereas agents must run on a Domino server.

Finally, you can write a standalone application that runs on a client; uses Java, CORBA, and IIOP to communicate with the Domino server; and with which you can access the Domino Object Model. Essentially, with CORBA and IIOP you can now almost write a replacement for the Notes client user interface in Java. A standalone application does not need a Web browser or the Notes client (although you probably need a client access license). Prior to release 5, you had to write this type of program using either C or C++, but now you can do it with Java.

Choosing a Language

With all these choices, which language should you use and why? This is a good question. The answer is: It depends. It depends primarily on what you're trying to do and your background and experience.

As I mentioned in the previous section, you are restricted to using certain languages for the various features in Notes and Domino. For example, to make an applet, you must use Java. For writing scripts for objects, you can use any of the other languages *except* Java. So the initial selection of language is done for you by the context.

In programming scripts for objects, though, you can still use LotusScript or JavaScript. If you're familiar with BASIC, go with LotusScript. Some pundits have spread rumors that LotusScript is going away. LotusScript is *not* going away. It will be around for a long time. There are probably millions of lines of LotusScript code available, and Lotus could not abandon LotusScript even if it wanted to.

If you're familiar with either JavaScript or JScript, use the JavaScript support in Notes. The world is moving more and more toward Internet standards. As JavaScript becomes more popular in general, there will be more programmers and programs available in JavaScript. JavaScript will hold a prominent place in Notes and Domino for the foreseeable future.

When programming agents, you can use LotusScript or Java (or formula language or simple actions), but you cannot use JavaScript. In this case again, use the tool most comfortable for you. If the situation is simple enough, use a simple action. For example, to replace a single value within a document, you could use a simple action. Usually, there are several ways to accomplish your goal, and you can pick any one of the options. If you're really ambitious, you can learn them all and pick the tool that seems just right for the occasion.

In the rest of this chapter, I give you some highlights of the three options—LotusScript, Java, and JavaScript—and show you the basics of using each.

Using LotusScript

Because LotusScript is a scripting language designed for controlling Notes and Domino, the way you write programs is slightly different from the way you write an application with a traditional programming language. When using traditional languages, the programmer writes the program, and when it runs, the application maintains control from start to finish. For example, a program might start, ask the user for some input, read a database, and print a report. These tasks are controlled and sequenced by the program that the application programmer creates. There is typically a "main" routine in this type of program.

Using a scripting language is slightly more complicated because two programs are actually involved. In this case, one program is Notes itself, and the other is the program written by the programmer in LotusScript. The LotusScript program and Notes work together; you might think of the Notes system as the primary program and the LotusScript program as a subsidiary. This is clearly different from the case given for traditional languages, in which the application program has complete control of the situation.

If you use one of the Microsoft Office products, such as Excel or Word, you can use Visual Basic for Applications (VBA) as the scripting language. The use of LotusScript with Notes is very similar.

As another example, consider the programming for an Internet Web browser, such as Netscape Navigator. Using the JavaScript language, a programmer can create one or more script programs to manipulate the browser. The script can process buttons, open new windows, and obtain data from input fields. LotusScript can be used in a somewhat similar manner within Notes. Separating the scripting language from the system to be controlled is a powerful concept that can be used in many contexts.

One primary benefit of using a language such as LotusScript is the ability to control whether the program code runs on the client or server. With LotusScript programs, you can create pieces of code that will execute on the client for faster response, and you can also create agents that will run on the Domino server. The choice is yours.

Figure 19.1 shows a simplified version of how Notes and Domino work with scripting languages. You can see how events in Notes or Domino can be used to trigger routines written in LotusScript, Java, or JavaScript. This intricate dance between Notes and scripting programs enables Notes to invoke your subroutines, and it enables your routines to access data and invoke services of Notes or Domino. For example, in Figure 19.1, after an event is triggered to the script program, it can get data from Notes/Domino. After the program has examined the data, it can send commands and data back to Notes/Domino. In this and future chapters, I show you how the events are triggered, how you get data from Notes/Domino, and how to invoke routines in Notes/Domino.

Figure 19.1
Lotus Notes/Domino and a script program.

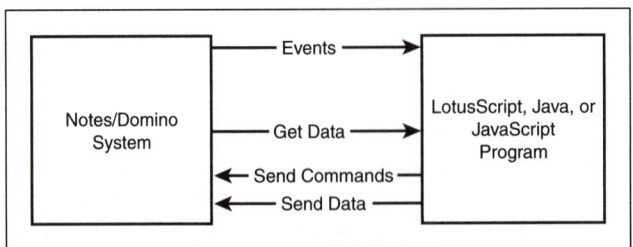

USING THE INTEGRATED DEVELOPMENT ENVIRONMENT

To begin our examination of Notes, we're going to create a simple program to display a message box. This single-line program is the simplest program we can make. I'll show you this example with both LotusScript and Java. Unfortunately, it will take us several steps to create the program, so follow along as we go. I'll cover LotusScript first.

USING THE INTEGRATED DEVELOPMENT ENVIRONMENT | 457

A LotusScript program cannot exist alone; we must create it in the context of a Notes database. The database is the outermost container for our program. Within a database, LotusScript programs can be associated with events, actions, buttons, and so on. These items can be used to trigger the invocation of a LotusScript program. You can think of these items as another container within the database. The LotusScript program resides within this smaller container. Typically, a LotusScript program will operate on the data within the database in which it is contained. It can, however, access data from other databases if necessary.

The Integrated Development Environment (IDE) is the environment you use to create and test your programs. The main area you will use, called the Programmer's Pane, is an area where you can edit your LotusScript programs. This pane is in the lower-right part of your screen. We'll cover this area and some of the other areas as we progress.

Okay, let's create our first LotusScript program. As mentioned, we need to be in the context of a database. You can use any database or you can create a new, blank database. If you want to follow along with a new database, open the Domino Designer. You will see the Domino Designer Welcome page.

From the Welcome page, you can click the Create a new database icon or you can use the menus. To use the menus, select File, Database, New. Enter the database Title `Script Test`, leave the type "Blank," and click OK. To accomplish our test, we will be using Domino agents. To create a new agent:

1. Click on the word Agents (with the light bulb) in the Design Pane on the left part of your screen. See Figure 19.2.

Figure 19.2
Use the New Agent action button to create your agent.

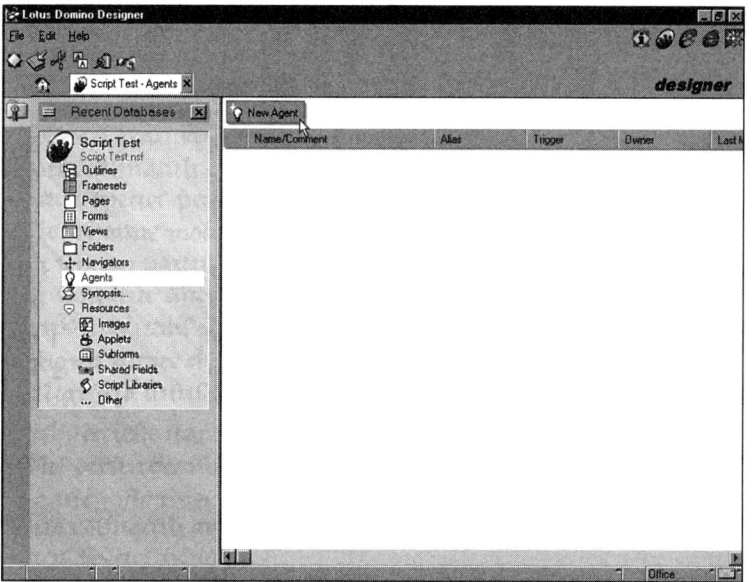

2. Click on the New Agent action button. A new, untitled agent will be created for you.
3. Give your new agent a name in the Name field. For our example, you can use the name HelloLS.
4. You can select when the agent should be run. In our case, we can leave the default Manually From Actions Menu.
5. You then select which documents the agent should act on. If you are writing an agent to process incoming mail, you might act on newly arriving documents. If you are creating an agent that will work within a view, you can act on documents selected by the user. In our case, click on the drop-down box and choose All documents in database.

Your screen should resemble Figure 19.3.

Figure 19.3
Creating a new agent for script testing.

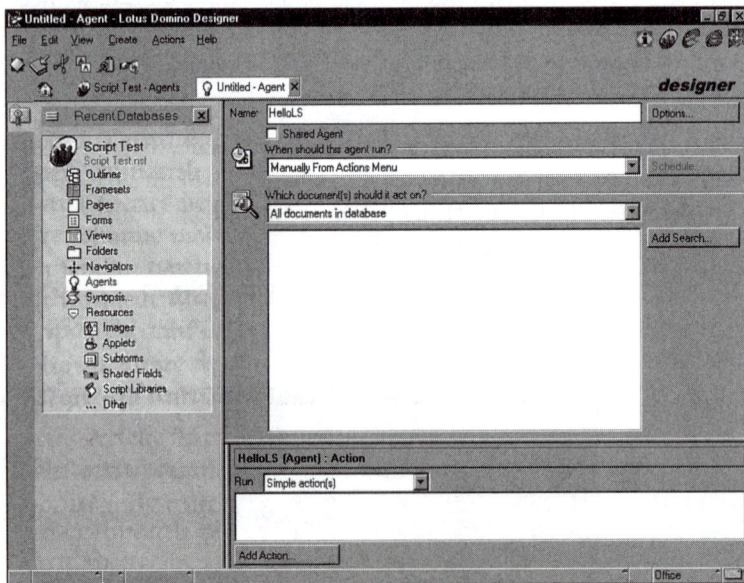

CREATING A LOTUSSCRIPT HELLO AGENT

In this chapter, I'm not going to go into the details of the LotusScript language, but I'll show you how to use the IDE. Our first example will be a little program to display the words "Hello, LotusScript". To create your first LotusScript program:

1. Click on the Run drop-down box in the Programmer's Pane in the bottom-right.
2. Select LotusScript. You'll see the information in the InfoList Pane appear. There will be four choices in the list: Options, Declarations, Initialize, and Terminate.
3. Select the name Initialize in the InfoList Pane. Notice that the IDE has automatically entered two statements for you in the Programmer's Pane: a Sub statement and an End

Sub statement. I cover these statements in more detail in Chapter 22, "LotusScript Subroutines, Functions, and Event Handlers." Here is what the Programmer's pane looks like:

```
Sub Initialize

End Sub
```

4. In the blank line in the middle, type the following:
   ```
   Msgbox "Hello, LotusScript"
   ```

5. Your completed program looks like this:
   ```
   Sub Initialize
   Msgbox "Hello, LotusScript"
   End Sub
   ```

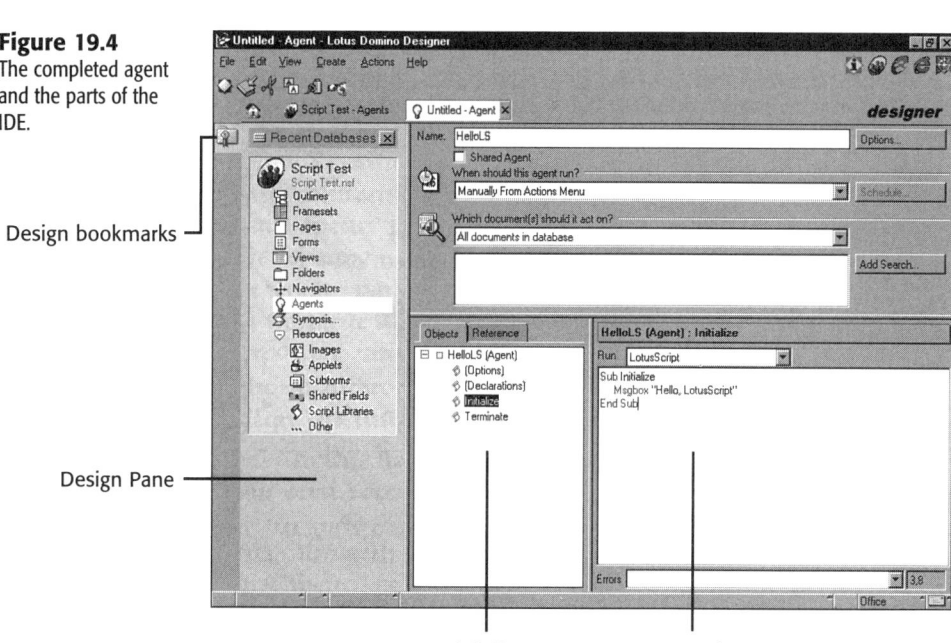

Figure 19.4
The completed agent and the parts of the IDE.

6. See Figure 19.4 to see your completed program and the names of the various parts of the IDE.

7. Now save the script by choosing File, Save.

8. You can now test your first LotusScript program by choosing Actions, HelloLS from the Actions menu. In Figure 19.5, you see the message box that pops up when you run the agent.

Figure 19.5
Testing the `HelloLS` agent.

Congratulations! You've created and tested your first LotusScript program. It's actually pretty easy. Let's recap what we've done. We created an agent, gave it a name, chose the LotusScript language, and supplied the program logic. We then saved the script and tested it.

CREATING A JAVA HELLO AGENT

Now that I have shown you how to create a LotusScript agent, let's take a look at a similar program using Java. To create your first agent in Java, do the following:

1. Click on the word Agents (with the light bulb) in the Design pane on the left.
2. Click on the New Agent action button. A new, untitled agent will be created for you.
3. Give your new agent a name in the Name field. For our example, you can use the name `HelloJava`.
4. You can select when the agent should be run. In our case, we can leave the default Manually From Actions Menu.
5. You then select which documents the agent should act on. If you are writing an agent to process incoming mail, you might act on newly arriving documents. If you are creating an agent that will work within a view, you can act on documents selected by the user. In our case, click on the drop-down box and choose All documents in database.
6. Click on the Run drop-down box in the Programmer's pane in the bottom-right.
7. Select Java (not Imported Java). You'll see the information in the InfoList Pane appear. There will be three levels of hierarchy in the list: `JavaAgent.java`, `JavaAgent`, and `NotesMain`.
8. In the Programmer's pane on the right, you will see an entire Java program template that has been constructed for you. In the middle there is a comment that says (Your code goes here).
9. You insert your code just below the comment line. The following text is case sensitive, so you must enter it exactly as shown. Enter the following:
   `System.out.println("Hello Java");`
10. Your program should look like Figure 19.6.
11. At this point you should save the script by selecting File, Save. In the Errors line, you should see the words `Successful compile`.

Figure 19.6
The `HelloJava` agent after we have entered our code.

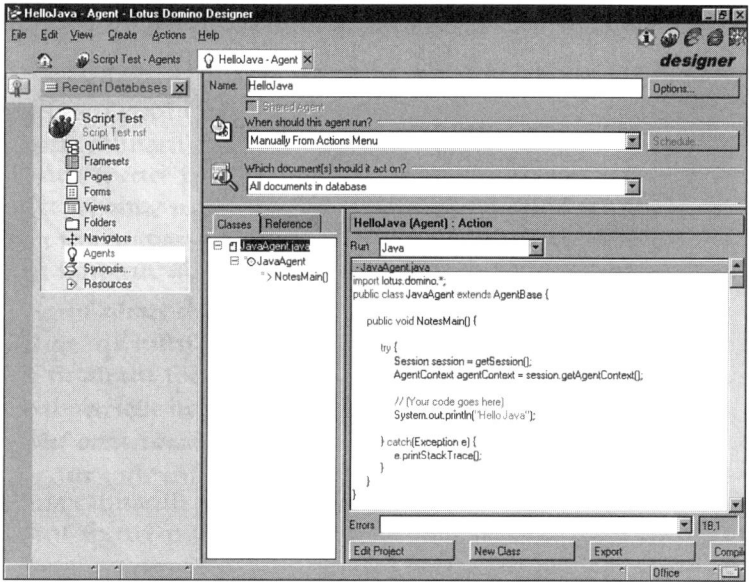

We're now ready to test our Java program. However, before we test it, I should explain a little bit about how output works with Java. Because Java is a platform-independent language, it has its own windowing model. The Abstract Windowing Toolkit (AWT) is at the foundation level in Java. There are also several windowing packages, such as the Swing package that uses AWT or performs similar functions.

Rather than explain all the details of the windowing model, for our purposes here, I've used the `println` routine. This routine writes line-oriented output (as opposed to windowing output) to the Java Debug Console. This is not quite as interesting as a dialog box, but our output here is not really too sophisticated.

To see our output, then, we must first display the Java Debug Console. After we display the Debug Console, we can test our routine. To test our Java agent, do the following:

1. Select File, Tools, Show Java Debug Console. The Java Debug Console window will appear.
2. Select Actions, HelloJava. Your screen should look like Figure 19.7.

Figure 19.7
The `HelloJava` agent with output in the Java Debug Console.

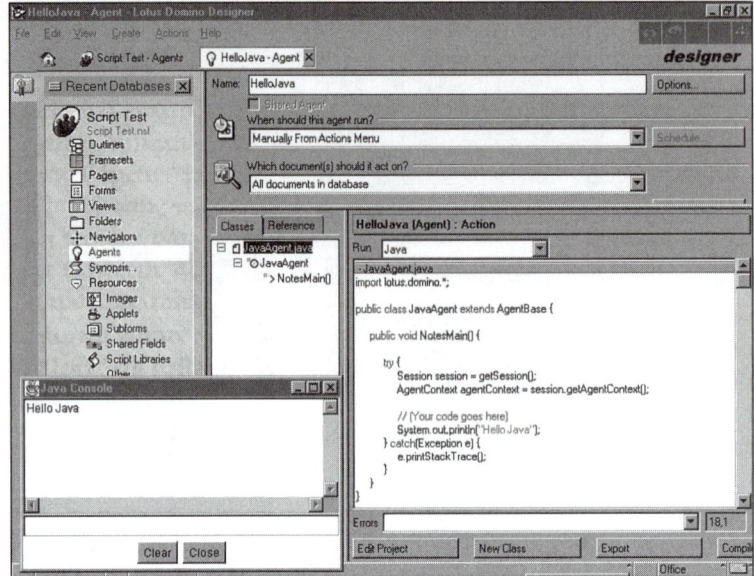

Getting Help

You have seen that we can create a very small program to display a message in both LotusScript and Java.

Both LotusScript and Java are very rich languages with many constructs and features. It might take you a while to become familiar with all their characteristics. What if you need a little help or reference material on a statement or function while you're using the IDE? Fortunately, help is right there, just a mouse-click away.

To see how to access this help, let's look at the HelloJava agent again. The InfoList Pane is the one just to the left of the Programmer's pane where our Java program appears. When we first create our program, the InfoList Pane is opened to the Classes tab. Reference material is available in the Reference tab. See Figure 19.8.

As you can see from Figure 19.8, a listing of the core Java classes and methods is available in the Reference tab. You can also find information about the Domino Object Model classes. If you are editing a LotusScript program, reference information relating to LotusScript becomes available.

Figure 19.8
The `HelloJava` agent with reference information.

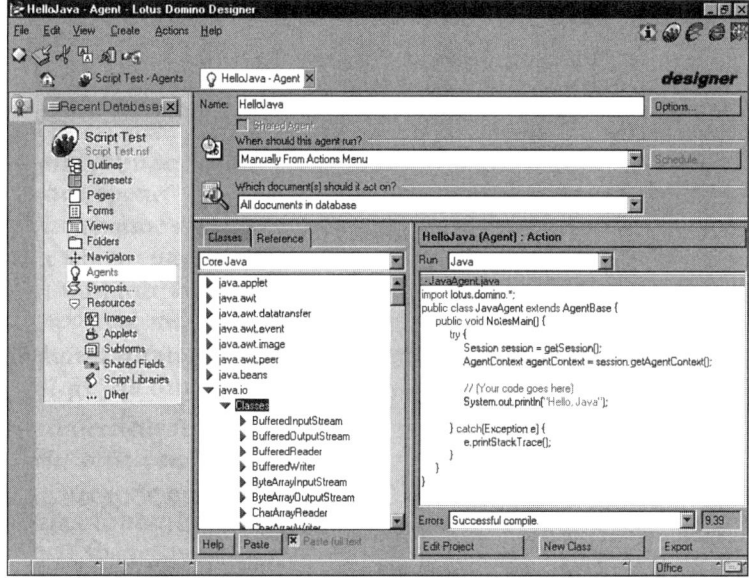

Figure 19.9
The `HelloLS` agent with reference information.

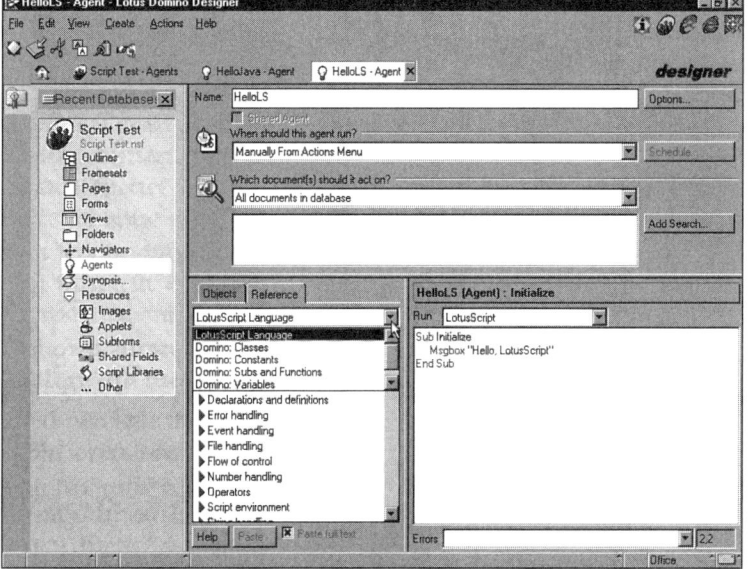

In Figure 19.9, I've edited our LotusScript agent to show you the LotusScript language reference. As you can see from the drop-down list, in addition to the language reference you can find out information about the Notes/Domino Object Model classes, subroutines, and more. If you select a line in the reference section, you can paste the selected line into your program in the Programmer's Pane. If you check the Paste full text option, the entire line will be pasted into your program, including various parameters and options. You can then edit this text and substitute your own variables. If you do not enable the Paste full text option, only the main keyword will be pasted into your program without all the parameters and/or options.

The InfoList Pane is useful for finding out the syntax of a routine or statement if you already know its name. On the other hand, it does not tell you what the function does or how to use it. You can find a lot of this information in the Domino Designer online Help database. To try this, select Help, Help Topics. Then in the Navigation pane on the left, select the topic that you want to see. An example is shown in Figure 19.10.

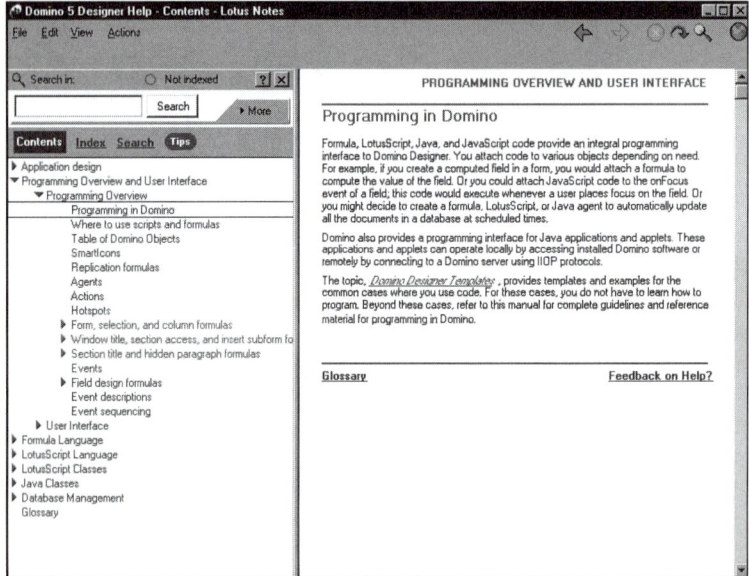

Figure 19.10
The Help Contents for the Domino Designer.

The Domino Designer Help database contains quite a bit of reference material about Java, LotusScript, JavaScript, and the formula language. You can browse this database or search for particular topics of interest.

ACCESSING THE DOMINO OBJECT MODEL

You have now seen how we can create and execute both a LotusScript and Java agent. Now let me show you how you can access the Domino Object Model from Java. LotusScript access is very similar, and we will cover it in great detail in later chapters. Look at Figure 19.11.

EVENT-DRIVEN PROGRAMMING | 465

Figure 19.11
You can access the Domino Object Model from Java.

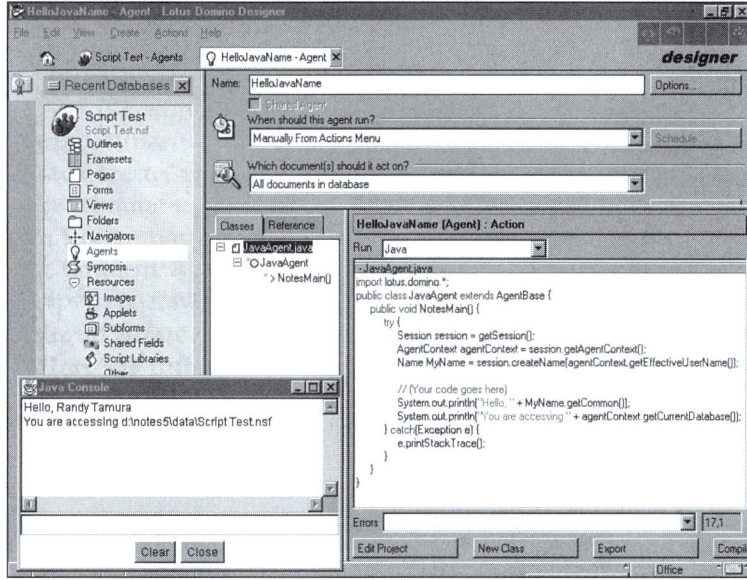

I have modified the Hello Java program to display both the username and the current database. The new Java agent is called HelloJavaName. The agentContext object contains the current database filename and the effective username. I use the effective username to obtain the common name. Here are the three important lines I've added:

```
Name MyName = session.createName(agentContext.getEffectiveUserName());

System.out.println("Hello, " + MyName.getCommon());
System.out.println("You are accessing " + agentContext.getCurrentDatabase());
```

The Domino Object Model is covered in the next chapter, but essentially, it enables you to access information from Domino. You can obtain information about the current user and the current database, and then you can access information within the database, such as view, form, and document data.

LotusScript access to the Domino Object Model has been available since release 4 and Java has been available since release 4.6, but with release 5, it is now much easier to write Java agents within the Domino Designer.

EVENT-DRIVEN PROGRAMMING

You might have heard the phrase *event-driven programming*. There are rumors that Ivan Pavlov might have coined this term as he programmed his dogs to drool at the sound of a bell. In computer programming, it's a very similar concept: When a particular event happens, it triggers a response. It even happens in humans. When the telephone rings, what do you do? If you're like most people, your first instinct is to pick up the phone to answer it. You've been programmed to implement that response to the phone-ringing event.

PART
IV
CH
19

What makes event-driven programming different from traditional application programming? It is mainly a question of control. In traditional programming, you write an application that maintains control. In event-driven programming, you write a series of subroutines, each one a response to a particular event. In event-driven programming, the user has much more control than in traditional programming. The user can control the flow of the application by clicking on buttons, selecting menu items, and so forth. User actions such as these create events. As the programmer, you create event handlers to process the events as they occur.

The event-driven model is used in both the Notes client and Web browser (JavaScript) interfaces. In LotusScript, the events have names such as QueryOpen, PostOpen, and Click. These events trigger LotusScript routines that the Notes client invokes. In JavaScript, events have names such as onMouseOver, onBlur, and onClick. Depending upon the language you choose, you can write your event handlers in either LotusScript or JavaScript.

What is the benefit of the event-driven programming model? Well, the main advantage is that it simplifies the task of programming more complex systems. Remember our Hello agents? All we needed to do was write one line of code to display our message. The agent was triggered by the user menu action. In a traditional language such as C++, this would have taken many more lines of code, and you would have to deal with much more complexity. Because each subroutine is focused on a single event, the programs are smaller and more manageable.

With release 5, the only complicating factor is that there are two types of events: LotusScript and JavaScript. You can actually mix and match the two event models, but I would not necessarily recommend it. The main reason for using both would be to handle the different client types. Remember that certain languages are available only in certain contexts. In particular, LotusScript is available only with a Notes client.

JavaScript, on the other hand, is available in both the Notes client and Web browser. If your intended audience will be using both Notes clients and browsers, you should consider JavaScript. If your audience will be using only Notes clients, you can stay with LotusScript.

Hello Again, and Again, and Again

Now that I've explained event-driven programming, let me show you an example that uses both LotusScript and JavaScript. In our previous agent example, we looked at LotusScript and Java. After this example, you will have seen all three languages: LotusScript, Java, and JavaScript.

For this example, we can use our existing Script Test database. Click on the Forms item in the Design Pane and click the New Form action button to create a new form. In my example, I've called this new form EventExample. You need to open the form properties box to give the form a name. Creating and naming forms was covered in Chapter 14, "Designing Pages, Forms, and Subforms." In this form, we are going to create two buttons: one LotusScript button and one JavaScript button. To create the LotusScript button:

1. If you haven't created the form, create one with the name EventExample. If you already have a form you like, you can just open it.
2. Select Create, Hotspot, Button. A new button will appear on your form.
3. In the button properties box, give the button the label LS Button.
4. In the Run drop-down box in the Programmer's Pane in the lower-right, select LotusScript. You will see six choices in the left InfoList Pane, and an empty (Click) subroutine will appear in the Programmer's Pane.
5. Enter the following text in the Programmer's Pane:
   MsgBox "Hello from the LotusScript button."
6. The complete text in the Programmer's Pane in the lower-right should be
   ```
   Sub Click(Source As Button)
   MsgBox "Hello from the LotusScript button."
   End Sub
   ```
7. Your screen should appear similar to Figure 19.12.

Figure 19.12
Using LotusScript, you can respond to user button clicks.

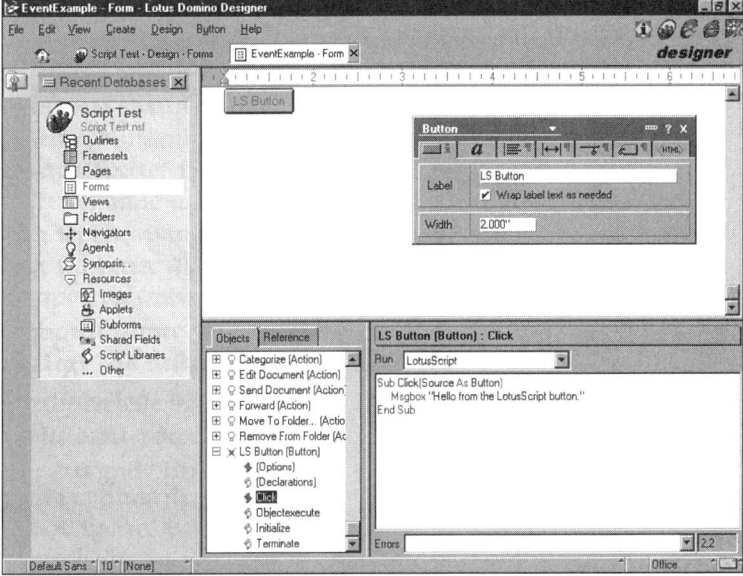

We have now completed the LotusScript button. Before we test this form, we will also create a JavaScript button. To create our JavaScript button, click in the work area just to the right of the existing button and click Enter to space down one line. To create our JavaScript button here:

1. Select Create, Hotspot, Button. A new button will appear on your form.
2. In the button properties box, give this button the label JS Button.

3. In the Run drop-down box in the Programmer's Pane in the lower-right, select JavaScript. You will see twelve choices in the left InfoList Pane. The `onClick` event will be highlighted and an empty (`onClick`) subroutine will appear in the Programmer's Pane.

4. Enter the following text in the Programmer's Pane:
   `alert("Hello from the JavaSript button.")`

> **Tip**
>
> JavaScript is case sensitive. The `alert` routine is built into JavaScript and will display a message dialog box. If you improperly capitalize the name (such as `Alert`), you will get a runtime error from the Web browser. The built-in names for JavaScript are all lowercase.
>
> Case sensitivity is a cause for frequent errors in JavaScript. It is extremely important to have a naming convention for your own routine names in JavaScript, because otherwise you will waste a lot of time. One easy convention is to use all lowercase names. Another possibility is to always use an initial capital letter. Pick a convention and stick to it.

5. Your screen should appear similar to Figure 19.13.

Figure 19.13
Using JavaScript, you can respond to user button clicks via the `onClick` event.

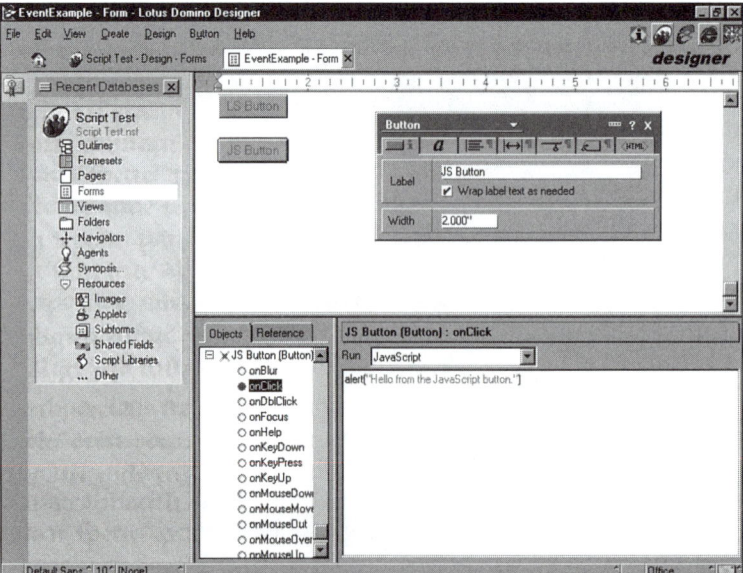

Now we can test our buttons. Here is how to test the buttons:

1. Select Design, Preview In Notes. If you are prompted to save the form, click Yes.

2. When testing with the Notes client, you will see both the LotusScript and JavaScript buttons. You can click either of the buttons to see the messages.

3. You can preview with the Microsoft Internet Explorer by clicking its icon in the upper-right corner of the screen. This icon will appear only if you have Internet Explorer installed on your machine.

4. You can preview with Netscape Navigator by clicking its icon in the upper-right corner of the screen. This icon will appear only if you have Netscape Navigator installed on your machine.

Figure 19.14 shows the Notes client, Netscape Navigator, and Microsoft Internet Explorer all previewing our form.

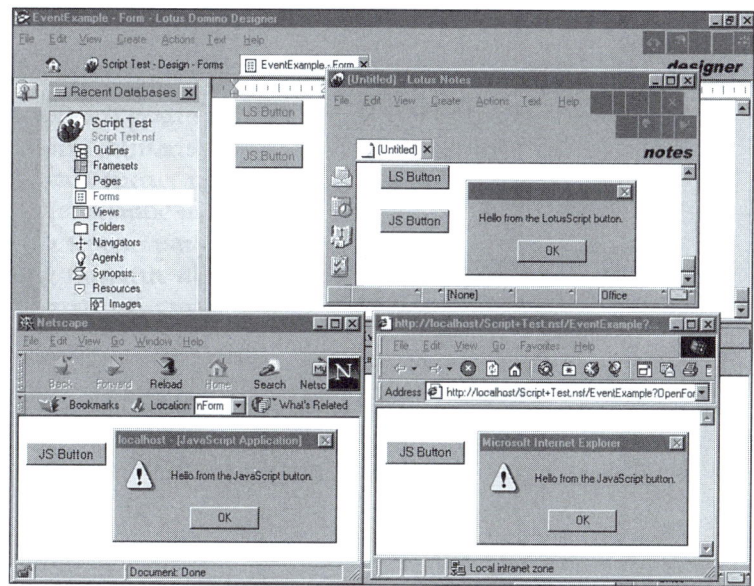

Figure 19.14
The button form previewed with three different clients.

Notice in the above figure that only the Notes client displays both buttons. I've clicked a button in each of the three different clients.

GETTING AN OPINION: REQUESTING INPUT

Now that we've taken a brief excursion into event-driven programming, let's examine one that requests input. This still shouldn't be too difficult, even if you are not an expert typist. We'll be using LotusScript for this example. To create a button that requests input:

1. Open your EventExample form by clicking Forms in the Design pane, and then double-clicking on the EventExample name.

2. Create a new button below the existing two buttons by selecting Create, Hotspot, Button.

3. In the properties box, give the button the label Opinion.

4. In the Run drop-down box in the Programmer's pane in the lower-right, select LotusScript. Enter the text in Listing 19.1.

LISTING 19.1 A PROGRAM THAT REQUESTS AND DISPLAYS A NAME

```
Sub Click(Source As Button)
MyName$ = Inputbox$("Please enter your name")
Msgbox "Hello " + MyName$
End Sub
```

As you can see, we have created a program to prompt for a name, and then we will display that name in the resulting message box. Your screen should look like the one in Figure 19.15.

Figure 19.15
A program that requests and displays a name.

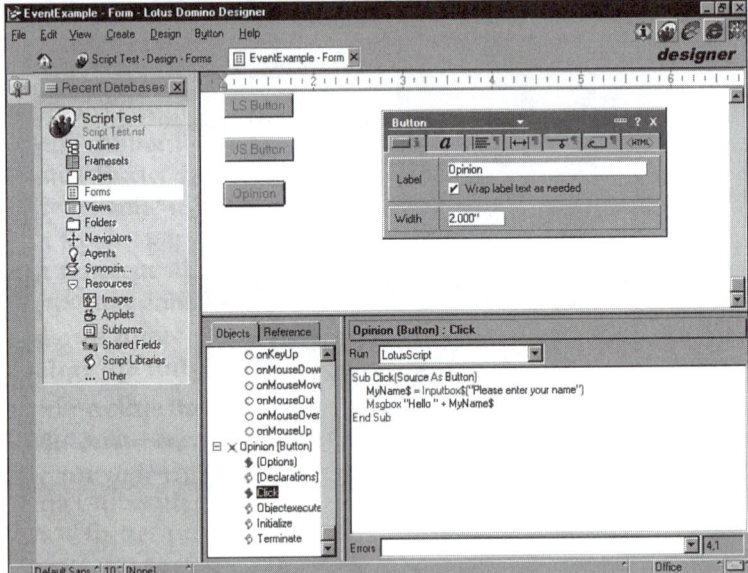

The new line calls the Inputbox function. The purpose of this function is to prompt the user for input and return the input to a variable within the program. In this case, I have defined a variable called MyName$. The $ at the end of the variable name signifies that the variable is a string variable. We'll cover variable declarations in more depth in Chapter 21, "LotusScript Variables and Objects." The Inputbox function also has a $ at the end to indicate that it is returning a string variable.

We have changed the Msgbox line to contain two parts. First is the constant "Hello " and second is the variable MyName$. The plus sign between them does not mean to sum these two words, which wouldn't make sense. Instead, in LotusScript, the plus sign between two strings means to concatenate them, or place one after the other, producing one large string.

Now, we can test this program in the Notes client. To do so, you can click the Notes Preview icon in the upper-right corner or select Design, Preview in Notes. After you click the Opinion button, you should see a prompt appear, as shown in Figure 19.16.

Figure 19.16
The Opinion button prompting for input.

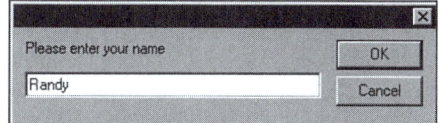

Enter your name as the program requests, and click OK. You should see the Hello dialog box appear with your name. If you want to try it again and use a different name, I won't tell anyone. In fact, you can try various options, including typing special characters or even no characters. Each of these various scenarios will cause a different output.

PUTTING IN YOUR TWO CENTS: INPUTTING NUMBERS RATHER THAN TEXT

I have shown you how to input, concatenate, and display strings. Now let's modify our program to work with a few numbers. Take a look at Listing 19.2.

LISTING 19.2   AN OPINION PROGRAM THAT DISPLAYS THE COST OF WISDOM

```
Sub Click(Source As Button)

MyName$ = Inputbox$("Please enter your name")
Msgbox "Hello " + MyName$
Amount% = Cint(Inputbox$("How much wisdom would you like?"))
Msgbox "OK. That will be " + Str$(Amount% * 2) + " cents."
End Sub
```

In Listing 19.2, I have added two lines. The first line asks how much wisdom you would like. The user should enter a number. The `Cint` function converts an expression to an integer. The value is then stored in the `Amount` variable. Just as the `$` suffix represents a string variable, a `%` suffix represents an integer variable. I'll cover all the suffixes and their meanings in a later chapter. After the user has input the amount, the program takes the amount and calculates the cost of the wisdom by charging two cents for each.

The expression

`Str$(Amount% * 2)`

calculates two cents for each item and then converts the resulting amount to a string. You must convert the number to a string for it to be concatenated with the other strings. After you have entered the program as shown in Listing 19.2, try it out.

> **Tip**
>
> If you are reading this book in a country other than the United States, you can use your own monetary names, such as yen, euro, peso, lira, or franc. In the United States, "putting two cents in" means stating your opinion. Another saying in the U.S. is "May I pay you a penny for your thoughts?" So when you're requesting an opinion, it is worth one cent; when you give your opinion to someone else, it is worth two cents. In your country, the value of your opinion might be worth much more or less.

From Here...

In this chapter, I have described scripting languages in general and told you how they can be used to control system operation. Many scripting languages are available, including many based on the BASIC language, such as LotusScript and Visual Basic. JavaScript is another language that can be used to control Notes and Domino as well as Web browsers. Java can be used to develop applets as well as full applications. I showed you a chart of which languages are available and told you when you should use each language.

When you're considering scripting languages, it's important to realize that typically two programs are involved: the system being controlled, which in this case is Lotus Notes or Domino, and the program written in the scripting language.

I showed you how to use the Integrated Development Environment (IDE) to create a simple LotusScript agent and an equivalent Java agent. We invoked this program from the menu.

I also covered the concept of events. You can associate a LotusScript or JavaScript routine with events such as opening a document or saving a document, or with the clicking of buttons. Many types of events have been defined in Notes, Domino, and Web browsers, and they are designed to give you, the programmer, control over the environment at key points in the processing of an application.

We created a form with two buttons: one using LotusScript and the other using JavaScript. Although the event names are different for these two languages, you can accomplish many of the same tasks. Remember that LotusScript provides you a powerful tool, integrated well with Notes and Domino, but is not available in Web browsers.

LotusScript, JavaScript, and Java are powerful languages. You can do much more than I have showed you in this introductory chapter, and in subsequent chapters I show you how to access and create information in Domino databases. Here are some suggestions for additional reading:

- Chapter 20, "Object-Oriented Programming and the Domino Object Model," gives you the background you need for object-oriented programming. It describes the general concepts and then covers the Domino Object Model in particular.
- Chapter 21, "LotusScript Variables and Objects," and Chapter 22, "LotusScript Subroutines, Functions, and Event Handlers," cover the LotusScript language. These chapters concentrate on the flow control, syntax, and built-in functions of LotusScript.

- Chapter 23, "Creating and Using Java Applets and Agents," describes the Java language and how you can use it to create Java applets and agents. You'll also learn about some unique features in Java, such as multithreading.
- Chapter 24, "Using the Lotus eSuite DevPack," puts Java to work. eSuite is an add-on package written in Java that can improve your productivity by giving you prewritten Java applets that can make your job of creating an application easier.
- Chapter 25, "The Session and Front-End Classes"; Chapter 26, "Database, View, and Document Classes in LotusScript and Java"; and Chapter 27, "Using Fields and Items in LotusScript and Java," all cover the Domino Object Model classes in detail. These chapters provide you a unique perspective by discussing the DOM using both the LotusScript and Java languages to compare and contrast the advantages of both languages.

CHAPTER 20

OBJECT-ORIENTED PROGRAMMING AND THE DOMINO OBJECT MODEL

In the preceding chapter, I showed you how to create some simple programs in LotusScript, Java, and JavaScript. In those examples, I showed some very elementary operations to interact with the user. This type of interaction is sometimes called the *front end*. If the front end typically means interacting with users, the *back end* means interacting with data. LotusScript and Java programming rely heavily on the use of object-oriented programming to access and manipulate Notes data.

In this chapter, I cover some of the basics of object-oriented programming and the Domino Object Model (DOM) classes so that you'll have the background to understand how to use them effectively. I'll tell you about the relationship between classes and objects, containers and collections, and class inheritance and data models. I'll cover events in LotusScript and the difference between the front-end and back-end classes, and I'll introduce you to the Domino Object Model. Prior to release 5, the interface to this model was sometimes called the Notes Object Interface (NOI).

A Bit of Object-Oriented Programming History

Surprisingly, object-oriented programming has been around for a long time. Many people think it is one of the newer innovations of computer science research, but actually object-oriented programming has been around since at least 1967; so as we approach the millenium, many of the concepts are over three decades old. At that time, in the late 1960s when flower children were blooming, Ole-Johan Dahl, Bjorn Myhrhaug, and Kristen Nygaard created the Simula language while working at the Norwegian Computing Centre in Oslo. Simula was an extension of the Algol 60 language, of an even earlier vintage.

In the 1960s when Simula was developed, the IBM 360 was the rage, and all computing was done on mainframe computers. It would be more than a decade before the first Apple and IBM personal computers would be created. The contributions, then, of Dahl, Myhrhaug, and Nygaard to create many of the ideas of object-oriented programming are all the more remarkable.

The main contribution of Simula was to introduce the concepts of classes, objects, and methods, which I'll describe shortly. The main approach of that language, as is true today of all object-oriented programming, is one of decomposition. It is a simple idea, really: Take a complex task, system, or project. Divide this job into smaller pieces, and then examine each piece and break it into yet smaller pieces. Break up these pieces until you have elementary ideas, tasks, or items you know how to handle.

Classes, objects, and methods are just some of the tools we can use to make our complex systems easier to handle. Decomposition enables us to mentally focus on only a small number of items at a time, and thus it should make our programs easier to write, understand, and debug. The decomposition should also allow our programs to be more reliable because each layer is simpler.

What Is Object-Oriented Programming?

Object-oriented programming (OOP) is, at its core, about managing complexity. It enables us to more easily create more complex systems by facilitating decomposition. We use the tools and techniques of OOP to break down larger problems into smaller, more manageable problems.

To bring this explanation back to reality a bit, when we use OOP with LotusScript, it enables us to create larger, more complex Notes applications with less work, and—we hope—more reliability. In essence, Lotus is providing a set of reusable tools we can build on to create applications.

As we examine the concepts of classes, objects, and methods in the sections to follow, keep in mind that our purpose is the management of complexity, and our means will be decomposition.

Traditional Programming Versus Object-Oriented Programming

The concepts of traditional programming go back even further than object-oriented programming and have many of their roots in mathematics. Because computers were first conceived to perform complex calculations more quickly than people, mathematics clearly had an important influence on the languages people use to communicate with computers.

One of the early programming languages, FORTRAN, which stands for formula translation, was designed to translate formulas from a language people could understand into a format a computer could execute. One characteristic of this language was the separation of data from functions. Functions in mathematics are supplied with their data in the form of parameters and yield numerical results.

Intellectually, it is appealing to separate functions or algorithms from the data on which they operate. After all, you can supply a value to a sine routine or a square root function, and it will calculate and return the result. The angle or number has nothing in particular to do with the way in which the computer calculates the sine or square root.

The problem, however, is that many complex systems don't behave as cleanly or purely as mathematics. The problem with the functional approach is that the function cannot retain *state* information. State information refers to the status of an object. For example, suppose you want to write a program to simulate an elevator. You need to keep track of whether the door is open or closed, which floor the elevator is on, and so forth.

In traditional programming, if you want to keep track of the state of an object, this task must be done separately from the functions themselves. By separating the data from the functions, you enable separate functions to access and modify global data. In a complex system, this modification of global data can make programs harder to write and debug. It also leads to programs that are less reliable than they should be.

I'll show you in the next section how you can use the concept of an object to encapsulate data with functions and keep track of state information at the same time.

Objects—Tangible Items

In our everyday world, we deal with objects all the time. One object is this book you are reading. Another might be your car, or your house, or the breakfast roll you ate this morning. In each of these cases, it is convenient to think of the item as a single object. But clearly, if you think about your car or house, you can easily see how that object can be decomposed into smaller subobjects.

A car, for example, can be simplistically decomposed into a body and four wheels. The body can be decomposed into the doors, windows, engine compartment, and so forth. A house can be decomposed into its constituent rooms. Each room, in turn, can be broken up into the walls, doors, and windows that make it a room. Even a breakfast roll is made up of flour, eggs, water, nuts, and other basic ingredients.

The word *object*, then, is used as a very generic word to represent any or all of these things. In the real world, of course, these objects are tangible things. They are items we can see, touch, hear, and recognize. In the programming world, we create objects to represent items in the real world.

If we are trying to describe objects, what kinds of characteristics should we use? In object-oriented programming, we use two kinds of characteristics. The first characteristic of an object is called its *properties*. The set of properties of an object can be used to describe it. For example, a property of the car might be its color, size, shape, weight, or even country of origin. A property of a house might be its address, the number of floors, the number of rooms, or its purchase price. A breakfast roll might have properties such as its weight or the number of raisins in it.

As you can tell, the properties of an object clearly depend on the type of object. For example, it might make sense to talk about the color of a car and the color of a house. But although it makes sense to talk about the number of raisins in a breakfast roll, it makes much less sense to talk about the number of raisins in your car (unless you have a two-year-old child, in which case there are probably at least a few raisins under the back seat of your car).

In addition to typically static attributes such as the color of the car, it is important to notice that a property can represent the state or status of an object. For example, the state of a car engine might be on or off; the car door is open or closed; the transmission is in low, neutral, drive, or reverse. This status is dynamic and can change over time. Other examples might be whether the windows of a car are rolled down or up, or whether the wheels are turning or not turning. In a house, the air conditioning might be on or off, a particular door might be open or closed, and the television might be tuned to a particular channel. All of these properties represent data associated with the object that can change over time, but that are set to a particular value at any given point in time.

The second characteristic we use to classify an object is its capabilities, which are really the actions it can perform. In the case of a car, it can perform many actions, such as starting, turning a corner, and stopping. Some of a car's subobjects can also perform actions. A car's headlights can turn on, the turn signals can flash, the horn can make a sound, and the wheels can turn. Within a house, the faucets can turn on, the kitchen stove can cook, and the stereo music system can play.

The actions an object can perform are called *methods* in object-oriented parlance. In object-oriented programming, an object's methods are also sometimes called subroutines, but OOP purists would recoil at this imprecise use of the word. I am not fanatically pure about OOP terminology in this book.

The basic idea of an object is that it encapsulates its properties and methods. These properties and methods are also sometimes called member variables or member procedures because the properties and methods are members of the object. This encapsulation enables you to group the data associated with an object with the operations to be performed on it. The properties and methods reflect both what an object is (properties) and what an object can do (methods).

When properties and methods are encapsulated together, the real power comes when there is more than one object of a particular type. For example, if you have two car objects, each object has its own copy of the property information, so each property can be set independently of the other. In traditional functional programming, it is much more work because you might have to keep track of multiple sets of data. Multiple sets of data are easily handled with object-oriented programming, because each object just manages its own data, no matter how many objects have been created. The next section dealing with classes shows how to handle multiple objects of the same type.

Classes—Describing Groups of Objects

Classes in object-oriented programming are a slightly more abstract concept than objects. Everyone can understand the concept of an object because an object can be related to something tangible. Whereas an object represents a particular item, a *class* is the description of a group of objects that share characteristics.

For example, let's go back to the example of a car. Suppose you own a red Ferrari (lucky you). This red Ferrari is a particular car; it's yours; it is an object. Suppose, however, that we wanted to describe all Ferraris, not just your car. In this case, the description would be the class definition, as illustrated in Figure 20.1.

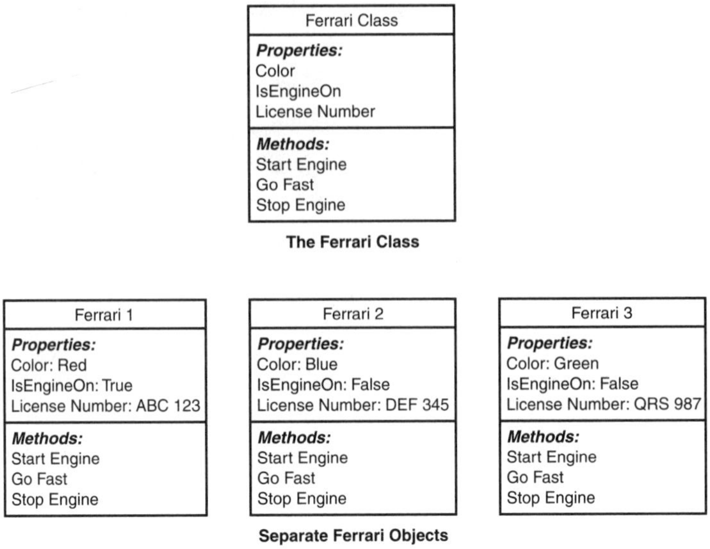

Figure 20.1
There can be many Ferrari objects based upon the `Ferrari` class.

Ferrari Class
Properties: Color IsEngineOn License Number
Methods: Start Engine Go Fast Stop Engine

The Ferrari Class

Ferrari 1	Ferrari 2	Ferrari 3
Properties: Color: Red IsEngineOn: True License Number: ABC 123	**Properties:** Color: Blue IsEngineOn: False License Number: DEF 345	**Properties:** Color: Green IsEngineOn: False License Number: QRS 987
Methods: Start Engine Go Fast Stop Engine	**Methods:** Start Engine Go Fast Stop Engine	**Methods:** Start Engine Go Fast Stop Engine

Separate Ferrari Objects

In the `Ferrari` class definition, we might describe the fact that the color is a property, and the weight, the license plate (tag) number, and other characteristics would also be properties. In the class definition, we do not give the properties specific values; we just describe the properties that the class contains. For example, we describe color as a property, but we do not prescribe a *particular* color.

If someone else owns a Ferrari of the same class, his car might be blue. Another person's Ferrari might be green. All of these cars are from the same class, but they represent different objects. Repeating again, an object represents a particular item, whereas a class describes a group of items that are similar.

It is important to emphasize here the difference between classes and objects. A class is just a definition. It describes the properties and methods shared by each object of the class. A class does not consume any computer memory. An object, on the other hand, is tangible. An object occupies memory in the computer, and for each separate object of the same class, separate memory is used.

As an example within Notes and Domino, there is a LotusScript class definition for a Notes document, called appropriately the `NotesDocument` class. This class represents the characteristics of all Notes document objects. The class has properties, such as the date the document was last modified, the size of the document, and the date the document was created. These properties are available for each document object, but they typically are different for each document object in the database. Methods of the `NotesDocument` class enable access to the document's fields, replacing values and removing the document from the database. There are many other properties and methods in this class and the other Notes classes.

Class Containment

I told you that decomposition is one of the important characteristics of object-oriented programming. I also gave examples of how a car is made up of subobjects, such as doors and wheels. This concept is called *containment* in OOP. When an object has subobjects, we consider the object to be like a container, with the subobjects being contained within it. Each subobject is typically considered to be a property of the class.

Using the house as an example, we might have a house object that contains 10 room objects. Each room object is separate and has different properties and methods. The relationship of the container to its subobjects is sometimes called the *Has-A* relationship. This can be expressed in words as the house Has-A kitchen or the house Has-A bedroom.

We describe these Has-A relationships when we define the class. After they have been described in the class definition, they normally do not vary from one object of the class to another. The class definition describes the structure for all objects of the class. The structure is the same for each object created from that class. For example, after we define that a car class Has-A steering wheel, each car object that is created will contain a steering wheel.

Collection Classes

When we are defining a car, it is relatively safe to say that each member of the car class, that is, each car object, will have 4 wheels. Unless there are some unusual circumstances, a car will not have 3 wheels or 37 wheels. In a case like this, we can create a class with a fixed number of wheel subobjects.

What happens, though, if we want to model a house, but each house object we create has a different number of rooms? For example, today we might be building a small house with 7 rooms. Tomorrow, however, we want to build a mansion with 23 rooms. How can we model this concept?

A *collection* class is a special kind of class. Its purpose is to hold a variable number of items within it. See Figure 20.2 for an illustration. Collection classes are also sometimes called *container* classes. When you define the class, you do not know how many objects will be contained inside it. For example, suppose you want to model a Notes database and within the database you want to have an unspecified number of document objects. It does not make sense to define 4, 10, 37, 2000, or any fixed number of documents in the database. Of course, you need the flexibility to have any number of documents in the database from a few to a few thousand. This class must allow documents to be added or deleted, but without the restriction of having a fixed number of items. The Notes database actually contains an element whose class is suitably named, the `NotesDocumentCollection` class.

A collection class typically has methods, such as add an item, delete an item, get the first item, and get the next item. These operations enable you to traverse the container, examining each element as you progress through the collection.

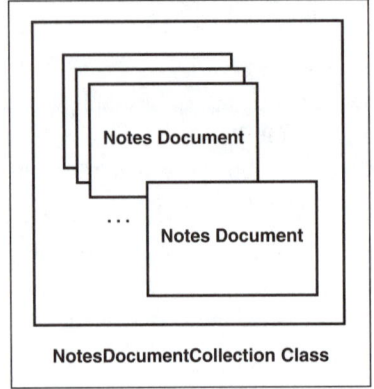

Figure 20.2
The `NotesDocument-Collection` class can contain an arbitrary number of `NotesDocument` elements.

Class Inheritance

I've told you about containment and collections. One other organizational tool is called inheritance. Inheritance is used in situations in which you want to define general classes, then progressively more refined classes. Each progressively more refined class is called a subclass of the original class.

For example, suppose you were to define a class called `Vehicle`. This class might represent any kind of vehicle, including trains, cars, and planes. You could create a subclass of the `Vehicle` class called `FourWheelVehicles`. This class might include cars, trucks, and minivans. You could then create a subclass called `Cars` as a subclass of `FourWheelVehicles`. A subclass called `Ferrari` could then be created, which would represent all Ferraris.

As you can see, each subclass gets progressively more refined, detailed, and specific. This type of modeling relationship is called the *Is-A* relationship. Recall that the Has-A relationship is what we used to model a car and its four wheels. A car has four wheels, but each wheel is not a car. On the other hand, a Ferrari Is-A Car, and a Car Is-A FourWheelVehicle, and a FourWheelVehicle Is-A Vehicle.

This Is-A relationship is also called *inheritance*. Just as a child inherits characteristics from its parents, a child class inherits the properties and methods of the parent class. Keep in mind the distinction between containment (Has-A) and inheritance (Is-A).

In the Notes classes, there is only one case of inheritance. The `NotesRichTextItem` class inherits from the `NotesItem` class. That is, any object that is a `NotesRichTextItem` object Is-A `NotesItem` object. All the other relationships within the Notes class hierarchy are ones of containment. So, for example, a `NotesDatabase` object Has-A `NotesDocumentCollection` object that represents the documents contained within the database. A `NotesItem` roughly corresponds to the data within a field on a form. A `NotesRichTextItem` can contain rich text information, such as fonts and size information. I cover all these classes in more detail later.

Object Models

I've used examples such as cars, houses, and breakfast rolls to illustrate some of the concepts of object-oriented programming, but to use OOP meaningfully, I now need to describe object models, which are also sometimes called data models. Object models are abstract concepts that help us organize data. These models group related information together, and in the case of the Domino Object Model, they are really just a set of object-oriented classes. The object model represents the logical hierarchy of classes and objects within Notes and Domino.

In Figures 20.3 and 20.4, you can see the classes contained in the Domino Object Model as implemented in LotusScript. The Java hierarchy is very, very similar, with only a few minor differences. The lines connecting the various classes signify containment. Notice that there are several instances of containment in the class definitions. For example, within a Notes database, there are views, forms, and documents. Within a Notes document, there are items and rich text items. All the high-level classes contain other, lower-level classes.

Figure 20.3
The Session, Workspace, and Database classes.

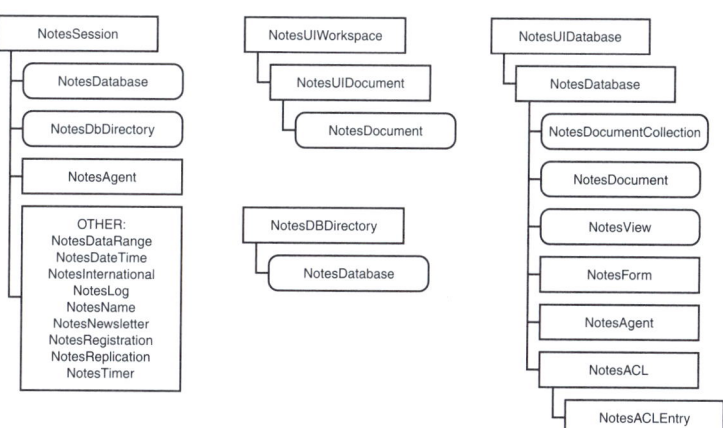

These classes represent a model of how Domino data is organized. It is important to realize that the Notes classes are not actually part of the LotusScript or Java languages. You can consider these classes to be an adjunct to the languages. They are accessible from the language but are not part of it. By separating the DOM from the programming languages, Lotus can implement the DOM once, and language bindings can be used to interface between different programming languages and the DOM routines. In addition, this separation allows usage of remote clients using CORBA, as we'll see in the next section.

Figure 20.4
The `View`, `Outline`, `Document`, and `RichText` classes.

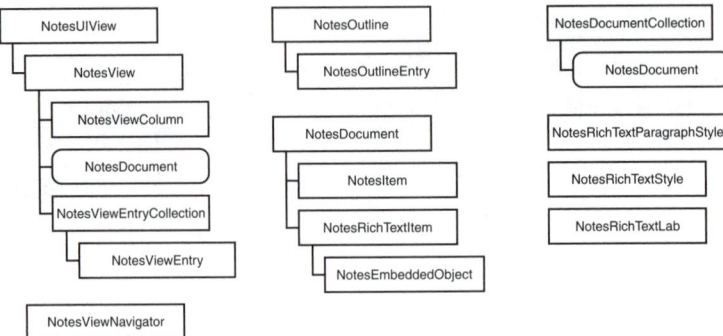

DOMINO OBJECT MODEL ARCHITECTURE

The interface to the DOM routines is through various adapters. By using the adapters, support for several programming languages is possible. In particular, LotusScript and Java can share the same underlying program code. See Figure 20.5.

Figure 20.5
The Notes client can access the Domino Object Model via LotusScript or Java.

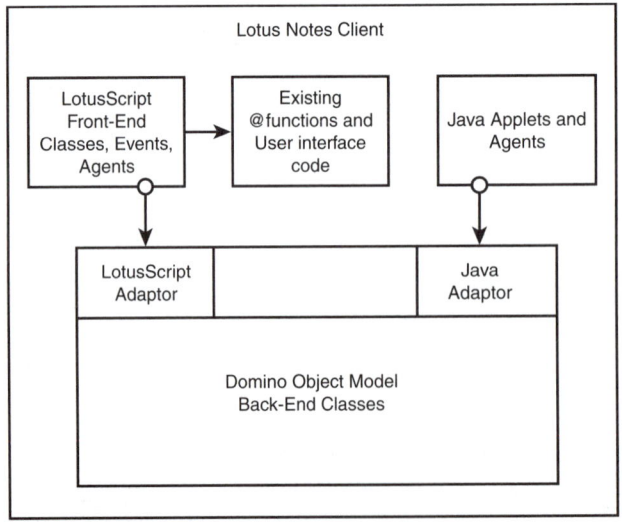

Figure 20.5 shows how both the LotusScript and Java languages can access the Domino Object Model. Notice that the LotusScript front-end classes consist of different code than the back-end classes. Also, notice that Java programs cannot access the front-end classes at all.

FRONT-END AND BACK-END CLASSES

A frequent source of confusion is the fact that Notes has both front-end and back-end classes. There are a couple of explanations for this setup. The first reason is that the front-end classes are wrappers that have been implemented around preexisting code in Notes to provide you with access to the existing features. The back-end classes have been implemented from new code. The back-end classes enable you to access data stored in Domino databases. These databases can reside on either the client or server.

In essence, the front-end classes make sense only in the context of the user interface. For example, there are events that deal with dragging and dropping. Only a user can accomplish these actions, and they cannot occur in the context of, for example, an agent running on a server. Similarly, issuing a dialog box and expecting a response when no user is present is not meaningful.

In Figure 20.6, you can see how Domino interacts with the DOM back-end Classes. Notice that it is similar but different from the Notes client interfaces. In this figure, you also see that a browser client can access the Domino Object Model.

Figure 20.6
Domino supports client/server access to the Domino Object Model via CORBA and IIOP.

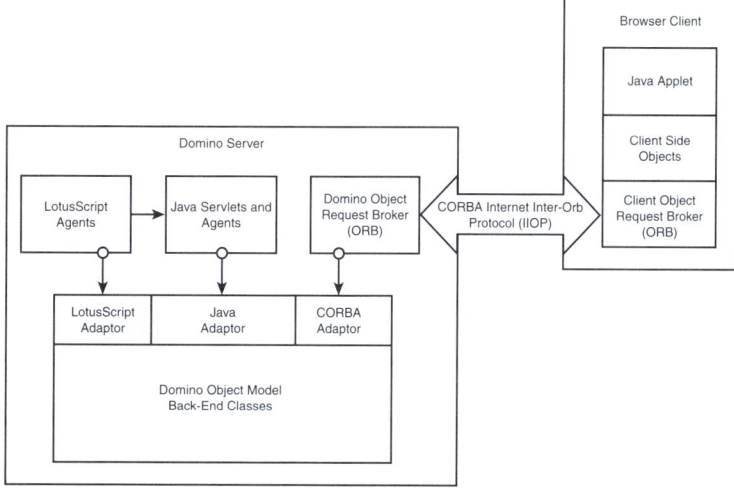

Refer to Figure 20.6 for the following discussion. On the Domino server, LotusScript programs can access the back-end classes, but not the front-end classes, because there is no real workstation user. The front-end classes are available only while there is a workstation user using the Notes client. Java is a very interesting case because there are a couple of different ways the Domino Object Model can be accessed, depending upon whether you are running the Java on Domino or on a browser client. If running on a Domino server, Java programs can go through the Java adapter directly to the DOM. In the browser implementation, the Java programs (on the client) interface with the client-side objects (CSOs). The client-side objects are implemented in Java and interface with a client-side Object Request Broker (ORB). This ORB then uses the Internet Inter-Orb Protocol (IIOP) to communicate with the Domino side ORB (on the server), which then uses the CORBA adapter to access the DOM.

I realize that this all may seem complicated, but key points to notice in this discussion are

- All the communication and remote procedure invocation is standards-based with CORBA, IIOP, and ORBs. By using these standards, future enhancements will be easier to implement, and the architecture is completely open.
- Because the communication between the browser client and the Domino server uses IIOP, they can each be located anywhere on the Internet. This is an extremely powerful connectivity statement. Also, because IIOP is a more powerful protocol than using HTML with browsers, complex client/server computing is enabled over the Internet.
- The browser client goes through the CSOs and the CORBA adapter to eventually get to the DOM. Java running on Domino goes through the Java adapter. This means that you may get minor differences in the implementation of these two methods. The CSOs implemented in the browser client have caching code to decrease the communication required and improve performance.
- The Notes client goes through the Java adapter in the same way as Domino. Again, this may mean slight differences in appearance or function between the Notes client and a browser client. Over time, however, Lotus can enhance the CSOs to obtain better functionality and come very close to implementing Notes client capabilities in a browser.

So the wizard behind the curtain has been uncovered. The way that Lotus has implemented Notes client functionality in a Web browser is via Java, CSOs, and CORBA. Although you may not be very familiar with this technology yet, it will be more and more important in the future because Lotus is implementing more and more front-end functionality with Java. As more of the client functionality is available in Java, using a Web browser instead of the Notes client will become more prevalent. In Chapter 23, "Creating and Using Java Applets and Agents," I go into more depth on Java and CORBA so you can see how to use this technology in your own Java applets. With CORBA, you will be able to create applications that use any Web browser as a client, the Internet (and IIOP) as the communications channel, and Domino as the server.

In the next two sections, I present an overview of the Notes front-end classes and the Domino Object Model (back-end) classes. This overview is meant not to give you a comprehensive description of the classes, but to acquaint you with the classes that are available and describe their primary functions. The classes are described in detail in Chapter 25, "The Session and Front-End Classes," Chapter 26, "Database, View, and Document Classes in LotusScript and Java," and Chapter 27, "Using Fields and Items in LotusScript and Java."

The Notes Front-End Classes

In deciding whether you want to use the front-end or back-end classes, consider whether the program you are writing will require user input, and if so, whether you want changes to be reflected in the user interface. If this is your situation, you should use the front-end classes. The front-end classes can emulate user input and perform actions, such as moving the cursor from one field to another.

Notes has seven front-end classes. Here are descriptions of these classes in alphabetical order with some of their major functions (more details on these classes are given in other chapters):

- `Button` This class represents button objects within forms and on Action Bars in views or forms.
- `Field` This class represents a field within a form. You can perform some processing when the user's cursor enters or exits the field.
- `Navigator` This class is used to handle user interactions with a navigator.
- `NotesUIDatabase` This class is used as a basis for accessing Notes databases. From this class, you can access the user views and documents contained in the databases. Database open and close events enable you to perform processing at these times.
- `NotesUIDocument` This class enables you to access the document that the user is viewing on the display. You can access information stored in the fields of the document. You can cut and paste and navigate through the document. In addition, the `Refresh` method enables you to update the display after you have made changes.
- `NotesUIView` This class enables you to access the documents contained in the view. It also contains the `NotesView` object back-end class. See the description in the following section for its functions.
- `NotesUIWorkspace` This class enables you to add a database to the workspace, compose (create) new documents, open a database, and refresh a view.

The four major classes have UI in the middle of the name to signify User Interface. Many of the actions taken by methods in these classes can be used to simulate user input, such as moving from one field to another or cutting and pasting information from one place to another.

Events

Before I discuss the LotusScript classes for Notes in more detail, I need to cover one more topic. *Events* in LotusScript are another characteristic of classes. Events are triggered in LotusScript when particular conditions are met. For example, an event occurs when a document in a database has just been opened. This event is called the `PostOpen` event.

For the most part, events are related to the front-end classes. This is because most of the events are triggered by user actions. The only exception is the `Alarm` event, which can be triggered on the `NotesTimer` back-end class.

When an event is triggered, a method within the class is called to handle the event. In older systems, these types of subroutines were sometimes called user-exits. In essence, the idea of the event is that it enables you, as a user of the class, a chance to perform some actions under certain circumstances.

For example, suppose that you want to perform some validity-checking whenever a document is opened in a particular database. You can supply a subroutine to handle the PostOpen event, and whenever a document is opened, your subroutine will be called. Similar events occur for opening a database, opening and closing views, and so forth.

The Domino Object Model Back-End Classes

The LotusScript DOM has 31 back-end classes, and the Java DOM has 32 classes. These classes are essentially the same for LotusScript and Java. The one additional class in Java is the AgentContext class. This class has properties and methods that are in the NotesSession class of LotusScript. In Chapter 25, I cover the Session and AgentContext classes in detail. Other than this one exception, though, the Java classes correspond very closely to the LotusScript classes. However, the names are slightly different, and their usage syntax is slightly different in the two programming languages. I cover these differences later, so for this section I'll use the LotusScript names. Here are the LotusScript DOM classes in alphabetical order:

- **NotesACL**   This class enables you to access and manipulate the Access Control List (ACL) for a database. You can create new ACL entries and traverse the existing entries.
- **NotesACLEntry**   This class represents a single ACL entry. You can query the properties of an object of this class to see whether the user can create documents, personal agents, or personal folders. You can also query whether the user can delete documents and find out about any associated Roles.
- **NotesAgent**   This class enables you to run an agent or query its properties, to find out such things as whether it is a public agent, whether it is enabled, and the associated server name.
- **NotesDatabase**   This class encapsulates methods and properties associated with a Notes database. You can obtain one of the views, query the ACL, get information about forms, grant or revoke access to the database, create and delete documents, and perform many other functions. This is one of the more important classes within the Notes class hierarchy.
- **NotesDateRange**   This is a utility class that contains a start date/time, an end date/time, and an associated string of text. This class is used to support the calendaring and scheduling feature.
- **NotesDateTime**   This class is used to represent a date and time within Notes. It can also be used to convert a date/time value to another time zone.
- **NotesDbDirectory**   This class is used to traverse the list of databases that are accessible on the local machine or on a server.

- `NotesDocument`   This is an important class, which enables you to add or remove items from a document, encrypt the document, and traverse the fields of the document. You can use this class to send the document via email or to save it to the database.

- `NotesDocumentCollection`   This class is used as a container for documents. Using this class, you can traverse the documents by getting the first document, the last document, the next or previous document, or the nth document.

- `NotesEmbeddedObject`   This class is used to represent an object that is embedded in a rich text field or directly within a document. Using this method, you can activate the object or execute some specific verb of the object. On Windows, this class supports object linking and embedding (OLE).

- `NotesForm`   The `NotesForm` class enables you to access attributes of the form, such as the fields, the form's name, and the users who are allowed to access the form. These attributes are not tied to any particular document in the database. You can also use the `NotesForm` method called `Remove` to remove a form from a database.

- `NotesInternational`   This class is used to return properties that might vary from one country to another. For example, the currency symbol in the United States is the dollar sign, but in Japan it is the yen sign, and in England it is the pound sign. In addition, different countries use different conventions for date formats, time formats (such as using 24-hour time notation), and even the thousands separator. It is common in some European countries, for example, to use a period separating each group of three digits and a comma to signify a "decimal point." The `NotesInternational` class provides support to handle these country-by-country differences.

- `NotesItem`   The `NotesItem` class represents an item (field) within a document. Each item in the document is a separate `NotesItem`. You can query the field name, type, value(s), and other properties. You can change the value of the item. A `NotesItem` can represent any type of item except a rich text item. Rich text items use the `NotesRichTextItem` class.

- `NotesLog`   The `NotesLog` class is a utility class that can be used to create log entries. If you have ever looked into the Notes Log database, you have seen entries that have been created with this class. You can log events, actions, and errors, as well as query some logging properties.

- `NotesName`   Frequently in Notes you must manipulate names. The `NotesName` class is a welcome addition to help you with these chores. There are usernames, server names, and names within Access Control Lists. Names are also found within groups and are associated with Roles. With the `NotesName` class, you can break a name into its component parts, such as the common name, and organization or organizational units.

- `NotesNewsletter`   The `NotesNewsletter` class represents a document that contains links to other documents. It can be created from a `NotesSession` object. When you create a `NotesNewsletter` object, you pass to it a `NotesDocumentCollection` object containing a collection of documents you want to be linked, and a new `NotesNewsletter` is created with links to each document in the collection. You can also use `NotesNewsletter` to create a rendering (picture) of a single document of a collection.

- `NotesOutline` This class is new in release 5. The `NotesOutline` class represents a control you can provide to users for traversal in your database. Outlines enable you to control the ordering, indentation, and traversal of the outline entries. Each entry represents a navigation destination. This class represents a collection of `NotesOutlineEntry` objects.
- `NotesOutlineEntry` This class is new in release 5. Each `NotesOutlineEntry` represents an item, such as a folder, view, page, frameset, or URL. Each entry controls what happens when a user clicks on the entry and what is displayed, whether the entry is expandable, and so forth.
- `NotesRegistration` This class enables you to manipulate the Domino directories. You can add users and servers, register new users, switch IDs, and cross-certify. This new class has many properties and methods to aid in the development of administration programs or agents.
- `NotesReplication` This class is new in release 5. This class can be used to set replication properties for the database in which the `NotesReplication` object appears. It can be used to set priorities, enable and disable replication, and control truncation of large documents during replication
- `NotesRichTextItem` This class is a special version of the `NotesItem` class. It has methods that are specific to rich text items, such as support for doclinks and embedded objects.
- `NotesRichTextParagraphStyle` This class is new in release 5. This class enables you to control the attributes that relate to an entire paragraph. For example, you can control the margin settings and the spacing above and below the paragraph. You can also control tab settings for the paragraph with this class.
- `NotesRichTextStyle` This class enables you to control the styling of the contents within a rich text field. It enables you to set properties, such as bold, italic, color, and font.
- `NotesRichTextTab` This class is new in release 5. This class enables you to control the position and type (center, decimal, left, or right) of a single tab within a paragraph.
- `NotesSession` The `NotesSession` class, in a sense, is the root class of the major hierarchy. This class represents a user session with Notes. When you create a `NotesSession` object, it is associated with a user Id, so the rights and privileges of that user will be used to access databases, run agents, run scripts, and so forth. The `NotesSession` class can also be used to access the list of Name and Address Books that are being used.
- `NotesTimer` This class enables you to trigger an event at specified fixed intervals. You set the timer interval, and the alarm event will occur each time the interval elapses. The time interval is not guaranteed because of other events that might be happening in the system, so the interval is approximate.
- `NotesView` The `NotesView` class enables you to traverse a view within a Notes database. You can do a full text search, get the first or last documents of the view, and go through

all documents of the view one-by-one. You can also find out information such as the view name and whether the view is the default view.

- `NotesViewColumn` `NotesViewColumn` represents one column of a view. A collection of these kinds of objects is stored in a `NotesView` object. Each column object contains attributes, such as whether the column is sorted, the position within the view, and the associated column formula.

- `NotesViewEntry` This class is new in release 5. This class represents one entry within a view. Among many properties, you can tell whether this entry has an associated document, whether the unread flag is on or off, and the full text search score for the entry.

- `NotesViewEntryCollection` This class is new in release 5. This class represents a collection of `NotesViewEntry` objects. Each of the entries in the collection will refer to a document, never a category or total type item. The list is always sorted.

- `NotesViewNavigator` This class is new in release 5. This class enables you to navigate within a `NotesViewEntryCollection`. You can issue a `GetFirst`, `GetNext`, `GetLast`, `GetNth`, and `GetParent` among several other navigational commands.

The LotusScript:Data Object

The LotusScript:Data Object (LS:DO) is an additional set of three classes that enable you to use Open Database Connectivity (ODBC) to access relational database systems. LS:DO is implemented using LotusScript Extension (LSX) technology.

LSX technology allows Lotus, third parties, or any other programmer to write extensions to the Notes classes. Because LS:DO is implemented using LSX technology, it is not really part of the core set of LotusScript classes. However, because LS:DO can be used almost interchangeably with the other classes, I will introduce them here. These are the classes:

- `ODBCConnection` The `ODBCConnection` class is used to establish a connection from your LotusScript program to a relational database. You must supply a data source and, optionally, a user ID and password. An ODBC connection can use either Auto-commit or transaction mode. You can check whether the underlying database supports transaction mode with the `IsSupported` method call.

- `ODBCQuery` The `ODBCQuery` class is used to store a SQL query, such as `Select * from customers`. You must supply an `ODBCConnection` object and the text string of your query to the `ODBCQuery` object. The query is used to specify which rows within a table are to be selected. The actual execution of the query is performed by the `Execute` method of the `ODBCResultSet`.

- `ODBCResultSet` The `ODBCResultSet` class enables you to execute a query and obtain the result of the query. After you create an `ODBCResultSet` object, you must supply the object with an `ODBCQuery` object, and then you can execute the query, access data, and change data.

Differences Between Java and LotusScript Implementations

I mentioned earlier that there were slight differences in the syntax and usage between the Java and LotusScript implementations of access to the Domino Object Model. The first difference is in the naming conventions of the classes.

In LotusScript, the classes are all named with a `Notes` prefix, as in `NotesSession`, `NotesDatabase`, and so forth. In Java, the classes use the same names, but without the `Notes` prefix. So the Java class `Session` corresponds to the LotusScript class `NotesSession`, and the Java class `Database` corresponds to the LotusScript class `NotesDatabase`. This convention applies to the rest of the class names as well. As mentioned previously, the Java class `AgentContext` contains the methods and properties that apply to agents from the `NotesSession` LotusScript class.

In addition to the class name differences, LotusScript properties and methods have a slightly different usage in Java. The LotusScript methods have Java counterparts, and the only difference might be in the capitalization of the names. LotusScript properties, however, are implemented differently in Java because Java does not have an equivalent properties concept. To simulate properties, the Java implementation of the DOM uses methods with a particular naming convention that will be described shortly.

In LotusScript, properties are implemented as two access subroutines. One subroutine implements a `get` of the property, the other subroutine implements the `set`. These subroutines are both associated with the property name. In LotusScript, the subroutines are implicitly called, and you can just use properties by referring to them.

For example, suppose a class has a property called `Name`, which represents the object's name. To obtain the value of this property, you could specify

```
Variable = MyObject.Name
```

To assign a new value to the property, you could use

```
MyObject.Name = value
```

The result of these two statements will be calls to the `get` and `set` routines for the property. Because Java does not have the property concept, access to properties must be made by explicitly calling the `get` and `set` routines.

The Java routine names for obtaining property values are prefixed by either `get` for generic properties, or `is` for Boolean properties. For example, you will find property access names such as `getUserName`, `getEnvironmentString`, `getFileSize`, `isHidden`, `isResponse`, and `isSorted`. You can tell that each of these is a property access routine by the name prefix.

Java routines to set property values begin with `set`. For example, `setDateTimeValue`, `setValueInteger`, `setReaders`, and `setFormUsers` are all names of routines to set properties within objects.

If you were to guess the Java syntax for the LotusScript examples above, the `get` routine would be

```
Variable = MyObject.getName()
```

To assign a new value to the property in Java, you could use

```
MyObject.setName(value)
```

Just remember that for Boolean values, the access routine typically is prefixed with `is`, not `get`. Here is the pair of calls for the ACL class, for example:

```
boolean = MyACLObject.isUniformAccess()
MyObject.setUniformAccess(boolean)
```

DOMINO OBJECT MODEL (DOM) OBJECTS

In my earlier explanation, I told you that classes are just definitions. They generically describe the characteristics of objects, but they are not actually objects. The difference between classes and objects can be very confusing when you are first learning object-oriented programming, so I have tried to emphasize the difference several times.

If the DOM classes are just definitions, how do you access real databases, documents, forms, and views? The answer is through the use of the DOM objects. These objects are the physical instantiation of the class definitions. That is, they are real objects. An object of a class is sometimes called an *instance* of that class, so *instantiation* just means you are creating an instance of the class. You can query the properties within the objects, and you can call methods and handle events. Variables and objects will be covered in more detail in Chapter 21, "LotusScript Variables and Objects."

You can consider the DOM classes to be like a containment hierarchy. Recall how a house is made up of rooms, and each room is made up of walls, doors, and so forth. The DOM classes are similar. At the top of the containment hierarchy is the `NotesSession` class, and contained within it are the various components of the current session.

SUMMARY

I told you a little about the history of object-oriented programming, and about some of the major concepts. You should understand the distinction between classes and objects. Classes are generic descriptions for all objects of a particular type. For example, the `NotesDatabase` class contains a property called `FileName`. Each object of the `NotesDatabase` class will contain the `FileName` property, but in general, each object will have a different value for this property.

I told you that properties, methods, and events are characteristics of classes. Properties are typically either static attributes or dynamic attributes of the objects of a particular class. Methods are really just another name for subroutines, and they contain the programs that operate on the properties contained within an object. Events are similar to methods, but are typically invoked automatically by the system rather than by program control. The user clicking on a button, for example, triggers an event such as the `Click` event. The event is not called from within the program itself.

I described a little bit of LotusScript as well as Java because the object-oriented concepts apply to both languages. The Domino Object Model (DOM) can be accessed from either language. In addition, I gave you an overview of the architecture for local and remote access to the DOM. The remote access is via CORBA and IIOP, which means that the client can be a Web browser and the Domino server can be connected via the Internet. This is a very powerful client/server model.

I gave you a quick overview of the DOM classes and their functions. In the following chapters, I give you more details on the classes and their usage.

From Here...

To read more about programming Notes and Domino, as well as the Domino Object Model, here are a few suggestions:

- Chapter 21, "LotusScript Variables and Objects," and Chapter 22, "LotusScript Subroutines, Functions, and Event Handlers," cover the LotusScript programming language. These chapters cover the important basics of the syntax and semantics of LotusScript.

- Chapter 23, "Creating and Using Java Applets and Agents," introduces the Java language as well as how to use it to create applets and agents.

- Chapter 25, "The Session and Front-End Classes"; Chapter 26, "Database, View, and Document Classes in LotusScript and Java"; and Chapter 27, "Using Fields and Items in LotusScript and Java," provide detailed information on the usage of the Domino Object Model. Examples are provided using both LotusScript and Java so you can learn a bit about both languages.

CHAPTER 21

LotusScript Variables and Objects

In this chapter, I cover the important aspects of variables, objects, and statements in LotusScript. If you are familiar with another programming language or if you are familiar with a dialect of BASIC, such as one of the versions of Microsoft Visual Basic, this material should be very easy for you. Even so, quickly review the material because you might find some information that's new or useful.

IDENTIFIERS

Identifiers are names you define and give to variables, classes, types, constants, subroutines, and properties in LotusScript. The first character of an identifier must be a letter. Identifiers in LotusScript are not case sensitive, so the initial letter can be in upper- or lowercase.

Identifiers can be up to 40 characters, and after the initial letter, can include any letter, digit, or the underscore (_). There are six data type suffix characters (%, &, !, #, @, and $). These characters will be discussed shortly. They are not included in the length limitation of 40 characters.

Here are some examples of identifiers:

MyName	Valid
myname	Valid—same identifier as first example
First_Name	Valid—contains underscore, which is okay
First1	Valid—begins with letter, contains a digit
My Name	Invalid—contains a space
_MisLeading	Invalid—begins with an underscore
1Time	Invalid—begins with a digit

Some ActiveX classes or external programs can define identifiers that include some characters that are illegal within LotusScript names. To use these names, you must use an escape character, which is the tilde (~) in LotusScript. The tilde must immediately precede the illegal character. For example:

MyVar = ActiveXClass.Go!	Invalid—ends with illegal character
MyVar = ActiveXClass.Go~!	Valid—tilde before illegal character

By preceding the illegal character with a tilde, you allow LotusScript to use the special character as part of the name.

IDENTIFIER SCOPE

Scope does not refer to a telescope, microscope, or even the scope on a rifle. In LotusScript, after you have created an identifier, the scope deals with how widely the identifier is known. With a small scope, the identifier is known only in a limited range, but with a larger scope, the identifier is more widely known and recognized. There are three levels of scope in LotusScript:

- Module scope
- Procedure scope
- Type or class scope

It is quite possible—almost likely—to have two identifiers with the same name. For example, you might have two identifiers called Amount. In this case, the identifier with the smallest or most limited scope is used. This is also sometimes called the innermost scope. Because of this definition, when you have two identifiers with the same name, the outer identifier is no longer accessible. This outer definition, referred to as *shadowed*, cannot be used by the inner program.

One way to visualize this is to think about a set of boxes of different sizes. A very small box is inside a larger one, which is inside a larger one, and so forth. When you refer to a variable in the innermost box, LotusScript will search from the inside outward until it finds a variable with the name you've given.

Because of these naming conflicts, you should carefully choose your identifier names. In fact, it is a good idea to follow naming conventions within all your LotusScript programs. Later, I'll describe some possible naming conventions you could use. In summary, however, good naming conventions allow you to quickly identify the type of the variable, and sometimes its scope as well.

Identifiers declared at the module scope are declared outside any procedure, class, or type definition. They are valid as long as the module is loaded. Procedure scope identifiers are declared within a subroutine (sub), function, or Property Get/Set routine. Identifiers at the type or class scope have meaning only within the definition of the type or class. Here is an example:

```
Dim Variable1 As Integer      '<-This is at module scope
Dim Variable2 As Integer      '<-This is at module scope

Sub Subroutine1               '<-Begins procedure level
Dim Variable1 As String       '<-This is at procedure scope
Dim Variable3 As Integer      '<-This is at procedure scope

Variable1 = "Hello"           '<-Uses procedure scope variable
End Sub                       '<-Ends procedure level
```

Notice that the same variable name (Variable1) is used both inside and outside the subroutine. They can even be declared as different types of variables. The innermost variable is used within the procedure.

Public and Private

Most identifiers can be declared as Public or Private. By default, identifiers are Private within a module, which means they are visible only within that module. Two Private identifiers with the same name but in different modules will not conflict.

Declaring an identifier Public makes it known to other modules. Public scope is also sometimes called global scope, which means that the identifier is known globally to all modules. A conflict will arise if the same Public identifier has been declared in separate modules.

Variables and Constants

Variables are really just programmer-defined names, or identifiers, for areas of the computer's main memory. You can also use named or unnamed constants in your program.

Data Types

Associated with each constant or variable is either an explicit or an implicit data type. The data type defines how the computer should interpret the bits that are stored in memory. Table 21.1 shows the data types allowed by LotusScript, along with the suffix character used for each type and the ranges for the numeric types.

TABLE 21.1   THE DATA TYPES IN LOTUSSCRIPT

Keyword	Suffix	Data Type	Range*
Integer	%	Integer value	−32,768 to 32,767
Long	&	Integer value	−2,147,483,648 to 2,147,483,647
Single	!	Floating-point value	−3.402823E38 to 3.402823E38
Double	#	Floating-point value	−1.7976931348623158E308 to 1.7976931348623158E308
Currency	@	Currency value internal format	−922,337,203,685,477.5808 to 922,337,203,685,477.5807
String Variant	$		Character strings can contain any of the preceding, plus date/time, Boolean, and objects

*Values for UNIX platforms might vary slightly. As you can see from the table, selecting the exact type of data you want can affect the range of values your variable can hold. Integers are stored exactly. Floating-point variables are like scientific notation. That is, they hold two components: a number and an exponent. By using a number and an exponential factor, the range of values that can be stored is much greater. Double-precision stores roughly twice the number of digits for the number, so it has greater accuracy for very large or very small (close to zero) numbers.

This list of suffixes can be applied to variable names or literal constants. For example, 3.7# represents a double-precision constant, whereas 3.7! represents a single-precision version of the same constant. Amount# is a double-precision variable, and Amount! is a single-precision variable with the same name. You cannot use both a single- and double-precision version of the same variable within the same scope.

Variants are a special kind of data type. A *Variant* variable is like a chameleon—it changes its character depending on the circumstance. If you assign an integer value to a Variant, the variable will keep it in its native integer format. If you assign a double variable, it will store the double value. You can also store date/time type values and Boolean (true/false) values. Variants can also store objects and can convert values from one format to another.

The main disadvantage of Variant variables is that because of their flexibility, they are less efficient than the other native variable types. As a general rule, you will get much better performance in terms of both space used and speed if you use a native type. You should use the Variant type sparingly when you really need the flexibility or power of the Variant (for example, when you need to store a date/time value).

Constants

Character string literal constants can be enclosed in one of three sets of delimiters: a pair of quotation marks (" "), a pair of vertical bars (¦ ¦), or an open and close brace ({ }). There are three sets of delimiters so that you can use one pair of symbols within another set. You cannot nest a pair of delimiters within another pair of the same type. If you want to include a character such as double quotation marks in a string, you can use another pair of delimiters for the string. For example, you could use a pair of vertical bars to create a string with an embedded double-quote character. See the second and third examples below.

Here are some examples:

```
"This is a literal string in quotes"
¦This is a string with double quote " embedded¦
{A brace string with a vertical bar ¦ enclosed inside}
```

Numeric constants are normally decimal notation. Integers do not include a decimal point. You can write floating-point constants by including an E, as in 314.159E-02. You can enter binary values by preceding the number with &B, octal with &O, and hexadecimal with &H. Here are some examples:

```
&B10101111
&O7342
&H0B31
```

You can define a named constant with the Const statement. You should always consider using Const statements to give names to specific constants instead of using literal constants within your program. By using named constants, you can easily later change your program by updating the Const statement. This enables you to change your program in only one place rather than searching completely through your source code for numeric or string constants.

Here are some examples:

```
Const dblInterestRate# = 0.075
Const strCompany$ = "First Federal"
Const curBaseAmount@ = 1000.00
```

SCALAR VARIABLES

LotusScript variables are defined with the `Dim` statement. Although you might think that the `Dim` statement is particularly unenlightened (pun intended), `Dim` is short for `dimension`. `Dimension` is a keyword of FORTRAN, and the creators of BASIC abbreviated the word `dimension` to `Dim`. Originally, in FORTRAN, the `dimension` statement was used only to define the size of array variables (which I'll discuss shortly), but in LotusScript the `Dim` statement is used to define not only arrays but all other variables as well.

A *scalar variable* means that the variable contains only a single value. Most variables in your program will be scalar variables. The term is usually used only to distinguish scalar variables from array variables, which can contain multiple values. In this book, I'll normally be discussing scalar variables when I use the plain term *variable*. When I'm referring to array variables, I'll usually just call them *arrays*.

Here are examples of declarations of some variables:

```
Dim intNoteIndex As Integer
Dim curAmount As Currency
Dim dblLoanRate As Double
```

ARRAY VARIABLES

An *array variable* can contain multiple values of the same type. You may have, for example, an `Integer` array, a `Double` array, or a `String` array. To identify a particular value within an array variable, you must specify which of the multiple values you want to access. This is done with an array *index*, or *subscript*. The subscript of an array has a lower bound and an upper bound. The lower bound is zero by default.

When you define the array variable with the `Dim` statement, you can either specify fixed dimensions that will not change or indicate a dynamic array. Memory for a dynamic array is allocated with the `ReDim` statement.

Following are some examples of array declarations:

```
Dim intValues(10) As Integer
Dim strNames(5,20) As String
Dim dblRates(1980 to 1999) As Double
Redim intVar(10) As Integer
Redim strAddrs(3,15) As String
```

In the first example, an integer array is defined with a lower bound of 0 and an upper bound of 10. Contrary to appearances, this actually means that 11 items are defined for this array. The second example shows a two-dimensional array. You can have up to eight dimensions. Again, the lower bound is assumed to be 0, so there are actually 6 times 21, or 126, elements in the array, not 100.

You can change the assumed lower bound for all arrays in a module with the `Option Base` statement. You can have only one `Option Base` statement within a module, and it must precede all array declarations. This is the format for the statement:

```
Option Base 0
```

or

```
Option Base 1
```

You can specify only values `0` or `1` in the `Option Base` statement.

You can also explicitly set a lower bound for an array, as shown earlier in the third example. In that case, the subscript for `dblRates` can be values from `1980` to `1999`, which might represent calendar years.

Values for subscripts must be between –32,768 and +32,767, inclusive. You are limited to a maximum of eight dimensions.

List Variables

A list variable is very similar to a one-dimensional array. A list can hold only values of the same type, but when you declare it, you do not need to specify the number of elements in the list. The list will grow or shrink automatically as items are added or removed.

The major benefit of a list is that you can use a `String` value rather than a subscript to access the elements of the list. This value, called a list tag, can be case sensitive or not case sensitive, depending on the setting of the `Option Compare` statement. The default is to use case sensitive comparisons. For example:

```
Dim strDictionary List as String
strDictionary("Lime") = "A Green fruit"
strDictionary("Plum") = "A Purple fruit"
strDictionary("Banana") = "A Yellow fruit"
strDictionary("Lotus") = "A Yellow computer company"
strDictionary("IBM") = "A Blue computer company"
strDictionary("Apple") = "A Red fruit or a rainbow computer company"
```

Notice that you can add values to the list with an assignment statement. To delete items, you can use the `Erase` statement, like so:

```
Erase strDictionary("Plum")      ' Erases one item
Erase strDictionary              ' Erases the whole list
```

User-Defined Type Variables

`Array` and `List` variables enable you to have a homogeneous collection of values of the same type. What if you want to give a name to a group of variables of different types? In this case, you could create your own type with the `Type` statement.

The `Type` statement can occur only at the module level and can be optionally prefixed with either a `Public` or a `Private` modifier. As an example, see Listing 21.1, which contains a type definition and two instances of `PersonType` variables.

LISTING 21.1 `PersonType` DEFINITION

```
Type PersonType
    m_strFirstName As String
    m_strLastName As String
    m_curSalary As Currency
End Type

Dim Person1 as PersonType, Person2 as PersonType
Person1.m_strFirstName = "Janet"
Person1.m_strLastName = "Trujillo"
Person1.m_curSalary = 55000.00

Person2.m_strFirstName = "John"
Person2.m_strLastName = "Hashimoto"
Person2.m_curSalary = 50000.00
```

If the member names of the `PersonType` data structure look odd to you, you can refer to the later section "Naming Conventions." In short, the m_ is used to signify that the variable is a member variable, and the three-letter prefix to the variable name indicates its type.

Variable Lifetimes

In addition to characteristics such as scope and data type, variables have a lifetime. The lifetime of a variable is related to its scope. Module scope variables are created when the module is loaded, and they retain their values while the module is active.

Procedure scope variables are normally created when the procedure is entered and are destroyed when control leaves the procedure. The exception to this rule is for variables that have been declared with the `Static` keyword. The keyword `Static` can be used only with procedure scope variables (not module or class scope). With `Static` variables, the value of the variable is saved between calls of the procedure. You can use this type of variable to store status information. For example, you could keep a count of how many times a subroutine has been called. This would be impossible with a regular variable.

Class scope variables have a programmer-defined lifetime. You create an object of a particular class with the `New` keyword. After it has been created, you can use the `Delete` statement to delete the object. An object variable is also deleted if control leaves the variable's scope.

Implicit Declaration

You can implicitly declare variables by just using them within a program. If you use a data-type-modifier suffix on the variable (such as #, $, !, %, @, or &), you must use that modifier every time the variable is used. If you do not use the type modifier, you cannot subsequently use one on a later reference to the same variable.

If you do not supply a type modifier, the variable will be a `Variant` type by default. A `Variant` variable is less efficient than a variable that you have declared to be of a particular type.

You can also control the implicit type of variables by using one of the `Deftype` statements. There are seven `Deftype` statements:

DefCur	Currency
DefDbl	Double
DefInt	Integer
DefLng	Long
DefSng	Single
DefStr	String
DefVar	Variant

Each of these statements has the same format. After the keyword, you supply one or more ranges of letters to be used. For example:

```
DefDbl A-H,O-Z
```

The preceding statement defines all variables that begin with any letter from *A* to *H* or from *O* to *Z* to be `Double` variables. `Deftype` statements must appear at the module level and will apply to all procedures and variables within the module. Any variable or procedure that is explicitly declared with a data type will use the explicitly defined data type rather than the default type for that letter.

> **Tip**
>
> Although the LotusScript language enables you to implicitly define variables, it is considered very poor programming style to use this feature. In general, variables should *always* be explicitly declared. The use of implicit variables makes it extremely easy to allow variables with misspellings to go unnoticed. In turn, these misspelled variables can cause your program to exhibit very strange behavior and will be very difficult to debug. You can turn off the implicit variable capability through the use of the `Option Declare` statement, which forces undeclared variables to generate a syntax error.

LOTUSSCRIPT LIMITATIONS

As in most programming systems, LotusScript has various size limitations in its implementation. LotusScript 4.0 (which is included with Notes/Domino 5.0) has greatly increased the size limitations. Table 21.2 lists the new maximums.

TABLE 21.2   LOTUSSCRIPT IMPLEMENTATION LIMIT IMPROVEMENTS

Type	Maximum
Number of strings	Limited by available memory
Total string storage	Limited by available memory
Length of string literal	16,267 characters (32,534 bytes)
Length of string value	2GB bytes
Total module string literals	2GB bytes

continues

TABLE 21.2 CONTINUED

Type	Maximum
Total size of an array	Limited by available memory*
Number of array dimensions	8
Dimension bounds	–32,768 to 32,767
Fixed-size data items with module scope	64KB bytes*
Number of source code lines per script	64KB lines
Number of symbols per module	64KB
Total module scope storage	Limited by available memory
Total class scope storage	64KB bytes
Total procedure scope storage	32KB bytes

Fixed-size arrays with module scope are limited to 64KB bytes.

Classes and Objects

In the preceding chapter, I discussed classes and objects. I introduced you to the class definitions for Lotus Notes. Most of your programming will involve the use of the Notes classes. In addition to the built-in classes, however, you can define your own classes and objects. Remember, the Class statement, like the Type statement, defines the class itself. The Class statement does not actually create any objects of the class.

The Class statement can be used only at the module level and cannot be used within a procedure or within another class.

Creating Classes

You create a class by using the Class and End Class keywords. Between them, you can define member variables and methods. To see an example, look through Listing 21.2.

LISTING 21.2 PersonClass **DEFINITION**

```
1    Class PersonClass
2       ' Member Variables
3       m_strFirstName As String
4       m_strLastName As String
5       m_curSalary As Currency
6
7       Sub New(strFirst As String, strLast As String, curSalary As Currency)
8          m_strFirstName = strFirst
9          m_strLastName = strLast
10         m_curSalary = curSalary
11      End Sub
```

```
12
13     Function FullName As String
14         FullName = Me.m_strFirstName + " " + Me.m_strLastName
15     End Function
16  End Class
```

In Listing 21.2, you'll notice a distinct similarity to Listing 21.1, which was a type definition for a person. You can now see that when you use a type definition as in Listing 21.1, you cannot define any methods. With a class definition, as in Listing 21.2, you can define methods, or operations on the data.

Referring to Listing 21.2, lines 2–5 represent the member variable declarations. Lines 7–11 are the New subroutine. This subroutine will be invoked when a new instance of a PersonClass object is created. Three parameters must be passed to the New method: the first name, last name, and salary. The method just fills in the member variables with the information.

Lines 13–15 are the FullName method. This method enables you to extract the full name, including first and last names, from the object formatted with one space between the names. Notice that the keyword Me is used to refer to the current object. This enables the same code within the class to be used, regardless of the name of the object that has been created.

CREATING OBJECTS

You create new objects by using the New keyword on the Dim statement or by using the Set statement. To create variables of the PersonType class defined previously, and then display the full name, you could use the following:

```
Dim person1 As New PersonClass("Sam", "Smith", 5000000)
Dim person2 As New PersonClass("John", "Jones", 500000)

Dim person3 As PersonClass
Set person3 = New PersonClass("Joan", "Johnson", 200000)

Messagebox person1.FullName
Messagebox person2.FullName
Messagebox person3.FullName
```

In this example, the first two statements declare, allocate PersonClass objects, and assign them to the object variables. In the third example, the Dim statement defines the type of variable, but does not allocate any storage for the variable. The storage is allocated by using the New keyword in a Set statement. You can use either method to allocate and initialize the storage for the object.

ASSIGNING OBJECTS

Although objects sometimes appear to be very similar to regular variables, there is one major difference that easily confuses novice LotusScript programmers. This aspect is very basic and occurs throughout LotusScript, so you should become very familiar with it.

This major difference between regular variables and objects is with the assignment statement. With regular variables, you use the `Let` statement, but with objects you use the `Set` statement. They appear very similar:

```
Let variable = expression
```

or

```
variable = expression
Set object1 = object2
```

or

```
Set object  = New classname(argList)
```

You should also be aware that the `Let` is optional and normally is not included in most programs.

If you do not include the `Set` keyword when assigning an object variable, you get an error message.

Much Ado About Nothing

There are three special values in LotusScript. They all have names that sound similar in purpose, so it is easy to get confused about them. These special values are `EMPTY`, `NOTHING`, and `NULL`.

Remarkable as it seems, the three values can be used to represent related concepts. The first value, `EMPTY`, is the initial value for `Variant` variables. If you declare a `Variant` variable and have not yet assigned it a value, it will be `EMPTY`. This type of value is pretty harmless because you can convert it to a string or number—in which case, it will just be the empty string or a zero value. Either of these values can then be used normally in operations, such as concatenation or arithmetic. After the `Variant` variable has a value, it will no longer be `EMPTY`. You can test to see whether a value is `EMPTY` with the `IsEmpty` function.

The second value, `NOTHING`, is used for object reference variables. Object reference variables are declared to be of a particular class, such as `NotesSession`. For example, suppose you declare a variable to be a `NotesSession` object or a `NotesDatabase` object. This kind of variable, before it is initialized with a real object, contains the value `NOTHING`. Remember, you will assign a value to this type of variable with the `New` keyword or by the `Set` statement.

If you allocate an object variable with the `New` keyword and then later delete the object with the `Delete` statement, the value of the object variable reverts to `NOTHING`.

Here is an example:

```
Dim session as NotesSession
Messagebox session.UserName
```

Notice in the preceding example that I did not include the `New` keyword before the class name `NotesSession`. I have declared a `NotesSession` variable, but I have not initialized it.

When the second line is executed, attempting to refer to the UserName property, I will get an error message saying `Object variable not set`. Although this error message does not tell you the variable name, remember that it just means you have not yet initialized some object variable within the statement.

The final value, NULL, really represents a situation that has arisen during execution rather than an initial value. It can indicate an error situation, and it sometimes represents missing data. If you are familiar with relational database systems, this NULL is analogous to a NULL value that the database system might return to you as a result of a query.

The value NULL is used because in some cases you want to distinguish between "no value" and, for example, a zero value. Suppose you are trying to retrieve the salary information for an employee. You really need to differentiate between NULL, which means the data is not in the database, and zero, which means that the salary is in the database but the employee is really a poorly paid individual.

So NULL will typically be the result of some query or request, and it indicates that no value is available. This really is different from EMPTY, which just means we haven't yet asked the question.

You probably now know more about NOTHING than you ever wanted to know, and although you understand the distinctions now, by next week, it will be NULL in your brain again. Just remember that you can look it up here in the book again when you need it next. Don't try to fill your brain with EMPTY concepts.

Naming Conventions

You have seen several cases of what might appear to be strange names for variables and member names. If you have been programming for only a short time, you might never have seen prefixes to variable names. If you are a seasoned Windows programmer, you might already be familiar with naming conventions commonly used for Windows programs.

The major advantage to using a naming convention such as the one employed in the previous examples is that it enables you, the programmer, to view parts of a program, sometimes out of context, and to know more information that might otherwise be available. For example, suppose you were to see just the following single statement:

```
m_strFirstName  = strFirst
```

Even though you don't have access to any of the declarations, you might be able to guess that both of these variables are string variables. You can guess this because each has a str prefix. This is important information. In addition, because of the m_ that appears before the first name, you can gather that the first variable is a member variable of some class. In essence, the assignment statement is copying a value from outside the class into a member variable of the class. You can make these observations without even referring to the variable names themselves. When you also include meaningful names such as FirstName, you can almost complete the picture.

In using LotusScript, you can abbreviate the built-in data types with the following prefixes:

Integer	int
Long	lng
Single	sng
Double	dbl
String	str
Currency	cur
Variant	var

In addition, it is a good idea to develop conventions for common user interface elements. For example:

Text field	txt
Numeric field	n
Rich text	rt
Button	btn

For objects created from the Notes classes, you can use the following object names (not prefixes):

NotesACL	acl
NotesDatabase	db
NotesDbDirectory	dbdir
NotesDocument	doc
NotesItem	item
NotesRichTextItem	rtitem
NotesSession	session
NotesUIWorkspace	uiws, or ws
NotesUIDocument	uidoc
NotesView	view
NotesViewColumn	column

By using a consistent set of names, you will make it easier to write, maintain, and debug your LotusScript programs. You can also use prefix modifiers to identify the following characteristics:

Static	s_
Public	g_ (for global)
Array	a
List	l

As I mentioned, these prefixes are just suggestions you can use as a starting point for a discussion of your own naming conventions. The actual letters you choose are not as critical as having a naming convention in the first place. As your library of programs grows, you will be very thankful if you have a naming convention. If you don't have one by the time your library gets large, *it will be too late to go back and implement one*. Start early with your naming convention, and stick with it.

LotusScript Statements

A LotusScript program consists of several lines of text. Each line of text can contain a part of a statement, one statement, or more than one statement. In most cases, your programs will have one statement per line.

You can continue statements by using the continuation character, the underscore (_). The continuation character must be preceded by at least one space or tab so that it is not confused with part of a variable name or another item on the line.

You can put multiple statements on a single line by separating them with the colon character (:). You can also have lines that are completely blank, which aids in readability, particularly within comments or between code sections.

If you do not end the line with the continuation character, the end of the line will be interpreted as the end of the statement.

Here are some examples:

```
Dim dblDip As Double    ' Ice cream with two scoops
Static sintCounter _    ' Continued
    As Integer          ' On the second line
intX = 0 : intY = 0 : intZ = 0  ' Three statements on a line
```

Comments

Comments are one of the most important aspects of your program, so you should liberally include comments. The easiest way to include comments is to use a single-quotation mark, or apostrophe ('). The apostrophe indicates that the rest of the line is a comment. If the apostrophe is the first nonblank character on the line, the entire line is a comment.

In addition to the apostrophe, you can create comments by using the older Rem statement. Following the Rem, you can include any text. All characters following the Rem are considered a remark and are ignored by LotusScript. You cannot continue a Rem statement with the continuation character.

Another way to include comments is to use the %Rem and %End Rem directives. You can initiate comments with %Rem. All lines following this line up to the %End Rem are ignored. You can end the set of comments with either %End Rem (with a space) or %EndRem (all one word). This method is useful for very long sequences of comments.

Here are some examples:

```
' This is a single-line apostrophe comment
Dim intSheepCount as Integer   ' Counter for insomniacs.
Rem This is a remarkable single-line comment
%Rem
Here are several remarkable lines.
These comments will not be used by LotusScript.
You should include meaningful information here.
%End Rem
```

Structured Programming

In the 1970s and perhaps even into the 1980s, there was a lot of interest in a concept called structured programming. Scholarly research was done, papers were presented, and of course many books were published on the topic. The interest in structured programming seems to have died down now—which is too bad, because there were several important core concepts in structured programming. These concepts are important because they provide a framework for organizing programs and thinking about how programs should flow.

The essence of structured programming is that the control flow of a program is important, and we should try to simplify the flow so that people reading the program can easily grasp it. I mention this because the original BASIC language was one of the early offenders and made it particularly difficult to simplify flow control.

Structured programming basically says that you should use only three types of flow control in your program:

- Sequential
- Selection
- Repetition

In particular, the structured programming advocates were opposed to "spaghetti" code, in which control would flow like strands of spaghetti, all over the place.

I'll use the three categories of flow control to organize my discussion of the LotusScript flow-control statements.

Sequential Flow Control

Sequential flow control is the easiest type of flow control. It is the default for LotusScript and most other programming languages. Sequential flow just means that after one statement has been executed, the next statement in sequence is executed.

Here is an example of sequential flow control:

```
Dim dblAmt1 as Double
Dim dblAmt2 as Double
Dim dblSum as Double
dblAmt1 = 5.2
dblAmt2 = 7.0
dblSum = dblAmt1 + dblAmt2
```

In this example, the three assignment statements are executed sequentially.

Selection Flow Control

Selection flow control means that when control reaches a particular point in the program, one of a set of alternatives is selected. You can control which of the alternatives is selected by testing a condition or evaluating an expression. The If-Then-Else and Select Case statements are examples of selection flow control.

If-Then-Else

There are two versions of the If-Then-Else statement. The first version must all fit on a single line. To use this format you would specify this:

```
If condition Then statement1 Else statement2
```

The condition is tested; *statement1* is executed if the condition is true, and *statement2* is executed otherwise. You cannot continue this statement on multiple lines. If you need to use multiple lines, you must use the If-Then-ElseIf statement. Following is an example:

```
If condition then
   ... statements
[ElseIf condition then
   ... statements]
   ...
[Else
   ... statements]
End If
```

In the preceding example, the optional parts are shown in square brackets. Each condition is sequentially tested, and when a condition is found to be true, the Then clause is executed. If no condition is found to be true, the Else clause is executed. Notice that you do not need to have an ElseIf clause or even an Else clause. Without these parts, the statement just conditionally executes the Then clause.

Select Case

The Select Case statement also implements the selection flow control. With this statement, an expression is evaluated, and the resulting expression is used to determine which of the groups of statements is executed. It is possible that the expression does not satisfy any of the statement groups, in which case the entire statement is just skipped. If more than one condition matches, only the first group is executed, and all other groups are ignored. Here is the syntax:

```
Select Case SelectExpression
   [Case conditionList
      [Statements]]
   [Case conditionList
      [Statements]]
   ...
   [Case Else
      [Statements]]
End Select
```

The *SelectExpression* is evaluated only once, and the value is saved. This value is tested in sequence against each of the conditions. For each Case, a *conditionList* is a list of conditions, separated by commas. Each condition within the list is tested against the saved value. If the test results in TRUE, the associated group of statements is executed.

Each condition can be in one of three formats:

- `ConditionalExpression` This is any expression. This expression is tested against the `SelectExpression` and results in `TRUE` if they match.

- `Expr1 To Expr2` This is a range. The test results in `TRUE` if the `SelectExpression` falls within the range. The range includes both the start and the end values.

- `Is CompareOperator Expression` The `CompareOperator` can be one of the following: <, <=, =<, =, =>,>=,>, <>, or><. For example, you might use `Is> 3`.

Example:

```
Select Case intYear
Case Is < 1970
   Print "Hippie"
Case 1971 To 1980
   Print "Yuppie"
Case 1981 To 1990
   Print "Generation X"
Case Else
   Print "Baby Echo Boom"
End Select
```

In this example, the variable `intYear` is examined. If it is less than `1970`, `"Hippie"` is printed, if it is from `1971` through `1980`, `"Yuppie"` is printed. If it is from `1981` through `1990`, `"Generation X"` is printed; otherwise, `"Baby Echo Boom"` is printed.

REPETITION FLOW CONTROL

Repetition is the third and final construct of structured programming. Typically, this construct is used to operate with a set of data in which each element of the set must be handled or processed. A loop consists of two things: a test to see whether the loop has finished, and the processing of one element of the set of data. The loop is repeated until the test that signifies the end of the loop has been satisfied.

The loop-ending test can be at the start or end of the loop, and it can consist of a counter for a fixed number of repetitions, or some condition such as whether a given value is greater or less than some limit.

LotusScript has four primary repetition constructs: `For/Next`, `ForAll/End ForAll`, `While/Wend`, and `Do While¦Until/Loop`. Each of these constructs consists of a beginning statement and a statement to mark the end of the loop. Each statement between the start and the end is repeated until the ending condition has been met.

For/Next Statements

The `For/Next` pair is typically used when you know how many iterations or repetitions should be performed. The syntax is as follows:

```
For counter = first To last [Step increment]
   [... Statements]
Next counter
```

In this syntax, *counter* represents a numeric variable. *first*, *last*, and *increment* represent numeric expressions. These expressions can be positive or negative. If *increment* is omitted, it is assumed to be 1.

Execution of the `For/Next` loop proceeds as detailed here:

1. The counter variable is initialized to the first value.

    Steps 2, 3, and 4 are repeated until the loop terminates in step 2.

2. If the counter is greater than *last* (and *increment* is positive), the loop is terminated. The loop also terminates if the counter is less than *last* and *increment* is negative. If the loop is terminated, execution continues with the statement after the `Next` statement.

3. If the loop does not terminate, the statements within the loop between the `For` and `Next` statements are executed normally. The counter variable can be referenced within the loop.

4. The increment is added to the counter variable.

You can leave the loop early with either an `Exit For` statement or a `GoTo` statement. An `Exit For` statement resumes execution immediately after the `Next` statement, and the `GoTo` transfers control to the specified label. The `GoTo` statement and labels are covered shortly. Here is an example:

```
Dim aintCountDown(10) As Integer
Dim I As Integer

For I=0 to 10
   aintCountDown(I) = 10 - I      ' 10, 9, 8, ...
Next I
Print "Blastoff"
```

This example fills in the eleven elements of the array with the values 10, 9, 8, and so forth down to zero, and then prints `"Blastoff"`. Notice the prefix `aint` means array of integers.

ForAll/End ForAll Statements

The `ForAll` statement is very useful when you have a collection but don't know how many items are contained in the collection. The `ForAll` statement essentially says to loop through the collection, exactly once for each item. Here is the syntax:

```
ForAll itemvariable in container
   [... Statements]
End ForAll
```

The container variable can be an array, a list, or a collection class object. Execution of the `ForAll/End ForAll` loop proceeds as explained here:

1. The *itemvariable* variable is initialized to the first item in the collection. This variable must *not* be declared with a `Dim` statement. The `ForAll` statement itself acts as the definition of the *itemvariable*. If you separately `Dim` this variable, you will get an error message. If the collection is empty, the rest of the loop is skipped.

   Steps 2 and 3 are repeated until the loop terminates in step 3.

2. If the loop does not terminate, the statements within the loop between the `ForAll` and the `End ForAll` statements are executed normally. The *itemvariable* variable can be referenced within the loop and represents the current item from the collection.

3. The next item from the collection is selected and placed into the *itemvariable* variable. If there are no more items, the loop terminates.

You can leave the loop early with either an `Exit ForAll` statement or a `GoTo` statement. An `Exit ForAll` statement resumes execution immediately after the `End ForAll` statement, and the `GoTo` transfers control to the specified label.

Here is an example that prints the name of each item (field) stored within a document.

```
Dim doc as NotesDocument

REM Set doc to the document you want to inspect...

ForAll I in doc.Items
   MsgBox "Field: " + I.Name
End ForAll
```

Note that the container must be an array, list, or collection within LotusScript. The `Items` property of a `NotesDocument` is an example. Some objects in the Domino Object Model seem like they would be collections, but they are not. For example, the `NotesDocumentCollection` class has its own methods, such as `GetFirstDocument` and `GetNextDocument`, for traversing the collection, and you cannot use `ForAll` with this type of object.

While/Wend STATEMENTS

The `While` statement is used when you want some condition to terminate the loop. This is the classic looping construct of structured programming. Here is the syntax:

```
While condition
  [... Statements]
Wend
```

Execution of the `While/Wend` loop proceeds in the following way:

1. The *condition* is tested before the statements in the loop are executed. If the condition is `TRUE`, the statements are executed. If the condition is `FALSE`, the rest of the loop is skipped. Execution continues with the statement after the `Wend`. It is possible that the statements within the loop will not be executed even once.

   Steps 1 and 2 are repeated until the loop terminates in step 1.

2. If the loop does not terminate, the statements within the loop between the While and the Wend statements are executed normally.

There is no version of the Exit statement to leave the While/Wend loop early and continue execution just beyond the Wend. If you want to do this, use the Do While loop described in the following section. You can use Exit Function or Exit Sub to leave the routine entirely, or you can leave the loop with a GoTo statement, which transfers control to the specified label.

Do While, Do Until, AND Loop STATEMENTS

The Do statement is a very general version of the While/Wend construct described previously. The Do statement is designed to execute a group of statements while a given condition is true, or while a given condition is false. There are two versions of the Do statement.

Here is the syntax of the first version:

```
Do [While ¦ Until condition]
   [... Statements]
Loop
```

And here is the syntax of the second version:

```
Do
   [... Statements]
Loop [While ¦ Until condition]
```

Execution of the Do statement proceeds as explained in the following paragraphs.

In version 1 of the syntax, the conditional test is performed before the loop. This means that the loop might be executed zero times. In version 2 of the syntax, the condition is tested following the statements within the loop, so the statements are executed at least once.

When the While clause is used, the statements within the loop are executed repeatedly while the condition is true. To use this case, you should set up the clause so that the condition is normally TRUE, and as soon as the condition is FALSE, the loop will terminate. For example, if you are using a counter and limit, you should use something like the following as a condition:

```
Do While counter < limit
  ' Perform operation on one element
  ' You can have multiple statements
Loop
```

If you use the Until clause, the loop is executed repeatedly while the condition is FALSE. It terminates as soon as the condition becomes TRUE, so you should set your condition to be normally FALSE. As an example, you could use this:

```
Do
    ' Search for a Needle, one at a time
    ' We assume that we know the needle is in the haystack.
Loop Until Needle=Haystack(item)    ' We found the needle
' Now, we know that we found the needle
```

The GoTo Statement and Labels

The `GoTo` statement is the black sheep of the flow control family. In the late 1970s, the rage in intellectual circles was to talk about `GoTo`-less programming. There were scholarly papers on how to transform a spaghetti program full of `GoTos` to one without any. There were even mathematical proofs that this was always possible. Many people even assumed that it was always desirable.

Well, we're here 20 years later, and we still have `GoTo` statements. I think that's because they are still useful, when used carefully, 20 years later. The syntax is simple:

```
GoTo label
```

`label` represents a label on a statement. You can label any statement by prefixing the statement with an identifier and a colon (:). This is the syntax for a label:

```
labelIdentifier: [statement]
```

A label can appear only at the beginning of a line, and there can be only one label per line. You can have more than one label for a particular statement, but the labels must be on separate lines. You cannot use the same label on more than one line in the same procedure.

Here is an example:

```
Do While counter < limit
    ' Access data
    If (data> maximum) Then Goto OutOfBounds
    ' Process normally
Loop
GoTo Contin
OutOfBounds:
    ' Handle error situation
Contin:
    ' Continue here
```

In this example, we use a `While` loop. Each time through the loop, we do a validity check on the data. If there is something wrong with the data, we do not want to continue processing. In this case, we go to the `OutOfBounds` label. After handling the error, we continue processing.

Summary

In this chapter, we covered a lot of ground. I showed you the rules for identifier names. I showed you how to create various kinds of variables and told you about variable lifetimes and scope. I covered classes and objects, as well as naming conventions for your variables. I strongly encouraged you to work with others to develop a naming convention for your company. Having such a convention is important when you are first starting out, because it will be very, very difficult to develop after you have implemented many applications.

I covered the core LotusScript statements, including variable declarations, comments, and flow of control statements. The three groups for flow of control are sequential, selection, and repetition. I gave specific examples of statements in each of these categories.

FROM HERE...

Here are some additional chapters you can read to learn more about programming Notes and Domino:

- Chapter 22, "LotusScript Subroutines, Functions, and Event Handlers," tells you more about how to segment your program, as well as describing some of the built-in subroutines and functions of LotusScript.
- Chapter 23, "Creating and Using Java Applets and Agents," gives you an introduction to the Java language and shows you how to use it with Notes and Domino.
- Chapter 25, "The Session and Front-End Classes"; Chapter 26, "Database, View, and Document Classes in LotusScript and Java"; and Chapter 27, "Using Fields and Items in LotusScript and Java," cover the Domino Object Model. These chapters start from the top of the class hierarchy and traverse down to the elementary level of fields and items within a Domino document.

CHAPTER 22

LotusScript Subroutines, Functions, and Event Handlers

In this chapter, I cover the various ways you can create and use subprograms in LotusScript. Subroutines are an important building block in LotusScript that enable you to modularize your program. LotusScript also includes several built-in functions that implement common functions that many programs need. I cover two of the most important areas in this chapter: string handling and file input/output (I/O).

Here are some of the highlights of this chapter:

- How to decide what to put into subroutines
- The different kinds of procedures: `Subs`, functions, `Property Get/Set` routines, and event handlers
- Characters, codes, and fonts
- General string handling
- File input and output in LotusScript

The Purpose of Procedures

Before we get into the details and syntax of procedures, I thought it would be helpful to reflect on where and why you should use them. I use the words *procedure* or *subroutine* here to refer generally to all the types of subprograms you can use in LotusScript. In LotusScript, you can use `Subs` (subroutines), functions, methods (subroutines in classes), events (event handlers in classes), and `Property Get/Set` routines (property access within classes). Not only are there various types, but each has a different purpose and context.

Of course, you use subroutines to modularize your program, but what criteria do you use to decide how to divide a program into parts? This is one of those areas that is a little subjective and depends a lot on your programming experience. Computer science research has been done on just what makes a "good" subroutine and what doesn't, but one important criterion is something called coherence. Coherence just means that all the elements of the subroutine are related and belong together.

Breaking Up Is Hard to Do

It might be easier to examine something that isn't coherent. Suppose you know that you need to write a program to accomplish a task. You sit down and start writing lines of code. You later discover that the module is too big and decide you must break it into smaller pieces. One way to do this is just to split the module in half. The first half of the statements go into one subroutine, the second half of them go in another, and you create a third routine that just sequentially calls the first and then calls the second. What's wrong with this scenario?

Well, first of all, I know you probably wouldn't write a program like that—it was just an example. The reason why the first and second subroutines are not coherent is that the lines within them don't necessarily have a common theme or purpose. The only thing they have in common is the fact that the lines that make them up were near each other before the split.

Coherence has to do with purpose. Another way to think about this subject is to look at the variables that are referenced. In our example here, it is very likely that some variables that are used in the first subroutine are also used in the second. To make them generally available to both routines, you have to place the variables in some global location so that both routines can use the variables.

In general, global variables are a bad idea, and you should avoid using them whenever possible. Using global variables is a bad idea because the number of possible routines that can modify the variables is large. A bug in one area of a program can have a ripple effect to a completely independent and unsuspecting part of the program. Frequently, the effects of a bug will show up only in an area of the program that has nothing to do with the cause. Global variables contribute to this kind of problem.

COHERENCE AND CLASSES

Well, you now have an example of what is not coherent. What *is* an example of coherence? Classes. Remember that classes combine both variables and methods. This combination greatly contributes to coherence because the variables needed are localized to the object. The need to store variables outside the object is greatly reduced, and, in turn, this makes debugging easier and programs more reliable because there are fewer global variables.

I conclude this section with a recap of my recommendations. A subroutine should have a well-defined purpose; it shouldn't be just a collection of program statements. You should use local variables and avoid global (`Public`) variables. You should declare and use classes and objects because this technique automatically helps you create more modular, coherent subroutines.

DIFFERENT TYPES OF PROCEDURES

Several types of procedures are available in LotusScript. The following subsections describe these various types.

Sub STATEMENT

The first type of subroutine uses the `Sub` statement. The syntax is as follows:

```
[Static] [Public ¦ Private] Sub Subname[([ParamList])]
    [... Statements]
End Sub
```

You can usually type the word `Sub`, followed by a name in most contexts in the Design Pane, and a new subroutine is created for you. If you specify `Static`, all the subroutine's local variables are saved between calls. When you specify `Public`, the name of the subroutine is known outside the current scope and is available to other modules.

The `ParamList` is a list of parameter declarations, separated by commas, to be passed to the subroutine. Each parameter within the list can be of the following form:

`[ByVal] parameter [() | List] [As type]`

If the `ByVal` keyword is used, the parameter is passed by value, which means that the value used by the subroutine is a copy of the original variable. Without this keyword, the parameter is a reference to the calling program's variable. (The topics of call by value with the `ByVal` keyword and by reference are discussed in detail later in this chapter.) `parameter` represents a programmer-supplied identifier. To specify an array, use (), and to specify a list, use the keyword `List`. The `As type` modifier at the end can be used to specify the data type of the parameter if a data type suffix is not used.

If the subroutine is defined within a class, it is also sometimes called a class method. A subroutine in module is private by default, whereas a class subroutine is public by default.

A subroutine exits and returns to the caller if control reaches the `End Sub` statement. You can also exit a subroutine with the `Exit Sub` statement before reaching the `End Sub` statement. Here is an example of the use of the `End Sub` statement:

```
Sub Caller
    Dim intVar as Integer       intVar = 3              ' Assign a value prior to call
    Call Incr(intVar)           ' Call the subroutine
    Print intVar        ' intVar now has a value of 4
End Sub

Sub Incr(intParam as Integer)
    intParam = intParam + 1     ' Increment the calling program's variable
End Sub
```

In this example, the name of the calling subroutine is `Caller`, and the called subroutine is `Incr`, which is short for increment. `intVar` is defined in the calling program and `intParam` is the name of the `Integer` parameter. The subroutine uses call by reference (the default), so the calling routine's variable is updated when this subroutine is called. See the section titled "Passing Arguments by Value or Reference," later in this chapter, for more details.

Function STATEMENT

A function is a special kind of subroutine. The purpose of a function is to compute and return a value. The type of the answer value is commonly a numeric value, but it can be any scalar data type, a variant, or a class. To return a value to the calling program, use a function. A subroutine does not return a value.

There are several built-in mathematical functions, such as `Sin` (sine), `Tan` (tangent), or `Sqr` (square root). There are also several string functions that return string values, such as `Mid$` (extract substring), `Left$` (extract leftmost substring), or `Right$` (extract rightmost substring). Some built-in functions return Boolean or true/false values. Examples of these functions are `IsDate` (test whether an expression is a date), `IsEmpty` (test whether an expression is `EMPTY`), or `IsNull` (test whether an expression is `NULL`).

Some LotusScript classes for Notes return class objects. For example, within the `NotesSession` class, you can use the `GetDatabase` function to return a `NotesDatabase` object. You can use the `GetDbDirectory` method to return a `NotesDbDirectory` object.

The syntax of the `Function` statement is as follows:

```
[Static] [Public ¦ Private] Function Functionname[([ParamList])] [As returnType]
    [... Statements]
End Function
```

You can usually type the word `Function`, followed by a name in most contexts in the Design Pane, and a new function is created for you. If you specify `Static`, all the function's local variables are saved between calls. When you specify `Public`, the name of the function is known outside the current scope and is available to other modules.

The `returnType` is the data type of the value to be returned by the function. It can be a built-in type, a variant, or a class. In particular, it cannot be a user-defined type that has been declared with the `Type` statement. If you need this type of functionality, use a class instead.

The `ParamList` is a list of parameter declarations, separated by commas, to be passed to the function. Each parameter within the list can be of this form:

```
[ByVal] parameter [() ¦ List] [As type]
```

If the `ByVal` keyword is used, the parameter is passed by value, which means that the value used by the function is a copy of the original variable. Without this keyword, the parameter is a reference to the calling program's variable. `parameter` represents a programmer-supplied identifier. To specify an array, use `()`, and to specify a list, use the keyword `List`. The `As type` modifier at the end can be used to specify the data type of the parameter if a data type suffix is not used.

If the function is defined within a class, it is also sometimes called a class method. A function in module is private by default, whereas a class function is public by default.

To assign the return value, just assign it to a variable that has the same name as the function name. The value that this variable contains when the function returns will be the value returned by the function to the calling program.

A function exits and returns to the caller if control reaches the `End Function` statement. You can also exit a function with the `Exit Function` statement before reaching the `End Function` statement. Here is an example of the use of the `End Function` statement:

```
Sub Caller
    Dim intVar as Integer     intVar = 3              ' Assign a value prior to call
    Print Incr(intVar)        ' We do not need a separate Call statement
    Print intVar       ' intVar still contains the value 3
End Sub
```

```
' The following function returns an Integer
Function Incr(ByVal intParam As Integer) As Integer
   Incr = intParam + 1       ' Increment but do not modify caller's variable
   ' Even if we modify intParam here, the caller's variable is NOT changed.
End Sub
```

In this example, the name of the calling subroutine is `Caller` and the called function is `Incr`, which is short for increment. Contrast this function with the one shown in the previous section. `intVar` is defined in the calling program, and `intParam` is the name of the `Integer` parameter. The function uses call by value, so the calling routine's variable is not changed when this subroutine is called. See the section titled "Passing Arguments by Value or Reference," later in this chapter, for more details.

Property Get/Set Statements

With the `Property Get` and `Property Set` statements, you can create the illusion of a variable. The user of a property refers to the name of the property and can get or set the value of the property as if it were a variable. At the point of reference, however, either the `Property Get` or the `Property Set` subroutine will be invoked to access the value.

A property can be defined at either the module level or the class level. Although I would expect a property to be used mostly within class definitions, it is possible that there could be uses for a property at the module level as well. A property within a module will have private scope by default.

This is the syntax of the `Property Get/Set` statements:

```
[Static] [Public ¦ Private] Property {Get ¦ Set} Propertyname [As Type]
     [... Statements]
End Property
```

You can usually type the words `Property Get` or `Property Set`, followed by a name in most contexts in the Design Pane, and a new function is created for you. If you specify `Static`, all the function's local variables are saved between calls. When you specify `Public`, the name of the function is known outside the current scope and is available to other modules.

The `Type` is the data type of the property. It can be a built-in type, a variant, or a class.

A property in a module is private by default, whereas a class property is public by default.

`Property Get` refers to the caller's perspective. That is, the caller is trying to get the value of the property from the routine. Thus, writing a `Property Get` routine is like writing a function. To assign the property value to be returned to the caller, assign it to a variable that has the same name as the property. The value that this variable contains when the routine returns will be the value used by the calling program.

The `Property Set` routine is invoked when the caller wants to set the value. To set and save the value, you must first access the value that the caller wants to save in the property. To obtain the property value in a `Property Set` routine, refer to a variable that has the same name as the property. The value that this variable contains when the routine starts is the value that the calling program wants to assign to the property. This convention is slightly different from using a named parameter.

A property routine exits and returns to the caller if control reaches the `End Property` statement. You can also exit with the `Exit Property` statement before reaching the `End Property` statement.

Event Handlers

Event handlers are declared with the same syntax as subroutines. They have a keyword `Sub`, followed by a name and optional parameters. The major difference between event handlers and a user-defined subroutine is that the names and parameters are specified by the class. You are not free to create and use your own name for the subroutine.

Further, although you can explicitly call event subroutines, they are typically called by the system in response to events that occur in the user interface.

You should be aware that there is a distinction between features of the LotusScript language and the classes defined by the Domino Object Model. The language does not specify any events. Events are characteristics of classes. The LotusScript DOM classes have been implemented separately from the language itself. We will see in a later chapter how this separation enables us to access the same DOM classes from Java as well as LotusScript.

Here is an example of an event handler. It handles the `Click` event from the `Button` class. To handle the event, you create a button on a page or form, and then fill in the code for the event handler in the IDE:

```
Sub Click(Source As Button)
   MsgBox "Hello, You pushed me."
End Sub
```

In this example, the `Click` event handler will be called automatically by Notes when the user clicks on the button. The `Button` class itself defines the `Click` event; you cannot change its parameter definition. Other classes, such as `NotesUIDatabase` or `NotesUIView` have other, different events that can be handled, based upon the user's actions.

Remember, the LotusScript language is a scripting language that can be used to write scripts for Microsoft Excel, as well as Notes or Domino. Thus, events such as `Click` cannot be defined in the LotusScript language. Conversely, Microsoft Visual Basic can be used to automate or script Notes using the LotusScript DOM classes. Try to keep in mind the separation of the LotusScript language and its features, such as the flow of control statements and the LotusScript DOM classes, which implement access to Notes databases.

Calling Subroutines and Functions

To call or invoke a subroutine, several methods are available. Each method has a slightly different syntax. The variety is allowed because various dialects of BASIC have used various forms over time. In each of the following descriptions, *subfunName* represents the name of a

LotusScript subroutine or function. If *functionName* is used, the name can refer only to a function and not to a subroutine.

Syntax version 1:

`Call subfunName [(argumentList)]`

Syntax version 2:

`subfunName [argumentList]`

Syntax version 3:

`subfunName (SingleByValArg)`

Syntax version 4:

`variable = functionName [(argumentList)]`

In the preceding descriptions, *argumentList* represents a list of values separated by commas. The values can be constants, variables, or expressions. Notice that the first three versions of the syntax can be used for either subroutines or functions. The fourth version can be used only for functions. In addition, although it is not explicitly shown in the fourth syntax, you can use the function reference within an expression.

When you use the `Call` keyword in version 1, you must use parentheses if there are any arguments. If there are no arguments, you can omit the parentheses.

In version 2, you can invoke the subroutine or function without using the keyword `Call`. In this case, you cannot use parentheses.

Version 3 is actually a variation of version 2. The supplied parentheses turn the variable name into an expression, which in turn causes the argument to be passed by value rather than by reference. See the next section for a detailed explanation of the difference.

Version 4 is used only for calling functions. Functions are a special kind of subroutine that returns a value. Subroutines in LotusScript do not return a value. If there are any arguments to be passed to the function, you must supply parentheses. If there are none, you can omit the parentheses when invoking the function. As mentioned previously, you can use version 4 of the syntax within an expression, not just a simple assignment statement. For example:

`strName = Trim$(strFirstName) & " " & Trim$(strLastName)`

`dblValue = Sqr(Sin(dblAngle)) + Sqr(Cos(dblAngle))`

In the preceding examples, more than one function is called per line, and in the second case, function calls are even nested.

Passing Arguments by Value or Reference

When passing arguments to a subroutine (or function) in LotusScript, values from the calling program are passed to the subroutine. This passing of values is a little like throwing them over an imaginary fence. Each side views the values a little differently. The values on the calling side of things are called *arguments*, whereas the names in the receiving subroutine are called *parameters*. Each argument on the calling side is matched with a parameter on the subroutine side.

Each parameter can be a call by value parameter or a call by reference parameter, the default. Call by value parameters are a little easier to understand. *Call by value* just means that on the calling side, before invoking the subroutine, the calling routine evaluates the argument expression, comes up with a final value, and then copies just the value into a temporary location for the subroutine to use. Thus, it is a call by value because only the value is passed to the subroutine.

Call by value is fine if you want to throw the values over the fence in only one direction. Suppose, however, you want to send the subroutine a variable containing a value, have the variable modified by the subroutine, and then send it back to the calling program. With a call by value mechanism, this is not possible, because the subroutine would be modifying a temporary copy, and the calling program wouldn't look at the value after the subroutine returned.

No, we need another mechanism. Fortunately, we have one, and it is called passing a variable by reference. *Call by reference* works by passing a reference, or address of a variable, rather than the value of the variable. Let me give you an analogy.

Suppose that you have a box of goodies that you want delivered to a friend across town. You could package the goodies, give them to the postman, and have them delivered across town for you. You're not really sure what happens to the goodies when they get there, but that's okay, because you've been assured by the post office that the delivery will reach the destination. This is call by value.

Now suppose that you really want an exchange of goodies because you want to eat some of your friend's goodies as well as give her some of yours. In this case, you give the postman your address on a slip of paper and you tell your friend, "I have some goodies here for you, here is my address, please come and get them. Don't forget to bring some goodies also."

The postman delivers your message—not the real goodies, but your address and message. Your friend comes to your house, and the two of you exchange goodies. This is call by reference. The goodies don't travel; just your address travels. There is a difference between passing the address of a variable (a reference to it) and the value of the variable.

Notice in the analogy that your friend comes to your house. This is similar to the way reference parameters work. The called subroutine is actually reading and writing directly to the caller's variable locations. This direct access to the variable locations might be exactly what you want, or it might not be. Whether you use this feature depends on your application and purpose. You could consider subroutines that you have not written as if they were strangers.

Whether you want to open your house to strangers depends on how much you know and trust them, and how much you want to get their goodies.

Now I can finally describe syntax version 3, shown previously. Suppose that when you have declared your subroutine, a particular variable is a call by reference variable. Normally, this would allow the called subroutine to access your variable and modify it. Suppose, however, that in this particular call you don't want to open your doors to a stranger. You don't want the called subroutine to modify your variable.

You can force LotusScript to create a temporary copy and pass a reference to the temporary copy variable (rather than your real variable) by enclosing a variable name in parentheses. These parentheses convert the variable into an expression. Any expression that is passed as an argument to a call by reference parameter is computed, and a reference to a temporary variable is passed instead. This is what happens with syntax version 3. It is actually a special case of version 2, with one argument variable that has been enclosed in parentheses. With this technique, an expression, and thus a temporary variable, is passed to the called subroutine.

Here are two small subroutines to show you the importance of how parameters are defined:

```
Sub Incr1(intCount As Integer)
   intCount = intCount + 1
End Sub

Sub Incr2(ByVal intCount As Integer)
   intCount = intCount + 1
End Sub

Sub Main
   Dim intTest As Integer
   intTest = 0
   Call Incr1(intTest)
   ' intTest now has 1
   Call Incr2(intTest)
   ' intTest still has 1, not 2
End Sub
```

In the example, the subroutines Incr1 and Incr2 are defined the same except that the parameter for Incr2 uses call by value. When the two subroutines are called by the main program, Incr1 can and will update the variable; Incr2 cannot because only the value is passed to the subroutine, not a reference to a variable that can be modified.

In LotusScript, there are rules for passing certain kinds of variables. Arrays, lists, user-defined Type variables, and objects must be passed by reference. Expressions and constants are passed by value so that the called program cannot mistakenly modify the value of a constant. A pair of parentheses converts a variable name into an expression, so it is passed by value, unless the variable is an array, a list, a user-defined Type, or an object. Because these types must be passed by reference, attempting to pass them by value causes an error.

Error Handling

Wouldn't it be nice if there were just no errors to handle? It would be great if we didn't have to think about all the possible things that might go wrong. There is an apocryphal story (in the United States, anyway) about a person named Murphy who made this law:

Anything That Can Go Wrong Will Go Wrong
I don't know about you, but in my experience with programming, there seems to be some truth to this saying.

Fortunately, LotusScript gives us a way, built into the language, to handle errors. This statement is called the `On Error` statement. The syntax is as follows:

```
On Error [errorNumber] {GoTo label ¦ Resume Next ¦ GoTo 0}
```

The scope of the `On Error` statement is the current procedure. The `On Error` statement is an executable statement, not a declaration, so control must flow through it for it to become effective. Also, you can change the `On Error` processing by executing a second `On Error` statement that overrides a previous statement.

The `On Error` statement tells LotusScript what to do if an error occurs. You can indicate a specific error by error number, or you can leave the number off, in which case the `On Error` will apply to all errors. These are the three actions associated with `On Error`:

- `GoTo label`   Transfer control to the given label if the error occurs.
- `Resume Next`   Just continue with the next statement after the error if an error occurs.
- `GoTo 0`   Do not handle the error in the current subroutine. If no *errorNumber* is specified, there will be no error handling in the current subroutine.

If no `On Error` is active in the current procedure, calling procedures will be examined, in order from the innermost calling procedure, until an `On Error` statement that applies has been found. If no `On Error` statement is active in any of the calling procedures, the default action is to display an error message box and stop execution.

In the actual error handling routine, you can issue the `Resume` statement, or you can use one of the `Exit` statements to leave the subroutine. The `Resume` statement syntax is as shown here:

```
Resume [0 ¦ Next ¦ label]
```

`Resume 0` means to resume execution on the statement that caused the error. `Resume Next` means to resume on the statement following the one that caused the error, and `Resume label` means to go to the specified label and continue from there.

GoSub AND Return

The `GoSub` and `Return` statements are actually artifacts of the long history of BASIC. They represent one of the original methods of writing subroutines in BASIC. Originally, a BASIC program was typically written as one large (usually very large) file. Each line of the program had a line number. The `GoSub` statement enabled the programmer to segment the program by allowing the programmer to transfer control to another area and then later return with the `Return` statement.

The syntax is as follows:

GoSub *label*

Return

In LotusScript, the `GoSub` and the `Return` statement must be contained within the same procedure and cannot be at the module level.

> **Tip**
>
> If you are familiar with another programming language (such as C or C++) you may be familiar with the `return` statement of that language. In LotusScript, the `Return` statement is not used exactly for the same purpose. It is similar, but different. Most likely in LotusScript, you really want to use the `Exit Sub` statement, which causes control to exit and return from a subroutine. Because you are most likely not using `GoSub`, you probably will not need to use the LotusScript `Return` statement, either.

String Handling

Strings are one of the most important data types in LotusScript. They are used extensively in the LotusScript DOM classes, and you will need to use them in your own programs as well. Before I cover the details of strings in LotusScript, however, let me digress into string handling in general.

Characters and Codes

Computers really can store only numbers. Every memory location in a computer is storing a binary value. Most computers can address every byte within their memory, and for most computers, a byte is typically 8 bits. This means that each memory byte can contain a value from 0 to 255, but you probably already know all this.

If memory bytes can store values from 0 to 255, how can they store characters, words, phrases, and even books? In Japan, computers can store Kanji, and in Korea, Hangeul. Actually, computers can store Arabic, Hebrew letters, Chinese, and Russian symbols as well. If you're a native English speaker, you probably don't even think about characters in many of these other languages, and you might not even think about how those numbers really store characters.

The basis for storing all these types of symbols in the computer is the concept of a code. A *code* is really just a standardized convention. There are several important codes, such as the ASCII code, the EBCDIC code (used on IBM mainframes), and the Unicode. What these codes have in common is that they are a convention. Within each convention, a particular symbol is assigned a *code point*. There are other codes as well, but these three will do for our explanation.

The numeric values of these code points are not as important as the fact that they are standardized and recognized. When they are standardized, you can use them or convert values to or from them.

In case you didn't know, the ASCII code was originally 7 bits but has now been extended to 8 bits. EBCDIC is an 8-bit code, and Unicode is a 16-bit code. Each of these codes is a convention for assigning code points to various symbols.

Take for example, the letter *a*. ASCII, EBCDIC, and Unicode all have numbers associated with this symbol. In ASCII and Unicode, the numeric value associated with the symbol is 97. In EBCDIC, the value is 129. You should be aware that the symbol *A* is different from the symbol *a*. That's because we typically want to differentiate a lowercase symbol from its uppercase equivalent. Uppercase *A* has value 65 in ASCII and Unicode, but value 193 in EBCDIC.

Well, why do you even care about all this information? Normally, you won't care too much about it. However, at some times, understanding the coding of the character set is important. For example, looking back at the code points, you'll notice that in ASCII, uppercase *A* is 65, and lowercase *a* is 97. This means that when you perform an ascending sort using the ASCII code, *A* will sort before *a*. In EBCDIC, lowercase and uppercase sorting will result in the opposite sort order. Neither method is necessarily right or wrong; they are just different.

It is also important to understand coding, because in the Unicode code, characters are actually represented by 2 bytes. These are sometimes called double-byte characters.

CODES AND FONTS

Notice in the coding discussion that I differentiated between lowercase *a* and uppercase *A*. If you have looked at most word processing, desktop publishing, or even Notes Rich Text fields, you'll notice that hundreds of fonts are available. Each font might have a different appearance for the lowercase *a*.

Does this mean that we have a different code point for each one? Does Times Roman need a code point for *a* that is different from a Courier *a*, which is different from the Helvetica *a*?

No. The fonts can all use the same code. A font is really a correspondence from a code, such as ASCII (or EBCDIC or Unicode), to a visual representation of the character. So with one set of code points, you can have hundreds of different and beautiful visual representations. I'm simplifying a little bit here because a discussion on fonts could be a complete volume by itself.

Within Rich Text fields, and similar types of data in other programs, you must specify both a font and a code point for each character. Typically, consecutive characters that are all in the same font typeface and size are grouped so that redundant data does not need to be specified.

Strings in LotusScript do not contain font information. They contain only code points. So you can manipulate strings, and after you have finished, you can display the resulting string in any font by associating the font with the string when you display or print the string.

Declaring Strings

Now that you understand the kind of data that is stored in a string, let's go back and discuss what you can do with strings. The syntax for declaring a string variable is this:

```
Dim stringvar as String [* length]
```

If the *length* parameter is specified, the string is a fixed-length string. It will contain the number of characters specified in *length*. Fixed-length strings are a little more efficient than variable-length strings. They are most practicable when used in a user-defined Type structure or when they are to be passed to an external subroutine or function.

If the length is not specified, the string is considered a variable-length string.

> **Caution**
>
> Using strings when calling external subroutines or functions is a frequent source of errors in programming. Many times, these external routines require you to pass a buffer and length. Be careful when you pass strings to these external routines. Make sure that you have allocated a string with enough space to store your results. If you pass a string that is too small, the called routine may write data beyond the end of your string, and your program may get a General Protection Fault (GPF) someplace well beyond where the problem occurs. This will be very difficult to debug.
>
> When passing the length of your buffer, use the Len built-in function to pass the length of your variable rather than hard-coding a length. This will ensure that the length you pass to the subroutine will always match the current length of your string buffer.

String Functions

After you have declared your string, you can turn your attention to the many functions you can use to manipulate it. Most of the time, you will be using variable-length strings. These are the most convenient to use because their length automatically varies, and the strings grow or shrink to your needs.

The basic operations on strings involve putting them together, extracting substrings, and comparing strings. Concatenation, or the attaching of one string onto the end of another string, is one of the most basic operations. You can concatenate strings using either the & operator or the + operator.

Here are some examples:

```
strName = strFirstName & " " & strLastName
strName = strLastName + ", " + strFirstName
```

You can use the Len function to determine the length of a string. The syntax is as follows:

IntegerVar = Len(*stringExpr*)

LotusScript has several built-in functions for extracting substrings from a string:

- Left$(*stringExpr, length*)   Extract leftmost *length* characters.
- Mid$(*stringExpr, start* [*, length*])   Extract *length* characters from within the string starting at character position *start*. The first character is position 1. If *length* is not specified, the substring continues to the end of the string.
- Right$(*stringExpr, length*)   Extract the rightmost *length* characters.
- StrLeft(*string1, string2* [*, flags* [*, occurrences*]])   Search *string1* from left to right and extract the characters in *string1* that appear to the left of *string2*. *flags* enables you to control case-sensitive and pitch-sensitive searching. *occurrences* is the number of occurrences of *string2* to find.
- StrLeftBack(*string1, string2* [*, flags* [*, occurrences*]])   Search *string1* from right to left and extract the characters in *string1* that appear to the left of *string2*. *flags* enables you to control case-sensitive and pitch-sensitive searching. *occurrences* is the number of occurrences of *string2* to find.
- StrRight(*string1, string2* [*, flags* [*, occurrences*]])   Search *string1* from left to right and extract the characters in *string1* that appear to the right of *string2*. *flags* enables you to control case-sensitive and pitch-sensitive searching. *occurrences* is the number of occurrences of *string2* to find.
- StrRightBack(*string1, string2* [*, flags* [*, occurrences*]])   Search *string1* from right to left and extract the characters in *string1* that appear to the right of *string2*. *flags* enables you to control case-sensitive and pitch-sensitive searching. *occurrences* is the number of occurrences of *string2* to find.

LotusScript has several built-in functions for trimming off leading or trailing blanks from strings:

- LTrim$(*stringExpr*)   Trims leading blanks from the expression.
- Trim$(*stringExpr*)   Trims both leading and trailing blanks from the expression.
- RTrim$(*stringExpr*)   Trims trailing blanks from the expression.

LotusScript has conversion routines that will convert data to strings:

- CStr(*Expression*)   Converts any expression to a string.
- Str$(*numExpr*)   Converts a numeric expression to a string.

- `StrConv(Expression, ConvType)`   Converts an expression to a string with various options. You can convert to uppercase, lowercase, proper case, wide (double-byte), narrow, katakana (Japanese), and hiragana (Japanese).

String variables can use the standard comparison operators: <, <=, =<, =, >=, =>, <>, and ><. String comparisons are affected by the `Option Compare Case` and `Option Compare Binary` statements. LotusScript has several built-in functions for string comparison:

- `StrCompare(string1, string2 [, method])`   Returns -1 if string1 < string2, 0 if they are equal, and 1 if string1 > string2. You can use this function if you want to override the comparison method specified in the `Option Compare` statement. `method` is 0 for case-sensitive comparison, 1 for non case-sensitive comparison, and 2 for platform collation sequence (binary).
- `InStr([beginpos,] strHaystack, strNeedle [, method])`   Tests to see whether `strNeedle` is found in `strHaystack`. You can specify a beginning position with `beginpos`, which must be a positive integer. If it is omitted, 1 is assumed. The method is specified as in `StrCompare`.
- `Expression Like Pattern`   Like is actually an operator. It is typically used in an `If` statement. `Expression` is a string expression. `Pattern` is a string that contains a pattern to be found. If the pattern is found within the string, the `Like` operator returns `True`; otherwise, it returns `False`. The rules for this operator are too complex to describe here, but following are some of the rules: ? matches any single character, * matches zero or more characters, and # matches a digit. For example, *Lotus* matches any string that contains `Lotus` anywhere within the string.

File Input/Output

You will almost assuredly need to access external files from LotusScript at some point. There are so many types of files and applications that it is impossible to cover all the aspects you might need. However, I'll try to cover the basics; from there, the best way to learn is to try it yourself.

File input/output (I/O) follows this simple model:

1. Open the file.
2. Perform file operations.
3. Close the file.

This model works for both reading and writing the file, as well as for random-access or sequential-access files. When you open the file, you must specify a file number. This file number is used on all subsequent file operations and when you close the file. This method enables you to have several files open at once.

Opening a File

Here is the syntax of the Open statement:

```
Open filename [For mode] [Access operations] [Lockmode]
   As [#]FileNum [Len = reclen]
```

mode can be one of the following: Random, Input, Output, Append, or Binary.

operations can be one of the following: Read, Read Write, or Write.

Lockmode can be one of the following: Shared, Lock Read, Lock Read Write, or Lock Write.

For Random and Binary files, you use the Get and Put statements to read and write the file. In a Random file, all records have the same length, specified by *reclen*. If omitted, the value assumed will be 128. If specified, the *reclen* must be between 1 and 32767, inclusive. Reclen is ignored for Binary files.

For Input files, you use the Input and Input # statements to read the file. If reclen is specified, the number indicates a buffer size, not the record length. The default buffer size is 512 bytes.

For Output and Append files, you use the Print # and Write # statements to output data to the file. The difference between Output and Append is that for Output mode, if the file exists it is replaced by the new data, whereas for Append, the new data is appended to the old data.

The Access clause, if specified, must be consistent with the For clause that you specify in the Open statement. For example, if the file is opened *For Output* mode, the Access clause must be *Access Write*.

Lockmode is used to lock the file from usage by other users on a network. Shared indicates no locking. Lock Read prevents other users from reading the file, although they can write to the file. Lock Read Write locks all other network users from reading and writing to the file. Lock Write prevents other users from writing to the file.

General File Operations

Several statements and functions are useful for reading or writing a file. The first function is the FreeFile function, which has the following syntax:

```
IntegerVar = FreeFile()
```

The FreeFile function returns a number that can be used as a file number on an Open statement. Generally, you will use the FreeFile statement just before executing an Open statement. It is considered a good programming practice to use FreeFile to obtain a file number instead of hard-coding a specific number into your program. When you use a specific number, it becomes harder to reuse your program, because the number you select might conflict with a routine written by someone else.

The `Seek` statement is used with `Random` and `Binary` files. It is used to set the current position within the file. In a `Binary` file, the position specified is the byte offset within the file. The first byte is 1. In a `Random` file, the record number is specified. The first record number is 1. Here is the syntax for the `Seek` statement:

`Seek #fileNumber, position`

You will typically use the `Seek` statement just before using a `Get` or `Put` statement with the file. The `Seek` statement sets the current position that is used by `Get` or `Put`.

FILE INPUT OPERATIONS

The `Read` operations are the `Get` and `Input` statements. `Get` is used for `Random` and `Binary` file modes. In either mode, you will probably also use the `EOF` function. The `EOF` function returns `True` if the specified file has reached the end of file.

Here is an example:

```
Dim intFile As Integer
intFile = FreeFile()

Open "Testfile.txt" For Input As intFile
Do Until EOF(intFile)
   ... File input and other processing statements
Loop
Close intFile
```

The `Get` statement is used for `Random` or `Binary` files. The syntax is as follows:

`Get #fileNumber, [recordPosition], variableName`

fileNumber is the number specified in the `Open` statement. *recordPosition* is optional; if it's left off, reading starts from the current position in the file. If specified for a `Binary` file, *recordPosition* represents the byte offset within the file. For a `Random` file, it represents the record number. *variableName* must be a scalar variable or a user-defined `Type` variable.

The `Input` statement is used for sequential `Input` files. The syntax is shown here:

`Input #fileNumber, variableNameList`

fileNumber is the number specified in the `Open` statement. *variableNameList* is a list of variable names separated by commas. Each variable must be a scalar variable. You cannot use arrays or user-defined `Type` variables; however, you can use individual array elements or scalar items within a user-defined `Type`.

You can also use the `Line Input` statement to read an entire line from a text file into a string variable. The syntax is as follows:

`Line Input #fileNumber, variableName`

fileNumber is the number specified in the `Open` statement. *variableName* is the name of a string or variant variable. An entire line is read into this variable.

FILE OUTPUT OPERATIONS

You can output to files using the `Put`, `Print#`, and `Write#` statements. The `Put` statement is used for `Random` and `Binary` files, whereas the `Print#` and `Write#` statements are used for sequential `Output` files.

This is the `Put` statement syntax:

`Put #fileNumber, [recordPosition], variableName`

fileNumber is the number specified in the `Open` statement. *recordPosition* is optional; if it's left off, reading starts from the current position in the file. If specified for a `Binary` file, *recordPosition* represents the byte offset within the file. For a `Random` file, it represents the record number. *variableName* must be a scalar variable or a user-defined `Type` variable.

The `Print` statement is used for sequential `Output` files. You can use this statement only if you have opened the file for `Output` or `Append` use. This statement is used for file output even though it is not sent to a printer. If you use the `Print` statement without a file number, the output is sent to the screen; if you use it with a file number, the output is sent to a file.

The syntax for screen output is as follows:

`Print [expressionList][, ¦ ;]`

expressionList is a list of expressions to be printed. The output is sent to the display. If you leave off the *expressionList*, LotusScript prints a blank line. A newline character is printed at the end of the *expressionList* unless the list ends with a semicolon or comma. If the list ends with a semicolon or comma, no newline character is appended.

If you use a comma to separate items in the list, each item is printed at the next tab stop. If you use a semicolon or space to separate the items, no space is printed between the two items.

The syntax for using the `Print` statement for file output is this:

`Print #fileNumber [, expressionList]`

fileNumber is the number specified in the `Open` statement. *expressionList* is a list of expressions to be written to the file. If you leave off the *expressionList*, LotusScript outputs a blank line.

If you use a comma to separate items in the list, each item is printed at the next tab stop. If you use a semicolon or space to separate the items, no space is printed between the two items.

The `Print` statement honors the width specified in the `Width` statement. If outputting a variable would cause the line to be longer than the specified width, a new line automatically is generated and the variable is output on the next line.

The format of the `Width` statement is as follows:

`Width #fileNumber, width`

fileNumber is the number specified in the Open statement. The width parameter can be from 0 to 255. Zero is the default and means an unlimited line length.

The Write statement is useful for creating files that will be used by other programs. It enables you to write a list of expressions to a file and have the delimiters between items. The most common version of this format is called a comma-delimited file. You can use this statement only if you have opened the file for Output or Append use. Following is the syntax for the Write statement:

```
Write #fileNumber [, expressionList]
```

fileNumber is the number specified in the Open statement. *expressionList* is a list of expressions to be written to the file. If you leave off the *expressionList*, LotusScript outputs a blank line. If you specify a list of expressions, each expression is evaluated and output to the file, separated by commas.

The Write statement ignores the current Width setting.

Reusing LotusScript Programs and Calling DLLs

One important aspect of programming is reusability. It is very valuable to be able to reuse code that either you or someone else has already written. Script libraries enable you to define declarations that can be used in several forms, views, or agents within a database. They enable you to share source code. Being able to call Dynamic Link Libraries (DLLs) from LotusScript enables you to reuse object code programs that you can buy commercially or that are written for a specific purpose.

Reusing Source Code

One of the most basic ways to reuse source code is to use the compile-time directive %include. This compile-time directive enables you to create LotusScript source code outside of Notes. This can be valuable if you want to perform source-code library maintenance on the code or if you want to share the same source code across several databases. The syntax of the %include statement is as follows:

```
%include filename
```

filename must be a string constant. It can be explicitly given within the %include statement, or it can be defined in a Const statement.

Following are some examples:

```
%include "c:\notes\source\appsubs.txt"
Const strSubs = "c:\source\Subs.lss"
%include strSubs
```

If you omit the suffix, LotusScript assumes the suffix .lss.

> **Note**
> When you use `include` files, you should remember that the source code will not be inside the database. This means that if you replicate the database, the source code will not be replicated with the database. This can be good or bad, depending upon your application. If you want security, this is good, because the replicating site will not have the source code. It is not good if someone at the replicating site needs to view the source code for debugging or some other purpose.

A second method for sharing code is with the Use statement and script libraries. Script libraries enable you to define declarations that can be shared among different LotusScript programs within a single database. Script libraries always contain at least (Options), (Declarations), Initialize, and Terminate procedures. A common use for script libraries is to use them for your Class and/or Type declarations and common subroutines. When you define declarations and routines in a script library, they can be used throughout your database.

You can have several script libraries within a single database. Each script library has its own name—the four sections described previously and any subroutines or functions that you add. You can define each separately and use each separately.

To access a script library, you use the Use statement. The syntax is as given here:

Use *scrlibName*

scrlibName can be either a string literal constant or a string constant that has been defined with a Const statement. You must create the script library in the database before you can use it.

REUSING OBJECT CODE

You can also reuse object code from LotusScript. Object code is code that has already been compiled by a compiler and link-edited together to form a module that can be loaded at runtime by LotusScript. The generic name for this kind of module is a Dynamic Link Library (DLL). A special form of DLL for use with LotusScript is called a LotusScript Extension, or LSX module.

You can use an LSX module by issuing the UseLSX statement. Here is the format for the UseLSX statement:

UseLSX *lsxDLLName*

lsxDLLName must be a character string literal constant or a string constant that has been defined with a Const statement. One important LSX is the LotusScript:Data Object or LS:DO. This LSX module is implemented in a DLL and implements the LotusScript classes for ODBC access from within LotusScript.

The final method for using DLLs is to declare and invoke them at a low level. This method is recommended only for technical users who understand the operating system and understand how modules are loaded and invoked. To invoke an external subroutine from

LotusScript, you must use the `Declare` statement so that LotusScript knows how to prepare the parameters; then you can invoke it with a syntax that is the same as a regular LotusScript subroutine call. The syntax for the `Declare` statement is as follows:

```
Declare [Public | Private] {Function | Sub} LSName Lib libName [Alias aliasName]
➥([parameterList]) [As returnType]
```

You must declare whether the routine is a function or a subroutine. This determines whether the routine will return a value. The *LSName* is the name you will use when invoking the routine from LotusScript. *libName* is specified as a string constant and represents the name of the DLL. *aliasName* is specified as a string constant, is optional, and is typically used when the name within the library is different from the name to be used from LotusScript. In Windows, the *aliasName* can be a pound sign (#) followed by a number to signify the ordinal number within the DLL. *parameterList* is the list of parameters to the routine (as described in the following paragraph). The *returnType* is the data type of the return value. It must be a scalar value and cannot be a variant, currency, or fixed-length string.

Each parameter declaration must be of the following form:

```
[ByVal] parmName As [LMBCS | Unicode] [dataType | Any]
```

parmName is the name of the parameter. You specify `ByVal` if you want LotusScript to pass the parameter by value. `LMBCS` stands for Lotus Multi-Byte Character Set. If either `LMBCS` or `Unicode` is specified, you must specify `ByVal` and `String` as the data type. The keyword `Any` is used if you want to disable type checking and pass any argument to the external routine.

SUMMARY

In this chapter, I explained the essence of subroutines and functions. I gave you some practical advice on how to break up larger routines into smaller, more coherent subroutines. Each routine should have a purpose, not just be a collection of sequential statements.

I explained the different kinds of subroutines and when you should use each one. Functions return values; subroutines don't. `Property Get/Set` routines can be used to allow callers to view the properties as variables but actually implement them as subroutines. Events are typically called by the system automatically in response to external events, such as a user action.

I told you about error handling, string handling, and file input and output. Lastly, I told you about some methods for reusing your source code, such as script libraries and `include` files, and reusing your object code through the use of LSX files and DLLs.

Using and reusing code in a modular manner is the cornerstone of good programming practice. It enables you to develop larger systems more effectively and efficiently. It enables you to reuse code that you or others have implemented and thus get your projects implemented more quickly.

From Here…

Here are some suggestions for further reading:

- To delve into the Domino Object Model and how it is used with LotusScript, read Chapter 25, "The Session and Front-End Classes," Chapter 26, "Database, View, and Document Classes in LotusScript and Java," and Chapter 27, "Using Fields and Items in LotusScript and Java."
- To learn about programming Notes and Domino with Java, read Chapter 23, "Creating and Using Java Applets and Agents."
- Chapter 24, "Using the Lotus eSuite DevPack," shows you how to use this Java-based set of applets to make programming Web-based applications easier.

CHAPTER 23

Creating and Using Java Applets and Agents

There are many reasons why you might want to use Java. Let's look at some of these reasons. First, maybe you've seen a lot of Web pages and they have spiffy animation, so maybe that appeals to you. Second, perhaps you want to do some simple calculations at the Web client, such as calculating sales tax. Third, you might be thinking about something much more sophisticated, such as creating a fancy user interface that is not possible with ordinary HTML. Lastly, you might be interested in distributing some Domino data to make your application more responsive to the Web end user.

In this chapter, I'm going to focus more on the business applications of Java rather than the spiffy animation. Of course you can do that also in Java, but there are plenty of other books that can show you how to do animation. I'll try to present some simple examples of how to get started with Java and how you can use Java in a way that enhances your usage of Domino in a Web-oriented business environment.

Setting Up the Java Environment

I want to clear up one point before we get started. If you are serious about using Java with Domino, you need a separate third-party development environment for Java. Although Lotus has made great strides with release 5, it still does not have enough features for serious Java development at this time.

There are many Java development environments, and you can probably choose any of them. Here are a few: IBM Visual Age for Java, Inprise (the company formerly known as Borland) Jbuilder, Symantec Visual Caf[as]e, and Java Workshop from Sun. There are probably hundreds of other options, and you can even download Sun's Java Development Toolkit (JDK) free from the Web. Sun's JDK package is extremely minimal, however, and for serious work, you'll probably want a real development environment.

A Java Overview

Some of you may be old hands at Java, but for those of you who are new to it, let me give you a quick overview. Java was originally conceived by Sun Microsystems as a language for embedded controllers (for example, for your microwave oven). It became extremely popular with the advent of the Web and because Netscape included it in its browser. It has quickly evolved, however, and now there are probably millions of Java programmers in the world.

Of course, you know that one of the main advantages of Java is that it is operating system–independent and hardware platform–independent. Sun's mantra is "write once, run anywhere." But how, exactly, does Java achieve this feat technically? The answer lies in another term that you may have heard: the Java Virtual Machine, or JVM. The JVM is a software program that simulates a real machine. The JVM accepts, as input, binary data that has been prepared by a Java compiler. This set of binary data corresponds to the machine-language codes that are used by traditional hardware, such as the Intel Pentium.

The binary codes are stored in files on the host operating system in class files. Groups of class files can be stored in a directory in the operating system, or they can be collected in a single file called an archive. There are several kinds of archive files available: JAR files, CAB files, and ZIP files. ZIP is a standard format for compressing a group of files and saving them as a single file. This extension is not normally used anymore, however, because it was confusing for some users who thought the ZIP files needed to be uncompressed. JAR files are the standard format for Java archives and are stored internally with the same format as ZIP files. CAB files were created by Microsoft and are used by its Internet Explorer.

Java achieves its machine and operating system independence by specifying the format for class files, archives, and the machine operations contained in the class files. There are several implementations of Java Virtual Machines. Each of the major Web browsers, as well as Notes and Domino, contains a JVM, and you can run standalone JVMs as well. A standalone JVM comes with Sun's JDK. With a standalone JVM, you can write a Java application that does not depend upon a Web browser.

THE CLASSPATH

So now we have a JVM and a class file that contains binary opcodes. Is there anything else we need? Well, yes, of course. The class file that you have developed probably needs to allocate and manage resources, such as memory and data. It probably needs to interact with a user via a user interface. There should be some capability of communicating over a network, and you need to have security programs. You probably don't want to write all this kind of code. Normally, these types of services are provided by an operating system. Well, we're in luck.

There are many, many programs that have been written in Java, and they are included in archive files that are distributed with the Java environment. They perform many of the routine tasks that are normally provided by any operating system environment. There is only one problem—how does the JVM find these files? The answer is the CLASSPATH environment variable.

The CLASSPATH environment variable is actually very similar in concept to the PATH variable that you may remember from the old days. The CLASSPATH variable tells the JVM where to find additional classes that are not included in the currently running class. Standard classes for user interface and many other functions are included in these libraries. In addition to the standard libraries, you can write your own Java programs, store them in archives, and include them in the CLASSPATH.

Lotus, in fact, has done this for many of the support functions required for Notes and Domino. Thus, in order to use these Lotus-written Java programs, you must include the Lotus archives in your CLASSPATH (for the Java development tool's use).

When Notes or Domino JVM is running, it actually uses an internal CLASSPATH variable. This variable is specified in the Notes.ini file and has the name JavaUserClasses. In order for Notes or Domino to be able to find any custom classes you write that are not stored within a database, you must make sure you have modified the `JavaUserClasses` variable in `Notes.ini`. Here is an example:

`JavaUserClasses=c:\Development\MyJavaClasses\`

You can specify more than one directory and separate them with semicolons.

> **Note**
> This section describing the `CLASSPATH` environment variable applies to version 1.1.x of the Java Development Toolkit. This is the version that ships with Notes and Domino. In Java version 2.0, class files are treated differently, as described in the next section.

JAVA DEVELOPMENT KIT VERSIONS

If you program a Windows application in C++, there are three separate and distinct concepts to work with: the programming language itself (C++), the compiler tool, and the Windows Application Programming Interface (API) . These same three concepts apply to Java programming. You need to know the Java programming language, you need to have a particular Java programming tool, and you need a programming API. The programming API is supplied by Sun Microsystems in the Java Development Kit (JDK), but it is almost always also supplied by the Java tool vendor when you purchase a Java programming tool.

The Java Development Toolkit provides an API that contains many of the programming features of a windowing operating system such as Windows. This is perhaps one of the reasons that Microsoft wants to portray Java as just a programming language. Although Java is a language, the JDK supplies the capability of creating windows and buttons, using networking, accessing databases, and many of the other features that we take for granted in Microsoft Windows. In addition, you can use the JDK on top of Windows, UNIX, Macintosh, or any other platform that supports the JVM. This includes Notes and Domino.

The JDK from Sun has undergone many revisions. At the time this is being written, there are two versions available: JDK 1.1.x, and JDK 2.0. The 1.1.x version is shipped with Notes and Domino due to the cycle of testing and quality assurance that goes into Domino prior to release. Java version 2.0 was announced by Sun on December 8, 1998, so there was not enough time to certify the Domino code with Java version 2.0, but I expect that it will be supported soon after it can be tested.

There are many new capabilities in version 2.0, including security enhancements and the inclusion of the Java Foundation Classes (JFC). The JFC includes the Swing components, the Java 2D graphics interfaces, drag-and-drop, accessibility, and many other application services. The Swing user interface components are an enhancement to the original Abstract

Windowing Toolkit (AWT) found in version 1.1 of the JDK. Although the AWT still works for compatibility, the Swing set of components is essentially a replacement.

As mentioned, in version 2.0, the `CLASSPATH` environment variable holds a less prominent role. In version 1.1.x, the setting of this variable caused a lot of setup problems (and is why I described it in the previous section). With version 2.0, system classes are found automatically by the JVM.

Here is your acronym test. I'll be using these acronyms later in the chapter so you should know the following: JVM, JDK, JAR, CAB, ZIP, AWT, JFC, and Swing. If you forget one or two of these, you can go back and review the previous sections. After a while, you'll get into the Swing of it.

THE JAVA LANGUAGE

The official Java language specification is over 700 pages, so it's pretty clear that I'm not going to be able to describe it all to you here. Instead, I'll provide you with a high-level description of the language so you can understand the examples, and then let you investigate the language in more detail if you desire.

Java has had a meteoric rise to fame. It has been around officially only since May, 1995, when it was introduced at the Sun World conference. Originally, Sun was going to call the product *Oak*, but the name was already trademarked and could not be used. Several of the Live Oak team members met for a brainstorming session and discussed many different possible names for the product. The final contenders were *Silk* and *Java*, but Java won the contest. You can read a very interesting account of the naming process at the `JavaWorld` magazine Web site at `http://www.javaworld.com/jw-10-1996/jw-10-javaname.html`.

Java is an object-oriented language that has a lot of similarities and a few differences from C++. It uses similar terminology with its classes, objects, and methods. Java lacks some of the more sophisticated, but error-prone, features of C++, such as pointers, templates, and multiple inheritance. Java adds some features that are not part of C++. For example, Java has automatic garbage collection, built-in multithreading, and the concept of the Java Virtual Machine.

JAVA IDENTIFIERS

Java programs are written using Unicode, which is upward-compatible from ASCII, but uses two-byte characters. Although keywords are in English, this enables programs to use identifiers written using the full Unicode character set, including Japanese and Chinese Kanji characters. This is useful for non–English-speaking programmers, but may make the programs less portable unless you happen to know Kanji.

The Java keywords are

abstract	default	if	private	throw
boolean	do	implements	protected	throws
break	double	import	public	transient
byte	else	instanceof	return	try
case	extends	int	short	void
catch	final	interface	static	volatile
char	finally	long	super	while
class	float	native	switch	
const	for	new	synchronized	
continue	goto	package	this	

Java keywords are reserved and may not be used for identifiers. The words `true`, `false`, and `null` are literal values and are therefore also restricted from being used as variable names. The keywords const and goto are reserved, but are not currently used by Java.

There is no limit within the Java language for the length of identifiers, so you have plenty of other choices for identifier names. In Java, identifier names are case sensitive; LotusScript ignores case.

An identifier must begin with a letter, but then may be followed by any number of letters, numbers, the underscore (_), and the dollar sign ($). You should not typically use the dollar sign because it is intended to be used only in mechanically generated code.

Java Comments

Java comments are similar to those found in C++. You can add a comment to the rightmost end of any line by using two forward slashes (//). You can enclose a block of lines by starting a comment with /* and ending with */. Here are some examples:

```
int iCount;      // Count of widgets
iCount = 1;      // Start with a single widget
/* In the following code, we'll count widgets
   We use a special algorithm that has been passed
   down for generations.
*/
```

In addition to normal comments, Java has an additional feature that can be used to process specially formatted comments. If you write comments in your code with these rules, the JavaDoc utility can be used to generate HTML pages documenting your code automatically. The JavaDoc utility is included with the JDK and can be downloaded free from the Sun Microsystems Java Web site (www.java.sun.com).

To use this feature, you use the block commenting format, and you must begin your comment with /** and end it with */. You can write a comment at the beginning of your class source file and before each of your methods. See Listing 23.1 for an example.

LISTING 23.1 A SAMPLE JAVA PROGRAM CONTAINING TAGGED COMMENTS FOR AUTOMATIC DOCUMENTATION GENERATION

```
***Tabs in code replaced with four spaces***
/** This is a sample class file. I'm using it to illustrate how you can
  use JavaDoc to process your source file to automatically generate HTML
  documentation.
  @see       Class
  @version   1.0, November 11, 1998
*/
public class Sample extends java.lang.Object
{
    int m_iMyValue;         // Saves a Value
    /**
    Constructor for Sample. Creates a new Sample object
    @see    Object
    */
    public Sample(){m_iMyValue = 0;};

    /**
    Return MyValue property. This routine returns the MyValue property.
    @see    int
    @return the MyValue property
    */
    public int getMyValue(){
        return(iMyValue);
    }

    /**
    Set the MyValue property. This routine sets the MyValue property.
    @see    int
    */
    public void setMyValue(int iMyValue){
        m_iMyValue = iMyValue;
    }

}
```

In Figure 23.1, you can see a display of the HTML that was automatically generated.

If you consistently comment your code and follow the relatively simple tagging conventions, you can get an automatic documentation generation for all your methods and classes, as well as an alphabetical listing and automatic hyperlinks between the various classes. The tags within the comments begin with @ and are followed by a keyword, such as see, and version. There are several tags you can use, and when used properly, the tags and JavaDoc enable you to turn comments within your code to useful documentation.

Figure 23.1
This documentation was automatically generated by the JavaDoc utility.

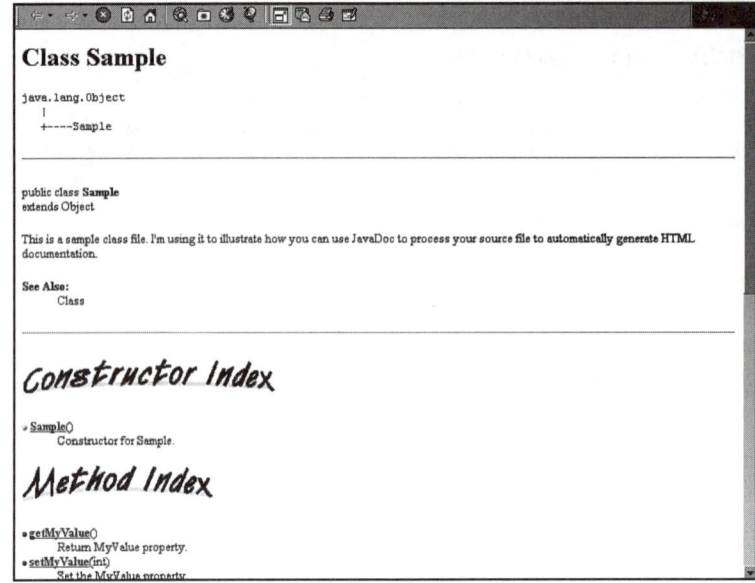

DATA TYPES

The built-in numeric data types for Java can be seen in Table 23.1.

TABLE 23.1	JAVA BUILT-IN DATA TYPES			
Type	**Description**	**Size**	**Minimum Value**	**Maximum Value**
Byte	Single-byte signed integer	8	−127	128
Char	Two-byte unsigned character	16	0	65535
Short	Short signed integer	16	−32768	32767
Int	Signed integer	32	−2147483648	2147483647
Long	Long signed integer	64	−9223372036854775808	9223372036854775807
Float	Single-precision floating-point	32	$-3.40282347 \times 10^{38}$	$3.40282347 \times 10^{38}$
Double	Double-precision floating-point	64	$-1.79769313486 \times 10^{308}$	$1.79769313486 \times 10^{308}$

In addition to the numeric types, there is a Boolean type that may be either true or false. A string type is represented as a built-in class. String constants are specified by using characters within double-quotation marks.

In addition to the basic data types, you can also create array variables of any of the built-in types.

OPERATORS AND EXPRESSIONS

The operators in Java are similar to those found in C++. The only operator in Java not found in C++ is the zero-extended shift-right operator >>>. You can see the list of Java operators in Table 23.2. The operators are listed in order of precedence; the highest-precedence operators are on the top of the table and are evaluated first.

TABLE 23.2   JAVA OPERATORS AND PRECEDENCE

Operators	Description
++ --	Postfix increment, postfix decrement
++ --	Prefix increment, prefix decrement
+ -	Unary plus, unary minus
~ !	Bitwise complement and logical complement
* / %	Multiplication, division, remainder
+ -	Addition, subtraction
<< >> >>>	Shift left, signed shift right, zero extended shift right
< <= >= >	Relational operators
== !=	Equality operators
&	Bitwise And
^	Bitwise Exclusive Or
|	Bitwise Inclusive Or
&&	Logical And
||	Logical Inclusive Or
? :	Conditional expression
Assignment, one of the following: = += -= *= /= %= &= |= <<= >>= >>>=	

Expressions in Java follow the normal rules of precedence. Operands are evaluated from left to right, and parentheses can be used to control the order of evaluation. For example:

a + b * c

This expression is evaluated by first multiplying (b * c), and then adding the result to a. Innermost parenthetical values are evaluated first. For example:

(a + b) * c

In this expression (a + b) is evaluated first because the parentheses override the natural precedence of the operators.

STATEMENTS

Statements in Java are very similar to those found in C++. Although there are a few exceptions, C++ programmers should feel very comfortable reading Java code. The list of statement types is found in Table 23.3.

TABLE 23.3 JAVA STATEMENT TYPES

Block	`{ BlockStatements }`
Local variable declaration	`Type VariableDeclarators;`
Expression statement	`StatementExpression ;`
If statement	`if ( Expression ) Statement` `if ( Expression ) Statement else Statement`

Switch statement	`switch ( Expression ) {SwitchStatements}`
	`SwitchStatements`
	`case ConstantExpression : Statement ;`
	`default : Statement ;`

While statement	`while ( Expression ) Statement`
Do statement	`do Statement while ( Expression ) ;`
For statement	`for ( ForInit ; Expression ; ForUpdate )` `Statement`
Break statement	`break [identifier];`
Continue statement	`continue [identifier];`
Return statement	`return Expression ;`
Throw statement	`throw Expression ;`
Synchronized statement	`synchronized ( Expression ) Block`
Try statement	`try Block catch ( parameter ) Block [ finally Block ]`

The table of statement types is not meant to be a formal syntax for Java. The actual formal reference in the Java specification takes 22 pages! Rather, you should use this table as a quick reference to the statements available. You need to consult a Java programming language reference (or use the online Web version at `http://java.sun.com/docs/books/jls/html/index.html`).

The statement here that may not be familiar to C++ programmers is the synchronized statement. This statement is for synchronizing multiple threads in Java. Because Java is natively multithreaded, the language itself has some constructs to aid in handling multiple threads. The synchronized statement behaves similar to a critical section lock, also sometimes called a monitor. When two threads synchronize on the same object, only one is allowed to process. The second thread automatically waits until the first thread is finished with its statement block.

Java Classes, Packages, and Archives

All programs in Java are a part of some class. Classes, as we have seen, are written in the Java source code language and then are translated to class files. Class files consist of machine-independent byte codes. The class file byte codes essentially represent machine operations to the Java Virtual Machine and are the instructions that get executed by the JVM.

As you might imagine, when you are doing large-scale development, you will quickly find that you need some methods to organize your class files, because you may quickly get hundreds of files to organize and manage.

Packages are hierarchical groupings of class files. They are a logical grouping and can be implemented physically in different ways. One simple and common way to organize the files in a package is with an operating system file directory structure. You simply use the hierarchical nature of file folders (directories) containing other nested folders to implement a hierarchical structure.

In Java, names are specified by a combination of identifiers and periods. The rightmost name represents the classname. All the other qualifiers in the name represent the package. For example, in `java.lang.Object`, `java.lang` represents the package name, and the name `Object` represents the classname. In the name `java.awt.event.ActionEvent`, the name `ActionEvent` is the classname and `java.awt.event` is the package name.

If you have the packages `java.awt`, `java.awt.datatransfer`, `java.awt.event`, `java.awt.image`, and `java.awt.peer`, you can imagine a directory folder structure that could accommodate this:

```
java
   awt
         datatransfer
         event
         image
         peer
```

In this case, there may also be other packages below the `java` level, such as `java.io`, `java.lang`, and `java.net`. When you have such a directory structure, all the classes in the `java.awt.event` package, for example, are stored in the directory that corresponds to that package.

When you are working by yourself on a small project, this structure is probably fine. You have everything you need, and it is all visible and easily accessible. However, suppose you are developing a large system and there are hundreds of components. It soon becomes much harder to manage multiple user access to hundreds of different files. Because of this, archive files were developed.

The original archive file format for Java was a ZIP file. This type of file was a de facto standard around the Internet, and many or most PC users have some sort of program, such as `pkzip`, `pkunzip`, or `winzip`, to create and extract files from ZIP files. By using a ZIP format, all the class files can be incorporated in a single file in the operating system. Also, the directory structure within the file can be preserved so that you can still have the hierarchical nature of the packages.

It was soon discovered, however, that users of these ZIP files did not realize that you could use the files within the ZIP archive and that you did not need to unzip the files in order to be used by Java. So a new format was created called the Java Archive (JAR) file. This essentially was just another name for a ZIP file, and all the ZIP file utilities can be used to create and extract from these files also. The only difference is that a JAR file should also contain a manifest file, which is like a table of contents and enables the members of the JAR file to have attributes. The attributes are stored within the manifest file in the JAR.

Finally, Microsoft decided that it wanted a format that was unique to its products. It already had a format called CAB, which stands for cabinet. It incorporated the CAB file format with its Internet Explorer. CAB files have an advantage in that they have a better compression algorithm, so the files are smaller. They have a disadvantage in that the files are in a Microsoft proprietary standard format and might not be supported on platforms other than Windows. If a product does support the CAB file format, it probably provides the same functionality as the JAR format.

For package files that are widely distributed, the packages should follow a naming convention outlined in the Java Language Specification. If two packages from different sources by chance had the same name, a user might have a very limited ability to fix the problem, because the source code might not be available. If the company producing the Java code has an Internet domain name, the first two levels of the package name should use them in reverse order. For example:

`com.ibm.CORBA.iiop`

`com.lotus.esuite.util`

`com.sun.java.swing`

`uk.acme.widgets.starter`

`gov.whitehouse.shredder.docs`

The highest-level qualifier of `java` (and `javax`) is reserved by JavaSoft for standard libraries and extensions, so you should never name your classes beginning with these names. If your packages do not begin with the domain type, you should probably use your company name as the high-level qualifier, as in

`lotus.chart`

`lotus.notes.addins`

`sun.net.ftp`

Sun recommends that if you are creating classes for local use, the first letter of your package should be lowercase.

There are no `#include` statements in Java. In C and C++, you use the `#include` statement to include additional source code modules. In Java, you use the `import` statement to accomplish a similar effect. The purpose of the Java `import` statement is slightly different than the `#include` statement of C++, however. The purpose of the Java `import` statement is to allow your programs to use a shorthand notation.

You can import a single class or an entire package. Here are some examples:

```
import java.awt.Graphics;
import java.applet.*;
import lotus.domino.*;
```

The first `import` statement is importing a single class, and the second two statements are importing entire packages. These two `import` statements allow a shorthand for all the classes in the respective packages.

You could refer to the `Applet` class as

`public class MyApplet extends java.applet.Applet`

or, if you have done the import, you can refer to the class as

`public class MyApplet extends Applet`

You can always refer to classes by their fully qualified names, so importing classes is not strictly required in any program, but it can make the program much more legible. You do not need to import the `java.lang` package, because all methods in that package are imported by default. The controlling factor on whether a class is found is the class path.

JAVA EXCEPTION HANDLING

Like C++, Java uses exception handling to handle runtime errors that occur in programs. In C++, exceptions were added as an innovation after the language was already in use, and as a result, there are many C++ programs that do not use exceptions. In contrast, Java has had exceptions since its origin, so you will probably find that most—if not all—Java programs use the exception handling model.

Exception handling involves the use of several different statements and objects. The essence of exception handling is that you group statements that might potentially cause an exception (including within called subroutines), and then if one occurs, you can catch it and handle it. Syntactically you use the `try-catch` statement for grouping. Here is the full syntax:

```
try {
      // This is the try block. Normal program statements are here
      // If an exception occurs, this block may be left early.
}
catch (Exceptiontype1 e1) {
      // This block catches exceptions of type Exceptiontype1
}
catch (Exceptiontype2 e2) {
      // This block catches exceptions of type Exceptiontype2
}

// More catch clauses can appear here

finally {
      // Here are statements that will be executed in all cases.
      // This block will execute whether or not there is an exception.
}
```

You can have as many different types of exceptions as you want to handle. The `finally` clause does not appear within C++. This is a very useful clause for cleaning up anything you initialize in the `try` clause. It is better to clean up in the `finally` clause than a `catch` clause, because then the cleanup will occur in both the error and nonerror cases. In the error case, the `finally` clause will be executed after the `catch` clause.

An exception is created with the `throw` statement. The syntax for the `throw` statement is

`throw expression;`

The *expression* must result in an object of the class `Throwable`. All exceptions are extended from this class. You can create your own exception classes, and throw and catch the exceptions. This technique is useful whenever you have a program that might detect an error situation several levels deep within subroutines, but if an error occurs, you want the program to "unwind" to a higher-level routine for processing. Java provides a language mechanism to do this gracefully without resorting to return codes.

Any exceptions that are generated by Notes or Domino use the `NotesException` class. This class extends the `java.lang.Exception` class and contains two fields: `id` and `text`. Within the exception handler (the `catch` block), you can refer to these fields. Here is an example:

```
try {
    ... Statements ...
}
catch (NotesException e) {
   System.out.println("NotesException: " + e.id + " ... " + e.text);
   e.printStackTrace();
}
catch (Exception e) {
   e.printStackTrace();
}
```

This code prints out the Notes error code and message along with the standard Java stack trace. For exceptions other than a `NotesException`, only the stack trace is printed.

> **Note**
>
> In release 4.6 of Notes and Domino, you used the `getErrorCode` method to extract the error code from the `NotesException` class. This method is no longer available. In release 5, you must use the `id` and `text` fields. Symbolic names for the codes may be found in the `NotesError` class.

Java Multithreading

In Java, multithreading is built into the language. This feature is one of the reasons why you may want to consider Java rather than LotusScript for certain agents. Some types of programs lend themselves more easily to multithreading than others. If multithreading is one of the requirements of your application, Java is a good choice.

The Java language provides a built-in class called, remarkably enough, `Thread`. The fully qualified name of this class is `java.lang.Thread`, so it exists in the `java.lang` package. Notes provides an important extension to this class called `NotesThread`. Let's take a look at both of these classes. I'll first describe `Thread` and then the extensions provided by `NotesThread`.

The `Thread` class is used to implement all threads in Java. You can implement your thread in two ways using the `Thread` class (there is one additional way with `NotesThread`). The first method is to write your own class that extends the `Thread` class. In this case, your class actually is a special case of a thread. You write your own class method called `run()` that overrides the base class method.

The second way to implement a thread involves two separate classes. With this approach, you create your own class that does not extend the `Thread` class. Rather, you implement an interface called the `Runnable` interface. This interface defines only one method, the `run()` method. You create an instance of your class, and then create an instance of the `Thread` class and pass your class to the `Thread` constructor. At the appropriate time, your `run()` method will be called.

Okay, so you now know that the code of your thread will exist within the `run` method. When does the code in the `run` method get invoked? You might think that it would start up as soon as your object is created, but it does not. If that were to happen, you wouldn't get much of a chance to initialize or set things up for your thread before it got off and running. So the creation of your thread and the running of it are separated. To start the code found in your `run()` method, you invoke the `start()` method of the thread. This gives you a chance to do some initialization prior to your invoking of the `start` method. It also means that if you forget to invoke `start`, your thread will never run.

The location of the `start` method depends upon which way you created the thread. If you derived your class (that is, you extended it) from the `Thread` class, your own class has the `start` method. If you created a separate class and implemented the `Runnable` interface, the `start` method is invoked on the `Thread` object you created separately.

Here is an example of the first method of implementing threads:

```java
public class MyMain1 {
   public static void main(String args[]) {
     try {
       ExtendedThread etMyThread = new ExtendedThread(); // My Thread
       etMyThread.start(); // This will eventually invoke my run();
       etMyThread.join();  // Wait for thread to finish
     }
     catch(InterruptedException e) {
     }
   }
}
public class ExtendedThread extends Thread {
   public void run() {
      System.out.println("ExtendedThread Running!");
   }
}
```

In this example, the `ExtendedThread` object is created with the `new` statement. The thread does not actually start until the `start` method is called. At that time, the `start` method initializes the thread and invokes its `run` method. Meanwhile, the original thread returns from the call to `start` and continues. At this point, it executes the `join` method, which causes the `main` thread to wait until the second thread has finished execution. When it does, the `main` thread wakes up again and finishes the program.

Here is an example of the second method of implementing threads:

```java
public class MyMain2 {
   public static void main(String args[]) {
     try {
       RunnableThread rtMyThread = new RunnableThread(); // My Thread
       Thread theThread = new Thread(rtMyThread);  // java.lang.Thread
       theThread.start();  // This will eventually invoke my run();
       theThread.join();   // Wait for thread to finish
     }
     catch(InterruptedException e) {
     }
   }
}
class RunnableThread implements Runnable {
   public void run() {
      System.out.println("RunnableThread Running!");
   }
}
```

In this second example, note that the class `RunnableThread` is not really a thread; it just runs on a separate thread from the `main` thread. You can think of the `run` method in this case as if it were a `main` program entry point.

In both of these examples, the `join` method is used to synchronize the `main` thread with the newly created thread. It would normally be considered a good programming practice for the main thread to wait until the subsidiary threads have finished before it finishes itself.

You might be asking when you should extend the `Thread` class and when you should use the `Runnable` interface. If you have complete control over all your classes, it doesn't matter too much which method you use. You can use either. Sometimes, however, you don't have complete control because you may be using some existing classes. In this case, you may not be able to take a class and have it extend the `Thread` class, because you can use only single inheritance in Java and the class you are working with may already be extending something else. In this situation, you should use the `Runnable` interface on your existing class, because you will not need to extend the `Thread` class. You need only to add the `run` method. Here is an example of the declaration:

```
public class MyClass extends MyBaseClass implements Runnable {
   // Here is your MyClass stuff

   public void run() {
      // Thread code here
   }
}
```

In this case, you don't need to modify any code in the `MyBaseClass` class. In fact, you may not even have the source code for that class. You just need to implement your extensions to the base class, implement one additional method (the `run` method), and pass your class to the `Thread` constructor. After that, the base class, as well as your extensions, will be run on a separate thread.

Notes and Domino Multithreading Using Java

You can use the threading mechanisms I described in the previous section within Notes and Domino. However, if you use them, you will not be able to access any Notes or Domino data. You can use the standard Java threading classes only if you are going to use them for animation or other standard Web kinds of processing in, for example, a standard Java applet. If you want to use threading and access Domino databases or services, you must use the `NotesThread` class.

Now that you've seen the two ways to implement threads with the standard Java libraries, let me show you the modifications necessary to use threads within Notes and Domino. Because `NotesThread` extends the standard Java `Thread` class, the first method you can use to create your thread is to extend `NotesThread`. It works similarly to regular Java, but rather than implement a `run()` method, you must implement a `runNotes()` method. The second way to implement threading with Notes is to implement a `Runnable` interface. In this case, you still implement a `run()` method, not a `runNotes` method. Here are the previous two examples, slightly modified for the Notes and Domino environment. As mentioned, you must supply a `runNotes` method for this approach to work. In `NotesThread`, the `run` method is specified as `final`, so you will not be allowed to override the `run` method even if you want to. You will get a compile-time error message if you attempt to use `run` instead of `runNotes`. Here is an example of the first method of implementing threads within Notes and Domino:

```
public class MyNotesMain1 {
   public static void main(String args[]) {
```

```
      try {
        ExtendedThread etMyThread = new ExtendedThread(); // My Thread
        etMyThread.start();  // This will eventually invoke my runNotes();
        etMyThread.join();   // Wait for thread to finish
      }
      catch(InterruptedException e) {
      }
   }
}
public class ExtendedThread extends NotesThread {
   public void runNotes() {
      System.out.println("ExtendedThread Running!");
   }
}
```

Notice that the main program is essentially identical to the version that we created for regular Java threading. The only changes are found in the ExtendedThread class, where it extends NotesThread instead of Thread and contains a runNotes method instead of a run method.

> **Note**
>
> You may see some Domino examples and documentation combine the two classes I've shown previously into a single class. This single class extends NotesThread (as in the ExtendedThread) and also has a static main method as well.
>
> I use two classes to illustrate and make clear that the main method is called on the caller's thread. The runNotes method is running on a newly created, separate thread. If you combine both the main and runNotes methods in one class, make sure you understand that main and runNotes will be running on separate threads, even though they are defined in the same class.
>
> The same note applies to combining the two classes in the following example.

Here is an example of the second method of implementing threads within Notes and Domino:

```
public class MyNotesMain2 {
   public static void main(String args[]) {
      try {
         RunnableThread rtMyThread = new RunnableThread(); // My Thread
         NotesThread theThread = new NotesThread(rtMyThread);  // NotesThread
extends java.lang.Thread
         theThread.start();  // This will eventually invoke my run();
         theThread.join();   // Wait for thread to finish
      }
      catch(InterruptedException e) {
      }
   }
}
class RunnableThread implements Runnable {
   public void run() {
      System.out.println("RunnableThread Running!");
   }
}
```

You can easily see by comparing the Notes/Domino version with the previous version that the interfaces are very similar. In the Notes version of the applications, it is even more critical for the `main` routine to wait until the secondary threads have finished (via the `join` method). This is because Notes or Domino will automatically terminate all the subsidiary threads when the `main` thread finishes. So the subsidiary threads cannot run longer than the `main` thread.

It should be apparent from the examples why the `NotesThread` version uses `runNotes` and the `Runnable` version uses the `run` method. When you extend `NotesThread`, your class is a `NotesThread`. That means it contains the prewritten Lotus code to implement `run`, and you cannot override and use this method. The Lotus code within `run` eventually calls your `runNotes` method after it initializes the Notes environment. On the other hand, when you implement the `Runnable` interface, your code is in a separate class, and your `run` method does not conflict with the Lotus version of the `run` method. By the time your `run` method is called, the `NotesThread` class has already set up the Notes environment. Here is the sequence of calls upon startup of a `Runnable` class:

>   `java.lang.Thread:start` creates a thread and calls (the new thread).
>
>   `NotesThread:run` initializes Notes environment and calls.

`YourClass:run` is your thread code in the `run` method. I mentioned that there was a third way to create a `NotesThread` besides the two that are normally available for all threads. This approach uses `static` methods within the `NotesThread` class to initialize Notes *on the currently running thread*. You use this approach if your program is invoked on a thread over which you have no control. In essence, rather than create a new `NotesThread` object, this approach initializes Notes without creating a separate `NotesThread` and turns the currently running thread into a pseudo-`NotesThread`.

This approach to initializing Notes can also be used if you write a standalone Java application that will use Notes classes. There is no particular reason for doing so, however, because either of the preceding two methods will also work.

If you do need to initialize Notes on the currently running thread, here is how you do it. First, you must call `NotesThread.sinitThread()` prior to using any other Notes/Domino classes. When you are finished with the Notes classes, you must call `NotesThread.stermThread()`. These two calls must be balanced. In particular, even if exceptions occur, you must be sure to call `stermThread` before your routine exits. Here is some sample code:

```
public class MyNotesMain3 {
   public static void main(String args[]) {
     try {
       NotesThread.sinitThread(); // Initialize Notes on the currently running
➥thread
       // Here you can place any Java code
     }
     catch(Exception e) {
       e.printStackTrace();      // Print a stack trace
     }
```

```
      finally {
        NotesThread.stermThread(); // This will be called in all cases
      }
    }
  }
}
```

Notice that in this code, I used the `finally` clause to house the `stermThread` call. By implementing the termination this way, the thread Notes environment will be terminated whether or not there is an exception. If you fail to properly terminate the Notes environment, your program can hang or cause an abnormal termination.

THE Session CLASS

We've seen so far how Notes and Domino use the `NotesThread` class to implement the startup and shutdown of the Notes and Domino environment. After this environment is set up, however, there is one additional class that must be used to initiate access to Domino. This class is the `Session` class, which corresponds to the `NotesSession` class of LotusScript.

The `Session` class is at the top of the Domino Object Model hierarchy. All other classes are obtained via the `Session`, either directly or indirectly. For example, from a `Session` object, you can get a `DbDirectory` object, through which you can access Domino databases. You can also obtain an `AgentContext` object (in an agent) from the `Session`, which gives you information about the current agent's context.

Okay, if the `Session` class is so important, how do you create one? Good question. There are two ways to get a `Session` object. You can either create one from scratch or you can obtain one from another class that happens to have one. When you are writing an agent, Notes will create a `Session` object for you, and you can just obtain it. When you are writing any other type of Java program, you have to create it from scratch. Creating a new `Session` in Java from scratch is very similar to using the LotusScript statement `Dim session As new NotesSession`. In Java, you use the `CreateSession` method of the `NotesFactory` class. Here is how you do it with Java:

```
Session s = NotesFactory.CreateSession();
```

> **Note**
> In release 4.6 of Notes and Domino, you used the `static Session.newInstance` method to create a new `Session` variable from scratch. The `NotesFactory` method now takes the place of `Session.newInstance`.

I mentioned that when you are writing code for an agent, you can obtain the `Session` object that was created for you. Within an agent context, you must do two things. First, your agent must extend the `AgentBase` class, and then you must have a `NotesMain` method. Within the `NotesMain` method, you use

```
Session s = this.getSession();
```

I'll describe this in more detail in the next section.

Java Agents, Applets, Applications, and Servlets

The Java language can be used in several different contexts with Notes and Domino. In particular, you can use Java in agents, applets, applications, and servlets. Each of these different contexts interacts differently with the Domino environment, so let me explain these contexts. In Chapter 19, "Using the IDE with LotusScript, Java, and JavaScript," I told you about the differences between these types of programs and when each language could be used. I'd like to examine each of the Java contexts now in more detail.

Some of the main characteristics of these different types of programs are how they are created, how they are invoked, and how they are terminated. In each section, I'll describe these characteristics.

Domino Java Agents

Java agents in Domino are really just special cases of the NotesThread class that we saw earlier. In order to create an agent, you extend the AgentBase class. However, the AgentBase class itself is just an extension of the NotesThread class, so without necessarily knowing it, your agent is also a NotesThread.

When I showed you how a NotesThread is started, I said that you need to provide only one routine, the runNotes method. When the NotesThread is started, the runNotes method is invoked automatically. In the special case of agents, however, the Notes system has some additional housekeeping chores to perform before it can start your code. So, in the case of agents, Notes commandeers the runNotes method, declares it final so you cannot use it, and substitutes the NotesMain method for your code. Here is how a Notes Java agent actually starts up:

> java.lang.Thread:start creates a thread and calls (the new thread).
>
> NotesThread:run initializes Notes environment and calls.
>
> AgentBase:runNotes initializes Agent environment and calls.
>
> YourAgent:NotesMain is your agent code.

The AgentBase runNotes method sets up an AgentContext object for you and creates a Session object for you. Because your agent extends the AgentBase class, you can use this.getSession to get the Session object that was created by runNotes.

If we look at the code that is automatically produced for you by the Domino Designer IDE for a Java agent, it should now be very clear. Notice that the getSession call omits the this qualifier. You can use either this.getSession or just plain getSession. It is important to understand the shorthand and why you don't need to use the this qualifier. (It's because getSession is defined in `AgentBase` and your agent extends `AgentBase`, so in effect your agent is an `AgentBase`.) Here's the code:

```
public class JavaAgent extends AgentBase {
   public void NotesMain() {
      try {
         Session session = getSession();
         AgentContext agentContext = session.getAgentContext();

         // (Your code goes here)

      } catch(Exception e) {
         e.printStackTrace();
      }
   }
}
```

Your Java agent automatically terminates when your `NotesMain` method ends. After it ends, control is returned in the reverse order to `AgentBase:runNotes` and then `NotesThread:run`. When `run` finishes, the thread itself is finished.

Also notice in the automatically generated code that an `AgentContext` is obtained for you. The `AgentContext` includes information such as the effective username, the current database, and the set of unprocessed documents that the agent should handle, along with several other agent properties.

Remember that an agent can run on either the Notes client or a Domino server. When the agent is running on the Notes client, the effective user is the current workstation user ID. However, when the agent is run on the server, the effective user is the user who last signed the agent. In addition, via the agent properties, you can also set up the agent to run with the identity of a Web user.

You can run a Java agent on a Domino server via a URL. You do this from a Web browser with the following syntax:

http://*server*/*database.nsf*/*agentname*

The database must exist, of course, and the specified agent must be a shared agent within the database. To send output back to the Web user, you must create a `PrintWriter` object by getting it from the `AgentBase` object. Here is how you do that:

```
Session s = getSession();
AgentContext ac = s.getAgentContext();
PrintWriter pw = getAgentOutput();    // Get AgentOutput
pw.println("<h1>Hello World</h1>");   // Send output back to browser
```

In order for this to work, make sure that your agent is declared as a shared agent. Note that you can specify this choice only when the agent is created. After it's created, you cannot turn a nonshared agent into a shared agent. You make an agent shared by checking the check box directly beneath the agent's name in the Create Agent dialog box.

The capability of running an agent on the server is similar to the servlet capability. There are a few differences, however. First, an agent is stored within a Domino database. Because of this, it can be replicated and can travel along with the database to another server. In addition, Java agents use the Domino security model and are more secure than servlets. Agents are written by extending `AgentBase` as previously described, and you use a `NotesMain` method for your agent code.

Java servlets are stored as Java class files within a directory on the server. Servlets can be initialized and stay active within the Domino server. When resident, a servlet can process many requests in a multithreaded manner from several Web clients at once. The capability of remaining in memory can provide servlets with an important performance advantage for certain applications. Because servlets may be handling many requests simultaneously, it is critical that servlets be threadsafe.

One common use for servlets is to access non-Domino databases via JDBC. You can also access Domino databases using the Java techniques described in previous sections. Servlets are an industry standard for server-side Java programming, whereas Agents are much more Domino-specific.

Domino servlets are implemented as extensions of the `lotus.domino.servlet` class. There is a full discussion of servlets in the section entitled "Java Servlets," later in this chapter.

JAVA APPLETS

An applet is a set of one or more Java classes that is downloaded to a Web browser and executed within the context of the JVM in the Web browser itself. Regular Java applets are independent of Notes and Domino. You can have Java applets that are created and served by a Web server, such as Domino or any other Web server.

Just as Domino Java Agents are special cases of the Java `Thread` class, with release 5 of Notes and Domino you can have specialized Domino applets as well. Let me first describe a regular Java applet, and then I'll explain how Domino Java applets are different.

An applet in Java is actually invoked by the Web browser. There is no main method in a Java applet. In fact, there are four important methods in a Java applet: `init`, `start`, `stop`, and `destroy`. Here are their definitions:

- `void init()`   This method is invoked when the applet is first loaded. It is called only once.
- `void start()`   This method is invoked after the `init` method. It is also invoked when the page comes into view or the browser is restored from an icon view.
- `void stop()`   This method is invoked when the page is left or when the browser is minimized into an icon.
- `void destroy()`   This method is invoked when the applet is no longer required. It is called after the `stop` method.

For completeness, I should mention that a Java applet is not actually a base class. As a matter of fact, it is four layers down in the hierarchy. The upper layers are `Component`, `Container`, `Panel`, and `Applet`. In other words, `Applet` extends `Panel`, which extends `Container`, which extends `Component`. These classes can be found in the java.awt package. It is beyond my scope here to explain all these other classes, but you should be aware of them. Suffice it to say that these other classes deal with user-interface characteristics, such as layout and the graphical appearance of the applet.

DOMINO JAVA APPLETS

What exactly is a Domino Java applet? A regular applet that is served by a Domino server to a Web browser might qualify, but that is not what I mean by a Domino Java applet. A Domino Java applet is an applet that has the capability of accessing the Domino Object Model. In other words, it can do everything that a normal applet can do, but it can also access Domino.

What does it mean to access Domino? This is an important question. Remember that a regular applet is a Java program running within the JVM in the Web browser. To clarify things, think about this hypothetical case. Suppose you have the newest gadget, a Web-enabled television set. This TV is a pure Java machine. It has a Java Virtual Machine (JVM) installed and can download and execute Java programs, but it certainly isn't a personal computer. Can you execute a Domino Java applet? Yes. In your Web television set, you can access Domino databases, traverse views, and use a Java program to perform functions that you might have used LotusScript for previously.

It is important to understand the capabilities of a Domino Java applet and to understand how this type of applet differs from a regular, ordinary Java applet. Let's take a look at a Domino Java applet.

A Domino Java applet is very similar in concept and implementation to a Domino Java Agent. If we want to create a Domino Java applet, we must extend the `AppletBase` class. This is analogous to extending the `AgentBase` class for agents. After we have extended `AppletBase`, there are four important methods for our Domino Java applet:

- void notesAppletInit()   This method is invoked when the applet is first loaded. It is called only once.
- void notesAppletStart()   This method is invoked after the `notesAppletInit` method. It is also invoked when the page comes into view or the browser is restored from an icon view.
- void notesAppletStop()   This method is invoked when the page is left or when the browser is minimized into an icon.
- void notesAppletDestroy()   This method is invoked when the applet is no longer required. This method is called after the `notesAppletStop` method.

I'm sure that you can see the immediate similarity to the four methods that are defined for a regular applet. Just as in the case for agents, the four `notesApplet` methods correspond to the underlying methods. I should also mention that the regular `init`, `start`, `stop`, and `destroy` methods are declared final within `AppletBase`, so you are not allowed to override them, and you should not call them directly.

There are two additional methods in the `AppletBase` class. The first method is another one similar to one found in `AgentBase`. It is our old friend `getSession`. Remember that we need to have a `Session` object to access the Domino Object Model. After we have this `Session` object, we can pretty much traverse the entire object model hierarchy. There are two forms for `getSession` within `AppletBase`:

```
Session s = getSession();    // Anonymous access
Session s = getSession(String userid, String password);
```

The first of these methods is used for anonymous access, and in the second method, you pass the user ID and password strings.

The last method in `AppletBase` is the `IsNotesLocal` method. This routine returns true if the applet is running within a Notes client and is accessing a local database. It returns false if you are accessing a remote server.

I have not described, until now, the magic that is used to implement Domino access from a Web-enabled television set. Hold on to your hats, here come the acronyms: CORBA and IIOP. These two technologies are important because they basically enable you to perform client/server computing, using Web browsers and Java over the Internet. The client can be any Java-enabled Web browser, and the server is Domino. I describe these technologies in more detail later in the chapter.

Java Standalone Applications

With Java, unlike LotusScript, you can create a standalone application and run it from a command-line prompt. There are a couple of scenarios here. First, you can access local Domino databases if you have Java and the Notes executable files present on your computer. This will typically be the configuration on your desktop or laptop computer if you are using the Notes client.

Second, with those magic components CORBA and IIOP, you can create a standalone Java application that runs on your desktop, but accesses a remote Domino server. In this case, all you need to have present on your local computer is a JVM and the appropriate class files. You do not need to have the Notes executable files present.

In the previous section, "Notes and Domino Multithreading Using Java," I showed you how to create a standalone Java application for Notes. As mentioned, a standalone application can extend `NotesThread`, or you can create a class that implements the `Runnable` interface. In either case, you must also have a `static` `main` routine. This `main` routine is invoked by the

JVM machine. Here is an example of a Java program that extends `NotesThread`. This is an example that must run locally. It does not use CORBA or IIOP:

```
public class MyNotesMain4 {
  public static void main(String args[]) {
    try {
      ExtendedThread etMyThread = new ExtendedThread(); // My Thread
      etMyThread.start();  // This will eventually invoke my runNotes();
      etMyThread.join();   // Wait for thread to finish
    }
    catch(InterruptedException e) {
    }
  }
}
public class ExtendedThread extends NotesThread {
  public void runNotes() {
    try {
       Session s = NotesFactory.createSession(); // Create a new Session
       String v = s.getNotesVersion();  // Notes version
       String p = s.getPlatform();      // Platform
       System.out.println("Running version " + v + " on platform " + p);
    }
    catch (Exception e) {
       e.prtinStackTrace();
    }
  }
}
```

Here is how this routine starts up:

> JVM calls `MyMain4:main`, which creates a thread and calls.
>
> `Thread:start` (`ExtendedThread:start`) initializes a thread and calls.
>
> `NotesThread:run` initializes Notes environment and calls.
>
> `ExtendedThread:runNotes` is the main code.

Note Do not confuse the `Thread:start` routine with the `Applet:start` routine. Although they have the same method name, they are completely different methods. `Thread:start` is a system routine that starts a thread; `Applet:start` is an optional user-written routine invoked by a browser when an applet starts.

The following example uses CORBA and IIOP. This `main` program can run on a client that does not have the Notes executables locally:

```
public class MyNotesMain5 {
  public static void main(String args[]) {
    try {
      RunnableThread rtMyThread = new RunnableThread(); // My Thread
      NotesThread theThread = new NotesThread(rtMyThread);  // NotesThread
➥extends java.lang.Thread
      theThread.start();  // This will eventually invoke my run();
```

```
      theThread.join();   // Wait for thread to finish
    }
    catch(InterruptedException e) {
    }
  }
}
class RunnableThread implements Runnable {
  public void run() {
    try {
      String IOR = lotus.domino.NotesFactory.getIOR("ACMESERVER");
      System.out.println("IOR='" + IOR + "'");
      Session s = NotesFactory.createSession(IOR, "John Doe/AcmeCorp",
➥"secretpassword");
      String v = s.getNotesVersion();   // Notes version
      String p = s.getPlatform();       // Platform
      System.out.println("Running version " + v + " on platform " + p);
    }
    catch (Exception e) {
      e.prtinStackTrace();
    }
  }
}
```

This code is an example of the `Runnable` interface. The major point to notice in this example is the fact that we have a new variable called `IOR`. `IOR` stands for Interoperable Object Reference. The `IOR` is specified as a string. If you print it out, you'll notice that it is a huge (and I mean huge), hexadecimal string. This string is used to set up the CORBA communication between the client and the server. If you are debugging online, you'll also notice a fairly long delay when you create the `Session` because of all the CORBA initialization. After the CORBA initialization has finished, however, the application will run fairly quickly.

The two examples `MyNotesMain4` and `MyNotesMain5` showed two different ways to create a standalone application. `MyNotesMain4` created an inherited thread, and `MyNotesMain5` created a `Runnable` class. You can use CORBA via either method.

One final note about this example: If you want to try this example yourself, you need to substitute your server name, your user ID, and your password at the appropriate points in the program.

JAVA SERVLETS

Java servlets are programs written in Java that run on a Domino server. A Web browser user can access them via a URL. When the URL for a servlet is invoked, the JVM in the Domino server starts the specified servlet. Here is an example of a servlet invocation:

`http://servername/servlet/Processit/the/pathvar?myquery=color`

Servlets are invoked with a path parameter and a query parameter. In this example, the servlet name is `Processit`, the path parameter is `/the/pathvar`, and the query parameter is `myquery=color`.

Servlets require some additional configuration to be able to execute in Domino, and you must have a copy of the Java Servlet Development Kit (JSDK). There are several major tasks to enable servlets:

1. Update the Domino Directory to enable servlets.
2. Create and compile your servlet Java programs.
3. Put your servlet's class files into the `Domino\servlet` directory under your main `Domino\Data` directory on your server. You may have to create the servlet directory, because it is not created by default. The complete path will be something like `d:\Domino\Data\domino\servlet`.
4. Type `tell http restart` on the Domino server console.

UPDATE YOUR DOMINO DIRECTORY

You must have administrator privileges to update the Domino Directory. To enable servlets

- In the Domino Administrator client, first choose the Domino server.
- Click on the Configuration tab.
- Click on the Current Server Document item in the Server section. You will see the current server's configuration document with a set of tabs across the top.
- Click on the Internet Protocols tab.
- Click on the Domino Web Engine subtab.
- There is a section entitled Java Servlets. In this section:
  - Make sure you are in edit mode and change the Java servlet support from None (the default) to Domino Servlet manager.
  - Leave the Servlet URL path `/servlet` (this is the default).
  - Leave the class path `Domino/servlet` (this is the default).
  - Leave all the other entries at their default value.
- Save and close the document.

CREATING A SERVLET

The JSDK defines the servlet APIs. The most basic servlet implements the `javax.servlet.Servlet` interface. Also supplied with the JSDK, however is an implementation of this interface called `javax.servlet.http.HttpServlet`. Most servlet implementations just extend this class. By default, servlets are multithreaded, but if you want your servlet to be single-threaded for some reason, you add `implements SingleThreadModel` to your class declaration. No extra coding is required for a single-threaded servlet.

The `javax.servlet.Servlet` interface defines just five methods `init`, `destroy`, `service`, `getServletConfig`, and `getServletInfo`. If you extend `HttpServlet`, you will be concerned with the following methods: `init`, `destroy`, and `getServletInfo` and then four higher-level routines: `doGet`, `doHead`, `doPost`, and `doPut`.

Processing an HTTP request involves two objects: the request object and the result object. The request object is of the class `HttpServletRequest`, and the result object is of the class `HttpServletResponse`. You can use the result object to obtain a `ServletOutputStream` object, and then you can call the `println` method.

Before you send back any response, you must set the content type. You do this with the `setContentType` method. Here is a sample servlet:

```java
import java.io.*;
import javax.servlet.*;
import javax.servlet.http.*;
import lotus.domino.*;

/* This is an example of a Domino Java HTTP Servlet.  */
public class PlatformServlet extends HttpServlet {
    public String getServletInfo() {
        return "Create a page that says Hello from Platform Servlet";
    }
    public void doGet(HttpServletRequest req, HttpServletResponse res) throws
➥ServletException, IOException {
        try {
            // Before sending output, set the content type.
            res.setContentType("text/html");

            // Initialize a NotesThread
            NotesThread.sinitThread();
            Session s = NotesFactory.createSession();
            System.out.println("Got past createSession");
            // Get the ServletOutputStream for sending response back
            ServletOutputStream out = res.getOutputStream();
            out.println("<HTML><HEAD><TITLE>Example Servlet</TITLE></HEAD>");
            out.println("<BODY>");
            out.println("<H1>Hello from Platform Servlet</H1>");
            out.println("<p>The server is running on the <B>" + s.getPlatform() +
➥"</B> platform");
            out.println("</BODY></HTML>");
            System.out.println("finished");
            out.close();
        }
        catch (Exception e) {
            e.printStackTrace();
        }
        finally {
            NotesThread.stermThread();
        }
    } // end doGet
} // end PlatformServlet
```

Finish Setting Up the Servlet

After you have created and compiled your Java servlet into a class file, place it into the `d:domino\data\domino\servlet` directory.

Finally, type `tell http restart` on the Domino server console. This is a new console command in release 5. It tells the HTTP server to reinitialize itself. Previously, you had to tell it to stop, and then tell it to load again. The restart command makes it a little easier. Note that if you are in a development cycle, the servlets are in memory, and the only way to flush them out is to restart the server. On occasion, I've also found that there are some disk caches (on the server and also possibly in the client-side browser) of the applet class files. If it seems as if your development changes are not having an effect, make sure to clear the caches and restart the HTTP task. You may also even have to restart the entire Domino server to clear out some caches.

INVOKING THE SERVLET FROM THE WEB BROWSER

Now you have finished creating and setting up your servlet. To test it from the Web browser, type a request in the following format:

`http://www.yourserver.com/servlet/PlatformServlet`

You must replace the server name with your real server name. The `/servlet` that follows matches the entry you made in the Domino Directory for Servlet URL path. Following that is the name of the servlet itself. In this case, we have named the servlet "PlatformServlet." Note that the name of the servlet is case sensitive, so be sure to use the proper case for the name or it will not be found.

NOTES AND DOMINO JAR FILES

There are several JAR files that come with Notes and Domino. Some of these JAR files contain Java support files, and some files are tied specifically to Notes and Domino. You may not see all of them because some of them reside on the server. The files will be located in the Notes executable directory for local access or will be in the `notes\data\domino\html` directory on the server if the files will be required to be served to a client.

The following files normally will appear in your Notes executable directory, which is either on your Notes client or on the Domino server:

- `rt.jar`   This JAR file contains the Java standard runtime environment routines. It contains `java.lang.*`, `java.io.*`, `java.util.*`, and `java.net.*`, as well as several other class libraries.
- `i18n.jar`   This JAR file contains class libraries for international language support.
- `tools.jar`   This JAR file contains classes for debugging and other support from Sun Microsystems. The classes in this library all begin with `sun.*`.
- `notes.jar`   This JAR file contains classes for the local operation of Java within the Notes client. It contains all the local (as opposed to CORBA) implementations of the Domino Object Model classes.

- `jsdk.jar` This JAR file contains the standard extension classes for servlets—`javax.servlet.*`—as well as some Sun classes—`sun.servlet.*`.
- `dservlet.jar` This JAR file contains the Domino servlet classes contained in the package `lotus.domino.servlet.*`.

The following files normally appear in the `Domino\Data\domino\java` directory on the server and in the `Notes\Data\domino\java` directory on the client. Notice that the archives exist in JAR format (the industry standard), in CAB format (the Microsoft version), and in ZIP format (an older version of the JAR format). This is so the server can serve up the version appropriate to your Web browser:

- `actionbar.jar/actionbar.cab/actionbar.zip` These archives hold the Action Bar Java applet.
- `editor.jar/editor.cab/editor.zip` These archives hold the rich text editor Java applet.
- `NCSO.jar/NCSO.cab/NCSOC.jar` These archives hold the Notes Client Side Objects classes. These classes implement the CORBA/IIOP implementations of the Domino Object Model. Because the Microsoft CAB format has better compression, it is only about one-third the size of the uncompressed JAR file. There is also a compressed JAR file that is called `NCSOC.jar`, and it is only a little bigger than the `NCSO.cab` file.
- `nvapplet.jar/nvapplet.cab/nvapplet.zip` These archives hold the view applet.
- `outline.jar/outline.cab/outline.zip` These archives hold the outline applet.

You should be aware that the Action Bar, rich text editor, view, and outline applets do not use CORBA to communicate with the Domino server. They use the HTTP protocol, which has the most likelihood of being able to pass through corporate firewalls. CORBA may be more appropriate for intranets because you control the communication within your corporation. CORBA may not make it from your server to a user behind another company's firewall.

CORBA and IIOP for the Acronym-Impaired

I've used the terms CORBA and IIOP several times in this chapter. I've also deferred a discussion of what these terms mean and their technical implications. Before I delve into those topics, though, let's back up the clock and look at how the regular Notes client communication with a Domino server is implemented.

The communication between a Notes client and Domino server during a user session is through a Notes proprietary interface. This interface was developed years ago, before standards such as CORBA and IIOP were invented. The Notes/Domino communication protocol works well and reliably to this day, but it has one major drawback, which is that only the Notes client and Domino server understand how to use it.

With the importance of the Internet, it is very desirable to allow any browser client to access a Domino server. This has been possible since the first release of the Domino server (at release 4.5), which converts Domino databases to HTML, which in turn can be rendered by a browser. This approach has the benefit that any browser can now be used as a client to a Domino server. You are no longer tied specifically to the Notes client. This approach, however, has a different drawback. That is, when using a browser, you lose some of the functionality that is provided by the Notes client.

So now we have two approaches. If we use the Notes client, we have extra functionality, but with the drawback that we cannot use a standard Web browser. If we use a Web browser, we lose some of the functionality of the Notes client. What are we to do?

Well, because you are an astute reader and you noticed the title of this section involves CORBA and IIOP, you certainly recognize that these technologies must be our strategy to solving these twin problems. By using CORBA and IIOP, we can gain the functionality of the Notes client, but we can have the ubiquity of the Web browser. Great! Now we know what problem the technology solves, but how does it do it?

CORBA stands for Common Object Request Broker Architecture. Notice that at the end of this name is the word *Architecture*. CORBA is not a product, like Notes, Domino, or Windows. It is not sold at your local computer store. Rather, CORBA is a standard specification that can be implemented within different products. The purpose of the specification is to allow different companies to write compliant products; and when the compliant products are used together, they will actually communicate.

So, by having a common architecture, defined by standards, clients and servers from different vendors can be used more successfully together. The ORB in the middle of CORBA stands for *object request broker*. You can think of an ORB in much the same way as a real estate broker, commodities broker, or stockbroker. The purpose of the broker is to bring together separate entities and enable them to make a transaction. In this case, the ORB brings together the client and the server.

So CORBA is used to define the mechanisms that enable clients and servers to transact. There still remains the detail of how they physically communicate. In real life, you might talk to your broker over the phone, see him or her in person, or just use a fax machine. The physical means you use to communicate is separate from the details of the transaction you are trying to accomplish.

The Internet Inter-ORB Protocol (IIOP) performs the same function as the phone network. IIOP is the protocol used by one ORB to talk to another ORB. So CORBA defines a higher-level interface for objects, methods, and properties, and the IIOP deals with communication issues between ORBs. The mechanism used by one ORB to talk to another ORB (IIOP) is independent of the topics of discussion (CORBA). In fact, CORBA can use other communications mechanisms, but by far the most interesting is the one that uses Internet standards (IIOP). This is the only one I will consider here.

Now that you understand about CORBA and IIOP, what is the tie-in to Domino? Lotus has implemented a set of Domino Java classes that can be downloaded to your Web browser. These are the classes that are held in the `NCSO.jar` archive. They are implemented using the CORBA/IIOP standards and they enable Java programs you have written as applets to interface through to the Domino server. You simply write the applet code and make calls to the normal Java Domino class interfaces, and the communication via CORBA/IIOP to the back-end classes is done for you automatically. So, in fact, you never even need to know that CORBA/IIOP is used on your behalf. The net effect is that your Java applets (and applications) can reside on a client workstation without Notes and can communicate to the Domino back-end classes. Thus, we are starting to be able to approach the Notes client level of functionality while using a browser interface.

There are a couple of caveats that may make this technology more suitable for intranets than Internet use at this time. First is that the `NCSO.jar` file is 1.5MB (the compressed versions are about 0.5MB), and on a 28.8 modem, this might take a while to download. With any fast communication protocol, this won't be a problem. Second, IIOP does not use the standard ports that are used by HTTP. In other words, IIOP opens up a separate communication channel from the client to the server. This improves efficiency, but it may cause problems if the clients and servers are separated by firewalls. Be careful to consider this possibility when you decide to use this technology.

DEBUGGING YOUR JAVA CODE

The Domino Designer environment now has the capability of creating Java agents via the IDE. You can create and compile Java source code. However, the Java IDE within the Domino designer does not contain any debugging facilities. You have a couple of choices. The first choice is to use a whole bunch of `println` calls in your program and open the Java console window. For very small agents, this might be entirely appropriate. For larger agents, this methodology will probably mean that your development will take longer than desirable. It would be very nice if you could debug your Java code within the third-party Java IDE you use to develop your code.

When you are developing an applet or application, you can use your Java IDE without a problem. As mentioned, you might want to use IBM Visual Age for Java, Inprise Jbuilder, or Symantec Visual Caf[as]e. Each of these Java IDEs contains a built-in debugger. You can debug your applets or applications because, in these environments, you are basically controlling the starting of your program, and your Java code obtains its own context starting from the `Session` object. This type of coding works from within a Java IDE. You can simply write your code, compile it, and interactively step through it with full debugging capabilities, such as breakpoints.

USING VISUAL AGE FOR JAVA 2.0

In this section, I describe details on how to use IBM's VA Java. This is a powerful Java development environment, and because of the ties between Lotus and IBM, I expect that this Java environment will be one of the first environments that is tested with Notes and Domino Java support. Our first step is to import the Domino Java class libraries. You import the class libraries by following these steps:

1. Import the appropriate JAR files into the VA Java environment. You do this by selecting File, Import.
2. When the dialog box comes up, select Jar file and click Next.
3. On the Import from a jar/zip file dialog box, locate the `NCSO.jar` file (for CORBA/IIOP support) or the `Notes.jar` file (for local database support) by clicking Browse on the Filename line. You can import both JAR files if desired.
4. Ensure that the class file check box is selected.
5. Under Project, type `Domino Java class library`.
6. Click Finish.

After the classes have been imported, you can have VA Java automatically set your classpath for you. You can have VA Java find and set your classpath as follows:

1. Create your class in a new project or one of your existing projects.
2. Right-click on the classname of your `main` class. Typically, this will be the one with the `static main` routine or the class derived from `Applet`. It also should have the little runner icon next to the classname. Select the Properties menu item.
3. When the dialog box appears, click on the Class Path tab.
4. Enable the "Include '.' (dot) in class path" option.
5. Click on the Compute Now button on the project path line. This is the magic that will search through the repository for the appropriate classes to automatically include in your class path.
6. After it has finished computing your class path, click OK.

USING THE AgentRunner TO DEBUG YOUR JAVA AGENTS

Although you can debug applets and applications within your Java IDE, you cannot easily debug agents. Why are agents different? Well, if you look back at the section on applets, agents, and applications, you'll remember that agents are extended from `AgentBase`, which itself is extended from `NotesThread`. Applets and applications create the `NotesThread` and then obtain the `Session`, but `AgentBase` works differently.

When an agent starts up, Notes or Domino starts the thread, which in turn starts up `AgentBase`. One of the tasks of `AgentBase` is to obtain the `Session` and initialize a context for the agent. By the time the agent starts at its `NotesMain` method, the `Session` and `AgentContext` have already been created and initialized.

Well, if you were to start your `NotesMain` method in the your Java IDE, guess what? Yes, the `Session` and `AgentContext` would not be properly initialized at the point when your

`NotesMain` method started. What can you do about this? One solution is to go back to the old `println` routine and write out your own debugging messages to the Java console. If you don't have any other tools, this is pretty much what you have to do.

A tool that ships with Notes and Domino is called `AgentRunner`. This tool consists of a Domino database called `AgentRunner.nsf` and a Java class that is included in `Notes.jar` called `AgentRunner.class`. By using the Java class and the `AgentRunner` database, you can debug your Java program using your favorite IDE.

Here is how it works. The following instructions assume that you are debugging your agent on a workstation that has the Notes executables installed. You need to know the path to these executables. Note that some of these instructions are for IBM Visual Age for Java 2.0, but it should be clear how to modify these instructions for another Java IDE. In VA Java, you should already have imported the Domino Java class library, as described in the previous section:

1. Update your `PATH` environment variable to point to the directory where the Notes executables (DLLs) are installed. This directory is typically `X:\Notes`, or `X:\path\Notes`, where path is a user-defined path. You may update your path by modifying your `Autoexec.bat` file in Windows 95/98 or by updating the Environment tab of the Systems Properties dialog box in Windows NT. You can access the System Properties dialog box by right-clicking on the My Computer Icon and selecting Properties. You may need to reboot after changing these settings.

2. Create a new Java agent in the Domino Designer. Give it the name you want to use for your agent. The Designer will give you a template agent. On the top line of your agent, change the agent to extend `DebugAgentBase` instead of `AgentBase`. You don't actually need to add any content to your agent at this point.

3. After you have created your agent and extended `DebugAgentBase`, you run it from within the Domino database where it will normally be run. The `DebugAgentBase` class is located in `Notes.jar`.

4. As your agent runs, `DebugAgentBase` will capture the current context and save it in the `AgentRunner.nsf` database. It won't actually try to run your agent code; it is only capturing the context and saving it in a Domino database. As a matter of fact, `getSession` will return null, and referencing it will generate an exception after the `AgentContext` document has been created. This will not matter, however, because the sole purpose in running the agent is to generate a context document.

5. Now you are ready to create your real agent and debug it.

Let's summarize what has happened here before we continue. We created a new agent and substituted `DebugAgentBase` for the real `AgentBase`. We then executed the agent. The `DebugAgentBase` code, rather than performing the normal initializations of `AgentBase`, captures the agent's context. This context information is then saved in a Domino database called `AgentRunner.nsf`. If the agent terminates with an exception after the context is generated, it's not a problem.

We're now ready to create and debug your agent. In essence, here is what happens next:

1. In your favorite Java Development environment (IBM VA Java, Symantec Visual Café, and so forth), create your Java agent. Do not put your agent into a package; leave it as a Java program without a package. You can cut and paste the Java template that was created for you by the Domino Designer into your Java IDE.

2. If you are using VA Java, and possibly some other IDEs, you must add a main program. You can use this one:

    ```
    import lotus.domino.*;
    public static void main (String[] args)
    {
       try {
          System.out.println("Starting AgentRunner");
          AgentRunner.main(args);
       }
       catch (Exception e) {
          e.printStackTrace();
       }
    }
    ```

3. This program contains a main program that will be invoked from the IDE, using parameters you specify. You must sometimes add your own main program because some IDEs do not allow you to use the main program from an included class (that is, AgentRunner.class). In this case, we just put a thin layer on top of the AgentRunner main class.

4. (VA Java) In Visual Age for Java, after you enter your program, you must set up the internal class path for this routine, so right-click on Main Class line (make sure it is not the main method line), and then click Properties. You enter the parameters (in the next step) on the Program tab. Click on the Class Path tab. Click on the button that says Compute Now. This computes the Class path that you need for this main class.

    The AgentRunner main program uses the parameters you specify (agent name, database name, and server name) to look up the agent context information in AgentRunner.nsf. Each Java IDE will have a different method for specifying the parameters to the main Java routine. In VA Java use the Program tab of the Properties dialog box to specify the parameters to the main routine. In the Command line arguments field enter the agent name, database name, and server name with a space separating the parameters. If you are using another Java IDE, consult your documentation for the method of supplying parameters to the main program.

5. Before you start your program, you may want to set a breakpoint at the beginning of your NotesMain routine.

6. Start the main program. After the AgentRunner main starts, and assuming the context information is found (if not, you will get an exception), the AgentRunner main will set up a simulated agent context from the information obtained from the AgentRunner.nsf.

7. The `main` program will then call your agent's `NotesMain` method, just as it would be invoked within the Notes or Domino environment.

If you're able to get this far, congratulations! You are now able to debug Notes and Domino agents within the comforts of your own Java IDE.

Summary

This chapter has covered a lot of ground. I've given you the 35,000-foot–level view of the Java language. In order to be useful, you will really need to try some examples and learn the language in more detail. I've given you the overview, however, so that this chapter can be read as a self-contained introduction to Java, applets, applications, agents, and servlets.

I told you about Java packages and classes. These are the organizational structures within Java, and it's important to understand them. You can use the `import` statement to make your programs more legible. Importing a class or package is not the same as using a C++ `#include` directive. The controlling force on whether packages are found is the `CLASSPATH` variable. If you ever receive an error message that a class cannot be found, your `CLASSPATH` variable (or one internal to your IDE) has not been set properly. See your IDE's documentation on how to properly set up your `CLASSPATH`.

I gave you details on how agents, applets, applications, and servlets can be written in Java. Each of these different types of Java programs starts up and behaves slightly differently within the Notes and Domino environments. Make sure you understand the differences and similarities between these different programming tools.

I gave you a high-level view of CORBA and IIOP. In essence, these two technologies enable you to write applet (or application) code that runs on a Java platform, calls the Domino back-end classes, and does not need the Domino executables available on the workstation.

Finally, I showed you how to use the `AgentRunner` tool. This tool simulates an agent's context from within your Java IDE. This enables you to step through your agent and debug it without resorting to a lot of `println` statements. It's a little complicated to set up, but after you do it, your debugging environment will be much more powerful.

From Here...

Here are some suggestions for reading about related topics:

- Chapter 24, "Using the Lotus eSuite DevPack," tells you how to use this set of Java applets with your Web-based applications. You can use the DevPack to save you development time, because the Java applets are already built and you just have to integrate them with the rest of your application.

- If you want to learn more about LotusScript, you can read Chapter 21, "LotusScript Variables and Objects," and Chapter 22, "LotusScript Subroutines, Functions, and Event Handlers."
- Chapter 25, "The Session and Front-End Classes"; Chapter 26, "Database, View, and Document Classes in LotusScript and Java"; and Chapter 27, "Using Fields and Items in LotusScript and Java," cover the Domino Object Model in depth. You'll learn about the use of these classes with both LotusScript and Java.

CHAPTER 24

USING THE LOTUS eSUITE DEVPACK

The Lotus eSuite version 1.5 is a Java-based set of programs and applets. It is packaged separately from Notes and Domino, but you can use it with Domino to build Web applications. There are two major parts of eSuite, designed for different audiences.

The first part of eSuite is called the eSuite Workplace. The Workplace is a set of applets that can be used with a standard browser to provide several common office functions. This set of applets includes an integrated desktop environment that end users can use for applications, such as spreadsheets, word processing, and presentation graphics.

The second part of eSuite is called the eSuite DevPack. The DevPack is a set of Java Applets that can be used by developers to incorporate into custom, line-of-business applications. This Java-based component approach is designed to enable developers to pick and choose small, fast components that can easily be combined with business logic to form custom applications rapidly. The general focus of this chapter will be on the eSuite DevPack, but I will provide a quick introduction to the Workplace.

The eSuite Workplace

The purpose of the eSuite Workplace is to lower the total cost of ownership (TCO) for office applications. Today, because most companies have a computer on every desktop, upgrading office applications can be a very costly proposition. If you have to visit each workstation to install a new version of client application software, the time for IT staff members can be very expensive.

The eSuite Workplace addresses this situation by using a client/server–based model with fairly minimal requirements for desktop software. Because the system is Java-based, the actual programs and applets can reside on the server, but be downloaded on demand to the workstations. This allows the latest software to be utilized, but you can still have processing distributed. Because the Java code is downloaded and executed on the workstation, the workload on the server is eased after the code has been downloaded.

You can use the Domino server as the HTML server along with the eSuite Workplace; however, you do not have to use Domino. You can use any Web server to serve the Java applets that comprise the Workplace. If you do use Domino, however, you gain the advantage of being able to use not only the Workplace, but the DevPack and all the other Domino features—all on the same server.

You can see the eSuite Workplace in Figure 24.1.

Figure 24.1 shows the full complement of eSuite applications. An administrator can limit the particular applications that a user may see. The eSuite Workplace supports only Windows NT as its registry server. The integration with Windows NT is very nice, however, and you can import users and groups directly from the Windows NT set of users and groups.

The eSuite Workplace

Figure 24.1
The eSuite Workplace desktop has configurable applications.

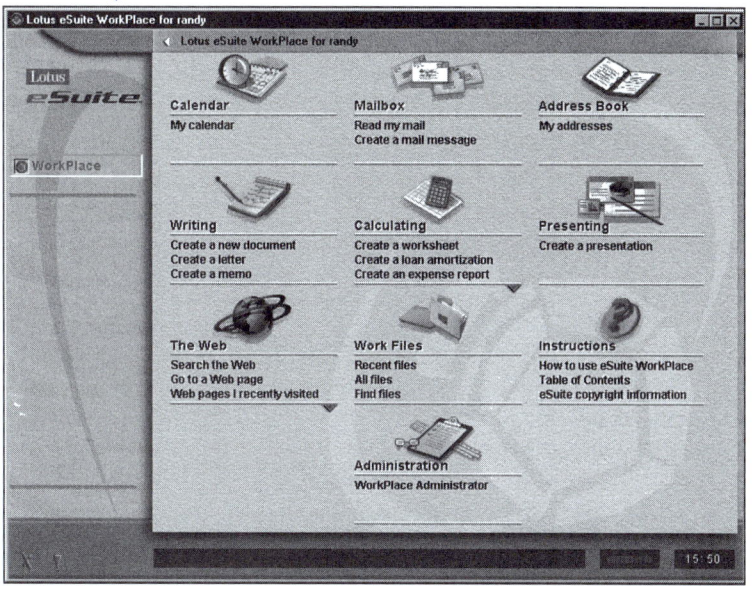

The applications provided by eSuite Workplace include

- Spreadsheet
- Word Processor
- Presentation Graphics
- Calendar
- eMail
- Address Book
- Web browser
- Work File Access

In addition, with the proper authority, you can also remotely administer the eSuite Workplace with the Administration applet. I will show you a few of the available applets that come with the eSuite Workplace.

The Calendar Applet

In Figure 24.2, you see an example of the Calendar applet. This applet enables you to see a day at a glance, as well as a three-month calendar on the right.

Figure 24.2
The eSuite Calendar applet.

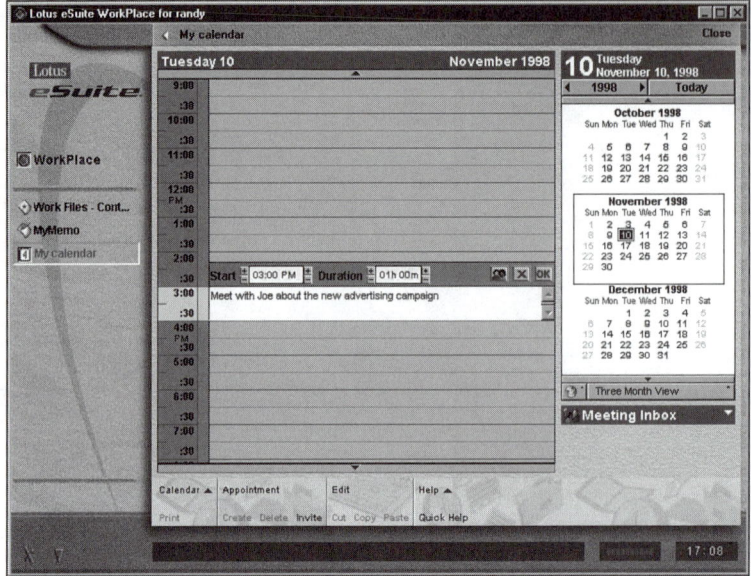

With the Calendar applet, you can perform most of the common functions of creating appointments, setting up meetings, and reviewing your schedule.

THE SPEADSHEET APPLET

In Figure 24.3, you see an example of the Spreadsheet applet. This applet supplies most of the important spreadsheet functions.

With the Spreadsheet applet, you can enter data, use simple formulas to total rows and columns, and provide formatting with different fonts.

THE WORK FILES APPLET

In Figure 24.4, you see an example of the Work Files applet. As you can tell, this applet enables you to navigate the file system, and it operates much like the Windows Explorer.

With the Work Files applet, you can navigate local directories or networked drives. If you locate a file, you can double-click on it to load it and the associated applet within the eSuite Workplace environment.

THE WORD PROCESSOR APPLET

In Figure 24.5, you see an example of the Word Processor applet, which enables you to create documents and change font size, style, and other attributes typically found in most word processors.

THE eSUITE WORKPLACE | 585

Figure 24.3
The eSuite Spreadsheet applet.

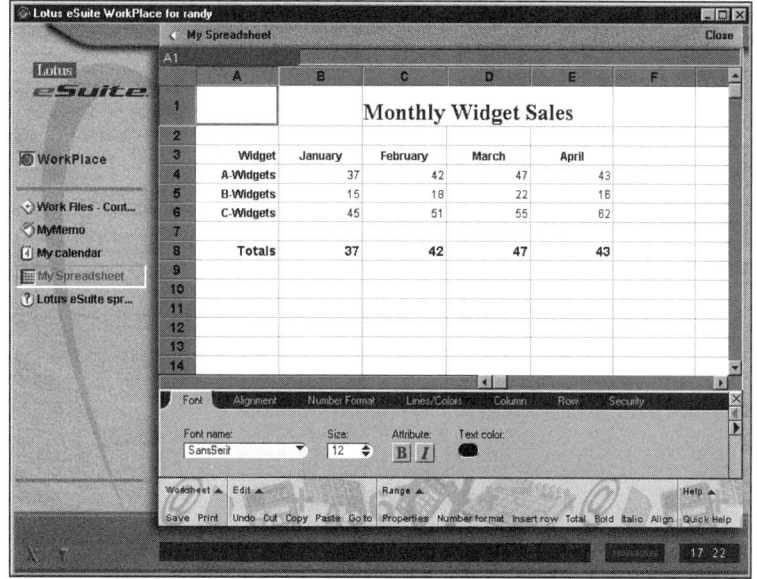

Figure 24.4
The eSuite Work Files applet.

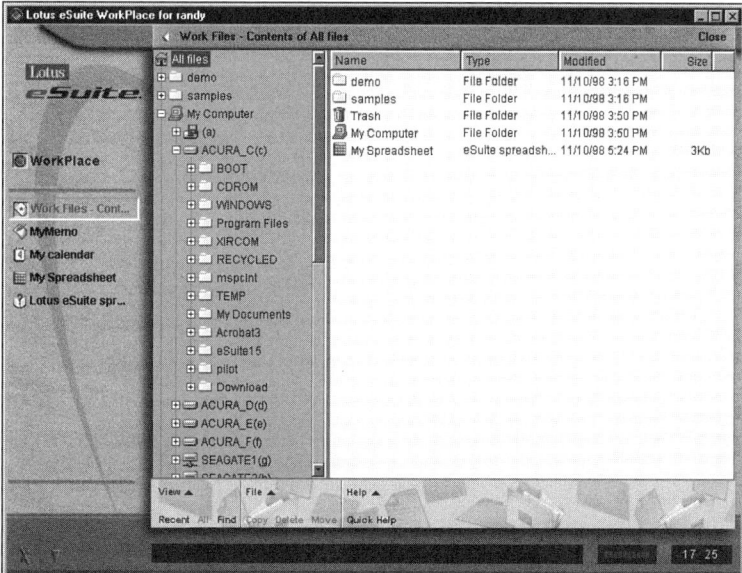

Notice the Check spelling feature, not because it is particularly unique in a word processor, but because of its technology.

Figure 24.5
The eSuite Word Processor applet.

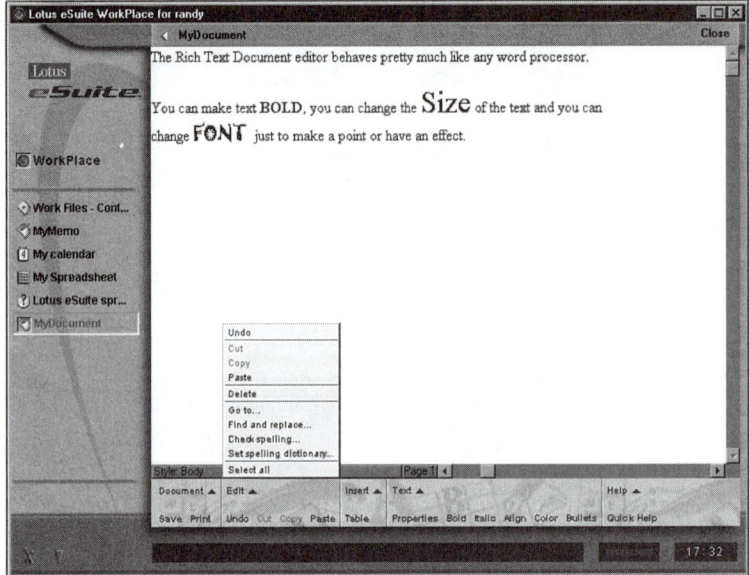

If you think about a spell-checker, you realize that there are several characteristics. First, you must have a spelling dictionary. Typically, this dictionary is very large. Second, the program that searches the spelling dictionary might be relatively compute-intensive. In the eSuite Java Workplace, downloading a very large dictionary to the client and then running a compute-intensive task is probably not going to result in very good performance. So this is not how spell-checking is done with eSuite.

In the eSuite Workplace environment, spell-checking is done on the server. This makes a lot of sense, given the characteristics of the application. Another interesting feature is that Lotus uses CORBA to implement the communication between the client and the server. I describe CORBA and IIOP in Chapter 23, "Creating and Using Java Applets and Agents." In essence, the CORBA technology provides a standards-based way to implement client/server communication in an object-oriented way. It enables the sharing of objects in a distributed-communication environment.

eSuite DevPack Overview

The eSuite Workplace that I showed you in the previous section was implemented using the eSuite DevPack. The DevPack is a series of Java applets that provides the core functionality of office applications. Some additional capabilities are found within the DevPack that are not exposed in the eSuite Workplace.

There are several methods to using the eSuite DevPack:

- You can use standard HTML, specify parameters (`PARAM` tags), and invoke the eSuite applets directly from your HTML.
- You can use the first method and augment it with the `ScriptHelper` applet. This applet enables you to write JavaScript code to add logic to the code that invokes the DevPack applets.
- You can use the JavaBeans versions of the eSuite applets and incorporate them into your Java IDE. From your IDE, you can embed them in your Java applets or applications just as any other JavaBean components.
- You can write your own Java program, use the InfoBus, and communicate directly with the eSuite components.

Unless you happen to be up on all the latest Java jargon, you may not be totally familiar with the terms *JavaBeans* and *InfoBus*. Let me explain these items.

What Are JavaBeans?

A JavaBean is simply a program or component that has been written in Java and follows certain conventions. The purpose of the JavaBeans specification is to enable components and containers to communicate. If you are familiar with Microsoft terminology, JavaBeans are similar to ActiveX controls. Because the interfaces have been standardized, tools such as Symantec's Visual Café, IBM's Visual Age for Java, and Inprise JBuilder can incorporate JavaBeans into their palettes of components.

You can create your own JavaBeans, use some that have been provided with your Java IDE, download them from the Internet, or purchase them from a third party. The advent of standardized components makes programming easier. With JavaBeans, a tool can inquire to the bean itself about its properties and methods. This introspection capability enables the tool to present property lists within a user interface.

Now that you know about JavaBeans, I can tell you that the eSuite DevPack components are supplied both as standard applets and as JavaBeans. You can use the applet versions within HTML code, and you can use the JavaBean versions from within a Java IDE environment, such as Visual Age for Java. In Figure 24.6, you can see the spreadsheet JavaBean component in the Visual Age for Java environment.

Notice in the figure that there are many properties shown in the properties box. These are the properties exposed by the JavaBean to allow user editing. You can see that one of the properties is called beanName. You can edit this property within the Java IDE environment to give this spreadsheet a name.

588 Chapter 24 Using the Lotus eSuite DevPack

Figure 24.6
The eSuite Spreadsheet JavaBean in Visual Age for Java.

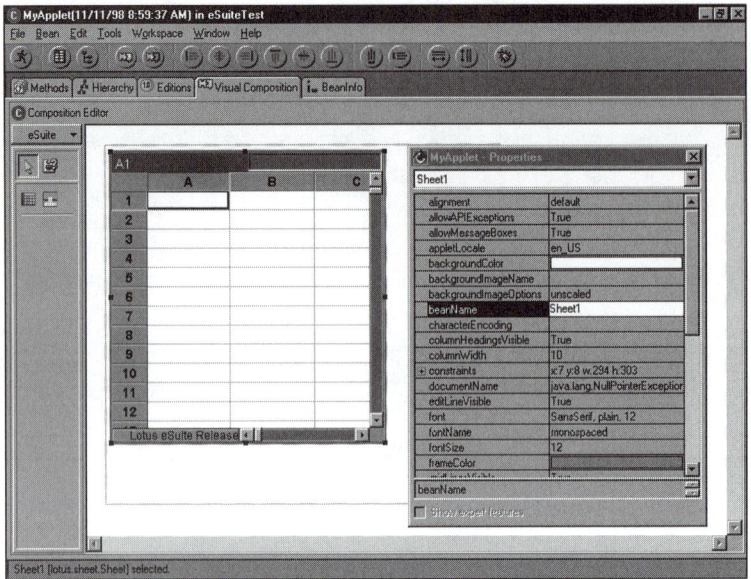

What Is the InfoBus?

The Java class hierarchy contains class definitions for events and event handlers. This event-handling model is used to process events, such as a button-click or mouse movement. With the native Java event-handling mechanism, you must write event handlers tied to specific components. For example, you write a button-click handler and associate it with a particular button. When the button is pushed, your handler is invoked.

For events such as button-clicks and mouse movements, this mechanism works fine. However, when you are writing higher-level components such as a spreadsheet, it would be convenient for these high-level components to communicate. For example, it would be nice if a spreadsheet could share data that has been calculated with a Chart applet so that the data could be presented visually in addition to numerically. The standard Java event mechanism cannot handle this, because the writer of the Java spreadsheet implementation would have no way of knowing what an end user might want to do with the spreadsheet itself.

The InfoBus technology is designed to solve this communication problem between Java components. The idea behind the InfoBus is similar to a hardware electronic bus. Information is placed on a shared bus, and components listen to the bus for data by name. Thus, components are not locked into relationships when the Java code is created; they can be dynamically linked while the application is running.

Suppose one component, such as the Chart applet, is listening for data named Q1Forecast. The spreadsheet component could put a named range of data onto the InfoBus with the name `Q1Forecast`, and the Chart applet would automatically pick up this data and display it. All other data that is placed on the InfoBus is ignored by the Chart applet.

The InfoBus technology is used extensively throughout eSuite as the means of communication. There are many different components that can produce or consume the data put on the bus. In addition, you can write your own InfoBus-aware components to place data on the bus or listen for data.

The InfoBus technology created by Lotus has been adopted by Sun as a standard extension to Java and is currently shipped by Sun as a part of the official Java environment.

The eSuite Applet Categories

Now that you know about some of the technology behind the eSuite applets, what can you do with them? There are three categories of applets: data presentation applets, data access applets, and utility applets.

The eSuite Data Presentation Applets

The data presentation applets enable you to enter, save, and display information in a variety of familiar formats. You can also use the data presentation applets in conjunction with the data access applets to obtain data from outside sources, such as databases to provide a front end for users.

The data presentation applets are

- Spreadsheet
- Word Processor
- Chart
- Project Scheduler
- Presentation Graphics
- Calendar
- Address Book

As mentioned previously, these applets can be used directly from HTML or from a Java development environment. If your Java development environment supports JavaBeans, you can conveniently drag and drop the components visually. This makes development much easier than trying to write the HTML code.

Spreadsheet

In Figure 24.6, I showed you an example of the Spreadsheet applet (bean). This component is probably one of the most versatile and one that you may frequently use. You can define cell formulas, lock cells, and use formatting, borders, and backgrounds.

You can provide task-specific user interfaces for your users. For example, suppose you have a forecasting model that you have developed. You can predefine the spreadsheet, have users enter specific values, and calculate and display answers to the users. All the user needs is a Web browser.

By using a spreadsheet component, you can do reasonably intensive calculations on the client without resorting to the JavaScript coding. Being able to develop a user interface with a spreadsheet will save you a lot of time and enable you to concentrate on the business logic involved, not the HTML, JavaScript, or Java necessary to accomplish your task.

The functions provided by the Spreadsheet applet include most of the common @functions, the capability of importing and exporting spreadsheet data from existing applications, and a 256×8192-cell area, which should be plenty for Web applications.

Here is some sample HTML code that includes the spreadsheet on an HTML page:

```
<HTML>
<HEAD>
<TITLE>Spreadsheet Example</TITLE>
</HEAD>
<BODY>
<H2>Spreadsheet Example<HR></H2>
   <APPLET CODEBASE="//localhost/C:/Dev/eSuiteDP15" CODE="lotus.sheet.Sheet"
        ARCHIVE="jars/devpack_infobus.jar,jars/devpack_shared.jar,jars/
        ➥devpack_sheet.jar"
        WIDTH=640 HEIGHT=350>
   <PARAM NAME = "cabinets"
        VALUE =
➥"cabs/devpack_infobus.cab,cabs/devpack_shared.cab,cabs/devpack_sheet.cab">
   </APPLET>

</BODY>
</HTML>
```

Figure 24.7 shows the result of this HTML code. In the HTML code, the HTML, HEAD, TITLE, BODY, and H2 tags should be self-explanatory. If you need a refresher, refer to Chapter 14, "Designing Pages, Forms, and Subforms," where I summarize the common HTML tags.

The APPLET tag is the only tag needed to incorporate the spreadsheet for this example. The CODEBASE parameter should specify the directory where you installed the eSuite DevPack. In this example, localhost refers to the local workstation. If you are running the DevPack from an HTTP server, the server name should appear. If you try the sample HTML, be sure to modify the CODEBASE parameter. The CODE parameter specifies the Java class to execute.

Because there are two different archive formats—one for Netscape and one for Microsoft—you must specify the archives twice. Lotus provides the classes in both formats: the JAR format and the CAB format. You specify the JAR format with the ARCHIVE parameter in the APPLET tag. You specify the CAB format by using a PARAM tag of cabinets with a value of the cabinet names.

THE eSUITE DATA PRESENTATION APPLETS | 591

Figure 24.7
The eSuite Spreadsheet invoked from plain HTML.

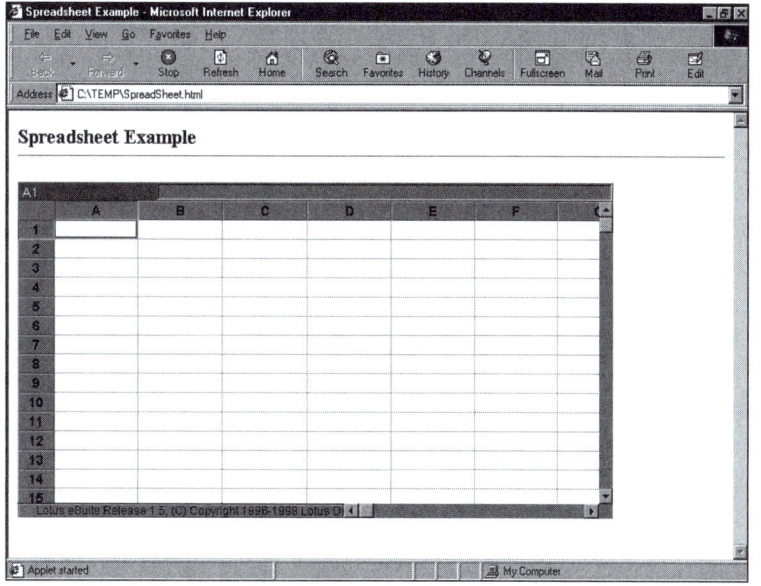

PART
IV
CH
24

The path components in both the JAR and CAB lists are directories relative to the CODEBASE parameter. So, for example, the infobus jar in the example shown will be found in

C:/Dev/eSuiteDP15/jars/devpack_infobus.jar

This is obtained by concatenating the CODEBASE parameter with the first JAR found in the list. The other JARs and CABs are located similarly.

WORD PROCESSOR

The Word Processor applet provides a rich text editor and container on a Web page. Here is some sample HTML:

```
<HTML>
<HEAD>
<TITLE>Word Processor Example</TITLE>
</HEAD>
<BODY>
<H2>Word Processor Example<HR></H2>

    <APPLET CODEBASE="//localhost/C:/Dev/eSuiteDP15"
➥CODE="lotus.fc.ac.AppletContainer"
    ARCHIVE="jars/devpack_infobus.jar,jars/devpack_shared.jar,jars/
    ➥devpack_ic.jar,jars/devpack_wp.jar" WIDTH=640 HEIGHT=350>
    <PARAM NAME="cabinets"

VALUE="cabs/devpack_infobus.cab,cabs/devpack_shared.cab,cabs/devpack_ic.cab,cabs/
➥devpack_wp.cab">
    <PARAM NAME="infoCenterVisible" VALUE="true">
```

```
            <PARAM NAME="applet0" VALUE="lotus.wp.WordProcessor">
            <PARAM NAME="name0" VALUE="wp">
            <PARAM NAME="wp.documentName" VALUE="WPExample.html-wp">
        </APPLET>

</BODY>
</HTML>
```

In this example, you see the same ARCHIVE and cabinets type of parameters. However, you see that we have a different CODE parameter and some additional PARAM values. Before I explain these additional parameters, look at Figure 24.8.

Figure 24.8
The eSuite Word Processing applet with the InfoCenter.

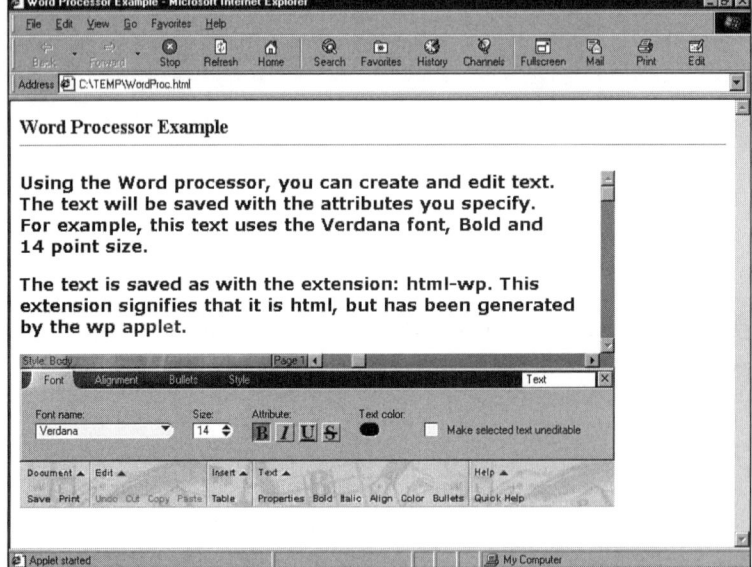

As you can see from Figure 24.8, the word processor is visible, but there is also a set of controls along the bottom of the window. This set of controls enables you to change properties, such as font, style, color, and so forth. The controls are provided by the InfoCenter applet.

Although it appears seamless to the user, there are actually several applets involved in this display to the user. Because we have two components that are displayed together in the window—word processor and InfoCenter—you use the AppletContainer applet. Notice that the CODE parameter specifies the AppletContainer.

The InfoCenter is specified by the archive devpack_ic.jar or devpack_ic.cab, depending upon your browser. When you include this applet, it provides the user with the ability to change formatting properties. You would typically make this available for word processing, but you may or may not want to make it available for spreadsheets if you provide a prebuilt spreadsheet template.

When you are using the AppletContainer, you no longer simply specify the applet in the CODE parameter as we did in our spreadsheet example. Because you may have more than one applet, you specify each applet with its own pair of PARAM tags. You must tell the AppletContainer which class to load and what name you want to give the applet. You can see this with the two tags:

```
<PARAM NAME="applet0" VALUE="lotus.wp.WordProcessor">
<PARAM NAME="name0" VALUE="wp">
```

Because the Word Processor is the first applet, you use the pair of parameters applet0 and name0. For the second applet, you use the pair applet1 and name1. You may have up to four applets within the AppletContainer.

Finally, look at the last PARAM line:

```
<PARAM NAME="wp.documentName" VALUE="WPExample.html-wp">
```

In this line, we are specifying the filename to be used by the word processing applet. This file will be loaded automatically when the word processor starts. If you don't specify a name, the user will see a blank, new document. The user can edit and save the default document or can specify and save the file under a new name.

Notice that the NAME is given as wp.documentName. The wp refers to the name0 value that we just specified. This enables you to have several word processing documents on the same page, but refer to them with different names. The extension type is given as html-wp. The file is saved as an automatically generated HTML file. It can be displayed by itself with any Web browser and can also be loaded back into the word processing applet.

Chart

The Chart applet must be used in conjunction with some source for the data. The Chart applet supplies the graphical representation of the data, but the user cannot enter the data directly into the Chart applet itself. The source can be another applet, a JavaScript program, or any other Java program that can put data onto the InfoBus. Here is a sample using a spreadsheet as the data source and Chart applet to show the data graphically:

```
<HTML>
<HEAD>
<TITLE>Sheet and Chart Example</TITLE>
</HEAD>
<BODY>
<H2>Sheet and Chart Example<HR></H2>

    <APPLET CODEBASE="//localhost/C:/Dev/eSuiteDP15"
➥CODE="lotus.fc.ac.AppletContainer"
      ARCHIVE="jars/devpack_infobus.jar,jars/devpack_shared.jar,jars/devpack_ic.jar,
            jars/devpack_sheet.jar,jars/devpack_chart.jar"
           WIDTH=640 HEIGHT=420>
    <PARAM NAME="cabinets"
       VALUE="cabs/devpack_infobus.cab,cabs/devpack_shared.cab,cabs/devpack_ic.cab,
```

```
                cabs/devpack_sheet.cab,cabs\devpack_chart.cab">
   <PARAM NAME="infoCenterVisible" VALUE="true">
   <PARAM NAME="applet0" VALUE="lotus.sheet.Sheet">
   <PARAM NAME="name0" VALUE="Mysheet">
   <PARAM NAME="Mysheet.documentName" VALUE="SheetExample.html-wk">
   <PARAM NAME="Mysheet.height" VALUE="160">
   <PARAM NAME="Mysheet.adornmentsVisible" VALUE="false">
   <PARAM NAME="applet1" VALUE="lotus.chart.Chart">
   <PARAM NAME="name1" VALUE="Mychart">
   <PARAM NAME="Mychart.height" VALUE="260">
   </APPLET>

</BODY>
</HTML>
```

See Figure 24.9 for the resulting output of this HTML. In this example, you can see that we have both the Spreadsheet applet and the Chart applet included within the AppletContainer. The Spreadsheet applet is defined as `applet0`, and its name is `Mysheet`. The Chart applet is `applet1` and its name is `Mychart`.

> **Caution**
>
> Note that the names for the applets are case sensitive. You must be very careful in supplying names. For example, `MyChart` is not the same as `Mychart`. This may be an easy cause of an error if you use two different types of capitalization in different parts of your HTML.

Figure 24.9
The eSuite Spreadsheet and Chart applets with the InfoCenter.

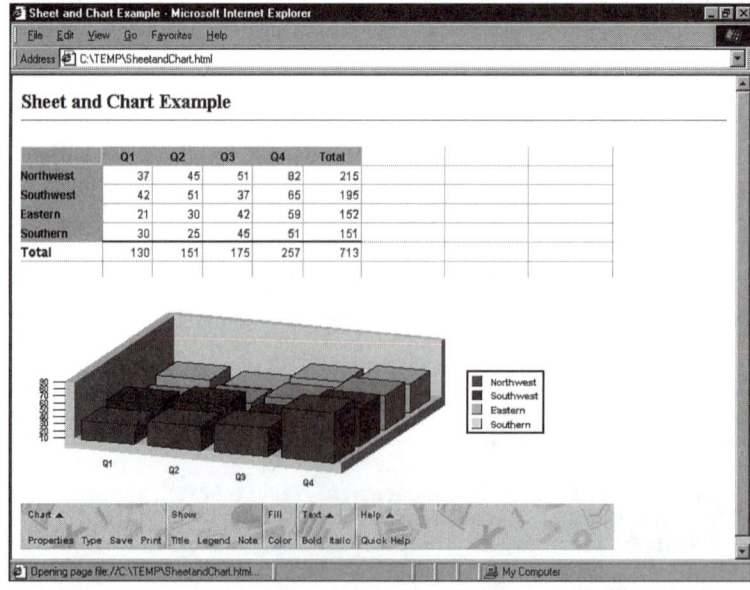

Besides the name, I have given several additional parameters for the spreadsheet. I have included a `documentName` parameter, which specifies where the spreadsheet should find the data to load. The height parameters for both the applets must add up to the height specified in the AppletContainer. In this case, `160` and `260` add up to the total of `420`. I've turned off adornments, which are the row and column labels in the spreadsheet, as well as the scrollbars.

Finally, there is one characteristic in the spreadsheet that you cannot see from the visual output. I have named a range within the spreadsheet. This range includes the column headers (`Q1`-`Q4`), the row headers, and all the numbers except the totals. I have named this range Mychart. This named range is important because the eSuite Spreadsheet applet puts this named range on the InfoBus. The Chart applet, which is named Mychart, looks for this name on the InfoBus and retrieves the data associated with the range.

The Chart applet is then able to display a legend and label the two axes for the chart from data that it obtains from the InfoBus. If you later change the contents of the values within the named range on the spreadsheet, the corresponding values in the chart will automatically change.

Multiple Applets

When you include more than one applet on a page, you have two options: You can use two applets within the AppletContainer as we did with the spreadsheet and chart example. Alternatively, you can use two separate `APPLET` tags in HTML to include two different applets. Here is the core of this type of HTML:

```
<APPLET CODEBASE="C:/Dev/eSuiteDP15" CODE="lotus.sheet.Sheet"
        NAME="Mysheet"
        ARCHIVE="jars/devpack_infobus.jar,jars/devpack_shared.jar,
                 jars/devpack_sheet.jar,jars/devpack_chart.jar"
        WIDTH=640 HEIGHT=350>
   <PARAM NAME = "cabinets"
        VALUE = "cabs/devpack_infobus.cab,cabs/devpack_shared.cab,
                 cabs/devpack_sheet.cab,cabs/devpack_chart.cab">
   <PARAM NAME="documentName" VALUE="SheetExample.html-wk">
   <PARAM NAME="infoBusName" VALUE="MyBus">
</APPLET>

<APPLET CODEBASE="C:/Dev/eSuiteDP15" CODE="lotus.chart.Chart"
        NAME="Mychart"
        ARCHIVE="jars/devpack_infobus.jar,jars/devpack_shared.jar,
                 jars/devpack_sheet.jar,jars/devpack_chart.jar"
        WIDTH=640 HEIGHT=350>
   <PARAM NAME = "cabinets"
        VALUE = "cabs/devpack_infobus.cab,cabs/devpack_shared.cab,
                 cabs/devpack_sheet.cab,cabs/devpack_chart.cab">
   <PARAM NAME="infoBusName" VALUE="MyBus">
</APPLET>
```

> **Caution**
>
> If you use two `APPLET` tags, you must be very careful with the `ARCHIVE` and `cabinets` tags because these tags must be *identical* in each Applet. The specific `jars/cabs` used, and their order, is used in determining the default InfoBus name. If the lists are different, a new InfoBus is created, and the applets will not be able to communicate with each other.
>
> When the `jars/cabs` lists are the same, the browser will load only one copy of the relevant `jars/cabs`. If the lists are different, new copies are loaded for each applet. Just having the same list of `jars/cabs` is not sufficient; the order must be identical also.

You can control the InfoBus that is used by a particular component. You might do this, for example, if you have two spreadsheets or two graphs on one page. In this case, you might have more than one InfoBus on a page. To specify an InfoBus name, you can use

```
<PARAM NAME = "infoBusName"   VALUE="yourInfoBusName">
```

To communicate, two or more components must be using the same InfoBus name. Differing names are considered separate InfoBuses.

Project Scheduler

The project scheduler enables you to incorporate a project schedule in your application. You can create and edit tasks and provide linkages between tasks, and it has a very nice Gantt chart display. Here is the HTML code for the next example:

```
<HTML>
<HEAD>
<TITLE>Project Scheduler Example</TITLE>
</HEAD>
<BODY>
<H2>Project Scheduler Example<HR></H2>
<BR>

<APPLET CODEBASE="//localhost/C:/Dev/eSuiteDP15"
 CODE="lotus.fc.ac.AppletContainer"
  ARCHIVE="jars/devpack_infobus.jar,jars/devpack_shared.jar,jars/devpack_ic.jar,
           jars/devpack_scheduler.jar"
              WIDTH=640 HEIGHT=335>
  <PARAM NAME="cabinets"
    VALUE="cabs/devpack_infobus.cab,cabs/devpack_shared.cab,cabs/devpack_ic.cab,
           cabs/devpack_scheduler.cab">
  <PARAM NAME="infoCenterVisible" VALUE="true">
  <PARAM NAME="applet0" VALUE="lotus.scheduler.Scheduler">
  <PARAM NAME="name0" VALUE="scheduler">
  <PARAM NAME="scheduler.documentName" VALUE="BookSchedule.lps">
</APPLET>
</BODY>
</HTML>
```

This code was used to generate the project schedule that you see in Figure 24.10.

THE eSUITE DATA PRESENTATION APPLETS | 597

Figure 24.10
The eSuite Project Scheduler applet with the InfoCenter.

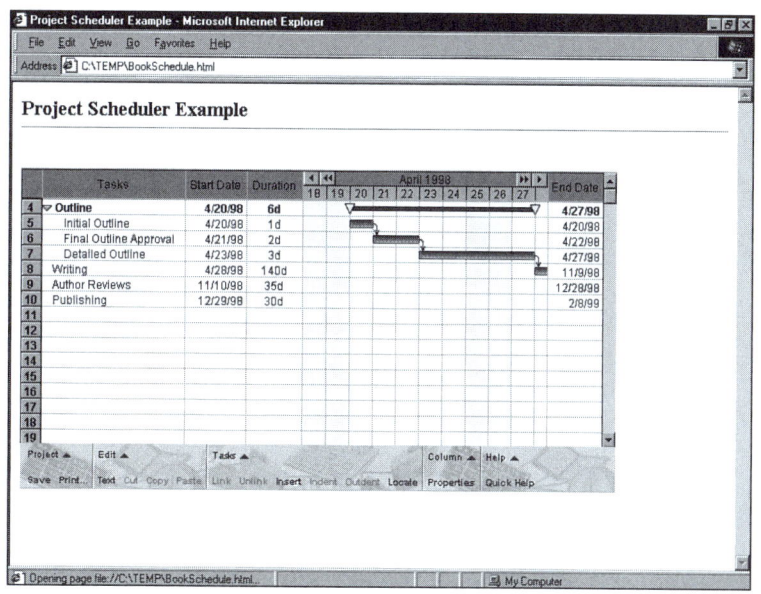

PART **IV**
CH **24**

PRESENTATION GRAPHICS

The Presentation Graphics applet enables you to create presentations similar to Freelance or Powerpoint presentations. This is a fairly simple applet. You can create presentations, add clip art and bulleted lists, and draw simple geometric shapes.

After your presentation has been created, you can print it or save it in one of three formats: a default format (.PG), Freelance format (.PRZ), or HTML.

You can also show your presentation in slideshow format after you have created and saved it. Remember also that because all you need is a Web browser to access this applet, you could conceivably use this applet to create and save a presentation on your Web server, and then access it from any client that is attached to the Web. This enables you to centralize your presentations and quickly update them, and then anyone in your sales force can access the newest presentation from anywhere on the Web.

CALENDAR

The Calendar applet enables you to provide a very user-friendly front end for any Java applet or application that wants to display appointment information. The Calendar applet has been imported into Visual Age for Java in Figure 24.11.

Figure 24.11
The eSuite Calendar applet in IBM Visual Age for Java.

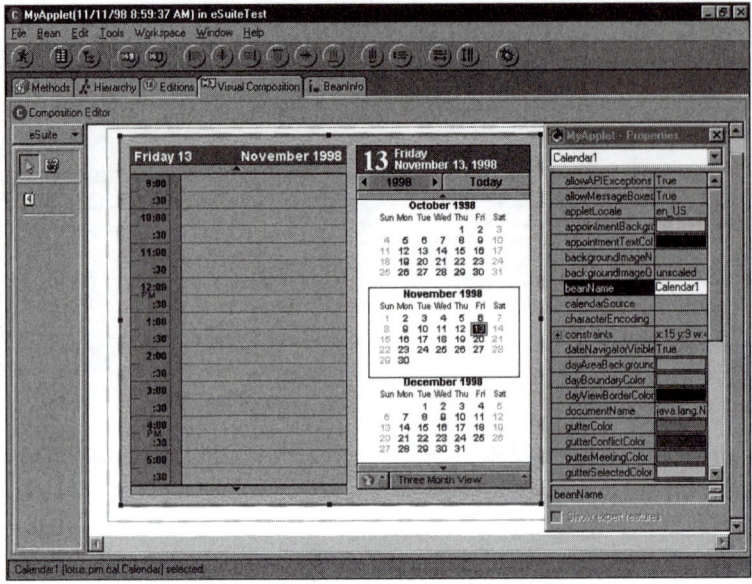

With the Calendar applet, you can set the date to display and control various visual properties, such as colors, for the many areas of the appointment display. You can also programmatically add and delete calendar entries by calling methods of the Calendar applet.

Address Book

The Address Book applet enables you to create and display an Address Book to the user. The Address Book sources can be either files stored locally or can be provided by a Lightweight Directory Access Protocol (LDAP) server. LDAP is an Internet standard, and there are several publicly available LDAP servers on the Internet, such as Bigfoot, InfoSpace, and SwitchBoard.

With the Address Book applet, you can add new entries into the Address Book, search entries, and delete entries.

The user interface for this applet can be in one of two modes: list mode or detail mode. When in list mode, it will display a list of Address Book entries. When it is in detail mode, it displays the details for a particular entry.

The eSuite Data Access Applets

The eSuite data access applets enable you to retrieve and save information from external data sources. You can access data from SQL databases, the file system, and HTML documents. You can also interface with CGI programs on your server to send data to the CGI program and retrieve the results.

THE eSUITE DATA ACCESS APPLETS

The data access applets are

- SQL/JDBC Database applet
- FormReader and TableReader HTML parsers
- CGI Gateway
- FileReader ASCII file reader applet

SQL/JAVA DATABASE CONNECTIVITY (JDBC)

The SQL/Java Database Connectivity (JDBC) applet is used to connect to existing SQL databases. JDBC is a standard extension to Java and works similarly to Microsoft's Open Database Connectivity (ODBC). In fact, one of the Java drivers available enables you to connect Java to ODBC. This driver enables you to use JDBC with your existing ODBC drivers to gain connectivity to existing databases.

The JDBC applet provides functions for reading and writing data to databases and publishing results to the InfoBus. Here are the major steps to obtaining data from the SQL/JDBC applet:

1. Load the JDBC driver (make sure it is in your Classpath).
2. Connect to the Database.
3. Execute a SQL command to query or update the database.
4. If reading data, publish the data to the InfoBus.

The JDBC applet also has a very useful feature that is enabled with the `allowUI` property. If this property is true, the JDBC applet will present a user interface for debugging. You should turn this interface on when initially developing your applet, and after it has been debugged, you can turn it off. When the interface is enabled, you can interactively control the loading of the database driver and the database connection, and you can type in an SQL query command.

> **Tip**
>
> If you are using Microsoft Internet Explorer, you may experience problems with the JDBC-ODBC driver, because Microsoft uses nonstandard calling conventions. By the time you read this, newer versions and/or patches to the software may be available, so be sure to apply any available fixes and try your code with the latest releases.

FORMREADER AND TABLEREADER

The FormReader and TableReader applets are used to parse and analyze HTML documents. The FormReader looks into a Form section within an HTML document, and the TableReader applet looks at tables. You can control the URL that these applets search, and you can tell the applets what to look for.

After the forms or tables have been parsed, the output is placed on the InfoBus and can then be read by other InfoBus applets, such as the Spreadsheet applet.

CGI Gateway

The CGI Gateway applet is used to send and retrieve data from a CGI server application. You can use the CGI applet to gather information from the InfoBus and then send it to the server. In addition, you can get information from the server and place it on the InfoBus so that other applets can use the information.

FileReader

The FileReader applet is used to read a file and place the information on the InfoBus. The data is placed on the bus in array format, which makes it useful for either the charting applet or the Spreadsheet applet.

The data within the files used by FileReader is simple ASCII with each field separated by a tab. The FileReader applet parses the data as it is read and then places it on the InfoBus for other applets.

The eSuite Utility Applets

The eSuite Utility Applets are used in conjunction with the presentation and data access applets to complete your application. The utilities provide additional functions that are useful across multiple applets or in conjunction with other applets.

AppletContainer and InfoCenter

You have seen several examples of the AppletContainer. This applet enables you to combine several (up to four) presentation applets in a single context. This context displays the InfoCenter at the bottom of the window, and the applets within the AppletContainer all use the same InfoBus.

When you include more than one applet within the AppletContainer, you can control the layout (for example, top-to-bottom or left-to-right), whether or not the InfoCenter is visible, and whether to use a compact version of the InfoCenter.

In Figure 24.12, you see a display of the InfoCenter for the Chart applet. The InfoCenter enables a user to save and open data files, change fonts, and control properties that are unique to an applet. For example, in the chart, you can change the type of chart from bar chart to pie chart, and so forth. Spreadsheets have other properties, such as named ranges. With the InfoCenter you can add and delete rows of the spreadsheet, insert a formula for a cell, and change the formatting.

Figure 24.12
The eSuite InfoCenter applet enables users to control applet properties.

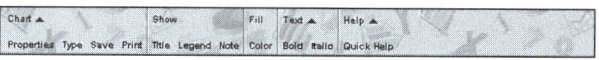

ScriptHelper

The ScriptHelper applet enables you to control various attributes of the eSuite applets via JavaScript instead of manipulating PARAM names and values. Listing 24.1 is an example of a JavaScript program used in conjunction with the Chart applet.

LISTING 24.1 A JAVASCRIPT PROGRAM TO GENERATE A RANDOM CHART

```
<HTML>
<HEAD>
    <TITLE>ScriptChart</TITLE>
</HEAD>

<BODY>
<FORM>

<INPUT type="BUTTON" name="mybutton" value="Create Chart" onclick="DoClick();">

<SCRIPT language="javascript">
function DoClick()
{
    // First create 4 InfoBusVectors, assign them to JavaScript variables
    vector1 = document.theHelper.createInfoBusVector();
    vector2 = document.theHelper.createInfoBusVector();
    vector3 = document.theHelper.createInfoBusVector();
    vector4 = document.theHelper.createInfoBusVector();

    // Now fill the vectors with random values between -10 to +10
    // The Math.random() function returns a value between 0 to 1
    // We add 10 values to each vector
    for (i = 0; i < 10; i++) {
        vector1.addValue(0, i, Math.random() * 20 - 10);
        vector2.addValue(0, i, Math.random() * 20 - 10);
        vector3.addValue(0, i, Math.random() * 20 - 10);
        vector4.addValue(0, i, Math.random() * 20 - 10);
    }

    // Publish the vectors to the InfoBus, with the respective names
    document.theHelper.publishVectorToInfoBus("vector1", vector1);
    document.theHelper.publishVectorToInfoBus("vector2", vector2);
    document.theHelper.publishVectorToInfoBus("vector3", vector3);
    document.theHelper.publishVectorToInfoBus("vector4", vector4);

    // Create 4 chart Series objects in the Chart applet
    document.theChart.createSeries();
    document.theChart.createSeries();
```

continues

LISTING 24.1 CONTINUED

```
    document.theChart.createSeries();
    document.theChart.createSeries();

    // Now get the 4 Series objects
    chartSeries0 = document.theChart.findSeries(0);
    chartSeries1 = document.theChart.findSeries(1);
    chartSeries2 = document.theChart.findSeries(2);
    chartSeries3 = document.theChart.findSeries(3);

    // Have each Series object go to the InfoBus for values.
    // Each one will be filled with the values we put there earlier.
    chartSeries0.setDataInputItemName("vector1");
    chartSeries1.setDataInputItemName("vector2");
    chartSeries2.setDataInputItemName("vector3");
    chartSeries3.setDataInputItemName("vector4");

    // Finally, refresh the chart
    document.theChart.refresh();
}

</script>

<applet
   codebase="//localhost/c:/Dev/eSuiteDP15/"
   code="lotus.scripthelper.ScriptHelper"
   name="theHelper"
   ARCHIVE="jars/devpack_infobus.jar,jars/devpack_shared.jar,jars/devpack_
➥scripthelper.jar,jars/devpack_chart.jar"
   width=1
   height=1>

   <param name="CABINETS"
      value="cabs/devpack_infobus.cab, cabs/devpack_shared.cab,cabs/
➥devpack_scripthelper.cab,cabs/devpack_chart.cab">
</applet>

<applet
   codebase="//localhost/c:/Dev/eSuiteDP15/"
   code="lotus.chart.Chart"
   ARCHIVE="jars/devpack_infobus.jar,jars/devpack_shared.jar,jars/
➥devpack_scripthelper.jar,jars/devpack_chart.jar"
   name="theChart"
   width=640
   height=350>
   <param name="CABINETS"

value="cabs/devpack_infobus.cab,cabs/devpack_shared.cab,cabs/devpack_scripthelper.
➥cab,cabs/devpack_chart.cab">

   <param name="yAxisScaleMin" value="0">
</applet>
```

```
    </FORM>
  </BODY>
</HTML>
```

Figure 24.13
An eSuite random chart generated by JavaScript.

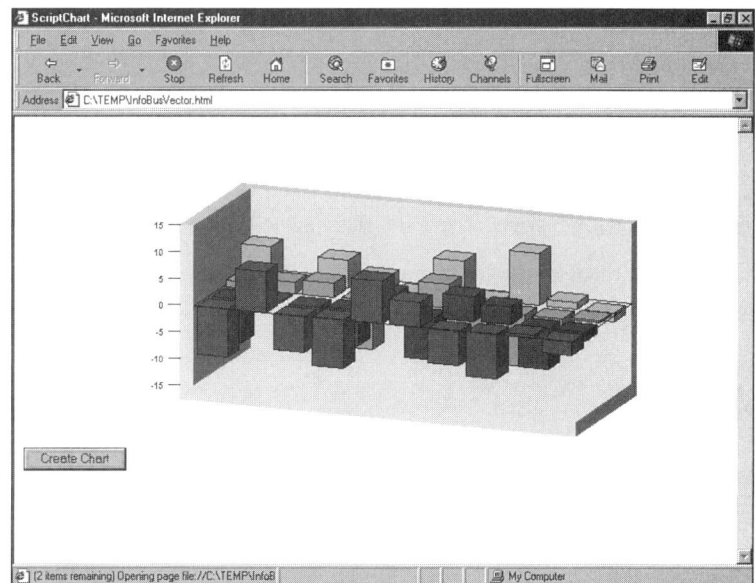

In this example, there are two applets, the ScriptHelper and the Chart applet. As you can see in Figure 24.13, there is one button, which is used to trigger the JavaScript program. When the JavaScript program `DoClick()` starts, it creates four `InfoBusVectors`. These are vectors that can contain multiple values. Each of the `InfoBusVectors` is then filled with 10 random numbers from –10 to +10. The `scripthelper` is then used to publish the four `InfoBusVectors` to the InfoBus, where the Chart applet picks them up and draws them.

You can browse through the code, but basically it does the following steps:

- Create four InfoBusVectors.
- Fill the InfoBusVectors with random numbers from –10 to +10.
- Publish the InfoBusVectors to the InfoBus.
- Create four Series objects within the Chart applet.
- Get the Series objects from the Chart applet.
- Fill each Series object with values from the InfoBus.
- Refresh the chart on the screen.

This example shows you how you can combine JavaScript program logic with the eSuite Java applets.

Messaging Feature

The messaging feature is comprised of several classes that work together to provide an eSuite application with messaging functions. The classes support the SMTP, IMAP4, and POP3 messaging standards. The messaging classes do not provide a user interface. They are designed to be used programmatically.

This set of classes includes the `MailStore` class, the `Folder` class, the `Message` class, and the `Part` class. The `MailStore` class is responsible for communication, logging in to the mail system, sending messages, and receiving messages. The `Folder` class is used to manage the eMail Inbox. The `Message` class represents one incoming or outgoing message. A message is composed of MIME parts. The `Part` class is used to represent these MIME parts.

You can scan through the list of messages in the `Folder`, and you can scan through the list of `Parts` within a `Message`.

Combining eSuite with Domino

Now that you have seen the technology available to you with eSuite, I'll now show you how you can combine eSuite technology with Domino. In fact, it's rather easy because Domino release 5 provides many of the features you need.

The first step in using eSuite with the Domino server is to install the eSuite DevPack on the Domino server. You must install it under the `data\domino\html` directory. So a typical directory for eSuite would be

`data\domino\html\eSuiteDP15\`

This directory then contains the two important subdirectories: `cabs` and `jars`. These subdirectories contain the Java class files that will be served to the clients.

After you have installed the DevPack on the server, you can use Domino to serve up the eSuite class files. When serving class files from Domino, the directory `data\domino\html` is considered the root directory. So, for the purposes of the `CODEBASE` parameter, you would specify `CODEBASE="/eSuiteDP15/"` if the eSuite directory were named as shown previously.

You can use the eSuite DevPack applets from Domino pages, forms, or subforms. One option to include the eSuite applets is to use the page or form properties option Treat page contents as HTML. See Figure 24.14 for an example.

If you use HTML tags, the methods for including the eSuite applets is essentially the same as the methods you use when coding native HTML.

COMBINING eSUITE WITH DOMINO | 605

Figure 24.14
An eSuite Spreadsheet on a Domino page with Treat page contents as HTML option.

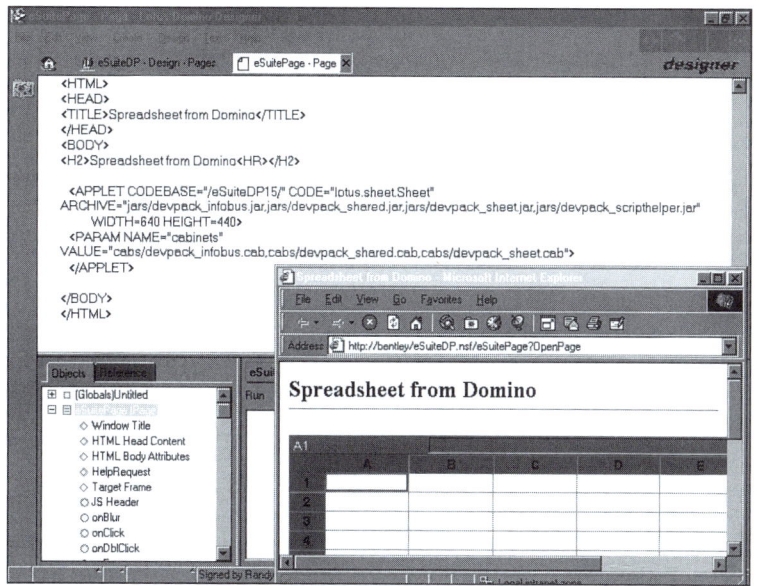

> **Note**
> If you use Treat page contents as HTML, you must be careful about the placement of your tags. Domino may insert extra
 (Break) tags into your text when serving them. If one is inserted in the wrong place, your HTML code will not work. In general, you should not split the `ARCHIVE` or the `cabinets` tags into two lines; keep them as a single line. To debug the generated HTML, use the View Source capability of your Web browser.

Another alternative to using HTML is to use the menu selection Create, Java Applet for either a page or form. When you use this menu command, you need to specify the same parameters as you would for HTML, but you will do it with dialog boxes. Here is an example that uses the AppletContainer with a spreadsheet inside:

1. Create a new page in the Domino Designer. You can also use forms, but for this example, we will create a page.
2. Select Create, Java Applet to create your Java applet in your page.
3. In the Create Java Applet dialog box, select the Link to applet on a Web server radio button.
4. In the Base URL box, enter `http://<yourserver>/eSuiteDP15/`, where `<yourserver>` represents your server name. The name `eSuiteDP15` represents the location where you have installed the eSuite DevPack under the `data\domino\html` directory.
5. In the class name box, enter `lotus.fc.ac.AppletContainer`. If you want to load a different applet, enter its class name here.
6. Click OK.

PART
IV
CH
24

7. Your applet will now be created in the designer. You can manipulate the size by dragging the lower-right corner.
8. Right-click on the applet area and bring up the Java Applet properties box. You'll notice that the information you entered in step 4 is shown here. See Figure 24.15.

Figure 24.15
Java applet properties and parameters.

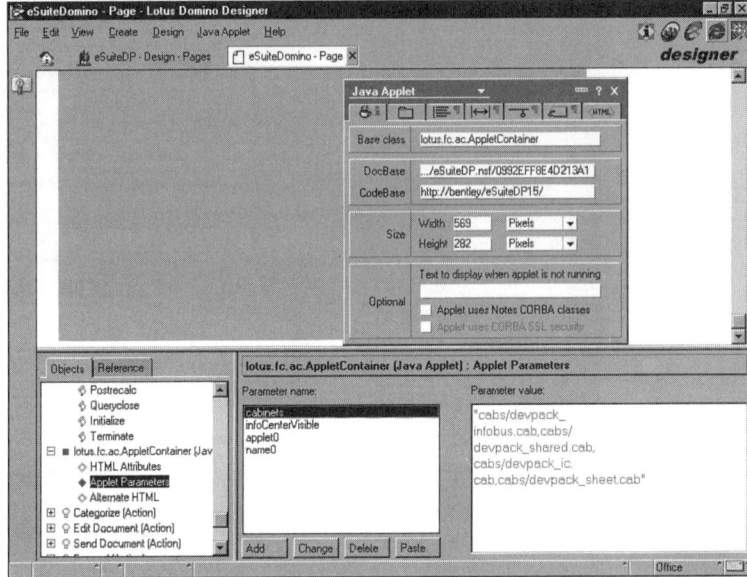

9. Click the <HTML> tab.
10. In the Other field, we need to add the information for Netscape Navigator. The archive locations are specified here. Enter the following:
    ARCHIVE="jars/devpack_infobus.jar,jars/devpack_ic.jar,jars/devpack_shared.jar,
    ➥jars/devpack_sheet.jar"
11. Click on the applet to highlight it. In the InfoList area at the bottom of the screen, click on Applet Parameters.
12. In the Programmer's Pane on the right, click Add to add a parameter. The first parameter will be the cabinets parameter. Enter cabinets for the parameter name and click OK.
13. In the parameter value area, enter the following (including the double-quotation marks):
    "cabs/devpack_infobus.cab,cabs/devpack_shared.cab,cabs/devpack_ic.cab,cabs/
    ➥devpack_sheet.cab"

14. For each of the following, enter a parameter name and value (be sure to include the double-quotes within the window):

```
infoCenterVisible          "true"
applet0                    "lotus.sheet.Sheet"
name0                      "sheet"
```

After you have entered all the parameter values, you can save the page and give it the name `eSuiteDomino`. If you created your database on your local machine, be sure to replicate it to your Domino server before trying to test it. Here is how you can test it. Enter the following string into your browser, substituting your server name and the name you used for your database:

`http://<yourserver>/<esuitedatabase>.nsf/eSuiteDomino`

You should see the Spreadsheet applet appear in your Web browser.

I have shown you the steps to include a single spreadsheet with the InfoCenter. However, by following the example, it should be clear how you can use this same technique to include the other eSuite applets.

Summary

In this chapter, I introduced you to the eSuite product from Lotus. It is made up of two major pieces: the eSuite Workplace and the eSuite DevPack. The Workplace is a ready-made set of applications that you can deploy. The built-in applets include a calendar, spreadsheet, word processing, eMail, and others. These built-in applets are actually implemented by utilizing the Java applets of the eSuite DevPack.

The DevPack is a set of Java applets that you can use in your own applications. You can deploy these applets with any Web server and use either Netscape Navigator or Microsoft Internet Explorer. The applets use a technology called the InfoBus to communicate with each other. You can also use the eSuite applets with the Domino server.

Install the eSuite DevPack under the `data\domino\html` directory. Then in the Domino designer, you can use Pass-Thru HTML, or you can reference the Java applet on the server.

The ability to include a spreadsheet or chart on your Domino Web pages is a very powerful feature, especially if you customize the applets with application-specific fields. You can also use JavaScript to programmatically control the applets and the InfoBus.

From Here...

You're now familiar with the usage of Java and how to use the eSuite DevPack to build applications. For more information on using the Domino Object Model, here are some suggestions:

- Chapter 25, "The Session and Front-End Classes," describes the top hierarchical levels of the Domino Object Model. It covers some of the similarities and differences between programming in LotusScript and Java with the DOM classes
- Chapter 26, "Database, View, and Document Classes in LotusScript and Java," covers some of the most important classes for developing Domino applications using the DOM classes. You'll learn how to access and organize your Domino data.
- Chapter 27, "Using Fields and Items in LotusScript and Java," describes the elementary items of a document. Read this chapter to learn how Domino organizes the fields of your documents as well as how to format rich text items for display.

CHAPTER 25

The Session and Front-End Classes

In this chapter and the next two, I cover the major Domino Object Model (DOM) classes for Notes and Domino. The DOM classes can be accessed from either LotusScript or Java. The syntax for accessing these classes is different between LotusScript and Java, but the classes themselves are pretty similar. Because there are more than 30 DOM classes for Notes and Domino with hundreds of properties and methods, it is not possible to cover all the classes in detail. Rather, I will cover the main aspects of the classes, working from the top of the hierarchy downward, which will get you started. After you become familiar with the main classes, the methods for using LotusScript and Java, and the debugging programs, the best way to learn will be with your own applications.

In this chapter, I cover the `Session` class for both LotusScript and Java and the front-end classes for LotusScript. I'll go through a few examples that you can try yourself.

As I explained in Chapter 20, "Object-Oriented Programming and the Domino Object Model," there are front-end and back-end classes. The front-end classes provide programmatic access to the Notes user interface, and the back-end classes deal only with the Domino databases. There is LotusScript support for both the front-end and back-end classes, but Java supports only the back-end classes. The `Session` class is at the top of the DOM back-end hierarchy and represents an important class. We'll start the chapter with this class.

THE `NotesSession`, `Session`, AND `AgentContext` CLASSES

In this section, I cover the `NotesSession` LotusScript class with the `Session` and `AgentContext` Java classes. The reason for covering all three classes is that when Lotus implemented Java support, it split the `NotesSession` LotusScript class into two classes: `Session` and `AgentContext`. In addition, there are a few properties of `AgentContext` that come from the LotusScript `NotesDatabase` class.

The `NotesSession` LotusScript class is used to access variables related to the current session. You can think of a session as being associated with a particular user Id and password. A session running on a Notes client is associated with the current user; for a session running in an agent on a server, the current user Id is the ID of the server itself.

The session in both LotusScript and Java is at the highest level of the back-end hierarchy. You use the session to get information about the current user, find out whether the program is running on a server, access environment variables, and create certain utility type objects, such as a `DateTime` object.

In LotusScript, you use both properties and methods. You can retrieve and assign properties with an assignment statement. In essence, properties behave like variables. Methods are invoked like function calls. In Java, all access is through method calls. In LotusScript, the names are not case sensitive, but in Java all names are case sensitive. Method names in Java usually begin with a lowercase verb.

A table of correspondence between the LotusScript properties and methods and the equivalent Java method names can be found in Table 25.1. An asterisk indicates the property is new in release 5 of Notes and Domino.

TABLE 25.1 MAPPING OF NotesSession PROPERTIES TO JAVA Session METHODS

LotusScript Properties		Java Methods	
NotesSession	**NotesDatabase**	**Session**	**AgentContext**
AddressBooks		getAddressBooks	
		getAgentContext	
CommonUserName		getCommonUserName	
CurrentAgent			getCurrentAgent
CurrentDatabase			getCurrentDatabase
DocumentContext			getDocumentContext
EffectiveUserName			getEffectiveUsername
International		getInternational	
IsOnServer		isOnServer	
LastExitStatus			getLastExitStatus
LastRun			getLastRun
NotesBuildVersion*			
NotesVersion		getNotesVersion	
Platform		getPlatform	
SavedData			getSavedData
		getServerName*	
		getURLDatabase	
UserName		getUserName	
UserNameList*		getUserNameList*	
		getUserNameObject*	
	UnprocessedDocuments		getUnprocessedDocuments

A table of the LotusScript methods and their equivalent Java methods can be found in Table 25.2.

TABLE 25.2   MAPPING OF `NotesSession` METHODS TO JAVA `Session` METHODS

LotusScript Methods		Java Methods	
`NotesSession`	`NotesDatabase`	`Session`	`AgentContext`
New		NotesFactory.createSession	
CreateDateRange		createDateRange	
CreateDateTime		createDateTime	
CreateLog		createLog	
CreateName		createName	
CreateNewsletter		createNewsletter	
		createRegistration	
CreateRichText ParagraphStyle*		createRichText ParagraphStyle*	
CreateRichTextStyle		createRichTextStyle	
CreateTimer		evaluate	
FreeTimeSearch		freeTimeSearch	
GetDatabase		getDatabase	
GetDbDirectory		getDbDirectory	
GetEnvironmentString		getEnvironmentString	
GetEnvironmentValue		getEnvironmentValue	
SetEnvironmentVar		setEnvironmentVar	
	UnprocessedFTSearch		unprocessedFTSearch
	UnprocessedSearch		unprocessedSearch
UpdateProcessedDoc			updateProcessedDoc

As you can tell from Tables 25.1 and 25.2, the vast majority of the `NotesSession` properties and methods map to similar `Session` methods. However, several properties and methods map to `AgentContext` as well as a few of the `NotesDatabase` properties and methods. Most of the other classes within the DOM have closer mappings between the LotusScript and Java classes.

In Chapter 23, "Creating and Using Java Applets and Agents," I showed you how to create a `Session` object in Java. To review, in a Java (standalone) application, you must first initialize a Notes environment with a `NotesThread`. After the environment has been created, you can use `NotesFactory.createSession` to create a `Session` from scratch. Alternatively, if you are creating a Java applet or agent, you can use the `getSession` method because a `Session` object has already been created for you by the base Java class.

In LotusScript, you create a new `NotesSession` object with the `New` statement, or in a `Dim` statement with the `New` keyword. For example:

```
Dim session As New NotesSession
```

or

```
Dim session As NotesSession
Set session = New NotesSession
```

Notice that because a `NotesSession` is an object, you must use the `Set` keyword. If you omit the `Set` keyword, you will get an error.

NotesSession Properties

The properties of the LotusScript class fall into two broad categories: properties about the environment and properties about the user. Properties about the environment include `AddressBooks`, which enables you to obtain a list of the Domino directories currently being used, and `NotesVersion`, `NotesBuildVersion`, and `Platform`, which provide information about the version and operating system environment.

User information includes `CommonUserName`, `UserName`, and `EffectiveUserName`. These three properties return information about an ID file in use. `CommonUserName` and `UserName` return information about the current workstation user or the server, depending upon where the current program is running. The only difference between these properties is the format of the result. `CommonUserName` returns the user ID in common username format, and `UserName` returns the fully distinguished name of the user ID. The `EffectiveUserName` property will also return a fully distinguished name. For a workstation user, it returns the same value as `UserName`, but for an agent running on a Domino server, `EffectiveUserName` returns the ID of the owner of the agent. The owner is the last person that modified and saved (signed) the agent.

The `International` property is used to obtain information about formatting that may vary from country to country—for example, the order of month, day, and year in date formats, currency symbols, and the character to use for a decimal separator. If you are writing an application that may be used in more than one country, you need to access the `International` class object. In Java, you use the `getInternational` method to obtain this object.

Where Do New DOM Class Objects Come From?

Now is a good time to review how new DOM class objects are created. There are actually several ways for the objects to be created, and different objects can be created only in certain ways. This is one of the confusing points about the DOM class objects, so let me describe the different ways objects are created. In LotusScript, there are three generic ways to get an object variable:

- Create it yourself with the `New` keyword.
- Call a method of an existing object.
- Access a property of an existing object.

Of these three methods, only the second method is available to create DOM objects in Java, with a few exceptions. The Domino Object Model in Java has a strict containment philosophy so that in general, objects are created by calling methods of other, existing objects. For example, the `Session` object has several methods, such as `createDateTime`, `createLog`, `createName` and so forth. These methods are used in place of the `New` keyword. The only exceptions to this policy are for creating the highest-level objects. Further, these high-level objects (`AgentBase`, `AgentRunner`, `AppletBase`, `NotesException`, `NotesFactory`, `NotesThread`) are typically created by Domino and not your application.

In LotusScript, all three methods of object creation are possible. Of the 38 classes in Notes 5.0, only 14 support creation with the `New` keyword. This means that objects for more than half of the LotusScript classes must be created by one of the other methods. Some classes support more than one method of creation. For example, you can create them with the `New` keyword, but you can also create them by calling a method or accessing a property of another class.

Objects Created with the New Keyword

Here are the classes that support creation with the `New` keyword: `NotesACLEntry`, `NotesDatabase`, `NotesDateTime`, `NotesDbDirectory`, `NotesDocument`, `NotesItem`, `NotesLog`, `NotesName`, `NotesNewsLetter`, `NotesRegistration`, `NotesRichTextItem`, `NotesSession`, `NotesTimer`, and `NotesUIWorkspace`.

These classes roughly break down into four categories:

- High-level classes, such as `NotesSession`, `NotesUIWorkspace`, `NotesDbDirectory`, `NotesDatabase`
- Major object items, such as `NotesDocument`, `NotesNewsLetter`, and `NotesRegistration`
- Low-level classes, such as `NotesACLEntry`, `NotesDateTime`, `NotesItem`, `NotesName`, and `NotesRichTextItem`
- Auxiliary classes, such as `NotesLog` and `NotesTimer`

In your LotusScript programs, you will probably create items of the high-level and major object classes so that you can access their properties and can use them to create objects lower in the hierarchy. The lower-level classes are typically used to do real work—in other words, to read and write information in your database. The auxiliary classes are for special-purpose use if you need them.

Objects Created by a Method or Property

Because less than half of the Notes classes of LotusScript can be created with the `New` keyword, the majority of the class objects are created by a method or property of an existing object. In addition, your program will typically start at the top of the hierarchy and traverse down, creating objects lower in the hierarchy as needed.

For example, you might first create a new `NotesSession` object, then access one of its properties, such as `CurrentDatabase`. You use this property to get a `NotesDatabase` object, from which you can extract forms, views, or the documents contained in the database. After getting a `NotesDocument`, you might access its fields to finally get data that you're looking for.

Because some objects are very generic and might be used throughout the hierarchy, their creation is done at the top `NotesSession` class. These are the class objects that are created by calling a method within the `NotesSession` class: `NotesDateRange`, `NotesDateTime`, `NotesLog`, `NotesName`, `NotesNewsLetter`, `NotesRichTextParagraphStyle`, `NotesRichTextStyle`, and `NotesTimer`. This is the same technique that is used in Java.

You'll notice that several of the classes can be created with the `New` keyword and also by calling a method of `NotesSession`. Almost all the rest of the classes that can be created with `New` can also be obtained from some other existing class. You may think this is just redundant, but it is not. Notes may be controlled by other OLE-compliant ActiveX controllers, such as Visual Basic, Visual Basic for Applications, and Delphi, among others. When used in this manner, the external controller does not have access to the `New` keyword of LotusScript. Typically, these foreign controllers can create a single type of object at the top of the hierarchy. After this object has been created, all other objects must be obtained from properties and methods of existing objects. Thus, while it may seem redundant in LotusScript, the capability of creating or obtaining objects from other objects is an important aspect of the Domino Object Model.

The `NotesInternational` class object can be obtained from the `International` property of the `NotesSession` class. This is the only place to get this object. A `NotesAgent` object can be obtained from a property of the `NotesSession` object or from a `NotesDatabase` object.

It's important to remember that when using a method or property to obtain an object, you must use the `Set` statement to assign the object value. This is what differentiates the assignment of an object from a regular assignment statement. An object assignment must use the `Set` keyword; a regular assignment cannot use the `Set` keyword. If you forget the `Set` keyword, you get the error message.

In the front-end, `NotesUIWorkspace` is at the top of the hierarchy. Prior to release 5, you could not programmatically create `NotesUIDatabase` and `NotesUIView` objects. With release 5, you can obtain these objects via the `CurrentDatabase` and `CurrentView` properties in the `NotesUIWorkspace` class. Alternatively, you can access the `NotesUIDatabase` and `NotesUIView` classes from events. You are passed an object of one of these classes if you write a `PostOpen` event, for example. After the user opens a database (or view), the PostOpen event is invoked, and an object of the appropriate type is passed to the event handler. The NotesUIDatabase and NotesUIView classes each have several events that are passed the respective objects.

This area is probably one of the more confusing areas of the LotusScript classes. The NotesUIDatabase class is meant to be used in the context of the user interface (UI), so the user action of opening and working with a database triggers the creation of the NotesUIDatabase object. The NotesDatabase object is used for almost all your normal database access requirements, such as getting and setting item values within the database.

The NotesView and NotesUIView objects have a similar situation. The NotesUIView is created by Notes when the user acts on the view, such as opening or closing it. The object is passed to you in an event handler. The NotesView class, in turn, can be obtained from a NotesUIView object. The NotesView class is used for most of your view traversal, such as getting the next or previous document and moving up or down the document hierarchy. When it's used in this manner, a user is present, and the NotesUIView represents the view a user has displayed.

A NotesView object can also be obtained from a NotesDatabase object. When used in this context, a user is not necessarily present. You might use this method to obtain a NotesView object in an agent running on a Domino server, for instance.

ARRAYS OF OBJECTS

Arrays can be declared and used in two ways in LotusScript. The first method is when you use the Dim statement and declare array bounds. This is the most straightforward and common use of arrays. When you declare array variables, however, you cannot use an aggregate assignment statement. For example:

```
Dim Array1(1 to 3) As Double
Dim Array2(1 to 3) As Double
Array2 = Array1     ' This is NOT allowed !
```

In the preceding example, you must create a loop of some sort and assign the elements of the arrays individually.

Another method for storing and using arrays is by using the Variant type. A Variant can hold data of any type, including arrays. In particular, you can declare a Variant and then copy an entire array with a single assignment statement. For example:

```
Dim Array1(1 to 3) As Double
Dim Var2 As Variant
Var2 = Array1     ' This IS allowed !
```

In the preceding example, when the assignment statement completes, Var2 will contain an array that is a copy of the original array. All the elements will be copied, and you did not need to copy each item individually.

What happens when you have an array of objects that are not elementary items, such as Doubles? Well, an array of objects behaves just like an array of Doubles in many ways. You cannot do an array assignment from one declared array to another. You can, however, do an array assignment from an array of objects to a `Variant`, just as you saw previously with `Var2`. Here's a concrete example:

```
Dim ndrArray1(1 to 3) As NotesDateRange
Dim ndrArray2(1 to 3) As NotesDateRange
Dim Var2 As Variant
ndrArray2 = ndrArray1    ' This is NOT allowed !
Var2      = ndrArray1    ' This IS allowed, No Set used !
```

As a last point, notice that the last assignment statement does *not* use the `Set` keyword. An array is not an object. You can have an array that contains objects within it, but the array itself is not an object. Because the array is not an object, a `Set` is not used when we do the assignment to the `Variant` in the last statement.

This distinction between a `Variant` holding an array of objects and holding an individual object is very important and often confused, even in the Lotus documentation. (It sometimes uses `Set` when referring to an array.) Here is another example:

```
Dim ndrArray1(1 to 3) As NotesDateRange
Dim ndr As NotesDateRange
Dim Var1 As Variant
Dim Var2 As Variant
Var1      = ndrArray1    ' This IS allowed, No Set used !
Set Var2  = ndr          ' Note: You must use the SET keyword !
```

Notice that in this case we have declared both `Var1` and `Var2` as a `Variant`, but when we do the assignment, one requires us to use `Set`, and in the other we cannot use `Set`. Why? Well in this case, we are assigning an object (a `NotesDateRange`) to `Var2`. Whenever you assign an object, you must use `Set`. In the first case with `Var1`, we are assigning an array. *An array of objects is not an object*. If you keep this simple rule in mind, you'll have a much easier time with LotusScript.

The reason why I'm spending so much time on this topic is that several LotusScript classes return arrays of objects. Let's take, for example, the `FreeTimeSearch` method of the `NotesSession` class. This method, as a matter of fact, happens to return an array of `NotesDateRange` objects. There are many other examples, but this one will illustrate the points:

```
Dim ndrArray(1 to 3) As NotesDateRange
Dim ndr As NotesDateRange
Dim Var2 As Variant
ndrArray = FreeTimeSearch( ... ) ' This is NOT allowed !
ndr      = FreeTimeSearch( ... ) ' This is NOT allowed !
Var2     = FreeTimeSearch( ... ) ' This IS allowed, No Set used !
Set ndr  = Var2(0)               ' Allowed: Subscript the array, we must use Set !
```

In the last line, we assign a single `NotesDateRange` object. We do this by subscripting the array and getting one element. Because this element (a `NotesDateRange`) is an object, however, we must use `Set`. If you're confused by this section, reread it. It may answer some questions you have had about why you sometimes need to use `Set` and other times cannot use it.

Time Out for Dates and Times

Before we move on to other topics, I need to stop and discuss date and time variables in LotusScript and the Notes classes. This topic is timely because there is currently a lot of concern over support for the year 2000. Notes supports dates up to, through, and well beyond the year 2000.

You should realize that the LotusScript language and the Domino Object Model class library are implemented separately and it is important to understand the difference. In fact, the LotusScript language was originally implemented by the office development group as an adjunct to Lotus 1-2-3; the DOM libraries were implemented by the Notes development team. One of the design goals of the LotusScript language was to be compatible with Visual Basic; DOM had to be consistent with the existing Notes code. It is not surprising that there are two different implementations of date/time (and a third for Java).

LotusScript, as you'll recall, is the language itself. Because it was implemented to be compatible with Visual Basic, there is a `Variant` data type that can hold data of various types. One of these types of values (type 7) is a date/time value. The date/time `Variant` value is the type of date that is built into the LotusScript language and is compatible with the Visual Basic implementation of dates and times. This is also the same format used by ActiveX automation, formerly known as OLE automation, so LotusScript can compatibly use ActiveX controls.

Date/time values in LotusScript are stored internally as double-precision floating-point numbers, with the integer part of the value representing the number of days since December 30, 1899, and the fractional part representing the time of day. A value of 1 indicates December 31, 1899, and a value of 2 is January 1, 1900. Negative values are allowed for the day portion, and dates can go back as far as January 1, 100 A.D. Dates can go into the future as far as December 31, 9999, well beyond any year-2000 problem. So, for Notes, I suppose we have a year 10,000 problem, but I'm not going to worry about it until at least after lunch.

What about Notes itself? Well, as you might imagine, Notes was originally developed independently from Visual Basic, and it has its own internal format for date/times. The Notes date/time format is made available through the `NotesDateTime` class and has support for time zones, daylight savings time, and time support for hundredths of a second. Internally, Notes counts days even farther back than LotusScript. Notes counts the days since January 1, 4713 B.C. If I recall correctly, this was even before the Intel 8088 was invented.

The time-zone support in Notes is important if you have data that will be used in multiple sites in different time zones. Because the time zone is recorded with the time, you can compare times that were generated in different locations, which is not possible with the LotusScript `Variant` form of date/time. Internally, Notes converts all date/time values to GMT for storage. With the GMT value and the time zone, Notes can convert the time to the local time. The LotusScript (`Variant`) date/time format really supports only what Notes calls local time, because the time zone is not stored.

As you might imagine, Java has its own format for dates. Java's format is different from both LotusScript and Notes. The Java date format is stored internally as a 64-bit (long) integer. It represents the number of milliseconds since January 1, 1970, GMT. The Java format does not store a time zone, so it cannot be converted automatically to local time. However, because it is based on GMT, Java's date/time value (unlike the LotusScript/Basic format) represents an absolute, not relative, date and time.

A new method in Release 5 of Notes and Domino in the Java `DateTime` class converts a Notes `DateTime` object to a Java `DateTime` object. This method is called `toJavaDate`.

In addition to enabling you to access the Notes date/time variables, the LotusScript `NotesDateTime` class can be used to convert from the LotusScript `Variant` form of date/time to the Notes format. If you understand the concepts of how the Notes classes are separate from the LotusScript and Java languages, it is easier to understand how and why there are three different date formats. Even if you understand the issue, however, it is easy to become confused about which format you're using. Just remember, if you are using a LotusScript language feature such as the `Cdat` built-in function, it expects a `Variant` date type, but if you are using a DOM class object, you can use a `NotesDateTime` class object. In Java, you'll use either the Java language date (`java.util.Date`) class or the `DateTime` class of Notes and Domino.

THE NotesUIWorkspace CLASS

Now that I've covered the `NotesSession` (LotusScript) and `Session` (Java) classes, I'd like to focus on the front-end classes of LotusScript. There are seven front-end classes: `NotesUIWorkspace`, `NotesUIDatabase`, `NotesUIView`, `NotesUIDocument`, `Button`, `Navigator`, and `Field`. Of these seven classes, I will be covering the first four classes. The `Button`, `Navigator`, and `Field` classes are fairly self-explanatory, and they represent the Notes concepts expressed in their names.

As I've mentioned, the front-end classes are not available in Java, but because they are an important part of the LotusScript class hierarchy, I will cover them as a group here. When I cover the back-end classes, I'll describe both LotusScript and Java features together, as I did for the `Session` class.

The `NotesUIWorkspace` class is at the top of the LotusScript front-end class hierarchy. This class represents the concept of the Notes user workspace. In the user interface, the primary functions you can perform in the workspace include adding databases to the desktop, opening databases, and editing documents. Each of these user actions has a counterpart in the `NotesUIWorkspace` class.

The following methods were available in release 4.6 and continue to be available in release 5: `AddDatabase`, `CheckAlarms`, `ComposeDocument`, `DialogBox`, `EditDocument`, `EditProfile`, `EnableAlarms`, `OpenDatabase`, `URLOpen`, `UseLSX`, and `ViewRefresh`.

In addition to these returning favorites, there are several new functions that are sure to be hits with existing Notes and Domino developers. To show off some of the new functions of the `NotesUIWorkspace` class, the next section has an interesting example.

Making Your Agent Play a Tune

This example shows you how to use two new methods: `PlayTune` and `GetListOfTunes`. These functions, of course are important new methods you can use for your business applications. Really.

To test these two new methods, open a test database and click on the Agents line in the Design Pane:

1. Create a new agent by clicking the New Agent action button.
2. Give the new agent the name `PlayTune`. Leave the trigger as manually from Actions menu and for the documents to act on, use All documents in database.
3. Change the Run drop-down in the Programmer's Pane to LotusScript.
4. Click the `Initialize` method and enter the following code in the Programmer's Pane:
   ```
   Sub Initialize
       Dim uiws as New NotesUIWorkspace
       Dim tunes as Variant
       tunes = uiws.GetListOfTunes()
       Forall tune in tunes
          MsgBox ("About to play " + tune)
          Call uiws.PlayTune(tune)
       End Forall
   End Sub
   ```
5. Select File, Save.
6. Select Actions, PlayTune.

This agent plays all the sounds that it can find in your Windows directory—assuming, of course that you have a sound card and speakers attached to your computer. If you don't have a sound card or speakers, I'm afraid that `PlayTune` will not work.

There are a few points that I want to make about the sample program. First, notice the `New` keyword that is found on the `Dim` line for the `NotesUIWorkspace` object. This keyword causes the `NotesUIWorkspace` object to be created and assigned to the named variable. This is a shorthand notation for

```
Dim uiws as NotesUIWorkspace
Set uiws = New NotesUIWorkspace
```

If you leave off the `New` keyword, you must use both statement lines and the `Set` keyword.

I declared the tunes variable as a `Variant`. This is because it will be returned from the `GetListOfTunes` method as an array. Notice that I do not use a `Set` keyword on the assignment of an array.

Finally, I use a `Forall` statement to loop through the list of items in the array. This is a very convenient construct of LotusScript. This statement type is not available in Java, but we can make good use of it here with LotusScript. Normally when you do some sort of loop, you need a counter, you must initialize it, and you must know the bounds of your array so that you don't go past the end. You don't need to do any of these things with the `Forall` statement.

The `Forall` statement in this example uses the variable tune and successively assigns it to each of the values found in the array. The first iteration through the loop uses the first value of the array. The second iteration uses the second array item, and so forth. The loop automatically stops when there are no more items in the array. The loop variable itself, in this case tune, must not be declared in a `Dim` statement in the program. The `Forall` statement acts as its declaration.

Of course, the middle of the loop displays the name of the tune about to be played and then plays it. On my computer, I have eight WAV files that are stored in my Windows directory. Each of these is played in sequence. If you have no WAV files stored in your Windows directory, you won't get any sounds.

Other ways to use the `PlayTune` method are to attach a WAV file to a form and then, within the `PostOpen` method, play the tune. The tunes don't have to be musical sounds. Any WAV file can be played. One real business use might be to have verbal instructions or help associated with a form. With a little imagination, you might come up with several other applications for this feature.

USING THE `OpenFileDialog` AND `SaveFileDialog` METHODS

The `OpenFileDialog` and `SaveFileDialog` methods of the `NotesUIWorkspace` class are new with release 5 and make it much easier than before to provide a dialog box for opening or saving files. Although in release 4.x of Notes you could use the `DialogBox` function to create your own simplistic open and save dialogs, it was typically too much trouble. With the two new functions, it is very easy to create file dialogs. Here is the syntax for `OpenFileDialog`:

```
uiws.OpenFileDialog(Multsel, [Title$ [, Filters$ [, Initialdir$ [,
➥Initialfile$]]]]) as Variant
```

The `Multsel` parameter is a Boolean and should be true if you want the user to be able to use multiple selections. The value should be false if you want the user to select only one filename from the dialog box. All the other parameters are string values.

The `Filters$` parameter is specified by pairs of items. The first string of the pair is the prompt that should appear in the dialog box; the second is the file specification. Each text string is separated from the others by a vertical bar. When specifying the files, be sure not to have any spaces, or the dialog box will not show your files.

In the following example, there are two pairs of items. The result will be an array of strings specifying the files that the user has selected. The result will be `Empty` if the user clicks Cancel. Here is some sample code:

```
Dim uiws as New NotesUIWorkspace
Dim files as Variant
files = uiws.OpenFileDialog(True, "Open Sesame", "Text Files¦*.txt¦HTML
➥Source¦*.html", "C:\Windows")
if IsEmpty(files) Then
   MsgBox "You clicked Cancel!"
   Exit Sub
End If
Forall file in files
   MsgBox "You selected " + file
End Forall
```

Figure 25.1 shows you the Open Sesame dialog box that is produced by Notes.

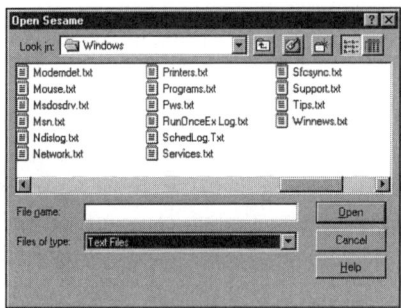

Figure 25.1
The Lotus Notes Open Sesame dialog box.

This example shows the Open Sesame dialog box, and then either displays a message if the user clicks Cancel or displays the list of files selected.

The `SaveFileDialog` is very similar to the `OpenFileDialog`. All the parameters except the first have the same meanings. Here is the syntax for the `SaveFileDialog` method:

```
uiws.SaveFileDialog(Showdir, [Title$ [, Filters$ [, Initialdir$ [,
➥Initialfile$]]]]) as Variant
```

The `Showdir` parameter is a Boolean and should be true if you want to show the user a directory dialog. The user will be able to select only a directory, but will not be able to specify a filename. The value should be false if you want the user to be able to specify a filename as well as the directory from the dialog box. All the other parameters are string values. The result will be `Empty` if the user clicks Cancel. Here is some sample code:

```
Dim uiws as New NotesUIWorkspace
Dim files as Variant
files = uiws.SaveFileDialog(True, "Save Salami", "Text Files¦*.txt¦HTML
➥Source¦*.html", "C:\Windows")
if IsEmpty(files) Then
   MsgBox "You clicked Cancel!"
   Exit Sub
```

```
End If
Forall file in files
    MsgBox "You selected " + file
End Forall
```

In this example, the `Filters$` is ignored, but I've included it to show how you would use it if the first parameter were false. Figure 25.2 shows you the Save Salami dialog box if the first parameter is set to `True`. Notice that you can specify only the directory.

Figure 25.2
The Lotus Notes Save Salami dialog box using the directory option.

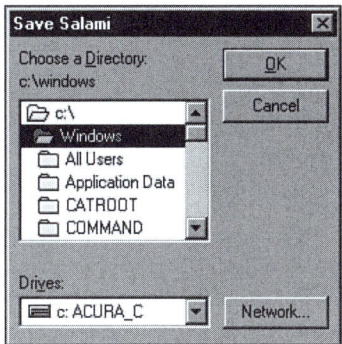

USING THE `PickListCollection` AND `PickListStrings` METHODS

In addition to the file dialog functions, two new methods of `NotesUIWorkspace` support a function similar to the `@PickList` function. These two new methods are called `PickListCollection` and `PickListStrings`. Both methods take as arguments a dialog type code, multiple selection Boolean, server, database, view, title, and prompt. `PickListStrings` also contains a column number as a last parameter. Here is the syntax for these methods:

Set *NotesDocumentCollection* = uiws.PickListCollection(Type%, Multsel, Server$,
➥DbFileName$, ViewName$, Title$, Prompt$, [, Category$])

StringArrary = uiws.PickListStrings(Type%, Multsel [, Server$] [, DbFileName$] [,
➥ViewName$] [, Title$] [, Prompt$] [, Column%])

`PickListCollection` returns a `NotesDocumentCollection` object of the documents selected. If you enable multiple selection, the collection may have more than one value. The Type field must be specified as `PICKLIST_CUSTOM`. All other fields except `Category$` are required. You may specify the `Server$` field as an empty string that indicates the local machine. You must include the database filename, even if the LotusScript program is running within the same database. If you include the optional `Category$` parameter, the view must be categorized, and the method will display only the single category specified. If you click Cancel from the dialog box, this method returns a `NotesDocumentCollection` with no elements. Otherwise, the method returns a `NotesDocumentCollection` containing the documents that were selected.

`PickListStrings` returns an array of strings. You can specify the following values for `Type`: `PICKLIST_NAMES`, `PICKLIST_ROOMS`, `PICKLIST_RESOURCES`, `PICKLIST_CUSTOM`. If you specify

PICKLIST_CUSTOM, all the optional parameters are required. The values for the strings are the values that are found in the specified column. If you enable multiple selection, the array may contain several values. Even if you turn off multiple selection (Only a single return value), the result will be an array with only one element. If you click on a category row within a categorized view (not a real document row), this method returns an empty string within the array. If you click Cancel from the dialog box, this method returns Empty.

> **Note**
>
> There is a difference among the three values Nothing, Empty, and Null. Nothing is used for object references (such as a NotesDocumentCollection) that are uninitialized. Regular variables, such as Variants, contain the value Empty when they are uninitialzed. Null is actually a valid value that is typically used to indicate "no answer." For more information, see Chapter 21, "LotusScript Variables and Objects," in the section titled "Much Ado about Nothing."

USING THE Prompt METHOD

The Prompt method is another useful method from the @formula language that has now been implemented in LotusScript. In the @formula language, @Prompt is useful for simple user prompts. The syntax in LotusScript is

```
Variant = uiws.Prompt(Type%, Title$ , Prompt$ [, default] [, values])
```

The Type% parameter may be one of the following values:

```
PROMPT_OK
PROMPT_YESNO
PROMPT_YESNOCANCEL
PROMPT_OKCANCELEDIT
PROMPT_OKCANCELLIST
PROMPT_OKCANCELCOMBO
PROMPT_OKCANCELEDITCOMBO
PROMPT_OKCANCELLISTMULT
PROMPT_PASSWORD
```

The Title$ parameter is the dialog box title, and the Prompt$ parameter is the prompt to display. The default value is used as the default input value. The values parameter is used to populate the dialog box options and is either a string or an array of strings.

The return value is an integer for Types PROMPT_OK, PROMPT_YESNO, and PROMPTYESNOCANCEL. Type PROMPT_OKCANCELLISTMULT returns an array of strings, and all the other Types return a string value. If you click Cancel, the return value will be Empty.

THE NotesUIDatabase CLASS

The NotesUIDatabase class represents the database that is currently being used by the workstation user. You can obtain a NotesUIDatabase object from the CurrentDatabase property of the NotesUIWorkspace class. Alternatively, and more commonly, the NotesUIDatabase class is used via event handlers.

Here are the `NotesUIDatabase` events:

- `PostDocumentDelete`   Called just after a document is deleted from the database. You are passed a `NotesUIDatabase` object.
- `PostDragDrop`   Called just after a drag-and-drop event in the database. You are passed a `NotesUIDatabase` object, the alias of the design element within the database, and a `continue` parameter.
- `PostOpen`   Invoked *after* the `QueryOpen` and `PostOpen` events of the `NotesUIView`.
- `QueryClose`   Invoked just before the database is about to close. You are passed the `NotesUIDatabase` and also a `continue` parameter. If you set the `continue` parameter to true, the database will close; if you return false for the `continue` parameter, the database will not close.
- `QueryDocumentDelete`   Called just prior to the deletion of one or more documents. You can obtain the documents that will be deleted by referring to the `Documents` property of the `NotesUIDatabase` class. If you return true in the `continue` parameter, the documents will be deleted; if you return false, the documents will not be deleted.
- `QueryDocumentUnDelete`   Called just prior to the undeletion of one or more documents. You can obtain the documents that will be undeleted by referring to the `Documents` property of the `NotesUIDatabase` class. If you return true in the `continue` parameter, the documents will be undeleted; if you return false, the documents will not be undeleted.
- `QueryDragDrop`   Called just before a drag-and-drop event in the database. You are passed a `NotesUIDatabase` object, the alias of the design element within the database, and a `continue` parameter.

In addition to the `Documents` property mentioned previously, you can also obtain the back-end `NotesDatabase` object by referring to the `Database` property of the `NotesUIDatabase` object.

You can open a view by calling the `OpenView` method of `NotesUIDatabase`.

THE `NotesUIView` CLASS

The `NotesUIView` class represents the view that is currently being used by the workstation user. You can obtain a `NotesUIView` object from the `CurrentView` property of the `NotesUIWorkspace` class. The `NotesUIView` class can also be accessed via event handlers. Several of the `NotesUIView` events occur only in a Calendar view. Therefore, you will not normally be concerned with these events.

THE `NotesUIView` EVENTS

Here are the `NotesUIView` events:

- `PostDragDrop` (Calendar view)   Called just after a calendar drag-and-drop operation.
- `PostOpen`   Occurs after the view has been opened.

- **PostPaste**   Called just after a document has been pasted within the view.
- **QueryAddToFolder**   Invoked prior to a document being added to a folder.
- **QueryClose**   Invoked just before the view is about to close. You are passed the `NotesUIView` and also a `continue` parameter. If you return true, the view will close; if you return false for the `continue` parameter, the view will not close.
- **QueryDragDrop (Calendar view)**   Called prior to a drag-and-drop operation. If you want to allow the drag-and-drop to continue, set the `continue` parameter to true. If it is set to false, the operation is aborted.
- **QueryOpen**   Called prior to opening a view. If you want to allow the view to open, set the `continue` parameter to true; if not, set it to false.
- **QueryOpenDocument**   Occurs prior to the opening of a document within a view. If you want to allow the document to open, set the `continue` parameter to true. If it is set to false, the document will not open.
- **QueryPaste**   Invoked to request permission to perform a paste operation within the view. It is allowed if `continue` is set to true.
- **QueryRecalc**   Invoked before a view is refreshed. You can perform operations at this point, and if you return true for the `continue` parameter, the view will be recalculated and refreshed. If you return false, the view will not be refreshed.
- **RegionDoubleClick (Calendar view)**   Called when a user double-clicks on a date within the Calendar view. You can find out the where the user double-clicked by obtaining the `CalendarDateTime` property of the `NotesUIView` class.

In addition to the `CalendarDateTime` property mentioned previously, you can also obtain the back-end `NotesView` object by referring to the `View` property of the `NotesUIView` object. The `Documents` property can be used to obtain the selected documents for the various events.

THE `NotesUIView` METHODS

Release 5 contains two new methods in the `NotesUIView` class. They are the `Print` method and the `SelectDocument` method. The `Print` method is used to print one or more documents from the current view. The `SelectDocument` method is used to select a document.

The syntax for the `Print` method is

```
Call notesUIView.Print([nCopies% [,fromPage% [,toPage% [, draft [, pageSeparator%
↪[, formOverride$ [, printView [, dateRangeBegin [,dateRangeEnd]]]]]]]]])
```

You can specify

- **nCopies**   Number of copies
- **fromPage**   Starting page, using 0 means all
- **toPage**   Ending page, using 0 means all
- **draft**   True to print the document in draft mode

- `pageSeparator` Specifies the page separator
- `formOverride` Specifies whether you want to override the documents form for printing
- `printView` True to print the view rather than the selected documents themselves
- `dateRangeBegin` Begin date of a Calendar view to print
- `dateRangeEnd` End date of a Calendar view to print

The `SelectDocument` method is used to select documents within a view. You can use the `SelectDocument` method in conjunction with the `Print` method for selecting and printing multiple documents from the view. The syntax for the `SelectDocument` method is

Call *NotesUIView*.SelectDocument(*document*)

THE NotesUIDocument CLASS

The `NotesUIDocument` class is probably one of the most important front-end classes (along with `NotesUIWorkspace`). The `NotesUIDocument` class represents the current document for the user. The front-end methods enable you to simulate operations of the user. For example, you can move among the various fields in the document, select strings, cut, copy, and paste information. You can also query the status for information, such as the current field, whether the document is in edit mode, and whether the document has been saved yet (that is, whether it is a `New` document).

Probably the most important feature of the `NotesUIDocument` class is the capability of getting and setting information into fields within the document. With this capability, in conjunction with the `NotesUIDocument` events, you can perform various field validations, calculations, or translations. Although you can perform validation and translation with field formulas, by using a `NotesUIDocument`, you can centralize all your consistency-checking logic in one place. This makes it easier to perform logic that may be based upon the contents of multiple fields. When you use field-validation logic, your code is spread among the various fields, and it is harder to read and debug the code.

Another point that may be confusing if you have not done much LotusScript programming is that the `NotesUIDocument` events are actually programmed while you are editing a form. In the Design Pane you select forms and you create a new form, but the InfoList for a form contains all the events for the `NotesUIDocument` class. Forms and documents are tied together, but if you are coming from the purely LotusScript programming side, you might wonder where you can find the `NotesUIDocument` events. Now you know.

Here is an example of calculating sales tax from document fields:

```
Sub QueryClose (Source As NotesUIDocument, Continue As Variant)
Dim dTotal As Double     ' Total sales amount
Dim dTaxRate As Double   ' You could also look the sales tax rate up from a table
➥or database
Dim dSalesTax As Double  ' Amount of sales tax
```

```
Dim strAmount as String   ' String field value
dTaxRate = 0.0675         ' Hard code this for the example
' Get first amount from field in document
strAmount = Source.FieldGetText("Amount1")
dTotal = CDbl(strAmount)  ' Convert to numeric
' Get second amount from field in document
strAmount = Source.FieldGetText("Amount2")
dTotal = dTotal + CDbl(strAmount)  ' Convert to numeric and add
dSalesTax = dTotal * dTaxRate  ' Calculate the Sales tax
strAmount = Format(dTotal, "Currency")  ' LotusScript Format function
strAmount = Source.FieldSetText("Total", strAmount)  ' Put it back in the document
strAmount = Format(dSalesTax, "Currency")  ' LotusScript Format function
strAmount = Source.FieldSetText("SalesTax", strAmount)  ' Put it back in the
➥document
Source.Save()  ' You MUST call Save to save these values back to the database
Continue = True  ' Continue with Close
```

In this simple example, I obtain two fields, add them, calculate the sales tax on the total, and save the result back to two fields in the document. This is not a polished application, because normally you would do much more error checking. Also, I've just supplied an arbitrary sales tax rate. You could look up a rate like this in a table or database.

A few points to notice about this example:

- The `NotesUIDocument` is already allocated and initialized prior to the entry to this routine.
- You can use the `FieldGetText` routine to get the value of a field in the document. The return value will be a string. If you will do computations on it, you must convert it to a number.
- You can use the `FieldSetText` routine to store the value back into the document.
- You must call `Save()` to save your updated document. If you forget to do this, the values you create will only affect the in-memory copy of the data and will not be stored back into the database.

SUMMARY

In this chapter, I covered the `NotesSession` LotusScript class as well as the `Session` and `AgentContext` Java classes. The `NotesSession` class is at the top of the Lotus implementation of the DOM, and the `Session` class is at the top of the Java implementation.

In LotusScript, `NotesSession` is used for foreground and background (agent processing). Properties relating to both are found in `NotesSession`. In Java, the `AgentContext` class is used to provide information about agents. Because this implementation came after the original LotusScript version, it is a little more coherently organized.

I told you about arrays of objects. This is one of the more confusing aspects of using LotusScript with the Domino Object Model classes. Remember that an array of objects is not an object itself. There are several formats for dates within Notes and Domino. Notes and Domino have an internal format, LotusScript has a separate format, and Java has a third format. You can use the `NotesDateTime` class to do some of the conversions among these formats.

There are seven front-end classes in LotusScript (and none in Java). The front-end classes are used to manipulate information currently being displayed to the end user. The primary four front-end classes are `NotesUIWorkspace`, `NotesUIDatabase`, `NotesUIView`, and `NotesUIDocument`. Of these four, you will most frequently use `NotesUIWorkspace` and `NotesUIDocument`.

You find the `NotesUIDocument` events in the InfoList while you are editing the Form. You can use these events to perform validation, calculations, or translations into standardized formats.

From Here...

We covered the highest level of the Domino Object Model in this chapter. Over the next two chapters, we'll traverse down the DOM hierarchy to the lower levels. You can find more information in the following chapters:

- Chapter 26, "Database, View, and Document Classes in LotusScript and Java," describes these very important DOM classes. Nearly every useful Domino program will need to access one or more of these classes, so reading this chapter is very important.
- Chapter 27, "Using Fields and Items in LotusScript and Java," shows you how to access the elementary data items of your documents. This chapter shows you with both Java and LotusScript examples of key concepts of document fields.

CHAPTER 26

DATABASE, VIEW, AND DOCUMENT CLASSES IN LOTUSSCRIPT AND JAVA

In this chapter, I cover the database, view, and document classes as well as a few others from the Domino Object Model (DOM). These classes form the core of the data model for Notes and Domino. In almost any program you write, you need to access an object of one of these classes.

Before we begin, let me clarify the terminology I'll be using in this chapter. I'm going to be discussing both the LotusScript and Java versions of the classes in this chapter. They represent the same conceptual model, so it shouldn't be too hard, but each language has a slightly different syntax. For example, in LotusScript, the classes all begin with the word `Notes`, so the database class is `NotesDatabase`. In Java, Lotus dropped the `Notes` prefix, so it is just the `Database` class in Java. I'll use the lowercase word *database* to refer to the Domino Object Model (DOM) conceptual class, the word `NotesDatabase` to refer to the LotusScript implementation, and the capitalized word `Database` to refer to the Java implementation. I'll use the fonts and the context within the chapter to try to make clear which version I'm discussing.

I won't show you all the methods for LotusScript and Java for each class, because that would be too redundant. I will instead show you some LotusScript and some Java using different methods of each so you can learn not only the classes, but the two different styles of programming. Let's begin with the database class because it is the container for the other classes.

The `NotesDatabase` LotusScript Class and the Java `Database` Classes

As discussed in previous chapters, the Domino Object Model is the conceptual framework for working with Domino objects. The database class gives you information about the database as a whole as well as providing functions to access the internal components of a database, such as its forms, views, and documents.

The `NotesDatabase` LotusScript Class

The LotusScript `NotesDatabase` class contains more methods and properties than any other LotusScript class, with almost 70 methods and properties. You can create a `NotesDatabase` object either with the `New` keyword or by accessing properties or methods from other objects. For example, you can use the `Database` property of the `NotesUIDatabase` class as mentioned previously, or you can use the `GetDatabase` method of the `NotesSession` class. As a matter of fact, you can create a new `NotesDatabase` object from an existing `NotesDatabase` object with one of several methods, such as `CreateReplica`.

Creating a New `NotesDatabase` Object

Before moving on, I want to clarify a point that might be confusing for some people. Suppose you create a `NotesDatabase` object with the `New` keyword, for example, like this:

```
Dim dbTemp as New NotesDatabase("","Temp")
```

The first parameter to the New NotesDatabase method is the server name, which in this case is empty, indicating the local drive. The second parameter is the Notes database name.

What happens here? Are you creating a new Notes/Domino database file on the disk or server? Are you creating a database file in memory that will later be stored on the disk or server?

The answer is that a new database file is *not* created. If you were using the preceding statement to attempt to create a new database on disk, you would be disappointed. A new disk file is not created as a result of the New keyword. An object of the class NotesDatabase is created in memory.

There is a difference between a Notes/Domino database file on disk and an object of the NotesDatabase class in memory, which is really a mechanism to manipulate the data found in a Notes database.

Creating a New Notes/Domino Database

Now that you know that a New keyword creates an object in memory but not a database on disk, how can you create a real database? You create it with the NotesDatabase Create method, of course. Assuming you have already created a NotesDatabase object in memory called dbobj, the Create method syntax is as follows:

```
Call dbobj.Create(strServer$, strDbFile$, boolOpen, [intMaxSize])
```

The first parameter is the server name, the second is the database filename, the third specifies whether the database file should be opened after it has been created, and the fourth parameter is an integer specifying the maximum size of the database in gigabytes. The fourth parameter is optional, and the maximum size you can specify is 4GB. This parameter applies only to databases that are created and saved in the Release 4.x format. Release 5 databases do not have a preset size limitation. You can create an R4.x database by giving the database an extension of .NS4 instead of .NSF.

You must be careful if you use the Create method, because this method causes the database to be created without a template, with no views or forms. The database is considered uninitialized. A normal database must have at least one view to be opened normally by a user. This implies that after you have used the Create method to create the database, you must also add at least one view (via the user interface) so that users can use the database. Forms and views cannot be created via the LotusScript Notes classes. They must be created manually with the Notes client user interface.

The third parameter, which specifies whether the database should be opened, is also important. After creating or obtaining a NotesDatabase object, you must first open the database before you can access any of the database properties or methods. Opening a database in this context is similar to opening a file with a program. Opening the database within LotusScript will not cause the database to be opened in the user interface.

The fourth parameter specifies the maximum size of the database in gigabytes. When the database is created, it does not actually take this amount of space; it is much smaller.

However, as documents are added, the maximum size is used as an absolute limit to the growth of the database file.

You can also create a Notes database on disk by calling one of the `CreateCopy`, `CreateFromTemplate`, or `CreateReplica` methods of the `NotesDatabase` object. These methods copy design elements, such as the forms and views, from the source database. Notes databases created with these methods typically contain at least one view and are considered initialized. After they are initialized, a database can be opened in the Notes user interface. Without a view, they cannot be opened by a user.

OPENING A NOTES/DOMINO DATABASE

If you have created the database with the `Create` method, you can open it directly with the third parameter. Suppose you create a `NotesDatabase` object like this:

```
Dim dbTemp as New NotesDatabase("","")
```

In this case, I have not specified a server or database filename. Does this create a new, empty database on disk? I hope you said no. This just creates a `NotesDatabase` object in memory. This object is not associated with any particular database file. If I later want to associate it with, for example, an existing database, I can use the `Open` method. This is the `Open` method's syntax:

```
Boolean = dbobj.Open(strServer$, strDbFile$)
```

After calling the `Open` method, I can access the methods and properties of the `NotesDatabase` object and obtain information about the Notes/Domino database.

You can also open an existing database by just creating the `NotesDatabase` object in memory with the `New` method. For example:

```
Dim dbTemp as New NotesDatabase("","MyData")
```

If the `MyData.NSF` database exists (the `.NSF` is assumed), this statement will both create the object *and open* the database. If `MyData.NSF` does not exist, you will not get an error. You can then later open an existing database by specifying an existing database name. Here is an example:

```
Dim dbTemp as New NotesDatabase("","NonData")    // No error if NonData does not
➥exist
Boolean = dbTemp.Open("", "MyData.NSF")          // Can open a different DB
filename
```

This example illustrates that you supply a database name on both the `Dim/New` statement and the `Open` method of the `NotesDatabase` class. However, if there is a discrepancy between the two names, the important name is the one supplied on the `Open` method, which will override the name supplied on the `Dim/New` statement.

As an alternative to the `Open` method, You can also use the `OpenIfModified` method. Following is the syntax for this method:

```
Boolean = dbobj.OpenIfModified(strServer$, strDbFile$, notesDateTime)
```

The `OpenIfModified` method examines the date specified in the third parameter and opens the file if it has been modified since that date. It returns `True` if the database was opened and `False` if not.

This method is useful if you want an agent to process only databases that have been modified since a particular date.

The `OpenWithFailover` method enables you to attempt to open a database, and if it does not exist on the specified server, Domino will attempt to find the database on another server within the cluster. You must be using clustered Domino servers for the `OpenWithFailover` method to be effective. The syntax for this method is

Boolean = dbobj.OpenWithFailover(strServer$, strDbFile$)

The `OpenByReplicaID` method enables you to open a database if you know its replica ID. Here is the syntax of its use:

Boolean = dbobj.OpenByReplicaID(strServer$, strReplicaID$)

I'll give you an example of `OpenByReplicaID` in Java in the next section.

THE `DbDirectory` AND `Database` JAVA CLASSES

In Java, you can open databases similarly to LotusScript; however, the access is slightly different. In Java, all classes are strictly hierarchical. This means that in order to access a lower-level object, you must have a copy of a higher-level object. All access begins at the top of the hierarchy with the Java `Session` class.

In LotusScript, The `NotesDbDirectory` class has only two methods (`GetFirstDatabase` and `GetNextDatabase`) and is used primarily just to traverse the available databases. In Java, however, the `DbDirectory` class is much more powerful and useful. In Java, the functions of creating and opening a database are within the `DbDirectory` class, rather than the `Database` class itself. The Java `Database` class is used to access data within the database, not to open it.

Here is the beginning of a Java agent:

```
public void NotesMain() {
   try {
      Session session = getSession();
      AgentContext agentContext = session.getAgentContext();
      // (Your code goes here)
      DbDirectory dbd = session.getDbDirectory("");
      dbd.createDatabase("MyJavaDb");
```

Notice that in this Java version we must first get a `Session` and a `DbDirectory` object before we can use `createDatabase`. The `AgentContext` object is not required for this example, but the IDE gives it to us free.

The `DbDirectory` class contains the `createDatabase`, `openDatabase`, `openByReplicaID`, and `openIfModified` methods that are found in the `NotesDatabase` class of LotusScript. The `createCopy`, `createFromTemplate`, and `createReplica` methods are contained in the Java `Database` class.

Here is an example of how you might use `openByReplicaID`.

```
Session session = getSession();
   AgentContext agentContext = session.getAgentContext();
   // (Your code goes here)
   DbDirectory dbDirLocal = session.getDbDirectory("");  // Local db directory
   DbDirectory dbDirServer = session.getDbDirectory("BENTLEY");  // Server db dir
Database dbLocal  = dbDirLocal.openDatabase("MyJavaDb"); // Open the local db
   // Now open the server replica of my local database
   Database dbServer=dbDirServer.openDatabaseByReplicaID(dbLocal.getReplicaID());
   // Now you can manipulate dbLocal and dbServer replica databases
   System.out.println("Local title="+dbLocal.getTitle());  //Print out the title
   System.out.println("Server title="+dbServer.getTitle());       //Print out the
➥title
```

In this example, I first open a local copy of a database. After the local copy is opened, I get the replica ID and use this to open the server replica of the same database. This is useful because it works even if the server copy has a different filename, different directory, and different database title. I don't need to know any of these properties of the server database as long as I know my local copy is a replica of the server version.

Table 26.1 shows the correspondence of the LotusScript and Java classes for databases. The first three columns contain LotusScript methods and the last three are Java methods.

DATABASE SECURITY

The major security mechanism for Domino databases is the Access Control List (ACL). ACLs are covered in detail in Chapter 17, "Access Control Lists (ACLs) and Application Security." In this section, I show you how you can programmatically obtain and change the ACL information for a database.

When your LotusScript or Java program runs, it is associated with a user ID. You will not be able to use your program to modify any ACL beyond any authority granted to the associated ID. As in the user interface, you must have manager access to be able to modify the ACL for a database. Assuming you have the proper authority, you can use the `NotesACL` class of LotusScript or the `ACL` Java class to create new ACL entries and traverse the existing entries.

In LotusScript, you can obtain the `NotesACL` class object via the `ACL` property of a `NotesDatabase`. After you have this object, you can get an entry via the `GetEntry` method or traverse with the `GetFirstEntry` and `GetNextEntry` methods of `NotesACL`. In Java, you get the ACL object via the `getACL` method within the `Database` class. The `getEntry`, `getFirstEntry`, and `getNextEntry` methods correspond to their LotusScript counterparts.

For each ACL entry, you use either the `NotesACLEntry` class in LotusScript or the `ACLEntry` class in Java. From the appropriate class, you can find the current level of the entry, you can get the associated roles, and you can query various authorizations for the entry.

TABLE 26.1 LOTUSSCRIPT AND JAVA DATABASE CLASSES

LotusScript			Java		
NotesSession	**NotesDbDirectory**	**NotesDatabase**	**Session**	**DbDirectory**	**Database**
GetDatabase			getDatabase		
GetDbDirectory			getDbDirectory		
	GetFirstDatabase			getFirstDatabase	
	GetNextDatabase			getNextDatabase	
		Create		createDatabase	
		CreateCopy			createCopy
		CreateFromTemplate			createFromTemplate
		CreateReplica			createReplica
		Open		openDatabase	
		OpenByReplicaID		openDatabaseByReplicaID	
		OpenIfModified		openDatabaseIfModified	
		OpenMail		openMailDatabase	
		OpenURLDb	getURLDatabase		
		OpenWithFailover		openDatabase (with failover parameter)	

Accessing Documents Within a Database

To access documents within a Domino database, you can search or traverse collections of documents. There are two different kinds of collections. The first kind of collection is a view. This is the traditional Notes/Domino concept that has been used to group documents. The LotusScript class is called `NotesView` and the Java class is called `View`. Although it is called the view class, it is used for both regular views and folders of Domino. You can use the `IsFolder` property of LotusScript or the `isFolder` method of Java to determine the type of object.

The second type of collection is simply called a document collection. This collection is dynamic and does not necessarily correspond to a folder or view of the database. It can contain any arbitrary set of documents and is not governed by a formula. The LotusScript class is called `NotesDocumentCollection`, and the Java class is called `DocumentCollection`. This type of class is generated automatically by Domino as the result of a full text search or a search by key.

There are several new classes in release 5 of Notes and Domino relating to views. These classes are the `NotesViewNavigator`, `NotesViewEntry`, and `NotesViewEntryCollection`. These classes are used to navigate and manipulate the entries within a view. These new classes were added because Lotus did not want to change the definitions of the existing view and document collection classes. If it changed the definitions, many existing programs would no longer work. As a result, the new classes are similar to the existing view and document collection classes, but they have added features that will be described shortly.

The LotusScript NotesView Class

You can use the `NotesView` class to traverse both folders and views. All the properties and methods are the same for both folders and views. There is one property called `IsFolder` that will be true for a folder and false for a view. Another property called `IsCalendar` will be true if the view is a calendar-style view.

The `NotesView` was available in prior releases of Notes and Domino. After reviewing the capabilities of this class, you should also review the `NotesViewEntryCollection` and `NotesViewNavigator` classes, discussed later. They provide a similar, but expanded, function for Notes and Domino release 5.

Navigating in the NotesView Class

The navigation methods for a view include `GetFirstDocument`, `GetLastDocument`, `GetNextDocument`, `GetNextSibling`, `GetNthDocument`, `GetParentDocument`, `GetPrevDocument`, and `GetPrevSibling`. Each of these methods returns a `NotesDocument` object. You will typically iterate through all the documents in a folder or view using these methods, processing or skipping each document as you go through them. You will typically use `NotesDocument` methods and properties to access individual items of the document itself.

You can use the `GetChild` method to traverse response documents within a view. `GetChild` returns the first response document to the specified document. You can find additional children by using the `GetNextSibling` method. Navigating through the responses in this manner presents the documents in the same order as they appear within the view. An alternative method for retrieving the immediate responses to a particular document is to use the `Responses` property of the `NotesDocument` class. This property is a `NotesDocumentCollection` object and contains all the responses in an arbitrary order, not necessarily the same as any particular view.

SEARCHING IN THE `NotesView` CLASS

You can filter a view by providing a full text search query string and invoking the `FTSearch` method. After you have called `FTSearch`, the `NotesView` object will refer only to the documents that meet the search criteria. You can use the `Clear` method to clear the previous search results. Here is an example:

```
Dim db As NotesDatabase
Dim view As NotesView
Set db = New NotesDatabase("","Cooking.nsf")
Set view = db.GetView("Recipes")
NumFound% = view.FTSearch("Chicken",0)
MsgBox "There were " + NumFound% + " chicken recipes"
Call view.Clear()
NumFound% = view.FTSearch("Beef",0)
MsgBox "There were " + NumFound% + " beef recipes"
```

The syntax for `FTSearch` is

NumFound% = viewname.FTSearch(SearchString$, MaxNum%)

The `FTSearch` method essentially filters the view to include only items matching the search string. The `GetFirstDocument`, `GetNextDocument`, and other traversal routines traverse only the found documents. *MaxNum* can be used to limit the number of documents you want to find. If you specify zero, all documents will be found. The result *NumFound* returns the actual number of documents found.

In addition to a full text search, you can also search for a single document by key(s) or obtain all the documents matching a set of keys in a view. To search for a single document by key, use the `GetDocumentByKey` method. Here is the syntax:

Set Notesdocument = viewname.GetDocumentByKey(keysStringarray [, boolExact])

You can specify multiple keys in the first parameter. Each key is an element of a string array. The keys are matched to the *sorted* columns of the view. The first document found will be returned. If no documents match the keys, the value `Nothing` will be returned. The second parameter is Boolean, is optional, and can be set to `True` to perform an exact search. If it is not supplied, `False` is assumed.

To retrieve all documents that match a set of keys, use the `GetAllDocumentsByKey` method. This method returns a `NotesDocumentCollection` object. Here is the syntax:

```
Set NotesDocumentCollection = viewname.GetAllDocumentsByKey(keysStringarray [,
➥boolExact])
```

The `GetAllDocumentsByKey` method returns the complete collection of all documents matching the keys found in the key array. As in the `GetDocumentByKey` method, only sorted columns are considered. They will be matched with the keys supplied in the string array. Exact matching can be requested by using a value of `True` for the second parameter. `False` is assumed if the second parameter is not supplied. The documents returned by `GetAllDocumentsByKey` are not sorted.

THE NotesViewEntry AND NotesViewEntryCollection CLASSES

Although Notes and Domino have had the `NotesView` class for several years, there are a few things that it doesn't provide. For example, you can use the `NotesView` class to traverse the documents in a view. As you go through each document, you receive a `NotesDocument` object. Although this is frequently sufficient, remember that a view can display more than just document fields. In particular, each column of a view can have a formula, which can be very complex. The `NotesView` class does not have a way to obtain the value that is actually presented in the view. This was previously accomplished using the `ColumnValues` property of the `NotesDocument`. It seems wrong to have view column values accessed through the document object, especially when the document can be in multiple views.

The `NotesViewEntry` and `NotesViewEntryCollection` classes of LotusScript and the `ViewEntry` and `ViewEntryCollection` classes of Java solve this problem and several more. A `NotesViewEntry` represents one row of a view. A row in a view, as mentioned, can contain much more than just document fields. The entry for each column can be a complex formula. A `NotesViewEntry` represents one row and contains the values shown in each column, after evaluating any formulas. A `NotesViewEntryCollection` represents a set of rows. The Java classes `ViewEntry` and `ViewEntryCollection` correspond to their LotusScript counterparts.

There are several useful properties of the `NotesViewEntry` class. You can obtain the number of direct children with the `ChildCount` property and the number of descendants with `DescendantCount`. Siblings are tallied by using the `SiblingCount` property.

The column values, as mentioned, can be obtained via the `ColumnValues` property. This property in LotusScript returns a `Variant` array, one value for each column within the view entry. The entries within this array are subscripted with a 0-origin. The corresponding Java method, called `getColumnValues`, returns a `java.util.Vector`. You should import `java.util.*` to make working with this vector more convenient. As in LotusScript, the vector subscripts begin at `0`.

Here is a Java agent that will cycle through rows of a view entry collection and print the contents of the second column:

```
import lotus.domino.*;
import java.util.*;

public class JavaAgent extends AgentBase {
public void NotesMain() {
```

```
try {
   Session session = getSession();
   AgentContext agentContext = session.getAgentContext();
   Database db = agentContext.getCurrentDatabase(); // Get from AgentContext
   View view = db.getView("MyView");
   ViewEntryCollection vec = view.getAllEntries();   // All rows
   ViewEntry ve;                                     // One view entry row
   int i;
   int  iCount = vec.getCount();         // Find out how many rows
   if  ( iCount>= 1) {                   // Do this only if there are rows
      ve = vec.getFirstEntry();          // The first row

      for(i = 1;   i <= iCount ;   i++) {    // Go through each row
         Vector cv = ve.getColumnValues(); // Get the column values
         System.out.println(cv.elementAt(1)); // Print second column (0-origin)
         ve = vec.getNextEntry(ve);        // Get the next row
      }
   }
} catch(Exception e) {
   e.printStackTrace();
}
}
```

Notice that for a Java agent you get the current database from the `agentContext` object, not the session object as you would with a LotusScript agent.

THE `NotesViewNavigator` CLASS

The `NotesViewNavigator` class is used to navigate through a view or a subset of a view. You can create a new view navigator from the `NotesView` class with a new method called `CreateViewNav`. The syntax is very simple:

`Set NotesViewNavigator = viewname.CreateViewNav()`

You can also create a view navigator from another view navigator, a category string, or from the children of a specified navigator. After you have a navigator, you can perform the standard navigations: `GetFirst`, `GetLast`, `GetNext`, `GetNextSibling`, `GetNth`, `GetPrev`, and `GetPrevSibling`. These methods get both documents and category items. You can also skip categories by using `GetFirstDocument`, `GetLastDocument`, `GetNextDocument`, and `GetPrevDocument`. You can get just the categories with `GetNextCategory` and `GetPrevCategory`.

The `ParentView` property can be used to get the `NotesView` object for the view that is associated with the view navigator.

Each of the navigation methods returns a `NotesViewEntry`. As discussed previously, a `NotesViewEntry` corresponds to a row within a view. Typically, as you navigate through the view, you will examine data found within each row of the view. You do this by using the `ColumnValues` property of the `NotesViewEntry` object.

The NotesViewColumn Class

Within the NotesView class, there is a property called Columns. The Columns property returns an array of NotesViewColumn objects. The NotesViewColumn class contains no methods, only properties. It includes properties such as Formula, IsCategory, IsHidden, IsResponse, IsSorted, ItemName, Position, and Title. These are properties of the view itself. With release 5 of Notes and Domino, over 25 additional properties are included in the NotesViewColumn class. These properties include formatting information, such as fonts, alignment, time, and date formatting. You can also now find out whether the class is sorted, and whether the column contains a field or a formula.

> **Tip**
>
> Do not take the values for IsField and IsFormula too literally. The intended definition is that a column value is either a formula or a field. When one is true, the other is false. However, sometimes even when the definition is a single field, Notes returns a true value for IsFormula with the formula definition just the name of the field. So a field name can sometimes be reported as a formula.

The NotesDocumentCollection LotusScript and the Java DocumentCollection Classes

The LotusScript NotesDocumentCollection class is very similar to the NotesView and the NotesViewEntryCollection classes. The primary purpose of the NotesDocumentCollection class is to be a container for documents. You can traverse the documents within the container, and you can perform certain operations on the entire collection of documents.

There are a few differences among these classes, so let me summarize them. The NotesDocumentCollection class can contain any arbitrary collection of documents. In fact, one of the most common ways to generate an object of this type is through one of the search methods, such as the database FTSearch. A NotesView and NotesViewEntryCollection, however, are both tied to a view, which means that the collection itself has a selection formula that dictates document inclusion within the collection.

Views are typically sorted, but a NotesDocumentCollection is not necessarily sorted. The only way a NotesDocumentCollection will be sorted is if it is the result of a full text search.

To traverse a NotesDocumentCollection, you can use these methods: GetFirstDocument, GetLastDocument, GetNextDocument, GetNthDocument, and GetPrevDocument. When you try to navigate to a nonexistent document, you receive the special value Nothing.

You can call the FTSearch method of NotesDocumentCollection to further refine a search. The collection will be narrowed to the set of documents that meets the search criteria. The Count property can be used to find the current number of documents within the collection. The Query property can be used to find the query that resulted in the document collection if the collection was generated by a search or full text search.

The `PutAllInFolder` is used to put all the documents of a collection into a specified folder. The `RemoveAllFromFolder` is used to remove documents of the collection from a given folder. You can delete all the documents within the collection completely from the database by using the `RemoveAll` method.

One useful method is the `StampAll` method. This enables you to store a value in a given field on each of the documents in the collection. Before you call the `StampAll` method, you must be sure to call the `Save` method on any documents that you have modified. You do not need to call `Save` after `StampAll`.

One important example of a `NotesDocumentCollection` is the `UnprocessedDocuments` property of `NotesDatabase`. In Java, you obtain this collection from the `AgentContext` class by calling the `getUnprocessedDocuments` method. This is one of the few differences in the logical class structure between LotusScript and Java. You can find out more about the differences in Chapter 25, "The Session and Front-End Classes."

The `UnprocessedDocuments` collection is used within either an agent or view action. For an agent, this collection represents the result of a search or is the set of documents that has been specified by the creator of the agent in the Which documents should it act on? criteria. For instance, if the agent is to operate on all unread documents, the unprocessed documents are the unread documents. In a view action, the collection contains the documents that have been selected by the user. After a document has been processed by an agent or view action, in LotusScript you must call the `UpdateProcessedDoc` method of the `NotesSession` class, and in Java you must call the `updateProcessedDoc` method in the `AgentContext` class.

Alternatively, you can call the `UpdateAll` method of the `NotesDocumentCollection` class or `updateAll` in the Java `DocumentCollection` class.

Here is a LotusScript sample agent that handles all unprocessed documents. The routine `HandleDoc` is a generic name for your routine that should process a document. Typically, you locate this routine in a script library:

```
Sub Initialize
Dim session As New NotesSession
Dim db As NotesDatabase
Dim dc As NotesDocumentCollection
Dim doc As NotesDocument
Set db = session.CurrentDatabase        ' Obtain current database object
Set dc = db.UnprocessedDocuments        ' All documents to be handled
Set doc = dc.GetFirstDocument()         ' Get first document of collection
Do Until (doc is Nothing)               ' While we have a valid document

   Call HandleDoc(doc)                  ' User subroutine to handle document
   Call session.UpdateProcessedDoc(doc) ' Indicate this one now handled
   Set doc = dc.GetNextDocument(doc)    ' Get the next one
Loop

End Sub
```

The NotesForm LotusScript and the Form Java Classes

The LotusScript `NotesForm` and the Java `Form` classes enable you to get information about a form in a Domino database.

In LotusScript, the `NotesForm` class has eight properties and only one method. These are the properties for this class:

- `Aliases` A string array containing the form's aliases
- `Fields` A string array of the field names
- `FormUsers` A list of users who can create documents using the form
- `IsSubform` A Boolean flag that is `True` if the form is a subform
- `Name` The name of the form
- `ProtectReaders` A flag that is set to `True` if the Readers list is protected from modification via replication
- `ProtectUsers` A flag that is set to `True` if the `FormUsers` list is protected from modification via replication
- `Readers` A list of users who can use the form to view documents

The only method of the `NotesForm` class is the `Remove` method. This method removes the form from the database.

Design Documents

In Domino databases, essentially all information is stored in documents. Clearly, the information you store and enter in databases is stored this way, but information about your views, forms, and so forth are also stored in a database in documents. These are special documents called design documents. For example, the definition of a Domino form is actually stored in a design document. This document has fields containing information about the form itself. As an example, look at Figure 26.1.

Figure 26.1 is an example from a Domino personal directory. The properties box displays the different fields of this design document. This properties box is different than what you'll see if you open the form for editing and request the properties. You can see from the figure that many of the fields begin with a dollar sign. This symbol signifies that this is an internal field used by Notes/Domino. In the figure, the $TITLE field has been highlighted. In the right side of the properties box, you'll see the form name as well as all the aliases for the form. In addition to the name, this form has four aliases: Server Connection, local, remote, and Connection.

When you access an object of the `NotesForm` class, you are really accessing data that is stored within the design document for the form. As another example, if you specify that you want to restrict who can create documents with the form, a new field is inserted in the design document for the form. This field has the field name $FormUsers. The FormUsers property of the NotesForm class enables you to retrieve or set this value. In essence, when you give it a new set of names, this field in the design document is updated with the values.

Figure 26.1
The design document properties for the Server Connection form.

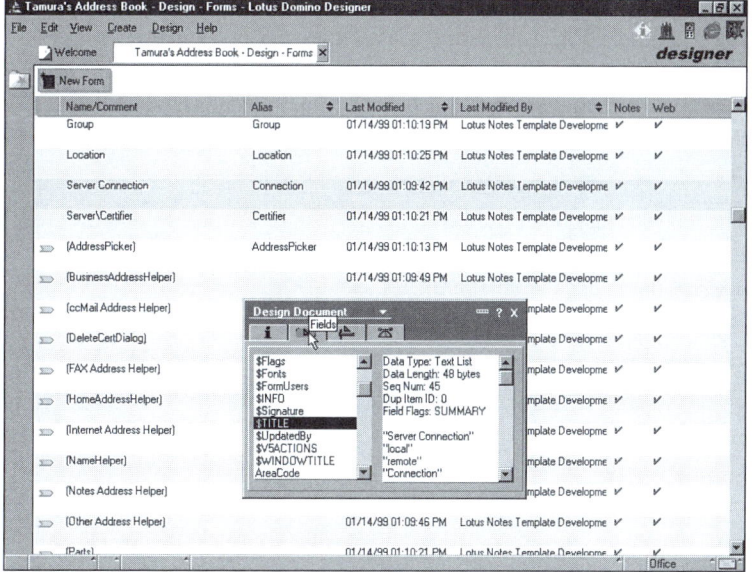

Just for fun, you might want to browse the design documents for some of the forms and views in some of your databases. You'll find it interesting to see some of the fields that have been created internally by Notes. Most of these internal fields are created as a result of property options set within the form or view properties. Other fields may track information, such as the time or user ID of users that edit documents.

THE NotesDocument LotusScript and Document Java Classes

The LotusScript NotesDocument class and the Java Document class are used to access data stored within a document in a Domino database. The document classes are important, because with these classes you can access and change information stored in the document fields. Although the LotusScript and Java classes are very similar, there are a few differences.

Creating a Document

One of the areas of difference between LotusScript and Java is in the way you create a document object. In essence, the Java methods are a subset of the LotusScript methods, so I'll cover the LotusScript methods first.

CREATING A NotesDocument OBJECT IN LOTUSSCRIPT

The NotesDocument class is back-end class that is used to manipulate values within a document in a Notes/Domino database. Because it is a back-end class, the NotesDocument class can be used in a Domino Agent running on the server, whereas the NotesUIDocument cannot.

You can obtain a NotesDocument class object in one of many ways. The first is through the Document property of the NotesUIDocument class. Another way to get a NotesDocument is by one of the methods of the NotesDocumentCollection class. The NotesDocumentCollection class has methods such as GetFirstDocument, GetNextDocument, and GetNthDocument. Each of these methods returns a NotesDocument object.

The NotesDatabase and NotesView classes have properties and methods that return NotesDocumentCollection objects. The document collection can represent all the documents in a database, all the documents in a view, or the result of a search of some sort. After you have the NotesDocumentCollection object, you can retrieve a NotesDocument object by using one of the traversal methods.

The NotesDatabase class also enables you to obtain a NotesDocument object via the document's NoteID (unique within a database) or the document's Universal ID (uniquely identifies the document in all replicas). These methods are GetDocumentByID and GetDocumentByUNID.

After you have obtained a NotesDocument object from one of the many possible methods, you can manipulate the items found in the document by using the NotesDocument properties and methods.

To create a new document within a database, you can use the New keyword with the NotesDocument class, or you can use the CreateDocument method of the NotesDatabase class. Note that this behavior is different from the behavior of the NotesDatabase class. With the NotesDatabase class, you cannot create a database with the New keyword. With the NotesDocument class, you can create a new document like this:

```
Dim session As New NotesSession
Dim db As NotesDatabase
Dim doc As NotesDocument
Set db = session.CurrentDatabase
Set doc = New NotesDocument ( db )
doc.Form = "MyForm"
Call doc.Save( True, True )
```

If you do not specify a form field value for the document, the document will not have a default form and will be displayed using the default form (if there is one) for the database. If there is no database default form, a document created this way cannot be displayed in the user interface. It is generally a good practice to include a field called Form and populate it with the form name. Also note that if you do not call the Save method at the end of the script, the newly created document will not be saved in the database.

Creating a Document Object in Java

In Java, there is no a equivalent to the front-end `NotesUIDocument`, so you cannot obtain a document this way. You can, however, use the `DocumentCollection`, `Database`, or `View` classes to obtain existing documents within the database.

As with LotusScript, the `DocumentCollection` class enables you to traverse the collection using methods such as `getFirstDocument`, `getNextDocument`, `getPrevDocument`, and `getLastDocument`. The `Database` class allows full text searching to obtain a `DocumentCollection`, and you can also get documents by unique ID or by URL.

In LotusScript, you can create a new document with the `New` keyword, as shown in the previous section. This method is not available in Java. Because a strict hierarchical structure is enforced in Java, you cannot create a document object outside a container. Thus, the only way to create a new document object is to use the `createDocument` method of the `Database` class. Here is a Java agent to create a new document in a database:

```
import lotus.domino.*;

public class JavaAgent extends AgentBase {
public void NotesMain() {
  try {
    Session session = getSession();
    AgentContext agentContext = session.getAgentContext();
    Database db = agentContext.getCurrentDatabase(); // Get from AgentContext
    Document doc = db.createDocument();       // Create the document
    doc.appendItemValue("Form", "MyForm");   // Add form field to document
    doc.save();                              // Be sure to save it in database
  } catch(Exception e) {
    e.printStackTrace();
  }
}
}
```

This example is very similar to the LotusScript example. Remember again, though, that in Java you obtain the `CurrentDatabase` from the `AgentContext` object, not the `Session` object. Also, the extended syntax form of assignment that is available in LotusScript is not available in Java. For example, in LotusScript, we can just specify

```
doc.Form = "MyForm"         ' In LotusScript we can use extended syntax
```

whereas in Java, we must call the `appendItemValue` method of the document object to store the value within the document. Here it is in Java:

```
doc.appendItemValue("Form", "MyForm");    // In Java we must call a method
```

Saving a Document

As mentioned, if you do not call the `Save` method after creating or changing a document, your changes will not be reflected in the database.

The syntax of the Save method is as follows:

```
SavedOK = documentvar.Save(boolForce, boolMakeResponse [, boolMarkRead])
```

If you do not want to check the return value, you can use the `Call` keyword to invoke the `Save` method, as shown in the preceding example.

All three parameters of the `Save` method are Boolean variables. The first two parameters control what happens if another user has modified the current document since you accessed it in your program.

If the first parameter of the `Save` method is true, the document will be saved even if another user has modified the document while the script is running. The `MakeResponse` parameter will then be ignored. If the first parameter is false and the `MakeResponse` parameter is true, the document will be saved as a new response document; but if the `MakeResponse` parameter is false, the save will be aborted. If the `MarkRead` parameter is true, the document will be marked as read. The return value will be true if the document was saved, and false if not. Assuming conflicting saves of the same document, the following table shows how the conflict is resolved, depending upon the parameters used for `Save`. The return value is `True` if the document was saved, and `False` otherwise.

Force	MakeResponse	Action
True	N/A	Current document overwrites other saved since document access.
False	True	Current document becomes a response to other document saved since access.
False	False	Save is aborted if there was another save since access.

In Java, you can call the save method using the following syntax:

```
SavedOK = documentvar.save( [Force [, MakeResponse [, MarkRead]]])
```

If you do not specify `Force` or `MakeResponse`, they are both assumed to be `False`. Notice that in Java, the `Force` parameter is optional, but in LotusScript, it is not. The operation and document save resolution works the same as for LotusScript.

Deleting a Document

You use the `Remove` method in LotusScript or the `remove` method in Java to delete a document from a database. Just as in the case of saving a document, the document may be modified by another user after you retrieve it and prior to your requesting a deletion. To handle this situation, you use the `Force` parameter. Here is the Java syntax:

```
RemovedOK = documentvar.remove(Force)
```

The LotusScript syntax is similar. If the `Force` parameter is `True`, the document will be deleted even if there were changes. If `Force` is `False`, the deletion will be aborted if there were any changes by another user.

In either case, the method returns `True` if the document was deleted and `False` if it was not.

Document Properties

You may occasionally need to query properties of a document. For example, you can query whether a document is new (that is, it has never been previously saved) by using the IsNewNote property of LotusScript or calling the isNewNote method in Java. Either one returns True if the document has not yet been saved in the database.

Two new document properties are available with release 5 of Notes and Domino. The first is called IsValid in LotusScript or isValid in Java. This property can be queried in LotusScript to tell whether an existing document has been deleted. You should use this when you first obtain the document and should not call this routine more than once. To find out whether a document has been deleted (most likely by another user) during the execution of your program, you can call IsDeleted.

IsValid returns a Boolean value that is True if the document is valid (has not been previously deleted). IsValid is False if the document is a deletion stub. IsDeleted returns True if the document is now deleted and False if it is not deleted.

The Size property returns a Long (32 bits) value that contains the size of the current document in bytes. This size includes any file attachments.

There are several time stamp properties of a document that you may find useful. The Created property is a time stamp of the date and time the document was created. The LastModified property is the date and time the document was last changed. The LastAccessed property is a time stamp of the last time the document was either read or written. Note that these three properties return dates in the LotusScript format, not the Domino Object Model format. Please see Chapter 25, in the section entitled "Time Out for Dates and Times," for a more complete discussion of the various date formats in Notes and Domino.

Document Hierarchy

Documents in Domino may be either main documents or response documents. Response documents can be considered children of the main document. Sometimes you may want to traverse documents based upon the document hierarchy.

The LotusScript IsResponse property of the NotesDocument class or the isResponse method in Java will let you know whether a particular document is a response to another document. If True, the document is a response document; otherwise, it is a main document. You can then obtain the parent document through a two-step process. First, use the ParentDocumentUNID property in LotusScript or the getParentDocumentUNID method of Java. Either of these returns a string version of the UNID (Universal ID). The second step is to use the UNID string with the database LotusScript method GetDocumentByUNID or the corresponding Java method. Remember that the UNID identifies the document uniquely in all replica databases.

To change the status of a main document to a response document, you can use the `MakeResponse` method. The single parameter to this method is a `NotesDocument` object that should become the new parent. You would use this method to move a document within a database to a new or different document hierarchy. One application for this method might be to create status documents for a given main document. When you change a document to a response document, you should also be sure to modify the form associated with the document to be a response form rather than a main form.

To find all the immediate response documents of a particular given document, you can use the `Responses NotesDocument` property. This property returns a `NotesDocumentCollection` that contains all the response documents. In Java, you use the `getResponses` method, which returns a `DocumentCollection` object. In either case, the responses returned will be only first-level responses. In order to obtain lower-level response documents, you must recursively obtain these documents or use a loop structure. To find out how many documents are in the document collection, you can use the `Count` property of the document collection. Alternatively, you can loop through the document collection contents until one of the methods returns `Nothing`.

Profile Documents

Profile documents have been in Domino since release 4.5, but they are not prominently described or used. These special documents were created to improve performance on per-user types of information. They are special documents because they are design elements, not regular documents. This means that profile documents will not appear in any view in the user interface.

Profile documents are cached on the Domino server and are accessed via a two-level hash key method. This is quite different than the normal lookup and indexing that is done for regular documents in a view within a database. The model for profiles is that a database can contain several different types of profiles, each one with a set of users. For example, one program might use profile documents for user interface preferences, another might use them for report options, and a third might use profile documents for per-user workflow information. All three types of profiles can be stored in the same database. To obtain a profile document, you specify the name of the profile and then a key, which is usually the username.

One last rather odd characteristic of profile documents is that there is no explicit call to create a profile document. The first time you reference a profile document, it is created. So, to create a profile document in LotusScript, you call the `NotesDatabase` method `GetProfileDocument`. In Java, you call the equivalent `getProfileDocument` method of the `Database` class. Here is the LotusScript syntax:

`NotesDocument = databasevar.GetProfileDocument(ProfileName$, UserName$)`

Notice that the `GetProfileDocument` is a method of the database class, not the document class.

After you have a document, you can query whether it is a profile document by using the `IsProfile` property in LotusScript or the `isProfile` method in Java. The `Key` method of the document class returns the key (username) associated with the profile document, and the `NameOfProfile` property returns the name of the associated profile.

Prior to release 5, there was no way to scan a database to find all the profile documents. Because you could not use a view (even a hidden view) to obtain them, it was possible for profile documents to become orphaned. With release 5, there are two new calls, `GetFirstProfileDoc` and `GetNextProfileDoc`, that enable you to traverse all the profile documents within a database. Here is the syntax:

```
NotesDocument = databasevar.GetFirstProfileDoc([ProfileName])

NotesDocument = databasevar.GetNextProfileDoc()
```

If you don't specify the profile name when you first call `GetFirstProfileDoc`, you will retrieve all the profile documents in the database.

The capability of using profile documents provides a powerful feature, but because all the data is cached on the server, you should use this facility with care so that you don't get thousands of profile documents cluttering up the server's cache.

Another feature available in release 5 is called single category views. These views are well suited for situations where you want to display per-user information to the user. In essence, it enables you to use a view to hold all the database information, but display only the user's small subset of information, which will be different for each user. See the section called "Single Category Embedded Views" in Chapter 15, "Developing Views and Folders," for more information on this feature.

Using Documents with Folders

Folders are very similar to views. The major difference is that the documents contained in a view are selected by a formula, and documents in a folder must be placed there explicitly. The documents included within a view change dynamically as new documents are added or changed in the database.

The documents in a folder are typically placed there by a user using the drag-and-drop facilities in the user interface. Alternatively, you can write LotusScript or Java programs that add or remove documents from a folder. You use methods of the document class to perform these operations. To add a document to a folder in LotusScript, you specify

```
Call documentvar.PutInFolder(Foldername$)
```

In Java, you use

```
documentvar.putInFolder(Foldername)
```

You specify the name of the destination folder. If the document is already in the folder, no error is generated and it remains in the folder. If the folder does not already exist, it is created and uses the default folder as the folder to clone.

To remove documents from a folder in LotusScript, you use

`Call documentvar.RemoveFromFolder(Foldername)`

In Java, you use

`documentvar.removeFromFolder(Foldername)`

The document will be removed from the specified folder. If it does not exist within the folder, no error will be generated.

In release 5, you can find out in which folders a document resides. This is useful, for example, if you want to keep a document in a database, but remove it from any folders. Previously, the only way to accomplish this was to go through all the folders of a database.

You can obtain the list of folder references by using the `FolderReferences` property. Here is the LotusScript syntax:

`StringArray = documentvar.FolderReferences`

Here is the Java you would use:

`java.util.Vector StringArray = documentvar.getFolderReferences()`

DOCUMENT SECURITY

Domino has many security features designed to protect documents. Two of these strong security features are document encryption and document signing. There are two types of encryption: one for documents using secret encryption keys; and the other for email, which uses public/private key encryption. Let me start with how the user interface works, and then follow with a brief summary of these capabilities and how to use encryption with LotusScript and Java.

Domino can encrypt documents using encryption keys. As mentioned, this facility is different from email encryption, which I'll cover shortly. Actually, when you encrypt a document, the encryption is done on a field-by-field basis. You can encrypt some fields within a document and leave others without encryption. In the user interface, this decision is up to a designer. So the phrase "to encrypt a document" really means to encrypt the encryptable fields within a document. It is also possible that even with encryptable fields, some documents are not encrypted at all. As a designer, the task is to define fields that might need to be encrypted by the user. Some, none, or all documents created with the form may actually encrypt data within the fields. As a designer, you can also specify default encryption keys to make encryption automatic for the user. As a LotusScript or Java programmer, you have some additional capabilities that are not available to an end user.

For any particular document, you can use several encryption keys. If a user has any of the keys available, he or she will be able to access the encrypted fields. So, after you create an encryption key, you must send it (usually via email) to any other user that will need to use it. The user's copy of the encryption key must be available in his or her User ID file. If it is not available, an encrypted field will not be accessible.

Here are the three roles: database designer, key creator, and key user. Of course, all three roles could be fulfilled by the same person.

Database Designer	Key Creator (User)	Key User
Define encryptable fields within database	Create encryption key(s)	Receive key(s) from creator
Specify default encryption keys	Send key(s) to any key users	Use key to encrypt or decrypt data
	Use key to encrypt or decrypt data	

Here are the steps to create encryption keys:

1. To issue encryption keys, select the following commands from the Notes client menus: File, Tools, User ID. After entering your password, select Encryption. On the Encryption menu, click the New button to create a new encryption key. See Figure 26.2. At this point, you can give the encryption key a name. The name you choose is important and will be used later. After the encryption key is created, it is stored in your User ID file.

Figure 26.2
Encryption keys are stored in your User ID file.

You can create more than one encryption key and have more than one encryption key in your User ID file. Typically, a key name will be associated with a particular group or function within your company, such as Sales or Engineering; or geography, such as Los Angeles; or a project, such as Manhattan Project. You could also use levels of keys, such as Top Secret, Medium Secret, and Indiscreet. Choose a name that will be informative to its users.

2. After your keys have been created, you can use the built-in facilities to email them to the appropriate people. Do this by clicking the Mail button on the Encryption dialog box while the key you want to send is highlighted.

Here are the steps to create encryptable fields in a Notes Form:

1. The designer first creates or edits a form.
2. For each field you want to encrypt, highlight the field and open the properties box for that field. Go to the Advanced tab (the one with a beanie hat).
3. Under the Security options section, click the drop-down box and enable the following option: Enable encryption for this field. Selecting this option makes the field encryptable, but does not actually encrypt any data.
4. As a designer, you can also specify default encryption for the form. If you do this, any documents created with the form will be encrypted automatically by default. To accomplish this, open the Form properties box, click on the Security tab (key icon), and specify one of the keys in the Default encryption keys field. This field will display only the encryption keys that are contained in your User ID file.

In the Notes client, a user can tell whether a particular field is encryptable, because the small corners for the field are red for encryptable fields and white for normal fields. Only encryptable fields will be encrypted. As a Notes user, here is how you can use keys to encrypt a document:

1. To encrypt a document, you must have keys stored in your User ID file. To use the keys with the user interface, create a document with a form with encryptable fields. You cannot encrypt fields unless they are encryptable.
2. Go to the Document properties box by selecting File, Document Properties.
3. Choose the Security tab (key icon). Under Secret Encryption keys, enable the keys you want to use by placing a check mark next to them. If you enable more than one key, if the receiver has any of the keys, he or she will be able to decrypt the document. The receiver does not need to have all the keys. Close the dialog box and the document. The document will be encrypted after it is saved.

These steps show you how to create keys, enable encryption in forms, and encrypt a document using the user interface. The model for encryption in LotusScript and Java is similar, but you have different capabilities with the programming interface.

With the programming interface, you cannot actually create the keys, and you cannot create forms with encryptable fields, but after keys have been created and are stored in an ID file, you can use the keys to encrypt a document. In fact, with LotusScript or Java, you can create documents and encrypt fields that have not been specified as encryptable with the user interface.

Here is a small example of an agent to illustrate how to encrypt a document:

```
Dim session As New NotesSession
Dim db As NotesDatabase
Dim doc As NotesDocument
Dim item As NotesItem
```

```
Set db = session.CurrentDatabase
Set doc = db.CreateDocument()
doc.Body = "Test Data"
doc.Form = "TestForm"
Set item = doc.getFirstItem("Body")
item.IsEncrypted = True
doc.EncryptionKeys = "Top Secret"
doc.Encrypt
Call doc.save(True,True)
```

There are several assumptions in this example:

- You must create and have the encryption key Top Secret installed in your User ID file.
- A form called TestForm has been created in your database with one field called Body.
- You have a view (the Default view is good enough) to view the document.

If you meet these assumptions, you can try the example. There are several points to notice in the example. To encrypt a field or set of fields:

1. You must set the IsEncrypted property of the item to True. This is what enables encryption for the field. This works even if the field has not been enabled for encryption in the user interface. In fact, the field does not have to appear in the user interface at all, so this may be a way to add additional protection for private data that you must keep within a document.

2. You must set the EncryptionKeys property of the document to either a string or an array of strings naming the encryption key(s). If you don't specify any encryption keys, the user's public key will be used to encrypt the document. After that, only the user who created the document will be able to decrypt the document (using his or her private key).

3. Call the Encrypt method of the document. This will encrypt the document. If you don't have the keys specified in the EncryptionKeys property associated with your user ID, you will receive an error message. Note that you must also save the document for the encryption to be stored within the database. If you don't call Save, the database will not be updated with the encrypted version of the document.

To recap document encryption, remember that encryption is normally performed using one or more encryption keys. This is called a single-key method of encryption as opposed to a dual-key or public-private key encryption. Both the creator and reader of the document must have the same encryption key(s) installed in their respective User ID files. In the user interface, you can encrypt only fields that have been made encryptable by the form designer. In LotusScript or Java, you can encrypt any document field by setting the IsEncryptable property of the item and by calling the document method Encrypt. You do not need to use document encryption to encrypt mail, which will be covered under the section called Mailing Documents.

Signing Documents

Another security issue is authenticity. How do you know when you are reading a document that it was actually created by the purported author? In the age of electronic documents, it is almost trivial to create electronic forgeries. Someone can create a document or email and pretend it was created by someone other than the stated author. How can we combat this form of electronic fraud?

The answer is with electronic signatures. These digital signatures use dual-key, public-private encryption to validate the authenticity of documents or email. In essence, a signature is a field that has been encrypted with the author's private key. It can be decrypted by anyone holding the author's public key. If the public key can successfully decrypt the field, you know that it was created by the authentic author.

You create signed documents in a manner very similar to encrypting documents, although it is even easier. In fact, it is just a single extra line of coding:

```
Call documentvar.Sign
```

Just call the `Sign` method of the `NotesDocument` class (or `Document` class of Java), and your document will be signed with your private key. If you execute this method on a server, the document will be signed with the server's ID, not the effective user ID. This is almost never what you want to do.

Note that in Java, as usual, the `sign` method is lowercase and Java is case sensitive.

After a document is signed, you can query information about the document. You can find out whether the document is signed in LotusScript by using the `IsSigned` property. In Java, you use the `isSigned` method.

You can obtain the fully distinguished name of the signer by accessing the LotusScript property `Signer` or by calling the Java method `getSigner`. Either version returns a string result.

Finally, you can use the `Verifier` property in LotusScript to obtain the fully distinguished name of the ID that certified (verified) the user. In Java, use the `getVerifier` method.

Mailing Documents and Mail Encryption

Mailing documents is very easy in Notes and Domino. After you have access to a document object, you just call the `Send` method. Mail automation in Notes and Domino is one of the factors that makes workflow applications easy to implement.

The syntax for sending mail in LotusScript is

```
Call documentvar.Send(boolAttachform, [recipientsStringArray] )
```

The first parameter is a Boolean variable. If `True`, the form associated with the document will be mailed, along with the document itself. This enables recipients to view the document from their mail database even if they don't have the form used to create the document. You can specify a string or array of strings for the second parameter. These are the recipients of the message. If you leave this parameter off the `Call` statement, you must supply a field within the document named `SendTo`. If the field is not contained in the document, you must supply the recipients in the `Call` statement. If both a field in the document and a list of recipients are supplied, the field contents are ignored and the recipients specified in the `Call` are used instead.

> **Note**
>
> Some Lotus documentation indicates that the document field will be used and the `Call` parameter ignored. This is incorrect. If both are specified, the field within the document will be ignored and the `Call` parameter will be used.

In addition to the `SendTo` field within the document, you can also include `CopyTo` and `BlindCopyTo` fields. These fields can contain one or more strings of user ids. The `CopyTo` field is for the cc: list, and the `BlindCopyTo` field is for the bcc: list.

In Java, unlike LotusScript, you can leave off the `Attachform` parameter. The four variations for the Java send method of the Document object are

```
void send(String recipient)
void send(java.util.Vector recipients)
void send(boolean attachform, String recipient)
void send(boolean attachform, java.util.Vector recipients)
```

If you leave off the *attachform* parameter, it is assumed to be `False`. As with LotusScript, you can include the `SendTo`, `CopyTo`, and `BlindCopyTo` fields within your document to control who receives the message. If you have both a `SendTo` and you specify recipients, the `SendTo` field in the document is ignored.

There are three LotusScript Boolean properties (and three corresponding Java methods) that control encryption, signing, and saving messages when they are sent:

- `EncryptOnSend`   If `True`, the message will be automatically encrypted with the recipient's public key when the message is sent. If there are multiple messages, each message will be encrypted with the specific recipient's public key.

- `SignOnSend`   If `True`, the message will automatically be signed with the sender's private key.

- `SaveMessageOnSend`   If `True`, the message will be automatically saved when it is sent.

Any time you send mail with the `Send` LotusScript method or the `send` Java method, Domino will add one extra field to the document called `$AssistMail`. This value is set to a 1 to indicate that the document was sent by a program.

On the receiving end, you can query the status of this field with the `SentByAgent` `NotesDocument` property. In Java, you use the `isSentByAgent` method to query. If `$AssistMail` is 1, you get a `True` result. This property is useful if you are generating automatic responses to incoming mail. For example, if you are writing an out-of-office agent, you can send responses back to people who have sent mail, but you can ignore any incoming mail sent by a program. This feature reduces the risk of two programs exchanging out-of-office messages and clogging up the mail system.

The final mail-oriented call is the `CreateReplyMessage` method. This method creates a reply message to the current document. The current document must contain a field called `From`. The syntax of the call is

```
Call documentvar.CreateReplyMessage(boolReplyToAll)
```

The `ReplyToAll` parameter is a Boolean variable. If it is `False`, the reply message will be sent only to the name found in the `From` field. If it is `True`, the current document's `CopyTo` and `BlindCopyTo` fields are copied over to the new reply message. The result will be that all recipients of the original message will receive the reply message.

Summary

In this chapter, I introduced the database, view, form, and document classes. I gave you some examples in both LotusScript and Java so you can see the various similarities and differences. For the most part, access to the classes is very similar. If you are using both LotusScript and Java, however, you should watch the session, dbdirectory, and database classes because some of the properties and methods are located in different classes. I've provided a table for you showing the corresponding methods within LotusScript and Java.

The database class is the repository that holds all your documents. After you have a database object, you can search and traverse its documents in many ways. The view and document collection classes are typically used to hold subsets of the database. You can use these classes to traverse documents. Sometimes information shown in a view is computed or otherwise derived from actual information within a document. If you need access to this information, you can use the new `ViewEntryCollection`, `ViewNavigator`, and `ViewEntry` classes to navigate through view entries.

Documents are the major unit of storage. All information is stored in documents, even design information. In addition to regular documents and design documents, you can have profile documents in your database. Profile documents enable you to store information that is typically per-user. They are a special kind of design document and will not show up in any view.

Finally, I gave you an overview of document and field security. I explained the difference between field encryption (using a single key) and mail encryption, which uses a public-private dual-key implementation. You can also sign documents to give the recipient an assurance of the authenticity of the document.

From Here…

You can find additional information in the following chapters:

- Chapter 27, "Using Fields and Items in LotusScript and Java," shows you how to access fields within documents. You'll learn how to read and write field-level information.
- Chapter 36, "Domino Security Overview," provides you with additional information on Domino security topics.
- Part V, "Developing Internet Sites with Domino," shows you how to make the most out of Domino for developing Web sites.

CHAPTER 27

USING FIELDS AND ITEMS IN LOTUSSCRIPT AND JAVA

In this chapter, I cover the Notes/Domino LotusScript and Java classes that deal with the real data in your documents. I also cover a few of the miscellaneous classes I have not covered in any of the other chapters.

Fields, Forms, Items, and Documents

In the Notes C API and internally within Notes and Domino, the terminology used is different from that normally used to describe Domino externally. This terminology is different for historical reasons, but it provides an interesting insight into a few of the external naming conventions. Databases use the acronym NSF, which stands for Notes Storage Facility. As you probably know, NSF is also the suffix used for Notes databases on your disk. One interesting fact you might not know is that views internally use the acronym NIF, for Notes Index Facility. There is a routine, for example, called `NIFOpenCollection`, which really just means to open a view.

Documents within a database are actually called *notes* internally. This isn't surprising, and of course this is probably how the product itself got its name. Internally, there are notes for just about everything there is to know about a database. There are design document notes, which hold attributes about forms, views, and other design elements. There are also notes for the database icon, the About and Using notes, and of course all the data notes (documents of the database).

This brings us to fields within a document. Although externally they are called fields, internally they are called items. If you know that regular fields are called items, you recognize that the name `RichTextItem` is just a special kind of item. Finally, it is a little clearer why the LotusScript class for this concept is called a `NotesItem`.

Because you've read through the entire text of this book up to this chapter (you have, haven't you?), and you've made it through the user-level descriptions of Notes and Domino, you deserve a little more detail here on the internal implementation of Notes. I always find that understanding how a tool is implemented enables me to use the tool a little more effectively.

As you know, a Notes document is made up of fields. Frequently, though not always, only one form is associated with a document. The form is our looking glass through which we can see information in the document itself. Thus, we typically think of the fields on the form as the fields of the document, but clearly they do not need to be in a one-to-one relationship. Relational database systems do not have the concept of data occurring within a document without a corresponding field. This is one of the unique features of Notes/Domino.

Notes and Domino internally use the word *item* to refer to the actual data within the document. The word *field* is used to represent fields on a form. So remember that forms contain fields, and documents contain items.

At the risk of oversimplifying, you can think of the items within a document as a list of name-value pairs. Of course, each item has several other attributes, such as its data type and modification date, but the most important characteristics of an item are its name and value.

Keep in mind that within a document, you can have more than one item with the same name. A document can contain two different items with the name `Subject`, for example—each with a different value. Arranging your documents this way is not normally considered a good programming practice, however. Typically, you should arrange your documents to contain items with unique names. If you need several values, remember that a single item can contain multiple values of the same type, and you can use separate fields to hold additional information.

> **Tip**
>
> The reason why the `NotesDocument` method is called `GetFirstItem` rather than just `GetItem` is because there might be multiple items with the same name. It also serves as a reminder so that in your programming you don't assume that there is only one item in your document with a given name.

A `NotesItem` Within A `NotesDocument`

The `NotesItem` class implements the concept of an item within a document. In LotusScript, you can create or get a `NotesItem` class object via several means. You can create a new `NotesItem` object with the `New` keyword, or you can obtain one via a method call of another object.

In the `NotesDocument` class, you can call `AppendItemValue`, `CopyItem`, `GetFirstItem`, or `ReplaceItemValue` to obtain a `NotesItem` class object. Here are some examples:

```
NotesItem = AppendItemValue(name, value)
NotesItem = CopyItem(item, newname)
NotesItem = GetFirstItem(name)
NotesItem = ReplaceItemValue(name, value)
```

`AppendItemValue` appends a new item to the document with the given name and value. If the name already exists, a separate item with the same name is created. `CopyItem` uses the new name and makes a copy of the original item's value. `GetFirstItem` returns the first item with the specified name. If there is more than one item with the same name, you must use the `Items` property of the `NotesDocument` class to traverse the list of items. `ReplaceItemValue` is usually preferable to `AppendItemValue`. `ReplaceItemValue` replaces an item's value with a new value. If the item does not exist, it is created.

Normally, when you refer to properties of an object, you use the "dot" notation. For example, within a `NotesSession` object called `session`, you could refer to `session.CurrentDatabase` to access the property. The `NotesDocument` class in LotusScript contains a special feature called "extended class" syntax that enables you to write programs that are a little easier to create and read.

With this syntax, you can refer to item names within a document as if they were properties of the class. For example, suppose you have a document in a `NotesDocument` object variable called *doc* that contains a field item called *LastName*. You can assign a value to this item with the following syntax:

```
doc.LastName = "Smith"
```

This is equivalent to the following line:

```
Call doc.ReplaceItemValue("LastName", "Smith")
```

Clearly, even though `LastName` is really not a property of the `NotesDocument` class, it is much simpler and more intuitive to use the first form of the assignment. You might have already used this syntax in one of your LotusScript programs without realizing that it was an extended class syntax.

Unfortunately, Java does not allow you to use the extended syntax, so you must use the `replaceItemValue` method. The reason is that Java checks the syntax of your Java program when it is compiled, not when it executes. At compile-time, there is no way for the compiler to know whether the item will exist in the document, and the Java language does not allow the extended syntax. Let's see how you would use an Item within a Java Document

A Java `Item` Within a Document

In Java, the `Item` class corresponds to the LotusScript `NotesItem` class. The `NotesItem` properties of LotusScript correspond directly to similarly named methods in Java. For example, the `IsAuthors` property of LotusScript corresponds to the `isAuthors` method of Java. Both return a `Boolean` value and indicate whether the item is an Authors item. `IsEncrypted`, `IsNames`, `IsProtected`, `IsReaders`, `IsSaveToDisk`, `IsSigned`, and `IsSummary` all have a similar correspondence between the LotusScript property and the Java method.

The properties of LotusScript I've just described are all read/write, so in LotusScript you can change the property's value by assigning it a new value. In Java, we must call a method to change the value. The methods to change the value all begin with the prefix set. Thus, the method to set the `IsAuthors` property is called `setAuthors` in Java. The methods `setEncrypted`, `setNames`, `setProtected`, `setReaders`, `setSaveToDisk`, `setSigned`, and `setSummary` all perform the set function for the corresponding property of the item.

Here is an example of obtaining and setting a property in Java:

```
Item it = doc.getFirstItem("Name");     // Get an Item object
boolean b = it.isAuthors();             // Check if is an authors item
it.setAuthors(true);                    // Set it to be an authors item
```

Setting and obtaining the value of a document item in Java presents unique problems that do not occur with other objects. The reason is that document items are similar to LotusScript variants. That is, the type of value that is stored in an item might be a number, a text string, a date, or even a multiple-value item. Java, on the other hand, is a strongly typed language where the data types must be defined at the time you compile your program.

The way the Domino Java implementation avoids some of these problems is to add some extra methods for getting and setting item values, each method with a particular type. For example, there is a getValueInteger method as well as a getValueDouble method. In addition to these, you can also get String and DateTime values as well. As you would predict, there are also setValueInteger and setValueDouble methods, as well as setValueString and setDateTimeValue, to set the corresponding data types.

There are several methods of the Item class in Java that have names that all sound as if they might do the same thing. Although these names appear to have a similar purpose, they perform different functions, so here is an explanation:

- getName   Returns the item name.
- toString   Appears in many of the Domino Java classes and overrides the Java definition in java.lang.Object. For an item, it returns the item's name, not its value.
- getText   Returns the text (string) representation of the value of the item. This method may be used to convert a numeric value to its string representation.
- getValueString   Is defined only if the item's value is a string. If so, it returns the string representation. If the item's value is another data type, the return value isn't defined.

CREATING A NEW NotesItem IN LOTUSSCRIPT

You can create a new NotesItem only within the context of a NotesDocument, because the item must reside inside a document. As with the other classes that support the New keyword, you can create a new NotesItem with the Dim keyword or with the New method:

```
Dim notesitemvar As New NotesItem(doc, name$, value, [special])

Dim notesitemvar As NotesItem
Set notesitemvar = New NotesItem(doc, name$, value, [special])
```

In the preceding examples, *doc* represents an object of the NotesDocument class, and *name$* is a string expression to be used as the name of the item within the document. *Value* represents the value you want to assign to the item. The data type of the document item depends on the data type of the value you assign. It behaves pretty much as you would expect. A string value causes the item to be a text item, an integer or floating-point value causes it to be a numeric item, and a LotusScript variant date/time causes it to store a date/time value in the item. This parameter might also contain an array. If so, all the values of the array are taken together and stored in the single item.

The *special* parameter, if supplied, is numeric and must be one of these constants: AUTHORS, NAMES, or READERS. AUTHORS and READERS specify names of users who are allowed to modify and read the document, respectively. Either of these values also implies that the value has the NAMES attribute. NAMES specifies that the item contains one or more usernames. See Listing 27.1 for an example.

> **Note**
>
> The code lines in some of the listings in this chapter will be preceded by numbers, as in Listing 27.1. These line numbers are there for ease of reference; they are *not* part of code, and should not be typed in as such.

LISTING 27.1   ADDING AN AUTHORS ITEM TO A DOCUMENT

```
 1: Dim uiws As New NotesUIWorkspace
 2: Dim doc As NotesDocument
 3: Set doc = uiws.CurrentDocument.Document
 4: Dim strAuthors( 1 To 3 ) As String
 5: strAuthors ( 1 ) = "Randy Tamura"         ' First Author
 6: strAuthors ( 2 ) = "Steve Kern"           ' Second Author
 7: strAuthors ( 3 ) = "Jane Calabria"        ' Third Author
 8: If doc.HasItem("docAuthors") Then
 9:     doc.removeItem("docAuthors")
10: End If
11: Dim itemAuthors As NotesItem
12:
13: Set itemAuthors = New NotesItem(doc, "docAuthors", strAuthors, AUTHORS)
14: Call doc.Save( True, True )
```

In lines 1–3, I obtain the current `NotesDocument` object via `NotesUIWorkspace`. Notice that the `CurrentDocument` property returns a `NotesUIDocument`, from which I can obtain the `NotesDocument`. The `strAuthors` variable is a string array containing three names. In lines 8–10, I check whether the document already has a `docAuthors` item. There is nothing special about this item name—you can choose another if you like. I just check to make sure I'm not creating two items with the same name. In lines 11–13, I create the new item in the document. The `New` method also returns a `NotesItem` object, but I don't need it for this routine. I have specified `AUTHORS` as the special value for the `NotesItem` parameter, so only the three people specified may edit the document.

Rich Text Items

Rich text items, implemented via the `NotesRichTextItem` class, are a very interesting special kind of item. Rich text fields handle extended text attributes, such as font, point size, color, and so forth. Notes and Domino distinguish between regular fields and rich text fields because rich text fields are more expensive in terms of storage space and processing time. This enables you to selectively use rich text fields. If you don't need the features of rich text, you can use regular items.

Drilling Down into Rich Text Items

In the United States, we use the term "drilling down" to mean "getting more details." After we have surveyed the landscape, we can drill down in a particular area to get more information about a particular topic of interest. Maybe if we drill down into "rich" text, we'll strike gold—or perhaps oil.

Rich text items are implemented internally as a big buffer that contains a sequence of CD records. CD stands for Composite Data, or Compound Document. Historians have not yet figured out which is the real original definition. In any case, there are CD records to define fonts, paragraphs, and text, as you might imagine. However, there are now over 100 different CD records, including items such as HTML object rendering, hotspots, tables, and graphics extensions.

The rich text field is how the Notes/Domino designers have added many extensions to the original Notes implementation. Layouts, hotspots, and doclinks are all implemented via rich text field CD records.

THE `NotesRichTextItem` CLASS

The `NotesRichTextItem` class is currently unique within the Notes/Domino class hierarchy. It is the only class that is derived from another class within the hierarchy. This derivation is also called inheritance. You might recall that in Chapter 20, "Object-Oriented Programming and the Domino Object Model," I described inheritance in the section titled "Class Inheritance."

If you don't remember Chapter 20, the key point about inheritance is that when one class is derived from another one, the derived class inherits properties and methods from the parent class. This means that the parent's properties and methods are available for use within the child class. Inheritance makes it easier to implement the derived class because basic properties and methods of the parent class do not need to be reimplemented.

In our `NotesRichTextItem` class, for example, the class inherits the properties `Name`, `Type`, and `Parent` (among many others). These properties specify the name and type of the item as well as the `NotesDocument` parent that contains the item. These are clearly properties that the `NotesRichTextItem` class, as well as the `NotesItem` class, needs. Because the properties and methods of a `NotesItem` are available within a `NotesRichTextItem`, we say that the `NotesRichTextItem` Is-A `NotesItem`. In other words, the `NotesRichTextItem` is just a special case of the `NotesItem`. Anything the `NotesItem` can do, the `NotesRichTextItem` can do, and more.

It is probably a good idea here to clear up any confusion about the word *parent*. In the case of the `NotesRichTextItem`, it is used in two different contexts and means two different things, so don't confuse the two meanings. In the first meaning, the parent of the `NotesRichTextItem` is the `NotesItem` from which it inherits its methods and attributes. I have just explained that this relationship means that the `NotesRichTextItem` Is-A `NotesItem`.

The second meaning of *parent* applies to any `NotesItem` and deals with the relationship Has-A. In this context, a `NotesDocument` object can contain a `NotesItem` object. We say that the `NotesDocument` Has-A `NotesItem`. This is a different relationship. It is clear that a `NotesDocument` is not a special case of `NotesItem` (or vice versa); it just contains one. The `NotesItem` `Parent` property then refers to the `NotesDocument` that contains it.

The `NotesRichTextStyle` Class

The `NotesRichTextStyle` class was introduced to Notes/Domino in Release 4.6. This class enables you to control the appearance of text within a rich text field. If you understand the concepts of the CD records outlined previously, you'll see that the use of this class just makes it easier to create and append CD records within a rich text field. This class is most easily described with an example. Take a look at Listing 27.2.

LISTING 27.2 USING THE `NotesRichTextStyle` CLASS

```
 1: Dim session As New NotesSession
 2: Dim uiws As New NotesUIWorkspace
 3: Dim uidoc As NotesUIDocument
 4: Dim doc As NotesDocument
 5: Set uidoc = uiws.currentdocument
 6: Set doc = uidoc.document
 7:
 8: Dim richText As New NotesRichTextItem(doc, "Body")
 9: Dim richStyle As NotesRichTextStyle
10: Set richStyle = session.CreateRichTextStyle
11:
12: Call richText.AppendText("Hello, world")
13:
14: richStyle.Bold = True
15: richStyle.FontSize = 24
16: richStyle.NotesColor = COLOR_RED
17:
18: Call richText.AppendStyle(richStyle)
19: Call richText.AppendText(" Hello, world, in Style")
20:
21: Call doc.Save(True, True)
```

To implement rich text attributes within a rich text field, you need two objects: one for the rich text field itself, and a second for the rich text style. In lines 1–6, I just declare and initialize the various objects required to access our document and field. In line 8, I create a new `NotesRichTextItem` object within the current document with the name `Body`. In lines 9 and 10, I declare and create a new `NotesRichTextStyle` object. Notice that I cannot use the `New` keyword with this class. I must create the object via the `NotesSession` class with the `CreateRichTextStyle` method.

In line 12, I add the text `"Hello, world"` to the rich text field without any attribute modification, so I'll get the default characteristics. In lines 14–16, I specify the characteristics I want the next phrase to have, and in line 18 I use the `AppendStyle` method to append a new style. In line 19, I append some extra text, which will be `Bold`, `RED`, and `24` points in size. Lastly, in line 21, I save the document. If the document is not saved, the changes will not be permanently stored in the database.

The properties for the `NotesRichTextStyle` class are `Bold`, `Effects`, `FontSize`, `Italic`, `NotesColor`, `NotesFont`, `PassThruHTML`, `StrikeThrough`, and `Underline`. The `Bold`, `Italic`, `StrikeThrough`, and `Underline` properties are Boolean properties, with `True` meaning that the property is on and `False` indicating off. The `PassThruHTML` property is also a `Boolean` property. You can turn on `PassThruHTML`, append text which will be treated as HTML, and then turn it off.

The `FontSize` property is just a number representing the font size in points. The `NotesFont` attribute can be one of four values: `FONT_COURIER`, `FONT_HELV`, `FONT_ROMAN`, or `STYLE_NO_CHANGE`. You use this last value if you want to change a `NotesRichTextStyle` object that changes the font to one that does not affect the font.

The `Effects` property can have the values `EFFECTS_EMBOSS`, `EFFECTS_EXTRUDE`, `EFFECTS_NONE`, `EFFECTS_SHADOW`, `EFFECTS_SUBSCRIPT`, and `EFFECTS_SUPERSCRIPT`.

Finally, the `NotesColor` property can be one of the following: `COLOR_BLACK`, `COLOR_BLUE`, `COLOR_CYAN`, `COLOR_DARK_BLUE`, `COLOR_DARK_CYAN`, `COLOR_DARK_GREEN`, `COLOR_DARK_GRAY`, `COLOR_DARK_MAGENTA`, `COLOR_DARK_RED`, `COLOR_DARK_YELLOW`, `COLOR_GREEN`, `COLOR_LIGHT_GRAY`, `COLOR_MAGENTA`, `COLOR_RED`, `COLOR_WHITE`, or `COLOR_YELLOW`.

THE `RichTextItem` AND `RichTextStyle` JAVA CLASSES

Here is the sample program from the previous section rewritten as a Java agent:

LISTING 27.3 USING THE `RichTextStyle` JAVA CLASS

```java
import lotus.domino.*;
public class JavaAgent extends AgentBase {
   public void NotesMain() {
      try {
         Session session = getSession();
         AgentContext agentContext = session.getAgentContext();
         DocumentCollection dc = agentContext.getUnprocessedDocuments();
         Document doc = dc.getFirstDocument();
         RichTextItem richText = doc.createRichTextItem("Body");
         RichTextStyle richStyle = session.createRichTextStyle();
         richText.appendText("Hello, world");

         richStyle.setBold(RichTextStyle.YES);       // Set bold on
         richStyle.setFontSize(24);                  // Set font size
         richStyle.setColor(RichTextStyle.COLOR_RED);   // Set it Red
         richText.appendStyle(richStyle);
         richText.appendText("Hello, world, in Style");

         doc.save(true, true);

      } catch(Exception e) {
         e.printStackTrace();
      }
   }
}
```

The program is mostly self-explanatory and operates similarly to the LotusScript version. One difference is that there are no front-end classes in Java, so you cannot access an equivalent to `NotesUIWorkspace` or `NotesUIDocument`. Instead, I refer to the `getUnprocessedDocuments` method of the `AgentContext` class.

THE `NotesRichTextParagraphStyle` AND `RichTextParagraphStyle` CLASSES

The LotusScript `NotesRichTextParagraphStyle` and the Java `RichTextParagraphStyle` classes are similar to the `RichTextStyle` classes, but they operate on complete paragraphs rather than just selected text. The properties that you can associate with the paragraph include alignment, the first line's left margin, interline spacing, left and right margins, spacing above and below the paragraph, and tab settings for the paragraph.

Here is an example in LotusScript:

LISTING 27.4 USING THE `NotesRichTextParagraphStyle` LOTUSSCRIPT CLASS

```
Dim session As New NotesSession
Dim uiws As New NotesUIWorkspace
Dim uidoc As NotesUIDocument
Dim doc As NotesDocument
Set uidoc = uiws.currentdocument
Set doc = uidoc.document

Dim richText As New NotesRichTextItem(doc, "Body")
Dim rtpStyle As NotesRichTextParagraphStyle
Set rtpStyle = session.CreateRichTextParagraphStyle

rtpStyle.Alignment = ALIGN_CENTER
Call richText.AppendParagraphStyle(rtpStyle)

Call richText.AppendText("Centralized Hello, world")

Call doc.Save(True, True)
```

THE `NotesEmbeddedObject` CLASS

The `NotesEmbeddedObject` class is used for two primary purposes. The first is to support file attachments to documents. The files can be attached directly to the document, or the attachments can be contained in rich text fields. The second purpose of a `NotesEmbeddedObject` is to support ActiveX Automation, formerly known as OLE Automation.

Attachment support is available on all Notes platforms, but ActiveX (OLE) support is available only on Windows platforms. You can attach a file on one platform and detach it on another platform, but the files must be in a format that is compatible between the two platforms, such as an ASCII text file.

You can get a `NotesEmbeddedObject` through the `EmbeddedObjects` property of either the `NotesRichTextItem` class or the `NotesDocument` class. The `NotesRichTextItem` property gives you an array of all the objects embedded within the specified field. The `NotesDocument` class returns all the objects within the entire document.

> **Note**
>
> There is a difference between the `EmbeddedObjects` property of the `NotesRichTextItem` class and the one in the `NotesDocument` class. The `NotesDocument` `EmbeddedObjects` property does not return attachments, only OLE 2 (ActiveX) objects. The `NotesRichTextItem` `EmbeddedObjects` property returns attachments as well as ActiveX objects.

The NotesTimer Class

The `NotesTimer` class is useful for generating events at specified intervals. You can create the `NotesTimer` object either with the `New` keyword or by calling the `CreateTimer` method of the `NotesSession` class. The latter method is useful if you are using ActiveX automation and are using the timer from a scripting language other than LotusScript, such as Visual Basic.

This is the syntax for creating a `NotesTimer` object:

```
Dim timervar as New NotesTimer(interval, [Comment$])
```

or

```
Dim timervar as Variant
Set timervar = New NotesTimer(interval, [Comment$])
```

You set the interval in seconds, but you are not guaranteed that your alarm will be triggered at exactly the time you specified, because of other activities that might be happening in your computer.

Keeping Track of Document Editing Time

Suppose you wanted to keep track of the editing time for each document. You could use the `NotesTimer` class as a mechanism to do this. Although the resolution of the `NotesTimer` is not extremely fine, you rarely want to know the document editing time with microsecond accuracy. Our accuracy here will be within a few seconds, which should be fine for this application.

Create a new form in the database by selecting Create, Design, Form. In the form, place the text `Timed Form` in 24-point, bold font.

Space down a couple of lines and enter the text `Total Document Editing Time (Sec.):`, followed by a field. Name the field `EditingTime`, make the type Number, and make the type Computed. In the Value event, make the formula `EditingTime`. Lastly, create a second field called `Body`, which should be defined as a rich text field. The `Body` exists so that when you create a new document with this form, the form will appear in edit mode. If you have no editable fields, the new document will appear in read mode. See Figure 27.1.

Figure 27.1
The timed form with the EditingTime field.

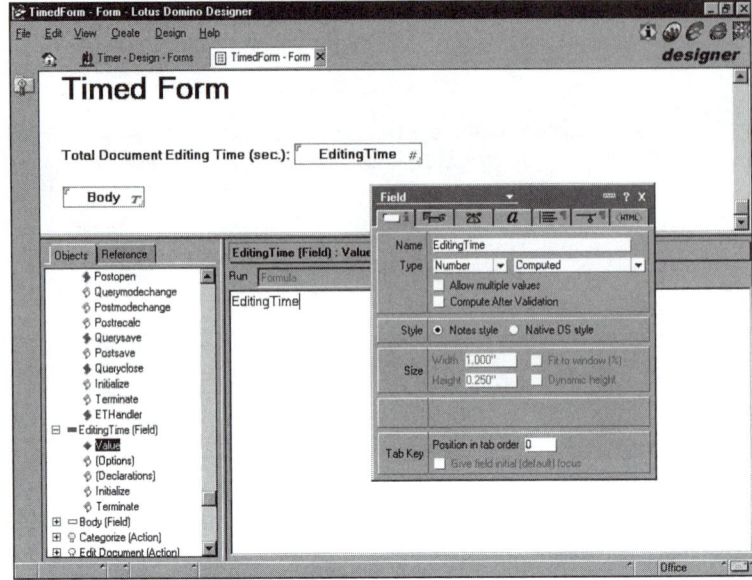

Save the form with the name `TimedForm`. Now, open the form for editing again, and in the Programmer's Pane at the bottom, select Define (Globals)TimedForm. Set the event to Declarations. In the Declarations section, enter two variables:

```
Dim timerEditing As NotesTimer    ' Editing Time NotesTimer object
Dim iEditTime As Integer ' Editing Time in Seconds
```

It is important that these variables are declared in the Globals section because they must be visible to several different routines within the form. Within the form, create two routines, the `PostOpen` routine and the `ETHandler` routine. To do this, first click on the plus sign on the TimedForm (Form) line. Then scroll down to find the PostOpen element. Click on PostOpen and enter the text in Listing 27.5.

LISTING 27.5   THE `PostOpen` AND `ETHandler` ROUTINES FOR TIMING DOCUMENTS

```
 1: Sub Postopen(Source As Notesuidocument)
 2:     Set timerEditing = New NotesTimer(1, "Document Editing time")
 3:     On Event Alarm From timerEditing Call ETHandler
 4:     Dim DocTime As Variant
 5:     DocTime = Source.Document.GetItemValue("EditingTime")
 6:     If DocTime(0) = "" Then
 7:         iEditTime = 0
 8:     Else
 9:         iEditTime = Cint(DocTime (0))
10:     End If
11: End Sub
12:
13:
```

```
14: Sub ETHandler(Source As NotesTimer)
15:     iEditTime = iEditTime + 1       ' Increment elapsed time in seconds
16: End Sub
```

> **Note**
>
> The `ETHandler` routine is not automatically created for you within the form window like `PostOpen`. Just type the header at the bottom of the `PostOpen` routine, and a new window opens into which you can enter the contents.

Before we move on, let's look at the routines we have created. Remember that the `PostOpen` routine will be called just after the document has been opened by the user. At this time (in line 2), we set the `timerEditing` variable with a new `NotesTimer` object. The first parameter is the duration between alarms, and the second parameter is just a comment. We set the duration to one second so that we'll get an alarm every second, which should be fine for tracking document editing time.

Line 3, the `On Event` line, specifies what should happen when the alarm event occurs in the `timerEditing` object. This line indicates that we should call the `ETHandler` routine.

Lines 4–10 of the routine are initializing the `iEditTime` variable. We first get the value of the field from the document, and we put it into a variant. The result of the `GetItemValue` routine is always an array, so we must obtain the first element. If this element is an empty string, we probably have a new document and the field does not yet contain a value. In this case, we just initialize the elapsed time to 0. If the variable already exists, we set the variable to the elapsed time so far. In this example, I ignore very large editing times that might overflow an integer variable. In your real application, you might want to handle this differently if your documents have the potential for long editing times.

The `ETHandler` routine will be called once a second. All we do in this routine is track the elapsed time. By using this method, we do not incur too much overhead because the processing for the routine is very simple.

Now, in the `QuerySave` and `QueryClose` routines, enter the source code given in Listing 27.6.

LISTING 27.6   THE `QuerySave` AND `QueryClose` ROUTINES FOR TIMING DOCUMENTS

```
Sub Querysave(Source As Notesuidocument, Continue As Variant)
  If Source.EditMode Then
    Call Source.FieldSetText("EditingTime",Cstr(iEditTime))
  End If
End Sub


Sub Queryclose(Source As Notesuidocument, Continue As Variant)
  If Source.EditMode Then
    Call Source.FieldSetText("EditingTime",Cstr(iEditTime))
  End If
End Sub
```

Notice that the code for each routine is the same. You could also enter this code once in a separate subroutine and call that subroutine from both the QuerySave routine and the QueryClose routine. This choice is a matter of style. Because there are only three lines, it is sometimes more convenient to enter the text, and then just copy and paste the code again to another routine. If the code were much longer than this, it probably would be a better idea to use a separate subroutine and call it from both places. This technique eases maintenance later when someone must make a modification; only one place needs to be changed.

The purpose of these two routines is to update the field in the document when it is saved or when the window is closed. We check to make sure that the document is in edit mode before attempting to save the value, because we will get an error if the document is in read mode.

Finally, let me say that this form does not really cover all the cases, and you will probably need to update it if you want to implement something like this form for yourself. The timer will work fine the first time the document is edited, but the form does not have all the logic necessary to handle the case of the user opening the document in read mode and changing it to edit mode. This enhancement is left as an exercise for the reader.

I have shown you this example just to get you started with implementing document timing. This example uses the time to keep track of the total editing time per document. You might put this type of code in a subform, and might want to hide some of the fields from users.

Finally, another extension would be to use the timer to autosave your documents in edit mode. You could keep track of the last time you saved the document and the elapsed time, and when appropriate you could automatically save the document. This code could also be placed in a subform with hidden fields so that your autosave feature could be added to several forms without the user seeing any additional fields. These are just a few examples of how you might use the NotesTimer facility.

THE NotesName, NotesACL, AND NotesACLEntry CLASSES

The NotesName class assists in parsing usernames. Several additional properties have been added to the NotesName class in R5, mainly to help parse Internet style names. The NotesACL and NotesACLEntry classes are used to implement control of the ACL list for a database.

THE NotesName CLASS

The NotesName class has only one method, the New method. You can create a NotesName class object either with the New keyword or by using the CreateName method of the NotesSession class. When you create a NotesName object, you must pass the routine a string containing a Notes user's name. The name is looked up in the Domino Directory (Name and Address Book), and you can then access properties of the NotesName object.

The properties of the `NotesName` object include different formats of the name: `Abbreviated` and `Canonical`. The properties also enable you to extract components of a hierarchical name: `Common`, `Country`, `Organization`, `OrgUnit1`, `OrgUnit2`, `OrgUnit3`, and `OrgUnit4`. Several of the properties are for handling industry standards and parsing other systems' names. For example, the `Surname`, `Generation`, `Given`, and `Initials` properties cannot be used to extract information from a regular Notes name. They can be used only if the name had specified these components separately.

The `Addr821` property is new with release 5 and corresponds to the RFC821 format for an Internet name: `UserName@Domain`. This is the most commonly used format for Internet naming. RFC822 has more components and can look something like this: `UserName@Domain<"User's real name">`, where the information within the quotes is called the Phrase and can be any text additionally describing the user.

The `NotesACL` Class

You use the `NotesACL` class in conjunction with the `NotesDatabase` class. After you have access to a `NotesDatabase` object, you can access the ACL property of the `NotesDatabase` object and obtain a `NotesACL` class object. You cannot create a standalone `NotesACL` object.

The `NotesACL` class enables you to add, delete, and rename roles within the ACL and to traverse the different ACL entries. You can also create a new ACL entry with the `CreateACLEntry` method. You must invoke the `Save` method of the `NotesACL` class after you make changes, or your changes will not be saved permanently in the database.

The `Roles` property returns an array of strings that represent all the roles within the database. The `GetEntry`, `GetFirstEntry`, and `GetNextEntry` methods enable you to traverse the ACL list. Each of the three methods returns an object of the `NotesACLEntry` class.

The `NotesACLEntry` Class

The `NotesACLEntry` class enables you to access and modify each entry within the ACL. Typically, you will use one of the `Get` routines within the `NotesACL` class to obtain a `NotesACLEntry` object. Alternatively, you can create a new `NotesACLEntry` with the `New` keyword or by calling the `CreateACLEntry` method of the `NotesACL` class.

After you have obtained a `NotesACLEntry` object, you can disable or enable roles associated with the entry. You can also allow or disallow the following privileges to the entry: Create Documents, Create Personal Agents, Create Personal Folders, and Delete documents.

From Here...

In this chapter, I covered several of the lower-level classes in the Notes object class hierarchy. I showed you how to use the `NotesItem` class to create a new item within a document. I explained the difference between a field in a form and an item in a document. I gave you examples in both LotusScript and Java.

With rich text fields, you can format text with several attributes, such as bold, italic, and underline. With the `NotesRichTextStyle` class, you can control the style of text within a rich text field. The `NotesRichTextParagraphStyle` class and its Java counterpart can be used to control the alignment and other characteristics of the paragraph.

The `NotesTimer` class can be used to keep track of how much time has been spent editing documents within a database. I gave you a simple example of doing this task. You could also use the timer to perform autosaves of your documents. You will probably need to update the example when you incorporate it into your own application, but I have shown you the basics of how to get started.

The `NotesName` class can be used to query usernames and to parse them into components. The `NotesACL` and `NotesACLEntry` classes can be used to manipulate the ACL for a database. Objects of these classes must always be associated with a `NotesDatabase` object. You access the `NotesACL` object by referring to the ACL property of a `NotesDatabase` object.

Now that you have learned how to use LotusScript and Java to develop your own applications, you can move on to developing your own intranet or Internet Web sites. In Part V, "Developing Internet Sites with Domino," you'll learn about the following:

- Chapter 28, "Building Your Own Web Site with Domino," will teach you how to use the power of Domino to develop informative and functional Web sites.
- Chapter 29, "Using External HTML Tools with Domino," shows you how Domino can work with other third-party HTML tools for Web site development.
- If you have not yet read the rest of the chapters in Part IV, "Using LotusScript, Java, and JavaScript," you should read them to learn about important aspects of programming the Lotus Notes and Domino Object Model.

PART V

Developing Internet Sites with Domino

28 Building Your Own Web Site with Domino

29 Using External HTML Tools with Domino

30 Moving to Electronic Commerce on Your Domino Site

31 Integrating Domino with Legacy Systems

CHAPTER 28

BUILDING YOUR OWN WEB SITE WITH DOMINO

Here's an oft-told story (the authenticity of which I have no reason to doubt), recently repeated by Lotus Vice President Mike Zisman:

> The chairman of Stanley Tools was set to address the yearly sales meeting. The various sales staff members had been assembled, and there was an air of jubilation. This had been a banner year—tool sales had set records—and everyone was in a great mood.
>
> The chairman entered the room with a doleful expression. He was obviously glum. He was slated to present a "fire-them-up" sales motivation speech…yet, something was obviously amiss.
>
> He approached the podium. "Ladies and gentlemen," he solemnly began, "we have a problem. People don't want our drills."
>
> The sales folks were taken aback. How could this be? Murmurs were heard throughout the assemblage: "People don't want our drills? This was our best sales year…what's he talking about?"
>
> The chairman went on: "People don't want our drills. What they want are *holes*."

Just as Stanley's chairman discovered that people want holes, not his company's product, the truth is that today people really don't want Lotus Notes, Netscape, Microsoft IIS, or any other *product*—what they want is information. What they want is a functioning Web site. They just want it to work, and the combination of Notes and the Web is a potent combination.

It wasn't always that way. It seems like only yesterday that Notes was Notes, and that's all there was to it. Way back in the old days (and gosh, that takes us back over two years!), we had Notes servers that served Notes databases to Notes clients, and that was that. Things have certainly changed since Notes first came on the scene, and the past couple years have seen unprecedented changes in Notes from the Internet standpoint.

The server is now the Domino server, and in addition to "serving" Notes clients, it can now host a wide variety of clients, including—most importantly for this chapter—Web browsers. In addition, besides delivering Notes databases, the server can now serve HTML, Java, native graphics, and more. The Domino server is now a full-fledged Web server, but it maintains its original charter; it still can serve Notes databases. You can now take a Domino server and use it to create a fully functional Web site. And, in a nutshell, that's what this chapter is all about: building a Web site with Domino.

We'll spend some time thinking about the philosophy of Web sites and talk about some of the design elements you should consider before you begin. We'll talk about design and implementation, and we'll discuss some of the challenges and benefits. We'll take a look at some of the ways you can bring Web-specific elements into your Notes database design and how you can implement this on the Web. We'll discuss some of the tools available to assist you in your efforts, and—hopefully—we'll wrap it up neatly before the chapter is through. But the bottom line is that we'll show you how to build a Web site on your Domino server.

The thing to keep in mind as you read through this chapter is that in a very real sense, we'll be borrowing from all the other chapters that precede or succeed this one in this book. We'll discuss how to employ the design tips you got from Randy Tamura and Don Child in Part III, "Introducing Domino Designer R5." We'll also discuss implementing the Domino server, which you'll learn more about in Parts VII, "Administering the Domino Servers," and VIII, "Advanced Domino Administration."

In a sense, this chapter will serve as an introduction to this very special aspect of the Notes/Domino story. But it also serves as a way to bring all the parts together into a working whole. The combination of Notes brings some remarkable capabilities to the Web, and the Web brings some remarkable capabilities to Notes as well.

For the past four years, I've been working almost exclusively with organizations that are using Notes/Domino in conjunction with the Web, whether for email connectivity, Web site content, or specific application development. I've helped build Internet sites, intranet sites, and a couple extranet sites, and Notes has been involved in all of them in one way or another.

BACKGROUND

With Notes/Domino R5, Notes and the Internet have become so closely aligned that it's hard to tell where Notes ends and the Web begins.

It wasn't always this way. As noted earlier, originally, we had just a Notes server. Then, along in 1996 came the Internotes family of products: Internotes Web Publisher (IWP), Internotes News, and Internotes Web Retriever. Each of these products was a separate, expensive, added cost add-in to the Notes server (if memory serves, Web Publisher originally sold for $9,500.00).

Web Publisher's goal was to allow Notes databases to be "published" to the Web; essentially, IWP allowed you to "save as HTML" from within a Notes database. You could set up a configuration document, not unlike a connection document, and schedule the frequency of this publishing on a database-by-database basis. The idea was that you'd have a Web server somewhere, and you'd use IWP to "publish" your Notes databases to that existing server. Notes, alone, had no Web-publishing capabilities.

> **Note**
> Interestingly, the "save as HTML feature" was slated to return with R5. There was to be an option to "publish" a Notes database as static HTML pages built directly into the Domino Designer client! The feature slipped out of the 5.0 release, but Lotus is saying it's supposed to see the light of day during the interim builds.

How far we've come! With Notes/Domino R5, Web browsers have become complete, fully functional clients of a Domino server (and conversely, Notes clients have become fully functional citizens of the Web, now able to access POP3 mailboxes, participate in NNTP newsgroups, and so on). No more scheduled publishing; the browser has the same potential capabilities of a Notes client. There are still some major differences between the two clients, and we'll take an in-depth look at that in a few pages.

In this chapter, we'll take a look at creating a Web site using Notes/Domino R5.

We'll walk our way through the philosophy of creating our site, which leads into a design discussion. We'll touch on the challenges and benefits and then discuss some of the specifics of creating the site and tools you can use.

But first, we'll have a quick discussion about the differences between a Notes client and a Web browser.

WEB BROWSERS VERSUS NOTES CLIENT

Obviously, there are a lot of differences between a Web browser and a Notes client. One of the biggest differences is patently obvious: Browsers are built solely on a point-and-click interface. The Notes client has the concept of "state."

In a browser, hypertext links within the HTML documents are clicked to take you to the next document. This works great, but there's no sense of "state" or "context." That is, even though you could hover over one of these links (and even though there could be some code that would change the color or the image as you hover), neither your browser nor the server has any sense that you're hovering over a particular link. It only gets that state when you actually click.

In the Notes client world, you can highlight a line in a view and simply press Enter: The Notes client understands that you "were on" a particular document; it even had that document's data in memory!

The upshot is simply this: In a view in Notes, you can reply to a given document because Notes maintains the idea of "being on" a particular document. From the browser's perspective, there's no concept of "being on" a document. From the browser's perspective, the document you're on is the view itself. You can't respond from the view because the browser is oblivious to what it would be responding to.

This makes life more difficult for us developers because we have to rethink some of our navigational options. A "respond" action button in a view is useless (in fact, even if you attempt to put one there, it won't be displayed). Even with the new R5 "view applet" (which we'll discuss in length later in this chapter), there's still no way to respond right from a view. There's still no "state."

Keep this issue of state (or context—I'll probably refer to it both ways) in mind as we look at some of the possibilities for building your Web site with Notes/Domino R5.

Philosophy

Although designing a Web site using Notes/Domino R5 isn't totally different from creating one in a "straight HTML" environment, we need to discuss your site's philosophy.

There are several ways to create a Web site in the Notes/Domino world. You could do any of the following:

- Create "normal" Notes databases and allow them to be accessed by Web browsers or specialized Notes databases with specific Web-oriented design
- Create "normal" Notes databases using some of the new R5 features such as View and Editor Applets, Pages, and Framesets and creatively add HTML to Notes forms, documents, views, and so on
- Create a hybrid of HTML documents and specialized databases

And so on. The different permutations here are endless, but in my experience, the "combo" choice tends to be the best. Although Notes/Domino R5 is far better at working the Web than its predecessors were, you will likely find that there are still some things that you're better off doing with HTML than with Notes's native design capabilities. Although, with R5, that list has gotten dramatically shorter than it was with previous Notes releases.

There are also some additional capabilities that can be found by using an HTML authoring tool such as Microsoft FrontPage or NetObjects Fusion. That option is explored at length in the next chapter, "Using External HTML Tools with Domino."

Let's spend a little time on each of the options outlined above.

Creating "Normal" Notes Databases to Be Accessed by Web Browsers...

If you listened strictly to the marketing hype, you'd be led to believe that you could take any normal, ordinary Notes database and allow Web browsers to access it.

Although this might technically be true, the results usually aren't very pretty. As shown in Figures 28.1 and 28.2, there's a different functionality in how the Notes client accesses a database versus how a Web client accesses it. The typical Notes spreadsheet-like view is generally inappropriate for Web usage. As we've mentioned numerous times already in this chapter, Notes/Domino R5 has made tremendous advances, but a "straight" Notes database probably will leave your Web clients cold.

> **Note**
> Beginning with Notes/Domino R5, you can now use a special Design feature known as a "View Applet" that gives the browser client some of the same capabilities in a view that a Notes client has. Specifically, it brings a small Java-based applet to the browser that has a "context" capability, among other things.
>
> We'll return to View Applets several times later in this chapter.

Figure 28.1
Notes view from a Notes client.

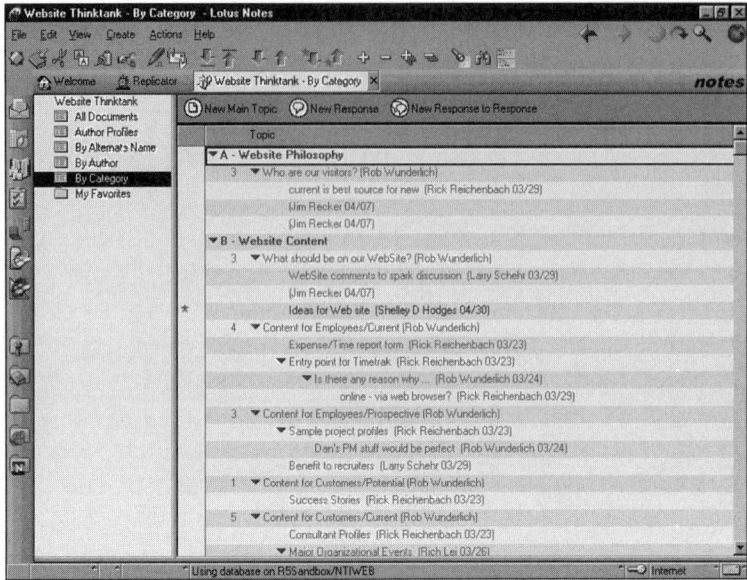

Figure 28.2
Notes view from a Web browser.

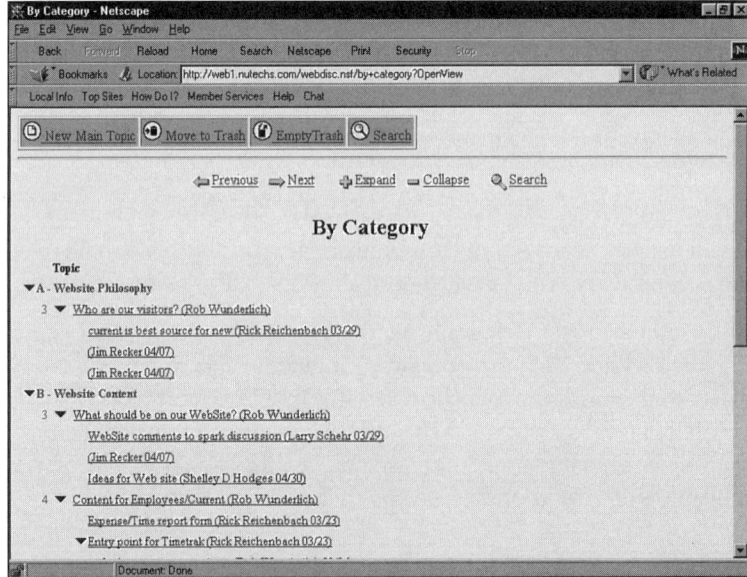

In addition to potential problems with views, there are also liable to be some problems with forms, agents, etc. If you want users to submit forms for the Web, without some intervention on your part, they'll get a grey screen with a "form processed" message—no hotlinks to take them anywhere, no nothing.

Although the "normal" Notes database does, indeed, work on the Web, the limitations are pretty severe. You'll quickly discover that a couple minor design features can make a big difference.

CREATING SPECIALIZED NOTES DATABASES WITH SPECIFIC WEB-ORIENTED DESIGN

If publishing "straight" Notes databases isn't the answer…you can try adding some minor modifications to make them more Web-friendly.

For example, I've always thought that the typical discussion database "By Author" view was inappropriate for Web use. As shown in Figure 28.3, the first "clickable" column is the date the document was created—what's *that* got to do with anything? From the Notes client, it doesn't seem so strange because you're actually clicking on the entire line in a view, but from a browser, it's the first noncategorized column. In the case of the By Author view, that's the Date column.

I've always suggested to my customers that we alter that view slightly so that the date comes in the second column, and the subject of the message comes in the first column. As shown in Figure 28.4, it seems like a far more intuitive item to click than the date.

Figure 28.3
Typical By Author view from Web.

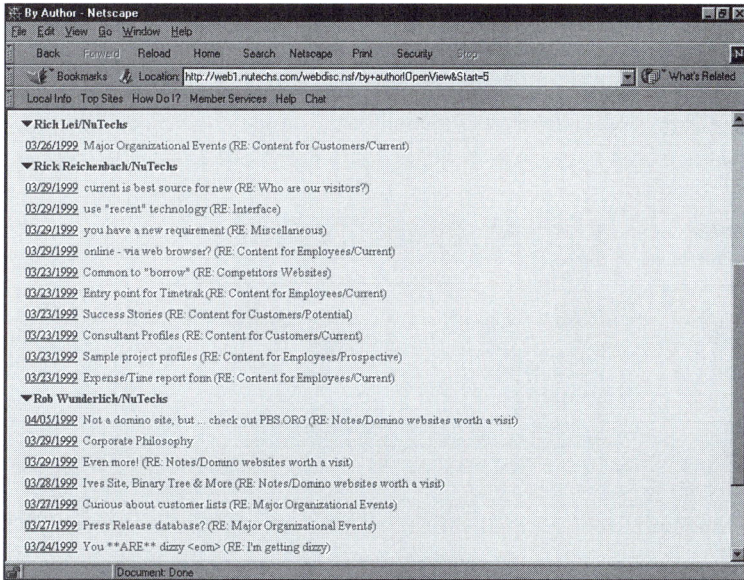

It's difficult to see in these black and white photos, but the first column in each of these screen shots is bright blue, indicating the hypertext link which will take you to the document indicated. Makes more sense to click on the topic, rather than the date, doesn't it?

Figure 28.4
Altered By Author view from Web.

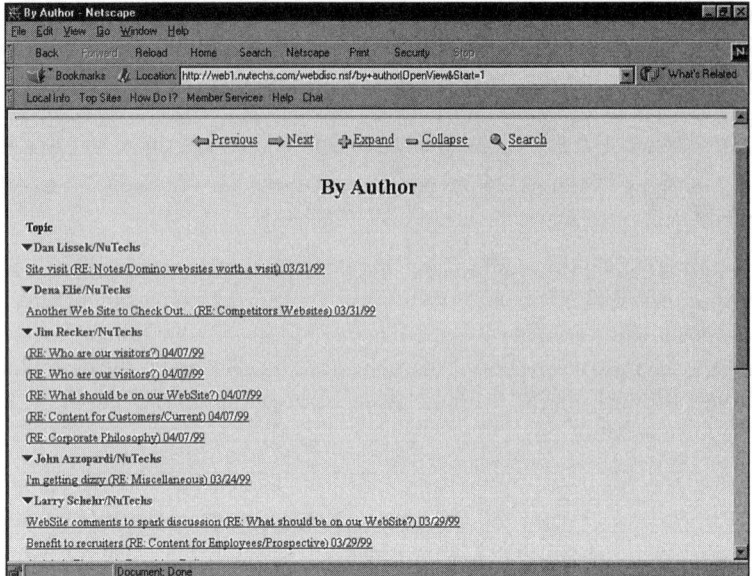

Another option to actually shift columns around is the Column Property box (found on the "beanie" tab) shown in Figure 28.5: "Show values in this column as links." By enabling this check box, you can make the second or third (or whatever) column be "clickable", not just the first. That way, people have the option of clicking on the subject, not just the date.

Figure 28.5
Property box with the Show values in this column as links option checked.

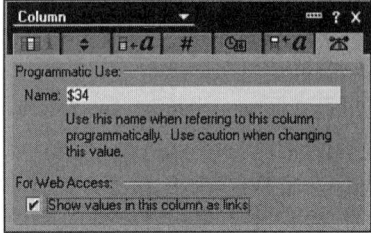

In addition to some minor column shifting and properties changing, R5 also offers a view applet that dramatically changes the way the view looks on the Web.

By simply clicking on an attribute in the properties for the view (shown in Figure 28.6), you can change the way the view looks by using the View Applet. In short, the View Applet downloads a small Java applet to the browser; Figure 28.7 below shows the outcome. The user now can use a view from a browser that looks and behaves much like its Notes counterpart.

So the second phase of our first option is to make minor changes in your design to cater to your Web visitors, turning on options such as Show values in this column as links, but doing nothing nearly as dramatic as adding HTML, for example, or truly taking advantage of all the new R5 features.

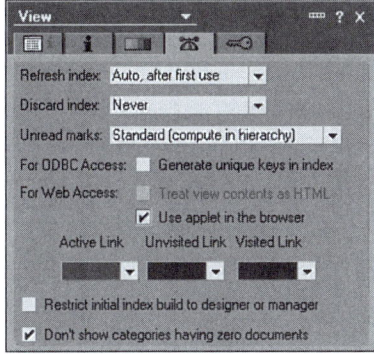

Figure 28.6
The View properties box.

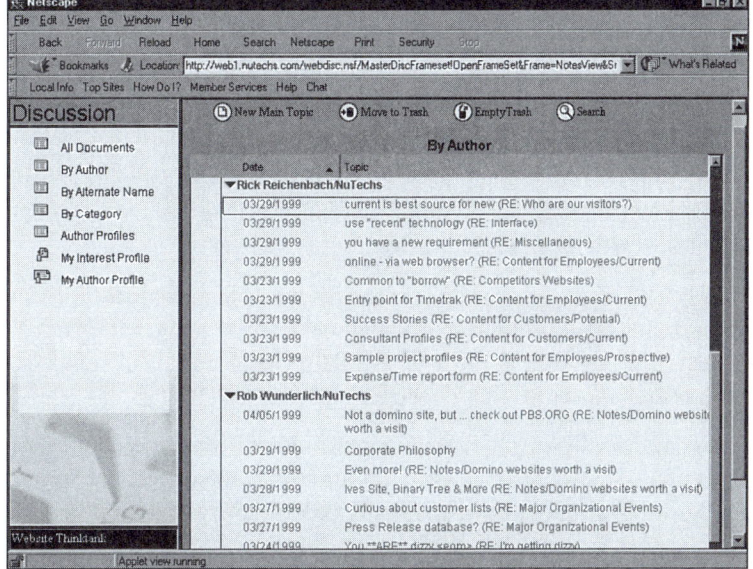

Figure 28.7
Discussion template with View Applet enabled.

CREATING "NORMAL" NOTES DATABASES USING SOME OF THE NEW R5 FEATURES

The second option goes several steps further than our first, yet it stays strictly within the realm of Notes itself. If our first option is to simply do "vanilla" Notes databases with an eye to the Web, our second option takes full advantage of the new features Notes/Domino R5 gives us. To the delight of Web-oriented developers, many of the features that debuted in R5 are directly applicable to Web site development.

Features such as View and Editor Applets, Pages, Framesets and Outlines—while not exactly useless in Notes itself—have their greatest value in a Web environment. View and Editor

Applets solve one of the most long-standing complaints: "You can't do the same stuff from a browser that you can do from a Notes Client." While that's still true, these two applets go a long way to solving the problem. Framesets were possible in R4, but only by doing a tremendous amount of HTML coding. Now, a couple simple clicks, and you've got a frameset. Likewise, pages. There have been many times in my development work where I wished that I had the opportunity to use multiple About Documents. I just wanted to put a "page" out there—not a form, not a document. Now, we have pages. And "Navigators" have grown into Imagemaps, which behave the same way in Notes as they behave in a browser.

We'll take a quick look at all these new features in this section of this chapter, but there are far more in-depth discussions on each of these new items elsewhere in this book.

Another new feature in R5 that doesn't fit directly into this discussion but is worth mentioning is the new way that images are handled in R5.

In previous versions of Notes/Domino, when you pasted a graphic into a Notes form or document, it was converted into the Notes metafile format. Even if it was a JPG or GIF file—which out of the box would be appropriate for Web users—the graphic was transformed into the Notes proprietary format. Then, when a browser client visited a Domino site, the server had to convert the graphic *back* into a Web-usable format. There were performance issues surrounding this, plus the graphic often suffered in quality by being converted to Notes and converted back again.

In R5, Notes is now storing the graphics in their native formats. If you paste in a JPG, Notes stores it as a JPG—no more conversions. That alone is important. Both performance and quality are enhanced simply due to that change.

In addition, images are now part of the resources of a database. You can add an image resource much like a subform or shared field, where you create it once and can reuse the element over and over in the database. Better yet, you actually can store an image once and use it over and over in *multiple* databases.

There are several benefits to this approach. First, from an economy standpoint, it's always nice to only store something once, not multiple times. Secondly, from a management standpoint, this gives a designer much better control over the images being used in their applications because you could change a logo in an entire application by simply changing one image resource. Third, from a housekeeping standpoint, it's great to have the images stored easily in a database rather than littering your ICONS folder. Granted, you could store images as file attachments in R4.x, but then to access them you needed to write a lengthy HTML <IMG> tag, and it would work only from a browser, not in the Notes world. Finally, from a "transportability" standpoint, with the images stored in the database itself, replication, clustering, and so on all become simple. I don't need to ship you a database and a ZIP file full of images; now I simply ship you the database, and the images are already there.

Working with image resources is detailed at length in Chapter 47, "Integrating Domino with Phone, Fax, and Image," but it's worth a mention here.

Our second, "middle ground" development option would still do vanilla Notes applications, but it would utilize these special features.

Let's walk through a simple scenario, and go through the specifics later.

Let's say that instead of having a database launch a view or an about document, we want it to open on a frameset. (Framesets are discussed in depth in Chapter 16, "Using Outlines, Framesets, and Navigators.")

We could design a three-frame frameset (keep the terminology in mind here; a *frameset* is a collection of individual *frames*), as shown in Figure 28.8. We could put an Outline in the bottom left frame, a corporate logo in the upper frame, and some sort of database view or imagemap in the third frame.

Let's start by creating a database and building the frameset. Create the database the usual way (File, Database, New), and use "blank" as the template. This gives us a clean slate to work from.

For the purpose of this example, let's say you've decided to create a Web-enabled application which is based on a three-frame frameset design. The leftmost frame will hold an outline for navigation purposes, the upper frame will simply have a company logo, and the lower right frame will hold the actual content. As someone clicks on one of the links in the outline in the left frame, the document they're requesting will show up in the frame at lower right.

In order to accomplish this, we'll need an outline, a frameset, and a couple pages.

To make matters simple for this discussion, let's make a couple simple pages and an outline quickly. We can come back to these later and make changes to make them more elegant or complex.

> **Note**
> The following discussion gives the short version instructions on creating pages, outlines, and framesets. These items are discussed in far greater depth in Chapter 16.

To create the first page, let's navigate to pages in the Designer. Click the New Page icon, and you're in business. Pages operate the way that About Documents do; you can add links, text, rich text, computed text, images, sections, tables—just about anything you can do on a form except fields. As shown in Figure 28.8, type something such as "This is our Home Page" across the top of the page. Save that page; when prompted, call it "Home".

Let's create a second page, and for simplicity's sake, we'll call it DetailPage1. Depending on what you were doing, you could easily create a series of pages for various departments in your organization or for the various segments or divisions of your Web site.

On DetailPage1, let's simply put a header stating "Company Information." Save that page.

Now, let's create an outline that will take you to these two pages. Switch to Outlines in Designer, and click New Outline. When you're in the process of creating the outline, you can create an outline entry by clicking the New Entry button at the top of the screen. You can connect this outline entry to the home page by picking it from the outline entry property box. You can give this outline entry a visual option by choosing an image to use. You can give it an alias, direct which frame should be populated when someone clicks on this outline item, and even handle hide-whens (potentially based on who the user is or what type of browser someone is using) for the item.

Figure 28.8
Creating a Home Page.

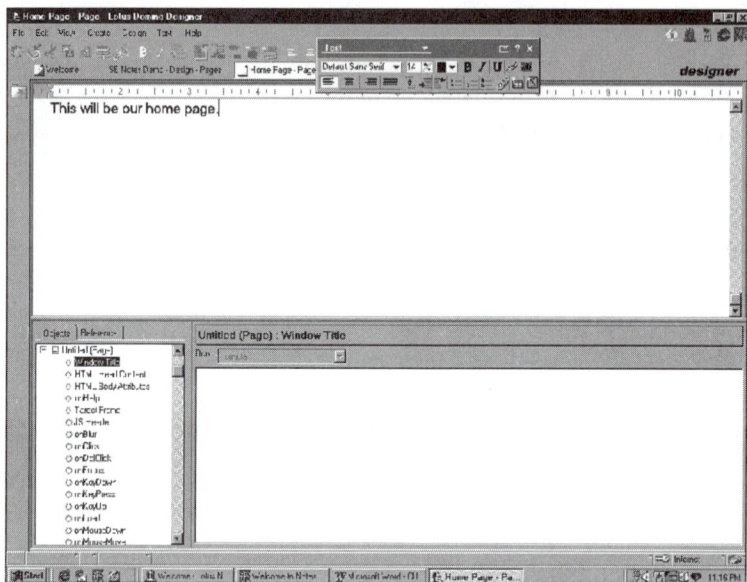

Connect your first outline entry to the home page; create a second and connect it to DetailPage1. To round things out, you might want to add additional items to connect to Notes-related Web sites.

Next, let's create a frameset. In Designer, go to Framesets and click New Frameset. The Create New Frameset dialog will appear. Choose how many frames you want (from two to four for starters—we'll choose three). That creates the frameset. From Frameset Properties, you can name it and choose any other properties that are appropriate. After you have named it, you can then use it as a launch option for the database itself.

Note

Just like practically every other design element, the database launch property has additional options in R5. By going to Database Properties (File, Database, Properties or click on the Properties SmartIcon), you can set the launch properties by going to the fifth tab (from the left), the one with the rocket ship.

You can set launch properties for Notes clients independently from Web clients, and the When opened in a browser options include opening a given frameset or a specific page.

Although this is a ridiculously simple example, in the course of a five-minute exercise, we've managed to build a simple Web application using elements found natively in the Domino Designer—nothing added from HTML, nothing from any sort of outside editing tool or product.

Our example—again, using Notes elements only—creates a simple but nice-looking Web application. Our opening frameset will display in the Notes client, as shown in Figure 28.9, virtually identical to how it displays from a Web browser, as shown in Figure 28.10.

Figure 28.9
Opening frameset shown in Notes client.

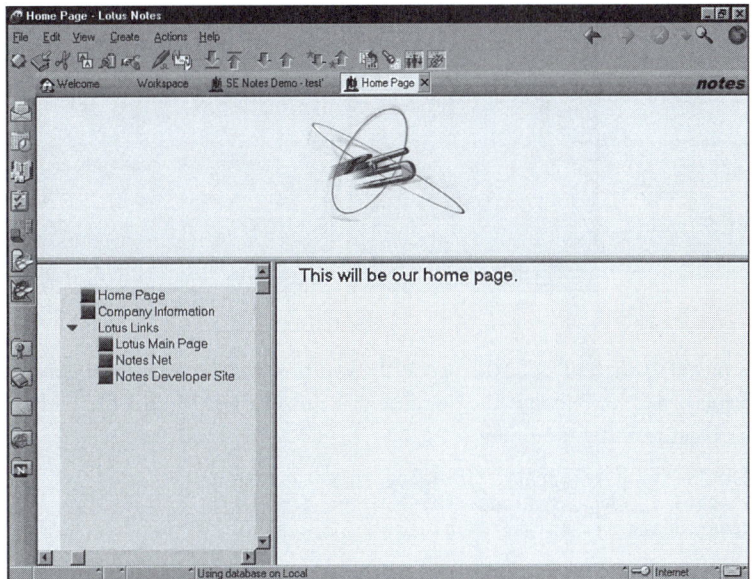

Adding HTML to Notes Forms, Documents, and Views

Another option is to get closer to a true Web implementation by employing HTML—the Hypertext Markup Language. This way, you neither have to rely solely on Notes nor solely on HTML.

We could create some HTML documents, or we can take our original Option B a couple steps further by adding HTML to the Notes design elements. For example, HTML can be used in forms and views to augment what you can do in Notes itself.

Here's a typical task that becomes much easier using a combo method. Let's say you wanted to employ a typical Web trick such as posting a "New" icon next to recently added items and an "Updated" icon next to items that have been recently modified. A savvy Webmaster can handle the task of adding the icon fairly easily, but removing the tag after it's no longer appropriate is an additional task. In a fluid, frequently changing Web site, this becomes a daunting task.

Figure 28.10
Opening frameset shown in browser.

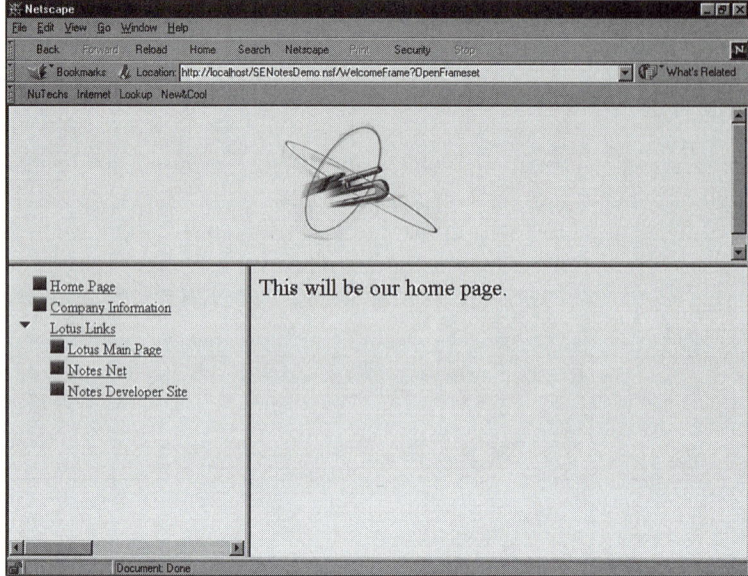

A nickel's worth of HTML can be thrown into the formula for a column in a view, which displays a "New" icon if the document is newer than 10 days old and an "Updated" icon if it's been recently modified:

```
REM "setting temporary variables to work with";
NewDate := @Adjust(@Today; 0; 0; -10; 0; 0; 0);
UpdatedDate := @Adjust(@Modified; 0; 0; -10; 0; 0; 0);
REM;
REM "Here's the statement that does the work";
REM "It'll display a NEW bitmap if the document is newer than ten days old";
REM "or a UPDATED bitmap if modified in the past ten days";
REM;
@If(@Created >= NewDate; "[<img src=../icons/new.gif>]";
@If((@Modified >= NewDate) & (UpdatedDate > @Created);
"[<img src=../icons/updated.gif>]"; ""))
```

> **Note**
>
> There are several ways that you add HTML to design elements in the Notes world.
>
> The first is to do as the example does above; add square brackets to enclose the HTML code (for example, in the final line above
>
> `"[<img src=../icons/updated.gif>]"`
>
> the square brackets enclose an HTML image tag that is passed directly to the browser). You can use this method in forms, views, pages, and documents. Domino recognizes the square brackets as a signal that HTML is enclosed and passes the HTML directly on to the browser. Domino itself doesn't attempt to act on the command; your browser does.

> The second is to transform the design element in Notes into HTML itself. That can be done in a view by using the view attribute Treat View Contents as HTML. In a form, you can select Treat Document Contents as HTML or Generate HTML for all fields.
>
> You could also have a field called HTML; Domino will recognize that as a special field and pass its contents directly to the browser.
>
> Additionally, you could create a style called HTML; any text flagged with that style will be automatically passed through to the browser.
>
> There are several excellent examples of each of these methods in Designer Help for R5.
>
> Any of these options would allow the developer to create HTML code that will be sent directly through to the browser.

Because the view in Notes will look terrible with the exposed HTML, you could easily hide the view from your Notes clients (you still can't do a "hide from Notes" at the column level, but you could hide the view itself from Notes clients).

By publishing the database with such a formula in a hidden view, the Web version of the database correctly identifies which documents are new and which have been recently updated. The Web view is shown in Figure 28.11. Or you could embed the view in a page and never need to bother with directing people to a view at all.

Figure 28.11
View showing "New" and "Updated" icons.

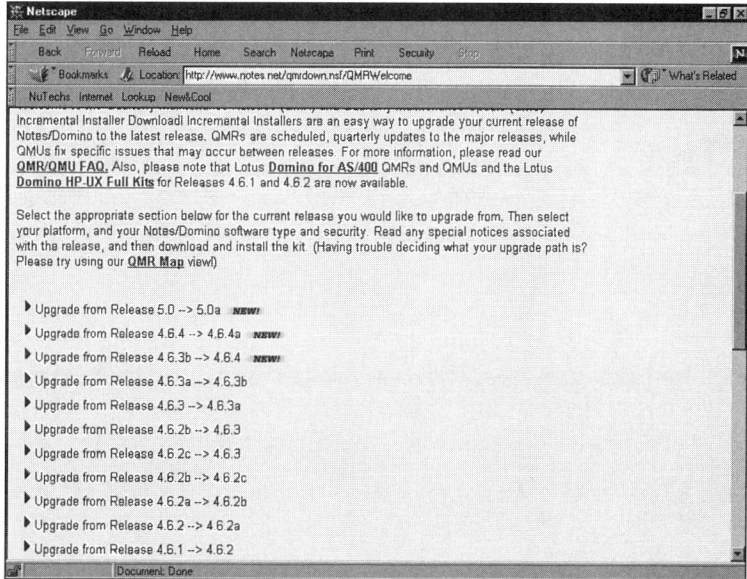

This is a simple example of the creative use of HTML in Notes database design. We're not building strictly in the HTML environment, but we're adding a touch of it here and there where it makes sense. There's no easy way in Notes to create a "new" or "updated" icon, yet the simple formula above is a lot easier than what a "conventional" Webmaster would have to do to achieve similar results.

Other places where you could utilize simple HTML within a Notes database would include loading graphics, specialized response messages such as within a $$Return field, text links (such as MailTo links), and more.

Further explanations follow:

- Loading graphics—As mentioned above, R5 handles graphics differently from HTML, but you can still use HTML to load images. If a particular icon (such as the "new" icon mentioned above) lives in the data/domino/icons directory, you can use the HTML Image Source tag to load the graphic from there via HTML pass through:
  `[<img src = "/icons/new.gif">]`
- $$ fields—There are a couple dozen Web-specific, reserved fields that begin with $$. See the Lotus Notes Help for more information.
- Links—You can build hot links to files, and you can create MailTo links, all of which can utilize HTML. Simply highlight the text you want to use for the highlight, and then click Create, Hotspot, URLLink or Create, Hotspot, Formula

Another simple way to add HTML to a more or less vanilla Notes database is to use the HTML Attributes event. Depending on where you are within the database, you can add HTML to do things such as add META Tags to a page. In R4 databases, HTML attributes were used to control things such as the size of a field.

> **Note**
> Once again, in R5 there's much less of a need to do things such as try to control the size of a field via HTML attributes. The new properties of Native OS and Size will allow you to control the sizing of fields without resorting to writing HTML!

You can also add HTML in the HTML Head Attributes event and the HTML Body Attributes event for the form itself. This gives you tremendous capabilities, adding META Tags, for example, for redirects or to give search engine robots additional search categorization criteria. In Figure 28.12, a simple META tag has been added to a Web site giving additional category and description tags, essential for search engines.

One of the other R5 options to be aware of is the capability to use an exclamation point (!) in lieu of the default of a question mark (?)as a separator within Domino-generated URLs.

The question mark is a "restricted" character as far as search engines are concerned. Because the question mark is used frequently in CGI programs, search engines are normally programmed to ignore URLs that have question marks in them—therefore rendering much of a typical Domino site unsearchable.

PHILOSOPHY | 695

Figure 28.12
Meta tags added in HTML Head Attributes event.

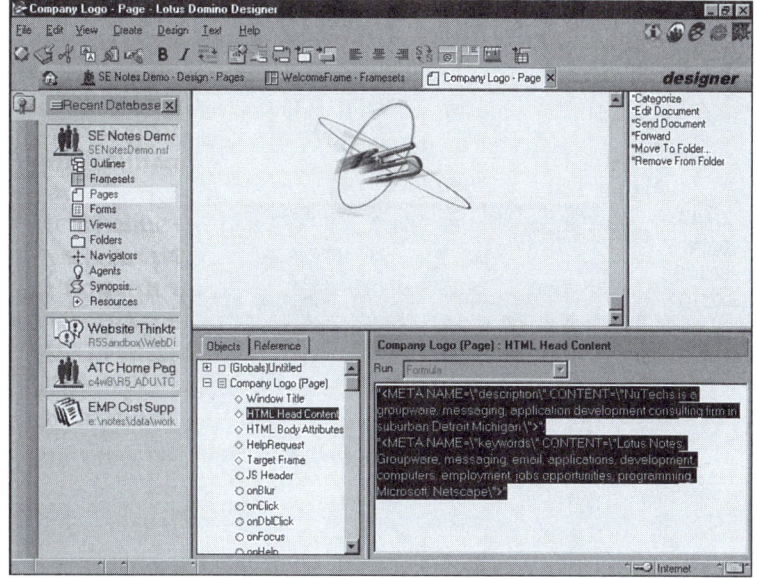

You can change the question mark to an exclamation point by going to your Domino Directory, opening the Server Document, and navigating to the Internet Protocols—Domino Web Engine tab. In the "conversion/display" section, there's an item reading Make this site accessible to Web search site crawlers. As shown in Figure 28.13, you can either enable or disable this property (it's disabled by default). By changing this to enabled, you'll substitute the exclamation point for the question mark.

One of the caveats about this property is that many existing Domino sites might already have links built, or HTML references, or be the subject of links from elsewhere that use the question mark.

CREATING HTML DOCUMENTS AND USING THE DOMINO SERVER TO SERVE THEM...

We're not going to spend much time on this particular part of our third option, mostly because if this is all you were going to do with a Domino server, you probably wouldn't have used Domino to begin with!

But, for the record, the Domino R5 server is pretty darn good as a straightforward HTTP server. There are several things you can do with a Domino server in the straight HTTP world that you can't do elsewhere (such as put ACL control on individual HTML files).

You absolutely could create HTML files in products such as Microsoft FrontPage, NetObjects Fusion, Adobe PageMill, Macromedia Dreamweaver, Netscape Composer,

PART
V
CH
28

SoftQuad HoTMetaL, Sausage Software's HotDog, and so on, and serve them on a Domino server. Just like you would serve a Web site from Microsoft Internet Information Server (IIS), Netscape Enterprise Server, or even an Apache HTTP server, Domino can serve "normal HTML," graphic images, CGI scripting, servlets, CORBA, Java applets, DHTML, Shockwave, and just about anything else.

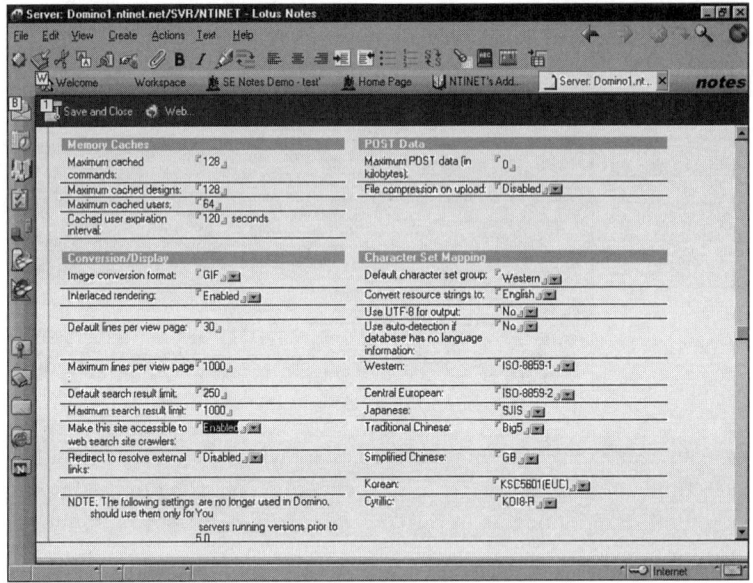

Figure 28.13
Server document showing the Make this site accessible... property.

If you were going to use a lot of HTML files in a Domino scenario, typically you'd put them in the html directory (data/domino/html) and/or a series of directories below that (data/domino/html/sales or data/domino/html/docs).

This would be particularly valuable for organizations that might be migrating a "straight HTML" Web site to a Domino-based site. They could move HTML files, images, CGI scripts, and so on. By default, images would go in the domino/icons directory and CGI scripts in the domino/cgi-bin directory, and so on, as per settings in the server document. However, there's no reason why the images can't go in an images directory immediately beneath the HTML directory (data/domino/html/images, for example).

Regardless of your decisions about the path, Domino is fine for serving straight HTML files.

But still, if we were going to do nothing but serve HTML, we really wouldn't be here, right? And, because Apache is *free*, we'd really be reading *Special Edition Using Apache Web Server* instead of this volume, wouldn't we?

...OR CREATING A HYBRID OF HTML DOCUMENTS AND SPECIALIZED DATABASES

There are some things that are better done in Notes; there are some things (still!) that are better done in HTML.

As indicated earlier, I'm working with a couple organizations where we have crafted elegant hybrid sites using HTML documents on the front end and Notes databases on the back end.

One of my customers has a wonderful site, originally done entirely with HTML pages. The firm, Electro-Matic Products, began to realize that there were several areas of their site that required constant updating: Job Opportunities, Technical Services, Customer Support, News and Information. Their site, at www.electro-matic.com, began to swap their hard-coded HTML pages in these areas for Notes databases.

We took the HTML code directly from the existing HTML pages and put it on Notes forms. That way, the head of the Human Resources department can add a new job posting simply by adding a new document in a Notes database. The woman who heads their marketing efforts can add additional customer support information with the click of a Notes submit button. Neither of these people have a clue about HTML, and they didn't need to learn another tool such as FrontPage or NetObjects Fusion.

One of the side benefits we began to realize from the transition to Notes was that the design elements of the site are now migrating to being Notes resources rather than loose HTML or image files littering the server. We can now make widespread changes by replicating to the Domino server, rather than needing to FTP into the file system of the server and drop image files, and so on.

The "front end" HTML files live in the data/domino/html directory; the Notes databases live in data/. Both the HTML and the Notes databases appear to be in the root of the server (for example, www.electro-matic.com/index.html and www.electro-matic.com/autoprgms.nsf both appear to be in the root of the server, despite the fact that in real life, they're nowhere near each other in the server directory structure).

A twist on this option is discussed in the following chapter. You can use an external tool, but save *that* as Notes. Read on....

CHALLENGES

Despite all the advancements made in the R5 client, there are still some issues revolving around what type of client your database is aimed at.

There are some distinct differences between a Notes client and a Web browser, and you'll need to keep these in mind as you develop your Web site.

Despite the advances that the Editor Applet and View Applet bring to Web designers, they still aren't as fully-featured as the Notes client. And, as much as they help a browser client gain functionality, they also take a while to load, and low-bandwidth sites might well elect not to use them for performance reasons.

There will still be some things that work great in Notes and look terrible from a browser. There will be more things that you do specially for a browser that look terrible from Notes. There will be additional things that seem to work fine in Notes and might work fine in Netscape, but don't work from Internet Explorer. Or vice versa.

The moral of the story: Experiment and test. Be sure to test under each browser and under most common screen resolutions (not everyone has a 19" monitor like you do, you know!).

Navigators will continue to be a thorn in the side, although R5's imagemaps will solve many of the problems. Likewise, although it was supposedly high on the R5 wishlist, Layout Regions still can't be seen by browser clients, so be careful what you do in a layout region.

There are other things that aren't supported from one side or the other: Lotusscript still can't be used behind fields, and the `refresh fields on keyword change` property only works in certain circumstances.

But R5 comes a long, long way toward eliminating many of the challenges and making for a great designer tool for creating Web applications.

Resources

Although this book (and, for the record, other offerings by the Que folks and others) goes a long way toward explaining some of the mysteries surrounding Notes and Domino, there are a number of resources you should be aware of:

- Notes Net, http://www.notes.net, is absolutely the first and foremost place to go for the latest information on Notes and the Web. You'll find an incredible wealth of information, as well as the latest incremental updates, and so on.

Other Web resources you might want to check out include the following:

- www.notesbench.org
- www.lotus-developer.com
- www.dominohive.com
- www.redbooks.ibm.com
- www.lotus-dev.net
- www.best.com/~cseh
- www.notes411.com
- www.keysolutions.com/

- www.garageworks.com/
- www.progtips.com
- www.rhizomatics.demon.co.uk/software/
- www.DominoCafe.com/
- www.itkey.com
- www.progtips.com

A couple great sites for learning more about HTML itself:

- www.htmlgoodies.com
- www.webmonkey.com

Summary

So, in a quick nutshell, that's the game plan for creating a Web site using the tools in Domino.

The individual pieces are outlined in detail elsewhere in this book; hopefully this chapter brings the disparate parts together.

In Chapter 29, we'll take a quick look at employing Microsoft FrontPage or NetObjects Fusion in conjunction with Domino, and in Chapter 30, we'll look at crossing the line between a normal site and a site doing electronic commerce.

ChAPTER **29**

USING EXTERNAL HTML TOOLS WITH DOMINO

The congruence of Notes and the Internet that has been going on for the last several releases has reached a pinnacle in R5.

The Notes client is now as full-fledged a citizen in the Web browsing world as you could ask for, and the Domino server is about as full-fledged a Web server as you could want. (Keep in mind, though, that Domino's market share lags far behind the leaders and that Apache—the "shareware" Web server—is still leading the pack with a whopping 56% market share, as reported by the Netcraft Web Server Survey at http://www.netcraft.com/survey.)

However, as good as it is, there are still some things that you may want to employ in a Web-based application that the Notes Designer itself can't offer. You may find yourself turning to "external" HTML authoring tools to do some of the more hard-core HTML work on your site. It might be that you want to use some of the HTML tools' built-in goodies (such as ticker-tape effects, rollover buttons, drop-down menus, time-based graphic display, and so forth), or maybe you just want to use the tool because you can control placement better, you can control frames and graphics better, you can do drag-and-drop page layout, and so on, and so on, and so on.

You also might find that the learning curve is easier by using one of the HTML tools. Instead of needing to get one of your developers up and running in Notes, he or she could get up and running more quickly in NetObjects Fusion or Microsoft FrontPage.

And, because we just happen to have mentioned NetObjects Fusion (hereafter NOF) and Microsoft FrontPage (MSFP), we happen to be in particular luck; there's a special integration between these two HTML authoring tools and the Domino server. In a sense, you can save-as-Domino from either tool, publishing your NOF or MSFP Web site into a Notes database to be served from Domino.

> **Caution**
>
> As this book goes to press, Lotus was in the process of updating the tools described in this chapter. Names, locations and even features might be completely different by the time you read this.
>
> Immediately above, we discussed NetObjects Fusion and Microsoft FrontPage being two HTML authoring tools that have a special integration with Domino. At press time, these were the only two HTML tools that have this special affinity with Domino, but Lotus has publicly announced that they're looking at supporting more tools.
>
> Not that this reviewer has any inside info, but I'd bet on Adobe PageMill and/or Macromedia's DreamWeaver being next on the list.
>
> Keep checking the Domino Design Components for Web Authoring Tools section on the Lotus Developer Web site (currently: http://www.lotus.com/dfc) for up to the minute info, downloads, etc.

> **Note:** A quick note about the parts. The official name for all the parts I discuss in the next few pages is Domino Design Components for Web Authoring Tools. For simplicity's sake, I'm going to generically refer to all these items as the Domino Design Components. See the sidebar "The Name Game" for specifics.

Why Use an HTML Tool?

Although the enhancements in the Notes R5 Designer's capabilities are substantial, its goal in life is not Web site building. Lotus may not forgive me for saying this, but Designer is still a Notes database designer, not a Web application development tool. Products such as NOF and MSFB were designed from the ground up to create Web pages and Web sites. They were optimized for that purpose, and, as such, do a better job.

The beauty for us Notes folks is in the combination of the tools. Use NOF or MSFP to create the Web site's structure, quickly prototype the site, and easily change the overall site look and feel; use Notes and Domino to provide the actual content.

One of the biggest problems that I've run across in my years working with Notes and the Internet is that on the Web it's often difficult to separate content from context, to separate the design from the data.

Notes has done this for a long time. A designer creates the forms and views; an end user creates the documents that use those design elements.

On the Web, however, it gets a lot stickier. The people who "own" the content for example, Eileen, the public relations person who wants to post a press release, or Samantha, the human resources person who wants to post job openings—don't have the tools to actually get the content to the Web. They don't know HTML and don't want to (and shouldn't need to learn it, because it has nothing whatsoever to do with what they really do for a living).

Word processors such as Word, WordPro, or WordPerfect don't help. Despite each of the office suites' claims that its word processor is an excellent HTML page creator ("revolutionary new Web technology built right in to Office 97 helps you quickly author exciting, multimedia Web pages directly from your Office 97 applications," enthuses Microsoft's Web site; "most advanced technology in the areas of Internet publishing, file compatibility, and speech recognition" promises Lotus), the truth is that while you might be able to take a document from a word processor and make a Web page from it, you can't make a Web site from one.

Think about the typical output from a word processing package. The content and the context are completely interwoven. Although you can start from a template (for example, "contemporary memo," "elegant fax," or "professional letter"), when you're done, there's no way to separate the design from the data. If you output it to HTML, you've got a single HTML document, and the originator is left with the questions of how to get it physically to the Web site, how to get people to it (that is, how do you create links from wherever to this page), and how to allow people to go somewhere from here.

In other words, even if the person who owned the content was capable by means of some word processing package to create an HTML page, then what? How does that person turn that into a Web site? How does he or she mimic the design of the site? create links? ensure security?

This brings up the dilemma of content versus context. I can make a page, but there's no delineation between the design and the data. Even if I do create it, how to I get it woven into the Web site?

Notes becomes the perfect solution. It enables developers to use Designer to create the forms and views, but enables the users who actually have the content to create the data.

For the Web, the combination of these HTML authoring tools and the Domino server is an even better solution: design (or context) left to the tools, data (or content) left to Notes/Domino.

So why would you want to use one of the HTML authoring tools?

First, additional capabilities. NOF offers a series of components (various applets such as the ticker tape mentioned earlier, rotating ad banners, and Dynabuttons) as well as built-in features such as the "screen-door" that debuted in NOF 4.0, which takes the capabilities of different browsers into account, automatically redirecting a recent browser to pages optimized with frames and older browsers to a different page that isn't dependent on frames. NOF also has a built-in site mapper, which functions similarly to the Notes Outline Applet, except that it's created automatically.

MSFP has similar, built-in capabilities. MSFP has its own set of components, including WebBots, scrolling text boxes, and so forth.

Second, as noted previously, the learning curve is much lower with one of these tools. Even though Notes Designer R5 has made such dramatic improvements, both MSFP and NOF are far more intuitive and user friendly than Notes Designer. Think of it as if Designer is out there for corporate developers, and NOF and MSFP are out there for end user developers or Webmasters.

Third, it's entirely possible now to design Notes databases for Web use without using the R5 Domino Designer at all. NOF and MSFP are capable of creating Notes databases for Web use without a Notes client in place.

> **Note**
>
> Although you *can* use NOF or MSFP to create Notes databases, be aware that the resultant database would be totally useless from a Notes client.
>
> The output of either NOF or MSFP in conjunction with a Domino server is, in fact, a Notes database, but it's a database full of HTML pages, as shown in Figure 29.1. The pages in the database are simply the HTML pages the tool would have stored as documents inside a Notes database. The Domino server treats them as pass-through HTML, virtually useless (if not unreadable) from the Notes client.
>
> Neither NOF nor MSFP should be considered as replacements for Notes Designer.

Figure 29.1
A typical page from an NOF-generated Notes database, full of HTML.

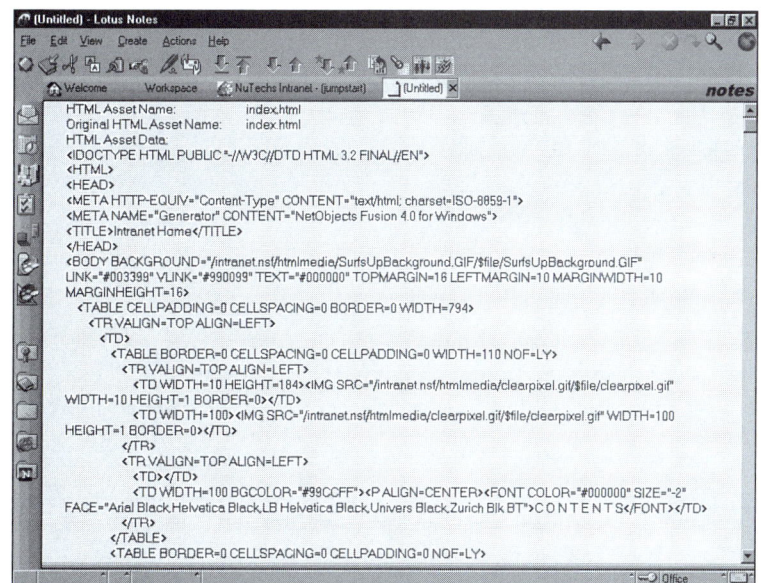

Regardless of whatever reason compels you to take a look at this combination, the HTML tool/Domino connection is a potent one.

Domino has as much to offer the HTML tools as they have to offer Domino. With Domino, I can offer dynamic content that even the best of these tools would have problems with. I can offer security that other servers can't duplicate, and because the result is a Notes database, I can replicate the Web site between servers (and take advantage of R5's HTTP clustering for load balancing and failover).

Using the HTML Tools with Domino

There are several steps involved in working with the HTML tools in the Domino world:

1. Have one of the authoring tools installed on your local machine.
2. Get "local" access to an up-and-running Domino server (to install the Domino Design Components—this doesn't need to be "permanent" local access to a server).
3. Download the Domino Design Components to get your HTML authoring tool to connect with the Domino server.
4. Install those components—the Design Components to your local machine and the Connector Components to your server.
5. Use special Domino Components in your HTML tool.
6. "Publish" the result to your Domino server.

Let's look at each of these steps in greater depth.

Installing the Authoring Tools

Obviously, my first assumption is that you have either NOF or MSFP installed on your machine. If not, install one of them!

NOF might be bundled with the Notes/Domino package you've purchased. Depending on the special promotion Lotus is running at any given time, it's been known to include this type of additional product in the package or to offer downloadable trial versions—or something.

> **Note**
>
> A fully functional 30-day timeout version of NOF can be downloaded from NetObjects' Web site: `http://www.netobjects.com/`.
>
> Microsoft no longer offers a free download of FrontPage, but you can find a ton of information and can order it online from the FrontPage home page on Microsoft's site: `http://www.microsoft.com/frontpage/`.
>
> FrontPage Express (the mini version of FrontPage, which ships with Internet Explorer) is not compatible with the Domino Design Components.

You install the developer portion of the Domino Design Components into your local authoring tool installation.

Getting Local Access to a Domino Server

One unfortunate side issue to getting all this to work is that you need to install the server portion of the Domino Design Components locally on the server. That is, you need to be physically at the server and install into your Domino server Data Directory, or you need to be able to map a drive to the Domino server's program and Data Directories if you're not physically standing at the machine.

One way or the other, you need to be able to install the executable and data files into the Domino program and Data Directories, respectively.

Downloading the Domino Design Components

Right now, there's only one guaranteed way to get the Domino Design Components and that's to download them. You can get everything from Lotus' Developer Central DDC Web site—`http://www.lotus.com/dfc`—and that's probably the best place to start and end the process, because there's a lot of other information there as well. There's online help, an FAQ database, a "water cooler" discussion database, and more.

However, the NOF Components can be downloaded from the NetObjects Web site:

`http://www.netobjects.com/products/html/3rdappserverdomino.html`

and the MSFP Components can be downloaded from Microsoft:

`http://www.microsoft.com/frontpage/3rdparty.htm`

As always, these URLs are subject to change. Keep in mind that the components might end up on a commercial Notes CD. They might end up in some sort of promotional package, so keep your eyes open. However, as discussed in the sidebar "The Name Game," these components are in a continual state of flux and you should keep checking back. Right now, however, they appear only online.

Regardless of where you find them, download the components and stash them in a temporary directory, ready to install.

The Name Game

The folks at Lotus are going through major trauma with the naming conventions for the various components involved with the HTML tool-to-Domino link.

Stick with me here for a moment. In the beginning (read: a year ago) we had DFC, the Domino Fusion Connector. Both the client components and the server components were called DFC, and the command to run the executable on the server itself was `load dfc`.

With the inclusion of FrontPage, calling the whole thing the Domino Fusion Connector was seen as kind of a problem, so the server piece became the Domino Import Service. The client pieces became Domino Fusion Connector (DFC) and Domino Design Components for MS FrontPage (DDCFP), respectively. Meanwhile, if you want to work with the NetObjects Authoring Server (which gives multiple developers working on a site check-in and check-out capabilities), you need Domino Design Components for NetObjects TeamFusion.

To make matters worse, the DFC right now has been upgraded to work with NOF 4.0 and Domino R5, but doesn't take advantage of the new R5 design elements (such as pages, framesets, or outlines). There's a DFC 2.0 waiting in the wings, except it'll be called Domino Design Components for NetObjects Fusion. And I'd bet at least $5.00 that there'll be a Domino Design Components for Adobe PageMill and a Domino Design Components for DreamWeaver before too long. But, as Dennis Miller says, "That's just my opinion and I could be wrong." Lotus would neither confirm nor deny my suspicions.

Installing the Domino Design Components on Your Local Machine and Server

Here's where we get confusing about names (see the sidebar "The Name Game"). Regardless of whether you're going to use NOF or MSFP, you need to install DIS (Domino Import Service) on the server.

You download the appropriate parts and should have two separate files, DIS.EXE for the server and another (either DFCXX.EXE for NOF, or DDC.EXE for MSFP) for your local machine.

It's relatively simple; open up the self-extracting ZIP files and follow the instructions. As shown in Figure 29.2, there's even an in-depth tutorial included in the download.

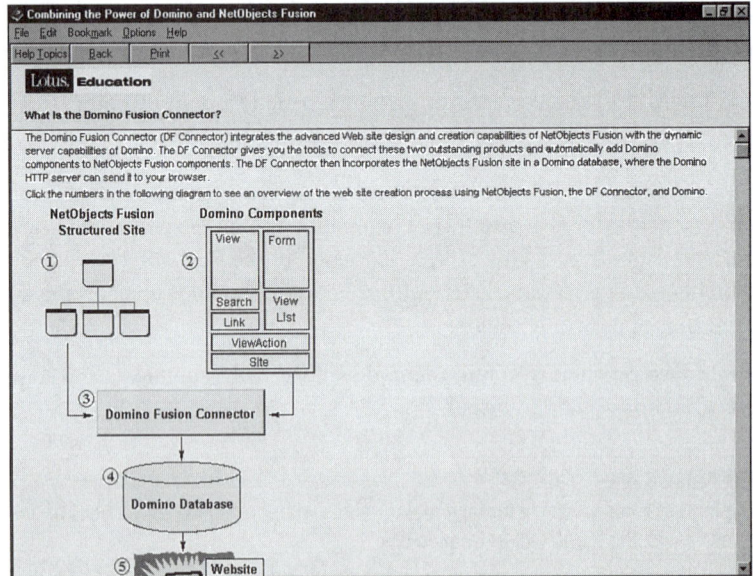

Figure 29.2
Tutorial included in the download.

The DIS component needs to be installed at the server (or from a machine that can map a drive to the server). You need to tell it where the Domino program and data directories are. The DIS install leaves behind a couple of executables and a couple databases. (Right now, the executables are still called DFC, not DIS.) The most important database is the template for the DFC configuration database. If you start DFC, a DFC configuration database will be created automatically. DFC will error out, because there's no preset configuration, but you can go into the database that gets created and set the configuration. You can also simply create the database yourself. Either way, this is where you set a few simple parameters to tell DFC how to operate (see Figure 29.3).

You need to tell DFC where its working directory is (and the directory needs to be created manually—this setup process does not create it). By default, it's expected to be domino\dfc,

INSTALLING THE DOMINO DESIGN COMPONENTS ON YOUR LOCAL MACHINE AND SERVER | 709

although it could be anything. You also need to tell it who has access to use the connector service; the default of blank means that anyone can use the service.

Figure 29.3
The Configuration document in the DFC configuration database.

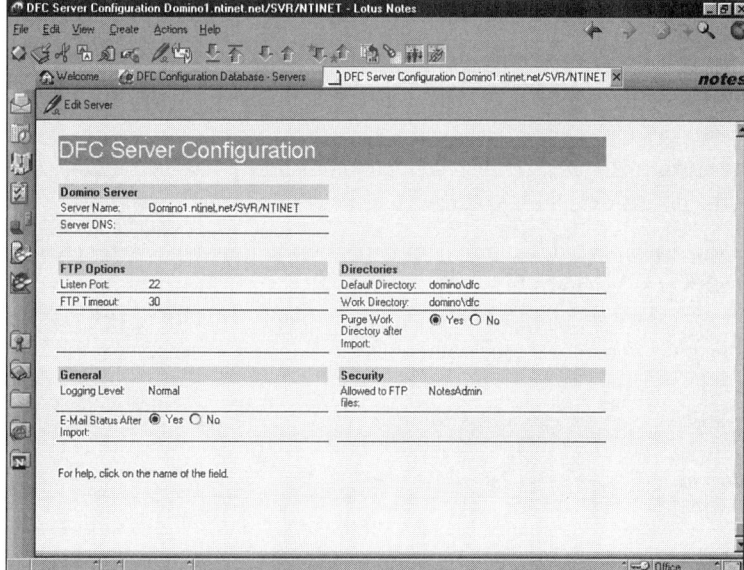

In personal use, I needed to change the default port, because on our server, the default port of 21 was already in use (by the server's "real" FTP server). As shown in Figure 29.3, I simply changed to port 22 and all was well (before anyone panics, port 22 is for SSH Remote Login Service and—whatever that is—we're not doing it, so the port was available).

On the NOF site, to alter the port setting, go to Publish Setup, pick your remote server, and click Edit; then click the Advanced button. As shown in Figure 29.4, the Server Port option is available there.

Figure 29.4
The port setting dialog from NetObjects Fusion.

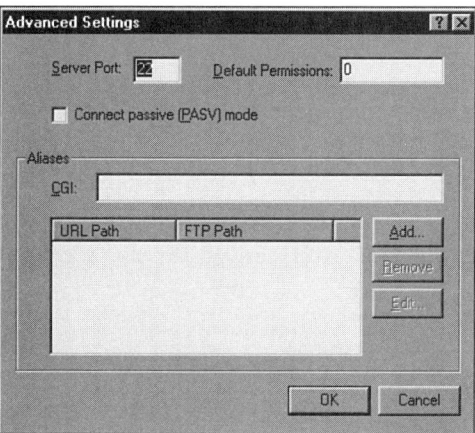

In order to start the service on the server, type `Load DFC` at the command line. You can also add DFC to the `Server Tasks=` line in the `NOTES.INI` file on the server. To stop the service, type `tell DFC quit`.

> **Note**
>
> The Domino Import Service V1.x server executable is still called DFC—that will change once V2.x is available.

Meanwhile, the DFC/DDC client components are installed locally, and need to be pointed at the directories where you have installed your HTML tool.

In my case, it asked one simple question: `Where is NOF 4.0 installed?` Then it installed itself there. As shown in Figure 29.5, the next time I opened NOF, when I clicked on Components, an additional toolbar was available to me: the Domino Components. We'll talk about how to use each component in the next section.

Figure 29.5
NetObjects Fusion with the Domino Components toolbar open.

Using the Domino Components in Your Authoring Tool

For the purposes of this discussion, I'm going to use NetObjects Fusion as the HTML authoring tool of choice. I'll use NOF in my examples; the screenshots herein will be from NOF. This is largely due to personal comfort levels; the NOF Connector was made available first and I've been working with it for much longer. However, what we're about to discuss works identically in MSFP.

There are seven Domino Design Components that are available to your authoring tool:

- Domino Site
- Domino Link
- Domino Form
- Domino View
- Domino View Action
- Domino View List
- Domino Search

Let's look at each for a moment.

Domino Site

The Domino Site component simply tells DFC what Notes database(s) you want to publish into. It's required; without it, you can't publish to a Domino server.

As shown in Figure 29.6, the Domino Site component can specify one or two databases: a source database for the HTML and an asset database for media, applets, and so on. The source database is a required property, but the asset database is optional. If you do not specify an asset database, the site's assets are stored in the source database. The database(s) specified are used until another Domino Site component is encountered within the site's hierarchy.

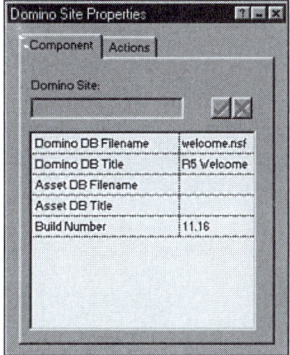

Figure 29.6
The Domino Site component being added to an NOF page.

Domino Link

The Domino Link component works on the URL level to enable you to link from a page in NOF to some other site. This can be a Web page, a Notes database—it doesn't matter. But you need to link to it via a URL.

When users click on a link directing them to the page containing the link, they're redirected to the Domino Link URL instead. This is particularly effective if you want to do a "site within a site." Suppose you were creating a corporate intranet site. One of the pages you create could be Human Resources, and you put a Domino Link component on that page pointing at the HR database. When a user clicks on the HR page, the Domino Link component takes you from the main part of the site to the human resource department's section, which could be another Notes database or even a series of HTML pages stored elsewhere.

The Domino Link can point at any valid URL, so anything you can call out within a Notes database is fair game: framesets, outlines, pages, views, documents, forms, and so forth. However, you have to give a specific URL for each. For several of the elements in a Domino database, there are easier ways to create the links.

Domino Form

The Domino Form component tells the DIS to create a form on the page where the Form component is placed. That is, you can create a form in NOF or MSFP, and the Import Service will treat it as if it were a form in a Notes database.

The Domino Form component is added to a page that you've created in your authoring tool by simply going to the Domino Components toolbar and selecting the Form icon, and placing it on the form in NOF or MSFP.

When your user clicks the Submit button, the resulting document gets saved into the Notes database, just as though it had been originally created there.

There are three properties to the Domino Form component: AutoCreate View, Success URL, and Failure URL. The AutoCreate View is used to tell Domino whether to actually create a form from the page; the Success URL and Failure URL are used much like the $$Return field in a Notes database. They specify which URL a user will be taken to upon submitting the form, based on whether the submission was successful.

Domino View

The Domino View component inserts a view from a Notes database into a page that you create in your authoring tool. This is similar to the embedded view element in Domino Designer, giving you a dynamic listing of documents from a Notes database.

Instead of having a series of hard-coded HTML links to hard-coded HTML documents, you can use the Domino View component to insert a view into a page, giving you the ability to design a nice-looking page with a Notes view in it.

Much like creating an embedded view in Notes, you simply need to specify what database and which view in that database you're targeting, as shown in Figure 29.7.

Figure 29.7
The Domino View component inserted in a page in NetObjects Fusion.

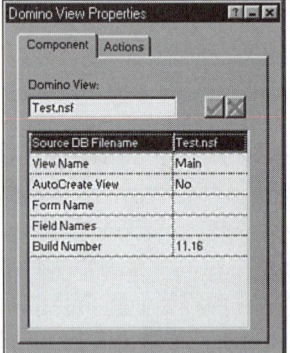

Domino View Action

If you insert a view, you should also insert the normal actions we associate with a view in Notes: Next, Previous, Expand, and so forth.

The Domino View Action component enables you to do just that: You can add a series of buttons across the top, bottom, or side of a view you've just included in a page via the View component. As shown in Figure 29.8, when you add the component, you have a choice of which of five actions this component will trigger.

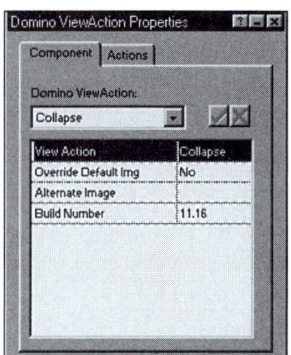

Figure 29.8
The View Action component added in NetObjects Fusion.

One of the side benefits to using this method from NOF or MSFP is that you can use alternative graphics for the standard action. Notice in the properties box in Figure 29.8 the line for Alternate Image. You use graphics other than the standard defaults, but you need to specify the image in order for it to work.

Domino View List

The Domino View List component displays a list of all the public views in the database. This is like the default Notes Web convention of displaying a view of views, except that you can add the list anywhere you want on a page.

Again, this is parallel to a normal Notes Web design trick, which is the $$ViewList field in a $$ViewTemplate form. To make sure we have our jargon correct, remember that the $$ViewList is also called an Embedded Folder Pane, as of Notes 4.6 and up.

There are no properties associated with the View List component.

Domino Search

The Domino Search component creates a search bar in your application. As shown in Figure 29.9, the Search component has only one property: which view to search from.

Publishing to Your Domino Server

After you build your application using NOF or MSFP, and after you tweak everything there is to tweak and polish everything there is to polish, it's time to publish.

In the normal NOF or MSFP worlds, when you publish, you simply create a series of HTML pages that you need to put on your Web server (in fact, each does a great job of publishing *to* the Web server via FTP services). In our scenario, because we put the Domino Site component on one of our pages, we end up publishing to a Notes database on the server, not to individual HTML pages.

As shown in Figure 29.10, when you click Publish, Settings, you need to indicate what server to publish to, a name, and a password. That user needs to have Create Database access to the server.

Figure 29.9
The Domino Search component added to our page.

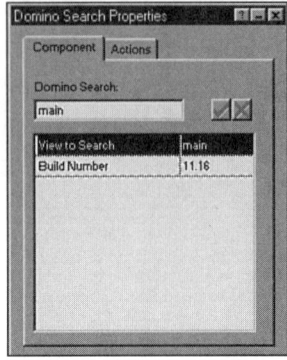

Figure 29.10
Publish settings from NetObjects Fusion.

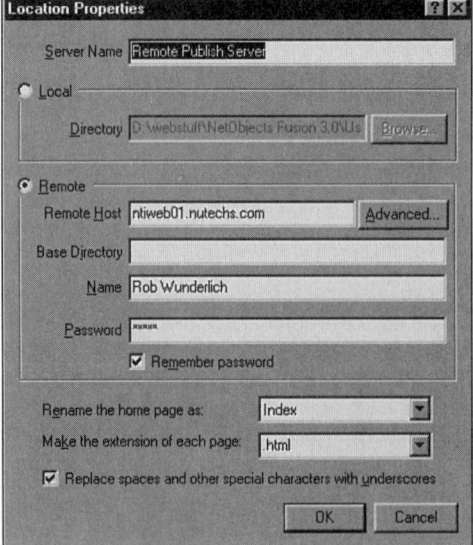

After you have the publishing settings correct, you can go ahead and publish. At this point, the Domino Site component and the publish settings action work in tandem; the first says what database to publish to, the second says what server it's on.

INSTALLING THE DOMINO DESIGN COMPONENTS ON YOUR LOCAL MACHINE AND SERVER | 715

In order to facilitate the actual publishing, be sure the server is running the DFC task (watch for error messages as you start the DFC task; they'll tell you if there are configuration problems). You can check whether it's running by typing show tasks at the server console; if it's not, simply type Load DFC. As shown in Figure 29.11, DFC loads, along with two additional tasks: DFCIMP, the actual import facility; and DFCFTP, the native Domino FTP task.

Figure 29.11
The server console as DFC loads.

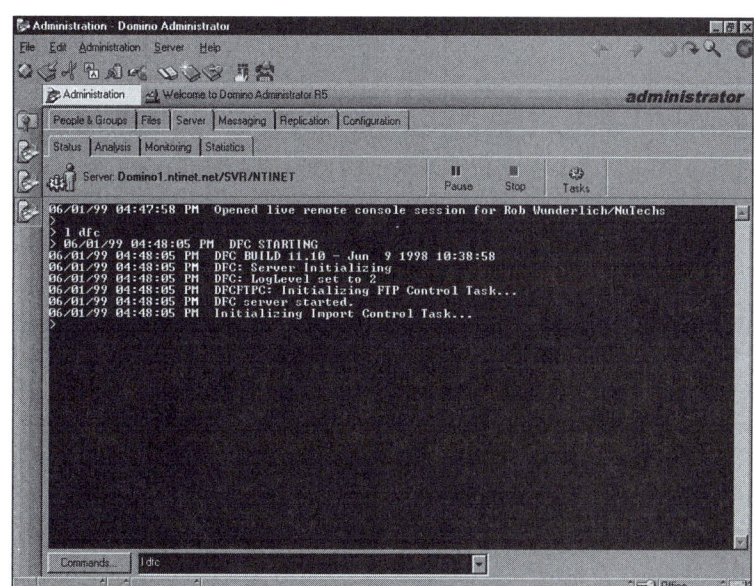

> **Note**
> You need the DFC task running during the import only—it doesn't need to be running constantly on the server. I tend to only run the task when I'm actively importing; my server has plenty of other tasks running the rest of the time anyway!

As you publish from NOF, the DFC service on the server connects with your local client, creates the NSF file (if necessary), and takes the HTML pages, graphics, and objects and inserts them into the NSF file.

> **Caution**
> Be sure to check the ACL on the resulting NSF file; the default is typically set too high. "Reader" should be sufficient for the default.

As you can see in Figure 29.12, the resulting Notes database is filled with individual pages, graphics files, applets, and so forth. It's essentially useless from Notes itself, but it becomes a rich container for all the elements that make up a Web site.

716 | CHAPTER 29 USING EXTERNAL HTML TOOLS WITH DOMINO

Figure 29.12
The "media" view of an NOF Website published into a Notes database.

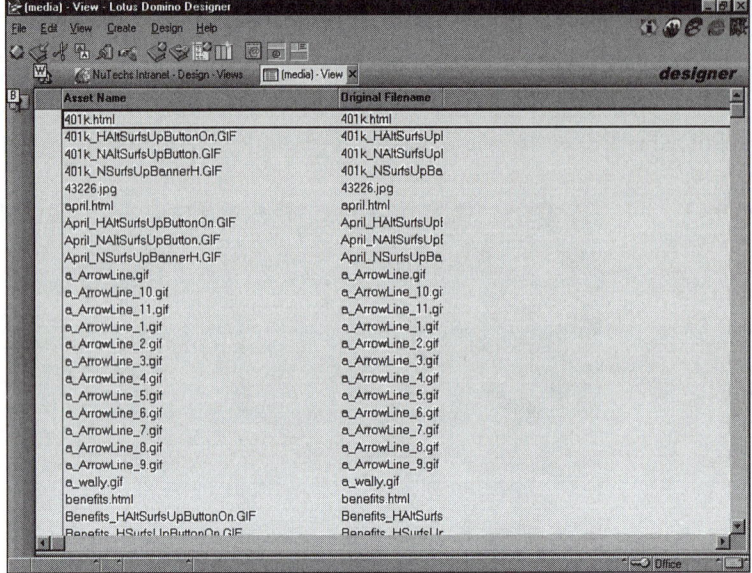

The obvious question is whether this is really all worth it.

Prior to R5, using one of the authoring tools was about the only way you could bring some of the elements, such as framesets, into a Notes environment. With R5's new native elements, it's not quite as difficult as it was, but these tools—designed and optimized to create Web sites—handle the task with greater grace and flexibility.

You can download a trial version of NOF from the NetObjects Web site, and you can download the DDC pieces from Lotus's site. Give it a try!

OTHER TOOLS: BEANMACHINE, AUTHORING SERVER, ESUITE

Thus far in this chapter, I've been discussing the integration of Domino with a couple major HTML authoring tools. But I really shouldn't stop before mentioning some additional options you have for dressing up a Web application based on Domino. These include several that come from NetObjects, the gang that gave us the HTML tool we've been using thus far in this chapter.

NETOBJECTS BEANBUILDER

Lotus created the BeanMachine around the beginning of 1998, and as part of the agreement with the NetObjects folks (IBM became a major investor in NetObjects), BeanMachine was transferred to them and renamed BeanBuilder.

BeanBuilder enables you to create Java-based site elements quickly and easily. These elements can be used in Web-based applications (regardless of whether they're in a Domino-based environment or not) or could be used in native Notes databases. You can create simple things such as rollover buttons in a matter of moments; more complicated elements take longer.

To create the rollover buttons is a snap; the BeanBuilder wizard walks you through the entire process, asking you for the filenames of the normal, mouseover, and clicked versions of the image.

When you're through, BeanBuilder compiles the buttons into a compact Java applet that can be inserted into your Domino application, either through the Domino Designer itself or via a tool such as NOF or MSFP.

You can use BeanBuilder to create a variety of Java-based elements, and there are a number of prebuilt samples that you can customize for your own use.

NetObjects TeamFusion and Authoring Server

In addition to BeanBuilder, there are several products that offer integration with Domino. NetObjects has a product called TeamFusion that offers groups of developers the ability to work on a Web site (giving check-out and check-in capabilities to Web design).

The integration between Domino and TeamFusion is similar to the single-user NetObjects Fusion integration. TeamFusion works with the Authoring Server, which handles the housekeeping chores of the check-in/check-out design elements for a Web site. When the site is completed, you can publish it to Domino from TeamFusion just like Fusion itself.

Because of the way Domino handles Pass-Thru HTML, virtually any HTML and/or Web tool can be used to create Web pages that are either served as HTML by Domino or are put into Notes databases as Pass-Thru HTML.

I use several tools—Allaire's HomeSite and SoftQuad's HotMetal for example—to assist in creating HTML. You can copy and paste into Notes and go to town!

Lotus eSuite

A few years ago, Lotus Components came on the scene. The Components were like mini–office suites, a mini–word processor, or a mini-spreadsheet.

eSuite is the Java-based successor to the Components, and it works great in Domino as well as on the Web.

Check out the eSuite home page on the Web:

http://www.lotus.com/home.nsf/tabs/esuite1

Other Products: Shockwave and More

Just because you're developing in Domino, doesn't mean that you can't do the same kind of exciting things that you'd do otherwise with a Web site.

Macromedia's Shockwave is a perfect example, and Domino is completely happy with Shockwave files being added to your site.

I won't go into this here—we're running up against the end of this chapter. But check out Iris Today on Notes Net (`http://www.notes.net/today.nsf/`) for tips on Java, Shockwave, and more fun things that you can add to your application.

Summary

Most of the tools that you'd use in "civilian life" to create a Web application are applicable in the Notes/Domino world, too.

The combination of the HTML authoring tools NetObjects Fusion and Microsoft FrontPage and the Domino server give each side of the equation capabilities they wouldn't have otherwise.

Additional Web-oriented tools such as BeanBuilder and Shockwave can offer additional depth and creativity to your site.

Have fun!

CHAPTER 30

Moving to Electronic Commerce on Your Domino Site

The boss walks into your office—you being the head Webmaster/Notes expert/troubleshooter—and hands you yet another new edit for what the organization's Web site should be like. Now the organization wants to conduct business on the Web! Imagine.

You've seen it before.

Actually, there's a fairly standard series of stages that most Web sites go through:

- Static
- Dynamic
- Commerce

This process usually begins just after the first site has been put in place.

BROCHUREWARE

At first, the boss was totally happy with "something about us" on the Web—a "presence" as they say. This type of Web site, referred to as a *static site* or *brochureware*, generally is heavy on the "about us" content and fairly light on products, job opportunities, and so forth. If it does have product listings, it's just that—a product listing. The organizations that are using this type of Web site tend to stay here for a relatively short time, because they quickly realize that visitors quit coming back if nothing seems to change.

> **Note**
>
> Let it not be said that I abhor static Web sites. They certainly serve their place in the Web world. Nor should it be inferred that I have never built a site falling into this category. Au contraire. One of the author's favorite pro bono creations was for the Ronald McDonald House of Detroit—and that site is about as static as they come. There's a quarterly newsletter that gets uploaded, but other than that single page, the site rarely changes. And it works just fine for the RMH—and the zero budget it has! You can check out that handiwork at `http://www.rmhdet.org`. Long live static sites!

DYNAMIC

At some point in the life of the static Web site, something happens. A customer makes some comment about the fact that the News page hasn't been updated in nine months, and the ball begins to roll. The sales department calls the Webmaster and points out that some of the information is awfully stale, and something has to be done. Now.

At this point, the metamorphosis to a more *dynamic site* is begun, with some sizable percentage of content that changes on some regular schedule, or changes as needed. Imagine a newspaper Web site that didn't change the stories it covered daily (or maybe weekly, depending on the type of publication). Imagine a job-posting site where the jobs never changed or a specials-of-the-week site where the specials never rotated. (Actually, I used to go to a particular restaurant where the "soup of the day" generally turned out to be the "soup of the month", but that's another story all together. Please refer to my *other* book, *Special Edition: Complete Guide to Eating Soup*. Just kidding.)

A dynamic site is the logical outgrowth of the static site, and depending on what your organization wants to do, it's generally an easy transition to make.

In the Chapter 29, "Using External HTML Tools with Domino," you learned about the difference between context and content; the dynamic site must be created in a way that the content providers within the organization can publish the information they have quickly and easily. Imagine a human resources person not having the ability to publish job openings—having to go through some HTML editor and a Webmaster every time there was a new job to post.

Domino, obviously, is the absolutely perfect answer for an organization that needs to create a dynamic Web site easily. Create a Notes database for the human resources department, and it can take care of business itself. The public relations department can post its own press releases. No HTML geek needed.

So the dynamic site is born.

It often goes through some changes, and at some point there's a subtle shift from being dynamic to interactive. At that point, the site ceases being one-way and begins being two-way. In the Notes world, we'd use Notes databases. Through these, we can allow our Web visitors to ask questions, apply for jobs, join in discussions, and so forth.

So, now the *interactive site* is born.

The logical extension of this is to allow your customers to do business over your site. This is the next logical step in the progression: a site that does electronic commerce.

Commerce

The idea of doing commerce electronically isn't new; manufacturers have had EDI systems for years, wherein an order from one of your customers can be directly input into your existing systems. The idea of doing commerce on the internet is fairly new, however. A scant five years ago, you probably wouldn't have considered the Internet as a viable alternative to a trip to the mall, but during the 1998 Christmas season, an estimated $3 billion worth of holiday sales was racked up online. That's just a drop in the proverbial bucket compared to the overall holiday sales totals, but it's an impressive number nonetheless.

That's why the boss wants to know more about moving your Web site toward a commerce site.

For the sake of this conversation, let's use a broad definition of commerce. In particular, let's *not* get stuck thinking of a commerce site strictly as a site where people can buy things. There are a lot of other ways you might conduct commerce on the Web.

You could allow customers to create work orders or create a job request. Maybe you want to allow customers to track the status of an existing order or check their balances. All these are examples of commerce, but not of browser-based product purchasing.

In some cases, the applications fall more into the extranet category: A company is linked with customers and/or suppliers over the Web, but with security in place so that the general public isn't allowed in. In some cases, it's "anyone welcome," with a red carpet rolled out.

So, as your Web site evolves from static to dynamic to commerce, there are additional concerns and issues to deal with.

In this chapter, we take a look at some of the issues and some of the products that are available off the shelf to help you conduct business online. First, we look at some of the non–product-oriented types of commerce, and then we zero in on some of the products that enable product sales online.

Chrysler SCORE—Commerce but Not Product Sales

In the opening of this chapter, the point was made that there are many types of online commerce that aren't product sales. Chrysler's SCORE program is a perfect example.

SCORE (Supplier Cost Reduction Effort) is an application developed by Chrysler to assist its suppliers in submitting money-saving recommendations about products. The program, widely touted in an IBM e-Business ad in 1998 (Businessman: "Chrysler saved over $2 Billion with its SCORE program running on Lotus Notes and Domino." Dennis Leary: "That's a nice start."), is really nothing more than an extranet application using Notes.

Chrysler gives a Notes client to each supplier, with a special ChryslerNet ID, allowing the supplier access to some special Domino servers at Chrysler. It's a simple process; yet, as the ad says, Chrysler has used it to save over two billion dollars.

> **Note**
>
> The Chrysler SCORE Program has been fairly well publicized, and if you're not familiar with the specifics, you might find them interesting.
>
> One of the better articles about SCORE was written for *InternetWeek* in 1997, and can be found online at
>
> `http://www.techweb.com/se/directlink.cgi?CWK19970428S0002`
>
> *Group Computing Magazine* also has a great article about SCORE at
>
> `http://www.groupcomputing.com/Issues/1998/98JulyAug/98JAp26_Chrysler/98jap26_chrysler.html`
>
> Lotus' Web site also features an article written by Chrysler's Debra Walker, supervisor of SCORE Systems and Measurements. Instead of giving you a typical foot-long URL (worse than the one for Group Computing), simply go to Lotus' site and search for `"SCORE"`. You'll find it.

Does the SCORE program sell products online? No way. Is it doing commerce over the Web? You bet. Two billion dollars worth!

So always keep in mind that there are ways to do commerce activities (that is, ways to conduct business) over the Web that have nothing to do with selling hard products:

- An ad agency might enable a customer to create a job order online that launches some sort of project plan (an advertiser issuing an ad placement order, for example).
- A design firm might use the Web to submit CAD drawings.
- Personnel firms could enable customers to create job requests.
- Product-oriented firms could enable you to check the status of your order.
- Repair shops could enable you to check the status of your repair.
- A builder might offer "virtual walk-throughs" of model homes.
- Newspapers and magazines could enable you to place ads, take subscriptions, respond to classifieds, respond to personals.

And on. And on.

All these, in a very real sense, are a form of electronic commerce on the Web. It might not be selling exactly, but it's certainly commerce!

To most people, electronic commerce means selling products, and Domino is more than happy to play in that market as well.

Selling Online

In the Release 4.x days, Lotus marketed a product called Domino.Merchant. The product is still out there, but Lotus has announced that it's not being revised for R5 and that the product itself will not be supported after January 1, 2000. The IBM/Lotus e-commerce solution is going to be Net.Commerce, which runs on a Domino server as of R5. More on Net.Commerce later.

A variety of vendors have created products that ride on a Domino server and enable you to create product catalogs, allow visitors to register (and you can then give certain user groups special discounts, and so forth), add products to a shopping cart, check out, and charge your purchase a variety of different ways.

At Lotusphere 99, there were nearly a dozen vendors offering merchant-like products, including some well-known names such as Binary Tree and EntreVision. Although this chapter is not intended to compare and contrast the various products, a brief overview is in order—and some product highlights as well.

> **Caution**
>
> One of the problems with even so much as mentioning any of these products is that this is what could tactfully be termed a "changing landscape." Several of these vendors didn't even exist a year ago; a few may no longer exist by the time you read this chapter. On the other hand, a couple of the vendors, such as Binary Tree and EntreVision, have been around for some time, and their merchant products are already on their second or third generations. Be sure to tread carefully when purchasing any shrink-wrapped product, merchant-oriented or otherwise. Check for customization capabilities, ongoing support, upgrades, and so forth.

Using a combination of the exhibitors at Lotusphere 99, the Lotus Guide, and the Lotus Partner Web site, there are slightly under a dozen vendors offering some sort of electronic-commerce, merchant-oriented application for Lotus Notes and Domino. Most of the Domino-based products fare well when compared against the "true e-commerce" products, such as iCat, SoftCart, Merchandizer or Cat@log.

> **Note**
>
> There are a number of places on the Web to find information about the "traditional" e-commerce products. A good starting point, other than Yahoo! or one of the other search engines, is Internet.Com's e-commerce section: `http://e-comm.internet.com/`.

Here are some of the products that you may want to investigate:

Product	Company Name	Phone	Web Site
ezMerchant	Binary Tree	212-248-4424	www.ezmerchant.com
Commerce Accelerator	Corporate Image Software	617-876-0514	www.cisoft.com
Ducat Commerce	Ducat	617-367-1182	www.healthctr.com
EntreVision Market	EntreVision	416-364-3590	www.entrevision.com
Net. Commerce	IBM	800-772-2227	www.software.ibm.com/commerce/net.commerce/
Hyper-Commerce	InterNoded	617-876-4007	www.internoded.com
Ecmarket.net	Nextgen	301-654-5555	www.ngsinc.com
Shopping ala Cart	Offer Solutions	202-955-9955	www.offersolutions.com
Ecommerce Suite	Uptime Computer Solutions	800-487-8460	www.uptimeone.com

These products range from the simple (Shopping ala Cart and ezMerchant) to the complex (Net.Commerce).

Depending on what you want to do with an electronic-commerce Web site, one of the more simple products might do.

ezMerchant, as an excellent example, takes the user through a series of setup steps, as shown in Figure 30.1. Similar to a Domino server setup, the ezMerchant setup asks a series of questions about where the application is to reside, what additional types of pages are to be included (want a discussion with your catalog?), and so forth.

Figure 30.1
One of the ezMerchant setup screens.

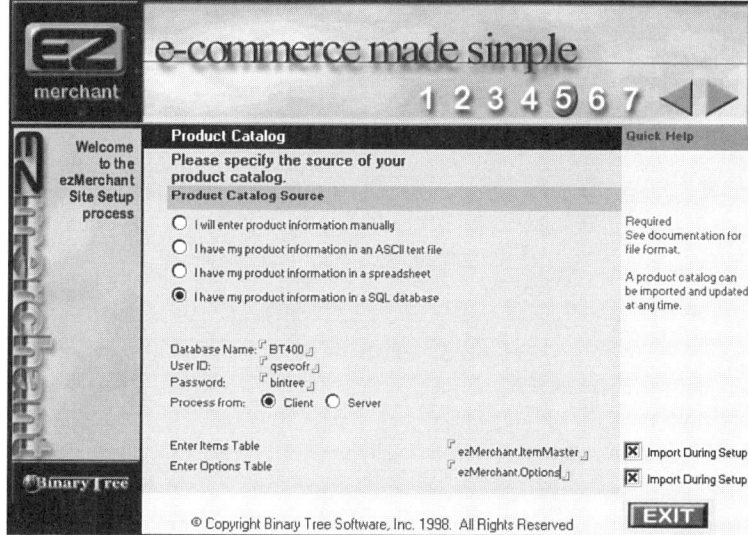

The folks at Binary Tree boast of sports product manufacturer Rawlings as one of the most visible ezMerchant sites out there: http://mail.rawlings.com/store/home.nsf. (Because you're reading this book, you should also be aware that dominobooks.com is also an ezMerchant site!)

The entire process for ezMerchant should take under 30 minutes to create a site, although populating it with data might take some time after that. ezMerchant automatically hooks into credit card processing systems, so there should be little additional work in that area. ezMerchant costs around $5,000, although recently one of my customers was quoted $25,000 for an ezMerchant setup. There was a reasonable (but not monumental) amount of customization in its site. In the long run, however, paying $25,000 for an e-commerce site is probably a steal compared with the salary and benefits for a full-time salesperson. On the other end of the spectrum is IBM's Net.Commerce. This is the product that cost Domino.Merchant its lease on life. Net.Commerce is a powerful, complex application that enables online shopping, but can easily allow a lot of other things. In essence,

Net.Commerce is nothing but a Web-oriented front end for a DB2 database, and the product ships with a complete DB2 server implementation on the CD. It also runs under Oracle or SQL, however.

Net.Commerce runs under Domino R5 on a variety of platforms, including the AS400. It connects with virtually anything, via MQSeries, so Net.Commerce is a perfect solution for firms that already have some sort of transaction system in place. Net.Commerce can tap directly into existing product catalogs, initiate product orders, and so forth.

Net.Commerce's robustness comes at a price, however. The single processor version of the Pro version costs $19,999, and IBM offers a product/consulting bundle wherein IBM Global Services will assist you in setting up your first storefront for $35,000. A consultant friend recently had a three-month Net.Commerce consulting engagement. Between the initial Net.Commerce purchase and the consulting fees, I'm sure the cost of the engagement totaled $75,000–100,000.

> **Note**
>
> Not necessarily included in these prices is one of the most important components in the e-commerce chain: the actual electronic credit card processing service. There are lots of credit card transaction vendors—the list of e-commerce payment vendors at about.com lists 35 companies:
>
> `http://ecommerce.about.com/msub10.htm?pid=2714&cob=home`)
>
> Yahoo! reports dozens (start at the following):
>
> `http://dir.yahoo.com/Business_and_Economy/Electronic_Commerce`
>
> Some of these vendors—notably CyberCash (`http://www.cybercash.com`) and Caledon WebTrans (`http://www.ccsinc.on.ca/products.html`)—are supported by a number of the products noted previously and work on the majority of platforms that Domino supports.
>
> It's important to research the credit card payment aspect of your e-commerce site, even as you're working your way through the design and configuration of the site itself. One of my customers was a week from putting a site online when it began an investigation and found out that merely getting a merchant number through one of these vendors takes several weeks.
>
> Normally, there's no up-front cost to these services; rather, they charge a nominal percentage on each transaction.
>
> If the organization already has a credit card transaction system, the e-commerce aspect is generally painless. But, check it out early in the process.

These costs need to be put into perspective. Although $35,000 or $50,000 seems like a lot of money (to me, anyway!), in comparison to a full-time salesperson's yearly salary (not to mention the expense account), this begins to seem like a pretty fair price to pay.

Incidentally, if you'd like to see Net.Commerce in action, IBM directs you to a few sites you might have heard of: L.L.Bean (www.llbean.com), or NHL stores (www.shop.nhl.com), for example. If you want to purchase software online from IBM, you use a Net.Commerce site.

Whatever you decide to do, the transition of your Web site from static to dynamic to commerce is all but inevitable. Take a look at your options carefully; the most expensive option might easily turn out to be the most economical. But, regardless of your product decision, and regardless of what type of commerce you end up doing, your Web site's move toward commerce is inevitable—and could be a whole lot of fun in the process.

Summary

The migration from a static site to an e-commerce site is becoming a more common occurrence and a more natural transition for organizations.

The rich assortment of products now supporting the Domino platform makes it relatively simple and cost-effective for organizations to take advantage of this natural extension of their Web presence.

CHAPTER 31

Integrating Domino with Legacy Systems

Lotus has gone to great lengths to shed the image of Domino as a standalone, proprietary system. One of the ways it's accomplished this, and continues to do so, is by providing a wide variety of tools for integrating Domino with an even wider variety of enterprise data sources. Additionally, several Lotus Business Partners have taken the lead in producing third-party tools for data integration. The depth of the product itself and the depth of its usage as a mission-critical Internet, intranet, and client/server development platform continue to increase. As a result, data integration will become both a standard practice and a specialization unto itself.

An in-depth treatment of this topic, and the host of tools and techniques available, could fill an entire book in itself. In this chapter, therefore, our aim is to provide, in one place, a survey of the options available to you.

What Do We Mean by Legacy Systems?

Legacy systems in common IT parlance usually refers to systems that are not cutting edge but nevertheless play a crucial and possibly central role in supporting the data needs of an organization. As with many terms in computing, the meaning has become more generic and encompassing over time. It's safe to say that legacy systems can refer to any existing data system, regardless of its age or sophistication. In fact, when we consider data integration in our organizations we may in fact be talking about integrating Domino with systems that aren't even in place yet—for example, "the new system for Human Resources." A more accurate phrase that encompasses all systems, old and new, is *enterprise integration*.

So what kinds of things do enterprises integrate? Systems, or sources of data, generally fall into one of these categories:

- Relational database systems
- Enterprise resource planning (ERP) systems
- Transactional systems
- Non–"system-based" sources

All these categories are fairly standard and well known. Let's cover them only very briefly, so that we're all on the same page, so to speak.

Relational Database Systems

Relational database management systems (RDBMS) are general-purpose data systems designed from the start to handle highly structured, table-oriented data. Familiar names from this arena are Oracle, Sybase, Informix, SQL Server, and DB2. RDBMS vendors, like nearly everyone else, have Web-enabled their products. Oracle in particular, with its WebServer product, is gaining use on intranets.

It's usually stated that Notes/Domino is not a relational system. This is true, but it is very possible to create applications that accomplish the same tasks as a relational system. In the right scenario—for example, relatively low-volume (tens of thousands of records, as opposed to hundreds of thousands or millions of records) and relatively small table depth (the number of table structures)—Domino is a viable option. Take both of these into account as you decide whether to implement a process in Domino or to integrate it as a front end to the process.

Enterprise Resource Plannning (ERP) Systems

ERP systems are all-in-one packages that are meant to support standard business functions throughout an organization. Human resources, asset management, purchasing, and so on are some examples. ERP systems provide a unified interface for performing these functions and generally use an RDBMS to store actual data. Familiar names in this arena are PeopleSoft, Baan, SAP R/3, and JDEdwards.

As central repositories for firmwide data, especially human resource information, it makes sense that workflow applications should be able to integrate with these systems. The gains in data integrity make the extra effort worthwhile.

Again, Domino applications have been used in numerous large organizations as ERP aystem equivalents. Probably the most important factor in deciding whether to build your own in Domino, or to integrate with an ERP package, is resources. Any system to support an enterprisewide function requires a long development and testing effort. This may not be feasible if your Domino staff is not large enough. The benefit of ERP packages is that, although their implementation may take as much time as Domino solutions, there are armies of consultants who specialize in their implementation and the business processes they address. In any event, the ability to integrate Domino with an ERP system enables developers to add its unique features, as well as make ERP data readily available on the Web.

Transactional Systems

Transactional systems, often referred to as transaction processing monitor systems, are the workhorses in business computing, particularly in finance. They may seem unexciting for those of us raised on GUI interfaces and point-and-click design, but they're complex, they're mission-critical, and they're everywhere.

The key to transactional systems is that they manage discreet and well-defined exchanges of data, in real-time, and can fully recover, at the transaction level, from a system failure. CICS, IMS, MQSeries, and BEA Tuxedo are some familiar systems.

Whereas Notes/Domino has been used successfully to implement semirelational systems and ERP-like systems, transaction processing systems represent an area where Domino has not been used. Notes/Domino, of course, was never meant to perform the functions that transactional systems perform, and it would be a definite mistake to try to jury-rig it into doing so. The good news is that Lotus has recognized this fact and has created products that nevertheless enable us to bring Notes/Domino into the mix.

Non–"System-Based" Data Sources

Data doesn't always reside in a "system." Files reside on servers, and data resides in text files, in spreadsheets, and so on. For many organizations, *this* constitutes legacy data too. OLE automation and regular old importing and exporting address this data, as well as several third-party products.

Now that we've covered the basic "arena" for enterprise integration, let's survey the options available to make integration possible. Because several of the tools and techniques we'll look at address integration with more than one of the types of systems we've just discussed, our survey will be "sorted" by tool.

Third-Party Tools

The third-party market for data integration tools is probably the most mature in the Domino world. Although you may tend to look only to Lotus products for integration solutions, you would be missing serious and solid contenders from other vendors. For this reason, let's first look at five products that have stood the test of time, and therefore are worthy of just as much attention as any Lotus product.

Replic-Action

Replic-Action, from Casahl Technology, is a robust product for integrating Domino and Domino data with a variety of relational databases. The model for Replic-Action, as you can tell from its name, is Domino-like replication. This means that data transfers can be one-way, two-way, selective (based on formula-like expressions), and field-level. This enables Replic-Action to transfer only records that have changed, as opposed to entire data sets.

Integration "applications" are created in the Composer, which is itself a Domino application. By filling out various forms, you establish data sources, tables, and columns to connect with, as well as the type of transfers to make. You also establish the kinds of monitoring you want performed on the Replic-Action server.

A strong point for Replic-Action is its close ties to Domino. By supporting doclinks and email, among other standard Notes features, Replic-Action fits well into an existing Domino environment. Casahl also provides LotusScript classes through its RADataTransfer LSX (LotusScript Extension). This gives developers fine-grained control over various aspects of a data rransfer object, such as data transformations and replication activity.

Replic-Action has also expanded on its base to create integration products outside the Domino-sphere. Casahl is a Lotus Premium Business Partner and has its own worldwide business partner network. For more information, visit its Website at www.casahl.com.

Support for Relational Databases

If a system is ODBC-compliant, Replic-Action supports it. It does so via ODBC (as opposed to native APIs), and includes its own ODBC Administrator. Besides the usual—Oracle,

Sybase, DB2, Informix, and MS SQL Server—Replic-Action supports dBase III, IV, and V; FoxPro; Paradox; Open Ingres; Teradata; and many more. ODBC drivers for these come with the product.

SUPPORT FOR ERP SYSTEMS

Replic-Action is actually a family of products. RA.ERP is the product that enables integration between Domino and all the standard ERP systems. It supports many of the same features as the Notes-specific product—for example, notifications, conflict resolution, and two-way replication.

SUPPORT FOR OTHER DATA SOURCES

Replic-Action can also work with spreadsheets, text files, and other Notes databases in much the same way as it does with relational databases.

PERCUSSION NOTRIX

Percussion Notrix from Percussion Software is another product with strong ties to Notes/Domino technology. Whereas Replic-Action runs on its own server, which has its advantages and disadvantages, Notrix runs as a server task on the Domino server itself. This means that as an add-in task it is extremely efficient and flexible.

Notrix has all the features you'd expect in a mature product, such as real-time access, action logging, and error recovery. Percussion also makes other Domino-related products, such as PowerFlow, a workflow development tool. This and the fact that Percussion Software is a Lotus Premium Partner show its commitment to Domino. For more information, visit its Web site at www.percussion.com.

Integration is configured using the provided Visual Workbench. This is a very graphical GUI that enables developers to get basic integration implemented without a stitch of programming. Figure 31.1 shows Visual Workbench.

SUPPORT FOR RELATIONAL DATABASES

Notrix supports any system that is ODBC-compliant. However, for Oracle, Sybase, Informix, DB2, Microsoft SQL Server, and even AS/400 Client Access, it provides access through each system's native API. This translates into better performance.

SUPPORT FOR OTHER DATA SOURCES

Notrix also supports integration with flat files using Notes column descriptor file (with the .col extension). A COL file is a simple text file you create that can include @functions and data typing to manipulate text data as it's imported into a Domino database. Even though COL files have been part of Notes for a long time and are pretty archaic, they can still be powerful, as Notrix proves.

Fifure 31.1
Visual Workbench.

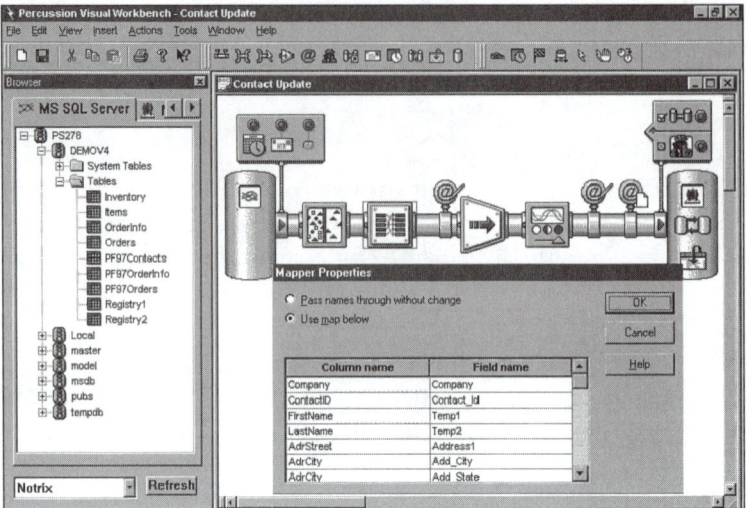

DataMirror SQL Pump

SQL Pump is one of several integration tools produced by DataMirror. SQL Pump is targeted specifically at integrating Domino with relational databases. Like the other products we've looked at so far, SQL Pump models its integration process after Domino-style replication. This means, for example, that only documents that have changed are targeted for replication, and only those fields that have changes are actually transferred.

SQL Pump has the standard features you'd expect from a basic Domino integration tool. As with the other data integration tools we have discussed so far, it enables data transformation using Notes formulas. Setup of integration tasks, as well as scheduling those tasks, is done using Notes forms. SQL Pump also enables email notification of system errors. For more information, visit www.datamirror.com.

Support for Relational Systems

As its name implies, SQL Pump is geared toward relational systems. Any ODBC-compliant system is supported. Although ERP systems aren't specifically supported, basic integration should still be supported for any ERP system using standard relational back-end data storage.

ZMERGE Power Tool for Lotus Notes

ZMERGE, from Granite Software, is a classic in the Notes/Domino world. It's been around a long time, it was created especially for integrating specific types of data with Domino, and it has a solid reputation for performing this task.

ZMERGE is a nuts-and-bolts tool tailored for importing, exporting, and merging flat files and Notes databases. If you're familiar with COL files, you'll feel at home with ZMERGE. Using a text file called a ZID file (ZMERGE Information Description file), you specify the rules for processing data from an external input file. The ZMERGE executable then reads from the ZID file and transforms your external data into Notes documents. It can also create response-type documents, doclinks, and transfer data between Notes databases. Here's an example of a simple ZID script taken from an ZMERGE database:

```
;This sample imports sample data (at the end of the script) into the sample
➥employee database.
;This script will create NEW documents only. No document matching or updating
➥occurs.
;
[
    /JOB_ID="Text to Notes Import"      // Identifies run
    /INP_FILE=*      // Use * to pull data from script (usually filename)
    /NSF_FILE=zmsampl1.nsf      // Target database
    /NSF_CREATE=YES      // Create database if not found
    /NSF_TEMPLATE=zmsampl1.ntf      // Create database from this template
    /NSF_TITLE="ZMerge Sample: Emp Review"      // Create database with this title
    /ON_SUCCESS="(start %Directory%\zmsampl1.nsf)"
]

DEFINE     KEY       PaymentCode PaySchedCode CASE_INSENSITIVE
DEFINE     TABLE     SchedByCode zmlookup.nsf;PaymentCodes

Form:          TYPE TEXT      VALUE "Employee"
FirstName:     TYPE TEXT      UNTIL ";"
MiddleInit:    TYPE TEXT      UNTIL ";"
LastName:      TYPE TEXT      UNTIL ";"
SocSec:        TYPE TEXT      UNTIL ";"
PhoneNumber:   TYPE TEXT      UNTIL ";"
StartDate:     TYPE DATE      UNTIL ";" FORMAT YYYY-MM-DD
PaySchedCode:  TYPE TEXT      UNTIL ";"
PayRate:       TYPE NUMBER    UNTIL ";"
PaySched:      LOOKUP         KEY:PaymentCode;TABLE:SchedByCode;PaySched
PaySchedTerms: LOOKUP         KEY:PaymentCode;TABLE:SchedByCode;PaySchedTerms
Comments:      TYPE RICH
UpdatedBy:     TYPE TEXT      VALUE "01. Text to Notes Import"


FORMULASTART NEW     // This formula evaluated against NEW documents only
SELECT @ALL;
FIELD FullName := @Trim(FirstName + " " + MiddleInit + " " + LastName);
FORMULAEND
```

Support for Other Data Sources

ZMERGE does one thing and does it well. It supports data from minis to mainframes in ASCII, EBCDIC, and binary format, as well as DBF files. Notes-to-Notes transfers are also supported.

ZMERGE is a no-frills tool for working with high-volume flat-file data. It was designed by a company with roots in Notes/Domino technology, so expect efficient processing. If your integration needs are focused on this type of integration, ZMERGE is the tool. For more information, visit www.gsw.com.

SENTINEL

Sentinel, by MayFlower Software, like Notrix, Replic-Action, and ZMERGE, is another example of a product developed specifically to address early shortcomings of Notes, and which has become a recognized tool in the Domino world. Like those others, it doubles as a data integration tool and a Domino data administration tool. All tasks, whether they're for integration or data administration, are entered using Notes forms. Figure 31.2 shows a typical setup form.

Figure 31.2
A typical Notes setup form.

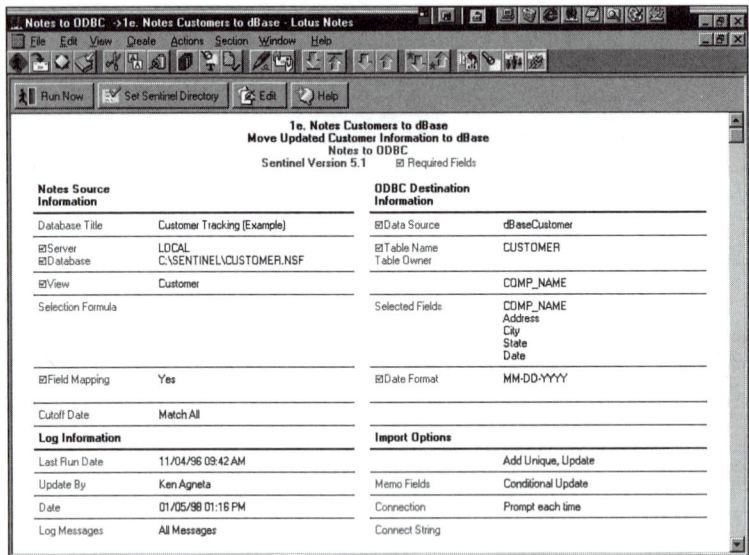

Although Sentinel does data integration, a majority of the product is devoted to Domino data administration, which, when done right, can provide added value to data integration solutions. It can also combine data from relational and flat-file sources at the same time.

SUPPORT FOR RELATIONAL SOURCES

If a data source is ODBC-compliant, Sentinel supports it. It does this using vendor ODBC drivers, as opposed to making native API calls.

SUPPORT FOR OTHER DATA SOURCES

Sentinel has extensive support for flat files (including EDI files) as well as batch importing of word processing files. Domino data administration features include totaling response document data into main documents and scheduled archiving of Domino data to other Notes databases or non-Notes databases.

Sentinel was built by Domino professionals to solve real-world problems. As such, it's very Domino-centric, which means the creators know the kinds of things Domino developers come across and have provided tools to address them. For more information, visit www.maysoft.com.

Tools from Lotus

Every one of the third-party products we just covered is worthy of attention as you search for integration solutions. Lotus has recognized the importance of integrating enterprise data with Domino. Its efforts have taken on various forms, from simple @functions to full-blown integration environments. In this section, we look at what Lotus has done or is in the process of doing.

Programming Solutions

In some circumstances, we need to access external data sources manually, perhaps in a custom agent, in a form event, or in a button. For these cases, Lotus provides both @functions and various LotusScript Extensions (LSXs).

ODBC versions of @DbColumn, @DbLookup, and @DbCommand

The ODBC versions of @DbColumn, @DbLookup, and @DbCommand have been around for some time. If you know how to work with the non-ODBC equivalents of @DbColumn and @DbLookup, you know basically how to use the ODBC versions. Other than the fact that you need to provide user ID and password information, the functions are equivalent. You specify a data source (server : database in Notes), a table and column (a view and column in Notes), and, in the case of @DbLookup, a key-column and key (a column number and key in Notes). A few options are provided, such as for sorting and returning unique values only, that aren't directly available in the non-ODBC versions, but they have simple equivalents (for example, the @Unique function).

Both @DbColumn and @DbLookup are simple read-only functions. @DbCommand, on the other hand, can be used to read and write data. Don't get excited, though. You're limited to sending a string that contains a SQL Select statement, a command that the data source system understands, or a stored procedure name. These functions are primarily meant to populate keyword lists. Non-ODBC equivalents tend to be pretty slow, so the ODBC will be even slower, because we've added the whole ODBC layer. Chances are, these won't suffice for your applications. For far better capabilities, and some improvement in performance, you need to use LotusScript.

LotusScript Extensions

A LotusScript Extension, or LSX, is a DLL file (or its equivalent) that contains definitions of various classes that you write to in LotusScript. By including a reference to this file in your code, those classes are made available, just as the standard Domino classes are. Each of the classes has methods and properties that can be used in code to implement extremely sophisticated integration.

LS:DO   LS:DO stands for LotusScript Data Object and refers to three classes provided in the ODBC LSX. These classes are `ODBCConnection`, `ODBCQuery`, and `ODBCResultSet`. With these classes are their properties and methods. You can access any ODBC-compliant data source, provided you have an ODBC driver for the external source.

OTHER LSXS   Lotus also has LSXs for DB2, SAP, and MQSeries. There's no magic in these LSXs. They function the same way as the LS:DO. You include a reference to the LSX in your LotusScript code, and then write to the system-specific classes provided in the LSX. A full exposition of all the classes is outside the scope of this book. Suffice it to say that the intention of providing these classes in the first place is to provide complete access to the external data sources, using methods that will be familiar to anyone who has experience in the external system. So, for instance, if you're familiar with MQSeries processing, you'll be familiar with how to use classes such as `MQQueue`, `MQQueueManager`, and `MQMessage`.

The difficult part of any of these is not the LotusScript coding, but understanding what you're doing on the external system. The classes insulate the developer to some extent from the native equivalents, but they don't eliminate the need to understand the external system.

NOTESSQL

As Domino developers we tend to think of our applications as the origin of integration—as the places into which external data is drawn. That doesn't have to be the case, though. Notes databases, particularly tracking or catalog applications, may very well serve as external sources to other systems. For this reason, Lotus provides its own ODBC driver for accessing a Notes database using SQL, as you would with other RDBMSs.

A common use for this is using a tool such as Crystal Reports to create sophisticated reports based on Notes data. Having a Notes database available as an ODBC source also enables developers to integrate it with other relational sources into a third system.

JDBC

In keeping with Lotus' objective of supporting Java, Domino ships with the tools to establish JDBC connectivity. A JDBC driver is provided so that Domino data can be accessed like any other relational system from within a Java applet or application. Also, agents written in Java can incorporate the classes contained in the `java.sql` package that Lotus provides.

LOTUS PRODUCT-BASED SOLUTIONS

Like any large software company, Lotus provides its own auxiliary products to enhance its core product, even when the functionality competes with third-party vendor partners. You can decide for yourself whether this is a good thing or not. The next sections cover Lotus' two primary integration products: NotesPump/Lotus Enterprise Integrator (LEI) and DECS.

NotesPump/Lotus Enterprise Integrator (LEI)

In keeping with its effort to appear nonproprietary, Lotus renamed NotesPump to Lotus Enterprise Integrator (LEI). This actually makes sense, beyond a strictly marketing move, because NotesPump was designed to integrate any supported data source with any other, regardless of whether either is a Domino database.

In terms of other third-party tools, LEI most resembles a combination of Replic-Action and Sentinel. It was designed to handle integration and Domino data administration. Integration tasks are configured using Notes forms residing in the NotesPump Administrator database. One of the ways in which it differs from the others is its support for various operating systems (in keeping with Domino's cross-platform support), such as Solaris, OS/2 Warp, and AIX, in addition to NT and others.

Support for Relational Sources

As with the other tools we've covered, LEI supports any ODBC-compliant relational system. It also supports Oracle, Sybase, and DB2 through its native APIs. Similar to Replic-Actions RADataTransfer LSX, there's a NotesPump LSX for gaining fine-grained programmatic control of the NotesPump engine.

Support for ERP and Transaction Systems

LEI doesn't support ERP and Transaction Systems as of this writing, but connectors (the new term for NotesPump Links) for these are in the works.

Support for Other Data Sources

LEI supports access to text files, HTML, and data transfer between Domino databases and servers. It also provides Domino data administration features, such as event polling and archiving.

Being the "mothership" (that is, Lotus) has its advantages. LEI is an extremely deep product with extensive data integration, Domino data management, and system management features. It is tailored for high-volume work and supports numerous environments. When support for transaction and ERP systems is in place, LEI will have a combination that's hard to beat.

Domino Enterprise Connection Services (DECS)

DECS, which comes bundled with Domino Server 4.6.3 and above, seems to confuse things a bit, because it apparently offers many of the same features as NotesPump. Actually, it is positioned almost as a NotesPump Lite, in that it supports and enhances the real-time features of NotesPump. It is also meant to support integration between external data sources and Domino only, as opposed to the wider scope of NotesPump, namely to integrate two or more non-Domino and/or Domino data sources.

Integration in DECS is configured by means of activities and connections. Figure 31.3 shows the DECS Admin screen. This should look familiar to Notes developers, because it's basically a Notes database. DECS supports integration with ODBC-compliant relational systems, ERP systems, and transaction systems—all through what Lotus calls Domino Connectors. Connectors are new objects, not enhanced LSXs. In fact, Lotus has a Connector LSX for accessing Connectors in LotusScript, as well as a Connector Toolkit for third parties to develop custom connectors.

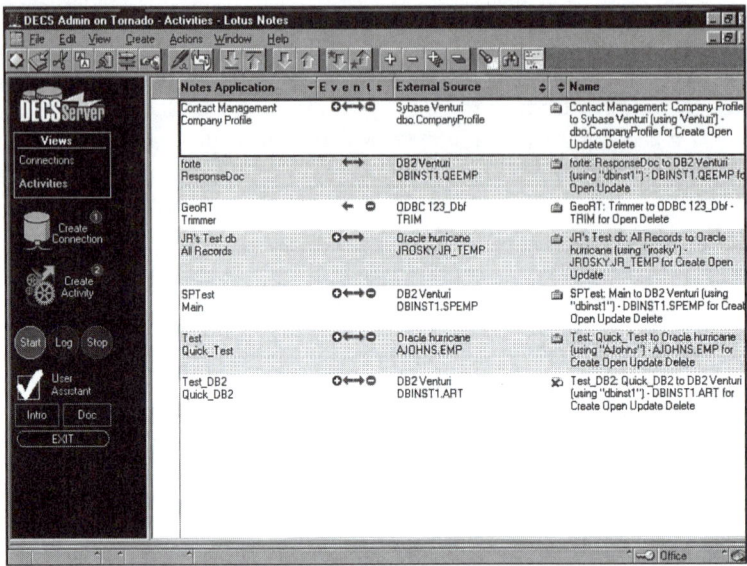

Figure 31.3
The DECS Admin screen.

The wide array of choices from Lotus may seem confusing. Fortunately, Lotus is in the process of simplifying matters as well as expanding options. Domino Connectors represent a unified architecture that will be used regardless of the specific tool or method you choose. For more information, visit the Lotus site at www.lotus.com. For integration-specific information, visit www.eicentral.lotus.com.

SUMMARY

As noted at the beginning of this chapter, the subject of data integration in Domino is huge, and worthy of an entire book. (In fact, IBM has a Redbook with 200+ pages that deals with nothing but implementing LEI.) We've only scratched the surface here. But the message is clear.

Not only can Domino be a mission-critical system itself, and not only can it be the glue that binds other mission-critical systems in your organization, but it also can be a vital part of your organization's overall information architecture. Wherever data resides in your organization, there are options available to integrate it with Domino and make it available on your intranet and/or Internet site.

From Here…

In this chapter, you surveyed several options for integrating Domino into your organization. The Websites I mentioned will provide more detail on individual products. The following parts and chapters will also help you further explore Lotus Notes and Domino R5's development and data integration capabilities:

- You can learn more about LotusScript and using Lotus Notes as a development platform in Part IV, "Using LotusScript, Java, and Javascript."
- Chapter 48, "Using NotesPump and Domino Enhanced Search," also provides more in-depth information on using Lotus Enterprise Integrator.

PART VI

Installing and Configuring the Domino Servers

32 Initial Planning and Installation

33 Upgrading from Domino R4.x to R5

34 Initial Configuration of Servers with the Domino Directories

35 Domino Security Overview

36 Firewalls, Virtual Private Networks (VPNs), and Internet Security

CHAPTER 32

THE DOMINO FAMILY OF SERVERS

The Domino server is at the heart of Lotus Notes. Without Domino, there would be no way for one Notes user to exchange information with another. There would be no replication, no email, no discussion databases, no workflow, no dynamic Web pages. In fact, without the Domino server, there would be no Lotus Notes. So just what is the Domino server?

Domino is a core of services that work together to deliver information to Notes workstations, to the Internet, and to other Domino servers in a Notes network. In this section of this book, you will look in greater detail at some of the services that run on the Domino server. This chapter provides an overview of those services and how they are combined to provide a family of Domino servers that can be scaled to meet the needs of organizations of all sizes.

The scalability of the Domino server is the primary factor behind the "family" in the title of this chapter. Lotus has three types of server licenses. The simplest form of the Domino server is the Domino Mail Server. With the same core services, the addition of the Web Application Server, and access to a wide variety of Notes and Web applications, you have the Domino Application Server. Add to that the ability to manage clustered servers and you have the Domino Enterprise Server, which provides bulletproof, large-scale reliability.

This chapter provides a summary of the features that distinguish the Domino family of servers:

- The Domino Mail Server
- The Domino Application Server
- The Domino Enterprise Server

Members of the Family of Domino Servers

There are three members of the Domino server family. All three have the same core of basic Domino services, with additional services for specific purposes, as described in this chapter. When you first set up a Domino server, you can select which member of the server family you want to install. The selection screen is shown in Figure 32.1.

Here are a few facts about the server family:

- The Domino Mail Server provides a Notes infrastructure that delivers email and simple Notes applications, such as discussions, calendaring and scheduling functions, and Web access. The Domino Mail Server is designed to be easy to deploy and manage.
- The Domino Application Server extends the messaging infrastructure of the Domino Mail Server to the Internet with an open Web Application Server. As you learn about the Domino Application Server, you will come to understand the true power of Domino.
- The Domino Enterprise Server provides the tools for scaling the Domino Application Server to a wider enterprise, with clustering, load balancing, and failover.

Figure 32.1
During setup, you select which member of the Domino server family you want to create.

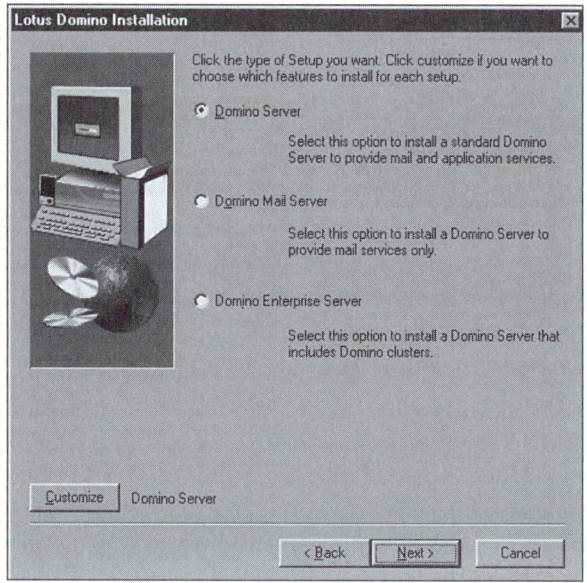

Details of the three members of the Domino server family are described in greater detail in the following sections.

The Domino Mail Server

The Domino Mail Server is appropriate for organizations that use Notes primarily for messaging, or those that want to use a Domino server specifically for mail routing.

It is the lowest common denominator among the Domino family of servers, providing the easiest way to implement a Notes infrastructure to manage your messaging needs. What types of messaging are included with the Domino Mail Server?

Email is the first and most obvious instance of messaging in an organization. It involves direct communication with another individual or with the individuals in a group. The Domino Mail Server handles the delivery of email within an organization, using the Domino Directory to determine where and how a message should be delivered, and using the Router task to move the message to the appropriate user's mail file. That is basic functionality that has been built into Notes from its earliest days. But beyond that basic functionality, what is it that makes Notes and the Domino server a world-class messaging system? In the words of the marketers, what makes it super.human.software?

Internet Messaging Standards

For starters, it is not just Notes mail, it is Internet mail. The Domino Mail Server is built on Internet standards, including native SMTP routing and native MIME content. That means that messages can be sent to other mail systems seamlessly.

Simple Mail Transfer Protocol (SMTP) is the standard used for relaying mail between networks on the Internet. By using this standard, the Domino server can route mail to any mail system on the Internet. Because the SMTP is native to Notes, it does the routing without having to convert between the Notes format and the Internet format using a separate message transfer agent (MTA), as was done in previous versions of the Domino server.

The Domino Mail Server also supports ESMTP (Extended SMTP), which makes it possible to receive delivery notifications. For example, you can send an email message over the Internet and receive a notification when the person receives (or fails to receive) the message. Notifications have always been a standard part of Notes email, but Notes 5.0 now provides similar functionality over the Internet.

The native MIME support (multipurpose Internet mail extensions) is another Internet standard that enables messages to include audio, video, international character sets, and multipart messages. MIME is the standard format for most messages on the Internet. With Notes and the Domino server 5.0, Notes messages are stored in MIME format. That means that there is no need to translate messages from one format to another as Notes messages are sent to people over the Internet. As a result, there is a gain in performance, and there is a gain in the fidelity of the messages themselves. In Notes 4.6, POP3 and IMAP clients could route messages through Notes in MIME format. In Notes 5.0, the Notes messages themselves are now stored in MIME format.

The use of the MIME standard goes beyond straightforward messages. The Domino Mail Server also supports S/MIME, the Internet standard for secure Internet mail. Secure connections that require a username and password can be made using TCP/IP, or you can make an encrypted connection with Secure Sockets Layer (SSL).

Addressing Messages

With traditional Notes addressing, Domino looks up the names of addressees in the Domino Directory. If an individual is listed in the directory, the location of his or her mail database is obtained from the Person record. If the person is not listed, an explicit path is required in the address, and connection documents are required to tell the Router how to deliver the message. In earlier versions of Notes, messages to the Internet had to be addressed to an Internet domain, and then the MTA would transfer the message.

With Notes 5.0, native Internet addressing is supported. There are two standards that are supported: RFC821 and RFC822. RFC821 is a straightforward Internet address. For example, under RFC821, my address would be don_child@datahouse.com. However, the RFC822 standard allows backward compatibility by including the user's distinguished name along with a bracketed Internet address. Under this standard, my address would appear as "Don Child/DataHouse <don_child@datahouse.com>".

One of the advantages of Internet addressing is the flexibility it provides. If users are constantly connected and use TCP/IP, the router can go directly to the user's domain and deliver mail to that person's Internet address. But if the user is sometimes disconnected, Notes can use connection documents and scheduled connections to deliver mail to the Notes address. In either case, the message ends up in the same mailbox in the same format. It provides an alternative that improves reliability and flexibility.

To ease the administrative burden, there is a special function in the Domino Administration client to convert Notes addresses into Internet addresses. Under the People & Groups tab, select People, People, Set Person's Internet Address to display the Set Internet Address dialog box (see Figure 32.2). Use the dialog to define parameters for creating Internet addresses from selected Person and Group records.

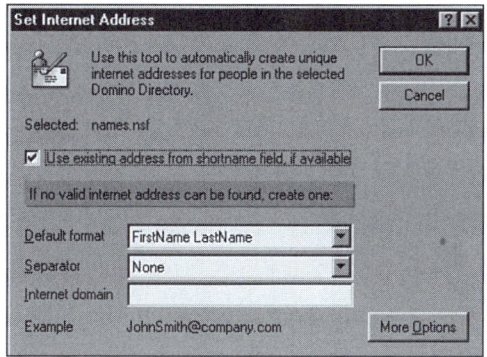

Figure 32. 2
Domino provides an easy way to convert Notes addresses to Internet addresses.

ROUTING MESSAGES

The Router task on the Domino Mail Server is used to deliver mail messages to the addressees. The Router has always been robust. It provides nearly instantaneous mail delivery for mail addressed to people on the same LAN and the same Notes Network (Domino servers that are in the same domain and use the same communications protocol) and uses rules for delivering messages to Domino servers in other domains.

With Domino server 5.0, there are some notable enhancements to the already-powerful Router. Using the Administration Client, you can tailor the Router to do the following:

- Limit who can route documents that are above a size set by the administrator.
- Have the Router refuse to deliver mail to databases that are over their size quota.
- Set controls so your server cannot be used for forwarding email from another domain. This prevents spammers from using your server to mask their mass emailings. You can also screen out mail from addresses you know are used by spammers—people who mail masses of unrequested (that is, junk) email.
- Give users the ability to "pull" mail using a temporary network connection.
- Provide support for multiple sessions to the same destination, multiple threads to deliver mail, and simultaneous agents running on incoming email.

In areas where clients don't have TCP/IP, SMTP routing will not work. But Notes has built-in Remote Procedure Calls (RPC) that enable you to route messages within the Notes environment using SPX, X.25, or NETBIOS protocols. Using non-Internet protocols provides one more layer of security for the data on your internal networks.

New to R5, in addition to many of the features already described, is the capability of delivering mail to multiple instances of the `mail.box` database, where delivered mail gets deposited. This eliminates a potential bottleneck, making the delivery of mail faster than ever.

The Domino Directory and Internet Directory Standards

For messaging in a Notes-to-Notes environment, the Domino Directory is the brains behind the organization. The Directory contains the names of all registered Notes users in the organization and contains information that tells the Router where and how to deliver email. The role of the Domino Directory has been described in detail elsewhere in this book.

Aside from the Domino Directory (which supports up to one million users in a single domain), the Domino Mail Server has two other directories to provide services to Notes users. Directory Assistance provides access to Domino Directories for an entire enterprise, and the Directory Catalog provides a compressed version of the information in one or more Domino Directories.

Directory Assistance was known as the Master Address Book in Notes 4.6, and earlier versions of Notes used cascading Address Books to provide some of the same functionality. In Directory Assistance, you can define trust relationships with other directories, enabling you to exercise greater control over your Domino Directory. For example, you can create a Directory Catalog that contains HTTP usernames, passwords, and X.509 certificates for people who need authenticated access to your Domino server through the Web. Using Directory Assistance, you don't have to put these people into the Domino Directory if they are not Notes users. And, using Directory Assistance, you can extend beyond the one-million–person limit in a single Domino Directory, making your enterprise directory as large as you want.

The Directory Catalog provides a compressed version of one or more Domino Directories, speeding up the process of name lookups and resolving mail addresses within organizations. You can put a subset of information into the Catalog for mail routing purposes, leaving it with a much smaller size than the Domino Directory. For example, the combined Iris/Lotus/IBM Domino Directory is 1GB in size, but the Directory Catalog is only 12MB, small enough that a mobile user could carry a complete catalog of everyone in the enterprise, if need be.

LDAP Authentication

The Domino Directory further underscores Domino's close ties to Internet standards. The Domino Directory is searchable over the Internet using Lightweight Directory Access Protocol (LDAP).

Domino supports LDAPv3, which provides authenticated read/write access, even enabling you to make updates to the Domino Directory over the Web using an LDAP client. This makes the Domino Directory available as an enterprise directory for any system that uses an LDAP client.

For example, a Windows NT BackOffice application in IBM DB2 uses an LDAP client, so all directory information can be stored in the Domino Directory, taking advantage of all the security and replication features of Domino. Because LDAPv3 allows writing to the Domino Directory as well as reading from it, the applications that store information about users can store that information in the Person record in the Domino Directory. The Person document has a customizable subform that can be used for adding new data needed by non-Notes applications for storage in the Domino Directory. In addition to the Person record, subforms are available in Group, Mail-in Database, Resource, and Certifier forms. These subforms are designed so that they are not modified during a design refresh, and the information in them will not get overwritten. The use of Domino as an LDAP directory has been tested with Microsoft, Netscape, IBM, and Novell.

Some of the features of the Domino Mail Server include

- Simplified administration using the Domino Administrator
- Outstanding support for mobile computing
- Built-in upgrade tools to move from other mail applications to Domino
- Standards-based Internet messaging
- Optional use of Lotus Notes mail or other popular email clients to access your mail on the Domino Mail Server
- Integrated services, such as calendaring and scheduling
- Integrated collaboration databases

The Domino Mail Server includes all the core Domino services that are embodied in all members of the Domino server family.

The Domino Application Server

The Domino Application Server provides all the basic services of the Domino Mail Server, including email, discussion databases, and calendaring and scheduling. In addition to discussion databases and mail databases, the Application Server can work with all other Domino databases. This includes databases built by application designers, databases used in workflow applications, and Notes application suites (many of them requiring additional licensing) such as LearningSpace and Domino.Doc.

One of the primary functions of the Domino Application Server is to serve Domino applications to Notes users. The server enforces security and provides communication services such as replication. All these features are available in some degree through the Domino Mail Server. But there is one service that truly distinguishes the Application Server from the Mail Server.

The Domino Application Server includes a Web Application Server that makes Domino Applications accessible from the World Wide Web. If you're familiar with earlier versions of Notes, you may well ask what is so special about that? Notes has been delivering documents to the Web on-the-fly since version 4.0. The difference with R5 is one of degrees. Not only are documents delivered to the Web on-the-fly, but they are done much more efficiently, and they are done with virtually full Notes functionality. There is very little that you can do in Notes that doesn't work equally well on the Web.

To help you understand the strength of Domino as a Web Application Server, I'll highlight some of the new Web server features in the Domino Application Server. The Web application services can be divided into three areas:

- Application design services
- Server enhancements
- Integration with IIS

Application Design Services

Part of the power of the Domino Application Server are the new features that have been added to the design of Notes applications, making Domino applications perfectly suited to the Web. These include the ease with which developers can move between different programming languages, including JavaScript, Java, HTML 4.0, and LotusScript. These languages are part of the IDE, not part of the server, but they make it possible to develop robust applications that can be delivered to either Notes or to the Web with full fidelity.

On the design side, the Domino Designer R5 includes its own Java editor and Java Virtual Machine for compiling Java applications. You can use JavaScript and HTML natively in the Notes client. This makes it possible to design applications that work the same way on the Web or within the Notes environment.

The other design enhancement that should be mentioned before looking more closely at the Domino Application Server is the Domino Enterprise Connection Services (DECS). DECS builds live links between Domino forms and relational databases. The DECS template enables you to associate fields and forms with external data and define settings for real-time connections. You can establish connections to DB2, Oracle, Sybase, EDA/SQL, and other databases. After the connections have been defined, the Domino Application Server takes over. An add-in task on the server passes instructions to the Domino Extension Manager, which monitors applications and waits for events that will trigger a real-time extension. For example, a user may want to perform a lookup on data that is stored in an external database. The Extension Manager then passes the query to the external database. The query is performed on the database; then the information is passed back to the Domino server and is displayed in the user's application. It takes place transparently, and users may not even be aware that the data they are seeing comes from a non-Notes source.

Domino 5.0 also includes the Common Object Request Broker Architecture (CORBA) support. CORBA technology is possible because of the Domino object model. Notes applications are created using object-oriented languages, and the Object Resource Broker (ORB) is able to deliver those objects to the end user in a dynamic environment. The user may be working with the objects using a Notes client or a Web browser. The user may be opening a local replica copy of the application or may be opening the application from a Domino server. The ORB transparently handles the object handling so that Web clients have access to virtually the same objects as Notes clients.

Ultimately, CORBA makes it possible to run Java applets that handle objects on the client side or the server side, depending on the type of client being used. Notes clients actually use the Java applet directly. For Web browser clients, the applet uses Internet Inter-ORB Protocol (IIOP) to talk to the Domino objects on the server. The end users see pretty much the same thing, whether they are using Notes or using the Web. But what they see is being accomplished in slightly different ways, with the same result.

CORBA moves as much of the processing as possible away from the Domino Application Server and onto the client, making R5 much more efficient. Domino services are projected to the client, and the end user works with the Domino objects locally.

Server Enhancements

One advantage of the integration between Notes and the Web is that Web applications can take advantage of the same robust security model that Notes uses. Domino R5 integrates SSL and can use X.509 certificates instead of Notes certificates, if desired. Domino also supports the Verisign Global Server IDs, which use a 128-bit cipher when communicating with International browsers and servers that use SSL with NNTP, LDAP, IMAP, or POP3.

Another security option that is new for Domino R5 is password quality testing. You can specify how complex passwords have to be, thus ensuring a certain level of security on the part of the end user, as well as enforcing security on the Domino server. The various security options enable you to reduce the complexity of security in your organization and minimize the duplication of data.

Perhaps the most visible enhancement to the Domino server is the Administrative client. This provides a standalone client for performing all administrative functions. The Administrative client features an extensive redesign that gives the Domino Administrator a multitude of options, using a graphical interface for controlling and tracking the Domino server.

Integration with IIS

The Domino server has delivered Domino documents to the Web since version R4. The Domino R5 HTTP engine has been enhanced, and it does an excellent job of rendering documents for both Web clients and Notes clients. As you have already seen, the built-in Java support makes the type of client nearly irrelevant to Domino. However, there are a few other Web server features that make Domino a world-class Web server:

- The capability of proxy servers and browsers of caching Domino pages and elements.
- Logging IP addresses or the hostname of the server that Web users request, which can be useful when looking at the statistics for virtual servers.
- Specifying how often a new Web log file is created. The default is for Domino to create new files daily.
- HTTP 1.1 byte-range serving, which enables users to download files in sections rather than all at once. This provides faster downloading of Web pages.
- The ability to write your own extensions to the Domino server using the Domino Web server Application Programming Interface (DSAPI).

Domino provides the numerous features and Web services, including serving up Web pages to the Internet. However, you do have the option of using Microsoft IIS as your HHTP stack instead of using Domino's own HTTP stack. You can still take full advantage of Domino's security, and have Domino serve up Web pages. This lets you use the strengths of the dynamic Domino environment, including features such as full text and view indexing, security, replication, and messaging—even while you are using Microsoft IIS to handle URL requests. Domino will continue to handle any URL requests that address Domino pages (URLs that include the .nsf extension). The two environments—Microsoft IIS and Domino—can run at the same time.

With IIS handling all the URL requests, the Domino server can be devoted to handling Notes requests. In this way, you get more mileage out of your server in environments where a single server has to handle a variety of tasks.

Let me summarize the Domino Application Server for you. The Domino Application Server provides all the services of the Domino Mail Server, plus it allows applications that go well beyond the simple discussion databases allowed when using the Domino Mail Server license. It includes the Web Application Server, which includes support for CORBA, making it possible to deliver the same functionality to clients who are using Notes or Web browsers. Among the key features are

- Enterprise system integration with Domino Enterprise Connection Services (DECS)
- Powerful collaboration between users, whether they are on Web browsers or Notes clients
- Simplified deployment and maintenance using the Domino Administrator, the Integrated Development Environment (IDE) of the Domino Designer, standards support, and robust features such as replication

The Domino Enterprise Server

Clustering on four or more processors is the feature that distinguishes the Domino Enterprise Server from the other members of the Domino server family. Clustering provides uninterrupted access to data and to Domino services through failover in both the Notes and the Web environments. Loads are balanced dynamically, ensuring optimum access to data.

With the Domino Enterprise Server, you can consolidate your Domino servers on larger machines through partitioning, and you can build clusters that run on a combination of Domino platforms across a LAN or high-speed WAN. The management of clusters is made simpler with the analysis tools that are built into the Domino Administrator. The analysis tools also can be used to track usage for billing, chargeback, and capacity planning purposes.

Clustering with the Domino Enterprise Server

One of the most frustrating things that can happen when surfing on the World Wide Web is nothing. You get no answer from a Web site, even though you know that you typed in the correct URL or followed a valid link. And it is rare that you have any idea why you get no response. Is the Internet choked with traffic? Did the Web site go out of business, or is the server offline for maintenance? Domino can't do much about the first two instances, but clustering with Domino servers makes the third alternative highly unlikely.

In this age of e-commerce, information has become probably the most important asset a company can have. As the importance of information becomes more apparent in today's global markets, so does the importance of 24/7 availability. You don't want to have any customers turned away by an unavailable server, the virtual equivalent of a busy signal in the online world.

Clustering on the Domino Enterprise Server has been available since Notes 4.0, which introduced Notes for Public Networks. Clustering provides bulletproof applications for Internet service providers and organizations that have large Notes deployments, sometimes in excess of 50,000 users. In clusters, replica copies of databases are maintained on the different servers. Then, if the server on which a user ordinarily accesses a database happens to be unavailable, Domino will failover to another available server in the cluster. This provides uninterrupted access to data and is transparent to the end user.

With Domino 5.0, clustering has been extended to the Internet with the Internet Cluster Manager (ICM) . ICM provides load balancing and failover for Notes and Web clients. The failover and balancing is done based on the type of content the user requests. The cluster uses event-driven replication to synchronize databases on the different servers.

The Domino Cluster Manager, a new server task, keeps tabs on all the servers in the cluster, including their availability and what replicas they have. The Cluster Manager routes users to the appropriate server, based on the information that is required and the current server load. For Internet requests, the ICM acts as a traffic director between HTTP requests and the different HTTP servers in the cluster. The ICM determines which server can best handle a particular HTTP request and passes the traffic to that server.

The ICM does the following:

- It monitors the servers in a cluster for availability.
- It monitors the Domino HTTP Web services for availability.
- It disallows connections to servers that are not currently in service.
- It provides failover to the best available server.

- It balances the load between servers in the cluster by monitoring availability thresholds.
- It supports virtual IP address and mapped ports.
- It provides content routing services for clients.

Basically, the ICM extends clustering services to Web clients as well as to Notes clients. If Web clients are using applications over an intranet or an extranet, they can be assured of the same reliable service they get from the Domino server when using Notes. The ICM handles HTTP and HTTPS requests to the Domino server, redirecting the requests until a session is established with the most suitable available server. ICM does not handle other protocols, including FTP, SMTP, or UDP.

The ICM should sit behind a firewall. From there, it can support the entire Domino security model for the Web. That includes logins and passwords. The ICM does not handle the security itself, but it can be configured to use SSL encryption to and from the servers in the cluster. As much as possible, the ICM is designed to be transparent to the system administrator. Note that each cluster must have its own ICM.

The Domino Enterprise Server is ideal for organizations that need a scalable computing platform. Additional servers can be added to a cluster at any time, making it easy to grow when additional computing power is required. The additional server can be a Windows NT, with each partitioned server running as a separate NT service; or you can add new partitioned servers on larger enterprise platforms, such as UNIX, AS/400, or S/390.

From Here...

Most of the remaining chapters in this book deal with one aspect or another of the Domino family of servers:

- Part VI, "Installing and Configuring the Domino Servers," deals with the details of setting up a Domino and Notes environment. The information in these chapters deals equally with every member of the Domino family of servers.
- Part VII, "Administering the Domino Servers," discusses the process of monitoring and administering a Domino environment. This also deals equally with all members of the Domino family of servers.
- Chapter 44, "Performance, Scalability, and Capacity Planning for Domino Servers," Chapter 46, "Using the Enterprise Domino Server with a Large Domino Network," and Chapter 48, "Using NotesPump and Domino Enhanced Search," deal primarily with the Domino Enterprise Server, but also include information relating to the Domino Application Server.
- Chapter 45, "Upgrading from cc:Mail, Microsoft Mail, and Exchange to Domino," and Chapter 47, "Integrating Domino with Phone, Fax, and Imaging Systems," deal with aspects of the Domino Mail Server and the use of Domino in an extended messaging environment.

CHAPTER 33

INITIAL PLANNING AND INSTALLATION

You have decided that Domino is for you. Now what? The first step to getting your Domino system up and running is planning. Planning is also probably your second and third step as well. With adequate planning, you'll find that your installation will be very smooth. Without it, you may find yourself doing extra work reorganizing and restructuring.

Domino is a very powerful system. Because installation is simple and the software is easy to use, you may think of Domino as an application, such as a spreadsheet program. But don't. Lotus Domino is more similar to a Windows NT or Novell Netware networking system in power and functionality.

So let's get started.

An Overview of Domino System Planning

When you first decide to implement a Domino system, you have many aspects to consider: managerial and financial, technical, and training issues. You should establish a team with people representing each of these various viewpoints. Many times, the people from different areas will be able to provide unique knowledge to the process. Here is a sample outline of how you might approach the planning and implementation process:

- Establish team
    - Management   Key management involvement improves the chances for successful deployment.
    - Technical   The Information Systems department can provide important technical information.
    - Users   The system exists to provide applications for users. Key users, especially power users, can supply information about which applications will produce the most benefit for the company.
- Establish strategy
    - Decide on initial and possible follow-on applications   Although email is probably one of your first applications, what will follow, and when?
    - Determine hardware and software requirements   Take into account not only your initial applications, but allow for growth in your follow-on applications.
    - Determine security requirements   Security should be an important consideration. Will your applications be used only internally or will you allow customers and partners to access your systems?
    - Determine training requirements   You must provide your users with training to work with any new systems. Training will almost always quickly pay for itself in increased productivity.
    - Determine human resource requirements, including the need for outside additional help, contractors, and consultants, if necessary.

- Divide team responsibilities and implementation
  - Financial, managerial   Typical tasks include budgeting and acquisition of hardware, software, and services.
  - Technical   Tasks involve the installation and deployment of the hardware and software.
  - Training   Training for users must be supplied either internally or externally.

Technical Planning for Your Domino Deployment

After you have outlined your company's plan for Domino deployment, you are ready to start the technical planning for the software itself. Here are some key questions:

- How many geographic locations will be involved? How many servers do you need?
- For each server, besides email, what applications will be used?
- How will you obtain software: purchase off the shelf, develop in-house, or contract with an outside firm to perform the initial development for you? Each option has different kinds of costs and benefits.
- Will you be doing Web serving from your Domino server?
- Will you be doing Internet News serving from your Domino server?
- Do you want to enable users to use additional Internet mail clients, such as Eudora or Microsoft Outlook Express?

After you have answered questions such as these, you are ready to consider how your organization will use Domino. Domino organizes servers and users with a concept called domains. Domain names such as lotus.com and microsoft.com are now familiar to most people. Although similar, Domino has its own concept of domain. To use Domino, you must first set up your own Domino domain.

Domino Domains

Domino uses the concept of domains to manage groups of servers. The information for all the users within one domain is stored in one Domino Directory, formerly called the Public Name and Address Book. This directory also contains information about your servers, connections, and configurations.

Normally, you will use one domain for your company, unless you have an exception, as described in the next section, "Naming Conventions." You should be aware that the Domino domain name is not necessarily the same as your Internet domain name. You can have a Domino domain with or without an Internet domain name. If you do have an Internet domain name, you may choose to use the same name for your Domino domain.

The major function of a Domino domain is for mail routing. Most small-to-medium deployments should use a single domain, because this will mean a single Domino directory to maintain. Even if you have multiple Domino servers, geographically separated, you should use a single Domino domain.

There are only a couple of specific cases where it may be advantageous to use multiple domains:

- You are using Domino as your Web server and you want to store external users in a separate Directory (Name and Address Book). The external users will then exist in a separate domain.
- You have a very large organization and you want to divide administrative responsibility into nonoverlapping groups. Each group will have its own domain and Domino Public Directory.

Naming Conventions

After you decide on your domain name, you need to consider the naming conventions for your company. Names in Domino are arranged in a hierarchical structure. The organization name, which is usually the company name, is at the top of the hierarchy. Within the organization, you can have up to four layers of organizational units (OUs). Figure 33.1 shows a hierarchy with one organization (Acme) and two layers of organizational units.

Figure 33.1
Organizations can contain organizational units and users.

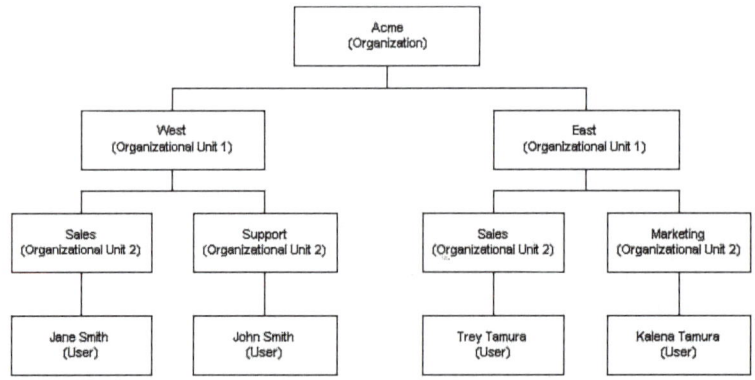

Notice in Figure 33.1 that two organizational units can have the same name if they are in different locations within the hierarchy. When you write a hierarchical name, you start from the bottom of the hierarchy. For example, in Figure 33.1, one user is John Smith/Support/West/Acme.

You do not have to have multiple layers of organizational units. In fact, you should probably limit yourself to the fewest number that is consistent with your actual organizational structure. For example, if you have a very small company and you are located in one physical location, you may not need any organizational units. The only required level in the naming convention is the organizational level. You can add users directly to this level if you like.

On the other hand, suppose you have three physical locations around the country. In this case, you might want to have the organization and three organizational units at the next level down, based on geographical location.

Even if you have a very large company, you should be able to manage with, at most, two levels of organizational units in addition to the Organization level. Having the right number of levels can ease your administrative burden, but having too many levels can add unneeded complexity and will generate extra work.

Organizational unit levels are important because usernames must be unique. If you have too many users within the organization or organizational unit, you increase the chances of having duplicate names. For example, you might have several users with the name John Smith. This is a problem if they are in the same organizational unit, but it is not a problem if they are in different OUs.

Hierarchical Names

I have shown you a user's hierarchical name:

```
John Smith/Support/West/Acme/US
```

This syntax is actually called the abbreviated format for the hierarchical name. In addition to the abbreviated format, you will sometimes see names in their canonical format. In canonical format, each name also has its component explicitly named. For example, here is the same hierarchical name shown in canonical format:

```
CN=John Smith/OU=Support/OU=West/O=Acme/C=US
```

In this syntax, CN stands for common name, OU stands for organizational unit, O stands for organization, and C stands for country. The CN component can have up to 80 characters, each OU can have 32 characters, the O component can have 3 to 64 characters, and the country code (C) can be omitted or have 2 letters. The country codes are fixed, and if used, they must match a valid country code. You may add a country code only if your country's clearinghouse for X.500 names has approved your organization name. The country code is frequently omitted.

As mentioned, you can have up to four OU components. The order in which they appear is significant. The rightmost OU is OU1; in the example, it would be West. The next OU to the left is called OU2, and in our example is Support. In the canonical name, you use the generic code OU. You do not include the number when specifying the name in canonical format. The numeric convention is used only so you can distinguish between the different organizational units for discussion.

Certification

How do User IDs get created? User IDs are files that are generated and then authorized through the certification process. In essence, a known entity, called the certifier, marks the

User ID file with an official stamp. This stamp is called a certificate and uses encryption technology to ensure that it could have been placed there only by a valid certifier. When servers and other users need to verify that the User ID is valid, they look at the certificate to make sure that they can trust the user.

For the organization and each different organizational unit, you need to have a certifier. Thus, if you use only the organizational level, you will have only one certifier ID. If you have many levels with many different organizational units (OU), you need a separate certifier for each OU. This is why many companies use geography as a basis for their organizational units. For example, suppose you have branch offices in North Haven, Connecticut; Denver, Colorado; and Irvine, California. With three organizational units, you could have a local administrator in each location, each using his or her own local certifier ID. Each administrator can update the common Domino Directory, and users can be conveniently added in each location. In this example, you would use the organization level and one organizational unit level. Example names might be Fred Smith/NHV/Acme, Sue Jones/IRV/Acme, or Tom Terrific/DEN/Acme.

When you first install Domino, you set up your first certifier ID, which can then be used to set up any additional OU certifier IDs if necessary.

> **Caution**
>
> The organization certifier ID file is probably the most important file in your Domino system installation. If a person can access this file and knows the password, he or she can access any database in your system. With the certifier ID file, the person can create additional user IDs, thus potentially impersonating anyone in the system, including you. Be very careful with this file from two perspectives:
>
> - Security   Do not allow unauthorized users to access this file.
> - System Integrity   Do not lose, fold, spindle, or mutilate this file. If you lose it, you cannot create a replacement file. Back this file up, and make sure you carefully control the backup copy of the file as well.
>
> You should use similar precautions for each of your OU certifier files as well.

Naming Convention Recommendations

Although the naming conventions may seem arbitrary, they are very critical, because if you decide to change the conventions at a later time, it may require a lot of work. If you change your organizational structure, you need to recertify all the User IDs that have been created and probably change the Access Control Lists (ACLs) for every database in your system. Save yourself some time and think about this topic carefully before you start. Here are some recommendations. The software does not require them, but experience shows they are very useful rules of thumb:

- Do not use spaces within any of your organization, organizational unit, or server names. If you use spaces, you need to supply double-quotation marks any time you refer to the names later.

- Your organization (and organizational unit) name(s) should be relatively short. They will be used very frequently. As a guideline, use at least three, and no more than eight, characters.

- If you are using geographically-based organizational units, include the location in the name. You could use city, state, or region abbreviations. Be careful in using city abbreviations if your office might move. For example, if you're located in Los Angeles, you might use LA as the organizational unit name. However, if you later move to San Francisco, all the names within the organizational unit may have to be changed. Another choice might be WEST instead of LA.

- An optional two-letter country code may be associated at the organizational level. The codes themselves are predefined and follow the X.500 naming conventions. You may use this component only if your organization name has been approved by your country's X.500 clearinghouse.

- The common name (CN—lowest in the hierarchy) for servers should be unique within the hierarchy. Although you can have duplicates because of the hierarchical nature of the names, do not depend on this to distinguish between servers. Other components of the operating system and networking software may use the common name only to identify the server.

- I would recommend at least one level of organizational unit (OU) below the organization level for most medium-sized companies. Even the largest companies can usually organize their naming conventions with no more than two levels of OU below the organization level. These are only guidelines, however, and your mileage may vary.

Before you actually start installing the Domino system files, you should develop your organizational naming scheme. While you are installing the system, you will be asked questions such as the name of your domain, your certifier, and so forth. If you have already mapped out your domain and naming conventions, answering these questions will be easy. Don't try to make up the answers as you fill in the blanks. Naming conventions are painful to change later, but they are easy to implement if done when you first install the system.

Initial Setup of the Installation Files

Okay, now that you have planned your Domino system, you have decided on your domain name and hierarchical names, and you understand certification, you are ready to install your Domino server. Lotus has greatly simplified the installation, so it is relatively simple. There are two separate phases to the installation:

1. Copy the files from the CD to your hard disk.
2. Run a Notes database application that customizes your installation and creates your ID files and initial databases.

You can install from a distribution CD, or you can access the installation files over a network. In either case, here is how to install Domino for Windows NT:

1. Locate the directory containing the installation files—either from the CD, hard disk, or network—and start the Setup program.
2. You will see an introduction screen. Click Next to see the license agreement. Read the license agreement carefully. Assuming you agree with the terms, click Yes.
3. You will then see a dialog box containing room for your name and company name. Fill in this box. You may also select an option to install a partitioned server. Partitioned servers are mainly for Internet service providers or others that want to support multiple Web sites from a single hardware platform. It essentially allows multiple logical servers on a single hardware box. Normally, you leave this option disabled. Click Next.
4. You now see a screen to enter the folder names for the Domino program files and Domino data. You should store the programs and data in separate folders. See Figure 33.2. I keep the data in a completely separate folder tree from the programs. This is because I sometimes need to replace all the programs, but I would rarely, if ever, need to replace the data files. Keeping them in separate folder trees allows me to manipulate the programs without affecting the data. After you have chosen the folders, click Next.

Figure 33.2
Choose the folders for the Domino programs and data.

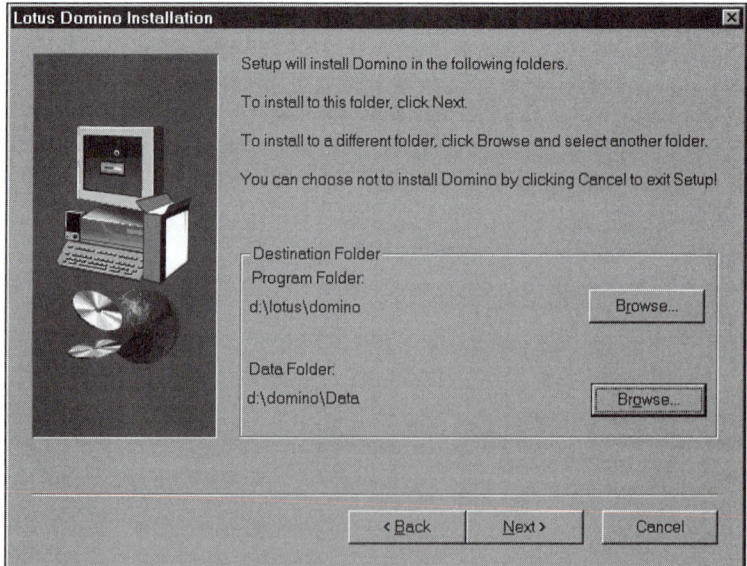

Tip

Some prior releases of Notes and Domino stored both the client and server software and data together. In release 5, however, the default is for the client software to be stored separately from the server software. The client data is data used by the Notes client software, but running on the same machine as the Domino server. In particular, this means two sets of file folders and two different Notes.ini files. I use \lotus\domino\ for server software, \lotus\notes\ for client software, \domino\data\ for server data, and \notes\data\ for client data. You, of course, can use any other names, but I would

INITIAL SETUP OF THE INSTALLATION FILES | 765

> recommend that you keep the client and server data separate. Also, you should keep each Notes.ini file in the file folder containing the programs that are associated with it. Do not store the Notes.ini file in the Windows directory, which was the convention of previous releases of Notes and Domino.

5. The next screen enables you to choose from the three different Domino servers: Domino Application Server, Domino Mail Server, and Domino Enterprise Server. The standard Domino server is also sometimes called the Domino Application Server. The install procedure for these three options is very similar, so I will describe only the standard Domino server. See Figure 33.3.

Figure 33.3
Choose the Domino server you have licensed.

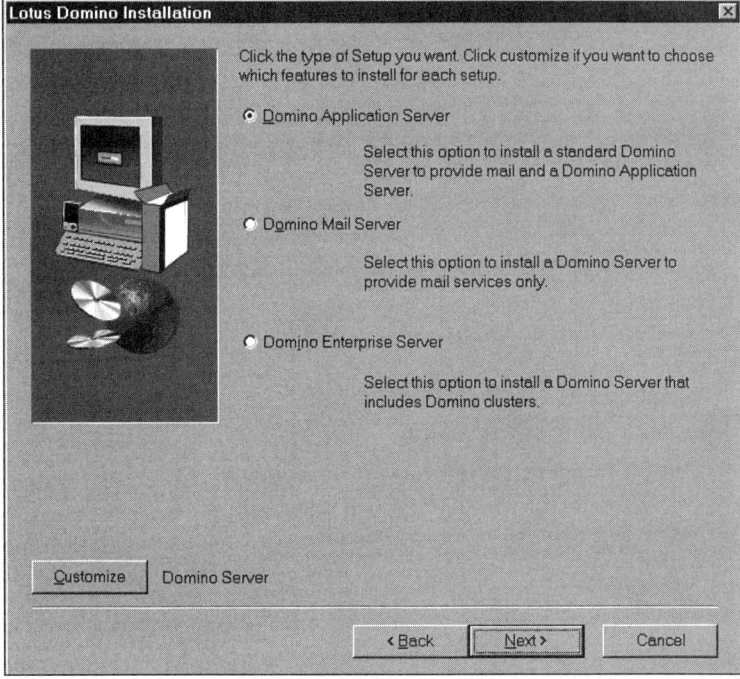

6. After you choose the radio button for the server you have licensed, you can click the Customize button to see additional options. See Figure 33.4.

7. You should normally install any files that have been selected by default. The option to run Domino as an NT service starts up Domino automatically when NT starts. If you choose this option, however, Domino starts up without a console window, so you will not be able to type any commands locally, nor will you be able to see any initial output. I recommend that when you are installing Domino for the first time, you leave this option disabled. Note that you can also start Domino automatically (with a live local console) by placing it in the Startup group of Windows NT. This is a security versus

PART
VI
CH
33

convenience issue. Some administrators prefer *not* to have a Domino console available at the server, and others prefer to have it available. After Domino has been installed, you can administer it from a Notes client, even if there is no console window open on the server.

Figure 33.4
You can add some optional features via Customize.

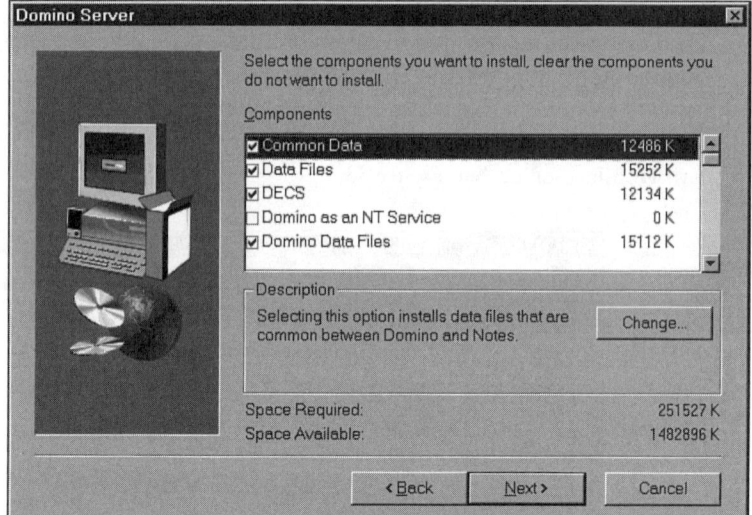

8. Click Next and you can specify a folder for the program icons. The default folder is Lotus Applications. You can use this folder or choose another. When you are ready to start copying files, click Next.

   Your files are now copied to the folders you have specified.

9. After your files are copied, you will see a dialog box to enter your registration information. Fill in this dialog box and click Next, or click Exit to skip the registration.

10. Click Finish to complete the initial phase of your installation. You will then be prompted to restart the operating system. Restart your operating system at this point.

Now that you have copied the files, start the Domino server by opening the folder containing the Domino server icon. Double-click on the icon to start the server. Alternatively, you can select Programs, Lotus Applications, Lotus Domino Server from the Windows menus. Actually, the first time you run the server, it invokes the Notes client to lead you through the setup.

After the Notes client starts, you see a screen similar to Figure 33.5.

Let's examine the installation of the first Domino server.

INSTALLING YOUR FIRST DOMINO SERVER | 767

Figure 33.5
The initial setup screen for Domino installation.

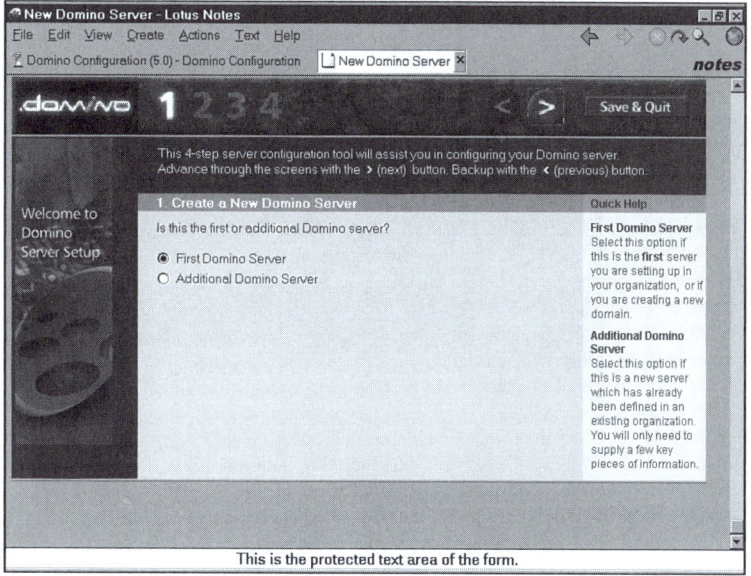

INSTALLING YOUR FIRST DOMINO SERVER

From the initial screen, select First Domino Server and click the Next button (>).

> **Note** Although there are only two options: First Domino server and Additional Domino server, you might have the following situation. You have a single Domino server running 4.x, but you want to upgrade it to 5.0. In this case, use the First Domino Server option. The Additional Domino Server option is reserved for the case when you are installing a second server while the original server is up and running. If you are upgrading a single server from 4.x to 5.0, you should take your 4.x server down while installing 5.0. As in any upgrade of major software, carefully consider your options before overlaying your running 4.x system with 5.0, however. See Chapter 34, "Upgrading from Domino R4.x to R5," for more details.

The second setup screen is shown in Figure 33.6.

The quick and easy setup uses several defaults for choices. This does not necessarily limit your installation, because you can always add and/or install features later, after you perform the initial installation. For now, let's just continue with the quick and easy installation. Click the Next button (>). See Figure 33.7.

The Domino server is always available to Notes clients. In addition to Notes clients, you can select from four optional additional client types. See Figure 33.7. These optional client types are

- **Web Browsers** For example, Microsoft Internet Explorer and Netscape Navigator. This establishes the HTTP protocol.

PART
VI
CH
33

- **Internet Mail Packages** For example, Lotus mail, Eudora, or Microsoft Outlook Express. This enables POP3 and IMAP. SMTP is always available.
- **News Readers** For example, Netscape Navigator or Microsoft Outlook Express.
- **Enterprise Connection Services (DECS)** This supplies access to non-Notes data via connections to external database systems, such as Oracle, DB2, ODBC, and so forth.

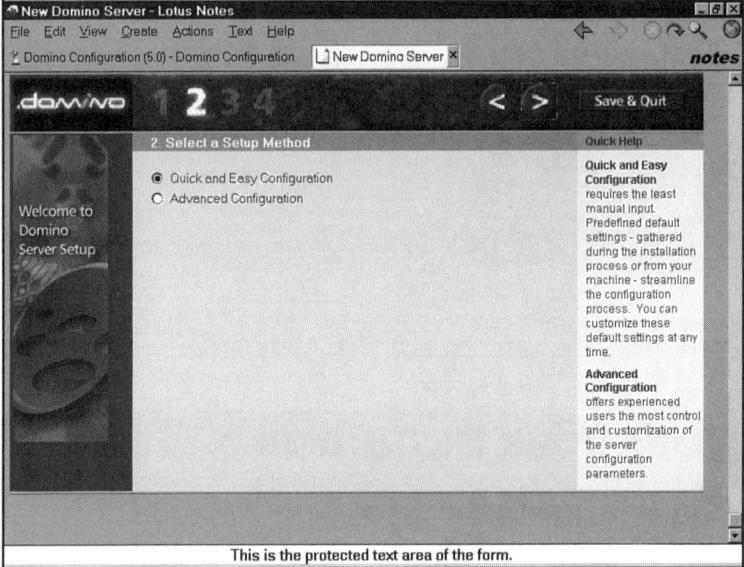

Figure 33.6
You can choose the quick and easy setup or the advanced setup.

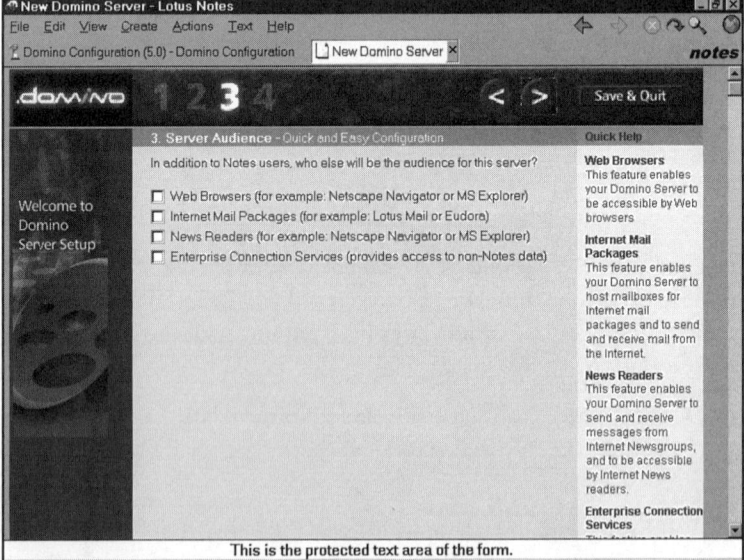

Figure 33.7
Choose the quick and easy setup to continue.

INSTALLING YOUR FIRST DOMINO SERVER 769

Choose the additional server audience features that you want to use and click the Next button (>). See Figure 33.8.

Figure 33.8
You must supply a few final parameters to set up your server.

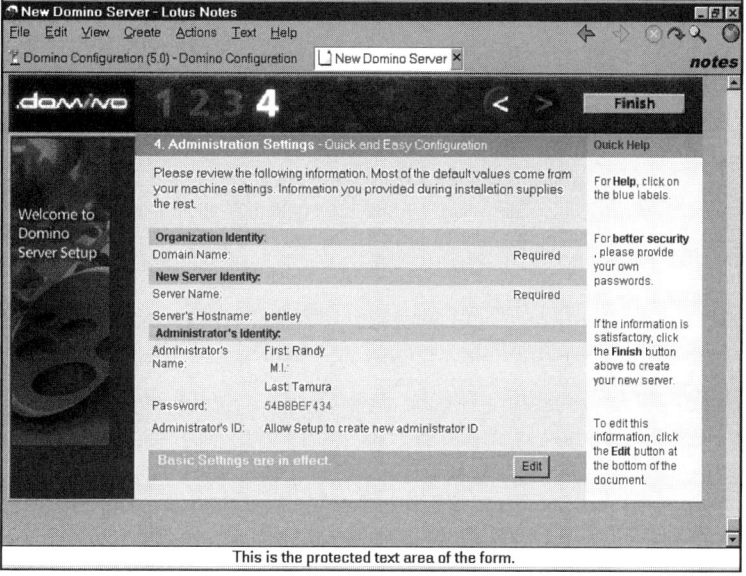

If your page is not in edit mode, click the Edit button in the lower-right corner of the window. See Figure 33.9.

Figure 33.9
Supply the domain name, certifier name, server name, and administrator's name.

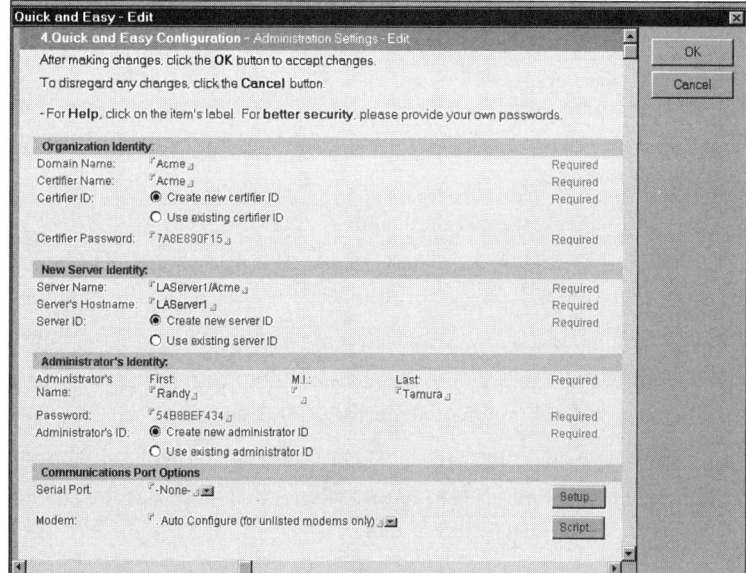

PART
VI
CH
33

In Figure 33.9, you see that you must supply the domain name, certifier's name, server name, and administrator's name. You can use the same name for both the domain and certifier if you like. The server name can be the same name as the server's hostname, but you should add the domain name as well.

> **Tip**
>
> When you create the administrator's ID file, you should normally leave off the middle initial, because the email ID consists of the fields you enter. If you include a middle initial, users must also include this initial when sending mail. Also, normally, it is easy to guess another employee's email address if it consists of only a first and last name. If you include the middle initial, it would be very hard to guess another employee's email address, because a user would have to guess (or know) the person's middle initial.

Click on Finish to finish your installation. It will take several minutes for the Domino server to set up your Domino Public Directory, certifier, server, and user ids.

After all the information has been set up, you will see the Congratulations screen. At this point, you can either initialize the ACLs for your databases or you can exit the installation. I recommend that you set the ACLs before exiting. This step enables you to control access to some of your key databases. You will be able to add an Administrators group and/or an Anonymous user ID setting. Follow the onscreen instructions and recommendations.

Congratulations. You have installed your Domino server. You can now start the server from the operating system. The Domino server will create a few databases when it first starts, and then the Domino server will be operational.

CREATING A CERTIFICATION LOG

Domino has the capability of logging the creation of all servers and users. By default, however, this logging is not enabled. To enable logging, you must create a certification log. In general, I recommend that you create this log, even though it is not required. By having a log, you create an audit trail, and you might find the information useful in the future. Creating the log is very easy:

1. In a Notes client, select File, Database, New.
2. In the New Database dialog box, choose the server name where you will register your users. You can click on the drop-down button or manually type the name of the server.
3. Click (enable) the Show Advanced templates check box at the bottom of the dialog box.
4. Click the Template Server button. Choose the name of your registration server or any other server that contains the Certification Log template.
5. In the Title field, enter Certification log or some name of your choosing.
6. For the filename, enter CERTLOG.NSF. Note that you *must* use the filename CERTLOG.NSF; you cannot choose a different name.

7. Click the OK button to create the certification log.
8. After it has been created, update the database ACL by adding administrators that will register users and servers. Give these administrators Editor level access to the database.

Creating Organizational Unit (OU) Certifiers

During the installation of your first server, Domino automatically creates a Server ID file, an organization certifier ID file, and a User ID file for the administrator. Remember from the previous discussion that OUs are part of the naming hierarchy for your organization. If you see a name such as `Clark Kent/Sales/West/Acme`, the names `Sales` and `West` represent organizational unit names. `Acme` is the organization name, and `Clark Kent` is the username.

To create and use hierarchical naming, you must create an OU certifier for each organizational unit. When you first register each user, you supply a certifier ID file. If you use the organizational certifier ID, the user is placed at the organization level. If you use a lower-level OU certifier ID file, the user is placed within that OU.

If you will be using at least one level of OU below the organizational level (normally recommended), you need to create an OU certifier ID file. Fortunately, this is very easy. To create an OU certifier, you start up the Domino Administrator client:

1. From the Domino Administrator client, click the Configuration tab.
2. In the Tools Pane on the right side of the screen, click on the Registration twistie and click Organizational Unit. You will be prompted to enter the password of the default certifier ID.
3. You can either enter the certifier ID password *or* you can click Cancel. If you click Cancel, you are prompted to locate another certifier ID. This other certifier ID can be located elsewhere in the organization's hierarchy. Enter the password for the ID file you choose. You will see the Register Organizational Unit Certifier dialog box. See Figure 33.10.
4. In the OU certifier dialog box, you can change the registration server by clicking the designated button. The Certifier ID button is used to change the location in the hierarchy where this OU will be located. In Figure 33.10, the organization certifier is specified, so the new OU will be the highest-level OU. You can change the location of the output ID file by clicking the Set ID File button. As mentioned, guard your certifier ID files carefully.
5. Enter the organizational unit name and password. The Password quality scale enforces passwords to be more or less difficult to guess, either manually or via program. The scale is from 0 to 16—the larger the number, the more secure the password.
6. At the bottom, choose the security type: North American or International. Also enter the name of the administrator that should receive certification requests. You can optionally include a location or comment.

Figure 33.10
You must create an OU certifier for each organizational unit.

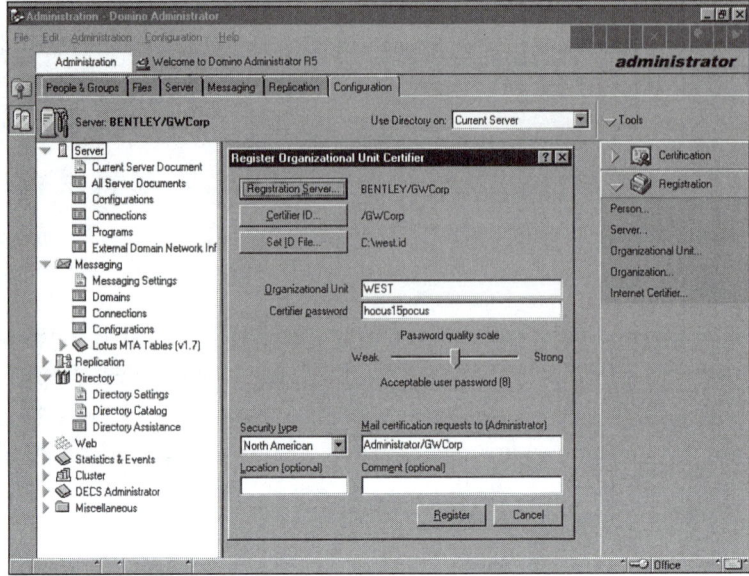

7. When you have finished filling in the dialog box, click Register. The process may take several minutes to complete, depending upon the speed of your processor.

After the process completes, you should see a message indicating that the ID file was created successfully.

After you create an organizational unit certifier, you can use this certifier ID to register other users. The certifier ID created in Figure 33.10 is /WEST/GWCorp. A sample user created with this ID file is John Doe/WEST/GWCorp.

INSTALLING ADDITIONAL DOMINO SERVERS

Lotus distinguishes between setting up the first server and setting up any additional servers, because there are some initial tasks required for setting up the first server that are not required (and should not be performed) for the second and subsequent servers.

In particular, here are some important tasks that are performed for the first server, but should not be performed again:

- The organization certifier ID is created. This is a one-time event. If this task is repeated, the second organization ID is considered a separate organization, *even if you use the same textual name.*

- The organization's Public Directory (Name and Address Book) is created and initialized. This task should not be repeated for subsequent servers or users.

There are actually two ways to register an additional Domino Server when you have at least one server running. Registration really consists of creating a server ID file and having the ID file certified. To register a new server, you can do one of the following:

- Use the Domino Administrator client to register the new server.
- Register the server when you actually install the software on the computer.

USING THE DOMINO ADMINISTRATOR TO REGISTER A NEW SERVER

To register a new server using the Domino Administrator client:

1. Open the Domino Administrator and click on the Configuration tab.
2. In the Tools Pane on the right, click on Registration, Server. You will see a dialog box requesting a certifier password.
3. You can either enter the certifier ID password *or* you can click Cancel. If you click Cancel, you are prompted to locate another certifier ID. This certifier ID can be located elsewhere in the organization's hierarchy. Enter the password for the ID file you choose. You will then see the Register Servers dialog box. See Figure 33.11.

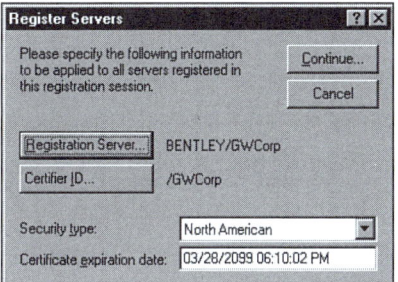

Figure 33.11
You can register a server via the Domino Administrator client.

4. From the dialog box, you can pick the registration server and the certifier ID. Click Continue to see the Register Servers dialog box shown in 33.12.

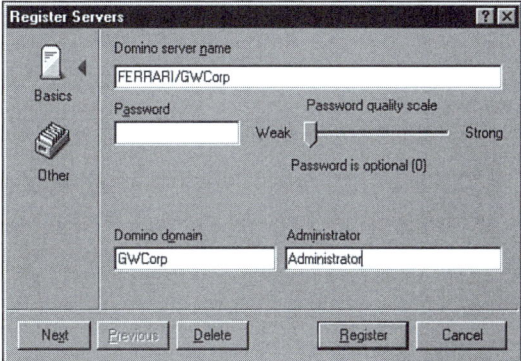

Figure 33.12
You can leave the password quality 0 for a server.

5. Enter the server's name and, optionally, a password, domain, and administrator. You may want to leave the password blank for a server. This enables the server to start up unattended. If you include a password, an operator must enter the password in order for the server to start up. Normally, you want to locate the server and server console in a locked environment, which enables you to configure the server to start without a password.

6. After you enter the basics, you may want to include some of the fields on the Other tab. These fields include the server title, network name, and information about where to store the server ID. When you have completed entering all your information, click the Register button and your server will be registered.

After the server is registered, the server's ID file is created. You need to use this ID file when you actually install the software from the CD-ROM.

Registering an Additional Server While Installing

When you install the code for a server, you can specify whether the server will be the first server or an additional server. In previous sections, I covered material for the first server.

Installing an additional server is very similar to installing the first server except that the Domino Public Directory (Name and Address book) is not created and a certifier ID is not created. Also, you first need to create a Server ID file and certify it, using the Administration client, prior to copying and configuring the server itself. You can create the ID file and save it to a file, or you can store it in the Public Directory. If you store it in the Public Directory, you must enter a password for the ID file.

The installation process copies the files from the CD-ROM or network to your hard disk, as described previously. Then you launch the Notes client, which will guide you through the customization database.

After the files have been copied to the server, the Notes portion of the server installation will start when you first start the server. On the first server setup screen, you click the radio button Additional Domino Server. See Figure 33.13.

At this point, you can choose either the quick-and-easy install or the advanced configuration. I've already shown you the quick-and-easy configuration, so let's now look at the advanced configuration screen. See Figure 33.14.

Basically, the advanced configuration screen enables you to specify which server tasks will be initialized when Domino starts up. There are seven sections in the advanced configuration:

- Standard Services are always installed and include Administration Process, Agent Manager, Indexer, Mail Router, and Replicator.
- Additional Services are commonly used, but are optional services, such as Calendar Connector, Event Manager, Schedule Manager, and Statistics.
- Web Browsers means that you will access the Domino server from browsers. In essence, this starts up the HTTP Web server. IIOP can also be selected if you will be creating applications that use Java to access Domino Databases from browsers. Usually, IIOP

will be most useful in intranet situations rather than the Internet, because the Java downloaded code is very large.

- Internet Mail Packages allow you to enable the mail protocols IMAP, POP3, or SMTP.
- Internet Directory Services allows you to enable LDAP.
- News Readers enables NNTP services.
- Enterprise Connection Services, DECS, enables Domino applications to easily access relational databases, such as Oracle or other SQL databases.

Figure 33.13
Click the Additional Domino Server button for the second and subsequent server installations.

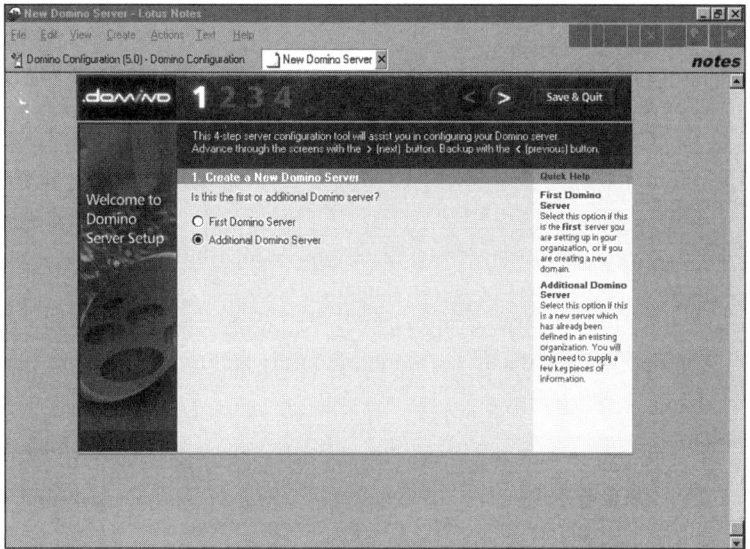

Figure 33.14
Choose which server tasks Domino will initialize at startup at the advanced configuration screen.

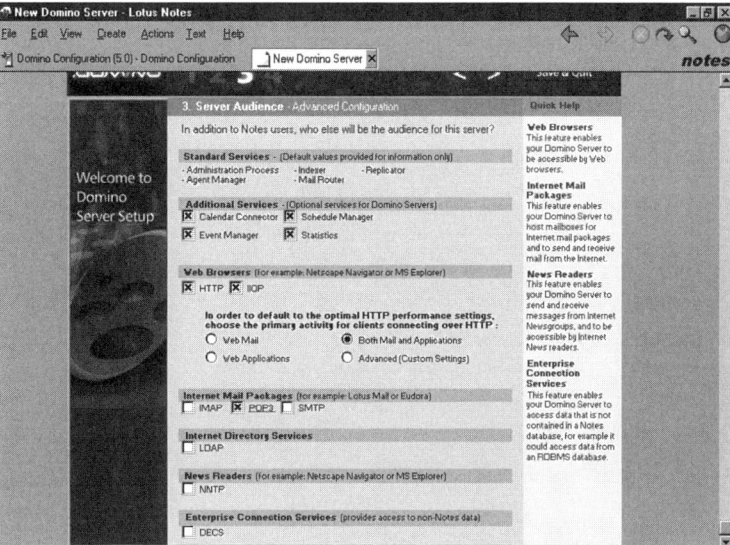

From Here...

In this chapter, I told you about the importance of planning your Notes and Domino installation prior to installing the software. Understanding domains and setting up a naming convention for your network are critical. After you have installed your system, you may want to find out additional information. Here are some additional topics you may find useful:

- Chapter 35, "Initial Configuration of Servers with the Domino Directories," gives you additional detailed information about your installation.
- Chapter 34, "Upgrading from Domino R4.x to R5," gives you essential information you need to know about upgrading.
- Chapter 36, "Domino Security Overview," provides you with information about the Domino security system and how you can configure and use it.
- Chapter 38, "Administering Users, Groups, and Certification," covers information about adding and removing users from your system and how to do it efficiently and effectively.
- Chapter 39, "Administering Electronic Mail," shows you how to set up your email system. If you are using Domino email, you should read this chapter.
- The additional chapters in Part VII, "Administering the Domino Servers," cover replication, files and databases, troubleshooting and more.

CHAPTER 34

UPGRADING FROM DOMINO R4.X TO R5

Having learned from the upgrade from R3 to R4, Lotus Development has carefully thought out the upgrade from R4.x to R5 to minimize the impact on your infrastructure. However, this also implies that you follow some key advice, which we will discuss in this chapter.

To start, Lotus ensures that the two environments, R4.x and R5, are entirely compatible, that coexistence should be painless, and that the upgrade should proceed without snags. Lotus claims that

- The Notes R4 client features are retained in the Notes R5 client. For example, you can decide to retain the R4 workspace environment as the Notes R5 startup page, so that it looks very similar to the R4 client, and still benefit from the bookmarking capability of R5.
- The Domino R5 Directory is built to respond equally to all R4 Notes clients and Domino servers. On the client side, both R4 and R5 Notes clients can access the R5 Domino Directory. On the server side, R4 and R5 servers can share the same directory, providing that you upgrade the R4 Public Address Book to the R5 Domino Directory design. In short, R4 clients work with Domino R5 servers, and Notes R5 clients work with Domino/Notes R4.x servers.
- All R4 applications can run on R5. However, as with all software upgrades, R4 clients cannot access new features of R5 applications. Before enhancing applications with R5 features, you should wait until all clients have been upgraded to R5.

Lotus has extensively tested the upgrade from all the different versions—4.1x, 4.5x, and 4.6x—so that you do not have to go, for instance, from R4.1 to R4.5 and then R4.5 to R5.0. According to Lotus, you can safely move directly from your current Domino/Notes version(s) to R5, without first upgrading to the latest R4.6x version.

An Overview of the General R4-to-R5 Upgrade Process

As with the upgrade from R3 to R4, it is strongly recommended that you upgrade your infrastructure in the following order:

1. R4 servers (which includes upgrading to the R5 Directory, formerly known as the Public Name and Address Book)
2. Notes R4 clients
3. R4 applications

Technically, this sequence brings resilience to your infrastructure. As mentioned earlier, R5 servers and clients are backward-compatible with their R4 counterparts. Additionally, your infrastructure automatically gains in functionality and performance without changing server configurations, topology, mail routing, or addressing. It also goes without saying that you cannot make changes to your topology at the same time.

Phase 1: The Server Upgrade Process

After completing your upgrade, your organization can immediately take advantage of R5's advanced features, such as more efficient searching, transactional logging for databases, and ESMTP. Or you may choose to redesign your mail routing scheme to take advantage of the availability of SMTP on every node.

Note, however, that new features, such as transaction logging and domain searching, are not enabled by default when you upgrade to R5. Your Notes/Domino network will be configured just as it was prior to the upgrade. Therefore, you decide if, and when, you need to enable these R5 features.

Upgrading Domino server software to R5 is a fast process. Most of the time is spent on compacting databases and rebuilding views, which is optional. Therefore, the time it actually takes to upgrade a server depends mostly on the amount of data on the server and the speed of the server's processor.

To minimize the upgrade's impact, upgrade your R4 servers in the following sequence:

1. Within your production environment, choose an isolated R4 server for the first upgrade, because you will be prompted to upgrade your organization's Public Address Book to the Domino R5 Directory. When you are assured about the R5 server backward-compatibility and at ease with the new Domino Administrator for server administration, move to the next step.
2. The safest next move is to upgrade your hub servers, because they are traditionally not accessed by users directly. Thus, users are less likely to be directly affected by any problems that might occur during the initial upgrade. This also enables you to benefit from R5's enhanced performance.
3. Upgrade your mail servers progressively.
4. Upgrade your application servers, after testing each application on an R5 server. For gateways and other third-party applications, Lotus Development recommends that you check with the software vendor to ensure that its applications support and interoperate with R5.

Phase 2: Client Upgrades

Client upgrades can be performed using the upgrade-by-mail capability; users receive an email that upgrades their desktop automatically, via a button. This functionality also enables the user to choose the most convenient time for the upgrade. When the user clicks on the button, the user's mail file, calendar, and Personal Address Book templates are upgraded automatically.

Administrators can configure the Notes R5 startup page to show the familiar R4 Workspace as the startup screen. This gives Notes users the familiar R4 look-and-feel to start with, thus reducing training time and letting users become accustomed to the new client gradually.

The good news is that when upgraded to R5, administrators can automatically gain more control over Notes users' desktops. With R5, a broad spectrum of client configuration information is maintained in the R5 Domino Public Directory and can be dynamically updated. These include

- Notes browser settings
- All proxies
- Search server
- Bookmarks
- Local replicas
- Mobile Directory setup
- Passthru server
- All Internet accounts
- Applet/Java security and settings

Phase 3: Application Upgrades

Existing R4 applications work on Domino R5 servers without modification. However, you should plan a testing phase of your critical and complex applications prior to deploying them to your user base.

After servers and workstations are running Domino and Notes R5, developers can safely begin to introduce new R5 functionality into existing applications, and can create new applications using features introduced in R5.

Notes R4 users who attempt to use parts of the application that are R5-based, such as tabbed tables, will be unable to see those features, and thus may experience confusing results. Such problems may also lead to an increase in end user calls to your internal support staff. Therefore, do not include R5 features in applications until all Notes clients have been upgraded to R5.

The Five Stages of Your Domino/Notes Upgrade

The upgrade of a mission-critical business utility such as your Domino/Notes messaging, groupware, and Internet infrastructure should not take place in one jolt; rather, it is more effectively executed in stages. There are five stages to a full upgrade: planning, testing, pilot, production, and leveraging.

Planning

Pre-upgrade planning is probably the most critical element of a successful upgrade.

Time invested in planning saves time later in the project and results in a quicker overall implementation with fewer unanticipated problems and headaches. During the planning stage, you should evaluate new features in Domino and Notes R5 and identify "big wins" for your organization, such as performance improvements and other enhancements that make your organization more efficient and productive. You should also create a detailed upgrade schedule.

Notes R5 is available on the Windows 95, 98, and NT, and MAC Power PC platforms. Users on other platforms need to stay with Notes R4.5x clients, move to a new operating system, or use a Web browser to access their Domino mail and applications. In addition, customers should consider the infrastructure benefits of new R5 features, such as those detailed in the following sections. Server R5 platforms include Windows NT4.0/Intel, Windows NT4.0/Alpha, AIX 4.3.1, HP-UX 11.0, Solaris/SPARC 2.6, Solaris/Intel 2.6, OS/2 Warp Server 4, AS/400 V4R2, and S/390 V2R6. Support for IBM OS/2 Warp Server 4 and Macintosh is available at the time of this writing. Releases for HP-UX 11.0, IBM AS/400, and IBM S/390 will be available at a later stage.

Public Address Book Changes

Upgrading the R4 Public Address Book is one of the first steps in an R4-to-R5 upgrade. The file format (ODS) for all databases, including the Public Address Book, is different in R5 than in R4, in order to support new features and improve performance and scalability. After upgrading the Directory, you should replicate the new Directory template to all other servers in the domain—both R4 and R5 servers. For ease of administration, you should install the new R5 Administration Client on at least one server, when the R5 Directory template is universally available.

Transaction Logging

Domino R5 offers superior data integrity. To maximize the efficiency of transaction logging, you should use a separate, single-purpose disk to hold the log files for transaction logging: minimal disk arm movement enables faster writes to the log. Note that transaction logging is disabled by default, so you decide how and when to best implement it.

New Network Configuration and Management Options

Domino R5 makes it much easier to configure and manage multiple Domino Domains. In particular, the new R5 "cross-domain" Administration Client enables you to move users and databases with drag-and-drop ease and access any server in any domain.

New Search Features

Domino R5's new domain search capability enables you to index and search an entire domain of Domino databases, including attachments to Notes documents and files stored in the file system. In R5, individual database indexes are larger than in R4 (as much as 50%, depending on the content indexed). However, if you eliminate indexes from several replica databases by using domain indexing, you save disk space overall because, in effect, you index only one replica of the database. If you choose to implement the domain index feature, you should dedicate a server as the Domain Catalog server. That way, the server can be fully dedicated as the indexing and search engine for the domain. A multiple-CPU system with adequate RAM and disk capacity will significantly increase search efficiency.

NEW DIRECTORY CATALOG

In R5, the Directory Catalog compresses one or more Domino Directories for fast, easy address lookups. For example, a 1GB Domino Directory can be compressed into a 12MB Directory Catalog—ideal for mobile users.

PASSWORD QUALITY CHECKING FOR NOTES CLIENTS

In R4, Notes clients checked only password length. Now the Notes client enforces both password length and quality, which means that users cannot reuse old passwords, and that passwords can be set to incorporate capital and lowercase letters as well as numbers. While upgrading to R5, organizations may also plan to upgrade Notes R4 security standards to optimize on cost savings.

SYSTEM TEMPLATE CUSTOMIZATIONS

If your organization has customized any R4 system templates or database files (such as the Name and Address Book and the mail template), you need to document these changes now, and, given the many new features in R5, evaluate whether the changes are still needed.

TESTING

In this phase, the upgrade team should set up a small test environment. In the pilot phase, you use this test environment to perform a test upgrade to R5. The test environment should resemble your R4 production environment as closely as possible. For instance, if POP3 users currently access one or more Domino servers for mail, the test environment should be configured to support POP3 users as well.

PILOT

After the testing phase, your upgrade team should conduct a pilot upgrade project to the test environment, to gain experience with the upgrade process. The pilot phase is different from your testing phase, because you perform an upgrade of mail and application servers within your production environment and then upgrade several predefined users to R5. This is a delicate phase, because you need to control the R5 environment to these predefined servers only. Your pilot phase should have several goals:

- To document your upgrade process for each type of server (mail and application) and client (LAN and mobile)
- To collect as much information as possible on what may impact your production environment

- To organize a detailed schedule of your server upgrade process and departmental users/clients
- To build a team of R5 experts

Members of the pilot phase should be carefully selected to include

- Pilot administrators   Ideally, these are different from the ones in your production environment. Their level of expertise is higher, and they will then train and assist your production administrators in due course.
- Power users   These are typically developers who can start upgrading your key applications to R5.
- Standard users   These are your end users. Ideally, you want to pick some from different departments. You will arrange to collect their feedback to assess your organization's level of resistance to change and prepare whatever training or end user informational sheets are required for a smooth client upgrade.

PRODUCTION

After your pilot rollout has been tested and documented, it is production-ready. You can start the R5 server deployment and move on to the client upgrade. Your planning and preparation should ensure that this transitional period proceeds quickly and without glitches, particularly if it occurs in the phased manner recommended previously.

LEVERAGING

After the Notes R5 client has been deployed across your organization, your IT department can begin to take full advantage of Domino R5's new features and capabilities. This stage mainly focuses on enhancing your critical applications with R5 functionality.

UPGRADING YOUR DOMINO SERVERS

When you upgrade a Domino server to R5, you gain added features, functionality, and performance without changing your server configuration, topology, routing, or addressing.

To upgrade a Domino server, you perform these steps, which are explained in more detail in the following sections:

1. Shut down the Domino server (by typing `quit` at the server console).
2. Back up important server files.
3. Upgrade the server's `MAIL.BOX`.
4. Remove the `Reporter` task from the `NOTES.INI` file.
5. Install the Domino R5 software.

6. Upgrade the Public Address Book to the Domino Directory.
7. Upgrade the Administration server for the Domino Directory.
8. Upgrade the Administration Requests database design.

BACKING UP IMPORTANT SERVER FILES

You must back up important Domino server files in case you encounter errors during upgrading. If you have problems during upgrading, you can use the backed-up copies to restore your files. Follow these steps to back up your critical server files:

1. Back up the Data Directory on your server (for example, C:\NOTES\DATA). This backs up DESKTOP.DSK, all ID files (including the server ID and certifier IDs), LOG.NSF, NAMES.NSF, MAIL.BOX, and any other Public Address Books located on the server.
2. Back up the contents of any directories pointed to by links (.DIR files) from your Data Directory.
3. Back up the NOTES.INI file for the server.
4. Back up any other Notes databases (,NSF), Notes templates (.NTF), and any databases pointed to by Directory links (.DIR).

UPGRADING THE SERVER'S MAIL.BOX TO R5

Upgrading MAIL.BOX gives you the performance advantages of the R5 ODS and MAIL.BOX template. Make sure you backed up the files on your server, as explained in the previous step. Use the server operating system to rename MAIL.BOX as MAIL.OLD in order to keep a backup of any mail that may still be in transit.

REMOVING THE Reporter TASK FROM THE NOTES.INI FILE

The Reporter task no longer exists in R5. The file statistics tasks performed by the Reporter task in R4 are handled by the Catalog. The R4 statistical analysis also performed by the Reporter is handled, in R5, by the Domino performance tools. Instead of Reporter, the Event task can monitor databases and generate an event that notifies the administrator. To remove the Reporter task:

1. Open the NOTES.INI file for the server you are upgrading in a text editor such as Microsoft Notepad.
2. Delete the entry Report from the ServerTasks= line of the file.
3. Save the file.
4. Close the text editor.

INSTALLING THE DOMINO R5 SOFTWARE

If you install Domino in the same directory as the previous version, you do not need to change the server configuration. If you install Domino in a new directory, the program prompts you to configure the server. During installation, select the server type for which you purchased a license. After installation, launch the Domino R5 server.

UPGRADING THE PUBLIC ADDRESS BOOK TO THE DOMINO DIRECTORY TEMPLATE

The Domino server prompts you to upgrade the Public Address Book template (PUBNAMES.NTF) after upgrading. The new Domino Directory template works with the Domino Administrator client to streamline directory and server administration. The Domino Directory is backward-compatible and is designed for use in mixed-release environments. Upgrade the design of your Address Book to the R5 Domino Directory template after you upgrade your server to R5 of Domino.

After you run the R5 installer, you launch the Domino Administrator client on the server and follow these steps:

1. When Domino asks whether you want to upgrade the Public Address Book design to the R5 template, press Y.
2. After you launch your R5 server, compact the Domino Directory twice. The first compaction enables the new database format (On-Disk Structure, or ODS) for R5, and the second compaction enables features in the new template that depend on the new ODS. Start compacting by typing the following:
   load compact names.nsf
   Press Enter to start compacting the Directory.
3. You now need to rebuild the views of the R5 Domino Directory. Install the Domino Administrator client on the workstation you use to administer the server.
4. Launch the Domino Administrator.
5. Choose File, Database, Open.
6. Select the Domino Directory you just compacted.
7. Click Open.
8. Enter information in the Directory Profile, as shown in Table 34.1.

TABLE 34.1 CONFIGURING THE DIRECTORY PROFILE FOR THE FIRST TIME

Field	Enter
Domain defined by this Directory	The Notes domain for this Directory. Domino completes this field automatically when you configure a new Domino server.
Directory Catalog file name for domain	The filename of a Directory Catalog set up for server access.

continues

TABLE 34.1 CONTINUED

Sort all new groups by default	Select Yes to automatically sort alphabetically the members of each new group you create. Domino Directory performance slows somewhat if you select Yes.
	Select No to display members of a group in the order in which you add them. If you select No, you can still override this option and sort members of a specific group.
Use more secure Internet passwords	Select Yes (the default) to use strong encryption for Internet passwords. Select No to use less-secure encryption.
Allow the creation of Alternate Language Information documents	Select Yes (the default) to allow you to create Alternate LanguageInformation documents for users in the Directory. These documents enable LDAP clients to use an alternate language when querying users in the Directory.
	Select No to prevent the creation of Alternate Language Information documents.

9. Rebuild the views by pressing Ctrl+Shift+F9.
10. Close the Domino Directory.

After you upgrade a server to R5, you can and should replicate the Domino Directory design to the Public Address Books on your organization's other servers, including R4 and R3 servers.

After replicating the new template to other servers, you must rebuild the views in the Domino Directories/Public Address Books on those servers. The view rebuild for the R5 template on an R4 or R3 server is time-consuming. Do not plan to do it during regular business hours!

OPTIONAL—UPGRADING DIRECTORY ASSISTANCE

After upgrading your Domino server and Domino Directory, upgrade your Directory Assistance database to R5. Follow these steps to upgrade your Directory Assistance to R5 only if you are using Directory Assistance in R4:

1. Start the Notes client.
2. Choose File, Database, Open.
3. In the Server box, select the server that contains your Directory Assistance database.
4. Select the Directory Assistance database.
5. Click Open.
6. Choose File, Database, Replace Design.
7. Click the Template Server button.

8. Select a Domino R5 server that has the new Directory Assistance template (DA50.NTF).
9. Click OK.
10. Select the Directory Assistance template (DA50.NTF).
11. Click OK.
12. When Notes asks whether you want to replace the template, click Yes.
13. Close the Directory Assistance database.

Upgrading the Administration Server for the Domino Directory

After you upgrade the first Domino server in your domain and replicate the new Domino Directory template to the other servers, upgrade the server that acts as the administration server for the Domino Directory. This enables you to take advantage of the new R5 Administration Process features. The new Administration Requests template is designed for backward compatibility on R4 and even R3 servers.

Upgrading the Administration Requests Database Design

After upgrading the administration server for the Domino Directory, you should process all requests in the Administration Requests database because it will quicken its upgrade process. Then, you must shut down the Administration Process and upgrade the design of the Administration Requests database on that server to the R5 template. The R5 Administration Requests template is designed for backward compatibility with the R4 Administration Process and use in mixed-release environments. You can and should replicate the new design to the Administration Requests databases on your organization's other servers:

1. Change to the Domino server console.
2. To process all Admin requests, type
   `tell adminp process all`
3. Press Enter. You may need to issue this command more than once, because some Administration Requests create others.
4. After the Administration Process finishes processing requests, shut it down by typing
   `tell adminp quit`

   Press Enter.
5. To upgrade the design of the Administration Requests database, launch the Domino Administrator client.
6. Choose File, Database, Open.
7. In the Server field, type the name of the upgraded administration server.
8. Select the Administration Requests (R4) database (ADMIN4.NSF) and click Open. If this is the first time you have opened the Administration Requests database, you see the About This Database document. Press Esc to close the document.
9. Choose File, Database, Replace Design.

10. Click Template Server.
11. In the Server field, enter the name of an R5 Domino server and click OK.
12. Select the Administration Requests (R5.0) template (`ADMIN4.NTF`) and click Replace.
13. When the Domino Administrator displays a warning about replacing the design, click Yes.
14. Close the Administration Requests database.
15. Replicate the new design to the other servers in your organization.

Upgrading an Internet Mail Server That Uses the SMTP/MIME Message Transfer Agent (MTA) to R5

The R4 server used a Message Transfer Agent (MTA) to route Internet mail. In R5, the Domino Router routes Internet mail over SMTP. Mail clients can use Internet mail with MIME or Notes mail in Compound Document format. Domino routes both formats natively and converts automatically between the two formats. Domino uses all R4 addressing and routing without change. You can implement R5 addressing and routing all at once, gradually, or not at all. You also have the opportunity to take advantage of some of the new advanced features of R5, such as anti-spam, ESMTP, and so forth.

You should consider conducting a pilot project to test your plans for upgrading your Internet mail servers before you begin moving your organization to R5. To upgrade an R4 MTA to an R5 Internet mail server, perform the following steps:

1. Back up important files.
2. Disable the SMTP/MIME MTA housekeeping.
3. Shut down the Router.
4. Shut down the inbound transport of messages.
5. Clear `SMTP.BOX`.
6. Clear messages from the outbound MTA queue.
7. Clear messages from the inbound MTA queue.
8. Shut down the MTA.
9. Upgrade `MAIL.BOX`.
10. Stop loading the MTA and remove the `Reporter` task from the `NOTES.INI`.
11. Install the Domino R5 software.
12. Upgrade the Public Address Book to the Domino Directory.
13. Set the server configuration for the Internet mail server.
14. Enable the SMTP listener task in the Server document for the Internet mail server.
15. If the upgraded server is the administration server for the domain's Domino Directory, also upgrade its Administration Requests database.

The following sections describe each of these steps in detail.

BACKING UP IMPORTANT FILES ON AN MTA SERVER

Back up important Domino server files in case you encounter errors during upgrading. If you have problems during upgrading, you can use the backed-up copies to restore your files.

Use the following steps to back up your files:

1. Shut down the server and workstation.
2. Back up the Data Directory on your server. This backs up DESKTOP.DSK, all ID files (including the server ID and certifier IDs), LOG.NSF, NAMES.NSF, MAIL.BOX, and any other Public Address Books located on the server.
3. Back up the contents of any directories pointed to by links (.DIR files) from your Data Directory.
4. Back up the NOTES.INI file for the server. This file is located in the system directory by default (for example, C:\WINNT40).
5. Back up any other Notes databases (.NSF), Notes templates (.NTF), and any databases pointed to by directory links (.DIR).

DISABLING SMTP/MIME MTA HOUSEKEEPING

Before upgrading an R4 MTA server, disable the MTA housekeeping. If you do not disable housekeeping and you clear the message queues during a time when the Compact task is set to run (2 a.m. by default), the MTA turns itself off, performs housekeeping tasks, and then turns itself on. This enables inbound and outbound transport, undoing the work of clearing the queues.

You must disable the SMTP/MTA housekeeping task prior to upgrading, as described in the following steps:

1. Make sure you backed up the critical files on the MTA server.
2. Launch the Lotus Notes client from which you administer the MTA server; open the server's Public Address Book and go to the Server/Servers view.
3. Select the Server document for the MTA server and click the Edit Server button on the Action Bar.
4. Expand the Internet Message Transfer Agent (SMTP MTA) section.
5. Under Control, click the down arrow next to the Enable daily housekeeping field.
6. Select Disable and click OK.
7. Click the Save and Close button on the Action Bar and close the Public Address Book.

Shutting Down the Router

You need to shut down the Router to ensure that no mail is routed to the server's SMTP.BOX. After you upgrade your server to R5, it will process messages that are already trapped when you copy messages from your old, backed-up MAIL.BOX to the newly created R5 mail.box.

Follow these steps to shut down the Router:

1. Change to the Domino server console.
2. To shut down the Router, type

   tell router quit
3. Press Enter. The server should show the Router task shutting down.

Shutting Down the Inbound Transport

Shutting down the inbound transport prevents the MTA from receiving SMTP messages addressed to recipients in your organization. The inbound transport moves messages into the Inbound Work Queue (SMTPIBWQ.NSF). Stopping inbound transport prevents the MTA from accepting inbound SMTP connections.

Follow these steps to shut down the SMTP/MTA inbound transport task:

1. Go to the Domino server console and type

   tell smtpmta stop inbound transport
2. Press Enter. The server should show the open Inbound Session Controllers and the Inbound Session Controller task (ISESCTL) shutting down.

Verifying That SMTP.BOX Has No Active Messages

You have shut down the Router and inbound transport tasks. You now need to verify whether the SMTP/MTA has any pending messages by opening the relevant SMTP/MTA databases. Please note that, ideally, you should have planned this upgrade for the least busy time—most probably, on a Sunday morning.

Follow these steps to add the relevant SMTP/MTA databases on your workspace:

1. Switch to the Lotus Notes client.
2. Choose File, Database, Open to add the server's SMTP MTA databases:
   - In the Filename field, type SMTP.BOX and click Add Icon.
   - In the Filename field, type SMTPOBWQ.NSF and click Add Icon.
   - In the Filename field, type SMTPIBWQ.NSF and click Add Icon.
3. Click Done.

Verify that there are no messages in the SMTP.BOX marked as Pending Conversion or Pending Transmission; wait for them to be processed and cleaned up by the Delivery Report

Task (DRT). To speed the cleaning-up process, type this line at the server console:

```
tell smtpmta housekeeping
```

CLEARING THE OUTBOUND WORK QUEUE

Clearing the Outbound Work Queue routes all remaining outbound SMTP messages to their destinations. Double-click the SMTP Outbound Work Queue (SMTPOBWQ.NSF) icon on your Notes workspace. Wait until all messages in the Outbound Work Queue are successfully processed by the MTA. There should be either no messages in the view or only messages marked Dead. Note that there may be some delay between message processing and the DRT removing the message from the view, due to the cycle time of the DRT.

CLEARING THE INBOUND WORK QUEUE

Clearing the Inbound Work Queue moves all SMTP messages addressed to recipients in your organization out of the Inbound Work Queue so they can be delivered. The MTA moves messages into either the Outbound Work Queue or MAIL.BOX, depending on who the recipients are. Messages in the Outbound Work Queue are cleared in the next step, and messages in MAIL.BOX wait until after the server is upgraded and restarted to be delivered.

Verify that all messages except those marked Dead are processed by pressing F9. Processed messages are removed from the view by the DRT. After clearing messages from the MTA, shut it down.

BACKING UP THE SMTP/MTA MAIL.BOX

Upgrading MAIL.BOX gives you the performance advantages of the R5 ODS and MAIL.BOX template—significantly faster than the R4 versions. If you still have messages pending in your MAIL.BOX, you can—after R5 server starts and creates a new R5 MAIL.BOX—copy these messages from your backup to the new mail.box. Use the server operating system to rename MAIL.BOX to MAIL.UPG.

STOPPING THE SMTP/MIME MTA AND THE Reporter TASK FROM LOADING

The R5 server provides native SMTP transport and MIME handling. Hence, you no longer need the SMTPMTA server task. As for the Domino R5 upgrade, you also need to remove the Statistics Report task.

Follow these steps to remove the SMTP/MTA and Report tasks from the server NOTES.INI:

1. Open the NOTES.INI file for the server in a text editor, such as Notepad.
2. Delete the entries SMTPMTA and Report from the ServerTasks= line of the file.
3. Save and close the file.

Installing Domino R5 on an MTA Server

Make sure that you have completed all the previous steps. Install the Domino R5 software. If you install Domino in the same directory as the previous version, you do not need to make any changes to the server configuration. If you install Domino in a new directory, the program prompts you to configure the server. During installation, select the Domino Mail server.

Upgrading the Public Address Book for an Internet Mail Server

The Domino server prompts you to upgrade the Public Address Book template (PUBNAMES.NTF) after upgrading. Upgrade the design of your Address Book to the R5 Domino Directory template after you upgrade your server to R5. If you have followed our upgrade sequence process, your SMTP server should already be using the R5 Domino Directory template. If not, upgrade its design when prompted.

If the server is already using the Domino Directory, you should have been through the process of compacting it twice and rebuilding the views. If not, follow the steps outlined in the section "Upgrading the Public Address Book to the Domino Directory Template," earlier in this chapter.

Setting the Server Configuration for an Internet Mail Server

You must enable native SMTP routing in the Server Configuration document to allow the upgraded mail server to route mail using SMTP. Edit the Server Configuration document that applies to the upgraded server, but be aware that this modification affects any other servers that use this Server Configuration document. If necessary, create a new Server Configuration document for your R5 Internet mail servers.

The Domino Directory for the domain must use the R5 template because the settings for native SMTP appear only in the R5 Domino Directory. Please note that relay host servers require additional configuration. The good news is that R5 relay host configuration is easier than in R4. You can select to route all mail with destinations outside the local Internet domain to a relay host, or not to use a relay host at all. Additionally, there is no need to route mail inside the local Internet domain to a relay host because Domino routes SMTP natively.

The "smart host," which lists users not in your Domino Directory, has functionality similar to a relay host, though its role is different. For more details on the Domino R5 SMTP relay functionality, refer to your Domino R5 Administration Help database.

Follow these steps to set the server configuration:

1. In the Domino Administrator, click the Configuration tab.
2. Expand the Server Configuration section.
3. Click Configurations. If you have a Server Configuration document that you want to use for this server, select it and click Edit Configuration. If not, click Add Configuration.

4. If you are creating a new configuration, do the following:
   - Enter a servername in the Basics section.
   - Select which Group or Server this configuration should apply to. Do not select Use for all unless you want every server to use SMTP to send messages to the Internet instead of going through an Internet mail server.
   - Click the Router/SMTP tab.
   - Click the down arrow next to SMTP used when sending messages outside of the local Internet domain.
   - Select Enabled and click OK.
   - Click the Save and Close button on the Action Bar. You should see the ternet;mail servers;configuring>new document in the view.

EDITING THE SERVER DOCUMENT FOR AN INTERNET MAIL SERVER

Edit the Server document for the upgraded server to enable the SMTP listener task. This tells the server to load the SMTP listener task at startup.

Make sure you set the server configuration to enable the server to route outbound SMTP mail. Remember that a Server Configuration document can apply to more than one server, so you may want to create more than one configuration document:

1. In the Domino Administrator, choose the Configuration tab.
2. Expand the Server Configuration section and choose All Server Documents.
3. Double-click the server document for the upgraded Internet mail server.
4. Click Edit Server.
5. On the Basics tab, click the down arrow next to SMTP listener task.
6. Select Enabled and click OK.
7. Click the Save and Close button on the Action Bar and close the Domino Directory.

> **Note:** Do not remove SMTP routing information from the Server document. Existing routing information enables you to route Internet mail in a mixed R4/R5 environment, or in an R5 environment that uses R4-style routing.

UPGRADING THE ADMINISTRATION REQUESTS DATABASE ON AN MTA SERVER

If the upgraded Internet mail server is also the administration server for the domain's Domino Directory, you now need to upgrade the design of its Administration Requests database to the R5 template as described earlier in this chapter in the section "Upgrading the Administration Server for the Domino Directory."

Internet Mail Routing in Mixed Release Environments
Domino R5 routes Internet mail (MIME) over both Notes RPC (Remote Procedure Calls) and SMTP. R4 servers do not support native MIME delivery or SMTP routing and use the MTA to accomplish these tasks. When an R5 server transfers a MIME message to an R4 server, it converts the message to Notes format and creates an attachment containing the original MIME. This is to preserve full message fidelity. That way, if an Internet mail client accesses the message, Domino sends the MIME from the attachment. The R4 server deposits both the CD record and the MIME attachment in a user's mail file for this reason. For these messages in a mixed environment, mail storage requirements and network utilization roughly double for each of these messages only.

In an all-R5 system, the Router delivers MIME messages directly to the recipient's mail file, because both Notes R5 and Internet clients can read MIME. If the message is in Notes format, the Router checks the Person document for each recipient. If the recipient accesses mail only via IMAP or POP3, the Router converts the message to MIME and delivers it to the user's mail file.

UPGRADING AN INTERNET MAIL SERVER TO USE MULTIPLE THREADS

After upgrading to R5, a mail server Router automatically supports multiple transfer threads to the same server. By default, the Router allows multiple threads based on configuration settings. You can change these settings to allow more or fewer multiple transfer threads. For instance, the `MailMaxConcurrentXferThreads` R4 `NOTES.INI` parameter, which specifies the maximum number of concurrent transfer threads per destination, is no longer configured within the `NOTES.INI`. It is a field in the Server Configuration document. The same applies to the `MailMaxThreads` parameter, which determines the maximum number of threads the mail Router can create to perform mail transfers. Without this variable, the default is one thread per server port. Increasing this number creates more threads to handle mail transfers. Again, you need to upgrade this parameter within the Server Configuration document.

POPULATING THE INTERNET ADDRESS FIELD IN PERSON DOCUMENTS

When upgrading to Domino R5, you can use the Internet Address tool to fill in the Internet Address field for all Person documents in which the field is blank in a Domino Directory.

Internet Mail Addresses in Domino R5
When looking up an address for Internet mail in the Domino Directory in R5, Domino checks the $Names view for an exclusive match of the address. If it finds the complete Internet address of the recipient in either the Short name or Internet address field, Domino delivers the message to the mail file of that person. In a mixed environment, Domino exhaustively searches $Names to ensure that any address generated by the R4 MTA for a user in your Directory is located properly. When the Directory is upgraded to R5, you can use the Internet Address field in the R5 Person document for better performance. To do so, you can use the tool that populates this field to standardize Internet addresses in your organization.

Follow these steps to populate the Internet Address field in the Person document of the R5 Domino Directory:

1. In Domino Administrator, click the People & Groups tab.
2. Select the server and Domino Directory for which you want to fill in the Internet Address fields.
3. Choose People—Set Internet Address tool.
4. In the Internet Address Construction dialog, choose a format for the Internet addresses. See Table 34.2 for details on the Internet address formats.

TABLE 34.2   R5 POSSIBLE INTERNET FORMATS

R5 Internet Address Format	Description
FirstName LastName	Contents of the First name field and the Last name field.
FirstName MiddleInitial LastName	Contents of the First name field, Middle initial field, and Last name field.
FirstInitial LastName	The First letter in the user's First name field and the contents of the Last name field.
FirstInitial MiddleInitial LastName	The first letter in the user's First name field, Middle initial field, and the contents of the Last name field.
LastName FirstName	Last name field and the First name field.
LastName FirstName MiddleInitial	Last name field, First name field, and Middle initial field.
LastName FirstInitial	Last name field and first letter in the user's First name field.
LastName FirstInitial MiddleInitial	Last name field, first letter in the user's First name field, and Middle initial field.
FirstName LastInitial	First Name field and the first character of the Last name field.
Use Custom Format Pattern	Custom Format Pattern enables you specify how to construct an Internet address.

5. Choose a separator for the Internet addresses. This character separates the items in the Format field. You can choose between an underscore, a dot or period, an equals sign, or no separator.
6. Enter the Internet domain for the company.

7. Optionally, click More Options and do any of the following:
    - Select Only for people whose Notes Domain is to set Internet addresses only for users in a given Notes domain.
    - Select Use secondary custom format pattern in case of error generating Internet address to specify a second Internet address pattern if Notes generates the same Internet address for two users. Specify the secondary pattern in the box.
8. The Internet Address Construction dialog box specifies the server and Domino Directory on which it runs. It also gives an example for each address and separator format.
9. The tool then checks all Person documents in the Domino Directory. When it finds a document without an entry in the Internet Address field, it creates an entry based on the rules given previously. It also verifies that the entry is a valid RFC 821 address and checks to ensure that the entry is unique by performing an exhaustive name lookup of the entry on all Domino Directories on the server. If the entry matches an Internet Address field, the tool leaves the field blank and enters an error in the Log (LOG.NSF). So, if you have a large Directory, it will take time!

INTERNET MAIL STORAGE FORMAT IN DOMINO R5

You should not need to change how users' Internet messages are stored when upgrading to R5. In a mixed R4/R5 environment, where some clients use native MIME messages on R5 servers, Domino will not deliver a native MIME message to an R4 client, mail file, or server, because native MIME is unreadable in R4. Domino converts the native MIME message to Notes format and a MIME attachment for R4 clients, mail files, and servers.

USING DIAL-UP WITH DOMINO SMTP R5

If you use a dial-up access to the Internet, you need to take additional steps before upgrading to R5 of Domino. Medium-to-large companies rarely use this setup, but if you need to do this, you can see the Administration Help database for more information before upgrading.

UPGRADING AN MTA SERVER AND NOTES.INI PARAMETERS

When you upgrade an MTA server to an R5 Internet mail server, the NOTES.INI file for the server may contain parameters that are not supported in R5. You do not need to change or remove these parameters—they are ignored by the server and do not interfere with its functionality in any way.

Upgrading sets configuration parameters for the settings most commonly used for Internet mail servers. The upgrade program does not convert R4 NOTES.INI settings to their R5 GUI equivalents. If you have configuration uniquely set through the NOTES.INI file in R4, you may need to reenable this configuration using the R5 Server Configuration and Server documents.

Upgrading Domino Clusters

To upgrade clustered R4 servers, you follow exactly the same processes as when upgrading a Domino R4 server to R5. If you are upgrading a clustered server that uses the R4 MTA to route Internet mail, refer to the section "Upgrading an Internet Mail Server That Uses the SMTP/MIME Message Transfer Agent (MTA) to R5," earlier in this chapter.

If you have mail files on a mixed R4/R5 cluster, be aware of the following issues:

- The R5 mail template uses features not available in R4, so if your mail file is converted back to R4, you cannot use these features. For instance, if you have mail rules set up in your R5 mail file to filter your mail, these rules will not work on the R4 server/mail file. By the same token, when your mail fails over the R4 server, and is delivered to that server, the rules do not filter or sort the mail according to the R5 rules.

- R4 servers do not support soft deletions. Your trash folder on an R4 server appears to contain all the documents in your mail file. You can ignore this.

- R5 servers can deliver native MIME, but R4 servers cannot. Thus, when a Notes client fails over to an R4 server from an R5 server, MIME messages are converted to Notes format documents and appear different than when viewed on the R5 server.

- If you attempt to send a MIME message through an R4 server, the message is converted to Notes format with an attachment containing the original MIME.

- Although failover is indicated in the Notes status bar at the bottom of the screen, if you do not monitor status bar messages, a failover from an R5 to an R4 server may not be apparent. However, as noted above, there are changes in functionality between R5 and R4 in clusters.

Upgrading to the R5 clients

R5 comes with three clients: the regular Notes client, the Domino Designer, and the Domino Administrator. Their upgrade is actually very similar to that described in this section. However, their upgrade sequence varies. After you upgrade your R4 Public Address Book to the R5 Domino Directory template, you should also upgrade your administration clients to the R5 Domino Administrator, because it is easier to administer your servers and Notes domain with the Domino Administrator. Note that the Domino Administrator is also designed to administer a mixed-release environment and works smoothly with R4 servers.

After you finish the servers and Domino Administrator upgrades, you can move to the R5 client deployment.

To upgrade Notes to R5, perform the following steps:

1. Set the default workstation security.
2. Back up important files.

3. Install Notes R5.
4. Launch the Notes client program.

Setting Default Workstation Security

Before starting the client upgrade, you should set the Administration Execution Control List (ECL) in the Domino Directory. The Administration ECL sets the default security on the Notes client when users start Notes for the first time after upgrading. Workstation security defines which group's applications can execute on a Notes client. If a group is not specified in the ECL for a client, Notes warns the user when an application created by the group attempts to run on that client.

Backing Up Notes Client Files

The rule is to always back up important Notes client files in case an error occurs during the upgrade process. Table 34.3 defines which files you need to back up.

TABLE 34.3 DOMINO ADMINISTRATOR KEY FILES

Domino Administrator Files to	Default Location Back Up
NOTES.INI (Notes Preferences on the Macintosh)	System directory (for example, C:\WIN95)
DESKTOP.DSK	Notes Data Directory (for example, C:\NOTES\DATA) C:\NOTES\DATA)
Personal Address Book	Notes Data Directory (for example, (NAMES.NSF by default)
User ID files (for example, JSMITH.ID)	Notes Data Directory (for example, C:\NOTES\DATA)
Local databases (.NSF)	Notes Data Directory (for example, C:\NOTES\DATA)
Local database directory links (.DIR)	Notes Data Directory (for example, C:\NOTES\DATA)
Any customized Notes database templates (.NTF)	Notes Data Directory (for example, C:\NOTES\DATA)

Installing the Notes R5 Software

To install the Notes R5 software, start by running SETUP.EXE. Follow the prompts on the InstallShield screens to properly install the software. Select the type of client for which you purchased a license. When you are finished, start Notes.

Notes sets up and upgrades the software automatically if you install R5 in the same directory as the previous release of Notes. If you install the R5 software in a different directory, Notes prompts you to complete the configuration process. If you install Notes in a different directory, note that the Setup program places NOTES.INI in the Notes Data Directory. Notes automatically upgrades your Personal Address Book to the R5 Domino Directory design. If you have Internet mail set up to work with POP3, Notes creates an Account document for that Internet mail configuration.

Setting Your Personal Address Book Preferences

Your Personal Address Book is automatically upgraded when you upgrade the client. When the upgrade is complete and you open your Personal Address Book for the first time, Notes asks you to enter your preferences into the Personal Address Book profile.

The R5 Personal Address Book has a number of new forms, views, subforms, agents, and script libraries, and has had some design elements deleted from the R4 template. For more details, refer to Chapter 7, "Contact Management with the Personal and Public Directories."

Creating Account Documents for Internet Mail

Notes R5 introduces Account documents, which contain information for accessing mail using POP and IMAP, and sending mail with SMTP. If your R4 Location document is set up to use POP or IMAP, Notes converts this information into an Account document for that setting. If you send mail to the Internet, Notes creates an SMTP Account document. The accounts are set for the Location that you set up for Internet mail.

> **Caution**
> Do not upgrade your mail file to the R5 template until your server has been upgraded. Added R5 functionality will not work on an R4 server.

R5 ID Files Security Issues

There are several points that you need to keep in mind regarding R5 ID files:

- ID files are not backward-compatible from R5 to R3. This means that IDs created with R5 are not usable with R3. So watch out! If you may have to create new accounts for users on R3, make sure to keep an R4 client to generate R4 ID files that can be used with R3. R3 files upgrade seamlessly to R5, and R3 users can continue to use them without any change in functionality.

- R5 servers and clients cannot create new flat ID files. If your organization's ID security is based on flat hierarchy, you must retain at least one R4 client to create new flat ID files. However, R5 fully supports flat ID file maintenance. You can renew certificates for existing flat ID files and issue new flat certificates to new hierarchical users who need access to servers with flat IDs. For increased security, you should consider upgrading to hierarchical ID files.

- The Password Checking feature that occurs during authentication requires that both workstations and servers run Release 4.5 or later. If you enable password checking on a server running a release prior to 4.5, authentication occurs without password checking.

If you enable password checking on a workstation running a previous release, authentication fails when the workstation attempts to connect to a server that requires password checking. Please note that the first time a user for whom password checking is required authenticates with a server, the user ID is altered and it cannot be used with a previous release.

Upgrading Databases and Applications

After upgrading a server to Domino R5, you can upgrade the databases to R5 database format (On-Disk Structure, or ODS) and design (template). The upgrade of the database format is independent of the upgrade of the database design. Because ODS does not replicate, you can leave the design of a database based on an R4 template and upgrade the database format on that server to R5 ODS. However, if you upgrade the database design to use R5 templates and features, pre-R5 clients will not be able to use R5 features.

Upgrading R4 Application Servers to R5

Upgrading R4 application servers follows the same process as when you upgrade a Domino server. However, please note that if any mission-critical application resides on that application server, make sure that its R5 pilot phase has been completed prior to upgrading.

To integrate applications with the R5 environment, you should compact them all so that they get converted to the new file structure. Be warned—it will take time. So make sure to leave enough lead time to give ample time to the conversion process. Should you decide to play your safe card and not convert your applications to R5 right away, make sure to change their file extension (.NSF) to NS4. This automatically protects their file structure.

When you upgrade an application server and its applications to R5 and decide to use features such as transactional logging, be sure to do the following:

1. Specify a drive with sufficient disk space for view rebuilds by setting the View_Rebuild_Dir variable in the NOTES.INI file to the correct drive for that disk. By default, this variable is set to the temp directory on the system. This drive holds the temporary files used to rebuild views. Clearly, a larger disk enables faster rebuilds and greater optimization. Note that view rebuilds can be as much as five times faster in R5 than R4. The size of the drive needed for view rebuilds depends on the size of the views you are rebuilding.

2. Use a separate, single-purpose disk to hold the log files for transactional logging. Minimal disk arm movement enables faster writes to the log. The default location for these files is the LOGDIR directory in the server's Data Directory, but without a separate disk, your server suffers a performance hit as it writes to different spaces on disk. The log requires at least 200MB disk space and can be set as large as 4GB. Using a dedicated mirrored drive is even better than a single disk for recoverability if the log disk fails.

Key Advantages of Upgrading Applications to R5

Upgrading databases and database servers to R5 brings a number of key benefits resulting in greatly increased performance. For example, the R5 database format (On-Disk Structure, or ODS) and templates offer much improved performance, especially for databases such as the Domino Directory and `MAIL.BOX`. Also, database operations require less I/O, and memory and disk space allocation are improved.

Transactional logging writes all changes to a database sequentially to a log file and does not physically alter the database until those changes are safely stored on disk. This enables you to recover data lost through database corruption or other problems by "rolling back" the database to a given point and replaying the changes to the database through the log. This also enables greatly improved backup of databases. R5 databases with transactional logging enabled do not need to have `Fixup` run on them. Be sure to use a separate, single-purpose, high-volume drive for the log files.

View rebuilds are as much as five times faster in R5 if you designate a separate drive for the temporary files for the rebuilds. The greater the space on the drive you dedicate to view rebuilds, the greater the increase in rebuild speed.

Multiple shared mail databases (single-copy object stores, or SCOS) allow fewer I/O transactions and reduce locking problems. Multiple `MAIL.BOX` databases enable you to spread the mail load over several databases.

The parallel indexer allows more than one indexing thread on servers with more than one CPU. R5 databases have an antidelete feature that you can enable. This feature performs "soft deletes" first, enabling you to undo a deletion. For example, R5 mail databases have this feature when operating in conjunction with an R5 Domino server.

Compaction of R5 databases occurs online and "in place" and does not require additional disk space. Users can read and modify the database while compaction occurs. R5 compaction is up to 10 times faster than R4 compaction. Also, R5 databases can be as large as 32GB.

Upgrading to R5 Improves Database Performance

The new database format used in R5 databases offers ways to improve database performance easily. These include

- Turning off unread marks
- Speeding up view rebuilds via bitmap optimization
- Turning off overwriting free space
- Removing specialized response hierarchies from views that don't use them
- Limiting the number of entries in the $UpdatedBy fields
- Limiting the number of entries in the $Revisions fields
- Turning off headlines monitoring

To access all these properties, open the database, choose File, Database, Properties, and click the Advanced tab, or press Alt+Enter. These options are available only for databases in the R5 database format.

Don't Maintain Unread Marks

Maintaining unread marks in a database slows performance. For some databases, such as the Domino Directory or the Domino log file, unread marks are not useful. If a database does not require tracking read and unread documents, consider disabling unread marks to improve performance.

Speeding Up View Rebuilds via Bitmap Optimization

Domino refers to tables of document information to determine which documents appear in an updated view. Selecting the Document table bitmap optimization property associates tables with the forms used by documents in each table. During a view update, Domino searches only tables whose views contain forms used by documents in that view. Although there is a slight performance cost to maintaining this association, this setting speeds updates of small views in large databases significantly.

To enable optimization using the table-form association, select Document table bitmap optimization. When you change this setting, compact the database to enable it. Make sure your system has sufficient disk space because this compact makes a temporary copy of the database. You can also use the `load compact` command with the `-F` or `-f` switch to enable or disable bitmap optimization.

Turning Off Overwriting Free Space

To prevent unauthorized users from accessing data, Domino overwrites deleted data in databases, which can reduce database performance. In the following situations, this security feature is not necessary:

- The database is physically secure—for example, on a password-protected server in a locked room.
- Space in the database is quickly reallocated—for example, in system databases, such as `MAIL.BOX`.
- Security is not an issue—for example, in an employee discussion database.

Removing Specialized Response Hierarchies from Views That Don't Use Them

Documents store information about their parent or response document, which is used only by the @functions @AllChildren and @AllDescendants. In databases that don't use these @functions in views, select the database property Don't support specialized response hierarchy to improve database performance.

When you change this setting, compact the database to enable it. Make sure your system has sufficient disk space, because this compact makes a temporary copy of the database. You can also use the `load compact` command with the `-H` or `-h` switch to enable or disable bitmap optimization.

LIMITING THE NUMBER OF ENTRIES IN THE $UpdatedBy FIELDS

A document stores the name of the user or server that made each change to it in the $UpdatedBy field. This edit history requires disk space and slows both view updates and replication. If you do not need to maintain a complete edit history, specify the number of changes that the $UpdatedBy field tracks with the database setting Limit entries in $Updated fields. When the $UpdatedBy field reaches this limit, the next edit causes the oldest entry to be removed from the list, which improves database performance.

LIMITING THE NUMBER OF ENTRIES IN THE $REVISIONS FIELDS

A document stores the date and time of each change saved to it in the $Revisions field. Domino servers use this field to resolve replication or save conflicts. The $Revisions field stores up to 500 entries by default. If you do not need to track changes this closely, specify the number of changes that $Revisions field tracks with the database setting Limit entries in $Revisions field. When the $Revisions field reaches this limit, the next edit causes the oldest entry to be removed from the $Revisions list.

However, note that it is recommended to set the number of entries in the $Revisions field to at least 10. If you don't, you risk increased replication or save conflicts in the database.

TURNING OFF HEADLINE MONITORING

Users can set up their headlines to search databases automatically for items of interest. If many users do this, database performance can slow. To prevent a database from being monitored, select Don't allow headline monitoring.

KEEPING A NEW DATABASE IN R4 FORMAT

Any Notes client can access a database hosted on a Domino server, regardless of what release the client or server is running or what release format the database uses. However, Notes clients cannot access or use database features from later releases. For instance, an R4 Notes client can access an R5 database on a Domino server, but it cannot access or use R5 features in that database.

If a database is stored on the local drive of a client, only clients of the same release and later can access it. A database in R4 format can be accessed locally by an R4 or R5 Notes client, but not by an R3 client.

Domino servers can host applications in only their release format and earlier formats. For example, an R4 server can host an R4 or R3 database, but not an R5 database. In turn, if an

R5 client compacts a local replica of an R4 database, the database moves to R5 database format and cannot be accessed by R4 clients.

To create an R5 application that can be accessed locally by R4 clients and stored on R4 servers, give it the extension .NS4 in the File Name field when creating the database. To keep a database in R4 format so it can be accessed locally by R4 clients or stored on an R4 server, change the database's extension to .NS4 via the operating system or make a new replica of the database using this extension.

To create a replica of a database in R4 format:

1. Choose File, Database, Open.
2. Select the database for which you want an R4 replica.
3. Click Open.
4. Choose File, Replication, New Replica.
5. In the File Name field, give the new replica the extension .NS4.
6. Click OK.

COMPACTING DATABASES IN A MIXED-RELEASE ENVIRONMENT

When you compact a database from an R5 Domino server, the server upgrades the database to the R5 ODS unless you specify R4 compacting or the database has an .NS4 extension. To specify R4 compacting, use the -r argument. When a database is upgraded to R5 format, you cannot convert it back to R4 format or move it to an R4 server. You can continue to replicate between an R5 replica and an R4 replica. Indeed, the R5 database format does not replicate, and R4 servers ignore unsupported R5 features, so you can safely replicate a database replica that has been upgraded to R5 with a replica that has not.

In addition, you can use the following arguments with Compact to preserve a mixed-release environment:

Compact Argument	Description
-r	Use for R4 compacting
-t	Disables transactional logging and uses R4 compacting
-T	Enables transactional logging and uses R4 compacting

Note that in R5, users experience an initial delay when accessing upgraded databases for the first time. This is due to all the database's views being rebuilt on initial access.

CONCLUSION

The upgrade of your R4 infrastructure to R5 should be an exciting time. The good news—and we cannot stress this enough—is that Lotus has learned considerably from its upgrade from Notes R3 to R4. Additionally—and this is even more important—you have never been so close to so much online help, thanks to the Web. The World Wide Web is clearly bringing you closer to the vendor, and the vendor now must listen to you and provide answers—fast.

The following is a list of resources that you should use to prepare for your upgrade.

- The R5 Release Notes, valuable information that ships with the newer releases of R5
- Certified Lotus training courses for customers and Business Partners on upgrading to Notes/Domino R5
- Lotus Business Partners, who are ready to assist with upgrades and rollouts worldwide
- Lotus-provided, Web-based white papers, articles, and other material on its own upgrade experience, available at www.lotus.com/R5
- The site at www.notes.net for the latest on R5
- Key niche printed publications on Domino, such as Universal net.Connect at www.netconnections.co.uk (why not subscribe?).

In any case, remember that the key success to your upgrade plan relies on what you learn from your pilot and the amount of testing that you are willing to perform. Good luck!

CHAPTER 35

INITIAL CONFIGURATION OF SERVERS WITH THE DOMINO DIRECTORIES

In Chapter 33, "Initial Planning and Installation," you walked through the necessary steps to successfully install your first Domino server. However, your job is not done yet. Now you need to further configure your new Domino server to optimize its performance and make it as trouble-free as possible. Basic configuration takes place in the Domino Directory database, formerly known as the Public Name and Address Book (NAB). The Domino Directory is the heart and soul of a Domino server, providing virtually all the information your server needs to operate. Without the Domino Directory, there is no Domino server.

This chapter covers the following:

- The importance of the Domino Directory in your Notes/Domino environment
- How you can use the various documents in the Domino Directory to configure and optimize the performance of your Domino server

The Importance of the Domino Directory

As stated earlier, the Domino Directory is the heart and soul of a Domino server. The Domino Directory really serves two main purposes for a Domino server. First, it acts as a simple directory service by providing a central repository for all user, group, and server documents in a Domino domain. Second, and more importantly, it provides a central location to manage a Domino server and the server's various services, such as replication, mail routing, Internet access, automated tasks, and a multitude of other information and processes.

When you set up your Domino server in Chapter 33, "Initial Planning and Installation," one of the operations that the installation process performed was the creation of the Domino Directory database (NAMES.NSF) in the Data Directory of your Domino server. When the Domino Directory was created, a Server document was also created in it, and the basic information you provided about your server was placed into this document.

When the Domino Directory database is initially created, the default access provided to the database is Author. In addition to the Default access, there are four other entries placed in the Access Control List (ACL) of the Domino Directory:

- The Administrator's name you specified during installation. This entry is a Person with Manager access and all roles assigned.
- The Server's name (a server should always have access to its own Domino Directory!). This entry is a Server with Manager access and all roles assigned.
- LocalDomainServers, a Server Group that should contain the names of all other servers in your Domain. This entry is a Server Group with Manager access and all roles assigned.
- OtherDomainServers, a Server Group that should contain the names of all servers outside your Domain that are allowed to access your server (such as for replication). This entry is a Server Group with an access level of Reader and no roles assigned.

There are numerous roles available for assignment in the ACL of the Domino Directory. These roles can be used to delegate administrative duties to other individuals or groups so that the administrative workload does not have to fall on the shoulders of one person. Here are the various roles available:

- GroupCreator can create new Group documents.
- GroupModifier can modify or delete existing groups, but cannot create new Group documents.
- NetCreator can create any document except Person, Group, or Server documents.
- NetModifier canmodify or delete all existing documents except Person, Group, or Server documents.
- ServerCreator can create new Server documents.
- ServerModifier can modify or delete existing Server documents.
- UserCreator can create new Person documents.
- UserModifier can modify or delete existing Person documents.

> **Note**
> The Domino Directory is the most critical component of your Domino server; therefore, you should provide users only the minimal access level necessary to successfully manage your Domino Directory. By using the roles defined previously, you can successfully delegate administrative tasks to other users without giving them the "keys to the kingdom."

There are many forms in the Domino Directory that provide you with an organized, task-oriented way to configure and manage your Domino server. These forms fall into two basic categories: Directory Services and Server Management. If you open the Domino Directory database and click the Create menu, you see all the available forms. The Server Management forms fall under the Server menu and include the following:

Certifier
Configuration Settings
Connection
Domain
External Domain Network Information
File Identification
Holiday
Mail-In Database
Program
Resource
Server
User Setup Profile

Now let's take a look at the most commonly used of these documents and explore how they can make your administration duties much easier.

THE SERVER DOCUMENT

The Server document is the most important document in the Domino Directory, because it defines everything there is to know about your Domino server. The Server document can be quite intimidating to a new administrator; however, let's break this huge document down tab-by-tab and cover the most important fields, which enable you to more thoroughly understand the basic configuration of your Domino server. Keep in mind that this chapter is not designed to cover every field on every tab of the server document; instead, it concentrates on the fields that either may be of interest to you or may need to be tweaked for optimal server performance.

THE BASICS TAB

Figure 35.1 shows the Basics Tab.

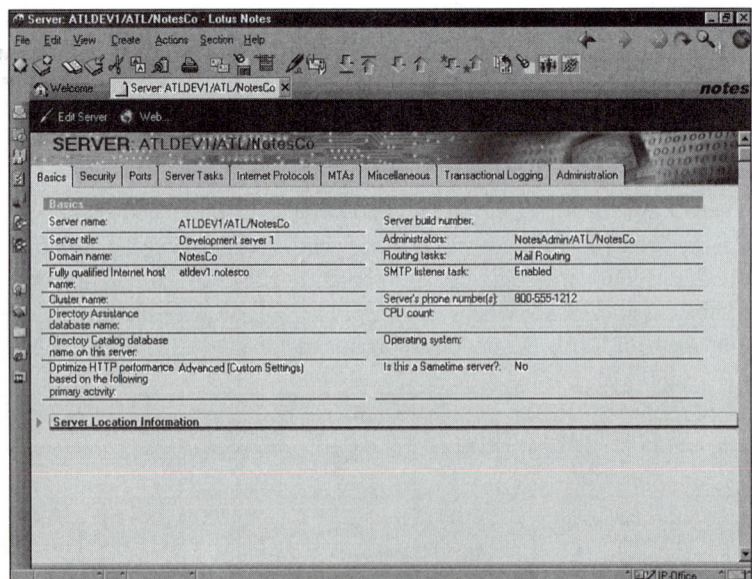

Figure 35.1
The Basics tab of the Server document enables you to configure the basic information about your Domino server.

The following fields on the Basics tab can be used to define the baseline information about your server:

> **Note**
> The field labels in the Server document usually have additional help available as a text pop-up. You can click the label to access the additional help.

- **Server name**   The Server name is a hierarchical name of the Domino server that was given during installation. This field is required and should not be modified unless you use the `ADMINP` process.

- **Server title**   The Server title is an optional descriptive title for the Domino server. This field enables you to enter a description that further identifies your Domino server in the Servers view.

- **Domain name**   The Domain name field contains the given domain name entered during the installation and registration process. This field is required. If a domain name is not provided during installation, this field defaults to the same name as the organization certifier. The domain name is very important for mail routing; therefore, changing this name takes careful consideration. If you do decide to change the domain name, please use the `ADMINP` process.

- **Directory Assistance database name**   The Directory Assistance database is a specialized database that enables users to browse and select names from multiple domains for efficient email addressing.

> **Note**
> In Lotus Notes/Domino R4.5x and earlier, the Directory Assistance database was known as the Master Address Book (MAB).

- **Administrators**   The Administrators field contains the names of users or groups of users who are allowed to administer your server. Anyone who is listed here can administer the server remotely using the Remote Server Console. Only the users listed here can create or update directory links, create or update full text indexes, designate an administration server for databases, or compact databases from the Administration Control Panel. Make sure that the individuals to whom you grant Administrator access are qualified to handle the responsibility, or you could encounter a great deal of pain when attempting to troubleshoot and correct the mistakes they make!

> **Tip**
> Create one or more Administrators groups and place the names of these groups into the Administrators field. Manage administrator access to your Domino server through this group, because this is much more convenient than continually updating one or more Administrator fields for your various server documents.

- **Routing tasks**   The Routing tasks keyword field specifies the various routing activities the server will execute. The default value for this field is Mail Routing, indicating normal Notes/Domino mail routing. If you have any other gateways installed (for example, X400 or cc:Mail) on this server, you may also specify them here.

- **SMTP listener task**   The Domino R5 server now includes native SMTP router code as a part of the server itself. The SMTP listener task keyword field either enables (Enabled) or disables (Disabled) this new feature.

> **Note**
>
> In releases of Domino prior to R5, the SMTP Gateway was an add-on server task. In Domino R5, the SMTP router code is now a part of the core Domino code, called the SMTP Listener.

- **Server's phone number(s)** If the Domino server supports dial-in access, the Server's phone number(s) field contains the phone number(s) that users dial to access the server remotely.

The Basics tab also contains the Server Location Information section, which is covered next.

THE SERVER LOCATION INFORMATION SECTION

The Server Location Information section of the Basics tab is divided into three groups of information: Phone Dialing, Additional Info, and Servers. Figure 35.2 shows the Server Location Information section of the Basics tab.

Figure 35.2
The Server Location Information section of the Basics tab enables you to specify location-specific information about the Domino server.

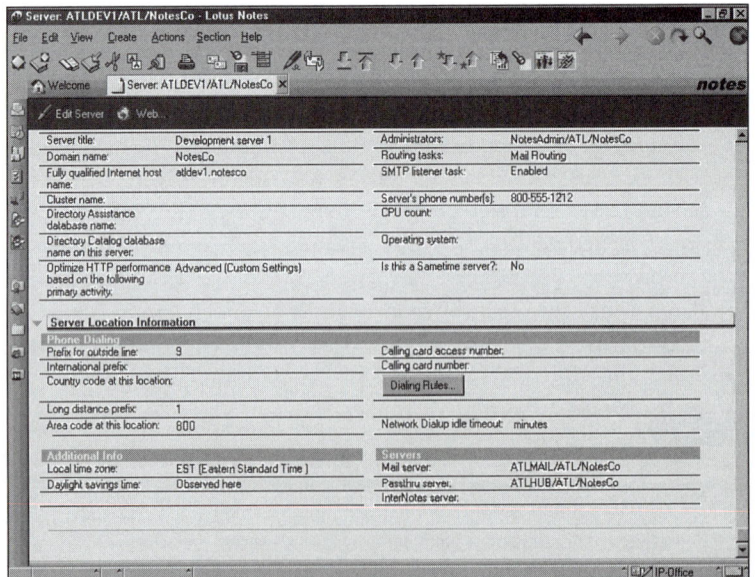

The Phone Dialing area is pretty self-explanatory. You can use the fields of the Phone Dialing area to enter additional calling information for the server, such as the number needed to dial an outside line or any needed long distance prefix.

The Additional Info area defines how your server operates with the time zone of your area, including daylight saving time. Because replication is a scheduled task, it is very important that you ensure your server is using the correct time. You can specify the local time zone of the server and whether it should observe daylight savings time.

The Servers area enables you to specify other servers that your server should use to perform certain tasks. The Mail server field contains the name of the server that is handling mail routing tasks for your server. Usually, a server does its own mail routing, so this field contains the name of the current server (such as in Figure 35.2). If your server uses a Passthru server to connect to other servers, you can specify the name of that server in the Passthru server field. Finally, if your organization is using an InterNotes server, you can specify its name in the InterNotes server field.

THE SECURITY TAB

The Security tab contains very important information concerning the security of your Domino server, especially if your Domino server also is an HTTP server. The Security tab provides a great deal of control over those who have access to your server, what information they have access to, how they access it, and what they can change about it. Figure 35.3 shows the Security tab.

Figure 35.3
The Security tab provides a great deal of control over the security of your Domino server.

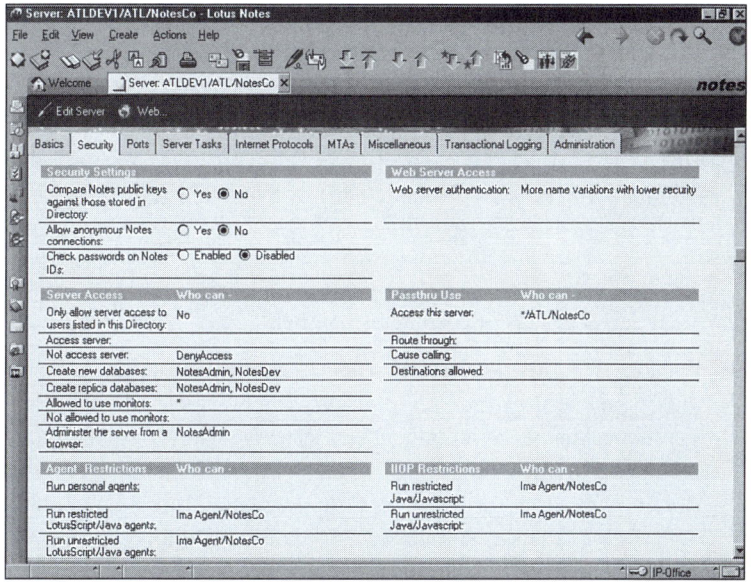

The Security tab is divided into 6 areas: Security Settings, Web Server Access, Server Access, Passthru Use, Agent Restrictions, and IIOP Restrictions.

THE SECURITY SETTINGS AREA

The Security Settings area contains the following fields:

- Compare Notes public keys against those stored in Directory   When this field is set to Yes, public key comparisons are made during user-to-server and server-to-server authentications. Therefore, the public key of the user or server that is being authenticated must be listed in the Domino Directory. If it is not, access is denied. The default value of this field is No.

- **Allow anonymous Notes connections** When this field is set to Yes, any Domino server or Notes client can connect with your server even if it cannot be authenticated. If you select Yes and there are entries in the Access server field of the Server Access area, add Anonymous as an entry to this field to allow anonymous access. If the Access server field is blank, you do not need to make this addition. If access is granted anonymously through this setting, it falls upon the databases on the server to enforce access control based on the Anonymous entry in the database's Access Control List (ACL). If there is no Anonymous entry, anonymous users have the access level granted to the Default entry of the ACL. The default value of this field is No.

> **Caution**
>
> For security reasons, *never* set the Allow Anonymous Notes Connections field to Yes on a server containing sensitive, proprietary, or confidential information. Doing so places your sensitive information in serious jeopardy of compromise.

- **Check passwords on Notes IDs** Setting this field to Enabled causes the Domino server to verify that the password provided by the Notes client to the Domino server is not expired and is the latest password according to the Person or Server document in the Domino Directory. The default value of this field is Disabled.

WEB SERVER ACCESS

The Web Server Access field contains one field:

- **Web server authentication** This field contains two settings. Fewer name variations with higher security requires all users authenticating via a Web browser to use their hierarchical name, common name, alternative name, or alias defined in the user's Person document. In order to use this setting, all your Domino servers must be using a Domino Directory based on the R5.x template. More name variations with lower security uses the same authentication routine as Domino R4.6x servers—that is, you may use all the previously mentioned name variations and also last name only, first name only, or Soundex value. This is the default setting.

SERVER ACCESS

The Server Access area contains the following fields:

- **Only allow server access to users listed in this Directory** If this field is set to Yes, only those individuals who have Person documents in this Domino Directory are allowed to access this server. If you set this field to Yes on a Web-enabled server, every person who accesses this server must have a Person document in the Domino Directory, which could be a pain to manage. You can set up a Web registration database so that users can automatically register themselves, which could alleviate this pain. Lotus has created a sample Web registration database that is available for download at http://www.notes.net. You should keep in mind that setting this field to Yes also denies access to all servers, even if they are listed in this Directory. You can get around this by placing the desired server names in the Access server field explicitly or entering a group name that contains the desired server names.

- Access server   The administrator can restrict access to the server to only the users, servers, and groups listed in this field. If this field is left blank, any user or server that can authenticate with the server can access the server (except those listed in the Not access server field). If this field does contain values, access is restricted to only those listed, and all others are denied access.

> **Tip**
> Maintaining access control for many servers can be very difficult, even when using groups. There are a few shortcuts that can make this a little easier, however. If you want to grant access to everyone listed in this Domino Directory, you can enter an asterisk (*). If you use an asterisk followed by a view name from the Domino Directory, everyone listed in that view is granted access. An asterisk followed by a slash and a certifier name grants access to everyone with that certifier. So, if you want to allow everyone with the /Falcons/NFL certifier to access your server, enter */Falcons/NFL in the Access Server field.

- Not Access Server   This field performs the opposite operation of the Access server field; anyone listed in this field is denied access to the server.

> **Tip**
> The most common entry in the Not Access Server field is a single group (I usually name it something like Deny Access) that contains the name of everyone whom you want to deny access, such as individuals who have been terminated from your organization. When you create this group in the Domino Directory, make sure you specify the group type as a Deny Access Group so the group can be used only for its intended purpose.
>
> An alternative to using a Deny Access Group is to use Notes ID Lockout in the Person document of the terminated person. Although more tedious, this prevents users from looking at a centralized list of everyone who has been terminated from your organization.

- Create new databases   This field lists all users, groups, and servers that are allowed to create databases on or copy databases to your server. If this field is left blank, any certified user who has access to the server can create databases on the server. If this field contains one or more values, only those named can create databases on the server. The default value of this field is blank.

- Create replica databases   This field lists all users, groups, and servers that are allowed to create replicas on your server. Unlike the Create new databases field, if this field is left blank, *no one* is allowed to create new replicas on your server. The default value of this field is blank.

> **Tip**
>
> You can prevent the uncontrolled proliferation of databases on your server by using the Create New Databases and Create Replica Databases fields to restrict database creation to only specified individuals.

- **Allowed to use monitors** Monitors are a new feature in Domino R5 that enable you to track certain events on a server and trigger specific events when the specified thresholds are crossed. Monitors can be set up to watch
    - Database information Access Control List changes, replication failures, file size, and so forth
    - Event statistics Communication, mail routing, and so forth
    - Server statistics Various server statistics

    Monitors are set up in the Statistics & Events database (STATREP5.NSF). Please refer to the documentation on this database for more information.

    The Allowed to use monitors field lists all users, groups, and servers that are allowed to establish Monitor documents in the Statistics & Events database. If this field is left blank, anyone with certified access to the server can set up a Monitor document; if this field contains one or more names, only those individuals are allowed to create monitors. The default value of this field is an asterisk (*), which enables anyone to create Monitor documents for your server.

- **Not allowed to use monitors** This field performs the opposite of the Allowed to use monitors field; anyone listed in this field is specifically forbidden from creating monitors. The default value of this field is blank.

- **Administer the Server from a Browser** This field contains the names of users or groups that are allowed to administer your server remotely through the Web Administration tool. During installation and setup, this field is automatically set to the name of the specified administrator. The default value of this field is blank.

> **Tip**
>
> If you have more than one administrator that will be working with your server, you can set up an administration group (I usually name mine Domino Administrators) and place the name of that group in the Administer the Server From a Browser field. Then you can manage administration access from one place for all your servers.

THE PASSTHRU USE AREA

The Passthru server is a powerful feature that was introduced in Lotus Notes R4. In the "old days" (that is pre-R4.x), a user who needed to remotely connect to multiple servers would set up Connection documents for each server. The introduction of the Passthru server feature changed that for the better. Now a user can call into one Passthru server, and that server provides connections to other servers in the network by passing information back and forth between the user and the target server. A Passthru server also enables users who are running one protocol—TCP/IP, for example—to connect to a server running a different protocol—SPX, for example—by managing the connection and passing of information itself. Please refer to the Lotus documentation for more information.

Configuring your server to be a Passthru server is pretty easy. First, make sure that your server can reach the destination server(s) through the network. Next, specify that your server is a Passthru server in the Server document (I cover that in a minute). Finally, create a Connection document that instructs other servers and Notes clients to connect to the Passthru server and then route through that server to their destination server. Connection documents are covered later in this chapter.

The Passthru Use area of the Security tab defines the details of your pass-through capability: who is allowed to use the server as a Passthru server, where they are allowed to connect, and how the connection is made.

THE AGENT RESTRICTIONS AREA

The Agent Restrictions area is used to determine who is allowed to run an agent on this server, and what type of agent they are allowed to run. There are two basic levels of agents in Notes/Domino: restricted and unrestricted. LotusScript and Java have access to some potentially dangerous areas on your server, such as file I/O, calling DLLs, and operating system commands. An *unrestricted* agent has access to all these capabilities and can perform any of these functions. A *restricted* agent can still perform database functions, but it cannot perform more dangerous actions, such as file I/O, or change the system time.

The following fields are used to restrict the execution of agents:

- Run personal agents   This field lists all users and groups that are allowed to run personal agents on your server. If there are no names listed in this field, anyone can schedule personal agents on this server. The default value of this field is blank.

- Run restricted LotusScript/Java agents   Anyone listed in the Run restricted LotusScript/Java agents field is allowed to run restricted agents, but not unrestricted agents. If this field is left blank, no one is allowed to run a restricted agent on the server. The default value of this field is blank.

- Run unrestricted LotusScript/Java agents   Anyone listed in this field is allowed to run restricted *and* unrestricted agents on your server. If this field is left blank, no one is allowed to run an unrestricted agent on the server. The default value of this field is blank.

> **Tip**
>
> I like to control what type of agents run on my servers, so I review each agent before it is "blessed" to run. I created a dummy user ID that I control called Ima Agent. I sign all scheduled agents with the Ima Agent ID, and I placed the name Ima Agent in the Run Restricted and Run Unrestricted fields. Another benefit of this technique is that all mail generated by the agent is from Ima Agent, not the original developer of the agent.

The IIOP Restrictions Area

The IIOP Restictions area is used to control who can run Java and JavaScript programs on your server. The fields in this area are similar to the fields listed in the previous area with regard to restricted and unrestricted programmatic access. If this field is left blank, no one is allowed to run unrestricted agents on your server.

The Ports Tab

The next tab on the Server document, the Ports tab, is important to your server because it defines the ports and addresses your server uses to communicate, as well as the Notes Named Networks (NNNs) to which your server belongs.

> **Note**
> A Notes Named Network (NNN) is nothing more than a group of servers that share the same network protocol. A server can be a member of multiple NNNs if it is running more than one protocol. For instance, a server that runs TCP/IP on one network card and SPX on another network card can be a member of two NNNs. The Database Open dialog box lists only servers that are in the same NNN. Servers that are members of the same NNN route mail without the use of Connection documents. NNNs are described in greater detail in the Domino Administrator's Guide.

The Notes Network Ports Subtab

The Ports tab is broken down into three subtabs: Notes Network Ports, Internet Ports, and Proxies. Let's begin by taking a look at the Notes Network Ports subtab, which is shown in Figure 35.4.

Figure 35.4
The Notes Network Ports subtab displays the Notes Network and communication port information about your server.

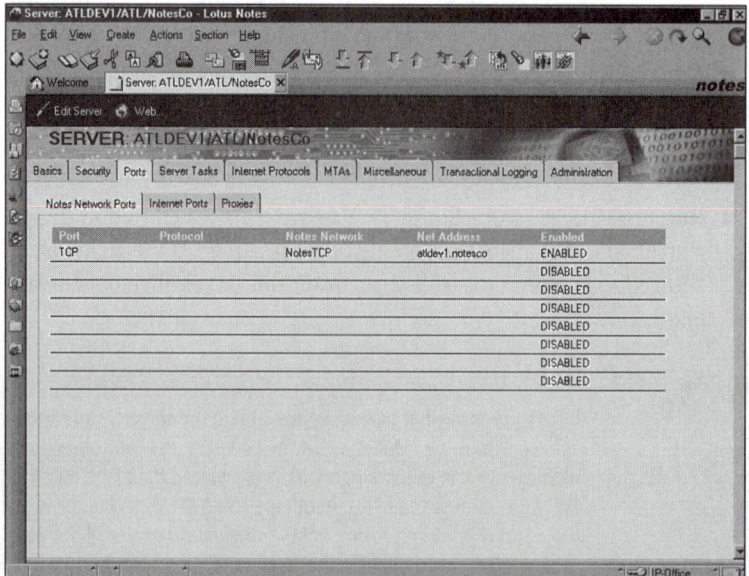

As you can see in the figure, the Notes Network Ports subtab is laid out in a tabular format, with each row representing a single NNN. The fields in the Notes Network Ports subtab are defined as follows:

- **Port**   This field is used to define a valid communications port for the server to use on a given NNN. For instance, if you are using the TCP/IP protocol and have that protocol assigned to a port named TCP, you enter TCP in the Port field. Remember, the ports for your Domino server are enabled through the File, Preferences, User Preferences dialog box, in the Ports area.
- **Protocol**   This field defines what protocol the named port is using.
- **Notes Network**   This field contains the name you give to each NNN.
- **Net Address**   This field contains the network address for the Domino server on the given network protocol. For TCP/IP networks, you can use either the DNS entry name for the server or the IP address of the server on that network.
- **Enabled**   This field indicates whether the port is enabled for your server.

THE INTERNET PORTS SUBTAB

The Internet Ports subtab is a rather busy subtab because it has an SSL settings area and then it actually has five subtabs of its own: Web, Directory, News, Mail, and IIOP. Figure 35.5 shows the Internet Ports subtab with the Web subtab showing.

Figure 35.5
The Internet Ports subtab enables you to configure the various Web access ports you use to interact with an intranet or Internet.

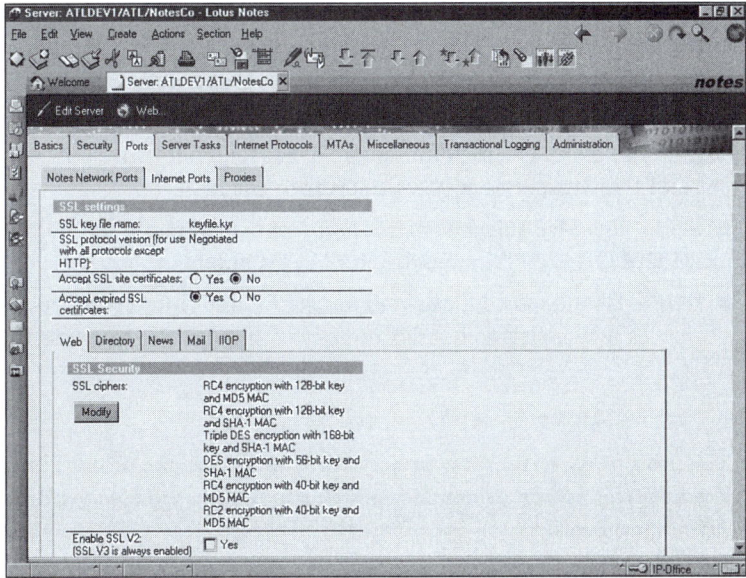

The SSL Settings Area

The SSL settings area enables you to define the criteria for your Secure Sockets Layer (SSL) protocol to use with secure, encrypted HTTP transactions (HTTPS). If you are not using SSL to provide HTTPS transactions on your Domino server, you can skip the SSL settings subsection. If you are using SSL for your Domino server, configure it here. The SSL key file name field is used to store the name of the file containing your site's SSL keys; the default value is KEYFILE.KYR. The SSL protocol version field enables you to specify which of the various SSL protocols are used for communication (for example, V2.0, V3.0); the default value is Negotiated, which means that the Domino server and the client being communicated with will attempt to determine which protocol they share. The Accept SSL site certificates field tells Domino to automatically acquire an SSL site certificate for use by the Domino Web Navigator server when it connects to an Internet host site. Although it makes it easier for Notes clients to access SSL secured sites, enabling this option can compromise security because Domino will not verify the remote server's identity. SSL certificates contain an expiration date. The Accept expired SSL certificates field tells Domino to accept an SSL certificate even though it has expired.

WEB, DIRECTORY, NEWS, MAIL, AND IIOP SUBTABS The Web, Directory, News, Mail, and IIOP subtabs all contain the same information that defines each of their various ports and protocols. Here is a brief explanation of each protocol:

- **Web** Defines the port information for the HTTP and HTTPS protocols.
- **Directory** Defines the port information for the Lightweight Directory Access Protocol (LDAP), which is used to communicate with LDAP directories such as Bigfoot and Four11. This protocol is also used for Web clients to access any Domino LDAP directories, otherwise known as the Lightweight Enterprise Directory.
- **News** Defines the port information for the Network Newsgroup Transfer Protocol (NNTP). NNTP is used to transfer newsgroup information from NNTP server to NNTP server and from NNTP server to client.
- **Mail** The Mail subtab contains protocol configuration for multiple mail protocols: IMAP, POP, SMTP Inbound, and SMTP Outbound.
- **IIOP** Defines port information for the Internet InterORB Protocol (IIOP). IIOP enables Java applets to interact directly with the server to access Domino databases.

The Proxies Subtab

If you use a proxy server on your network, you can use the settings in the Proxies subtab to tell your server how to communicate with and use the proxy server for various Internet services and protocols.

THE SERVER DOCUMENT | 821

> **Note**
> A proxy server is a computer running proxy software sitting between your internal network and the Internet. A proxy server accepts user requests for Internet services and retrieves the requested information on behalf of the user. Proxy servers have three main benefits: They block access to the internal network, they mask the IP address of the user by submitting requests using their own IP address, and they can cache requests to make Internet access quicker.

Figure 35.6 shows the Proxies subtab.

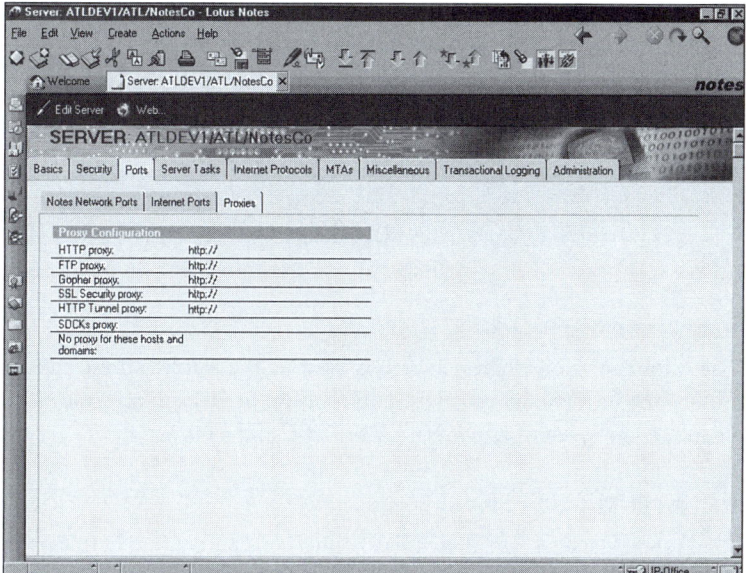

Figure 35.6
The Proxies subtab enables you to define how your Domino server communicates with the proxy server.

Configuring the Proxies subtab is relatively simple. If you are using a proxy server for any of the protocols listed, simply enter the DNS name or IP address of the proxy server responsible for the protocol.

THE SERVER TASKS TAB

The Server Tasks tab contains configuration information for various administrative tasks that the server handles for you automatically. The Server Tasks tab is broken down into six subtabs: Administration Process, Agent Manager, Domain Indexer, Directory Cataloger, Internet Cluster Manager, and Web Retriever. Let's begin by examining the first subtab, Administration Process, which is shown in Figure 35.7.

PART
VI
CH
35

Figure 35.7
The Administration Process subtab determines when and how the ADMINP process handles tasks.

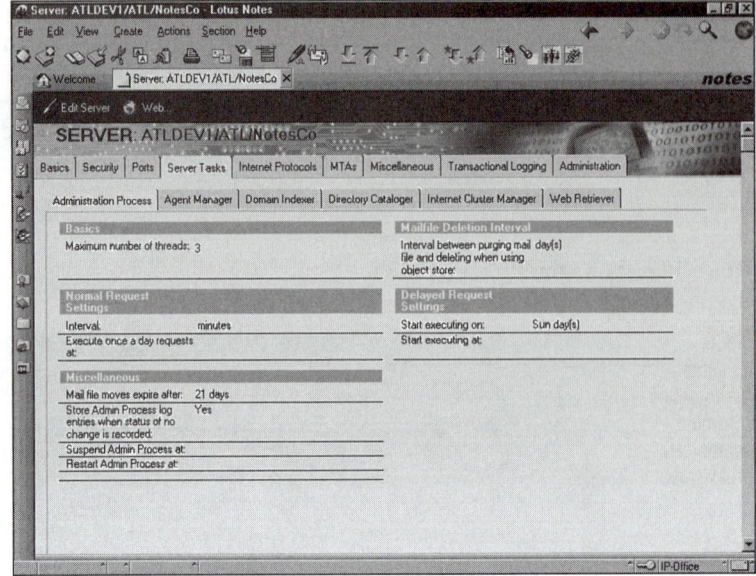

THE ADMINISTRATION PROCESS SUBTAB

The Administration Process subtab is used by the Administration Process (ADMINP) to determine when to carry out requests. Each setting in this subtab controls threshold information when specific types of requests are executed, and so forth.

THE AGENT MANAGER SUBTAB

The Agent Manager subtab enables you to configure a number of options that determine when scheduled agents can run, how many can run, and for how long. Figure 35.8 shows the Agent Manager subtab.

The Basics subsection contains only one field: Refresh agent cache. The Domino server contains a list of agents that can run during the current day. For example, agents set to run If Documents Have Been Pasted and On Schedule Hourly can run each day and appear in the Agent Manager list each day; On Schedule Monthly agents show up in this list only one day each month. The time value entered in this field tells the Domino server when to update the list of agents in the cache.

The next subsections in the Agent Manager section, Daytime Parameters and Nighttime Parameters, enable you to control how much of the Domino server's resources are used to run agents. By default, the daytime parameters are set so that agents consume less resources than they do at night.

The Server Document

Figure 35.8
The Agent Manager subtab is used to configure when and how scheduled agents run on your server.

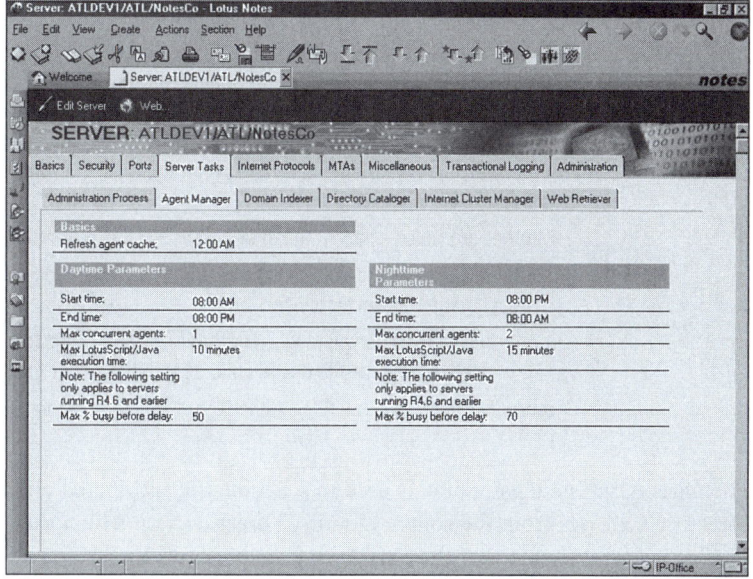

The Domain Indexer Subtab

The Domain Indexer subtab contains only one major field, Domain wide indexer. The Domain wide indexer field has two choices available: Enabled and Disabled. This field enables the Domain Search feature for your Domino domain. The default for this field is Disabled. Figure 35.9 shows the Domain Indexer subtab in all its splendor.

Figure 35.9
The Domain Indexer subtab is used to enable the Domain Search feature.

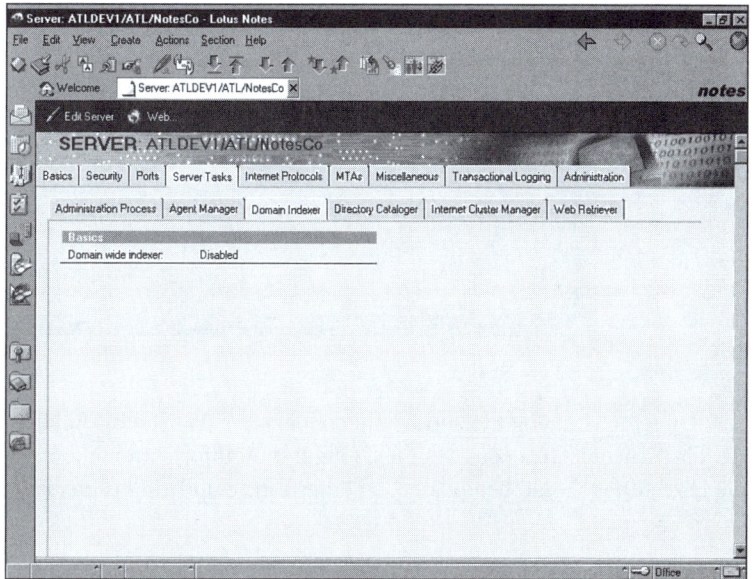

THE DIRECTORY CATALOGER SUBTAB

> **Note**
>
> The Directory Catalog feature is new to Domino R5, and is a compressed version of one or more Domino Directories. The Directory Catalog contains entries for users, groups, and mail-in databases only. Directory Catalogs use the Lightweight Directory Access Protocol (LDAP) protocol to achieve the information compression. The Directory Catalog feature provides these benefits:
>
> - Entries are much smaller (100 bytes versus 10KB in a normal Domino Directory).
> - When a Directory Catalog is maintained locally, name lookups are dramatically faster, and a lookup to a server is not needed.
> - You can still use encryption when addressing from a Directory Catalog; the encryption is resolved at the time the document is sent to the server for delivery.
>
> For more information please refer to the Lotus Domino documentation.

The Directory Cataloger subtab is used to schedule the automated updating of the Directory Catalogs from the source Domino Directories on which they are based. Figure 35.10 is a perfect example of the Directory Cataloger subtab.

Figure 35.10
The Directory Cataloger subtabfeature is used to schedule the updating of the Directory Catalogs on your server.

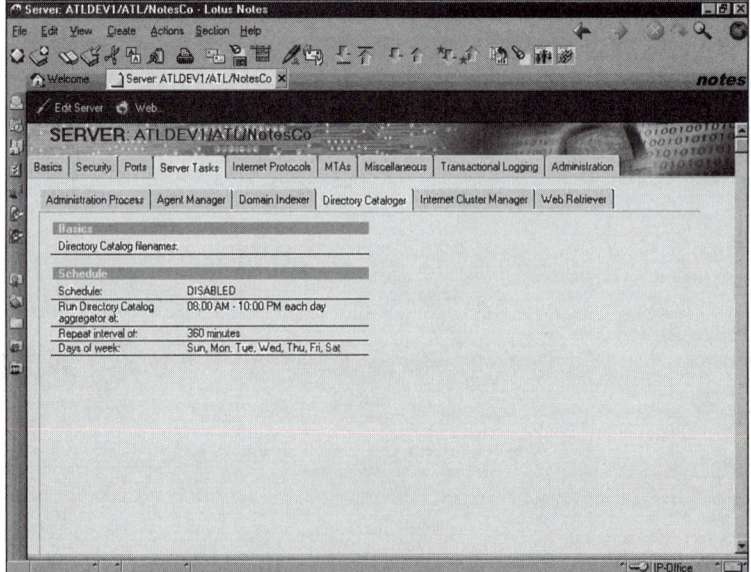

The Directory Catalog filenames field contains the name(s) of the directories to be updated. The Schedule area contains the configuration information about what days and times the Directories should be updated, whetherfeature updating is enabled, and so forth.

The Internet Cluster Manager Subtab

The Internet Cluster Manager (ICM) is a featurenew feature in Domino R5 that extends the capabilities of enterprise clustering to Domino-based Web (HTTP) servers. Now you can provide failover and load balancing to your Web browser clients.

The ICM sits between the Web (HTTP) clients and a Domino server cluster. The Web clients send HTTP requests to the ICM. Because the ICM knows all the vital information about the servers in the cluster, it can make the decision as to which cluster server is best suited to handle the request, and it passes the request to the appropriate server.

The ICM is a server task that must be started separately. The ICM does not have to run on a server in the cluster, but it must run on a server in the same domain as the cluster. The ICM is configured in the Internet Cluster Manager subtab of the Server Tasks tab in the Server document. Figure 35.11 shows the Internet Cluster Manager subtab.

Figure 35.11
The Internet Cluster Manager subtab contains the configuration information for your ICM.

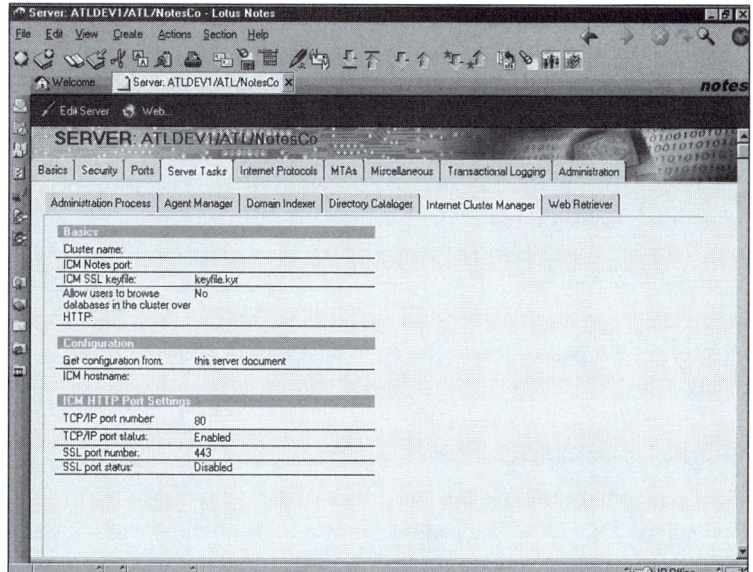

The Web Retriever Subtab

The Web Retriever subtab applies only to installations that use the Web Retriever to retrieve and store HTTP, FTP, and Gopher information in a Notes database for Notes users. The Web Retriever can be very handy if you don't have the IP protocol on your network or don't want to give direct Internet access to each user. Figure 35.12 displays the Web Retriever Administration section of the Server document.

Figure 35.12
The Web Retriever subtab configures the environment that enables the server to retrieve Web pages for the users.

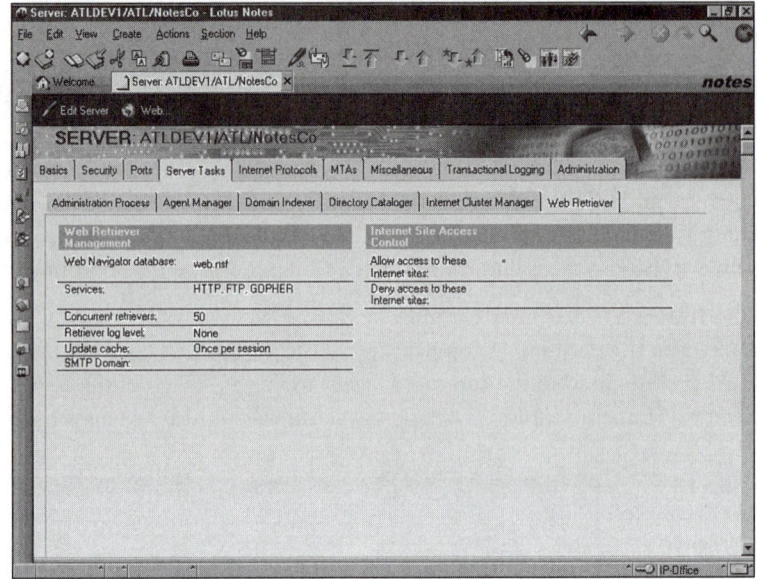

The Web Retriever subtab can also be used to restrict access to specific Internet sites through the fields located in the Internet Site Access Control area. You can specify specific site URLs or IP addresses that you want to allow your users to access in the Allow access to these Internet sites field; the default value of an asterisk (*) allows your users to access any site on the Internet. The Deny access to these Internet sites field enables you to explicitly list sites you do not want your users accessing (such as http://www.dilbert.com). The default value is blank, which indicates that there are no sites you want to deny your users.

THE INTERNET PROTOCOLS TAB

The Ports subtab contains the basic information your server needs to use various Internet protocols and services. The Internet Protocols tab builds upon that information by defining the environment your server uses when using these Internet protocols. The Internet Protocols subtab is divided into five subtabs: HTTP, Domino Web Engine, IIOP, LDAP, and NNTP. Let's begin by taking a look at the HTTP subtab.

THE HTTP SUBTAB

If you are planning to use your Domino server to handle HTTP requests either over the Internet or a corporate intranet, the HTTP subtab is very important to you. As you can see in Figure 37.13, the HTTP Server subtab is quite large and is divided into several subsections.

THE SERVER DOCUMENT | 827

Figure 35.13
The HTTP subtab is key to configuring your Web server for optimal performance.

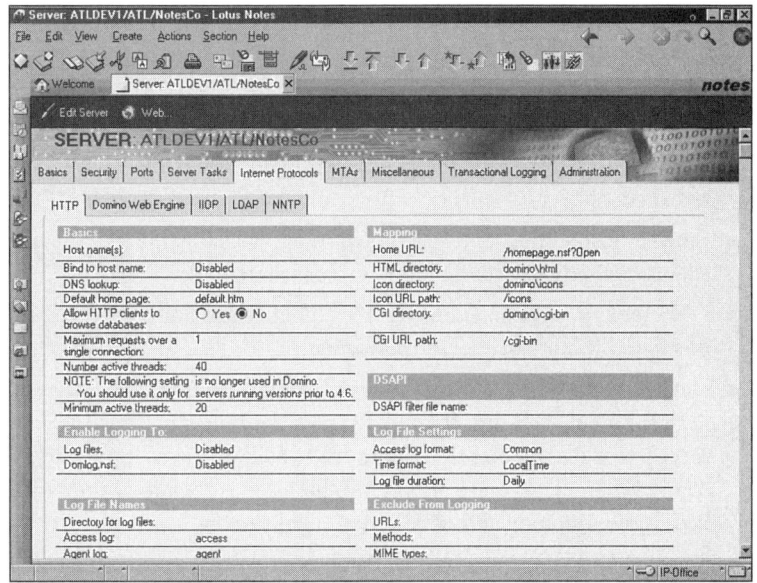

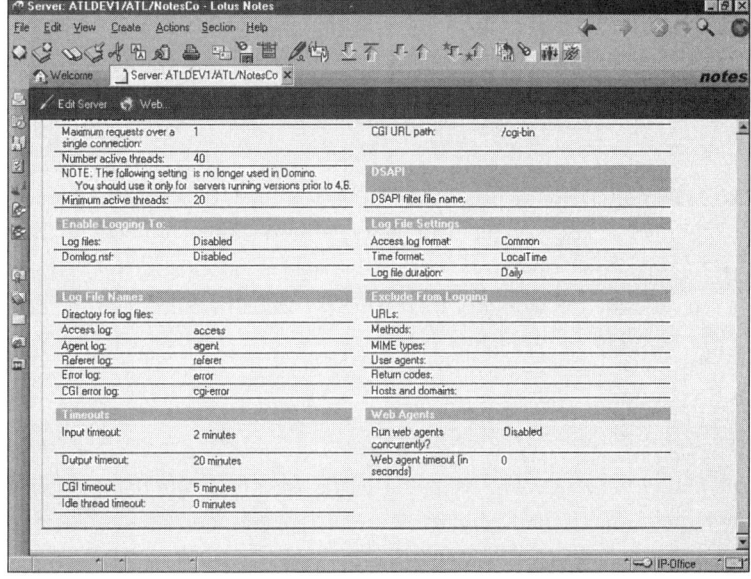

PART
VI
CH
35

THE BASICS AREA Because the first subsection, Basics, is the most important, let's start there. It contains the following fields:

- Host name(s)   Use this field to enter the host name(s) you want returned to a client's browser. The host names can be either DNS names or IP addresses. You can enter up to 32 separate names. If the field is left blank, the name of the current machine is returned.
- Bind to host name   Select Enabled to allow aliases for the host name. If disabled, clients can only use the Domino server name, but not aliases.
- DNS lookup   When enabled, DNS lookups are done for logging purposes. Turning this field off increases server performance.
- Default home page   This field tells Domino what HTML page to use as the home page for your Web site. If you want to use a Notes database as your default home page, specify that database in the Home URL field of the Mapping area and leave this field blank. If you elect to use an HTML file, it must reside in the HTML directory specified in the Mapping subsection, described shortly.
- Allow HTTP clients to browse databases   When set to Yes (which is the default), this field enables browser users to get an FTP-style listing of databases on a Domino server (the HTTP equivalent of the Open Database dialog box in Notes).

> **Tip**
> In almost every instance, setting this field to Yes is *bad, bad, bad,* because it allows hackers to see all the databases on a Domino server! Be very judicious when allowing database browsers. Personally, I would never enable this option.

- Maximum requests over a single connection   This field tells your server the maximum number of requests that can be served by a single connection. The default value is one.
- Number active threads   This field enables Domino to determine how much memory to set aside for Domino. Increasing the value to more than the default of 40 causes Domino to consume more memory.

The Minimum Active Threads field should only be used for servers running releases prior to 4.6. It is not used by Domino R5.

THE MAPPING AREA   The Mapping area is used to define the directories that are used by the Domino server to access various items, such as icon files, CGI programs, HTML pages, and so forth. You can also designate the Notes database you want to use as the default home URL for your Domino server. If you want to use an HTML page as your default home page, use the Default home page field in the Basics area to specify the HTML filename and leave this field blank.

The Home URL field takes precedence over the Default home page field, so if you specify both, Domino will use the Home URL field. All paths in the Mapping section are relative to the Domino data directory (for example D:\Domino\Data). If an entry begins with a "/" then it is located in the data directory. The full path for a Home URL `/homepage.nsf?Open` for this example would be D:\Domino\Data\homepage.nsf. URLs will normally use forward slashes while directory specifications will typically use back slashes.

DSAPI, ENABLE LOGGING TO, LOG FILE NAMES, TIMEOUTS, LOG FILE SETTINGS, EXCLUDE FROM LOGGING, AND WEB AGENTS AREAS   The DSAPI (Domino Web Server Application Programmer's Interface) area is used to define the filter program to be used for DSAPI access to your Domino server. The filter program is notified when specific events occur such as web page retrieval or authentication.

The logging feature has been greatly improved in Domino R5, including the capability of logging the IP address or host name of the requests made by users.

The Enable Logging To area contains two fields: Log files, which enables or disables logging; and Domlog.nsf, which enables the Web Server log database.

The Log File Names area is used to define the filenames of the various log files to be used and the directory where these logs are stored.

The fields in the Timeouts area enable you to tell Domino how long it should try various operations before it decides that enough is enough and gives up. For each of the four fields (Input timeout, Output timeout, CGI timeout, and Idle thread timeout), simply enter the time (in minutes) that Domino should wait for an operation to complete before timing out and freeing the resources in use. The Log File Settings area determines the Access log format (common or extended common) and the Time format, which is a keyword field that enables you to time-stamp log entries with either the local time zone information or with the current Greenwich Mean Time information.

The Exclude From Logging area enables you to enter a list of IP addresses or DNS names for various protocols and services (URLs, Methods, MIME types, User agents, Return codes, Hosts and domains) that should *not* be logged. Note that if you enter DNS names in these fields, you must have the DNS lookup feature in the Basics subsection enabled. The Web Agents area is used to indicate whether Web agents are allowed to execute concurrently—that is, at the same time. You can also specify a timeout period so that stalled agents do not prevent other agents from starting, if you have not allowed concurrency.

THE DOMINO WEB ENGINE SUBTAB

Like the HTTP subtab, the Domino Web Engine subtab contains quite a few areas. Most of these areas are self-explanatory and the default settings are fine, so you probably will not need to modify the settings in this tab. If you need more information concerning the use of this tab, please refer to the Domino Administration documentation for more information. Figure 35.14 is provided to awe you with the amount of data on the Domino Web Engine subtab.

Figure 35.14
The Domino Web Engine subtab provides granular control of your Domino caches.

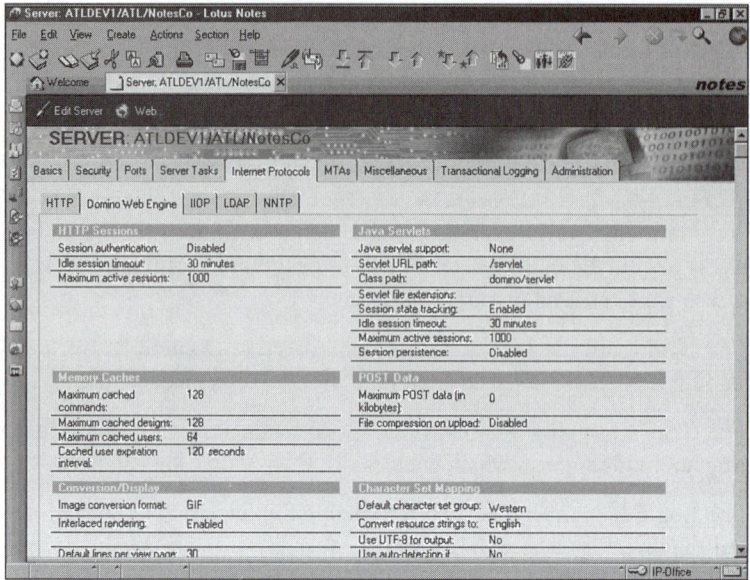

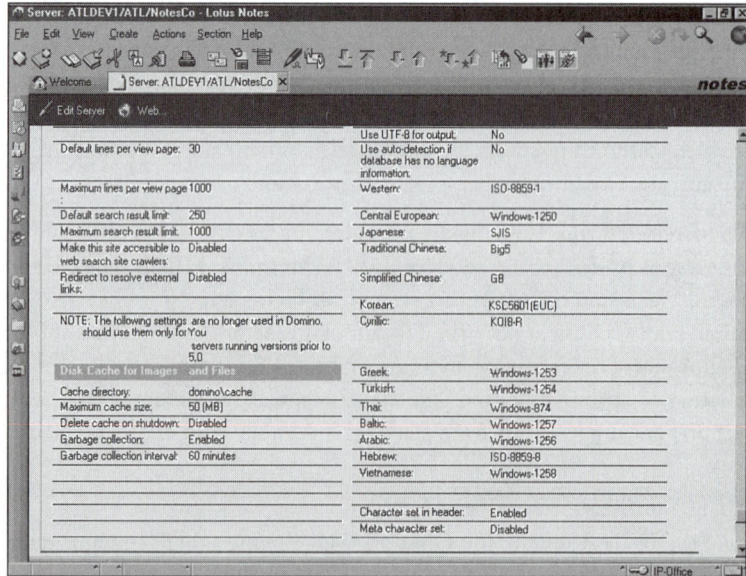

The IIOP Subtab

The IIOP subtab contains one field for the Internet InterORB Protocol (IIOP), Number of Threads. The Number of Threads field defines the maximum number of IIOP threads the server can have open at any given time.

The LDAP Subtab

The LDAP subtab gives instructions on where to go to configure LDAP settings.

The NNTP Subtab

The NNTP subtab contains three areas that define the configuration and administration for Network Newsgroup services: Basics, News Reader Parameters, and News Feed Parameters (see Figure 35.15).

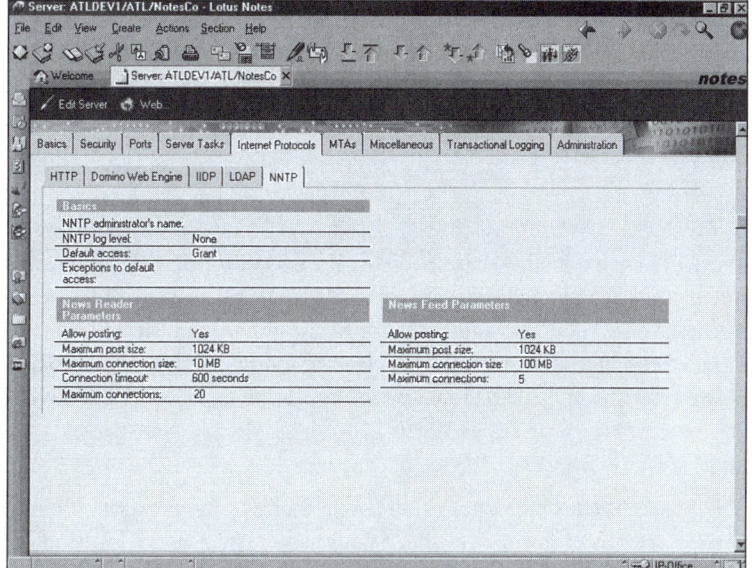

Figure 35.15
The NNTP subtab is used to configure your Web server for network newsgroup services.

The Basics Area

The NNTP administrator's name field contains the name of a user or group that is allowed to administer the NNTP features, such as editing an NNTP database profile document. The NNTP log level field tells the server how much information to log about the NNTP service: None, Terse, or Verbose. The Default access field tells the server whether to allow the average user to access the NNTP services. The Exceptions to default access field lists IP addresses that have an access level other than the default access level to newsgroups.

The News Reader Parameters Area

The News Reader Parameters area defines the connection settings for newsgroup readers that access your server. The Allow posting field is set to Yes to allow newsreader clients to post articles, and No to prevent all newsreader clients from posting articles. The Maximum post size field tells the server, in kilobytes, the maximum allowed size of newsgroup posts. The Maximum connection size field defines the maximum combined size, in megabytes, of postings in one session. The Connection timeout field defines the length of time, in seconds, that the server should keep an idle newsgroup readers session open. The Maximum connections size field tells the server the maximum allowed number of concurrent newsgroup sessions.

The News Feed Parameters Area

The News Feed Parameters area defines the connection settings for connections between your server and other NNTP servers. The Allow posting field indicates whether users are allowed to create posts in the provided newsgroups (some businesses allow read access to newsgroups for reference, but do not allow posts to newsgroups). The Maximum post size field tells the server, in kilobytes, the maximum allowed size of newsgroup posts from another server. The Maximum connection size field defines the maximum combined size, in megabytes, of postings in one session from another NNTP server to your server. The Maximum connections field tells the server the maximum allowed number of concurrent NNTP server sessions.

The MTAs Tab

The MTAs tab contains three subtabs: R4.x SMTP MTA (R4.x Internet Message Transfer Agent), X.400 MTA (Message Transfer Agent), and cc:Mail MTA (Message Transfer Agent). These subtabs contain data only if you installed the MTA in question when you installed the Domino server. If you need to configure the Domino R5 SMTP feature, please refer to the Server/Domain Configuration and Server/Server Configuration forms.

The Miscellaneous Tab

The Miscellaneous tab contains one area, Contact Information. This area enables you to enter descriptive information about your server, such as the location of the server, department that uses the server, and so forth.

The Transactional Logging Tab

Transaction-based logging and recovery, commonly referred to as transactional logging, is a new feature in Domino R5 databases. This feature enables all updates to an R5 database to be captured and logged, which enables a database to be recovered quickly and fully in the event of a system crash. The Transactional Logging tab is used to define the parameters used for transactional logging, and is shown in all its glory in Figure 35.16.

The Transactional logging field enables or disables transactional logging for all R5 databases on your server. Remember, transactional logging works only on R5 databases or R4.x databases that have been converted to the R5 On-Disk Structure (ODS).

The Log path field tells the server where it can find or create the transactional log file. It is highly recommended that you place the transactional log file on its own disk, for a number of reasons. Two of the most notable reasons are because it will read/write to the file often, so a dedicated disk will be faster, and because transactional logs can get quite large—you don't want to run out of disk space.

THE SERVER DOCUMENT | 833

Figure 35.16
The Transactional Logging subtab configures transaction logging, a new feature of Domino R5.

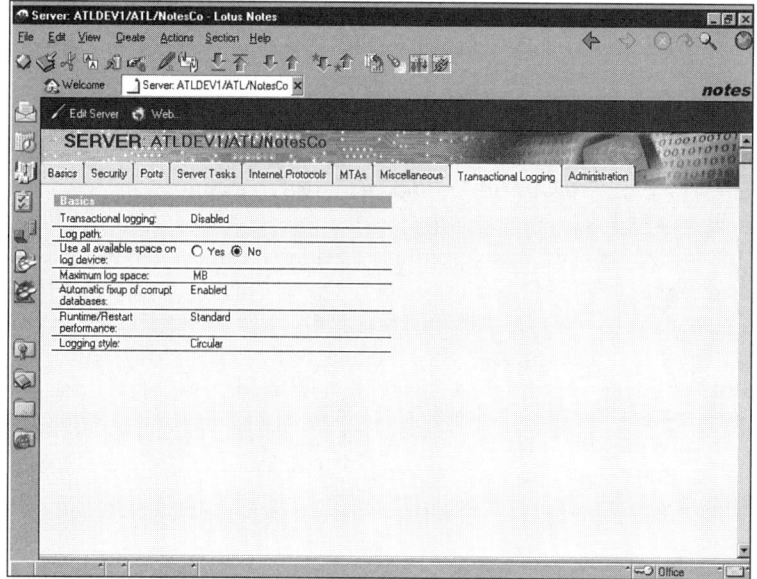

The Use all available space on log device field tells the Domino server that it can use all free space on the drive indicated in the Log path field. Because this should be a dedicated device, this is a recommended option.

The Maximum Log Space field should contain the maximum amount of space you want to provide on the drive indicated in the Log path for logging. Once again, if you take my recommendation and use a dedicated drive, this field should contain the disk size, but no more than 4GB—that is the maximum size of a log file. In any case, the amount of space allowed should be over 200MB, and even this amount will get used up fairly quickly.

The Automatic fixup of corrupt databases field enables a task that, when a corrupt database is detected, attempts to correct the errors using the information stored in the log file. This is a very useful feature for mission-critical systems, because it keeps the system integrity intact (as much as possible).

The Runtime/Restart performance field enables you to control where you take the transactional logging performance "hit." When you set this field to Favor Runtime performance, more of the transactional log is kept loaded in memory, enabling faster access times. When you set this field to Favor Restart Recovery Time, the server keeps less of the transaction log in memory and makes updates to the file on disk more often. This means that (usually) a more current "snapshot" of the database's recent transactions are stored in the file, enabling the transaction log to recover faster because it has to reconstruct fewer transactions. The default value of Standard is a compromise and checkpoints occur regularly. The default value of Standard is recommended.

The Logging style field enables you to indicate whether you want the transaction log to begin overwriting itself when it gets full, or whether you want to archive old transaction

PART
VI
CH
35

logs. Archiving old transaction logs gives you more of the transaction history for recovery, and Circular takes up less disk space.

THE ADMINISTRATION TAB

Well, we finally made it to the last tab of the Server document (whew!), the Administration tab. The Owner field is an Authors field used to identify the person to whom the server belongs—and more importantly, the person who can edit this Server document. The Administrators field is also an Authors field that can be used for additional users and groups who can modify the Server document. The last two fields, Certified Public Key and Change Request, are used by the Administration Process (ADMINP) when changing a server's name. During this process, ADMINP adds the hierarchical certificate to the Certified Public Key field and a change request to the Change Request field of the Server document.

Now it is time to move on and take a look at some of the other documents available to the administrator in the Domino Directory. The next document we will look at is the Connection document.

THE CONNECTION DOCUMENT

Another very important part of configuring your Domino server using the Domino Directory is the Connection document. Connection documents are required to define and establish mail-routing and replication schedules. Connection documents also enable you to define how a server should talk to another server.

> **Note**
> Connection documents are not necessary for mail routing between Domino servers on the same Notes Named Networks (NNNs).

There are currently eleven types of connections defined in the Connection Type field:

- Local Area Network
- Notes Direct Dialup
- Passthru Server
- Network Dialup
- X.25
- SMTP
- X.400
- cc:Mail
- SNA
- Hunt Group
- News/NNTP Feed

Fortunately, creating Connection documents, regardless of type, is fairly straightforward. Because most people use only the first four types, those are the only ones we examine in detail in this chapter. For details on the other seven types, see the Domino Administrator's Guide or the Admin Help database.

The Local Area Network Connection

Let's start by examining the most common connection type: the local area network (LAN) connection.

Much like Server documents, Connection documents are divided into logical tabs that present different options, depending on the parameters needed for a particular type of connection. Because of the similarity of the information required by the different types of connections, I cover only the differences, starting with the most common type of connection, LAN. The LAN connection type has three primary sections (there is also one tab called Miscellaneous, but it has only one field for comments).

The Basics Tab

The Basics tab defines the servers to be connected and how they will connect. Notice that this section remains fairly constant for all eleven types of connections (there are some slight variations). The fields in the Basics section for the LAN Connection document are as follows:

- Connection Type   This keyword list enables you to set the type of connection you want to establish (choose from the eleven types listed earlier).
- Source Server   This field specifies the name of the server that will be establishing the connection. Always use the fully qualified name of the server here.
- Source Domain   This field specifies the domain from which the connection will be established.
- Use the Port(s)   This field enables you to define which ports should be used when attempting to establish this connection. You can click the Choose Ports button to choose from a list of valid ports on your server.
- Usage Priority   This field is a keyword list with two choices: Normal and Low. When a Connection document is set to Low priority, it is used only after all attempts to connect over the LAN have been exhausted.
- Destination Server   This field specifies the name of the server to which you are attempting to connect. As with the Source Server field, it's best to enter a fully qualified name here.
- Destination Domain   This field specifies the name of the domain in which the destination server resides.
- Optional Network Address   You can use this field to enter the destination server's address as it appears on the network. For servers running TCP/IP, you can also enter the IP address here.

The Routing and Replication Tab

The Routing and Replication tab of the Connection document is used to define what should happen when the source server connects to the destination server. The fields in this section are as follows:

- Routing Task   This keyword field tells the Domino server what to do when a connection is established between the servers using this Connection document. There are five choices: Mail Routing, X.400 Mail Routing, SMTP Mail Routing, cc:Mail Routing, and None. Of the five, you are most likely to use Mail Routing (for native NotesMail). The choices you make here affect which fields are displayed in the rest of this section because some fields are not relevant to some of these choices. Try choosing different options to see the effect.

- Route at Once If   If you have Mail Routing enabled, you can use this field to set a threshold for message queuing. When the threshold value is reached, a connection is established using this Connection document; the outbound mail will automatically be routed, regardless of the schedule (remember that mail routes automatically in the same NNN). The default value of this field is 5 messages.

- Routing Cost   This field can be used to associate a "cost" with this connection. This cost is taken into account when trying to connect to the destination server. For example, you may want to give a Connection document that uses an Internet connection a cost of 1, a WAN connection a cost of 5, and a dial-up modem calling long distance a cost of 10 so that the dial-up connection is always tried last.

- Router Type   This field defines what types of request are made to the other server when routing mail. The choices are Push-Wait (the server waits for a call from the other server before sending mail), Push-Only, Pull-Push, Pull-Only.

- Replication Task   This field enables or disables the replication task.

- Replicate Databases of x Priority   This keyword field offers three choices: High, Medium & High, and Low & Medium & High. The Replication Priority of a database is set in the Replication Settings dialog, under the Other area. These choices can be used to determine which databases are replicated when a connection is established. For example, you may elect to replicate only high-priority databases over a costly connection, but you want to replicate all databases over an inexpensive connection.

- Replication Type   This is another keyword field with four choices: Pull-Pull, Pull-Push, Pull-Only, and Push-Only. These choices enable you to control which ends of the connection replicate and which server(s) do the work. A Pull-Pull replication means that each server "pulls" changes from the other server and thereby shares the workload. A Pull-Push replication dictates that the server establishing the connection does all the work (first it pulls changes from the destination server, and then it pushes changes to the destination server). A Push-Only replication is one-way (it only pushes changes from the source server to the destination server). A Pull-Only replication is the opposite of the Push-Only option (it only pulls changes from the destination server). The default is Pull-Push, which means that the source server does all the work. You can use this option to help balance the workload among servers.

> **Note**
>
> If you use Pull-Pull and Pull-Push replication, you need only one Connection document for databases to be synchronized between the source and the destination server. If you use Push-Only or Pull-Only, each end needs a Connection document. Mail routing, on the other hand, requires a Connection document on both ends because it is a one-way process.

- **Files/Directories to Replicate** You can use this field to control which files or directories are replicated during the connection. Enter the list of filenames and directories (separated by commas) you want to replicate.
- **Replication Time Limit** This field can be used to determine how long a replication session can take place. Setting a time limit can be useful in ensuring that one server doesn't consume your server's replication resources.

THE SCHEDULE TAB

The Scheduled Connection section of the Connection document is used to determine when the source server will attempt to connect to the destination server and how often:

- **Schedule** This keyword field has only two choices: Enabled and Disabled. When a Connection document is enabled, the source server calls the destination server based on the schedule defined in the next few fields. If the connection is disabled, the source server does not use this Connection document to call the destination server. Note that if the connection is over a LAN, there will not actually be a phone call. The word call is used to mean that the source server should initiate a connection.
- **Call at Times** This field expects a time, or a range of times, at which the connections should be established. For example, entering a time of `12:30 PM` tells the source server to "call" the destination server at 12:30 p.m. each day. If a range of times is entered (for example, `6:00 AM - 7:00 AM`), this tells the source server to call the destination server within the time range specified based on the Repeat Interval.
- **Repeat Interval** This field enables you to define the number of minutes the source server should wait before calling the destination server. For example, if you enter a value of `0`, the source server calls only once. If you enter a value of `120`, within the Call at Times range, every 120 minutes the source server attempts to call the destination server.

  To help explain this concept, consider the following scenario: If the Call at Times field is set to `7:00 AM - 7:00 PM` and the Repeat Interval field is set to `60` minutes, the source server attempts to call the destination server at 7:00 a.m. The server then attempts to call again 60 minutes after replication has finished, so if replication takes 10 minutes, the next call should begin at 8:10 a.m., and so on.
- **Days of the Week** This is another keyword field that enables you to choose the days of the week on which the connection schedule should be observed. For example, to have this connection made three out of seven days of the week starting on Sunday, enter `Sun, Tue, Thu`.

The Notes Direct Dialup Connection Type

Now that you've seen what a Connection document for a LAN connection looks like, let's take a look at a Connection document for a dial-up modem. You'll notice some immediate changes to the Basics section. Notice that the Choose Ports button is missing from the Notes Direct Dialup version of the Connection document. You have to manually enter the port to which your modem(s) are connected. Additionally, you'll notice that the following fields have been added to the Basics section:

- Always Use Area Code   Set this keyword field to Yes if you want the Domino server to always dial the area code you have supplied when using this connection.
- Destination Country Code   Use this field to enter the country code of the country in which the destination server resides. For example, if you are connecting to a server in Germany, enter 49.
- Destination Area Code   This field is self-explanatory. Enter the area code for the location in which the destination server resides.
- Destination Phone Number   Another self-explanatory field. Enter the phone number the Domino server must dial to reach the destination server.
- Login Script File Name   If you have to run a script file to log in after the modems have connected, enter the name of the script file here.
- Login Script Arguments   You can use these fields to pass up to four arguments to your login script.

The Passthru Server Connection Type

The next type of Connection document you are likely to encounter is the Passthru Server Connection document. Notice right off the bat that the only difference between the Passthru Server and Local Area Network Connection documents is that there is no Ports field in the Passthru Server document. Instead, it a has a field labeled Use Passthru Server, which is used to name a Domino server that has been configured for pass-through use.

The Network Dialup Connection Type

The final type of Connection document covered in this chapter is the Network Dialup Connection type (formerly known as the Remote LAN Service document). If you are using dial-up networking, you can have your Domino server make connections to other Domino servers using this server.

Here is the difference between the Notes Direct Dialup and the Network dialup connection types. Both of these connections might use a modem, so it is important to understand the distinction. When you use the Notes Direct Dialup connection, Notes actually takes charge of the modem and controls it on both sides of the communication link. When using this type of connection, other programs on both the client and server cannot use the modems, even if they are not currently active within the Notes program.

The Network Dialup connection, however, uses operating system facilities to manage the modem. One common example is Microsoft's Dial-up Networking (DUN). When using this connection type, the operating system controls the modem and Notes shares it with other programs. Thus, if Notes is not currently using the modem, another program can use it for another purpose.

A Network Dialup Connection document is much like a LAN Connection document except that you must complete the configuration information specific to your dial-up networking service. This information is completed in the Network Dialup tab. The Choose a Service Type button displays a dialog box that enables you to choose Microsoft Dial-up Networking, Macintosh PPP, or AppleTalk Remote Access. The Configure Service/Edit Configuration button displays a dialog box that enables you to configure the options for the service you have chosen. For instance, if you choose Microsoft Dial-up Networking, the dialog box contains the following fields: Dial-Up Networking Name, Login Name, Password, Phone Number, Area Code, Country Code, and Dial-back Phone Number. When you enter this information, the data is displayed in the computed fields shown under Configuration area. If you chose AppleTalk or Macintosh PPP, you see slightly different options.

There are two new Connection types available in Domino R5: Hunt Group and News/NNTP Feed. The Hunt Group connection type is basically a specialized Notes Direct Dialup connection type. The News/NNTP Feed Connection sets up a connection with an NNTP server to exchange newsgroup information.

Domain Documents

In Notes/Domino terminology, a *domain* is a group of users and servers that all share the same Domino Directory. Within a domain, mail routing is easy because all users share the same Domino Directory.

Often, the need arises to allow communications between domains, either within the same company or between companies. This is where Domain documents come into play. There are seven different types of Domain documents: Foreign Domain, Non-Adjacent Domain, Adjacent Domain, Foreign X400 Domain, Foreign SMTP Domain, Foreign cc:Mail Domain, and Global Domain. Let's briefly examine each here.

As you've seen with the other documents in the Domino Directory, the Domain document is divided into tabs; choosing the Domain type determines the rest of the choices in the document. Let's start with the Foreign Domain type.

The Foreign Domain Type

In addition to Domain type, the Basics tab contains the Foreign domain name field, which is used to give a name to this foreign domain, and the Domain description field, which is used to enter a description of the foreign domain.

The Restrictions Tab

The Restrictions tab of the Domain document can be used to prevent mail from routing through your domain to other domains. The Restrictions section contains two fields: The Allow mail only from domains field contains the names of foreign domains that can route mail through your domain, and the Deny mail from domains field enables you to enter domain names from which mail *will not* be permitted.

The Mail Information Tab

The Mail Information tab contains two fields. For mail routing to a foreign domain, enter the name of the mail server in the foreign domain in the Gateway server name field; enter the name of the mail file in the Gateway mail file name field.

The Calendar Information Tab

If you want to do calendaring and scheduling with a foreign system, such as IBM's Office Vision, just enter the name of the foreign calendar server in the Calendar server name field and use the Calendar system field to choose the type of foreign calendar system: OfficeVision or Organizer 2.x. You may also another supported system by typing its name.

The Non-Adjacent Domain Type

Non-Adjacent Domain documents are used to enable communication with another Notes domain through an intermediary domain. For example, you want to send mail to Robin Oliver in the Bobbin domain, but you don't have a direct connection to that domain; however, you do have a connection to the Buddy domain, which communicates with the Bobbin domain. A Non-Adjacent Domain document specifies the route to Bobbin through Buddy.

The are four tabs in a Non-Adjacent Domain type document: the ever-present Basics tab, the Restrictions tab, the Calendar Information tab, and the Administration tab. Because the Restrictions tab is identical to the Restrictions tab of the Foreign Domain type document, we'll look at the Basics tab and the Calendar Information tab. The Administration tab specifies the owners and the administrators of the document.

The Basics Tab

In addition to the Domain Type and Domain Description fields, the Basics section of the Non-Adjacent Domain document contains the following fields: The Mail sent to domain field is used to enter the name of the destination domain and the Route through domain field is used to define the domain through which the mail will pass. The domain entered in the Route through domain field must have a physical connection to both the source and the destination domains. Using the preceding example, enter Buddy in this field.

THE CALENDAR INFORMATION TAB

The Calendar Information tab contains one field, the Route requests through calendar server field. This field is used to indicate the intermediary server that will route calendar information from your server to the destination calendar server.

THE ADJACENT DOMAIN TYPE

The Adjacent Domain type document enables you to limit what mail can route between two adjacent domains. An *adjacent domain* is a domain to which your server has either a physical network connection or dial-up connection. This is important because in pre-R4 version of Notes, an adjacent domain could route mail through your domain as well as pass through mail from other domains, making you incur additional costs and overhead.

The Adjacent Domain document contains four tabs: Basics, Restrictions, Calendar Information, and Administration. The Restrictions section is used to determine which mail can route through your domain. The Basics section varies slightly from the other Domain document types; in addition to the Domain type and Domain description fields, the Basics section of the Adjacent Domain document contains the Adjacent domain name field, which is used to name the adjacent domain.

The Calendar tab contains one field, Calendar server name. This field is used to enable adjacent domains to exchange calendaring information. Simply enter the name of the calendar server in the Calendar server name field and you're ready to go. The Administration tab specifies the owners and the administrators of the document.

THE GLOBAL DOMAIN DOCUMENT

The Global Domain document has a special role on your Domino server: It provides a set of rules that determine how your SMTP task converts Notes addresses into Internet addresses. Additionally, it lists the Notes domains that are considered members of the global domain. The Global Domain document does not play any part in the routing of mail; it only determines how Notes Mail addresses are converted to Internet addresses.

Please refer to the Domino Administrator's Guide for more information on the Global Domain type document.

THE FOREIGN SMTP, X.400, AND cc:MAIL DOMAIN TYPES

The Foreign SMTP, X.400, and cc:Mail Domain type documents work hand-in-hand with Global Domain type documents and are essential for routing SMTP, X.400, and cc:Mail mail.

These Foreign Domain document types are very similar to the other types of domain documents. The Basics tab contains only one field, the Domain type field. The Routing tab contains two areas: Messages Addressed to and Should be Routed to. These two areas work hand-in-hand and enable you to control outbound mail routing to different hosts.

New Server Configuration Documents

There are three new Server Configuration documents that IBM/Lotus/Iris has added to make administering a Domino server even easier:

- External Domain Network Information documents The External Domain Network Information document enables users to more easily connect to servers outside their domain without using their own Connection documents.
- Holiday documents The Holiday document enables you to define all holidays that your organization recognizes. These holidays are then available for users in group calendaring and can be imported into their local calendars.
- Resource documents The Resource document enables you to define a room or other resource that is available for reserving and scheduling through group calendaring and scheduling.

Other Important Server Configuration Documents

In addition to the Domino Directory documents discussed in detail in this chapter, you will want to learn about a number of other documents in the Domino Directory to make your Notes/Domino environment perform optimally (and to help you maintain your sanity). The following list briefly describes these additional documents:

- Configuration documents These documents can be used to simplify working with the Notes INI file by allowing you to choose from a list of the available INI file parameters and then setting specific values. It also tracks the changes made to the INI file. Remember that documents in the Domino Directory are replicated, while settings in a particular computer's NOTES.INI file are unique to that computer.
- Certifier and Cross-Certifier documents These documents identify each certificate's ancestry. Certifier documents are crucial to the security of a Notes/Domino installation because they are used to verify the identify of both servers and users.
- Program documents These documents can be used to automatically start server tasks, batch programs, or API programs. For example, if you wrote an API program to transfer data from an Access database to a Notes database and wanted it to run each night, you could create a Program document that would run the program at the specified interval.
- User Setup Profile documents These documents enable the administrator to define a common set of setup elements that can then be applied to multiple users. Profile documents can make adding new users to the system significantly less complicated and time-consuming. For example, if you want everyone in a certain OU, such as Accounting, to be configured exactly the same, you can create a Profile document that enables you to build a common set of configuration parameters for this group.

- Mail-In Database documents These documents enable the administrator to configure a database to receive mail messages. For example, you may have a sales rep on the road compose an expense-report form in his or her mailbox, and then route the document using mail to a common database that serves as a repository for all expense reports.

Summary

Configuring your Domino server is crucial to establishing a smooth-running and effective Notes/Domino environment. This can happen only after you have a thorough understanding of the key role the Domino Directory and the documents it contains play in managing your domain. Make sure you pay particular attention to the Server, Connection, and Domain documents in your Domino Directory.

Each release of Notes/Domino gains new, useful features. This means that you, as an administrator, must constantly learn new things! Lotus strives to make it easier for you to administer your environment. For instance, Lotus has added a great deal of Internet protocol support in Domino R5. Spend some time learning about the many intricacies of both the Domino Directory and your Notes/Domino servers, and your career will run much more smoothly.

You will find the following to be excellent resources for learning about the Domino Directory and Domino servers: the Domino Administration Help database; the Notes/Domino Knowledgebase, which can be accessed as either a Notes database (available only to Lotus Business Partners) or from www.lotus.com; and the Lotus Notes/Domino Administrator's Guide.

From Here...

Here are some additional chapters for you to read if you are interested in these topics:

- Chapter 36, "Domino Security Overview," explains how the major Domino security features work.

- Chapter 37, "Firewalls, Virtual Private Networks (VPNs), and Internet Security," continues the security discussion with important topics for connecting to the external world.

- Part VII, "Administering the Domino Servers," contains six chapters that discuss the administration of users, groups, mail, databases, and replication. You'll also learn about troubleshooting and monitoring your system.

CHAPTER 36

DOMINO SECURITY OVERVIEW

You may be familiar with that shot from the TV sitcom *Get Smart*. Secret Agent Maxwell Smart walks down a long corridor blocked by numerous security doors. Each door is as heavy as the door to a bank vault. The doors magically swing open as Smart approaches, then slam behind him as he exits.

Get Smart makes a nice metaphor for Notes and Domino security. There are a number of security doors that you must open in order to work with data. First, you have to be able to communicate with the Domino server. You have to be able to open an application. The security continues all the way down the level of individual fields. You or other users, including other Domino servers, can be stopped at any one of these security doors. In this chapter, you learn about the various doors—and how to lock or unlock them.

Keeping Your Password Secure

If someone gets your user ID and can guess your password, that person is you, as far as the Domino server is concerned. Your valid Notes ID is your key to unlock the data that is stored securely inside the Domino server. If you leave your ID lying around on a disk or on the hard drive of an unattended workstation, anyone could steal it. But guessing or stealing a password is not easy, because Notes has a built-in defense system.

When you type the password for your user ID, Notes displays a random number of Xs to make it difficult for the casual observer to determine how many characters there are in the password.

Notes also displays a series of hieroglyphic symbols as you type your password. The glyphs change as you type. These hieroglyphics make it more difficult to spoof the system—trick it with a fake password dialog box that captures your password for the thief. Every password generates a different pattern of glyphs. To mimic the password dialog box, the techno-thief would have to develop a different program for every user in the organization.

In addition to the antispoofing hieroglyphics, Notes has a timeout period after an unsuccessful entry. The timeout period gets longer in random intervals, hopefully frustrating the would-be password guesser.

A third password-security feature is the capability of requiring multiple passwords for an ID.

In Notes 4.5, additional password security was added in the form of password expiration. The Notes Administrator can specify an expiration period or date for user ID files. If a password has expired, the user is informed during authentication, and he is required to select a new password before he can access the server. In addition, a list of previous passwords is maintained, and users can be prevented from reusing the previous *n* number of passwords.

An Overview of Notes Security

As I mentioned, there are several levels at which Notes and Domino security can be enforced. Each level refines the previous level, moving from physical security right down to a single field on a single document.

Think of security as if you were building a pyramid. The base level of security entails protecting the physical and logical access to the Domino server and the Notes network. As you move up the pyramid, you control access to the Domino server. When a user has access to the server, you can limit access to individual Domino applications. Within the applications, you can control access to specific views, forms, actions, and other design elements. Finally, using Author and Reader fields, you can control access to individual documents, and even to individual sections within the documents. Figure 36.1 graphically illustrates the path that you must take, from the bottom of the pyramid to the top, to get to your data.

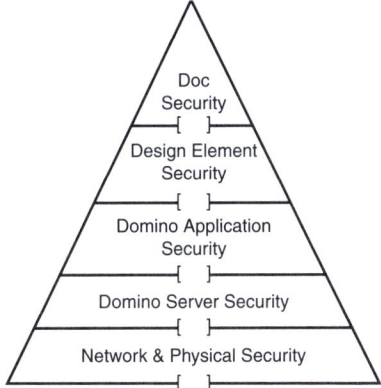

Figure 36.1
Notes and Domino security has several layers to protect your data.

NETWORK PHYSICAL AND LOGICAL SECURITY

As part of network security, I'm including the physical security of the Domino server, as well as the security features that are built into the logic of the Domino software.

The Domino servershould be located in an area where casual users cannot physically access it. As mentioned previously, you can locally encrypt databases and enforce access control, and you can protect ID files with multiple passwords, but physical-access security is still vitally important. If someone has physical access to your server, that person is a big step closer to being able to breach security at the operating-system level.

You might also want to consider a couple of other, less obvious, logical access-security issues. Domino 5.0 is an ideal tool for Internet as well as intranet applications, but you should create a firewall. For example, you can do this by creating a Domino server specifically for handling all external communications, and communicate with internal servers using a communication protocol other than TCP/IP. Ensure that you know what you are doing before you open your databases to the Internet.

Workstations on the network must also be secure, because data can be accessed through the workstations.

> **Tip**
>
> For the security of your Notes network, have in place a plan to ensure each of the following:
> - Keep a backup of all your vital files.
> - Do not rely solely on replication to another Domino server as a form of backup.
> - Keep your Domino servers in a locked area that is accessible only to authorized personnel.
> - Keep your Notes certifier IDs safe in a secure location so that unauthorized people cannot gain access to your network by creating their own ID.
> - Do not leave Notes workstations logged in and running if they are in a publicly accessible area.

Domino Server Security

When a Domino server is first set up, ID files are generated. These ID files are an integral part of the security structure. Those ID files are one of the primary focuses of this chapter because they are the cornerstone of security in a Notes environment. The ID files used with Notes and the Domino server include the following:

- The server ID, which gives each Domino server its own unique identity.
- The administrator ID, which is a user ID that provides administrative access to the Domino server. This is a regular user ID, but it is the first one created to ensure that there is a registered user who can administer the Domino server in order to set up the rest of the Notes environment.
- The certifier ID, which is used to register additional servers, organization certifiers, and users within the Notes organization.
- The user ID, which is issued to each user in the Notes organization.

In the Domino Directory, there is a document for every user and server that is allowed to access a particular Domino server via a Notes client. The IDs created for these users and servers are used in authentication and Domino server security. This is discussed in detail later in this chapter.

Domino Application Security

Assuming you have gained access to Domino applications (see Chapter 17, "Access Control Lists (ACLs) and Application Security"), you need to be aware of security at the application level. The databases in which applications reside (NSF files) can be secured in the following ways:

- **Local encryption** You can select simple, medium, or strong encryption from the Database properties dialog box, or when you first create a new application. To access an encrypted application, you must have the user ID that was used to encrypt the application in the first place. Because your user ID should always be password-protected, if your user ID was used to encrypt the application, you need your user ID and password to access the encrypted application. This is an excellent way to protect an application on a laptop computer. Just be aware that if you lose your Notes user ID and do not have a backup, you will no longer be able to access the encrypted application.

- Access Control List security   Every Domino application has an Access Control List (ACL) that defines which privileges users and servers have in the application. Although the ACL is usually thought of in terms of applications on Domino servers, Notes also provides a means to enforce ACL security on all replicas of an application database, no matter whether the replica is on a Domino server or on a local workstation. The database manager (the person with Manager access in the ACL) can enforce local ACL security by placing a check mark next to Enforce a consistent Access Control List across all replicas of this database on the Advanced page of the Access Control List dialog box.

Design and Document Security

The remaining security features are concerned with the design of the Domino application, and generally are refinements of access security. Not all these features are true security measures, but each contributes to security in its own way. Among other things, you can lock the design of an entire database. You can define who is allowed to use certain forms, and under what conditions. You can restrict the use of certain views. You can define who has access to create or modify data on a particular document. You can restrict access to a section within a document. And although it is not a true security measure, you can hide a field under certain conditions, including hiding fields from certain users. Design and document security features represent the top of the security pyramid depicted earlier in Figure 36.1. The use of these features is described in detail in chapters dealing with database design.

The Role of Notes IDs in Security

Despite the layer upon layer of security features, the security that really counts within Notes is the interaction of the various Notes ID files with one another, and the interaction of the server and user ID files with ACLs in individual applications. When you have the correct ID and the correct password, you probably will not even be aware that you are going through so many layers of security. The remainder of this chapter looks at the role of Notes user IDs in greater detail.

Notes IDs

Four types of ID files are involved in security:

- The certifier ID, created when the first server is set up, provides a unique identity to every server and every user in a Notes organization. The certifier ID is used to create certificates that establish the authenticity of IDs for users and servers.
- The organizational unit (OU) certifier ID provides a way that your organization can expand its use of Notes. An OU certifier ID can be used to create new servers and users in your organization, delegating some administrative work. OU certifier IDs are hierarchical, so you will not find them in organizations that use a flat naming scheme.

- The server ID uniquely identifies a server within the organization. Each server has its own ID that contains certificates from the organization certifier ID or OU certifier ID used to create the server.

- The user ID uniquely identifies every Notes user in the organization. The user ID, like the server ID, holds hierarchical certificates. The user ID is used to authenticate with Domino servers, and to identify the user in various security roles, such as database ACLs, server access lists, and in Reader and Author fields.

Server and User IDs

The server and user IDs are binary files that hold the following information:

- The name of the user or server
- A Notes license number
- A password (optional, depending on how the administrator has defined the minimum password length on registration)
- A private key, which is used to encrypt and decrypt data
- Encryption keys generated by designers to encrypt database data
- Certificates that identify the server or user's place within the organizational hierarchy

Think of a certificate as being like the official seal that is stamped onto your driver's license or passport. Because you recognize the authority that issued the driver's license, you accept the document as being valid. Without that authority, the document cannot be trusted. Likewise, when two IDs each have at least one certificate that they both recognize as valid, the two IDs trust each other enough to begin the process of communicating with one another. There is no peer-to-peer communication between Notes users, so the previous sentence assumes that at least one of the IDs is a server ID.

Organization and OU Certifier IDs

The certificates associated with your user ID are created by a Notes certifier ID. The certifier ID is the identity of your Notes organization. Any user or server created using the certifier ID (or any of its organizational unit certifiers) is automatically trusted by all other servers and users in the organization. It may be a good idea to require multiple passwords to access the organizational certifier IDs and organizational unit (OU) certifier IDs, thereby ensuring that multiple administrative personnel are aware whenever the Notes certifier ID is being used. You also want to be sure to store the ID in a safe place.

The certifier ID is used to register new users and new servers. In most organizations, it is an OU ID that is used to register users and servers, but in a smaller organization, the organization certifier ID may well be used to create users and servers. The certifier ID is also used to issue certificates that enable external organizations to communicate with you, usually at an OU level. If two server IDs or a user ID and a server ID have a certificate issued by the same certifier ID, they can potentially talk to each other.

When an OU certifier ID is used to issue a certificate, the certificate is hierarchical. A hierarchical certificate carries the name of both the organizational unit and the organization.

For example, the Sales OU certifier ID could be used to create a certificate for a new user, John Doe. John Doe's username identifies the full hierarchy of certificates issued to him, in a format such as `John Doe/Sales/Marketing/West/Acme`, where `Acme` is the organizational certifier ID and `West`, `Marketing`, and `Sales` are all OU certifier IDs. In this instance, Acme created the OU certifier ID West/Acme, which in turn created the OU certifier ID Marketing/West/Acme, which in turn created the OU certifier ID Sales/Marketing/West/Acme. A user can have up to four OU certificates in their hierarchical name.

THE ROLE OF NOTES IDS IN PROTECTING SERVER ACCESS

When a user (or another server) attempts to initiate a session with a server, the Domino server validates the ID file, and then goes through a process known as *authentication*.

Validation is a process of establishing trust. The server examines the certificates on the ID of the server or user trying to establish a session. If the ID contains a certificate that has the same hierarchical ancestor ID as the server, the ID can be trusted. If there is not a common ancestral ID, the Domino server looks at cross-certificates in the Domino Directory, and trusts the ID if there is a valid cross-certificate.

When an ID is trusted by the server, authentication takes place. For example, John Smith wants to access Server1/Acme. When he contacts the server, the server initiates an authentication dialog with the John Smith ID, as follows:

1. Server1/Acme   Here is my name and my public key. You can trust me because I have an Acme certificate.
2. John Smith/Acme   I have an Acme certificate too. Therefore, I trust you. Here is my name and my public key.
3. Server1/Acme   To make sure you aren't an impostor, let me give you a test. I'm thinking of a number between 1 and 10. I'll send you the number, and I challenge you to encrypt it with your private key.
4. John Smith/Acme   That's easy. I'll use my private key to encrypt the number. Now, here it is back.
5. Server1/Acme   Using your public key, I can see that you sent me back the same number, encrypted with my public key. Let's talk.
6. John Smith/Acme   Not so fast. I want to make sure you aren't an impostor. Now I'll send you a number.

The dialog is reversed until both IDs are satisfied with each other's identity, and communication is then fully established. The authentication remains in place as long as the session lasts, even when the user closes one database and opens another. But if the user logs off or changes to another ID, the authentication is no longer valid. The server databases and server functions can no longer be accessed.

LDAP Authentication on the Web

Notes 5.0 enables you to use LDAP Directories in addition to Domino Directories. This enables you to authenticate Web clients without having to set them all up in your Domino Directory with HTTP usernames and passwords.

LDAP authentication is implemented using a Directory Assistance application, created using a Directory Assistance template (DA50.NTF). Create an LDAP document in the Directory Assistance application. In this document, you need to set up rules and select Yes in the Trusted Credential field. This is illustrated in Figure 36.2.

Figure 36.2
In the LDAP document in Directory Assistance, set up rules and indicate that you trust credentials from this Directory.

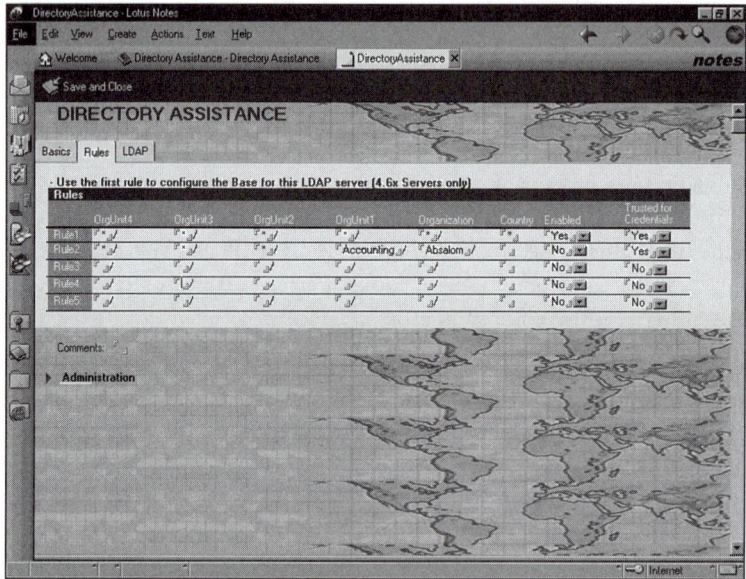

The Domino server searches the Domino Directory for a username and password, but if a name is not located, it looks for trusted domains in the LDAP Directories after looking in any secondary Domino Directories.

When a hierarchical name is returned, Domino checks it to make sure that the organization and organizational units match an enabled, trusted rule in the LDAP document in Directory Assistance, or a name in a secondary Domino Directory.

Cross-Certification

Every Notes organization has its own certifier ID, and an ID must have a certificate from the organization certifier before it can authenticate with any of the organization's servers. Within the organization, this does not present any problems; the organization certificate is part of every server ID and every user ID in the organization. But what about another organization that wants to communicate with your servers?

For example, the Acme Corporation is teaming up with a subcontractor, XYZ Corporation, on a project. They need to discuss project issues and share progress reports, email, and so on. They don't want to do it over the Internet, so they decide to set up cross-certification between their Notes organizations. To communicate directly with Acme using Lotus Notes, XYZ needs a certificate that is recognized as valid by Acme, and Acme needs a certificate that is recognized as valid by XYZ.

When you attempt to establish communication with a server in another organization, the first thing the server looks at are the certificates on your ID. If there are no certificates recognized as valid, the Domino server looks for a Cross-Certificate document. If there are no certificates or cross-certificates recognized by the server, you cannot authenticate, and therefore cannot access the server.

Cross-certification involves exchanging certificates between two organizations. You can cross-certify at the organizational level, at the organizational unit level, or at the user level. No matter which level you cross-certify at, both sides must exchange certificates.

For example, suppose Jane Doe in the Sales Department at Acme has reason to access a server in the XYZ Corporation:

1. She sends a *safe copy* of her user ID to the Notes administrator of the XYZ organization, requesting cross-certification.

    The safe ID used in the cross-certification process is not a complete ID. It contains just enough information to be able to collect certificates, but it is useless for any other purpose.

2. The XYZ administrator certifies (usually using an OU certifier ID to create a certificate for) the safe ID.

    This creates a cross-certificate document in the XYZ Domino Directory, where the cross-certificate is stored.

3. Meanwhile, the server to be accessed within XYZ has to be certified on Jane Doe's side, so XYZ sends a safe copy of the server ID to Acme.

4. The organizational certifier or an OU certifier from Acme certifies the safe copy of the XYZ organizational certifier ID and stores it in a cross-certificate document in the Acme Domino Directory.

    Now each organization has a cross-certificate in its own Domino Directory.

5. Jane Doe copies the cross-certificate from XYZ into her Personal Address Book.

When Jane Doe communicates with the XYZ server, the XYZ server looks in the XYZ Domino Directory and finds Jane Doe's cross-certificate, and therefore lets her continue with the authentication process. Conversely, when XYZ communicates with Jane Doe, Notes looks in her Personal Address Book to see whether there is a cross-certificate available.

In summary, the following cross-certificates are created during cross-certification so that a Notes user from XYZ can access a server in another organization (Acme):

- A safe copy of a user ID from XYZ is cross-certified by an Acme certifier ID and placed in the Acme Domino Directory as a cross-certificate.
- A safe copy of an Acme certifier ID is cross-certified by a certifier ID from XYZ and placed in the XYZ Domino Directory.
- The user who needs to access an Acme server places a copy of the Acme cross-certificate (from the XYZ Directory) into her Personal Address Book. Every user or server that wants to cross-certify must have a local copy of the cross-certificate.

When a Domino server checks to see whether another user or server ID is valid, it looks at the ID to see whether it contains a certificate that can be trusted. Trust is established only if the other ID holds at least one certificate issued by a trusted certifier. Therefore, in the scenario described previously, Acme trusts Jane Doe because the Acme Domino Directory contains a safe copy of Jane Doe's ID, which has been cross-certified by an Acme certifier ID.

> **Caution**
>
> If you cross-certify at the Organization or Organization Unit level, you should use server-access restrictions to ensure that the other organization has access only to those servers you mean to let them access. If you want to access servers in another organization but do not want to allow them access, make sure that you have restricted access to all servers in your organization. Note that if you cross-certify a specific user in another organization, all users in the other organization at that user's organization level or below can potentially authenticate with your server.

How to Cross-Certify

How you cross-certify depends on the circumstances. There are four ways to cross-certify, all of them having the same goal—certifying a safe ID and generating a cross-certificate from that ID. The only difference in the techniques lies in the mechanics. The four ways to cross-certify are described in the following four sections.

Using Notes Mail

You can use Notes mail to cross-certify. This is probably the most common method. To cross-certify, you do the following:

1. Display the User ID dialog box by selecting File, Tools, User ID. Click on the Certificates icon and the Request Cross-certificate button. The dialog box is shown in Figure 36.3.
2. Select the ID to be cross-certified. The ID must be a hierarchical ID.
3. The request is in the form of a mail memo. Address the request to the administrator in charge of certification in the other organization and send it. The request dialog box is shown in Figure 36.4.

Figure 36.3
Request a cross-certificate from the Certificates page in the User ID dialog box.

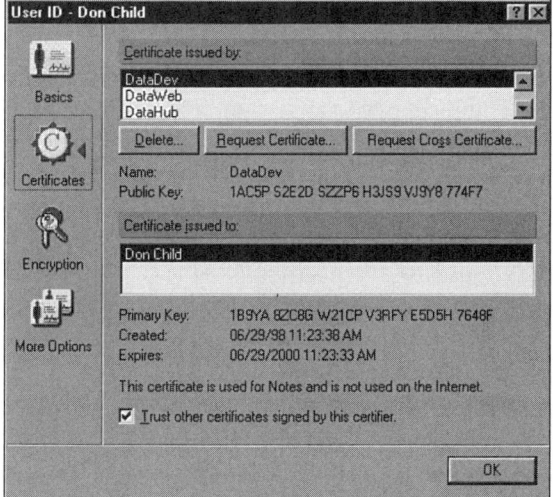

Figure 36.4
Email your request for a cross-certificate to the administrator of the system with which you want to cross-certify.

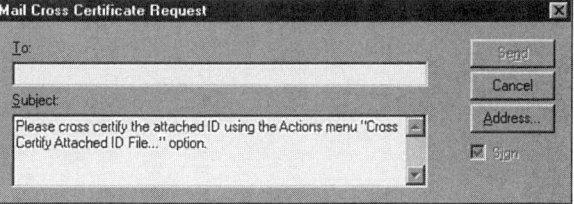

4. The administrator in the other organization opens the request in his or her mail file, and from the Actions menu selects Cross-certify Attached ID File, selects the certifier ID to use, and enters the password for the ID. The Cross Certify ID dialog box is then displayed, as shown in Figure 36.5.

Figure 36.5
After the certifier selects the certifier ID and enters a password, he or she can cross-certify the ID.

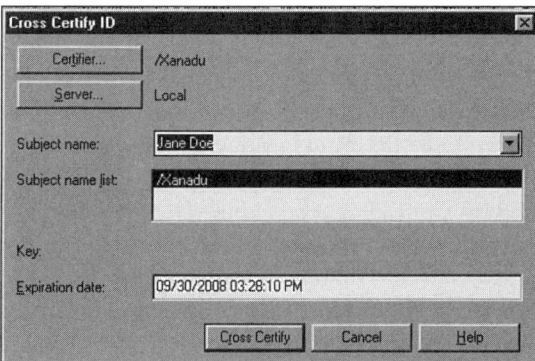

5. In the Subject name field of the dialog box, the administrator enters the name of the certifier, user, or server being cross-certified.

6. Click on Cross Certify to complete the process on this end. The same process must be repeated in the other direction before the complete cross-certification is effective.

USING SNAIL MAIL OR "SNEAKER NET"

The first time two organizations exchange cross-certificates, they may not be able to communicate via computers until after cross-certificates are exchanged. Therefore, they may need to use disks to exchange safe IDs created by the system administrator.

A safe server or certifier ID can be created as follows:

1. Start the Domino Administration client, go to the Configuration tab, and select the Configuration, Certification, ID Properties menu.

2. Select the certifier ID or a safe ID certified by the certifier ID, and enter a password if necessary.

3. Select the More Options icon and click on the Create Safe Copy button. Name the safe ID something like ACMESAFE.ID and save it on a disk. On a UNIX server, transfer the file to a disk or through a utility such as FTP.

4. Send the safe copy of the ID to the administrator responsible for certification in the other organization. The administrator will repeat steps 4–6 in the previous section on cross-certifying via email.

Note It is also possible, but not very practical, to cross-certify via telephone. This involves correctly transcribing a long public key string. For details, refer to Notes online help or the Domino help manuals.

CROSS-CERTIFYING ON DEMAND

If you have a hierarchical ID and try to access a hierarchical server in another organization for which you are not cross-certified, Notes prompts you to see whether you want to cross-certify. You have the option of creating a cross-certificate for the root certifier of your organization, of declining to cross-certify, or of creating a cross-certificate for a certifier ID. You can then put the cross-certificate in the Domino Directory by selecting a registration server. Note that you must have at least Editor access in the Domino Directory before you can do this. You could also store the cross-certificate in your Local Address Book—in which case, you don't need Editor access to the Domino Directory. Note that the other organization must also have demanded or generated a cross-certificate for authentication to occur.

HOW TO EXCHANGE FLAT CERTIFICATES

Whenever possible, you should use hierarchical certification and communicate with other organizations through cross-certification. But there may be times when an organization with flat certification has to communicate with a hierarchically certified or flat certified organization. In this case, the two organizations must exchange safe server IDs (or a server and a user ID), each of which is certified by the other organization, and then the certified IDs are returned and merged into the regular server or user ID. To do this, the hierarchical organization must create a flat certifier to use in the process.

Safe IDs are created by selecting File, Tools, User ID from the server, ensuring that you are using the server ID. Click the More Options icon and select Create Safe ID. After the safe ID has been certified and returned, merge the certified safe ID back into the server ID from the same screen.

Because a certificate gives everyone from the other organization an open door into your Notes network, you should turn off Trust on certificates issued by certifiers outside your organization. With trust turned off, the other organization can communicate only with the particular server that has the certificate in its ID. This protects the rest of your organization from unauthorized intrusion by untrusted users.

Securing the Server Console with a Password

There is another aspect to server security that Notes administrators need to be aware of. On the Domino server, there are two icons for launching Notes. One icon launches the server process itself, and the other launches the Notes client workspace on the server. The administrator communicates with the Domino server process primarily by entering commands via a text-based console, or by using the same commands via a remote console from a Notes client, which can be the Notes client on either the server machine or a workstation. There is a special administrative window on the Notes client that groups all administrative functions together, including certifying servers and users, and accesses the remote console function. This administrative client must be selected during installation. The Server document in the Domino Directory already defines who has administrative rights. Only those with administrative rights can use the remote-console function.

A limited number of administrative functions are also accessible from the Web.

To prevent unauthorized individuals from using the server-console commands, the administrator can protect the console with a password. Password protecting the console increases security, especially in the case where someone gains physical access to the server.

To secure the console, enter the following command:

SET SECURE *password*

where *password* is the password you want to use to secure the console. The console password does not have to be the same as the administrative password and, in fact, should not be the same.

The following commands cannot be used while the console is secured with a password:

LOAD

TELL

```
EXIT
QUIT
SET CONFIGURATION
```

To use these commands, you must remove console security by again entering

```
SET SECURE password
```

There is one small loophole here that can be sealed only by denying physical access to the Domino server. The password used to secure the console is stored as an environment variable in the `NOTES.INI` file. You can edit the file and delete the line that contains the console password. This is great for the forgetful system administrator, but does provide a back door for anyone attempting to gain direct-disk access to your server. In short, protect your server by securing the console, but do not turn around and hand out the key by allowing people physical access to your Domino server.

PEOPLE RESPONSIBLE FOR NOTES SECURITY

There are a number of individuals involved in Notes security at various levels, from the person who initially sets up the system to the individual who decides to encrypt an email message. Some of the key security functions are described here, with a description of the person who performs that function.

At the most explicit level of security, as already mentioned, is the *individual user* who can, for example, decide to encrypt a particular mail message. The individual user plays another, more pivotal role, however—protecting his or her Notes user ID. The individual user should be taught to lock his or her ID out of the system whenever he or she gets up from the desk. If the user leaves a workstation unattended without locking the ID (in other words, logs off Notes by pressing F5 or selects File, Tools, Lock ID), anyone can access the server without having to locate a valid Notes ID and enter a password. It is as if the user had installed new locks on his or her house, and then left the house without locking the door. Locking the user ID is the first line of defense when it comes to keeping intruders out of the Notes network.

The second line of defense is the *application developer*, the person who designs Domino applications. Applications are teeming with potential security features that the designer can choose to use or not. Some of these features include form and view formulas, read and compose access, enabling fields for encryption, hiding information under certain circumstances (more for convenience than for security), creating sections that can be edited only by particular users, determining how users will enter data into fields, and so on. Not all of these are absolute security measures, but they do determine how easy it is to use the database and how much can be done by the casual user.

The other person involved in security at the application level is the *application manager*. Every application can have a different manager (the user with Manager access in the ACL). The manager is the one who determines which level of access other users will have. If users have too high a level of access, an application is subject to misuse and could eventually become unwieldy from too many replication or save conflicts, because there are too many people capable of editing the same documents.

At the system level, there is only one type of individual involved with Notes security—the *system administrator*. But this role can be broken down into two major divisions: the system administrator and the administration certifier, the person responsible for the certifier ID. Beyond that, specific administrative roles can be delegated. Roles can involve creating and editing a variety of documents in the Domino Directory.

The system administrator is the person (or persons) with Manager access to the Domino Directory. By default, the system administrator is the person you name as administrator during the setup of the first server in the organization. Other users can later be assigned this role by the original administrator. Common sense says that you should have more than one person capable of changing access privileges in the Domino Directory. If your lone system administrator gets hit by the proverbial bus on the way to work, you would have little choice but to break down your Notes network and set it up again from scratch, because nobody would be able to gain administrative access. If you had to set up the Notes organization a second time, you would probably be a little smarter, and assign a team of users to an administrative group.

Another administration role is that of *server administrator*. The server administrator can use the remote console to issue commands to the Domino server. His or her Notes username must be entered into the Administrators field on the server document in order to use the remote console.

A common approach to server administration is to create a group with a name something like Administrators, and add to the group any users who should have administrative privileges on the organization's servers. Presumably, you would not add people to this group until they had been certified as system administrators or had at least taken system administration classes from a Certified Lotus Instructor (CLI). And then, you would want to trust them to use discretion when they make changes that can easily affect every user in the organization.

If you understand how a Notes network is set up and how servers and users are added to the Notes organization, you realize the crucial role played by the *administration certifier*. This is the person responsible for the organization's certifier ID.

If the certifier ID falls into the wrong hands, you can no longer trust any of the users who access your servers. It cannot be overemphasized—you should keep your certifier ID (and one or more backup copies of it) safe from loss, safe from theft, and safe from unauthorized use. Consider keeping the certifier ID in a safe deposit box. Consider protecting it with multiple passwords so that at least two people have to be present in order to create new users or servers.

In addition to the administrative functions described previously, Notes provides an easy way to delegate authority by creating and assigning *roles* to individual users. As long as users have at least Author access, they can normally create documents or edit the documents they have created. The notable exception to this is in the Domino Directory, where you would expect that only the system administrator could create or modify documents. But in a large organization, the administrator cannot be everything to everyone. Figure 36.6 illustrates the roles assigned by default to the system administrator. Roles are defined on the Roles page of the Access Control List dialog box, but they are actually assigned or removed on the Basics page.

Figure 36.6
Roles can be used to restrict the functions assigned to a particular system administrator.

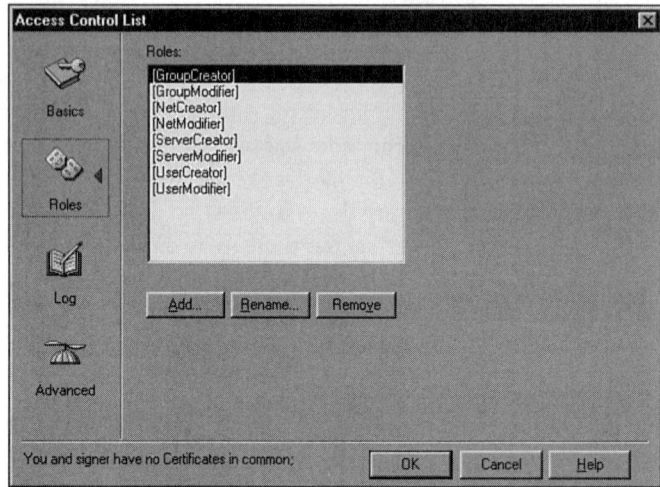

Modifier roles can be assigned to anyone with at least Author access in the ACL. Creator roles have to be explicitly assigned before individuals can perform those roles, regardless of their access privileges. Notes has eight default roles defined:

- GroupCreator is a user or group of users who can create new groups.
- GroupModifier is a user or group of users who can modify or delete existing group documents, but cannot create new groups unless assigned as a GroupCreator as well.
- NetCreator is a user or group of users who can create all documents except Person, Group, and Server documents.
- NetModifier is a user or group of users who can modify all existing documents except Person, Group, and Server Documents.
- ServerCreator is a user or group of users who can create new Server documents.
- ServerModifier is a user or group of users who can modify existing Server documents.
- UserCreator is a user or group of users who can create new Person documents. The administration certifier would have to be assigned this role in order to perform his or her job of creating new users.
- UserModifier is a user or group of users who can modify existing Person documents.

Use these roles wisely; the Domino Directory is vital to your Notes organization. Plan out who will do what, and make sure that all administrative functions are adequately covered by assigned roles. It is easy to give all managers an equally high level of access, but it may be a foolish approach.

Encryption in Lotus Notes

Encryption gets a lot of press. The U.S. Congress wants to limit the export of encryption, calling it a weapon. Legislators fear that powerful encryption will be used to hide illegal activities. And until recently, they required that encryption on software shipped overseas had to put a certain number of bits of data in escrow...leaving a key that the government could use to help it decrypt data.

There is still a difference in how North American (U.S. and Canadian) versions of Notes and International versions handle encryption. But the difference, for most users, is insignificant.

What is significant is that Notes uses public key encryption.

Understanding Public Key Encryption

Traditional encryption, the kind you see in spy movies, entails both the sender and receiver having access to the same secret key, which is used to encrypt a message on one end and decrypt it on the other end. If the secret key is intercepted, the message is no longer secure.

Notes uses another form of security called public key encryption, based on RSA's Cryptosystem.

Here is how public key/private key encryption works. Each person gets two keys: one public key and one private key. The public key is made publicly accessible (stored in the Person document in the Domino Directory)—hence its name. The private key is kept secret as part of the user ID.

All encrypted communications use only public keys. The private key is never sent to anyone over the network, and it is never exchanged with anyone. You don't have to worry about the secret key being intercepted. You don't have to worry about someone eavesdropping on your communications. The encrypted message can move across publicly accessible channels, and the public key is easily obtainable. But here's the key. The only person who can decrypt the message is the person who owns the private key associated with the public key that was used to encrypt the message.

Digital Signatures

With electronic documents, you cannot go to a notary public and have him or her put a seal on a document to verify witnessing your signature. But encryption does provide a way to exchange secure digital signatures that are recognized by many organizations as legally valid signatures.

A digital signature ensures that a document was actually sent by the person whose name appears on the document. In addition, the digital signature ensures that the document has not been tampered with since its creation.

A digital signature is created using the sender's private key. To sign a mail memo, create the memo and click on the Delivery Options button. Click on the Sign check box. Then, when the memo is mailed, your private key (not a full, usable private key, but just enough information to create the digital signature) will be encrypted and attached to the document.

When a user receives a document that has a digital signature attached, the sender's public key is retrieved from the Public Address Book to decrypt the signature. If the decryption is successful, the recipient can be sure that the document was sent by the person identifying himself or herself as the sender.

If someone in another Notes domain sends you a message and you do not have that person's public key in any of your address books, you can still read the message. However, Notes displays a message box that says `You and the signer have no Certificates in common; signer cannot be assumed to be trustworthy`. Although you can still read the document, you cannot accept the digital signature as a legal signature. See the section "The Execution Control List (ECL)," later in this chapter.

Encrypting Outgoing Email

Using the same public key-private key encryption technology in a slightly different way, you can encrypt the email you send to another user. For example, when a Notes user, Mary, wants to send an encrypted message to her co-worker Stuart, this is what happens:

1. Mary creates a memo using her Notes Mail. Before she sends the memo, she clicks on the Delivery Options button on the Action Bar, checks Encrypt, and then sends the memo.

2. The mailer on Mary's workstation looks for the Person document for Stuart in the Domino Directory and uses Stuart's public key to encrypt the memo. The memo is then sent via regular communication channels, which could be over a local area network, over a phone line, or over the Internet.

3. Stuart receives the memo. When he opens the message to read it, it looks just like any other memo. Notes used the private key that is part of Stuart's Notes user ID to decrypt the memo automatically at the time he opened it.

Encrypting Incoming Mail

The Mail page in the User Preferences box (File, Preferences, User Preferences) has two check boxes concerned with encryption. One check box causes all outgoing mail to be encrypted so you don't have to open the Delivery Options dialog box every time. If you are sending mail to someone who has a Person record in the Domino Directory, the mail is encrypted. If no public key is available for the addressee, you will see a message telling you that message cannot be encrypted. The message is sent in unencrypted form if you okay that option.

The second check box in the User Preferences box enables encryption of all incoming mail. This option uses your public key to encrypt mail before it is stored. The mail cannot be read subsequently unless your Notes ID and its private key is available.

The system administrator can also encrypt mail for all mail files on a Domino server by setting the system parameter `MailEncryptIncoming=1` in the server's `NOTES.INI` file.

What happens if your organization is using an optional shared copy object store (SCOS) database for storing the nonsummary portion of shared email messages? You will not be able to use the shared object store if you encrypt incoming mail, but don't encrypt outgoing mail. Instead, you receive the full email message, which is stored in your personal mailbox.

Encrypting All Network Data over a Network Port

If your organization needs to ensure that all data transmissions over a particular network port are secure, you can elect to encrypt all data traffic through that port. This prevents someone with a network sniffer from intercepting messages. The messages get encrypted at the network port, and they remain encrypted while they are being transported. After the traffic is received and stored on the other end, the data is no longer encrypted.

The data needs to be encrypted only on the sending end. A different encryption algorithm is used for this form of encryption. There is little difference in performance with this type of encryption, except that transmission speed may be slowed because the encrypted data cannot be compressed.

To set up encryption for a network port, open the Ports page of the User Preferences box (File, Preferences, User Preferences), select a network port, and click on Encrypt Network Data.

The Role of Encryption in Authentication

Authentication between a user and a server, or between two servers, uses encryption to verify the identity of the other party. The two exchange digital signatures that guarantee that the other party is not an impostor.

Consider for a moment what could happen with the earlier secret key encryption technology. If someone obtained the secret key by stealth, he or she could create a message and claim to be the legitimate user of the secret key. There was no way to guarantee the identity of the sender on the other end.

With public key-private key encryption, the digital signature exchanged between the two systems is guaranteed to be authentic. A short mathematical message is encrypted using the public key of the other system. The other system then decrypts the message with its private key and sends it back in unencrypted format to verify that the right mathematical message was decrypted. The process is then reversed until both systems recognize each other as authentic.

This exchange of encrypted data takes place every time two Notes systems authenticate each other.

Encrypting Documents and Fields Within Documents

Field encryption can be used only at the option of the application designer. Fields on a Domino form can be defined with encryption enabled for the field. This is done in the Security Options field on the "beanie" page of the Field Properties InfoBox, shown in Figure 36.7.

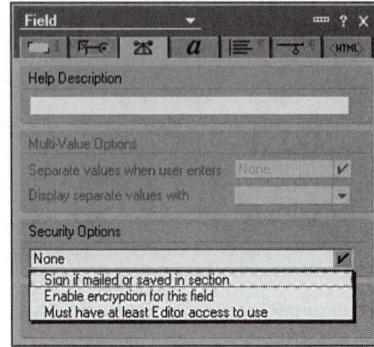

Figure 36.7
The application designer can enable encryption for individual fields.

The database designer can enable fields for encryption and can assign a default encryption key that will automatically encrypt the enabled field when a document is created and saved.

If no default encryption key has been assigned to the form properties by the designer, users can decide whether to encrypt enabled fields. The brackets around encrypted fields are displayed in red to distinguish them from unencryptable fields, which, by default, have gray brackets around them.

When you save a document with encryption-enabled fields, you are asked whether you want to encrypt the fields. If you say yes, you are asked which encryption key to use. You can encrypt the fields on the document by selecting an encryption key. Any users who need to read the data in the encrypted fields need to have a copy of the same encryption key that you assigned to the document, and they have to merge the encryption key into their Notes user IDs.

Encrypting an entire document is similar to encrypting individual fields within a document. Again, the database designer is responsible for enabling encryption for all the individual fields. When encryption has been enabled, a document may be encrypted automatically as soon as it is saved, or the user may have the option of encrypting the document, depending on how the designer has enabled the form you used to create the document.

All the fields enabled for encryption in a document can be encrypted in any of the following ways:

- A form attribute can be selected (on the security page of the Form Properties InfoBox) whereby the designer assigns one or more encryption keys to the form. Users must have one of those encryption keys before they can read documents created with the form.

- The user can encrypt a document that has one or more fields enabled for encryption by displaying the Document Properties InfoBox and selecting an encryption key to apply to the document, using a field on the security page of the InfoBox.
- The designer can include a field named SecretEncryptionKeys on the form. This field can be blank, enabling users to assign their own encryption keys. The field can have a default value that is the name of an encryption key. The field can be hidden or visible. The field can use a formula to determine whether the data should be encrypted, based on the conditions set by the designer.

It is also worth reminding you that local applications can be encrypted from within the Database Properties InfoBox, or at the time the application is created. You have three methods of encryption—simple, medium, and strong. Simple encryption is simplest and provides the quickest access, and the encrypted database can be compressed.

Medium encryption is the default. A database with medium encryption cannot be compressed, but it can be accessed faster than a strongly encrypted database, and should be sufficient for most uses.

A strongly encrypted database has all the security encryption can provide, but the strong encryption has a price in terms of database access and performance.

CREATING AND SHARING ENCRYPTION KEYS

Encryption keys are created by selecting File, Tools, User ID. Enter your password to display the User ID dialog box, and then click on the Encryption Navigator to move to the encryption page (See Figure 36.8).

Figure 36.8
Work with encryption keys in the User ID dialog box.

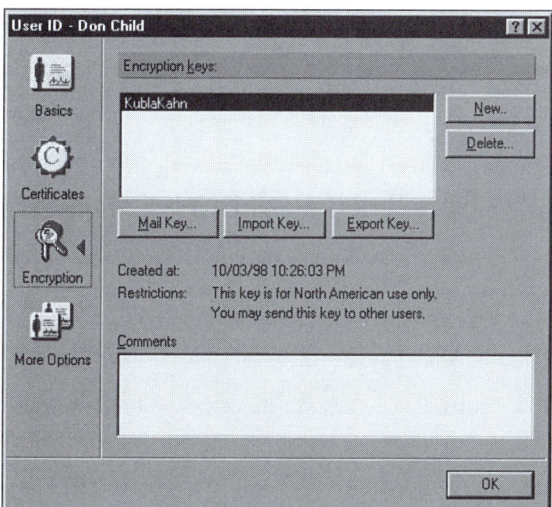

To create a new encryption key, click on the New button. Notes displays just the encryption key name field, a comment field, and gives you the option of creating a key for North American use or for International use.

> **Caution**
>
> If you are sending encrypted documents to a user outside the United States or Canada, you must create an International encryption key to encrypt your data. International licensees cannot decrypt data encrypted with a North American license. However, a user with a North American license can decrypt data created with either a North American or an International encryption key.

To send the encryption key to another user so that user can decrypt documents created with it, click on the Mail button. An addressing dialog will be displayed. Address the user you want to send the encryption key to and click on Send. The user will receive the key as an email attachment, along with instructions to select Accept Encryption Key from the Actions menu. Clicking Accept merges the encryption key into the recipient's Notes user ID.

If you want to export the encryption key to a file, click on the Export button. A dialog box is displayed with a field where you can enter a password to protect the exported encryption key file. There is a second field where you must retype the password to confirm what you have entered. You can also click on a Restrict Use button and enter the exact name of the only person who is authorized to use the exported key. When you have entered a password (required) and entered the optional name of the person who can use the key, click on OK. Notes creates an encryption key file named with a .KEY extension.

To import a key that has been sent to you as a file, you do the opposite of exporting. Click on the Import button and identify the file you want to import. Enter the password that protects the file, and Notes will display information about the encryption key in the file and give you the option of accepting the key. Click on the Accept button to merge the key into your Notes user ID. When the key is part of your ID, you can read any documents encrypted using that key.

Added Security Features for the Internet

The integrated Notes client blurs the line between the Notes environment and the Internet. This presents security problems. The dedicated Notes environment is very secure, but security on the Internet is still evolving. Notes 5.0 has to ensure security, whether data resides in a Domino application, on a Web page, or in a data warehouse on an enterprise system.

Notes handles security in this diverse environment using some of the tools described in the following sections.

The Execution Control List (ECL)

You can determine what actions a Notes document can perform on your workstation by setting up the Execution Control List (ECL) as part of your workstation security. Using the

ECL, you control how much of your system the embedded program can touch. If a colleague created the document that has an embedded program, you can probably trust that person. If the document was retrieved from the Internet and you don't know the person or company who created it, maybe you should withhold your trust.

When you first open a document, Notes checks the ECL to see whether the document's Author is trusted to perform specific actions on your workstation, such as accessing the current application. If the Author isn't listed in the ECL for that specific action, Notes displays a dialog box that gives you the following options:

- Trust Signer modifies the ECL to accept the current action from the Author of the current document in the future without warning you.
- Execute Once performs the action this one time, but you will be warned the next time a document from the same signer attempts to perform the same action.
- Abort prevents the action from being performed, but the document might still open if the action isn't essential.

You control what can be done on your workstation by documents that were created by others. You have considerable control over what actions can be executed on your workstation.

In addition to choosing to trust the signer of a document or to execute an action only once for that signer, you can define a variety of actions from the ECL. To view the ECL, select File, Preferences, User Preferences and click the Security Options button on the Basics page. The ECL dialog box is shown in Figure 36.9.

Figure 36.9
Use the ECL to refine what actions documents created by other users can perform on your workstation.

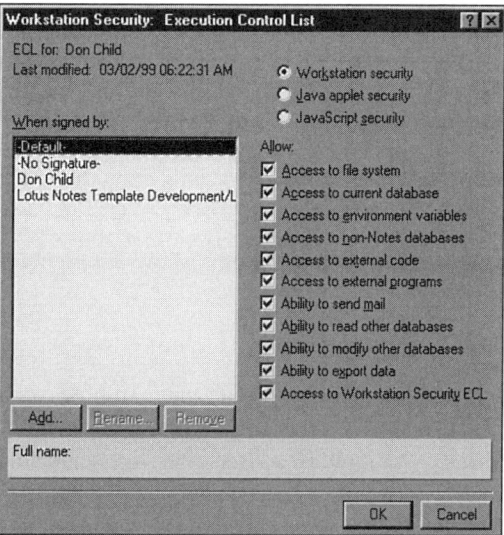

In many instances, you can use Default and No Signature to protect your system from intrusion by unwanted agents. The degree of protection is very much in your hands. It's a small price to pay for the rich complexity of Notes documents culled from enterprise systems, the Internet, and fellow Notes users.

In Notes 5.0, you can also set execution security for Java applets. In the world of Internet computing, there is an increasing use of Java applets as interfaces to back-end systems. You may very well want to be more restrictive with Java applets than you are with signed agents. To set the ECL for Java applets, click on the Java applets radio button and click on the check boxes that you want to allow, or unclick those actions you want to block.

> **Tip**
>
> In a view, you can display an icon next to documents that contain attachments. To do this, create the following View column formula:
>
> `@If(@IsAvailable($Title);n;"")`
>
> n can be any number between 1 and 170. Each number displays a different icon. You can also view the icons online by looking under "Displaying an icon in a column" in the Notes Help database. Be sure that you have Display Values as Icons selected in the Column Properties box. Then you will be able to see in advance that a document has an attachment and can set up the ECL accordingly.

JAVA APPLET SOURCE SPECIFICATION

In addition to the ECL, you have other options for working with Java applets. The built-in Web Navigator enables Java applets from the Web to run on your computer. To prevent unwanted applets from executing on your workstation, you can define which locations are acceptable sources of Java applets. For example, you could decide not to retrieve Java applets unless they're hosted on Web servers located inside your firewall.

By default, all hosts can run Java applets on your system, but no hosts are allowed to access system resources—such as password files, environment variables, and files—regardless of their capability of running applets.

You can modify the list of trusted Java applet hosts in location documents in your Personal Address Book.

In the Advanced section of your Location document, shown in Figure 36.10, click on the Java Applet Security tab.

Four fields are used to set Java Applet Security:

- **Trusted hosts**   Enter the IP address or domain name of hosts that can load Java applets on your computer. You can specify wildcards, as in `123.45.678.*` or `*.lotus.com`. Note that if a host name maps to multiple IP addresses or vice versa, intended hosts might not be included in your wildcard. If you leave this field blank, all hosts are considered to have the type of access defined for network access for untrusted hosts.
- **Network access for trusted hosts**   This is the level of network access you want to give to trusted hosts. Options include the following:
  - **Disable Java**   The trusted host cannot run applets on your system.

- **No access allowed** Lets the host run an applet on your system but doesn't let it make network HTTP connections on any host.
- **Allow access to any originating host** The applet can make network HTTP connections on the host from which the applet was retrieved.
- **Allow access to any trusted host (the default selection)** The applet can make network HTTP connections on trusted hosts only.
- **Allow access to any host** The applet can make network HTTP connections on any host.

■ **Network access for untrusted hosts** This determines the level of access for all other hosts—those not selected as trusted hosts. Options are the same as the first three options just discussed. Allow access only to originating host is the default.

■ **Trust HTTP Proxy** This field is used if you specified an HTTP proxy in the Web proxy field on the location document. Yes indicates that you want the proxy to resolve the host for you. Otherwise, you won't be able to resolve the host name or run Java applets.

Figure 36.10
Define Java Applet Security in the Location document.

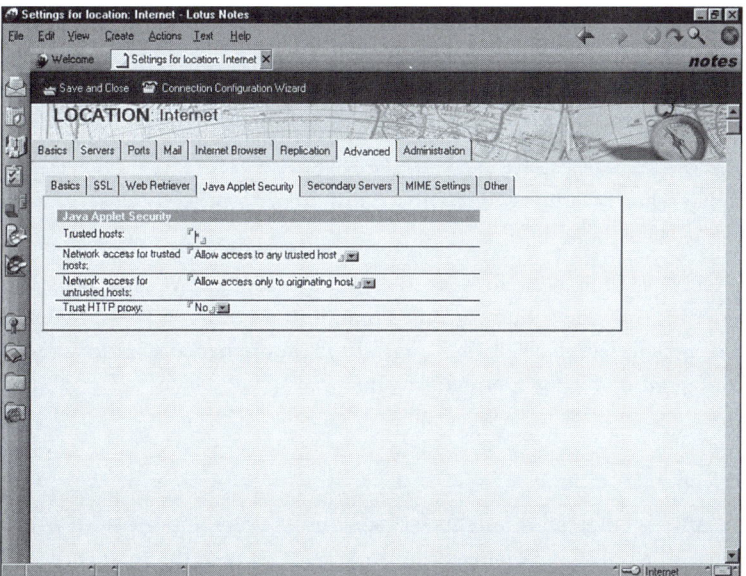

Securing Files from Web Browsers

In Notes 5.0, you can secure files from Web browsers, adding an extra layer of security to a vulnerable area. You can decide in advance which files you don't want Web browsers to access and protect those files. This is done in the Domino Directory as follows:

1. Open the Servers/Servers view and highlight the server on which you want to protect files.
2. Select Actions, Web, Create File Protection.

3. If you have virtual servers defined, enter the IP address for the server you are protecting. Otherwise, leave the default of All Web Servers protected.

4. Enter the full pathname of a Directory relative to the Domino Directory—for example, `c:\notes\data\projects`.

5. Enter the name you want users to see when they try to access the Directory and are prompted for a password.

6. Set Access Control for the Directory. You can define individual users or groups. You can give them GET and HEAD access, which lets them browse and start programs, or you can give them POST, which is used to send data to a CGI file.

   A File Protection Document with no name entered in the Access Control setting is not accessible to anyone. It is the same as setting No Access.

Additional Internet Security

Notes 5.0 provides additional Internet security options, including the capability of securing SMTP connections using TCP/IP or a TCP/IP port secured with Secure Sockets Layer (SSL).

You can authenticate with a name and password for both TCP/IP and TCP/IP secured with SSL. You can also authenticate servers, including message validation and data encryption for TCP/IP secured with SSL.

Notes 5.0 also supports VeriSign Global Server IDs. These Global Server IDs use a 128-bit cipher when communicating with international browsers and servers using SSL over NNTP, LDAP, IMAP, and POP3.

If you have SSL set up for your Internet protocol and your browser supports the Global Server ID, Domino automatically communicates using a 128-bit cipher. Ciphers are the keys SSL uses to secure data when transmitted on the network. You don't have to do any special configuration for the Domino server.

From Here...

Security is enforced throughout Notes and the Domino server. If you are interested in specific security issues, you may want to look at some of the following sections in this book:

- Chapter 17, "Access Control Lists (ACLs) and Application Security," provides an overview of application security.
- Chapter 14, "Designing Pages, Forms, and Subforms," and Chapter 15, "Developing Views and Folders," describe specific techniques for enforcing application security using Reader and Author restrictions.
- Chapter 37, "Firewalls, Virtual Private Networks (VPNs), and Internet Security," provides more detail on some of the security features mentioned in this chapter.
- Part VII, "Administering the Domino Servers," provides numerous details on security and the Domino server.

CHAPTER 37

Firewalls, Virtual Private Networks (VPNs), and Internet Security

The meteoric rise of Internet-based networking continues to spawn new possibilities and new vulnerabilities related to remote communication and collaboration. The overwhelming potential for new productivity is matched by an equally overwhelming potential for lost productivity, service outages, and data corruption or theft, to name just a few of an endless litany of security risks.

As corporations grow comfortable with placing critical reliance on the Internet, the security administrator's job becomes exponentially more difficult. Mission-critical systems deployed on Internet-based or Web-centric networks demand creative security measures that must guard against increasingly complex threats, while facilitating growing numbers of users with diverse access needs.

The purpose of this chapter is to examine the range of options available for securing your network from outside intrusion, extending your private network beyond the boundaries of the firewall, and guarding yourself from the Internet's security threats.

This chapter explores, in three sections, the latest generation of security solutions that you can deploy with Notes and Domino. The first section deals with firewalls, and is followed by a section on Virtual Private Networks. The final section concludes the chapter with an overview of Internet security issues.

Firewalls

Think of firewalls as your network's friendly bouncers—minus the tattoos and nose rings, of course. Firewalls stand squarely in the doorway of your network and decide who gets in and who doesn't. You need a firewall because, believe it or not, some people think your network is a totally rocking place and they'll do anything to get in.

The term "firewall" can refer to a specific server or application, but is often used generally to refer to an overall solution made up of servers, routers, proxies, and third-party applications. Just to make sure there's no confusion, this chapter covers the whole range of firewalls and firewall components that relate to or work with Lotus Notes/Domino.

Corporations deploy firewalls to keep unwanted intruders from raiding internal computers and data. Firewalls allow users on the internal network to access the Internet, but do not allow external users to see or access the computers and servers of the internal network. Firewalls greatly reduce the threat of unauthorized access to your internal network.

As you'll see in the following sections, today's firewall and proxy configurations can do a great deal more than simply block traffic in one direction. The firewall section of this chapter will show you how to combine the power of Notes/Domino with the power of proxies and third-party add-ons to create a firewall solution that serves as well as it protects.

How Firewalls Work

The original firewall concept, still popular today, consists of a computer with two network cards, each with its own IP address. One network card connects to the Internet, the other network card connects to your internal network. The internal network card accepts requests from the internal network and forwards them to the card connected to the Internet. At the same time, the card connected to the Internet refuses to forward any requests that do not originate from the internal network. Because of this, those on the Internet—all the hackers, crackers, and ne'er-do-wells—cannot see or reach any destination on the other side of your firewall. To the denizens of the outside, the computers and servers on the internal network are invisible. See Figure 37.1 for an illustration of a simple firewall model, often referred to as a Dual Homed Host, or packet-filtering firewall.

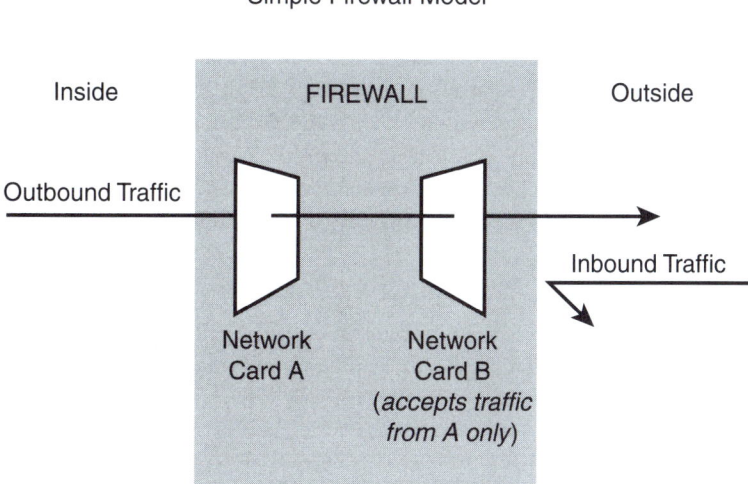

Figure 37.1
A simple Dual Homed configuration employs tandem network cards and simple packet filtering to control traffic.

Today's emerging commercial firewall solutions consist of increasingly sophisticated suites of integrated applications working together to protect an organization's private network. With advanced features, such as automatic logging, reporting, and notification, these firewalls work in conjunction with routers and third-party proxy applications to impose control on both directions of traffic: limiting outsiders from accessing internal resources, but also monitoring and limiting what users inside the network are allowed to access.

More and more third-party vendors are offering proxy applications that add useful functions, such as virus scanning and Web site filtering. We'll explore these additional services in detail later on. Figure 37.2 shows a more advanced firewall configuration with a variety of proxy services.

Figure 37.2
An advanced firewall scheme complemented by a range of proxy services.

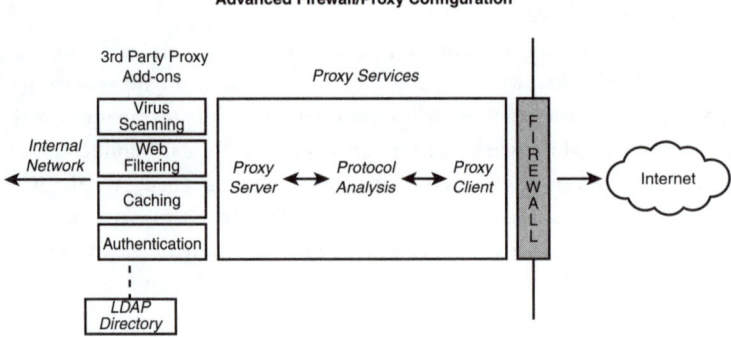

Setting Up a Firewall

Setting up a firewall requires a number of crucial choices that will affect your entire network. The following sections take you down the path of setting up the right firewall for your organization. For starters, you select the right firewall type for your organization and decide how your firewall will work with any proxies you decide to implement. Then you'll be faced with the chore of selecting the right firewall products from a confusing array of vendors. You'll learn how to cut through the marketing hype and get a solid solution. I'm starting to sound like a seminar speaker, so we'd better go ahead and get started.

Choosing a Firewall Type or Configuration

You should be aware of the different types of firewalls available today and how they can each work with Notes/Domino. For the purposes of Notes/Domino deployments, there are three types of firewall solutions:

- Dual Homed Host
- Screened Host
- Screened Subnet

Each of these firewalls is discussed in further detail in the next few sections.

Dual Homed Host Firewalls

The simplest firewall configuration, Dual Homed Host provides a basic packet-filtering service based on two network cards, as shown previously in Figure 37.1. Don't be misled by the simplicity of this system. A Dual Homed configuration can serve as the basis for a Notes Passthru server, capable of providing proxy service for all Notes clients and Domino servers in your internal network.

SCREENED HOST FIREWALLS

A Screened Host configuration works somewhat differently by relying on a router to dictate what network segments or machines can communicate with each other or other entities. These configurations are used primarily to limit or control who is allowed to communicate with the remote network.

SCREENED SUBNET FIREWALLS

The Screened Subnet firewall invokes the concept of network segmentation to isolate sensitive services and systems. Rather than relying on a single server or application, this method uses routers to separate the internal network into segments. Typically, a single Screened Subnet will be isolated from both the Internet and the "private" internal network (sometimes referred to as the demilitarized zone or DMZ).

Why would you want to divide your network like this? If your organization uses a diverse set of Internet and private network-based servers and applications, segmenting your network will strengthen your security while giving your users more flexibility to use services they might not otherwise be allowed to use.

For example, if you needed to protect several UNIX servers with sensitive data, you probably would not want to allow Telnet on your network. Your users complain because they need Telnet to access some executive management information from another server or remote site. Solution? Separate your network into several zones, one being the Internet zone where all Web and mail servers reside. Users are allowed to use FTP, Telnet, and other applications in this zone. Your more vulnerable and sensitive assets, such as the UNIX servers, reside in other zones that prohibit Telnet, FTP, and so forth.

The routers that separate each segment or zone follow specific rules regarding which kind of traffic can pass between segments and which protocols can be used to communicate across segments. Figure 37.3 shows an example of a segmented network topology.

Figure 37.3
A Screened Subnet firewall segments the network into zones or virtual LANs to provide flexibility and increased security for sensitive data.

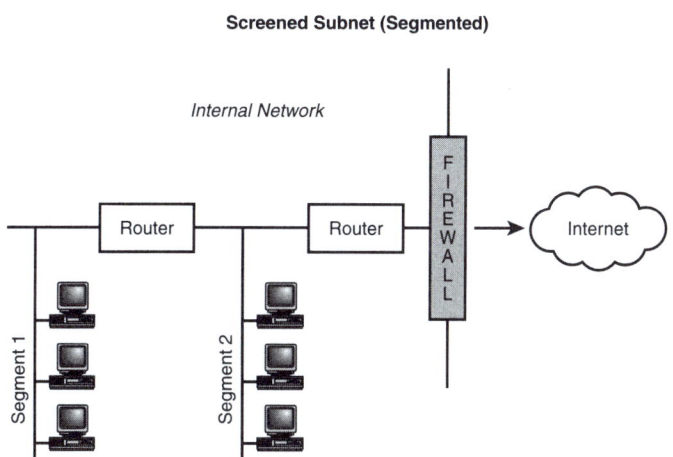

Which Firewall Should I Use?

In most midsize to large organizations, the Screened Subnet firewall is preferred because of its capability of dividing your network into areas with varying security constraints. As more and more organizations develop increasingly complex information management needs, the flexibility offered by Screened Subnets makes it a favorite of network administrators (and users for that matter).

Firewalls and Proxy Servers

Firewalls and proxy servers can compensate for each other's weaknesses and provide a solid solution when combined.

Firewalls screen network packets based on their origin, destination, and port. They effectively block outsider access to your internal network, but present several drawbacks.

Firewall Drawbacks

Firewalls hinder your ability to trace network activity to individual computers on your network. For example, let's assume you have a program that logs users' FTP access to a certain server. Instead of showing the individual IP addresses of each user's computer, your log file will show only one IP address: the firewall's. This drawback can hinder a number of logging, troubleshooting/tracking, and monitoring activities.

Another problem with firewalls is that they offer an all-or-nothing approach. Either everyone has access, or no one has access. Opening a port on the firewall so your trusted friend can use a chat program or have special access opens that port to every unscrupulous hacker in the world. Sure, the port number may be obscure, but it can be discovered quickly and exploited by anybody armed with any one of a number of freely available utilities.

Proxy Types

Proxy servers act as intermediaries, providing controlled access through the firewall. Instead of connecting directly through the firewall, you connect to the proxy server, which then connects to your intended destination and handles your data transfers. Proxy security is particularly strong, because proxies can eliminate any and all direct IP routes from the Internet to computers on the internal network. Proxy servers can also take advantage of caching (keeping copies of previously accessed documents) to reduce network traffic and improve response time for frequently used documents.

Proxies come in two types: application-level proxies, which, as their name suggests, function as applications on a server; and circuit-level (or network) proxies, which function at the network level.

SOCKS is an example of a circuit-level proxy. The SOCKS protocol uses sockets (a network connection method) to track each connection made through the proxy server. Like all circuit-level proxies, SOCKS can provide proxy services at the network level (instead of at the application level) for a variety of different communication applications: HTTP, MIME, FTP, and more.

Application-level proxy servers, by contrast, have a reputation for sometimes being very slow, due to the way they must examine each network packet. Think of these proxies as assembly-line inspectors who must lift each packet off the conveyor belt and examine it before placing it back on the conveyor belt and allowing the packet to continue. Because these proxies are applications, each packet of data must travel upward from the network stack's low-level protocols to the application space, where the proxy operates. Only then can the proxy conduct its protocol analysis, inspecting each packet's header and data.

Surrounding your firewall and proxy servers with routers can help minimize the traffic that needs to be analyzed and reduce the proxy server's impact on network performance.

Proxy Add-ons

More recent proxies offer compatibility with third-party plug-ins that add a variety of useful functionality to your proxy configuration. For example, Secure Computing offers SmartFilter (`http://www.smartfilter.com`), a Web filtering application that works with Netscape's proxy server. Web filtering and several of the more common proxy add-ons are described later in this chapter.

Authentication Authentication essentially verifies a user's identity and matches that identity with a set of access privileges. More companies are using centralized authentication schemes for all the logins to various applications. A single Directory server keeps track of all usernames, passwords, and access privileges. When a user logs in to any of the applications, servers, or workstations he or she has access to, the authentication proxy service refers to the Directory server to determine what access privileges this user should be granted.

Web Caching Web caching saves time and bandwidth by maintaining copies of frequently used Web pages. When a user requests a certain Web page, the caching proxy first checks the cache to see whether this Web page has already been downloaded. If it has, the proxy serves up the cached copy, rather than going out to the actual site to access it. Of course, the caching proxy will retrieve the page from the remote site, if necessary.

Web Filtering Web filtering proxy add-ons restrict access to Web pages deemed unfit by corporate policy. This could include restricting access to sites offering pornography, hate speech, criminal skills, gambling, chat, or what is typically referred to as worthless content. The Web filter compares a requested Web site or page URL against a control list of sites that are off limits.

A good Web filtering application enables you to restrict or allow either individual URLs or entire categories of URLs—sex, racism, humor, and online selling, to name a few. Your restrictions or allowances for individual URLs will overide any categorical restrictions or allowances. For example, you might categorically restrict all chat sites, but exempt your own chat site, allowing users to visit only your chat site.

Typically, Web filtering applications require that you regularly download a new control list in order to restrict users from the latest crop of undesirable Web sites.

VIRUS SCANNING   Similar to Web filtering, a virus-scanning proxy add-on examines incoming traffic for suspicious files and attachments. As with Web filtering, the control list must be kept up-to-date to effectively prevent the introduction of viruses into your network.

You should keep in mind that all these proxy add-ons represent extra steps that each network packet must go through before reaching its destination. Implementing any one or all of these could significantly slow your network traffic.

PROXY/FIREWALL INTEGRATION WITH DOMINO

If you need to handle Notes RPC connections, you can take advantage of Domino's built-in Notes Passthru services to create a proxy server. The Notes Passthru services enable a Domino server to serve as an application-level proxy server for securing Notes RPC (Remote Procedure Call) data transfers. Remember, because it is an application-level proxy, it will slow down network traffic to some degree.

This is not the only way you can integrate a proxy with your firewall. Instead of handling RPC connections, maybe you need to manage IP traffic. We'll refer to the next two methods as the 1-box and 2-box configurations (using the term "box" to describe the server machine).

In the 1-box firewall/proxy configuration, the firewall application and the proxy both reside on the same box (server machine). See Figure 37.4 for an illustration.

Figure 37.4
The firewall and the proxy applications may reside on a single physical box.

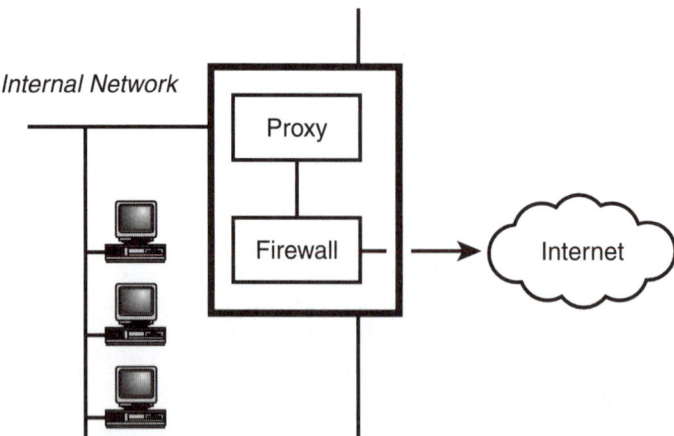

In the 2-box configuration, the firewall and the proxy server each have their own box and are linked together. The firewall server machine uses a SOCKS server (which is bound to the proxy server in the other box) to process requests.

Figure 37.5 shows a typical 2-box firewall/proxy configuration, often called a *socksified* proxy server.

Figure 37.5
A socksified proxy, consisting of a proxy server linked to a SOCKS server residing on the firewall.

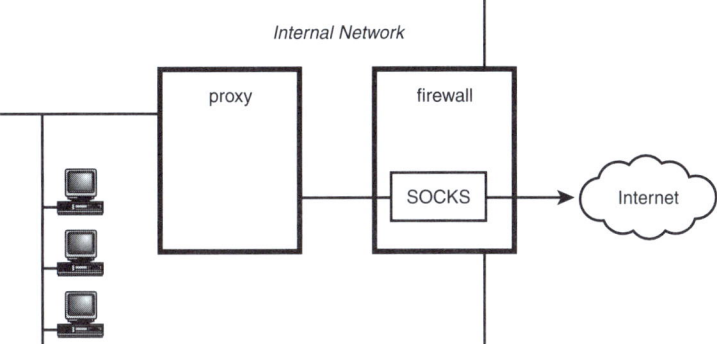

SELECTING FIREWALL PRODUCTS

Because your firewall provides the foundation of your Internet security, exercise extreme caution when choosing firewall products. Look for firewall solutions that have a proven track record and are certified by the International Computer Security Association (ICSA).

ICSA CERTIFICATION

ICSA's Firewall Certification Program certifies firewall products that pass a rigorous set of standardized security attack tests. During these tests, the firewalls must demonstrate the capability of providing a comprehensive array of network services to both internal and external users—while under attack. Too numerous to include here, the services include SSL access, SMTP mail delivery, DNS, and more. Security attacks are mounted not only from the external side, but also the internal side to simulate the conditions that occur when a hacker breaches the firewall.

These stiff requirements are intended to ensure that ICSA-certified firewalls provide robust protection from a range of security attacks while operating under real-world conditions.

ICSA publishes a list of the firewalls that successfully complete their "firewall boot-camp" certification program. According to ICSA, 31% of the firewall products submitted for certification fail their first attempt.

The "From Here" section at the end of this chapter provides a URL to ICSA's list of certified firewall vendors and products.

FIREWALL WRAP-UP

Although Notes offers very strong application-level security, you need a firewall to provide your network-level security.

Domino can function as a component in a variety of firewall types: packet filtering, circuit-level proxy, and application-level proxy, to name a few.

This section explored the range of options available for securing your network from outside intrusion. You looked at different types of firewalls and what you should know before setting one up.

Certain firewall or proxy configurations may have an impact on the speed with which Domino is able to respond to requests from Web browsers or other clients. For more information on Domino performance topics, see Chapter 44, "Performance, Scalability, and Capacity Planning for Domino Servers."

The next section, Virtual Private Networks, shows you how to extend your network beyond your firewall to remote users without leasing expensive network lines.

Virtual Private Networks

Several years back, I had to spend some time on business in London, along with several colleagues. During our stay there, we made daily dial-up connections (yep, with one of those chirpy 2400-baud modems) from London to our home office in the Washington D.C. metro-area. As you can imagine, the phone bill was pretty horrific. Too bad we didn't have a Virtual Private Network (VPN).

What's a VPN?

Not too long ago, companiesneeding to extend their private corporate networks simply resigned themselves to the recurring costs of expensive leased lines or long distance dial-up connections.

Ah, but what if you could just form your own private network from the existing bandwidth of the Internet? Along came VPNs and a new world of networking possibilities was born—at a new low price. Because they enable secure, private data transfers over the Internet, VPNs provide significant cost savings over the more-expensive leased lines traditionally used for secure private networks.

A VPN could have saved us a lot of money when we were in London. Instead of dialing long distance, we could have dialed in to a local ISP and established secure connections with the home office—over the Internet instead of metered phone lines.

How Can VPN Be Secure?

How can your data be secure when it is traveling across the wild and wooly Internet?

VPN security uses special methods of handling and concealing data while it is in transit across the Internet. Three different methods, called protocols, were developed by several groups of networking and software companies and submitted to the Internet Engineering

Task Force (IETF). Figure 37.6 shows a logical view of a VPN. Currently, VPNs can secure data using one of three protocols:

- Point-to-Point Tunneling Protocol (PPTP)
- Layer 2 Tunneling Protocol (L2TP)
- IP Security Protocol (IPSec)

The next few sections describe each of these protocols in further detail.

Figure 37.6
VPNs encrypt data before it is sent and decrypt it upon arrival. For additional security, the network addresses of the sending and receiving parties can also be encrypted.

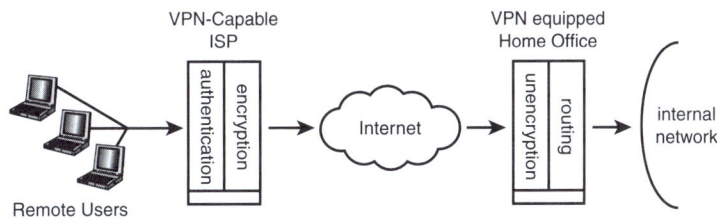

THE POINT-TO-POINT TUNNELING PROTOCOL (PPTP) The Point-to-Point Tunneling Protocol creates private "tunnels" through the public Internet, enabling your data to pass securely to its destination. A cousin to the well-known dial-up protocol, PPP (Point-to-Point Protocol), PPTP provides a method for tunneling the PPP through an IP network.

A PPTP-enabled VPN allows a remote user with PPP to dial in to a local Internet service provider (ISP) and establish a secure connection to the home office several thousand miles away.

Proposed by a consortium of Microsoft and several companies to the IETF (Internet Engineering Task Force), PPTP is currently in draft form and likely to become a standard, or the basis for the standard. Microsoft NT 4.0, Win95, and Win98 all currently support PPTP. However, in June 1998, Counterpane Systems, a cryptography and security firm, announced that they had successfully defeated the security mechanisms of Microsoft's implementation of PPTP, specifically their Windows NT PPTP Server. Microsoft has subsequently announced that Windows NT 5.0 (renamed Windows 2000) will support not only PPTP, but also L2TP and IPSec protocols, described in the next two sections.

If you're interested, or just can't sleep, you can take a look at the PPTP Specification at

`http://www.ietf.org/internet-drafts/draft-ietf-pppext-pptp-08.txt`

If you can't find the draft at this location, the draft number (the last number in the URL) has probably been updated. Use IETF's handy search engine instead:

`http://search.ietf.org/search/brokers/internet-drafts/query.html`

The Layer 2 Tunneling Protocol (L2TP)   The Layer 2 Tunneling Protocol (L2TP) is designed to free ISPs from the traditional limitation of being tied to specific registered IP addresses. L2TP promises a "virtual dial-up" service that allows the use of unregistered (privately addressed) IP addresses, as well as support for existing network protocols (IP, IPX, AppleTalk, and so forth). Like the other two VPN protocols, L2TP also provides secure connections across the Internet.

For further information, see the L2TP IETF Draft available at

http://www.ietf.org/internet-drafts/draft-ietf-pppext-l2tp-14.txt

As noted previously, you can also quickly find drafts using the IETF search located at

http://search.ietf.org/search/brokers/internet-drafts/query.html

The IP Security Protocol (IPSec)   The IPSec protocol provides security at the packet-processing (network) layer rather than the application layer of the network communications model. Because its security works independently of client computers or applications, IPSec is truly platform/application-independent.

IPSec offers two security modes. The Authentication Header (AH) provides sender authentication, but does not encrypt the data. The Encapsulating Security Payload, as the name implies, both authenticates the sender and encrypts the data. These modes are specified, along with any separate key protocols, in the network packet header.

The IP Security Document Roadmap, which provides an overview of the IETF documents that describe IPSec, is available here:

http://www.ietf.org/internet-drafts/draft-ietf-ipsec-doc-roadmap-02.txt

---

The Internet Engineering Task Force

The Internet Engineering Task Force brings together network administrators, architects, and researchers for the purpose of guiding the evolution of the Internet's architecture and operational methods.

Companies and other groups submit proposed standards for new protocols to the IETF for approval and standardization. The IETF meets three times a year and has a policy of open membership to any interested individual. IETF members, who span the globe, are divided into working groups which, in turn, are grouped into areas. Members collaborate with other members of their working group, performing most of the technical analysis by corresponding through mailing lists and referring to the IETF Web site, where literally hundreds of proposed drafts and working papers are posted.

For more information about the IETF, visit their Web site at

http://www.ietf.org

To Be Forewarned

Be aware that deploying VPN services will more than likely require you to reconfigure the filtering schemes in your routers and firewalls. VPN solution providers may require the installation of various servers and components, some more intrusive than others. Before making a purchase decision, make sure you understand the exact impact a VPN solution will have on your existing network topology.

On a similar note, if your network employs Network Address Translation (NAT) to maintain a private addressing scheme, you need to comply with some detailed rules dictating how network addresses are managed in the communication process between the VPN packet processor and your NAT implementation. Be sure to discuss these issues with your VPN provider.

VPN Wrap-up

VPNs provide increasingly elegant solutions for leveraging the public Internet to save communication costs. More vendors are announcing support for VPN and many or all of its associated standards.

VPN's chief drawback lies in its reliance on the Internet, which cannot guarantee any level of bandwidth on demand. In spite of this, more companies are finding ways to take advantage of VPNs. Because VPNs operate transparently to Notes and Domino, they provide no conflicts or compatibility problems for organizations seeking to extend their network to remote Notes/Domino users. For a real-world example of a VPN integrated with a Notes/Domino environment, visit the Upper Manhattan Empowerment Zone at http://www.umez.org.

Internet Security

Internet-capable since 1993, when Lotus implemented TCP/IP support in Notes R3, Notes has a long history of Internet security experience, often implementing good security concepts long before the rest of the industry.

Take, for example, the Notes system of cryptographic authentication using .ID files. Charles Kaufman, security project leader for Lotus Notes and Domino 5.0, provided the most succinct description of cryptographic authentication's value in a recent interview. Instead of exposing passwords by sending them over networks to an authenticating server, cryptographic authentication "lets the user prove knowledge of a secret without revealing it."

Kaufman notes that cryptographic authentication, a cornerstone of Notes security since the beginning, has only recently, with the advent of SSL version 3, begun to be deployed in other environments. (for the full Kaufman interview with Patricia Kennedy, see "Secure Communication on the Non-secure Internet," at http://www.lotus.com).

In addition to cryptographic authentication, Domino has also supported encryption outside the firewall, enabling the exchange and distribution of public keys for decryption across the firewall. Domino also supports digital signatures on both sides of the firewall.

The following sections present highlights of Domino's more important Internet security concepts.

Authentication

Domino's authentication provides a system for positively verifying each user's identity. In keeping with Domino's consistent and scalable security, Domino offers authentication services for Web browsers as well as client/server environments.

Browsers

Domino uses Secure Sockets Layer (SSL), the standard authentication protocol for Web clients, to authenticate browser users. Based on the X.509 public key infrastructure, SSL verifies the identity and credentials of both clients and servers, and uses encryption to ensure private data transfers.

Client/Server

Domino performs its client/server authentication in accordance with its own RSA-based public key infrastructure.

Domino's client/server authentication—who has access to what—can be controlled either by the user or by system settings configured by the administrator.

Granularity

No, granularity isn't a new high fiber cereal. It is one of Domino's key security features, which gives us complete control over security—down to the tiniest level. Domino's control access granularity enables us to deny access to a single field in a specific document on a specific server on a specific network. That's granularity.

Other security schemes, by contrast, are not so granular. They might enable you to restrict access to a network segment, or a directory or document, but not to a specific field inside a document. Not from a centralized console, either.

Encryption

Notes and Domino support RSA public key encryption as well as several implementations of private key encryption. The difference between public key and private key encryption lies in the keys—the alphanumeric strings used to encode and decode.

Public key encryption enables you to give others a public key so they can create encrypted documents that only you can read. Why are you the only one who can decrypt the documents? Because you are the only one who possesses the private key. The public key can encrypt the data, but only the private key can decrypt it.

The reverse of this, private key encryption, means that a single key is capable of both encryption and decryption. The key must be guarded closely, because it contains the data needed to decrypt your private documents.

What Can Go Wrong

In the security world, the old adage has been upgraded: What can go wrong can also go really wrong unless you understand Internet security issues and how to handle them. The next few sections provide an overview of the security threats that can originate from the Internet and what you can do about them.

Setting up any type of Internet connection, particularly if you decide to set up a Domino server outside your corporate firewall, means you have some serious security planning to do.

Any connection to the Internet should include a plan for securing your Domino server(s) and internal network. Domino can work in tandem with a firewall, but Domino itself does not constitute a firewall solution.

The following sections will help you think about the security issues involved when you are connected to the Internet. The safest operating assumption is that whether you are outside or inside the firewall, everything needs its own security. There is no protection or security otherwise. The server, the applications on the server, and the connection between the server and the rest of your network should all have their own airtight security.

You Need a Security Policy

Your organization needs a security policy that defines acceptable use of your Internet resources. In addition, your security policy should stipulate the use of the best available security technologies, specify how security risks will be handled, and make provisions for the segregation of operations documentation from user documentation.

A well-planned security policy should also be complemented by an established process for dealing with new security issues as they arise.

In my experience, many organizations understand on a basic level the need for security, but have a very difficult time handling the scenarios that develop. Large organizations, in particular, often face conflicts that pit user requirements (or desires for new Web/network products) against established security practices. Without a predetermined framework for arbitrating these security-related disputes, your organization will suffer from stalled decision-making and degraded Internet security.

For example, if you decide to use a Screened Subnet firewall configuration, as discussed earlier in the firewall section of this chapter, you should construct a matrix that shows what types of traffic and protocols (email, FTP, HTTP, Telnet) will be allowed to communicate across the different segments of your network. This matrix will guide your network and security policy decisions and will be the basis for user documentation and procedures.

To start developing your security policy, or to make sure your current policy addresses the security issues your organization will face, you need a method for assessing and categorizing the security threats. DataHouse, a recognized Internet Enterprise consulting firm (and my employer), has developed a Security Risk Classification Model for this purpose. The next few sections take you through a simplified version of this useful model.

SECURITY RISK CLASSIFICATION MODEL

The Security Risk Classification Model helps us accurately categorize security risks and determine the best actions to deter them. There are numerous risks present in any enterprise, and a classification system helps us concentrate our preventative efforts on those security risks that pose the greatest threat or are most likely to occur. The Security Risk Classification Model is shown in Figure 37.7.

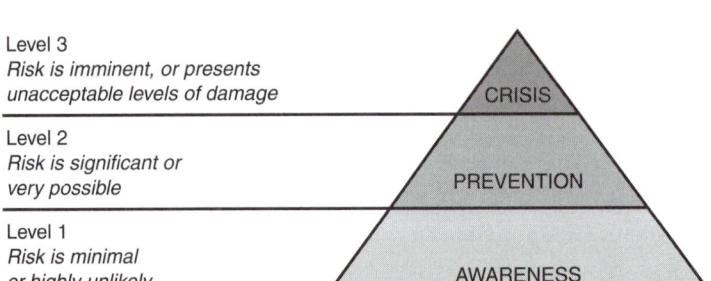

Figure 37.7
The Security Risk Classification Model categorizes security risks and recommends appropriate measures for each category.

The three levels on the left show levels of risk severity. When assessing any security risk, we attempt to determine

- The likelihood of the risk
- The severity of damage it would cause

By examining these factors, we are able to categorize a given risk into one of the three levels in the Security Risk Classification Model. After we determine the level of a security risk, we then are better able to determine the type of precautions that are most appropriate for this particular risk. The pyramid of the model shows the three corresponding levels of security precautions. The bottom level, Awareness, is the most basic level and is fundamental to any security prevention effort. The next level, Prevention, requires awareness in order to work. If prevention and awareness measures are not implemented, or if they fail, the final and most serious scenario may develop. Crisis refers to instances where a grave security threat is very imminent or has already occurred, and the strongest security or security response measures are required.

The next sections provide specifics on each security risk level and the type of measures that each level requires.

Level 1: Awareness Measures

Security threats that are either highly unlikely or represent only minimal risk to the operations and security of your organization usually call for basic awareness measures. Make your users aware of the risk and what specific activities expose them to this risk. Give them guidelines for ensuring that their activities do not escalate the risk to a higher level. Where needed, provide training or orientation briefings to inform them.

Let's look at a possible scenario where awareness measures might be appropriate. Suppose a Web browser vulnerability is discovered that, under certain circumstances, might allow a hacker to view data on a user's computer. You, or another knowledgeable person, determine that the degree of difficulty and the large number of required conditions for the vulnerability to be exploited make this a highly unlikely scenario. Because of these factors, you decide to enact awareness measures. You advise your users of the Web browser vulnerability and of activities that increase their exposure to risk. Specifically, you might advise them to not store sensitive data on their computer hard drives.

Level 2: Prevention Measures

Level 2 security threats pose significant risk to your operations and security, and due to the number of users and computers active in your organization, present a high likelihood of occurrence if prevention measures are not taken. Prevention measures differ from awareness measures because they not only make the users aware of a risk, but also require the user to do something. You may require your users to take a prevention measure such as refraining from launching email attachments from the browser. A few other examples of preventative measures include standard backup procedures, scheduled purchase or upgrade of new hardware and software, and running antivirus tools. Failure to practice these measures may lead to a situation where crisis measures are required. Implementing effective prevention measures requires clear communication and some form of training.

Level 3: Crisis Measures

A Level 3 security risk presents the imminent possibility that critical data, operations, systems, or confidentiality is in grave danger of being violated, seriously degraded, or destroyed. When a risk is categorized as a Level 3, the strongest precautionary measures are appropriate. Crisis measures put top priority on effective protection or immediate restoration of critical data, systems, and operations. This includes redundancy measures and emergency procedures. Recognizing a risk as a Level 3 means that you believe your organization would be seriously jeopardized if this risk were to become reality, and therefore are willing to prioritize the prevention of this risk over other normal functions. Crisis measures might include system shutdown, dismissal of certain employees, immediate backup or restoration of data, or immediate purchase and implementation of new hardware or software. Crisis measures always require the involvement of your organization's top management, your security officer, and CIO.

Building a Strong Defense

The first step is to assess your security risks, using the Security Risk Classification Model. The Model doesn't dictate anything; it simply helps you organize your security policy. You decide what kinds of risks deserve what kinds of measures, based on their impact on your organization.

After you assess your security risks, create a security policy that spells out what measures are required to avoid or respond to each type of security risk. If you have been careful to address every potential risk, you will have a comprehensive security policy.

After this, you can select a firewall solution, choosing a type that best matches your security policy. (If you already have a firewall, you must ensure that your current solution meets the requirements of your security policy.) On top of the firewall solution, you also build your network security, your application security, workstation security, and so forth. Figure 37.8 shows the process, in the proper order of importance, for building the strongest possible security defense.

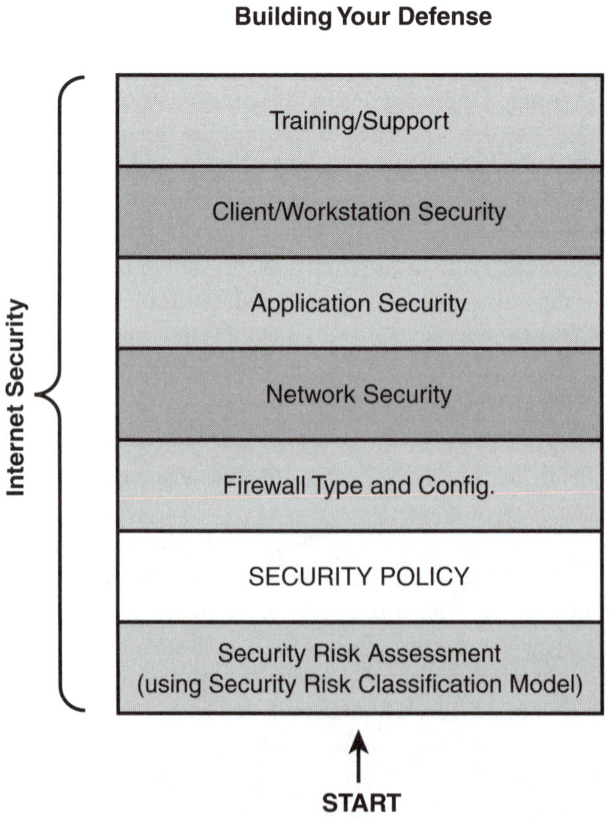

Figure 37.8
Build a strong defense by first assessing risks, and then building a security strategy that will guide the configuration of all your security measures.

Building Your Defense

Training/Support
Client/Workstation Security
Application Security
Network Security
Firewall Type and Config.
SECURITY POLICY
Security Risk Assessment (using Security Risk Classification Model)

Internet Security brace covers: Firewall Type and Config., Network Security, Application Security, Client/Workstation Security.

START ↑

Responding to an Attack

Your security strategy needs to include a plan for responding to security attacks. Besides your predetermined action plan, your logs will be one of the most important factors impacting your ability to respond. In the event of an attack, you should be able to access the HTTP logs and any logs created by FTP servers, proxy servers, or Web filtering software.

Lotus recognized this need and provided Domino with comprehensive logging and auditing capabilities. The Domino server logs all accesses and errors (which can provide clues to unsuccessful attacks) from both Web and Notes Clients.

Internet Security Pitfalls

Now that you've looked at the process for constructing a solid security policy and defense, let's turn to prevention. The following sections provide information you need in order to avoid some of the more common security vulnerabilities that may occur when your Domino servers are connected to the Internet.

The Objects of Your Disaffection

Some security administrators often use the term "unwanted object" to label undesirable items that enter networks attached to incoming email messages or Web pages. Unwanted objects can include applets, mail bombs, macros, Trojan horses, viruses, and so forth.

Even if you have a virus-scanning proxy, your firewall may be helpless to spot or stop these objects. The only foolproof solution for preventing these unwanted objects is to reject any and all email messages, Web pages, or applets—hardly a feasible idea.

Domino alleviates this risk significantly by giving you the ability to decide whether an object should be allowed to execute or not. This feature, called the Execution Control List (ECL), enables you to set parameters that guide how unknown or suspicious objects will be handled.

Unauthorized Email Forwarding and Spamming

Several methods exist for unscrupulous individuals to exploit your Domino server for the purpose of sending unwanted email (spam) to users all over the Internet. Spammers, usually marketeers sending unsolicited email, often seek to cloak their identity with bogus return email addresses in the messages. They further hide the origin of their messages by often passing their mail through another domain—maybe yours. The resultant email messages appear to have originated from your domain.

You can prevent this in two ways. First, change your domain settings to prevent mail from being routed from your domain.

The domain settings that control this can be easily set in Domino's Domain Document. Failing to take this step leaves your server vulnerable to exploitation by spammers.

Second, be cautious about running multiple services on a single server that is accessed by the Internet. Some combinations of services present security problems. With the advent of cheaper RAM and more powerful servers, administrators are able to run more services on a single box. However, it is important to understand the security implications of running multiple services from the same server. For example, a Domino Web server sharing a server with Notes SMTP MTA might run fine and save money. It could also allow someone to use your server to spam thousands of email users.

When Scripts Attack

CGI scripts, popular on many Web sites, can open a serious security hole in your otherwise well-protected system. CGI scripts have the capacity for several risky behaviors:

- They can be easily "tricked" into displaying or mailing sensitive data, such as password files.
- They can allow Denial of Service attacks by facilitating large file uploads.
- They can allow the upload of executable files.
- They can overload memory and allow the execution of commands that otherwise would be prohibited.

If you decide to use CGI scripts, you should restrict the number of people in your organization who have access to the `cgi-bin` directory (and related directories) where CGI files and scripts reside. In addition, you should limit the number of people who are allowed to create and upload CGI scripts. The best practice is to have a predetermined set of CGI scripts that have been tested and found safe. Provide your users and departments with instructions for including the appropriate calls in their Web pages so they can access these scripts and put them to good use.

Organizations that make the mistake of allowing anyone to develop and upload CGI scripts are running the risk of server outages—due to Denial of Service attacks—or unauthorized access.

Fortunately, Domino enables you to control who is able to access the various files (including scripts) that reside on your server.

Restricting Telnet Access

For years a mainstay of the online world, Telnet is now recognized as a potential security problem for corporate networks. Administrators almost universally agree that allowing Telnet access to your server will dramatically increase your chances of a security attack. Using Telnet, hackers can execute programs, make system changes, and cause outages or denial-of-service attacks. An abundance of hacker documentation freely available on the Web provides simple tricks that can cause system damage or failure using Telnet.

For example, one simple method involves the use of several directory and naming commands to start a process that continuously creates new directories until the system memory overloads and the server crashes, resulting in a very difficult recovery. This attack, and most others like it, can be accomplished without root privileges.

Because of risks like these, most firewall administrators close down the Telnet port on the firewall, thus configuring the firewall to refuse Telnet connections.

Security Wrap-up

Domino's built-in security features best serve your organization when they are an integral part of an overall Internet security plan. Internet security is more than a set of configurations. It always involves one or more persons whose job is to follow prescribed security policy to ensure the operational integrity of the system and its data. Good solutions, such as Notes/Domino, can never replace a qualified network administrator who understands how to implement and maintain a secure system.

From Here...

This chapter provided information needed for understanding and setting up a firewall. You examined the potential cost savings, protocols, and issues involved with Virtual Private Networks. Finally, you explored Internet security issues and how to use the Security Risk Classification Model to assess your security threats and develop an appropriate security policy.

If you are interested in learning how to set up your own homemade firewall, Mark Grennan has provided a detailed tutorial for setting up a simple packet-filtering firewall. This helpful guide can be accessed at

http://electron.phys.dal.ca/Firewall-HOWTO.html

For a list of ICSA-certified firewalls, check out

http://www.icsa.net/services/consortia/firewalls/certified_products.shtml

For SOCKS information and download, see

http://www.socks.nec.com/

PART VII

Administering the Domino Servers

38 Administering Users, Groups, and Certification

39 Administering Electronic Mail

40 Replication and Its Administration

41 Administering Files and Databases

42 Managing Your Domino Server Configuration

43 Troubleshooting and Monitoring Domino

CHAPTER 38

ADMINISTERING USERS, GROUPS, AND CERTIFICATION

With the evolution of the Notes server from the preeminent client/server Groupware application host to Domino, the highly functional Internet application server, the roles of user management, group management, and certification management have taken on entirely new meanings. The Domino server hosts both Notes users and Internet users. It services Notes and SMTP Internet mail requests, Web and News requests, and Domino and Internet (LDAP) Directory requests. It hosts standard Notes databases and Post Office Protocol Version 3 (POP3) and Internet Mail Access Protocol Version 4 (IMAP) message store databases. Paralleling this increase in functionality is a complexity in Domino server administration.

This chapter covers three major topics relevant to systems administrators: user management within the Domino domain, group management within the Domino Directory, and certification management. Each section consists of subsections detailing major aspects of the topic. In the areas of user management, this entails the process of registering users, setting up Internet (Web, News, and LDAP Directory) users, managing user accounts, and integrating user account administration with Windows NT. In the areas of group management, this entails managing groups, creating groups, editing groups, and deleting groups. In the areas of certification, this covers topics of certify, cross-certify, cross-ertify key, multiple passwords, recovery information, and ID file.

Each subsection of the chapter provides a descriptive overview of the task at hand. It follows with a procedural outline of the steps to follow to complete the task. These descriptions attempt to summarize the most important steps required in the specific topic of Notes/Domino administration. Where necessary, it concludes with an example for the particular task.

Introducing the Domino Administrator

As in previous releases, much of the administrative functionality discussed in this chapter can be accomplished in a variety of ways. The most common of these originate from granular action buttons associated with each of the major groupings within the Domino Directory. For example, within the Group, Location, or Person view of the Domino Directory, the administrator has the facility to Add, Edit, or Delete a particular Group, Location, or Person. Notes Domino R5 introduces a much more powerful and efficient means to perform these and other administrative functions. This is the R5 Domino Administrator, evolving from the Administrative Control Panel of the R4.x releases. The task-oriented Domino Administrator panel is shown in Figure 38.1.

The R5 Domino Administrator creates a central environment within which administrators can perform administrative tasks. When initialized by starting the Domino Administrator independently or, if installed, by selecting the Domino Administrator icon or by traversing the File, Tools, Server Administration menu option within the Notes client, the Domino Administrator consists of two areas. In its left column, it shows the typical client icons. If the Server icon is selected, the Administrator displays a directory tree consisting of all the servers, the certificate hierarchy, and networks from a specific domain or multiple domains.

The right pane divides Domino administration tasks into "areas," giving each its own tab. Depending on the tab or task selected, the right pane is further subdivided into two or three areas: information regions and, for all but one tab, a collapsible Tools Pane section consisting of actions relevant to the major tab and embedded tab combination. The administrator can quickly switch between servers on the one hand and from people and group management, to file management, to replication, messaging, server, or configuration management on the other.

Figure 38.1
The Domino Administrator, showing the directory tree in the left pane with the servers, clusters, and networks in a specific domain, and details regarding the selected view in the right pane.

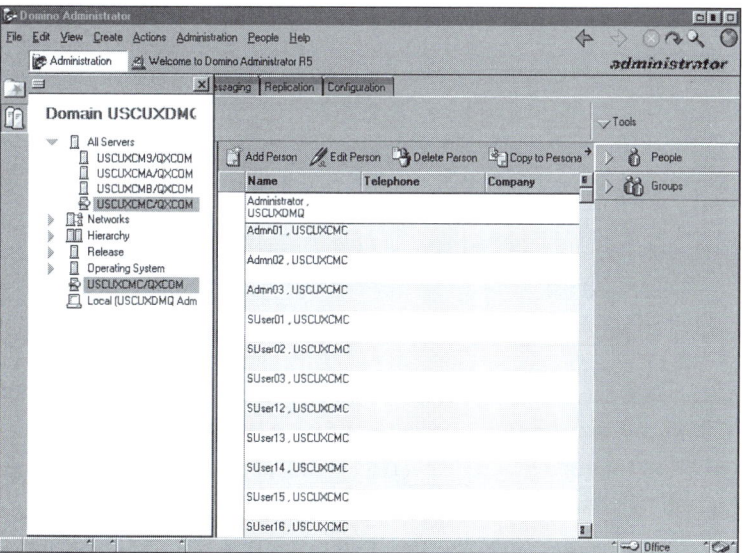

The Domino Administrator introduces the use of drag-and-drop technology to facilitate the administration and management of the Domino domain. To change a user's home server, for example, the administrator can drag and drop his or her name onto the new server. To move or copy databases from one server to another; to add or remove users to and from groups; or to run tools such as Compact, Fixup, Full Text Indexing, and so on; the administrator can simply drag and drop them to their desired targets.

The R5 Domino Administrator supports the following six areas: People & Groups; Configuration; Files; Server with embedded tabs to cover Status, Analysis, Monitoring, and Statistics; Messaging with embedded tabs to cover Mail and Tracking Center; and Replication.

People & Groups

The People & Groups tab facilitates actions relevant to person or user management, group management, certification management, mail-in database management, setup profile management, and the registration of persons, servers, organizational units, organizations, and internet certifiers. Most of the functions associated with this tab serve as the topic of the current chapter.

FILES

While displaying the directory and its contents in its two subordinate panes, the Files tab facilitates actions relevant to the display of disk information, directory and directory link creation and removal, and database tools. It enables administrators to quickly find information about the databases on their servers and then easily manage them. The administrator is able to see all the servers in the domain and all the files on those servers. To move, copy, or replicate a database from one server to another, the administrator can simply drag it from one server and drop it on another. The administrator is also able to change database properties and ACLs for multiple databases at once.

SERVER

The Server tab consists of a set of four embedded tabs:

- The Status tab enables the administrator to submit console commands relevant to tasks (for example, Tell, Load, or Quit), to Users (for example, Broadcast or Drop), or to the Server (for example, Properties, Replicate, Route Mail, Port Information, Secure Console, Quit).
- The Analysis tab presents views of the Domino log (log.nsf), the database catalog (catalog.nsf), the statistics reporting database (statrep.nsf), and the administration request database (admin4.nsf). It enables the administrator to perform a log analysis or a cluster analysis, or to decommission a server.
- The Monitoring tab enables the administrator to analyze service availability by service and by time line, thereby determining availability of a server.
- The Statistics tab enables the administrator to view real-time statistics of selected servers.

These embedded tabs enable the administrator to monitor servers, their tasks, statistics, and IP services. In this way, the administrator can see not only that the server is up or down, but that specific tasks are no longer functioning. The administrator can define multiple status indicators per server—one for each configured service—and can see a history of state changes for the server's services. The administrator can then analyze why a server is not responding, access a server's log, access Server and Connection documents, run remote console, access help on status indicators, and determine the probable cause and solutions for errors reflected by the status indicators.

MESSAGING

The Messaging tab contains two embedded tabs:

- The Mail tab enables the administrator to view properties pertaining to mailboxes on selected servers, shared mail attributes, mail routing status, mail routing events, and a mail routing topology map. It also allows the administrator to submit a mail trace, route mail, and start and shut down the router.

- The Tracking Center tab enables the administrator to track messages from a source point to a target. This feature enables the administrator to see where messages are in the network at any point in time. Using it, the administrator can look in the message-tracking database and troubleshoot problems pertaining to mail delivery. As part of this, the administrator can track messages across Notes domains, across pre-R5 Domino servers, and even across the Internet, if the destination server is running Domino R5.

Replication

The Replication tab enables the administrator to view the Replication schedule, Replication topology map, Replication events, and Replication cycles of selected servers within the selected Domino domain.

Configuration

The Configuration tab enables the administrator to view the Server Configuration, Messaging Configuration, Replication Configuration, Directory Configuration, Web Configuration, Statistic & Events Configuration, and Cluster Configuration from a selected server's Address Book.

Administering Users Within the Domino Directory

The People & Groups tab within the Domino Administrator serves as the control point for administering users within the Domino Directory. From this tab, you can perform all actions relevant to user management, group management, mail-in database management, setup profile management, certification management, and registration of persons, servers, organizational units, organizations, and internet certifiers. The People & Groups tab within the Domino Administrator is shown in Figure 38.2.

Previous chapters discuss the fundamentals of creating the Domino infrastructure and registering a new user to the Notes/Domino network. To review, this entails the following:

- Designing a hierarchical name scheme based on your organizational structure
- Creating a Certification Log to record how you register additional users
- Creating additional certifier IDs, if required by your hierarchical name structure, and distributing the certifier IDs to administrators at other sites
- Adding users by registering them with the appropriate certifier ID

Registering Notes Users

To set up users with hierarchical names, you must register them with the appropriate certifier ID according to where they belong in your organization. Registration is the process for adding users to your Domino system, and IDs are created with appropriate certificates. The appropriate certifier ID enables that user to authenticate with a server in any branch of the hierarchical name tree. It also enables a user to validate signed mail received from another user in any branch of the hierarchical name tree.

Figure 38.2
The People & Groups tab within the Domino Administrator, showing the currently selected Domino Directory on the left and the expanded People and Groups sections on the right.

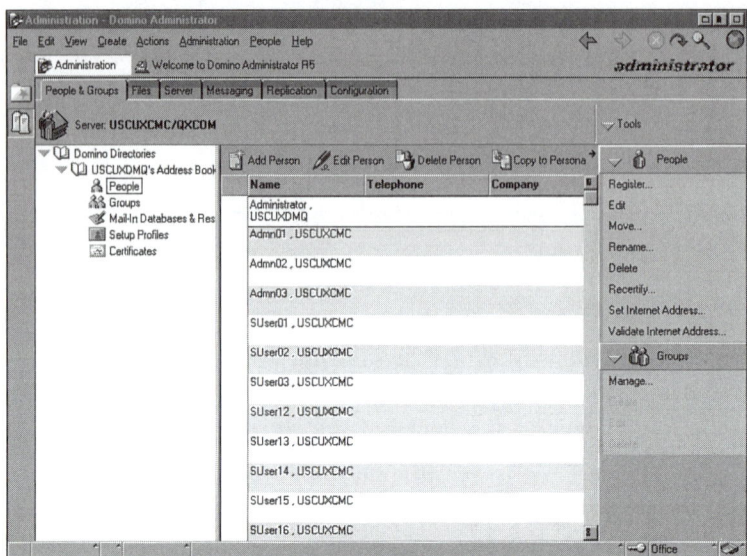

During registration, the entire name of the certifier ID is stored in a certificate with the entire name of the entity that is being registered. In addition, all the certificates originating from the certifier are added to the ID file. For example, the name `John Smith/Sales/New York/Acme` shows the hierarchy of certificates on John Smith's user ID, going from the lowest to the highest in the hierarchy. The last certificate name is `Acme`, identifying the organizational certificate that is at the top of the hierarchical name scheme. Then there is organizational unit certifier, `New York/Acme`. At the lowest end is the organizational unit certifier `Sales/New York/Acme`, just above the common name, `John Smith`. Such a combination of certifiers enables John Smith to communicate with others sharing the same certificates.

Preparing for Registration

Two configuration elements assist in the registration process and the subsequent installation/setup of the registered user's workstation environment: User Setup Profiles and workstation Execution Control Lists (ECLs), respectively. You create User Setup Profiles to set up default workstation settings and set up a default workstation ECL to establish a prescribed workstation data security.

Creating a User Setup Profile You create a User Setup Profile to create workstation defaults for users, including Internet settings, Passthru server settings, and the databases that appear on their workspaces. User Setup Profiles facilitate user registration and guarantee a level of administrative consistency in users' settings. They also make individual user setup tasks easier. You can create a User Setup Profile by opening the Domino Administrator, selecting the Domino Directory to which you want to add the Setup Profile, selecting Setup Profile, then clicking the Add Setup Profile button. In the form provided, you can specify the following:

1. In the Basics tab, enter the name of the profile and, optionally, the name of the Internet Browser used from this location and where users retrieve their Web pages.

2. In the Databases tab enter, optionally, the databases that you want to add automatically to the users' workspace, the databases that you want to add automatically as new replica to the users' workspace, and the enterprise directory databases that you want to add automatically to the users' workspace.

3. In the Dial-up Connections tab, enter, optionally, the server name, country code (if necessary), and phone numbers of the users' default Passthru server and remote servers that users need to access. The setup program creates Connection documents for the servers specified here.

4. In the Accounts tab, enter, optionally, the account names, server addresses, protocols, and Secure Sockets Layer (SSL) connections to Internet servers that users need to access. The setup program creates Connection documents for servers specified here.

5. In the Name Servers, Applet Security, Proxies, and MIME tabs, enter, optionally, the names and addresses of secondary TCP/IP and NDS Domino name servers, trusted hosts and network access for trusted and untrusted hosts, and proxy servers.

SETTING UP A WORKSTATION EXECUTION CONTROL LIST Complementing the User Setup Profile is the Execution Control List definition inherited by the individual's workstations from the Administration ECL. By default, a workstation ECL is created by the Setup program by copying the Administration ECL in the Domino Directory to the workstation. The resulting workstation ECLs limit the actions of another user's formulas or scripts when they run on the workstation. For example, an ECL could limit an executable from running on a computer and damaging or erasing data. The ECL accomplishes this by looking for the signature on applications or templates before they open on the workstation. The ECL then checks the signature against its settings to determine whether to grant or deny access. Hence, by carefully editing the values in the Administration ECL, you can determine what is and what is not permitted to execute on individual workstations.

You can edit the Administration ECL by opening the Domino Directory, choosing Actions, Edit Administration ECL, and assigning the desired access levels to accounts within the Directory. It is of particular importance to assign workstation access values to the -Default- and -No signature- accounts. However, you can also add users, groups, and servers to the ECL as well. Finally, if you want to allow users to modify their own ECLs, you can select the Allow user to modify button on the Administration ECL panel.

REGISTERING USERS

Registration formally adds users to Domino by creating IDs stamped with appropriate certificates. The user registration process performs three tasks. It creates a Person document in the Domino Directory, a user ID, and a server-based mail file if your site uses Notes, POP3, or IMAP4 mail. If you are using Windows NT, you can also create Windows NT user accounts during the registration process, if your account has rights on the target server to create users.

As you register users, you should be aware of the organization's hierarchical naming scheme and where within that scheme the user should be positioned. This helps you know which server to use when you register each user. As part of the registration process, you must also have access to each server that you are using, the certifier ID files that you will be using during registration, and their passwords.

You can register users at the end of the Domino server setup following initial installation and configuration. You can also register users at any time from within the Domino Administrator panel; you proceed by selecting the People & Groups tab and expanding the Register section in the right pane.

At this point, you can register new users either individually or from a text file. You choose the former when you have only a few users to register, or when each requires a different basic configuration. You choose the latter when you have many users to register and you want to standardize the registration for them. Either way, you can concurrently create Windows NT user accounts.

REGISTERING USERS INDIVIDUALLY The registration process requires that you have access to the user's certifier ID, you know its password, and you have at least Author-level access with `CreatorModifier` and `UserModifier` roles to the Domino Directory. The individual User Registration dialog consists of two tabs for Basic registration and three additional tabs if the Advanced check box is selected. The total of five tabs consist of the following: a Basics tab for username and password settings; a Mail tab for mail settings; an ID tab for ID settings; a Group tab for group settings; and an Other tab for such settings as adding a user profile or adding users to NT.

As you create registration documents for users, Domino enters the user into its User Registration Queue. The queue is actually a database, the `USERREG.NSF`, holding users pending registration. The User Registration Queue enables you to view users, identify their registration status, and assign values to non–user-specific fields to multiple users. Non–user-specific fields are such fields as username and password unique to the individual.

To perform basic user registration, you must complete the Basics and Groups panes. To perform more advanced registration, you must complete the Mail, ID Info, and Other panes as well. Complete the following steps to register an individual user:

1. Initiate the Domino Administrator, click the People & Groups tab, select the Domino Directory to which you want to register users, and click People.
2. From the Tools Pane, click Registration, Person.
3. Click Yes if you have purchased a user license. You will be presented with a Browse dialog box enabling you to select the desired certifier ID.

4. Browse to the selected certifier ID, and then, when prompted, enter the administration password for the specified certifier ID and click OK.

    This opens the Register Person—New Entry dialog box. Figure 38.3 shows the dialog box inset atop the Directories tab of the Domino Administrator, used to register new Notes Domino users, with the Advanced registration functionality selected.

Figure 38.3
The Register Person–New Entry dialog box, displaying the Advanced functionality available to an administrator when registering new Notes Domino users.

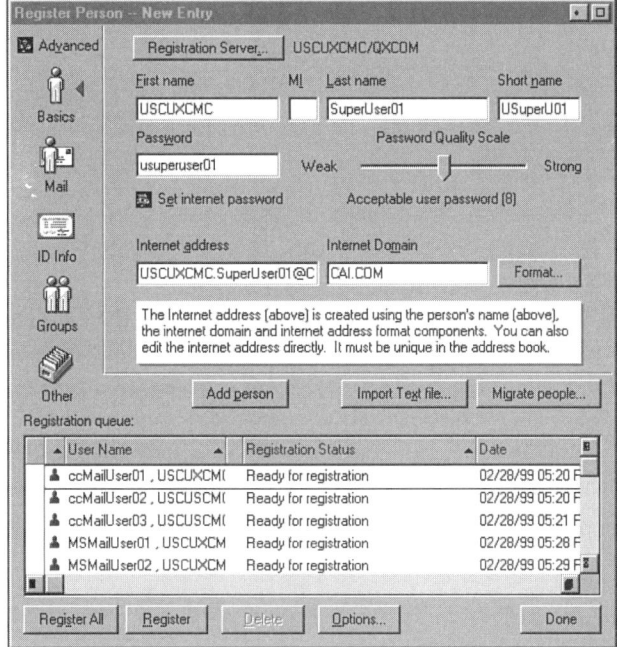

5. If the local server is not the registration server, you can change the registration server by selecting the Registration Server button, selecting an alternative server for registration, and clicking OK.
6. Enter the user's first name, middle initial, last name, and short name.
7. Enter a case-sensitive password for the user and the password quality level, and select whether to set an Internet password.
8. Review the Internet address and Internet Domain fields. An Internet address is generated for the user in the Internet address field from the person's name and the Internet address components specified on the pane. You can modify the format by selecting the Format button and choosing options from the lists available in both the Address name format and Separator fields.
9. Click Mail and then do the following:
    - Select the mail server and the appropriate mail system.
    - If you select Lotus Notes, POP, or IMAP, select the mail file template, enter the name of the user's mail file, define the mail file owner access, and select whether

you want to create the mail file now or in the background. The default name of the mail file is the first character of the first name, followed by the last name. You can also set the database quota, the warning threshold for the mail database, and whether to create a full text index.

- If you select Other or Other Internet, enter the user's forwarding address.
- Selecting None as the mail system requires no further input.

10. Click ID Info to specify information relevant to the selected certifier ID and individual user license.

11. If the certifier ID highlighted is not the desired ID, you can select a different certifier ID and press Enter. You will then be prompted for the certifier ID password; then click OK.

12. Select either the North American or International Security type.

13. If you want to change the expiration date, enter the date in mm-dd-yy format in the Certificate expiration date field.

14. Select how you want to store the user's ID file—in the Domino Directory or in a file. If you store the ID in a file, click Set ID file, specify the filename and path and double-click. If you do not select an ID storage type, a Notes ID is not created unless the mail type is Notes Mail. Most organizations view the storage of the ID files in the Domino Directory as highly insecure, because anyone with Reader access can detach them, so it is recommended to store them in a file in a secure directory location.

15. Click Groups and select the Groups to which you want the user added.

16. Click Other to specify additional Directory information:

    - Enter the desired setup profile, a unique organizational unit for the user, and a location—for example a region, district, city, or office.
    - Enter a local administrator and comment about the user.

17. If you use Windows NT, you can create a Windows NT account for the user by selecting Add this person to Windows NT and specifying the Windows NT username. In the NT Group Name field, you can enter the name of the Windows NT group in which you like to add all user accounts created in this session. By leaving the field blank, you place the user in the default Windows NT user group, Users.

18. If necessary, you can differentiate between two users with the same name, certified by the same certifier ID, by adding another level to the name in the User unique organizational unit box.

19. You can then click Add person to add the user to the User Registration Queue. You are then able to proceed to add another user to the queue.

20. After you have completed the documents for all users you want to register, click Register All or Register.

21. Click Done to exit.

If, during the registration process, you choose to create user accounts in Windows NT, the accounts include the following information:

- **Windows NT User Name**   Created from the entry made in the NT User Name field in the Other Pane of the Register Person dialog. The default is the user's short name.
- **Full name**   Created by combining the user's first name (if supplied) and last name.
- **Password**   Created by using the Notes password. If the Notes password exceeds 14 characters, the Windows NT password consists of the first 14 characters of the Notes password.
- **NT Group Name**   Created by using the name specified in the Register Person dialog or the default Windows NT user group, Users.

During registration, Domino copies the Windows NT User Name to the Network account name field in the Person document in the Directory. This facilitates the matching of Person documents within the Domino domain with user accounts in the Windows NT User Manager. This aids the synchronization of information when altering or deleting a record in one product and propagating the changes to the other product.

If, while creating user accounts, Domino encounters a Windows NT error (for example, you are not a Windows NT Administrator or Account Operator), it returns an appropriate message to the log file (`LOG.NSF`). If an error occurs that prevents the creation of an account in the User Manager, the user is still registered in Notes. Windows NT errors have no effect on the Domino registration process.

Note that you can create Windows NT users accounts only while registering Notes users. You cannot create a Windows NT user by manually adding a Person document to the Directory.

EXAMPLE INDIVIDUAL USER REGISTRATION   As an example, let us examine how you would register John Smith who has recently joined the Acme Corporation. He is working out of the New York office, which falls under the responsibility of the `New York/Acme` certifier. He is working in the Sales office, so the ultimate responsibility for registering him as a user on the system falls to the administration certifier responsible for the `Sales/New York/Acme` certifier ID.

If John Smith were to be registered by the top-level Acme certifier, he would be given automatic access to any databases that include `*/Acme` in the ACL at Reader access or higher. That includes databases in all divisions within all regions of the company. In short, if the top-level Acme certifier registered John Smith, John would have access that was too broad.

On the other hand, if John is registered with the `Sales/New York/Acme` certifier ID, you ensure that he is not accidentally included in Access Control Lists for divisions and regions for which he is not responsible. By using the `Sales/New York/Acme` certifier ID, John can access the Sales databases, the New York databases, and the Acme databases using a wildcard

`*/Sales/New York/Acme` that creates a de facto group for anyone with a certificate from the `Sales/New York/Acme` certifier ID.

John Smith, whose full name is `John Smith/Sales/New York/Acme`, can enter his name in a shortened form as `John Smith/`. The slash following his name means that the entire hierarchy, his full username, is intended.

Notes refers to names in several different ways. A fully canonical name includes location markers, for example `CN=John Smith/OU=Sales/OU=New York/O=Acme`, where `CN` is the common name, `OU` is an organizational unit, and `O` is the organization. This is how Notes stores the name, with all its components labeled. The abbreviated distinguished name is how the user might see it displayed, such as `John Smith/Sales/New York/Acme`. However, many fields on Notes forms contain input translation formulas that simplify the name so that only the common name is displayed, such as `John Smith`.

Registering John has automatically created the Person record and displayed the abbreviated fully distinguished name in the User Name field, along with his common name. This means that John can be addressed by just his common name, and the Notes Router will find his mailbox. Hence, everyone can send John Smith email addressed simply to `John Smith` and it will get to him.

REGISTERING A GROUP OF USERS FROM A TEXT FILE Complementing individual user registration, the Domino Administrator also enables you to register a group of users from a text file. To accomplish this, you need to be an administrator with at least Author-level access with `CreatorModifier` and `UserModifier` roles to the Domino Directory. As with individual user registration, you can concurrently create Windows NT user accounts, if you use Windows NT, at the same time that you are registering Notes users—again, if you have the proper administrative rights to the NT server.

To register a group of users from a text file, start by creating or automatically generating a semicolon-delimited file with the following information about the person: last name, first name, middle initial, organizational unit, password, ID file directory, ID filename, home server name, mail file directory, mail filename, location, comment, forwarding address, profile name, local administrator, Internet address, short name, alternate name, and mail template file.

After the text file has been created or generated, complete the following steps:

1. Initiate the Domino Administrator, select the People & Groups tab, and from the Tools Pane, click Registration, Person.
2. Select Register Users From File.
3. Enter the certifier password.
4. If the local server is not the registration server, you can change the registration server by selecting an alternative server for registration and clicking OK.
5. Click Import Text File, select the text file, and click Open. Because you can reconcile problems generated during the import process by editing individual documents

displayed in the User Registration Queue described previously, click OK for any status messages received.

6. If necessary, modify any user settings by editing individual documents displayed in the User Registration Queue.

7. Click Register All or Register. Domino uses default settings or settings defined in the global registration preferences for any options not defined.

REGISTERING NOTES USERS WITH WINDOWS NT USER MANAGER Just as you are able to register Windows NT user accounts within Notes, you can also register Notes users from the Windows NT User Manager. You can accomplish this by creating new Windows NT accounts and adding the users simultaneously in Notes, or registering existing Windows NT users in Notes, or adding both new and existing Windows NT groups to Notes, registering the group members as Notes users simultaneously.

Whichever way you choose to register a user in Notes from the Windows NT User Manager, the process creates a Person document, a user ID, a password, and mail file for the user, as with the traditional Notes registration process. Optionally, you can add the user to Notes as an Internet-only user. This creates a Person document and a Notes Internet password, but does not create a Notes ID or a mail file for the user.

You prepare and complete the Notes registration process by performing four actions within the Notes menu in the Windows NT User Manager:

1. Set up the registration options.
2. Create new Windows NT user accounts and register Notes users simultaneously.
3. Register existing Windows NT user accounts as Notes users.
4. Register members of Windows NT groups as Notes users.

SETTING UP WEB, NEWS, AND INTERNET (LDAP) DIRECTORY USERS

Whether you are using the Domino Administrator or the Windows NT User Manager to register Notes users or pure Internet users within the Domino domain, you have made it possible for them to authenticate themselves with Domino servers. It is possible however to set up Web, News, and Internet (LDAP) Directory users who remain anonymous to Domino servers. Hence, you, as an administrator, are able to set up two types of Internet users: users who you want to authenticate with servers and anonymous users.

SETTING UP AUTHENTICATED USERS

Authenticated users require a name and password when accessing the server or use client authentication with Secure Sockets Layer (SSL). For this, you must create a Person document for the user. You can accomplish this by registering the person as an Internet user, as described above, or you can just create the Person document directly in the Directory and enter information about the user's name, password, and SSL certificate without following any form of user registration.

Setting Up Anonymous Users

Anonymous users, on the other hand, do not even require Person documents. However, you do need to ensure that anonymous users can access the server and databases on a server. To do so, you must enter Anonymous into the desired database ACLs and assign it the proper access level.

Setting and Validating Internet Addresses

The Domino Administrator also enables you to set and validate Internet addresses. The Set Internet Address tool fills in the Internet Address field for all Person documents in which the field is blank in the selected Domino Directory. The Validate Internet Address field verifies the uniqueness of all Internet Address fields.

To set the Internet Address field, complete the following:

1. Open the Domino Administrator, select the People & Groups tab, highlight the People view for the given directory to be modified, open the People section within the Tools Pane, and select Set Internet Address.
2. In the Internet Address Construction dialog, choose a format for the Internet addresses.
3. Choose a separator for the Internet addresses.
4. Enter the Internet domain for the company.
5. If you want to set addresses only for users in a given Notes domain or use a secondary custom format pattern in case an error is generated using the first address construction format, click More Options and select either of the advanced features.

The Set Internet Address tool checks all Person documents in the Domino Directory. It creates an entry based on the rules specified, verifies that the entry conforms to RFC 821 address syntax, and then validates that the entry is unique. If a duplicate entry is found in the Directory, the tool leaves the field blank.

Managing Usernames

Periodically, it's necessary for you to rename and delete users in your organization. Because the Administration Process in Domino R5 automates this process to a large extent, it is best to utilize its functionality when performing such changes to names within your Domino Directory. You can accomplish all this from within the Domino Administrator.

Changing Notes Usernames with the Administration Process

In order to change a Notes user's common name or move a Notes user's name to a different branch of the organization name hierarchy, initiate the Domino Administrator, select the People & Groups tab, highlight the People view for the given Directory, and then open the People section within the Tools Pane and select either the Rename or Move buttons.

This initiates the Administration Process to automate changing the name throughout databases in the Domino domain by generating and carrying out a series of requests posted in the Administration Requests database (ADMIN4.NSF). The Administration Process can change names only if the database is assigned an administration server. It also automates changing the names only of Notes users. You must manually change the name of an Internet user who has a Person document in the Directory—for example, a Web browser user.

CHANGING A NOTES USER'S COMMON NAME WITH THE ADMINISTRATION PROCESS

You can use the following steps to rename the common name component of a hierarchical username when Domino servers are set up to use the Administration Process. To accomplish this, you must have the UserModifier role or Editor access, as well as Create Documents access to the Directory, and you must also have at least Author with Create Documents access to the Certification Log.

1. Within the Domino Administrator, select the People & Groups tab, open the People view for the chosen Directory, and select the person to be renamed.
2. In the Tools Pane under People, choose Rename.
3. Click Change Common Name.
4. Select the certifier ID that certified the user's ID and press Enter. For example, to rename John Smith/Sales/New York/ACME, use the certifier ID /Sales/New York/ACME.
5. Enter the password for the selected certifier and click OK.
6. Either accept the default certificate expiration date (two years from the current date) or enter a different date.
7. Change the user's first name, last name, and middle initial, as necessary.
8. If you want to differentiate this user from another user, you can enter a qualifying Organizational Unit. This extends the canonical name by adding a component that appears between the common name and the certifier name.
9. If you want to update the Windows NT user account name while renaming the user, select Rename NT User Account.
10. Click Rename.

Figure 38.4 shows the Rename Selected User dialog box, which is used to assign new common name values to the selected user.

Figure 38.4
The Rename Selected User dialog box within the Domino Administrator used to change the common name for a given user.

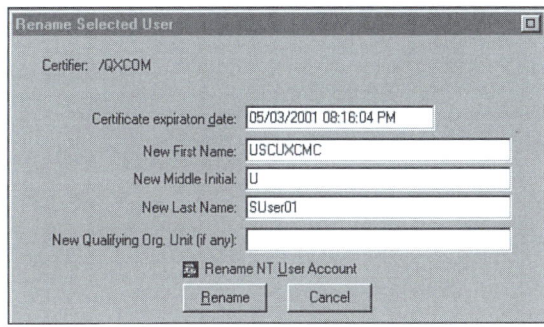

Moving a Notes User's Name in the Hierarchy with the Administration Process

As with changing a Notes user's common name, you can affect a rename that moves a Notes user's name from one organization to a different organization. To accomplish this, you must have the UserModifier role or Editor with Create Documents access to the Domino Directory. In addition, you must have at least Author with Create Documents access to the Certification Log and at least Editor access to the Administration Requests database. Figure 38.5 depicts the Request Move For Selected Entries dialog box, which is used to assign a new certifier to the selected users.

1. From the Domino Administrator, select the People & Groups tab, open the People view within the chosen Directory, and select the person to be moved.
2. In the Tools Pane under People, choose Rename.
3. Click Request Move to New Certifier.
4. Select the certifier ID and press Enter.
5. Enter the certifier ID password and click OK.
6. Enter the name of the certifier to use to recertify the user's hierarchical name in the New Certifier field.
7. Click Submit Request.
8. Open the Administration Requests database.
9. Choose View, Name Move Requests and select the name(s) to move.
10. Choose Actions, Complete Move for selected entries.
11. Select the certifier ID that will recertify the name(s) and press Enter.
12. Enter the certifier ID password and click OK.
13. Accept the default certificate expiration date (two years from the current date) or enter a different date.
14. If you want to differentiate this user from another user, you can enter a qualifying Organizational Unit. This extends the canonical name by adding a component that appears between the common name and the certifier name.
15. Click Certify.

Figure 38.5
The Request Move For Selected Entries dialog box used to assign a new certifier to the selected users.

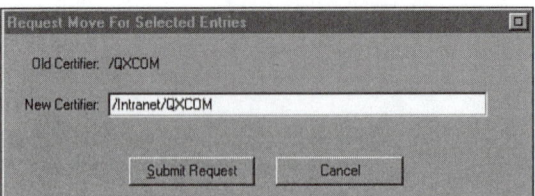

Changing Notes Usernames Manually

If you don't use the Administration Process, you can manually rename the hierarchical user using Notes mail or without Notes mail. You can also manually move a user's name in the name hierarchy. To do this, you must recertify the ID.

Because the Administration Process is generally used whenever possible with manual renames infrequent, consult either the online help or relevant administrative guides to assist in manually changing a Notes user's common name.

Sample Individual User Rename and Move

You will recall that the user's name is part of his or her Notes identity, and the hierarchical name, in effect, lists the certificates that enable him or her to access servers and databases within the Notes organization. When a name is changed, the user risks losing the ability to access databases, both on the server and on the local computer. When the user's name has changed or the user has been moved to a new hierarchical certificate (for example, been given a new certificate or set of certificates), the user ID is changed, so data encrypted with a different hierarchical certificate may be lost. If a backup of the old ID was not saved so that the user can decrypt the data, the encrypted data is lost forever (unless someone else has a copy of the same data that they are willing to share).

Let's examine what happens when John Smith gets married and decides to hyphenate his name or moves from the Sales office in New York to the corresponding office in San Francisco. Recall that his name, as far as Notes Domino is concerned, is `John Smith/Sales/New York/Acme`.

First, John gets married to Jane Jones. They decide to hyphenate their name to Smith-Jones. Here is how the administrator changes his name. The administrator initiates the Domino Administrator, highlights the People & Groups tab, selects John within the People view, and expands the People section within the Tools Pane. The administrator then selects the action Rename user. The administrator then selects Change Common Name, selects the certifier ID used originally to certify the person, changes any defaults, and clicks Certify. The Change Common Name dialog box appears. The administrator completes the fields for the Certificate Expiration Date, the New First Name, the New Middle Initial, the New Last Name, and the New Qualifying Organization Unit (if any), and then selects whether to rename the NT User Account.

A record is made in the Certification Log and in the Administration Requests database. When the Administration Process runs on the server that night, all instances of the original name are replaced with the new name. The only place the name cannot be changed is in the Personal Address Book of individual users and in databases on local hard drives. John still has all his original certificates, but the common name component of his ID has thus been changed.

Then a few months later, John Smith-Jones and his wife Jane decide to relocate to San Francisco from New York. The administrator must move John from one part of the company to another. The administration certifier must also move his name within the hierarchical naming scheme. This is done by recertifying him with his new hierarchical name. The name change is made in one place, and then the Administration Process takes over and automatically changes the name throughout the Domino network. John retains his John Smith-Jones common name, but now he has a new certificate hierarchy and hence a new Notes distinguished name, which affects his ability to access data throughout the organization, including on his own desktop or mobile computer. To rectify this, John's entry must also be updated in the Access Control Lists of any databases with which he needs to interface.

By changing John's name through renaming, he is automatically moved within the Domino organization, including a name change in his Person document in the Directory, in all groups to which his name has been added, and in the ACL of all databases to which he has been added. If the name were not changed in all databases and groups, he could end up losing access to some databases.

The one thing that isn't changed is the user's mail file. John wants his mailbox moved to a San Francisco server. To accomplish this, the mail file must be replicated to the new home server, and the name of the home server should be changed in John's Person document in the Directory. When John arrives in San Francisco, he can use his renamed user ID, open his mail, and have access to local copies of all the databases he is accustomed to.

The Domino R5 Administrator facilitates this move by providing a Move user option under the People section within the Tools Pane of the People & Groups tab. To move a user and the corresponding mail file from one server to another, select the Move tool within the People section and specify the server to which you want the user moved. In order to complete this successfully, you must have either Editor access or Author access and `UserModifier` role to the Domino Directory and `CreateReplica` rights to the new mail server and to the old mail server.

STUDYING THE IMPACT OF NAME CHANGES ON A MOBILE USER

The Administration Process minimizes the impact of changes to a user ID on a Domino server. However, changing the user ID does have consequences for the mobile user:

- If the user changes his or her own name, rather than submitting a request to the administrative certifier, he or she is unable to access any servers, encrypted databases, and encrypted documents. There is no back door. The system administrator cannot help. The data is irretrievably lost. Also, the user cannot open local replicas on which the ACL is enforced. If the user's name is changed on the server by the administrative certifier, he or she can still access all databases on the server, but must either change his or her name on the ACLs of local databases, or wait for them to replicate with the server if ACLs are locally enforced. Of course, if the Administrator has kept an archive copy of the mobile user's ID file, this could be given back to the user to access the data created with the former ID.

- If the user is recertified but remains in the same organization, he or she loses access to local databases on which ACLs are locally enforced until the databases replicate with the server and get updated ACLs. The user can still read locally encrypted databases and documents. However, as the manager of his or her own mail database file, the user can go in and change the ACL of that database locally.

Deleting a Username

Aside from changing a user's common name and moving the user to a different organizational hierarchy, you can also delete him or her from the Domino Directory. You can accomplish such entry deletion in one of the following ways: by using the Domino Administration Process, by deleting the username within the Windows NT User Manager, or by deleting a username manually.

Deleting a Username with the Domino Administration Process

To delete a username with the Domino Administration Process, complete the following steps:

1. From the Domino Administrator, select the People & Groups tab, highlight the People view for the given directory to be modified, and open the People section within the Tools Pane.
2. Choose the user's Person document to be deleted.
3. Within the Tools Pane, click the Delete Action button.
4. Click Delete Person and click Yes to continue.
5. Optionally select one or both of the following:
    - Delete user in ACL?
    - Delete mail file?
6. Click OK.
7. Determine whether to delete all references to the person within the Domino Directory immediately or based on the configured Administration Process interval by selecting one of the following:
    - Click Yes if you want to delete all references to the person in this Directory replica and to post a Delete in Access Control List request immediately.
    - Click No if you want to post a Delete in Address Book request in the Administration Requests database and to have the Administration Process delete references to the person in the Directory and database ACLs, according to the Interval setting for the Administration Process.
8. Determine whether to delete the user's mail file.
    - If you choose to have the Administration Process delete the user's mail file, examine and, in edit mode, approve the Approve File Deletion request in the Pending Administrators Approval view of the Administration Requests database.

- If you choose not to have the Administration Process delete the user's mail file, delete the file manually.

9. Deny the user access to all servers by adding the user to some form of Deny Access group.

Figure 38.6 depicts the Delete Person dialog box, which is used to delete selected users from the Domino Directory.

Figure 38.6
The Delete Person dialog box displayed when the user selects to delete person documents for selected users from the Domino Directory.

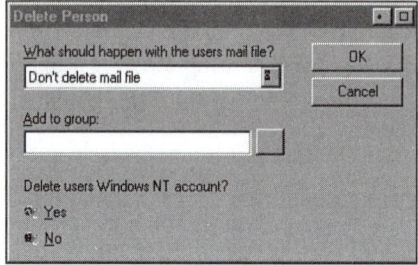

DELETING A USERNAME WITH WINDOWS NT USER MANAGER

As with deleting a Notes user entry within the Domino Administrator, you can also delete a Notes user entry from the Windows NT User Manager while removing the user's NT user account. You can also automatically delete the user's mail file if you want. Prior to deleting the NT user account within the Windows NT User Manager, ensure that Notes User/Group deletion is enabled. Furthermore, ensure that you have configured the correct server containing the Domino Directory from which you want to delete the Person document and whether you want to delete the user's mail file in the Notes, Delete/User Synch Options within the Windows NT User Manager. Then proceed to delete the user account in accordance with the Windows NT documentation.

DELETING A USERNAME MANUALLY

If you have not set up the Adminstration Process, you can manually delete a username from the Domino domain. Consult either the online help or relevant administrative guides to manually delete a Notes user from the Domino domain.

EXAMPLE INDIVIDUAL USER DELETION
John Smith-Jones decides it's time to explore other vocational opportunities. He gives his notice. The usual separation interview is done, and his last day comes to an end. He turns over his Notes user ID and walks out the door for what seems to be his last day. As John Smith-Jones leaves, the system administrator adds John to a group that has been named NO_ACCESS. The group is included in the Not Access Server field on every server in the organization. As soon as the Directory is replicated around the organization, John Smith-Jones can no longer access any server, even if he has retained a copy of his Notes user ID.

Because it is uncertain whether another copy of John Smith-Jones' Notes ID exists, the administrator locked John out of the system via the NO_ACCESS group mechanism. Following corporate policy, however, the administrator archived the Notes ID John gave him. The administrator does not immediately delete the user from the system using the Administration Process, by using the Domino Administrator's Person management delete action. John may, after all, have a change of heart and return to Acme.

If he had selected to delete John, the administrator would have opened the Domino Administrator, selected the People & Groups tab, highlighted the People view for the given directory to be modified, opened the People section within the Tools Pane, selected John's Person document, and clicked Delete. This would have given him the option to delete the person from the Directory immediately. If he had selected this option, all references to John would have been removed immediately. Otherwise, the references would be removed only after the normal running of the Administration Process. Similarly, the administrator would have had to decide whether to remove John's mail file.

Instead, after adding John to the NO_ACCESS group, the administrator simply forces replication of the Directory to all servers in the organization to ensure that the change is distributed throughout the organization as quickly as possible.

RECERTIFYING A HIERARCHICAL NOTES ID WITH THE ADMINISTRATION PROCESS

The final administrative action required on Notes IDs is recertification or extension of their expiration date. When a certificate on an ID is due to expire, you must recertify the ID. As with the administrative actions surrounding the renaming and deletion of user IDs, the Administration Process also automates actions involved in the recertification of hierarchical IDs.

RECERTIFYING A NOTES USER ID WITH THE ADMINISTRATION PROCESS

Follow these steps to use the Administration Process to recertify a hierarchical ID that is due to expire. You must have Author with Create Documents access and the UserModifier role or Editor access to the Directory. You must also have at least Author with Create Documents access to the Certification Log:

1. Initiate the Domino Administrator, select the People & Groups tab, and highlight the People view for the given directory to be modified.
2. From the Tools Pane, expand the People section.
3. Select all the users to be recertified with the same certifier.
4. If the certifier ID is on a disk, insert the disk in the disk drive.
5. Select the Recertify button.
6. Select the certifier ID originally used to certify the selected users and click OK.
7. Enter the password for the selected certifier ID and click OK.

8. Accept the default certificate expiration date (two years from the current date) or enter a different date.
9. Click Certify, and then click OK.

Recertifying a Notes User ID Manually

If you don't use the Administration Process to recertify an ID with a hierarchical certifier ID, you can do so manually. You need to recertify an ID when its certificate is due to expire or when you want to move a name to a different name hierarchy. Consult either the online help or relevant administrative guides to manually recertify a Notes user's ID.

Sample Individual User Recertification

Just a few months after his resignation, John Smith-Jones decides to return to Acme. Because he is resuming his position within the Sales division in the San Francisco territory, he will retain his Notes hierarchical designation. However, his certificate has expired. To extend the expiration date on the certificate, the administrator initiates the Domino Administrator, selects the People & Groups tab, expands the People section, and clicks Recertify. Taking the certifier ID file archived upon John's resignation, the administrator selects it, provides its password, and enters the new expiration date. The administrator proceeds to click Certify. John's user ID file has been recertified. To be activated, all that remains for the administrator is to remove John from the NO_ACCESS group.

Integrating User Account Administration with Windows NT

For organizations that have standardized on a Windows NT environment, Domino R5 has several enhanced features. These features include single password logon, directory synchronization so that the Directory can be managed from Notes or from NT, and event logging on the NT event log.

Using the NT Single Logon Feature

With the single logon feature, the NT service is accessed with the NT password, and the same password is used to unlock the Notes ID file. This gives the NT user secure access to all Notes messaging features—including data encryption and digital signatures from Notes or from third parties—without having to log on separately to Notes. This feature is available only to Notes users on NT workstations.

Clarifying Directory Synchronization Between Notes and NT

As delineated in the previous sections, when the Domino server is running in a Windows NT environment, you have the option of managing and administering those directories either from the Windows NT User Manager for Domains or the Domino Administrator. Furthermore, you can configure an automatic directory synchronization of user and group information between Domino and Windows NT. This enables you to perform many administrative tasks from one place and have the changes duplicated in the other product.

CLARIFYING EVENT LOGGING ON WINDOWS NT

Events such as replication and mail routing are routinely logged in Notes as information events, or as alarms if there is a failure. When the Domino server is running in a Windows NT environment, the administrator can redirect logging to the Windows NT Event Logger. In this way, the NT administrator can monitor both Notes events and NT events from a single vantage point.

ADMINISTERING GROUPS WITHIN THE DOMINO DOMAIN

Extensive group management functionality is also available within the People & Groups tab of the Domino Administrator. The Group section enables the administrator to

- Manage groups, enabling the administrator to add or remove users, servers, or groups to or from groups by selecting the desired users, servers, or groups and clicking buttons or dragging the entry to the target group
- Create groups, enabling the administrator to add groups to the Domino Directory
- Edit groups, enabling the administrator to add and delete user, server, or group entries within individual groups
- Delete groups, enabling the administrator to remove the entire group from the Domino Directory

MANAGING GROUPS

To manage groups within the Domino Administrator, complete the following steps:

1. From the Domino Administrator, select the People & Groups tab, highlight the Group view for the given directory to be modified, and open the Group section within the Tools Pane.
2. Within the Tools Pane, choose the Manage button. You will be presented with the Group Management dialog, as shown in Figure 38.7.
3. Under the People and Groups section of the dialog, select the Domino Directory serving as the source of the modifications. Note that you can view this list either alphabetically or by organization, and that you can display the Person, Server, or Group document for any of the entries by either double-clicking the entry or highlighting the entry and selecting the Details button.
4. Under the Group Hierarchies section, select the Domino Directory to be modified. Note that you can display this list either by group or member hierarchies and that you

can select which type of group to display. Note that you can also display the Group document for any of the entries by either double-clicking the entry or highlighting the entry and selecting the Details button.

Figure 38.7
The Manage Groups dialog box used to display current group and member hierarchies and to add users and/or groups to or remove them from groups within the Domino Directory.

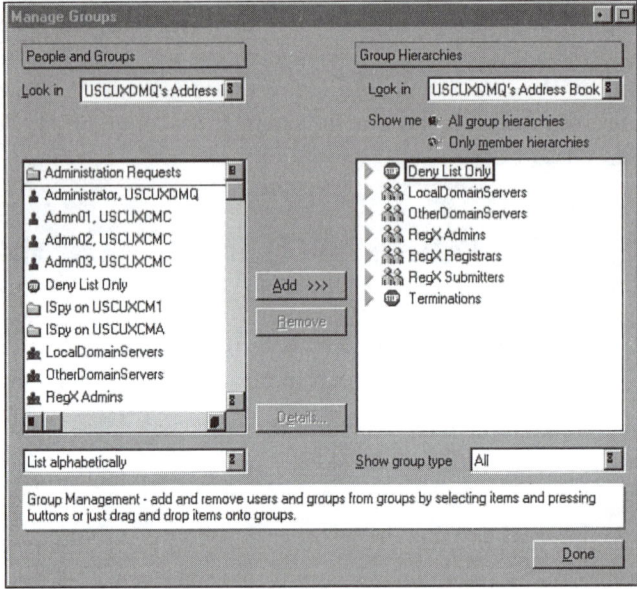

5. To add a user, server, or group to a target group, select the group from the Group hierarchies list, select the user, server, or group to be added to the list, and either drag the entry to the target or click the Add button.

6. To remove a user, server, or group from a target group, select the entry from the Group Hierarchies list and click the Remove button.

7. Select the OK button to save your changes.

CREATING GROUPS

To create groups within the Domino Administrator, complete the following steps:

1. From the Domino Administrator, select the People & Groups tab, highlight the Group view for the given directory to be modified, and open the Group section within the Tools Pane.

2. Within the Tools Pane, choose the Create button. You will be presented with a New Group document, as shown in Figure 38.8.

3. Complete the Group name, select the Group type, provide a brief description for the Group, and then add the desired members to the Group from the Names dialog presented to you by selecting the down arrow.

ADMINISTERING GROUPS WITHIN THE DOMINO DOMAIN | 919

Figure 38.8
The Group creation dialog box consisting of a New Group document.

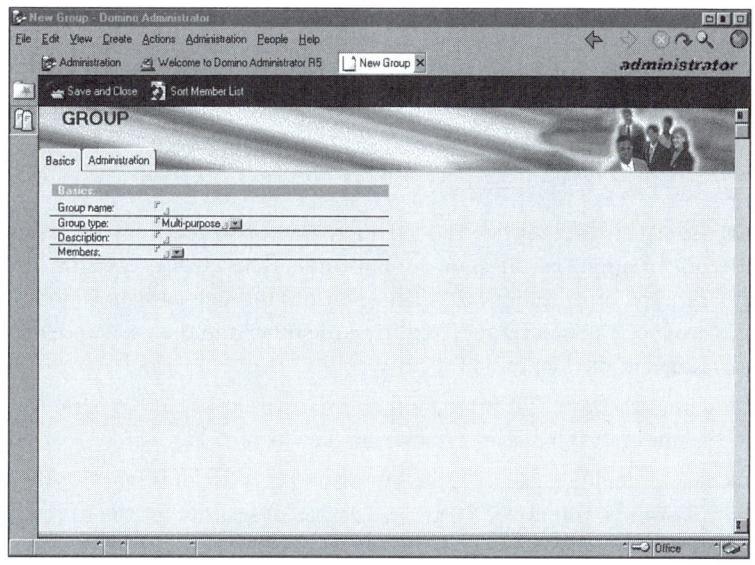

4. Under the Administration section, select, optionally, whether Foreign directory sync is to be allowed for the Group entry.

5. Select the Save and Close button to save the document.

MODIFYING GROUPS

To modify groups within the Domino Administrator, complete the following steps:

1. From the Domino Administrator, select the People & Groups tab, highlight the Group view for the given directory to be modified, select the Group to be modified, and open the Group section within the Tools Pane.

2. Within the Tools Pane, choose the Edit button. You will be presented with the Group document for the selected Group.

3. Perform whatever modification is desired to the selected Group document.

4. Select the Save and Close button to save the document.

DELETING GROUPS

To delete groups within the Domino Administrator, complete the following steps:

1. From the Domino Administrator, select the People & Groups tab, highlight the Group view for the given directory to be modified, select the Group to be deleted, and open the Group section within the Tools Pane.

2. Within the Tools Pane, choose the Delete button. You will be presented with the Delete dialog to confirm the deletion of the selected groups.

3. Select Yes to confirm the deletion, or No to abort the deletion.

Administering Certification

Extensive certification management functionality is also available within the People & Groups tab of the Domino Administrator. The Certification action allows the administrator to

- Add a selected Certify to IDs.
- Issue a cross-certificate to a certifier, user, or server, from a safe copy sent from another organization's certification administrator. This enables users in different hierarchically certified organizations to verify identities through authentication. Each organization cross-certifies an ID received from the other and then stores the cross-certificate it has issued in the Domino Directory.
- Cross-certify an ID from another organization when that organization's certification administrator has sent its name and key to you.
- Assign multiple passwords to an existing certifier or server ID. By assigning multiple passwords, you provide a greater degree of security for the selected certifier and server IDs.
- Set up ID file recovery and prepare IDs for recovery.
- Examine the contents of selected ID Files.

Summary

This chapter has introduced you to several important aspects of Domino administration. It has provided a general overview of the new task-oriented Domino Administrator and given a brief description of each of the Administrator's major functions. It has then turned to the central topic of the chapter and discussed in greater detail user management and administration, group management, and certification management. Within each of these areas, you have seen an increased level of complexity corresponding to the rich functionality provided by Domino, the Internet application server. Concurrently, you have observed that your role as administrator of this enterprise has assumed an ever-greater scope and responsibility. This will become increasingly clear as you explore the other chapters within the sections on administering the Domino servers and advanced Domino administration.

From Here...

You can find material related to Domino server administration in the following chapters and parts:

- Part VI, "Installing and Configuring the Domino Servers," discusses the different Domino server types, their initial installation and configuration, and the upgrade paths from R4.x to R5. It also provides an overview of Domino security, firewalls, Virtual Private Networks (VPNs), and Internet security. This represents fundamental information for administering a Domino enterprise.

- Chapter 39, "Administering Electronic Mail," provides you with the basics in establishing your Domino messaging infrastructure.
- Chapter 40, "Replication and Its Administration," gives you an overview of the steps required to configure and maintain a successful replication schedule between servers within your Domino domain.
- Chapter 41, "Administering Files and Databases," covers management and administration of disk information, files, directories, and databases; updating database designs; and rolling out databases to users. It summarizes information pertinent to systems administrators who also perform database administration.
- Chapter 42, "Managing Your Domino Server Configuration," discusses general Domino server administration, maintaining server configuration documents and running server tasks, modifying networks and domains, and analyzing and monitoring server performance.
- Chapter 43, "Troubleshooting and Monitoring Domino," introduces the tools available within Domino to analyze problems and perform corrective action.
- Part VIII, "Advanced Domino Administration," gives you specialized information about topics, such as performance and capacity planning, upgrading from other email systems, and integration with phones, fax, and image.

CHAPTER **39**

ADMINISTERING ELECTRONIC MAIL

The Lotus Domino R4.5x and R4.6x releases introduced a rich Internet mail functionality within Notes Mail, thereby providing standardized support of audio, video, international character sets, and multipart messages and enhanced Internet mail routing. With the advent of the Domino R5 mail server, the integration of Internet functionality within Notes Mail has reached an entirely new dimension. The Domino messaging server has become an Internet messaging server. With a primary objective of becoming the enterprise-grade messaging server for any size organization, Notes Mail has been enriched and complemented with a fully integrated Internet functionality. As such, Domino R5 now supports native Internet addressing, native multipurpose Internet mail extensions (MIME) content, native Simple Mail Transfer Protocol (SMTP) routing and Extended SMTP functionality, and native Internet messaging security.

With native Internet addressing, the Domino messaging server understands and interprets Internet addressing rules. This provides users with a consistent naming scheme across the Notes and Internet world. It also improves Domino performance, making it unnecessary for the server to convert addresses in either direction.

With native MIME content support, Domino now stores message content as MIME content. It no longer translates mail when sending Internet mail to the Notes client. This improves message fidelity and interoperability.

With native SMTP routing and Extended SMTP support, the Domino router now combines support of SMTP to route Internet messages natively with additional support for such SMTP service extensions as 8BITMIME functionality, SMTP Pipelining and Message Size Declaration, and Delivery Status Notifications.

Native support of SMTP reduces message conversion overhead by eliminating the encoding and decoding required by an independent SMTP MTA process. Support of the 8BITMIME SMTP service extension enables the Domino server to exchange messages that include a body consisting of a MIME message containing arbitrary octet-aligned material. SMTP command pipelining and message size declaration service support enables the Domino server to combine a sequence of SMTP commands and negotiate the maximum message size supported for a given client/server connection, thereby streamlining the protocol exchange between peer server processes and clients and servers. The delivery status notification extension enables the Domino server to provide a high-quality, end-to-end delivery reporting mechanism.

Such Extended SMTP support increases the overall messaging infrastructure performance of the Domino server.

With native Internet messaging security, Domino supports Secure/MIME, the Internet Engineering Task Force (IETF) standard for secure Internet mail delivery ensuring the privacy and integrity of email, regardless of recipient client type.

In this way, the Domino R5 messaging server represents a fully functional, standards-based messaging platform.

This chapter focuses on the major capabilities of this Domino R5 messaging server and summarizes the facilities available to administer electronic mail. The chapter covers five major topics relevant to mail administration. It begins with an overview of the messaging administration tools within the Domino Administrator. Then we turn to the topic of configuring and administering the R5 messaging server itself, introducing the section with a brief summary on mail routing within the Domino network. Finally, you look at administering Shared Mail, administering the Domino Post Office Protocol Version 3 (POP3) message store server, and administering the Domino Internet Mail Access Protocol message store server.

Each section consists of subsections detailing major aspects of the topic. Each subsection provides a descriptive overview of the task at hand. It follows with a procedural outline of the steps to follow to complete the major tasks relevant to the specific area. These descriptions attempt to summarize the most important steps required in the specific topic of Notes/Domino administration. Where necessary, it concludes with an example for the particular task.

Administering Electronic Mail Within the Domino Administrator

The Messaging and Configuration tabs within the Domino Administrator serve as the control point for administering electronic mail within the Domino Directory. The Messaging tab, shown in Figure 39.1, consists of a set of two subtabs: a Mail tab and a Tracking Center tab.

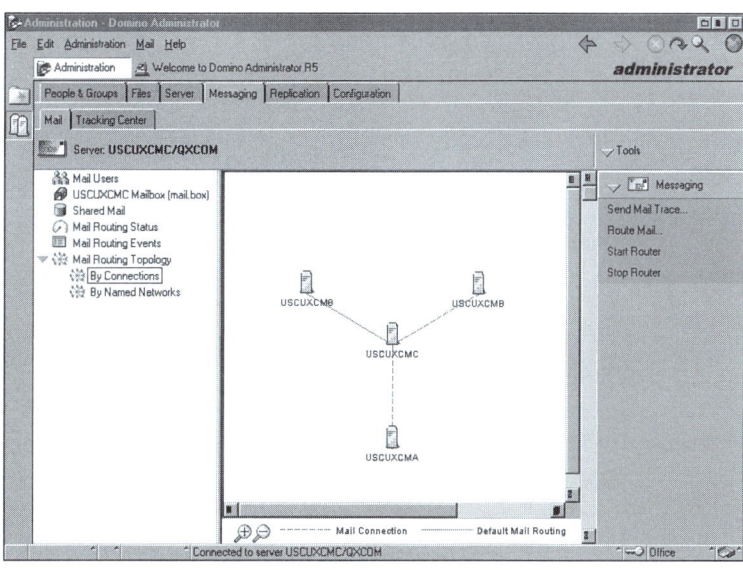

Figure 39.1
The Messaging tab within the Domino Administrator, with subtabs for Mail and Tracking Center, showing the Mail entries on the left and the actions available to the administrator—Send Mail Trace, Route Mail, Start Router, and Stop Router—on the right.

The Messaging, Mail embedded tab provides the administrator with a series of informational views on the selected server's messaging infrastructure. First, it enables the administrator to view the mail users on a selected server, from which individual Person documents can be added, edited, or deleted. Next, it provides a view pertaining to the selected server's `mail.box` or `mail.boxes`, from which messages can be deleted, dead messages can be released, and selected held messages can be released or released for a final time. Third, it provides a view of the Shared Mail attributes, if shared mail has been enabled on the selected server. Fourth, it provides an odometer reading on the `MAIL.Dead` and `MAIL.Waiting` Mail Routing Status counters on the selected server. Fifth, it provides the Mail Routing Events view of the selected server's log file. Sixth, and finally, it provides two alternative Mail Routing Topology maps: By Connections and By Named Networks. The Tool Pane associated with this tab also enables the administrator to send mail trace, start and stop the router, and route mail.

The Messaging, Tracking Center embedded tab allows the administrator to track messages from a source point to a target. This feature enables the administrator to see where messages are in the network at any point in time. Using it, the administrator can look in the message-tracking database and troubleshoot problems pertaining to mail delivery. As part of this, the administrator can track messages across Notes domains, across pre-R5 Domino servers, and across the Internet, if the destination server is running Domino R5.

The Configuration tab, shown in Figure 39.2, includes a Messaging configuration in addition to Server, Replication, Directory, Web, Statistics & Events, Cluster, and Miscellaneous configuration sections.

Figure 39.2
The Configuration Tab within the Domino Administrator showing the Messaging Settings, Domain, and Connections for the selected server.

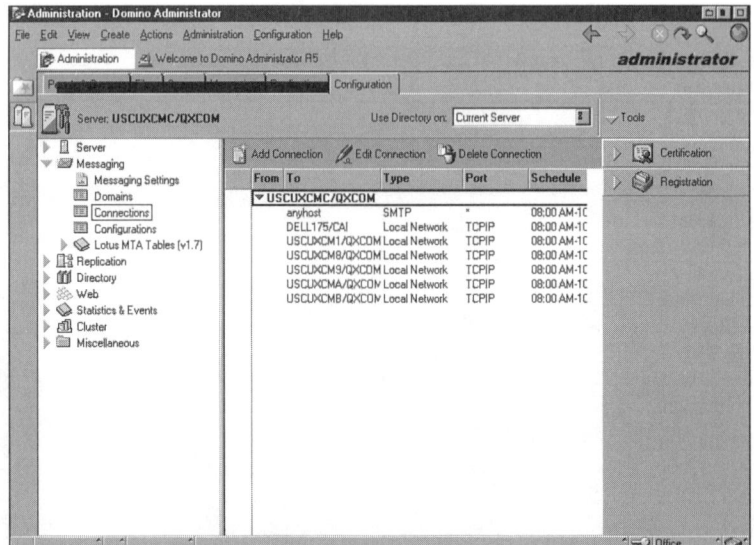

The Messaging subsection of the Configuration tab consists of the current Messaging Settings document within the directory on the selected server and views of the current Domain documents, Connections documents, and Configurations documents within the same directory. The latter three views enable you to add, edit, and delete the respective object to the directory, whether this is a domain, connection, or configuration. The subsequent two sections provide general overviews of Domino domain administration and connection administration.

Configuration administration is discussed in Chapter 35, "Initial Configuration of Servers with the Domino Directories," and Chapter 42, "Managing Your Domino Server Configuration."

Configuring Domains

The Domino Domaindocument defines the name, location, and access to adjacent and non-adjacent Domino domains and non-Domino or foreign domains. The document consists of four tabs: a Basics tab specifying the domain type and supplementary information required by the specific type, a Restrictions tab allowing and denying access to specified domains for the particular domain, a Calendar Information tab specifying the Calendar server for the particular domain, and an Administration tab detailing the Owner(s) and Administrator(s) of the given document.

Configuring Connections

The Domino Connection document provides server and domain information for connecting a server for mail routing and replication. The document consists of five tabs: a Basics tab specifying the connection type, source and destination server and domain information, and supplementary information required by the specific type; a Routing/Replication tab specifying whether the particular connection is for routing, replication, or both, and the accompanying parameters for one, the other, or both; a Schedule tab specifying with what frequency the connection should occur; a Comments tab enabling comments to be recorded; and an Administration tab detailing the Owner(s) and Administrator(s) of the given document.

Administering the Domino Mail Server

Domino Mail uses the Directory and a Mail Router process to deliver documents to user mail files and to databases that have been mail-enabled. The Mail Router process can also deliver mail through gateways, to routers in other Notes domains, and to other non-Notes message transfer agents, and hence to external mail systems, such as cc:Mail and X.400.

Understanding the Basics of Mail Routing

Routing within a Domino infrastructure is easy to understand if you think of it as functioning analogously to the post office. Using this analogy, you write a letter and put it in the mailbox. It is picked up by the mail carrier and deposited at the central post office, where it is sorted according to which route the addressee lives on. If the mail is local, it is sent out, under ideal situations, immediately on the carrier's route and put into the addressee's mailbox. If the addressee lives in another neighborhood, the letter goes into a bin. As soon as the bin is full (or sooner, if a truck is going that way), the mail is delivered to a branch office nearer to the addressee and is then delivered to the addressee's mailbox. On the other hand, if the addressee lives out of town, the mail goes to the airport and is sent to a post office in another town, where the local post office looks at the address, determines the route, and delivers the mail.

The situation is similar to this in Lotus Notes and Domino. Within Notes and Domino, a task called the Mailer (running on a local workstation) looks up the addressee's name and address in the Personal or Domino Directory, or both, to see whether the user's name is valid, then puts the mail message into a database on the Domino server called MAIL.BOX.

The Mail Router then takes over. The Mail Router determines where the addressee's home server is located by looking at the Person document in the Domino Directory. The home server is the Domino server on which their mail database is stored. The Router then puts the message into the user's mail database if the database is on the local server, or places it in the MAIL.BOX database on a server elsewhere in the same Notes Named Network for the other server's Mail Router to deliver. Servers share the same named network if they share a common LAN protocol, have the same Notes Network name in the Notes Named Network embedded tab within the Ports tab of the Server documents, and are constantly connected to that network.

If the user's mail database is in another Notes Named Network, the Mail Router looks for a Server Connection document to determine how and when to route the mail. If there are multiple Connection documents, the least expensive and most direct route to the other server is used. The order of precedence used by Notes is to route through the local area network, a remote LAN service, a dial-up modem, and then a Passthru server.

If the addressee is in another Notes domain, the Mail Router has no way to verify the user's address in the local Directory and in secondary Domino directories or LDAP directories without Directory Assistance. Therefore, the mail is routed to a MAIL.BOX file in the other domain using Connection documents and, if necessary, gateways or Message Transfer Agents connecting Notes to external systems. At the other end, the router from the other domain picks up the message and delivers it.

To prevent routing loops during this message transfer process, Domino sets a default maximum hop count of 25 for each message. That is, a mail message can make up to 25 server stops before the Mail Router returns the message to the sender. Each time the message passes through a server, the hop count decreases, until the count reaches zero.

The way that Domino routes mail from one server to another depends on the system topology and on the relationship between the locations of the sender's and the addressee's home server. Routing can be simple and quick. Or it can require that a message make multiple hops from server to server as it finds its way to the addressee's home server.

You set up mail routing based on the server topology you have established within your Domino network. To review, server topologies can be hub-and-spoke, chain, ring, or mesh. In a hub-and-spoke topology, one hub server schedules and initiates all mail routing requests to all other servers, or spokes. This is the most efficient way to set up mail routing. In a chain topology, two or more servers are set end-to-end, where Server A calls Server B, Server B calls Server C, and so on down the line. In a ringtopology, the chain is closed, with the last member of the chain calling the first member of the chain, forming a closed loop. In a mesh topology, every server exchanges mail with every other server.

DEFINING GENERAL GUIDELINES FOR MAIL ROUTING

Whether you decide to use a hub-and-spoke, chain, ring, or mesh topology, the resulting configuration has significant performance consequences. Some of the guidelines you should consider in defining your mail routing topology include

- Setting up replication so that the Domino Directory replicates frequently to all servers in the Domino domain. This ensures that the Server, Connection, and Domain documents reflect consistent data for all servers.
- Assigning roles to restrict who can create Connection documents in the Domino Directory.
- Minimizing the number of Connection documents by designating only two or three servers in each Domino-named network responsible for routing mail to other Domino networks or external systems.
- Creating two separate Connection documents to schedule separate repeat intervals for mail routing and replication. This differentiates between the parameters for mail routing and replication and assists your troubleshooting efforts when mail routing and/or replication problems occur.
- Determining whether to use Shared Mail and thereby store only a single copy of widely distributed mail messages in a server's central database, rather than multiple copies in the individual user's mail file.
- Ensuring the scheduling of mail routing over a dial-up modem connection during a range of time between midnight and 6:00 a.m.
- Using the Mail Trace feature to locate and debug mail routing problems.
- Ensuring that at least one Mail Router task is running by using the Show Tasks server command to see which server tasks are currently running.
- Checking the server's log file for the summary of mail routing events. You can record additional information in the log file by editing the Server Configuration document and including the `Log_MailRouting` setting. This setting determines the amount of information recorded in the log file for messaging events. Setting 10 displays only the errors, warning, and major routing events. Setting 20 displays the previous messages and includes successful deliveries and transfers. Setting 30 additionally displays thread information. Setting 40 adds the display of transfer messages, message queues, and full document information for the `MAIL.BOX`.

Connecting Servers for Mail Routing

You connect servers for mail routing differently, depending on whether the servers are in the same Domino Named Network and/or the same Domino domain.

Setting up mail routing between servers in the same Domino Named Network does not require you to configure any Connection documents. Mail is automatically routed between servers sharing the same named network.

Setting up mail routing between servers in different Domino Named Networks, but the same Domino domain, requires you to create two Connection documents, one in each direction. This guarantees two-way, server-to-server communication.

Setting up mail routing between two servers within two distinct domains that can establish some form of network connection, otherwise known as adjacent domains, requires you to create Connection documents in the Directory of each Domino domain.

Setting up mail routing between servers within two distinct domains that have no possible way of establishing a network connection, otherwise known as non-adjacent domains, requires that you complete two configuration steps. First, you create Connection documents in the Domino Directories of the servers within the two domains that are directly connected. You then create Non-adjacent Domain documents for the respective domains that you want to reach via the directly connected Domino servers. Though not necessary, you can also create Adjacent Domain documents between the domains that are directly connected, in order to make the mail routing more explicit.

Setting up mail routing between a Domino server and a non-Domino server in a foreign domain, such as a cc:Mail or X.400 domain, requires that you create a Connection document and a Foreign Domain document in the Directory of your Domino domain.

If the servers within the participating domains do not share a common hierarchical ancestor, it is necessary to cross-certify your Domino servers within the respective domains, in addition to creating the required Connection documents for the adjacent, non-adjacent, or foreign domains. Such cross-certification establishes a level of trust between the communicating servers and enables servers to authenticate each other.

To exchange cross-certificates, you need to create a safe copy of the ID file to be cross-certified by your peer administrator, and then you need to issue a cross-certificate for the safe copy of the ID file provided to you by your peer administrator. You do both within the Domino Administrator. To create a safe copy of the ID file to be cross-certified:

1. Initialize the Domino Administrator, select the Configuration tab, expand the Certification section under the Tools Pane, and choose ID Properties.
2. Select either the server or certifier ID file, click Open, and, if the certifier requires it, provide the password.
3. Click More Options and select Create Safe Copy. You can then enter the path and name of the safe copy. A safe copy of the ID file is stored in the path specified.

You can then transmit the safe copy of the certifier ID file to your peer administrator.

After you have received a similar safe copy from your peer administrator, you need to add a cross-certificate for the safe copy. To do this, complete the following steps:

1. Initialize the Domino Administrator, select the Configuration tab, expand the Certification section under the Tools Pane, and choose Cross Certify.
2. Select the certifier ID file that you want to issue the cross-certificate, for example, the certifier ID for your organization or organizational unit. Click OK, and, if necessary, provide its password.
3. Select the safe copy of the certifier ID file provided to you by your peer administrator and click OK.
4. Enter the name of the organization or organizational unit certifier to be cross-certified in the subject name, an optional alternative name identifying the certifier ID, the date when the cross-certificate expires, the filename of the certifier ID, and the name of the server within whose Domino Directory you want the cross-certificate to be stored.
5. Click Cross Certify. A cross-certificate is placed in the Server-Certificates view of the Domino Directory specified in the previous step.

ROUTING WITHIN THE SAME DOMINO NAMED NETWORK

When routing mail within the same Domino Named Network, the Notes client determines the recipient's address by a name lookup in the Domino Directory. The Mail Router retrieves the location of the recipient's mail file from the address and performs one of two actions:

- It delivers the document to the recipient's mail file, if that mail file resides on the same server as the sender's mail file.
- It transfers the document immediately to the MAIL.BOX on the server, where the recipient's mail file resides. The Mail Router on the recipient's server in turn delivers the document to the recipient's mail file.

ROUTING BETWEEN DIFFERENT DOMINO NAMED NETWORKS IN THE SAME DOMINO DOMAIN

When routing mail between different Domino Named Networks in the same Domino domain, the Mail Router determines how to route the message by looking at the Connection documents in the Domain's Directory. It then performs one of two actions based on routing tables it has built with the information within the given Connection documents:

- It transfers the message to the server that connects to the other Domino-named network, if a single direct connection exists between the two servers on the differently named networks.
- It computes the least-cost route to the destination server and transfers the message to the next hop in that route, if more than one route exist to the destination server.

Routing Between Adjacent Domino Domains

When routing mail between adjacent Domino domains, the Mail Router looks in the Domino Directory for a Connection document connecting a server in the local domain to a server in the remote domain. Upon the next mail routing connection to that remote server, the local server transfers the mail to that remote host. Upon receipt of this mail by the server in the remote domain, the Mail Router on that server retrieves the mail server information for the recipient from the Domino Directory and delivers it to that server.

If you are using cascaded directories by storing copies of other domains' directories on your Domino server, or if you are using Directory Assistance to assist directory lookups and mail routing, some of the name- and address-checking takes place before the mail gets routed to the other Domino domain. If you are not using either of these methods, you can still send mail to other Domino domains by appending the appropriate domain name after the username or group name. The Mail Router transfers the message to the Domino server servicing the connection for that domain. The receiving server, in turn, expands the groups and translates the names.

Routing Between Non-adjacent Domains

When routing mail between non-adjacent Domino domains, the Mail Router determines, via the configured Connection and Domain documents within the Domino Directory, that a message addressed to a non-adjacent domain is to be routed through an adjacent domain. This information is stored in the Non-adjacent Domain document, which conveys an adjacent domain as the "route-through" domain. In this way, the Mail Router uses an intermediary, adjacent domain to route mail to the non-adjacent domain.

Creating Connection Documents for Mail Routing

To create Connection documents to route mail between two servers in the same Domino domain but in different named networks, or to route mail between two servers in adjacent Domino domains, complete the following steps:

1. Initiate the Domino Administrator, click the Configuration Tab, select the Domino Directory to which you want to add the Connection, expand the Messaging view, and select Connections.
2. In the right pane, select the server to be administered.
3. Choose Action, Add Connection, and the Basics tab of the Connection document is presented, as shown in Figure 39.3.
4. Complete the fields on the Schedule embedded tab:

    Ensure that ENABLED is selected in the Schedule field.

    Enter a range of time—for example, 12:00 AM - 2:00 AM—or specific times—for example, 12:00 AM, 3:00 AM—when you want the source server to connect to the destination server in the Call at times field. Separate multiple specific times with a comma.

If you enter a range of time to connect then in the Repeat interval of field, enter, optionally, how soon after a successful connection the source server attempts to connect again. The default is 360 minutes.

Enter the days of the week that you want the source server to connect to the destination server in the Days of week field. The default is every day of the week.

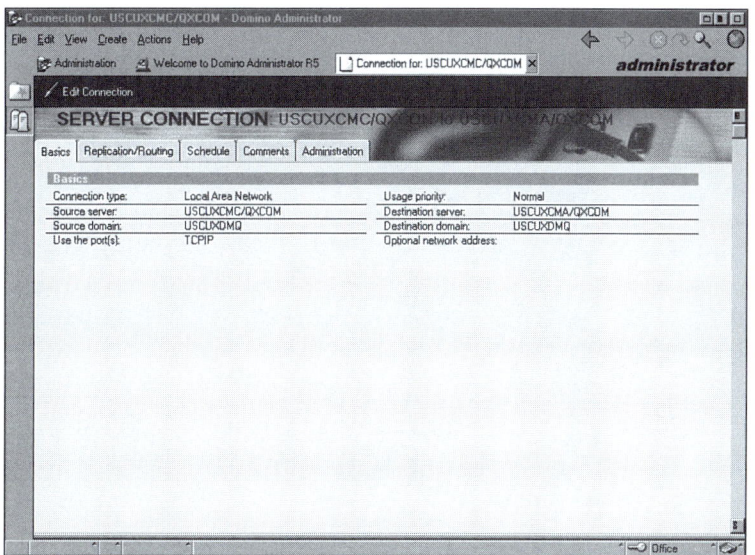

Figure 39.3
The Basics tab of the Connection document.

5. Complete the fields on the Replication/Routing embedded tab:

    Ensure Mail Routing is selected in the Tasks field.

    Enter a value to determine the number of pending, normal-priority mail messages that force mail routing to occur in the Route at once if field. In the Routing cost field, specify a value of 1 to 5 with 1 being the least-cost and preferred route. A LAN connection is low in cost; a dial-up modem connection is high in cost. Initially, by default, each LAN connection has a cost of 1. Each dial-up modem connection has a cost of 5. Domino uses this field to build its routing tables and determine the least-cost route.

6. Save and close the Connection document.

CONFIGURING NON-ADJACENT DOMINO DOMAINS

To enable mail routing between Domino domains that are not directly connected, you must identify an intermediary Domino domain serving to connect the two unconnected domains. You accomplish this by creating a Non-adjacent Domain document in each of the unconnected domains' Directories. You subsequently create the necessary Connection documents to route mail through this middle Domino domain to the non-adjacent domains.

A sample Non-adjacent Domain document is shown in Figure 39.4. It specifies a Domino domain that is connected to both the source and destination Domino domain. This serves as the intermediate or route-through domain to the non-adjacent destination domain.

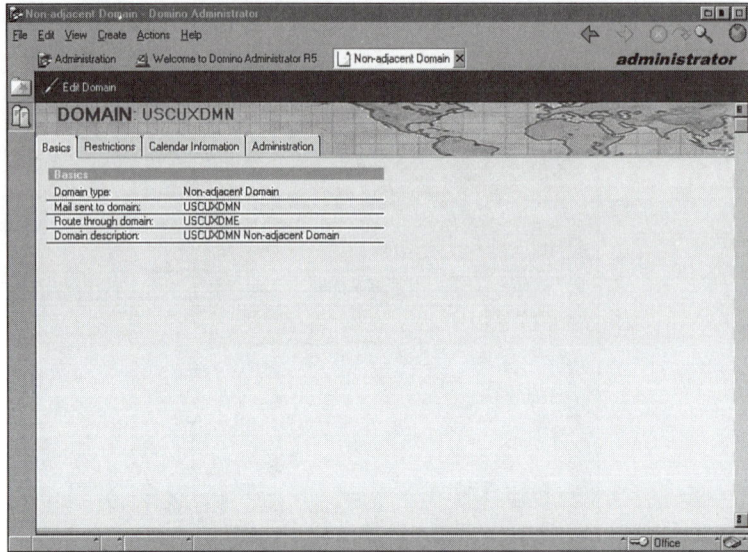

Figure 39.4
The Non-adjacent Domain document.

To enable bidirectional mail routing between servers in non-adjacent domains, you create Connection documents for the three participating servers, namely the two unconnected servers and their intermediary. This provides the communication path to and from the non-adjacent domains through the middle, adjacent domain.

If, for example, you are trying to connect Server A to Server C through Server B, each with its own Domain of A, B, and C, you complete the following configuration documents: For Server A/Domain A/Domino Directory A, you create Connection documents to Server B and to Server C. You create a Non-adjacent Domain document for Domain C, specifying Server B's domain. Server B's Domino Directory has Connection documents to Server A and Server C, respectively. For Server C/Domain C/Domino Directory C, you create Connection documents to Server A and to Server B. You create a Non-adjacent Domain document for Domain A, specifying Server B's domain. In this way, Server A connects to Server B, in order to route mail to Server C. Though not necessary, you can create Adjacent Domain documents between A and B, between C and B, and between B and both A and C to make the mail routing path even more explicit.

ALLOWING AND DENYING MAIL ACCESS ACROSS DOMINO DOMAINS

Within the Restrictions tab of the domain documents for a given server, you can allow and deny mail access across Domino domains. As part of restricting communication between Domino domains, you can specify that only certain domains can route mail to this domain.

You do this in the Allow mail only from domains field on the Restrictions tab. Similarly, you can enter the names that cannot route mail to this domain in the Deny mail from domains field.

RESTRICTING EXPLICIT MAIL ROUTING

You can also use the allow and deny mail access features to restrict explicit mail routing. Because Adjacent Domain documents are unnecessary to route mail between servers in physically connected domains, you can use an Adjacent Domain document as a mail routing security feature to prevent users from taking advantage of "explicit routing" to bypass restrictions specified in the Deny mail from domains field in a Non-adjacent Domain document.

If, for example, you are trying to restrict mail from Server A going any further than Server B, but you want Server B to communicate to Servers C and D, with each server within its own Domain A, B, C, D, respectively, and Domain A adjacent to Domain B, Domain B adjacent to Domain C, and Domain C adjacent to Domain D, you complete the following configuration documents.

Within the Domino Directory on Server B, you create an Adjacent Domain document for Domain C, listing Domain A in the Deny mail from domains field on its Restrictions tab. Within the same Directory, you create a Non-adjacent Domain document to Domain D listing Domain A in the Deny mail from domains field on the Restrictions tab. When a Mail Router in Domain B sees mail destined for Domain C that originated from Domain A, the Mail Router checks the Adjacent Domain document for Domain C and routing is denied. In this way, a user cannot circumvent the interdomain restrictions by specifying explicit routing, such as `John Smith @D @C @B`.

ROUTING MAIL BY PRIORITY LEVEL

The Router routes mail based on its priority level. Users can specify one of three priority levels: high, normal, or low. The priority level determines how rapidly the server processes the message.

- The Mail Router routes high-priority mail immediately.
- It routes normal-priority mail at the next scheduled interval, based on the configuration setting in the server's Connection document. This is the default priority.
- It routes low-priority mail between midnight and 6 a.m. within the same Domino-named network or between Domino-named networks by default. It routes low-priority mail at this time, even if such mail is pending when it routes high- or normal-priority mail. You can change the default setting by entering the value for the `MailLowPriorityTime` setting in the `NOTES.INI` configuration settings for the given server.

You can also completely disable mail priority on a server by setting the `MailDisablePriority` parameter to 1 in the `NOTES.INI` configuration settings for the given server. This causes the

Mail Router on that server to ignore the delivery priority of mail messages and to treat all messages as normal priority. This does not modify the messages themselves, only their processing by the given server.

Forcing Unscheduled Mail Routing

To force the Mail Router to route all pending mail, regardless of priority, you can specify the route server command. This may be necessary when you encounter problems and need to troubleshoot your messaging environment.

Note that hierarchically named servers whose names contain spaces must be enclosed in quotation marks (" "). Hence, to route mail immediately to "Server A/Sales/New York/Acme", enter the following command:

```
route "Server A/Sales/New York/Acme Corporation" .
```

at the server console.

Configuring Alternative Route Selection

The Domino Mail Router builds internal routing tables from which it derives routing costs to specific destinations. It uses this information to select the optimal, least-cost route for mail messages between source and destination servers.

The Server, Domain, and Connection documents within the Domino Directory serve as the basis for the Mail Router's calculations. From these, it builds its internal routing tables. It initially calculates a LAN connection as 1, or low in cost. It calculates a dial-up modem connection as 5, or high in cost. During the course of processing, however, when network connections fail or are intermittently interrupted, the Mail Router selects an alternative path, if one is available. At the same time, it maintains a history for the failed connection, reevaluates the cost of the connection by adding to the connection cost a cost bias, and subsequently reroutes messages to alternative paths where required.

The Mail Router calculates its routing decision in the following way:

1. Based on the information stored in its internal routing tables, it calculates and selects the route with the least cost.
2. If the selected route fails, the Mail Router adds the cost bias (one) to the cost of the failed route. This increases the total cost of the given route for any subsequent comparisons. Note that the cost bias is never more than one.
3. Upon subsequent comparisons, the Mail Router selects an alternative path, if there is one that is equal in cost with fewer hops or if there is one simply less in cost.
4. The cost bias for a given path is reset under three circumstances: when the server receives an inbound connection from the failed server, when the dynamic cost reset interval occurs, or when the Mail Router is reinitialized.

The Mail Router stores the internal routing information in memory-resident tables. It rebuilds its list of routes and cost biases, when the server is restarted or the Connection, Server, or Domain documents are modified within the Domino Directory.

Connecting Domino Servers with Foreign Domains

The Domino messaging server communicates and exchanges mail with external, non-Notes mail systems, either via gateways or message transfer agents (MTAs). Gateways consist of encoding and decoding processes that translate the messages to and from native Notes or Internet messaging format prior to transferring them to their respective host servers. MTAs can perform the role of a gateway as well as of a native mail server. In this way, MTAs can both translate messages prior to message transfer or send them natively in Notes and Internet format.

To enable the exchange of mail between Domino and non-Notes mail systems, you must install and configure the necessary gateway or MTA software and create a Foreign Domain document for the non-Notes mail system with which you want to exchange mail. The non-Notes mail system is perceived by Domino to be a group of computers in a foreign domain.

Defining a Foreign Domain Within the Domino Directory

To define a foreign domain within the Domino Directory, complete the following steps:

1. Initiate the Domino Administrator, click the Configuration Tab, select the Domino Directory to which you want to add the Foreign Domain document, expand the Messaging view, and select Domains.

2. Select the Add Domain action.

3. On the Basics tab, in the Domain Type field, select Foreign Domain.

4. In the Foreign Domain Name field, enter the domain name of the foreign mail system. This name was chosen when the gateway or MTA was installed.

5. On the Mail Information tab, in the Gateway server name field, enter the name of the Domino server where the gateway resides. In the Gateway mail file name field, enter the gateway's mail filename. You should be able to obtain this from the documentation that came with the gateway.

6. On the Restrictions tab, in the Allow mail only from domains field, you can specify that only certain domains can route mail to this foreign domain. In the Deny mail from domains field, you can restrict use of this domain by naming specific domains that cannot route mail to this foreign domain.

7. Save and close the Domain document.

Connecting Domino to a cc:Mail System   The Lotus Notes cc:Mail MTA is an MTA-facilitating directory synchronization and mail exchange between Domino servers and Notes workstations with cc:Mail systems. To establish connectivity to cc:Mail systems, you need to install and configure the cc:Mail MTA software. The configuration process includes creating a cc:Mail Foreign Domain document, a cc:Mail Post Office Server document, and a Connection document between the Domino server and the cc:Mail Post Office server.

Connecting Domino to an X.400 System   The Lotus Notes X.400 MTA is an MTA facilitating mail exchange between Domino servers and Notes workstations with X.400 systems. To establish connectivity to the X.400 network, you need to install and configure the X.400 MTA software. The configuration process includes creating an X.400 Foreign Domain document, an X.400 Server document, and a Connection document between the Domino server and the X.400 MTA.

Disabling Mail Routing

Mail routing can be disabled either temporarily or permanently. To disable it temporarily, enter the command `Tell Router Quit` or `Tell Router Exit` at the console. To disable it permanently, remove the Router task from the list of tasks on the `ServerTasks` setting within the `NOTES.INI` file.

Configuring Multithreaded Mail Routing

If you have sufficient memory on your computer system, you can increase the number of threads used by the Mail Router. This allows the server to initiate mail routing connections to multiple servers at the same time. You do this by altering the `MailMaxThreads NOTES.INI` configuration settings for the given server. This setting defines the maximum number of transfer threads the Mail Router can create per port. Its default value is one.

Tools for Monitoring Mail Routing

Because the messaging infrastructure is vital to an organization's success, you must monitor its functioning constantly. Domino includes a number of tools to monitor mail routing. The most important of these include the following:

- Mailbox   A `MAIL.BOX` database is located in the Domino data directory on every server. It holds pending mail and dead mail documents. Pending mail is mail awaiting delivery to other users or servers. Upon failure to deliver mail, Domino attempts to send a Delivery Failure Report to the sender of the message detailing why it failed to be delivered. Similar information is recorded in the log (`LOG.NSF`). If Domino is unsuccessful in sending the Delivery Failure Report, it stores a report as a dead mail document. You should periodically check the `MAIL.BOX` for pending mail or dead mail documents.

- Log file   The Domino log (`LOG.NSF`) also stores valuable monitoring and troubleshooting information. Domino records mail routing problems in the Mail Routing Events, Miscellaneous Events, and Phone Calls view of the log. The Mail Routing Events view shows information about specific events, whereas the Miscellaneous Events view shows high-level routing information. By adjusting the `Mail_Log_To_Miscevents` and `Log_MailRouting NOTES.INI` configuration settings, you can determine what, if any, information is stored where. For example, if you do not want to use the Mail Routing

Events view, you can set the `Mail_Log_To_Miscevents` to 1. Similarly, by increasing the setting value of the `Log_MailRouting` parameter, you can display more detailed mail routing information in both the Mail Routing Events and Miscellaneous events views.

- **Reporter or Collector task** By running the Reporter and Statistics Collector tasks, you can generate a variety of mail statistics in the statistics reporting database (`STATREP.NSF`). You can complement this by configuring the generation of alarms when specified thresholds are exceeded.

- **Event task** By running the Event task and configuring Event Monitor documents, you can report potentially problematical mail events. An example is to create an Event Monitor document for mail messages that are classified as Fatal, Failure, and Warning.

    You can obtain further information regarding the Reporter, Collector, and Event tasks in Chapter 43, "Troubleshooting and Monitoring Domino."

- **`Tell server` command** The `Tell server` command allows you to issue a set of commands to a specific Domino server task—in this case, the Mail Router. You can, for example, tell the Router to show statistics, perform mailbox file compaction, and shut down.

- **The Domino Administrator Messaging tab** Within this tab, you can monitor Mail Routing Status, Mail Routing Events, and Mail Routing Topology, and send a test message for tracking and troubleshooting purposes. Figure 39.5 shows the New Tracking Request dialog box used to analyze message tracing across Domino servers and domains.

Figure 39.5
The New Tracking Request dialog box used to analyze message tracing across Domino servers and domains.

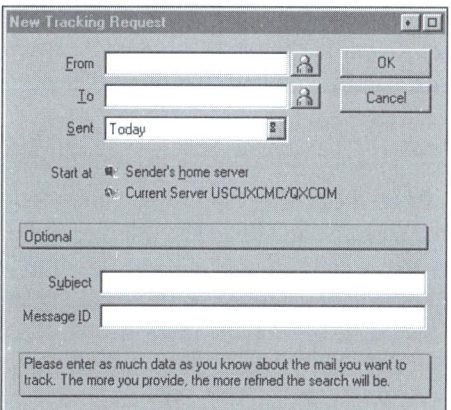

Administering Shared Mail

Within the Domino messaging server, the Mail Router stores a copy of the same document in each personal mail file, if the document is sent to groups of users. This can eventually lead to storage problems as mail databases expand. To overcome this problem, Domino R5 enables the system administrator to set up shared mail using a single-copy object store (SCOS), which is a specialized database that holds nonsummary data (the body of a mail memo and any file attachments) for all messages received by more than one user.

When the router receives a message addressed to more than one user on the same server, the message header—containing the To, From, Cc, Bcc, and Subject fields—is placed in each user's mail file, along with a pointer to the object store. The body of the message is saved just once in the object store. When the user opens the memo from his or her desktop, Domino displays the header from the mail file and the nonsummary data from the object store as a single message. The user is not even aware that the two parts of the document are stored in different places.

If a message is subsequently edited by a user, Domino places the entire message in the user's mail database and deletes any pointers to the original message. Domino also places the entire message in the user's mail database if the user encrypts incoming mail or if the user makes a local replica of the mail database.

Domino keeps track of how many users still have a header pointing to a particular object in the object store. When all users have deleted the message from their mail databases, namely the header for a particular memo, there is no longer a need to keep the nonsummary portion of the memo. A server task, Collect, runs automatically at 2 a.m. by default. This task deletes unused messages in the object store, deletes all links, and compacts the database to reclaim the unused space.

Reviewing Security Considerations

A user's email is confidential, protected by many of the same guarantees of privacy as a letter sent through the postal service. By default, the security for the user's mail file makes each user the manager of his or her own database, and no one else has access. However, the information in the object store is shared. To protect the confidentiality of the information in the object store, only the Notes Router has access. No users can open the database. The database does not show up in the database catalog. It is not listed when the user selects File, Database, Open. It does not have any views.

If a user selects to encrypt incoming mail, the Router encrypts incoming mail with the user's public key. Because others would not be able to read the encrypted, nonsummary data, the object store will be bypassed for this user, and he or she will receive the entire memo in his or her mail file. On the other hand, if an encrypted message is sent to users, an encryption key is generated and included in the header portion of the message. The encrypted body of the message is stored in the object store in encrypted format, and the encryption key stored in the header is used to decrypt the body of the message when the user opens the mail memo.

Setting Up Shared Mail

If you are running a Domino server and all your users have Notes R4.x-or-later client workstations, you can set up shared mail. You set up shared mail by issuing a server-console command to the router, which must be running. At the server console, type Tell Router Use SHARED.NSF, where SHARED.NSF is the full name and path to the object store database you want to create.

The Router will create the shared mail database you have specified, along with another database called MAILOBJ.NSF, which goes into the Notes data directory. MAILOBJ.NSF is actually just a traffic director and contains a pointer to the shared mail database currently in use.

After the object store database has been created, you may want to change the configuration for it. By changing the value of the Shared_Mail setting in the notes.ini or by using the Set Config command at the server console, you can alter what resides in the common object store. The Shared_Mail setting is given a default value of 2. This means that all mail is automatically placed into the object store, and users receive only header information, even if they are the only ones to receive the message. You might want to change the value of this setting to 1, which means that only shared messages are placed into the object store. A setting of 0 disables the object store. When shared mail is set up, you can link existing mail files to the store. Otherwise, only new messages are placed in the store. To link a user's mail database to the shared mail file, enter the server console command Load Object Link USERMAIL.NSF SHARED.NSF, where USERMAIL.NSF is the name of the user's mail file and SHARED.NSF is the name of the object store database. You can enter a directory instead of a filename for USERMAIL.NSF, in which case all mail files in the directory will be linked. The currently active common object store, in this case SHARED.NSF, keeps track of pointers, and if more than one user has the same memo, the nonsummary portion of the memo will be put into the object store, and only the header will be stored in the user's mail file. If a user has more than five documents to be linked, his or her mail database will be compacted automatically to reclaim unused space. You may want to link a few users at a time and monitor the growth of the shared mail file.

If the shared mail file grows too large, you can create another file by issuing the server console command Load Object Create NEWOBJ.NSF where NEWOBJ.NSF is the name of the new object store. You then issue the command Tell Router Use NEWOBJ.NSF. MAILOBJ.NSF will still recognize older object store databases. If you want to delete old object stores, there is a console command to unlink the old database and relink to the new one, after which the old database can be deleted.

Moving and Unlinking User Mail Files

If you make a file copy of a user's mail database and place it on another server, the Router can no longer resolve links to the shared mail object store. Each mail file looks only at the object store on the home server, the server on which the mail file is stored. All the user sees in a copy of the database is the summary data in the header of his or her mail messages.

The problem of moving a mail file is compounded if you delete the user's mail file from the original server, because deleting a mail file without unlinking it makes it so that the object store database cannot be purged of the documents the user left behind.

To move a user's mail to another server if he or she is using shared mail, do the following:

1. Replicate (make a replica copy) of the user's mail database on the new server.
2. On the new server, issue the console command Load Object Link USERMAIL.NSF NEWSHARED.NSF, where NEWSHARED.NSF is the name of the object store on the new server.

3. On the original server, issue the console command `Load Object Unlink USERMAIL.NSF` to delete pointers from the common object store to the user's mail database.
4. Delete the user's mail database from the original server.

COLLECTING GARBAGE FROM THE OBJECT STORE DATABASE

The `Collect` server task, which by default runs at 2 a.m., purges unlinked messages from the object store. If users have deleted headers from their mail databases, the common object store keeps track of how many other users are linked to the message. When there are no links remaining, the message is purged. If you want to compact the database after obsolete messages have been purged, you have to use the `-COMPACT` option with `Collect`.

USING SHARED MAIL WITH MOBILE USERS

The shared mail database works only on a per-server basis for mail databases that are stored on that server. Mobile users can still use shared mail, but only when they are accessing their mail directly from their home server.

If mobile users have a replica of their mail on their mobile or remote workstation, the entire message (summary information and the body) is replicated to them, exactly as it was with earlier versions of Notes and Domino. If messages were copied from the server-based mail instead of being replicated, users would receive only summary information, and the pointers to the body of the messages would no longer function.

MANAGING A SHARED MAIL DATABASE

In order to manage a shared mail database, you need to

- Purge obsolete messages from a shared mail database to keep the size of the shared mail database small.
- Back up and restore shared mail to reduce the amount of shared mail that could be lost if the shared mail database is corrupted or destroyed.
- Delete a shared mail database when it is no longer in use.
- View shared mail statistics at the server console.

ADMINISTERING THE DOMINO POP3 SERVER

POP3 is an Internet mail protocol. It facilitates the retrieval of mail by such POP3 clients as Netscape Navigator and Outlook Express from host systems also running POP3 servers. You set up a Domino server to be a POP3 host server by running the POP3 server task.

As with other server tasks, you can start the POP3 messaging server at the console by typing `Load POP3` or by adding it to the `ServersTasks` line in the `notes.ini` file. You can stop the POP3 server temporarily by issuing the console command `Tell POP3 quit`, or permanently by removing it from the `ServerTasks` setting.

Understanding Domino POP3 Server Requirements

No special software and hardware requirements exist for the Domino POP3 server. Because POP3 is an Internet application protocol, however, the Domino POP3 server does require that you configure TCP/IP. Furthermore, because POP3 is an Internet message-retrieval protocol only, you must also configure mail routing by creating the necessary Connection and Domain documents in the Domino Directory. This enables the Domino mail server to transfer both incoming and outgoing mail from POP3 clients to other Internet host servers, as well as to serve up mail to POP3 clients via the POP3 server task.

Example Internet Client Configuration

To enable such supported POP3 clients as Netscape Navigator or Outlook Express, you must provide varying configuration information. For example, for the Microsoft Internet Explorer, as part of the Outlook Express configuration, you must provide the following information:

- Outgoing Mail (SMTP) server name, consisting of the Internet domain name of the Domino server hosting Internet mail
- Incoming Mail (POP) server name, consisting of the Internet domain name of the Domino server running the POP3 server task
- Account name, consisting of the Internet Address within the given individual's Person document in the Domino Directory
- Password, consisting of the Internet password within the given individual's Person document in the Domino Directory

Figure 39.6 shows a sample configuration using Outlook Express as Microsoft Internet Explorer's Internet mailer.

Figure 39.6
A sample server's configuration screen within Microsoft's Outlook Express server as Internet Explorer's Internet mailer.

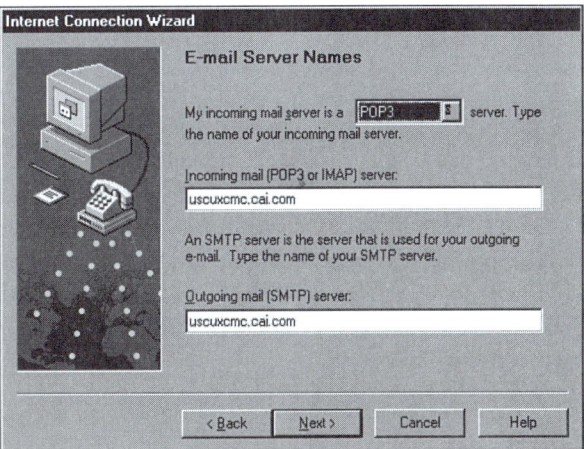

Administering the Domino IMAP Server

IMAP is also an Internet mail protocol. IMAP-enabled clients can manipulate mail in different modes. They can retrieve messages from the IMAP message server and store them locally, much like POP3. They can also access messages directly from the server or copy messages for offline use. You set up a Domino server to be an IMAP host server by running the IMAP server task.

As with other server tasks, you can start the IMAP messaging server at the console by typing Load IMAP or by adding it to the ServersTasks line in the notes.ini file. You can stop the IMAP server by issuing the console command Tell IMAP quit or by removing it from the ServerTasks setting.

As with all IMAP servers, the Domino IMAP server enables IMAP clients to access their messages. It is not involved in the message-transfer activities of the messaging server. These functions are handled by the Domino messaging server itself and require the standard Connection and Domain documents for mail routing in the Domino Directory.

Understanding Domino IMAP Server Requirements

No special software and hardware requirements exist for the Domino IMAP server. Because IMAP is an Internet application protocol, however, the Domino IMAP server does require that you configure TCP/IP. Furthermore, because IMAP is an Internet message store-and-retrieval protocol only, you must also configure mail routing by creating the necessary Connection and Domain documents in the Domino Directory. This enables the Domino mail server to transfer both incoming and outgoing mail from POP3 clients to other Internet host servers, as well as to serve up mail to POP3 clients via the POP3 server task.

Summary

This chapter has introduced you to several important aspects of the Domino messaging server and its administration. The Domino messaging server enables the flow of documents throughout your organization. It also enables the flow of documents between your system and outside organizations. It consists of server-side processes providing mail routing for local area network and remote users. It supports rich text and graphics, images, audio, and video directly within a document and the inclusion of live data from non-Notes applications using object linking and embedding (OLE). It is highly robust, providing a single-copy object store for reduction of mail storage requirements. Finally, it represents a highly open messaging server. You can set up a Domino server to include a Post Office Protocol Version 3 (POP3) server or Internet Mail Access Protocol (IMAP) server. In short, it has evolved into a premier Internet messaging server.

From Here...

You can find material related to Domino server administration in the following chapters and parts:

- Part VI, "Installing and Configuring the Domino Servers," discusses the different Domino server types, their initial installation and configuration, and the upgrade paths from R4.x to R5. It also provides an overview of Domino security, firewalls, Virtual Private Networks (VPNs), and Internet security. This represents fundamental information for administering a Domino enterprise.

- Chapter 38, "Administering Users, Groups, and Certification," introduces you to the R5 Domino Administrator. It then discusses user, group, and certification administration within the Domino Directory.

- Chapter 40, "Replication and Its Administration," gives you an overview of the steps required to configure and maintain a successful replication schedule between servers within your Domino domain.

- Chapter 41, "Administering Files and Databases," covers management and administration of disk information, files, directories, and databases; updating database designs; and rolling out databases to users. It summarizes information pertinent to systems administrators who also perform database administration.

- Chapter 42, "Managing Your Domino Server Configuration," discusses general Domino server administration, maintaining server configuration documents and running server tasks, modifying networks and domains, and analyzing and monitoring server performance.

- Chapter 43, "Troubleshooting and Monitoring Domino," introduces the tools available within Domino to analyze problems and perform corrective action.

- Part VIII, "Advanced Domino Administration," gives you specialized information about topics such as performance and capacity planning, upgrading from other email systems, and integration with phones, fax, and image.

CHAPTER 40

REPLICATION AND ITS ADMINISTRATION

The explosion of the Internet during the past decade has introduced one of the most rapid forms of information dissemination known in the world. The Internet-enabled household, small business, research center, and domestic or international corporation has voluminous amounts of internal and external data to assist in personal or corporate growth. Information exchange has become vital to existence. Many technologies are emerging to assist in information exchange and concurrently moving it from an asynchronous activity carried on in email, bulletin boards, and discussion databases into virtual chat rooms assisted by streaming audio and video.

One of the oldest and most important technologies supporting information exchange is replication. Replication makes information of all sorts—whether it be objects, applications, documents, attachments, or hyperlinks—available to users anywhere in the world so that members of a workgroup can share information and work on local copies of objects, no matter where they are physically located. The Lotus Domino R5 server has one of the most sophisticated of these replication mechanisms.

This chapter introduces the Domino Administrator and the major concepts underlying replication. As part of this introduction, it provides a brief overview of the tools within the Lotus Domino R5 server product assisting the Administrator in replication management. The major portion of the chapter summarizes the most important procedures to be followed as part of replication administration.

The chapter consists of six subsections: The first subsection includes a general introduction to replication and the administrative tools assisting replication administration. The subsequent five subsections delineate administrative procedures covering the following topics: creating database replicas, enabling selective replication of database components, setting up and initiating replication, creating and customizing replication, and monitoring replication and maintaining database replicas.

Each subsection provides a descriptive overview of the task at hand. Where necessary, it follows with a procedural outline of the steps to follow to complete the task. These descriptions attempt to summarize the most important steps required in the specific topic of Notes/Domino administration. Where necessary, it concludes with an example for the particular task. As such, the chapter attempts to assemble the most important information required by the Domino Administrator to administer replication within the Domino enterprise.

UNDERSTANDING REPLICATION

Replication is the process of synchronizing two databases that are special copies of one another. Replication can be either automated or manually initiated by the administrator. Replication can also take place between a workstation and a server, either as an event scheduled on the workstation or as an event initiated by the user from a workstation. The Domino server cannot initiate replication with a workstation, and workstations cannot communicate directly with each other (peer-to-peer).

Within Domino, synchronization takes place at the field level. After the initial replication, when a replica copy of a database is first made, subsequent replication has to synchronize information only in fields in which data has been added or modified since the last successful replication. This makes replication between two databases very fast.

Prior to delving into the specifics of replication administration, the next several paragraphs examine, in general terms, the functionality of the replica task, what it processes, the fundamental role played by access control in the replication process, and the administrative tools available within Lotus Domino R5 to assist in the management of the replication process.

Introducing the Replica Task

In Domino, `Replica` is the name of a task that runs on the server to perform replication between Domino servers. It is referred to as the `Replica` task in the `NOTES.INI` and the `Replica` or `Replicator` task within the Domino server console environment. When the server is started up, an instance of `Replica` is also started, and it remains idle until there is a scheduled replication or a replication is initiated from the server console or the Notes workspace. As soon as a replication is initiated, `Replica` wakes up and begins a replication cycle.

Understanding Server-to-Server Replication

In server-to-server replication, the initiator—for example Server A—can connect and initiate a replication with a responder—for example Server B. Such a replication can take place between servers in adjacent rooms, in different districts of the city, in different states, or in different parts of the world.

The first server, Server A, can do any of the following:

- **Pull-Pull replication**   Server A pulls changes from Server B and then tells Server B's replicator to pull changes from Server A. The two processes can take place simultaneously.

- **Pull-Push replication**   Server A can pull changes from Server B and then push changes back to Server B. In this case, only Server A's replicator is involved in the process, and it writes information in the replica databases on both servers. All the burden is on Server A, which could be a specialized server that does nothing but replicate, so other servers in the organization can more efficiently support other Domino functions. Pull-Push replication is the default configuration between Domino servers.

- **Push-Only replication**   Server A pushes changes to Server B. Changes are not pulled or pushed back to Server A from Server B. This scenario is ideal for a server topology, where all changes are made centrally and are then replicated to the distributed remote servers.

- **Pull-Only replication**   Server A pulls changes from Server B. No changes are pulled by Server B or pushed by Server A back to Server B. This scheme enables all the distributed remote servers to do all the work, and the central server is left free to perform other tasks.

UNDERSTANDING WORKSTATION-TO-SERVER REPLICATION

In workstation-to-server replication, the replication process achieves the same results as in server-to-server replication, with one vital difference. The replicator on the server remains passive in workstation-to-server replication. Replication is initiated by the workstation, although the workstation has no `Replica` task. The workstation does all the work, copying changes from databases on the Domino server and sending changes back to the server.

DEFINING THE OBJECTS OF REPLICATION

Practically every element in Domino can be thought of as a container for an increasingly smaller object. The Domino kernel is the back end or core of the Domino system. The Notes user interface is the outermost container. Within the client interface, applications are realized in the forms of databases.

Within each database are many objects, but not necessarily just the user-created documents. There are other objects whose framework is hidden from the user, but these are elements that are nonetheless vital to the database. These include the Access Control List (ACL), replication settings, and definitions for other database properties and design elements—including forms, subforms, views, folders, tables, action buttons, pages, framesets, outlines, navigators, and agents, each of which is a specialized object. Within these objects, there is another level of properties, fields, and actions. And, of course, within this framework, there are documents, defined as a related collection of data that fits into the fields on a form and the properties of that data.

It would take too much time to copy all this information every time replication occurs, so the replicator is very selective in the information it pulls from another database. Here is what happens when replication occurs between two Domino servers using the `Replicate` command initiating a Pull-Push replication between servers:

1. After one server calls the other to replicate, the two servers compare replica IDs on all databases to determine which ones they have in common (including database templates or database design copies, which are specialized databases containing the database design elements for the given application).

2. Databases are replicated in numerical, then alphabetical, order. The exception to this is the Domino Directory, which is replicated before all the other databases are considered. The Domino Directory is the first to be replicated, because changes in it could affect what is replicated or even whether replication can take place during subsequent scheduled events. If, for example, the server-access fields or Connection documents were changed to deny or disable replication between servers, subsequent replication between servers would be disallowed.

3. For each database, design changes and database properties are pulled, including the Access Control List, from the database on the other server. The ACL is actually a design document and is the first document pulled. If the ACL has changed on the other end, it could determine which documents can be pulled.

Understanding Replication

4. The replicator looks at the date and time of the last successful replication with this database, held in the Replication History window, which can be displayed from the Basics page of the Document Properties InfoBox. This history is used to determine what has changed, and therefore what should be replicated during the next replication event. An example of the Replication History dialog box is shown in Figure 40.1. It compares this date to the document-creation date for each document in the source database (the one being pulled from). If the document was created after the last successful replication, it will be pulled. If the database's replication history is cleared, Domino no longer has a record of when replication occurred last. Hence, on a subsequent replication cycle, Domino replicates all documents modified after the database's cutoff date, rather than replicating only what has changed since the last replication. The cutoff date is specified in the Only replicate incoming documents saved or modified after box on the Other panel of the Replication Settings dialog box. If no cutoff date is specified, Domino replicates all documents.

Note that you need Reader-or-higher access in the database ACL to display the Replication History. You need Manager access to clear it.

Figure 40.1
The replication history for a database, listing the last time replications occurred between Domino servers and workstations.

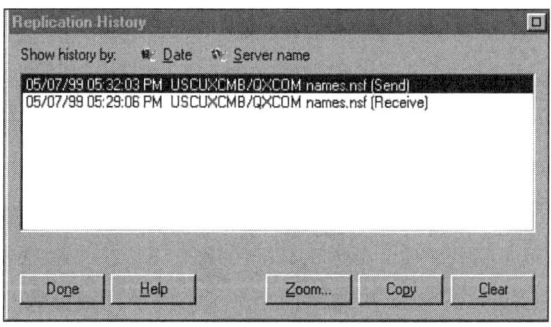

5. If the document in the source database has been modified since the last successful replication, there are several options related to field-level replication:
   - Each field in the document has a sequence number. If the field was modified since the last replication, its sequence number is incremented by 1. Domino compares the sequence number of each field in the source document with the sequence number in the same field in the target document. If a source field has a higher sequence number than the same field in the target document, the contents of the field are pulled by the replicator and merged into the target document.
   - If the sequence numbers in a field in both databases are the same, the contents of the field are ignored.
   - If the field has been modified in both the source and target databases, the source document is pulled in as the main document, and the document from the target database is saved in what is termed a replication conflict. Both versions of the document are then available.

6. The application developer can have Domino attempt to merge documents even if a potential conflict arises. This is done on a form-by-form basis. By selecting one of the versioning options (new versions become responses, prior versions become responses, or new versions become siblings) on the first page of the Form properties InfoBox, the application developer can have Domino automatically generate new documents when a document is edited. By checking the Merge Replication Conflicts option on the first page of the Form Properties InfoBox, the application developer can have Domino reduce the number of replication conflicts by automatically merging several conflict documents into one.

Establishing the Desired Access Control for Replication

As with everything in Domino, the proper access control is a prerequisite for proper functioning. Most people familiar with Domino are aware of how the ACL affects what a user can do in a database. Anyone with at least Reader access can read documents in a database. Users with Author access or higher can create documents and can edit documents they have created. Editors or higher can modify any document in the database. Designers can make design changes to the database, and only Managers can make changes to the ACL. These settings are generally true, but some options can be set; for example, in some instances, by creating a Readers field to the form, Reader access to all documents created from that form can be restricted. Additionally, persons, servers, or groups listed with Author-level access to a database can be explicitly listed in an Author Names field on a form within the database, and thereby can edit documents created from that form.

Database access levels for servers are the same as for users, except that the access level assigned to a server in a replica's ACL controls what, if any, changes that server can replicate to the replica.

The server can be considered an agent for the user, an agent that goes out and retrieves data, creates documents, and modifies documents created by the user. Basically, the server can do anything the user can do, depending on how the ACL is set up.

From a server perspective, this means that if you want Server A to replicate with Server B, you must grant Server A access to Server B. If, for example, the ACL on Server A lists Server B as a Reader, Server B can read documents (in other words, can pull documents or accept documents that are pushed by Server A), but it cannot send any new documents or modifications to Server A.

If Server B is an Author in Server A's ACL, Server B can send new documents to Server A, and it can send modifications to documents that were originally created on Server B.

If an administrator on Server B wants to make changes to the ACL on a database that is being replicated to Server A, Server B must be listed as a Manager in the ACL of that database.

As such, Domino servers have the same access as though they were people. If you want someone to act as a courier and deliver a message to someone you trust, you have to trust the courier as well. If the courier cannot be trusted to carry the message, the person on the other end will not receive the message. Likewise, if a Domino server does not have sufficient access privileges, the local Database Manager will not be able to receive messages.

As a rule of thumb, always list internal servers (servers in a group known as `LocalDomainServers`, included by default in all database ACLs) as Managers in the ACL, and you will have no problems. If replication is scheduled serially—from Server A to Server B, then from Server B to Server C—Server C is limited by what Server B can do on Server A. Therefore, try to give all intermediary servers Manager access unless there is an overriding reason not to. And with external servers (servers in a group known as `OtherDomainServers`, included by default in all database ACLs), you can limit their access using the ACL, if there is a reason to give them access to your servers.

Introducing Replication Administration Tools

As with all administrative tasks within Lotus Domino R5, the Domino Administrator serves as the focal point for replication administration. Although much of the actual configuration is done through documents accessible by alternative means, the Domino Administrator serves as the central control point from which all administrative actions can be initiated. As such, the Domino Administrator's Configuration, Server, and Replication tabs facilitate the configuration and administration of replication:

- The Configuration tab facilitates the modification of configuration settings within the `NOTES.INI` and Connection documents relevant to replication.
- The Replication tab itself assists in monitoring replication schedules, replication topology, and replication events.

Creating Database Replicas

Databases cannot replicate until you have created a replica of the database. This task must be done only once; however, it must be done before you replicate for the first time. After the replica database has been created, keeping replica copies of the database synchronized is usually a matter of refining what is to be replicated and the replication schedules themselves.

Being replicas of each other does not mean that the two databases are identical. It means that the two databases have the same replica ID. Every database has a replica ID made up of two eight-character strings separated by a colon. If the replica IDs for two databases match exactly, they are replicas of each other. Replica databases can be given different filenames, they can have different icons, and one can have only a subset of documents of the other, but they are still replicas as long as their replica IDs are identical. On the other hand, just because two databases have the same name and the same icon on different servers, it does not necessarily mean that they are replicas of each other.

The difference lies in how a database copy was created. Replica databases can be created in any of the following instances:

- One database is created using the command File, Replication, New Replica, and the other database is selected on the desktop.
- Both databases are copied from the same install disk (or at least from two install disks that have identical files on them) during setup.
- One of the two databases is created by copying the other at the operating-system level, or both are copied from a common ancestor database at the operating-system level.
- A new replica of the Domino Directory is created automatically when an additional server or workstation is set up on the network.

Unlike replicas, copies of databases can be created by selecting File, Database, New Copy from the pull-down menu. In so doing, the newly created database is not a replica. It has a different replica ID from the original database and cannot replicate with the original.

You can tell whether two databases are replicas of each other in two ways. The first way is to look at their replica IDs. The replica ID is found on the Information page of the Database Properties InfoBox, and in the database catalog (CATALOG.NSF) on a Domino server.

The other way to tell whether two databases are replicas is to place them both on your workspace and select View, Stack Replica Icons. If the icons are stacked on top of each other (a small drop-down arrow will be displayed in the upper-right corner of the top icon), they are replicas of each other.

After the replica database has been created, keeping replica copies of the database synchronized is usually a matter of deciding how often to replicate, and establishing a schedule so that the replication occurs automatically.

Enabling Selective Replication of Database Components

By default, two replicas exchange all edits, additions, and deletions if the servers the replicas are on have the necessary access. However, you can customize replication—for example, to save disk space—by preventing the transfer of documents that are not pertinent to your site.

There is a lot of flexibility in determining which parts of a database are replicated and which aren't. For example, you can replicate selected documents or parts of documents. You can select the documents by formula, by view or category, or by date. You can replicate specific design elements.

All these selections are made from a single Replication Settings dialog box, displayed by opening the database within the Files tab of the Domino Administrator and selecting File, Replication, Settings. The Space Savers page of the dialog box appears, as shown in Figure 40.2.

ENABLING SELECTIVE REPLICATION OF DATABASE COMPONENTS | 955

Figure 40.2
The Space Savers page of the Replication Settings dialog box.

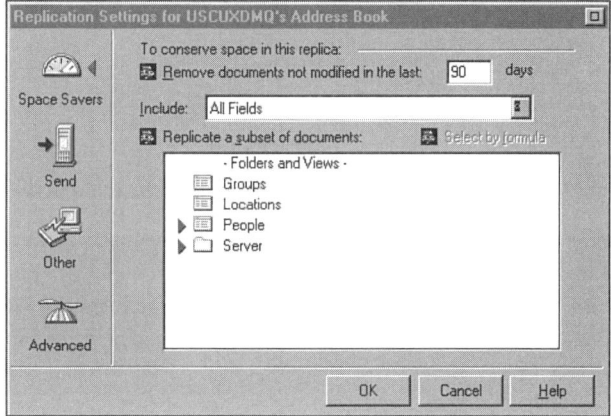

All the selections on this page can be used to save space in the local replica of the selected database. The selections include the following:

- **Remove documents not modified in the last *n* days** If you select this option, replication completely removes a document from the local replica if it was not modified in the number of days specified. This gets rid of older documents. As long as the documents still exist in another replica copy of the database, you can later change this setting and get the old documents back from the other replica.

- **Replicate a subset of documents** If you select this option, you can click a view or folder, and only the documents in that view or folder will be replicated.

- **Select by formula** You can select by formula only if you first click the Replicate a subset of documents option. A formula screen will be displayed with the default SELECT @All formula. You can enter a variety of formulas in this screen. Some examples include

    - SELECT Author = @UserName, where @UserName returns the name of the current user
    - SELECT Form = "formname", where formname is the name of any form in the database
    - You can also create formulas to select documents based on the content of any field, as long as the field is not a computed for a display field or a rich-text field.

The Space Savers settings are specifically useful for mobile users. The settings enable such users to save disk space and time during replication to their local replicas.

On the second page of the Replication Settings dialog box, you can specify what not to send from your local replica to the replica on the server. There are three options available on this page.

PART
VII
CH
40

First, you can elect not to send deletions made in this replica to other replicas. You can then safely delete documents locally and not worry about the deletions being copied to other replicas throughout your organization.

Second, you can elect not to send changes in database title and catalog information to other replicas of the database. You can then change the title of your own local database or database catalog settings without affecting other replicas of the same database.

Third, and finally, you can elect not to send changes in local security to other replicas. You can then safely make changes to the local-access control without affecting other replicas of the same database. This is important if you want to enforce local security, but you do not want to replicate your ACL changes to the server-based copy of the database.

On the third page of the Replication Settings dialog box, marked Other, you can temporarily disable replication of this copy of the database, set the replication priority, filter incoming documents based on their modification date, and set a CD-ROM publication date. For example, with respect to the first option, you might be making design changes on a replica sitting on one server, and you want to ensure that the changes are not replicated to replicas on other servers until your design changes have been thoroughly tested.

The second option enables you to determine the replication priority of the database. Different replication schedules can be set up for databases, based on their priorities. For example, you might want to replicate a high-priority database every two hours, but low-priority databases only once a week.

The third option enables you to establish a cutoff date and receive documents that were created or modified only after the cutoff date.

Fourth, if you publish the database on a CD-ROM, you can specify the publication date. The database can then be published on that date. Users can make a copy of the database from the CD, and then they have to replicate only documents created or modified since that date.

The fourth page of the Replication Settings dialog box, labeled Advanced, enables a system administrator to create selective replication settings for other servers from a central location. The Advanced page is used to administer replication settings from a central location.

On this page of the Replication Settings dialog box, the administrator can specify selective replication settings between any two Domino servers in the domain, or specify the server from which the local server should receive documents.

You can also specify which database elements can be received from other databases during replication, including whether to accept incoming deletions from other databases.

SPECIFYING REPLICATION SETTINGS

You can specify replication settings at various points in the administrative cycle. You specify them when you create a replica. You can specify them following the creation, if you have Manager access in the ACL of the replica. You can also specify some replication settings for multiple replicas at once from a central source replica.

Specifying Replication Settings from One Replica

To specify replication settings from one replica, you must have Manager access to the database. If you are creating the replica, click Replication Settings in the New Replica dialog box. If you are modifying replication settings on an existing replica, select or open the replica and choose File, Replication, Settings. Then, proceed to select or deselect the options listed in the Space Savers, Send, Other, and Advanced panels, as outlined previously.

Specifying Replication Settings from a Central Source Replica

You can specify replication settings for multiple replicas of a database from one central source replica and then replicate these custom settings to the appropriate replicas. To accomplish this, first ensure that you have Manager access in the ACL of the central source replica and that the central source replica has Manager access in the ACL of all destination replicas.

Using such centralized management, you can specify Replicate a subset of documents to control which documents a replica receives, and Replicate incoming to control which non-document elements a replica receives.

If you are creating the replica, click Replication Settings in the New Replica dialog box to specify replication settings for a new central source replica. If you are modifying replication settings in an existing replica, select the central source replica, and then choose File, Replication, Settings.

From this point, click the Advanced panel and proceed to follow the procedures as outlined previously in the section "Enabling Selective Replication of Database Components."

Note that changing centrally administered replication settings requires two replications for the changes to take effect: the first replication to replicate the new settings from the source server to the destination servers, and a second replication to replicate based on the new settings.

Setting Up and Initiating Replication

In order to establish the necessary infrastructure within which replication between servers and workstations can occur, you need to define the desired underlying system topology, define connections between your servers, and set the replication schedule.

Scheduling Replication Based on System Topology

Your server topology determines to a large extent your replication schedule and setup. There are four common replication strategies:

- With a hub-and-spoke topology, a central hub server communicates with disparate distributed spoke servers. Replication is scheduled and initiated between the hub and individual spokes.

- With an end-to-end topology, two or more servers are connected end-to-end to form a chain. The replication scheduling is similarly configured between servers.
- With a ring topology, three or more servers are connected to form a closed loop. Again, the replication schedule corresponds to the underlying connections established.
- With a mesh topology, each server possesses Connection documents for all other servers in the domain.

The most common of these topologies is that of hub-and-spoke. In a hub-and-spoke topology, either the hub or spoke server initiates replication with the other.

The hub server performs the role of control center. It monitors server resources and guarantees that replications occur with each spoke. In short, it ensures that all changes are replicated to its distributed servers.

Connecting Servers for Replication

You create a Connection document in the Domino Directory to connect servers for replication. The Connection document details the specifics regarding the information exchange. Based on your underlying network infrastructure connecting your servers, you can establish a connection for servers over a Local Area Network (LAN), over the Internet, over an intermittently connected serial line, such as a dialup modem or Remote LAN service, or through a Passthru server.

Note that as with mail routing, in order for replication to occur successfully, your Domino server must either be in the same Domino organizational hierarchy as the Domino server with which it wants to replicate or share a common certificate. A common certificate establishes a level of trust between the communicating servers and enables servers to authenticate with each other. If this is not the case, you need to cross-certify the servers so that they can then, in turn, authenticate with each other. The steps to accomplish this are detailed for mail routing between servers in Chapter 39, "Administering Electronic Mail."

Creating a Connection Document for Replication

You create one Connection document to connect each pair of servers for replication. An example of a Connection document is shown in Figure 40.3.

To create a Connection document to enable replication between two Domino servers, complete the following steps:

1. Initiate the Domino Administrator, click the Configuration tab, select the Domino Directory to which you want to add the connection, and expand the Replication view.
2. Highlight Connections.
3. Click the Add Connection button. A Server Connection document consisting of five tabs is displayed.

Figure 40.3
The Basics tab of the Server Connection document used for scheduling replication.

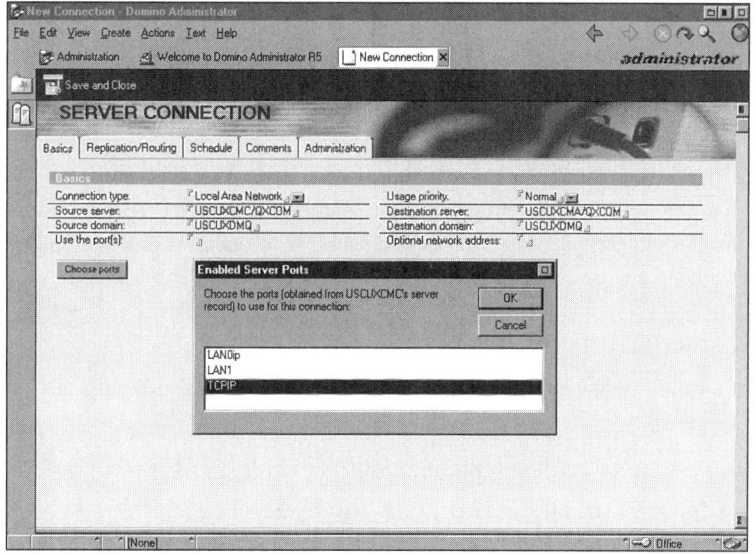

4. On the Basics tab of the Server Connection document, in the Connection Type field, select the type of network connection to be used—for example, Local Area Network, Notes Direct Dialup, Passthru Server, Network Dialup, X.25, SMTP, X.400, cc:Mail, SNA, Hunt Group, News/NNTP Feed.67t

   Complete the source server/domain and destination server/domain information.

   Optionally, select the Usage priority. For example, select Normal to force the server to use the network information in this document to make the connection.

   Select the Choose ports button and select the port obtained from the server record to be used for this connection.

5. On the Replication/Routing tab, ensure that -None- is selected for the Routing task and that the Replication task is enabled.

   Optionally, select High, Medium & High, or Low & Medium & High in the Replicate databases of Priority field. The default is Low & Medium & High.

   Optionally, select Pull-Pull, Pull-Push, Pull-Only, or Push-Only in the Replication Type field. The default is Pull-Push.

   Optionally, specify to replicate only certain databases or directories of databases in the Files/Directories to Replicate field.

   Optionally, enter a time limit for the replication in the Replication Time Limit field.

6. On the Schedule tab, ensure that the Schedule is Enabled.

   In the Call at times field, specify a specific hour, such as 8:00 a.m.; set of hours; or a range of hours—for example, 10:00 a.m.–6:00 p.m.

   In the Repeat interval field, specify how often to repeat the call.

   In the Days of week, specify which days for the replication to occur.

7. On the Comments tab, enter any relevant comments pertaining to the configured replication.
8. Save and Close the document.

Scheduling Times for Replication

As noted briefly while enumerating the steps required to create a Connection document, you can schedule replication between servers to occur at one specific time, for a set of times, or during a time range with a repeat interval.

Scheduling Replication for One Specific Time

You can schedule replication for a specific time when addressing one of the following situations:

- You are scheduling replication of low-priority databases.
- You believe daily updates of databases are sufficient.
- You are relatively confident that calls being made will be successful after just a few retries.

To schedule replication for a specific time, enter the desired time in the Call at times field in the Connection document. Enter 0 for the repeat interval. The Repeat interval field is applicable only when a time range is specified. Based on this setting, the server calls at the specific time. If unsuccessful, it retries for an hour. Following the course of an hour, the next call does not occur until the specific time on the next day, regardless of whether replication was successfully completed.

Scheduling Replication for a Set of Times

You can schedule replication for a set of times when addressing one of the following situations:

- You are scheduling replication of medium-to-low–priority databases.
- You believe that a few daily updates of databases are sufficient.
- You are relatively confident that calls being made will be successful after just a few retries.

To schedule replication for a set of times, enter the desired set of specific times in the Call at times field separating the individual times by a comma in the Connection document. Enter 0 for the repeat interval. The Repeat interval field is applicable only when a time range is specified. Based on the settings given, the server calls at the first time specified. If unsuccessful, the server continues to retry for up to an hour. Regardless of whether the call succeeds, the server initiates the next call at the next scheduled time. This continues through the set of times provided.

Scheduling Replication for a Time Range with a Repeat Interval

You can schedule replication for a time range both with and without a repeat interval. To schedule replication with a repeat interval, enter a time range in the Call at times field and enter a number of minutes in the Repeat interval field in the Connection document. If unsuccessful upon the initial attempt, the server retries periodically until it successfully establishes a connection and replicates or it reaches the end of the time range specified. If the server successfully replicates, it calls again, following the number of minutes specified in the repeat interval.

For example, let's assume that you accept the default replication time setting between two servers Server A and Server B, that schedules Server A to call Server B from 8 a.m. to 10 p.m. with a repeat interval of 360 minutes. If Server A calls and replicates successfully with Server B at 8:30 a.m., Server A does not place the next call until 2:30 p.m. that afternoon. If the replication is unsuccessful, however, it continues to connect and replicate periodically until the end of the time range specified.

Scheduling Replication for a Time Range Without a Repeat Interval

You can schedule replication for a time range without a repeat interval when addressing one of the following situations:

- You are scheduling replication of medium-to-low–priority databases.
- You believe daily updates of databases are sufficient.
- You know that a long retry period is necessary.

To schedule replication for a time range without a repeat interval, enter a time range in the Call at times field in the Connection document. Enter 0 for the repeat interval. Based on this setting, the server attempts the first call at the start of the time range. If unsuccessful, the server tries again for the entire call range, with the time between each unsuccessful call attempt increasing. Following a successful exchange of information, the server ceases the calls until the next cycle.

Customizing Replication

With the desired Connection documents in place, you can customize replication in a number of ways and then test the resulting replication. Some of the more useful means of customizing replication include

- Specifying replication direction to indicate whether replication is one-way or two-way between servers
- Replicating only specific databases rather than all databases common to the participating servers
- Replicating databases by priority
- Limiting replication time

- Refusing replication requests from other servers
- Disabling replication to prevent changes from being replicated
- Forcing immediate replication to replicate changes to critical databases
- Scheduling replication from a workstation
- Testing the replication schedule

Specifying Replication Direction

In the Replication Type field on the Replication/Routing tab of the Connection document, you can specify replication direction. The value of this field determines whether the server(s) involved simply send, receive, or both send and receive updates during the replication cycle.

As delineated in the earlier section, "Understanding Replication," Domino offers four forms of replication direction: Pull-Pull; Pull-Push, the default replication direction; Push-Only; and Pull-Only. Both Push-Only and Pull-Only forms of replication, because they are one-way as opposed to two-way forms, take less time than the Pull-Push and Pull-Pull alternatives.

You can similarly affect the replication direction by altering the server console command you execute when you force replication. For example, instead of using the `Replicate` command, you can use either the `Push` command or `Pull` command. In this way, you could use the Push-Only or Pull-Only method when there is an update in a Domino Directory on one server and you want to manually propagate that change to the other servers.

Replicating Only Specific Databases

In the File/Directories to Replicate field on the Replication/Routing tab of the Connection document, you can limit the scope of replication between servers. The default scope is all databases. To limit this scope, enter the directory or database names that you want to replicate, separating the individual entries with semicolons.

For individual databases, enter the filename of the database, including its full path relative to the Domino data directory—for example, `SALES\TRACKING.NSF`.

For entire directories, including subdirectories within the directory, enter the directory name relative to the Domino data directory—for example, `SALES\`.

This setting pertains to Pull-Push, Push-Only, and Pull-Only replication directions. It does not pertain to Pull-Pull. If the replication direction selected in the Connection document is the latter, only the initiating server receives the specified databases during replication. The responding server receives all databases in common with the initiating server.

Replicating Databases by Priority

To enable Domino administrators to schedule replication for databases based on priority, Database Managers can assign a replication priority to them within the Other tab of the Replication Settings dialog box.

After such a priority has been assigned—for example, high priority to such business-critical databases as the Domino Directory—you can schedule it to replicate frequently during the day. Conversely, you can schedule low-priority databases to replicate during off-peak hours.

To replicate databases by priority, create separate Connection documents for your low-, medium-, and high-priority databases. To differentiate the priority levels, edit the Replicate databases of field on the Replication/Routing tab in the Connection document. The default setting is Low & Medium & High. With this setting, Domino automatically replicates all databases that two servers have in common. During the replication process, Domino uses the priority assigned to the replica on the calling server, if the respective replicas possess different priorities.

Limiting Replication Time

If you need to limit the cost of replication with servers in remote sites, you should decrease the time limit a server has to replicate with another server. Be aware, however, that if you underestimate the time limit, you can cause an incomplete replication cycle. This leads to replication terminating prematurely when the time has been reached. Although a message indicating termination is written in the server's log file, it relates that the replication was successful, thereby providing an inaccurate record of replication activity.

You can limit replication time by setting the Replication Time Limit field on the Replication/Routing tab in the Connection document to a nonzero value.

The default value of blank enables Domino to use as much time as necessary to complete the replication cycle.

Refusing Replication Requests

You can configure a server to refuse replication requests by setting the `ServerNoReplRequests` NOTES.INI Configuration Setting parameter to 1. This prevents a server from accepting a replication request. It does not, however, prevent the server from initiating replication with other servers.

Disabling Replication

You can disable replication temporarily or permanently. To disable replication temporarily, tell the Replica task to quit (`tell replica quit`). To disable replication permanently, remove the `Replica` task from the `ServerTasks` line in the NOTES.INI. You can also disable the replication for a given connection by setting the Replication task field to Disabled on the Replication/Routing Tab of the Connection document for the given connection.

Forcing Immediate Replication

You can force immediate replication between servers after you have configured the necessary replication Connection documents. By using the `Replicate` server command, you can have Domino perform a Pull-Push replication and thereby replicate changes to databases in both directions. By using the `Pull` or `Push` server command, you can have Domino perform either a pull or push and replicate changes in only one direction. You can force replication with a console command either from the Domino Administrator or from the server's console.

Figure 40.4 shows the Replicate from dialog box, entered within the Domino Administrator by selecting the Server tab, expanding the Tools Pane, and clicking the Replicate action.

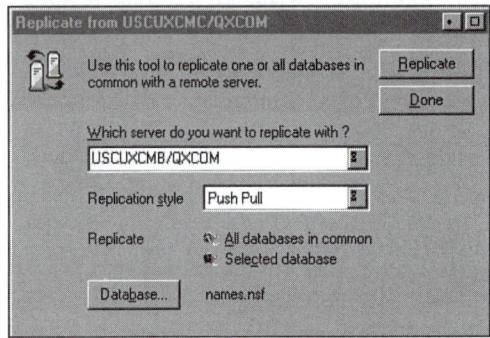

Figure 40.4
Forcing replication from the Domino Administrator.

To force replication of selected databases between two servers from the Domino Administrator, complete the following steps:

1. Initiate the Domino Administrator.
2. Click the Servers tab.
3. Expand the Server section.
4. Select the Replicate action. The Replicate from dialog box will display.
5. Enter the name of the server with which you want to replicate.
6. Enter the style of replication.
7. Select the database or databases to be replicated.
8. Click the Replicate button.

    The server will initiate replication with the target server you have identified in the console command.

Alternatively, you can enter a console command within the Servers tab by selecting a server and clicking the Console button.

Server console commands consist of the replication command, the name of the server you want to replicate with, and, optionally, the names of any specific databases you want to replicate. Valid replication commands include `Replicate` (Pull-Push Pull), `Pull`, or `Push`. For example:

- `Replicate Server B/Acme` executes a full two-way replication with Server B/Acme.
- `Pull Server B/Acme names.nsf` pulls changes to the Domino Directory on Server B/Acme, but no other replication occurs.
- `Push Server B/Acme *.nsf` sends all changes in all replica databases from the initiating server to Server B/Acme, but no modifications are pulled from Server B/Acme, and no modifications to Domino template files (`*.ntf`) are sent.

Scheduling Replication from a Workstation

Replication between a Notes client workstation and a Domino server can be initiated only from the workstation. Scheduling the replication is similar to scheduling replication between servers, except that the replication schedule is maintained in Location documents on the workstation. There is a Server Connection document in the Personal Address Book on the workstation, but it is used only to provide specific information for connecting with a server.

Because you can have several different Location documents, you can create replication schedules that are specific to the needs of each location. For example, you might want to replicate a number of databases to your Home location if you regularly telecommute from home. If you are traveling with a laptop computer, you will probably want to replicate only databases that you know you will need while you are on the road. When you switch to a different location from the status bar, you will automatically activate the replication schedule for that location.

The replication schedule portion of a Location document is shown in Figure 40.5. The fields are the same as they are in the Scheduling portion of the Server Connection document on the Domino server. However, there are no options on the Location document to select which databases will be replicated. Instead, this is done from the Replicator page on the Notes desktop.

Initiating Replication from the Desktop

The Replicator page provides a graphical way to manage replication on the Notes workstation from a single screen, with each replica database potentially residing on different servers.

Replication can take place in the background, enabling you to continue working while replication occurs. With background replication enabled, you can continue working in Notes while replication takes place. If you elect, however, to replicate a database using one-time options (for example, by highlighting the database icon and selecting File, Replication, Replicate, and then selecting Replicate with options), the replication takes place in the foreground, and you must wait for the replication to finish before you can resume working.

Figure 40.5
The Location document showing a replication schedule between the workstation and a server.

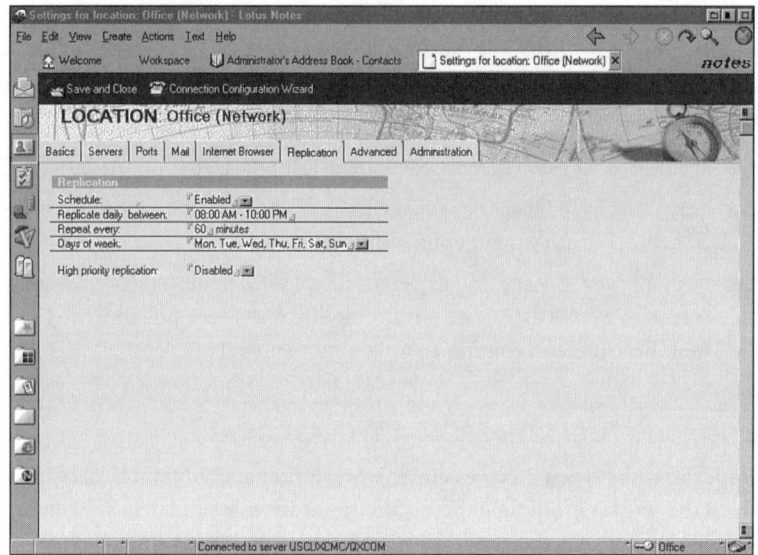

Depending on the type of location you have set up, the basic elements of the Replicator page may vary slightly. For example, if you have a location document that gives you a remote network connection over TCP/IP, you do not need an option to automatically hang up the phone as you would with a modem connection. But whatever your location setup, you will have options to enable scheduled replication, to replicate templates, and to replicate any databases that have a replica copy on the desktop.

Each of the horizontal rows in the Replicator page represents a possible action during replication. You can turn the action on or off by clicking the check box on the left. The first row, Start Replication At, is used to enable a replication schedule. The next rows are databases that will replicate with the server. The next row will replicate template files that have been modified or added. The last row is a database that is currently being replicated. When a replication event is in progress, a pointer icon indicates the database that is currently being replicated, and the status of the current database replication is illustrated at the bottom of the screen.

Domino estimates the time it will take for the initial replication to complete, based on the documents it has pulled so far and the total number of documents that remain to be pulled. However, Domino constantly recalculates as more documents are pulled in. After the initial replication, regular replications are likely to take considerably less time, because you only replicate the fields that have been modified and any new documents that have been added. Each row on the Replicator page has a check box, icon, text, and button. To the right of the button is more text, reporting on the status of the last replication. If you want a row to be a part of the next replication, make sure that it is checked. Only checked rows are considered during replication.

The buttons on each row can be used to tailor the replication action on that particular row. For example, if you click the button with the Clock icon on the line labeled Start Replication At, Domino opens the current Location document so that you can set up a replication schedule for that particular location. If you click the button for a database, you can determine which server you prefer to look on for a replica of the database, whether to send documents, and whether to replicate full documents or only a summary and up to 40KB of rich text.

The database icons on the Replicator page can be placed there in two ways. If you manually replicate a database by highlighting the database and selecting File, Replication, New Replica, the icon will be placed on the Replicator page automatically. Alternatively, you can drag a database icon and drop it on the tab for the Replicator page. The original icon remains on the workspace page where you found it, and a row is added to the Replicator page for that database.

You can specify the order in which databases are replicated by pointing to a row and dragging it to a new location in the replication process.

If you want to remove a row from the Replicator page, highlight the row and press the Delete key. Notes removes the database from the Replicator page. This does not affect the database icon on other workspace pages. You cannot remove the Start Replication At entry or the Templates entry, although you can uncheck these to make them inactive. If you delete entries such as Hang Up from your Replicator page, you can add them by selecting them from the Create menu.

Other options can be initiated from the action buttons at the top of the Replicator page, from the Action menu, or by clicking the right mouse button. The buttons on the Action Bar have the following effects:

- **Start** replication. You can initiate replication manually at any time, whether or not you have set up a replication schedule.
- **Send & Receive Mail** Routes mail that is held in your outgoing mailbox to the server and retrieves any new mail from the inbox in your server-based mail file. No replication takes place. Mail routing is a completely different task within Domino, but the two tasks share enough functionality that they have been grouped together on the Replicator page and on Connection documents.
- **Other Actions** Enables you to replicate all your high-priority databases, replicate with a specific server, replicate only the database you have selected on the Replicator page, or send outgoing mail without replicating or receiving incoming mail.

TESTING REPLICATION

You can test replication between servers after you have configured the necessary replication Connection documents. Begin by creating a new replica of a database; alter it in some way and then force replication with a replica of this database on another server.

You can track the results of your replication tests for individual databases or collectively for all the databases replicated. The replication history for an individual database records replication events with servers and workstations. You can access this information by selecting the target database and selecting File, Replication, History. The Replication Events view of the Domino log file (LOG.NSF) provides you collective information regarding the replication cycle. You can access this from the Replication tab within the Domino Administrator.

MONITORING REPLICATION AND MAINTAINING REPLICA DATABASES

In order to monitor replication and maintain replica databases on your various servers within your Domino environment, you need to familiarize yourself with the various monitoring tools available to the Domino Administrator and the methods to resolve replication conflicts if and when they arise.

MONITORING REPLICATION OF SPECIFIC DATABASES

The following tools are available to assist you in monitoring replication and troubleshooting replication problems within your Domino server:

- The `Replication` task within the Domino Administrator.
- The replication history of each database, recording each successful replication session for the given database.
- The Replication Events view of the log file (LOG.NSF), showing details about replication events between servers.
- Replication Monitors, notifying you when replication of a database hasn't occurred within a specified time period. You create Replication Monitors as a part of configuring the `Event` task.
- The Database Analysis tool, enabling you to collect such information as the replication history, the replication events from the log file, and other information specific to a database and store it in a results database for subsequent analysis.

UNDERSTANDING THE REPLICATION TAB WITHIN THE DOMINO ADMINISTRATOR

The Replication tab within the Domino Administrator provides three information views, detailing the replication schedule, replication topology map, and replication events of servers. The Replication tab is shown in Figure 40.6. A summary of each of these views follows:

- Replication Schedule summarizes the contents of Connection documents pertinent to replication tasks for servers within the selected Domain.
- Replication Events provides a summary listing of the Replication Events view of the selected Domino server's `log.nsf`.

MONITORING REPLICATION AND MAINTAINING REPLICA DATABASES | 969

Figure 40.6
The Domino Administrator Replication tab highlighting the three administrative selections: replication schedules, events, and topology map.

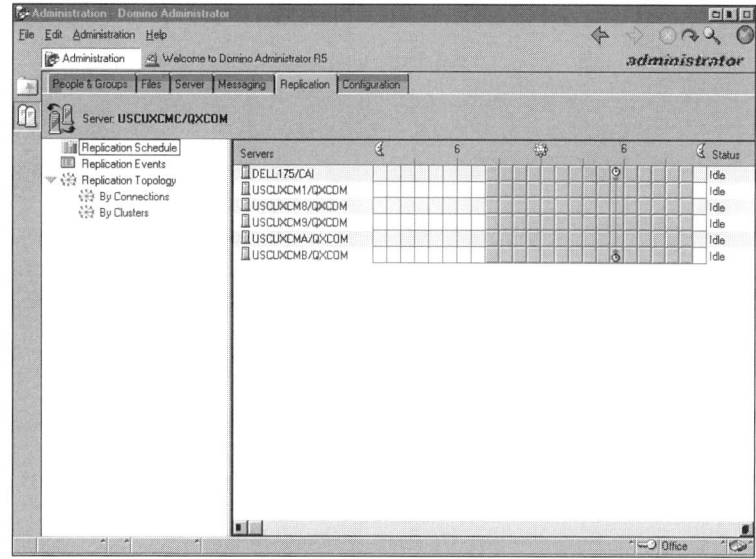

- Replication Topology provides a graphical depiction of the underlying Replication configuration between servers within the selected Domain. By double-clicking connections between servers, you can view the particulars of the Connection document for the selected calling and answering Domino servers. Similarly, by highlighting either endpoint of the connection, you can view the details of the selected server's replication configuration. A sample replication topology is shown in Figure 40.7.

Figure 40.7
A graphic display of replication topology within the Domino Administrator.

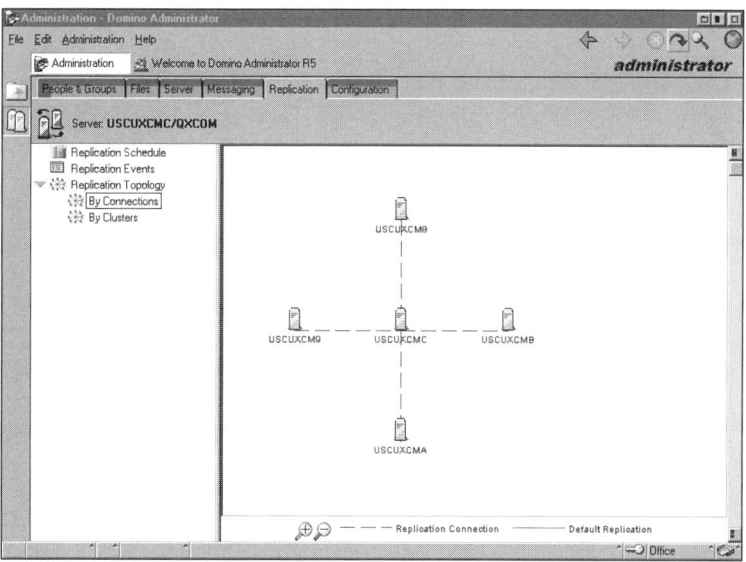

PART
VII
CH
40

Viewing the Database Replication History

Recall that you can view a database's replication history by opening the database and selecting File, Replication, History. Domino records an entry in the history the first time one server replica successfully replicates with a replica on another server. The entry consists of the name of the peer server and the date and time of the replication. Domino subsequently creates separate entries when a replica sends information and when a replica receives it.

Viewing Replication Events in the Log File

The Replication Events view of thelog file (LOG.NSF) provides comprehensive information on the replication of databases between servers. A replication log document shows the following information for each database replicated on a given server:

- The access the server has to the database
- The number of documents added, deleted, and modified
- The size of the data exchanged
- The name of the replica that this database replicated with

Above this individual database information, you can find the Events section within the replication log document. It records any problems that occurred when replication was attempted for specific databases. This includes such information as whether the database access control is set to not allow replication or whether replication is disabled.

Use the Domino Administrator to view a replication log:

1. Initiate the Domino Administrator and select the server to be administered.
2. From the Domino Administrator, select the Replication tab.
3. Click the Replication Events view of the Notes Log.
4. Open a recent replication log.

Creating Replication Monitor Documents

You can create a Replication Monitor document to alert yourself or another adminstrator when replication between specific databases fails to occur according to the schedule you established. To prompt this:

1. Initiate the Domino Administrator, select the server to be administered, and click the Configuration tab. In the left pane, expand the Statistics & Events, Monitors, and Replication sections.
2. Select the New Replication Monitor action button.
3. On the Basics tab
    - Type the name of the database or databases you want to monitor next to the File Name label.

- Specify servers to monitor by clicking the Only the following button and selecting the servers by clicking the Servers button.
- Alternatively, retain the All in the domain default setting.
- Enter a time, in hours, next to the timeout label. This indicates a time after which you want the Event server task to generate a report if replication has not occurred.

4. On the Other tab
    - Click the arrow next to the Generate a Replication event of severity label, select a severity level, and click OK.
    - Click OK to save the Replication Monitor.

Analyzing Replication Using the Database Analysis Tools

You can compile replication information for a database or set of databases by performing a database analysis. This assembles the replication history for the selected database(s) as it has been recorded and any additions, updates, or deletions as reported in the log file. To capture this information:

1. Initiate the Domino Administrator, select the server to be administered, and click the Files tab. The Notes data directory is displayed in the left pane, and the contents of the selected subdirectory is displayed in the middle pane.
2. Highlight the file or files for which you want to collect replication information.
3. Under the Tools section, expand the Database section and select Analyze. The Analyze Database dialog box appears.
4. Under Replication, select one or both of Find replicas on other servers and Replication history. Find replicas reports information from other replicas in addition to the database(s) on the selected server. Replication history reports successful replications of the database(s), as reported in the replication history for the database(s).
5. Specify the number of days of activity to collect.
6. Click the Results button and designate the results database.
7. Click OK to initiate the analysis. Upon completion, review the contents of your results database.

Resolving Replication or Save Conflicts

A replication conflict or save conflict arises when more than one user concurrently edits the same document in different replicas between replication sessions or the same document in one copy of a database.

Understanding Replication Conflicts

A replication conflict represents the first condition: when more than one user edits and saves the changes in different replicas between replications. Under these circumstances, Domino stores the results of one session in a main document and the results of the second and subsequent editing sessions in response documents. Domino adheres to some basic precepts to determine the main and response document hierarchy. First, it makes the document that has been edited and saved the most number of times the main document, with the others becoming Replication Conflict documents. Second, if all documents have been edited the same number of times, it makes the most recently edited document the main document, with the others becoming Replication Conflict documents.

UNDERSTANDING SAVE CONFLICTS

A save conflict represents the second of the two conditions: when two or more users open and edit the same document at the same time on the same server. Under these circumstances, the first document saved becomes the main document. All subsequently saved documents become Save Conflict documents.

PREVENTING REPLICATION OR SAVE CONFLICTS

In order to reduce or eliminate replication or save conflicts from occurring, database designers and system administrators have the following options:

- In design mode, the database designer can select the Form property Merge replication conflicts on the bottom of the Information tab. This option triggers an automatic merge of Replication conflicts into one document if no fields conflict.
- Again in design mode, the database designer can specify one of the Versioning options on the Information tab. This option specifies how the various versions of the same document are treated—as responses or siblings.
- The system administrator can assign users Author access or lower in the database ACL, thereby preventing users from editing other users' documents.
- The system administrator can construct LotusScript agents which attempt to resolve the conflicts.
- Finally, the system administrator can simply keep the number of replicas to a minimum, if that is a possible alternative.

CONSOLIDATING REPLICATION OR SAVE CONFLICTS

The process of consolidating a replication or save conflict is relatively straightforward: You merge information into one primary document and remove the secondary document(s). If you want to save the main document, copy any information from the replication or save conflict documents into the main document, save it, and delete the conflict documents. If you want to save one of the replication or save conflict documents, copy any information from the main and other response documents, savethe selected document, and delete the others.

Summary

Owing to the importance of maintaining synchronicity of information within a Domino Domain, replication administration is one of the key roles performed by Domino administrators. This chapter provided insights into the most important aspects of replication administration. It provided a general introduction to Lotus Domino Replication. Following the overview, it provided administrative procedures and examples of creating database replicas, enabling selective replication of database components, and setting up, initiating, and customizing replication. It concluded with a section on monitoring replication and maintaining replica databases.

From Here...

You can find material related to Domino server administration in the following chapters and parts:

- Part VI, "Installing and Configuring the Domino Servers," discusses the different Domino server types, their initial installation and configuration, and the upgrade paths from R4.x to R5. It also provides an overview of Domino security, firewalls, Virtual Private Networks (VPNs), and Internet security. This represents fundamental information for administering a Domino enterprise.

- Chapter 38, "Administering Users, Groups, and Certification," introduces you to the R5 Domino Administrator. It then discusses user, group, and certification administration within the Domino Directory.

- Chapter 39, "Administering Electronic Mail," provides you with the basics in establishing your Domino messaging infrastructure.

- Chapter 41, "Administering Files and Databases," covers management and administration of disk information, files, directories, and databases; updating database designs; and rolling out databases to users. It summarizes information pertinent to systems administrators who also perform database administration.

- Chapter 42, "Managing Your Domino Server Configuration," discusses general Domino server administration, maintaining server configuration documents and running server tasks, modifying networks and domains, and analyzing and monitoring server performance.

- Chapter 43, "Troubleshooting and Monitoring Domino," introduces the tools available within Domino to analyze problems and perform corrective action.

- Part VIII, "Advanced Domino Administration," gives you specialized information about topics, such as performance and capacity planning, upgrading from other email systems, and integration with phones, fax, and image.

CHAPTER 41

ADMINISTERING FILES AND DATABASES

Maintaining the integrity of application data is a chief responsibility of the Domino Administrator. Such maintenance entails a wide range of activities. Among the most important preventative maintenance activities are backing up the server on a regular basis; fixing up corrupted databases; monitoring files, databases, and directories; and, in general, monitoring disk space.

This chapter focuses on issues relevant to the Domino Administrator performing the role of disk, file, directory, and database administrator. It consists of five major sections. The first section covers the aspects within the Domino Administrator facilitating the collection of general disk information, specifically general disk capacity and disk usage information. The second section covers aspects within the Domino Administrator of managing files and directories, file and directory creation and deletion, and database and directory link creation and deletion. The third section covers the extensive facilities to manage and maintain databases. The fourth section provides a brief descriptive overview reviewing the concepts of updating database designs. The fifth and final section describes the general procedure involved in rolling out databases to an end user population.

Files is the generic term within the Lotus Domino Administrator for the administration of files, databases, directories, and links. Databases are the cornerstone of Lotus Domino application environment. From design to deployment, database applications are influenced by various parts of a corporation, from systems analysts, through systems architects and designers, to the database application developer, Database Manager, and system administrator.

When the database designer has completed the application and it is ready for production, it is time to move it to the Domino server. At this point, the responsibility for the database is taken over by the system administrator and the Database Manager. The Database Manager is responsible for seeing that database security is enforced and that users have access to the data they need. The system administrator, on the other hand, is responsible for the impact of the database on the Domino system, and the impact of the system on the database.

Among other things, databases must be monitored for usage and size. Corrupted databases must be repaired and put back into production. View and full text indexes require updating. Databases have to be moved to a new location or replicated so that they are accessible by users in other locations. These tasks are the responsibilities of the system administrator. Within Lotus Domino R5, the majority of these tasks can be accomplished under the Files tab within the Domino Administrator.

Upon selection, the Files tab displays the Domino Data Directory for the selected server. By default, the display contains only the databases. You can alter what is shown by selecting one of the appropriate options from the Show drop-down at the top of the database display. The available options include Databases only, Templates only, Mail Boxes only, All database types, All Files, Database links only. You can also customize the display by selecting from a set of file types to view.

As shown in Figure 41.1 with its expanded tasks or actions, the Files tab does not contain any embedded tables. Instead, it provides a set of three tasks or actions: Disk Space, Folder, and Database.

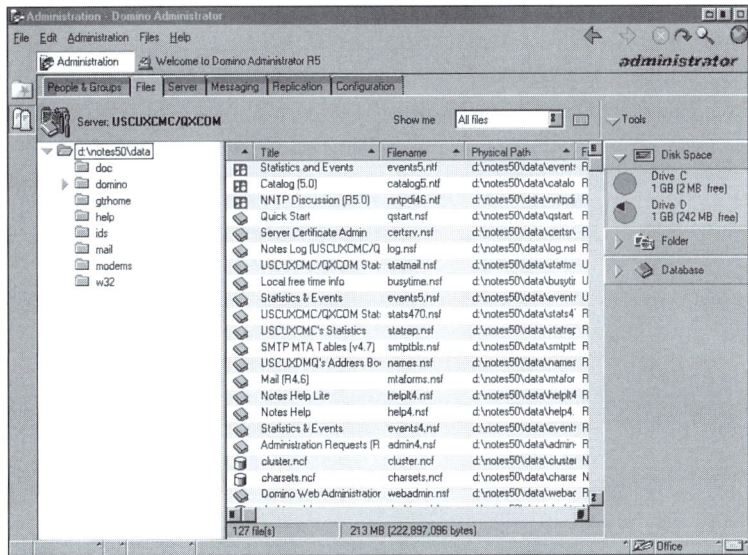

Figure 41.1
The Files tab within the Domino Administrator displaying its three tasks or actions of Disk Space, Folder, and Database, with the first expanded to show general disk capacity and usage information.

The following three sections provide detail on each of these three actions.

MANAGING GENERAL DISK INFORMATION

The General Disk Information task or action displays the size and free space of all partitions configured on the server. This provides the administrator, at a glance, with the disk size and free space for each disk partition on the server.

MANAGING FILES AND DIRECTORIES

The Folder task or Action Bar, shown in Figure 41.2, facilitates the creation of new folders, creation of new links to folders or databases, updating of existing links, or deletion of folders, databases, or links to either. Creating links to folders and databases enables the administrator to increase security within the Domino environment. The administrator accomplishes this by placing entire folders or individual or groups of databases outside the normal Domino data directory structure. During the creation of the link to the external folder or database, the administrator then specifies those users who should be able to access the link. Furthermore, external to Domino, the administrator can define operating system

978 CHAPTER 41 ADMINISTERING FILES AND DATABASES

specific access control limitations. As a result, Domino users can see the linked folder as a subdirectory or the database as an entry under the Domino data directory but cannot access either one unless they have been given access permission.

Figure 41.2
The Folder task or Action Bar displaying the action buttons to create a new folder, create a new link to a folder or database, update an existing link, or delete entries, whether such entries are folders, databases, or links to either or both.

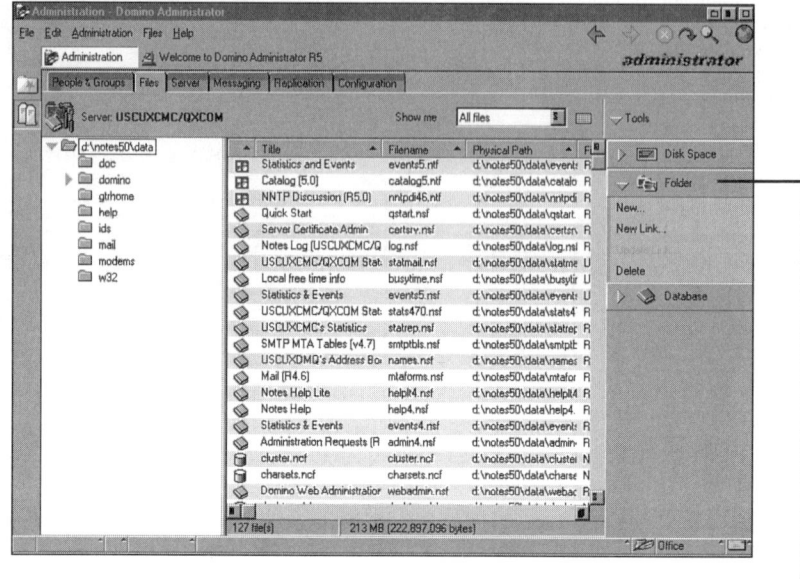

Folder Action Bar

The following paragraphs delineate the Domino Administrator procedures for creating and deleting folders, and creating, updating, and deleting folders, databases, and links to either or both.

To create a folder, complete these steps:

1. Within the Domino Administrator, select the server to be administered from the Server icon in the far left of the Domino Administrator screen.
2. Click the Files tab. The selected server's Domino Data Directory is displayed in the left pane. Expand the Folder task under the Tools selection.
3. Position yourself where you want to create the new directory.
4. Select New. The Create New Folder Dialog box is displayed.
5. Enter the name of the new folder.
6. Click OK. The new Directory is created as a subdirectory under the Directory highlighted in the left pane.

MANAGING FILES AND DIRECTORIES | 979

To delete a folder, complete these steps:

1. Within the Domino Administrator, select the server to be administered from the Server icon in the far left of the Domino Administrator screen.
2. Click the Files tab. The selected server's Domino Data Directory is displayed in the left pane. Expand the Folder task under the Tools selection.
3. Select the folder you want to delete. A Folder icon differs from a Link icon because it does not display an arrow.
4. Click Delete. The Delete Folder dialog box appears.
5. Click Yes to delete the folder.

As mentioned in the introductory paragraph, you can manage and maintain links to folders and databases external to the Domino Directory to increase security by creating folder or database links, modifying folder or database links, and deleting folder and database links.

To create a folder link, complete these steps:

1. Within the Domino Administrator, select the server to be administered from the Server icon in the far left of the Domino Administrator screen.
2. Click the Files tab. The selected server's Domino Data Directory is displayed in the left pane. Expand the Folder task under the Tools selection.
3. Click New Link. The Create New Link dialog box appears, as shown in Figure 41.3.

Figure 41.3
The Create New Link dialog box prompting for filename, whether it is a folder or database link, what the link points to, and who can access the link.

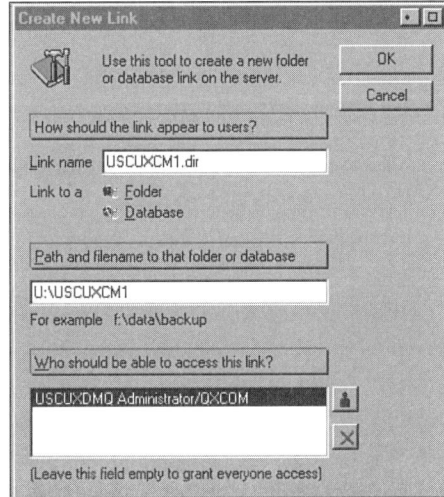

PART
VII
CH
41

4. In the Link name box, enter a name for the folder link.
5. Select Folder. Domino appends the `.dir` extension to the link name specified.
6. Enter the path to the folder to which the link points.
7. Optionally, under Who should be able to access this link?, enter the names of users. This restricts access to the linked directory. You can also retrieve these from the current Directory by clicking the Person icon.
8. Click OK.

To create a database link pointing to a single database outside the Domino data directory, complete these steps:

1. Within the Domino Administrator, select the server to be administered from the Server icon in the far left of the Domino Administrator screen.
2. Click the Files tab. The selected server's Domino Data Directory is displayed in the left pane. Expand the Folder task under the Tools selection.
3. Click New Link.
4. In the File box, enter a name for the database link.
5. Select Database. Domino adds the extension `.nsf` to the link name you specified.
6. Enter the complete path to the database to which the link points.
7. Optionally, under Who should be able to access this link?, enter the names of users. This restricts access to the linked database. You can also retrieve these from the current Directory by clicking the person icon.
8. Click OK.

To modify a folder or database link, complete these steps:

1. Within the Domino Administrator, select the server to be administered from the Server icon in the far left of the Domino Administrator screen.
2. Click the Files tab. The selected server's Domino Data Directory is displayed in the left pane. Expand the Folder task under the Tools selection.
3. Select the icon for the link within the displayed Domino Data Directory. A Link icon displays an arrow.
4. Click Update Link.
5. Change the filename for the link, the path to the directory or database it points to, or the access list.
6. Click OK.

To delete a folder or database link, complete these steps:

1. Within the Domino Administrator, select the server to be administered from the Server icon in the far left of the Domino Administrator screen.
2. Click the Files tab. The selected server's Domino Data Directory is displayed in the left pane. Expand the Folder task under the Tools selection.
3. Select the icon for the link within the displayed Domino Data Directory. A Link icon displays an arrow.
4. Click Delete Link. The Delete Link dialog box is displayed.
5. Click Yes.

Managing and Maintaining Databases

When databases are in production, they must be monitored and maintained. Although many of the maintenance tasks can be scheduled to run automatically by setting parameters in the NOTES.INI file, in server Configuration documents, or in Program documents, certain tasks still require a certain level of administrative intervention. The Domino Administrator provides a central location for such activity.

Under the Database task or Action Bar, shown in Figure 41.4, the Domino Administrator facilitates the following Database actions, expanded from the earlier Database Tools: Manage ACL, Create Replica(s), Compact, Full Text Index, Multi-Database Index, Advanced Properties, Quotas, Move, Sign, Replication, Fixup, Cluster, Analyze, and Find Note.

Figure 41.4
The Database task or Action Bar expanded to list the actions available from within the Domino Administrator.

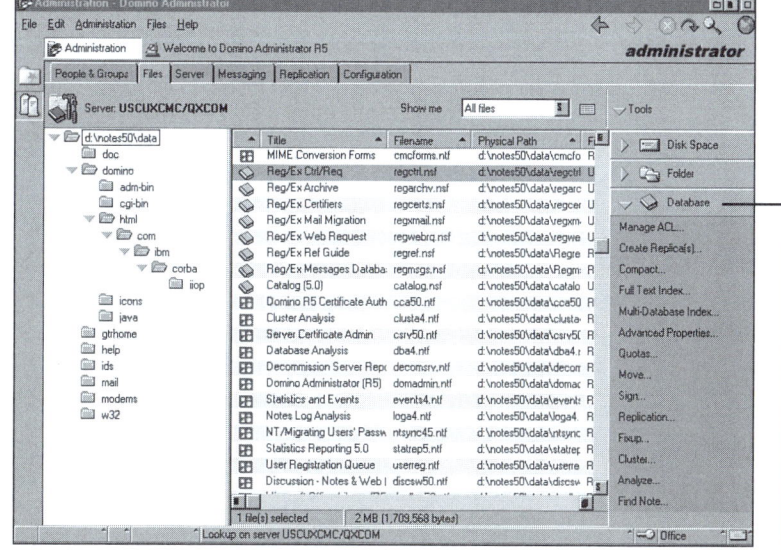

Database Action Bar

The following paragraphs detail the background and procedures for each of the tools associated with these actions. Where not specifically stated, the procedures assume that you are performing the role of Domino administrator and are listed in the ACL with the user type of Manager.

COMPACTING DATABASES

Adding and deleting documents to and from a database during normal processing leaves blocks of unused space. When a document is deleted, a deletion stub is put in its place. This occupies only a percentage of the space of the original document. The remaining unused space is now available. Because it is difficult to populate these chunks of unused space, the database becomes fragmented over time and server performance decreases. Compacting is the process of removing this unused whitespace.

It is generally recommended to compact databases that have 10% or more unused space. Further, it is also recommended to run Compact at least once a month on all databases on the server.

To determine whether a specific database has reached 10% unused space, complete the following steps:

1. Within the Domino Administrator, select the server to be administered from the Server icon in the far left of the Domino Administrator screen.
2. Click the Files tab. The selected server's Domino Data Directory is displayed in the left pane.
3. Select and open the database from the list of databases provided in the left pane.
4. From the Domino Administrator's main drop-down menu, select File, Database, Properties.
5. Click the Information tab.
6. Click the % used button. The database's current used percentage is displayed.

Because compacting large databases can consume a great deal of time, it is recommended to run Compact during off-peak hours. In this way, you do not overburden your servers with administrative processing during the normal business day. Furthermore, because compacting databases can require the creation of a duplicate copy of the database being compacted, based on the option selected, the server must also have enough disk space to store the copy during the process.

To compact databases, you can use the Domino Administrator or load the Compact task from the server console. You can also use a program document. When you load Compact as a server task or have it run as a program document, it runs under the auspices of the server. You can also compact an individual database by clicking the Compact button in the Database Properties InfoBox.

To compact a database within the Domino Administrator, complete the following steps:

1. Ensure that you have at least Designer access to the databases you want to compact. Then, within the Domino Administrator, select the server to be administered from the Server icon in the far left of the Domino Administrator screen.
2. Choose the Files tab. The selected server's Domino Data Directory is displayed in the left pane.
3. Expand the Database task under the Tools selection.
4. In the Databases box, select the database(s) to compact.
5. Select Compact. The Compact Databases dialog box is displayed.
6. Select the desired options for the compaction. These include
    - Specifying for compaction to take place only if unused space is greater than a certain percentage.
    - Discarding any built view indexes.
    - Setting a maximum size of the database to 4GB.
    - Keeping or reverting the database back to R4 format.
    - Archiving the database.
    - Defining the compaction style. The compaction styles include in-place compaction recovering unused space without reducing the file size, in-place compaction recovering unused space with file size reduction, copy style with the options of allowing access while compacting and ignoring errors during compaction.
7. Click OK to complete the compaction.

You should note that compacting an R4 database results in the database being converted to R5 format. To prevent this, you can give your R4 databases the .NS4 extension.

MONITORING FULL TEXT INDEXING

Full text indexing enables users to search databases for information. Physically on disk, the full text search represents a set of files stored in a subdirectory of the database being indexed. Domino names this subdirectory by appending .FT to the filename of the database excluding the .NSF extension. All the files for the full text index are stored in this directory. Every time the full text index is updated, Domino adds an index file into the index subdirectory.

Because full text indexes can consume significant disk space, you should ensure that you have adequate disk space before creating the full text index. Depending on the content of the database and the indexing options selected, the full text index can approach 75% of the size of the text in the target database. The index's size depends on the following factors:

- The percentage of text in your database in comparison to nontext items, such as bitmaps and graphics.
- The full text options chosen. For single-database indexes, these include Case Sensitive Index; Index Attachments; Index Encrypted Fields, Index Sentence and Paragraph breaks and Exclude Words in Stop Word File; Index Word Breaks Only; and Index Word, Sentence, and Paragraph breaks. The meaning of those options is enumerated in the following list:
  - The Case Sensitive Index option includes in the index an entry for each word each time a different capitalization scheme for the word is encountered. This can increase the size of the full text index by up to 10%. For example, "computer" and "Computer" both appear in the index as different words so that searches can locate occurrences of one but not the other.
  - The Index Attachments option indexes the text in any attachments while building the index.
  - The Index Encrypted Fields option encrypts the index so that only those users who have the correct decryption key can search the index.
  - The Exclude Words in Stop Word File option excludes the words specified in the stop word file from being included in the index. By minimizing the words included in the index, this option can effectively decrease the index's size up to 20%. Domino provides a default stop word file, DEFAULT.STP. This can be easily edited for a particular environment. The same stop word file must be provided on all servers replicating the full text indexed database or their indexes will vary in size.
  - The Index Word Breaks Only option creates an index suitable for performing searches on a word-by-word basis. The option results in a smaller index, but disables the use of proximity operators in full text searches.
  - The Index Word, Sentence, and Paragraph Breaks option enables the use of proximity operators. Such operators locate multiple words in the same sentence or paragraph. For example, the following query finds documents in which cat and mouse are in the same paragraph: cat paragraph mouse. Similarly, the following query finds documents in which cat and mouse are in the same sentence: cat sentence mouse.

CREATING, UPDATING, AND DELETING FULL TEXT INDEXES

You can create, update, or delete a full text index by completing the following steps:

1. Ensure that you have at least Designer access to the target database or databases for which you want to create a full text index. Then, within the Domino Administrator, select the server to be administered from the Server icon in the far left of the Domino Administrator screen.

MANAGING AND MAINTAINING DATABASES | 985

2. Choose the Files tab. The selected server's Domino Data Directory is displayed in the left pane.

3. Expand the Database task under the Tools selection.

4. In the Databases box, select the database for which you want to manage the index.

5. Select Full Text Index. The Full Text Index dialog box is displayed. This is shown in Figure 41.5.

Figure 41.5
The Full Text Index dialog box providing selections for delimiting the nature and contents of the resulting index.

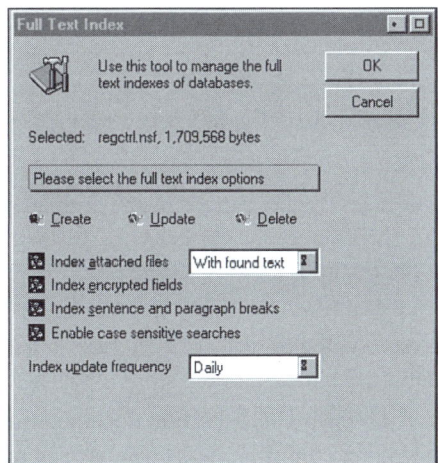

6. Select Create, Update, or Delete.

7. Select one or more of the following options: Index attached files (With found text or With file filters), Index encrypted fields, Index sentence and paragraph breaks, Enable case sensitive searches.

8. Specify the Index update frequency of Hourly, Daily, or Scheduled.

9. Select OK. A full text index is created with your specifications.

CREATING REPLICA COPIES OF DATABASES

Replica copies of databases are special copies that are identified by their replica IDs. As detailed in Chapter 40, "Replication and Its Administration," you can create such replica copies of databases in a number of ways. One of the most facile means is provided by the Database actions within the Domino Administrator. With the Domino Administrator, you can use the Administration Process to create replicas on servers in the same Domino domain or in another Domino domain. To create a replica copy of a database in the same Domino domain, complete the following steps:

1. Ensure that the necessary Administration Process and access control has been established. This entails the following: the Administration Process is running on both the

PART
VII
CH
41

source and destination servers, you have Create Database access to the destination server or servers and at least Reader access to the database on the source server, the source server has Create Replica access in the Server document of the destination server, and the destination server has at least Reader access in the ACL of the source replica database.

Within the Domino Administrator, select the server to be administered from the Server icon in the far left of the Domino Administrator screen.

2. Choose the Files tab. The selected server's Domino Data Directory is displayed in the left pane.
3. Expand the Database task under the Tools selection.
4. In the Databases box, select the databases for which you want to create replica copies.
5. Select Create Replica.
6. Specify the server or servers on which you want to install a replica copy. You can also set the path and filename for the given replica by selecting the Set Path and filenames button and completing the Destination file path setting.
7. Click OK to accept the path and filename settings, and then click OK to submit the Create Replica request. To create a replica copy of a database on a server in another Domino domain entails additional configuration.

You must have an outbound Cross Domain Configuration document in the Administration Requests database on your source server. Similarly, you must have an inbound Cross Domain Configuration document in the Administration Requests on the destination server. The former enables the Administration Process on the source server to export Create Replica requests to the destination server. The latter enables the Administration Process on the destination server to import Create Replica requests from the source server.

Furthermore, you must have a Connection document for mail routing configured on your server to one server in the domain of your destination server. Finally, if they do not share a common certifier, you must have cross-certified the two servers in order for them to authenticate with each other.

MOVING AND DELETING DATABASES

Within the Domino Administrator, you can use the Administration Process to move non-mail databases from one server to another server by completing the following steps:

1. Ensure that the necessary Administration Process and access control has been established. This entails the following: the Administration Process is running on both the source and destination servers, you have Create Database access to the destination server or servers and at least Manager with Delete documents access in the ACL of the database on the source server, the source server has Create Replica access in the Server document of the destination server, and the destination server has at least Reader access in the ACL of the source replica database.

Within the Domino Administrator, select the server to be administered from the Server icon in the far left of the Domino Administrator screen.

2. Choose the Files tab. The selected server's Domino Data Directory is displayed in the left pane.
3. Expand the Database task under the Tools selection.
4. In the Databases box, select the databases that you want to move.
5. Select Move. The Move Database dialog box is displayed.
6. Specify the server or servers to which you want to move the database. You can also set the path and filename for the given move by selecting the Set Path and filenames button and completing the Destination file path setting.
7. Click OK to accept the path and filename settings, and then click OK to submit the Move Replica request.

Chapter 38, "Administering Users, Groups, and Certification," discusses the procedures to follow when moving a user's mail file from the People & Groups tab within the Domino Administrator.

Analyzing a Database

You can analyze a database or set of databases by completing the following steps:

1. Within the Domino Administrator, select the server to be administered from the Server icon in the far left of the Domino Administrator screen.
2. Choose the Files tab. The selected server's Domino Data Directory is displayed in the left pane.
3. Expand the Database task under the Tools selection.
4. In the Databases box, select one or more databases to analyze.
5. Select Analyze. The Analyze Database dialog box is displayed. This is shown in Figure 41.6. The dialog box consists of a set of options enabling you to customize the scope of the database analysis. You can analyze
   - Changes in Data documents and/or Design documents. The first provides a report on document additions, edits, and deletions. The second provides a report on changes to the database ACL and design.
   - User activity, consisting of User reads and/or User writes. For User reads, the report details the total times users opened documents and servers read documents. For User writes, it reports the total times users and servers created, modified, or deleted documents, and the total number of mail messages delivered to the database.
   - Replication events, by finding replicas on other servers and/or viewing the selected database's replication history. This reports on the replicas on other servers and the successful replications, as logged in the replication history for the database.

- Miscellaneous Events view and/or Database usage view, as recorded in the respective views of the Domino log file. This reports the events relating to the database from the Miscellaneous Events view and the Usage—By User view of the log.

6. Specify the number of days that you want the analysis to include.
7. Click Results and specify the server, database title, and database filename where you want to store the results. You should create the results database on your local workstation rather than on your server. This prevents overwriting another administrator's work. You can also optionally either Overwrite the contents of the database or Append to it.
8. Click OK to select the Results database, and then click OK to begin the database nalysis.

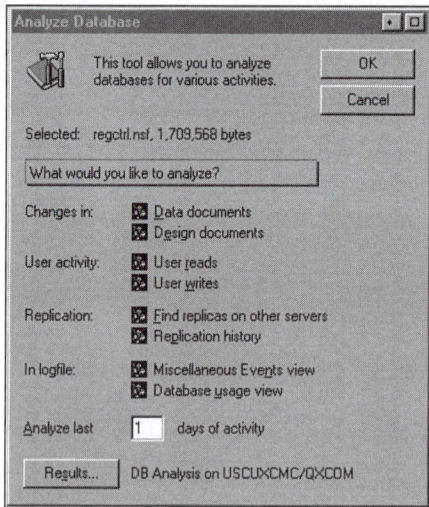

Figure 41.6
The Analyze Database dialog box.

VIEWING THE RESULTS OF A DATABASE ANALYSIS

After you run the Database Analysis, you can view its results by completing the following steps:

1. Open the results database.
2. Choose View and then choose one of the following subviews:
    - By Date, providing a view with documents categorized by the date the reported event happened
    - By Event Type, providing a view with documents categorized by the type of event described.
    - By Source, providing a view of documents categorized by the source server on which the event occurred

- By Source Database, providing a view of documents categorized by the source database for the event

3. Select a document within the view.

Each analysis document contains the following fields:

- The Date the event occurred
- The Time the event occurred
- The Source of Event Information, whether it is the analyzed database, its replicas, or the log file on the server
- The Event Type, whether it is Activity, Mail Router, Data Note, Design Note, or Replicator:
    - Activity event types are recorded if you select User reads and User writes options. They represent the number of user or server reads and writes, as noted in the database user activity report.
    - Mail Router event types are recorded if you select the User writes option. They represent the number of documents delivered to the database.
    - Data Note event types are recorded if you select the Changes to documents option. They represent details about document creations, edits, or deletions.
    - Design Note event types are recorded if you select the Changes to design option. They represent details about changes to the database Access Control List or design.
    - Replicator event types are recorded if you select the Replication History option. They represent replication history as reported in the database replication history indicating successful replications.
- The Source Database, which is the database from which documents were read or from which documents were pulled, in the case of database replication events
- The Source, which is the server that hosts the database containing documents that were read or written, or the server that hosts the database from which information was pulled, in the case of database replication events
- The Destination, which is the database within which documents were updated or to which information was pushed, in the case of database replication events
- The Destination machine, which is the server that hosts the database that was updated or to which information is pushed in the case of replication events
- The Description of the event

Setting Database Quotas

One of the major responsibilities of Notes Domino administrators is to monitor the size of the database and set quotas based on this information.

Monitoring Database Size

You can monitor database size in the Notes log by examining the Database Usage, Database Sizes, and Usage By User views. Individual databases can be monitored by examining the Information page in the Database Properties dialog box. You can also use the Statistics Reporting database and monitor unused space in databases, or run Compact on databases that fall below a specific threshold.

Setting Database Quotas

You can also set up quotas for database size and generate warnings at thresholds you determine. When you define a specific quota for a database, you are specifying a maximum size the database can grow. When it exceeds this quota, the message Cannot allocate database object—database would exceed its disk quota appears in the Miscellaneous Events view of the log file. It is also displayed to users attempting to open the database.

Similarly, when you define a warning threshold, you are specifying that, when the database reaches the threshold size, the warning message Warning, database has exceeded its size warning threshold be written to the Miscellaneous Events view of the log file.

Complete the following steps to set quotas on one or more databases:

1. Within the Domino Administrator, select the server to be administered from the Server icon in the far left of the Domino Administrator screen.
2. Choose the Files tab. The selected server's Domino Data Directory is displayed in the left pane.
3. Expand the Database task under the Tools selection.
4. Select the database or databases to which you want to assign a quota or warning threshold.
5. Select Quotas.
6. At this point, you can obtain the current settings by clicking the More Info button. The Database Quota Information dialog for the selected database is displayed. Click OK to return to the Set Quotas dialog.
7. Select the Set database quota to button and specify a size limit that does not exceed the maximum database size set for the selected database(s).
8. Select Set warning threshold to and specify a size at which a message appears in the log file.
9. Click OK to activate the quota and threshold defined.

Enabling or Disabling Replication of Databases

You can enable or disable replication for a database or set of databases by completing the following steps:

1. Within the Domino Administrator, select the server to be administered from the Server icon in the far left of the Domino Administrator screen.
2. Choose the Files tab. The selected server's Domino Data Directory is displayed in the left pane.
3. Expand the Database task under the Tools selection.
4. In the Databases box, select the databases for which you want to enable or disable replication.
5. Select Replication.
6. Click Enable or Disable.
7. Click OK.

Managing Databases Within Clusters

The Cluster action within the Database tools of the Domino Administrator enables you to manage database availability within a cluster. There are three database attributes associated with such availability: Out of service, In service, Pending delete:

- By marking the database Out of service, you are preventing subsequent open requests for the database. If it is possible, such open database requests failover to a replica in the cluster. If no such replica exists, access to the database is denied.
- All current open connections remain intact, until users close their sessions with the database. As this occurs, Domino prevents subsequent opens, as stated previously. The database is brought to an out-of-service state without disruption to the active users.
- By marking the database as In service, you can restore access to it. In so doing, it becomes fully operational to users again.
- By marking the database as Pending delete, you can set a database to be deleted only after every active user has finished using the database. The database is marked Out of service. No subsequent open requests are accepted. After all active users have closed their sessions with the database, any changes are replicated to a replica in the cluster and the database is deleted.

Complete the following steps to mark a database out of service, in service, or pending delete:

1. Within the Domino Administrator, select the server to be administered from the Server icon in the far left of the Domino Administrator screen.

2. Choose the Files tab. The selected server's Domino Data Directory is displayed in the left pane.
3. Expand the Database task under the Tools selection.
4. Select Cluster.
5. In the Databases box, select the databases that you want to mark out of service, in service, or pending delete.
6. Click OK.

LOCATING NOTES WITHIN DATABASES

Each document within a Notes database has an 8-character ID. This number uniquely identifies the document within a single database. Each document also has associated with it a 32-character ID. This "universal" qualifier uniquely identifies it within all replicas of the given database. This value is generally referenced in the Domino log (`log.nsf`) when recording events. To analyze such documents reported in the log file and to troubleshoot problems pertaining to them, you can utilize the Find Note action. This action enables you to track which document the Note ID or UNID references and review the document's properties. Complete the following steps to review a given note's properties:

1. Within the Domino Administrator, select the server to be administered from the Server icon in the far left of the Domino Administrator screen.
2. Choose the Files tab. The selected server's Domino Data Directory is displayed in the left pane.
3. Expand the Database task under the Tools selection.
4. In the Databases box, select the databases that you want to search.
5. Select Find Note under the actions. The Find Note dialog box is displayed. This is shown in Figure 41.7.
6. Select Note ID or UNID and copy the hexadecimal value from the log file into the appropriate field.
7. Click OK.

The Notes Document Properties and Fields are displayed in the respectively labeled boxes.

MULTIDATABASE INDEXING

The Multi-Database Index action allows you to enable or disable multiple database indexing for a database or set of databases. If enabled, the database can then be included in the configuration of a Search Site database that enables users to search multiple databases for information. Enabling the database for multidatabase indexing is the first of five steps in the creation of this multidatabase searching infrastructure. The subsequent four steps consist of creating a search site database, configuring a search scope, creating a multidatabase full text index, and notifying users of the search site database.

MANAGING AND MAINTAINING DATABASES | 993

Figure 41.7
The Find Note dialog box.

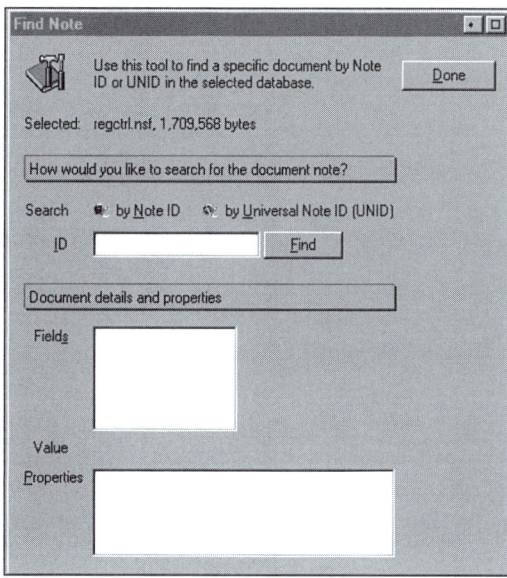

To enable multiple database indexing for a database or set of databases, complete the following steps:

1. Ensure that you have Manager access in the ACL of the databases to be enabled for multidatabase searching. Within the Domino Administrator, select the server to be administered from the Server icon in the far left of the Domino Administrator screen.
2. Choose the Files tab. The selected server's Domino Data Directory is displayed in the left pane.
3. Expand the Database task under the Tools selection.
4. In the Databases box, select the databases you want to enable for multidatabase indexing.
5. Select Multi-Database Indexing.
6. Click Enable, and then click OK.

DISABLING MULTIDATABASE SEARCHING OF A DATABASE

Follow these steps if you've enabled a database for multidatabase searching and now want to disable this property:

1. Ensure that you have Manager access in the ACL of the databases to be disabled for multidatabase searching. Then, within the Domino Administrator, select the server to be administered from the Server icon in the far left of the Domino Administrator screen.

PART
VII
CH
41

2. Choose the Files tab. The selected server's Domino Data Directory is displayed in the left pane.
3. Expand the Database task under the Tools selection.
4. In the Databases box, select the databases you want to disable for multidatabase indexing.
5. Select Multi-Database Index.
6. Click Disable, and then click OK. Update.

Upon disabling multidatabase searching of a database, you want to update the contents of the search site database by updating the contents of the search site database configurations.

SIGNING DATABASES WITH CERTIFICATES

Design elements within databases and database templates possess the signature of the creator's or last modifier's certificate. It may be necessary to modify this signature to enable the database or selective components within it to function properly within your environment.

You can accomplish this by completing the following steps:

1. Ensure that you are using the correct certified user ID to sign a template or database. Then, within the Domino Administrator, select the server to be administered from the Server icon in the far left of the Domino Administrator screen.
2. Choose the Files tab. The selected server's Domino Data Directory is displayed in the left pane.
3. Expand the Database task under the Tools selection.
4. In the Databases box, select the databases that you want to sign.
5. Select Sign.
6. Specify whether you want to sign every design note, a specified design class, or a specified design note. If you select a specified design class, select which class to sign from the list of policy, form, view, icon, design note, ACL, Help Index, Help, Agent, Shared Field, or Replication Formula. If you select a specified design note, specify the hexadecimal Note ID to sign.
7. Click Sign.

FIXING CORRUPTED DATABASES WITH FIXUP

Databases can become corrupted during an improper shutdown of the system or by an external program that accesses the database incorrectly. Whenever Notes detects a database that has been closed improperly, it examines every field in every document and deletes documents that are damaged. This ensures that the damaged document is not replicated to other copies of the database. It may be that users can live with this simple solution, enabling Notes to automatically fix documents.

However, it is the system administrator's job to ensure that the system is running as efficiently as possible. The job of examining databases and fixing any corrupted ones takes time and system resources. This task can therefore be scheduled to run once for all databases on the server, and the task can be scheduled for the middle of the night, when there are few users on the system. The program that does this is the Fixup task.

Corrupted databases can be restored (after corrupted documents have been deleted) through replication, by manually copying and pasting the deleted documents from another copy of the database, or by deleting the database and replacing it with a backup copy.

Fixing Corrupted Views

Corrupted views can result in the information in documents and views being out of synchronization. Sometimes, you will be unable to open a view that is corrupted, odd characters may appear in the view, documents may be missing, or you may find messages in the Notes log.

You can repair corrupted views in the following ways.

First, you may be able to rebuild the view from the workstation by opening the view and pressing Shift+F9. Alternatively, you can press Ctrl+Shift+F9 to rebuild or refresh all views in a database.

You can run the Updall task on a specific database and include the -r flag to rebuild the corrupted view. Enter the following at the server console:

```
Load Updall filename -r
```

Other options include restoring a view by copying the view from a backup copy of the database or by creating a replica copy of the original database.

If you choose to create a new replica to fix corrupted views, but you want to make sure that users can still access the database without having to delete the old icon and reopen the new replica, follow these steps:

1. Back up the database with a corrupted view and rename the copy.
2. Create a replica of the original database, giving it the same server and directory as the original, but giving the new replica a different name temporarily.
3. Create the new replica immediately and copy the ACL. Make sure that you replicate all documents (for example, turn off the indicator that replicates documents created only after a certain date).
4. Delete the original database and then rename the new replica with the filename of the original database.

You can also use the Fixup action within the Database tools panel to fix up a database or set of databases on a selected server:

1. Within the Domino Administrator, select the server to be administered from the Server icon in the far left of the Domino Administrator screen.
2. Choose the Files tab. The selected server's Domino Data Directory is displayed in the left pane.
3. Expand the Database task under the Tools selection.
4. In the Databases box, select the databases that you want to fix up.
5. Select Fixup. The Database Fixup dialog box is displayed.
6. Select from a number of options, including
   - Report all processed databases to logfile   Fixup logs every database it opens and checks. The default is to log only actual problems.
   - Exclude views (faster)   This option results in Fixup skipping views.
   - Perform quick fixup   This option results in a less thorough check of the documents within the database, but it is quicker. If this is not selected, Fixup checks the entire document.
   - Scan only since last fixup   This option results in Fixup checking only documents modified since the last Fixup run. Without this, Fixup checks all documents.
   - Optimize user unread lists   This option results in Fixup reverting the unread note tables for the target databases to the previous release format.
   - Don't purge corrupted documents   This option prevents Fixup from purging corrupted documents. They are left intact so that information can be salvaged if necessary.
   - Fixup transaction-logged databases   This option results in Fixup running on R5 format databases enabled for transaction logging.
7. Click OK.

Setting Advanced Database Properties

The Domino Administrator enables you to reset a number of advanced database properties to optimize database performance and reduce database size. These settings include

- Don't maintain unread marks   This option enables you to disable maintaining unread marks in databases for which they aren't useful. Examples of such databases include reference databases and databases constantly being updated.
- Document table bitmap optimization   This option results in Domino more efficiently updating and rebuilding views. It does this by associating tables with the forms used by the documents the tables contain. For the view being rebuilt and updated, Domino searches the tables associated with the forms used by documents.

- **Don't overwrite free space** This option prevents Domino from overwriting deleted data on disk with a specific pattern to secure it from unauthorized viewing via some form of disk utility.
- **Maintain LastAccessed property** In general, the document property Accessed (in this file) shows the date a document was last modified or read. The Maintain LastAccessed property option controls whether the Accessed (in this file) property is updated if the last document access is a read. By default, it is not selected.
- **Disable transaction logging.**
- **Allow soft deletions.**
- **Don't support specialized response hierarchy** This option disables response hierarchy information in databases. It can be selected for databases that do not use the @functions @AllChildren and @AllDescendants, which utilize such response hierarchy information in view selection and replication formulas.
- **Don't allow headline monitoring** This option prevents users from setting up a headline to automatically monitor databases for information.
- **Limit entries in the $UpdatedBy fields** This option enables the administrator to specify the number of entries that the $UpdatedBy field can contain. When this limit is reached, the oldest entry is replaced by a new entry. By default, every document stores the name of the user and server associated with each document editing session in the $UpdatedBy field. Because this can become quite large, limiting it can conserve disk space and improve performance.
- **Limit entries in the $Revisions fields** This option enables the administrator to specify the number of entries that the $Revisions field can contain. When this limit is reached, the oldest entry is replaced by a new entry. By default, the $Revisions field can maintain a list of 500 sessions.
- **Undelete Expire Time.**

You modify these settings by completing the following steps:

1. Ensure that you have at least Designer access in the database ACL. Then, within the Domino Administrator, select the server to be administered from the Server icon in the far left of the Domino Administrator screen.
2. Choose the Files tab. The selected server's Domino Data Directory is displayed in the left pane.
3. Expand the Database task under the Tools selection.
4. Select the database or databases whose Advanced properties you want to set.
5. Select Advanced Properties. The Advanced database properties dialog box is displayed.
6. Select the options desired.
7. Click OK.

Modifying ACL Settings

You can perform a number of ACL management actions within the Manage ACL action of the Domino Administrator's Database tools. In general, the ACL Management action facilitates

- The adding, renaming, and removing of people, servers, and groups to the ACL of a selected database or databases. Concurrently, it enables you to specify user type and access.
- The adding, renaming, and removing of roles in the ACLs of a selected database or databases.
- Updating the current Administration Server setting, the consistent ACL setting, and the current Internet name & password setting.

To modify the ACL parameters of databases in any of these areas, complete the following steps:

1. Ensure that you have Manager access in the database or set of databases to be modified, in order to edit, delete, and rename entries in the ACL. Then, within the Domino Administrator, select the server to be administered from the Server icon in the far left of the Domino Administrator screen.
2. Choose the Files tab. The selected server's Domino Data Directory is displayed in the left pane.
3. Expand the Database task under the Tools selection.
4. Select the database or databases whose ACLs you want to manage.
5. Select Manage ACL. The Basics screen of the Manage ACL dialog box, shown in Figure 41.8, is displayed.
6. Within the Basics section, define a set of one or more ACL actions you want to have applied to the ACLs of the selected database or databases. These discrete actions include adding entries, renaming existing entries, or removing existing entries. The tasks associated with the given entry are displayed in the inset box below the action buttons.
7. Within the Roles section, define a similar set of one or more actions to add roles, rename existing roles, or remove existing roles from the ACLs of the selected database or databases. Again, the tasks associated with the given entry are displayed in the inset box below the action buttons.
8. The first setting within the Advanced section pertains to the Administration Server for the selected database or databases. The Administration Process automates a number of routine administrative tasks, including maintaining the Access Control Lists and Reader and Author fields within databases. Before you can make use of it on any given database, however, you must ensure that the Administration Process is running on the

MANAGING AND MAINTAINING DATABASES | 999

server and specify an administration server for that database. Determine whether to keep the current Administration Server setting, set it to None, or define a new server.

Figure 41.8
The Basics Pane of the Manage ACL dialog box.

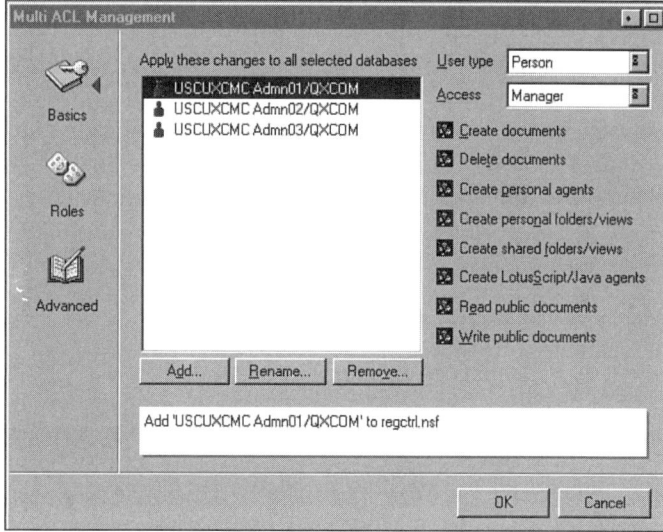

The second setting within the Advanced section pertains to the Consistent ACL setting. By enforcing a consistent ACL across all replicas of the selected database or databases, you can ensure that the ACL remains the same when users replicate the database or databases to their workstations, or when a database or databases are accessed from the server workstation. If you do not select the Enforce consistent ACL option, users have Manager access to the local replicas of server databases. This enables users to change access levels and other ACL settings on local replicas. It does not, however, enable them to replicate those changes back to the server. To keep the ACL the same across all server replicas of a database, you must have Manager access to the database and select this setting on a replica whose server has Manager access to the other replicas. If this is not the case, replication fails. Without Manager access, the server has inadequate access to replicate the ACL.

The third and final setting within the Advanced section pertains to the Maximum Internet name & password setting. This controls the maximum type of access that Internet or intranet users have to a database with a browser. The list contains the standard Notes user access levels. It applies to users accessing the server either via name-and-password authentication or anonymously. It does not apply to users with certificated IDs.

9. Click OK to update the ACL settings for selected database or databases.

PART
VII
CH
41

Updating Database Designs

You can refresh the design of databases if they are linked to a specific design template residing on the same server as the database itself by running the Design task. The Design task runs by default at 2 a.m. every morning and updates the database's design with the database's controlling design template. To enable this to perform effectively, you should distribute a copy of the design template to all servers that have a copy of the database and place the design template in each server's respective Domino Data Directory. Alternatively, you can refresh or replace the design of a database manually by selecting the Database icon or opening the database and selecting Files, Database, Refresh Design or Files, Database, Replace Design.

Rolling Out Databases

The final section of this chapter reviews how to add databases to a production Domino environment. It includes a sketch of the production database organizational structure and the creation of database libraries to rapidly locate your database applications.

In order for your user population to access application databases, you generally have to replicate them from the development/test environment into the production environment. Prior to this production release, however, you generally coordinate with the database administrative team and decide which of your application servers are most aptly suited, both from a location perspective and a software perspective, to host the newly developed application. Some of the factors influencing your plan include the type of the database application being rolled out, the size of the databases involved, the number of users and their locations, and the underlying replication schedules between proposed participating servers.

In general, you complete the following during the rollout cycle:

1. Determine which servers will host the application databases and where the replicas should reside.

2. Review the configurations for the servers involved in the rollout, verify that the necessary Connection documents exist and are enabled between all servers in the rollout, and create them if they don't.

3. Place an image of the application databases on the initial server and create replicas of the production database from this source production server.

As part of the aforementioned step, you also work with the database administrator to determine where the application databases should be stored within the Domino data's directory structure. The default location for all databases is in the Domino Data Directory, defined in the NOTES.INI file (for example, Directory=C:\NOTES\DATA). If you create a subdirectory for the database, the directory is automatically placed beneath the data directory. If you create a database and give it the name MYDATA\SALES.NSF, the database is placed on the Domino server as C:\NOTES\DATA\MYDATA\SALES.NSF.

In short, you have a number of alternatives for where to locate your application databases. You can place them at the root of the Domino data directory. Alternatively, you can construct application-relevant subdirectories—for example, Sales, and place them there. As discussed earlier in this chapter, you can even place them completely outside the Domino Data Directory hierarchy, using the folder or database link technology. In this way, you can take advantage both of the heightened security of the given environment and of the additional space offered by it.

Regardless of where you place the application databases, you can make it easier for your user population to locate them by using the Domino database catalog and database library.

Creating a Database Catalog

To maintain an inventory of databases on your server, you can create a database catalog (CATALOG.NSF). All databases within your Domino Data Directory are listed in the catalog by default, except those databases whose Design Property List in Database Directory has been deselected.

The Catalog server task creates and maintains the catalog. The task runs by default on a server at 1 a.m. every day and updates the entries for all databases when changes occur. For example, if a database is moved to another server, the Catalog server task updates the database entry with the new location.

You create the database catalog from the Database Catalog template (CATALOG.NTF), following the standard database creation process and assigning it a server location, title, and filename. The Database Catalog template is an advanced template, which is displayed by selecting Show Advanced Templates at the bottom of the New Database dialog box. When you create a database catalog, you have Manager access by default.

Following the database creation, you should adjust the database catalog's ACL to give Manager access to all administrative users and similar access to servers who host the catalog or a replica copy of it. While modifying the ACL, you should give the Default group Reader access.

You can then create replicas of the database catalog on the desired servers within your Domino environment. In this way, the catalog contains information on the databases on all the selected servers.

Creating a Database Library

The database library feature is similar to the database catalog, but it lists only those databases published to the library by the library's Database Manager or librarian. When a user attempts to open a database from the library, Notes searches for the database using the replica ID. It searches first on the local hard drive, then on the user's home server, and then on other servers. The first occurrence of the database is opened.

A library is created by creating a new database using the `DBLIB4.NTF` template. After creating the database, you can create a list of librarians in the Librarians view. You can publish a database in the library if you are a librarian and have the library on your desktop:

1. Highlight the Database icon you want to publish and select File, Database, Publish.
2. Enter an abstract describing the database in the dialog box displayed by Notes. This creates a document for the database in the library.

If a user has only reader access to the database library and attempts to publish a database, a Notes agent automatically generates mail to the librarian, who can then decide whether to publish the database. This check must be done because readers do not have access to create or modify documents on their own.

Summary

This chapter has focused on issues of administering files and directories relevant to the functioning of the Lotus Domino server. It first covered the aspects within Domino providing general disk information, providing general disk capacity and disk usage information. It then covered aspects of managing files and directories, file and directory creation and deletion, and database and directory link creation and deletion. The third section covered the extensive facilities to manage and maintain databases. The fourth section provided a brief description reviewing the concepts of updating database designs. Finally, the fifth described the general procedure involved in rolling out databases to your end user population and making them accessible through the database catalog and library mechanisms.

From Here...

You can find material related to Domino server administration in the following chapters and parts:

- Part VI, "Installing and Configuring the Domino Servers," discusses the different Domino server types, their initial installation and configuration, and the upgrade paths from R4.x to R5. It also provides an overview of Domino security, firewalls, Virtual Private Networks (VPNs), and Internet security. This represents fundamental information for administering a Domino enterprise.
- Chapter 38, "Administering Users, Groups, and Certification," introduces you to the R5 Domino Administrator. It then discusses user, group, and certification administration within the Domino Directory.
- Chapter 39, "Administering Electronic Mail," provides you with the basics in establishing your Domino messaging infrastructure.
- Chapter 40, "Replication and Its Administration," gives you an overview of the steps required to configure and maintain a successful replication schedule between servers within your Domino domain.

- Chapter 42, "Managing Your Domino Server Configuration," discusses general Domino server administration, maintaining server configuration documents and running server tasks, modifying networks and domains, and analyzing and monitoring server performance.
- Chapter 43, "Troubleshooting and Monitoring Domino," introduces the tools available within Domino to analyze problems and perform corrective action.
- Part VIII, "Advanced Domino Administration," gives you specialized information about topics such as performance and capacity planning, upgrading from other email systems, and integration with phones, fax, and image.

CHAPTER 42

Managing Your Domino Server Configuration

Administering Domino servers is one of the most multifaceted assignments of the Domino administrator. It covers the entire breadth of server administration, from server installation, configuration, and maintenance, to ongoing monitoring and troubleshooting. It entails ensuring that servers are installed, configured, and maintained at an optimal level to perform the specific function required by their organizations.

This chapter focuses on issues relevant to the Domino Administrator performing the role of server administrator. The first section covers general aspects of Domino server administration. It discusses the administrative tasks involved in Domino server administration, the tools facilitating the administrative process, and the basics of utilizing these tools in performing the general tasks of Domino server administration. The second section focuses on maintaining configuration documents and running server tasks. It introduces the major documents within the Domino Directory pertinent to server administration and outlines the configuration of each. It also describes the major Domino server processes and their execution. The third section provides an overview of the procedures to follow when modifying networks and domains. It details the tasks required in merging two Domino domains, splitting a single Domino domain into two, or moving a Domino server from one domain to another. The fourth and final section focuses on the tools available to analyze and monitor server performance.

ADMINISTERING DOMINO SERVERS

To ensure the stability, accessibility, and reliability of any one particular Domino server and the Domino network in general, administrators are responsible for the following tasks:

- To install and configure new servers.
- To run, monitor, and troubleshoot existing servers by monitoring the Domino log and statistics databases.
- To back up databases and files on a regular basis.
- To optimize server performance by setting and configuring the NOTES.INI settings on the Domino server, compacting databases, fixing corrupted files, and enabling the server to run at maximum efficiency.
- To manage the Domino Directory by creating and updating server-relevant documents within the Directory.
- To oversee Directory Assistance, manage cascading address books, and administer LDAP.
- To configure, monitor, and troubleshoot mail routing by setting up and maintaining shared mail, setting mail thresholds, rerouting dead mail, and configuring POP3 and IMAP clients and files. Chapter 39, "Administering Electronic Mail," details many of the specifics regarding Domino messaging administration.
- To configure, monitor, and troubleshoot replication. Chapter 40, "Replication and Its Administration," details many of the specifics regarding the administration of replication in the Domino environment.

- To enable calendaring and scheduling within the organization.
- To configure, monitor, and troubleshoot connectivity and network security to servers within the domain or outside the domain over the intranet, Internet, or extranet.
- In the case of Domino Advanced Services, to configure clustering, billing and monitoring, failover, load balancing, and partitioned servers.

Understanding the Domino Administration Tools Available

Domino provides the administrator with a number of tools with which to perform the tasks enumerated in the last section. The tools consist of processes and applications, databases, console commands, and configuration settings. The most important of these include

- The Domino Administrator, specifically the Server and Configuration tabs within the Domino Administrator, from which all other tools are accessible or whose function can be achieved. The Configuration tab is shown in Figure 42.1.

Figure 42.1
The Configuration tab within the Domino Administrator.

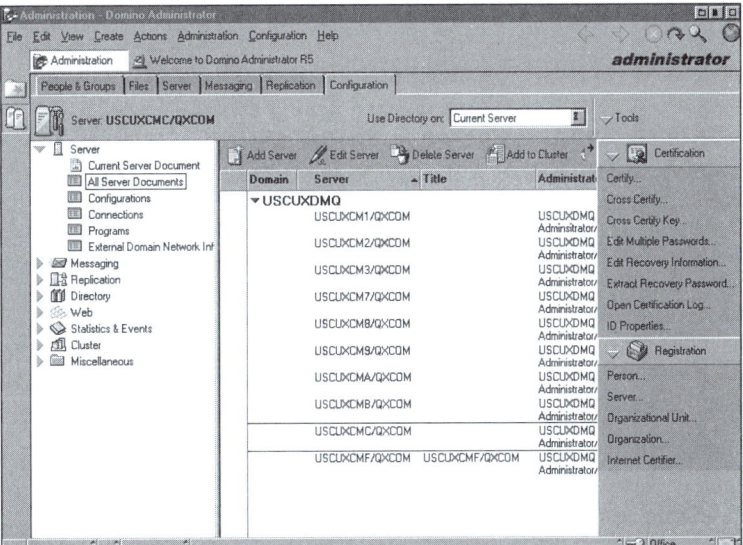

- The Web Administration tool facilitating the performance of administration tasks through a Web browser.
- The Administration Process automating such administrative tasks as the recertification, renaming, deletion, and upgrading to hierarchical naming of users and servers.
- Server programs automating such administrative tasks as the compaction of all databases on a server, the updating of all view indexes within databases on a server, or the refreshing/replacement of the design of all databases given specific design templates on a server.

- The Agent Manager task controlling who can run agents and when they can run on each server.
- Administration databases facilitating the collection and analysis of data about the system. These include the log file (LOG.NSF), the Administration Requests database (ADMIN4.NSF), the Statistics database (STATREP.NSF), the Certification Log (CERTLOG.NSF), the Database Catalog (CATALOG.NSF), and the MAIL.BOX file:
    - The LOG.NSF records server-specific information on replication, mail routing, database activity, and network and modem communications. A sample log file record is shown in Figure 42.2.

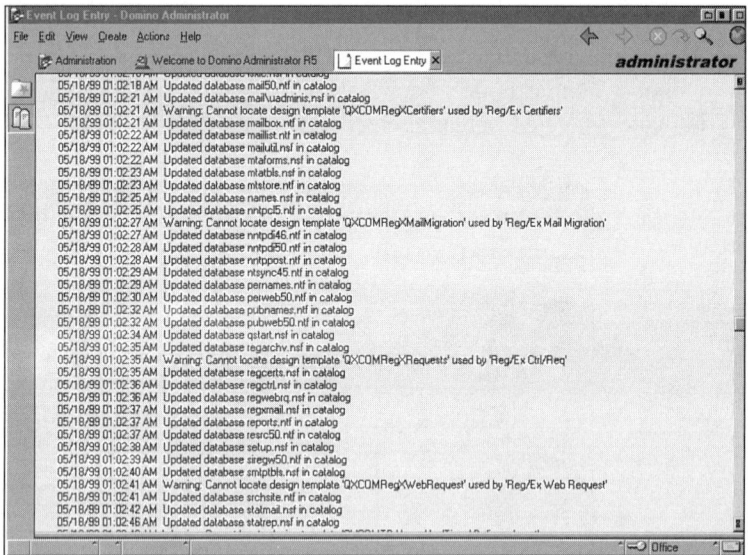

Figure 42.2
A sample log file record.

    - The ADMIN4.NSF posts all requests and responses to those requests associated with the Administration Process.
    - The STATREP.NSF tracks server statistics and records reported events.
    - The CERTLOG.NSF lists certification events pertaining to users and servers with their given certificates.
    - The CATALOG.NSF catalogs all major database attributes, including general database parameters, replication settings, full text index settings, and ACL settings.
    - The MAIL.BOX contains a listing of dead and pending mail.
- Server commands performing tasks such as shutting down or restarting a server.
- The NOTES.INI configuration settings defining how the Domino server runs.

Automating Many Administrative Tasks via the Administration Process

Of the tools mentioned, the Administration Process is the one most responsible for automating routine administrative tasks. Although the process runs by default at server start-up, you still must enable it for the domain. To do so, you begin by designating a particular server, preferably a central or hub server, to perform the role of administration server for the Domino Directory. When established, the designated server can maintain the Access Control List (ACL) within the Directory, perform name changes and removals, and replicate these to other servers.

The Domino Administration Process requires the following database and processing infrastructure on each server on which it is to run:

- A Certification Log database has been created on each server performing the role of administration server for selected databases. This Certification Log database keeps track of all users and servers in the organization and the certificates they have.
- An Administration Requests database has been created on each server performing the role of administration server for selected databases. The Administration Requests database, ADMIN4.NSF, is created automatically the first time you run the Administration Process on a server. The views available within the Administration Requests database are shown in Figure 42.3.
- At least one hierarchically certified server exists within your Domino domain. If your naming scheme is flat and you do not have any hierarchically certified servers, manually certify one server with a hierarchical name. The Administration Process can be run only on a hierarchically named server.
- The Administration Process is running as a task on the selected server.
- You have designated yourself and other administrators to have the authority to modify Person and Server documents in the Domino Directory.
- As noted previously, you have specified an Administration Server for the Domino Directory.

After you have ensured that the necessary infrastructure for the Administration Process exists on your selected servers and you have established an administration server for your Domino Directory, you can proceed to assign administration servers for all other databases which you want the Administration Process to maintain. In this way, when you make modifications to user or server accounts using the Administration Process, the Administration Process in turn propagates these changes to all such target databases for which there exists an administration server.

Figure 42.3
The views within the Administration Requests database.

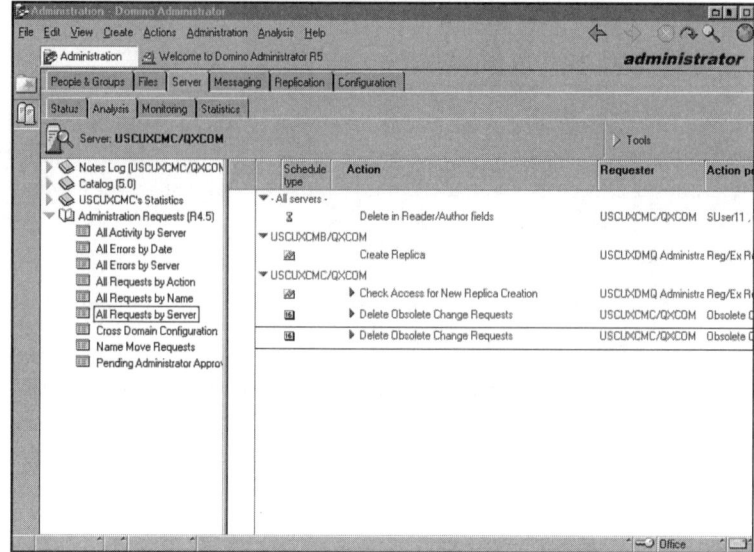

To assign an administration server for a particular database or set of databases, complete the following steps:

1. Ensure that you have Manager access in the database or set of databases for which you want to assign an Administration Server.
2. Choose the Files tab. The selected server's Domino Data Directory is displayed in the left pane.
3. Expand the Database task under the Tools selection.
4. Select the database or databases for which you want to assign an administration server.
5. Select Manage ACL. The Basics screen of the Manage ACL dialog box is displayed.
6. Move to the Advanced section.
7. The first setting within the Advanced section pertains to the Administration Server for the selected database or databases. Select the Modify Administration Server setting, choose the server from the list provided or add the target server desired, and, optionally, select whether you want the server to Modify fields of type Reader or Author. Keep in mind, however, that the Administration Process must be running on the target server and that the network connectivity infrastructure must also be in place between the designated target server and the Administration Server of the target server's Domino Directory.
8. Click OK to assign the target server as the Administration Server of the selected database or databases.

Chapter 38, "Administering Users, Groups, and Certification," provides extensive examples on how you use the Administration Process in renaming, deleting, and recertifying users within the Domino Directory. A subsequent section of this chapter provides a similar example on using the Administration Process to rename servers.

Becoming Familiar with the Major Documents Within the Domino Directory

The Domino Directory contains documents that manage directory and server-to-server communications. Many documents in the Domino Directory appear automatically from tasks that are performed by an administrator. For example, a new Person document is created automatically upon user registration, and a new Server document is created automatically upon server registration. Other documents can be generated as needed. For example, a Connection document can be created to connect a server for mail routing or replication.

Each document in the Domino Directory contains an Administration section to control edit access at the document level. The Administration section contains two fields: an Owners field and an Administrators field. By default, the Owners field contains the name of the person who created the document. The Administrators field is used to assign edit rights to individuals or groups at the document level.

The following lists the major document types accessible from the Servers view within the Domino Directory:

- Server\Certificates view displays the available Certifier documents which describe a certifier ID, including public key information.
- Server\Clusters view displays the available clusters and the servers belonging to those clusters.
- Server\Configurations view displays the available Configuration Settings documents, which contain server parameters and NOTES.INI settings.
- Server\Connections view displays the available Connection documents that provide server and domain information for connecting a server for mail routing and replication.
- Server\Deny Access Groups view displays the list of group documents designated as Deny List only within the Domino Directory.
- Server\Domains view displays the available Domain documents, which define name, location, and access to adjacent and non-adjacent Domino domains and non-Domino domains.
- Server\External Domain Network Information view displays the available External Domain Network Information documents, which contain names and addresses of servers from a secondary domain. These documents enable Notes clients to connect to servers in the secondary domain.
- Server\File Identification view displays the available File Identification documents, which contain the file attributes for application and multimedia types used by the Domino server.

- Server\Holidays view displays the available Holiday documents, which identify a date and repeat interval as a holiday.
- Server\Licenses view displays the list of users and servers currently registered within the Domino Directory.
- Server\Mail Users view displays the list of users, their mail addresses, and their mail file location per server within the Domino Directory.
- Server\Mail-In Databases and Resources view lists the currently configured Mail-In Database documents, which define the location and properties of a database that can receive mail and Resource documents that define the name, capacity, type, and resource database for a room or other type of scheduled item.
- Server\Networks view displays the list of networks configured in the Server documents within the Domino Directory.
- Server\Programs view displays the list of configured Program documents, which schedule server programs to run at times you specify.
- Server\Servers view lists the currently configured Server documents, which provide security, network (ports), server tasks, Internet protocols, configured MTAs, and miscellaneous settings for the servers within the Domino Directory.
- Server\Setup Profiles view lists the available User Setup Profile documents, which define a standard set of databases, dial-up connections, accounts, name servers, applet security, proxy, and MIME settings that you provide for users when you register them.
- Server\V3 Stats and Events view lists the currently configured Monitor documents.
- Server\Web Configurations view lists the currently configured File Protection Settings for the Domino servers within the Domino Directory.

Maintaining Server Configuration Documents and Running Server Tasks

There are two distinct areas of server configuration for which the system administrator has responsibility: documents within the Domino Directory, such as those described in the previous section, and the scheduling and running of server tasks.

Using the Domino Administrator to Maintain Documents Within the Domino Directory

The set of tasks subsumed under the Configuration tab within the Domino Administrator facilitates the administration of Domino server documents. Under this Configuration tab, there are eight categories: Server, Messaging, Replication, Directory, Web, Statistics & Events, Cluster, and Miscellaneous.

The Server Configuration category is particularly relevant to configuration of server documents. This provides subordinate categories or views for the Current Server Document, All Server Documents, Configurations, Connections, Programs, and External Domain Network Information.

Current Server Document

The Current Server Document category displays the document for the current server. It enables the administrator to perform a set of Create actions from the Domino Administrator Create drop-down menu: Create Server Certifier, Configuration Settings, Connection, Domain, External Domain Network Information, Holiday, Mail-In Database, Program, and Resource. The complete set of Create actions available when positioned on a given server within the Domino Administrator is shown in Figure 42.4. It also enables the administrator to edit the current server document, add the server to a cluster, or perform a set of Web-related Create actions: Create Virtual Server, Create URL Mapping/Redirection, Create File Protection, and Create Realm.

Figure 42.4
The complete set of Create actions relevant to Domino server administration available to the administrator within the Domino Administrator.

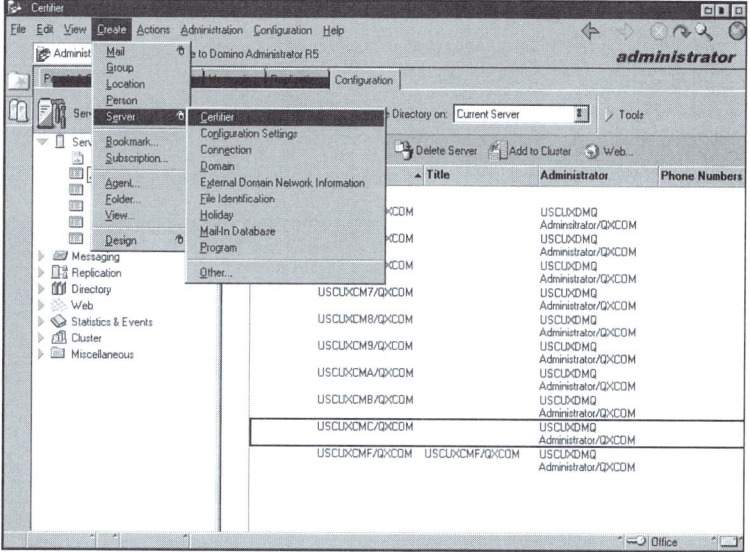

When positioned on the Current Server Document within a specific domain, the Domino Administrator Actions drop-down menu also enables the administrator to perform the Edit Server action. The same action can be initiated by clicking the Edit Server button above the current selected document. The Current Server Document in edit mode is shown in Figure 42.5.

Figure 42.5
The server document entered in edit mode by selecting the Edit Server button above the viewed Current Server document.

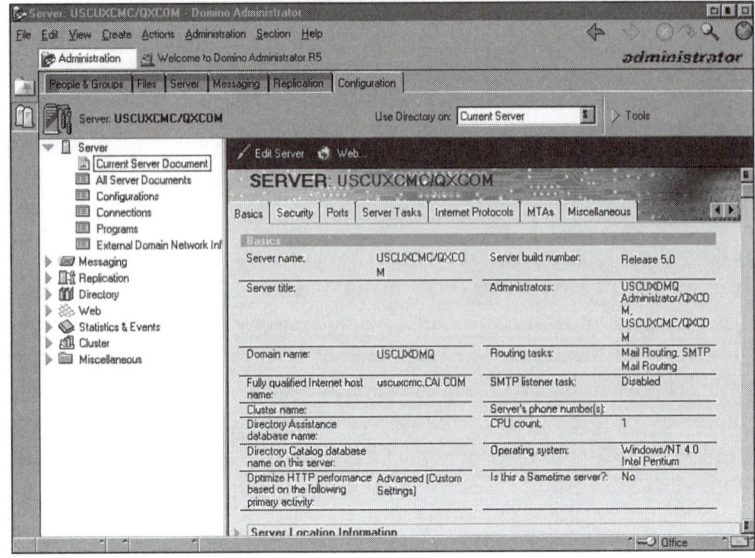

SERVER DOCUMENT

The Server Document contains nine embedded tabs, as shown in Figure 42.6. These cover the following areas:

Figure 42.6
The Server document displaying its nine embedded configuration tabs.

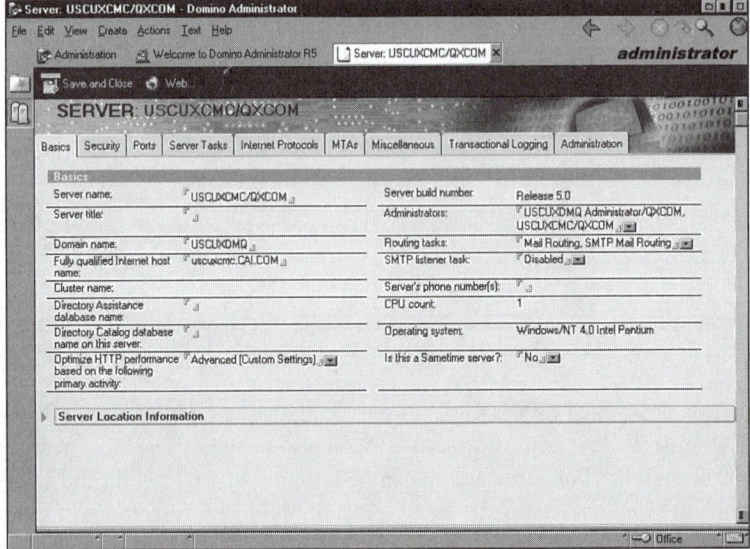

- Basics
- Security
- Ports
- Server Tasks
- Internet Protocols
- MTAs
- Miscellaneous
- Transactional Logging
- Administration

One document must be set up for every server in your organization. The Server Name field, the Domain field, and the Administrators field are required, and are filled in automatically based on the information you supply when the server is first registered.

On the Basics tab, you specify server location information, including the telephone numbers and dialing rules to use for dialing, and any additional information, such as which mail server, Passthru server, or InterNotes server to use.

On the Security tab, you specify settings for general server access, HTTP access, use of the server for pass-through, agent execution restrictions, and restrictions on the use of the Notes Object Interface (NOI) by Java or JavaScript agents.

On the Ports tab, you specify the active Notes Network ports, the SSL settings for Internet ports, and the standard and SSL port parameters for each of the major Internet server tasks: Web, Directory, News, Mail, and the NOI.

On the Server Tasks tab, youspecify the parameters for each of the major server tasks: the Administration Process, the Agent Manager, the Domain Indexer, the Directory Cataloger, the Internet Cluster Manager, and the Web Retriever.

On the Internet Protocols tab, you specify the server task configuration parameters for the major Internet server tasks: HTTP, Domino Web Engine, IIOP, LDAP, and NNTP.

On the MTAs tab, you specify the configurations for the R4.x SMTP MTA, the X.400 MTA, and the cc:Mail MTA. On the Miscellaneous tab, you specify general contact and administration information.

On the Transactional Logging tab, you enable or disable transactional logging.

A detailed explanation of each of the field settings within the Server document is provided in Chapter 35, "Initial Configuration of Servers with the Domino Directories."

All Server Documents

The All Server Documents category displays a view containing the Domain, Server, Title, Administrator, Phone Numbers, and Routing Tasks for each server. It also enables the administrator to perform the same set of server configuration create and action verbs as described for the individual server document itself.

Configuration Documents

The Configuration Documents category displays a view containing the Configuration documents for the given domain. It provides a view consisting of the servername for the given configuration, the configuration parameters for the given server, and when the document was last updated.

Understanding Server Configuration Documents in the Domino Directory

Using a Server Configuration document in the Domino Directory, you can specify parameters pertaining to the LDAP task, the Router/SMTP task, MIME conversions, and NOTES.INI settings for a single server, a group of servers, or for all servers in a domain. A server Configuration Settings document, shown in Figure 42.7, enables you to centralize server administration and thereby modify server settings remotely from one location.

Figure 42.7
The Server Configuration document displaying its six embedded configuraton tabs of Basics, LDAP, Router/SMTP, MIME, NOTES.INI Settings, and Administration.

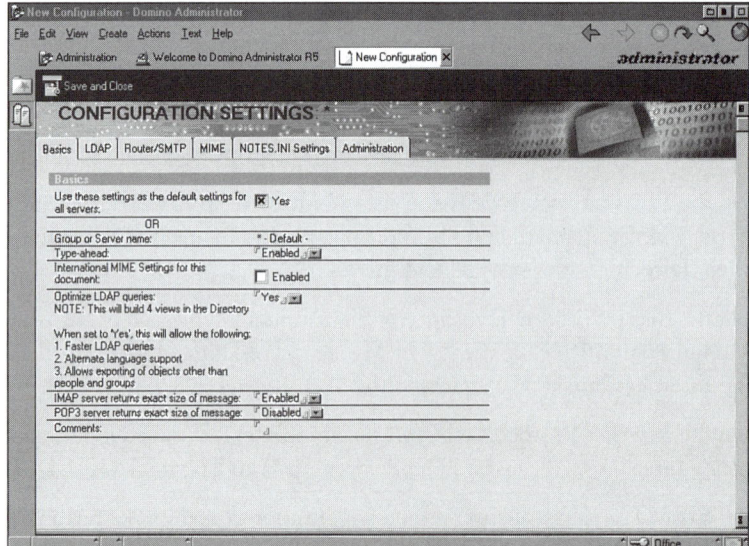

In general, servers evaluate Server Configuration documents in the following order: The individual server ranks documents specific to itself with the highest precedence. Second, it ranks documents containing a group specification, within which it is an individual member. Finally, it evaluates the documents pertaining to all servers within the domain.

Understanding How a Server Updates Its Configuration Settings

Whenever the individual server reinitializes or starts up, it scans the Domino Directory for Server Configuration documents pertaining to it. The server then reads these settings into memory and updates the NOTES.INI file accordingly. Approximately every five minutes thereafter, it checks the Domino Directory for modifications to the configuration documents. When it encounters a new or modified configuration setting, it reads the new or modified settings into memory and updates the NOTES.INI file. The latency is approximately five minutes. When updating the configuration settings for remote servers, this delay can be increased. This stems from the fact that a replication cycle must occur between the local and remote servers. Furthermore, upon completion of the replication cycle, the receiving server must update its views containing the documents. The delay usually averages twenty minutes following the last replication cycle before the configuration settings take effect on the remote servers.

PREPARING TO CONFIGURE MULTIPLE SERVERS

By grouping your servers into functional sets, such as mail servers, database servers, and Internet application servers, you can create configuration documents for each group, assigning them the same settings. In this way, you increase your administrative accuracy and efficiency.

CREATING A SERVER CONFIGURATION DOCUMENT

To create a Server Configuration document for a single server, a group of servers, or all servers within the domain, complete the following steps:

1. Within the Domino Administrator, select the server to be administered from the server icon in the far left of the Domino Administrator screen.
2. Choose the Configuration tab and select the Configuration view.
3. Choose Create, Server, Configuration or Actions, Add Configuration from the main drop-down menu, or click the Add Configuration button within the central pane of the Configuration tab.
4. On the Basics tab, specify whether the settings are to be used as the default settings for all servers, whether they apply to a Group of servers, or whether they apply to an individual server. In the Server name field, you can enter the name of a server or a group of servers. If you specify that this is to be used as the default settings for all servers, the asterisk (*) is placed in the Server name field and becomes the default configuration. If you create more than one default document, the server does not check for duplicates and usually uses the first document encountered. You then complete the Basics tab by specifying the following:
    - Whether to enable International MIME Settings for this document   This works in collaboration with the International Character Set definitions you provide on the subordinate tabs under the MIME tab. You must enable this parameter for the International MIME settings to take effect.
    - Whether to optimize LDAP queries   When selecting Yes, Domino constructs four hidden views in the Domino Directory: $LDAPS, $LDAPG, $LDAPCN,

and $LDAPHIER. These improve searches on both Person documents and Server documents. Specifically, they improve searches on common name, last name, and first name, and on documents within the Domino Directory created from custom forms. The optimization also facilitates the display of search results to LDAP clients according to the name hierarchy in the Directory tree.

- Whether to enable the IMAP server to return exact size of messages   When selecting Enabled, the IMAP server calculates the exact size of the message upon receipt of such a request from the IMAP client; otherwise, it returns an estimated size. Enabling this option may impact performance.
- Whether to enable the POP3 server to return exact size of message   When selecting Enabled, the POP3 server returns the exact size of the message in response to the STAT command. This means that the entire message is converted and this may lead to timeouts of the PASS command.

5. On the LDAP tab (visible for default configurations), specify the following:
    - The queriable fields that anonymous LDAP users can access   By default, anonymous LDAP clients can access a set of fields in both Person and Group documents in the Domino Directory and search the FullName field within the Certifier documents. You can alter this configuration by adding or removing fields from the list for the supported forms. Open the LDAP Field List dialog box by clicking the <<>> button. Select the form that you want to grant query access and and click the Show Fields button. The list of fields for the selected form are displayed. Select the fields desired and then click Add. Click OK. Note however that LDAP clients cannot search information for several form types—among them, Location, Domain, External Domain Network Information, Holiday, User Setup Profile, Configuration Settings, Connection, and Cross Certificate.
    - Whether to grant LDAP users write access   You enable this option to grant authenticated LDAP clients the ability to add, delete, or modify entries in the Domino Directory within which this Configuration Settings document resides. Note that the LDAP clients must have the proper access within the ACL of the Domino Directory. This entails Editor access to Add entries, Editor access or Author access with the modifier role to modify entries, and the Delete documents privilege to delete entries.
    - The maximum number of seconds Domino allows a search query to take before timing out.
    - The maximum number of entries Domino returns to an LDAP search query.
    - The minimum number of characters permitted for a wildcard search.
    - Whether to allow alternate language processing. This enables the Domino server to support LDAP client operations specifying alternate language information.
    - Entry modification rules to follow when Domino encounters multiple entries matching the distinguished name being compared or modified. You can select

from not modifying any entries, modifying the first, or modifying all matches of the distinguished name.

6. On the Router/SMTP tab, specify Basic configuration parameters, Restrictions and Controls parameters, Message Tracking parameters, and Advanced parameters.

   On the Basics subordinate tab, specify the following:

   - A number from 1 to 10 to set the Number of MAIL.BOX files for each server using this Configuration document.
   - Whether to enable SMTP to be used when sending messages outside the local Internet domain Enabling such routing allows SMTP to route mail outside the local Domino domain. Disabling such routing prompts Domino to use Notes routing based on SMTP Foreign Domain documents and Connection documents.
   - Whether to have Domino use SMTP to transfer messages within the local Internet domain When specifying MIME messages, Domino uses SMTP routing to route mail to other Domino servers within the same named network capable of receiving SMTP mail. When specifying All messages, Domino uses SMTP routing to route Notes and MIME format messages. This causes Domino to convert Notes format messages into MIME format, which may lead to a loss of fidelity and performance. When specifying Disabled, Domino uses Notes routing between servers in the same named network.
   - Whether to have Domino use SMTP routing to route mail to other Domino servers configured to receive incoming SMTP mail within the same local Internet domain or use Notes routing to route mail to other servers in external Notes named networks When specifying Always, Domino uses SMTP routing to route mail to other Domino servers configured to receive incoming SMTP mail within the same Internet domain. When specifying Only if in same Notes Named Network, Domino uses Notes routing to route mail to other servers in external Notes Named Networks.
   - What part of the name Domino uses to perform a non–case sensitive match during Address lookup When specifying Fullname and then Local Part, Domino first performs a non–case sensitive match for the entire Internet address and, upon failure, follows with a match for only the part preceding the @. Similarly, when specifying Fullname only, Domino performs a non–case sensitive match for the entire Internet address; or when specifying Local Part, Domino performs a non–case sensitive match for only the part preceding the @.
   - Whether to perform an exhaustive lookup during a Directory search When enabled, Domino searches all directories to ensure that there are no duplicate recipients. When disabled, Domino searches until it finds the first Directory instance of the recipient.
   - What, if any, name to use as a relay host for messages leaving the local Internet domain When specified, this host name or domain name is used to send

messages outside the local Internet domain. This could represent a firewall or Internet service provider.
- What, if any, name to use as a host name for the local Internet domain smart host When specified, Domino routes mail to SMTP recipients who are not in the local Domino Directory to this smart host.
- Whether to route all incoming SMTP messages to a smart host When enabled, Domino routes all incoming SMTP messages to the smart host for name lookup. When disabled, Domino routes only messages with recipients not found in the local Domino Directory to the smart host.
- Whether to use Dynamic lookup only (DNS only), local lookup only (hosts file only), or Dynamic and then local for the Host name lookup for host name resolution. Dynamic lookup utilizes only the server's DNS server. Local lookup utilizes the server's host file.

On the Restrictions and Controls subordinate tab, specify the following:
- Router Restrictions delimit the domains, organizations, and organizational units from which the Domino router should allow mail or deny mail. They also include a maximum message size parameter, whether to send messages between certain sizes as low priority, and whether to obey database quotas.
- SMTP Inbound Controls delimit the external Internet domains and hosts from which the Domino server allows or denies relaying service, both to the local Internet domains and to other external Internet domains. It also includes parameters for Inbound Connection Controls in the form of hostname connection verification and allowing and denying connections from specific hostnames or IP addresses. Similarly, Inbound Sender Control parameters exist to verify the sender's domain and allow or deny messages based on Internet addresses or domains. Finally, Inbound Intended Recipient Controls allow or deny access to specific Internet addresses.
- SMTP Outbound Controls delimit the Internet addresses or Notes addresses allowed to send or denied access from sending messages to the Internet.
- Delivery Controls define a set of server inbound processing parameters. They delimit the maximum number of delivery threads, whether to encrypt all delivered mail, and whether to impose an execution timeout on any predelivery agents.
- Transfer Controls define a corollary set of outbound processing parameters. These include the maximum number of transfer threads and concurrent transfer threads, the maximum hop count, the low priority mail routing time range, the initial transfer retry interval, and the expired message purge interval.

On the Message Tracking subordinate tab, specify whether to enable message tracking for the given configuration. If enabled, list any users or servers for which you do not want to track messages. Specify the message tracking collection interval. This number equates to how often message tracking activity is logged in the Mail Tracking Store database. Decide whether to log message subjects, and, if enabled, for whom you do not want to log subjects. Finally, specify which users and servers are allowed to track messages and subjects. If you want to track messages across multiple servers, you have to include all participating servers in the latter two lists.

On the Advanced subordinate tab, specify which Inbound and Outbound SMTP Commands and Extensions are enabled and general controls pertaining to logging level, transfer controls, name lookup restrictions, cluster failover, and failure message files. The Inbound SMTP Commands and Extensions include the following:

- SIZE to reject inbound messages greater than the maximum size specified.
- Pipelining to send multiple SMTP commands in the same network packet thereby improving performance.
- DSN to generate, upon request, Deliver Status Notifications to a messsage's sender for an SMTP message.
- 8-bit MIME to send multinational characters without encoding if enabled, or with encoding if disabled.
- HELP to support the HELP command.
- VRFY to support the VRFY command to verify usernames.
- EXPN to support the EXPN command to expand mailing lists to show individual usernames.
- ETRN to support the ETRN command enabling the server to accept inbound requests to send queued outbound messages.
- SSL negotiated over TCP/IP port to enable the server to connect securely to another server by creating an SSL channel over the TCP/IP port.
- The Outbound SMTP commands and extensions include the outbound derivatives of the SIZE, Pipelining, DSN, and 8-bit MIME extensions.
- The failure message files configuration enables you to specify text files with customized messages for specific failures. The customized message is appended to the default text for the message. The failures whose messages can be augmented in this way include Transfer, Delivery, Message expiration, Domain, Server, Username, Size, and Restriction failures.

7. On the MIME tab, specify Basic configuration parameters, Conversion options, Settings by Character Set Groups, and Advanced configuration parameters.

8. On the Basics subordinate tab, specify the primary character set and any secondary character set groups to be supported. All International MIME settings rely on enabling the International MIME settings for this document parameter on the main Basics tab.

9. On the Conversions Options tab, specify the General parameter of whether to return receipts. For the Inbound parameters, specify the length of the inbound message line and whether to autodetect the character set if the message carries no such character set

information. For the Outbound parameters, specify whether to use Base64, QuotedPrintable, Uuencode, or BinHex as the attachment encoding method to use on outbound conversions and whether to convert tabs to spaces. Additionally, specify the length of the outbound message line and whether to look up Internet addresses for Notes addresses when the Internet address is not in the document.

10. On the Settings by Character Set Groups tab, define font options for Inbound HTML and Plain Text and Outbound Header and Body Character Sets and Encoding methods.

11. On the Advanced tab, specify the Advanced Inbound Message Options and Advanced Outbound Message Options. The inbound options include the following: whether re-sent headers take precedence over original headers, whether to remove group names from headers, whether to add a recipient address to the BCC line in the address header if it does not appear in any address header, what 8-bit character set is to be assumed to be the character set for non-MIME messages or MIME messages with an unknown character set, and mappings between character set aliases and supported character sets. The outbound options include the following: whether to use AppleDouble or BinHex4.0 encoding method for Macintosh attachment conversion; which RFC822 display name format, if any, to use for outbound recipient naming; whether to include nonstandard or private items necessary for Notes clients running such applications; a list of Notes item names to be removed from the message header prior to transmission; which character set to use when converting a multilingual message to MIME; and outbound character set alias mapping between supported character sets and known aliases.

12. On the NOTES.INI Settings tab, select the Set/Modify parameters button. The Server Configuration Parameters dialog box opens. Open the Select a Standard Parameter dialog by clicking the Item arrow. Select one of the standard parameters—for example, the ADMINPINTERVAL specifying the interval cycle for when the Administration Process performs request handling—and click OK. Assign it a value—for example, 30 (minutes). Click next to assign another standard parameter or OK to return to the main NOTES.INI Settings tab.

13. On the Administration tab, review and, if desired, modify the Owner and Administrators fields.

14. Save and close the document.

A further explanation of the configuration settings is provided in Chapter 35.

UNDERSTANDING SETTINGS YOU CANNOT SPECIFY IN A SERVER CONFIGURATION DOCUMENT

You cannot edit every parameter in the NOTES.INI using a Server Configuration document. You must enter some configuration settings using the Server document. This maintains the integrity of Domino security. You should also refrain from editing the NOTES.INI file directly to specify these settings. This can lead to server errors. The parameters that cannot be updated using a Server Configuration document include

- Any parameter beginning with $
- ServerName
- Server_Title
- Type
- Form
- Names
- Allow_Access
- Deny_Access
- Create_File_Access
- Create_Replica_Access
- Admin_Access
- Allow_Passthru_Access
- Allow_Passthru_Targets
- Allow_Passthru_Clients
- Allow_Passthru_Callers
- Ports
- KitType
- Domain
- MailServer
- MailFile
- Server_Console_Password (You can set this parameter only at the server console.)

MODIFYING THE NOTES.INI

In addition to editing the NOTES.INI parameter settings using either a Configuration Settings document or a Server document as detailed in the preceding sections, you can edit the NOTES.INI in two further ways:

- You can use the Set Configuration server command at the console to write a specific setting to the NOTES.INI file. This setting is written to the Server Configuration document specific to the server, if one exists, or a new document is created.
- You can edit the NOTES.INI file directly in a text editor. If you do edit the NOTES.INI file directly, however, make sure to make a backup copy of the file in case you encounter

problems and want to recover your previous version. Because directly editing the NOTES.INI can lead to file errors and impair the operation of the Domino server, it is not a recommended practice.

CONNECTION DOCUMENTS

The Connections category displays all current Connection documents. It provides a view consisting of the destinations for the given connection, the connection's type, the port being used, the schedule for the given connection, the interval between successful connections, the tasks associated with the given connection, what (if any) priority databases are to be replicated, and whether the connection is direct or dial-up.

UNDERSTANDING SERVER CONNECTION DOCUMENTS

You use Connection documents to configure servers to route mail and to replicate databases. Replication between servers requires a single Connection document. Mail routing requires two Connection documents, one document for each direction. Within the Connection document, you can specify the times, days, and intervals between scheduled connections for two servers, and whether this is for mail routing, replication, or both. You can also create multiple Connection documents between two servers, which enables you to schedule mail routing and replication separately.

A detailed explanation of Connection documents is provided in Chapter 35, Chapter 39, and Chapter 40.

PROGRAM DOCUMENTS

The Programs category displays all current program documents. It provides a view consisting of the programs, their command lines, whether they are currently enabled, and their repeat interval.

UNDERSTANDING PROGRAM DOCUMENTS IN THE DOMINO DIRECTORY

You create a Program document to schedule tasks and programs to run at a regularly scheduled time or at server startup on your Domino servers. A sample of a program document is shown in Figure 42.8. Using a Program document gives you greater control over when programs run. Instead of being limited to specifying the exact hour of the day when a program runs, as is necessary in the NOTES.INI file, you can specify a range of times, a day of the week, and a regular interval when the program runs on the server within a Program document.

MAINTAINING SERVER CONFIGURATION DOCUMENTS AND RUNNING SERVER TASKS | 1025

Figure 42.8
The server Program document used to schedule Notes tasks.

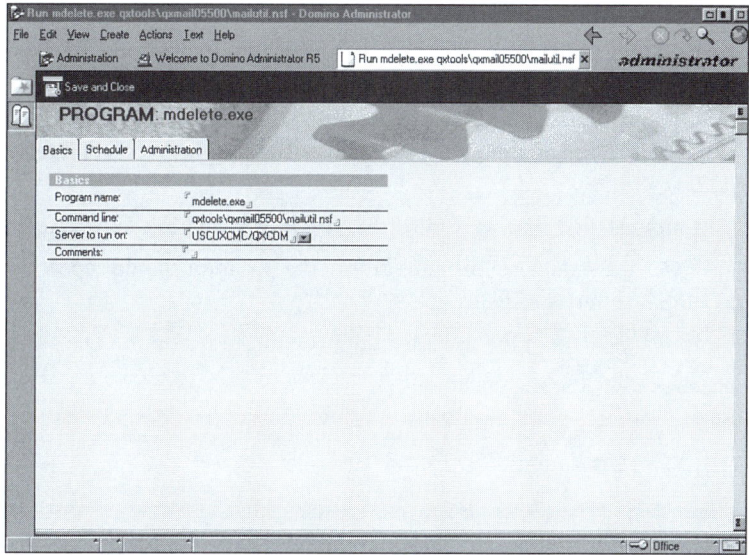

USING A PROGRAM DOCUMENT TO SCHEDULE PROGRAMS

To create a Program document to schedule tasks and programs on your Domino server, complete the following steps:

1. Within the Domino Administrator, select the server to be administered from the server icon in the far left of the Domino Administrator screen.
2. Choose the Configuration tab and select the Programs view.
3. Choose Create, Server, Program or Actions, Add Program from the main drop-down menu, or click the Add Program button within the central pane of the Configuration tab.
4. On the Basics tab, enter the name of the server program or script to run in the Program name field. You can use the following characters: A–Z, 0–9, & (ampersand), - (hyphen) , . (period), _ (underscore), ' (apostrophe), / (forward slash). You can also use spaces.

   In the Command line field, enter the command to start the program and any arguments required by the command.

   In the Server to run on field, enter the full hierarchical name of the server on which to run the program.

   Specify any program description or comments in the Comments field.

5. On the Schedule tab, select ENABLED or STARTUP ONLY, depending on whether you want to specify a specific schedule or only want the program to run when the server starts.

   If you specified ENABLED, enter the schedule when you want the program to execute. This includes providing values for the Run at times, Repeat interval, and Days of week fields.

   Enter the first time of day for the program to run in the Run at times field.

   Enter the number of minutes before the program should repeat its execution in the Repeat interval of field.

   Enter the days of the week for the program to run in the Days of week field.

6. Save and close the document.

Running Server Tasks

Administering the server also means ensuring that full-time server tasks such as the replicator and the mail router start up when the server starts. In addition, other server tasks can be scheduled to run on a periodic basis from the `NOTES.INI` file, from a Server Configuration document, or from a Program document. Tasks can also be run manually from the server console on an as-needed basis.

Depending on the functions the server performs, various tasks are initiated at startup or run periodically. Some of the more important tasks include those from the following list:

- `Adminp`   The Administration Process task automates many routine administrative tasks. By default, `Adminp` is included in the `ServerTasks NOTES.INI` setting to run at server startup.

- `Amgr`   The Agent Manager controls who has the authority to execute agents on a specified server. By default, `Amgr` is included in the `ServerTasks NOTES.INI` setting to run at server startup.

- `Catalog`   The `Catalog` task updates a database catalog (`CATALOG.NSF`) that is created on a server the first time the `Catalog` task runs. The catalog lists all databases available to users of that server. It includes such database attributes as the database location, indexing configuration, ACL properties, search and result forms, file system configuration forms, and the database's nearest replica. By default, `Catalog` is included in the `ServerTasksAt1 NOTES.INI` setting, meaning that the task will run at 1 a.m.

- `Collect`   The `Collect` server task summarizes statistics from one or more servers. The statistics collected cover the following areas: system information, such as disk and memory usage, server configuration, and load; messaging performance; database and replication performance; communications and networking performance; and calendaring and scheduling. By configuring a Server Statistic Collection Profile document, you can designate a particular server to collect statistics from a list of specified servers. The default for this, however, is to collect data only from the server on which the server `Collect` task resides. Unless otherwise specified, the `Collect` task creates a `STATREP.NSF` as its repository where the statistic reports reside. You can load `Collect` at the server console, or you can schedule it to run at startup by including it in the `ServerTasks NOTES.INI` setting.

- `Compact` The `Compact` server task gets rid of unused whitespace in databases. Blocks of whitespace are left in the database after documents are deleted. Compact recovers that whitespace. You can load `Compact` at the server console, or you can schedule it to run at a set time in the `NOTES.INI` file or a Program document.

Additional information on `Compact` is provided in Chapter 41, "Administering Files and Databases."

> **Caution**
>
> When you run `Compact` on a Notes R4 database, the database is converted to R5 format unless the database has been named with an `.NS4` file extension. You can revert to R4 format by running `Compact` with an `-r` flag (for example, `Load Compact DATABASE.NSF -r`, where *DATABASE.NSF* is the filename of the database to revert to R4 format).

- `DECS` The Domino Enterprise Connection Services task provides dynamic access to a host of relational databases. Using the `DECS` Administrator template, you can map fields in forms directly to fields in relational database tables, making these accessible to your users without storing any data within native Domino databases. You can load `DECS` at the server console, or you can schedule it to run at startup by including it in the `ServerTasks NOTES.INI` setting.

- `Design` The `Design` task updates the design of databases with changes made to the templates on which the database design is based. The `Design` template should be placed in the Notes Data Directory and should be replicated to all servers on which the database resides. The `Design` task runs by default at 1 a.m. and should be followed by the `Updall` task to rebuild views changed during the `Design` task.

Additional information on the `Design` task is provided in Chapter 41.

- `Event` The `Event` task is an optional task used for event reporting. When `Event` is loaded for the first time at the server console, or when it is put into the `ServerTasks` setting in the `NOTES.INI` file, an `EVENTS5.NSF` database is created automatically to collect server statistics and event documents. Events are specific, system-performance statistics that surpass predefined parameters.

- `Fixup` The `Fixup` task fixes corrupted databases by locating corrupt documents and removing them completely from the database, including the document-deletion stub. If a replica of the database exists, the document can be replicated back into the database after the document has been completely deleted. `Fixup` runs at startup and fixes the Notes log, but it does not locate and rebuild corrupted views. You can schedule `Fixup` to run using a Program document or a `NOTES.INI` setting, but be aware that it takes significant CPU resources to run. Therefore, avoid running `Fixup` from the server console during the day unless absolutely necessary.

Additional information on the Fixup task is provided in Chapter 41.

- `ICM` The Internet Cluster Manager server task coupled with native Domino clustering extends failover and load balancing to Web browser clients utilizing HTTP or HTTPS services. The ICM maintains information about availability of servers in the cluster and the distribution of databases. HTTP clients direct requests for Notes databases to the `ICM` via the Domino HTTP server. The `ICM` ensures that the clients are connected to an appropriate server and the workload is balanced across the servers in the cluster. You can load `ICM` at the server console, or you can schedule it to run at startup by including it in the `ServerTasks NOTES.INI` setting.

- `HTTP` The Domino Hypertext Transfer Protocol servertask provides standard HTTP access to Web browser clients. You can load `HTTP` at the server console, or you can schedule it to run at startup by including it in the `ServerTasks NOTES.INI` setting.

- `IMAP` The Domino Internet Mail Access Protocol server provides support for the IMAP protocol. IMAP-enabled clients can thereby retrieve messages from the IMAP server and store them locally, access messages directly from the server, or copy messages for offline use and then later synchronize with mail on the server. You can load `IMAP` at the server console, or you can schedule it to run at startup by including it in the `ServerTasks NOTES.INI` setting.

- `LDAP` The Lightweight Directory Access Protocol server task provides standard LDAP Directory access to clients running the LDAP protocol. LDAP-enabled applications can thereby query and, with the proper access permissions, modify entries in Domino Directories on the LDAP server. You can load `LDAP` at the server console, or you can schedule it to run at startup by including it in the `ServerTasks NOTES.INI` setting.

- `NNTP` The Network News Transport Protocol server task enables users to participate in private discussion groups or public USENET newsgroups using the Notes client, a standard NNTP newsreader, or a Web browser. You can load `NNTP` at the server console, or you can schedule it to run at startup by including it in the `ServerTasks NOTES.INI` setting.

- `POP3` The Post Office Protocol Version 3 server task provides standard POP3 Internet Mail support to clients running POP3. It enables such clients to retrieve mail from the host server running POP3. You can load `POP3` at the server console, or you can schedule it to run at startup by including it in the `ServerTasks NOTES.INI` setting.

- `Replica` The `Replica` task serves to replicate data between servers or between servers and clients. It starts at system startup by default, and then remains idle until there is a scheduled replication, a replication request from the server console, or a request for a replication from another server. It is possible to have a database server that allows other servers to perform only Pull-Push replication—in which case, the `Replica` task is not

- Router   The Router task is used to route mail, as well as documents automatically generated by other tasks, such as the Event task, and by workflow applications that send documents to mail-in databases. By default, the Router task is included in the ServerTasks NOTES.INI setting to run at server startup.

- Update and Updall   The server indexer tasks, Update and Updall, update database views and full text indexes. They also detect and rebuild any corrupted indexes. The Update task updates all active views in a database when a user or server task, such as the Replicator, updates any documents in the database. It also updates the full text index if one has been created for the database. The Updall task updates view indexes and full text indexes on all databases on the server. As documents are added to databases, views need updating, and full text indexes get out-of-date because new documents are not automatically added to the index. The Updall task can be run on specific databases that may have damaged view indexes as one way to repair the view. (Another way is to create a new replica of the database and then delete the original that has the damaged view index.)

  By default, the Update task is included in the ServerTasks NOTES.INI setting to load at server startup; the Updall task is included in the ServerTasksAt2 setting to run at 2 a.m.

  You can use a number of optional flags to control what is updated. Note that the flags are all optional. Updall can be run without any arguments. The following table describes these flags:

Flag	Description
-f	Updates full text indexes without updating views.
-s	Updates full text indexes that have an Immediate or Hourly update frequency, and scheduled update frequencies if the Updall task is initiated from a Program document.
-m	Same as -s, but updates scheduled update frequencies even if no Program document exists for Updall.
-h	Updates full text indexes only if they have Immediate or Hourly update frequencies.
-l	Updates all view and full text indexes.
-x	Rebuilds full-text indexes.

Modifying Networks and Domains

To set up an additional server in an organization, you register the server, run the setup program, verify your ports, modify Connection documents, and set up access security. All these changes are replicated throughout the organization because they are all contained in the

Domino Directory. But what happens to existing servers when you merge or split Domino domains?

MERGING DOMAINS

The Domino Directory provides a unified identity for all the Domino servers and users who share it. It is associated with a domain used for mail routing. The domain name and the organization name are usually the same.

If your company is merging with another company, you will probably want to merge Domino Directories to simplify administration. Otherwise, you would have to address some users within your own corporation, using an explicit path to the other domain (for example, `John Smith/Sales/New York/Acme @ XYZ`).

To merge two domains, decide which Domino Directory will be used for the single domain. Copy from the other Domino Directory into the primary one all Person and Server documents you want to have in the merged domain. Determine whether you need any of the other documents (such as Connection documents and Group documents) and copy those as well. Edit them to reflect the setup in the new domain. For example, make sure that the servers in the old domain are now part of the `LocalDomainServers` group and no longer part of the `OtherDomainServers` group. When all the documents you require have been copied over, determine whether you need to recertify or cross-certify users and servers so that all users and servers can communicate within the single domain. When everyone can communicate successfully, delete the old Domino Directory (or rename it and save it until everything has been thoroughly tested). Edit the `Domain=` line in the `NOTES.INI` file on servers that have moved from the old domain so that the line reflects the name of the new domain.

SPLITTING DOMAINS

On occasion, you may want to split a single domain into multiple domains. For example, your company may have grown too large, and you decide to create multiple domains to more effectively delegate administration. Or you may be spinning off part of the organization.

Splitting a domain is essentially the reverse of merging two domains: Make a nonreplica copy of the Domino Directory and delete Person and Server documents from each Directory until it contains only the users and servers that belong in that domain. Change the name of the mail domain in the relevant Person documents, and the name of the domain and the network in the Server documents.

Edit and create Domain and Connection documents for the new domain to make sure that the new domain can communicate with the old domain (if appropriate). Change the administrator names and edit the `LocalDomainServers` group. Edit the `Domain=` line in the `NOTES.INI` file, and then shut down the server by typing e or q at the server console. Start the server again by clicking the Server icon. This process reinitializes the server with the new information in the `NOTES.INI` file. When the server is running again, replicate the Domino Directory to other servers in the domain.

MOVING A DOMINO SERVER WITHIN THE ORGANIZATION

The process of moving a server within an organization is virtually the same as moving a person within the organization. The administrator requests certification for the server and selects the new certifier ID. The Administration Process handles the remainder of the process, changing the name of the server throughout the Domino Directory.

To be specific, one method of renaming a hierarchically named server consists of the following steps:

1. Within the Configuration tab of the Domino Administrator, expand the Server selection and select the All Server Documents view.
2. In the middle pane, select the Server document or documents to be recertified.
3. From the Actions menu, select the Recertify Selected Servers action. A Choose Certifier dialog box appears. Select the desired Certifier ID and click Open. The Renew Certifiers in Selected Entries dialog box appears.
4. Optionally, supply a value in the Only renew certificates that will expire before field, and click Certify.

The request is automatically posted in the Adminstration Requests database and in the Certification Log database on the server where the request was made. If this is not the server listed as the administration server for the Domino Directory, the Administration Requests database is replicated to the administration server.

At this point, the Administration Process on the administration server updates the Server document in the Domino Directory with the new certificate, and the Domino Directory is then replicated throughout the domain. The Administration Process also automatically changes the ACLs in the Domino Directory and in other databases to correspond to the new name. Further, it updates any documents in the Directory where the previous name appeared.

Such updates can include the home-server information in each Person's user document, if the server is a home server for some users. Similarly, it can include changes in the Security section of the Server documents and in pass-through Connection documents, if the server is a Passthru server or is the destination of a Passthru server.

Because moving to a new Domino organizational infrastructure may make available alternative communication paths, the administrator may want to reprioritize ports and review the lowest-cost routing connections configured for the renamed servers. For example, the server may now be able to communicate using TCP/IP over a local area network connection rather than having to dial in directly, now that the server is part of the organization it was formerly calling.

CHAPTER 42 MANAGING YOUR DOMINO SERVER CONFIGURATION

> **Note**
>
> Renaming a server that has a flat certificate is essentially the same as renaming a server that already has a hierarchical name, except that you must be aware that the Administration Process can be run only from a hierarchically named server. In place of the Recertify Selected Servers action, you use the Upgrade Server to Hierarchical action.

ANALYZING AND MONITORING SERVER PERFORMANCE

In addition to facilitating the configuration of the server, the Domino Administrator also facilitates the analysis and monitoring of Server performance.

Under the Servers tab, there are four embedded tabs: Status, Analysis, Monitoring, and Statistics. These are shown in Figure 42.9.

Figure 42.9
The Servers tab within the Domino Administrator displaying its four embedded tabs of Status, Analysis, Monitoring, and Statistics.

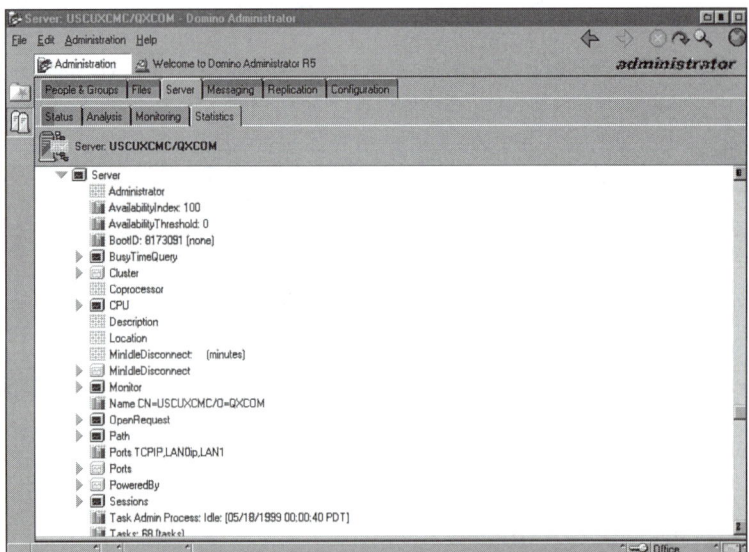

The Status embedded tab includes two views: one displaying Tasks and current Activity, and the other for Users with Databases Open and Minutes Idled.

The Status embedded tab also includes console actions facilitating the server console commands of User Broadcast, User Drop, Task Tell, Start, Stop, Replicate, Route Mail, Setup Ports, Secure Console, Stop Port, and Shutdown:

Command	Description
User Broadcast	Send a message to specified users or to all users of the server.
User Drop	Close one or more server sessions.

Command	Description
Task Tell	Issue a command to a server task.
Task Start	Load and run a specified server task. The program must be in the server's search path.
Task Stop	Shut down a specified server task on the server.
Replicate	Force replication between two servers: the destination server specified and the source from which the command is entered.
Route Mail	Send mail immediately to a specific server on another network.
Setup Ports	Configure the network adapter card or communications port.
Stop Port	Disable transactions (or messages) on the given port. This enables the administrator to make changes to the port to take effect immediately following a subsequent Start Port command.
Secure Console	Password-protect the console.
Shutdown	Shut down the server.

The Analysis embedded tab facilitates the analysis of the Notes Log, the Database Catalog, and server statistics and views within the Administration Requests databases. The statistics subcategory includes a comprehensive set of folders and views. These include Statistic Reports views (including Calendaring & Scheduling, Clusters, Commmunications, Mail & Databases, Network, System, and Web Server & Retriever); an Alarms view; an Events view; a Spreadsheet Export view; Graphs views (including System Loads, System Resources, and System Statistics); Trouble Tickets views (Alarm and Event); an Analysis Report view; a File Statistics view; and a Single Copy Object Store view.

The embedded tab also includes console actions facilitating the server console commands of Analyze Log, Analyze Cluster, and Decommission Server.

Analyze Log

The log analysis tool enables the administrator to search the log file on one or more servers for specific keywords and direct the output of this search to a specific database. In this way, the administrator can view a single Log Analysis database as opposed to multiple Domino log files. The search string specified can represent any length containing any type of character. It is not case sensitive. For example, when searching for all documents containing such words as warning, error, and fatal, Domino places any document containing one of these words, regardless of case, in the results database specified.

The results database contains one view, Log Events, categorized by server and capable of being sorted in ascending or descending order by server, date, or message. The view shows the date and time of events, their source (event or console message), and the text of the messages.

Analyze Cluster

Cluster analysis provides a mechanism for the administrator to generate a set of reports verifying that a server cluster is set up correctly. As part of the analysis, the administrator can specify the type(s) of analysis to be run and where the results are to be placed. For example, the administrator can evaluate the number of cluster members, consistent domain membership, consistent protocol support among cluster members, required server tasks running, consistent ACLs, disabled replication, consistent replication formulas, and existence of replicas within the cluster.

Decommission Server

Decommission Server provides a report on the steps to take an existing server out of service permanently. The Decommission Server Analysis creates a results database with detailed information comparing the source server and the target server. Any inconsistencies between the source and target servers are marked in the results database. The information in the results database serves as a guide for the administrator of what needs to be done before the source server can be decommissioned, such as adding protocol support, databases, server tasks, and so on, to the target server.

The Monitoring embedded tab provides two summary status displays of the servers and their processes within your currently selected domain: By State and By Timeline. The displays provide alternative depictions of server state. They include current task status and statistics on the number of users, the amount of dead mail, the amount of mail queued for processing, and the memory allocated.

The Statistics embedded tab provides a comprehensive report of the statistics gathered by the Domino server, categorized by task or functional area.

Summary

This chapter has focused on issues relevant to the Domino Administrator. It first covered general aspects of Domino server administration. It discussed the administrative tasks involved in Domino server administration, the tools facilitating the administrative process, and the basics of utilizing these tools in performing the general tasks of Domino server administration. It then focused on maintaining configuration documents and running server tasks. It introduced the major documents within the Domino Directory pertinent to server administration and outlined the configuration of each. It also described the major Domino server processes and their execution. The third section provided an overview of the procedures to follow when modifying networks and domains. It detailed the tasks required in merging two Domino domains, splitting a single Domino domain into two, or moving a Domino server from one domain to another. The fourth and final section focused on the tools available to analyze and monitor server performance.

FROM HERE...

You can find material related to Domino server administration in the following chapters and parts:

- Part VI, "Installing and Configuring the Domino Servers," discusses the different Domino server types, their initial installation and configuration, and the upgrade paths from R4.x to R5. It also provides an overview of Domino security, firewalls, Virtual Private Networks (VPNs), and Internet security. This represents fundamental information for administering a Domino enterprise.

- Chapter 38, "Administering Users, Groups, and Certification," introduces you to the R5 Domino Administrator. It then discusses user, group, and certification administration within the Domino Directory.

- Chapter 39, "Administering Electronic Mail," provides you with the basics in establishing your Domino messaging infrastructure.

- Chapter 40, "Replication and Its Administration," gives you an overview of the steps required to configure and maintain a successful replication schedule between servers within your Domino domain.

- Chapter 41, "Administering Files and Databases," covers management and administration of disk information, files, directories, and databases, updating database designs, and rolling out databases to users. It summarizes information pertinent to systems administrators who also perform database administration.

- Chapter 43, "Troubleshooting and Monitoring Domino," introduces the tools available within Domino to analyze problems and perform corrective action.

- Part VIII, "Advanced Domino Administration," gives you specialized information about topics such as performance and capacity planning, upgrading from other email systems, and integration with phones, fax, and image.

CHAPTER 43

Troubleshooting and Monitoring Domino

As our networked world continues to grow in power and usefulness, the complexity of the systems used to build these networks become increasingly complex. Lotus Notes/Domino is one of the most powerful, and therefore intricately complex, computer network systems in the world. As more features are added to Domino, the workload for Domino administrators has likewise increased. Domino R5 is no exception. In Domino versions prior to R5, the task of analyzing and monitoring a Domino network was very daunting because tools were scattered all over the place. However, Domino R5 strives to rectify this problem, and does so nicely. Domino R5 is equipped with a powerful, unified, and centralized interface for monitoring and administering your entire Domino enterprise.

This chapter covers the following topics:

- Monitoring servers with the Domino Administrator   An introduction to the monitoring features of the new Domino Administrator Client.
- Troubleshooting Domino   A review of the more common techniques used to troubleshoot problems you may encounter with your Domino servers, including analysis of the various log files.

Tips are scattered throughout the chapter to help make your administration experience as painless as possible. Let's begin by reviewing one of the most exciting features in Domino administration, the Domino Administration Client.

Monitoring Servers with the Domino Administrator

Lotus Notes/Domino R5 introduces a powerful new interface for Domino Administrators, known as the Domino Administrator Client (Admin Client). The Admin Client replaces the Server Administration interface found in R4.x. The Admin Client is very complex, and we will not cover all its features here; instead, we concentrate on the Server tab and its related subtabs, plus a few other areas that can prove highly useful in staying on top of your Domino network performance. Let's start our review with the Server tab.

Server Tab

The Server tab of the Domino Administrator is used to monitor the status of the currently selected Domino server, perform statistics analysis, monitor the servers of your Domino network, and monitor the up-to-date statistics of the currently selected Domino server. Let's begin with the Status subtab.

Status Subtab

Figure 43.1 shows the Status subtab.

Monitoring Servers with the Domino Administrator 1039

Figure 43.1
The Status subtab of the Server tab provides continuous task information and access to the server console.

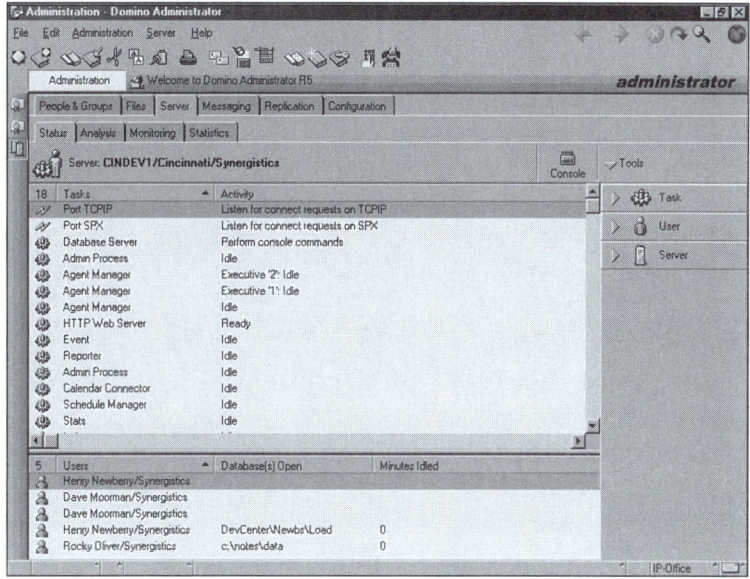

The Status subtab is divided into two major areas: Tasks and Users. The Tasks area displays all the tasks that are loaded on the Domino server and their respective status. The information displayed in the Tasks area is basically the same information that is displayed when you use the console command SHOW TASKS (SH TA). But although the SH TA command gives you a snapshot of what tasks are doing at any given time, the Tasks area shows the status of each task continuously, in real time.

> **Tip**
> You can right-click a task listing to access a pop-up menu that enables you to issue Tell Task (send the command to the selected task), Stop Task (end the selected task), or Start New Task commands to the server.

The Users area displays a list of all users that are currently connected to the server, what databases they are accessing, and how long they have been idle. The information displayed in the Users area is the same as the information provided by the console command SHOW USERS (SH U). However, the SH U command provides only a snapshot of the user status, and the Users area shows the current status of each user connected to the server.

> **Tip**
> You can right-click a user listing to access a pop-up menu that enables you to issue a broadcast message to the selected user or all users (Broadcast Message), or you can drop the user's connection to the server (Drop).

The Status subtab also provides access to the remote server console if you click the Console button. The Console area is shown in Figure 43.2.

Figure 43.2
The Console area of the Status subtab enables you to remotely access the server console.

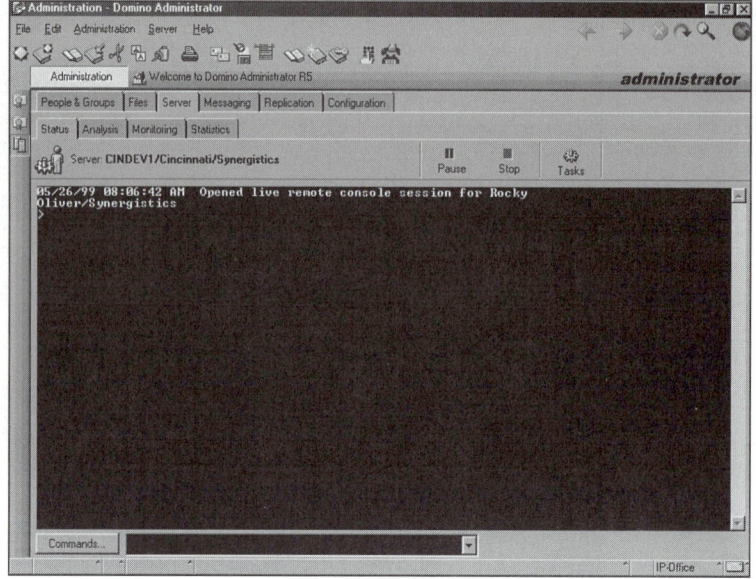

There are three buttons available in the Console area:

- Pause, which pauses the output of the console
- Stop, which provides you a live console connection or ends a live console connection
- Tasks, which returns you to the Tasks/Users area of the Status subtab

The Status subtab contains a Tools button that enables you to toggle between showing and hiding the tools panel. The Tools panel provides access to the following commands for Users, Tasks, and the Server:

- Task: Tell, Start, Stop
- Users: Broadcast Message, Drop
- Server: Replicate, Route Mail, Setup Ports, Secure Console, Stop Port, Shutdown

The next tab in our tour is the Analysis tab.

ANALYSIS SUBTAB

The Analysis subtab provides a centralized location to access the server's log database, catalog database, statistics database, and admin requests database. The Analysis subtab also enables you to analyze the log database, clusters, and decommissioning of a server. Figure 43.3 illustrates the Analysis subtab.

MONITORING SERVERS WITH THE DOMINO ADMINISTRATOR | 1041

Figure 43.3
The Analysis subtab provides a central location to access and analyze log and statistics databases.

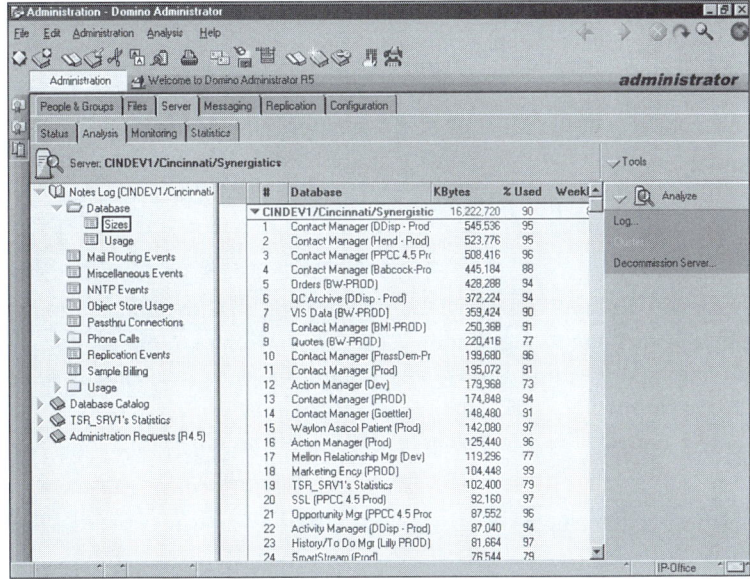

MONITORING SUBTAB

By far the most useful tab for monitoring the performance of your Domino network is the Monitoring subtab. Before we dive into the Monitoring subtab, let's take a look at a Figure 43.4 for reference.

Figure 43.4
The Monitoring subtab provides a powerful monitoring system for your Domino Network.

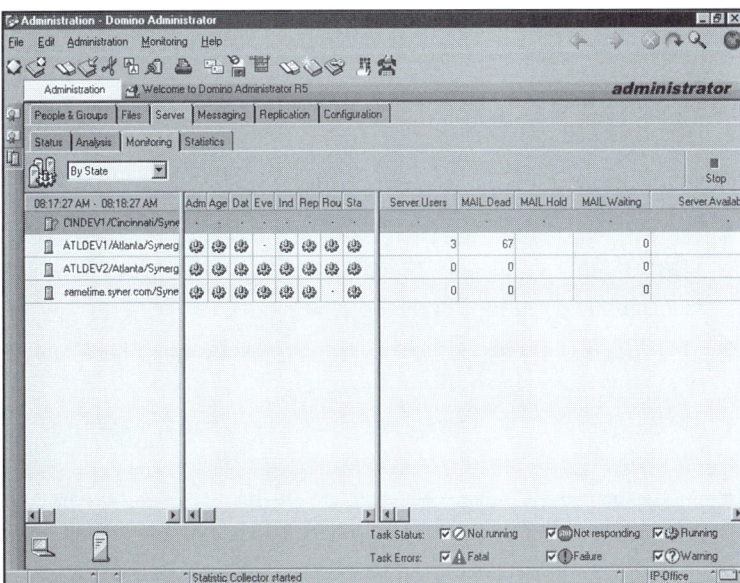

The Monitoring subtab enables you to monitor all the servers in your Domino network by periodically polling the major areas of your servers, such as memory usage, dead mail, the number of connected users, and much more.

The main area of the Monitoring subtab looks similar to a view. This view area displays the state information for each service (for example, Admin Process, Agent Manager, and so forth) or by timeline. The polling period can be set from as often as every minute to as infrequently as once every 60 minutes. Let's take a look at displaying information By State first.

BY STATE   To begin monitoring, make sure you click the Start button in the upper right corner of the monitoring window. Once you have started monitoring, the Start button will turn into a Stop button. The first column of the view area contains a listing of all the servers in your Domino network. The server entry can be expanded or collapsed. When collapsed, the row contains the monitoring information from the last polling period; when expanded, all the polling information rows are displayed for that server.

The next eight columns display the status of the following server tasks: Admin Process, Agent Manager, Database Server, Event, Indexer, Replicator, Router, and Stats. The columns show the current status of each task; the statuses that can be displayed are

- Running
- Not Running
- Not Responding
- Warning
- Failure
- Fatal

You can select what statuses to watch for at the bottom of the Monitoring tab, as shown at the bottom of Figure 43.4.

The following are the major server statistics:

- Server.Users   Number of users currently connected to the server.
- MAIL.Dead   Number of dead (undeliverable) messages in the server's MAIL.BOX file that cannot be returned to the original sender.
- MAIL.Hold   Number of messages being held waiting for a replication cycle to transfer to another server in an adjacent domain.
- MAIL.Waiting   Number of mail messages currently waiting for transfer in the server's MAIL.BOX file.
- Server.AvailabilityIndex   The relative availability of the server based on workload. This value is a number from 0 to 100, where 100 is a lightly loaded server.
- Trans.Server.ElapsedTime   Time since server was started.

BY TIMELINE The By Timeline display shows the same information as the By Service display, except that the information is "flipped" so that the polling intervals are the columns, and the tasks and statistics are the rows, collapsed under each server name. Figure 43.5 shows the Monitoring subtab displayed By Timeline.

Figure 43.5
When the Monitoring subtab is displayed By Timeline, the polling intervals are sorted by task.

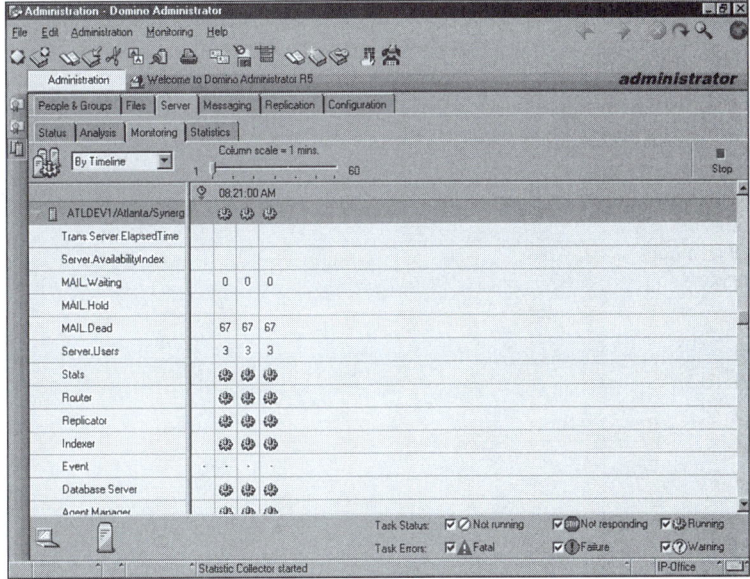

The tasks and statistics that are monitored in the Monitoring subtab can be selected by using the Monitoring, Monitor New Task for Selected or Monitoring, Monitor New Statistics for Selected menu items. The Monitor New Task dialog box is shown in Figure 43.6.

Figure 43.6
The Monitor New Task dialog box enables you to determine what tasks are monitored by the Administrator for the selected Domino server.

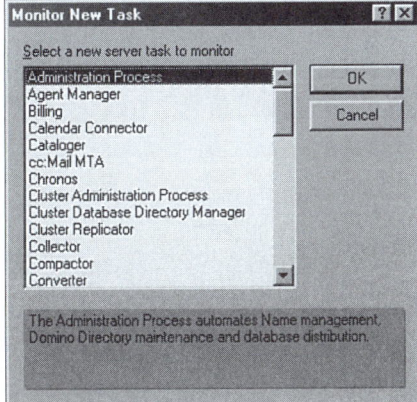

When you select a particular task for monitoring, a brief description of the task is given in the Monitor New Task dialog box.

STATISTICS SUBTAB

The Statistics subtab displays all the real-time statistics for the selected server in your Domino network. Notice that the statistics that aren't available in the Statistics subtab shown in Figure 43.7 are grayed out; statistics that are available appear in color.

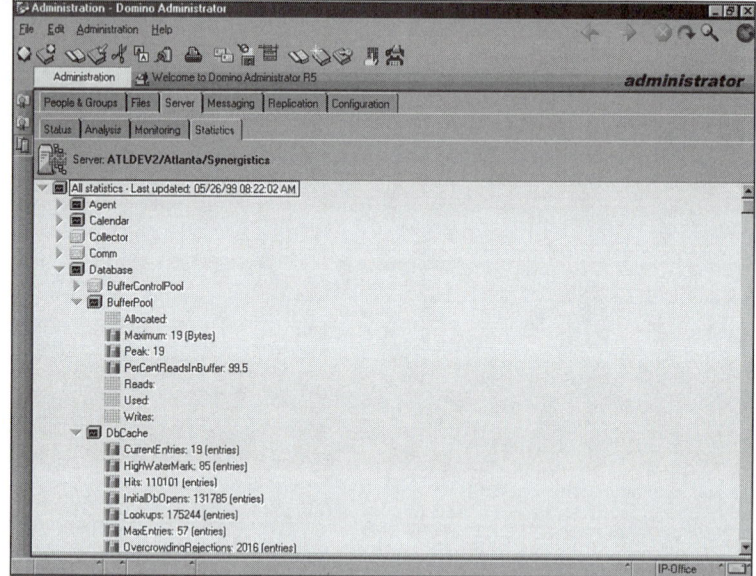

Figure 43.7
The Statistics subtab enables you to access an abundance of statistical information about a server in your Domino network.

The statistics are displayed in a tree format. Some of the more usable statistics that are available include

- Agent (Daily and Hourly)
- Calendar (Appointments, Reservations, Resources, and Users)
- Database (Various pool sizes, both peak size and used size)
- Disk (All drives, free and total space)
- Domino (Build information, Commands, Requests/time interval)
- Mail (a ton of statistics, such as AverageDeliverTime, AverageSizeDelivered, and so forth)
- Memory (Allocated, Availability, and so forth)
- Replica (Cluster info, Doc info, Failed, Successful)
- Server (Administrators, Name, BusyTime, Sessions, Trans, Users, and so forth)
- SMTPMTA
- Stats

These statistics are retrieved from the Statistics & Events database and are continuously updated. The directory tree organization enables an administrator to quickly "drill down" to the desired statistic. Selecting any of the statistics provides you a brief description in the status bar of the Domino Administrator.

There are other monitoring tools available to you in some of the other tabs. These tools are covered next.

OTHER MONITORING TOOLS

Almost all the tabs in the Domino Administrator Client contain some type of monitoring tool. These tools are covered in the following sections, organized by tab.

FILES TAB

The Files tab has a Disk Information tool that displays a pie graph showing the total disk space, disk space used, and disk space free.

The Files tab also displays all the databases and/or templates on the selected server with statistical information, such as Title, Filename Size, Max Size, Created Date, Last Fixup Date, and so forth.

REPLICATION TAB

The Replication tab contains two great tools for planning and managing your replication topology. The first tool is a graphical representation of your replication schedule, as shown in Figure 43.8. This tool can show you any contradictions, dead times, or overlaps in your replication scheduling.

Figure 43.8
The Replication tab provides your replication schedule in a user-friendly format.

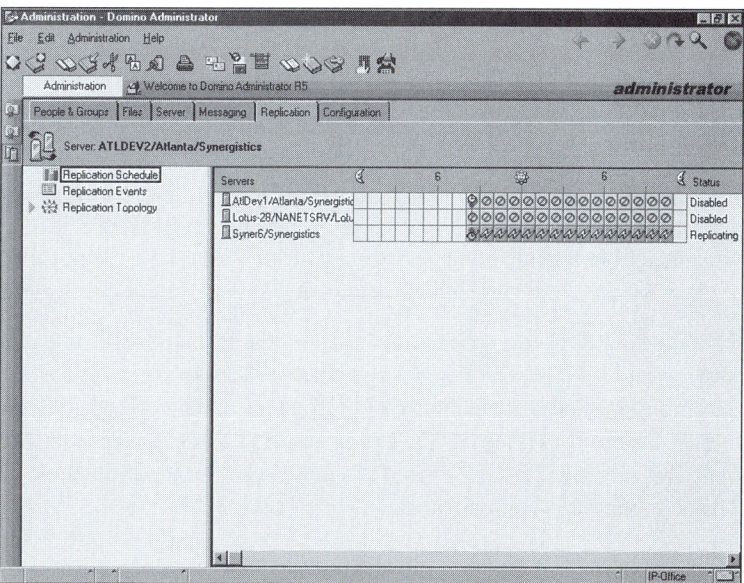

The other tool is a replication topology map, as shown in Figure 43.9. The replication topology map graphically displays the replication connections in your Domino network, which helps you identify redundancy or holes in your replication process. It also greatly enhances your ability to plan the most streamlined replication topology possible.

Figure 43.9
The Replication tab also shows your replication topology for efficient replication planning.

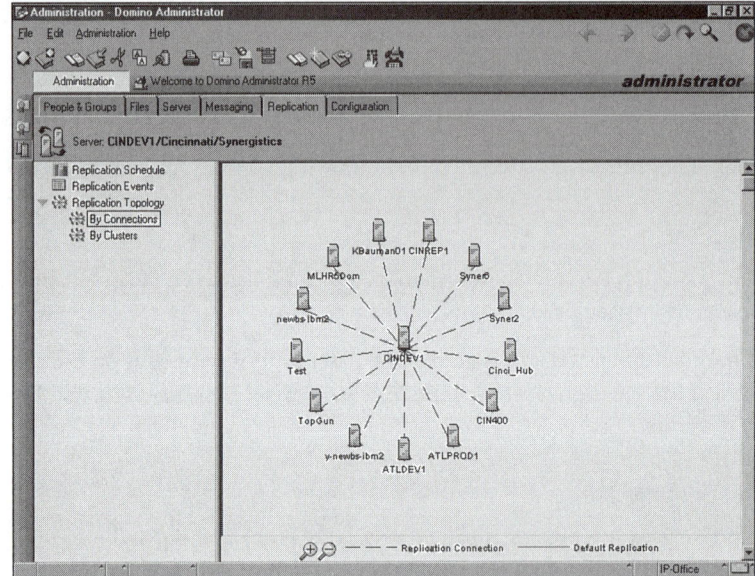

MESSAGING TAB

The Messaging tab contains three tools to assist you in monitoring and troubleshooting your NotesMail messaging infrastructure: Mail Routing Status, Mail Routing Topology map, and the Tracking Center. The first tool, the Mail Routing Status gauges, displays the dead and waiting mail counts in a speedometer-style interface. The Mail Routing Status feature is shown in Figure 43.10.

The second tool in the Messaging tab is the Mail Routing Topology map. This feature displays a graphical map of your mail topology, as shown in Figure 43.11. A topology map is a valuable tool in planning and analyzing your mail routing topology, because it can assist you in identifying holes or unneeded redundancy in your mail routing connections.

The Tracking Center is a great new feature that enables you to track email, *even if it has already been sent!* The Tracking Center shows all tracking requests, status, and so forth. Mail tracking is enabled by loading the Mail Tracking Collector or MTC server task. Information collected by the MTC task is stored in a special report database known as the Mail Tracking Store database (`MTSTORE.NSF`). See the Domino documentation for more details on the Mail Tracking feature.

Figure 43.10
The Mail Routing Status feature of the Messaging tab displays dead and waiting mail.

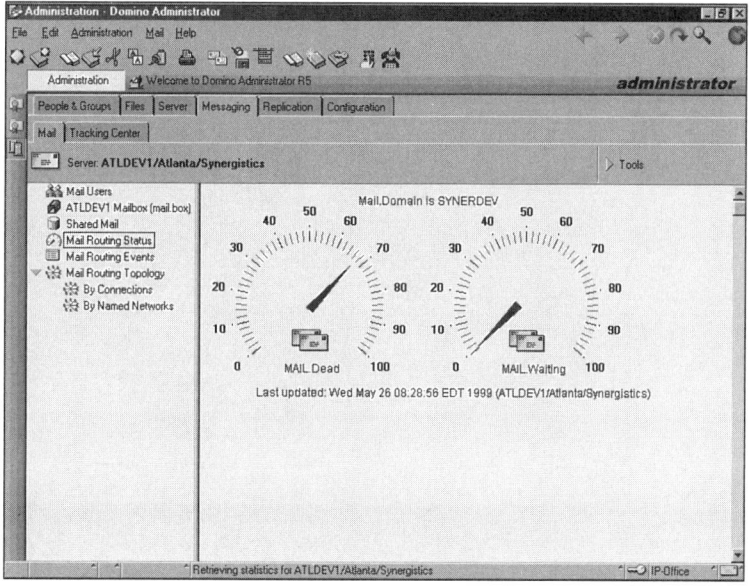

Figure 43.11
The Mail Routing Topology map is a great feature for planning and analyzing your mail routing topology.

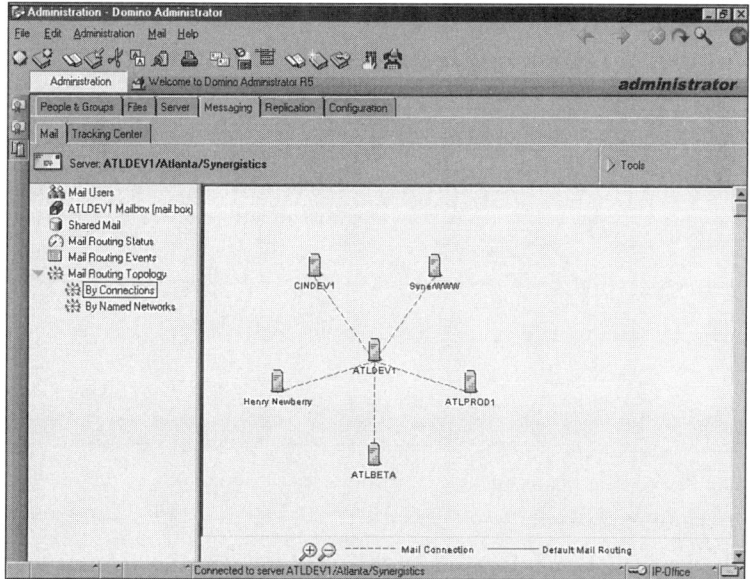

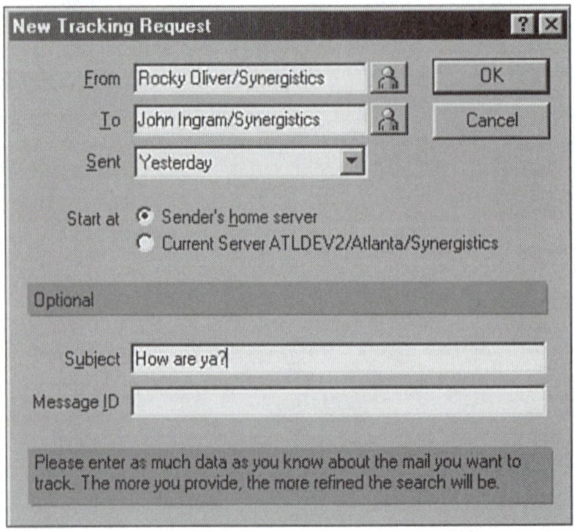

Figure 43.12
You can track mail based on the sender, recipient, date, and optionally on text in the subject line.

Figure 43.13
The Tracking Center is where you initiate requests to track email.

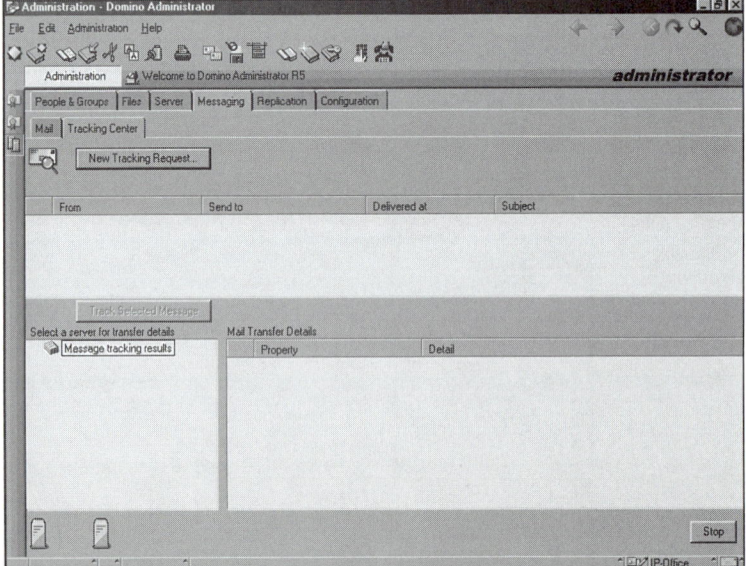

CONFIGURATION TAB

The Configuration tab provides access to all configuration information for your server, including server, cluster, Directory, Web, messaging, and statistic/events. You can use this interface to quickly adjust and tweak your Domino environment based on the wealth of information provided to you in the other monitoring areas of the Domino Administrator.

Now that you are familiar with the new monitoring features of Domino Administrator Client in Domino R5, it is time to learn a few troubleshooting techniques and hints to further enhance your ability to be a successful administrator.

Troubleshooting Domino

This section provides some techniques for troubleshooting the most common problems found with a Domino network. This list is not intended to be comprehensive; with a system as complex as Domino, listing all the known problems and their solutions could fill many, many books. Instead, I take a look at some of the more common problems and point you in the right direction for finding a resolution. In this section, we explore the following areas:

- Security issues
- Passthru issues
- Server issues
- Replication issues
- Modem issues

Security Issues

There are quite a few security fields on the Server document for your Domino server. These fields are set by default so that they will not immediately cause security blockages that were open by default in previous versions of Notes/Domino. If you choose to use them, however, you should understand how users will be notified when they cannot proceed past one of these checkpoints.

These are the main security fields in the Server document:

- Check Passwords on Notes IDs—Security Tab
- Authentication Options\Anonymous (formerly Allow Anonymous HTTP Connections)—Ports tab, Internet Ports subtab, in all the protocol subtabs
- Allow HTTP Clients to Browse Databases—Internet Protocols tab, HTTP subtab, Basics area

Problems with Checking Passwords

When you enable the Check Passwords on Notes IDs feature on the Server document, the feature is not completely enabled. You must enable it for individuals by modifying their Person documents to allow password checking for them. To do this for multiple people, use the Administration Process (ADMINP) to make the task easier. Or write your own agent that modifies the field on the Person document for selected documents.

Password checking is an optional feature for every server. If it is enabled on one server, but not a second, the second server does not check passwords and the first one does.

After this feature has been enabled for a user, the first time he or she authenticates with a server that requires password checking, Notes alters his or her ID so it cannot be used with earlier versions of Notes.

Do not enable this feature for any IDs to which you have applied multiple passwords. The feature works only for IDs with one password.

If a user has multiple copies of his or her ID with different passwords, the password that is valid is the one on the ID that was first used to access the server doing the password checking. The passwords on the other IDs should be changed to match the valid password.

Up to 50 previous passwords will be cached to prevent reuse. You can, however, clear the Password Digest field on a Person document to clear this history.

If you specify a grace period and a user's password expires, the user will not be allowed to authenticate with a server until he or she sets a new password or the administrator clears the Password Digest field on his or her Person document.

Problems with Web Browser (HTTP) Connections

If a user is being asked for a user ID and password when first accessing a site, the request is caused by one of two features. It is impossible to tell from the password prompt alone why a user is being denied access without a password. Knowing the causes enables you to check the correct places for a solution.

First, the Server document might have the Authentication Options\Anonymous (formerly Allow Anonymous HTTP Connections) option set to No. This forces authentication immediately upon access of the server.

Second, the database being accessed on the server might be configured so that its ACL does not allow anonymous access. You implement this by setting the Default or Anonymous entries to No Access in the ACL. The Default entry applies to either Notes or Web clients. The Anonymous entry applies primarily to Web clients; the exception is if the server is set to Allow Anonymous Notes Connections (Security tab) in the Server document.

The other HTTP setting, Allow HTTP Clients to Browse Databases, is not likely to cause problems on its own (enabled or not) unless it is enabled for a default Server document in which the HTTP section's Home URL field is still set to its default value.

This feature controls the ability of a user to see the equivalent of the File, Database, Open dialog box, listing all the databases and directories under the Notes Data Directory on the server.

If this setting is enabled, the default home page that will be served to clients is this list of databases. This is because the Home URL field in the Internet Protocols tab\HTTP subtab contains the value ?Open. It is this single value, ?Open, that is controlled by this security setting. Other URLs lead directly into a known place in a database. The error code that identifies this condition is `Error 403: HTTP Web Server: Database Browsing Not Allowed`.

If you enable this feature, be sure to change the Home URL field, because Error 403 is certainly not a nice home page. After this is done, the security setting will occur only when someone who knows?Open enters it into his or her browser in an attempt to bypass the home page you've set up and browse the contents of the server. I usually create a simple home page that informs the user that the browsing of databases is not permitted, or I place the default home page URL here so the user is automatically sent to the desired home page. For instance, if you had a database that serves as the main menuing site for your database, you would place the URL HTTP://www.mysite.com/mainmenu.nsf in the Home URL field.

> **Tip**
>
> Generally speaking, I do not think that the Allow HTTP Clients to Browse Databases option should ever be set to Yes. It leaves the door open too wide for a security breach, so my recommendation is to set this option to No.

PASSTHRU PROBLEMS

Passthru servers are a great tool to provide a central connection point for one or more of your Domino servers. However, if you decide to use Passthru, you may encounter problems related to your restriction settings or to network routing problems. Let's take a look at these issues first.

There are also four parameters that have counterparts in both the Server document and the NOTES.INI file; if you don't set a standard, such as always putting the entries in the Server document only, you might forget about settings you made that affect the behavior of Passthru.

> **Tip**
>
> Try to restrict setting parameters to either the Domino Directory (the preferred method) or the NOTES.INI, but not both (whenever possible). This makes it easier to keep track of what you have configured.

PASSTHRU RESTRICTION–RELATED PROBLEMS

If you find that users and servers attempting Passthru cannot complete their connections, check the server documents' Passthru Use sections, found in the Security tab. The first three of the four fields in this section (Access this Server, Route Through, and Cause Calling), if left empty, allow no one to perform those activities. The fourth field, Destinations Allowed, is used by that server in determining the remote servers to which it may route using Passthru; if the field is blank, there are no restrictions, and the Domino server can route to any server to which it has access.

For other servers and users, you have control over three things: Who can access this server using Passthru, who can route through this server using Passthru, and who can cause this server to call other servers while using Passthru. You must explicitly list users, servers, or (better yet) groups for any other entities to be able to use this server for Passthru. Make sure that you use the fully qualified names for people and server entries. If you want to allow everyone to use your server as a Passthru server, you can enter an asterisk (*).

Another security measure that may affect Passthru is the field in the Security tab of the Server document named Compare Notes Public Keys Against Those Stored in the

Directory. Enabling this field forces this server to compare the public key contained in an ID with the public key stored in the Domino Directory document for that ID. Passthru will fail if this comparison fails. Although this is an authentication problem, it may at first appear to be a communication problem.

Passthru Routing Problems

A server that is being used for Passthru may not be able to determine the route to a destination server being requested. This may be caused by several factors: The network name resolution systems might not be functioning correctly, the Domino Directory might not contain enough information for Domino to determine the route, or this server may not be configured for Passthru.

Depending on your protocol, your network routing system has a method for resolving computer names into network addresses. If this system develops problems, when Domino asks for the network address for a server name it won't get a response, and the server will not be reachable. In this case, an error would be returned to the Passthru client saying that a route to the server that the user was attempting to reach could not be found. The most typical instance of this type of problem occurs in TCP/IP networks. Computers connected to a TCP/IP network normally rely on a domain name services (DNS) server to resolve computer names into IP addresses. If a DNS server is not available for computer name resolution, the computer will look on its file system for a file known as a HOSTS file. A HOSTS file is similar to a local phone book. It is simply a file that contains the names of computers that are accessed often and their IP addresses. The HOSTS file generally speeds up connection time and enables the computer to find another computer on the network with the need for a DNS server.

If your Domino Directory doesn't have the required information, Passthru won't be able to find a complete path to the server the user is trying to reach. This might be caused by a simple condition in which the Domino Directory on the Passthru server hasn't replicated the most current documents from the hub server, or it might be that certain values were either forgotten or mistyped. Settings to look for include missing Connection documents for servers not directly reachable on the network, wrong values for the Passthru Server field on the Server document or users' Location documents, or invalid Passthru Connection documents.

Passthru Connection documents are usually not required, but if they are entered, they take precedence over the network name resolution process. If a server's address is changed, the server is physically moved to another network, or is renamed, then the Passthru Connection documents referencing that server must be changed.

Passthru Parameters in NOTES.INI

The parameters in Table 43.1 correspond to fields on the Server document. They are used only if you've created entries for them in the NOTES.INI file and the related fields on the Server document are empty. If there is a conflict between the NOTES.INI setting and the Server document field, the Server document takes precedence.

TABLE 43.1 Passthru PARAMETERS AND THEIR CORRESPONDING FIELDS

NOTES.INI Variables	Server Document Fields
Allow_Passthru_Access	Access This Server
Allow_Passthru_Callers	Cause Calling
Allow_Passthru_Clients	Route Through
Allow_Passthru_Targets	Destinations Allowed

SERVER ACCESS

Several factors control who can access a server. Authentication occurs between Notes ID files. Depending on how these files have been certified, access may not succeed. As mentioned earlier, the Server document also contains entries governing access based on names entered in these fields. The following sections look at various methods and techniques you can use to control access over specific ports.

AUTHENTICATION AND CERTIFICATION

When two Notes entities (servers or workstations) attempt to communicate, the first hurdle is authentication. A comparison of Notes IDs reveals whether the two sides trust each other. There are two distinct methods of authentication. The first involves the older, nonhierarchical ID structure, in which an ID file contains one or more certificates. The second involves the newer, hierarchical ID structure, in which an ID contains one certificate that gives it a hierarchical name, adding at least an organization name to the common name on the ID, and perhaps additional organizational units as well.

FLAT CERTIFICATION: MISSING CERTIFICATES OR LACKING TRUST

During authentication, under nonhierarchical certification, these certificates are compared against those held by the other's ID. The two must each find a trusted certificate in each other's ID file. If this does not happen, authentication fails.

By examining the ID files and looking at the certificate lists, you can determine what must be done to resolve the situation. Either a certificate is missing, or the trust flag has been disabled on one or more of the certificates.

EXPIRED CERTIFICATES

Every certificate given to an ID file has its own expiration date. By default, users expire in two years and servers expire 100 years after the date of certification. These initial values can be modified at the time the certificate is issued.

When the expiration date nears, starting at 90 days from expiration, Notes issues a message indicating the expiration date. For a server, this message appears at the console (and thus in a Miscellaneous Events document of the log).

When the expiration date is reached, the certificate is no longer valid; unless there are other flat certificates available on the ID file that are also trusted, the ID becomes useless.

By simply recertifying the ID file, it once again becomes viable. If the expiration date has been reached, the file must be physically transported to the administrator for recertification. It is easier to use Notes Mail before the expiration date to send the ID to the administrator, who can then recertify it and send it back through Notes Mail.

CROSS-CERTIFICATION PROBLEMS

Authentication failure under the hierarchical scheme is easier to debug and resolve. The error message that results informs you of the nature of the problem. First, however, when does authentication work under the hierarchical structure? It succeeds when both IDs have a common ancestor, or when both IDs have been cross-certified to access the other organization. This chapter doesn't explain the details of cross-certification; instead, it describes how to resolve the problem resulting from a lack of it. Refer to Chapter 36, "Domino Security Overview," for more information on configuring cross-certification.

For servers and/or workstations who lack cross-certificates, you must decide at what level you want to cross-certify and then proceed to accomplish that. Here is a list of the possible levels:

- Between server and server or workstation
- Between server and organization/organizational unit
- Between organization and organizational units

CROSS-CERTIFICATION AT THE WORKSTATION

For users to communicate with a server in another organization, they must hold a cross-certificate to that server or organization in their Personal Address Book. Without it, half the puzzle is missing (assuming the server already has a cross-certificate for the user).

When a user attempts to communicate with such a server, Domino R5 displays a message that explains the lack of cross-certificates and enables the user to fix his or her half of the authentication problem by issuing an appropriate cross-certificate in his or her Personal Directory. This cross-certificate is not the same as the organization-to-organization cross-certificate that exists in the Domino Directory. It is usable only by the user who generates the document. Additionally, this works only when the two organizations have cross-certified at the organization and organizational-unit levels.

Even though the user can proceed with this "fix," it does not change the potential lack of a cross-certificate in the Directory on the server. It is likely that the user still will not be able to access the server unless that server has already been cross-certified with the user's organization.

Authorization: You Are Not Authorized to Access the Server

When the You Are Not Authorized to Access the Server message appears, you know one fact: Authentication has succeeded, and you are being denied access not because your ID file is invalid or because of cross-certification, but because the Server document or a parameter in the server's NOTES.INI file has an entry that specifies that you should be denied.

The key word in the message is authorized. A Notes/Domino term similar to *authorization* is *authentication*. Authentication, however, is the verification process that takes place between two Notes ID files. Authentication verifies your identity. Once your identity has been established, Domino determines whether you are authorized to access the server. Authorization is a comparison between the ID file accessing the server and the restriction parameters that have been configured on that server.

Server-Document Restrictions

Every Server document has a Restrictions section, which contains a number of fields in which you can specify server-specific access rights for users or groups. Two fields on this document may be causing the authorization failure.

The Access Server field (Security tab), if it is empty, allows access to any ID file certified under the same organization certifier, or to any ID that has been properly cross-certified. In other words, if authentication succeeds, the ID is allowed access to the server. However, if this field contains one or more entries, access is limited to only those users or groups. If the ID attempting to access the server is not specifically listed and is not a member of a group that is listed, it is denied access.

The other server document field that affects authorization is the Not Access Server field (Security tab). Entries listed here are specifically denied access. This field overrides any entries from the Access Server field, if any duplicate entries exist.

> **Tip**
>
> The list of individuals that are allowed access and denied access to your servers (such as those employees that are terminated) is much easier to maintain in a Group document. Create two Group documents called something like Allow Access and Deny Access and place these group names in the Access Server and Not Access Server fields, respectively. By using a Group to manage this list, you do not have to shut down your server to have changes take effect.

Each time you change the server access lists, the server must be shut down and restarted, unless you use groups to manage the contents of these fields.

NOTES.INI Restrictions (Port Level)

Some parameters not found in the Server document can be added to the NOTES.INI file to affect authorization. These entries are ALLOW_ACCESS_*portname* and DENY_ACCESS_*portname*.

For example, to allow the Developers group access to the Dev1 server over the TCP/IP port, the entry would read as follows:

`ALLOW_ACCESS_TCPIP=Developers`

To deny access to the OtherDomainServers group over the COM2 port, the entry would read as follows:

`DENY_ACCESS_COM2=OtherDomainServers`

The `ALLOW_ACCESS_portname` parameter, like the Access Server field in the Server document, allows access across that port to the listed users or groups only. The `NOTES.INI` file does not contain this entry initially; you have to add it. If this parameter exists and your name is not specified (individually or through a group name), you cannot use that port.

On the other hand, the `DENY_ACCESS_portname` field, if present in the `NOTES.INI` file, specifically denies access across that port to any user or group listed. This entry overrides the `ALLOW_ACCESS_portname` entry.

Depending on the various settings, you may be able to access the server over one port but not another.

Server Issues

Let's begin by looking at a couple of common server issues that you'll probably encounter at some point. First, we'll discuss an error message: Server not responding. This occurs when your workstation cannot reach the server; we'll look at the reasons. A second common server issue occurs when you have difficulty getting your server to start; we'll explore some possible reasons for this.

Message: Server Not Responding

The Server not responding message occurs when the server is not reachable from a client or another server. The reasons for this message can vary depending on the protocol being used; sometimes it occurs when there are not enough network sessions.

For TCP/IP, the resolution of the server name to an IP address happens either through a local HOSTS text file or through a network Domain Name Service (DNS). If you are using the HOSTS file method, and the file is missing or has been edited in such a way that the server's name has been removed, the name resolution will fail. If you are using DNS, check to see whether the name table has been changed. Check the DNS to make sure it is operational. Try using the `Ping` utility to ping the server by name, or using the `TRACERT` utility to trace the connection path from the source to the target server. If these fail, Notes will not be able to reach the server either. Resolve the DNS issue, and the server will reappear.

For SPX, the name resolution is handled by a NetWare server. If no server responds to the Domino request, the name is never resolved into an SPX address, and the server becomes unreachable. Examine your NetWare servers for problems. Examine your Domino server for SPX connectivity outside the Domino server task. Try rebooting the Domino server if all SPX functionality is available elsewhere.

For NetBIOS, determine whether you have ever been able to see the server. If so, ensure that no routers exist between the workstation and the server—or if they do, that they have the capability of routing NetBIOS packets and that they have been configured to do so. Most routers cannot route NetBIOS. Try rebooting the server, if possible. If both the client and the server are running Novell's NetBIOS, they may not be running the same frame type.

CONDITION SERVER FAILS TO START

If your Domino server shuts itself down shortly after you start it, check for the following:

- The server document may have been corrupted or deleted. Without this document, the server cannot identify itself properly, and it may shut down.
- The server may not have been configured properly during setup before launching the server task. Finalize the setup of the Domino server through the client first. Do this by launching the Notes client and filling out the installation documents.

SERVER STABILITY

If your server tends to crash frequently, how can you explore the possible causes? Notes/Domino has a process for creating a special file (NOTES.RIP) when a crash occurs. This file contains information about the state of the system at the time of the crash. Let's look at this process and an example of using the RIP file to find the problem.

SERVER CRASHES, RIP FILES, OR UNIX CORE DUMPS   At times, a server or workstation may crash. Not all crashes are fatal to Notes/Domino, but most are. Rare and isolated incidents aren't worth worrying about, but a server that crashes repeatedly must be investigated. When a crash occurs, Notes/Domino invokes a program commonly known as *Quincy* (for QNC.EXE). Depending on platform type, Quincy generates either a NOTES.RIP file or (in the case of UNIX) a core dump file. This file is appended to, not overwritten, each time a crash occurs.

> **Tip**
>
> For Trivial Pursuit fans, someone observed that the name Quincy comes from the popular 1980s TV show about a curious coroner (starring Jack Klugman)—hence the use of the extension .RIP for the output file.

A RIP file consists of several sections. Although much of the file is in the form of a hex dump, you can determine the cause of many crashes with some careful reading. At the top of the file is some basic information, such as the general condition that occurred, the amount of free memory, and if applicable, swap-file space. The contents of the registers are displayed, followed by the main section: the stack trace.

The stack trace has two parts. On the left is the hex dump of the stack contents. To the right of the hex dump is the ASCII representation of the hex codes. By perusing the ASCII section, you can often determine what program or task was executing before the crash. Not far below the name of the task, you can often find the filename of the database that was in use.

As an example, let's say you find that your server is generating RIP files every morning just after 5 a.m. By looking at the RIP, you may see that the UPDALL server task was running, and the last database referenced was the NAMES.NSF file (the Domino Directory). This may indicate that the Domino Directory (or the database that is referenced) has one or more corrupted views. You can often fix the problem by loading UPDALL with the -R switch to rebuild the indexes of that database:

```
LOAD UPDALL -R NAMES.NSF
```

Without looking at the RIP file, you may have determined that, because your NOTES.INI file contains UPDALL in the ServerTasksAt5 entry, UPDALL is causing the problem. You wouldn't know, however, which database is causing trouble for UPDALL.

API PROGRAMS Suppose that your server is crashing every morning at 7 a.m. You peruse your configuration looking for the culprit. The INI file yields no clues; you can't find a ServerTasksAt entry for 7 a.m.

If your environment requires the development and use of custom API server add-in programs, you may encounter situations like this where the API program is causing the server problems.

Using the RIP file and comparing the time with your Program documents in the Domino Directory, you may find that an API program seems to be the culprit.

Turn off one or more of the suspect API programs for a short period and determine whether the problem disappears. If so, your only recourse is to take this information back to the API developers and wait for a fix.

It is a good idea to have API developers run their tasks on a development server that cannot affect the contents or schedule of your production servers. Often, however, these custom tasks behave well in a limited development environment and misbehave only in a loaded server. Try copying the databases being used by the API programmers to the development server, complete with all the contents so that their code is tested under load. You should also enable many background macros and other server tasks to put the development server under a load to simulate your production server.

SERVER VISIBILITY

The *visibility* of your servers is manifested through the dialog boxes used on workstations. A user may want to open a new database (using File, Database, Open); how can you control which servers they can see in this dialog box?

What is happening if you suddenly see a different list of servers on your File Open dialog list than you normally expect?

First, let's talk about the File, Database, Open menu command. Essentially, there are two different server lists in R5.

Troubleshooting Domino

> **Tip**
> You can also open a database by clicking the right mouse button somewhere on your workspace (not on an icon). Then choose the Open Database item from the resulting context menu that appears.

This command initially brings you to a directory of the Notes Data Directory on the local drive. In the drop-down list is a list of servers, which is determined from the collection of icons you have on your desktop and the list of server Connection documents in your Domino Directory. If you have icons from three different servers that you access through a network port somewhere on the desktop, and you have a Connection document to another server that you communicate with through a modem port, the list contains Local plus four other server names. This quick, local lookup means that the File Open dialog box and the server list typically perform very quickly.

> **Tip**
> You may find that even after you've removed all icons that refer to a particular server, this server still shows up in the initial list. To remove this server name from the File Open list (if you have no references to it any longer, you probably don't need it in the list), do this: Open the Server Connections view in your Personal Directory and remove the Connection document to that server.

The second server list appears when you choose Other from the initial server list. If you are connected to a network or are online with your modem, the Notes client reaches out and asks your home server (or the one you're connected to with the modem) for a list of available servers. The resulting list is then a combination of the first list and any other available servers to which you don't have local references. This search is called a Name Server lookup; your home server is acting as Name Server, providing you with this list.

What determines the list that the server returns to you? The list is determined by the Notes Named Network settings in the Server documents in your domain. The list contains those servers that belong to the same Notes Named Network as your Name Server. Notes builds the list by looking at all servers in the same Notes Named Network as the user's home server.

If a user's home server goes down, Domino uses a fallback method to obtain the server list. The method used depends on the network protocol. In general, the workstation looks for another Domino server from which it can get its list. This list reflects all the servers in the same Notes Named Network as the fallback server; the list may be completely different than the one the user normally sees.

Replication Issues

A number of factors control which documents replicate. The most important fact to know and remember is that most replication controls affect the documents being received, not those being sent. The controls for the documents being sent can be found in the remote database. Yet the controls, which are set locally, specify the name of the remote entity (server or workstation).

> **Tip**
>
> To capture detailed information about the replication process, try using the server configuration parameter LOG_REPLICATION=3. This parameter causes the Replicator to report detailed information about the documents that replicate, including which fields replicated. This additional information is recorded in the Notes log in the Replication Events documents.

TOO FEW DOCUMENTS REPLICATE

Think of this question when resolving replication issues: "What can the other entity do to this replica, based on the local settings?" Or, to simplify the question, become the database: "What can the other entity do to me?"

It is important to remember that, to Notes/Domino, servers are "people" too. Notes ID files simply give a license number a name that you reference in the system. It is not known or distinguished whether an entity is a server or a workstation; the entity is identified simply as a trusted Notes name that has been granted a certain level of access to a database.

SERVERS AND THE ACL   A database's Access Control List (ACL) is fairly straightforward. It contains a list of servers, people, or groups and assigns one of seven levels of access to each entry.

Realize, however, that every replica of every database has its own ACL. As you deploy many servers, it becomes important to consider the settings on each replica. You can think of the multiple replicas of a single database as an ACL topology: Which server will be the master for design and ACL changes?

Consider this: How many replication hops are there from this ACL hub down to the last replica? That is, does the ACL hub copy replicate with all other copies, or does it replicate with some intermediary copies? At each intermediate step, these servers must have sufficient access in the next replicas to pass ACL and design changes.

You may want to consider using the feature that enables you to maintain a consistent ACL throughout all replicas. To use this feature (under the Advanced Settings of the ACL dialog for a database), you set two items: the administration server, and the check box labeled Enforce Consistent ACL Across All Replicas of this Database. All other replicas must use the same settings. Then, any local changes to an ACL are overwritten with the settings from the "master" database. The administration server must be listed in this ACL with Manager access.

SERVERS AND AUTHOR ACCESS   You should generally avoid giving a server Author access. Because servers are not used to create and edit documents, they are not listed as the Authors of documents. Notes/Domino refuses to receive edits to a document from a user or a server if that name isn't listed in the document as the Author.

In the case of users, Author access is useful in preventing those who can make local changes to a document from passing those changes back illegally to the server replica. Servers, however, are often in the role of distribution agents; that is, they pass documents (including changes) back and forth between them.

A server that is listed as an Author cannot write changes to documents. This typically comes to an administrator's attention because certain users, in conversation, determine that they aren't looking at the same document in their respective replicas. The user who edited the document will be confused about why his or her associates are reporting that they don't see the changes.

Along with the Author access level, there are two important access flags that can also affect the number of documents that replicate. The `Create documents` flag allows the named entity to write new documents in the replica. The `Delete documents` flag allows the entity to write document-deletion stubs.

SELECTIVE REPLICATION FORMULA Databases can also control what is received based on one or more Selective Replication formulas. This formula, which is written much like the Selection formula for a view, receives only those documents that meet the criteria specified in the formula.

A Selective Replication formula also acts as a Selection formula for the local database. Any local documents that do not meet the criteria are removed. If the formula is changed, at the next replication, the set of allowed documents also changes. This may result in too many documents being received or in too many documents being removed from the local replica.

To test your formula, consider using a selection agent that contains the same formula to see whether the correct documents are being marked for replication; or build a view with the desired replication formula to see whether the desired documents will be replicated.

DOCUMENT-LEVEL ACCESS LISTS AND ROLES The ACL is a broad classification of what a named entity can do. It applies across all the documents in the database. Notes also provides for document-level access lists. These lists can contain names of users, groups, or roles. They act to reduce the level of access for members of the database ACL, but do not grant more rights than those given in the ACL.

Document-level access lists, otherwise known as Readers and Authors fields, can be applied in a number of ways. They are usually applied by designers, but users can also apply Read access lists to particular documents independent of the form design. Forms can have Create and Read access lists. Views and folders can have Read access lists.

If a user or server is listed in the database ACL but not in document-level access lists, those documents may not replicate. It is important to remember server names when access lists are defined. Server names affect the planning of administrators, who must know of and educate users of the factors that affect replication, and designers, who must include a mechanism that enables servers to replicate documents regardless of the document-level access that users apply.

> **Tip**
>
> A useful way to ensure that servers are allowed to replicate documents is to create one or more roles just for servers, and then use these roles throughout the database design, such as in access lists or Readers/Authors fields (which control document access).

TIME LIMIT Connection documents contain a field specifying the maximum time limit allowed for replication. This field can be used to efficiently schedule many replication jobs. At any particular time, however, it may appear to affect the amount of data that gets replicated. If a replication is halted for time considerations, those documents not replicated must wait for the next cycle. Depending on the frequency of replication with that server, users may find that new documents or changes aren't present at a particular time. You may get complaints about "failures" that are "fixed" with the next replication. You can view the replication schedules of your Domino servers in the Domino Administrator Client, Replication tab.

USER TYPE ACL entries are simply text strings that Notes/Domino compares against the name from an ID file or the text strings of names in Group documents. This means that it is possible to create or modify a group in the Domino Directory with the same name as an ACL entry (say, LocalDomainServers), entering your username in that group, and then be allowed access to the database based on the group name entry. Notes doesn't know or care whether an ID is a server or a user. This is the reality, because Notes/Domino does this for compatibility with previous database versions.

However, R4-and-later versions of Notes/Domino have a provision for specifying the type for an ACL entry. The choices for the user type are Person, Server, Mixed Group, Person Group, or Server Group. This provision prevents this kind of aliasing problem. In an R4-or-later database in which the user types have been applied, the LocalDomainServers group would be identified as a Server group. If a username has been entered into this group, that user is not allowed access based on the LocalDomainServers group. Notes/Domino sees that the user's ID is a user-type ID, and that the group should contain only server-type IDs; therefore, it ignores the username entry in the group. If LocalDomainServers is defined as a Mixed Group, however, the user is allowed. The only other user type that exists is Unspecified, which basically leaves the user type undefined, allowing any entity of the specified name access to the database, regardless of user type (for example, server or user).

If you intend to use the server's workstation to perform administration tasks, you add that server to the ACLs of any databases you will work on, defining the server entry as Unspecified, and not as Server. The server ID as seen from the workstation process is seen as a User; if you've told the ACL that ID is a Server, you won't be allowed to make changes.

DOCUMENTS DISAPPEAR AFTER REPLICATION

After a replication is complete, it is possible that documents present before replication began are now missing. Several factors can play a part in the removal of documents.

As discussed previously, a Selective Replication formula (if it has been modified since the last replication) may now not allow certain documents that had been allowed by the previous formula.

Suppose that you have a Status field (whose values can be Open or Closed), and you also use a Selective Replication formula that selects only documents for which `Status=Open`. If a document that had been Open replicated in and was subsequently changed to Closed, the Selective Replication formula causes this document to disappear from this replica copy after it replicated.

In addition, there is a pair of replication settings that work in concert to keep a replica database small. These are known as the purge interval and the cutoff date. The purge interval is measured in number of days. The setting is called Remove Documents Not Modified in the Last __ Days. The purge interval is the number that fills the blank. Every one-third of the number of days entered here, Notes/Domino purges documents that are older than the purge interval. If the purge interval is 30 days, every 10 days Notes trims documents that are 30 or more days old.

More specifically, every one-third of the purge interval, the cutoff date is updated. It is the setting in the cutoff date that determines the date boundary for removing documents. The cutoff date is identified as the field called Only Replicate Incoming Documents Saved or Modified After ____, specifying a date and time.

To recover documents that have been purged, you can manually reset the cutoff date. Replicate again, and this cutoff date is used as the date boundary for determining the documents to replicate. The purge interval will take over again, however.

If the replication cycle has completed propagating deletion stubs to all replica copies of the database, and the purge interval has passed, you can no longer recover documents; all copies have been deleted.

Another reason for losing documents is that they were actually deleted. If the ACL settings on the various replicas allow deletions, the deletion stub for a document will replicate to each copy of the database.

Note
Domino R5 has introduced a powerful new feature known as transactional logging. Similar to transaction logging in relational database systems, transactional logging tracks all changes to a database for a specified period of time. If you accidentally delete documents from a database that has transactional logging enabled, you should be able to recover ("undelete") it.

REPLICATION BETWEEN SERVERS NOT OCCURRING OR FAILING TO FINISH

If replication between a pair of servers continually fails or even fails to occur, what can you look for?

First, make sure that replication has not been disabled for this database. Look in the Replication Settings dialog box under the Other icon for an entry labeled Temporarily Disable Replication. If this setting is enabled on either of the replica copies in question, the database will not replicate.

Second, determine whether replication is failing to occur or failing to finish. By using the Notes log, you can determine the answer to this question. If the servers communicate asynchronously, you can check the Miscellaneous Events, Phone Call, and Replication Events documents. For network replication, you can check the Miscellaneous Events and Replication Events documents.

Let's investigate some reasons for the servers' failure to replicate. First, by looking at Connection documents, determine which of the servers is supposed to make the call.

Verify that the parameters of the Connection document are correct:

- Is the connection enabled?
- Is the port specified indeed the correct port?
- Are the source and destination server names spelled correctly?
- Is the phone number correct (including extra dialing rules)?
- Does the Tasks field contain the replication task entry as it should, or does it just include mail routing?

> **Tip**
>
> A sneaky problem could be that there are one or more files specified in the Files to Replicate field. This precludes all other files from replicating. If these filenames are incorrect, no files will replicate.

If the network or serial port that is specified for the connection between the two machines isn't working, replication will fail.

Before two Notes entities can communicate, they must first authenticate. If the two machines are not certified under the same organization or cross-certified, it would be a breach of security to let replication occur. Miscellaneous Events and the Replication Events documents reflect this security issue.

Additionally, servers may fail to obey their own schedule for the following reasons:

- A low memory situation exists.
- There is not enough disk space.
- The server activity load is too high to permit replication to take place.
- All allowable replicators are busy.

The first two of these conditions generate a message on the console (and thus in the log). The second two just cause the Replicator to skip the job without notification.

If the replication schedule is lengthy, it is possible that the server cannot get to the Connection document in question before a new day begins or the end of the scheduled range has passed.

If you have schedules that overlap by one minute or more, replication occurs randomly; replication may even skip parts of the schedules. This overlap may be between multiple entries in one document or between schedules specified on multiple documents.

Let's look at an example: You have Low priority databases scheduled to replicate between 1 a.m. and 5 a.m. (document #1), and Medium and High priority databases are scheduled to replicate between 5 a.m. and 11 a.m. (document #2). The overlap at 5:00 a.m. causes a problem; at the least, change the schedule in document #1 to 1 a.m. to 4:59 a.m.

If you have multiple Connection documents telling your server to call another server, and the document that references databases of the same or lower priority tells the server to make a call, but another document is scheduled to make a call within the next hour, the first replication is suppressed in favor of the document referencing the higher-priority databases. What should you do? Spread out your replications further than one hour, or do as I mentioned previously so that lower-priority documents aren't ignored. Give each a wider range so that at some point in their schedules, they are not within an hour of each other.

Here's another related issue. If you have Connection documents going in both directions for the same two servers at the same time, one server is going to call the other for replication, and the second schedule will be ignored.

REPLICATION CONFLICTS

At times, youour your users will notice replication conflict documents in some databases. These conflicts occur when a document is edited in multiple replicas between replications. When this database replicates, the Replicator doesn't know how to resolve changes to both documents, so it creates a conflict document as a response to the other. The "winner," or main document, is the one that has been edited more recently or has been saved more times.

More specifically, each document contains a sequence number and a sequence time. When you update a document, the sequence number increments by 1, and the sequence time is recorded from the system clock. Thus, the winner has the higher sequence number; if these are the same, the winner is the document with the more recent sequence time.

How can you resolve replication conflicts? First, resolve the conflicts in only one replica, or you will likely create more conflicts. Second, you must manually review both documents and decide on a course of action. Can one document be saved and the other deleted? Do you have to cut and paste to merge information into one of them? Your review of the documents will tell you this.

To actually perform the resolution, it is best if you can keep the main document, merging all updates into it and then deleting the conflict response. The main document is usually the preferred document to keep, because this is the document that is known to other replicas. If you keep this document and replicate, only the changes to the main document are replicated. If you delete the main document and keep the conflict response as the main document, the entire new document is replicated and the main document is deleted, causing more replication transactions than necessary. If there are more changes to the conflict response and you would rather keep that document, before you do any editing, edit this document and resave it. Resaving the conflict response makes the document a main document. Then you can safely cut and paste and finally delete one of them.

How can you prevent conflicts? Use field-level replication. With field-level replication, in addition to the document's sequence number and time, every field has its own sequence number. When that field is modified and the document is saved, the field sequence number is incremented to 1 greater than the previous document sequence number, and the document sequence number is incremented by 1. The document sequence number is then equal to that of the field(s) that just changed.

During replication, in addition to comparing document sequence numbers, the Replicator also compares field sequence numbers. If it turns out that different fields have been modified, the potential exists for the documents to be merged instead of generating a conflict. The reason this is a potential instead of an automatic event is that the database designer must have enabled a property called Merge replication conflicts for this form in the database.

Field-level replication speeds up replication because less data has to replicate, and it can also reduce the number of replication conflicts.

Another way to reduce replication conflicts is to cause them! This sounds contradictory, but let's explore it further. There is a feature called *document versioning*. This form property tells Notes to create a new document each time a document is modified. This new document can either be created as a response document or it can become the new main document while the earlier versions become responses (or siblings). In essence, you are creating a new "conflict," but this is a proactive step instead of a reactive step. This conflict, or version, gives you an audit trail.

When this method is used, if the document is edited in multiple replicas, all the versions add up during replication and no replication conflict appears.

Clearing Replication History

When a replication is successful, Notes updates the replication history in a database. You can see this history by selecting the File, Replication, History menu option. If replication is occurring in both directions (as opposed to a Pull-Only or a Push-Only), you see two entries for a particular server: one entry for send and one entry for receive. Notes also stamps the time and date from the other server into the history on the current server.

The next time this database is replicated between these two servers, Notes takes this time stamp as the starting point to speed up the process.

In rare cases, documents may get saved during a replication, after Notes has determined the set of documents to replicate at that time. That document's time stamp is slightly older than the history stamp that is written in the history upon the successful completion of that replication. At the next replication, Notes uses the history time stamp as the starting point, ignoring the document in question.

When will you find out about this? Notes doesn't announce this behavior; in fact, it doesn't know it happened. Typically, your users discover that they aren't seeing the same set of documents in their respective replicas.

To fix the problem, you can clear the replication history by clicking the Clear button on the Replication History dialog box. Notes informs you that clearing the history makes the next replication with all servers take much longer, and that you should clear the history only if you suspect a time problem as just described. But by clearing the history, you force the Replicator to look at all documents without regard to a history time stamp, and the lost documents reappear. Be aware that you need Manager access to clear the replication history (unless you access a replica locally on a server).

Modem Issues

In an ideal world, the modems you've configured for your Domino servers would always work. Let's take a look at a couple of issues you might encounter. If you walk up to your console and observe that the server seems to be continually querying a modem at all the available speeds but never getting an answer, that modem is not operational. Or what if you notice that your modems just don't seem to be working—what can you do?

Your Server Is Cycling Through the Available Modem Speeds

If you see your server continually try to communicate with a modem, cycling through each of the speeds in order, your server isn't communicating with the modem. If a modem is not available but the port is enabled, the server continually attempts to access the modem. If the modem is connected, cycle the power to it; if Domino still cannot access it, you may have a damaged port, or the system may just need to be rebooted. If this happens repeatedly, try using a different port, if one is available. Try another modem or modem cable. Consider replacing the port. Make sure that another task on that machine hasn't been configured to use that port, which would prevent Notes from having access to it.

Modem Connections Are Not Working

If you are experiencing a problem across multiple ports with a set of modems of the same brand, try checking the following:

- Look in the Miscellaneous Events documents for evidence that modem commands are being sent and acknowledged by the modems. Look carefully at the responses being received during any connection attempts with other servers.

- Examine the modem file (or switch to an alternative) for setup-string errors. Try simplifying the setup strings to one line that states SETUP=AT&F for factory-default settings.

- Check the settings on your modem. If it has dip switches, compare the current settings with those recommended in the manual. Try setting the switches to the most basic settings described in the manual; you can slowly improve them after reaching a known good combination.
- Check the cable and the port. Try alternatives if they are available.

From Here...

This chapter introduced you to the new monitoring features found in the Domino Administrator Client. You also looked at some of the more common problems found in a Domino server network and explored solutions to these problems. Here are some other chapters that may be of interest to you.

- Chapter 38, "Administering Users, Groups, and Certification," covers information you need to know to add and change user and group information.
- Chapter 39, "Administering Electronic Mail," gives you more detailed information on electronic mail and its administration.
- Chapter 40, "Replication and Its Administration," covers the details of replication. It shows you how to optimize your replication schedules and connections.
- Chapter 41, "Administering Files and Databases," tells you about compacting database, full text indexing, and performing database analysis.

Advanced Domino Administration

44 Performance, Scalability, and Capacity Planning for Domino Servers

45 Upgrading from cc:Mail, Microsoft Mail, and Exchange to Domino

45 Using the Enterprise Domino Server with a Large Domino Network

45 Integrating Domino with Phone, Fax, and Imaging Systems

45 Using Lotus NotesPump/Lotus Enterprise Integrator

Epilogue

CHAPTER 44

PERFORMANCE, SCALABILITY, AND CAPACITY PLANNING FOR DOMINO SERVERS

Domino R5 offers an improved high-performance infrastructure that takes Domino's already impressive openness and scalability to a new level.

For years, Domino has demonstrated its potential to provide high-performance and high-availability service to thousands of users. However, Domino's performance can be degraded severely by poor scalability and capacity planning, and by configuration factors that are often not understood by network or server administrators.

This chapter is divided into three sections. The first section explains the factors that affect Domino's performance and provides guidance for making Domino perform at its best. The other two sections of this chapter explore scalability issues and capacity planning.

R5 Performance

The NotesBench Consortium has released preliminary findings that set R5 performance at 3–5 times faster than that of R4, with possibly greater gains for the Enterprise-class servers. Other improvements enable you to keep track of up to a million users in a single domain directory, and maintain exponentially larger databases. Lotus tested R5 databases up to 32GB (16GB on NT), but has not specified a size limit on R5 databases. By contrast, R4 domain directories supported a maximum of 150,000 users, and R4 database sizes could not exceed 4GB.

Lotus also fine-tuned Domino R5's reindexing and incremental view indexing for faster displays. Other R5 performance enhancements include

- NameLookup cache, which provides faster name resolution
- Better memory and I/O utilization
- Multiple `mail.box` databases

Domino Performance Issues

"Why is it so slow?" If you've set up more than one Domino server, you've probably heard or asked this question at least once. Improperly configured, Domino can take an intolerably long time to load a view or Web page to display. Domino performance is affected by a complex array of related factors, but this chapter gives you a comprehensive overview of what causes those excruciating slowdowns and how to realize Domino's maximum performance potential.

Performance problems are not always the fault of Domino itself, and are not necessarily caused by the applications Domino may be running. The solution to better performance is not necessarily to make Domino just "run faster." For example, Domino may be shooting out responses and Web pages at its peak capacity, but the results won't be apparent to users who are connected via a poorly configured network.

The following sections explain in detail how your server configuration, your network, your databases, and other factors affect Domino's performance.

How the Server Affects Domino Performance

Your server platform, CPU speed, disk drive, and memory play crucial roles in Domino's overall performance.

Platform

Domino R5, at the time of writing, is available for the following server platforms:

- AIX 4.3.1
- AS/400 V4R2
- HP-UX 11.0
- OS/2 Warp Server 4
- S/390 V2R6
- Solaris/Intel 2.6
- Solaris/SPARC 2.6
- Windows NT4.0/Alpha
- Windows NT4.0/Intel

Note This list could change if operating system vendors ship new versions.

The system architecture and scalability of the UNIX servers gives them an edge over NT servers. But Lotus offers more comprehensive support and resources for NT servers. Similarly, OS/2 provides a well-integrated solution that performs well. The downside is that you might have a difficult time finding someone with OS/2 expertise to manage the server.

Platform choice is only one (and perhaps the least significant) of all the numerous factors that impact Domino's performance. An NT version running on a well-tuned server and network provides more satisfactory response times than a beefy UNIX version hampered by a poor configuration or network problems.

If you are planning to support small-to-midsize organizations, NT servers with single or multiple CPUs, or clusters of NT servers will provide adequate service. If you are planning to support a large enterprise, you should take a close look at the AS/400 platform and the Enterprise Domino Server. For more detailed information on this topic, see Chapter 46, "Using the Enterprise Domino Server with a Large Domino Network."

CPU

Predictably, your server's CPU speed and number of processors have a large impact on Domino's potential to serve heavy loads. You should definitely buy a server that has the capacity for dual or multiple processors. In my experience, the 200MHz (or lower) Pentium class servers probably won't have sufficient power for your needs, unless you are serving a very small group of users.

Pentium II or P6 systems are popular choices among many Domino vendors.

Memory

At startup, Domino obtains approximately a quarter of the available system memory for its operations. As the load increases, Domino dedicates more memory. If you have insufficient memory, Domino will be forced to "make do" with smaller chunks of memory allocated per user. This also leaves less memory for other system operations and tasks. The Scalability and Capacity Planning sections that follow provide detailed memory-planning tips.

Disk Drives

Your disk drives can impact Domino's performance in two ways. The speed of your disk drive directly or indirectly affects several other aspects of Domino's performance, so it's wise to take advantage of the newer, faster hard drives. With falling prices and speeds approaching 8,000rpm, the new disk drives make solid investments for just about any enterprise.

Having only a single disk drive, instead of several, can slow Domino's performance by forcing the entire I/O (input/output) workload to be handled by a single device.

I/O distribution significantly impacts Domino's performance. Having the operation system, Domino's executable, and data files all on a single disk drive poses a less than ideal I/O configuration. If you have multiple drives, consider dividing the I/O workload among them. For example, try placing the Domino executable on one drive, the operating system on another, and your Domino databases on a third drive.

How the Network Affects Domino Performance

After you have properly configured your server for optimum performance, you want to examine your network's impact on Domino.

Network Protocol

If your network isn't already IP-compliant, you should consider switching to IP. Aside from the recognized advantages for general networking, using IP can greatly enhance Domino's performance.

Network Segments

Implementing network segments (or virtual LANs) can help you balance your network load and isolate a heavy traffic area, minimizing its adverse affects on the rest of your network. Segmenting your LAN makes sense, particularly if you have multiple Domino servers serving different departments. Your individual user groups will enjoy better response times from their own Domino servers.

Network Bandwidth and Speed

Your internal network's bandwidth and speed can impact Domino response times by slowing the delivery of requested data. The NotesBench Consortium, which provides recommended performance practices and is discussed later in this chapter, reports that its vendors are upgrading their 10Mbps networks to 100Mbps. Bandwidth and speed issues also affect the delivery of data over the Internet or phone lines, neither of which can guarantee a specific level of performance.

FIREWALLS, DOMAIN NAME (DNS), AND PROXY SERVERS

Firewalls, DNS and servers;DNS;(Domain Name Service)>proxy servers, athough often critical to operations and security, can negatively impact Domino's performance, sometimes severely. Troubleshooting a problem of this nature will probably require a "sniffer" and some assistance from your network administrator. For more detailed information about firewalls and their impact on Domino, see Chapter 37, "Firewalls, Virtual Private Networks (VPNs), and Internet Security."

PORT ENCRYPTION

A useful security option, port encryption enables you to protect your data while it is in transit across your network. Although port encryption has no effect on a Notes client, it can slow data transfer times on a Domino server.

Network Monitoring Applications

Network monitoring applications can help you get a better idea of what factors are impacting your network's performance at any given time. A critical component of any network, monitoring tools provide services that fall into two categories: polling and analysis.

Polling monitors ping (send a single data packet and listen for a response) whatever network nodes you specify at regular intervals and provide a real-time or near real-time view of what network services are working. The purpose of polling monitors is simply to let you see the current status of your network—which servers are up and which are down. Some products page or email the administrator if a server doesn't respond to the pings for a specified period. Although you can sometimes use this polling data to draw conclusions about a certain hub or server's performance, polling monitors do not provide the comprehensive analytical data that large networks often need. A trial version of one of the better polling monitors, Ipswitch's What's Up Gold, can be downloaded from `www.ipswitch.com`.

Analysis monitors, on the other hand, are designed to provide the more comprehensive data used to troubleshoot problems in complex networks. These solutions, often packaged as suites of applications, cost several times more than the simpler polling tools priced in the hundreds of dollars.

HOW YOUR DATABASES AFFECT DOMINO PERFORMANCE

Domino Release 5 offers several new database properties settings that can help improve performance. To change these settings, right-click the Database icon and select Properties. In the properties dialog box, select or deselect the settings as recommended in the following sections. The R5 Release Notes provides full details on these settings.

DON'T MAINTAIN UNREAD MARKS

Selecting Don't maintain unread marks improves performance by freeing system resources that would otherwise be used for keeping track of the unread marks.

Document Table Bitmap Optimization

Selecting Document table bitmap optimization streamlines the processes Domino has to go through when updating views. It may be particularly beneficial if you have a lot of large databases.

Remember that your view-rebuilding response time is lengthened if you do not have enough disk space available in your temp directory. When Domino rebuilds a view, it stores a number of temporary files. You may want to specify a directory other than your standard temp directory for the view rebuilds.

Don't Overwrite Free Space

Domino has a security feature that protects deleted data by overwriting it with a pattern. This process of overwriting is processor-intensive and can slow things down. Selecting Don't overwrite free space in the database property settings turns this feature off. Recognize that there may be situations where security concerns dictate that you want this feature to remain active.

Maintain LastAccessed Property

The property Maintain LastAccessed property is not selected by default. Selecting it requires extra read/write activity that could impact performance, particularly on a server with a heavy workload.

Select this property only if you need to keep track of the date when a particular document was last read. The document deletion tool uses this property to automatically delete documents that haven't been read for a certain number of days.

Don't Support Specialized Response Hierarchy

Select Don't support specialized response hierarchy to relieve Domino of the task of tracking parent or response relationships between documents. Selecting this property improves performance and does not affect hierarchical views or replication formulas, as long as you do not use the `@AllChildren` or `@AllDescendants` functions for view selection or replication formulas.

Remember that selecting this property requires you to compact the database. This operation requires enough disk space to make a temporary duplicate of your database(s).

Limit Entries in $UpdatedBy Fields

Selecting Limit entries in $UpdatedBy fields enables you to limit the number of entries that can be saved in the $UpdatedBy field. Every time a document is edited, the username or servername responsible for the modification is stored in the $UpdatedBy field. Over time, this history of edits can grow large enough to consume a significant amount of disk space and cause your replication and view updates to lag.

LIMIT ENTRIES IN $REVISIONS FIELDS

The Limit entries in $Revisions fields property follows the same principle as the previous property setting. Again, this field stores the time and date of every document-editing session, for up to 500 sessions. This field helps Domino prevent save and replication conflicts, using the time and date to arbitrate situations where a document was opened and edited simultaneously by two users. But 500 edit session entries take up several megabytes or more of disk space and slows performance. The Lotus R5 Release Notes recommend reducing this number to no less than 10 entries.

DATABASE POLICY

Because Domino database properties can significantly impact Domino performance, you may want to consider adopting a database policy that guides the creation and configuration of all Domino databases in your organization. A set of recommended or required property settings and configurations that enhance performance will benefit just about any size organization. For heavily trafficked Intranets or Web sites, database policies are a necessity.

OTHER FACTORS

You should always make sure you are running the latest version of Domino, as well as the latest Notes Clients. Older versions have rather severe limitations on the number of active users they can support.

The same holds true for operating systems. Upgrading to the latest version helps prevent unnecessary performance bottlenecks.

PERFORMANCE TROUBLESHOOTING PROCEDURES

You now have an overview of all the many things that could possibly go wrong and cause performance problems. Let's put this information to work.

If you are experiencing performance problems with your Domino server, follow a structured process of elimination to find the problem. Troubleshooting Domino performance problems means sorting out whether the problem is being caused by Domino, an application, or some other external factor. The following procedure eliminates possible performance factors in their order of probability and proximity to the server:

1. Check the Domino databases and applications.
2. Check the server software and system configuration.
3. Check the server hardware and specs.
4. Check the network configuration (in your local area/segment/VLAN first, then outward).
5. Check firewalls, DNS servers, and proxies.

There is a good reason for this order. By starting with the Domino databases and applications, you are eliminating problems within your domain of responsibility before working outward into domains controlled by others (network, firewall, and so forth). The order is also geared to increase your chances of solving the performance problem without having to make configuration changes to mission-critical assets that affect other people. The goal is to eliminate the problem with as little impact as possible on the overall enterprise.

The Domino troubleshooting procedures should be understood and agreed upon ahead of time by your operations staff. Correctly ordered procedures help prevent counterproductive finger-pointing and keep the troubleshooting process on track.

PREREQUISITES FOR TROUBLESHOOTING DOMINO PERFORMANCE

This checklist shows the basics you probably need in order to figure out what is degrading your Domino server's performance:

- The assistance of your network administrator (or your network documentation)
- A sniffer or a network monitoring application (see previous sidebar, "Network Monitoring Applications")
- Configuration details of your server hardware
- Access rights to Domino applications

Using NT's Built-in Performance Monitors
If you are running Windows NT on your server, you can use the NT Performance Monitor to track your Domino server's performance. The NT Performance Monitor offers a simple method for adding a "performance counter" representing your Domino Server to its list of monitored functions.

PERFORMANCE WRAP-UP

The preceding sections provided an overview of the performance factors affecting Domino, with guidelines for troubleshooting performance problems on an existing system. The next two sections will help you plan for optimum performance on new or growing Notes/Domino deployments.

SCALABILITY

The following sections guide you through the process of planning for future growth. You start with an overview of general scalability issues, and then home in on Domino's scalability, with particular focus on Domino's clustering capabilities.

A CLOSER LOOK AT SCALABILITY

A favorite buzzword in recent tech-press hype, the term *scalability* gets thrown around quite a bit by conference speakers and new-product press releases. These advertising messages often imply that scalability is an infinite capacity to meet unforeseen and open-ended requirements. This kind of scalability doesn't exist. It may be more realistic to think of scalability in terms of being able to reach specific targets.

For our discussion, let's define scalability as the capacity to accommodate a fairly specific set of growth expectations.

The Basic Scalability Model in Figure 44.1 shows the three necessary components of scalability:

- Known current configuration.
- A projected growth expectation.
- A scalability strategy for accommodating the specified future growth. The strategy will typically be broken into stairsteps that correspond either to long-term phases or stages of implementation or growth.

The purpose of this model is to show an objective view of the issues involved in real-world scalability. Notice the small letters *a* and *b* situated on either side of the delta. *a* refers to the point where the solution is more than adequate, and *b* refers to the inevitable point where the solution is less than adequate. *a* is preferred over *b*, and the midpoint of the two is best of all. Of course, in real-world situations, the magic middle point, where a system is perfectly sized to meet the current load, is difficult, if not, impossible to maintain.

Because the three components of the Basic Scalability Model each play a critical role in your approach to scalability, they are examined in some detail in the next few sections.

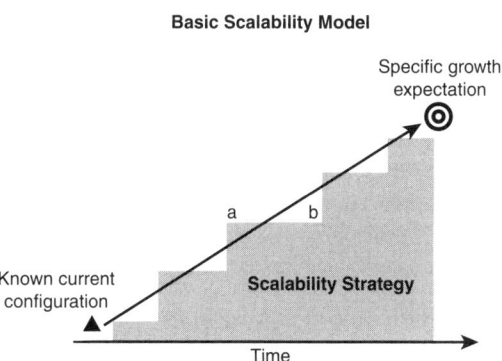

Figure 44.1
The Basic Scalability Model establishes the required components for scalability planning.

The first element of the Basic Scalability Model, Known current configuration, may seem elementary, but you need to take the time to make sure you know your Domino server and network's current configuration and what it is truly capable of supporting. The purpose of this step is to determine whether your user's needs are truly outstripping your server's capacity. Or is something else degrading the performance of an otherwise adequate server? Working through the performance sections at the beginning of this chapter is a good starting point for this exercise.

The second step is to determine the specific growth expectation to which you are going to scale. This helps you set the objectives of your scalability strategy. The first question you need to ask is What exactly is growing or changing? Figure 44.2 shows possible scalability scenarios and the unique issues that accompany them.

Figure 44.2
Different scenarios typically present unique issues that need to be considered when developing growth expectations and scalability strategies.

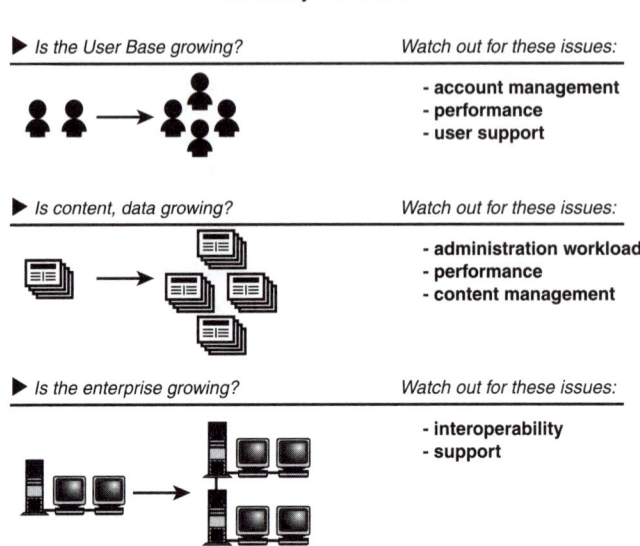

Is the Enterprise/Platform Growing?

Let's say a larger company acquires your company, and suddenly your enterprise grows from a small LAN to a large WAN. This kind of a scalability scenario requires you to determine whether your number of users will grow or whether you will continue to operate as a small unit. You also need to determine what coordination is needed between the managers of your information assets and those of other units. As the operations of your two companies are merged, interoperability and support issues also dominate this scalability scenario.

A closely related scenario might have you moving from a small-to-medium–capacity server to a high-end Enterprise server. The reasons for this could include increased users, a growing enterprise, and so forth, but the focus in this scenario would be on moving existing data and applications from one platform to another with minimal service disruption.

Is the Content/Data Growing?

Your client wants to turn its Domino-powered Web site into a full-blown extranet, adding a new range of online publications and data for its customer base. The number and size of databases is expected to grow dramatically in the near future and at cyclical intervals each year. This scenario requires an examination of the data (is it structured or unstructured? is it relational?) and a focus on content management procedures as they relate to the creation and maintenance of Domino databases and services.

Are the Requirements Growing?

Your company's fast growth is expected to double the number of Notes/Domino users you must support. In a similar scenario, your number of users remains constant, but new requirements are spawned by the rollout of an Intranet that offers a new range of services for your users. This scenario requires careful attention to performance and capacity planning.

This should give you a flavor of the different kinds of scalability scenarios you may be faced with. In each case, before you start planning the scalability strategy, you want to nail down the growth expectation. What exactly is growing and what exactly will the Domino server be required to support?

After this has been determined, you can move to the third component of the Basic Scalability Model: the Scalability Strategy.

Domino R5 and Your Scalability Strategy

Domino has a well-established reputation for platform scalability. Domino can run on everything from Windows 95 and NT (versions 3 and 4) all the way to AS/400s and even IBM mainframes. In addition, Domino's system architecture enables it not only to simply run on high-end systems, but also to actually take full advantage of their resources. Real-world Notes/Domino configurations have proven that they can support large enterprises with thousands of email accounts, Web servers with over a million hits day, and hundreds of concurrent Notes client users. Domino also has proven its appeal to organizations seeking scalable solutions, with a need to control or reduce procurement and ownership costs.

You'll never find a one-size-fits-all perfect strategy for scalability. Each company must examine its own needs and its own ability to make use of Notes/Domino scalability solutions. Figure 44.3 shows a sample scalability strategy for a company that expects to grow from 100 users to 100,000 users. The growth scale is exaggerated to show the range of scalability that Notes/Domino can support. Remember this is only a sample—don't stake your next promotion on it!

Figure 44.3
This example scalability strategy presents a simplified plan for meeting specific growth expectations over time.

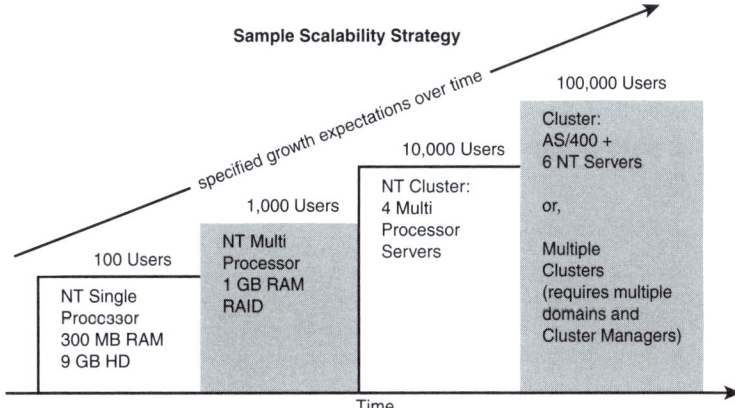

Strategy Tips

The purpose of a scalability strategy is to keep from painting yourself into a corner, so to speak. Nothing could be worse than not being able to scale, due to unenlightened previous decisions or oversights.

First, if you cannot afford larger Enterprise-class servers, choose servers that enable you to add processors when they are needed later. You should also be aware of the scalability of servers and platforms. For example, an AS/400 is more scalable than an NT or OS/2. You could possibly run up to a dozen or more Domino servers with ease on a single AS/400.

Second, always think about scalability in terms of the following:

- Future directory services
- Future user population
- Future bandwidth
- Future administrator workload (when an environment scales, the administration tasks may multiply exponentially)
- Future user requirements and capabilities
- Future network architecture

Third, keep in mind that advanced users have a definite tendency to use more system resources. The immediate post-rollout period, when users are still learning how to use Notes, will not reflect the normal usage patterns of users. As they become more proficient, they are more likely to make full use of Notes/Domino capabilities.

Likewise, users with newer, more powerful computers tend to use more system resources, taking advantage of their extra RAM and processing power to run multiple applications, browser windows, and client features simultaneously.

And finally, be sure to have a transition plan for moving from one level to the next, and decide ahead of time what will trigger your move to the next level. This will involve outside factors and nontechnical issues, such as funding, space, possibly hiring new positions, training, increased support requirements, and so forth.

R5 Scalability Features

Your scalability strategy should outline how you plan to use Notes/Domino scalability features as your requirements grow.

Domino R5 scalability features include

- The Internet Cluster Manager (ICM), which enables support for HTTP server clusters, allowing Webmasters to distribute Web traffic across multiple Web servers. The ICM follows Domino's model of clustering servers to provide high availability.
- Integrated support for POP3, IMAP4, and SMTP mail; LDAPv3 directories; MIME, S/MIME, HTML, and Java.

- Directory support for up to one million users.
- Improved administration console and management tools.
- New system-level features and options that enhance scalability on UNIX platforms.
- For Release 5, Lotus redesigned the architecture of its Server Networking Model to provide better scalability and overall performance.

The following sections examine the concepts behind clustering and how Domino's clustering can support your scalability strategy.

Symmetric Multiprocessing with Domino R5

Symmetric multiprocessing (SMP) refers to the collaborative activity of a group of processors that share common resources (operating system, memory, or I/O bus). A single copy of the operating system manages the group of processors.

SMP, popularly dubbed the "shared everything" architecture, is the direct opposite of MPP (massively parallel processing), which is often referred to as a "shared nothing" architecture. In contrast to MPP's redundant copies of system resources and databases, SMP offers dynamic workload balancing and reduced cost of ownership through shared usage of scalable resources.

For mission-critical applications, Lotus offers an SMP version of Domino that leverages the power of multithreading and multiprocessing. Domino product specifications note that the SMP Domino server is designed to simultaneously support a wide variety of tasks and demands:

- High user loads
- Concurrent server-to-server mail routing
- Concurrent server-to-server replication
- Traffic encryption
- Indexing
- Scheduling
- HTTP
- POP3 support

Lotus applies the power of SMP using Domino clusters (groups of servers that share a workload) to provide high availability. The next few sections discuss the concept of clustering.

About Clustering

Clustering applies the old adage "Many hands make light work" to servers and networks. One of the biggest scalability advantages of Domino R5, clustering is a method of grouping redundant Domino servers to provide a higher level of reliability than could be provided by a single server. Each cluster of servers is synchronized by a Cluster Manager. Amazingly, clustered servers can reside on different operating systems and hardware platforms. A cluster might include a Domino server running on an AS/400, complemented by three Domino servers running on NT servers.

CLUSTERING ADVANTAGES

Since 1995, the Domino server's Advanced Services option has provided built-in support for clustering and partitioning for maximum reliability. By clustering up to six (maximum limit) Domino servers per domain in a LAN, administrators can provide the performance advantages discussed in the following sections.

HIGH AVAILABILITY High availability attempts to guarantee uninterrupted access to mission-critical services, even if major disruptions occur in the network. Lotus's Domino server clustering is just one of a growing number of high-availability strategies. The advantage of Domino clustering is that it uses standardized components and does not require that all clustered servers run on the same operating system or hardware platform.

FAILOVER SUPPORT Notes R5, for the first time, includes browser client failover support, so if a database goes down or fails to respond to a request, the requesting client is automatically forwarded to a replica of the unavailable database.

WORKLOAD BALANCING Workload balancing enables you to specify the level of traffic you will allow on a server before redirecting traffic to another less-utilized server.

CLUSTER REPLICATION Cluster replication enables you to set a schedule for replicating databases. Replication can be prompted by either conditions/events or by time settings. For example, you might want replication to occur when 10 documents have been updated in a particular database.

THE INTERNET CLUSTER MANAGER

The Internet Cluster Manager (ICM), which supports HTTP and HTTPS protocols, synchronizes the clustered servers and controls incoming traffic to balance the workload among the individual servers. For example, if one server in a cluster reaches its capacity or fails, the ICM coordinates the redirection of requests for a certain database to another server containing a replica of the same database. The redirection is transparent to the user.

The ICM must reside in the cluster's domain, but does not need to be running on one of the servers in the actual cluster. Figure 44.4 depicts a cluster of four NT servers and one AS/400 Enterprise Notes server.

To set up the ICM, install clusters according to normal procedures (see www.notes.net or your Domino documentation for full details), and then install the ICM.

The ICM must reside in the cluster's domain, but does not need to be running on one of the servers in the actual cluster.

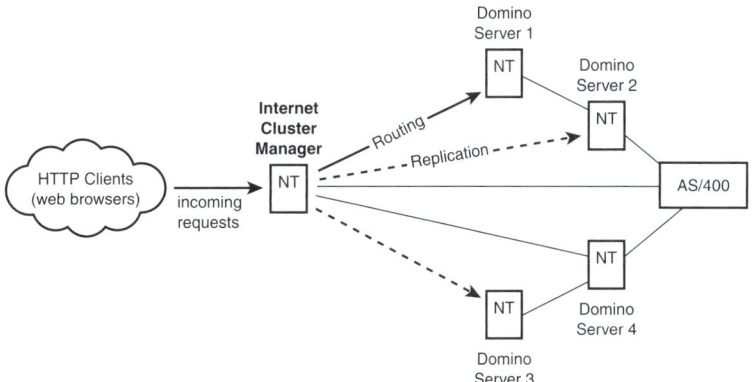

Figure 44.4
The Internet Cluster Manager redirects incoming requests from HTTP clients to balance the workload.

SCALABILITY WRAP-UP

We've examined the important issues of scalability and how Domino can provide a scalable enterprise solution. Next, we put our scalability knowledge to work with a little capacity planning.

CAPACITY PLANNING

"How big of a server do you need?" The sound of the question is always tinged with suspicion, as if you're up to something. You'd love to reply "The biggest we can find!" But that's probably not what your purchasing department or boss wants to hear. Domino's product documentation doesn't help your case either. It says the minimum requirements are a 1GB drive and 64MB of RAM. You think to yourself, there's no way. How do you find out what you really need—and justify it?

This section tears the wraps off the heretofore black art of planning a server configuration that matches your organization's needs. We start with a simple capacity planning exercise that helps you cover all the issues, and then examine capacity planning tools, memory issues, and more.

CAPACITY PLANNING EXERCISE

The following exercise asks questions and provides guidelines designed to help you remove the guesswork from your planning efforts and focus on the scalability and performance issues that are most important to your enterprise.

SETTING A SCOPE FOR SCALABILITY

What exactly needs to be scalable? Your email and applications? Your Web site? All of the above? Without a scope that prioritizes what must be scalable, it is difficult to meet specific objectives. Write a sentence that states exactly what you intend to make scalable.

Set Your Horizon

How many years out are you planning? A 6-month plan will dramatically differ from a 2-year or 5-year plan. The shorter the timeline, the easier it will be to predict growth in requirements. Write down the time period during which you will ensure scalability and adequate performance.

Set a General Platform Direction

Does your organization prefer UNIX? NT? OS/2? Each of these choices presents radically different ramifications for your scalability planning. Write out your organization's platform direction.

Set Growth Expectations

Be able to state specifically what kind of growth you are preparing for. What exactly will grow? Write out one or more sentences stating the growth you are planning to accommodate. For example, you might write, "We expect to add 500 email users, 40 new databases, and 3 new Web sites." Or, "Our network will grow from 5 servers to 20."

List Dependencies or Limitations

If scalability is contingent on external factors, such as the bandwidth of your network or your budget, you should evaluate and, if possible, resolve these issues before going any further. For your scalability effort to succeed, try to determine early the things that could impact, limit, or derail your plans. Write a list, and decide whether anything on your list requires you to adjust your scope or horizon.

Set an Objective

Now that you have completed the previous steps, you are ready to state your scalability objective. To the sentences you have already written, add one more. Write what services you will provide and how many users you will support. Be specific. Here's an example: "We will build and maintain a system that will provide the following services for no more than 600 users: Email, Web Browser access to Domino databases, Notes Client access to Domino databases."

Congratulations! You've given yourself a tremendous headstart and increased your chances of planning a properly sized server. Now it's time to look at the tools you'll need.

Capacity Planning Tools

Lotus provides several tools and services that can help you select the Domino configuration that best matches your organization's requirements.

NotesBench

As the name denotes, NotesBench is a set of tools designed to provide standardized testing procedures and benchmark information. NotesBench's independently audited performance findings are published at the NotesBench Web site (www.NotesBench.org). The NotesBench Web site's reports and data help vendors and customers make intelligent Notes/Domino configuration and platform choices.

The NotesBench toolset itself is made available to qualified and trained vendors and Lotus Business Partners. These vendors and partners can, if needed, create customized benchmarks for customers who need to determine whether a solution fits their specific requirements.

DOMINO SERVER.PLANNER

Domino Server.Planner helps you identify the right server size and capacity for your requirements. This capacity-planning tool enables you to specify different workloads and uses Lotus vendor benchmark data to recommend a server configuration.

For more information about Server.Planner, visit the NotesBench Consortium Web site (www.NotesBench.org). You can download Server.Planner from http://www.notes.net.

PLANNING MEMORY REQUIREMENTS

My advice is to buy as much as you can afford! But you need something more than my advice to go on. How much do you really need? What if you already know how much memory you have, and you want to know how many users you can realistically expect to support? It helps to understand how Domino uses memory.

Domino, by default, obtains 25% of the available system memory at startup. If your server has 240MB of RAM, Domino starts off with 60. If increased usage requires more memory, Domino obtains whatever amount is needed.

If you're running a server with a large number of users, you have the option of specifying that Domino start with more than 25% of available memory. The NSF_BUFFER_POOL_SIZE setting in the NOTES.INI file enables you to set the amount of memory you want Domino to start with.

How much RAM should your Domino server have? Recommendations vary between 300KB–1MB of RAM per user. A series of excellent Domino performance tests conducted by James Grigsby, Carol Zimmet, and Susan Florio recommended that you plan 1MB of RAM for each user, assuming that you have average-to-advanced users. As mentioned previously, advanced users use more server resources than beginners or sporadic users. The complete findings from these tests have been published in a two-part article "Optimizing Your Server Performance," which can be found on Notes.net (www.notes.net).

If you can afford it, I recommend following the 1MB-per-user rule of thumb provided by Grigsby, Zimmet, and Florio. This means 1MB per Notes client, or for each user who will use a Web browser to access and work with databases on your server.

Does this rule apply to a Web site that could possibly attract hundreds of thousands of visitors? Probably not. Most Web sites, even corporate sites, have to work very hard to stand a chance of attracting this kind of traffic, and those that do usually find that their traffic falls into two categories: serious users and casual visitors.

To illustrate, let's do some experimental math. In accordance with our guidelines, we'll follow a rule of 300KB of RAM for casual users and 1MB of RAM for serious users. We'll make an assumption that 75% of your traffic will be from visitors who are browsing through your site. The other 25% of your traffic will come from your internal users, who will be updating content, sharing calendars, and accessing databases. Assuming 1,000 visitors a day, you conclude that 250 of them (or 25%) will require 1MB of RAM each, and the others should have 300KB each. This calls for 475MB of RAM for this particular server.

Users also differ in another way. Users who work directly on the server rather than replicating databases to their own computers constantly require the server's resources. Users who replicate databases to their workstations instead of working directly on the server free Domino processing resources for other operations.

Planning Your Directory Services

Directory services represent another critical issue for capacity planning. As your enterprise grows, what kind of directory services will be needed? Fortunately, Domino now provides a new range of scalable options for managing your Directory.

Domino R5 includes full support for the Lightweight Directory Access Protocol (LDAPv3). A full treatment of the LDAP protocol resides at

`http://idm.Internet.com/foundation/ldap.sHTML`

Domino's LDAP support enables users to access and update the Domino Directory (in previous versions, called the Public Address Book) using any client that supports LDAP. The Notes client is an example of an LDAP-compatible client. Microsoft, Netscape, and Novell have all announced support for LDAP.

LDAP support enables Domino to authenticate users by looking at their certification information in other LDAP directories. By the same token, other directory services can authenticate users listed in the Domino Directory.

In addition, Domino R5's Directory has increased its capacity so it can now handle up to one million users per directory. This means enterprise directory service can handle a practically unlimited number of users.

What If I Have to Make Do?

Capacity planning is not always a joyous occasion. Sometimes, instead of getting the brand new superserver of your dreams, you get to figure out how you're going to support more users or requirements with your current configuration. Besides handing in your resignation, you can do a couple of things.

First, use the capacity planning tools discussed in the previous sections to test specific loads against your server. These tools can help you determine the optimum configuration for your particular situation. You may find solutions that do not require you to buy anything.

Second, try implementing as many of the NotesBench vendor practices as you can. The NotesBench Consortium reports that an analysis of NotesBench reports for 1997 revealed a number of standard practices among vendors attempting to maximize their capacity. Although some of these practices involve purchasing new equipment, the purchases are often relatively manageable (such as buying a faster hard drive), and many of the practices involve making changes to an existing configuration. The NotesBench vendor practices are listed here in order of priority:

1. Allocated 300–400KB per active user, setting the NSF_BUFFER_POOL_SIZE to the maximum for its memory configuration.
2. Distributed I/O across separate devices (putting the operating system on one drive, Domino on another, and so forth). Some even changed the log= parameter (in the Notes.INI file) to offload logging to a directory other than the default.
3. Improved the I/O subsystem by moving from EISA or EISA/PCI to faster PCI controllers, and used striping, a process of distributing data across the array drives. Also used multiple I/O controllers to logically distribute databases. (Note: Because Domino R4.6-and-later versions do not allow RAID0 to be used for publishing data, you may not be able to use striping as a means of improving performance on your server).
4. Moved from 5400rpm disk drives to 7200rpm drives.
5. Used proper Strip size (8KB for Digital systems, 16KB for IBM Netfinity). Not all Strip size results were disclosed.
6. Chose faster CPUs, ignoring 100–200MHz processors and showing a preference for P6-based systems over Pentium II systems for high-end Domino server loads. As user loads increased, level 2 cache amounts also increased from 256KB, to 512KB, all the way up to 2MB for servers with multiple processors.
7. Increased network bandwidth (10Mbps to 100Mbps) and segmented their LANs.
8. Over the past two years, made IP their network protocol of choice, moving away from SPX and NetBIOS.
9. Upgraded to the latest available Domino versions, taking advantage of performance and capacity improvements.
10. Using Domino Server Partitioning, hosting multiple servers on a single, more powerful machine, such as an AS/400. This enables each server to take advantage of the superior performance of these machines (multiple I/O controllers connected by fiber OS to CPU binding, and so forth).

SUMMARY

This chapter started with an overview of Domino performance issues, examining what factors impact Domino's performance. You then moved on to a discussion of scalability and the solutions offered by Notes/Domino. The final section, "Capacity Planning," provided a capacity planning exercise, an overview of tools, memory issues, and what to do if you are forced to plan for a less than ideal configuration.

From Here...

You can access History of Lotus Notes and Domino at the following address:

`http://www.notes.net/history.nsf/`

The entire history is worth perusing, but the sections titled "Release 4.6" and "Release 5.0" give you a concise technical comparison of the two versions.

Check out the NotesBench Consortium Web site at

`http://www.notesbench.org/Action/HomePage.nsf?OpenDatabase`

The NotesBench Consortium is an independent, nonprofit organization that provides Notes/Domino benchmark test results, as well as tips for optimizing your servers. You need to register.

You can reach the Domino Release 5.0 discussion forum at

`http://www.notes.net/r5`

CHAPTER 45

Upgrading from cc:Mail, Microsoft Mail, and Exchange to Domino

This chapter focuses on issues relevant to upgrading to Lotus Notes Domino R5. It consists of four major sections. The first covers general issues regarding the upgrade process itself, providing a rationale for the upgrade and then explaining some of the most critical issues to be encountered during the upgrade. The second section addresses the upgrade path from previous releases of Notes and Domino. The third section introduces the general features and functionality of the upgrade and migration facilities provided by the Domino Upgrade Services. The final three sections of the chapter focus on the specifics of the upgrade facilities offered for cc:Mail, MS Mail and Exchange, and LDAP Interface File Format migrations and conversions as representative samples of the upgrade facilities provided by Domino R5. Each of these final three sections outline procedural descriptions of upgrading users from one environment to the next.

Upgrading to Notes and Domino R5

In general terms, an upgrade marks an improvement, whether to become more advanced in one's profession, more knowledgeable, or more productive. Upgrading your technology and tools assists you in reaching these objectives.

Understanding the Rationale for the Upgrade

Lotus Notes and Domino R5 is one such technology. Notes and Domino R5 build on the rich Internet-enabled groupware functionality introduced in R4.5 and advanced in R4.6 to provide a completely integrated solution for mail, calendaring and scheduling, and discussion forums. The R5 technology, however, transcends the traditional groupware application arena, providing corporations of all sizes a set of tools in an array of disciplines from Web application development frameworks to enterprisewide data integration frameworks, elaborate extended search engines, and secure infrastructures.

In short, Lotus Notes and Domino R5 provide

- A server-agnostic and easy-to-use multiprotocol Notes, HTTP, POP3, IMAP, LDAP, and NNTP client in the Lotus Notes client
- A client-agnostic, enterprise-grade multiprotocol Lotus Domino server equally servicing native Notes, HTTP, POP3, IMAP, LDAP, and NNTP client requests
- A functionally rich messaging server for companies of all sizes in the Lotus Domino mail server
- An open and secure Web application server in the Domino Internet and Web application server
- Simple and flexible administration in the Domino Administrator
- An advanced knowledge management application infrastructure
- Enterprise data integration with the most popular relational and object-oriented database systems in the form of the Domino Enterprise Connection Services and Enterprise Integration products

- Domino Extended Search
- An open Public Key Infrastructure implementation in the Domino Certificate Server

Notes and Domino R5 offer the infrastructure and technology required to develop applications from the asynchronous world of email, calendaring, and scheduling into same-time intranet and extranet collaboration, rapidly becoming a prerequisite of secure electronic commerce.

Understanding the Critical Issues in the Upgrade

Whether you are migrating from cc:Mail with Organizer calendaring capabilities or Microsoft Mail and Exchange, or importing users from LDAP-compliant directories to Lotus Notes and Domino R5, the migration process is complex. In fact, customer migration from one system infrastructure to another represents much more than mail migration. It entails the migration of calendaring and scheduling elements, document libraries, document translation, bulletin boards, and business-specific applications. It requires a well-conceived, well-organized, and well-orchestrated program with a rich set of tools to assist the varying aspects of the upgrade and migration efforts.

Lotus, with its Messaging Upgrade Program, its close working ties with the extended IBM community, its consulting division, and its diverse Business Partner program, provides a number of migration and coexistence solutions. The latter product offerings are relatively inexpensive to obtain and easy to deploy. The recently enhanced migration packages, discussed in this chapter, and others available from Lotus Business Partners assist customers to move from legacy systems to the advanced technology of Notes and Domino in an efficient, orderly manner.

To ensure the successful migration and upgrade process to Lotus Notes and Domino R5, Lotus complements its product offerings by formulating an upgrade and migration methodology outline. No matter how small or large the migration effort is, the upgrade process goes through various phases—from auditing through planning, deployment and coexistence—and ultimately concludes with migration and postmigration processes. With this in mind, the methodology abstracts four phases for a smooth migration: planning, preparation, conversion, and postconversion.

During the planning phase, you gather a thorough understanding of your environment's messaging requirements. As part of this period, you prepare a potential timeline for the migration effort, devise a budget, define the necessary resources, and set the expectations for your client.

Auditing your existing messaging environment represents a key initial step of the planning phase. Such a review enables you to verify the degree to which the hardware and software components within your system are functioning optimally. It also helps you understand the specific business requirements from which your current messaging topology evolved.

The following are some of the questions to be considered in performing your audit during the planning phase; you also need to document additional information relevant to your installation's specific configuration and business requirements:

- **Planning**   Does an overall plan for the upgrade exist? What is the anticipated timeframe for the upgrade? Does a computer system or business process design exist for the infrastructure? What customizations have been made in your environment? Do you plan on running a pilot project?
- **Time frame**   How long will the migration process last? During the period of overlapping or coexisting systems, what messaging, calendaring, and scheduling tools will you need? Will you use gateways, switches, message transfer agents (MTAs), calendar agents, or directory synchronization agents, or do you require a combination of all of them?
- **Users**   What is the size of your user population? How is the population distributed geographically? What is the computer system hardware and software being used? What percentage of the population is mobile or remote?
- **Network**   What is the underlying network architecture? Will this remain stable during the migration? Do you plan to develop or upgrade your network architecture as you move?
- **Services**   Do you have sufficiently trained resources to complete the migration? Is outsourcing all or part of the migration an alternative?
- **Tools**   What technology is available to assist you during the migration? Which of the tools available should be deployed?

The second phase of the migration, the preparation phase of the project, consists of three major activities. The first involves installing and configuring the Domino servers. The second involves streamlining and running maintenance on your legacy system's message repositories or message stores to prepare them for the pending migration. The third covers developing the training materials to assist in preparing your user population for the new environment.

During this phase, you must consider the steps required to deploy Lotus Notes Domino. After you have deployed a startup Domino network, you can establish coexistence with your legacy network and begin the process of migrating users to the Notes Domino environment. To deploy Notes Domino during this preparation phase, you perform the following steps:

1. Assemble a Notes Domino rollout team.
2. Verify the status of legacy post offices.
3. Identify the users who will be migrating to Notes messaging and those who will be making use of only Notes Domino applications, if the two groups are not identical.
4. Assess hardware and software needs for initial deployment of Notes Domino.
5. Consider how the new Notes Domino system should be structured.

6. Plan the hierarchical naming syntax you will use in the Domino Directory.
7. Prepare for Notes Domino support and administration by training your information managers and engineers on the technology and basic administration of that technology.
8. Deploy one or more Domino Servers at each site.
9. If you set up multiple named networks, create the appropriate connection records to enable and schedule mail routing and replication.
10. Set up User Profile documents in the Domino Directory.

After deploying the initial Notes Domino network, you are then ready to connect Notes Domino messaging with the legacy system, whether that represents cc:Mail, MS Mail, MS Exchange, Internet SMTP, POP3, IMAP4, or whatever. Coexistence requires some form of gateway, message switch, or message transfer agent. Domino R5 offers message transfer agents for cc:Mail and X.400. With native support of Internet addressing and routing in Domino R5, an SMTP MTA for Internet messaging connectivity is no longer required. Gateways and message switches to and from other legacy mail systems, such as MS Mail and MS Exchange, are available from either other divisions within Lotus or from Lotus Business Partners.

The conversion phase is the core of any messaging system migration and upgrade. The conversion phase consists of the actual directory and messaging migration. It consists of three activities: migration of the legacy system's directory and mailbox data, installation and configuration of the Notes client at the workstations, and training.

After a startup Notes Domino network has been deployed and interconnected with the legacy system with some form of messaging gateway, switch, or message transfer agent, you can begin migrating users to the Notes Domino messaging and application environment using the available migration tools for the given legacy system. For the most popular platforms, such as cc:Mail, MS Mail, or MS Exchange, migration tools exist that fully automate or assist in the automation of the process. With their assistance, you can migrate users individually or in groups following the migration schedule earlier devised.

During the postconversion phase, you verify that every user and, where necessary, user mailbox has been converted successfully. You compare the legacy directory with the Domino Directory to ensure that all users have been upgraded to Notes Domino. You provide ongoing support to the users beyond the initial training. You can then remove the messaging gateways, switches, or message transfer agents, and, finally, any legacy post offices or routers within your network environment.

Upgrading from Previous Releases of Notes and Domino

Upgrading infrastructure software systems, such as the Notes Domino R5 messaging and Internet application server system, represents a complex task. Even though the R4 and R5 environments are completely compatible, with all R4 features retained in R5; all R4 applications running without modification in R5; and all R4 and R5 servers, clients, and databases interworking; you should still proceed methodically. In so doing, you minimize disruptions and maintain accessibility for both your pure Notes and intranet/Internet/extranet users to Domino messaging and application services.

Chapter 34, "Upgrading from Domino R4.x to R5," details the critical planning issues and administrative procedures to completing a successful upgrade from R4.x to R5. The following sections summarize the salient points with respect to such an upgrade.

Understanding the Critical Issues

Your phased upgrade from R4 to R5 will include most, if not all, of the following steps:

1. Establish a test or pilot environment and, if necessary, application development environment.
2. Upgrade your R4.x Name and Address Book to the R5 Domino Directory.
3. Upgrade your server population and, if necessary, begin compatibility testing and upgrading of your applications within the new R5 environment.
4. Upgrade your client population.
5. Deploy your applications.

In this way, your applications will not make use of R5 features before your user population can access them. Similarly, users with R5 clients will not attempt to use R5 features not available on pre-R5 servers.

To provide greater detail to the previously formulated upgrade outline, you should first install the software, set up a test environment and, if necessary, set up an application development environment. Setting up an isolated cluster of servers and clients enables you to become familiar with the new functionality of the system. Likewise, it enables your application development team to begin experimenting with the compatibility of its applications within the R5 framework. Such testing and migration of the applications continue throughout your upgrade period until their deployment during the final stage of the upgrade process.

When you have become comfortable in your test environment of running pure Domino R5, you can begin the upgrade of your R4.x Name and Address Book to the R5 Domino Directory. You can do this in a number of ways, depending on the complexity of your Domino network. If you have not customized the R4 Name and Address Book or simply plan to use the R5 Domino Directory, you can replace the copy of the NAMES.NSF following your Domino R5 install in your test environment and allow Domino to update its design upon initialization. If you plan to customize the R5 Directory, you should create a backup of your R4 design, copy a version of the NAMES.NSF following your Domino R5 install, and allow Domino to update its design upon initialization. After you have tested that Domino R5 runs with your version of NAMES.NSF, you can then apply the modifications desired.

If you do not encounter problems during your verification testing of either the vanilla or your modified version of the R5 NAMES.NSF, you are ready to migrate the chosen directory template to your production system. If you have modified the NAMES.NSF, create a PUBNAMES.NTF template from it.

At this point, you should install and configure an R5 Domino Administrator or full Notes Client. Next, select one of your hub or centralized servers to perform the role of the administrative server for the Domino Directory. This serves as the initial control point for your R5 network. You should also alert your user population that you will be upgrading the R4 Name and Address Book to the R5 Domino Directory. At this point, you can assure them that no R5 features prevent R4 servers from operating, and that R4 clients can interact with R5 directories even though some views may appear to be askew from an R4 client.

On the selected administrative server, complete the following steps:

1. Back up the Domino server files, the Data Directory, any links (.DIR files) contained within the Data Directory, and the NOTES.INI.
2. Rename the MAIL.BOX to MAIL.OLD.
3. Remove the Report task from the ServerTasks line within the NOTES.INI.
4. Install the Domino R5 software. If you use the same program and Data Directory as your previous version of Domino, you do not need to alter your server configuration. If you install Domino R5 in a new directory, the installation will prompt you to configure the R5 server.
5. When the Domino 5 software is installed, you should replace the standard administrative templates with any customized templates previously tested during the test or pilot period—for example, the PUBNAMES.NTF. Before starting the server, perform a consistency check on the Domino Data Directory by running NFIXUP -v within a command shell.
6. Launch the Domino R5 server. It will prompt you to upgrade the design of your Domino Directory. Answer Y for Yes. When it is launched, compact the Domino Directory twice by entering load compact NAMES.NSF at the server console. The first compaction enables the new database format (On Disk Structure or ODS). The second compaction enables features using the new ODS.
7. Because the R5 Domino Directory is backward-compatible with R4 and is designed for use in a mixed-release environment, you can now replicate the newly designed Domino Directory throughout your network.
8. Finally, perform a verification test of the nightly tasks, such as Design, Catalog, Updall, and any third-party software. If you encounter problems with these and cannot find a resolution, restore to a previous working version of the software.

You are now prepared to follow the same basic steps for the rest of your server population. The Domino server upgrade should proceed with the remaining hub servers or servers with the least direct impact on the end user population. Then it should proceed to user mail and application servers and, finally, upgrade servers running other products, if that is feasible given the compatibility requirements of other servers. The only additional steps you should take for your mail servers beyond those enumerated previously should be the following:

1. Copy any existing messages from the MAIL.OLD database to the newly created MAIL.BOX following R5 installation. When the R5 server has successfully delivered these messages, delete the MAIL.OLD. The R5 installation will have created a new MAIL.BOX without UNREAD marks, note hierarchy, or deleted space recovery. Note that Domino R5 supports multiple MAIL.BOX databases to improve server performance. This enables multiple server threads to deposit mail into one of the available MAIL.BOX databases not currently marked as in use by a companion thread. You define this parameter on the Basics subordinate tab of the Router/SMTP tab within the Configuration Settings document. For more information regarding the Configuration Settings document, refer to Chapter 42, "Managing Your Domino Server Configuration."

2. Refrain from upgrading the design of the individual mail databases until you have completed the client installation.

If you are running an SMTP MTA on a Domino R4 server, the upgrade to R5 automatically configures that server to route SMTP mail without affecting the mail-routing topology, the design of the network, or the flow of mail. Prior to the upgrade process however, you should complete the following administration:

1. Back up the program and data files on your SMTP MTA server.

2. Disable the SMTP/MTA housekeeping setting within the Internet Message Transfer Agent section of the Server document for the SMTP MTA server.

3. Shut down the Router by issuing the command TELL ROUTER QUIT at the Domino server console.

4. Shut down the inbound transport of messages by issuing the command TELL SMTPMTA STOP INBOUND TRANSPORT at the Domino server console.

5. Clear all messages from the SMTP.BOX, the outbound queue, and the inbound queue, and rename the MAIL.BOX to MAIL.OLD.

6. Shut down the Domino server by issuing the command QUIT at the Domino server console.

7. Edit the NOTES.INI to remove the SMTPMTA and Report tasks from the ServerTasks line.

8. Install the R5 Domino server software and upgrade the Domino Directory as enumerated in the previous steps.

9. Following installation, enable the native SMTP routing within the Router/SMTP tab in the Server Configuration Settings document for the selected server to allow the upgraded mail server to route mail using SMTP.

10. Finally, enable the SMTP listener task in the Server document for the Internet mail server and restart your Domino R5 server.

You can follow the same basic process as those detailed for your generalized hub servers to upgrade your spoke servers.

After you have completed the R5 server deployment, you can install the R5 software on your client workstations and deploy your applications. As with the Domino R5 upgrade process in general, you upgrade your client populations using the following steps:

1. Back up the Notes client files, primarily the NOTES.INI, the DESKTOP.DSK, the Personal Address Book (NAMES.NSF), any user ID files, any local databases or customized templates, and any additional databases or templates pointed to by directory links (.DIR).

2. Install the Notes R5 software by running SETUP.EXE. If you install the R5 in the same directory as the previous release of Notes, Notes upgrades the software automatically. If not, Notes prompts you to complete the configuration process. It also places the NOTES.INI in the Notes Data Directory, not in the system directory as with previous releases.

Following the installation, you can begin to use such R5 features as the Bookmark navigational model, the configurable Headlines page, and Native MIME messages.

Migrating Users to Notes and Domino R5: An Overview

The migration process entails creating user accounts and moving user mailboxes, mail, and addresses from one system to another. Notes and Domino R5 provide two sets of tools to assist in the migration process: an administrative tool and an end user tool. Both tools, denominated generically as the Domino Upgrade Services, install a custom option as part of the full Notes client or Domino Administrator installation. The primary or administrative tool enables an authorized administrator to

- Import users from a server-based directory.
- Register imported users.
- Create Notes mail files for registered users.
- Convert messages from mailboxes in the legacy post office into Notes format.

The Domino Administrator provides Domino Upgrade Services for Lotus cc:Mail and Organizer 2.x for cc:Mail, Microsoft Mail, Microsoft Exchange, Microsoft Windows NT Server, LDIF (LDAP Data Interchange Format) files, Novell GroupWise 4, Novell GroupWise 5, and Netscape Messaging Server.

The second or end user tool provides a wizard that end users can run at their workstations. The wizard complements the administrative migration tool by enabling the user to migrate private distribution lists and locally stored message archives. The upgrade wizards support migrating personal mail data from cc:Mail, Microsoft Mail, and Microsoft Exchange/Outlook.

Use the following general steps to migrate users from any of these environments to Notes and Domino R5:

1. Install the Domino Administrator client with the custom migration tools component on the administrative workstation serving as the designated migration workstation.
2. Import the users from the external directory, such as a cc:Mail post office directory, a Microsoft Mail post office address list, an Exchange directory, a Windows NT domain list, an LDIF file, a Novell GroupWise directory, or a Netscape Directory Server.
3. Set basic and advanced migration options.
4. Queue the users for registration.
5. Register the users, create their Notes mail files, and migrate their messages.

Figure 45.1 depicts the People and Groups Migration dialog box.

Figure 45.1
The People and Groups Migration dialog box.

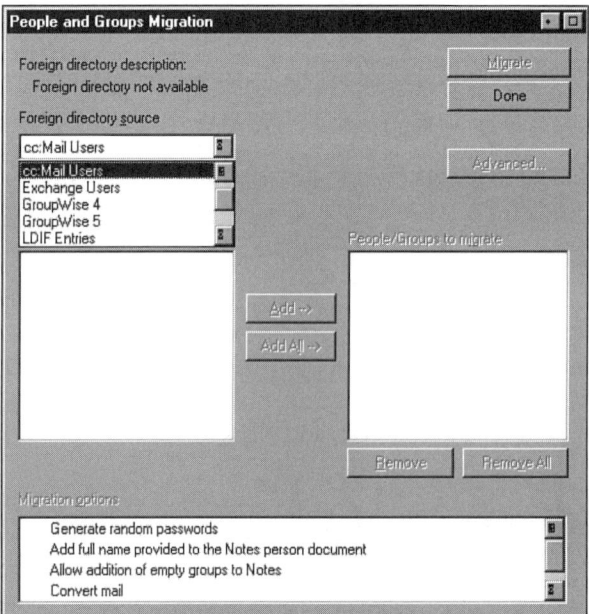

Owing to the unique attributes of each of the environments supported, configuring the Domino Upgrade Service for that particular system and migrating users from that system to Notes and Domino R5 have equally specific requirements. The configuration procedures for cc:Mail, Microsoft Mail and Exchange, and LDIF are outlined in the following three sections of this chapter. These provide a representative sample of the upgrade services available. Similar procedures are followed for the Windows NT, Novell GroupWise 4, Novell GroupWise 5, and Netscape Messaging Server upgrade services.

Upgrading from cc:Mail to Notes and Domino

You can upgrade a cc:Mail user to Notes Domino either as part of the registration process using the Domino Upgrade Services or by performing a standalone migration effort.

Upgrading from cc:Mail Using the Domino Upgrade Services

Using the cc:Mail to Notes migration tools provided with R5, you can upgrade Lotus cc:Mail users/groups to Notes Domino by completing the following steps:

1. Prepare to migrate the cc:Mail users. This includes the following administrative tasks:
    - Ensuring that the Domino Administrator client serving as the migration administrative workstation contains the cc:Mail migration tool component. A custom installation is necessary to install the migration tools.
    - Determining what types of cc:Mail data to migrate and the amount of disk space required.
    - Mapping a drive on your migration administrative workstation to the cc:Mail post office from which you are migrating users.
    - Verifying that the Notes administrative ID to be used during the migration has the required level of access to the Domino Directory on the Registration Server, the target mail server, and the organizational and organizational unit certifier IDs to be used. The Notes ID must have Editor, Designer, or Manager access rights to the Domino Directory on the Registration Server, Create database access on the target mail server, and the necessary passwords to the certifier IDs to be used.
    - Cleaning up the cc:Mail message store by having users archive or delete unnecessary mail.
    - Removing inactive accounts from the cc:Mail post office directory.
    - Taking the post office offline.
    - Ensuring that all cc:Mail user accounts to be migrated have a non-null password value.
    - Clearing all post office message queues and router express calls.
    - Backing up the post office, and then streamlining it by running CHKSTAT (DB6) or MSGMGR (DB8) to delete unnecessary messages, followed by RECLAIM to recover disk space from the deleted messages.
    - Concluding the administrative preparation by backing up the Domino Directory, the administrative client's DESKTOP.DSK and NOTES.INI files, and any ID files to be used during the migration process.
2. If you plan to migrate Organizer data for the cc:Mail users, complete the following additional preparation steps:

- Mapping a drive on your migration administrative workstation to the directory containing the Organizer (OR2) files.

- Verifying that at the operating system level you have full access rights to the directories containing the OR2 files and Read access to Organizer OR2 files to be migrated. Similarly, verifying that you have Editor-or-higher access to the Notes mail files to contain the migrated Organizer information.

- Instructing the Organizer end user population to record information about included sections, to process meeting notices, to remove data that does not need to be migrated, and to archive data to be migrated. The migration tool does not migrate included sections. By recording their names, users can create links between the migrated documents in Notes. The migration tool also does not migrate pending meeting invitations. These must be processed prior to migration. Finally, because migration of Organizer data can be very time- and disk-intensive, having the individual users perform basic administrative archiving and compacting routines improves migration performance.

- Disconnecting Organizer users from the directory containing the Organizer (OR2) files and disabling the Organizer scheduling agents.

- Concluding this phase of the administrative preparation by compacting Organizer data files.

3. Within the Domino Administrator, click the People & Groups tab, select the Domino Directory to which you want to migrate the users, click People, and select Register.

4. Click the Migrate People button.

5. Select the cc:Mail Users option from the Foreign directory source keyword list. The cc:Mail Post Office Information dialog box is displayed. Complete the fields for the Post Office Name, the Post Office Path consisting of the drive letter and directory path to the post office, and the Post Office Password, and click OK. The contents of the post office directory is displayed in the Available people/groups box. Figure 45.2 depicts the cc:Mail Post Office Information dialog box.

Figure 45.2
The cc:Mail Post Office Information dialog box.

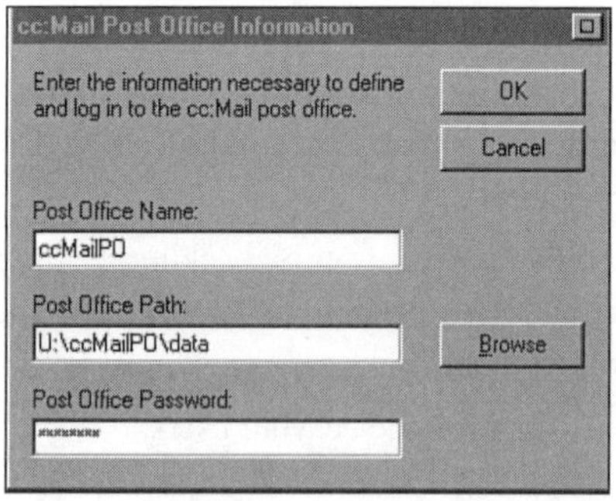

6. Highlight the people/groups you want to register and click the Add button. Alternatively, click the Add All button. The people/groups you add appear in the People/Groups to migrate box.
7. Set the Migration options. Select from such options as Generate random passwords, Add cc:Mail name to Notes person document (required for cc:MTA), Allow Addition of empty groups to Notes, Convert mail, and Convert mail ONLY (person document must already exist).
8. Click Advanced. The cc:Mail Upgrade Advanced Settings dialog box is displayed. Three such settings are available: Conversion settings, Gateway settings, and Other settings. By default, all the Conversion settings are enabled, except Convert Bulletin Boards to Notes discussion databases. The settings include Mail private mailing lists as attachments, Convert Organizer .OR2 scheduling files to Notes, Convert alias entries, and Convert Bulletin Boards to Notes Discussion database. It may also be necessary to set the code page to use when migrating a DB6 post office. The code page defaults to the current language version of the post office. The Gateway settings map the names of cc:Mail gateway post offices to Notes domains enabling the newly migrated users to reply to mail from external gateways, such as the Internet. The Other settings include Upgrading to cc:Mail 6.3 Client for Domino, Specifying the post office for routing mail to Notes, and Specifying an error threshold.

> **Note**
>
> Note that conversion of Organizer 2.x Group Scheduling information residing in OR2 files is enabled by default. If Organizer information exists and the administrative workstation being used for the migration is connected to the appropriate Organizer data directories, the Organizer information is migrated to locations in the Notes mail file, Personal Journal database, and Personal Name and Address Book.

9. Click the Migrate button. This creates registration documents for each of the specified users in the People/Groups to migrate box and stores them in the registration queue.
10. Click OK at the status message that displays errors and successes. You can rectify errors in the User Registration screen.
11. Click Done to return to the main User Registration screen.
12. Following the successful import of users into the registration queue, you can register them and complete the migration. Depending on the options selected, you can create a Notes Person document and Notes ID for each migrated user, create a Notes mail file, and migrate messages and other data from the cc:Mail mailbox. Figure 45.3 shows a registration queue with the Mail Pane registration options being reviewed for the queued users.

Figure 45.3
The registration queue with the Mail Pane registration options being reviewed for the queued users.

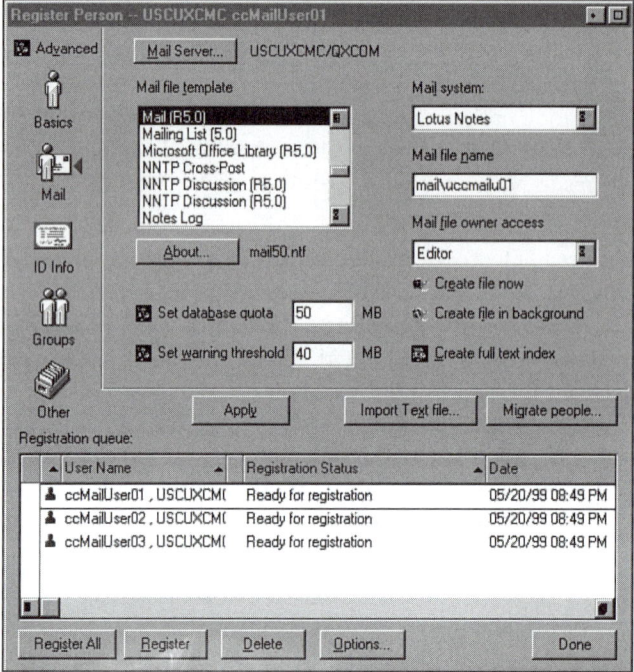

13. Prior to registration, view the registration information for each user in the registration queue.

14. Select the registration options to apply during this session by clicking Options beneath the Pending Registrations box and selecting those desired.

15. Returning to the Registration status box, select the users to register and click Register.

Depending on the number of users and options selected, the registration process can take a considerable amount of time. At its conclusion, a message box appears, which summarizes the status of the registration. For any failed registrations, correct the information in the registration document and attempt to register the user again.

Upgrading from cc:Mail Independent of the Domino Administrator

In R4, and now complementing the integrated upgrade/migration features within R5, the most common method used to migrate a cc:Mail user population involves deploying a combination of the Lotus Notes cc:Mail MTA, the Lotus cc:Mail to Notes migration tools, and, where calendar and scheduling conversion is necessary, the Organizer migration tool within the Organizer 97 GS product.

Understanding the Role of the cc:Mail MTA

The Lotus Domino cc:Mail MTA is an loptional message transfer agent (MTA) for use with the Domino Server. It serves to integrate Lotus cc:Mail and Lotus Notes networks by transparently exchanging messages and directory information between the two messaging systems. When integrated within a Lotus Domino environment, it can serve as a hub for cc:Mail networks, improving their scalability, performance, and manageability.

The cc:Mail MTA is integrated with Domino management, routing, directory, security, log/trace, transport, and message conversion services. It serves both as a gateway and an MTA. Like a gateway or connector, it can function as a message translator between cc:Mail and Notes. In addition to this, however, the MTA supports native message relaying using cc:Mail protocols. This means that Domino with the cc:mail MTA can route messages in cc:Mail format. It does not need to convert each incoming or outgoing message between Notes and cc:Mail.

Understanding the Role of the cc:Mail to Notes Migration Tools

The cc:Mail to Notes migration tools consist of two components: the Admin tool and the User tool, both of which can be run as either a standalone executable or as a Domino server add-in task. Together, the tools facilitate the migration of mailboxes and post offices from cc:Mail to Notes Mail files and servers. The resulting migration process builds upon the Domino distributed architecture. This enables the migration of large numbers of mailboxes simultaneously using multiple Domino servers. As a result, multiple POs can be migrated to a single Domino server, or a single PO can be split and migrated to different Domino servers. In addition, the cc:Mail shared message store can be retained by enabling the Shared Mail feature on the Domino server.

The Admin tool accomplishes Directory Migration, Message Migration, and User Migration by the Administrator:

- Directory Migration provides migration of the directory components of a PO. This can be either an entire PO or specific users within the PO. It includes batch registration of Notes users, automatic mail file creation, and the conversion of aliases, bulletin boards, and public mailing lists. This process migrates all the cc:Mail names from the PO to the Domino Directory.
- Message Migration provides migration of the message components of a PO. Similar to Directory Migration, this can be either an entire PO or specific users within the PO. It includes automatic migration of folders, private mailing lists, and messages with attachments. The post office to be migrated can be either a LAN-based PO or a cc:Mail Mobile PO. If the Shared Mail feature has been enabled on the target Domino server, the cc:Mail single message store can also be retained.

    User Migration provides migration of user's local information. It includes such information as Private Directory, Mobile PO, and Archives for the end users.

The User tool provides message and user migration. It can be used by either an end user or by an administrator:

- Message Migration provides the migration of message components within a user's Mobile PO. This includes folders, private mailing lists, private bulletin boards, and messages with attachments.
- User Migration provides migration of user's local information. It includes such information as Private Directory, Mobile PO, and Archives.

Understanding the Role of the Organizer 97 GS Migration Tool

The Lotus calendar migration tool ships with the Organizer 97 GS product. Although the tool is designed for users who plan to use Organizer 97 as a front end to the Notes calendar, it can also be used to migrate data for users who will use the Notes calendar interface.

The Organizer 97 GS migration tool can be run by the administrator to do bulk migration or by an individual user to migrate his or her own data. Migration consists of converting the data from the OR2 file into the proper format and inserting it into the user's Notes mail file. Information from the address section is formatted for inclusion in the Notes Personal Address Book and is mailed to the user for processing.

The first step in upgrading an Organizer 2.x user to Notes is to register the user to Notes. The user must be listed in the Domino Directory as a Notes user and have a Notes mail file before Organizer 2.x calendar data can be migrated.

The Organizer migration utility makes use of the following fields in the Person document of the Domino Directory: `OrganizerCalendarPath`, the LAN path to access the Organizer OR2 files; `OrganizerCalendarServer`, the LAN file servername and volume where the OR2 file is stored; `OrganizerAgentName`, the name of the Organizer 2.x scheduling agent; `OrganizerEntryType`; and `CalendarDomain`. These fields are added to the Domino Directory when you synchronize the cc:Mail directory with the Domino Directory. They are maintained when the cc:Mail to Notes migration is performed.

The presence of these special Organizer fields within the Domino Directory provides the Organizer migration utility with the necessary information on which users are candidates for calendar migration and where the Organizer 2.x data is located. After migration, the cleanup phase of the tool updates the contents of these fields in the Domino Directory.

With the exception of Organizer data residing in links between an address section and another section, file links in the address section, address section filters, and notepad references, all data in Organizer data files is converted to Notes during the migration process.

Complete the following general procedures to upgrade Organizer v2.x Data to Notes:

1. Install the Organizer 97 GS client code on the Domino server machine.
2. Invoke the `ORGMIGRT.EXE` from the source directory after stopping the Domino server.

3. Archive any old data that does not need to be migrated.
4. Process all unprocessed meeting notices.
5. Close all OR2 files.
6. Back up all user's Personal Address Books, mail files, and OR2 files.
7. Ensure that the Domino server can access all OR2 files to be converted and update access to the Domino Directory.
8. Run the migration utility.
9. Perform the cleanup process.
10. Clear the Calendar Domain field within the Person documents.
11. Uninstall the Organizer 97 GS Migration Utility.

Upgrading from Microsoft Mail and Exchange to Domino

Using the Microsoft Mail and Microsoft Exchange to Notes migration tools provided with R5, you can easily upgrade Microsoft Mail and Microsoft Exchange users/groups to Notes/Domino.

To convert Microsoft Mail users to Notes as part of the registration process using the Domino Upgrade Services, you complete the following steps:

1. Prepare to migrate the Microsoft Mail users. This includes the following administrative tasks:
    - Ensuring that the Domino Administrator client serving as the migration administrative workstation contains the Microsoft Mail migration tool component. A custom installation is necessary to install the migration tools.
    - Mapping a drive on your migration administrative workstation to the Microsoft Mail post office from which you are migrating users.
    - Verifying that the Notes administrative ID to be used during the migration has the required level of access to the Domino Directory on the Registration Server, the target mail server, and the organizational and organizational unit certifier IDs to be used. The Notes ID must have Editor, Designer, or Manager access rights to the Domino Directory on the Registration Server, Create database access on the target mail server, and the necessary passwords to the certifier IDs to be used.
    - Sending any pending Microsoft Mail messages.
    - Backing up the Microsoft Mail post office. Refer to the Microsoft Mail Administrator's Guide for further information.

- Concluding the administrative preparation by backing up the Domino Directory, the administrative client's DESKTOP.DSK and NOTES.INI files, and any ID files to be used during the migration process.

2. Within the Domino Administrator, click the People & Groups tab, select the Domino Directory to which you want to migrate the users, click People, and select Register.

3. Click the Migrate People button.

4. Select MS Mail Users from the Foreign directory source keyword list. The MS Mail Initialization dialog box is displayed. Complete the fields for the Postoffice path, consisting of the drive letter and directory path to the post office; the Administrator's name; and the Administrator's password. Click OK. The contents of the MS Mail Postoffice are displayed in the Available people/groups box. Figure 45.4 depicts the MS Mail Initialization dialog box.

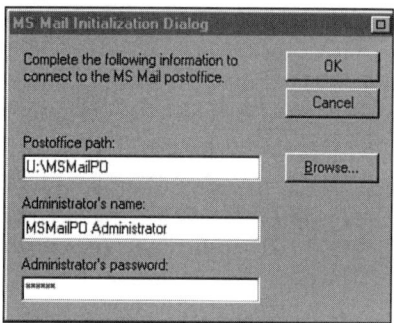

Figure 45.4
The MS Mail Initialization dialog box.

5. Highlight the people/groups you want to register and click the Add button. The people/groups you add appear in the People/Groups to migrate box.

6. Set the Migration options. Select from such options as Generate random passwords, Add full name provided to the Notes person document, Allow addition of empty groups to Notes, Convert mail, and Convert mail ONLY (Notes user and mail file must already exist).

7. Select the advanced upgrade settings by clicking Advanced from the People and Groups Migration dialog box. The Advanced settings consist of three options: The first allows you to enable or disable Migrating the Microsoft Mail Personal Address Book. If selected, a temporary Notes Personal Address Book will be created and placed in a message in the Inbox of the user's mail file. Users can then run an upgrade wizard at the Notes client to copy this information from this document to their own Notes Personal Address Book. The second specifies the number of errors to be tolerated when migrating messages from mailboxes in the Microsoft Postoffice to Notes mail files. The migration tool by default allows an unlimited number of errors and completes the

migration successfully regardless of error count. You can prevent this by setting the error threshold. The third option specifies the language code page to use when converting characters from the Microsoft Postoffice to Notes. The migration tool by default uses the current code page of the Postoffice.

8. Click the Migrate button. This creates registration documents for each of the specified users in the People/Groups to migrate box and stores them in the registration queue.

9. Click OK at the status message that displays errors and successes. You can rectify errors in the User Registration screen.

10. Click Done to return to the main User Registration screen.

11. Following the successful import of users into the registration queue, you can register them and complete the migration. Depending on the options selected, you can create a Notes Person document and Notes ID for each migrated user, create a Notes mail file, and migrate messages and other data from the Microsoft Mail Postoffice.

12. Prior to registration, view the registration information for each user in the registration queue.

13. Select the registration options to apply during this session by clicking Options beneath the Pending Registrations box and selecting those desired. Figure 45.5 depicts the Advanced Person Registration Options dialog box, showing the options active for the queued users.

Figure 45.5
The Advanced Person Registration Options dialog box, showing the options active for the queued users.

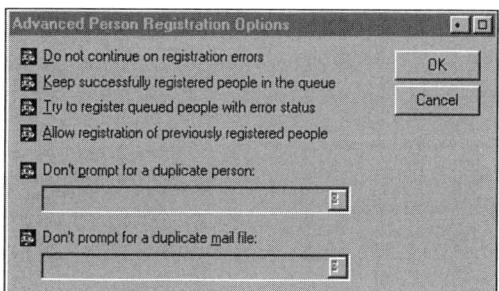

14. Returning to the Registration status box, select the users to register and click Register.

Depending on the number of users and options selected, the registration process can take a considerable amount of time. At its conclusion, a message box appears, which summarizes the status of the registration. For any failed registrations, correct the information in the registration document and attempt to register the user again.

To convert Microsoft Exchange users to Notes as part of the registration process using the Domino Upgrade Services, you complete the following steps:

1. Prepare to migrate Microsoft Exchange users. This includes the following administrative tasks:
   - Ensuring that the Domino Administrator client serving as the migration administrative workstation contains the Microsoft Exchange migration tool component. A custom installation is necessary to install the migration tools.
   - Ensuring that the migration administrative workstation has an Outlook or Exchange client installed and an Administrator mail profile pointing to the Exchange server. This mail profile is used to connect to the Exchange server during the migration process. It must contain an Administrator account which has the Service Account Administrator role for the Exchange site and server. This gives the account full access to all accounts and mailboxes in the Exchange server directory.
   - Verifying that the Notes administrative ID to be used during the migration has the required level of access to the Domino Directory on the Registration Server, the target mail server, and the organizational and organizational unit certifier IDs to be used. The Notes ID must have Editor, Designer, or Manager access rights to the Domino Directory on the Registration Server, Create database access on the target mail server, and the necessary passwords to the certifier IDs to be used.
   - Sending any pending Microsoft Exchange messages.
   - Ensuring that the Exchange directory to be migrated is complete by performing an Exchange Directory Synchronization.
   - Concluding the administrative preparation by backing up the Domino Directory, the administrative client's DESKTOP.DSK and NOTES.INI files, and any ID files to be used during the migration process.
2. Within the Domino Administrator, click the People & Groups tab, select the Domino Directory to which you want to migrate the users, click People, and select Register.
3. Click the Migrate People button.
4. Select Exchange Users from the Foreign directory source keyword list. The Choose Profile dialog box is displayed. Select the administrator mail profile created in the first step and click OK. The contents of the Exchange Directory are displayed in the Available people/groups box.
5. Highlight the people/groups you want to register and click the Add button. The people/groups you add appear in the People/Groups to migrate box.
6. Set the Migration options. Select from such options as Generate random passwords, Add full name provided to the Notes person document, Allow addition of empty groups to Notes, and Convert mail.
7. Click the Migrate button. This creates registration documents for each of the specified users in the People/Groups to migrate box and stores them in the registration queue.
8. Click OK at the status message that displays errors and successes. You can rectify errors in the User Registration screen.

9. Click Done to return to the main User Registration screen.
10. Following the successful import of users into the registration queue, you can register them and complete the migration. Depending on the options selected, you can create a Notes Person document and Notes ID for each migrated user, create a Notes mail file, and migrate messages and other data from the Microsoft Exchange server mailboxes.
11. Prior to registration, view the registration information for each user in the registration queue.
12. Select the registration options to apply during this session by clicking Options beneath the Pending Registrations box and selecting those desired. If you are converting mail files, ensure that you specify information in the Mail Pane of the registration dialog box.
13. Returning to the Registration status box, select the users to register and click Register.

Depending on the number of users and options selected, the registration process can take a considerable amount of time. At its conclusion, a message box appears, which summarizes the status of the registration. For any failed registrations, correct the information in the registration document and attempt to register the user again.

Importing from an LDAP Directory

With the widespread acceptance of the Lightweight Directory Access Protocol as the de facto access protocol for corporate directories, it has become mandatory for systems to interoperate using (LDAP). In addition to providing an LDAP interface to the Domino Directory, Lotus Notes and Domino R5 facilitate the exchange of information with LDAP-compliant directories by supporting an import facility for LDAP Interface File Format files.

Understanding the LDAP Interface File Format Import Facilities Within the Domino Administrator

Using the LDAP Data Interchange Format (LDIF) to Notes Import tool, you can easily create Notes users by importing directory entries from an LDIF file.

The LDIF format conveys directory information taken from the LDAP format directory. An LDIF record consists of a sequence of lines describing a directory entry. From this, a registration document can be placed in the registration queue and processed for registration in a method identical to the regular registration process.

To migrate users defined in an LDIF file, you complete the following steps:

1. Prepare to migrate users from an LDIF file. This includes the following administrative tasks:
    - Ensuring that the Domino Administrator client serving as the migration administrative workstation contains the LDIF Administrative migration tool component. A custom installation is necessary to install the migration tools.

- Mapping a drive on your migration administrative workstation to the LDIF file from which you are migrating users.
- Determining whether the LDIF entries are to be registered Notes users or directory entries only. If the entries are to be registered Notes users, create a separate LDIF file for each organization and/or organizational unit represented.
- Verifying that the Notes administrative ID to be used during the migration has the required level of access to the Domino Directory on the Registration Server, the target mail server, and the organizational and organizational unit certifier IDs to be used. The Notes ID must have Editor, Designer, or Manager access rights to the Domino Directory on the Registration Server, Create database access on the target mail server, and the necessary passwords to the certifier IDs to be used.
- Concluding the administrative preparation by backing up the Domino Directory, the administrative client's DESKTOP.DSK and NOTES.INI files, and any ID files to be used during the migration process.

2. Within the Domino Administrator, click the People & Groups tab, select the Domino Directory to which you want to migrate the users, click People, and select Register.
3. Click the Migrate People button.
4. Select LDIF Entries from the Foreign directory source keyword list. The Select LDIF File dialog box is displayed. Specify the LDIF file to import and click OK. Figure 45.6 depicts the Select LDIF File dialog box.

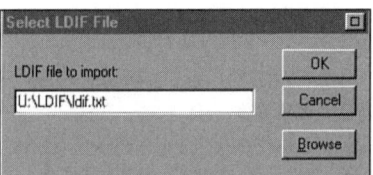

Figure 45.6
The Select LDIF File dialog box.

5. Set the Migration options. Select one of two options: Generate random password, and Add full name provided to the Notes person document. If you are only adding the LDIF entries to the Domino Directory and not registering them as Notes users, you must select the second option. This instructs the migration tool to add the user's complete LDAP distinguished name as the primary entry in the username field of the Person document.
6. Click the Migrate button. This creates registration documents for each of the specified users in the People/Groups to migrate box and stores them in the registration queue.
7. Click OK at the status message that displays errors and successes. You can rectify errors in the User Registration screen.
8. Click Done to return to the main User Registration screen.

9. Following the successful import of users into the registration queue, you can register the available users or add the users to the Domino Directory as directory entries only. If you decide to register the available users, you can create a Notes Person document and Notes ID for each migrated user and create a Notes mail file.

10. Prior to registration or simple Directory import, view the registration information for each user in the registration queue.

11. Select the registration options to apply during this session by clicking Options beneath the Pending Registrations box and selecting those desired. For those users in the registration queue whom you want to add to the Domino Directory only, you must ensure that certain fields have been set to None or have been cleared. To do this, complete the following steps:

    - Select the Advanced Check box. The Mail, ID Info, and Other configuration Panes appear.
    - On the Mail Pane, select None in the Mail System box and click Apply.
    - On the ID Info Pane, clear the boxes under the Store user ID section and click Apply.

12. Returning to the Registration status box, select the users whom you want to register or simply add to the Domino Directory and click Register.

Depending on the number of users and options selected, the registration process can take a considerable amount of time. At its conclusion, a message box appears, which summarizes the status of the registration. For any failed registrations, correct the information in the registration document and attempt to register the user again.

Summary

This chapter focused on issues relevant to upgrading to Lotus Notes Domino R5 from some of the major platforms in the market today, namely Lotus Notes and Domino R4, cc:Mail, Microsoft Mail and Microsoft Exchange, and interoperating with LDAP-compliant directories. It first reviewed the rationale for the upgrade itself, providing the salient reasons to begin the transition to Lotus Notes and Domino R5. It then focused on specific upgrade paths, whether from previous releases of Notes and Domino, from cc:Mail, or from MS Mail or Exchange. Each of these outlined procedural descriptions of upgrading users from one environment to the next. The final section of the chapter described the similar procedural available to import, migrate, or add users stored within an LDAP directory into Domino R5 environment.

From Here...

You can find material related to Domino server administration in the following chapters and parts:

- Part VI, "Installing and Configuring the Domino Servers," discusses the different Domino server types, their initial installation and configuration, and the upgrade paths from R4.x to R5. It also provides an overview of Domino security, firewalls, Virtual Private Networks (VPNs), and Internet security. This represents fundamental information for administering a Domino enterprise.

- Chapter 38, "Administering Users, Groups, and Certification," introduces you to the R5 Domino Administrator. It then discusses user, group, and certification administration within the Domino Directory.

- Chapter 39, "Administering Electronic Mail," provides you with the basics in establishing your Domino messaging infrastructure.

- Chapter 40, "Replication and Its Administration," gives you an overview of the steps required to configure and maintain a successful replication schedule between servers within your Domino domain.

- Chapter 41, "Administering Files and Databases," covers management and administration of disk information, files, directories, and databases; updating database designs; and rolling out databases to users. It summarizes information pertinent to systems administrators who also perform database administration.

- Chapter 42, "Managing Your Domino Server Configuration," discusses general Domino server administration, maintaining server configuration documents and running server tasks, modifying networks and domains, and analyzing and monitoring server performance.

- Chapter 43, "Troubleshooting and Monitoring Domino," introduces the tools available within Domino to analyze problems and perform corrective action.

- Part VIII, "Advanced Domino Administration," gives you specialized information about topics, such as performance and capacity planning, upgrading from other email systems, and integration with phones, fax, and image.

CHAPTER 46

Using The Enterprise Domino Server with a Large Domino Network

There is an old adage that craftsmen recite to young apprentices quite often: "Measure twice, cut once." The same advice can be useful when approaching the initial setup of your Domino network. Although most administrators would never haphazardly create their main network, many times a Domino network is created as an afterthought. This usually winds up costing many dollars and person-hours to correct problems that could have been avoided with the proper plan of attack. This chapter is intended to inform you of the newest features and options available in Domino servers, and then give some solid bits of advice that should provide you enough "clues" to successfully plan your corporation's Domino network. This chapter covers

- Forming a game plan
- Teamwork: sharing the responsibility
- Designing your network
- Planning your server infrastructure
- Planning your communications infrastructure
- Topology types
- Mail routing topology
- Replication topology
- Passthru topology
- The domain and the Domino Directory
- Incorporating mail gateways
- Monitoring your Notes servers

Let's begin by discussing some guidelines to use when planning your Domino network.

Forming a Game Plan

Forming a solid game plan for your network is a critical step toward success. The easy installation of a Domino server tends to oversimplify the importance of the early decisions you need to make. In fact, if you use some of the examples provided in the dialog boxes during setup, you can establish an unwieldy naming scheme. Use the following steps as a guide:

1. **Plan for administrative teamwork**   Use Notes/Domino to assist your administrative team. Establish open lines of communications and develop a clear process for establishing standards and resolving conflicts.

2. **Plan your network infrastructure**   Your servers will cause you fewer headaches if you provide adequate hardware. Modem technology has greatly improved, yet many modem combinations still refuse to work or perform poorly together. Check with forums, the Knowledgebase, and your peers to determine which hardware works best for running a Domino server.

3. Plan your topologies carefully. Many aspects of Domino administration can be thought of as a topology. Because Notes doesn't draw pictures, develop topology maps for your administrative team. It will help you make sense of the contents of your domain's Domino Directory.

4. Plan to monitor your system. Through careful monitoring, you can often detect minor conditions that might actually be symptoms of more serious problems.

Teamwork: Sharing the Responsibility

Notes/Domino solves many problems with regard to information sharing and distribution. How widely spread are your offices or employees? Do your business units function as separate companies? You can choose to control your Domino environment centrally, or more likely (and recommended), you and your team of administrators will share the responsibility (perhaps geographically).

Developing Standards

The topic of standards touches nearly all the functionality of the system. Before you can create meaningful standards, you must have a firm grasp of the components of the system, as well as the tools at your disposal. Although it is not within the scope of this chapter to lay out everything you need to develop a thorough standards document, you can take the high-level structure presented here to get you started.

Some of the more crucial standards to establish involve the items that the public will see. Your servernames are visible to others who connect to your domain; you use these names when you perform console commands such as REPLICATE SERVERNAME. Your domain names are visible to anyone sending email to your users. Your organization name is visible to anyone reading documents you compose; it could be your email memos or documents in a discussion database that replicates around the world. Think ahead and determine just how you want your company's name to be seen. Keep the names short and avoid spaces.

Distributed Management of the Domino Directory

In a large network, it is virtually impossible for one administrator to manage the entire environment. Requests are often generated so rapidly that they pile up quickly; fulfillment sometimes requires a local presence. A team of administrators must work together to fulfill requests and, ultimately, maintain the documents of the Domino Directory (formerly known as the Public Name and Address Book).

It has been observed, however, that in established Notes networks, local changes are often implemented without consideration for the impact on the other servers that depend on the same book. "Way back when," R3 did little to facilitate safe local changes. Enabling administrators to have Editor access to the book gave them free rein over all the documents. R4 added tools to the Public Address Book to enhance its maintainability in a large, distributed environment. R5 takes that a step further by providing numerous roles in the Domino Directory that enable you to more finely assign roles to other administrators.

Creating the Administrative Process

To manage the maintenance of the Domino Directory, create a list of the types of changes (additions, modifications, and deletions) that will be necessary in your domain. Design a request-and-approval process that will facilitate the best balance of administration among all your administrators. Reaching agreement not only on the methods for maintaining the directory, but also on the resolution process for any related management issues (such as maintaining this request/approval process) will enable your administrative team to perform with confidence.

Document Adds, Moves, and Changes

If changes must be made to documents (such as groups) that can affect users and servers at other sites, consider forming a policy requiring that change requests are submitted and reviewed before they are implemented. However, this review does not need to fall on one person, but instead can be put up for examination by all administrators. An administrator who notices a detrimental effect can voice the concern before the change is made. Review the various types of changes that may be made and classify them as to which can be made without review.

Creating a Request and Approval Process

You might consider creating an administrative facilitation database; it could contain a request/approval workflow process, a discussion section, tips and tricks, perhaps even a Knowledgebase. It should define your company's standards for handling the routine chores of the Domino Directory. The request types should include creating and modifying users and creating and modifying groups. You can also use a similar procedure to promote new databases from test servers to production servers. I use my own version of this type of database to accept such requests; this enables me to review, approve, and delegate the changes that need to be made in a documented, expedient manner.

Notifications

Use Notes Mail to notify administrators of a new request (include a DocLink). After a request has been approved, a notification could be mailed to the requester informing of a change with regard to that request.

Grant and Reject Requests with Reasons and Suggestions

If your environment is one in which you have a hierarchical request process, use an email to inform the requester of the decision. Offer suggestions if appropriate, especially for a rejection.

Designing Your Network

In a large Domino network design, you evaluate the pros and cons of several different topics. Should you model your network after the political or geographic makeup of your company? How should you plan for your servers to communicate? How many domains would make sense for you? What should you consider in creating your hierarchical naming conventions? How should you configure the topologies for mail routing, replication, and other features, such as passthru? As your Domino Directory grows in size and distribution, what are the effective ways to manage it? How should you plan for additional gateways or mail transfer agents? Do you have a need for a Domino Internet/intranet presence? If so, how should that be implemented with your internal Domino network?

Let's consider each of these individually, realizing that many decisions on one topic are dependent on the decisions made in another area.

Naming Users and Servers

Notes/Domino provides a way to associate each resource (a user or server) with a component of your company. This is best accomplished using hierarchical names. Not only is it a convenience to know what part of your company a user is associated with, but it also enhances your company's security if you can isolate access to branches of your company. The rules of naming Notes users descends from the X.500 protocol.

> **Note**
>
> If you are into reading dry, boring, and arcane technical standards abstracts, you can read more about the X.500 schema standard at
>
> `http://www.cis.ohio-state.edu/htbin/rfc/rfc2256.html`

Although it is difficult to give hard and fast rules to what the hierarchies should be in your company, there are guidelines to follow. It is important to remember that hierarchies associated with users are flexible, whereas hierarchies associated with servers are much less flexible. The following are the rules of hierarchical naming:

- At least one level of naming must be established. This is referred to as the organization or O.
- The country code is married to the organization. It is a two-character, predefined value.
- After the O, the hierarchy can be four additional levels deep; each level is referred to as the organizational unit (OU*n*), where *n* is the level.
- Each user and server has a common name associated with it.
- The common name, organizational units, and organization define the name of the resource, in this format:
  Common Name/OU1/OU2/OU3/OU4/O
- Each organizational unit at each level as well as the organization itself is associated with a discrete certifier ID.
- In order to secure your system, at least one level of OU should be implemented.

Consider the company D. J. Cohen, Inc. The firm has 45 employees worldwide. I would recommend that it use its short-form name for the organization—DJCOHEN—because it will be repeated over and over again in the domain. I would also recommend that it choose its locations as first-level OUs (OU1) because the company is location-based. Company officials chose ATL for Atlanta, LON for London, and TOR for Toronto. Finally, I recommend that it use a separate OU for its servers. Company officials chose SRV for servers. Debi Bailey in Atlanta has the name Debi Bailey/ATL/DJCOHEN. The servers are named sequentially by function. HUB01/SRV/DJCOHEN is the first hub server.

Using these rules, guidelines are simple. When setting up a naming scheme, remember that this is internal to the company. People communicating with members of your company with email use the common name of the person and domain name to get the mail to the user. Domino resolves the name within your company to getto the proper destination.

Guidelines for Naming

These are general guidelines to use when determining your user and servernames. These guidelines make managing these names easier, and make it easier for your users to type them:

- No component should have a space in it. This would require referring to the resource with quotation marks around it when referring to this name at the server console, for instance.
- The O name should be at least three characters long.
- If country codes are implemented, refer to them in an OU to keep all IDs under the same certificate. Because the country code is associated with the organization, a new organization certifier (the top), has to be created for each country.
- O names should be the "short form" of your company. Because this component is going to be referred to whenever a name is represented in Notes, it is cumbersome to use a long name. For example, the company International Business Machines is known as IBM. Instead of using International Business Machines in every name, using IBM makes a better reference.
- The total number of characters in the OU levels should not exceed 15 for users. If you choose to have many (two to four) OU levels, make the names short. Remember that each time you refer to a resource in your domain, you will be using the entire name, including the hierarchy.

> **Note**
> The maximum characters allowed in a name is 274: 80 max for Common Name (CN), 32 max for each Organizational Unit (OU) with up to 4 OUs, 64 max for Organization (O), and 2 max for country.

- Servers should be isolated in their own branches of the hierarchy. Changing the name of the server is difficult because all users have to change icons in their bookmark file

(R5) or on their desktops (R4 and before), and we all know how much users love change.

- Keep in mind that, internally, all resources will be able to authenticate (access each server and sign documents); externally, you can isolate branches of your hierarchy for authentication. Remember that you manage external access to your servers through the use of cross-certificates.

Designing a Scheme for Using the Guidelines

First, investigate other software packages in your company that use hierarchical naming (for example, Microsoft Exchange or Novell 4.0, using Directory Name Services). You can save time if you implement a plan similar to what is already being used.

You should treat servers and users separately. First, ask your users, "How do you know Lisa Phillips is in your company?" Is it because she is in the marketing department or because she is in San Francisco? This should be your first-level OU. For example, if the answer to the question is "We know her because she is in marketing," the first level should represent departments. Don't limit yourself to thinking of departments or location; companies have also implemented the first-level OU based on skill set. You may just have one OU level for users.

For servers, create an OU indicating that they are servers—for example, SVR. You may want to plan for external servers and internal servers by creating a second level separating the two. You don't have to implement the external servers' OU right away; if you have a plan, using it in the future will be easier.

The common name of the server should indicate its function in the company and a number for future growth. For example, your first hub is HUB01; when you add additional hubs because your company is growing at a phenomenal rate, the next hub would be HUB02, and so on.

Because some protocols used by Domino look only at the common name of the servername, servers should be uniquely named in their common name. That is, don't depend on the hierarchy to define the server uniquely. As well, each server's certifier will indicate that it is a server as a component of its name. It is unnecessary to include this in the common name of the server. For example, MKT01/SVR/BIGCO is an appropriate name, whereas MKTSVR01/SVR/BIGCO is redundant.

One of the main reasons to choose a good hierarchical naming scheme is to delegate responsibility to others. Most corporations are regional, with servers located in the regions as well as in corporate headquarters. If administrative support is available in the regions for the regional users, it makes sense to have regional administrators responsible for their own minidomain.

The global administrator can delegate the responsibility to a number of degrees. If all responsibility is to be delegated—that is, creating users, setting up servers, managing mail distribution, and ensuring replication—the global administrator can give the OU certifier for the region to the local administrator. This, along with delegation of authority in the Domino Directory (discussed later in this chapter) enables the local administrator to create IDs for users, enables them to access their regional servers, and updates Connection documents. The global administrator should hold onto the server OU certifier and grant access to the Server document to the appropriate local administrator or administrative group. This enables the global administrator to leave the regional tasks in the regions.

Now that we have standards and naming conventions out of the way, it is time to plan our infrastructure.

Planning Your Server Infrastructure

Typically, Notes/Domino implementations start with servers performing two tasks: supplying access to databases and routing mail. When a critical mass of users starts using Notes/Domino, you may need to streamline your servers by function. You should consider this streamlining early in the process because certain efficiencies can be achieved. The types of servers to consider are mail, database, Passthru, external, and firewall.

Mail Servers

Mail servers provide access to mail files only. The server replicates with the rest of the domain to keep the Domino Directory and Directory Catalogs in synch. The mail server has only mail databases and these directories located on it.

Using mail servers is the most efficient use of single copy object stores (SCOS), otherwise known as Shared Mail. Shared Mail stores the body of mail messages in a central database; the header (address) and pointer to the body are located in the individual mail files. Each mail file has just pointers and headers. If mail is centralized on one server, fewer Shared Mail databases are required. Consult your Domino Administration documentation for further information on installing and using Shared Mail.

Note

Shared Mail was not considered usable by many Domino Administrators in R4.x. However, Lotus has greatly improved the efficiency and capability of Shared Mail for Domino R5, so it warrants another look if your infrastructure could benefit from Shared Mail.

In order to use the resources on a mail server efficiently, create a replication schedule that replicates the Domino Directory only between the mail servers and the rest of the servers in your domain.

Mail servers should be used in conjunction with Passthru servers so that remote users need to make only one phone call to get their mail and databases.

Mail servers should be frequently backed up and be high-end machines to provide maximum access. Domino Administrators need to have full access to mail servers. There should be at least one mail server per Notes Named Network so that users can easily access their mail servers.

Database (Application) Servers

Database servers (commonly referred to as application servers) hold databases for users. Applications residing on database servers depends on who is accessing the server. For example, if the marketing department accesses one server, all the databases for that department should be located there.

Placement of database servers in your environment can enhance network traffic. If the databases are streamlined so that users are using the servers closest to them with regard to the network, Notes/Domino operates more efficiently.

Placement of databases on servers can also have an effect on the amount of disk space used by a database. If your replication topology requires databases to exist on the hub in order for it to be distributed to several spokes, you may want to reconsider placing a database on several spokes. Another consideration is to implement a schedule for the database in question directly between spokes.

It is difficult to control how many users are accessing the databases. On busy servers, you may restrict access to certain users only to prevent slow access. For example, users with the last name *A* through *F* access one server; all others access another server for the same database.

You may want to consider placing reference databases on only a few servers for access.

Passthru Servers

If remote users access both database and mail servers, it may be necessary to implement Passthru servers for dial-in purposes. This enables users to make only one call to access both their mail and the databases they need. A Passthru server acts as an ambassador for the user and makes the connections for the user.

Passthru servers can be mail servers or database servers. Users specify their mail servers in the Location documents of their mail files and the names of the servers to act as ambassadors.

The receiving server must also have passthru enabled in order for it to act on behalf of the user to find the target server.

When users call in to get their mail, the Passthru server is really called; then the connection is made by the Passthru server. If the Passthru server can connect to the database server, the user can execute a database replication at the same time.

Passthru servers have a layer of security limiting who can use the server to get to other servers.

Passthru servers should have enough modems on them to ensure efficient connectivity to the other servers.

External Servers

Servers that communicate to outside organizations should be planned for in advance. The idea is to isolate nonsecret information on these servers to provide access to the pertinent information and, at the same time, not to risk company data.

External servers should be isolated in their own branches of the naming hierarchy you have in place so that you can provide access just to those servers easily through cross-certification.

External servers should have bare-bones Domino Directories on them so that companies outside your organization do not know how your domain is connected and how it is set up. This is done by changing documents in this server manually.

External servers contain Directory Catalogs for ease of mail addressing to outside domains. When building external servers, plan for denying and allowing access to specific servers/people from outside companies by implementing them with entries in the allow and deny access groups.

Firewall Servers

The term firewall comes from Internet connectivity and refers to servers that allow access to data without letting the other company have access to the rest of the network. It is important to understand that access to a Domino server does not mean that the user has access to the company network. The nature of Domino provides access to data on top of the current network layer; this does not allow access to the network.

A firewall in Domino prevents access to other servers in the Domino network. The following are recommendations for setting up a firewall Domino server:

- Cross-certify based on the servername only. As soon as you provide access to a complete branch of your hierarchy, you risk placing a server with insecure data in that branch.
- Use allow/deny access groups to limit who can access the server specifically.
- Limit what is in the Domino Directory and Directory Catalog on the firewall server.

With our basic understanding of the server types available to us, it is time to explore the communications infrastructure options.

Planning Your Communications Infrastructure

You need to design a communications infrastructure that supports communications between your servers and between remote users.

Modem

The most common method for connecting servers and users is to use modems. They are inexpensive and can use the well-established worldwide analog phone line system.

Certainly for remote or laptop users, modems are still an attractive option. Other methods, such as ISDN or X.25, require more hardware and software, not to mention support, to make them work.

It pays to bear in mind, however, that the analog system differs in quality around the world. As your users travel, they may dial back to your network from many locations where line quality is poor. You may have to suggest to some users that they reduce line speed to achieve a reliable connection.

Modem Through ISP

More and more companies are providing their disconnected users with a national Internet service provider (ISP) account to reduce remote connection/long distance costs. Because the Internet is IP-based, users connect to the Internet via the local Point-of-Presence (POP) in the city they are in. The Notes client then connects to the external Passthru server over the IP connection, which authenticates the user. Because the external server is a Passthru server, the user then has full access to the Domino network, all on the cost of a local call.

Three of the most popular and reliable national ISPs are IBM Global Services (http://www.ibm.net), Mindspring (http://www.mindspring.com), and AT&T WorldNet (http://www.att.net). Contact them for more details.

ISDN

For servers or users at fixed remote sites, such as those who work from their homes, ISDN services are becoming attractive. Increasingly, providers are offering a wider array of ISDN services at lower price points.

ISDN is not to be taken lightly, however. The installation and support required to establish and maintain a single ISDN link can create a cost far greater than that imposed by the use of a modem. Until these procedures are simplified, ISDN should be considered only in cases where the costs are justified.

That said, Notes/Domino performs wonderfully over ISDN. The Notes software knows only which protocol it is speaking; it isn't concerned with the underlying hardware that enables that protocol. You can run Notes over IP very effectively using ISDN.

ADSL

Asymmetrical Digital Subscriber Line (ADSL)services are the latest high-speed connectivity option for users and corporations. ADSL is a modem technology that enables common phone lines to be used for ultra–high-speed Internet access (up to 8Mbps downstream and 1Mbps upstream, as compared to ISDN, which is only up to 128Kbps upstream/downstream). Costs for ADSL are much lower than ISDN services, so ADSL may be an attractive alternative to ISDN.

As with ISDN, Notes/Domino works wonderfully with ADSL, because it provides an IP connection just like any IP network.

Check with your local phone company to services determine whether ADSL is available in your area. You can also read more about ADSL at http://www.adsl.com/adsl_forum.html.

WAN

Lotus Notes/Domino ADSLworks well in a WAN environment. If your decision to implement a WAN hinges solely on Domino, however, it is often not worth the extra cost, because a Domino WAN can be implemented more cheaply with modem, ISDN, and/or ADSL technology.

A WAN still operates on certain network protocols. Again, Domino makes use of these protocols to communicate; it doesn't distinguish the underlying architecture. However, remember that Domino servers cannot be included in the same Notes named network unless they share the same protocol and are constantly connected (modem connections are technically allowed, but are not sufficient).

TOPOLOGY TYPES

A *topology* is a layout or schematic of a series of controls in a system. For Lotus Notes/Domino, this applies to many aspects of the system: mail routing, replication, and passthru, to name a few. Let's look at some different types of topologies; they can be applied where appropriate against the various portions of a Domino system.

PEER-TO-PEER

A topology in which communications are established among a series of servers without designating a single master server can be called a peer-to-peer topology. For example, a New York server calls Dallas, which calls San Diego, which calls New York.

Peer-to-peer can be scheduled in an end-to-end fashion or as a mesh. This method is generally used when only a few servers are involved and a hub-and-spoke system would be overkill, perhaps requiring more hardware than necessary to meet the communication needs.

Though we use the term peer-to-peer, this does not apply to workstations. Just remember this: Workstations cannot answer connection requests; they always initiate them. This implies that workstations cannot call one another.

END-TO-END

In an end-to-end setup, servers call each other in an orderly fashion, making a series of calls to form a calling loop. For example, a New York server calls Dallas, which calls San Diego, which calls Chicago, which in turn calls New York. If a server goes down, however, the replication of databases around the loop is slowed significantly. For a document to replicate its way back upstream, for instance, it takes several more cycles. Note that all servers have to have a replica copy of all databases being replicated. You should use the `LocalDomainServers` group or an equivalent, assigning it Manager access in each replica.

Mesh

The mesh method is an end-to-end schedule with a twist. Instead of calling only one other server, some of them make two or more calls, creating a crisscross pattern. If one server goes down, it does not affect the replication among the other servers.

With this method, the number of Connection documents grows almost exponentially as the number of servers increases. It is only practical when there is a small number of servers (no more than 4 or 5).

Hub-and-Spoke

The most common and efficient topology in a large network is called hub-and-spoke. It is most prevalent largely because of its scalability.

The simplest hub-and-spoke arrangement is this: One server acts as the hub and coordinates the flow of information to other subhubs. The subhubs talk to production servers. As the number of production servers grows, more subhubs or even new layers of subhubs can be added to serve more production servers. The simplest arrangement is a single hub with 8 or 9 spoke servers.

One factor that is solved best by the hub-and-spoke method is the number of hops that a piece of data must make to travel from one end of the network to the other. Other topologies often require many more hops, slowing the communication process for the users. This topology can move a mail message or a replicated document quickly anywhere within your network or even to other companies.

The principal benefits for using the hub-and-spoke model include the following:

- Centralized communication costs
- Enhanced security (hub will have restricted access)
- Centralized replication and backups
- Alleviation of overlapping replication schedules

You may also want to consider implementing a backup hub server that replicates with the hub and that can quickly be reconfigured into becoming the hub server if the primary hub goes down.

Now that we have a general understanding of basic network topologies, it is time to take a look at the various topologies specific to a Domino network.

Mail Routing Topology

Let's look at how you can use Notes Mail to configure your domain for efficient mail routing, which is critical to satisfying your users.

Minimizing Hops

The simplest factor for efficient mail routing is the number of hops a message must make to reach its destination. This is not only a factor for speed, but troubleshooting as well. Each server has its own schedule for routing mail; two factors, the schedule and the message count threshold, determine how quickly messages route through a server.

The schedules are specified in Connection documents in the Domino Directory, along with the method of connecting (such as the COM port and phone number). You can specify days of the week, times to attempt connections (as either single times or ranges), and—for time ranges—how often to call during the range.

> **Note**
> In Domino R5, you can also specify how mail replication takes place, using Push-Wait (wait until the other mail server calls this server, and then send the mail), Pull-Push (receive new mail, and then send mail), Pull-Only (receive new mail), and Push-Only (send new mail).

The most efficient method of routing mail uses the hub-and-spoke topology. Messages travel one or two hops to the hub, then one or two hops down to thef recipient's mail server.

Minimizing Cost

If some of your servers are connected by modem, you bear a communication cost for each phone call. Your goal is to make as few phone calls as possible. Instead of calling for each message that uses that route, you can let messages accrue in the `MAIL.BOX` file, and then pass them all at a scheduled time.

There is a field called Route at Once if X Messages Pending on the Connection document. By putting a threshold number in this field, the router will force a call if and when the threshold is reached. Otherwise, it will wait until the next scheduled calling time to route the messages.

Non-Adjacent Domains

To simplify addressing for your users, you can create non-adjacent Domain documents that enable the sender to specify the recipient's domain but not the intermediate domain needed to route the message. Suppose that your design specifies that you will use an "external" domain for mail routing outside your company. A message intended for someone at another firm must be addressed to that user at that user's domain at your external domain (`User @ UserDomain @ ExternalDomain`). This tells the servers in your internal domain to first forward the message to the external domain, where a connection is found and established to the recipient's domain (`UserDomain`).

A non-adjacent Domain document specifies that any message addressed to a particular domain must first pass through another domain (for example, to route to `UserDomain`, first route through `ExternalDomain`).

You can use other fields on a non-adjacent Domain document to secure the use of this feature. You may not want users from other domains to be able to take advantage of this route simplification, so you can specify who should or should not be allowed to route mail to this domain by using the fields Allow Mail Only from Domains or Deny Mail from Domains.

ADJACENT DOMAINS

An adjacent domain is a domain to which your Domino server has a physical connection, and a non-adjacent domain is a domain to which your server lacks a physical connection. Connection documents are the link between adjacent domains. The Adjacent Domain document is a security measure that enables you to close down mail routing holes that may exist because of explicit routing. If a user relies on a non-adjacent Domain document to route a message, the Allow and Deny fields you've set up there will allow or prevent the message from routing.

However, if a user explicitly routes a message (for example, `Lisa Phillips @ DomainA @ DomainB`), no non-adjacent Domain documents are used by the router. If you want to prevent routing to `DomainA` from `DomainB`, you can create an Adjacent Domain document that prevents using `DomainB` to route to `DomainA`.

One reason for wanting this security would be to prevent users from other companies from using your mail infrastructure to route mail to other domains that are also connected to your domain—in other words, messages that are not destined for users in your domain, but for users in one of your adjacent domains. By allowing such activity, you may bear substantial communication costs for routing those messages.

REPLICATION TOPOLOGY

Your replication topology depends on many factors. Consider the number of databases that need to replicate, how much information each database contains, what type of information is being replicated (documents containing large objects or documents containing only text fields), how often the databases need to replicate, and where they need to replicate.

DATABASES

Initially, users should be allowed to create databases freely. The reason is to get people interested in Lotus Notes/Domino and comfortable with using the product. When the enterprise grows, however, data flow becomes more important. In a large enterprise, databases are not just placed on a server and accessed by users. You should consider the following:

- Who should access the database? Is it on the servers they need to access? Because replication is the means to distribute databases, allowing a database for users sometimes requires that replica copies of the database be located on several servers. If this is the case, ensure that all servers used to distribute the information also have the database. For example, in a hub-and-spoke situation, if the database is to be located on multiple spokes, it also needs to be located on the hub for distribution.

- Who needs to update the design? How will the design be implemented? Typically, changes to a design of a database are located in a database template, and the template is then used to propagate design changes. The person updating the design needs to have at least Designer access to the database. The servers propagating the design changes need to also have Designer access to the database.

- Who will be responsible for data distribution? This issue comes into play when a database is used as a reference—a company phone book or Directory Catalog, for example. The user responsible for adding data to the database needs to have access to do so. Any server distributing data needs to have access as well.

- What other databases are required by the database? Notes enables you to look up data in other databases to provide information for the current database. Wherever the database is being used, the lookup database must also be available.

- What company standards for databases will be implemented? The person who creates a database needs to create it in such a way that the design can be modified easily by another designer. Standards for databases are difficult to have in place, because the perception is that they are restrictive. In the long run, however, the cost of maintaining the database will go down considerably if standards are followed. Standards have to be flexible and documented in order to get buy-in from the database developers in your company. A suggestion is to standardize basic elements, such as ACLs, keyword listings, form names, and database names. As the first databases get implemented, document the design. Use the design documentation as a basis to develop new standards.

IMPLEMENTING DATABASES

In a large enterprise, it is the administrator who places the database on a public server (hub) and who can be the gatekeeper for database design adherence. The job of the administrator primarily is to ensure that the database is replicated throughout the environment correctly. Second, because the database is being checked anyway, the administrator can also ensure that the database adheres to company standards. You will explore these roles later in the section. First, let's look at how a database is published on a server. The process in a large network should be as follows:

- The database is developed by the designer to meet users' needs.

- The database is staged on a server that few people can access for testing. Consider this your pilot of the database.

- The database is modified and versioned; then a template is drawn for future revisions. Versioning a database in an enterprise is important. A Notes database can be quite nebulous from a design perspective. It is very easy to "fix" something and end up ruining something else. When a change is made to a database, it should be documented and reported to the users. The scope of the change should also be considered.

- The database is implemented, which means that the database is placed in the environment in such a way that the data can be distributed to the users. In a hub-and-spoke

situation, the database is placed on the hub and replicas are made on the spoke. It is at this point that the administrator checks the database for standards.
- The database is published in a library for logical access. A catalog is generated by the server and tracks all databases in a domain. A library is a grouping of documents pointing to databases on the server. The group is decided arbitrarily.

Ensuring Data Flow

The ACL of any database needs to be standardized so that servers can replicate data appropriately. The rules are generally the following:

- All servers changing ACLs need to have Manager access—this means servers on which design changes originate.
- All servers changing other design elements need to have Designer access. Servers on which design changes originate need to have Designer access to the database.
- All servers propagating documents should have Editor access to the ACL.
- All servers receiving data only should have Reader access to the ACL.
- A back door should be put in place to enable the administrator to change the ACL on the server. This back door is a group in the ACL that has Manager access. The administrator need only add his or her name to the group in the Domino Directory to gain access to the database.
- All ACLs for a database should be the same; exceptions to this rule should be verified by the administrator.

Using these rules, let's examine a possible scenario—a database used as a reference. The database is implemented in a hub-and-spoke topology on all spokes. A recommended ACL should have the hub as Manager, the spokes as Reader, default as Reader, the group of people updating as Author, and the back door group as Manager.

To make the job of the administrator easier, the ACL standard should be published so that the databases come with the ACLs set properly. The administrator needs only to check the access. Tools exist in the new Domino R5 Administration tool that enable you to set the ACLs of databases remotely.

Not all databases need to go through this test in a distributed environment. If the database is located on only one server in the domain, it is unnecessary to check the ACL because data propagation is not an issue. In fact, if you have implemented a plan in which administrators in regions are responsible for their own database replication on servers in their regions, they are responsible for the ACLs in their regions. It is only databases that go public that need to adhere to the ACL standards.

The standards should be published in a database available to all database developers. To aid in buy-in, the developers should be allowed to comment on and change standards. The reason for publishing standards is to speed up implementation of databases. If a database is held at the checking phase, interest in it will diminish.

PUBLISHING THE DATABASES

When a database is available, users need to access it. This can be done by the user accessing the server and loading the database. This becomes problematic in organizations in which users move around in job functions frequently. Knowing which databases to access is half the battle when training a user to do a job. This is where database libraries come into play.

A database library is a collection of database links. You, the librarian, publish the database to a library. The users add the database library to their bookmarks (or workspaces, if any of your users are still using the R4 workspace) and use the links to load the icons to the database list in their bookmarks.

When new people start, they need only to add the database library bookmark to have access to the groups of databases in their locations.

REPLICATION CONTROLS

There are four replication controls that you can configure on a Connection document to optimize and tune your replication topology: the overall schedule, the database priorities to replicate, specific filename(s), and a time limit on the call.

SCHEDULING   Determined through your Connection documents, scheduling is an important facet of your replication topology. An overworked server often results from lack of schedule planning. Draw a timeline for each server depicting the calls for replication that it makes. Plot the starting times and durations of the various connections. Balance the calls against the busy times for that server. Use the Statistics Reporting database or the Domino Administration tool to determine the busy times using the Graph views.

PRIORITY   A limited control is the database priority. Each database can be given a priority of High, Medium, or Low. Your Connection documents can specify that only databases of certain priorities replicate. This setting applies to all the databases on the server. Managers can set the priority level by using the Properties dialog box of a database.

You might want to have one Connection document for each priority level. Your choices for priority levels are High, Medium & High, or Low, Medium & High.

As you can see from these choices, High-priority databases are always included, so you can use the first two choices to narrow down the number that replicate.

Database managers can set the priority of a database in the Replication Settings dialog box (select File, Replication, Settings, in the Other section).

SPECIFIC FILES   A better control is the field for specifying individual database filenames or directories. One or more files can be listed, or a directory of databases can be listed, effectively narrowing the focus of the Connection document to just the items in the list (no other files will replicate). This enables you to specify different schedules for each of your databases. Make sure that you plot these on your timeline.

TIME LIMITS Given the varying nature of the data contained in Notes databases, time limits give you more control over your replication schedule planning. For each Connection document, you can specify a time limit in minutes. If this limit is reached during replication, the document in progress is finished and replication stops. Using this control, you can more closely plan and manage your replication timeline.

REPLICATION OF ACLS

It is important that you recognize and plan for replication of database Access Control Lists (ACLs) . The ACL behaves differently from normal documents in a database. The ACL is considered first in replication and is overwritten if a change is implemented. The initiating server's ACL is the one that is checked to see whether there is a change.

The ACL is actually a "document" in the database, albeit not a data document that you can use in a view. During replication, the ACL replicates first in case any changes to the settings would prevent further replication. The ACL "document" that is newer between the two replicas will overwrite the older if the newer one has been modified since last replication. This is a time-sensitive feature, and if the clocks on the two servers are not very near each other in time (we can't expect perfect synchronization), you might experience cases in which the newer ACL does not update the older version because the clock on that server is a few minutes behind the clock on the other server. This situation usually occurs only when you are attempting replication manually after making changes. If you encounter this problem, check the clocks on the servers and compare them with the time stamps on the ACLs. You can resave the newer ACL, wait until the lagging server passes the time of the last change on the older ACL, and then replicate again.

CENTRAL MANAGEMENT FOR DATABASE ACLS

Plan to manage the ACL of every database. This doesn't mean that you need to manage each ACL yourself; it means that you should have a plan for each database agreed on by your administrative team. Ideally, each database's ACL will be maintained on one server. If you plan to use the administration process, make use of the Administration Server setting on the ACL dialog box. This lets the administration process make changes to the ACL on the server specified in this field. Each replica of this database should have the same setting.

The administration process consists of a server task (`ADMIN.EXE`) and a series of steps initiated in the Domino Directory by an administrator using the Actions menu. An administrator can initiate a change, such as renaming a user. That action writes a document into the Administration Requests database.

The administration process server task sees that request, and it takes action on the Domino Directory. In the case of renaming a user, it puts the pending request into the user's Person document.

When that user next accesses the server, Notes alerts him or her to the pending request and asks the user to accept the change. Upon accepting the change, another request is generated in the Administration Requests database, and the administration process server tasks takes action again—this time by propagating the new name throughout other documents in the Domino Directory.

The Enforce a consistent access control list across all replicas of this database option, under the Advanced section of the ACL dialog box, does what it says: One replica copy is listed as manager in all other replicas. On this copy only, enable this setting. The managing replica forces its ACL into every other replica, including those that reside on workstations or laptops.

This process should not be used on separate replica copies of the Domino Directory, but should be used on only one replica, which is specified in the Administration Server field on the Replication Settings dialog box in the Advanced section. If this procedure is not followed, either the administration process on the other servers will ignore the requests, or replication conflicts will result.

> **Note**
> The Statistics & Events database in Domino R5 now contains a new document, ACL Monitor, which was formerly known as the Database Monitor. The ACL Monitor document enables you to define one or more databases to watch for ACL changes, and then notifies you if the ACL is changed. You can use this in conjunction with an Event Monitor document to also log the change to the Events view of the Statistics & Events database.

Passthru Topology

Under R3, a Notes server was always an endpoint on a network; it performed no routing of protocols. Notes R4 introduced the concept of passthru topology, which is essentially just that: protocol routing. By accessing a known, reachable Domino server, another Domino server or Notes client can route through that server to reach another. This feature is fully configurable in the Server document, including the capability of disabling it. Please review Chapter 35, "Initial Configuration of Servers with the Domino Directories," for more information on Passthru servers.

Task-Specific, Dedicated Servers

Passthru enables servers to be truly dedicated in their tasks. In the old days (R3.x), a user could reach one server with a phone call; if a database resided on a different server, it either must have been replicated to the dial-in server or the user had to hang up and redial that other server.

With passthru topology, however, the Domino server can route the caller to other Notes servers on the network in one phone call. This enables you to segment your server types without wasting precious drive space for replica copies. A database can live on one server and be accessed easily by both network and remote clients.

Protocol-Specific Servers

Another benefit of using passthru is the capability of streamlining your protocols. Suppose that you have many users working under SPX, but a server in another area is using TCP/IP. Rather than enabling TCP/IP on the SPX users' machines, you can enable this protocol on a server running SPX. Using passthru, the SPX clients can reach the TCP/IP server by routing through their normal SPX servers.

Let's take another powerful example. Domino R4.x introduced a server task called the Web Retriever, or WEB. This task reaches out to the World Wide Web and retrieves HTML pages, putting them into a Notes database called the Web Navigator. Access to the Web normally requires TCP/IP at the desktop, but by using a Passthru server to provide access to a server running the WEB server task, your clients do not need TCP/IP. They can communicate with the Domino server over SPX while the server itself communicates with the Web using TCP/IP.

Segmenting your protocols can greatly reduce the expense of adding protocols to single-protocol desktops.

Mapping Your Passthru Topology

Draw a chart showing all your servers, their connections, and their protocols. Determine which servers should allow the passthru topology. You can control passthru with four fields on each Server document: Access Server, Route Through, Cause Calling, and Destinations Allowed. As with other fields on a Server document, use groups or wildcards rather than individual user or servernames so that minimal changes will be required. Please refer to Chapter 35 for more information on setting up a Passthru server.

The Domain and the Domino Directory

The glue of a Notes domain is the Domino Directory, formerly known as the Public Name and Address Book (NAB). The larger your network, the more crucial the management of this instrument. Your users will depend on it for addressing mail (along with the Directory Catalog); your servers need it for identification, security, and task scheduling. Management of this book should be planned in advance so that emergencies can be avoided through routine maintenance.

Notes Domains

As you've learned, a domain is defined as a group of servers that replicate their primary Domino Directories. The components of that domain are all defined in that Domino Directory. Each server knows its place in the network as well as the roles of, and communications paths to, each of the other servers.

However, this is not necessarily the best method for setting up a large network, although this doesn't imply that it is wrong. Simply stated, the evaluation of several factors can help you determine whether to use one domain or to split your organization into multiple domains.

SIMPLICITY VERSUS EFFICIENCY A single Domino Directory eases mail addressing, but as this Domino Directory grows large, efficiency for each of the servers using that book decreases.

Multiple domains (each has its own Domino Directory) are each more efficient for lookups, but they make addressing harder; they require a separate combined Domino Directory. In the pre-Domino R5 days, this was a real pain for both administrators and users. R5 introduces a new database known as a Directory Catalog. A Directory Catalog is an LDAP-based database that contains an entry for all users and groups of the specified domains. Even though a Directory Catalog can contain hundreds of thousands of names, it remains *very* small because of the LDAP technology used. It is small enough for users to keep a local replica for disconnected addressing.

ROLES

The Domino Directory provides various roles stratified to match the most common administrator functions in such an environment. The users and groups listed in the ACL are assigned to appropriate roles that grant them rights according to their assigned responsibilities. You can enable some administrators to create and modify only groups but not users or servers; likewise, you can allow some to create users but not modify groups. In this way, it is possible to distribute the maintenance responsibilities without releasing control to each and every administrator.

These are the roles that are in the Domino Directory:

- GroupCreator allows creation of Group documents.
- GroupModifier allows modification of Group documents.
- NetCreator allows creation of all documents except Groups, Servers, and Person.
- NetModifier allows modification of all documents except Groups, Servers, and Users.
- ServerCreator allows creation of server IDs and Server documents.
- ServerModifier allows modification of Server documents.
- UserCreator allows creation of user IDs and Person.
- UserModifier allows modification of Person.

ADMINISTRATION GROUPS

The documents in the Domino Directory make it easier to facilitate local changes in a distributed environment. Using the Administrators field, you can specify, per document, those groups that are allowed to modify it. This enables you to allocate specific sets of documents to the control of a local administrator; that person will be allowed to maintain those documents, yet you haven't relinquished control of the other documents.

Incorporating Mail Gateways

Domino R5 can host two types of Mail Gateways: cc:Mail and X.400. The SMTP gateway is now built into Domino R5, and can be configured in the Server document of your server. The cc:Mail and X.400 MTAs must be installed later. They are available free on the World Wide Web at http://www.lotus.com/notesmta for many platforms.

The MTA architecture is a robust mechanism, not only for translating messages as they travel into or out of a Notes Mail environment (as previous "gateways" did), but also for hosting true message-transfer capabilities for transient messages (those that are simply routing from one non-Domino system to another). This architecture uses standard message routing protocols as opposed to the Domino message router protocol, which implies excellent coexistence with standards-based mail environments.

The MTAs analyze the routing fields and intelligently transfer messages. For instance, with the SMTP gateway, you can use "business card" addressing—that is, by specifying an address using the format user@domain.com without including any Domino-specific items, such as a Notes domain name. Thus, because the SMTP gateway observes and handles such addresses appropriately, it does not matter whether they exist in a Notes Mail message or are from another system.

Additionally, the MTAs will seamlessly encapsulate Notes Mail messages so they can be routed from one Notes domain to another using the MTAs while retaining the original formatting. On reaching the destination Notes Mail user, the messages appear without loss of fidelity.

All MTAs can run on a single Domino server, although it is recommended that such a server not be simultaneously used to support user activity, such as mail accounts and production databases. You might want to set up a single server for each MTA, however, because this technique avoids the problem of a single point of failure.

Configuration of the MTAs requires planning and forethought. Because it is not in the scope of this chapter to detail the installation steps, read the respective Administrator's Guide database (which ships with each MTA). The example configuration documents are especially helpful for verifying and troubleshooting your configuration.

Monitoring Your Notes Servers

Domino R5 introduces a completely new Administrator client, replacing the R4.x Administration Panel. The Domino Administrator client is installed as a separate client from the Notes client, and it can be accessed independent of the Notes client from within the Notes client.

The Domino Administrator client provides a centralized, robust interface to manage your Domino network. You can centrally control virtually everything about your Domino servers: files, Directories, ACLs, replication, user registration, and much more.

Please review Part VII, "Administering the Domino Servers," for more information on the Domino Administrator client.

Statistics and Events Server Tasks

Domino R5 provides you with a way to collect statistics and trap events that occur on your servers. You can have this collection feedback to one central database from all your servers. And in Domino R5, you can set up various Monitor documents to watch for specific events, and then perform some action based on that event.

Statistics collection enables you to observe the behavior of a server over time, monitoring usage, disk space, memory, and tasks at specified intervals. Special graphing views in the Statistics database (STATREP5.NSF) give you a visual representation of some of these statistics.

Simply collecting statistics will not alert you to trouble conditions. By creating various Monitor or Event documents in the Statistics & Events database (EVENTS5.NSF), you can actually receive notification of thresholds that have been exceeded or of events as they occur.

Summary

As with any network, a Domino network has the potential to grow very large and to become unmanageable. By carefully planning the management of the system before you implement, you can ease the cost of ownership and provide truly useful groupware services for your company:

- Through administrator teamwork, use Notes/Domino to assist your administrative group as you maintain and expand your Domino environment.
- Create a good infrastructure. Your servers will behave better if you provide adequate hardware.
- Plan your topologies carefully, drawing topology maps for your team. It will help you make sense of the contents of your domain's Domino Directory.
- Plan to monitor your system so that you can detect conditions that might lead to serious problems.

Through careful planning and implementation, your groupware deployment can be a resounding success.

From Here...

To read additional information about administering your Domino system, you can read Parts VI and Part VII. Here are some chapters that may interest you.

- Chapter 38, "Administering Users, Groups, and Certification," covers information about the addition and removal of users and groups from your Domino directory.
- Chapter 39, "Administering Electronic Mail," provides you with critical information about email, one of the most important applications for Domino.

- Chapters 36, "Domino Security Overview," and Chapter 37, "Firewalls, Virtual Private Networks (VPNs), and Internet Security," cover Domino security. These chapters can help you secure your system.
- Database Replication and Administration are covered in Chapter 40, "Replication and Its Administration," as well as Chapter 41, "Administering Files and Databases."
- Chapter 43, "Troubleshooting and Monitoring Domino," provides you with information to help you debug problems in your system and to keep it running smoothly.

CHAPTER 47

Integrating Domino with Phone, Fax, and Imaging Systems

One of Domino's greatest strengths is its capability of supporting multiple types of data to deliver integrated business solutions. This chapter introduces you to unified messaging and explores ways to integrate phone, fax, and imaging technologies with the Domino server.

Unified Messaging

Unified messaging combines all types of message media—including electronic mail, fax, and voice mail—in one message store or message database. The Notes electronic mail database is a message store. There are great advantages to using unified messaging, including a higher degree of efficiency and better productivity, largely related to better and easier communication.

With unified messaging, all your messages are stored in a single place and can be accessed via a personal computer using a Notes client, a Web browser, or a telephone. Electronic mail messages are read to you over the telephone by converting the text into speech using a synthesized voice, which reads the message to you. Voice mail can be heard on the PC, provided you have a sound card and speakers on the PC, or on a standard telephone. Unified messaging is comprised of voice, paging, fax, imaging, and electronic mail.

There are advantages to unified messaging built on the Domino infrastructure for both end users and for database and mail administrators:

- **One place**   All messages are stored in one place. When access is gained, all messages can be retrieved, regardless of message type.
- **Single login, single password**   End users have one login to one system with one password.
- **Message management**   Regardless of message type, messages can be grouped, for example, in one Notes Mail Folder. Additionally, messages can be stored, copied, forwarded, and categorized, and can take advantage of all Notes/Domino functions, such as archiving and agents. For example, an intelligent agent can be set up to send a page when an urgent voice mail or electronic mail message is sent to you.
- **Unified administration**   Administrators have one system to manage.

Because unified messaging is built on Domino, you have an additional advantage of using portable or hand-held devices, such as PDAs, notebooks, or Web television to enhance your unified messaging system. The features and limitations of the device determine the extent to which you can do this. For example, some hand-held devices do not have voice capability and have limited storage.

VOICE MAIL SYSTEMS

Generally speaking, conventional voice mail systems do not integrate well with electronic messaging systems such as Domino. Integration problems are related to

- **Two storage systems**—Voice mail in the voice mail message store, electronic mail in the electronic mail database.
- **Independent management**—Each system requires separate maintenance, administration, and management.
- **Duplicate Address Books**—Each system requires a separate Address Book even though the systems are used by the same group of people.

Keep in mind that some conventional voice mail systems do not allow you to access messages except by telephone. An additional limitation of a conventional voice mail system is that there are normally storage limits, such as the number of days the end user can keep a message.

In contrast, with an integrated voice system built on Domino, you have all the advantages of a conventional voice mail system combined with the advantages of a Domino server. It is easier, and most of the time less expensive, to increase drive space, expand the system, and integrate the technology with other infrastructure components.

> **Caution**
>
> Newer versions of some conventional voice mail systems have an electronic mail interface. This is a nice feature, but it is not true unified messaging. Electronic mail capabilities enable you to forward a voice mail message to an electronic mail address. However, you still cannot access electronic mail messages via the telephone. That is, you cannot call your voice mail system and have electronic mail messages read to you.
>
> A similar trend is occurring with voice systems that add fax capabilities. Remember that one of the criteria of true unified messaging is that you have access to a single message store.

PLANNING FOR INTEGRATED VOICE MAIL

When planning to integrate a voice mail system with your Domino server, it is very important to understand how to size a system. All voice mail systems are sized based on the number of ports you purchase. The number of ports determines the number of simultaneous connections the voice server will handle. Unlike conventional PC software, most voice systems are not licensed by user, but are licensed per port.

Formulas for how to size the system range by manufacturer, but most conventional systems have an 8:100 ratio of ports to number of users. For basic planning purposes, you should use a 1:10 ratio, but additional factors can have a dramatic impact on this number.

For your system, you need to take into consideration how many people will be dialing in to the voice server to access the voice system. If the majority of people will be accessing their voice mail through a personal computer, you need fewer ports, because access to messages is accomplished through the network infrastructure, not the phone system. Conversely, if most of the people will be using the phone to check their messages, either from within the office or from remote locations, you need more ports.

Although every case is different, the price tag to add a small voice server system to Domino, including all hardware and software, starts at about $10,000. As of now, the pricing of integrated voice systems is along the same lines as conventional proprietary voice mail systems.

Hardware and Network Infrastructure

For all but the smallest installations (under ten people), use a separate PC server box for the voice server. The messages are stored in the users' mail databases on the Domino server, so your Domino server should have plenty of drive space.

A typical voice server has the following components:

- Operating system   Microsoft Windows NT 4.0.
- Lots of RAM   96MB or more depending on expected load and product specifications.
- Drive space   Because all messages are stored on the Domino mail database server and not the voice server, disk space required depends on the voice system software manufacturer's specifications. Usually this is quite low, so small disk drives are adequate. However, as with all servers, you should plan on mirroring drives or using RAID to protect the voice server from drive failures.
- Voice card   A card specifically designed to interface with phone systems. Voice cards are specially designed to work with all types of phone lines (PBX, regular telephone lines, ISDN, T1). There are different models for different line types. They are designed to detect touch-tones and record-and-play digitized sounds, and to handle high-performance text-to-speech (TTS) conversion. There are only a handful of products on the market today, most notably from Dialogic and Natural MicroSystems.
- Voice software   Software that controls the voice cards and runs the voice applications, from vendors such as Phonesoft and Big Sky (described in more detail in the next section).

> **Caution**
> Voice cards are not modems. You cannot use a voice modem instead of a voice card in your server, because voice cards have dedicated digital signal processors (DSP) that provide the extra processing power needed. Voice cards are not limited by serial port restrictions as modems are.

Voice Mail Software

As mentioned earlier, voice, electronic mail, and fax messages are stored in the users' mail databases, and administration of the voice system is usually handled through the Domino Directory. However, special voice software enables integration to take place by controlling the voice card and managing user features:

- Auto attendant   The feature that answers the phone with a recorded greeting, routes calls to individuals or departments with a known extension, and enables searching of the user directory by spelling the desired name.

- Scripting   Used to set up intelligent branching of calls through cascading menus or based on time of day, such as different messages played while the office is open and when it is closed.

- Leaving a message   Callers are given options if they call and you do not answer your phone, such as leaving a voice mail message, sending a message to a pager, being placed on hold, and forwarding to another extension. When users leave a message in your mailbox, they have the option of replaying it, rerecording it, and setting priorities, such as urgent.

- Access via phone   Enables you to review messages in the order they were received—older first—by person, by category, by message type, or even by the contents of the subject line.

- Access via PC   In order for your messages to be played back on any PC, they must be in WAV file format or another format supported by users' PCs. If your PC does not have sound hardware, some products can ring your phone and play the messages over the phone.

- Message playback   You can choose to skip, save, delete, forward, rewind, or replay the message from the beginning. You can also send copies of the message preceded by an introductory greeting to other users. Some systems enable you to control the way you hear the message with forward and rewind controls.

- Call Pursuit/Find Me   If you don't answer the call, the system can try to find you by calling a list of phone numbers. When you are found, the system can transfer the call to you.

- Support for fax and pager gateways   If you already have a fax or pager gateway installed, most voice software can support it.

- Telephone integration   Support for message waiting indicators (MWI) and other programmable telephone system features.

- Growth/expansion options   As you grow, so should your voice system. Ports should be able to be added in reasonable increments.

Interactive Voice Response Applications (IVR)

Interactive Voice Response (IVR) applications are used as a means for gathering information over the telephone via touch-tone keypad entries or voice. Any application that interacts with a user over the telephone is an IVR application. Phonesoft, for example, has a software development kit available to enable developers to create customized IVR applications. Some examples of IVR applications are

- Voice mail
- Auto attendant
- Filing federal payroll tax forms
- Accessing bank and credit card balances
- Registering for conferences
- Help desk, queue systems
- Fax-on-demand

Paging

Paging can be integrated into Domino messaging via one of two ways: if the paging provider (such as SkyTel) offers messaging services through the Internet, or through the use of pager gateway software, such as Lotus Pager Gateway.

Both Lotus Pager Gateway and Internet pager messaging can be used to support two-way pagers and using a Web browser to send and receive pages. Some additional features of the Lotus Pager Gateway are alphanumeric pages that can be automatically converted into abbreviated and shortened words to reduce the size, support for pagers that don't have Internet messaging capabilities, and support for wireless real-time access to Domino.

Less Paper: Moving Toward a Paperless Office

Every time a person in an organization touches a piece of paper, it costs money. In fact, storing documents also costs money. Therefore, many companies have made it a priority to replace paper-based systems with electronic systems. At the same time, companies want to encourage collaborative activities through the use of knowledge management.

It is important to reduce paper without reducing necessary business communication, as well as with minimal disruption. Careful evaluation of the business processes and the people that make those processes work is necessary. You should reduce your internal paper before you reduce your external paper. Primarily, this is because you control all the paper you generate. When you reach a measurable point of paper reduction, you can contact the customers, suppliers, and organizations that you interact with to figure out ways to reduce the paper they provide to you.

The first steps to achieving a paperless office is to implement a "less paper" policy.

Integrating a fax and an imaging system into your infrastructure significantly reduces paper volume.

Although integrated voice systems may not reduce large quantities of paper handling directly, some IVR applications do. For example, consider this scenario: Customers call a credit card company to obtain balance or transactional information, and a synthesized voice provides them with this information. Because the process is completely automated, no paper is generated.

A less-paper office can be a reality if you have both a fax and imaging system built on the Domino infrastructure. Electronic mail eliminates the need for a lot of postal mail; imaging eliminates the need for document file storage, photocopying and distribution; fax software eliminates the paper-intensive side of the fax process. If all three are integrated in the same Domino platform, it is easier to manage and administer than if these three are separate.

There are some instances of necessary paper. For example, documents that require hardcopy signatures, notarization, or some other form of certification or authentication for validity can be imaged or faxed electronically, but they lose their validity. Some government organization paperwork such as original payroll tax reporting forms cannot be eliminated due to legal or audit reasons. The type of industry you are in will also have an impact on your ability to go paperless. For example, architectural firms may have some difficulty converting large-scale blueprints to an imaging system with conventional equipment.

INTEGRATING FAX WITH DOMINO

Since its introduction, the fax has revolutionized the business world. Integrating faxes with the messaging system is the next logical step in achieving either a less-paper or paperless office.

There is immediate benefit in removing a fax machine and replacing it with a fax server. Remember that a fax machine is another piece of equipment that needs service, paper, and toner, and eliminating it saves money. (A fax server *never* runs out of paper or needs toner!)

With a fax server, people can send and receive faxes from their desktops without leaving their desks. They do not waste time going down the hall to the fax machine, dialing numbers, and waiting for the fax to go through. A fax server enables people to fax directly from their application software using a print-to-fax driver (word processor, spreadsheet, business graphics, accounting systems, and so forth) instead of printing hard copy and then faxing.

The benefits increase exponentially when you integrate the fax server with your Domino infrastructure.

PLANNING FOR INTEGRATED FAX

In order to plan a fax solution, measure the volume of faxes sent and faxes received. If you send a lot of hand-written faxes or other non–computer-generated faxes, you should select a scanner that is able to handle the volume of paper faxes you want to send.

Hardware and Network Infrastructure

For all but the smallest installations (fewer than 10 people), use a separate server as your dedicated fax server. The fax server is separate from your Domino server but should be integrated into your network infrastructure. Phone lines go directly to the fax server.

The fax server handles all incoming and outgoing fax transmissions, document and message conversion, fax routing, and other fax management and fax administration tasks. The requirements for your fax hardware depend on the recommendations of the manufacturer of the fax software and the volume and types of faxes you will be sending and receiving.

The typical fax server has the following components:

- Operating system   Microsoft Windows NT 4.0.
- Lots of RAM   64MB or more, depending on expected load and product specifications.
- Drive space   Depends on the volume of faxes, but minimally should be about 500MB. Faxes can be stored on the Domino mail database server in individual mail databases, so your Domino server must have enough capacity to handle storing them.
- Fax card(s)   A board specifically designed for faxing. Cards are specifically designed to work with all types of phone lines. One card can support one or more telephone lines. Two well-known fax card brands are Brooktrout and GammaFax.
- Fax software   The software that controls the fax card and faxing features, such as the Lotus Domino Fax Server, RightFAX, TopCall, and many more (described in more detail in the next section).

> **Caution**
> Fax cards are not modems. With most products, you cannot use a fax modem instead of a fax card in your server, because fax cards have dedicated processors for extra processing power. Fax cards are not limited by serial port restrictions as modems are and can support many lines per card and different types of lines (analog, DID, T1, and so forth). Fax cards are preferred, especially where many phone lines and types of lines are required.

Fax Software

There are two types of fax solutions: desktop-based solutions and client/server solutions. Currently, most fax solutions that integrate with Domino are client/server.

Desktop-based solutions are designed for single users and are not designed for companywide use. Even if the fax software is stored on a file server, it is typically configured to work with small groups of people and typically has limited or no integration capabilities.

Fax Server Software

The fax server manages all fax activities. Products such as RightFAX, TopCall, Lotus Domino Fax Server and others support integration with the Domino infrastructure. It is important to get a product that interfaces with your personal Directory and public Domino

Directory. If you want to have your faxes read to you over the telephone as a component of unified messaging, the fax server software has to support Optical Character Recognition (OCR).

The fax server software has the following user features:

- **Inbound fax routing** The fax server can automatically route an incoming fax to a person's electronic mail address. There are several common methods of achieving inbound routing:
    - **DID and DNIS (Direct Inward Dial and Dialed Number Identification Service)** Each user gets his or her own personal fax number. All the fax numbers point to the same group of phone lines on the fax server. For example, you could have 100 users, each with his or her own number, directing all incoming faxes to four lines plugged into the fax server. The fax server software then routes to the designated party based on that user's fax number.
    - **Line/channel routing** Faxes can be routed based on the phone line they came in on. All the faxes coming into the fax server on one specific line gets routed to one individual's electronic mail box.
    - **DTMF routing (Dual Tone Multi Frequency)** Commonly known as touch tone, fax routing is controlled by the sender who presses a button on the phone to route to a specific individual after the fax server answers. For example, the sender might hear, "To send a fax to Max, press 1. To send a fax to Charlie, press 2. To send a fax to Thomas, press 3." This type of routing is not as practical because most senders use a conventional fax machine or a computer-based fax solution where user options are not expected.
    - **OCR routing** Another way to automatically route is to use OCR. The fax server will scan the first page and look for a user's name or extension or other information that you specify during setup and route the fax using this information.
    - **Manual routing** Faxes go to a general mailbox, and an administrator routes them manually into a user's mailbox.
- **Address Books** Enables users to select either individual names or a group name from a list to distribute the fax. In the case of a fax solution that is integrated with Domino, the Address Book is the public Domino Directory or personal directory.
- **Broadcast or distribution lists** Fax broadcasting is widely used to send the same information to many people with one send task. This is especially useful for sending newsletters, special bulletins, news releases, and other similar wide-scale distributions.

    A fax server that is integrated with Domino makes broadcasting easy and powerful because distribution lists can contain individual electronic mail addresses and fax numbers. When you send a broadcast fax using one single broadcast list, the receiver receives the message as an email or as a fax, depending on how it was listed in your Address Book.

- **File attachment conversion** To make sending files via fax easier, most fax servers enable you to email a file in its original format, because the fax server converts the file into a fax image before sending it. This is useful for sending different types of files, such as a word processing document and a spreadsheet, at one time in a single fax.

  Unfortunately, some fax server products do not do the best job in maintaining original file formatting, so extensive testing should be done to check the quality of the conversion. For files that are not converted accurately, you should use a print-to-fax driver.

- **OCR** Because faxes are simply images or graphic data, they cannot be edited or pasted as text into your own documents. The fax has to be converted into an editable text format first. OCR is the process that converts an image into editable text.

  RightFAX, a fax server product, automatically uses the OCR process on an incoming fax before it sends the fax to the receiver's email address. The designated receiver's email includes both an image file containing the original fax and a text file that was created by the OCR process. This can be a great time-saver, because the OCR feature can be used for automatic routing and the text file from the OCR can be full text–indexed by Domino for fast and easy searching of faxes and emails.

- **Load balancing** The fax workload can be automatically balanced across multiple phone lines and multiple fax servers. System performance is maximized by automatically balancing the load. If you have high-volume and/or time-sensitive faxing requirements, this is a critical feature.

- **Cost management** Most fax server products enable you to manage the costs associated with sending faxes, such as off-hour sending usually based on schedules or delivery priorities, restricting the number of pages, or the total number of faxes sent by a particular user.

- **Least cost routing** If you have several fax servers in your company in different locations or departments that are connected via a wide area network (WAN) or the Internet, least cost routing can save you money.

  Least cost routing distributes a fax the least expensive way possible. For example, a company connects its offices in New York (NY) and Los Angeles (LA) via the Internet. Each office has its own fax server. When a user in LA sends to a user in NY, the fax server in LA routes the fax via the Internet directly to the fax server in NY. The public switched telephone network is bypassed, and therefore the cost of the long distance phone call is eliminated.

  Least cost routing can also be very helpful even if the recipient is not at the second site, but is in close proximity. Using the same example, the user in LA sends a fax to a recipient in Newark, NJ. The fax server routes from LA to NY over the Internet, and then initiates a call from NY to Newark over the public switched telephone network. The cost of sending the fax is the call from NY to Newark, not from LA to NJ.

Fax Client Software

The client software that you install on the desktop largely depends on the fax server you use. However, the people that send and receive faxes may be interested in having certain features, as described in the following:

- **Sending faxes**   Some fax products provide you with the option to use one or several sources for Address Books: your email Address Book, any MAPI or Mail API–compliant Address Book, any ODBC or Open Database Connectivity–compliant database, or the fax server's own Address Book.

    Faxes can be sent via electronic mail, via a Web browser, or by printing from an application. To send a fax from email, you use a special addressing syntax that tells Domino and the fax server where to send the message. An example of a fax address used in the To: field of a Notes mail message would be

    ```
    Logan Straub  @ 1-609-555-1234 @ Fax
    ```

    The name listed in the fax address is the intended recipient, and it appears on the automatically generated fax cover sheet. The number is the number of the recipient's fax machine. The word Fax at the end of the address lets the Domino server know to route the message to the fax server.

    Most products also support the capability of sending a fax directly from any application by printing to a specially installed printer driver. To send the fax, you select the print-to-fax (PTF) driver from the printer list in your application. When you print, you are prompted for the person's name, fax number, and other information. The printout is then sent to the fax server, which transmits it to the fax machine.

    Using the print-to-fax (PTF) driver is useful if you have an existing file that you want to fax. Using PTF maintains all the original formatting you used in your file, because the fax is actually generated by the application itself. An added benefit is that you can also preview the file with the PTF driver before sending it, if your application has a print preview feature.

- **Receiving faxes**   Depending on the fax server product you choose, faxes can be received in email or in a fax-only mailbox. Faxes can be viewed, printed, sent to another user or fax machine, merged with other faxes or documents, and sometimes even annotated and converted into text.

- **Web access**   Through the use of Domino's built-in Web capabilities, users can access their faxes in their mail databases, along with email, via a Web browser. Faxes that are routed to an email address appear as just another mail message.

    The mail message contains a file attachment of the fax image, which is viewable with an image viewer, if the viewer is compatible with the fax image format used by the fax server. Most fax servers deliver the image in TIF format. Faxes can also be sent via the Web browser using the mail database by addressing a mail message in the same way you would do in mail if you were using Notes.

In addition to using the Domino mail database to access faxes via the Web, some fax server products also support other interfaces to send and receive faxes using a Web browser. For example, RightFAX has a Web client that enables users to manage their RightFAX mailboxes directly.

- Fax client   Some fax server products have their own client, which is used to manage all your faxing activities. The fax clients also enable you to use faxing separately from Domino.

INTEGRATING IMAGING TECHNOLOGY

As previously mentioned, reducing or removing paper has numerous benefits. Paper is generally difficult to manage because of conventional, but not necessarily practical, approaches. For example, copying with intent to distribute results in the "cannot find my desk" syndrome. The common practice of storing information in notebooks, and putting the notebooks where everyone has access to them, results in comments such as, "Is this manual up-to-date?" or "Where is the manual?"

As mentioned in the previous section, "Less Paper: Moving Toward a Paperless Office," it is beneficial to remove paper from your organization, but you cannot lose vital business communication in the process. When images are stored in a Notes database, they can be categorized so that people can find them quickly. Multiple users can share images simultaneously. Images can be mailed electronically and managed through purge agents.

Images consist of text, photos, diagrams, blueprints, handwritten notes, or drawings, and can be either black-and-white or color.

An example of an imaging solution would be to create a Notes database to replace a file cabinet. All the paper contents would be scanned, and the Notes documents would be be categorized by the file folder names. The paper would then be destroyed, and the file cabinet removed.

Existing Notes applications become extremely powerful when they are image-enabled. For example, a Notes database that keeps track of the computer inventory in your company can now contain images of the purchase orders, invoices, warranties, and schematic diagrams of the printed circuit-board components. An HR application that assists with managing employees can now include an image of tax forms or other working papers.

PLANNING INTEGRATED IMAGING

When you are planning on incorporating imaging into your organization, you should understand the differences between the types of imaging solutions before you make a decision.

However, the volume of paper your company uses is probably the biggest factor. If your organization is highly paper-intensive—you store or manage large volumes of paper—you need a client/server solution. If your paper use is only casual or you have the need for occasional imaging, a desktop imaging solution may be the answer for you.

Questions you should ask include the following: Are you going to scan in a warehouse of existing paper? Do you need a large system with the capability of migrating data to and from optical disks? How long are you going to keep the paper?

The other factor that will help you determine the type of solution you need is whether you have a requirement that people outside your network are going to view the image as remote users over the Internet. In that case, you probably cannot use a client/server application out of the box.

A client/server imaging solution usually uses a proprietary file format, which is visible using only the proprietary image viewer. Some client/server imaging products are adding Web browser support to extend their products.

If your needs are more casual—that is, a relatively low volume of paperwork that people can use whenever and however they want—you may need a more flexible solution without investing in an imaging server. In this case, you should investigate desktop-based imaging software.

Desktop-based imaging requires no image server. You can still route the image via electronic mail to anyone, including over the Internet. You can access the image via a Web browser, which means that you can easily access the image from anywhere in the world, anytime, using a standard Internet browser. This is because the image is stored in a standard format.

Because the images are stored in a Domino database with a desktop-based imaging system, the database can get very large very quickly. There are no hierarchical storage management capabilities, and therefore there is no support for optical drive migration.

Hardware and Network Infrastructure

If you choose a desktop-based imaging solution, you need only a client that connects to the network and that meets the minimum requirements of the software provider. If you choose a client/server solution, your hardware and network infrastructure largely depends on the volume of paper you will be managing.

Scanners

Whether you use client/server imaging software or desktop imaging software, you have to have a scanner. It can be anything from a personal-size scanner connected to your keyboard to a large high-speed scanner. Check your software specifications for any limitations or recommendations of scanner choice. TWAIN is a standard interface for scanners, and most imaging software and most scanners support TWAIN. Other factors involved in your scanner choice include speed, feeder capacity, automatic document feeding add-ons, and the size of the documents to be scanned.

Imaging Software

As already mentioned, there are two types of imaging solutions: client/server imaging systems and desktop-based imaging systems.

Client/Server Imaging System

The imaging *server* manages the images and the storage system, typically an optical storage system with hundreds of gigabytes of storage capacity. This server is not your Domino server nor your file server, but a separate server that is integrated into the network. The server has an optical jukebox that loads the correct disk as the image is needed. A motorized robotic arm finds the disk, pulls it, loads it into the player, and then removes it when it is no longer needed. Imaging server software is stored on this machine's hard drive, and data is stored on both the hard drives and optical drives.

The imaging server has the capability of managing the optical jukebox, conventional hard drives, and tape. Hierarchical storage migration (HSM) capabilities enable the system to move data from one medium to another based on a schedule set by the network administrator. HSM is critical for organizations that manage large volumes of images. Image purging is another component of HSM.

The *client* software has to be installed on every desktop that is either going to scan or view images in the same proprietary format. There could be a separate client for each function, or the client could be configured to perform both functions.

The client software may also have the capability of putting notes on images, drawing red circles, attaching notes to images, and performing other image administration. The viewer enables you to zoom and print the documents, and may include the capability of using OCR on the image to turn it into editable text.

Integrating Client/Server Imaging with Domino   In general, the Domino application serves as a front end to the imaging system. The end users have access to supporting information input into Notes fields. In many cases, the supporting information is sufficient information, but the image is stored in the database as additional reference material. Imaging systems are typically limited in their capabilities of categorizing documents by date, subject, author, and document title. The Domino application, however, can have significantly more categories.

There are two ways to integrate imaging into a Domino application. The first way stores an OLE link in a Notes Rich Text Field (RTF). When the user wants to view the image, he double-clicks on it; that launches an imaging client that retrieves the image from the server. This enables you to create a link anywhere there is an RTF, such as the body of an email.

A more user-friendly way to integrate imaging into the applications is to add scripting to buttons in the Action Bar, buttons in the form, or in an agent. Users can link and view images easier because the Notes client seamlessly brings up the imaging client or server. This solution is critical if you are going to use imaging to have workflow features because of categorizing and security.

Desktop-based Imaging

Because there is no server, all application function is done on the desktop. Images are stored in the Domino database.

To view an image, you can use the standard viewer in the operating system using standard image formats such as TIF, JPG, and GIF. Windows 95, Windows 98, and Windows NT come with an image viewer in the operating system, so you do not have to go out and buy separate software if all you are going to do is view images.

You can also use the Notes built-in file viewer or the Lotus Image Viewer to view images. The Lotus Image Viewer is a separate program that has to be installed on the desktop, but it is provided free for every Notes client.

To scan the image, you can typically use the scanning software that comes with your scanner. You can also use the more sophisticated solution Lotus Notes Document Imaging (LN:DI) and store it in any RTF in any Lotus Notes database. LN:DI Professional has annotation capabilities, OCR, and minor image manipulation, such as cleaning noise out of the image, retouching, and enabling you to merge several pages into one image.

From Here...

In this chapter I have covered the exciting areas of integrating phone, fax, and imaging systems with Domino. I've given you important ideas to consider when you are planning an integrated system.

Here are some additional chapters that may be of interest:

- Chapter 39, "Administering Electronic Mail," covers important topics in the administration of regular Domino electronic mail.
- Chapter 5, "Using Electronic Mail," covers the use of the Domino email system.
- Chapter 9, "Using Sametime Collaboration," covers another exciting technology: Sametime. This technology provides a capability similar to an online chat.
- If you will be developing your own telephony or image applications, read Part III, "Introducing Domino Designer R5," to find out about application development.

Whatever your imaging needs—large, small or casual—integration with Domino results in significantly more powerful and useful applications.

CHAPTER 48

Using Lotus NotesPump/Lotus Enterprise Integrator

Domino and Notes provide an excellent platform for building applications. However, Domino is never the only database and application platform that is used within an organization. Enterprise resource planning (ERP) and other business systems based on relational databases, such as DB2, Oracle, Sybase, Informix, and so forth, are often among the most critical IT systems in use in an organization.

When an organization identifies a need to extend those existing database systems with Internet/Web, workflow, and remote/mobile capabilities using Domino and Notes, a database integration technology is required. A technology such as Lotus NotesPump/Lotus Enterprise Integrator enters the picture at this point. There are also many other third-party integration products on the market, such as Casahl Replic-Action, Percussion Notrix, Mayflower's Sentinel Data Integrator, and others. This chapter focuses on how one firm, InterFusion, used NotesPump to deliver a solution to one of our customers.

What Is the Lotus NotesPump/Lotus Enterprise Integrator?

Lotus NotesPump and its replacement, Lotus Enterprise Integrator (LEI), are database integration tools. They are used to integrate other database systems with Domino. They act as a data distribution server for high-volume transfers and data synchronization between Domino, relational database management systems (RDBMS), enterprise resource planning (ERP) systems, directories (LDAP, NDS, and so forth), transaction processing systems, and file system sources.

Technically speaking, these types of tools can be used to integrate any database with any other database, and are not necessarily Domino-specific. But, of course, for the purposes of this book, I am talking about integrating other database systems with Domino.

Enterprise Integrator is the latest version of—and new name for—NotesPump. The two products are really the same thing and can be used interchangeably. As of this writing, Enterprise Integrator v3.0 is the current version, and NotesPump v2.5a is the previous version.

Lotus Enterprise Integrator (LEI) extends the Domino Enterprise Connection Services (DECS) functionality, which is built into Domino R5 and in Domino R4.63 or later. DECS provides real-time access to enterprise database systems from Domino and Notes applications. DECS was actually created from a piece of the technology that is in NotesPump.

Enterprise Integrator is a server product that can run on an existing Domino server or its own server. It includes the same real-time capabilities of DECS and has the following additional features:

- Batch download and synchronization of large volumes of data
- A visual data mapping tool to establish integration between data sources, including the capability of initiating event-driven or scheduled high-volume data transfers

- Supports relational databases, ERP, and transaction processing system sources
- The capability of customizing activities and data transfers using LotusScript or Java
- Includes a set of database, directory, and file system connectors, plus metaconnectors
- Includes a completely redesigned Notes-based user interface that allows forms-based Activities to be created containing instructions for the LEI Server
- Server provides scheduling, logging, remote management, and automatic character set translation
- Notes-based administration and control of the NotesPump/LEI infrastructure
- SNMP-based management of the NotesPump/LEI servers providing integration with Lotus NotesView–based management networks and other SNMP-capable monitoring systems
- Java-based console for remote server management

Operating Systems Supported

Here are the operating systems supported by Lotus Enterprise Integrator 3.0:

- Windows NT 4.0 (Intel)
- Windows NT 4.0 (Alpha)
- Windows 95/98
- OS/2, Warp 4
- HP-UX
- Sun Solaris on SPARC
- Sun Solaris Intel Edition
- IBM AIX
- IBM OS/400
- IBM OS/390

Database Systems Supported

Enterprise Integrator supports many different types of data sources. Each supported system can be a source of data and a destination. Because of the flexibility of these kinds of tools, you could move data from DB2 to Oracle, without Domino even being involved.

Support for the various data sources are provided via a component called a Lotus Domino Connector. You can develop your own additional Connectors or you can obtain them from a third party.

The following list of Connectors that are marked Basic are included with Domino for use with DECS. Connectors marked LEI are included in LEI, along with the Basic Connectors. Connectors marked Premium are for ERP and transaction systems and are sold separately.

Various other Connector development efforts are under consideration or may be underway by third parties. The list contains several Connectors that were under development when this was written in March 1999. Visit the Lotus Web site for the latest list of Connectors.

Database Connectors (Basic)

- Lotus Domino databases
- IBM DB2
- Oracle Server
- Sybase SQL Server
- ODBC
- IBI EDA/SQL

File System Connectors

- File System (Basic)
- Zmerge Text (LEI)

Directory Connectors (LEI)

- Domino Directory Services
- Lightweight Directory Access Protocol (LDAP)
- NetWare Directory Services (NDS)

ERP Connectors (Premium)

- SAP R/3
- JD Edwards One World/Purchasing
- Oracle Applications/Financials
- PeopleSoft
- Lawson

Transaction System Connectors (Premium)

- BEA Tuxedo
- IBM MQSeries Enterprise Integrator
- IBM CICS

Metaconnectors (LEI)

The Lotus Enterprise Integrator provides a concept called a Metaconnector. This is a component that encapsulates a regular Connector and provides additional capability. The Metaconnector does not require any changes in the Connector itself or the tool that is using the Metaconnector. For example, the Order Metaconnector can provide a canonical or consistent method for sorting keys. Here is a list of some Metaconnectors:

- Order   Imposes a consistent sort order on retrieved records. The Order Metaconnector can be used to resolve mismatches in heterogeneous replication using text keys that are sorting differently.
- Collapse/Expand   Transforms multiple records into a single record with multivalue fields and vice versa. This Metaconnector can be used to automatically collapse several RDBMS records to a single Notes document or expand one Notes document to several RDBMS records.
- Meter   Tracks and reports on data moving to and from a Connector. You can tabulate the results based on record counts, data size, and data contents.
- Connection Broker   Enables data transfers to go to and from different sources and targets, depending on the data being transferred. The connections can be based on data fields contained in the individual records.

NotesPump/LEI Activities

NotesPump and Lotus Enterprise Integrator can do many different types of tasks, called Activities. Activities can be executed in a number of ways, including scheduling, command-line, Web/HTTP interfaces, Java interfaces, and so forth.

Activities provide support for a variety of data integration methods, including Direct Transfer, Replication, RealTime Notes, Polling, Archive, Command, DPROPR, scheduled LotusScript or Java programs, and LEI administrative actions. The following table describes these Activities:

Activity Type	Description
Command Activity	Command Activities enable an action to be performed against any NotesPump/LEI Link. Actions include initiation of relational database stored procedures and Lotus Domino/Notes agents.
Direct Transfer Activity	With direct transfer, NotesPump/LEI users can schedule the transfer of data from any NotesPump/LEI data source to any supported destination, according to user-defined conditions created through SQL queries and Domino/Notes formulas.
DPROPR Activity	The DPROPR Activity transfers data between IBM Data Propagator Consistent Change Data (CCD) DB2 databases and NotesPump/LEI-supported databases.
Polling Activity	NotesPump/LEI uses Polling Activities to define conditions to monitor in Domino/Notes or relational database sources. When a condition is satisfied, NotesPump/LEI immediately initiates a specified Activity to perform data exchange.

continues

continued

Activity Type	Description
Realtime Activity	A Realtime Activity catches and handles Domino/Notes events as they occur. Using the Realtime Activity established by the system administrator, end users can open or update Domino/Notes forms, causing real-time queries or updates to back-end–supported NotesPump/LEI sources. This capability can be accessed from a Notes client or via a Web browser accessing a Domino server.
Replication Activity	NotesPump/LEI supports two different types of Replication Activities, whose purpose is to ensure the synchronization of relational data from different sources.
	Type one is called Primary Key replication, which enables the NotesPump/LEI administrator to specify a primary key in the metadata that is used to determine which documents and records are to be replicated.
	Type two is called Primary Key/Timestamp replication, which allows faster synchronization of data sources, based upon additional time stamp criteria.
Scripted Activity	LotusScript can be used to run data manipulation and conditional processing routines. The Scripted Activity executes the LotusScript language commands directly entered in the Activity or executes a Domino/Notes Agent.
Java Activity	A Java Activity executes a Java Application. NotesPump/LEI defines a set of Java classes that enable you to extend beyond the functionality available with other Activities. In situations where you need more complete control over data transfers, or want to perform data manipulation or evaluation during transfer, Java classes can be used to construct those customized routines.
Archive Activity	An Archive Activity moves data from one database to another, deleting the original records as they move. Selection of records to archive can be done with either a condition or a relative time stamp.
Administrative Activities	Admin-Backup Activity can be used to back up the Administrator database. Admin-Purge Log Activity can be used to purge the log of documents older than a given number of days.

Executing Activities

After Activities have been defined, you must specify when they should occur. Activities are normally scheduled, which means that they will occur at specified time intervals or when a particular business condition occurs. Activities can also be initiated from the command line of the server or via the Web by using the CGI interface.

Scheduling

NotesPump/LEI has extensive scheduling capabilities and configuration options for determining where and when an Activity is executed. Activities can be scheduled for repetitive days, times, or selections of times. Multiple Activities can be scheduled to execute as dependent processes. Polling Activities can be used to allow the execution of an Activity based on any business condition. An example of this flexibility would allow NotesPump/LEI to run an Activity on the last business day of the month.

COMMAND-LINE EXECUTION

NotesPump/LEI allows Activities to be executed from the system command line of a running NotesPump/LEI Server. This feature allows programs with the capability of executing system commands to start NotesPump/LEI Activities.

COMMON GATEWAY INTERFACE FOR WEB APPLICATIONS

NotesPump/LEI supports a common gateway interface (CGI) which allows it to be integrated into any Hypertext Transfer Protocol (HTTP) server for Web applications. Using the NotesPump/LEI CGI provides Web applications with controlled access to any NotesPump/LEI supported database.

ALL THE TOOLS YOU NEED

In addition to NotesPump and Lotus Enterprise Integrator, Lotus provides many other ways to integrate other data sources into Domino and Notes applications. The following lists several database connectivity solutions available to developers and users of Domino and Notes:

Connectivity Solutions	Description
DECS (Domino Enterprise Connection Services)	Declarative data mapping tool. Provides live access to enterprise data and applications, including relational databases, transactionprocessing systems, and ERP systems.
LS:DO (LotusScript Data Object)	Access to any ODBC-compliant data sources from LotusScript.
JDBC (Java Database Connectivity)	Access from Java agents to relational data. A JDBC-to-ODBC bridge is part of Domino.
Lotus Domino Connectors	Modulesthat provide native connectivity to enterprise data sources. These Connectors can be accessed from DECS, LEI, LotusScript, or Java.
	Connectors to DB2, Oracle, Sybase, Text, and file-based systems EDA/SQL and ODBC are provided with the Domino server. Premium Connectors to ERP applications, transaction processing systems, and directory systems will be available separately.
Lotus Domino Connector Classes	A consistent object-oriented interface for programmatically accessing enterprise data and applications. The classes can be accessed using either the LotusScript or Java programming languages.

continues

continued

Connectivity Solutions	Description
Lotus Enterprise Integrator	Data distribution server for the high-volume transfer and data synchronization between Domino and RDBMS, ERP, Directory, Transactionand File enterprise sources.
Domino Connector Toolkit	A toolkit for creating native connections to enterprise systems. Connectors developed with the Domino Connector Toolkit can be accessed through DECS, LEI,LotusScript, or Java.

Case Study: InterFusion Energy

The best way to understand how to use a technology can be to learn about how someone else used it to solve a real problem. With that in mind, I am going to focus on how our firm, InterFusion, used NotesPump/Enterprise Integrator to solve a customer's real business problem.

InterFusion is a Lotus Premier Partner that develops customer software applications in Domino and Notes. The customer is a utility company, which we will call InterFusion Energy.

InterFusion Energy is a utility company that offers natural gas service to customers through a pipeline system located in the Northeastern U.S., partially owned by the utility. Some of its customers are other energy companies that market and resell its natural gas. Other customers are large end users, such as factories, plants, and bakeries.

What's the Business Problem?

InterFusion Energy needs a secure extranet that its customers can use to download usage and billing information. The customers that are energy companies marketing and reselling its products need this information so that they can, in turn, bill *their* customers.

For example, ABC Energy Co. sells many types of energy products to its customers. ABC markets and sells electricity, heating oil, and natural gas. The natural gas comes from InterFusion Energy, the electricity from ABC's own generation facilities, and the heating oil from a petroleum company. Part of the value-added service that ABC offers its customers is a consolidating billing system, so customers don't need to receive and pay three separate bills for all three types of energy products. To make this possible, ABC must integrate usage and billing data from its electricity division, the petroleum company, and InterFusion Energy into a single billing system. ABC requires InterFusion Energy to provide it with billing data in an electronic format, which it can integrate into ABC's billing system without manual data entry.

An Industry in Transition

On top of customer demands for better service from InterFusion Energy, the utility industry is being deregulated all across the country. One of the primary objectives of deregulation is to open up competition in the utility industry.

Act Now or Else!

In InterFusion Energy's home state, the utility commission has set regulatory requirements that all utility companies are required to meet in early 1999. Part of the requirements being enforced by the utility commission is that tariffs, usage, and billing data must be able to be received electronically by customers.

Although the commission does not specify the exact method of electronic delivery, InterFusion Energy has decided that the best way to deliver this data is via an Internet Web site.

Service the Customer

The increased competition that deregulation creates also means that all utility companies must be able to better serve their customers. In a business such as the utility industry, where usage data equals money, billing is the end game. To streamline this core business process means automating metering systems to deliver usage data in a just-in-time fashion, and then delivering that usage data electronically to customers in the form of billing.

For InterFusion Energy, that means that billing data must be delivered electronically to its customers every day. InterFusion Energy determined that the best way to deliver that data is via the Internet, at a secured Extranet Web site.

Information Systems at InterFusion Energy

InterFusion Energy, like most companies, has many information systems in place.

AS/400s Rule!

At InterFusion Energy, IBM AS/400s are used extensively for many different core business systems. Its accounting and customer service systems, including billing, all run on the AS/400. Large amounts of data are stored in the AS/400's native relational database system (RDBMS), DB2.

The data used in the core business systems on the AS/400 comes from several sources, including metering systems that monitor usage and collect usage data from meters located throughout their gas distribution pipeline and at customer sites. The metering data is collected by a metering server and imported into the billing system on the AS/400. The data on the AS/400 is also used by many PC-based reporting and analysis programs.

The Beast: Dumping the Legacy System

Before the new Internet Web-based customer billing download system was developed and put in place, a legacy system was used to provide a subset of the data download functionality for customers. This legacy system was a PC bulletin board system (BBS).

The legacy BBS system ran on a PC under DOS. Billing data was processed into files and passed over to the BBS. Customers could then dial in to the BBS, log in, and download the files.

Another function that the BBS was used for was to distribute messages to customers regarding service issues, notices, and so forth. Messages were posted to a message forum on the BBS that customers could read when they dialed in to it.

The bulletin board system had several problems and limitations:

- BBS was very cumbersome to use because it supported only simple text-only terminal emulation and dial-up connections. The BBS was not very user friendly.
- BBS was difficult to maintain and expand with new users.
- To support Internet access, the BBS would have required a large system upgrade.
- BBS could not be easily integrated into the many new Internet-based applications that InterFusion Energy wanted to implement.
- BBS supported only some types of customers and did not provide access to all types of billing data that customers needed.

InterFusion Energy decided that the BBS needed to go—and be completely replaced by a secure Internet Web site.

The Savior: Domino to the Rescue

Lotus Domino and Notes was implemented at InterFusion Energy for electronic mail and calendaring in the previous year, 1998. Domino was also used to host the first Web site that InterFusion Energy put online.

InterFusion Energy also used the AS/400's OfficeVision system for electronic mail, so Domino and OfficeVision were integrated to provide a seamless messaging environment.

Integration between Domino and OfficeVision allowed AS/400-only users with AS/400 terminals to have their mail account on OfficeVision. PC users could have their mail account on Domino and use Notes clients. The integration makes it transparent as to which system a particular user is on. As needed, users could be migrated from OfficeVision to Domino/Notes, and the move would also be transparent.

Incoming Internet mail for InterFusion Energy's entire Internet mail domain was handled by a single Domino server. This Domino server would deliver the mail to either the Notes mail account or the OfficeVision system, depending on which mail system the user's account was on. This makes the two systems transparent to the outside world as well, because regardless of which system the user's mail account was on, mail was always sent to the same Internet domain.

The initial Web site contained some basic content, including general information about the company, information for customers on services offered, and copies of tariffs. Posting the tariffs on a Web site was a requirement of the utility commission. Figure 48.1 illustrates the existing information systems before NotesPump.

Figure 48.1
InterFusion Energy's integrated Domino and AS/400 OfficeVision messaging systems.

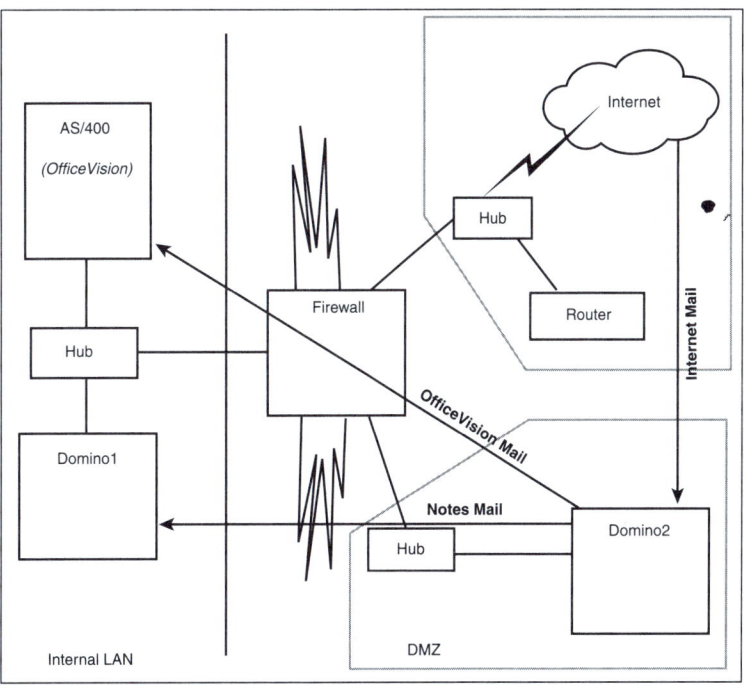

THE SOLUTION

Based on their early experience with using Domino for their initial Web site and research into the IBM and Lotus technologies available for the AS/400 and Domino, InterFusion Energy decided that it would use Domino as its platform for Web applications.

The solution would be a self-service Web site that would enable customers and partners to access any information they may require. The Web site would be secured, and each customer would be provided with an account name and password to access the secured area of the site. Lotus Domino would be the platform for all the Web applications needed.

Extending the Business via the Internet

A Web site based on Domino would be able to provide InterFusion Energy with many benefits that other technologies could not:

- The Web site would be universally accessible via the Internet. Many companies already have access to the Internet, and the continuing growth of the Internet makes it the preferred method of accessing information electronically.
- IBM, Lotus, and every other computer company have already implemented support for the Internet, and support for the Internet in systems and software is growing at a blazingly fast pace.
- An Internet Web solution based on Domino would provide a solid platform on which to integrate several applications and add new applications to in the future.
- Building the Web applications on Domino would allow InterFusion Energy to use a single directory and security system to manage access to all Web applications, simplifying administration and support.
- Lotus NotesPump/Enterprise Integrator would be used as the database integration platform to integrate the AS/400 DB2 databases and other databases in use with Domino. The flexibility, scalability, and cross-platform support of NotesPump/LEI makes it an excellent solution for all the applications needed today, and any applications needed in the future.

Security, Performance, and Bears—Oh My!

Security is also a huge concern in any technology environment, but additional attention to it is especially important when you are dealing with the Internet and with sensitive customer data. With Domino's enterprise class directory and security support, it was the obvious solution.

Another security and performance issue centered around the AS/400. NotesPump/LEI and Domino enable you to build an application that can query data in real-time directly from the AS/400. Also, some AS/400 business applications enable you to give access to applications and data from the Internet.

The advantages to real-time access to the AS/400, or any business system, are

- Up-to-the-minute data is available to users.
- Batch processing and synchronization of data are unnecessary because users can access the real data directly.

The disadvantages to real-time data access are

- Security becomes an even bigger concern. Often the people responsible for the AS/400 or other business systems, as well as company management, are understandably worried about people directly accessing the system.

- Performance on the AS/400 or other business system will be impacted by additional Internet users accessing it and conducting real-time queries on it.
- Availability is often an issue with a core business system. There are usually planned downtime periods in the late evenings or the middle of the night that are used to run many batch processes and backups. With a self-service Internet Web site, users expect the site to be available all the time—24 hours per day, 7 days per week.
- Management of the AS/400 or other business system becomes more complex. In some cases, it would be necessary to create and maintain several user accounts, one on each system, for every customer. Keeping all these accounts and security profiles in sync would be a potentially significant administrative expense and could introduce more potential security holes.

InterFusion Energy decided to implement batch processing of data synchronization to Domino, using NotesPump/LEI. This eliminates any concerns and problems with security, performance, availability, and management.

The downside to this strategy for application development and implementation is that it can increase the initial development and management of the applications. We implemented a way to compensate for these issues by building into the applications as much activity logging and automatic monitoring as possible. This makes identifying and resolving problems that might occur much easier.

INTERFUSION ENERGY'S NETWORK AND SERVER CONFIGURATION

InterFusion Energy has two Domino servers, Domino1 and Domino2, both running Windows NT v4.0. Domino1 is used on the internal network for email and calendaring and is accessed only by internal Notes clients. Domino2 is used for access to and from the Internet and handles Internet SMTP email routing, HTTP Web services, and runs the NotesPump/LEI server. The IBM AS/400s are, of course, connected to the internal network only.

The firewall prevents access from the Internet to any computer on the internal network. Domino2 can be accessed from the Internet and is protected by the firewall, which allows only specific types of access to Domino2. The firewall is configured with a DMZ network where the Domino2 server is connected. The firewall is configured to provide the following:

- Allow Internet users to access the Domino2 server via Web browsers using HTTP
- Allow Internet SMTP mail to be sent and received by the Domino2 server
- Allow Domino2 to communicate to the Domino1 server and the AS/400 on the internal network
- Allow Internet SMTP mail to be sent from the AS/400
- Allow internal network users to access the Internet.

The NotesPump/LEI server running on Domino2 accesses the AS/400 using the ODBC driver that is part of the AS/400 PC client software. When the databases are transferred from the AS/400 to Domino2, they are processed by the Domino applications on Domino2. All the Web applications that support the Internet Web site are hosted on Domino2. Figure 48.2 illustrates InterFusion Energy's network and server configuration.

Figure 48.2
InterFusion Energy's network and server configuration.

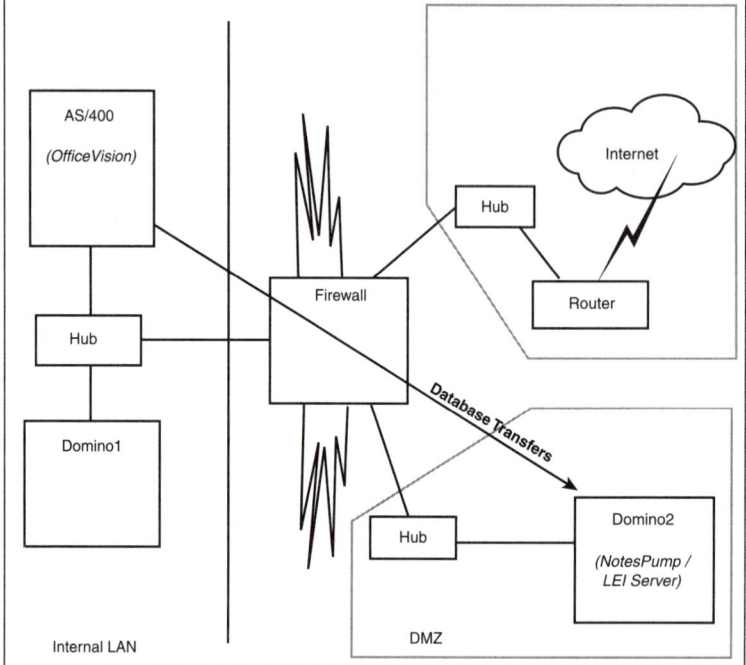

Getting the Data from the AS/400

One of the first steps in any application development project is to identify the required outcomes. In other words, what data do the customers need, how will they use it, and in what format do they need it?

After the outcomes are identified, we can identify the inputs that we need to accomplish the outcomes. This is where the old data processing saying, "Garbage in, Garbage out (GIGO)," comes from. That's why identifying outcomes required and then identifying inputs needed are the first two steps in application development.

The inputs are the databases that we need to get from the AS/400 using NotesPump/LEI. The data is then processed into the format needed by customers.

Case Study: InterFusion Energy

The Outcomes   Customers need to be able to download files containing their own billing data. The records in the downloaded files must contain details down to the day. The files must be formatted in standard comma-delimited ASCII text and Data Interchange Format (DIF). These formats can then be imported into just about any application, including database systems, spreadsheets, word processors, and more.

The Inputs   The data we need to create these outcomes are detailed data records by customer and by day. We need one big database table that contains all billing data by customer and day. This data can then be processed to create separate files for each customer in the formats required. Additional database tables are required that contain miscellaneous tables to support the batch processing routines that will be run.

Setting Up Lotus NotesPump/Lotus Enterprise Integrator   After installing NotesPump/LEI on the Domino2 server, several setup and configuration steps are required:

1. Install and configure the ODBC driver for the AS/400 on the NotesPump/LEI server.
2. Create an ODBC Link document for the AS/400.
3. Create a Notes Link document for each Notes database.
4. Create Direct Transfer Activity documents for each database transfer.

The ODBC Link document links NotesPump/LEI to the AS/400 via an ODBC driver installed on the Windows NT server running the NotesPump/LEI server (see Figure 48.3).

Figure 48.3
The NotesPump ODBC Link document.

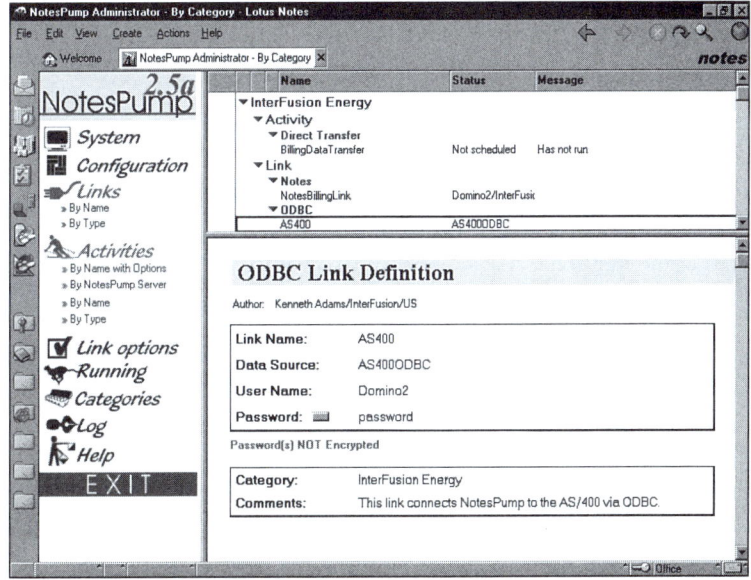

The following are important fields in the ODBC Link document:

Field	Description
Link Name	Use to uniquely name the Link.
Data Source	Enter the name of the ODBC Data Source that was created in Windows NT to access the AS/400.
User Name	Username of AS/400 account used to transfer data to Domino.
Password	Password of AS/400 account used to transfer data to Domino.

The Notes Link document is used to link NotesPump/LEI to the database used to hold the raw AS/400 data. When in the Domino database, the data is processed into downloadable files (see Figure 48.4).

Figure 48.4
The NotesPump Notes Link document.

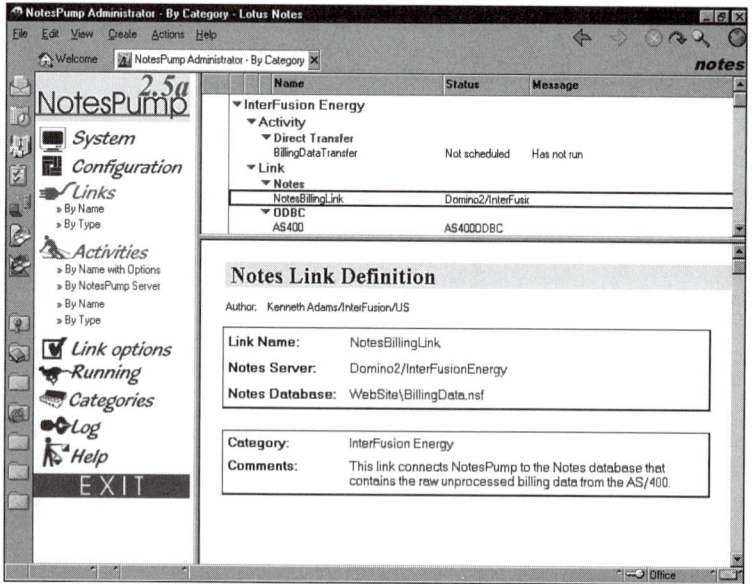

The following are important fields in the ODBC Link document:

Field	Description
Link Name	Use to uniquely name the Link.
Notes Server	The name of the Domino2 server that hosts all the Domino Web applications.
Notes Database	The pathname of the Domino database that contains the raw database transferred from the AS/400.

CASE STUDY: INTERFUSION ENERGY | 1173

The Direct Transfer Activity document is used to perform the actual data transfer process. This Activity document uses the link documents to identify the database source and destination. The document also allows you to schedule the Activity and control a number of specific details about the transfer process. Figure 48.5 shows this document.

Figure 48.5
The NotesPump Direct Transfer Activity document.

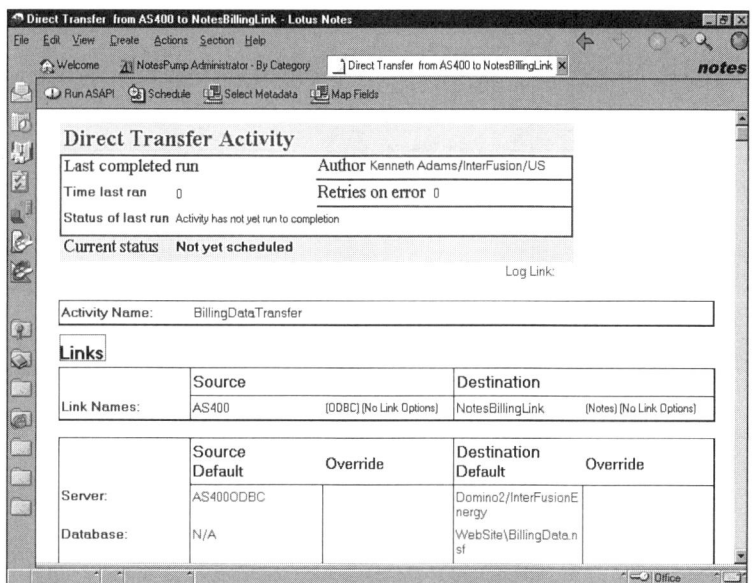

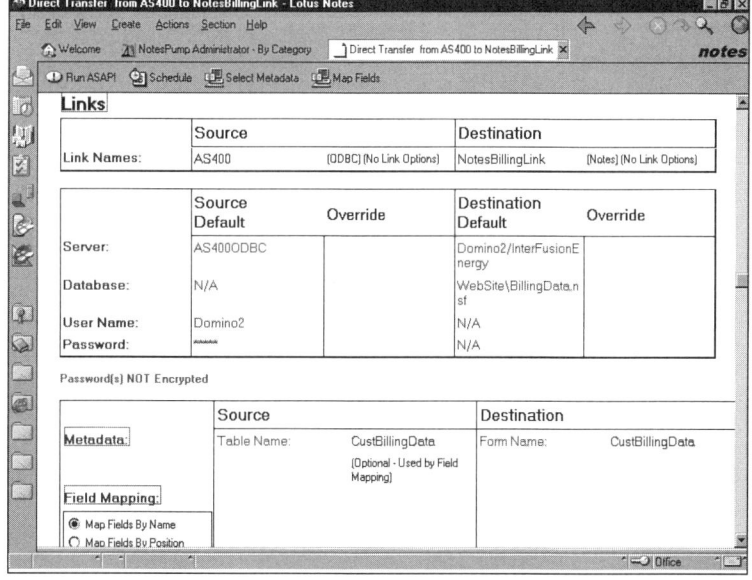

1174 CHAPTER 48 USING LOTUS NOTESPUMP/LOTUS ENTERPRISE INTEGRATOR

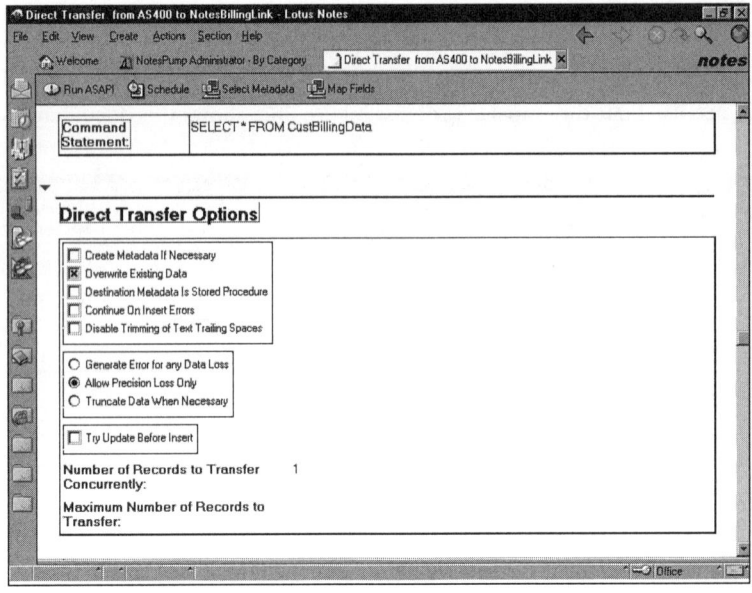

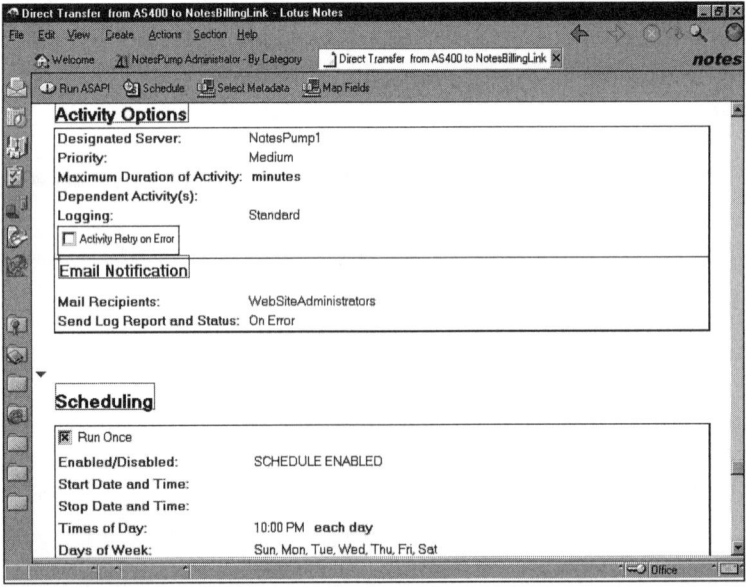

The following are sections of the Direct Transfer Activity document:

Field	Description
Activity Name	Use to uniquely name the Activity.
Links section	Use to identify the database source and destination for the Activity. The main setting selects the link documents used for the source and destination. Additional fields for MetaData and Field Mapping enable you to control exactly which tables and forms are used and which source data fields will be transferred into which destination fields.
Direct Transfer Options section	Gives you additional control over how the transfer process will be done, including whether to overwrite existing data, how many records to transfer, and so forth.
Activity Options section	Enables you to control specifics, such as which NotesPump/LEI server to run the Activity on, priority, and so forth. Logging and email notification are especially useful to keep an eye on the process and alert you via email if anything goes wrong.
Scheduling section	Gives you a lot of flexibility in controlling when the Activity will run.

PROCESSING THE DATA FOR CUSTOMERS

After the main databases are brought over to Domino from the AS/400, that's when the fun begins. The databases transferred from the AS/400 contain records for every customer for every day. The customers need to download data in ASCII text and DIF-formatted files that, of course, contain data for only that customer.

DOMINO AGENTS—HARD WORKERS   All the batch processing required to create the downloadable files for users is done with Domino agents. Several agents were created to complete the tasks described in the next two sections.

The parsing agents process the raw data from the AS/400 and create the downloadable files for customers. Parsing agents complete the following tasks:

1. Files are created in comma-delimited ASCII text and Data Interchange Format (DIF) formats.
2. New documents are created or existing documents updated in the database that is actually accessed by customers over the Web.
3. Key fields are populated and the files are attached to the document.
4. Security is set in the document using reader fields, and the document is saved to the Domino database.

The purging agents are used to delete old downloadable files from the Domino databases. After the files are downloaded by customers, they aren't really needed again. Purging is controlled by InterFusion Energy through profile documents that enable them to specify after how many days to purge both read and unread documents.

ACTIVITY LOGGING—THE TRAIL OF BREADCRUMBS Two types of logging are important in this application. The first type of logging involves the internal processes used to implement the application. These back-end agents are the parsing and purging agents. The second type of logging involves information about end user usage of the system.

LOGGING THE PARSING AND PURGING ACTIVITY Both the parsing and purging agents log everything that they do into a specially designed Agent Log database. This database provides an exact and detailed audit trail of everything that any agent does. This eliminates any questions or problems regarding the agents.

The system administrators can always know exactly what's going on. The agents can also send email notifications on all activity and errors that might be encountered during agent processing.

InterFusion Energy needed the capability of having an exact audit trail of what users did on the Web site. This audit trail needed to be much more sophisticated and easier to use than the standard Domino Web activity logging could provide. So it developed agents that would log specific Web user activity in a specially designed usage logging database.

Every time a Web user reads a file download or message document, the usage log agent logs it into the Usage Log database. This usage data is also used to control the purging agent, which purges based on whether the customer has read a file download document.

To make the Web site even easier to use, the usage data is also used to dynamically generate a single Web page that shows the Web user only what he or she hasn't read yet. This single Web page means the Web users don't have to surf through mounds of links to get their work done. This is something we cannot use unread marks to accomplish, because Domino does not support unread marks with Web browsers.

DAY-TO DAY-MANAGING

The daily management of the system is pretty simple. Because the solution is designed to alert an administrator if it has a problem, there really is no daily care and feeding required.

Email notifications of both activity status and error conditions are built into NotesPump/LEI. All the agents that were developed by InterFusion that do all the automatic processing were designed with email notification also.

The notification enables anyone to get emails every single day, which provide a summary of the processing done by NotesPump/LEI and the Parsing and Purging agents—sort of like a daily health check of what's going on. InterFusion Energy also has the option of being emailed only about errors. It can even send the status and error emails to different people, providing a way to automatically escalate attention to the system if an error occurs.

The extensive activity-logging in both NotesPump/LEI and the Domino applications provides extensive detail on everything that is done by the entire system. This make troubleshooting and auditing significantly easier.

The only management the system really needs is the addition of or change of a customer's account. Even that has been designed to be simple on the Domino side. For example, adding a new user requires the following steps:

1. Create a new Person document in the Customer Public Address Book. Set the username and Internet password and give them to the customer.
2. If the Person's account is for a new company, create a new group for that company's ID number (company ID numbers are used to control security). Then add the Person to the group for that company ID.

Done!

Other Information Resources to Check Out

There are many sources of information on NotesPump/Enterprise Integrator. Lotus and IBM have many White Papers and Redbooks on the subject.

Information can be found at the following Web sites:

Lotus Enterprise Integration Web site	www.edge.lotus.com
IBM Redbooks Web site	www.redbooks.ibm.com

Check out these IBM Redbooks:

Title	Part Number
Lotus Solutions for The Enterprise, Volume 1: Lotus Notes: An Enterprise Application Platform	SG24-4837-00
Lotus Solutions for the Enterprise, Volume 2: Using DB2 in a Domino Environment	SG24-4918-00
Lotus Solutions for the Enterprise, Volume 3: Using the IBM CICS Gateway for Lotus Notes	SG24-4512-00
Lotus Solutions for the Enterprise, Volume 4: Lotus Notes and the MQSeries Enterprise Integrator	SG24-2217-00
Lotus Solutions for the Enterprise, Volume 5: NotesPump: The Enterprise Data Mover	SG24-5255-00

continues

Title	Part Number
Enterprise Integration with Domino.Connect	SG24-2181-00
Implementing Lotus Domino Connector and J.D. Edwards' OneWorld on IBM Netfinity	SG24-5308-00
Enterprise Integration with Domino for S/390	SG24-5150-00
Lotus Solutions for the Enterprise Links between VSE/ESA and Lotus Notes	SG24-2037-00

From Here...

In this chapter I have given you an overview of NotesPump and its successor, Lotus Enterprise Integrator. You can use this tool to manage the transfer of data between dissimilar systems. I gave you a real-life example of how this system can be used to provide back-end data from a legacy system to a Domino web-based front-end. This is a very typical application of this technology.

You may be interested in reading some of these other chapters:

- Chapter 31, "Integrating Domino with Legacy Systems," provides you with a high level overview of some of the other options you have for legacy data integration.
- Chapter 30, "Moving to Electronic Commerce on Your Domino Site," tells you about some additional things to consider before making your Web site commercial.
- Chapter 37, "Firewalls, Virtual Private Networks (VPNs) and Internet Security," contains important information about securing your Web site.

Epilogue

Completely covering products as rich and diverse as Notes and Domino is becoming nearly impossible. It is amazing to know that after including well over a thousand pages of information, I still have not been able to include everything. In this book, I used a couple of important principles in deciding what to include. I tried to emphasize new features of R5—and the most important features.

I think I succeeded, but you are the ultimate judge. I am proud of the result, but know that there is always room for improvement. One of the feedback comments I received from one of my previous books, *Lotus Notes and Domino Server 4.5 Unleashed*, was that the softcopy of the book should be provided in a Notes database so that it could be used on multiple platforms. This suggestion was used in the next edition of that book and this book.

Over time, I've received feedback about typographical errors, as well as other kinds of errors, and suggestions for improvement, additional topics to be covered, and so forth.

I appreciate all feedback about the book, read all the comments I receive, and try to take them into consideration for the next book. If you would like to send me any comments on this book, you can send them to me via email at RandyTamura@gwcorp.com. You can also visit the Graphware Corporation Web site at www.gwcorp.com.

For now, I thank you for purchasing this book and I hope it has been useful to you. I also hope that you will find a continuing use for this book as a companion reference in your work. Best wishes in your Domino Deployment.

Randall A. Tamura

April, 1999

PART IX

Appendixes

A Notes/Domino Class Reference

B Function and @Command Listings

APPENDIX

Notes/Domino Class Reference

The purpose of this appendix is to provide a quick, easy-to-use reference for the Domino Object Model classes. The classes are organized by front end and back end, and are sorted in alphabetical order. Each class has its inheritance, containment, properties, methods, and events listed, if applicable.

The Inheritance sections list the parent class from which a subclass inherits its properties, methods, and events.

The Containment sections list the objects of other classes from which an object of the current class can be obtained, or the classes for objects that can be obtained from the current class.

The Properties sections list the public properties of the current class, but not the inherited properties. Properties are listed in this fashion:

`PropertyName As DataType`

In this syntax, `PropertyName` is the name of the property, and `DataType` is the datatype or class of the property.

The Methods sections list the public methods of the current class, but not the inherited methods. Methods are listed in this fashion:

`MethodName( parameter1, parameter2, ... , parameterN [, optionalparameter1 [, optionalparameter2 [, ... [,optionalparameterN ]...]]) As ReturnType`

In this syntax, `MethodName` is the name of the method, `parameter1` through `N` are the required parameters, `optionalparameter1` through `N` are the optional parameters, and `ReturnType` is the datatype the method returns, if applicable.

The Events sections list all the events for the current class. Events are listed in this fashion:

`EventName( parameter1, parameter2, ... , parameterN)`

In this syntax, `EventName` is the name of the event, and `parameter1` through `N` are the parameters for the event.

An asterisk (*) indicates that this item is new or changed for release 5.

> **Note**
>
> The classes are shown in LotusScript syntax, but they are almost identical to the Java equivalents. The major difference for Java access is that Java does not support properties, so getting and setting property values is done via method calls. Here are a few general guidelines for Java:
> - Class names in Java do not use the `Notes` prefix. The Java class name is just the LotusScript name without the prefix.
> - To access a property, generally prefix the property name with `get`. If the property name begins with `Is` or `Has`, you do not use the `get` prefix.
> - To set a property, generally prefix the property name with `set`. If the property name begins with `Is` or `Has`, drop that and substitute `set`.

LOTUS NOTES FRONT-END CLASSES

> • You will need to import the `lotus.domino.*` classes. You should no longer import `lotus.notes.*`, and you should try to use the `lotus.domino.*` version instead. Most code will work, but you may need slight modifications.

LOTUS NOTES FRONT-END CLASSES

The front-end classes pertain to objects represented in the Notes user interface (UI). These classes are not available in scheduled agents because there is no UI for scheduled agents.

THE Button CLASS

The `Button` class represents LotusScript actions, buttons, and hotspots in forms or views.

EVENTS

```
Click(Source as Button)
ObjectExecute(Source as Button, Data)
```

THE Field CLASS

The `Field` class represents a field on a form. The entering and exiting events are available only when the field is editable.

EVENTS

```
Entering (Source as Field)
Exiting (Source as Field)
```

THE Navigator CLASS

The `Navigator` class represents a button or hotspot in a navigator.

EVENTS

```
Click( Source as Navigator)
```

THE NotesUIDatabase CLASS

The `NotesUIDatabase` class represents a database opened to the UI.

CONTAINMENT

```
Contained by: NotesUIWorkspace
Contains: NotesDatabase, NotesDocumentCollection
```

PROPERTIES

```
Database As NotesDatabase
Documents As NotesDocumentCollection
```

Methods
```
OpenNavigator( navigatorName$ [, fullWindow] ) *
OpenView( ViewName as String [, key$ [, newInstance]]) *
```

Events
```
PostDocumentDelete( Source as NotesUIDatabase)
PostDragDrop( Source as NotesUIDatabase, EntryName$, Continue as Variant) *
PostOpen( Source as NotesUIDatabase)
QueryClose( Source as NotesUIDatabase, Continue as Variant)
QueryDocumentDelete( Source as NotesUIDatabase, Continue as Variant)
QueryDocumentUndelete( Source as NotesUIDatabase, Continue as Variant)
QueryDragDrop( Source as NotesUIDatabase, EntryName$, Continue as Variant) *
```

The NotesUIDocument Class

The NotesUIDocument class represents a document opened to the UI.

Containment
```
Contained by: NotesUIWorkspace
Contains: NotesDocument
```

Properties
```
AutoReload As Boolean
CurrentField As String
DialogBoxCanceled As Boolean *
Document As NotesDocument
EditMode As Boolean
FieldHelp As Boolean
HiddenChars As Boolean
HorzScrollBar As Boolean
InPreviewPane As Boolean
IsNewDoc As Boolean
PreviewDocLink As Boolean
PreviewParentDoc As Boolean
Ruler As Boolean
WindowTitle As String
```

Methods
```
Categorize( [CategoryName$ ])
Clear()
Close()
CollapseAllSections()
Copy()
CreateObject( [name$ [,type$ [,filepath$]]]) As Variant
Cut()
DeleteDocument()
DeselectAll()
ExpandAllSections()
FieldAppendText( fieldName$, text$ )
FieldClear( [ fieldName$ ] )
FieldContains( fieldName$, textValue$ ) As Boolean
FieldGetText( [ fieldName$ ] ) As String
```

Lotus Notes Front-End Classes 1187

```
FieldSetText( fieldName$, textValue$ )
FindFreeTimeDialog( reqPeopleItem$, optPeopleItem$, reqRoomItem$, optRoomItem$,
➥reqResourcesItem$ optResourcesItem$, removedPeopleItem$, startDateItem$,
➥endDateItem$ ) as Boolean
FindFreeTimeDialogEx( reqPeopleItems$, optPeopleItems$, reqRoomItems$,
➥optRoomItems$, reqResourcesItems$ optResourcesItems$, removedPeopleItems$,
➥startDateItem$, endDateItem$ ) as Boolean *
FindString( fieldName$ ) *
Forward()
GetObject( name$ ) As Variant
GetSelectedText( [fieldName$ ] ) As String *
GotoBottom()
GotoField( fieldName$ )
GotoNextField()
GotoPrevField()
GotoTop()
Import( [filter$ ] [, filename$] ) *
InsertText( textValue$ )
NavBarSetText( urlText$, windowTitle$)
NavBarSpinnerStart()
NavBarSpinnerStop()
Paste()
Print( [numCopies%] [, fromPage%] [, toPage%] [, draft] )
Refresh( [includeRichTextItems%] ) *
RefreshHideFormulas()
Reload()
Save()
SaveNewVersion()
SelectAll()
Send()
SpellCheck() *
```

EVENTS

```
PostModeChange( Source as NotesUIDocument )
PostOpen( Source as NotesUIDocument )
PostRecalc( Source as NotesUIDocument )
PostSave( Source as NotesUIDocument ) *
QueryClose( Source as NotesUIDocument, Continue as Variant )
QueryModeChange( Source as NotesUIDocument , Continue as Variant )
QueryOpen( Source as NotesUIDocument, Mode as Integer, IsNewDoc as Variant,
➥Continue as Variant )
QuerySave( Source as NotesUIDocument , Continue as Variant )
```

THE NotesUIView CLASS

The NotesUIView class represents a view opened to the UI.

CONTAINMENT

```
Contained by: NotesUIWorkspace
Contains: NotesDocumentCollection, NotesView
```

PROPERTIES

```
CalendarDateTime As Variant
CaretCategory As Variant *
```

```
Documents As NotesDocumentCollection
View As NotesView
ViewName As String *
```

METHODS

```
Print( [numCopies%] [, fromPage% ] [,toPage%] [, draft] [, pageSeparator%]
➥ [, formOverride$] [,printView] [, dateRangeBegin] [, dateRangeEnd]) *
SelectDocument( notesDocument )
```

EVENTS

```
PostDragDrop(Source As Notesuiview)
PostOpen(Source As Notesuiview)
PostPaste(Source As Notesuiview)
QueryAddToFolder(Source As Notesuiview, Target As Variant, Continue As Variant)
QueryClose(Source As Notesuiview, Continue As Variant)
QueryDragDrop(Source As Notesuiview, Continue As Variant)
QueryOpen(Source As Notesuiview, Continue As Variant)
QueryOpenDocument(Source As Notesuiview, Continue As Variant)
QueryPaste(Source As Notesuiview, Continue As Variant)
QueryRecalc(Source As Notesuiview, Continue As Variant)
RegionDoubleClick(Source As Notesuiview)
```

THE NotesUIWorkspace CLASS

The NotesUIWorkspace class represents the Notes workspace.

CONTAINMENT

`Contains: NotesUIDatabase, NotesUIView, NotesUIDocument`

PROPERTIES

```
CurrentCalendarDateTime As Variant
CurrentDatabase As NotesUIDatabase *
CurrentDocument As NotesUIDocument
CurrentView As NotesUIView *
```

METHODS

```
AddDatabase( server$ , filename$ )
CheckAlarms()
ComposeDocument( [ server$ [ , file$ [ , form$ [ , windowWidth# [ , windowHeight#
➥]]] ] ] ) As NotesUIDocument
DialogBox( form$ [ , autoHorzFit [ , autoVertFit [, noCancel [, noNewFields [,
➥noFieldUpdate [, readOnly [, title$ [, notesDocument ]]]]]]]] ) As Boolean
EditDocument( [editMode [, notesDocument [, notesDocumentReadOnly]]] )
➥As NotesUIDocument
EditProfile( profileName$ [ , userName$] ) As NotesUIDocument
EnableAlarms( enable ) As Boolean
Folder( [folderName$] [, moveOrCopy] ) As Variant *
GetListOfTunes( ) As Variant *
New() As NotesUIWorkspace
OpenDatabase( server$, file$ [, view$ [, key$ [, newInstance [, temp]]]] )
```

```
OpenFileDialog( multipleSelection [, title$] [, filters$] [, initialDir$]
➥ [, initialFile$] ) as Variant *
OpenFrameset( FramesetName$ ) *
OpenPage( PageName$ ) *
PickListCollection( type% [, multipleSelection] [, server$] [, databasefilename$]
➥ [, viewName$] [, title$] [, prompt$] [, column%]) as NotesDocumentCollection *
PickListStrings( type% [, multipleSelection] [, server$] [, databasefilename$]
➥ [, viewName$] [, title$] [, prompt$] [, column%]) as Variant *
PlayTune( tuneName$ ) *
Prompt( type%, title$, prompt$ [, default ] [, values]) as Variant *
RefreshParentNote( ) *
ReloadWindow ( ) *
SaveFileDialog( multipleSelection [, title$] [, filters$] [, initialDir$]
➥ [, initialFile$] ) as Variant *
SetCurrentLocation( [location$] ) *
SetTargetFrame( targetFrame$ ) *
URLOpen( Url$, reload, urlList, charset$, webusername$, webpassword$, ➥
proxywebusername$, proxywebpassword$ )
UseLSX( lsxLibraryName$ )
ViewRefresh()
```

LOTUS NOTES BACK-END CLASSES

The back-end classes pertain to objects not directly represented in the Notes UI. These classes are available in any LotusScript module.

THE NotesACL CLASS

The NotesACL class represents the Access Control List (ACL) for a Notes database.

CONTAINMENT

```
Contained by: NotesDatabase
Contains: NotesACLEntry
```

PROPERTIES

```
InternetLevel As Integer*
Parent As NotesDatabase
Roles As Variant
UniformAccess As Boolean
```

METHODS

```
AddRole( name$ )
CreateACLEntry( name$, level% ) As NotesACLEntry
DeleteRole( name$ )
GetEntry( name$ ) As NotesACLEntry
GetFirstEntry As NotesACLEntry
GetNextEntry( notesACLEntry ) As NotesACLEntry
RenameRole( oldName$, newName$ )
Save()
```

The NotesACLEntry Class

The NotesACLEntry class represents an entry in the ACL of a Notes database.

Containment
Contained by: NotesACL

Properties
```
CanCreateDocuments As Boolean
CanCreateLSOrJavaAgent As Boolean *
CanCreatePersonalAgent As Boolean
CanCreatePersonalFolder As Boolean
CanCreateSharedFolder As Boolean *
CanDeleteDocuments As Boolean
IsAdminReaderAuthor As Boolean *
IsAdminServer As Boolean *
IsGroup As Boolean *
IsPerson As Boolean *
IsPublicReader As Boolean
IsPublicWriter As Boolean
IsServer As Boolean *
Level As Integer
Name As String
Parent As NotesACL
Roles As Variant
UserType As Integer *
```

Methods
```
DisableRole ( name$ )
EnableRole ( name$ )
IsRoleEnabled( name$ ) As Boolean
New( NotesACL, entryName$, level% ) As NotesACLEntry
Remove()
```

The NotesAgent Class

The NotesAgent class represents an agent in a Notes database.

Containment
Contained by: NotesSession and NotesDatabase

Properties
```
Comment As String
CommonOwner As String
HasRunSinceLastModified As Boolean *
IsEnabled As Boolean
IsNotesAgent As Boolean *
IsPublic As Boolean
IsWebAgent As Boolean *
LastRun As Variant
Name As String
```

```
Owner As String
Parent As NotesDatabase
Query As String
ServerName As String
Target As Integer*
Trigger As Integer*
```

METHODS
```
Remove()
Run()
RunOnServer()As Integer *
Save()
```

THE NotesDatabase CLASS

The NotesDatabase class represents a Notes database.

CONTAINMENT
```
Contained by: NotesSession, NotesDbDirectory, and NotesUIDatabase
Contains: NotesACL, NotesAgent, NotesDocument, NotesDocumentCollection,
```
➥NotesForm, NotesOutline, NotesReplication, NotesView

PROPERTIES
```
ACL As NotesACL
Agents As Variant
AllDocuments As NotesDocumentCollection
Categories As Variant
Created As Variant
CurrentAccessLevel As Integer
DelayUpdates As Boolean
DesignTemplateName As String
FileName As String
FilePath As String
FolderReferencesEnabled As Boolean *
Forms As Variant
IsDirectoryCatalog As Boolean *
IsFTIndexed As Boolean
IsMultiDbSearch As Boolean
IsOpen As Boolean
IsPrivateAddressBook As Boolean
IsPublicAddressBook As Boolean
LastFTIndexed As Variant
LastModified As Variant
Managers As Variant
MaxSize As Long *
MaxSizeV5 As Double *
Parent As NotesSession
PercentUsed As Double
ReplicaID As String
ReplicationInfo As NotesReplication *
Server As String
Size As Double
SizeQuota As Long
```

TemplateName As String
Title As String
UnprocessedDocuments As NotesDocumentCollection
Views As Variant

METHODS
```
Compact( ) As Long
Create( server$, dbfile$, openFlag [, maxsize%] ) *
CreateCopy( newServer$, newDbFile$ [, maxsize%] ) As NotesDatabase *
CreateDocument As NotesDocument
CreateFromTemplate( newServer$, newDbFile$, inheritFlag [, maxsize%] )
➥As NotesDatabase *
CreateOutline( outlineName$ [,generateDefaultOutline%] ) As NotesOutline *
CreateReplica( newServer$, newDbFile$ ) As NotesDatabase
EnableFolder( folderName$ ) *
FTDomainSearch( query$, maxDocs% [,sortoptions% [, otheroptions%]
➥ [, start&][, count%]], entryForm$ ) As NotesDocument *
FTSearch( query$, maxDocs% [,sortoptions [, otheroptions]] )
➥As NotesDocumentCollection
GetAgent( agentName$ ) As NotesAgent
GetDocumentByID( noteID$ ) As NotesDocument
GetDocumentByUNID( unid$ ) As NotesDocument
GetDocumentByURL( URL$ [ , reload ] [ , urllist ] [ , charset$ ]
➥ [ , webusername$ ] [ , webpassword$ ] [ , proxywebusername$ ]
➥ [ , proxywebpassword$ ] ) As NotesDocument
GetForm( name$ ) As NotesForm
GetOutline( outlineName$ ) As NotesOutline *
GetProfileDocCollection( [profilename$] ) As NotesDocumentCollection *
GetProfileDocument( profilename$ [ , username$] ) As NotesDocument
GetURLHeaderInfo( URL$ , headername$ [ , Webusername$ ] [ , Webpassword$ ]
®[ , Proxywebusername$ ] [ , Proxywebpassword$ ] ) As String
GetView( viewName$ ) As NotesView
GrantAccess( name$, level% )
New( server$, dbfile$ ) As NotesDatabase
Open( server$, dbfile$ ) As Boolean
OpenByReplicaID( server$, replicaID$ ) As Boolean
OpenIfModified( server$, dbfile$, notesDateTime ) As Boolean
OpenMail()
OpenURLDb() As Boolean
OpenWithFailover( server$, dbfile$ ) As Boolean
QueryAccess( name$ ) As Integer
Remove()
Replicate( serverName$ ) As Boolean
RevokeAccess( name$ )
Search( formula$, notesDateTime, maxDocs% ) As NotesDocumentCollection
UnprocessedFTSearch( query$, maxDocs% [,sortoptions [, otheroptions]] )
➥As NotesDocumentCollection
UnprocessedSearch( formula$, notesDateTime, maxDocs% ) As NotesDocumentCollection
UpdateFTIndex( createFlag )
```

THE NotesDateRange CLASS

The NotesDateRange class represents a range of dates and times.

Containment

Contained by: NotesSession
Contains: NotesDateTime

Properties

EndDateTime As NotesDateTime
StartDateTime As NotesDateTime
Text As String

The NotesDateTime Class

The NotesDateTime class represents a date and time and provides a way to convert between Notes and a LotusScript date/time value.

Containment

Contained by: NotesDateRange, NotesSession

Properties

DateOnly As String
GMTTime As String
IsDST As Boolean
IsValidDate As Boolean *
LocalTime As String
LSGMTTime As Variant
LSLocalTime As Variant
TimeOnly As String
TimeZone As Integer
ZoneTime As String

Methods

AdjustDay(n% [, preservelocaltime])
AdjustHour(n% [, preservelocaltime])
AdjustMinute(n% [, preservelocaltime])
AdjustMonth(n% [, preservelocaltime])
AdjustSecond(n% [, preservelocaltime])
AdjustYear(n% [, preservelocaltime])
ConvertToZone(newzone, dst)
New(dateexpr$) As NotesDateTime
SetAnyDate()
SetAnyTime()
SetNow()
TimeDifference(notesDateTime) As Long
TimeDifferenceDouble(notesDateTime) As Double *

The NotesDbDirectory Class

The NotesDbDirectory class represents the available databases on a local machine or a Domino server.

CONTAINMENT
Contained by: NotesSession
Contains: NotesDatabase

PROPERTIES
Name As String

METHODS
GetFirstDatabase(fileType%) As NotesDatabase
GetNextDatabase As NotesDatabase
New(server$) as NotesDbDirectory

THE NotesDocument CLASS

The NotesDocument class represents a document in a Notes database.

CONTAINMENT
Contained by: NotesDatabase, NotesDocumentCollection, NotesNewsletter,
➥NotesUIDocument, NotesView, NotesViewEntry
Contains: NotesEmbeddedObject, NotesItem, NotesRichTextItem

PROPERTIES
Authors As Variant
ColumnValues As Variant
Created As Variant
EmbeddedObjects As Variant
EncryptionKeys As Variant
EncryptOnSend As Boolean
FolderReferences As Variant*
FTSearchScore As Integer
HasEmbedded As Boolean
IsDeleted As Boolean *
IsNewNote As Boolean
IsProfile As Boolean
IsResponse As Boolean
IsSigned As Boolean
IsUIDocOpen As Boolean
IsValid As Boolean *
Items As Variant
Key As String
LastAccessed As Variant
LastModified As Variant
NameOfProfile As String
NoteID As String
ParentDatabase As NotesDatabase
ParentDocumentUNID As String
ParentView As NotesView
Responses As NotesDocumentCollection
SaveMessageOnSend As Boolean
SentByAgent As Boolean
Signer As String
SignOnSend As Boolean

```
Size As Long
UniversalID As String
Verifier As String
```

METHODS

```
AppendItemValue( itemName$, value ) As NotesItem
ComputeWithForm( doDataTypes, raiseError ) As Boolean
CopyAllItems( notesDocument [, replace] ) As Boolean
CopyItem( notesItem, newName$ ) As NotesItem
CopyToDatabase( notesDatabase ) As NotesDocument
CreateReplyMessage( all ) As NotesDocument
CreateRichTextItem( name$ ) As NotesRichTextItem
Encrypt()
GetAttachment( fileName$ ) As NotesEmbeddedObject
GetFirstItem( name$ ) As NotesItem
GetItemValue( itemName$ ) As Variant
HasItem( itemName$ ) As Boolean
MakeResponse( notesDocument )
New( NotesDatabase) as NotesDocument
PutInFolder( folderName$ [, createFolderonFail] ) *
Remove( force ) As Boolean
RemoveFromFolder( folderName$ )
RemoveItem( itemName$ )
RenderToRTItem( notesRichTextItem ) As Boolean
ReplaceItemValue( itemName$, value ) As NotesItem
Save( force, createResponse [ , markRead ])   As Boolean
Send( attachForm [, recipients ] )
Sign()
```

THE NotesDocumentCollection CLASS

The NotesDocumentCollection class represents a subset of documents from a Notes database.

CONTAINMENT

```
Contained by: NotesDatabase, NotesSession , NotesUIDatabase, NotesUIView
Contains: NotesDocument
```

PROPERTIES

```
Count As Long
IsSorted As Boolean
Parent As NotesDatabase
Query As String
```

METHODS

```
AddDocument( noteID$ ) *
DeleteDocument( notesViewEntry ) *
FTSearch( query$, maxDocs% )
GetDocument( notesDocument ) As NotesDocument *
GetFirstDocument() As NotesDocument
GetLastDocument() As NotesDocument
GetNextDocument( notesDocument ) As NotesDocument
```

```
GetNthDocument( n% ) As NotesDocument
GetPrevDocument As NotesDocument
PutAllInFolder( folderName$ [, createFolderonFail] ) *
RemoveAll( force )
RemoveAllFromFolder( folderName$ )
StampAll( itemname , value )
UpdateAll()
```

THE NotesEmbeddedObject CLASS

The NotesEmbeddedObject class represents an embedded object, a linked object or file attachment in a Notes document, or a rich-text item.

CONTAINMENT

```
Contained by: NotesDocument and NotesRichTextItem
```

PROPERTIES

```
Class As String
FileSize As Long
FitBelowFields as Boolean *
FitToWindow as Boolean *
Name As String
Object As Variant
Parent As NotesRichTextItem
RunReadOnly As Boolean *
Source As String
Type As Integer
Verbs As Variant
```

METHODS

```
Activate( show ) As Variant
DoVerb( verb$ ) As Variant
ExtractFile( path$ )
Remove
```

THE NotesForm CLASS

The NotesForm class represents a form in a Notes database.

CONTAINMENT

```
Contained by: NotesDatabase
```

PROPERTIES

```
Aliases As Variant
Fields As Variant
FormUsers As Variant
IsSubForm As Boolean
Name As String
ProtectReaders As Boolean
ProtectUsers As Boolean
Readers As Variant
```

Methods
Remove()

The NotesInternational Class

The NotesInternational class represents the international setting for the current machine's operating system.

Containment
Contained by: NotesSession

Properties
AMString As String
CurrencyDigits As Integer
CurrencySymbol As String
DateSep As String
DecimalSep As String
IsCurrencySpace As Boolean
IsCurrencySuffix As Boolean
IsCurrencyZero As Boolean
IsDateDMY As Boolean
IsDateMDY As Boolean
IsDateYMD As Boolean
IsDST As Boolean
IsTime24Hour As Boolean
PMString As String
ThousandsSep As String
TimeSep As String
TimeZone As Integer
Today As String
Tomorrow As String
Yesterday As String

The NotesItem Class

The NotesItem class represents a field in a Notes document.

Inheritance
Inheritance parent of: NotesRichTextItem

Containment
Contained by: NotesDocument

Properties
DateTimeValue As NotesDateTime
IsAuthors As Boolean
IsEncrypted As Boolean
IsNames As Boolean
IsProtected As Boolean
IsReaders As Boolean

```
IsSigned As Boolean
IsSummary As Boolean
LastModified As Variant
Name As String
Parent As NotesDocument
SaveToDisk As Boolean
Text As String
Type As Long
ValueLength As Long
Values As Variant
```

METHODS

```
Abstract( maxAbstract&, dropVowels, useDictionary ) As String
AppendToTextList( newValue )
Contains( value ) As Boolean
CopyItemToDocument( notesDocument, newName$ ) As NotesItem
New( NotesDocument, itemName$, Value [, type%] ) as NotesItem
Remove
```

THE NotesLog CLASS

The `NotesLog` class represents an object that enables you to record a script's execution, progress, and results.

CONTAINMENT

Contained by: NotesSession

PROPERTIES

```
LogActions As Boolean
LogErrors As Boolean
NumActions As Integer
NumErrors As Integer
OverwriteFile As Boolean
ProgramName As String
```

METHODS

```
Close()
LogAction( description$ )
LogError( code%, description$ )
LogEvent( message$, queuename$, type%, severity% )
New(programName$) As NotesLog
OpenAgentLog()
OpenFileLog( path$ )
OpenMailLog( recipientsV, subject$ )
OpenNotesLog( server$, dbfile$ )
```

THE NotesName CLASS

The `NotesName` class represents a user's or server's name and hierarchy.

Containment

Contained by: NotesSession

Properties

```
Abbreviated As String
Addr821 As String *
Addr822Comment1 As String *
Addr822Comment2 As String *
Addr822Comment3 As String *
Addr822LocalPart As String *
Addr822Phrase As String *
ADMD As String
Canonical As String
Common As String
Country As String
Generation As String
Given As String
Initials As String
IsHierarchical As Boolean
Keyword As String
Language As String *
Organization As String
OrgUnit1 As String
OrgUnit2 As String
OrgUnit3 As String
OrgUnit4 As String
PRMD As String
Surname As String
```

Methods

```
New( name$ [, language$]) as NotesName
```

The NotesNewsletter Class

The `NotesNewsletter` class represents a collection of Notes documents and can create documents that render or link to the Notes document collection.

Containment

Contained by: NotesSession
Contains: NotesDocument

Properties

```
DoScore As Boolean
DoSubject As Boolean
SubjectItemName As String
```

Methods

```
FormatDocument( notesDatabase, index% ) As NotesDocument
FormatMsgWithDoclinks( notesDatabase ) As NotesDocument
New(notesDocumentCollection) As NotesNewsletter
```

THE NotesOutline CLASS*

The NotesOutline class represents the outline class. You can add, remove, and traverse the outline entries within the outline.

CONTAINMENT
Contained by: NotesDatabase
Contains: NotesOutlineEntry

PROPERTIES
Alias As String
Comment As String
Name As String

METHODS
AddEntry(newNotesOutlineEntry, [,referenceNotesOutlineEntry] [, addAfter%] [, AsChild%])
CreateEntry(outlineEntryName$) As NotesOutlineEntry
GetFirst( ) As notesOutlineEntry
GetLast( ) As notesOutlineEntry
GetNext(notesOutlineEntry) As notesOutlineEntry
GetNextSibling(notesOutlineEntry) As notesOutlineEntry
GetParent(notesOutlineEntry) As notesOutlineEntry
GetPrev(notesOutlineEntry) As notesOutlineEntry
GetPrevSibling(notesOutlineEntry) As notesOutlineEntry
MoveEntry(notesOutlineEntry, referenceNotesOutlineEntry
➥ [, moveAfter% [, AsChild%]])
RemoveEntry(notesOutlineEntry)
Save() As Boolean

THE NotesOutlineEntry CLASS*

The NotesOutlineEntry class represents a single entry within a Notes outline object. You can query various properties about the entry

CONTAINMENT
Contained by: NotesOutline

PROPERTIES
Alias As String
Database As NotesDatabase
Document As NotesDocument
EntryClass As Long
Formula As String
FrameText As String
HasChildren As Boolean
ImagesText As String
IsHidden As Boolean
IsInThisDb As Boolean
IsPrivate As Boolean
Label As String

```
Level As Long
NamedElement As String
Type As Long
URL As String
View As NotesView
```

METHODS

```
New(notesDocument) As NotesOutlineEntry
SetAction( Formula$ ) As Boolean
SetNamedElement(notesDatabase, elementName$, entryClass& ) As Boolean
SetNoteLink(notesDatabase [, notesView, [ notesDocument]]) As Boolean
SetURL(URL$) As Boolean
```

THE NotesRegistration CLASS

The `NotesRegistration` class represents an object that enables users to be registered through LotusScript.

PROPERTIES

```
CertifierIDFile As String
CreateMailDB As Boolean
Expiration As Variant
IDType As Integer
IsNorthAmerican As Boolean
MinPasswordLength As Integer
OrgUnit As String
RegistrationLog As String
RegistrationServer As String
StoreIDInAddressBook As Boolean
UpdateAddressBook As Boolean
```

METHODS

```
AddCertifierToAddressBook( idFile$ [, certPW$ [, location$ [, comment$]]])
➥As Boolean
AddServerToAddressBook( idFile$ [, server$ [, domain$ [, userPW$ [, network$
[, adminName$ [, title$ [, location$ [, comment$]]]]]]]]) As Boolean
AddUserProfile( userName$, profileName$ )
AddUserToAddressBook( idFile$, fullName$, lastName$ [, userPW$ [, firstName$
➥ [,middle$ [, mailServer$ [, mailDBPath [, fwdAddress$ [, location$
➥ [, comment$]]]]]]]]) As Boolean
CrossCertify( idFile$ [, certPW$ [, comment$]]) As Boolean
DeleteIDOnServer( userName$ , isServerID )
GetIDFromServer( userName$, idFilePath$ , isServerID)
GetUserInfo( userName$ [, mailServer$ [, mailFile$ [, domain$ [, mailSystem
➥ [, profile$ ]]]]])
New() As NotesRegistration
ReCertify( idFile$ [, certPW$ [, comment$]]) As Boolean
RegisterNewCertifier( organization$, idFile$ [, certPW$ [, country$]]) As Boolean
RegisterNewServer( server$, idFile$, domain$ [, serverPW$ [, certPW$ [, location$
➥ [, comment [, network$ [, adminName$ [, title]]]]]]]) As Boolean
RegisterNewUser( lastName$, idFile$, mailserver$ [, firstName$ [, middle$
➥ [, certPW$ [, location$ [, comment$ [, mailDBPath$ [, fwdDomain$
```

```
➥ [, userPW$ [, userType% ]]]]]]]]) As Boolean *
SwitchToID( idFile$ [, UserPW$] )   As String
```

THE NotesReplication CLASS*

The `NotesReplication` class represents the replication settings of the database. Note that there is only one `NotesReplication` class per `NotesDatabase` class. You must call the `Save` method to make property values persistent.

CONTAINMENT
```
Contained by: NotesDatabase
```

PROPERTIES
```
Abstract As Boolean
CutoffDate As Variant
CutoffDelete As Boolean
CutoffInterval As Long
Disabled As Boolean
DoNotBrowse As Boolean
DoNotCatalog As Boolean
HideDesign As Boolean
IgnoreDeletes As Boolean
IgnoreDestDeletes As Boolean
MultiDbIndex As Boolean
NeverReplicate As Boolean
NoChronos As Boolean
Priority As Long
```

METHODS
```
ClearHistory()
Reset ()
Save( )
```

THE NotesRichTextItem CLASS

The `NotesRichTextItem` class represents a rich-text field in a Notes document.

INHERITANCE
```
Inherits from: NotesItem
```

CONTAINMENT
```
Contained by: NotesDocument
Contains: NotesEmbeddedObject
```

PROPERTIES
```
EmbeddedObjects As Variant
```

Methods

```
AddNewLine( n% [, forceParagraph ])
AddPageBreak( notesRichTextParagraphStyle ) *
AddTab( n% )
AppendDocLink( linkTo, comment$ [, hotSpotText$ ]) *
AppendParagraphStyle( notesRichTextParagraphStyle ) *
AppendRTItem( notesRichTextItem )
AppendStyle( notesRichTextStyle )
AppendText( text$ )
EmbedObject( type%, class$, source$, [ name$ ] ) As NotesEmbeddedObject
GetEmbeddedObject( name$ ) As NotesEmbeddedObject
GetFormattedText( tabstrip, lineLength% ) As String
New(notesDocument, itemName$) As NotesRichTextItem
```

The NotesRichTextParagraphStyle Class*

The `NotesRichTextParagraphSytle` class represents a formatting style that can be appended to a `NotesRichTextItem` object.

Containment

Contained by: NotesSession

Properties

```
Alignment As Integer
FirstLineLeftMargin As Long
InterLineSpacing As Integer
LeftMargin As Long
Pagination As Integer
RightMargin As Long
SpacingAbove As Integer
SpacingBelow As Integer
Tabs As Variant
```

Methods

```
ClearAllTabs()
SetTab( position& , type% )
SetTabs( number%, startPosition&, interval& [,type%] )
```

The NotesRichTextStyle Class

The `NotesRichTextStyle` class represents a style that can be appended to a `NotesRichTextItem` object.

Containment

Contained by: NotesSession

Properties

```
Bold As Integer
Effects As Integer
FontSize As Integer
```

Appendix A Notes/Domino Class Reference

```
Italic As Integer
NotesColor As Integer
NotesFont As Integer
PassThruHTML As Integer *
Strikethrough As Integer
Underline As Integer
```

THE NotesRichTextTab CLASS*

The NotesRichTextTab class represents a single tab in a NotesRichTextItem object.

CONTAINMENT
Contained by: NotesRichTextParagraphStyle

PROPERTIES
```
Position As Long
Type As Integer
```

METHODS
Clear ()

THE NotesSession CLASS

The NotesSession class represents the user of the current machine and the Notes configuration.

CONTAINMENT
Contains: NotesAgent, NotesDatabase, NotesDateRange, NotesDateTime, ➥NotesDbDirectory, NotesDocumentCollection, NotesInternational, NotesLog, ➥NotesNewsletter, NotesRichTextParagraphStyle, NotesRichTextStyle, NotesTimer

PROPERTIES
```
AddressBooks As Variant
CommonUserName As String
CurrentAgent As NotesAgent
CurrentDatabase As NotesDatabase
DocumentContext As NotesDocument
EffectiveUserName As String
International As NotesInternational
IsOnServer As Boolean
LastExitStatus As Long *
LastRun As Variant
NotesBuildVersion As Long *
NotesVersion As String
Platform As String
SavedData As NotesDocument
UserName As String
UserNameList As Variant *
```

LOTUS NOTES BACK-END CLASSES

METHODS
```
CreateDateRange As NotesDataRange
CreateDateTime( dateTime$ ) As NotesDateTime
CreateLog( programName$ ) As NotesLog
CreateName( name$ ) As NotesName
CreateNewsletter( notesDocumentCollection ) As NotesNewsletter
CreateRichTextParagraphStyle() As NotesRichTextParagraphStyle *
CreateRichTextStyle() As NotesRichTextStyle
CreateTimer() As NotesTimer
FreeTimeSearch( windowNotesDateRange, duration%, names [, firstfit%] ) As Variant
GetDatabase( server$, dbfile$ [,createOnFail]) As NotesDatabase *
GetDbDirectory( serverName$ ) As NotesDBDirectory
GetEnvironmentString( name$ [ , system ] ) As Variant
GetEnvironmentValue( name$ [ , system ] ) As Variant
New() As NotesSession
SetEnvironmentVar( name$, valueV [, issystemvar] )
UpdateProcessedDoc ( notesDocument )
```

THE NotesTimer CLASS

The NotesTimer class represents a mechanism for triggering an event for every given length of time.

CONTAINMENT
```
Contained by: NotesSession
```

PROPERTIES
```
Comment As String
Enabled As Boolean
Interval As Integer
```

METHODS
```
New([interval% [,comment$]]) As NotesTimer
```

EVENT
```
Alarm( Source as NotesTimer )
```

THE NotesView CLASS

The NotesView class represents a view in a Notes database.

CONTAINMENT
```
Contained by: NotesDatabase, NotesUIView
Contains: NotesDocument, NotesViewColumn, NotesViewEntry,
```
↪NotesViewEntryCollection, NotesViewNavigator

Properties
```
Aliases As Variant
AllEntries As NotesViewEntryCollection *
AutoUpdate As Boolean
BackgroundColor As Integer *
ColumnCount As Integer *
Columns As Variant
Created As Variant
HeaderLines As Integer *
IsCalendar As Boolean
IsCategorized As Boolean *
IsConflict As Boolean *
IsDefaultView As Boolean
IsFolder As Boolean
IsHierarchical As Boolean *
IsModified As Boolean *
IsPrivate As Boolean *
LastModified As Variant
Name As String
Parent As NotesDatabase
ProtectReaders As Boolean
Readers As Variant
RowLines As Integer *
Spacing As Integer *
TopLevelEntryCount As Integer *
UniversalID As String
```

Methods
```
Clear( query$, maxDocs% )
CreateViewNav() As NotesViewNavigator *
CreateViewNavFrom( docOrViewEntry ) As NotesViewNavigator *
CreateViewNavFromCategory( category$ ) As NotesViewNavigator *
CreateViewNavFromChildren( docOrViewEntry ) As NotesViewNavigator *
CreateViewNavFromDescendants( docOrViewEntry ) As NotesViewNavigator *
FTSearch( query$ [, maxDocs%] ) As Long
GetAllDocumentsByKey( keyArray [ ,exact ] ) As NotesDocumentCollection
GetAllEntriesByKey( keyArray [ ,exact ] ) As NotesViewEntryCollection *
GetChild( notesDocument ) As NotesDocument
GetDocumentByKey( keyArray [ , exact ] ) As NotesDocument
GetEntryByKey( keyArray [ ,exact ] ) As NotesViewEntry *
GetFirstDocument() As NotesDocument
GetLastDocument() As NotesDocument
GetNextDocument( notesDocument ) As NotesDocument
GetNextSibling( notesDocument ) As NotesDocument
GetNthDocument( index& ) As NotesDocument
GetParentDocument( notesDocument ) As NotesDocument
GetPrevDocument( notesDocument ) As NotesDocument
GetPrevSibling( notesDocument ) As NotesDocument
Refresh()
Remove()
```

The NotesViewColumn Class

The NotesViewColumn class represents a column in a Notes view.

CONTAINMENT
Contained by: NotesView

PROPERTIES
```
Alignment As Integer *
DateFmt As Integer *
FontColor As Integer *
FontFace As String *
FontPointSize As Integer *
FontStyle As Integer *
Formula As String
HeaderAlignment As Integer *
IsAccentSensitiveSort As Boolean *
IsCaseSensitiveSort As Boolean *
IsCategory As Boolean
IsField As Boolean *
IsFomula As Boolean *
IsHidden As Boolean
IsHideDetail As Boolean *
IsIcon As Boolean *
IsResize As Boolean *
IsResortAscending As Boolean *
IsResortDescending As Boolean *
IsResortToView As Boolean *
IsResponse As Boolean
IsSecondaryResort As Boolean *
IsSecondaryResortDescending As Boolean *
IsShowTwistie As Boolean *
IsSortDescending As Boolean *
IsSorted As Boolean
ItemName As String
ListSep As Integer *
NumberAttrib As Integer *
NumberDigits As Integer *
NumberFormat As Integer *
Position As Integer
TimeDateFmt As Integer *
TimeFmt As Integer *
TimeZoneFmt As Integer *
Title As String
Width As Integer *
```

THE NotesViewEntry CLASS*

The NotesViewEntry class represents a single entry within a view.

CONTAINMENT
```
Contained by: NotesViewEntryCollection, NotesViewNavigator
Contains: NotesDocument
```

PROPERTIES
```
ChildCount As Integer
ColumnIndentLevel As Integer
```

```
ColumnValues As Variant
DescendantCount As Integer
Document As NotesDocument
FTSearchScore As Integer
IndentLevel As Integer
IsCategory As Boolean
IsConflict As Boolean
IsDocument As Boolean
IsTotal As Boolean
IsValid As Boolean
NoteID As String
Parent As NotesView
SiblingCount As Integer
UniversalID As String
```

METHODS
```
GetPosition( separator$ ) As String
```

THE NotesViewEntryCollection CLASS*

The NotesViewEntryCollection class represents a collection of NotesViewEntry objects.

CONTAINMENT
```
Contained by: NotesView
Contains: NotesViewEntry
```

PROPERTIES
```
Count As Long
Parent As NotesView
Query As String
```

METHODS
```
AddEntry( NotesViewEntry )
DeleteEntry( NotesViewEntry )
FTSearch( query$, maxDocs% )
GetEntry( NotesViewEntry ) As NotesViewEntry
GetFirstEntry() As NotesViewEntry
GetLastEntry() As NotesViewEntry
GetNextEntry( NotesViewEntry ) As NotesViewEntry
GetNthEntry( NotesViewEntry ) As NotesViewEntry
GetPrevEntry( NotesViewEntry ) As NotesViewEntry
PutAllInFolder( folderName$ )
RemoveAll( force%)
RemoveAllFromFolder( folderName$ )
StampAll( ItemName,  value)
UpdateAll()
```

THE NotesViewNavigator CLASS*

The NotesViewNavigator class represents a class that can be used to navigate within a NotesView object.

CONTAINMENT
```
Contained by: NotesView
Contains: NotesViewEntry
```

PROPERTIES
```
MaxLevel As Long
ParentView As NotesView
```

METHODS
```
GetChild( currentNotesViewEntry) As NotesViewEntry
GetEntry( currentNotesViewEntry) As NotesViewEntry
GetFirst() As NotesViewEntry
GetFirstDocument() As NotesViewEntry
GetLast() As NotesViewEntry
GetLastDocument() As NotesViewEntry
GetNext( currentNotesViewEntry) As NotesViewEntry
GetNextCategory( currentNotesViewEntry) As NotesViewEntry
GetNextDocument( currentNotesViewEntry) As NotesViewEntry
GetNextSibling( currentNotesViewEntry) As NotesViewEntry
GetNth( index& ) As NotesViewEntry
GetParent( currentNotesViewEntry) As NotesViewEntry
GetPos( position$, separator$ ) As NotesViewEntry
GetPrev( currentNotesViewEntry) As NotesViewEntry
GetPrevCategory( currentNotesViewEntry) As NotesViewEntry
GetPrevDocument( currentNotesViewEntry) As NotesViewEntry
GetPrevSibling( currentNotesViewEntry) As NotesViewEntry
```

ODBC DATA ACCESS CLASSES

The ODBC data access classes provide a LotusScript method for reading to and writing from ODBC data sources.

> **Note**
> To use these classes, add the line USELSX "*LSXODBC" in the options event of the programmable object.

THE ODBCConnection CLASS

The ODBCConnection class represents an ODBC data source.

CONTAINMENT
```
Contained by: ODBCQuery
```

PROPERTIES
```
AutoCommit As Boolean
CommitOnDisconnect As Boolean
```

DataSourceName As String
GetLSDOMasterRevision As String *

SilentMode As Boolean

METHODS

CommitTransactions( ) As Boolean *
ConnectTo(dataSourceName$ [, userID$, password$]) As Boolean
Disconnect As Boolean
GetError As Integer
GetErrorMessage ([errorValue%]) As String
GetExtendedErrorMessage (errorValue%) As String
IsConnected As Boolean
IsSupported(option%) As Boolean
ListDataSources As Variant
ListFields([tableName$]) As Variant
ListProcedures([dataSourceName$ [, userID$, password$]]]) As Variant
ListTables([dataSourceName$ [, userID$ [, password$]]]) As Variant
RollbackTransactions( ) AsBoolean

THE ODBCQuery CLASS

The ODBCQuery class represents a query to an ODBC data source.

CONTAINMENT

Contained by: ODBCResultSet
Contains: ODBCConnection

PROPERTIES

Connection As ODBCConnection
QueryExecuteTimeOut As Integer
SQL As String
UseRowID As Boolean *

METHODS

GetError As Integer
GetErrorMessage ([errorValue%]) As String
GetExtendedErrorMessage (errorValue%) As String

THE ODBCResultSet CLASS

The ODBCResultSet class represents the results of a query to an ODBC data source.

CONTAINMENT

Contains: ODBCQuery

PROPERTIES

CacheLimit As Long
CurrentRow As Long
FetchBatchSize As Long

```
MaxRows As Long
Query As ODBCQuery
ReadOnly As Boolean
```

METHODS

```
AddRow As Boolean
Close( option ) As Boolean
DeleteRow ( tableName$ ) As Boolean
ExecProcedure( procedureName$ , arguments ) As Variant *
Execute( DB_CANCEL ) As Boolean
FieldExpectedDataType( column , dataType ) As Integer
FieldID( column$ ) As Integer
FieldInfo( column_id% or column_Name$ ) As Variant
FieldName( column_id ) As String
FieldNativeDataType( column_id% or column_Name$ ) As Integer
FieldSize( column_id% or column_Name$ ) As Integer
FirstRow As Boolean
GetError As Integer
GetErrorMessage ([errorValue%]) As String
GetExtendedErrorMessage (errorValue%) As String
GetParameter( parameter_index% ) As Variant
GetParameterName( parameter_index% ) As String
GetRowStatus As Integer
GetValue( column_id% or column_Name$ [ , variable ] ) As Variant
HasRowChanged As Boolean
IsBeginOfData As Boolean
IsEndOfData As Boolean
IsResultSetAvailable As Boolean
IsValueAltered( column_id% or column_Name$ ) As Boolean
IsValueNull( column_id% or column_Name$ ) As Boolean
LastRow As Boolean
LocateRow ( column_id% or column_Name$ , value , [ column_id2% or column_Name2$ ,
➡ value2 , [column_id3% or column_Name3$ , value3 ] ] ) As Boolean
NextRow As Boolean
NumColumns As Integer
NumParameters As Integer
NumRows As Integer
PrevRow As Boolean
SetParameter ( parameter_index% , value$ ) As Boolean
SetValue ( column_id% or column_Name$, value ) As Boolean
UpdateRow As Boolean
```

APPENDIX

@Function and @Command Listings

@Function Listing

Here is a listing of the @functions that are available in release 5. An asterisk (*) means that the function is new or changed in release 5.

Mathematical Functions

The mathematical functions work with numbers and are used for calculation. These functions are included in Notes and Domino for those random requirements. I would not recommend using them for a complex math job, but if you need to commit an occasional sin, these functions are here to oblige:

@Abs
@Acos
@Asin
@Atan
@Atan2
@Cos
@Exp
@Integer
@Ln
@Log
@Max
@Min
@Modulo
@Pi
@Power
@Random
@Round
@Sign
@Sin
@Sqrt
@Sum
@Tan

String Handling Functions

You will probably make pretty heavy use of the string handling routines. You can already concatenate strings with the + operator. With these functions, you can extract substrings, search for matches, and explode or implode lists to and from strings. Don't confuse @ReplaceSubstring with @Replace, which operates on lists:

@Abstract
@Begins
@Char
@Contains
@Date
@Ends
@Explode
@Implode
@Left
@LeftBack
@Length
@Like

@LowerCase
@Matches
@Middle
@MiddleBack
@NewLine
@ProperCase
@Repeat
@ReplaceSubstring
@Right
@RightBack
@Text
@Trim
@UpperCase
@Word

Conversion Functions

These functions are not used for religious conversion, just conversion of the various data types. `@Text` is pretty useful for converting anything into a string. `@Integer` is used to truncate numeric values to their whole number, leaving off any decimal fractional digits. `@TextToNumber` converts a string to a number, and `@TextToTime` converts a string to a time value. `@Narrow` and `@Wide` are used to support national languages that require 2-byte characters, such as in Japanese:

@Ascii
@Char
@Explode
@Implode
@Integer
@IsNumber
@IsText
@IsTime
@Narrow *
@Soundex
@Text
@TextToNumber
@TextToTime
@Wide *

List Functions

Lists are used to store multiple values in a single variable. You can perform operations on lists in either a pair-wise or permuted manner. See the previous section on lists and list operations for more details. With these functions, you can find out whether an item is a member of a list or replace members with `@Replace`. Don't confuse `@Replace` with `@ReplaceSubstring`, which operates on strings:

@Elements
@Explode
@Implode
@IsMember
@IsNotMember
@Keywords
@Member

```
@Replace
@Subset
@Unique
```

Date and Time Functions

The date and time functions are used mainly to extract components from a time-date value. For example, you can extract the month or year from a date. You can also add a specified amount of time by using the `@Adjust` function:

```
@Accessed
@Adjust
@Created
@Date
@Day
@Hour
@Minute
@Modified
@Month
@Now
@Second
@Text
@Time
@Today
@Tomorrow
@Weekday
@Year
@Yesterday
@Zone
```

Database Access Functions

The database access functions enable you to access data contained within the same or different Domino databases or other ODBC sources:

```
@DbColumn
@DbCommand
@DbExists
@DbLookup
```

Current Document and View Selection Functions

The functions in this section are useful in the context of a single document or for view selection. Note that in release 5 the `@DeleteDocument` can be used for soft deletion, meaning that the document can later be recovered with `@UndeleteDocument`. `@HardDeleteDoc` overrides this and causes a hard deletion:

```
@AddToFolder *
@All
@AllChildren
@AllDescendants
@Attachments
@AttachmentLengths
@AttachmentNames
@Author
```

@Function Listing 1217

```
@Certificate
@DeleteDocument *
@DocFields
@DocLength
@DocMark
@DocumentUniqueID
@InheritedDocumentUniqueID
@IsAvailable
@IsDocBeingEdited
@IsDocBeingLoaded
@IsDocBeingMailed
@IsDocBeingRecalculated
@IsDocBeingSaved
@IsDocTruncated
@IsModalHelp
@IsNewDoc
@IsReponseDoc
@IsUnavailable
@IsValid
@NoteID
@Responses
@UndeleteDocument *
```

Column Formula Functions

The following functions are useful in column formulas, which evaluate to form the text that will be shown within a particular column of a view or folder:

```
@DocChildren
@DocDescendants
@DocLevel
@DocNumber
@DocParentNumber
@DocSiblings
@IsCategory
@IsExpandable
@Responses
```

Document Field Manipulation Functions

The following functions and keywords are useful within the context of a single field. Use @DeleteField in conjunction with the FIELD keyword to delete a field from a database. @GetProfileField and @SetProfileField can be used to get and store information within profile documents of a database:

```
DEFAULT
@DeleteField
FIELD
@GetDocField
@GetProfileField
@SetDocField
@SetField
@SetProfileField *
@Unavailable
```

Part IX
App B

1218 Appendix B @Function and @Command Listings

Internet Access Functions

The Internet functions are used to access WWW sites via their URLs, get information about the browser, and validate Internet addresses:

```
@BrowserInfo *
@URLGetHeader
@URLHistory
@URLOpen
@ValidateInternetAddress *
```

User Interaction

The `@Prompt` function is the easiest way to display a message box to the user and optionally request a response. You can use the `@DialogBox` function to exert more control over the formatting of the dialog box to the user:

```
@DialogBox
@PickList *
@Prompt
@SetTargetFrame *
```

Mail Functions

Mail functions enable you to control various preferences for mail:

```
@MailDbName
@MailEncryptSavedPreference
@MailEncryptSentPreference
@MailSavePreference
@MailSend
@MailSignPreference
@OptimizeMailAddress
```

User Attribute and International Functions

Several functions have been added in release 5 to look up and control user attributes. In particular, support has been added for national languages. You can use the `@Locale` function to return information about the user's national language, if any:

```
@FormLanguage *
@LanguagePreference *
@Locale *
@Name *
@NameLookup *
@UserAccess *
@UserName *
@UserNameLanguage *
@UserNamesList *
@UserPrivileges
@UserRoles
@V3UserName
@V4UserAccess *
```

Security and Execution Control List (ECL) Functions

The Execution Control List (ECL) controls various aspects of the environment for program execution. It is used to control security and authorization for program execution:

@EditECL
@EditUserECL
@Password
@RefreshECL *
@UserAccess *
@V4UserAccess *

Database and Environment Functions

The functions in this section can be used to obtain information about the current database and operating system environment:

@CheckAlarms
@ClientType
@DbManager
@DbName
@DbTitle
@Domain
@EnableAlarms
ENVIRONMENT
@Environment
@FontList *
@GetPortsList
@IsAppInstalled *
@IsAgentEnabled
@LaunchApp *
@Platform
@SetEnvironment
@Version
@ViewTitle

Dynamic Data Exchange (DDE) Functions

The functions are used to exchange data between Notes/Domino and other processes that are running on the Windows platform. These functions are not supported on UNIX or the Macintosh:

@DDEExecute
@DDEInitiate
@DDEPoke
@DDETerminate

Control Flow Functions

The functions in this section control execution flow within a formula:

@Do
@If
@Return
@V2If

Constants and Other Functions

Functions in this section represent constants and other miscellaneous @functions:

```
@Command
@Error
@Failure
@False
@IsError
@No
@PostedCommand
REM
SELECT
@Select
@Set
@Success
@True
@Yes
```

@Command Listing

In the following sections, the square brackets are left off the names. They must be used when you use the @Command function itself. The command names are grouped roughly according to their functions. Any command with an asterisk (*) is new or changed in release 5:

Administration

```
AdminCertify
AdminCreateGroup
AdminCrossCertifyIDFile
AdminCrossCertifyKey
AdminDatabaseAnalysis
AdminDatabaseQuotas
AdminIDFileClearPassword
AdminIDFileExamine
AdminIDFileSetPassword
Administration
AdminNewOrganization
AdminNewOrgUnit
AdminOpenAddressBook
AdminOpenCatalog
AdminOpenCertLog
AdminOpenGroupsView
AdminOpenServerLog
AdminOpenServersView
AdminOpenStatistics
AdminOpenUsersView
AdminOutgoingMail
AdminRegisterFromFile
AdminRegisterServer
AdminRegisterUser
AdminRemoteConsole
AdminSendMailTrace
```

@Command Listing

```
AdminStatisticsConfig
AdminTraceConnection
```

Agent

```
AgentEdit
AgentEnableDisable
AgentLog
AgentRun
AgentSetServerName
AgentTestRun
```

Attachment

```
AttachmentDetachAll
AttachmentLaunch
AttachmentProperties
AttachmentView
```

Calendar

```
CalendarFormat *
CalendarGoTo
FindFreeTimeDialog
```

Create

```
Compose
CreateAction
CreateCreate
CreateControlledAccessSection
CreateEllipse
CreateFolder
CreateForm
CreateLayoutRegion
CreateNavigator
CreatePolygon
CreatePolyline
CreateRectangle
CreateRectangularHotspot
CreateSection
CreateSubForm
CreateTextbox
CreateView
```

Design

```
DesignDocumentInfo
DesignFormAttributes
DesignFormFieldDef
DesignFormNewField
DesignForms
DesignFormShareField
DesignFormUseField
DesignFormWindowTitle
DesignHelpAboutDocument
```

DesignHelpUsingDocument
DesignIcon
DesignMacros
DesignRefresh
DesignReplace
DesignSharedFields
DesignSynopsis
DesignViewAppendColumn
DesignViewAttributes
DesignViewColumnDef
DesignViewEditActions
DesignViewFormFormula
DesignViewNewColumn
DesignViews
DesignViewSelectFormula

EDIT

EditBottom
EditButton
EditClear
EditCopy
EditCut
EditDeselectAll
EditDetach
EditDocument
EditDown
EditEncryptionKeys
EditFind
EditFindInPreview
EditFindNext
EditGoToField
EditHeaderFooter
EditHorizScrollbar
EditIndent
EditIndentFirstLine
EditInsertButton
EditInsertFileAttachment
EditInsertObject
EditInsertPageBreak
EditInsertPopup
EditInsertTable
EditInsertText
EditLeft
EditLinks
EditLocations
EditMakeDocLink
EditNextField
EditOpenLink
EditPaste
EditPasteSpecial
EditPhoneNumbers
EditPrevField
EditProfile
EditResizePicture
EditRight

```
EditSelectAll
EditSelectByDate
EditShowHideHiddenChars
EditTableDeleteRowColumn
EditTableFormat
EditTableInsertRowColumn
EditTop
EditUndo
EditUntruncate
EditUp
InsertSubForm
V3EditNextField
V3EditPrevField
```

File

```
AddBookmark *
AddDatabase
AddDatabaseRepID
DatabaseReplSettings
FileCloseWindow
FileDatabaseACL
FileDatabaseCompact
FileDatabaseCopy
FileDatabaseDelete
FileDatabaseInfo
FileDatabaseRemove
FileDatabaseUseServer
FileExit
FileExport
FileFullTextCreate
FileFullTextDelete
FileFullTextInfo
FileFullTextUpdate
FileImport
FileNewDatabase
FileNewReplica
FileOpenDatabase
FileOpenDBRepID
FilePageSetup
FilePrint
FilePrintSetup
FileSave
FileSaveNewVersion
RenameDatabase
```

Folder

```
ChooseFolders
Folder
FolderCollapse
FolderCustomize
FolderExpand
FolderExpandAll
FolderExpandWithChildren
FolderMove
```

Appendix B @Function and @Command Listings

```
        FolderProperties
        FolderRename
        RemoveFromFolder
```

Form

```
        FormActions
        FormTestDocument
```

Help

```
        Help
        HelpAboutDatabase
        HelpAboutNotes
        HelpFunctions
        HelpIndex
        HelpKeyboard
        HelpMessages
        HelpRelease3MenuFinder
        HelpReleaseNotes
        HelpTableOfContents
        HelpUsingDatabase
```

HotSpot

```
        HotSpotClear
        HotSpotProperties
```

Layout

```
        LayoutAddGraphic
        LayoutAddText
        LayoutElementBringToFront
        LayoutElementProperties
        LayoutElementSendToBack
        LayoutProperties
```

Mail

```
        MailAddress
        MailComposeMemo
        MailForward
        MailForwardAsAttachment
        MailOpen
        MailRequestCrossCert
        MailRequestNewName
        MailRequestNewPublicKey
        MailScanUnread
        MailSend
        MailSendCertificateRequest
        MailSendEncryptionKey
        MailSendPublicKey
        V4MailAddress *
```

NAVIGATE
    NavigateNext
    NavigateNextHighlight
    NavigateNextMain
    NavigateNextSelected
    NavigateNextUnread
    NavigatePrev
    NavigatePrevHighlight
    NavigatePrevMain
    NavigatePrevSelected
    NavigatePrevUnread
    NavigateToBackLink

NAVIGATOR
    NavigatorProperties
    NavigatorTest

OBJECT
    ObjectDisplayAs
    ObjectOpen
    ObjectProperties

OPEN
    OpenCalendar
    OpenDocument
    OpenFrameset *
    OpenHelpDocument *
    OpenNavigator
    OpenPage *
    OpenView

PASTE
    PasteBitmapAsBackground
    PasteBitmapAsObject

REFRESH
    RefreshHideFormulas
    RefreshParentNote *

REPLICATOR
    Replicator
    ReplicatorReplicateHigh
    ReplicatorReplicateNext
    ReplicatorReplicateSelected
    ReplicatorReplicateWithServer
    ReplicatorSendMail
    ReplicatorSendReceiveMail
    ReplicatorStart
    ReplicatorStop

Section

    SectionCollapse
    SectionCollapseAll
    SectionDefineEditors
    SectionExpand
    SectionExpandAll
    SectionProperties
    SectionRemoveHeader

ShowHide

    ShowHideLinkPreview
    ShowHideParentPreview
    ShowHidePreviewPane
    ShowProperties

SmartIcons

    SmartIconsFloating
    SmartIconsNextSet

Text

    TextAlignCenter
    TextAlignFull
    TextAlignLeft
    TextAlignNone
    TextAlignRight
    TextBold
    TextBullet
    TextCycleSpacing
    TextEnlargeFont
    TextFont
    TextItalic
    TextNormal
    TextNumbers
    TextOutdent
    TextParagraph
    TextParagraphStyles
    TextPermanentPen
    TextReduceFont
    TextSetFontColor
    TextSetFontFace
    TextSetFontSize
    TextSpacingDouble
    TextSpacingOneAndaHalf
    TextSpacingSingle
    TextUnderline

Tools

    ExchangeUnreadMarks
    ToolsCall
    ToolsCategorize
    ToolsHangUp
    ToolsMarkAllRead

```
ToolsMarkAllUnread
ToolsMarkSelectedRead
ToolsMarkSelectedUnread
ToolsRefreshAllDocs
ToolsRefreshSelectedDocs
ToolsReplicate
ToolsRunBackgroundMacros
ToolsRunMacro
ToolsScanUnreadChoose
ToolsScanUnreadPreferred
ToolsScanUnreadSelected
ToolsSetupLocation
ToolsSetupMail
ToolsSetupPorts
ToolsSetupUserSetup
ToolsSmartIcons
ToolsSpellCheck
ToolsUserLogoff
```

UserID

```
UserIDCertificates
UserIDClearPassword
UserIDCreateSafeCopy
UserIDEncryptionKeys
UserIDInfo
UserIDMergeCopy
UserIDSetPassword
UserIDSwitch
```

View

```
ViewArrangeIcons
ViewBelowFolders
ViewBesideFolders
ViewCertify
ViewChange
ViewCollapse
ViewCollapseAll
ViewExpand
ViewExpandAll
ViewExpandWithChildren
ViewHorizScrollBar
ViewMoveName
ViewNavigatorsFolders
ViewNavigatorsNone
ViewPageDown
ViewPageUp
ViewRefreshFields
ViewRefreshUnread
ViewRenamePerson
ViewShowFieldHelp
ViewShowObject
ViewShowOnlyCategories
ViewShowOnlySearchResults
ViewShowOnlySelected
ViewShowOnlyUnread
```

ViewShowPageBreaks
ViewShowRuler
ViewShowSearchBar
ViewShowServerNames
ViewShowUnread
ViewSwitchForm

Window

ReloadWindow *
WindowCascade
WindowMaximize
WindowMaximizeAll
WindowMinimize
WindowMinimizeAll
WindowNext
WindowRestore
WindowTile
WindowWorkspace

Workspace

WorkspaceProperties
WorkspaceStackReplicaIcons

Other

DebugLotusScript
DialingRules
EmptyTrash
Execute
GoUpLevel
PictureProperties
PublishDatabase
SetCurrentLocation
StyleCycleKey
ZoomPreview

Deleted

The following @Commands from R4.x are no longer supported in R5:

AdminNewCertifier
ViewPageDown
ViewPageUp
WindowCascade
WindowNext
WindowTile

INDEX

Symbols

& (ampersand), 1025
' (apostrophe), 509, 1025
* (asterisk), 108, 145, 334, 815, 1017, 1051, 1184, 1214, 1220
*/ (asterisk, forward slash), 548
@Adjust function, 377, 443
@ (at symbol), 304
@BrowserInfo function, 392
@Command, functions, 446-447
   administration, 1220-1221
   agent, 1221
   attachment, 1221
   calendar, 1221
   create, 1221
   deleted, 1228
   design, 1221-1222
   edit, 1222-1223
   file, 1223
   folder, 1223-1224
   form, 1224
   help, 1224
   HotSpot, 1224
   layout, 1224
   mail, 1224
   miscellaneous, 1228
   navigate, 1225
   navigator, 1225
   object, 1225
   open, 1225
   paste, 1225
   refresh, 1225
   replicator, 1225
   section, 1226
   ShowHide, 1226
   SmartIcons, 1226
   text, 1226
   tools, 1226-1227
   UserID, 1227
   view, 1227-1228
   window, 1228
   workspace, 1228
@Created function, 443
@DbColumn, 737
@DBColumn function, 354, 446
@DbCommand, 737
@DbLookup, 444-446, 737
@DbName function, 444
@DialogBox function, 444
@Environment function, 438
@Explode function, 443
@formula
   function, 387
   language, 346
@functions
   column formula, 1217
   constants, 1220
   control flow, 1219
   conversion, 1215
   current document, 1216-1217
   database, 1216, 1219
   date and time, 1216
   DDE (dynamic data exchange), 1219
   document field manipulation, 1217
   ECL (Execution Control List), 1219
   environment, 1219
   international, 1218
   Internet access, 1218
   list, 1215-1216
   mail, 1218
   mathematical, 1214-1215
   security, 1219
   string handling, 1214
   user attribute or interaction, 1218
   view selection, 1216-1217
@if function, 442
@Implode function, 443
@Left function, 442
@LowerCase function, 442
@PickList function, 444
@PostedCommand function, 446-447
@Prompt function, 443
@Right function, 442
@SetEnvironment function, 438
@Subset function, 443
@Trim function, 442
@UpperCase function, 442
@UserAccess function, 444
@UserName function, 346
@UserNamesList function, 444
@UserRoles function, 444
\ (backslash), 434
{ } (braces), 499
[ ] (brackets), 303, 434, 692, 1220
: (colon), 509, 953
, (comma), 219
$ (dollar sign), 548
. (dot), 795
%End Rem directives, 509
= (equals sign), 795
! (exclamation point), 144, 694-695
/ (forward slash), 1025
/* (forward slash, asterisk), 548
// (forward slashes), 548
- (hyphen), 1025
%include statement, 538
$MediaTypes field, 320
, (mobile computing), 219
(number sign), 343, 348
+ operator (Addition), 435
:= operator (Assignment), 435
+ operator (Concatenation), 435
/ operator (Division), 435
= operator (Equal), 436
: operator (List concatenation), 435
& operator (Logical AND), 436
| operator (Logical OR), 436
* operator (Multiplication), 435

!= OPERATOR

!= operator (Not equal), 436
=! operator (Not equal), 436
*+ operator (Permuted addition), 436
*+ operator (Permuted concatenation), 436
*/ operator (Permuted division), 435
*= operator (Permuted equal), 436
** operator (Permuted multiplication), 435
*!= operator (Permuted not equal), 436
*=! operator (Permuted not equal), 436
*- operator (Permuted subtraction), 436
- operator (Subtraction), 436
! operator (Unary logical NOT), 436
- operator (Unary negative), 435
+ operator (Unary positive), 435
( ) (parentheses), 551
. (period), 795, 1025
+ (plus sign), 145, 377
? (question mark), 694-695
" " (quotation marks), 434, 550, 936
%Rem directives, 509
$Revisions field, 263, 803
; (semicolon), 546, 906
~ (tilde), 496
_ (underscore), 509, 548, 795, 1025
$UpdatedBy field, 263, 803
% used button, 982
| | (vertical bars), 499

A

\<A\> tag (HTML), 307
abbreviated formats, hierarchial names, 761
About documents, updating, 270-271
absolute size limitation, 261
Abstract Windowing Toolkit (AWT), 461, 547
accelerators, extended for keyboards, 94

Accept button, 866
Accept Encryption Key command (Actions menu), 866
access control for replication, establishing, 952-953
Access Control List dialog box, 269, 860
Access Control Lists. *See* ACLs
access lists (views), 371-372
Access server field (Security tab of Server document), 815
access via PC or phone software, 1145
access-controlled sections on forms, 338-339
accessing
　database documents, 638
　Domino databases, 256
　Domino Object Model, 464-465
　formulas, 433
　LotusScript files, 534-538
account administration of users, integrating with Windows NT, 916-917
accounts, Windows NT, creating for users, 904-905
Accounts Settings view (personal address book), 76
Accounts view (personal address book), 76
ACL
　class (Java), 636
　dialog box, 415, 418, 421-422, 426
　Monitor, 1134
　Monitor document, 423
　property, 636
ACLs (Access Control Lists), 113, 849, 950, 982 1133
　Administration server, 423-425
　browsers, 427
　Create personal folders/views, 347
　Domino databases, 636
　Domino Directory, 808-809
　entries, 268-269, 675
　groups, 416-417
　levels, 414-415, 419-420
　mobile computing, 229
　monitoring, 423
　people, 416-419
　replication, 426-429, 1133-1134
　restrictions, group/users, 417

　roles, 421-422
　servers, 417, 428-429, 1060
　settings, in databases, 998-999
　unspecified users, 427-428
acquire scripts, modems, 213
Action Bar (Replicator page) buttons, 967
Action entries, outlines, 387
Action Hotspot properties dialog box, 407
Action Pane, 334
actionbar.cab files, 573
actionbar.jar files, 573
actionbar.zip files, 573
actions
　creating, 333-335
　defining, 334
　formulas, 432-433
　graphics, 335
　predefined, 334
　shared in Domino Designer Resources twistie, 287
　views, 373-374
Actions
　button, 180
　menu, 54
Actions menu commands
　Accept Encryption Key, 866
　Add Connection, 932
　Add Recipients, 118
　Cross-certify Attached ID File, 855
　Empty Trash, 90
　Folder, 160
　Forward, 251
　Internet Options, 242
　PlayTune, 620
　Recertify Selected Servers, 1031
　Tools, 77, 117, 169
　　Add Sender to Address Book, 153, 156
　　Add Sender to Personal Address Book, 118
　　Import Holidays, 181
　　Out of Office, 118
　　Visit Web Page, 161
ActiveX
　Automation, supporting, 670-671
　enabling in Notes browsers, 92
activities, logging, 1176
Activities
　Admin-Backup, 1162
　Admin-Purge, 1162
　Archive, 1162

Agent Manager

Command, 1161
Direct Transfer, 1161
DPROPR, 1161
Java, 1162
NotesPump/LEI, 1161-1163
Polling, 1161
Realtime, 1162
Replication, 1162
Scripted, 1162

Add @Func button, 58

Add Command button, 58

Add Condition button, 343

Add Configuration button, 1017

Add Connection
button, 958
command (Action menu), 932

Add Group button, 162

Add Mailing List button, 162

Add Program button, 1025

Add Recipients command (Actions menu), 118

Add Role dialog box, 422

Add Sender
to Address Book (Tools command, Actions menu), 156
to Personal Address Book (Tools command, Actions menu), 118

Add User dialog box, 417

add-ons, proxy servers, 877

adding
fields, 327
SmartIcons, 56
users to ACLs, 417, 419

Addition operator (numeric values), 435

Additional Domino server
button, 775
option, 767

Additional Options (user preference), 90

Additional Setup dialog box, 211

Address book. *See also* **directories; Personal Address Book**
applets (eSuite), 598
contacts, list of, 74

addresses
email, Randall A. Tamura, 1180
Internet, 794-795, 908
Notes, converting to Internet addresses, 749

addressing email, 104-105, 748-749

Adjacent Domain documents (Domino Directory), 841, 930

adjacent domains, 932, 1129

Adjust function, 377, 443

Admin Client (Domino Administrator Client), monitoring servers, 1038-1048

Admin screen, 740

Admin tool, 1105

Admin-Backup Activity, 1162

Admin-Purge Activity, 1162

ADMIN4.NSF file, 1008

Administer a server from a browser field (Security tab of Server document), 816

administering
certification, 920
document groups, 1136
Domino Directory, 1118
Domino servers, 1006-1012
email
Domino Administrator, 925-927
Domino IMAP server, 944
Domino POP3 server, 942-943
shared mail, 939-940
groups, 917

administration
@Command functions, 1221
certifiers, security, 859
client, servers, 22-24, 38-40
databases, analyzing data, 1008
function, @Command functions, 1220
servers
for databases, assigning, 1010
for Domino Directory, upgrading from R4 to R5, 787
real-time status, 22
upgraded software systems, 1097
systems (Domino), tasks, 22
tools, 953, 1099

Administration ECL (Execution Control List), 798, 866-868, 1219

Administration Process, 1007
Administration Requests database, 1009
Certification Log database, 1009
Notes
IDs, recertifying, 915-916
usernames, changing, 908, 910-913
servers, hierarchically certified, 1009

subtab (Server Tasks tab in Server document), 822
task (Domino servers), 1026
usernames, deleting, 913-914

Administration Requests database, 1009
upgrading, 787-788, 793
views, 1010

Administration section (Domino Directory documents), fields, 1011

Administration server (ACLs), 423-425

Administration tab
Domino Administrator, 1022
Domino Connection or Domain documents, 927
Server document, 834

Administrative client, 753

Administrative Process, Domino servers, 1009-1011

Administrator. *See* **Domino Administrator**

administrators. *See also* **system administrators**
administration groups, 816
ID files, 770, 848
security, 859

Administrators field (Basics tab of Server document), 811

ADSL (Asymmetrical Digital Subscriber Line), 1125-1126

Advanced database properties dialog box, 997

Advanced page (Replication Settings dialog box), 956

Advanced Person Registration Options dialog box, 1109

Advanced section (Calendar Preferences screen), 170

Advanced tab
Domino Administrator, 1022
Domino database properties, 277
Table properties dialog box, 317
view properties, 366-371

agent function, @Command functions, 1221

Agent Log database, parsing or purging agent, Interfusion Energy (case study), 1176-1177

Agent Manager, 1008
subtab (Server Tasks tab in Server document), 822
task (Domino servers), 1026

1232 AGENT RESTRICTIONS

Agent Restrictions (Security tab of Server document), 817
AgentContext class, 488, 492, 610-611, 613, 643
AgentRunner, Java agents, debugging, 576, 578-579
agents, 453-454
    ACL restrictions, 420
    creating, 620
    disabling Domino database, 274
    Domino Designer, 286, 293-294
    Enable Scheduled Local Agents (user preference), 90
    Java
        applets, comparing, 296
        creating, 36
        debugging with AgentRunner, 576-579
        Hello agent example, 460-462
        help settings, 462
        in Domino, 563-565
    LotusScript
        Hello agent example, 457-460
        help settings, 462-464
    NotesUIWorkspace class, playing tunes, 620-621
    parsing or purging, Interfusion Energy (case study), 1175-1177
    restricted, 817
    reviewing, 817
    synopsis, 286
    writing programming languages, 294
AH (Authentication Header), 882
Alarm event, 487
alarms, options for appointments, 175
Alarms section (Calendar Preferences screen), 170
aliases
    folders, Simple Action, 403
    outline entries, 386
    views, 362
alignment, fields, 332
All Documents (email), 103
All Server Documents, (Configuration tab, Domino Administrator), 1015
Allow anonymous Notes connections field (Security tab of Server document), 814
Allowed to use monitors field (Security tab of Server document), 816

Alt+Enter keyboard shortcut, 312, 802
Alt+P keyboard shortcut, 64
Alt+Tab keyboard shortcut, 193
alternative route selection configuration for email, 936-937
Always Use Area Code field (dial-up modems of Connection document), 838
America Online (AOL), agreement with Lotus, 14
Amount variable, 471
ampersand (&), 1025
Analysis embedded tab (Servers tab, Domino Administrator), 1033
Analysis subtab (Server tab, Admin Client), monitoring servers, 1040
Analysis tab (Domino Administrator), 898
Analyze Database dialog box, 971, 987-988
analyzing
    databases, 971, 987-989
    Domino server performance, 1032-1034
    networks, monitoring, 1075
anchors, 404. *See also* links
anniversaries on calendars, creating, 181-182
Anonymous ACLs (Access Control Lists)
    access, 417
    entries, 268-269
anonymous users, setting up, 908
AOL (America Online), agreement with Lotus, 14
API (Application Programming Interface), 546, 1058
apostrophe ('), 509, 1025
Append files, LotusScript, 535
Append New Column command (Create menu), 350
AppendItemValue, 663
AppleTalk, mobile computing, 209
<APPLET> HTML tag, 91, 596
AppletContainer applets (eSuite), 600, 605-607

applets. *See* Java applets
application designers, encrypting fields, 864
application developers, security, 858
application managers
    applications, ACLs (Access Control Lists), 414
    security, 858
Application Programming Interface (API), 546
application-level proxy servers, 876-877
applications
    ACLs (Access Control Lists), 414, 849
    Administration server, multiple, 425
    AppShare Content Window, 202
    bundles, 13
    creating with Domino Designer, 19-20
    databases, bookmarks, 83, 85
    design services of Web Application Server, 752-753
    Directory Assistance, 416
    Domino
        databases, 257
        security, 848-849
    eSuite Workplace, 583
    for intranets (Domino Designer)
        agents, 286, 293-294
        forms, 285, 290-292
        framesets, 285, 288
        image resources, 295
        Java applets, 295-296
        navigators, 286, 293
        outlines, 285, 287-288
        pages, 285, 289-290
        resources, 294
        script libraries, 297
        sharing fields, 296-297
        views, 286, 292
    Host Control Panel, 202
    IVR (Interactive Voice Response), 1146
    Java, standalone, 567-569
    local encryption, 848
    mail. *See* email
    network monitoring, 1075
    programming in C++, 546
    Sametime, sharing, 202-203
    servers, upgrading R4 to R5, 800-801
    Share Frame window, 202
    standalone, languages, 454

students driving, 202-203
tools for writing, 14
upgrading R4 to R5, 778- 780, 800
Web CGI (common gateway interface), 1163

Appointment forms, 172

appointments
   alarm options, 175
   Mark Private, 175
   Notify me, 175
   Pencil in, 175
   scheduling, 172-173, 175

AppShare Content Window, applications, sharing, 202

architecture
   Domino server, new features, 37-38
   shared nothing, MPP (massively parallel processing), 1083

Archive Activity, 1162

archive files, 545, 573

<ARCHIVE> HTML tag, 596

Archive Profile, 117

Archive Settings
   button, 117
   dialog box, 273

ARCHIVE tag, 596

archives
   Java, 553-555
   Lotus, including inCLASSPATH, 545

archiving
   Domino database documents, 273-274
   email, 117

arguments, 527
   Compact in mixed-release environment, 804
   LotusScript subroutines, passing, 526-528

arrays
   of objects, 616-617
   variables, LotusScript, 500-501
   Variant type, 616

arrowheads (small), 145

AS/400
   data, Interfusion Energy (case study), 1170-1176
   rule, 1165

Ascending sorts, documents, 355-356

ASCII code, 531

Assign Style to Keyboard dialog box, 136

Assign to Keyboard button, 136

Assignment operator, 435

asterisk (*), 108, 145, 334, 815, 1017, 1051, 1184, 1214, 1220

asterisk, forward slash (*/), 548

Asymmetrical Digital Subscriber Line (ADSL), 1125-1126

asynchronous collaboration, 191

at symbol (@), 304

Attach command (File menu), 105, 141

attachform parameter, 657

attachment function, @Command functions, 1221

Attachment icon, 145

attachments
   email, paper clip icon, 356
   files, in rich-text fields, 141
   Mime Conversion, 247

attacks on computers, responding to, 889

attributes
   <FRAME> tag, 392
   framesets, 390
   of fields, changing, 331-332

auditing
   messaging environments, 1093-1095
   trails, data, Interfusion Energy (case study), 1176

authenticated users, setting up, 907

authentication, 851, 1055
   encryption, 863
   Internet security, 884
   LDAP (Lightweight Directory Access Protocol), 750-751, 852
   proxy servers, 877
   signing documents, 656
   troubleshooting, 1053

Authentication Header (AH), 882

Author access
   ACLs, 429
   servers, troubleshooting, 1060-1061

Author ACLs (Access Control Lists)
   fields, 421
   levels, 414

authoring tools
   Domino Design Components, 710-714
   installing, 706
   MSFP (Microsoft FrontPage), 702-707

authorization, troubleshooting, 1055

authors fields, 330

AUTHORS item, documents, adding to, 666

auto attendant software, 1145

Auto Spellcheck option, sending email, 107

auto-type, mobile computing mail, 216

Automatic fixup of corrupt databases field (Transactional Logging tab of Server document), 833

automating tasks, administering Domino servers, 1009, 1011

Autoprocess section (Calendar Preferences screen), 170

awareness (real-time collaboration key term), 190-191

AWT (Abstract Windowing Toolkit), 461, 547

B

<b> tag (HTML), 307

Back button, 54

back-end
   classes, 485-486, 488-491
   operations, 476

Background tab (Page properties dialog box), 304-305

backgrounds
   colors, views, 364
   graphics of Web pages, 304-305
   images in Personal Address Book, 153
   navigators, 399-400
   table/cell, 314, 316

backing up
   files, 784, 789, 798
   SMTP/MTA MAIL.BOX, 791

backslash (\), 434

bandwidth, networks, Domino R5, 1074

Banyan VINES, mobile computing, 209

Basic connectors (Database Connectors), 1160
Basic Scalability Model, 1079-1083
basic user preferences, 89-94
Basics option (User Preferences dialog box), 88
Basics page (Access Control List dialog box), 860
Basics pane (Manage ACL dialog box), 999
Basics tab
 Connection document, 835, 838, 927, 932-933
 Delivery Options dialog box, 106-107
 Domino Administrator, 1017-1018
 Domino database properties, 273-274
 Domain documents, 839-840, 927
 Page properties dialog box, 303-304
 Server Connection documents, 959
 Server Documents, 810-813, 1015
 User ID dialog box, 65
 view properties, 362-363
batch processing, documents, 144
BBS (bulletin board system), 1166
BeanBuilder (BeanMachine), 717
beveled headings, views, 366
bidirectional languages, 261
binary codes, storing, 545
Binary files, LotusScript, 535
Binary Tree, ezMerchant
 setup screens, 725
 Web site, 724
bitmapping fonts, 290
BlindCopyTo fields, 657
<BODY> tag (HTML), 389
Bookmark command (context menu), 250
bookmarks, 85
 Domino Designer window, 284
 folders, 61, 83-84
 icons, 61, 89
 Notes client, 31
 Workspace, 84

Bookmarks file, mobile computing locations, 220
Border tab (Table properties dialog box), 312
borders in tables, 312-313
BR tag (HTML), 308
braces ({ }), 499
brackets, [ ], 303, 692, 1220
brochureware, Web sites, 720
BrowserInfo function, 392
browsers. *See* Web browsers
browsing
 offline, 82
 Web pages, 234
buddy lists, 191, 198
bulletin board system (BBS), 1166
bundles of applications, 13
Business Partners, 1093
business problems, Interfusion Energy (case study), defining, 1164-1165
Business section (Contact form), 154
Button class, 487, 1185
Button properties dialog box, 406
buttons
 % used, 982
 Accept, 866
 Action Bar (Replicator page), 967
 Actions, 180
 Add @Func, 58
 Add Command, 58
 Add Condition, 343
 Add Configuration, 1017
 Add Connection, 958
 Add group, 162
 Add Mailing List, 162
 Add Program, 1025
 Additional Domino Server, 775
 Archive Settings, 117
 Assign to Keyboard, 136
 awareness (red or green), 191
 Back, 54
 Calendar helper, 173
 Cancel, 54
 Categorize, 157
 Certifier ID, 771
 Certify, 916
 Chat, 199
 Check Calendar, 179
 Choose a Service Type, 839
 Choose ports, 959

 Clock helper, 173
 COM5 Options, 211
 Compact, 983
 conditions (Search Builder dialog box), 345
 Configure Service/Edit Configuration, 839
 Console, 1039
 Copy from, 348
 Create, 141, 918
 Create Safe Copy, 856
 Create Stationery, 116
 Customize, 149
 Default Fonts, 89
 Delete, 919
 Delete Action, 913
 Delivery Options, 106, 177, 862
 Drive, 203
 Edit, 127, 919
 Edit Icon, 58
 Edit Server, 1014
 Empty Trash, 109-110
 Enable/Disable, 118
 Enable Web Ahead, 242
 Export, 866
 Float, 193
 Folder, 159
 Folder Action Bar, 978
 Footer, 149
 Formula, 58
 Forward, 54
 Generate Default Outline, 384
 Go Back, 238
 Go Forward, 238
 Header, 148
 hotspots, 406
 Icon Size, 57
 Import, 304, 322, 866
 Indent Entry, 389
 Link to applet on a Web server, 605
 List, 198-199
 Manage, 917
 Migrate, 1103, 1109
 Migrate People, 1102, 1108, 1110
 More Info, 990
 Move, 908
 Move to Folder, 160
 navigation, Sametime, 194
 navigators, 400
 New, 866
 New Agent, 457, 620
 New Entry, 386, 690
 New Folder, 348
 New Form, 326
 New Group Calendar, 184
 New Image Resource, 322
 New Memo, 103, 117
 New Outline, 384
 New Page, 301, 305
 New Replication Monitor, 970

New Rule, 119
New To Do Item, 182
New View, 343, 346
Next, 232, 767
Open URL, 239
Other Actions, 967
Outdent Entry, 389
Paste, 304
Pause, 1040
Preview, 67
Previous, 232
Printer, 67
radio, 329
Recertify, 915
Redefine Styles, 136
Refresh, 54, 239
Registration Server, 903
Remove forms Trash, 110
Rename, 908
Replicate, 964
Reply, 110
Request Cross-certificate, 854
Request Information, 179
Respond, 179
Respond with Comments, 178-179
Restrict Use, 866
Results, 971
rollover, creating, 717
Save and Close, 919
Save Set, 57
Schedule Meeting, 160
Scheduler, 176-177
Search, 54, 239
Security Options, 94, 867
Send, 105, 199
Send & Receive, 967
Send and File, 159
Send and Receive Mail, 225
Set database quota to, 990
Set ID File, 771
Set Password, 64
Set Path and Filenames, 987
Show Status, 234
Start, 967
Stop, 239, 1040
Style, 315
Submit, 201
task, 60-61
TCP/IP Options, 233
Template Server, 770, 786
Tools, 110, 169, 181, 1040
Trace, 234
Use Outline, 396
User Dictionary, 89
Write Memo, 158
By Field option (Search Builder dialog box), 345
ByVal keyword, 522-523

C

C++, windows applications, programming, 546
CA (Certificate Authority), 244-245
CAB (cabinet) files, 545, 554
cabinets tag, 596
caching Web pages, 82, 877
calculating sales tax, 627-628
Caledon WebTrans Web site, 726
calendar and mail database, 77-79
Calendar
  applets, 583, 597-598
  Entry command (Create menu), 172
  Entry forms, 160, 169, 172
  function, @Command functions, 1221
  helper button, 173
  icon, 172
  Information tab (Domain documents), 840-841, 927
  Preferences, 169-171
  views, 168-169, 183-184, 362-363
calendaring
  Notes databases, 187-188
  overview, 168-169
  server tasks, 187
  using with other software, 187
  while traveling, 185-186
calendars
  anniversaries, 181-182
  appointments, 172-175
  Calendar Entry forms, 169
  Calendar view, 169
  delegating reading or editing, 171
  elements, 169
  entries, 78, 172
  events, deleting, 182
  Group Calendars, 169, 184
  meetings, 175-181
  Meetings view, 169
  preferences, setting up, 169-171
  reminders, creating, 182
  Resource Reservations database, 186
  To Do lists, managing, 182
  Trash view, 169
  viewing, 183-184
Call at Times field (Schedule tab of Connection document), 837

call by reference or value parameters, 527
Call Entry command (Create menu), 225
Call keyword, 526
call parameter, 657
call pursuit/find me software, 1145
Call statement, 656
calling, LotusScript subroutines, 525-526
calling cards, mobile computing, 218
Cancel button, 54
canonical formats, hierarchial names, 761
capacity planning, servers, 1085-1089
cards
  fax, 1148
  voice, 1144
Casahl Web site, 732
cascading style sheets (CSS), 303
case sensitivity
  JavaScript, 468
  of methods, 610
  names of rows, 320
  passwords, 51, 63-64
case studies. *See* Interfusion Energy
Catalog
  servers, mobile computing locations, 215
  task (Domino servers), 1026
CATALOG.NSF file, 1008
catalogs
  Directory Catalogs, 1124, 1136
  Domino databases, 275
  for databases, creating, 1001
categories in documents, 334, 371
Categories field, sorting documents, 355
Categorize
  button, 157
  dialog box, 158
categorized documents, 145-146
categorizing email contacts (Personal Address Book), 156-158

cc:Mail

cc:Mail
  Domain documents (Domino Directory Domain documents), 841
  free downloading, 1137
  MTA, 937
  to Notes migration tools, 1101-1104
  Post Office Information dialog box, 1102
  Upgrade Advanced Settings dialog box, 1103
  upgrading, 1104-1107
  users, migration preparations, 1101-1102

CD (Composite Data or Compound Document), 667-669

CD records, 667

Cell Borders tab (Table properties dialog box), 312

cells in tables, 314-316

Certificate Authority (CA), 244-245

certificates
  cross-certification, 852-854, 1054
  expired, troubleshooting, 1053-1054
  IDs, 65, 850-851
  servers, accessing, 65
  signing databases, 994
  SSLs (Secure Socket Layers), 244-245

Certificates
  page (User ID dialog box), 855
  tab (User ID dialog box), 65

certification
  administering, 920
  cross-certification, 852-856
  for Domino domains, 761-762
  flat
    certificate exchange, 856-857
    troubleshooting, 1053
  ICSA (International Computer Security Association) Certification for firewalls, 879
  logs, creating, 770-771
  troubleshooting, 1053

Certification Log database, 1009

Certified Lotus Instructor (CLI), 859

Certifier documents (Domino Directory), 842, 1011

Certifier ID button, 771

certifier ID file, 848-851

certifiers
  for OUs (organizational units), 762, 771-772
  User IDs, 761

Certify button, 916

certifying Notes IDs, 915-916

CERTLOG.NSF file, 1008

CGI (common gateway interface)
  Activities (NotesPump/LEI), 1163
  scripts, Internet security, 890

CGI Gateway applets (eSuite), 600

chain topology, 929

chairpersons of meetings, actions, 179-181

characters, LotusScript, 530-531

Chart applets (eSuite), 593-595

charts, random (eSuite), generated by JavaScript, 603

Chat (Java applet), 194, 199

Chat button, 199

chat rooms, 199

Check All Schedules, invitees, viewing, 177

check boxes, 57, 329

Check Calendar button, 179

Check passwords on Notes IDs field (Security tab of Server document), 814

Check spelling, 585

Check Subscriptions (user preference), 89

ChildCount property, 640

children, inheritance, 482

Choose a Service Type button, 839

Choose Certifier dialog box, 1031

Choose ports button, 959

Choose Profile dialog box, 1110

Chrysler, SCORE (Supplier Cost Reduction Effort), 722-723

Cint function, 471

ciphers, 870

circles
  drawing navigator object, 401
  JavaScript, 36

circuit-level proxy servers, 876-877

Class keyword or statement, 504

classes, 479-480
  AgentContext, 488, 492, 610-611, 613
  back-end, 485-486, 488-491
  Button, 487, 1185
  collections, 481
  creating, 504-505
  Database, 492
  Domino Object Model, 1184-1185
  Field, 487, 1185
  class files, 545
  front-end, 485-487, 669
  inheritance, 482, 667
  Item, 664-665
  Java, 553-555, 632
    ACL, 636
    AgentContext, 610-613, 643
    Database, 635-636
    DbDirectory, 635-636
    Document, 645-658
    Form, 644-645
    Session, 610-613
    View, 638
  Java/LotusScript comparisons, 637
  LotusScript, 523, 632
    date and time variables, 618-619
    Java comparisons, 492-493
    NotesACL, 636
    NotesDatabase, 632-635
    NotesDocument, 645-658
    NotesDocumentCollection, 642-643
    NotesForm, 644-645
    NotesSession, 610-611, 613
    NotesView, 638-640
    NotesViewColumn, 642
    NotesViewEntry, 640-641
    NotesViewEntryCollection, 640-641
    NotesViewNavigator, 641
    subroutines, 521
  lowercase letters, 555
  Navigator, 487, 1185
  Notes, 618-619, 1185
  NotesACL, 488, 675, 1189
  NotesACLEntry, 488, 675, 1190
  NotesAgent, 488, 1190-1191
  NotesDatabase, 488, 492, 1191-1192

NotesDateRange, 488, 1192-1193
NotesDateTime, 488, 1193
NotesDbDirectory, 488, 1193-1194
NotesDocument, 480, 489, 663-664, 671, 1194-1195
NotesDocumentCollection, 481, 489, 1195-1196
NotesEmbeddedObject, 489, 670-671, 1196
NotesException, fields, 556
NotesForm, 489, 1196
NotesInternational, 489, 1197
NotesItem, 482, 489, 663-667, 1197-1198
NotesLog, 489, 1198
NotesName, 489, 674-675, 1198-1199
NotesNewsletter, 489, 1199
NotesOutline, 490, 1200
NotesOutlineEntry, 490, 1200-1201
NotesRegistration, 490, 1201-1202
NotesReplication, 490, 1202
NotesRichTextItem, 482, 490, 666-667, 671, 1202-1203
NotesRichTextParagraphStyle, 490, 670, 1203
NotesRichTextStyle, 490, 668-669, 1203-1204
NotesRichTextTab, 490, 1204
NotesSession, 490, 492, 610-615, 1204-1205
NotesThread, 559
NotesTimer, 490, 671-674, 1205
NotesUIDatabase, 487, 616, 624-625, 1185-1186
NotesUIDocument, 487, 627-628, 1186-1187
NotesUIView, 487, 625-627, 1187-1188
NotesUIWorkspace, 487, 619-624, 1188-1189
NotesView, 490, 616, 1205-1206
NotesViewColumn, 491, 1206-1207
NotesViewEntry, 491, 1207-1208
NotesViewEntryCollection, 491, 1208
NotesViewNavigator, 491, 1208-1209
objects, 613-617
ODBC (open database connectivity), 1209
ODBCConnection, 491, 1209-1210

ODBCQuery, 491, 1210
ODBCResultSet, 491, 1210-1211
parameters, 445-446
parent, 667
RichTextItem, (Java), 669-670
RichTextParagraphStyle, (Java), 670
RichTextStyle, (Java), 669-670
Runnable, 561
scope, 497
Session, 492, 562-563, 610-613
Thread, 557-559

CLASSPATH (Java environment variable), 545-546

clauses
Else, ElseIf, or Then, 511
Until or While, 515

Clear
command (Edit menu), 350
method, 639

CLI (Certified Lotus Instructor), 859

Click
event handler, 525
formulas, hotspots, 320

clicking actions, navigators, 402-403

client-side objects (CSOs), 486

clients
accessing DOM, 485-486
administration, new features, 38, 40
Administrative, 753
authentication, 884
client functionality, 191
Domino, administration, 22-24
Domino Administrator, 14
Domino Designer, 14
  applications, creating, 19-20
  new features, 32-37
  tools, 19
imaging technology integration, client/server integration, 1154
Notes, 13-14
  bookmarks, 31
  browsing the Web, 18
  drop-down actions, 30-31
  email, 29-31
  framesets, opening, 691
  IDs, 51
  installing, 46, 48-50
  logging on, 51-52
  new features, 28-31
  Notes view, 684
  passwords, 51-52
  upgrading R4 to R5, 778-783, 797-800

  versus Web browsers, 682
  welcome page, 28-29
software, imaging technology integration, 1154
types, 47-48, 767-768
upgraded software systems, 1099
upgrading R4 to R5, 797
Windows NT, passwords, 63

Clipboard, graphics, 304

Clock helper button, 173

Close command (File menu), 108, 146, 271

clustering
with Domino Enterprise Server, 755-756
ICM (Internet Cluster Manager), Domino R5, 1084
scalability, Domino R5, 1083-1084
servers, 1084

clusters
analysis, Domino server performance, 1034
databases, managing, 991-992
Domino Directory, 1011
Domino servers, upgrading, 797
managing, 755

CN (Common Name), 1120

code
code point, 531
HTML (Hypertext Markup Language)
  [ ] (square brackets), 692
  multiple applets (eSuite), 595
  Project Scheduler applets (eSuite), 596
  Spreadsheet applets (eSuite), 590
  spreadsheet on HTML page, 591
  Word Processor applets (eSuite), 591
Java, debugging, 575-578
LotusScript, reusing code, 538-540
Notes and Domino sharing, 13
SMTP router, 812

coherence, LotusScript subroutines, 520-521

COL files, 733

collaboration
asynchronous, 191
real-time, key terms, 191
Sametime, 203-204
synchronous, 191

Collaboration options page

Collaboration options page, 243
collaborative learning
   applications, sharing, 202-203
   Chat (Java applet), 199
   chat rooms, 199
   driving applications, instructors revoking control, 203
   Follow tool, 203
   participants, knowing who is online, 198-199
   Private Message (Java applet), 200
   quiz boxes, 202
   quizzes, 201
   Sametime, 190-193
   students, 199-200
   whiteboards, 195-198
Collapse/Expand Metaconnector (LEI), 1161
collapsible tables, 317-318
collapsing
   categorized documents, 145
   Text Properties InfoBox, 128
   twisties, views, 363
Collect task, 940-942, 1026-1027
collections, 481
   document, 638
   UnprocessedDocuments, 643
Collector task, email routing, 939
colon (:), 509, 953
colors
   backgrounds, table/cell, 314-316
   fonts, 128
   views, 364-365
Colors tab (Table properties dialog box), 315
COLS attributes, framesets, 390
column formula functions, 1217
Column properties box, 350
Column Properties
   command (Design menu), 358
   dialog box, 351, 358
columns
   defining, 349
   Delete Special, 311
   icons, 356, 358
   in tables, 310-314
   Insert Special, 311
   small arrowheads, 145
   sorting documents, 354-356
   triangles (small), 144
   view columns, 144

   view properties, 348-350
   views
      color, 365
      creating, 350
      date formatting, 360-361
      deleting, 350
      extending, 365
      fonts, 358-359
      HTML links, 361-362
      naming columns, 361
      numeric formatting, 359-360
ColumnValues property, 640
COM5 Options button, 211
combo boxes, 330
Command Activity, 1161
Command function, 446-447
command-line execution, Activities (NotesPump/LEI), 1163
commands
   @Command functions
      administration, 1220-1221
      agent, 1221
      attachment, 1221
      calendar, 1221
      create, 1221
      deleted, 1228
      design, 1221-1222
      edit, 1222-1223
      file, 1223
      folder, 1223-1224
      form, 1224
      help, 1224
      HotSpot, 1224
      layout, 1224
      mail, 1224
      miscellaneous, 1228
      navigate, 1225
      navigator, 1225
      object, 1225
      open, 1225
      paste, 1225
      refresh, 1225
      replicator, 1225
      section, 1226
      ShowHide, 1226
      SmartIcons, 1226
      text, 1226
      tools, 1226-1227
      UserID, 1227
      view, 1227-1228
      window, 1228
      workspace, 1228
   Actions menu
      Accept Encryption Key, 866
      Add Connection, 932
      Add Recipients, 118
      Cross-certify Attached ID File, 855

      Empty Trash, 90
      Folder, 160
      Forward, 251
      Internet Options, 242
      PlayTune, 620
      Recertify Selected Servers, 1031
      Tools, 77, 117-118, 169
      Tools, Add Sender to Address Book, 153, 156
      Tools, Add Sender to Personal Address Book, 118
      Tools, Import Holidays, 181
      Tools, Out of Office, 118
      Tools, Visit Web Page, 161
   context menu, Bookmarks, 250
   Create menu
      Append New Column, 350
      Calendar Entry, 172
      Call Entry, 225
      Contact, 154
      Design, 671
      Embedded Element, 378, 409
      Folder, 159
      Horizontal Rule, 323
      HotSpot, 137, 404
      Hotspot, Link Hotspot, 113-114
      Image Resource, 323, 408
      Insert Shared Field, 333
      Java Applet, 605
      Layout Region, 335
      Mail, 103, 172
      Memo, 103
      Page Break, 324
      Picture, 321, 408
      Reservation, 186
      Section, 323, 338
      Server, 1017, 1025
      Site Profile, 186
      Special menu, 113
      Special, Link Message, 113
      Subscription, 86
      Table, 138, 310
      To Do, 182
   Database menu
      New Copy, 265
      Refresh Design, 277
   Design menu
      Column Properties, 358
      Preview, 468
      Remove Graphic Background, 400
   Edit menu
      Clear, 350
      Copy, 146
      Copy as Link, 113, 137, 387
      Cut, 333
      Paste, 113, 146, 333
      Properties, 312, 378
      Unread Marks, 89, 108

CONFIGURING 1239

File menu
   Attach, 105, 141
   Close, 108, 146, 271
   Database, 80, 689, 770, 785-786, 802-804, 954, 1000-1002, 1058
   Document Properties, 654
   Import, 576
   Mobile, 208, 235
   Preferences, 88-89, 105, 140, 210, 243
   Preferences, SmartIcon Settings, 55, 58
   Preferences, User Preferences, 57, 121, 233
   Print, 66, 147
   Replication, 223, 804, 954, 957
   SendTo, 93
   Tools, 63, 854
Help menu, Help Topics, 464
Pull, 962, 964-965
Push, 962, 964-965
Replicate, 950-952, 965
replication, 965
server, 1008, 1040
Start New Task, 1039
Stop Task, 1039
Table menu
   Delete Selected Row(s), 311
   Merge Cells, 316
   Split Cells, 316
   Table Properties, 312
Task, 1040
tell http restart, 572
Tell Router Exit, 938
Tell Router Quit, 938
Tell server, email routing, 939
Tell Task, 1039
Text menu
   Named Style, 135
   Pass-Thru HTML, 301
   Permanent Pen, 129
   Text Properties, 301
Users, 1040
View menu
   Design, 271
   Expand/Collapse, 145
   Refresh, 109
   Stack Replica Icons, 954
Welcome Page menu, Create New Page style, 71

comma (,), 219

comments
Java, 548-549
LotusScript, 509
views, 362

Comments tab
Domino Connection documents, 927
Server Connection documents, 960

commerce, electronic, 720-721
Chrysler's SCORE (Supplier Cost Reduction Effort), 722-723
credit cards, 726
Internet.Com, e-commerce section, 724
Net.Commerce (IBM), 725-726
products, 724-725
selling online, 723-727

Common Name (CN), 1120

Common Object Request Broker Architecture (CORBA), 21, 94, 573-575, 753

CommonUserName property, 613

communications
faxes, integrating, 1147-1152
imaging technology, integrating, 1152-1155
IVR (Interactive Voice Response) applications, 1146
messaging, unified, 1142
paging, 1146
paper, reducing usage, 1146-1147
voice mail, 1143-1145

Compact
arguments in mixed-release environment, 804
button, 983
Databases dialog box, 983
task (Domino servers), 1027

compacting databases, 804, 982-983

company address book. *See* **Public Directory**

Compare Notes public keys field (Security tab of Server document), 813

comparing
agents and Java applets, 296
Domino and Microsoft Exchange, 16
forms, documents, and Web pages, 325-326

compiled languages, 453

computed
fields, 330-331
subforms, 338

concatenation, text, 437

Concatenation operator (text values), 435

conceptual models, Domino Object Model, 21-22

Condition drop-down box (Search Builder dialog box), 344

Configuration documents, 709
Configuration tab, Domino Administrator, 1016-1024
Domino Directory, 842

configuration settings of servers, updating, 1016-1017

Configuration Settings documents (Domino Directory), 1011

Configuration tab
Admin Client, servers, monitoring, 1048
Domino Administrator, 899, 925-927, 1007
   All Server Documents, 1015
   Configuration Documents, 1016-1024
   Current Server Document, 1013-1014
   document maintenance, 1012-1013
   replication, 953
   Server Configuration, 1013
   Server Connection documents, creating, 958
   Server Document tabs, 1014-1015

configurations
current (Basic Scalability Model), 1079
mobile computing, 207
   Location document, 214-220
   modems, 211-213
   Passthru servers, 220-222
   Personal Address Book, 213-214
   ports, 208-211
   protocols, 209-210
   replication, 222-223

Configure Service/Edit Configuration button, 839

configuring
alternative route selections for email, 936-937
connections for email, 927
Directory Profile, 785
domains for email, 927
Domino servers, 1012
firewalls, 1169
Internet clients with Domino POP3, 943
Internet mail servers, 792
multithreaded email routing, 938

1240 CONFIGURING

networks, Interfusion Energy (case study), 1169-1170
Non-adjacent Domino domains, email routing, 933-935
server documents, 1012-1013
servers
   Interfusion Energy (case study), 1169-1170
   multiple servers, 1017
SSLs (Secure Socket Layers), 244-245
Web Retriever Configuration, 245-246

Conflict Checking section (Calendar Preferences screen), 170

conflicts, save or replication, 971-972

connecting databases, solutions, 1163-1164

Connecting document, 1011

Connection Broker Metaconnector (LEI), 1161

Connection documents, 76, 834, 928-930, 986, 1011
Basics tab, 835, 932-933
creating, 958, 960
database replication, 958
dial-up modems, 838
email routing, 932-933
LANs (local area networks), 835
Network Dialup connection, 838-839
Passthru servers, 221, 838
Routing and Replication tab, 836-837
Replication/Routing tab, 962-963
Schedule tab, 837

connections. *See also* **mobile computing**
configuring for email, 927
mobile computing, 227
to servers, tracing, 99

Connections Documents (Connections tab, Domino Administrator), 1024

Connections tab (Domino Administrator) Connections Documents, 1024

Connectors (Lotus Domino), 1159-1161

Console button, 1039

Const statement, 499, 538-539

constants
formulas, 434
functions, 1220
LotusScript variables, 499-500

Contact
command (Create menu), 154
form, 154-156

contacts, email
adding to Personal Address Book, 153-158
background images in Personal Address Book, 153
categorizing in Personal Address Book, 156-157
creating mailing lists, 162-163
folders, 159-160
group sorting in Personal Address Book, 153
help adding to Personal Address Book, 154-155
LDAP (Lightweight Directory Access Protocol) queries in Personal Address Book, 153
keeping track of, 159
managing, 152, 164-165
Personal Address Book, 74, 152
personal preferences, 152-153
scheduling meetings, 160
sending, 158, 161-162

Contacts By Category view, 157

Contacts view, 157

containers, 481

content/data growth, scalability, 1080

context, concept for hypertext links, 682

Context Icons check box, 57

context menu commands, Bookmark, 250

context sensitive
Actions menu, 54
menu bars, Domino Designer window, 284
SmartIcons, 55

continuation character, 509

control flow
functions, 1219
repetition, 512-516
selection, 510-512

Controlled Access dialog box, 338

Controlled Access Sections, ACL roles, 421

controlled mode (whiteboards), 197

controls, replication topologies, 1132-1133

conversation tools (real-time collaboration key term), 191

conversion functions, 442, 1215

Conversions Options tab (Domino Administrator), 1021

cookies, 92

copies, replicas of databases, 985-986

Copy as Link command (Edit menu), 113, 137, 387

Copy command (Edit menu), 146

Copy Database dialog box, 266

Copy from button, 348

copying
documents, 146
Domino databases, 264-266
email, preventing, 107
ID files, safe copying, 930-931

CopyItem, 663

CopyTo field, 657

CORBA (Common Object Request Broker Architecture), 21, 94, 573-575, 753

core dumps (UNIX), troubleshooting, 1057-1058

Corporate Image Software Web site, 724

corrupted databases, repairing, 994-996

Count property, 650

Counterpane Systems, PPTP (Point to Point Tunneling Protocol), 881

CPUs, Domino R5, 1073-1074

crashes of servers, troubleshooting, 1057-1058

Create
button, 141, 918
documents privilege (ACLs), 420
menu, 54
method, NotesDatabase class, 633-634
new databases field (Security tab of Server document), 815
personal agents or folders/views privileges (ACLs), 420
privileges (Domino Directory), 156

replica databases field (Security tab of Server document), 815
shared folders/views privilege (ACLs), 420
Create Folder dialog box, 83
create function, @Command functions, 1221
Create Java Applet dialog box, 605
Create LotusScript/Java agents privilege (ACLs), 420
Create menu commands
Append New Column, 350
Calendar Entry, 172
Call Entry, 225
Contact, 154
Design, 671
Embedded Element, 378, 409
Folder, 159
Horizontal Rule, 323
HotSpot, 137, 404
Hotspot, Link Hotspot, 113-114
Image Resource, 323, 408
Insert Shared Field, 333
Java Applet, 605
Layout Region, 335
Mail, 103, 172
Memo, 103
Page Break, 324
Picture, 321, 408
Reservation, 186
Section, 323, 338
Server, 1017, 1025
Site Profile, 186
Special, Link Message, 113
Special menu, 113
Subscription, 86
Table, 138, 310
To Do, 182
Create New Folder Dialog box, 978
Create New Frameset dialog box, 393, 690
Create New Link dialog box, 979
Create New Page Style command (Welcome Page menu), 71
Create Paragraph Style dialog box, 135
Create Safe Copy button, 856
Create Stationery button, 116
Create Table dialog box or Smarticon, 138
Create View dialog box, 346

CreateCopy method, 634-635
Created
function, 443
property, 649
CreateDocument method, 635, 646
CreateFromTemplate method, 634-635
CreateReplica method, 634-635
CreateReplyMessage method, 658
CreateTimer method, NotesTimer object, 671
credit cards, electronic commerce, 726
Cross Certify ID dialog box, 855
Cross Domain Configuration document, 986
cross-certification, 852-853, 1054
on demand, 856
Domino servers, 930-931
with email, 854-856
with snail mail, 856
by telephone, 856
Cross-Certifier documents (Domino Directory), 842
Cross-certify Attached ID File command (Actions menu), 855
CSOs (client-side objects), 486
CSS (cascading style sheets), 303
CStr function, 533
Ctrl+B keyboard shortcut, 128
Ctrl+C keyboard shortcut, 146
Ctrl+E keyboard shortcut, 127, 146
Ctrl+I keyboard shortcut, 128
Ctrl+M keyboard shortcut, 103
Ctrl+O keyboard shortcut, 80
Ctrl+P keyboard shortcut, 66
Ctrl+Shift+F9 keyboard shortcut, 995
Ctrl+U keyboard shortcut, 128
Ctrl+V keyboard shortcut, 113, 146
Ctrl+W keyboard shortcut, 108, 146
Currency data type, 498
current configuration (Basic Scalability Model), 1079

current document functions, 1216-1217
Current Server Document (Configuration tab, Domino Administrator), 1013-1014
customers, Interfusion Energy (case study), 1171, 1175-1176
Customize button or dialog box, 149
customizing
replication of databases, 961-968
SmartIcons, 55, 57
system templates, 782
welcome pages, 71-73
Cut command (Edit menu), 333
CyberCash Web site, 726
Cycle SmartIcon, 136

D

daily management, data, Interfusion Energy (case study), 1176-1177
data
activity logging, 1176
displaying in documents, 124-125
encrypting, 863
integrating, tools, 733-740
organizing, 323-324
real-time, 1168-1169
sources, non-system-based, 732
data access applets (eSuite), 598-600
Data Interchange Format (DIF), 1171
data models (object models), 483-484
data presentation applets (eSuite)
Address Book applets, 598
Calendar applets, 597-598
Chart applets, 593-595
multiple applets, 595-596
Presentation Graphics applets, 597
Project Scheduler applets, 596
Spreadsheet applets, 589-591
Word Processor applets, 591-593
data types
Currency, 498
Double, 498
fields, 126-127, 328, 330

DATA TYPES

for fields, 124
Integer, 498
Java, 550-551
Long, 498
LotusScript variables, 498-499
Single, 498
Variant, 498

Database Action Bar (Domino Administrator, Files tab), 981-982

Database
    class, 492, 635-636
    command (File menu), 80, 689, 770, 785-786, 802-804, 954, 1000-1002, 1058

Database Connectors, Basic, 1160

Database Fixup dialog box, 996

Database Manager, 119, 976

Database menu commands
    New Copy, 265
    Refresh Design, 277

Database Monitor (ACL Monitor), 1134

Database Properties dialog box, 272, 990
    Advanced tab, 277
    Basics tab, 273-274
    Design tab, 275-276
    Information tab, 274-275
    Launch tab, 276
    Printing tab, 275

Database Properties InfoBox, 865
    email, archiving, 117
    Printer tab, 148

Database property, 632

Database Quota Information dialog box, 990

databases. *See also* **documents**
    access functions, 1216
    accessing with Web browsers, 683-685
    ACLs (Access Control Lists), 636, 982
        managing, 1133-1134
        settings, 998-999
    administration, analyzing data, 1008
    Administration Requests, 1009
        upgrading, 787-788, 793
        views, 1010
    administration servers, assigning, 1010
    Agent Log database, parsing or purging agent, 1176-1177
    analyzing, 971, 987-989

bookmarks, 83, 85
catalogs, creating, 1001
certificates, signing, 994
Certification Log, 1009
clusters, managing, 991-992
compacting, 982-983
components, selective replication, 954, 956
connecting, solutions, 1163-1164
corrupted, repairing, 994-996
creating, 20, 689, 816
Database Action Bar (Domino Administrator, Files tab), 981-982
default location, 1000
designs, updating, 1000
Document table bitmap optimization property, 1076
documents, 324, 342, 638, 662
Domino Administrator, 976
Domino R5, 1075-1077
Don't maintain unread marks property, 1075
Don't overwrite free space property, 1076
Don't support specialized response hierarchy property, 1076
email, shared mail, managing, 942
forms, 662, 671
full text indexes, 983-9845
functions, 1219
HTML (Hypertext Markup Language), 697
indexes, size factors, 984
KM (knowledge management), 18-19
libraries, 1001-1002, 1132
Limit entries
    in $Revisions fields property, 1077
    in $UpdatedBy fields property, 1076
links, 980-981
LotusScript, NotesDatabase class, 632-635
mail and calendar, 77-79
MAIL.BOX, 938
Maintain LastAccessed property, 1076
maintaining, 981-982
managing, 22, 976, 981-982
moving, 986-987
multidatabase indexing, 992-994
Notes
    calendaring and scheduling, 187-188
    HTML documents, 697

    R5 features, 687-689, 691
    Web-oriented designs, 685-687
notes, locating, 992
ODS (On-Disk Structure), 800
opening, 237, 1058-1059
parameters, 445-446
personal address book, 74-76
Personal Web Navigator, 82-83
printing, testing, 66-67
properties
    policies for, 1077
    setting, 996-997
Public directory, 80-82
quotas, setting, 989-990
R4
    preventing conversion to R5, 983
    replicating, 804
    upgrading to R5, 800-804
relational, 18
    Percussion Notrix, 733
    Replic-Action, 732
replication, 20
    access control, establishing, 952-953
    administration tools, 953
    Connection documents, 958-960
    copies, 985-986
    customizing, 961-962
    direction, specifying, 962
    disabling, 963
    finding, 85
    forcing, 964
    history, 951
    IDs, 953
    initiating, 957
    maintaining replicas, 968
    managing, 991
    monitoring, 968-972
    objects, defining, 950-952
    priorities, 963
    Pull-Only, 949
    Pull-Pull, 949
    Pull-Push, 949
    Push-Only, 949
    refusing requests, 963
    Replica task, 949
    Replicate command, 950-952
    scheduling, 957-960, 965-966
    scope of, 962
    servers, 948-949, 958
    settings, 956-957
    testing, 967-968
    time limits, 963
    topologies, 1129-1131
    troubleshooting, 1059
    workstation-to-server, 950
    workstations, 948

Resource Reservations, 186
rolling out, 1000-1001
SCOS (shared copy object store), 863
servers, planning, 1123
standard, 73
Statistics & Events, 1134
status of, 991-992
subscriptions, 86-87
systems integration, 1158-1164
tables (Interfusion Energy case study), 1171
10% unused space, determining, 982
User Registration Queue, 902
Web registration, downloading, 815

databases (Domino), 256
About documents, updating, 270-271
accessing, 256
ACLs (Access Control Lists), 267-268, 347
agents, disabling, 274
copying, 264-266
design elements, 269-270
documents, 256-257, 350
 archiving, 273-274
 folders, 342
 inheritance, 351-353
 response, 351
 response to response, 353-354
 sorting, 354-356
 views, 342
embedding elements, 409-410
fields, 256-257
folders, 342, 348
forms, saving, 274
frames, 391-392, 395
framesets, 389-398
full text indexes, 277
graphics, 274
hotspots, 403-408
items, 256
JavaScript, 274
navigators, 399-403
ODS (On-Disk Structure), 257
outlines
 Action entries, 387
 creating, 384-385
 entries, 385-386
 hiding entries, 388-389
 inserting in pages, 395, 397
 Link entries, 387
 moving entries, 389
 Named Element entries, 387-388
 URL entries, 388
programs, 257
properties, 272-277

refreshing, 277
relational database comparisons, 256-257
release 5, 257-258
replacing, 278
replication, 266-267
SSL (Secure Socket Layer), 274
templates, 259-264
Using document, updating, 271-272
views
 access lists, 371-372
 accessing through ODBC, 369
 actions, 373-374
 aliases, 362
 browsers, 369-371
 Calendar, 362-363
 categories, 371
 color, 364-365
 column properties, 348-350
 comments, 362
 creating, 342-343
 creating columns, 350
 date formatting, 360-361
 default settings, 363-364
 deleting columns, 350
 document selection, 343-346
 embedded, 374-378
 fonts, 358-359
 hiding, 362
 HTML links, 361-362
 icons, 356, 358
 indexes, 366-368, 371
 naming columns, 361
 numeric formatting, 359-360
 opening, 343
 private, 346-348
 properties, 362
 shared, 346-348
 Single Category embedded, 379-380
 unread marks, 368

Databases folder, Workspace, 84
DataMirror, 734
date and time
 field, 329
 functions, 1216
 variables, 618-619
Date Picker, embedding, 410
dates
 formatting, 331-332, 360-361
 functions, 208, 443
 values, formulas, 434
Day of the Week field (Schedule tab of Connection document), 837

DBColumn function, 354, 446
DbDirectory class, (Java), 635-636
DbLookup function, 444-446
DbName function, 444
DDCFP (Domino Design Components for MS FrontPage), 707
DDE (dynamic data exchange) functions, 1219
debugging Java, 576-579
declaring
 LotusScript strings, 532
 variables, 502-503
DECnet Pathworks, mobile computing, 209
Decommission Server, Domino server performance, 1034
DECS (Domino Enterprise Connection Services), 738-739, 752, 1158, 1163
 Admin screen, 740
 Domino server tasks, 1027
Default Fonts button, 89
DEFAULT keyword, formulas, 438
Default Value formula, 332-333
defaults
 background images in Personal Address Book, 153
 Domino Administrator files, location backup, 798
 location of databases, 1000
 Notes as Web browser, 93
 settings, views, 363-364
 timeout interval (TCP/IP), 233
 welcome pages, 70-71
 Workstation security, setting, 798
Defaults section (Calendar Preferences screen), 169
defense building, Internet security, 888-889
defining
 actions, 334
 columns, 349
 email preferences, 110-113
 hotspots, 290
 local directories, 164
 Notes documents, 124
 objects of replication, 950-952
 ports, mobile computing, 210-211
 public directories, 164

DEFINING

rich text, 290
roles, ACLs, 421
TCP/IP ports, 232, 234

Deftype statement, 503

delegating functions, email, 79, 112-113

Delegation section (Calendar Preferences screen), 171

Delete Action button, 913

Delete
button, 919
documents privilege (ACLs), 420

Delete Folder dialog box, 979

Delete Link dialog box, 981

Delete Person dialog box, 914

Delete Selected Row(s) command (Table menu), 311

Delete Special (rows and columns), 311

Delete statement, 506

deleted function, @Command functions, 1228

deleting
calendar events, 182
columns, from views, 350
documents, 143-144, 160, 347
Domino databases, 263
email documents, 109
folders, 979
full text indexes, 984-985
groups, 919
links to databases or folders, 981
shared email messages with Collect task, 942
SmartIcons, 56
soft deletions, 348
usernames, 913-915

delimiters, constants, 499

Delivery Options
button, 106, 177, 862
dialog box, 106-107, 178

Delivery Priority option, sending email, 107

Delivery Report option, sending email, 106

Deny List documents (Domino Directory), 1011

deployment, Domino, technical planning, 759

Depositor, ACLs (Access Control Lists)
access, 429

level, 414

DescendantCount property, 640

Descending sorts, documents, 355-356

Descriptions check box, 57

Design command
Create menu, 671
View menu, 271

design documents, 644-645

design elements. See Domino Designer

design function, @Command functions, 1221-1222

Design Icon dialog box, 272

Design menu commands
Column Properties, 358
Preview, 468
Remove Graphic Background, 400

Design pane (Domino Designer window), 283, 285

Design tab, Domino database properties, 275-276

Design task (Domino servers), 1027

Designer (Domino). See Domino Designer

designing
Domino databases, 269-270
forms, 324-325
intranet applications, Domino Designer elements, 285-297
networks, 1119
Notes databases
R5 features, 687-689, 691
Web-oriented, 685-687
View Applets, (Java), 683
Web pages, Domino Designer, 282-297
Web site navigation, 33

DESKTOP.DSK file, saving views, 347

desktops
eSuite Workplace, 583
imaging technology integration, desktop-based imaging, 1155
Notes, Replicator page, 965, 967
Web pages, opening, 248

Destination Area Code field (dial-up modems of Connection document), 838

Destination Country Code field (dial-up modems of Connection document), 838

Destination Domain field (Basics tab of Connection document), 835

Destination Folder dialog box, 47

Destination Phone Number field (dial-up modems of Connection document), 838

Destination Server field (Basics tab of Connection document), 835

developers, applications, security, 858

development environments, Java, 544

DevPack (eSuite)
applet categories, 589
InfoBus, 588-589
installing, 604
JavaBeans, 587

DFC (Domino Fusion Connector), 707
Configuration document, 709
DIS (Domino Import Service), installing, 708
loading, 715

dial modes, mobile computing, 212

dial-up, Domino SMTP R5 server, 796

dial-up modems (Connection document), 838

Dial-up Networking (DUN), 839

dialing
mobile computing locations, 218-219
modem configurations, 213

dialog boxes
Access Control List, 269, 860
ACL, 415, 418, 421-422, 426
Action Hotspot properties, 407
Add Role, 422
Add User, 417
Additional Setup, 211
Advanced database properties, 997
Advanced Person Registration Options, 1109
Analyze Database, 971, 987-988
Archive Settings, 273
Assign Style to Keyboard, 136
Button properties, 406
Categorize, 158
cc:Mail Post Office Information, 1102

Directory Assistance 1245

cc:Mail Upgrade Advanced Settings, 1103
Choose Certifier, 1031
Choose Profile, 1110
client type selection, 47
Column properties, 351, 358
Compact Databases, 983
Controlled Access, 338
Copy Database, 266
Create Folder, 83
Create Java Applet, 605
Create New Folder, 978
Create New Frameset, 393, 690
Create New Link, 979
Create Paragraph Style, 135
Create Table, 138
Create View, 346
Cross Certify ID, 855
Customize, 149
Database Fixup, 996
Database Properties, 272-277, 990
Database Quota Information, 990
Delete Folder, 979
Delete Link, 981
Delete Person, 914
Delivery Options, 106-107, 178
Design Icon, 272
Destination Folder, 47
Document properties, 654
ECL (Execution Control List), 867
Edit Icon, 58
Embedded Outline, 397
Embedded Outline properties, 384
Enter Password, 51-52
File Open, 1058
Find Note, 992
Folder, 159
Form properties, 350-351, 373
Frame properties, 397
Free Time, 176
Full Text Index, 985
Group creation, 919
Hotspot Pop-up properties, 405, 407
Hotspot Rectangle properties, 402
Hotspot Resource Link properties, 404-405
Import, 322
Import from a jar/zip file, 576
Insert Row/Column, 311
Internet Address Construction, 795-796, 908
Locations, 235
Lotus Notes Installation, 48

Mail Preferences, Preferences InfoBox, 110-112
Manage ACL, Basics pane, 999
Manage Groups, 918
Monitor New Task, 1043
Move Database, 987
MS Mail Initialization, 1108
Names, 152, 418, 918
New Database, 260, 770
New Layout Region, 335
New Replica, 267, 957
New Tracking Request, 939
Notes Preferences, 140
Open, 322
Open Database, 80
Open Sesame, 622
OU certifier, 771
Outline Entry properties, 386-389, 397
Page properties, 303-305
People and Groups Migration, 1100, 1108
Picture Info properties, 409
Ports preferences, 98-99
Print, 67, 147
Proxy Server Configuration, 236
Register Organizational Unit Certifier, 771
Register Person, 905
Register Person-New Entry, 903
Register Servers, 773
Rename Selected User, 909
Repeat Options, 173
Replace Database Design, 278
Replicate from, 964
Replication History, 951, 1067
Replication Settings, 954-956, 963, 1064
Request Move For Selected Entries, 910
Reschedule, 180
Save Salami, 623
Search Builder, 343-345
Section properties, 324
Select LDIF File, 1112
Set Internet Address, 749
Set Password, 64
SmartIcons, 56-58
SmartIcons Formula, 58
Table, 319
Table properties, 312-317
User ID, 64-66, 855, 865
User Preferences, 88, 96-98, 233, 243
User Preferences, 210
Workstation Security, 94-95
dialog list field, 329
DialogBox function, 444

dictionaries, spelling, User Dictionary button, 89
DIF (Data Interchange Format), 1171
digital signal processors (DSP), 1144
digital signatures, 107, 656, 861-862
Dim
    keyword, NotesItem class, creating, 665
    statement, 500
Direct Transfer Activity, 1161, 1173-1175
directives, %End Rem or %Rem, 509
directories
    Directory Assistance, 750
    Directory Catalog, 750
    Domino, 22, 750
        Create privileges, 156
        document groups, administering, 1136
        domains, 1135-1136
        Internet mail addresses, 794
        managing email contacts, 164-165
        roles, 1136
        updating, 570
        upgrading Domino servers from R4 to R5, 785-786
    Domino Public Directory, 152
    email names, 104
    eSuite, 604
    Internet directory standards, 750
    LDAP (Lightweight Directory Access Protocol), 852, 1111-1113
    local, defining, 164
    Notes Personal Directory, 152
    Public, 772
        defining, 164
        Groups section, 81
        location documents, 82
        People section, 81
        reviewing, 80, 82
        Server section, 82
    services, planning, 1088
    synchronizing between Notes and Windows NT, 916-917
Directory Assistance, 750
    application, 416
    database name field (Basics tab of Server document), 811
    LDAP documents, creating, 852
    upgrading Domino servers from R4 to R5, 786-787

Directory Catalog

Directory Catalog, 258, 750, 1124, 1136, 782

Directory Cataloger subtab (Server Tasks tab in Server document), 824

Directory Connectors, 1160

Directory Migration, 1105

Directory Name Services (DNS), 1052

Directory Profile, configuring, 785

DIS (Domino Import Service)
DFC (Domino Fusion Connector, 707
installing, 708

disabling
agents, Domino database, 274
email routing, 938
SMTP/MIME MTA housekeeping, 789

Discussion document, data display, 124-125

Discussion Threads (email), 103

DiscussionNotes and Web (R5.0) template, 259

disk drives, Domino R5, 1074

disks, partitions, General Disk Information (Domino Administrator, Files tab), 977

Display section (Calendar Preferences screen), 170

displaying
fields, 331
formulas, 433
mobile computing locations, 208

dithering, graphic images, 92-93

Division operator, 435

DLLs (dynamic link libraries), 538-540

DNS (Directory Name Services), 1052, 1075

DO (Data Object), LotusScript, 491

Do statement, 515

Doc Library Notes and Web (R5.0) template, 259

DocLinks, creating, 113-114

Document class (Java), 645
folders, 651-652
hierarchies, 649-650

objects, creating, 647
profile documents, 650-651
properties, 649
Remove method, 648
Save method, 647-648
security, 652-658

Document Properties
command (File menu), 654
InfoBox, 148, 654, 865

Document property, 646

Document table bitmap optimization property, 802, 1076

document-level access lists, troubleshooting, 1061

document-specific versus static text, 125-126

documents, 324, 350-351. *See also* databases
account for Internet mail, 799
ACL
*Monitor, 423, 1134
restrictions, 420*
Adjacent Domain, 841, 930
AUTHORS item, adding, 666
batch processing, 144
Calendar Preferences, 169
categories, 145-146, 334
cc:Mail Domain, 841
Certifier, 842, 1011
clusters, 1011
collection, 638
comparing with forms and Web pages, 325-326
Configuration, 709, 842
Configuration Settings, 1011
Connecting, 1011
connection, 76, 928, 986
Connection, 834, 930 1011
*Basics tab, 932-933
creating, 958-960
database replication, 958
dial-up modems, Basics tab, 838
email routing, 932-933
LANs (local area networks), 835
Network Dialup connection, 838-839
Passthru server connection, 838
Replication/Routing tab, 962-963*
Cross Domain Configuration, 986
Cross-Certifier, 842
data, displaying, 124
deleting, 143-144, 648

Deny List, 1011
design documents, 644-645
digital signatures, 861-862
Direct Transfer Activity, 1173-1175
disappearing after replication, troubleshooting, 1062-1063
Discussion, data display, 124-125
document-specific text, 125
domain, creating, 187
Domain, 839-841, 1011
Domino Connection, tabs, 927
Domino databases, 256-257, 342, 638
Domino Directory, 809, 1011-1013
Domino Domain, tabs, 927
editing, 334, 671-674
8-character IDs, 992
email, 107-109
External Domain Network Information (Server Configuration documents), 842, 1011
fields, 332, 627-628, 662, 864-865
File Identification (Domino Directory), 1011
File Protection Settings (Domino Directory), 1012
files, attachments, 141, 670-671
folders, 160, 334, 348
fonts, colors, 128
footers, creating for printing, 147-149
Foreign SMTP Domain (Domino Directory Domain documents), 841
forms, 124-127, 291, 325-339, 662
forwarding, 334
Global Domain (Domino Directory Domain documents), 841
graphics, 139-141, 688
groups, administering, 1136
headers, creating for printing, 147-149
Holiday (Server Configuration, 842, 1012
HTML (Hypertext Markup Language), 599, 682, 691-696
icons, 144-145
items, 662-665
Link
*Notes, 1172
ODBC, 1171-1172*
location, 76-77, 82

Location
*Internet Browser page,
   235-236*
*Java Applet Security tab,
   868-869*
replication schedules, 965-966
setting up Web browsers, 235
*viewing in Personal Address
   Book, 234*
Mail-In Database (Domino
   Directory), 843, 1012
main, 350
Mark Documents Read (user
   preference), 90
Monitor (Domino Directory),
   1012
on networks, changing, 1118
Non-adjacent Domain
   (Domino Directories), 930
Non-Adjacent Domain
   (Domino Directory Domain
   documents), 840-841
not replicating, troubleshooting, 1060
notes, 124, 662
Notes, 124
NotesEmbeddedObject class,
   (LotusScript), 670-671
NotesItem class
   *creating in LotusScript,
      665-666*
   *in NotesDocument class,
      663-664*
NotesRichTextItem class,
   666-667
NotesRichTextParagraphStyle
   class, (LotusScript), 670
NotesRichTextStyle class,
   668-669
opening in Web browsers, 232
organizing, 342
paper, reducing usage,
   1146-1147
paragraphs, properties, 670
Person, 1011
   email routing, 928
   *Internet Address field,
      794-796*
previewing, 67
printing, 66-67, 149
Program (Domino Directory),
   842, 1012
Replication Monitor, creating,
   970-971
Resource (Server Configuration
   documents), 842
response, 350-354
response to response, 350
rich text items, 666-667
RichTextItem class, (Java),
   669-670

RichTextParagraphStyle class,
   (Java), 670
RichTextStyle class, (Java),
   669-670
in Sametime, controlling, 192
SaveOptions field, 320
SaveOptions:="0" statement,
   321
saving, 647-648
Scan for Unread (user prefer-
   ence), 89
sending, 334
Server, 1012
   Administration tab, 834
   Basics tab, 810-813
   *Internet Protocols tab,
      826-832*
   Miscellaneous tab, 832
   MTAs tab, 832
   Ports tab, 818-820, 928
   Security tab, 813-818
   Server Tasks tab, 821-826
   *Transactional Logging tab,
      832, 834*
Server Configuration, 792-793
   *configuring multiple servers,
      1017*
   creating, 1017-1022
   *External Domain Network
      Information document, 842*
   Holiday document, 842
   *NOTES.INI file modifica-
      tions, 1023-1024*
   Resource documents, 842
   *server configuration settings
      updated*
   *settings unspecified,
      1022-1023*
Server Connection, 928,
   959-960
server documents
   displaying, 1013-1014
   *restrictions, troubleshooting,
      1055*
sorting, 354-356
static text, 125
tables, 137-139
text
   document-specific, 125
   editing versus viewing, 127
   fields, 126-127
   rich text, 127-137, 668-669
   static, 125-126
User Setup Profile (Domino
   Directory), 842, 1012
versioning, 1066
view columns, 144
views, 346
   actions, 373-374
   column properties, 348-350
   creating columns, 350

date formatting, 360-361
deleting columns, 350
embedded, 374-378
fonts, 358-359
HTML links, 361-362
naming columns, 361
in Notes, 141-149
numeric formatting, 359-360
private, 346-348
selecting for, 343-346
shared, 346-348
*Single Category embedded,
   379-380*
*Treat View Contents as
   HTML, 693*
X.400 Domain (Domino
   Directory Domain docu-
   ments), 841

dollar sign ($), 548

**DOM (Domino Object Model),
484, 610**
   accessing Java, 485-486
   back-end classes, 488-491
   class objects, 613-617
   objects, 493, 614
   Session class, 610
   strings
      LotusScript, 530-534
      modems, 212
      *string handling functions,
         1214*

**Domain documents, 187,
839-841, 1011**

**Domain Indexer subtab (Server
Tasks tab, Server document),
823**

**Domain name field (Basics tab,
Server document), 811**

**Domain Name Service (DNS),
1075**

**domain search servers, mobile
computing locations, 215**

domains, 839
   adjacent, 932, 1129
   configuring for email, 927
   Domino, 759-763, 932
   foreign, connections for email
      routing, 937-938
   merging, 1030
   modifying, 1029
   non-adjacent, 932, 1128-1129
   Notes, 1135-1136
   splitting, 1030-1031
   upgrading Domino servers and
      Notes clients from R4 to R5,
      781

Domino

Domino, 13-14
administration, 22, 24
Administrator, 12
clusters, upgrading, 797
databases, replicating, 20
deployment, technical planning, 759
Designer, 12
directories, 22
domains, 759-763
email server, 16
eSuite, combining, 604-607
firewalls and proxy servers, integrating, 878-879
HTML (Hypertext Markup Language), tools, 706-707
JAR files, 572-573
Java
  agents, 563-565
  applets, 566-567
Microsoft Exchange
  comparing, 16
  converting to Notes, 1109-1111
Microsoft Mail, converting to Notes, 1107-1109
multithreading with Java, 559-562
new features, 318, 322
Notes, code sharing, 13
pages with Treat page contents, eSuite spreadsheets, 605
servers, 13, 121-122
  adding user IDs, 46
  certification logs, creating, 770-771
  client types (optional), 767-768
  installing, 763-775
  OU (organizational unit) certifiers, creating, 771-772
  registering while installing, 774-775
  upgrading R4 to R5, 778-788
systems
  administration, tasks, 22
  planning, 758
  strategy, 758
  teams, 758-759
tools, programming, 21
troubleshooting, 1049
  modems, 1067-1068
  Passthru servers, 1051-1053
  replication, 1059-1067
  security, 1049-1051
  server access, 1053-1056
  servers, 1056-1059

upgrading, resources, 805
URLs (uniform resource locators), 694-695
Web browsers versus Notes client, 682
Web sites
  background, 681-682
  challenges, 697-698
  creating, 683
  HTML (Hypertext Markup Language), 691-697
  Notes databases, 683-691
  resources, 698-699

Domino Administrator, 14, 797, 896-897, 1007, 1137-1138
ACLs (Access Control Lists), 982
Administration tab, 1022
Advanced tab, 1022
anonymous users, setting up, 908
authenticated users, setting up, 907
Basics tab, 1017-1018
certification, administering, 920
Configuration tab, 899, 925-927, 953, 958, 1007, 1012-1024
Connections tab, 1024
Conversions Options tab, 1021
databases, 976
  ACLs (Access Control Lists) settings, 998-999
  analysis results, 988-989
  analyzing, 987-988
  catalogs, creating, 1001
  certificate signing, 994
  cluster management, 991-992
  compacting, 982-983
  corruption repair, 994-996
  default location, 1000
  designs update, 1000
  full text indexes, 984-985
  indexes, size factors, 984
  libraries, creating, 1001-1002
  links, 980-981
  maintaining, 981-982
  managing, 981-982
  moving, 986-987
  multidatabase indexing, 992-994
  notes locations, 992
  preventing R4 converting to R5, 983
  property settings, 996-997
  quota setting, 989-990
  replication, 985-986, 991
  rolling out, 1000-1001
  status of, 991-992

disk partitions, monitoring, 977
documents, maintaining, 1012-1013
Domino servers, performance, 1032-1034
dragging and dropping technology, 897
email, 925-927
files, 798, 976
Files tab, 898, 971, 976
  Database Action Bar, 981-982
  Folder Action Bar, 977-981
  General Disk Information, 977
folders, 978-981
groups, 917-919
icon, 896
Internet, users, setting up, 907-908
LDAP tab, 1018-1019
Messaging tab, 898-899, 925-926
MIME tab, 1021
Notes
  IDs, recertifying, 915-916
  usernames, changing, 908-913
  users, registering, 899, 901-907
NOTES.INI Settings tab, 1022
People & Groups tab, 897-900, 1102
Programs tab, 1024-1026
replication logs, viewing, 970
Replication tab, 899, 953, 968-969
replication topology, displaying, 969
Router/SMTP tab, 1019-1021
Server tab, 898, 964
servers
  registering, 773-774
  tasks, 1026-1029
Servers tab, 1032-1033
Settings by Character Set Groups tab, 1022
10% unused space, determining, 982
user account administration, integrating with Windows NT, 916-917
usernames
  deleting, 913-915
  managing, 908

Domino Administrator Client (Admin Client), monitoring servers, 1038-1048

Domino Administrator Messaging tab, email routing, 939

Domino Directory 1249

Domino Application Server, Web Application Server, 751-754
Domino Components toolbar, 710
Domino Connection document, tabs, 927
Domino Connector Toolkit, 1164
Domino Data Directory, 976
Domino databases, 256
  About documents, updating, 270-271
  accessing, 256
  ACLs (Access Control Lists), 267-269, 347, 636
  agents, disabling, 274
  copying, 264-266
  design elements, 269-270
  documents, 256-257, 350
    accessing, 638
    archiving, 273-274
    folders, 342
    inheritance, 351-353
    response to response, 353-354
    response, 351
    sorting, 354-356
    views, 342
  embedding elements, 409-410
  fields, 256-257
  folders, 342, 348
  forms, saving, 274
  frames, 391-392, 395
  framesets, 389-398
  full text indexes, 277
  graphics, showing, 274
  hotspots, 403-408
  items, 256
  JavaScript, 274
  Lightweight Directory, 258
  navigators, 399-403
  ODS (On-Disk Structure), 257
  outlines, 384-389, 395-397
  programs, 257
  properties, 272-277
  refreshing, 277
  relational database comparisons, 256-257
  release 5, 257-258
  replacing, 278
  replication, 266-267
  SSL (Secure Socket Layer), 274
  templates, 259-264
  Using document, updating, 271-272
  views, 346
    access lists, 371-372
    accessing through ODBC, 369
    actions, 373-374
    aliases, 362
    browsers, 369-371
    Calendar, 362-363
    categories, 371
    color, 364-365
    column properties, 348-350
    comments, 362
    creating, 342-343
    creating columns, 350
    date formatting, 360-361
    default settings, 363-364
    deleting columns, 350
    document selection, 343-346
    embedded, 374-378
    fonts, 358-359
    hiding, 362
    HTML links, 361-362
    icons, 356-358
    indexes, 366-368, 371
    naming columns, 361
    numeric formatting, 359-360
    opening, 343
    private, 346-348
    properties, 362
    shared, 346-348
    Single Category embedded, 379-380
    unread marks, 368

Domino Design Components, 703
  authoring tools, 710
  Domino Form, 712
  Domino Link, 711
  Domino Search, 713-714
  Domino Site, 711
  Domino View, 712
  Domino View Action, 712-713
  Domino View List, 713
  downloading, 707
  installing, 708-710
  MS FrontPage (DDCFP), 707
  publishing to servers, 713-715

Domino Designer, 14, 797
  agents, 286, 293-294
  applications, creating, 19-20
  data, organizing, 323-324
  databases, creating, 20
  design elements, 285-287
  fields, sharing, 296-297
  folders, 286, 292
  forms, 285-286, 290-292, 326
  framesets, 285, 288, 393-394
  graphic images, image resource library, 322-323
  icon, 282
  IDE (Integrated Development Environment), Java agents, 36
  image resources, 295
  Integrated Development Environment (IDE), 20
  Java applets, 295-296
  navigators, 286, 293
  new features, 32-37
  outlines, 285-288
  pages, 285, 289-290
  Pages design, Web pages, creating, 300-303
  pictures, embedding or importing, 321-322
  resources, 294
  Resources twistie, 286-287
  script libraries, 297
  starting, 282-283
  synopsis, 286
  tables
    borders, 312-313
    cells, 316
    collapsible, 317-318
    columns, 310-314
    creating, 309
    margins, 312-313
    nesting, 318
    programmatic control, 318, 320
    properties, 312
    rows, 310-311
    special effects, 317-318
    tabbed, 317
    table/cell backgrounds, 314, 316
    timed, 318
  tools, 19
  views, 292, 344
  Views design, 343
  Web pages, 300-305
  Web sites, creating, 20
  window, 283-287

Domino Directory, 750, 759, 808-810, 1135
  ACL (Access Control List), 418, 808-809
  certification, administering, 920
  Certifier documents, 842, 1011
  clusters, 1011
  Configuration documents, 842
  Configuration Settings documents, 1011
  Connection document, 834-835, 838-839, 1011
  Create privileges, 156
  Cross-Certifier documents, 842
  Deny List documents, 1011
  documents, 809, 930
    Administration section fields, 1011
    Certifier, 1011
    Configuration Settings, 1011
    Connectings, 1011

Domino Directory

Connection, 1011
Deny List, 1011
Domain, 1011
External Domain Network Information, 1011
File Identification, 1011
File Protection Settings, 1012
groups, administering, 1136
Holiday, 1012
Mail-In Database, 1012
Monitor, 1012
Person, 1011
Program, 1012
Server, 1012
User Setup Profile, 1012
Domain documents, 839-841, 1011
domains, 1029-1031, 1135-1136
Domino Administrator
   All Server Documents, 1015
   Configuration Documents, 1016-1024
   Configuration Documents, Server Configuration documents, 1016
   Connections Documents, 1024
   Current Server Document, 1013-1014
   document maintenance, 1012-1013
   Programs Documents, 1024-1026
   Server Configuration, 1013
   Server Document tabs, 1014-1015
Domino servers, moving within the organization, 1031
email, contacts, 104, 164-165
External Domain Network Information documents, 1011
File Identification documents, 1011
File Protection Settings documents, 1012
forms, 809-810
groups, 917-919
Holiday documents, 1012
Internet mail addresses, 794
LDAP (Lightweight Directory Access Protocol), LDIF (LDAP Data Interchange Format), 1111-1113
Mail-In Database documents, 843, 1012
managing, 1117-1118
Monitor documents, 1012
Monitors, 816
Program documents, 842, 1012

registered users and servers, 1012
roles, 1136
Server Configuration documents, 842, 1016-1024
Server documents
   Administration tab, 834
   Basics tab, fields, 810-813
   Internet Protocols tab, 826-832
   Miscellaneous tab, 832
   MTAs tab, 832
   Ports tab, 818-821
   Security tab, 813-818
   Server Tasks tab, 821-826
   Transactional Logging tab, 832, 834
Server documents, 1012
servers, mobile computing locations, 215
updating, 570
upgrading Domino servers from R4 to R5, 785-786
User Setup Profile documents, 842, 1012
users
   account administration, integrating with Windows NT, 916-917
   administering, 899
   mail information, 1012
   Notes IDs, recertifying, 915-916
   Notes users, registering, 899-907
   setting up, 907-908
   usernames, 908-915

Domino Domain document, tabs, 927

Domino domains, adjacent and non-adjacent, email routing between, 932

Domino Enterprise Connection Services (DECS), 739, 752, 1158

Domino Enterprise Server, 754-756

Domino Extension Manager, 752

Domino Form (Domino Design Component), 712

Domino Fusion Connector (DFC), 707

Domino IMAP server, email, 944

Domino Import Service (DIS), 708

Domino Link (Domino Design Component), 711

Domino log, LOG.NSF file, 938-939, 1008

Domino Mail server
email, 748-749, 927-938
Internet, 747-750
LDAP (Lightweight Directory Access Protocol), authentication, 750-751
Router, 749-750

Domino messaging server, 924

Domino Named Networks, email routing, 931

Domino Object Model (DOM), 21-22, 610
classes, 1184-1185
Java access, 464-465
LotusScript access, 465

Domino POP3 server, email, 942-943

Domino Public Address Book, 22

Domino Public Directory, 152

Domino R4 and R5 servers, MIME messages, transferring, 794

Domino R5
capacity planning, 1085-1089
cc:Mail, upgrading to, 1101-1104
CPUs, 1073-1074
databases, policies for properties, 1077
disk drives, 1074
Document table bitmap optimization property, 1076
Don't maintain unread marks property, 1075
Don't overwrite free space property, 1076
Don't support specialized response hierarchy property, 1076
Internet mail, storage format, 796
Limit entries in $Revisions fields property, 1077
Limit entries in $UpdatedBy fields property, 1076
Maintain LastAccessed property, 1076
mail interface (Notes), 17
memory, 1074
networks, 1074-1075

new features
  bookmarks, 31
  Domino Designer client, 32-33
  Domino server, 37-38, 40
  drop-down actions, 30-31
  email, 29, 31
  framesets, 32, 34
  graphic image storage, 322
  HTML 4.0 support, 35, 37
  Java support, 35, 37
  JavaScript support, 35, 37
  nesting tables, 318
  Notes client, 28
  outlines, 32, 34
  subscriptions, 86-87
  Web pages, 32, 34
  welcome page, 28-29
NotesBench Consortium rating, 1072
NT Performance Monitor, 1078
performance, 1072-1078
platforms, 1073
readers, feedback to authors, 1180
scalability, 1078-1085
software, installing, 784, 792
users, migrating to, 1099-1100

Domino Search (Domino Design Component), 713-714

Domino security. *See* security

Domino Server Planner tool, 1087

Domino servers, 746-747
administering, 1006-1012
ADSL (Asymmetrical Digital Subscriber Line), 1125-1126
choosing, 747
communications infrastructure, planning, 1124
configuring, 1012
cross-certifying, 930-931
database servers, planning, 1123
documents
  All Server Documents, 1015
  Configuration Documents, 1016-1024
  Configuration Documents, Server Configuration documents, 1016
  Connections Documents, 1024
  displaying, 1013-1014
  Programs Documents, 1024
  Programs Documents, schedul-
  ing Notes tasks, 1025-1026
  Server Document tabs, 1014-1015
domains, 1029-1031
Domino Administrator, 1137-1138
Domino Directory, 1135-1136
email, shared mail, 939-942
events, trapping, 1138
external servers, planning, 1124
firewall servers, planning, 1124
functions, 896
infrastructure, planning, 1122
ISDN (Integrated Services Digital Network), 1125
ISPs (Internet service providers), 1125
licenses, 746
location security, 847
Mail Gateways, 1137
mail servers, planning, 1122-1123
mobile computing
  connections, 227
  Internet connections, 227-228
  Location document, 214-220
  locations, selecting, 227
  modems, 211-213
  Passthru servers, 220-222
  Personal Address Book, 213-214
  ports, 208-211
  protocols, 209-210
  replication, 222-226
  security, 229
  sending mail, 228-229
modems, planning, 1124-1125
moving within the organization, 1031
networks, 1029, 1116-1122
new features, 37-40
Passthru servers, planning, 1123
performance, 1032-1034
renaming, 1032
scalability, 746
Server Configuration documents (Domino Directory), 1016-1024
statistics, 1138
tasks, 1026-1029
topologies
  end-to-end, 1126
  hub-and-spoke, 1127
  mail routing, 1127-1129
  mesh, 1127
  passthru, 1134-1135
  peer-to-peer, 1126
  replication, 1129-1134
WAN (wide area network), 1126

Domino Site (Domino Design Component), 711

Domino SMTP R5 server, using dial-up, 796

Domino Upgrade Services
Microsoft Exchange, converting to Notes, 1109-1111
Microsoft Mail, converting to Notes, 1107-1109
tools, 1099

Domino View (Domino Design Component), 712

Domino View Action (Domino Design Component), 712-713

Domino View List (Domino Design Component), 713

Domino Web Engine subtab (Internet Protocols tab in Server document), 829-830

Domino Web server Application Programming Interface (DSAPI), 754

Domino.Merchant, 723-724

Don't maintain unread marks property, 1075

Don't overwrite free space property, 1076

Don't support specialized response hierarchy property, 1076

dot (.), 795

Double data type, 498

downloading
cc:Mail, 1137
Domino Design Components, 707
files by customers (Interfusion Energy case study), 1171
graphics, mobile computing, 220
JavaDoc utility, 548
MSFP (Microsoft FrontPage), 707
NOF (NetObjects Fusion), 707
Web registration database, 815
X.400 MTAs, 1137

DPROPR Activity, 1161

dragging and dropping technology in Domino domain, 897

drawing navigator objects, 400-401

drawing tools (Sametime), 196-197

Drive button, 203

DRIVERS

drivers
  JDBC-ODBC on Internet Explorer, 599
  verifying for TCP/IP ports, 234
drives
  disk, Domino R5, 1074
  space for voice mail, 1144
driving applications, 202-203
drop-down
  actions, Notes client, 30-31
  boxes, Position, 57
DSAPI (Domino Web server Application Programming Interface), 754
dservlet.jar files, 573
DSP (digital signal processors), 1144
Dual Homed Host firewalls, 873-874
Ducat Web site, 724
DUN (Dial-Up Networking), 839
dynamic Web sites, 720-721

E

EBCDIC code, 531
ECL (Execution Control List), 798, 866-868, 1219
e-commerce, 720-721
  Chrysler's SCORE (Supplier Cost Reduction Effort), 722-723
  credit cards, 726
  Internet.Com, e-commerce section, 724
  Net.Commerce (IBM), 725-726
  products, 724-725
  selling online, 723-727
  Web site, 726
Edit button, 127, 919
Edit Document SmartIcon, 127, 146
edit function, @Command functions, 1222-1223
Edit Icon, button or dialog box, 58
Edit menu, 53
Edit menu commands
  Clear, 350
  Copy, 146
  Copy as Link, 113, 137, 387
  Cut, 333
  Paste, 113, 146, 333
  Properties, 312, 378
  Unread Marks, 89, 108
edit mode, 127, 287
Edit Server button, 1014
editing
  calendars, delegating task, 171
  documents, 146, 334, 671-674
  fields, 330-331
  mobile computing locations, 208
  Server Configuration document, 792-793
  SmartIcons, 57, 59
  text versus viewing, 127
Editor access, ACLs, 429
Editor Applets, 687
Editor level, ACLs, 415
editor.cab files, 573
editor.jar files, 573
editor.zip files, 573
editors
  email, alternative editors, 121
  icon editor, Domino databases, 272
  outline, Web site navigation design, 33
  Outline Editor, creating outlines, 384-385
EffectiveUserName property, 613
Effects property, 669
Egyptian hieroglyphics and passwords, 52
8-character IDs, documents, 992
EICentral Web site, 740
Electro-Matic Products Web site, 697
electronic commerce. *See* e-commerce
electronic mail. *See* email
ellipses
  drawing navigator object, 400
Else clause, 511
ElseIf clause, 511
email, 15-17. *See also* Internet; protocols; Web browsers; Web pages; Web sites; WWW (World Wide Web)
  * (asterisk), 108
  account documents, 799
  ACLs (Access Control Lists), 113
  Actions menu, tools, 118-119
  addresses, 794, 1180
  Adjacent Domain documents, 930
  administering in Domino Administrator, 925-927
  All Documents, 103
  archiving, 117
  calendars, 77-79, 171
  cc:Mail MTA, 937
  closing, 108
  Collector task, 939-940
  Connection documents, 928, 930
  Contact form, 154-156
  contacts
    adding to categories, 157-158
    adding to Personal Address Book, 153-156
    categorizing, 156-157
    creating mailing lists, 162-163
    folders, 159-160
    help adding to Personal Address Book, 154-155
    managing, 152, 164-165
    messages, 158-159
    personal preferences, 152-153
    scheduling meetings, 160
    visiting Web pages, 161-162
  cross-certifying organizations, 854-856
  Database Manager, sending messages to, 119
  databases, SCOS (shared copy object store), 863
  delegating, 79
  deleting, 109, 940
  Discussion Threads, 103
  DocLinks, creating, 113-114
  documents
    deleting, 109, 160
    forwarding, 334
  Domino Administrator Messaging tab, 939
  Domino and Microsoft Exchange, comparing, 16
  Domino directories, 104
  Domino Directory, Create privileges, 156
  Domino IMAP server, 944
  Domino Mail server
    alternative route selection configuration, 936-937
    Connection documents, 932-933
    disabling, 938
    forcing unscheduled routing, 936

EMAIL

Internet messaging standards,
  747-748
monitoring tools, 938-939
multithread configuration,
  938
Non-adjacent Domino
  domains configuration,
  933-935
priority level routing,
  935-936
routing, 927-932
Domino messaging server, 924
Domino POP3 server, 942-943
Domino R5 storage format,
  796
Domino servers, 16, 121-122,
  930-931
drop-down actions, 30-31
editors, alternatives, 121
encryption, documents,
  656-658
Event task, 939
Extended SMTP, 924
files
  attaching, 105
  naming, 102
Folders, 103
functions, 1218, 1224
hop counts, 928, 1128
IETF (Internet Engineering
  Task Force) standard, 924
Inbox, 102, 108
incoming, encrypting, 862-863
interfaces, voice mail systems,
  1143
international preferences,
  changing, 97-98
Internet
  directory standards, 750
  messaging server, 924
  protocols, 121-122
Link Messages, creating,
  113-114
links to Web pages, 114
lists (email), creating, 162-163
Location documents, defining
  local and public directories,
  164
LOG.NSF file, 938-939
Mail Address Assistant, 155
Mail Gateways, 1137
Mail Router, 928
Mail Routing Status, 1047
Mail Routing Topology map,
  1047
MAIL.BOX, 938
Mailer, 928
mailing lists, 162
memos, 104-107

messages
  addressing, 748-749
  delivering, 749-750
  folders, 159-160
  keeping track of, 159
  reading, 107-108
  replying to, 110
  sending, 103-104, 158
  students in Sametime sending
    to instructors, 200
messaging standards, 121-122
MIME (multipurpose Internet
  mail extensions), 924
mobile computing locations,
  216-217
names, looking up, 104
Non-adjacent Domain docu-
  ments, 930
Notes
  client, 29-31
  R5 mail interface, 17
  SendTo (Microsoft Office 97),
    93
notifications of request
  approvals or rejections,
  sending, 1118
opening, 107
Out of Office, setting up, 118
outgoing, encrypting, 862
packages, 768
paper clip icon, 356
Personal Address Book, 104
  adding recipients or senders,
    118
  background images, 153
  contacts, 152-158
  group sorting, 153
  LDAP (Lightweight Directory
    Access Protocol) queries, 153
  managing contacts, 152
  owners, 152
Phone Messages, creating, 115
POP3 (Post Office Protocol
  Version 3), 925
preferences, defining, 110-113
preview panes, opening, 103
Private, delegating reading or
  editing, 171
protocols, 17
recipients, adding, 118
red exclamation points, 106
replication, 1128
Reporter task, 939
Retain View column sorting, 92
routing, 927
  alternative route selection
    configuration, 936-937
  between adjacent Domino
    domains, 932
  between Domino Named
    Networks, 931

  between non-adjacent Domino
    domains, 932
  Collector task, 939
  Connection documents,
    932-933
  costs, minimizing, 1128
  disabling, 938
  domains, adjacent and non-
    adjacent, 1128-1129
  Domino Administrator
    Messaging tab, 939
  Domino domains, 760
  Event task, 939
  forcing unscheduled routing,
    936
  foreign domain connections,
    937-938
  guidelines, 929
  hops, minimizing, 1128
  LOG.NSF file, 938-939
  MAIL.BOX, 938
  monitoring tools, 938-939
  multithread configuration,
    938
  Non-adjacent Domino
    domains configuration,
    933-935
  Person document (Domino
    Directory), 928
  priority levels, 935-936
  Reporter task, 939
  server connections, 930-932
  Tell server command, 939
  topologies, 1127
  within Domino Named
    Networks, 931
rules for handling, 119-121
SCOS (single-copy object
  store), 939-942
senders, adding, 118
sending, 106-107, 225, 228-229
Sent, 103
Server Connection documents,
  928
Server documents, Ports tab,
  928
servers
  planning, 1122-1123
  topologies, 929
  upgraded software systems,
    1098
shared mail, 939-942, 1122
SMTP (Simple Mail Transfer
  Protocol), 790-791, 924, 1098
Stationery, 103, 115-117
Tell server command, 939
tools, 118-119
topologies, defining, 929

tracking, 1048
Tracking Center, 1046-1048
Trash, 103, 109
Typeahead, 104
unread marking, 108
user information, Domino Directory, 1012
views, 103
X.400 MTA, 938

Embedded Element command (Create menu), 378, 409

Embedded Outline dialog box, 384, 397

EmbeddedObjects property, comparing in NotesRichTextItem class and NotesDocument class, 671

embedding, 409-410
outlines, 395-397
pictures, 321-322
views, 374-380

Empty Trash
button, 109-110
command (Actions menu) or folder (user preference), 90

EMPTY value, 506-507

Enable JavaScript (user preference), 91

Enable Scheduled Local Agents (user preference), 90

Enable Unicode Display (user preference), 94

Enable Web Ahead button, 242

Enable/Disable button, 118

Enabled field (Ports tab of Server document), 819

Encapsulating Security Payload, 882

Encrypt
method, 655
option, sending email, 107

encryption
documents, 652-655, 864
Domino databases, 261, 266
fields, 652-655
Internet security, 884
keys
    creating, 653-654
    International, 866
    User ID dialog box, 865
local, of applications, 848-849
mail encryption, 656-658
mobile computing, 229
Notes
    authentication, 863
    digital signatures, 861-862

document fields, 864-865
email (outgoing), 862
keys, 865-866
network data, 863
private keys, 861-862
public keys, 861-862
port, Domino R5, 1075
views, 371

Encryption tab (User ID dialog box), 65

EncryptionKeys property, 655

End Class keyword, 504

End ForAll statement, 513-514

End Function statement, 523

End Property statement, 525

End Sub statement, 522

end user tool (Domino Upgrade Services), 1099

end-to-end topology, 958, 1126

Enter Password dialog box, 51-52

enterprise integration
ERP (enterprise resource planning), 731
non-system-based data sources, 732
RDBMS (relational database management systems), 730
transactional systems, 731

enterprise resource planning (ERP), 1158

enterprise/platform growth, scalability, 1080

EntreVision Web site, 724

entries
ACLs (Access Control Lists), 268-269, 675, 808
in calendars, creating, 172
outlines, 385-389
$Revisions fields, limiting, 803
$UpdatedBy fields, limiting, 803

Entry Hide When tab (Outline Entry properties dialog box), 388-389

envelope icons, 144

Environment function, 438

ENVIRONMENT keyword, formulas, 438-439
CLASSPATH, 545-546
PATH, updating, 577

environments
development, Java, 544
functions, 1219

mixed-release, compacting databases, 804
variables, 438-439

Equal, 436

equals sign (=), 795

Erase statement, 501

ERP (enterprise resource planning), 731, 1158
Connectors, Premium, 1160
Replic-Action, integrating data, 733
Transaction System Connectors, 1160

errors, LotusScript, On Error statement, 529

ESMTP (Extended SMTP), 748, 924

eSuite
Calendar applets, in IBM Visual Age for Java, 598
Chart applets, with InfoCenter, 594
data access applets, 598
CGI Gateway applets, 600
FileReader applets, 600
FormReader applets, 599
SQL/Java Database Connectivity (JDBC) applets, 599
TableReader applets, 599
data presentation applets, 589
Address Book applets, 598
Calendar applets, 597-598
Chart applets, 593, 595
multiple applets, 595-596
Presentation Graphics applets, 597
Project Scheduler applets, 596
Spreadsheet applets, 589-591
Word Processor applets, 591-593
DevPack
applet categories, 589
InfoBus, 588-589
installing, 604
JavaBeans, 587
directories, 604
Domino, combining, 604-607
Project Scheduler applets, with InfoCenter, 597
random chart, generated by JavaScript, 603
Spreadsheet applets, with InfoCenter, 594
spreadsheets, on Domino page with Treat page contents, 605
Utility Applets
AppletContainer applets, 600
AppletContainer applets, spreadsheets, 605-607

FIELDS 1255

InfoCenter applets, 600
messaging, 604
   ScriptHelper applets, 601-603
Word Processing applets, with InfoCenter, 592-593
Workplace, 582
   applications, 583
   Calendar applet, 583
   desktop, 583
   SpreadSheet applet, 584
   Windows NT, 582
   Word Processor applet, 584-586
   Work Files applet, 584

ETHandler routine, 673

Event task (Domino servers), 939, 1027

event-driven programming, 465
EventExample Hello agent, 466-469
input requests, 469-472

EventExample Hello agent, 466-468
input requests, 469-471
numeric input requests, 471-472

events, 488
Alarm, 487
on calendars, deleting, 182
generating at intervals, 671
handlers, LotusScript subroutines, 525
HTML Head Attributes, meta tags, 695
JavaScript, 36, 466
logging, redirecting from Notes to Windows NT Event Logger, 917
LotusScript, 466
NotesUIDatabase class, 625
NotesUIView class, 625-626
PostDragDrop, 625
PostOpen, 487, 625
PostPaste, 626
QueryAddToFolder, 626
QueryClose, 626
QueryDragDrop, 626
QueryOpen, 626
QueryOpenDocument, 626
QueryPaste, 626
QueryRecalc, 626
RegionDoubleClick, 626
trapping, 1138

exceptions
handling in Java, 555-556
NotesException class, 556

exclamation point (!), 144, 694
red, 106
replacing question marks, 695

Execution Control List (ECL), 798, 866-868, 1219

Exit For statement, 513

Exit Property statement, 525

Expand/Collapse command (View menu), 145

expiration periods, password security, 846

expired certificates, troubleshooting, 1053-1054

explicitly declaring, variables, 503

Explode function, 443

Export button, 866

Expression, 534

expressions
formulas, 433, 435-436
Java, 551

extended accelerators for keyboards, 94

extended class syntax (LotusScript), 663-664

Extended SMTP (ESMTP), 748, 924

extensions, NTF, 275

External Domain Network Information document (Server Configuration documents), 842

External Domain Network Information documents, 1011

external servers, planning, 1124

extranet applications, ACLs, 427

ezMerchant
setup screens, 725
Web site, 724

F

failover support for clustering servers, 1084

FarSite Viewer (Java applet), 194

Favorite Bookmarks folder, subscription results, 87

favorites. *See* **bookmarks**

fax client software, 1151-1152

faxes
cards, 1148
integrating
   fax client software, 1151-1152
   fax server software, 1148-1150

   hardware infrastructure, 1148
   network infrastructure, 1148
   planning, 1147
   software, 1148
server software, 1148-1150

features, new. *See* **new features**

feedback to authors, 1180

Field class, 487, 1185

FIELD keyword, 434, 439

fields, 124-126, 434, 662
Access server (Security tab of Server document), 815
ACL roles, 421
Administer a server from a browser (Security tab of Server document), 816
Administration section (Domino Directory documents), 1011
Administrators (Basics tab of Server document), 811
alignment, 332
Allow anonymous Notes connections (Security tab of Server document), 814
Allowed to use monitors (Security tab of Server document), 816
Always Use Area Code (dial-up modems of Connection document), 838
authors, 330
Automatic fixup of corrupt databases (Transactional Logging tab of Server document), 833
Basics tab (Server document), 810-812
BlindCopyTo, 657
By Field option (Search Builder dialog box), 345
calculating sales tax, 627-628
Call at Times (Schedule tab of Connection document), 837
Categories, sorting documents, 355
Check passwords on Notes IDs (Security tab of Server document), 814
Compare Notes public keys (Security tab of Server document), 813
Connection type (Basics tab of Connection document), 835
CopyTo, 657
Create new databases (Security tab of Server document), 815
Create replica databases (Security tab of Server document), 815

FIELDS

data types, 124, 126-127
date/time, 329
dates, formatting, 331-332
Day of the Week (Schedule tab of Connection document), 837
Destination Area Code (dial-up modems of Connection document), 838
Destination Country Code (dial-up modems of Connection document), 838
Destination Domain (Basics tab of Connection document), 835
Destination Phone Number (dial-up modems of Connection document), 838
Destination Server (Basics tab of Connection document), 835
dialog list, 329
Directory Assistance database name (Basics tab of Server document), 811
Domain name (Basics tab of Server document), 811
Domino databases, 256-257
   $Revisions field, 263
   $UpdatedBy field, 263
email memos, 104
Enabled (Ports tab of Server document), 819
encryptable, 652-655
encrypting, 864-865
Files/Directories to Replicate (Routing and Replication tab of Connection document), 837
fonts, 332
Foreign Domain (Basics tab Domain documents), 839
on forms, 124, 325-326, 662
   adding, 327
   attributes, changing, 331-332
   computed, 330-331
   data types, 328- 330
   displaying, 331
   displaying information, 291
   editable, 330-331
   formulas, 332-333
   naming, 327-328
   shared, 333
   single-use, 333
formula, 330
help text messages, 332
hidden, 127
HTML (Hypertext Markup Language), 332
id (NotesException class), 556

input, 126
Internet Address (Person Document), 794-796
Log path (Transactional Logging tab of Server document), 832
Logging style (Transactional Logging tab of Server document), 833
Login Script Arguments (dial-up modems of Connection document), 838
Login Script File Name (dial-up modems of Connection document), 838
Maximum Log Space (Transactional Logging tab of Server document), 833
$MediaTypes, 320
multiple value separators, 332
names, 330
Net Address (Ports tab of Server document), 819
Not access server (Security tab of Server document), 815
Not allowed to use monitors (Security tab of Server document), 816
Notes Network (Ports tab of Server document), 819
number, 329
numbers, formatting, 332
Only allow server access to users in Directory (Security tab of Server document), 814-815
Optional Network Address (Basics tab of Connection document), 835
password, 330
placing information, 627
Port (Ports tab of Server document), 819
Protocol (Ports tab of Server document), 819
readers, 330
Repeat Interval (Schedule tab of Connection document), 837
Replicate Databases of x Priority (Routing and Replication tab of Connection document), 836
Replication Task (Routing and Replication tab of Connection document), 836
Replication Time Limit (Routing and Replication tab of Connection document), 837

Replication Type (Routing and Replication tab of Connection document), 836-837
$Revisions, limiting entries, 803
rich-text, 330
   file attachments, 141
   graphics, 139-141
   links, 136-137
   tables, 138
Route at Once If (Routing and Replication tab of Connection document), 836
Router Type (Routing and Replication tab of Connection document), 836
Routing Cost (Routing and Replication tab of Connection document), 836
Routing Task (Routing and Replication tab of Connection document), 836
Routing tasks (Basics tab of Server document), 811
Run personal agents (Security tab of Server document), 817
Run restricted LotusScript/Java agents (Security tab of Server document), 817
Run unrestricted LotusScript/Java agents (Security tab of Server document), 817
Runtime/Restart performance (Transactional Logging tab of Server document), 833
SaveOptions, 320
Schedule (Schedule tab of Connection document), 837
security, 332
Security Settings (Security tab of Server document), 813-814
SendTo, 657
Server Access (Security tab of Server document), 814-816
Server name (Basics tab of Server document), 811
Server title (Basics tab of Server document), 811
Server's phone number(s) (Basics tab of Server document), 812
shared in Domino Designer Resources twistie, 286
sharing, Domino Designer, 296-297
SMTP listener task (Basics tab of Server document), 811
Source Domain (Basics tab of Connection document), 835

Source Server (Basics tab of Connection document), 835
symbols, 291
text, 329
text (NotesException class), 556
time, formatting, 331-332
Transactional logging (Transactional Logging tab of Server document), 832
$UpdatedBy, limiting entries, 803
Usage Priority (Basics tab of Connection document), 835
Use all available space on log device (Transactional Logging tab of Server document), 833
Use the Port (Basics tab of Connection document), 835
view column properties, 349
views, document selections, 344-345
Web Proxy (Location document), 236
Web Server Access (Security tab of Server document), 814
Web server authentication (Security tab of Server document), 814

File Identification documents (Domino Directory), 1011

File menu, 53

File menu commands
Attach, 105, 141
Close, 108, 146, 271
Database, 80, 689, 770, 785-786, 802-804, 954, 1000, 1002, 1058
Document Properties, 654
Import, 576
Mobile, 208, 235
Preferences, 88-89, 105, 140, 210, 243
  SmartIcon Settings, 55, 58
  User Preferences, 57, 121, 233
Print, 66, 147
Replication, 223, 804, 954, 957
SendTo, 93
Tools, 63, 854

File Open dialog box, 1058

File Print icon, 57

File Protection Settings documents (Domino Directory), 1012

File System Connectors, 1160

file upload control, embedding, 410

File-Tools-SmartIcons icon, 57
FileReader applets (eSuite), 600
files
actionbar.cab, 573
actionbar.jar, 573
actionbar.zip, 573
ADMIN4.NSF, 1008
administrator ID, 770, 848
archive, 545, 573
attachments
  to documents, 670-671
  to email, 105
  in rich-text fields, 141
backing up
  on MTA (Message Transfer Agent) servers, 789
  upgrading Domino servers from R4 to R5, 784
CAB, 545
CATALOG.NSF, 1008
certifier ID, 848-851
CERTLOG.NSF, 1008
class, 545
COL, 733
control, replication topologies, 1132-1133
DESKTOP.DSK, saving views, 347
Domino Administrator, 798, 976
Domino databases, naming, 261
downloading by customers (Interfusion Energy case study), 1171
dservlet.jar, 573
editor.cab, 573
editor.jar, 573
editor.zip, 573
email, naming, 102
function, @Command functions, 1223
i18n.jar, 572
ID, 62-63, 848
  certificates, 65
  cross-certifying, 931
  safe copying, 930-931
  security, 799-800
  User ID dialog box, 64
installation for Domino servers, 763-766
JAR, 545, 572-573
Jar (Java Archive), 554
JavaUserClasses, 545
jsdk.jar, 573
log
  database replication, viewing replication events, 970
  record, 1008

LOG.NSF, 938-939, 1008
LotusScript, 534-538
MAIL.BOX, 1008
modems, 213
NCSO.cab, 573
NCSO.jar, 573
NCSOC.jar, 573
Notes clients, backing up, 798
NOTES.INI, 1008
  modifying, 1023-1024
  removing Reporter task, 784
  upgrading for MTA server, 796
notes.jar, 572
nvapplet.cab, 573
nvapplet.jar, 573
nvapplet.zip, 573
organization certifier ID, 762
organizational unit (OU) certifier ID, 849-851
outline.cab, 573
outline.jar, 573
outline.zip, 573
RIP, troubleshooting servers, 1057-1058
rt.jar, 572
server ID, 848, 850
STATREP.NSF, 1008
system access, Java applets, 96
text, registering users, 906-907
tools.jar, 572
user ID, 848, 850
user mail files, moving and unlinking, 941-942
  from Web browsers, Internet security, 869-870
ZID, 734
ZIP, 545, 554

Files tab
Admin Client, servers, monitoring, 1045
Domino Administrator, 898, 971, 976-977
Database Action Bar, 981-982
databases
  ACL (Access Control List) settings, 998-999
  analysis results, 988-989
  analyzing, 987-988
  certificate signing, 994
  cluster management, 991-992
  compacting, 982-983
  corruption repair, 994-996
  full text indexes, 983-985
  moving, 986-987
  multidatabase indexing, 992-994
  notes locations, 992
  property settings, 996-997

quota setting, 989-990
replica copies, 985-986
replication management, 991
Folder Action Bar, 977-981
General Disk Information, 977

Files/Directories to Replicate field (Routing and Replication tab of Connection document), 837

filtering Web pages, 877-878

Find Note dialog box, 992

firewalls, 872, 879-880
choosing type or configuration, 874
concept, 873
configuring, 1169
drawbacks, 876
Dual Homed, 873
Dual Homed Host, 874
ICSA (International Computer Security Association) Certification, 879
networks, Domino R5, 1075
products, 879
proxy servers, 237, 876-879
proxy services, 874
Screened Host, 875
Screened Subnet, 875-876
security, 847
servers, planning, 1124
setting up, 874

First Domino server (option), 767

Fixup
corrupted databases, repairing, 994-996
task (Domino servers), 1027-1028

flat certification
exchange, 856-857
troubleshooting, 1053

Float button, 193

floating
Java applets, 193
menu (Text Properties InfoBox), 128
pictures, 140

flow control
repetition, 512, 516
selection, If-Then-Else statement, 511
sequential, 510
structured programming, 510

Folder Action Bar (Domino Administrator, Files tab), 977-981

Folder
button, 159
command
Actions menu, 160
Create menu, 159
dialog box, 159

Folder pane, embedding, 410

FolderReferences property, 652

folders, 342
ACL restrictions, 420
aliases, Simple Action, 403
bookmarks, 61, 83-84
creating, 348, 978
Databases, Workspace, 84
deleting, 979
documents, 160, 334, 651-652
Domino Designer, 286, 292
for email messages, 159-160
Empty Trash, 90
Favorite Bookmarks, subscription results, 87
Folder Action Bar (Domino Administrator, Files tab), 977-981
function, @Command functions, 1223-1224
links, 979-981
Local Database Folder (user preference), 90
Personal Web Navigator, 241-242
properties, ACL roles, 421
Trash, 109, 347

Folders (email), 103

Follow tool, 203

font style indicator (status bar), 59

fonts
bitmapping, 290
colors, 128
Default Fonts button, 89
Enable Unicode Display (user preference), 94
in fields, 332
LotusScript, 531-532
rich text, Text Properties InfoBox, 128-130
view columns, 358-359

FontSize property, 669

Footer button, 149

footers, creating for printing, 147-149

For statement, 513

ForAll statement, 513-514, 621

Force parameter, 648

foreign domain connections for email, 937-938

Foreign Domain field (Basics tab of Domain documents), 839

Foreign SMTP Domain documents (Domain documents), 841

Form class, (Java), 644-645

Form properties dialog box, 351, 373

Form Properties InfoBox, 864

Form= conditions, View selection property, 372

formats
abbreviated, hierarchial names, 761
canonical, hierarchial names, 761
Internet addresses, 795
R4 for databases, replicating, 804
storing Internet mail in Domino R5, 796

formatting
dates, 331-332
mail, mobile computing, 217
numbers, 332
paragraphs, 130-131
time, 331-332
view columns, 358-361

FormReader applets (eSuite), 599

forms, 124
actions, 333-335
Appointment, 172
Calendar Entry, 160, 169, 172
comparing with documents and Web pages, 325-326
Contact, 154-156
creating, 326, 671
data, displaying, 124
designing, 324-325
documents, 350
inheritance, 351-353
response to response, 353-354
response, 351
sorting, 354-356
Domino database, saving, 274
Domino Designer, 285, 290-292
Domino Directory ACL (Access Control List), 809-810
embedding elements, 409-410
fields, 124-127, 291, 325-333, 662
formulas, 373, 440-441
function, @Command functions, 1224

hotspots, 403-408
HTML (Hypertext Markup Language), 691-695
layout regions, 335-337
Meeting Invitations & Reservations, 175-176
Notes setup, 736
pages comparisons, 410-411
properties, ACL roles, 421
sections, 338-339
subforms, 286, 337-338
text
   editng versus viewing, 127
   rich text, 127-137
   static versus document-specific, 125-126
views, 374-376, 693

Formula button, 58

Formula language, 454

formulas, 432, 452
Default Value, 332-333
expressions, 435-436
folders, 342
field, 330
for fields, 332-333
forms, 440-441
function, 387
Input Translation or Validation, 332-333, 441
keywords, 438-440
lists, 437-438
objects, 432-433
operators, 435-436
pair-wise operations, 437-438
permuted operations, 437-438
pop-up hotspots, 406-407
subforms, computed, 338
syntax, 433-434
text concatenation, 437
values, 434-435
view column properties, 350
views, 342-343, 372-373
window title, 441

Forward
button, 54
command (Actions menu), 251

forward slash (/), 1025

forward slash, asterisk (/*), 548

forward slashes (//), 548

forwarding
email, unauthorized, 889-890
documents, 334

Frame properties dialog box, 397

FRAME tag (HTML), 390, 392

frames, 391-392, 411
adding to framesets, 394
content, 395

deleting from framesets, 395
links, 395-397

FRAMESET tag (HTML), 390-391

framesets, 389-391, 411, 688-689
creating, 392-393
Domino Designer, 32- 34, 285, 288
frames, 394-395
nested, 390-391
opening, 691-692
pages, inserting, 397-398
Web pages, creating, 690

free space, overwriting, turning off, 802

Free Time
dialog box, 176
section (Calendar Preferences screen), 170

FreeFile function, LotusScript, 535

front end
classes, 485-487, 669
operations, 476

FrontPage, MSFP (Microsoft FrontPage), 702-707

FTF (Rich Text Field), 1154

FTSearch method, 639

Full Text Index dialog box, 985

full text indexes
creating or deleting, 984-985
Domino databases, 262, 277
monitoring, 983-984
updating, 984-985

FullName method, 505

Function statement, 522-524

functions, 441-442
@Adjust, 377, 443
@BrowserInfo, 392
@Command, 446-447
   administration, 1220-1221
   agent, 1221
   attachment, 1221
   calendar, 1221
   create, 1221
   deleted, 1228
   design, 1221-1222
   edit, 1222-1223
   file, 1223
   folder, 1223-1224
   form, 1224
   help, 1224
   HotSpot, 1224
   layout, 1224
   mail, 1224

   miscellaneous, 1228
   navigate, 1225
   navigator, 1225
   object, 1225
   open, 1225
   paste, 1225
   refresh, 1225
   replicator, 1225
   section, 1226
   ShowHide, 1226
   SmartIcons, 1226
   text, 1226
   tools, 1226-1227
   UserID, 1227
   view, 1227-1228
   window, 1228
   workspace, 1228
@Created, 443
@DBColumn, 354, 446
@DbLookup, 444-446
@DbName, 444
@DialogBox, 444
@Environment, 438
@Explode, 443
@formula, 387
@functions
   column formula, 1217
   constants, 1220
   control flow, 1219
   conversion, 1215
   current document, 1216-1217
   databases, 1216, 1219
   date and time, 1216
   DDE (dynamic data exchange), 1219
   document field manipulation, 1217
   ECL (Execution Control List), 1219
   environment, 1219
   international, 1218
   Internet access, 1218
   list, 1215-1216
   mail, 1218
   mathematical, 1214-1215
   security, 1219
   string handling, 1214
   user attribute, 1218
   user interaction, 1218
   view selection, 1216-1217
@if, 442
@Implode, 443
@Left, 442
@LowerCase, 442
@PickList, 444
@PostedCommand, 446-447
@Prompt, 443
@Right, 442
@SetEnvironment, 438
@Subset, 443

FUNCTIONS

@Trim, 442
@UpperCase, 442
@UserAccess, 444
@UserName, 346
@UserNamesList, 444
@UserRoles, 444
Cint, 471
column formula, 1217
constants, 1220
control flow, 1219
conversion, 1215
CStr, 533
current document, 1216-1217
databases, 1216, 1219
date and time, 1216
DDE (dynamic data exchange), 1219
document field manipulation, 1217
ECL (Execution Control List), 1219
email, delegating, 112-113
environment, 1219
formulas, 434
FreeFile, 535
GetDatabase, 523
Inputbox, 470
InStr, 534
international, 1218
Internet access, 1218
IsDate, 523
IsEmpty, 506
IsEmpty, 523
IsNull, 523
Left$, 522, 533
Len, 533
list, 1215-1216
LotusScript
    FreeFile, 535
    strings, 532-534
    subroutines, 522-526
LTrim$, 533
mail, 1218
mathematical, 1214-1215
Mid$, 522,533
Right$, 522,533
RTrim$, 533
security, 1219
Str$, 533
StrCompare, 534
StrConv, 534
string handling, 1214
StrLeft, 533
StrLeftBack, 533
StrRight, 533
StrRightBack, 533
Trim$, 533
user attribute or interaction, 1218
view column properties, 349
view selection, 1216-1217

G

Garbage in, Garbage out (GIGO), 1170
gateways, Mail Gateways, 1137
General Disk Information (Domino Administrator, Files tab), 977
Generate Default Outline button, 384
Generate HTML for all fields view, 693
get routines, 492-493
Get statement, LotusScript, 536
getACL method, 636
GetAllDocumentsByKey method, 639-640
GetChild method, 639
GetDatabase
    function, 523
    method, 632
GetDbDirectory method, 523
GetDocumentByID method, 646
GetDocumentByKey method, 640
GetDocumentByUNID method, 646
GetEntry method, 636
GetFirstEntry method, 636
GetFirstItem, 663
GetListOfTunes method, 620-621
getName method, 665
GetNextEntry method, 636
GetNextSibling method, 639
getParentDocumentUNID method, 649
GetProfileDocument method, 650
getResponses method, 650
getText method, 665
getUnprocessedDocuments method, 643
getValueString method, 665
GIGO (Garbage in, Garbage out), 1170

Global Domain documents (Domain documents), 841
Globe icon, 248
Go Back button, 238
Go Forward button, 238
GoSub statement, LotusScript, 530
GoTo 0, On Error statement, 529
GoTo label, On Error statement, 529
GoTo statement, 516
Granite Web site, 735
granularity, Internet security, 884
graphics
    for actions, 335
    backgrounds
        navigators, 399-400
        Web pages, 304-305
    buttons, 400
    Clipboard, 304
    Domino database, showing, 274
    images, 688
        dithering, 92-93
        image resource library, 322-323
        graphic, Web sites, 688
        scanning or viewing, 1155
    manipulating in Picture Properties InfoBox, 139-141
    mobile computing locations, 220
    pictures
        embedding, 321-322
        floating, 140
        importing, 321-322
        inserting versus importing, 140
        on Web sites, 140
    in rich-text fields, 139-141
Graphware Corporation Web site, 1180
Greater than operator, 436
Greater than or equal operator, 436
green lights, users names on buddy lists, 198
Grennan, Mark, 891
Group Calendars, 169, 184
Group Computing Magazine Web site, 722
Group creation dialog box, 919
group scheduler, embedding, 410

GroupCreator
  Domino Directory ACL (Access Control List), 809
  role, 860

grouping statements, syntax, 556

GroupModifier, Domino Directory ACLs (Access Control Lists), 809

GroupModifier role, 860

groups
  ACLs (Access Control Lists), 268, 416-417
  administering, 816, 917
  creating, 918-919
  deleting, 919
  of email contacts, creating mailing lists, 162-163
  managing, 917-918
  modifying, 919
  in Personal Address Book, sorting, 153

Groups
  section (Public directory), 81
  view (Personal Address Book), 162

groupware. *See Sametime*

growth expansion options software, 1145

guidelines
  email routing, 929
  naming users and servers for networks, 1120-1122
  planning networks, 1116-1117

H

H.323 standard, 190

Hand (Java applet), 194

Hand icon, 199

handshake icon, 145

hanging up
  mobile computing, 208
  replication, 225

hardware
  independence, 13
  infrastructure
    for voice mail, 1144
    imaging technology integration, 1153
    integrating faxes, 1148

Has-A relationships, 481

Head Attributes event (HTML), meta tags, 695

Header button, 148

headers, creating for printing, 147, 149

headings, views, customizing, 366

headline monitoring
  Domino databases, 263
  turning off, 803

headline pages (welcome pages), 28-29

height, embedded views, 378

Hello agent example
  Java
    creating, 460-462
    help settings, 462
  LotusScript, 457
    creating, 458-459
    help settings, 462-464
    testing, 459-460

help
  contacts, adding to Personal Address Book, 154-155
  email, Mail Address Assistant, 155
  function, @Command functions, 1224
  Java reference material, 462
  LotusScript reference material, 462-464
  Microsoft Mail Administrator's Guide, 1107
  NotesPump/LEI, resources, 1177-1178
  students getting in Sametime, 200-201
  text messages for fields, 332

Help (Java applet), 194

Help menu, 54

Help menu commands, Help Topics, 464

Help Topics command (Help menu), 464

hidden
  columns, sorting documents by, 356
  fields, 127

hiding
  formulas, 433
  outline entries, 388-389
  paragraphs, 133-134, 332
  rich text, 134
  views, 362

hierarchies
  certified servers, 1009
  documents, 649-650
  Domino
    databases, response hierarchies, 263
    domains, 761

  names, 416-417, 761
  response, removing, 802-803
  response documents, 364
  storage migration (HSM), 1154

hieroglyphic symbols, password security, 846

Highlighter, rich text, Text Properties InfoBox, 130

highlighting navigator objects, 402

HiLite tab, 401

histories
  database replication, 970
  replications, 951, 1066-1067

Holiday document (Server Configuration documents, 842, 1012

Home (Notes Direct Dialup) location, mobile computing, 213

Home pages, creating, 690

home servers, mobile computing locations, 215

hop counts (email), 928, 1128

Horizontal Rule command (Create menu), 323

horizontal rules, data, organizing, 323

Host Control Panel, 202

HotSpot
  command (Create menu), 113-114, 137, 404
  function, @Command functions, 1224

Hotspot Pop-up properties dialog box, 405, 407

Hotspot Rectangle properties dialog box, 402

HotSpot Resource Link
  Infobox, 137
  properties dialog box, 404-405

hotspots, 400, 403, 411
  action, 407
  buttons, 400, 406
  Click formulas, 320
  defining, 290
  drawing, 401
  formula pop-ups, 406-407
  imagemaps, 407-408
  links, 90, 404-405
  navigators, 399-400
  pop-ups, 405-406

housekeeping, SMTP/MIME MTA, disabling, 789

Housekeeping page, 243
HSM (hierarchical storage migration), 1154
HTML (Hypertext Markup Language)
  code
    [ ] (brackets), 692
    multiple applets (eSuite), 595
    Project Scheduler applets (eSuite), 596
    Spreadsheet applets (eSuite), 590
    spreadsheet on HTML page, 591
    Word Processor applets (eSuite), 591
  documents
    concepts of state or context, 682
    Domino server, 695-696
    New icon, 692-693
    and Notes databases, 697
    parsing and analyzing, 599
    Updated icon, 692-693
  Domino Design Components, downloading, 707
  fields, 332
  frames, 391-392
  framesets, 389-391
  Generate HTML for all fields view, 693
  generating with JavaDoc, 549-550
  Head Attributes event, meta tags, 695
  links, view columns, 361-362
  MSFP (Microsoft FrontPage), 704
  NOF (NetObjects Fusion), 704-705
  Notes, 691-695
  question marks, changing to exclamation points, 695
  tags, 301, 309
    <A, 307
    <APPLET>, 91, 596
    <ARCHIVE>, 596
    <b>, 307
    <BODY>, 389

, 308
    <cabinets>, 596
    <FRAME>, 390-392
    <FRAMESET>, 390-392
    <I>, 307
    <IMG>, 308
    <INPUT>, 308
    <LI>, 308
    <NOFRAMES>, 390-392
    <OL>, 308
    <OPTION>, 308
    <P>, 308
    <S>, 308
    <SELECT>, 308
    syntax, 306-307
    <TEXTAREA>, 308
    <U, 308
    <UL>, 308
  tools, 703-707
  Treat Document Contents as HTML view, 693
  Treat page, 605
  Treat View Contents as HTML view, 693
  views, embedded, 378
  Web browsers, 306
  Web pages, 301-309
  Web sites, 691-697
HTML 4.0, supporting, Domino Designer, 35, 37
HTTP (Hypertext Transfer Protocol) Domino server tasks, 1028
  HTTP subtab (Internet Protocols tab in Server document), 826-829
  HTTPS (HTTP transactions), 820
  requests, processing, 571
  servers, CGI (common gateway interface), 1163
  Web browser connections, troubleshooting, 1050-1051
hub-and-spoke topology, 929, 957, 1127
Hunt Group connection, 839
hypertext links. See links
Hypertext Markup Language. See HTML
Hypertext Transfer Protocol. See HTTP
hyphen (-), 1025

I

<I> tag (HTML), 307
i18n.jar files, 572
IBM
  Net.Commerce, 725-726
  Redbooks Web site, 1177-1178
  Visual Age for Java with Calendar applets (eSuite), 598
  Web site, 724, 1125
ICM (Internet Cluster Manager), 38, 755-756, 825, 1028, 1082-1084
Icon Bar check box, 57
Icon Color Scheme (user preference), 89
icon editor, Domino databases, 272
Icon Size button, 57
icons
  Attachment, 145
  bookmarks, 61
  Calendar, 172
  Create Table SmartIcon, 138
  Cycle SmartIcon, 136
  Domino Administrator, 896
  Domino Designer, 282
  Edit Document SmartIcon, 127, 146
  envelope, 144
  File Print, 57
  File-Tools-SmartIcons, 57
  for documents, 144-145
  Globe, 248
  Hand, 199
  handshake, 145
  International (User Preferences dialog box), 96-97
  Mail and News (User Preferences dialog box), 97-98
  navigation, 54
  New, HTML documents, 692-693
  Open URL, 54
  paper clip, 356
  paperclip, 145
  pencil, 198
  Ports, 233
  Print SmartIcon, 147
  pushpin, 248
  Replicator, 61
  Server, 896
  SmartIcons, 55-59
  Spacer, 56
  square, 70
  string around a finger, 145
  Tabbed Table, 317
  Updated, HTML documents, 692-693
  view columns, 356, 358
ICSA (International Computer Security Association)
  Certification for firewalls, 879
  certified firewalls Web site, 891
id field (NotesException class), 556
ID files
  safe copying, 930-931
  security, 799-800

INFORMATION SYSTEMS 1263

IDE (Integrated Development Environment), 20, 35, 282, 456
Domino Designer
agents, 286, 293-294
design elements, 285-287
fields
 sharing, 296-297
folders, 286, 292
forms, 285
subforms, 290-292
framesets, 285, 288
image resources, 295
Java applets, 295-296
navigators, 286, 293
outlines, 285-288
pages, 285, 289-290
resources, 294
script libraries, 297
starting, 282-283
views, 286, 292
window, 283-285
Java, 460-462, 575
LotusScript, 456-464

identifiers, 496
Java, 547-548
Private, 498
Public, 498
scope, 496-498

IDs. *See also* **passwords; security**
ACLs (Access Control Lists), 414
administrator files, 770
authentication, 851, 1053
certification, 850-851, 1053
8-character for documents, 992
files, 62-65
logging on to Notes client, 51
Notes security, 849-851
organization certifiers, 762, 772
replication, 223, 953
servers, ciphers, 870
users
 adding to Domino server, 46
 certifiers, 761
 creating, 761
security, 846

IETF (Internet Engineering Task Force), 190
standard, 924
Web site, 881-882

if function, 442

If-Then-Else statement, 511

IIOP (Internet InterORB Protocol), 21, 486, 573-575, 753, 820
Restrictions (Security tab of Server document), 818
subtab (Internet Protocols tab in Server document), 830
subtab (Ports tab in Server document), 820

IIS integration with Web Application Server, 753-754

Image Resource command (Create menu), 323, 408

image resources
Domino Designer, 295
library, graphic images, 322-323

Image Resources (Domino Designer) in Resources twistie, 286

imagemaps, 411. *See also* **navigators**
hotspots, 407-408
importing, 408

images. *See* **graphics**

imaging technology, integrating
client software, 1154
client/server imaging, 1154
desktop-based imaging, 1155
hardware infrastructure, 1153
imaging servers, 1154
imaging software, 1154-1155
network infrastructure, 1153
planning, 1152-1153
scanners, 1153

IMAP (Internet Mail Access Protocol), 121
Domino server tasks, 1028
servers, email, 944

<IMG> tag (HTML), 308

implicitly declaring, LotusScript variables, 502-503

Implode function, 443

Import
button, 304, 322, 866
command (File menu), 576
dialog box, 322

Import from a jar/zip file dialog box, 576

Import Holidays (Tools command, Actions menu), 181

Importance option, sending email, 106

importing
classes, 555
imagemaps, 408
from LDAP (Lightweight Directory Access Protocol), LDIF (LDAP Data Interchange Format), 1111-1113
packages, 555
pictures, 321-322

INPUT tag (HTML), 308

inbound transport, shutting down, 790

Inbound Work Queue, clearing, 791

Inbox
email, opening and reading, 108
view, 102

Indent Entry button, 389

independence, of hardware and operating systems, 13

indexes
array, 500
Domino databases, 262, 277
full text, 983-985
size factors, 984
views, 366-368, 371

indexing, multidatabase, 992-994

individual users, security, 858

InfoBoxes
Database Properties, 865
Document Properties, 148, 865
Form Properties, 864
opening, 138
Picture Properties InfoBox, 139
Property, opening, 138
Table Properties InfoBox, 138

InfoBus, 588-589
controlling, 596
FileReader applets, 600

InfoCenter
applets (eSuite), 600
with Chart applets (eSuite), 594
with Project Scheduler applets (eSuite), 597
with Spreadsheet applets (eSuite), 594
with Word Processing applets (eSuite), 592-593

InfoList Pane, 462, 464

information
awareness, 190
framesets, 390
sharing in real-time, 191-192

information systems, Interfusion Energy (case study)
AS/400 rule, 1165
BBS (bulletin board system), 1166
data, managing, 1175-1176
integrated messaging systems, 1166-1167
Web site (self-service), 1167-1177

Information tab, Domino database properties, 274-275

infrastructures
  hardware
    imaging technology integration, 1153
    integrating faxes, 1148
    for voice mail, 1144
  networks
    imaging technology integration, 1153
    integrating faxes, 1148
    for voice mail, 1144
  servers
    communications, 1124-1126
    database, planning, 1123
    external, planning, 1124
    firewall, planning, 1124
    mail, planning, 1122-1123
    Passthru, planning, 1123
    planning, 1122

inheritance, 482
  in classes, 667
  documents, 351, 353
  Domino databases, 275, 264-265
  properties in NotesRichTextItem class, 667

innermost scope, 497

input
  fields, 126
  LotusScript requests, 469-472
  statement, LotusScript, 536
  translation formulas, 441
  validation, formulas, 441

Input Translation formula, 332-333

Input Validation formula, 332-333

Inputbox function, 470

Insert Row/Column dialog box, 311

Insert Shared Field command (Create menu), 333

Insert Special (rows and columns), 311

installation files for Domino servers, 763-766

installing
  authoring tools, 706
  DevPack (eSuite), 604
  DIS (Domino Import Service), 708
  Domino Design Components, 708, 710
  Domino R5 software, 784, 792

  Domino servers, 768-770
    additional servers, 772-775
    installation files, 763-766
    options, 767
    registering while installing, 774-775
  Notes client, 46, 48-50
  Notes R5 software, 798-799

instances, 493. *See also* **objects**

instant messaging (real-time collaboration key term), 191

instantiation, 493

InStr function, 534

instructors
  drawing tools (Sametime), 196
  Follow tool, 203
  Sametime
    quizzes, 201
    sharing applications, 202-203
  students driving applications, revoking control, 203
  whiteboard presentations, preparing and showing, 196

Integer
  data type, 498
  parameter, 522

Integrated Development Environment. *See* **IDE**

Integrated Services Digital Network. *See* **ISDN**

integrating
  data, tools
    Lotus, programming solutions, 737-738
    Percussion Notrix, 733
    Replic-Action, 732-733
    Sentinel, 736-737
    SQL Pump, 734
    third-party tools, 732
    ZMERGE, 734-735
  database systems, 1158-1164
  faxes, 1147-1152
  firewalls and proxy servers with Domino, 878-879
  imaging technology, 1152-1155
  messaging systems, Interfusion Energy (case study), 1166-1167
  user account administration with Windows NT, 916-917
  voice mail, 1143-1145
  Web browsers, 237

interactive site, 721

Interactive Voice Response (IVR), 1146

interfaces
  Notes R5 mail, 17
  user, comparing workspace and Web browsers, 70
  Web browsers, 238-239

Interfusion Energy (case study)
  business problems, defining, 1164-1165
  customers, files, downloading, 1171
  data, 1175-1176
  databases, 1164, 1171
  files, customers downloading, 1171
  information systems, 1165-1167
  NotesPump/LEI, 1171-1175
  Web site (self-service), 1167
    AS/400 data, 1170-1176
    audit trails, 1176
    daily management, 1176-1177
    extending business, 1168
    network configuration, 1169-1170
    parsing agent, 1176-1177
    performance, 1168-1169
    purging agent, 1176-1177
    security, 1168-1169
    server configuration, 1169-1170

international
  functions, 1218
  preferences, 96-99

International Computer Security Association (ICSA), 879

International encryption keys, 866

International icon (User Preferences dialog box), 96-97

International option (User Preferences dialog box), 88

International property, 613

International Telecommunications Union (ITU), 190

Internet, 13-14. *See also* **email; protocols; Web browsers; Web pages; Web sites; WWW (World Wide Web)**
  access functions, 1218
  addresses
    formats, 795
    setting up and validating, 908
  clients, configuring with Domino POP3, 943

directory standards, 750
ESMTP (Extended SMTP), 748
firewalls, 872, 879-880
   choosing type or configuration, 874
   concept, 873
   configuring, 1169
   drawbacks, 876
   Dual Homed, 873
   Dual Homed Host, 874
   ICSA (International Computer Security Association) Certification, 879
   products, 879
   proxy servers, 876-879
   proxy services, 874
   Screened Host, 875
   Screened Subnet, 875-876
   setting up, 874
ICM (Internet Cluster Manager), 755-756
ISP (Internet Service Provider), 232
Java applets, security, 246-247
mail servers, 788-796
messaging
   server, 924
   standards, 747-748
MIME (multipurpose Internet mail extensions), 748, 794
Mime Conversion, 247
mobile computing, 214, 227-228
MTA (message transfer agent), 748
Notes
   addresses, converting to Internet addresses, 749
   client, integrated, 237
parameters, 244-247
Personal Web Navigator, 239
   folders, 241-242
   Internet Options screen, 242-247
   opening, 240
   setup summary, 247-248
   views, 241-242
S/MIME, 748
Secondary servers, 247
security, 870, 883, 891
   authentication, 884
   CGI scripts, 890
   defense building, 888-889
   ECL (Execution Control List), 866-868
   email forwarding and spamming unauthorized, 889-890
   encryption, 872-884
   firewalls, 872, 879-880
   granularity, 884
   Java applets, 868-869
   pitfalls, 889
   policies, 885-886
   problems, 885
   Security Risk Classification Model, 886-887
   Telnet, 890
   unwanted objects from networks, 889
   VPNs (Virtual Private Networks), 880-883
   from Web browsers, 869-870
SSLs (Secure Socket Layers), 244-245, 748
standards, RFC821 and RFC822, 748
URLs (uniform resource locators), 239
users, setting up, 907-908
VPNs (Virtual Private Networks), 880-883
Web Retriever Configuration, 245-246
Web Tours, 240
workgroups, 240

Internet Address
Construction dialog box, 795-796, 908
field (Person document), 794-796
tool, Internet Address field (Person document), 794-796

Internet Browser page (Location document), 235-236

Internet Cluster Manager (ICM), 38, 755-756, 825, 1082, 1084

Internet Engineering Task Force. *See* **IETF**

Internet Explorer
Internet mailer, Outlook Express server, 943
JDBC-ODBC driver, 599
mobile computing, 217

Internet Inter-ORB Protocol. *See* **IIOP**

Internet Options
command (Actions menu), 242
screen, 242-247

Internet Ports subtab (Ports tab in Server document), 819

Internet Protocols tab (Server document), 826-832, 1015

Internet service providers (ISPs), 17, 232, 1125

Internet.Com, e-commerce section, 724

InternetWeek **Web site, 722**

InterNoded Web site, 724

InterNotes Web Browser (now Server Web Browser), 237, 240

Internotes Web Publisher (IWP), 681

interpretive languages, 452

intranets, applications, Domino Designer, 285-297

invitations to meetings
chairpersons, actions, 179, 181
issuing, 175, 177-179, 181
Respond with Comments button, 178-179
tracking, 178-179

IP Security Document Roadmap, 882

IPSec (IP Security Protocol), 882

Ipswitch Web site, 1075

IPX, mobile computing, 211

Iris Today on Notes Net Web site, 718

Is-A relationships, 482

IsCalendar property, 638

IsDate function, 523

IsDeleted property, 649

IsEmpty function, 506

ISDN (Integrated Services Digital Network)
mobile computing, 213
server communications infrastructure, 1125

IsEmpty function, 506, 523

IsEncrypted property, 655

IsField method, 642

IsFolder property, 638

IsFormula method, 642

Island (Disconnected) location, mobile computing, 214

isNewNote method or property, 649

IsNull function, 523

IsProfile property, 651

ISPs (Internet service providers), 17, 232, 1125

isResponse method or property, 649

isSentByAgent method, 657
IsSigned property, 656
issues, upgrades, 1093-1099
isValid property, 649
Item class, methods, 665
Items property, 663
itemvariable variable, 514
ITU (International Telecommunications Union), T.120 standards, 190
IVR (Interactive Voice Response), 1146
IWP (Internotes Web Publisher), 681

J

JAR files, 545, 554, 572-573
Java (object-oriented language), 454, 547
   ACLs (Access Control Lists), 636
   agents, 563-565
      ACL restrictions, 420
      creating, 36
      debugging with AgentRunner, 576-579
   <APPLET> tag, 91
   applets, 453-454, 565-567
      Address Book (eSuite), 598
      agents, comparing, 296
      AppletContainer, 600, 605-607
      Calendar, 583
      Calendar (eSuite), 597-598
      categories, 589
      CGI Gateway, 600
      Chart, HTML code, 593
      Chart (eSuite), 593-595
      Chat, 194, 199
      data access (eSuite), 598-599
      data presentation (eSuite), 589-598
      Domino Designer, 286, 295-296
      Editor Applets, 687
      enabling, 91
      FarSite Viewer, 194
      file system access, 96
      FileReader, 600
      FormReader, 599
      floating, 193
      Hand, 194
      Help, 194
      InfoCenter, 600
      Internet security, 868-869
      List, 194
      multiple, (eSuite), 595-596
      parameters, 606
      Presentation Graphics (eSuite), 597
      Project Scheduler (eSuite), 596-597
      Private Message, 200
      properties, 606
      View Applets, 683, 687
      ScriptHelper, 601-603
      security, 96, 246-247
      Send, 194
      SpreadSheet, 584
      Spreadsheet, HTML code, 590
      Spreadsheet (eSuite), 589-591, 594
      SQL/Java Database Connectivity (JDBC) (eSuite), 599
      TableReader, 599
      toggling, 193
      Utility (eSuite), 600
      View Applets, 683, 687
      views, 369-370
      Word Processing (eSuite), 591-593
      Word Processor, 584- 586, 591
      Work Files, 584
      toggling, 193
   applications, standalone, 567-569
   archives, 553-555
   back-end classes, 488-491
   BeanBuilder, 717
   binary codes, storing, 545
   CAB files (cabinet), 554
   classes, 553-555, 632
      ACL, 636
      AgentContext, 610-613, 643
      Database, 635-636
      DbDirectory, 635-636
      Document, 645-658
      Form, 644-645
      LotusScript comparisons, 492-493, 637
      Session, 610-613
      View, 638
   CLASSPATH, (environment variable), 545-546
   code
      debugging, 575-578
   comments, 548-549
   CORBA (Common Object Request Broker Architecture), 573-575
   data types, 550-551
   development environments, 544
   DOM (Domino Object Model), 464-465, 485-486, 614
   enabling access from JavaScript, 92
   eSuite
      applet categories, 589
      InfoBus, 588-589
      JavaBeans, 587
      Workplace, 582-586
   EventExample Hello agent, 466-469
   exceptions, handling, 555-556
   expressions, 551
   front-end classes, 669
   Hello agent example, 460-462
   IBM Visual Age with Calendar applets (eSuite), 598
   IDE (Integrated Development Environment), 36
   identifiers, 547-548
   IIOP (Internet Inter-ORB Protocol), 573-575
   importing classes or packages, 555
   Item class, 664-665
   JAR files, 554, 572-573
   JavaDoc utility, downloading, 548
   JDK (Java Development Kit), 546-547
   JSDK (Java Servlet Development Kit), 570
   keywords, 548
   method calls, 610
   methods, 610, 664
   multithreading, 557-562
   operators, 551
   overview, 544-545
   packages, 553-555
   properties, obtaining and setting, 664
   replaceItemValue method, 664
   RichTextItem class, 669-670
   RichTextParagraphStyle class, 670
   RichTextStyle class, 669-670
   servlets, 569-572
   Session
      class, 562-563
      methods, mapping of NotesSession methods, 612
   Session MethodsLotusScript properties, mapping of NotesSession properties, 611
   statements, 552-553
   supporting Domino Designer, 35, 37
   tags, <APPLET>, 91

Thread class, 557-559
views, 369-370
ZIP files, 554

Java Activity, 1162

Java Applet command (Create menu), 605

Java Applet Security
mobile computing locations, 220
tab (Location document), 868-869

Java Archive (JAR) file, 554

Java Database Connectivity (JDBC), 599

Java Development Kit (JDK), 546-547

Java Foundation Classes (JFC), 546

Java IDE, 575

Java Servlet Development Kit (JSDK), 570

Java Virtual Machine (JVM), 544

JavaBeans, 587

JavaDoc
source files, generating HTML (Hypertext Markup Language), 549-550
utility, downloading, 548

JavaScript, 452- 454
circles, 36
Domino database, 274
Enable JavaScript (user preference), 91
enabling Java access, 92
EventExample Hello agent, 466-469
events, 36, 466
random chart (eSuite), 603
security, 97
supporting, Domino Designer, 35, 37

JavaUserClasses file, 545

JavaWorld Web site, 547

JDBC (Java Database Connectivity), 599, 738, 1163

JDBC-ODBC driver on Internet Explorer, 599

JDK (Java Development Kit)
API (Application Programming Interface), 546
AWT (Abstract Windowing Toolkit), 547

JFC (Java Foundation Classes), 546

join() method, 558

Jscript, 452

JSDK (Java Servlet Development Kit), 570

jsdk.jar files, 573

JVM (Java Virtual Machine), 544-545

K

Kaufman, Charles, 883

Kennedy, Patricia, 883

Key method, 651

key parameter, 445

key terms, real-time collaboration, 191

keyboard shortcuts
Alt+Enter, 312, 802
Alt+P, 64
Alt+Tab, 193
Ctrl+B, 128
Ctrl+C, 146
Ctrl+E, 127, 146
Ctrl+I, 128
Ctrl+M, 103
Ctrl+O, 80
Ctrl+P, 66
Ctrl+Shift+F9, 995
Ctrl+U, 128
Ctrl+V, 113, 146
Ctrl+W, 108, 146
Shift+Tab, 108

keyboards, accelerators, extended, 94

keys
encryption, 652-654, 865-866
NotesView class, 639
private or public, 244

keywords
ByVal, 522-523
Call, 526
Class, 504
Dim, NotesItem class, creating, 665
End Class, 504
FIELD, 434
formulas, 434, 438-440
Java, 548
New, 505-506, 620, 632, 646, 663
creating class objects, 614
NotesTimer object, creating, 671
Search Builder dialog box, 345
Set, 613- 615
Static, 502

KM (knowledge management), databases, 18-19

L

L2TP (Layer 2 Tunneling Protocol) Web site, 882

labels, repetition flow control, 516

languages
@formula, 346
bidirectional, 261
Domino databases, 256, 276
object-oriented. *See* Java
scripting. *See* LotusScript

LANs (local area networks), Connection document, 835

LastAccessed property, 262, 277, 649

LastModified property, 649

launch properties, 690

Launch tab, Domino database properties, 276

launching Chat (Java applet), 199

Layer 2 Tunneling Protocol (L2TP), Web site, 882

layout function, @Command functions, 1224

Layout Region command (Create menu), 335

layout regions on forms, 335-337

LCCOV (Lotus Calendar Connector for OfficeVision), 187

LS:DO (LotusScript Data Object), 738

LDAP (Lightweight Directory Access Protocol), 598, 750, 820, 824
directories, importing from, 1111
documents, creating in Directory Assistance, 852
Domino server tasks, 1028
LDIF (LDAP Data Interchange Format), 1111-1113
queries in Personal Address Book, 153
security, authentication on the Web, 852
subtab (Internet Protocols tab in Server document), 831
tab (Domino Administrator), 1018-1019

LDAP V2 Protocol RFC1777, 121

LDAPv3

LDAPv3 (Lightweight Directory Access Protocol), 1088
  standard, 751
LDIF (LDAP Data Interchange Format), 1111-1113
learning, collaborative, Sametime, 192-193
leaving a message software, 1145
Left function, 442
Left$ function, 522, 533
legacy systems
  defined, 730
  ERP (enterprise resource planning), 731
  non-system-based data sources, 732
  RDBMS (relational database management systems), 730
  transactional systems, 731
LEI (Lotus Enterprise Integrator), 739, 1158. *See also* NotesPump/LEI
  Database Connectors, Basic, 1160
  Directory Connectors, 1160
  File Systems Connectors, 1160
  Metaconnectors, 1160-1161
  relational sources, supporting, 739
  Web site, 1177
Len function, 533
length parameter, 532
Less than operator, 436
Less than or equal operator, 436
Let statement, 506
letterheads, email, defining, 111
letters, lowercase for packages, 555
Level 1, awareness measures (Security Risk Classification Model), 887
Level 2, prevention measures (Security Risk Classification Model), 887
Level 3, crisis measures (Security Risk Classification Model), 887
levels, ACLs (Access Control Lists), 414
  assigning, 415
  privileges, 419-420
leveraging upgrading Domino servers and Notes clients, R4 to R5, 783

<LI> tag (HTML), 308
libraries
  database library, 1132
  for databases, creating, 1001-1002
  image resources, graphic images, 322-323
  script, Domino Designer, 287, 297
licenses, servers, 746
lifetimes, LotusScript variables, 502
lights, red or green, users names on buddy lists, 198
Lightweight Directory (Domino databases), 258
Lightweight Directory Access Protocol (LDAP), 598, 750, 820, 824
Lightweight Directory Access Protocol (LDAPv3), 1088
Like operator, 534
Limit entries in $Revisions fields property, 1077
Limit entries in $UpdatedBy fields property, 1076
Line Input statement, 536
lines, view headings or rows, 366
Link
  documents, 1171-1172
  entries, outlines, 387
Link Hotspot (Hotspot command, Create menu), 113-114
Link Messages (email), creating, 113-114
Link Properties InfoBox, links, 114
Link to applet on a Web server button, 605
links
  creating for Web pages, 251
  to databases, 980-981
  to folders, 979-981
  frames, 395, 397
  hotspots, 404-405
  hypertext, concepts of state or context, 682
  in rich-text fields, 136-137
  to Web pages, creating, 114
  view columns, 361-362
List (Java applet), 194
List
  button, 198-199
  concatenation operator, 435

listings
  Opinion Program That Displays the Cost of Wisdom, 471
  PersonClass Definition, 504-505
  PersonType Definition, 502
  Program That Requests and Displays a Name, 470
lists, 131
  boxes, 330
  buddy lists (real-time collaboration key term), 191
  formulas, 437-438
  functions, 443, 1215-1216
  To Do, managing, 182
  values, formulas, 435
  variables, LotusScript, 501
LN:DI (Lotus Notes Document Imaging), 1155
loading
  DFC, 715
  stopping, SMTP/MIME MTA or Statistics Reporter, 791
Local Database Folder (user preference), 90
local directories, defining, 164
local encryption of applications, 848
LocalDomainServers group, 417, 428
Location documents, 76-77. *See also* locations
  email, defining local and public directories, 164
  Internet Browser page, 235-236
  Java Applet Security tab, 868-869
  mobile computing, 214-220
  Passthru servers, 221-222
  Public directory, 82
  replication schedules, 965-966
  TCP/IP, 234-237
  viewing in Personal Address Book, 234
  Web browsers, setting up, 235
  Web Proxy field, 236
locations. *See also* Location documents
  Bookmarks file, 220
  browsers, 217
  dialing in, 218-219
  graphics, downloading, 220
  idle times, 220
  mail, 216-217
  mobile computing 208, 213-214, 227

LOTUSSCRIPT 1269

multiple users, 220
naming, 215
ports, 215
prompt (user preference), 89
replication, 217-218
Secure Sockets Layer, 220
servers, 215

Locations dialog box, 235

locking workstation, 96

Lockmode, LotusScript files, 535

log analysis, Domino server performance, 1033

log files
database replication, viewing, 970
record, 1008

Log path field (Transactional Logging tab of Server document), 832

LOG.NSF file, 938-939, 1008

logging
Domino database transactions, 262-263
event logging, redirecting from Notes to Windows NT Event Logger, 917
on to Notes client, 51-52
transactions, upgrading Domino servers and Notes clients from R4 to R5, 781

Logging style field (Transactional Logging tab of Server document), 833

Logical AND operator, 436

Logical OR operator (|), 436

logical values, formulas, 435

Login Script Arguments field (dial-up modems of Connection document), 838

Login Script File Name field (dial-up modems of Connection document), 838

logs
ACLs, viewing changes, 423
certification, creating, 770-771

Long data type, 498

loops. *See* repetition control flow

Lotus
agreement with AOL (America Online), 14
archives, including in CLASSPATH, 545

tools
for integrating data, 737
product-based solutions, 738-740
programming solutions, 737-738
Web site, 722, 740

Lotus Business Partners, 14

Lotus Calendar Connector for OfficeVision (LCCOV), 187

Lotus Developer Web site, 702

Lotus Domino Connectors, 1159, 1163

Lotus Enterprise Integrator. *See* **LEI**

Lotus eSuite, Web site, 717

Lotus Notes. *See also* **Notes**
Connect (mobile computing), 209-210
Document Imaging (LN:DI), 1155
Domino, deploying, 1094-1095
Installation dialog box, 48
Internet Cookbook Web site, 228

Lotus Organizer 97 GS, 187

Lotus Web site, 309, 805, 883, 1137

LotusScript, 452-456
ACLs (Access Control Lists), 636
agents, ACL restrictions, 420
back-end classes, 485, 488-491
classes
creating, 504-505
date and time variables, 618-619
Java comparisons, 492-493, 637
NotesACL, 636
NotesDatabase, 632-635
NotesDocument, 645-658
NotesDocumentCollection, 642-643
NotesForm, 644-645
NotesSession, 610-611, 613
NotesView, 638-640
NotesViewColumn, 642
NotesViewEntry, 640-641
NotesViewEntryCollection, 640-641
NotesViewNavigator, 641
comments, 509
DO (Data Object), 491
Domino Object Model, 465

EventExample Hello agent, 466-469
events, 466, 487-488
extended class syntax, 663-664
files, 534-538
GoSub statement, 530
Hello agent example, 457
creating, 458-459
help settings, 462-464
testing, 459-460
IDE (Integrated Development Environment), 456-457
identifiers, 496-498
input requests, 469-471
methods, case sensitivity, 610
NotesACL class, 675
NotesACLEntry class, 675
NotesEmbeddedObject class, 670-671
NotesItem class, creating, 663-666
NotesName class, 674-675
NotesRichTextItem class, 667
NotesRichTextParagraphStyle class, 670
NotesRichTextStyle class, 668-669
NotesTimer class, 671-674
NotesUIDatabase class, 624-625
NotesUIDocument class, 627-628
NotesUIView class, 625-627
NotesUIWorkspace class, 619-624
NotesUIWorkspace class agents playing tunes, 620-621
numeric input requests, 471-472
objects, 505-506
On Error statement, 529
OOP (object-oriented programming), 477
properties, comparing to Java methods, 664
Return statement, 530
reusing code, 538-540
scope, 496-498
size limitations, 503-504
statements, 509
strings, 530-534
subroutines
calling, 525-526
classes, 521
coherence, 520-521
event handlers, 525
functions, 522-524
passing arguments, 526-528
Property Get, 524-525

Property Set, 524-525
Sub statement, 521-522
variables, 521
syntax, Domino Object Model classes, 1184
values, 506-507
variables
array, 500-501
constants, 499-500
data types, 498-499
implicitly declaring, 502-503
lifetimes, 502
list, 501
naming, 507-508
scalar, 500
user-defined type, 501-502

LotusScript Data Object. *See* LS:DO

LotusScript Extensions (LSXs), 737-738

LowerCase function, 442

lowercase letters for packages, 555

LS:DO (LotusScript Data Object), 1163

LSXs (LotusScript Extensions), 539-540, 737-738

LTrim$ function, 533

M

MAB (Master Address Book). *See* Directory Assistance

machines, Domino Design Components, installing, 708, 710

macro languages. *See* LotusScript

mail. *See* email

Mail, Calendar view, 168

Mail Address Assistant, 155

Mail and News
icon (User Preferences dialog box), 97-98
option (User Preferences dialog box), 88

Mail
button, 866
command, Create menu, 103, 172

Mail Gateways, 1137

Mail Information tab (Domain documents), 840

Mail Preferences dialog box, Preferences InfoBox, 110-112

Mail Router, email, 928

Mail Routing Status, 1047

Mail Routing Topology map, 1047

Mail subtab
Messaging tab, Domino Administrator, 925-926
Ports tab in Server document, 820

Mail tab (Domino Administrator), 898

Mail-In Database documents (Domino Directory), 843, 1012

MAIL.BOX
database, 938
file, 1008
SMTP/MTA, backing up, 791

Mailer, email, 928

main documents, 350

Maintain LastAccessed property, 1076

Make this site accessible property, 696

MakeResponse
method, 650
parameter, 648

Manage ACL dialog box, Basics pane, 999

Manage button, 917

Manage Groups dialog box, 918

Manager level, ACLs (Access Control Lists), 415-416

managers, application security, 858

managing
ACLs (Access Control Lists), databases, 1133-1134
daily, data of Interfusion Energy (case study), 1176-1177
databases, 22
Domino Directory, 1117-1118
groups, 917-918
schedules, 169
To Do lists, 182
usernames, 908

manually
changing Notes usernames, 911
deleting usernames, 914
recertifying Notes IDs, 916

mapping
NotesSession methods to Java Session methods, 612
NotesSession properties to Java Session MethodsLotusScript properties, 611
passthru topologies, 1135

margins
setting, Text Properties InfoBox, 133
in tables, 312-313

Mark Documents Read (user preference), 90

Mark Private (appointments), 175

MarkRead parameter, 648

marks, unread
maintenance, 802
viewing documents in Notes, 143

massively parallel processing (MPP), 1083

Master Address Book (MAB). *See* Directory Assistance

mathematical functions, 522, 1214-1215

Maximum Internet name & password (ACLs), 427

Maximum Log Space field (Transactional Logging tab of Server document), 833

Mayflower Software Web site, 737

Meeting Invitations & Reservations form, 175-176

meetings
canceling, 180-181
chairpersons, actions, 179-181
confirming, 180
invitations, 178-179
participants, viewing status, 180
people, inviting, 175-181
rescheduling, 180
Resource Reservations database, 186
Sametime, 203-204
scheduling with email contacts, 160

Meetings view, 169

member variables, 479

Memo command, Create menu, 103

memory
Domino R5, 1074
requirements for servers, 1087-1088

memos, email, 103-104

menu bars, 53-54, 284

menus
Actions, 54
Create, 54
Edit, 53

File, 53
floating (Text Properties InfoBox), 128
Help, 54
Tools, 53
View, 53

Merge Cells command (Table menu), 316

merging
cells in tables, 316
domains, 1030

mesh topology, 929, 958, 1127

Message Migration
Admin tool, 1105
User tool, 1106

message playback software, 1145

Message Transfer Agents (MTAs), 748, 788, 832, 1105, 1137

messages. *See* **email, messages**

messaging
environments, auditing, 1093-1095
instant messaging (real-time collaboration key term), 191
services
   faxes, integrating, 1147-1152
   imaging technology, integrating, 1152-1155
   IVR (Interactive Voice Response), 1146
   paging, 1146
   paper, reducing usage, 1146-1147
   unified messaging, 1142
   voice mail, 1143-1145
standards for email, 121-122
standards of Internet, 747-748
systems, integrated, Interfusion Energy (case study), 1166-1167
unified, 1142
Utility Applets (eSuite), 604

Messaging tab
Admin Client, monitoring servers, 1046
Domino Administrator, 898-899, 925-926

Messaging Upgrade Program, 1093

meta tags, HTML Head Attributes event, 695

Metaconnectors (LEI), 1160-1161

methods, 632
calls, 610
case sensitivity, 610
classes, 480
Clear, 639
Create, NotesDatabase class, 633-634
CreateCopy, 634-635
createDatabase, 635
CreateDocument, 646
CreateFromTemplate, 634-635
CreateReplica, 634-635
CreateReplyMessage, 658
CreateTimer, NotesTimer object, 671
creating class objects, 615-616
Encrypt, 655
FTSearch, 639
FullName, 505
getACL, 636
GetAllDocumentsByKey, 639-640
GetChild, 639
GetDatabase, 632
GetDbDirectory, 523
GetDocumentByID, 646
GetDocumentByKey, 640
GetDocumentByUNID, 646
GetEntry, 636
GetFirstEntry, 636
GetListOfTunes, 620-621
getName, 665
GetNextEntry, 636
GetNextSibling, 639
getParentDocumentUNID, 649
GetProfileDocument, 650
getResponses, 650
getText, 665
getUnprocessedDocuments, 643
getValueString, 665
IsField, 642
IsFormula, 642
isNewNote, 649
isResponse, 649
isSentByAgent, 657
Item class, 665
Java, 492, 664
join(), 558
Key, 651
LotusScript, 492
MakeResponse, 650
New, NotesItem class, 665
New NotesDatabase, 633
NotesDocument, GetFirstItem, 663
NotesSession, mapping to Java Session methods, 612
NotesUIView class, 626-627

objects, 479
Open, NotesDatabase class, 634-635
OpenByReplicaID, 635-636
openDatabase, 635
OpenFileDialog, 621-623
OpenIfModified, 634-635
OpenWithFailover, 635
PickListCollection, 623-624
PickListStrings, 623-624
PlayTune, 620-621
PostOpen, 621
Print, syntax, 626
Prompt, 624
Remove, 644, 648
RemoveAll, 643
replaceItemValue, 664
run(), 557, 559
runNotes(), 559
Save, 643, 647-648
SaveFileDialog, 621-623
SelectDocument, 627
Send, 656-657
Session, mapping of NotesSession methods, 612
Sign, 656
StampAll, 643
start(), 557
toString, 665
UpdateProcessedDoc, 643

Microsoft
Exchange
   converting to Notes, 1109-1111
   Domino, comparing, 16
FrontPage, MSFP (Microsoft FrontPage), 702-707
Mail, converting to Notes, 1107-1109
Mail Administrator's Guide, 1107
Office 97, SendTo, 93
Office Library (R5.0) template, 259
Web site, 706-707

Mid$ function, 522, 533

Migrate button, 1103, 1109

Migrate People button, 1102, 1108-1110

migration
cc Mail users, preparing, 1101-1102
Directory Migration, 1105
Message Migration, 1105-1106
tools, 1105-1107
User Migration, 1105-1106
users, 1099-1100

MIME

MIME (multipurpose Internet mail extensions), 121, 748, 794, 924
   conversions, mobile computing locations, 220, 247
   messages, transferring on Domino R4 and R5 servers, 794
   tab (Domino Administrator), 1021

Mindspring Web site, 1125

miscellaneous function, @Command functions, 1228

Miscellaneous tab (Server document), 832

mixed-release environments, compacting databases, 804

Mobile command (File menu), 208, 235

mobile computing, 207-208
   connections, 227-229
   Location document, 214-215
      Bookmarks file, 220
      browsers, 217
      dialing in, 218-219
      graphics, 220
      idle times, 220
      Java Applet Security, 220
      mail, 216-217
      MIME conversions, 220
      multiple users, 220
      ports, 215
      replication, 217-218
      secondary servers, 220
      Secure Sockets Layer, 220
      servers, 215
      Web Retriever, 220
   locations, selecting, 227
   modems, 211-213
   Passthru servers, 220-221
   Personal Address Book, 213-214
   ports, 208-211
   replication, 222-226
   Replication Settings dialog box, Space Savers page, 955
   security, 229
   shared email, 942
   usernames, change impact, 912-913

models
   Basic Scalability, 1079-1083
   Domino Object Model, 21-22
   Security Risk Classification Model, 886-887

modems
   ISPs (Internet service providers), 1125
   mobile computing, 211-213, 225-226
   planning, 1124-1125
   troubleshooting, 1067-1068
   voice, 1144

modes, whiteboards, controlled or uncontrolled, 197

module scope, 497, 502

Monitor documents (Domino Directory), 1012

Monitor New Task dialog box, 1043

monitoring
   ACLs (Access Control Lists), 423
   Domino databases, headline database, 263
   networks, applications, 1075
   servers (with)
      Admin Client (Domino Administrator Client), 1038
      Analysis subtab (Server tab, Admin Client), 1040
      Configuration tab (Admin Client), 1048
      Files tab (Admin Client), 1045
      Messaging tab (Admin Client), 1046
      Monitoring subtab (Server tab, Admin Client), 1041-1044
      Replication tab (Admin Client), 1045-1046
      Server tab (Admin Client), 1038
      Statistics subtab (Server tab, Admin Client), 1044-1045
      Status subtab (Server tab, Admin Client), 1038-1040

Monitoring subtab (Server tab, Admin Client), 1041-1044

Monitoring tab (Domino Administrator), 898

monitoring tools for email routing, 938-939

Monitors, 816

Mood stamp option, sending email, 107

More Info button, 990

More Options tab (User ID dialog box), 66

mouse
   calendar entries, displaying, 78
   drawing navigator objects, 400
   highlighting navigator objects, 402

Move button, 908

Move Database dialog box, 987

Move to Folder button, 160

moving
   databases, 986-987
   documents to folders, 334
   Domino servers within the organization, 1031
   outline entries, 389

MPP (massively parallel processing), 1083

MS Mail Initialization dialog box, 1108

MSFP (Microsoft FrontPage), 702-707

MTAs (message transfer agents), 748, 788, 832, 1105, 1137
   cc:Mail, upgrading, 1105
   inbound transport, shutting down, 790
   servers
      file backups, 789
      installing Domino R5 software, 792
      NOTES.INI file upgrades, 796
      upgrading Administration Requests database, 793
   tab (Server document), 832, 1015

multidatabase indexing in databases, 992-994

multiple
   applets (eSuite), 595-596
   servers, configuring, 1017
   threads, upgrading Internet mail servers, 794
   value separators for fields, 332
   windows, opening, 60

Multiplication operator, 435

multipurpose Internet mail extensions. *See* **MIME**

multithreading
   configuration for email routing, 938
   in Java, 557-562
   servlets, 570

My News welcome page, 29

MyName$ variable, 470

N

NAB (Public Name and Address Book). *See* Domino Directory

NAME attribute, FRAME tag, 392

Named Element entries, outlines, 387-388

Named Style command (Text menu), 135

NameOfProfile property, 651

names
   classes, LotusScript, 492-493
   domains, 760-763
   email files, 102
   email, looking up, 104
   fields, 327-328
   files, Domino databases, 261
   mobile computing locations, 215
   Notes users, X.500 protocol, 1119
   replicated databases, 267
   of rows, case-sensitive, 320
   searching, mobile computing mail, 217
   servers, renaming, 1032
   SmartIcons sets, 56
   usernames, parsing, 674-675
   users and servers for networks, 1119-1122
   variables, 507-508
   view columns, 361

Names dialog box, 152, 418, 918

names fields, 330

NAT (Network Address Translation), 883

navigate function, @Command functions, 1225

navigation, 411
   buttons, Sametime, 194
   creating, 399
   Domino Designer, 286, 293
   embedding, 409
   frames, 390-392, 395
   framesets, 389-398
   function, @Command functions, 1225
   graphic backgrounds, 399-400
   hotspots, 403-408
   icons, 54
   imagemaps, 407-408, 411
   navigators, 399-403
   NotesView class, (LotusScript), 638-639
   objects, 400-403
   outlines, 384-389, 395-397
   Web site, designing, 33

Navigator class, 487, 1185

NCSO.cab files, 573

NCSO.jar files, 573

NCSOC.jar files, 573

NDS (Novell Directory Services), 81

nested framesets, 390-391

nesting tables, 318

Net Address field (Ports tab of Server document), 819

Net.Commerce (IBM), 725-726

NetBIOS, mobile computing, 209

Netconnections Web site, 805

Netcraft Web Server Survey Web site, 702

NetCreator, Domino Directory ACL (Access Control List), 809

NetCreator role, 860

NetModifier, Domino Directory ACL (Access Control List), 809

NetModifier role, 860

NetObjects Fusion. *See* NOF

NetObjects' Web site, 706

Netscape, mobile computing, 217

NetWare SPX, mobile computing, 209

Network Address Translation (NAT), 883

Network Dialup connection (Connection document), 838-839

Network preferences page, 243

networks
   adjacent Domino domains, email routing between, 932
   bandwidth, Domino R5, 1074
   communications infrastructure, 1124-1126
   configuring, Interfusion Energy (case study), 1169-1170
   data, encrypting, 863
   designing, 1119
   DNS (Domain Name Service),, 1075
   documents, changing, 1118
   Domino Administrator, 1137-1138
   Domino Directory, 1117-1118, 1135-1136
   Domino Named Networks, 931
   Domino R5, performance, 1074
   events, trapping, 1138
   firewalls, 1075
   infrastructure
      imaging technology integration, 1153
      integrating faxes, 1148
      for voice mail, 1144
   modifying, 1029
   monitoring applications, 1075
   MTAs (message transfer agents), 1137
   naming users and servers, 1119-1122
   NNNs (Notes Named Networks), 818
   non-adjacent Domino domains, email routing between, 932
   planning guidelines, 1116-1117
   ports, encrypting data, 863, 1075
   protocols, 1074
   proxy servers, 1075
   requests, approval or rejection notification, 1118
   security, physical and logical, 847-848
   segments, 1074
   servers
      infrastructure, 1122-1124
      naming, 1119-1122
   speed, 1074
   standards, 1117
   statistics, 1138
   teamwork responsibility, 1117
   topologies
      end-to-end, 1126
      hub-and-spoke, 1127
      mail routing, 1127-1129
      mesh, 1127
      passthru, 1134-1135
      peer-to-peer, 1126
      replication, 1129-1134
   unwanted objects, 889
   users, naming, 1119-1122

New Agent button, 457, 620

New button, 866

New Copy command (Database menu), 265

New Database dialog box, 260, 770

New Entry button, 386, 690

new features
   Directory Catalog, 824-825
   document versioning, 1066
   Domino Designer client, 32-37

Domino server, 37-40
graphic image storage, 322
ICM (Internet Cluster Manager), 825
Monitors, 816
nesting tables, 318
Notes
   client, 28-31
   window, 53
subscriptions, 86-87
task buttons, 60-61
transactional logging, 832
welcome pages, 14

New Folder button, 348

New Form button, 326

New Group Calendar button, 184

New icon, HTML documents, 692-693

New Image Resource button, 322

New keyword, 505-506, 620, 632, 646, 663
creating class objects, 614
NotesTimer object, creating, 671

New Layout Region dialog box, 335

New Memo button, 103, 117

New Method, NotesItem class, 665

New NotesDatabase method, 633

New Outline button, 384

New Page button, 301, 305

New Replica dialog box, 267, 957

New Replication Monitor button, 970

New Rule
button, 119
screen, 119-120

New To Do Item button, 182

New Tracking Request dialog box, 939

New View button, 343, 346

news
international preferences, changing, 97-98
readers, 768

News subtab (Ports tab in Server document), 820

News/NNTP Feed Connection, 839

newspaper style columns in tables, 313-314

Next button, 232, 767

Next statement, 513

Nextgen Web site, 724

NIF (Notes Index Facility), 662

NNNs (Notes Named Networks), 818

NNTP (Network News Transport Protocol), 122
Domino server tasks, 1028
subtab (Internet Protocols tab in Server document), 831-832

No Access, ACLs, 414, 429

NOF (NetObjects Fusion), 702-703
components, 704
downloading, 707
HTML (Hypertext Markup Language), 705

NOFRAMES tag (HTML), 390-392

NOI (Notes Object Interface), 476

Non-Adjacent Domain documents (Domain documents), 840-841, 930

non-adjacent domains, 932-935, 1128-1129

non-Internet protocols, 750

non-system-based data sources, 732

Not access server field (Security tab of Server document), 815

Not allowed to use monitors field (Security tab of Server document), 816

Not equal operator, 436

NoteID, 646

Notes, 12-14, 124, 662
addresses, converting to Internet addresses, 749
browsers, ActiveX or plugins, enabling, 92
cc:Mail, upgrading to, 1101-1104
classes
   Button, 1185
   date and time variables, 618-619
   Field, 1185
   Navigator, 1185
   NotesACL, 1189
   NotesACLEntry, 1190

   NotesAgent, 1190-1191
   NotesDatabase, 1191-1192
   NotesDateRange, 1192-1193
   NotesDateTime, 1193
   NotesDbDirectory, 1193-1194
   NotesDocument, 1194-1195
   NotesDocumentCollection, 1195-1196
   NotesEmbeddedObject, 1196
   NotesForm, 1196
   NotesInternational, 1197
   NotesItem, 1197-1198
   NotesLog, 1198
   NotesName, 1198-1199
   NotesNewsLetter, 1199
   NotesOutline, 1200
   NotesOutlineEntry, 1200-1201
   NotesRegistration, 1201-1202
   NotesReplication, 1202
   NotesRichTextItem, 1202-1203
   NotesRichTextParagraphStyle, 1203
   NotesRichTextStyle, 1203-1204
   NotesRichTextTab, 1204
   NotesSession, 1204-1205
   NotesTimer, 1205
   NotesUIDatabase, 1185-1186
   NotesUIDocument, 1186-1187
   NotesUIView, 1187-1188
   NotesUIWorkspace, 1188-1189
   NotesView, 1205-1206
   NotesViewColumn, 1206-1207
   NotesViewEntry, 1207-1208
   NotesViewEntryCollection, 1208
   NotesViewNavigator, 1208-1209
client
   bookmarks, 31
   browsing the Web, 18
   drop-down actions, 30-31
   email, 29, 31
   new features, 28-31
   framesets, opening, 691
   IDs, 51
   installing, 46, 48-50
   logging on, 51-52
   Notes view, 684
   passwords, 51-52
   TCP/IP (Transmission Control Protocol/Internet Protocol), 232-237
   upgrading R4 to R5, 778-800

NOTESDOCUMENTCOLLECTION 1275

versus Web browsers, 682
Web browsers, 238-248
Web pages, 248-251
welcome page, 28-29
databases
   accessing with Web browsers, 683-685
   calendaring and scheduling, 187-188
   HTML documents, 697
   R5 features, 687-689, 691
   Web-oriented designs, 685-687
as default Web browser, 93
desktop, Replicator page, 965-967
directories, synchronizing with Windows NT, 916-917
documents
   8-character IDs, 992
   defined, 124
   HTML (Hypertext Markup Language), 691-695
   viewing, 141-149
Domino, code sharing, 13
encryption, 861-866
event logging, redirecting to Windows NT Event Logger, 917
exploring, 52
forms, HTML (Hypertext Markup Language), 691-695
formulas. *See* formulas
Internet, security, 866-870
JAR files, 572-573
menu bar, 53-54
Microsoft
   Exchange, converting with Domino Upgrade Services, 1109-1111
   Mail, converting with Domino Upgrade Services, 1107-1109
migration tools, cc:Mail, upgrading, 1105-1106
multithreading with Java, 559-562
navigation icons, 54
Organizer 2x, upgrading to, 1106-1107
R5 mail interface, 17
security
   cross-certification, 852-856
   Domino applications, 848-849
   flat certificate exchange, 856-857
   IDs, 849-851
   network physical and logical security, 847-848
   overview, 846-847
   pyramid of security, 847

   responsible people, 858-861
   server console passwords, 857-858
SendTo (Microsoft Office 97), 93
servers, Domino Administrator, 1137-1138
setup form, 736
SmartIcons, 55-59
status bar, 59
tasks, scheduling with Program Documents, 1025-1026
tools, programming, 21
users
   migrating to, 1099-1100
   naming, X.500 protocol, 1119
   registering, 899-907
   usernames, 908-913
views, 684, 691-695
Web site, 698, 815
window, new features, 53
workflow capabilities, 20
workstation, security options, 94-96

Notes Client Configuration Wizard, 49

Notes domain, Domino Directory, 1135-1136

Notes IDs, recertifying, 915-916

Notes Index Facility (NIF), 662

Notes Link document, 1172

Notes Mail
contacts, adding to Personal Address Book, 156
notifications of request approvals or rejections, sending, 1118

Notes Named Networks (NNNs), 818

Notes Network field (Ports tab of Server document), 819

Notes Network Ports subtab (Ports tab in Server document), 818-819

Notes Object Interface (NOI), 476

Notes Personal Directory, 152

Notes Preferences dialog box, 140

Notes Storage Facility (NSF), 662

NOTES.INI file, 1008
Passthru parameters, troubleshooting, 1052-1053
modifying, 1023-1024
upgrading for MTA server, 796

removing Reporter task, 784
restrictions (port level), troubleshooting, 1055-1056
Settings tab (Domino Administrator), 1022

notes.jar files, 572

NotesACL class, 488, 636, 675, 1189

NotesACLEntry class, 488, 675, 1190

NotesAgent class, 488, 1190-1191

NotesBench Consortium
Domino R5 performance rating, 1072
Web site, 1087

NotesBench
toolset, 1086
Web site, 1087

NotesDatabase
class, 488, 492, 1191-1192
   Create method, 633-634
   NotesDatabase object, creating, 632-633
   Open method, 634-635
object, 482, 506, 632-633

NotesDateRange class, 488, 1192-1193

NotesDateTime class, 488, 1193

NotesDbDirectory class, 488, 1193-1194

NotesDocument
class, 480, 489, 645, 1194-1195
   containing NotesItem class, 663-664
   creating objects, 646
   EmbeddedObject property, comparing with NotesRichTextItem class, 671
   extended class syntax, 663-664
   folders, 651-652
   hierarchies, 649-650
   profile documents, 650-651
   properties, 649
   Remove method, 648
   Save method, 647-648
   security, 652-658
method, GetFirstItem, 663

NotesDocument EmbeddedObjects property, 671

NotesDocumentCollection
class, 481, 489, 642-643, 1195-1196
object, 482, 639

NotesEmbeddedObject class

NotesEmbeddedObject class, 489, 670-671, 1196

NotesException class, fields, id and text, 556

NotesForm class, 489, 644-64, 1196

NotesInternational class, 489, 615, 1197

NotesItem
class, 482, 489, 1197-1198
creating in LotusScript, 665-666
in NotesDocument class, 663-664
parent classes, 667
object, 482

NotesLog class, 489, 1198

NotesName class, 489, 674-675, 1198-1199

NotesNewsletter class, 489, 1199

NotesOutline class, 490, 1200

NotesOutlineEntry class, 490, 1200-1201

NotesPump/LEI (Lotus Enterprise Integrator). *See also* LEI (Lotus Enterprise Integrator)
Activities, 1161-1163
database systems integration, 1158-1161
Interfusion Energy (case study)
Direct Transfer Activity document, 1173-1175
Notes Link document, 1172
ODBC Link document, 1171-1172
setting up, 1171
resources, 1177-1178

NoteSQL, 738

NotesRegistration class, 490, 1201-1202

NotesReplication class, 490, 1202

NotesRichTextItem class, 482, 490, 666-667, 1202-1203
EmbeddedObject property, comparing with NotesDocument class, 671
parent classes, 667
properties, inherited, 667

NotesRichTextItem EmbeddedObjects property, 671

NotesRichTextItem object, 482

NotesRichTextParagraphStyle class, 490, 670, 1203

NotesRichTextStyle class, 490, 668-669, 1203-1204

NotesRichTextTab class, 490, 1204

NotesSession
class, 490-492, 610, 1204-1205
objects, creating, 615
properties, 613
methods, mapping to Java Session methods, 612
object, 506
properties, mapping to Java Session MethodsLotusScript properties, 611
variable, 506

NotesSQL, 369

NotesThread class, 559

NotesTimer
class, 490, 671-674, 1205
object, creating, 671

NotesUIDatabase class, 487, 616, 624-625, 1185-1186

NotesUIDocument class, 487, 627-628, 1186-1187

NotesUIView
class, 487, 625-627, 1187-1188
objects, 616

NotesUIWorkspace class, 487, 619, 1188-1189
agents playing tunes, 620-621
OpenFileDialog method, 621-623
PickListCollection method, 623-624
PickListStrings method, 623-624
Prompt method, 624
SaveFileDialog method, 621-623

NotesView
class, 490, 616, 639-640, 1205-1206
object, 487, 616

NotesViewColumn class, 491, 642, 1206-1207

NotesViewEntry class, 491, 640-641, 1207-1208

NotesViewEntryCollection class, 491, 640-641, 1208

NotesViewNavigator class, 491, 641, 1208-1209

NOTHING value, 506-507

notifications of request approvals or rejections, 1118

Notify me (appointments), 175

Novell Directory Services (NDS), 81

NSF (Notes Storage Facility), 662

NT Performance Monitor, 1078

NTF extensions, 275

NULL value, 506-507

number field, 329

number sign (#), 343, 348

numbers, formatting, 332

numeric
formatting, view columns, 359-360
input requests (LotusScript), 471-472
values, formulas, 434

NumFound results, 639

nvapplet.cab files, 573

nvapplet.jar files, 573

nvapplet.zip files, 573

O

O (Organization), 1120

Object Request Broker (ORB), 486

Object Resource Broker (ORB), 753

object-oriented languages. *See* Java

object-oriented programming. *See* OOP

objects, 478-479
class, 613-617
code, LotusScript, reusing code, 539-540
containers, 481
creating, 505, 615
Document class, creating, 647
DOM (Domino Object Model), 493, 614
formulas, 432-433
function, @Command functions, 1225
models, 483-484
navigators, 400-403
NotesDatabase, 482, 506, 632-633
NotesDocument class, 646
NotesDocumentCollection, 482, 639
NotesItem, 482
NotesRichTextItem, 482

NotesSession, 506
NotesTimer, 671
NotesUIView, 616
NotesView, 487, 616
of replication, defining, 950-952
Set statement, 505-506, 615
shared objects (real-time collaboration key term), 191
unwanted from networks, 889

ODBC (Open Database Connectivity), 599, 1209
accessing Domino databases, 369
classes, 1209-1211
Link document, 1171-1172
versions of @DbColumn, @DbLookup, and @DbCommand, 737

ODBCConnection class, 491, 1209-1210

ODBCQuery class, 491, 1210

ODBCResultSet class, 491, 1210-1211

ODS (On-Disk Structure), 800, 832
absolute size limitation, 261
Domino databases, 257, 275

Offer Solutions Web site, 724

Office (Network Dialup) location, mobile computing, 213

Office Library (R5.0) template, 259

offline browsing, 82

Ohio State Web site, 1119

<OL> tag (HTML), 308

On Error statement, LotusScript, 529

On-Disk Structure. *See* **ODS**

online sales, 723-727

Only allow server access to users in Directory field (Security tab of Server document), 814-815

OOP (object-oriented programming), 477
classes, 479-480
collections, 481
containers, 481
DOM (Domino Object Model), 493-494, 614
history of, 476
inheritance, 482
LotusScript, 477
object models, 483-484

objects, 478-479
traditional programming comparisons, 477-478

Open Database Connectivity. *See* **ODBC**

Open Database dialog box, 80

Open dialog box, 322

open function, @Command functions, 1225

Open method, NotesDatabase class, 634-635

Open Sesame dialog box, 622

Open statement, LotusScript, 535

Open URL
button, 239
icon, 54

OpenByReplicaID method, 635-636

openDatabase method, 635

OpenFileDialog method, 621-623

OpenIfModified method, 634-635

opening
documents, 146
email, 107
folders, Simple Action, 403
InfoBoxes, 138
links, Simple Action, 403
multiple windows, 60
navigators, Simple Action, 403
Personal Web Navigator, 240
preview panes for email, 103
Property InfoBox, 138
URLs, Simple Action, 403
views
default settings, 364
Domino databases, 343
Simple Action, 403
Web pages
from desktop, 248
from Personal Web Navigator, 248, 250

OpenWithFailover method, 635

operating systems
database systems integration, 1159
independence, 13

operators
formulas, 434-438
Java, 551

Opinion Program That Displays the Cost of Wisdom (listing 19.2), 471

Option Base statement, 501

Option Compare statement, 501

OPTION tag (HTML), 308

Optional Network Address field (Basics tab of Connection document), 835

Options tab, view properties, 363-364

ORB (Object Request Broker), 486

ORB (Object Resource Broker), 753

Order Metaconnector (LEI), 1161

Organization (O), 1120

organization certifier IDs, 762, 772

Organizational Unit (OU), 760-762, 771-772, 849-851, 1120

organizations
cross-certifying Notes, 852-856
Domino servers, moving within, 1031

Organizer 2.x
Group Scheduling information, 1103
upgrading to Notes, 1106-1107

Organizer 97 GS migration tool, upgrading, 1106-1107

organizing
contacts in personal address book, 74
data, 323-324
documents, 342
Domino database documents, 342

Other Actions button, 967

Other page (Replication Settings dialog box), 956

Other tab (Replication Settings), 963

OtherDomainServers group, 417, 428

OU (Organizational Unit), 760-762, 771-772, 849-851, 1120

OU certifier dialog box, 771

Out of Office, 118

Outbound Work Queue, clearing, 791

Outdent Entry button, 389

outgoing mailbox, mobile computing, 228
Outline Editor, creating outlines, 33, 384-385
Outline Entry properties dialog box, 386-389, 397
outline.cab file, 573
outline.jar file, 573
outline.zip file, 573
outlines
    Domino Designer, 32-34, 270, 285-288, 384, 411
    embedding, 409
    entries, 385-389
    inserting in pages, 395, 397
    Web pages, creating, 689-690
Outlook Express server as Internet Explorer's Internet mailer, 943
Output files, LotusScript, 535
overviews
    Java, 544-545
    time management, calendaring and scheduling, 168-169
overwriting
    Domino databases, 262
    free space, turning off, 802
owners, Personal Address Book, 152

P

<P> tag (HTML), 308
packages
    classes, lowercase letters, 555
    Java, 553-555
    Java AWT, 461
Page Break command (Create menu), 324
page breaks, organizing data, 324
Page Minder, 83, 242
Page properties dialog box
    Background tab, 304-305
    Basics tab, 303-304
pages. *See* Web pages
pagination, rich text, Text Properties InfoBox, 131-133
paging, 1146
Paint, SmartIcon, creating, 58-59
pair-wise operations, formulas, 437-438

palettes, Web (user preference), 93
panes
    Action, 334
    Basics (Manage ACL dialog box), 999
    Design (Domino Designer), 283-285
    InfoList, 462-464
    Programmer, 292, 457
    View Navigation, 384
    Work, Domino Designer window, 285-287
paper, reducing usage, 1146-1147
paper clip icon, 145, 356
paragraphs
    formatting rich text, Text Properties InfoBox, 130-131
    hiding, 133-134, 332
    properties, 670
parameters, 527
    attachform, 657
    Call, 657
    class, 445-446
    database, 445-446
    Force, 648
    FRAME tag, 392
    Integer, 522
    Internet, 244-247
    Java applets, 606
    key, 445
    length, 532
    MakeResponse, 648
    MarkRead, 648
    NotesDatabase object, 633
    Passthru in NOTES.INI, troubleshooting, 1052-1053
    ReplyToAll, 658
    view, 445
ParamList, 522-523
parent classes, 667
ParentDocumentUNID property, 649
parentheses ( ), 551
parents, inheritance, 482
ParentView property, 641
parsing
    agents for data, 1176-1177
    usernames, 674-675
Participant Status, sorting, 180
participants
    in meetings, viewing status, 180
    in Sametime, knowing who is online, 198-199

Pass-Thru HTML
    command (Text menu), 301
    text property, alternative, 303
passing arguments, LotusScript subroutines, 526-528
Passthru servers, 816-817
    connection (Connection document), 838
    mobile computing, 215, 220-222
    planning, 1123
    troubleshooting, 1051-1053
passthru topologies, 1134-1135
Passthru Use (Security tab of Server document), 816-817
password field, 330
passwords. *See also* IDs; security
    case sensitive, 51, 63-64
    changing, 62-65
    creating, 63
    Egyptian hieroglyphics, 52
    logging on to Notes client, 51-52
    mobile computing, 229
    quality scale, 771
    quality testing, 753
    security, 52, 846
    server consoles, 857-858
    single logon (Windows NT), 916
    spoofing, 52
    troubleshooting, 1049-1050
    upgrading Notes clients from R4 to R5, 782
    User ID dialog box, 64
    Windows NT, 63
Paste
    button, 304
    command (Edit menu), 113, 146, 333
paste function, @Command functions, 1225
pasting documents, 147
PATH environment variable, updating, 577
Pattern, 534
Pause button, 1040
peer-to-peer topologies, 1126
pencil icon, 198
Pencil in (appointments, 175
People & Groups tab (Domino Administrator), 897-900
    anonymous users, setting up, 908
    authenticated users, setting up, 907

certification, administering, 920
groups, 917-919
Internet
  addresses, setting up and validating, 908
  users, setting up, 907-908
Notes
  IDs, recertifying, 915-916
  usernames, changing, 908-913
  users, registering, 899-907
user account administration, integrating with Windows NT, 916-917
usernames, 908, 913-915

people (ACLs), 416
  adding, 417- 419
  assigning roles, 422
  roles, 421
  unspecified users, 427-428

People and Groups Migration dialog box, 1100, 1108

People and Groups tab (Domino Administrator), 1102

People section (Public directory), 81

People-Set Internet Address tool, 795

percentages, view columns, 360

Percussion Notrix
  COL files, 733
  integrating data, 733
  relational databases, supporting, 733
  Visual Workbench, 734
  Web site, 733

performance
  databases, 802-803
  Domino R5, 1072-1078
  Domino servers, 1032-1034
  Interfusion Energy (case study), Web site (self-service), 1168-1169

period (.), 795, 1025

Permanent Pen, 129

Permuted addition operator (numeric lists only), 436

Permuted concatenation operator (text lists only), 436

Permuted division operator (lists only), 435

Permuted equal operator (lists only), 436

Permuted greater than operator (lists only), 436

Permuted greater than or equal operator (lists only), 436

Permuted less than operator (lists only), 436

Permuted less than or equal operator (lists only), 436

Permuted multiplication operator (lists only), 435

Permuted not equal operator (lists only), 436

permuted operations, formulas, 437-438

Permuted subtraction operator (lists only), 436

Person documents, 1011
  email routing, 928
  Internet Address field, 794-796

Person records, 751

Person with Manager access, Domino Directory ACL (Access Control List), 808

Personal Address Book, 74-76, 104
  ACLs, adding users, 418
  Address book, contacts list, 74
  background images, 153
  Calendar Entry form, 160
  connection documents, 76
  Contact form, 154-156
  contacts
    adding, 153-158
    categorizing, 156-157
    creating mailing lists, 162-163
    folders, 159-160
    help, 154-155
    managing, 152, 164-165
    messages, 158-159
    organizing, 74
    personal preferences, 152-153
    scheduling meetings, 160
    visiting Web pages, 161-162
  Contacts By Category view, 157
  Contacts view, 157
  group sorting, 153
  Groups view, 162
  LDAP (Lightweight Directory Access Protocol) queries, 153
  Location documents, 76-77, 234
  mobile computing, 208, 213-220
  owners, 152
  Passthru servers, 221-222
  preferences, setting, 799
  Profile, 153
  recipients, adding, 118

senders, adding, 118
switcher control, 75
template, 259

personal information manager (PIM), 187

Personal Journal (R4) template, 259

personal preferences, email contacts, 152-153

personal views (private views), 346-348

Personal Web Navigator, 82-83, 239-240
  folders, 241-242
  Internet Options screen, 242-247
  Internet parameters, 244-247
  opening, 240
  screens, 241
  setup summary, 247-248
  template, 259
  URLs (uniform resource locators), 239
  views, 241-242
  Web pages, opening, 248, 250

PersonType variable, 501-502

Phone Messages (email), creating, 115

Phones section (Contact form), 154

PickList function, 444

PickListCollection method, 623-624

PickListStrings method, 623-624

Picture command (Create menu), 321, 408

Picture Info properties dialog box, 409

Picture Properties InfoBox, 139-141

pictures. *See* graphics

pilot upgrades, upgrading Domino servers and Notes clients R4 to R5, 782-783

PIM (personal information manager), 187

ping, 1075

pitfalls, Internet security, 889-890

planning
  capacity for servers, 1085-1086
    directory services, 1088
    memory requirements, 1087-1088
    tools, 1086-1087

PLANNING

capacity for serves, 1088-1089
Domino systems, 758-759
guidelines, for networks,
1116-1117
technical planning for deployment, 759
servers
communications infrastructure, 1124-1126
infrastructure, 1122-1124
upgrading Domino serves and Notes clients, R4 to R5, 780-781

platforms
Domino R5, 1073
enterprise/platform growth, 1080

PlayTune
command (Actions menu), 620
method, 620-621

Please Reply By option, sending email, 107

plugins, enabling in Notes browsers, 92

plus sign (+), 145, 377

Point to Point Tunneling Protocol (PPTP), 881

Point-of-Presence (POP), 1125

policies
Internet security, 885-886
properties in databases, 1077

polling, monitoring networks, 1075

Polling Activity, 1161

polygons, drawing navigator object, 401

polylines, drawing navigator object, 401

POP (Point-of-Presence), 1125

pop-ups, hotspots, 405-406

POP3 (Post Office Protocol Version 3), 122, 925, 942-943, 1028

port encryption, networks, 1075

Port field (Ports tab of Server document), 819

ports
international preferences, changing, 98-99
mobile computing, 208
configurations, 213
locations, 215
protocols, 209-210
networks, encrypting data, 863

settings, 709
TCP/IP (Transmission Control Protocol/Internet Protocol), 232-234
UCP/IP, enabling, 233

Ports icon, 233

Ports option (User Preferences dialog box), 88

Ports preferences dialog box, 98-99

Ports tab (Server Document), 818-821, 928, 1015

Position drop-down box, 57

Post Office Protocol Version 3. 122, 925, 942, 945, 1024

PostDragDrop event, 625

PostedCommand function, 446-447

PostOpen event, 487, 625

PostOpen method, 621

PostPaste event, 626

PPP protocol stacks, 228

PPTP (Point to Point Tunneling Protocol), 881

PPTP Specification Web site, 881

predefined actions, 334

preferences
calendars, 78-79, 169-171
email, 110-113
mail users, setting, 78
Personal Address Book, setting, 799
personal, email contacts, 152-153
user
basic preferences, 89-94
changing, 88
international, changing, 96-97
international, mail and news changing, 97-98
international, ports changing, 98-99
Internet Options screen, 243-244
security options for workstation, 94-96

Preferences command (File menu), 88-89, 105, 140, 210, 243
SmartIcon Settings, 55, 58
User Preferences, 57, 121, 233

Preferences InfoBox (Mail Preferences dialog box), 110-112

Presentation Graphics applets (eSuite), 597

Presentation page, 243

Presentation Whiteboard, 195
instructors preparing, 196
students' roles, 197

Prevent Copying option, sending email, 107

Preview
button, 67
command (Design menu), 468

preview panes for email, opening, 103

previewing
documents, 67
Web pages, 302

Previous button, 232

Print
command (File menu), 66, 147
dialog box, 67, 147
method, syntax, 626

Print SmartIcon, 147

Print statement, LotusScript, 537

Printer button, 67

Printer tab (Database Properties InfoBox), 148

printers, setting up, 66-67

printing
documents, 66-67, 147, 149
footers or headers, creating for printing, 147-149
previewing, 67
testing, 66-67

Printing tab, Domino database properties, 275

priorities
levels, email routing, 935-936
replication
control, replication topologies, 1132
of databases, 963
mobile computing, 218
sending email, 106-107

Private identifiers, 498

private keys, 244, 861-862

Private Message (Java applet), 200

private views, 346-348

PROTOCOLS 1281

privileges
  ACLs, 419-420
  Create (Domino Directory), 156
procedure scope, 497, 502
procedures. *See* subroutines
product-based solutions, integrating data, 738-740
production, upgrading Domino servers and Notes clients R4 to R5, 783
products
  electronic commerce, 724-725
  for firewalls, 879
profile documents, 650-651
Program documents (Domino Directory), 842, 1012
Program That Requests and Displays a Name (listing 19.1), 470
programmatic
  column names, view columns, 361
  control of tables, 318-320
Programmer's Pane, 292, 372, 457
programming
  event-driven, 465
    EventExample Hello agent, 466-469
    input requests, 469-471
    numeric input requests, 471-472
  languages, writing agents, 294
  object-oriented programming. *See* OOP
  solutions, integrating data, 737-738
  structured programming, 510
  tools, 21
  windows applications in C++, 546
programs
  actions, 333-335
  Domino databases, 257
  servlets, 453
Programs Documents (Programs tab, Domino Administrator), 1024-1026
Programs tab (Domino Administrator), 1024-1026
Project Scheduler applets (eSuite), 596-597
projected growth (Basic Scalability Model), 1080-1081

Prompt function, 443
Prompt method, 624
properties, 478
  ACL, 636
  ACL roles, 421
  ChildCount, 640
  classes, 480
  ColumnValues, 640
  CommonUserName, 613
  Count, 650
  Created, 649
  creating class objects, 615-616
  Database, 632
  of databases, setting, 996-997
  DescendantCount, 640
  Document, 646
  Document table bitmap optimization, 802, 1076
  Domino databases, 272-277
  Don't maintain unread marks, 1075
  Don't overwrite free space, 1076
  Don't support specialized response hierarchy, 1076
  EffectiveUserName, 613
  Effects, 669
  EmbeddedObjects, comparing in NotesRichTextItem class and NotesDocument class, 671
  EncryptionKeys, 655
  FolderReferences, 652
  FontSize, 669
  hotspots, 404-409
  inherited in NotesRichTextItem class, 667
  International, 613
  IsCalendar, 638
  IsDeleted, 649
  IsEncrypted, 655
  IsFolder, 638
  IsNewNote, 649
  IsProfile, 651
  IsResponse, 649
  IsSigned, 656
  IsValid, 649
  Items, 663
  Java, 492, 664
  Java applets, 606
  Java Session MethodsLotusScript, mapping of NotesSession properties, 611
  LastAccessed, 262, 277, 649
  LastModified, 649
  launch, 690
  Limit entries in $Revisions fields, 1077

  Limit entries in $UpdatedBy fields, 1076
  LotusScript, 492, 664
  Maintain LastAccessed, 1076
  Make this site accessible, 696
  NameOfProfile, 651
  NotesDocument EmbeddedObjects, 671
  NotesRichTextItem EmbeddedObjects, 671
  NotesRichTextStyle class, 668-669
  NotesSession, 611-613
  objects, 479
  ParentDocumentUNID, 649
  ParentView, 641
  Pass-Thru HTML text, alternative, 303
  policies for databases, 1077
  Responses, 650
  SentByAgent, 657
  SiblingCount, 640
  Size, 649
  tables, 312
  UserName, 507, 613
  Verifier, 656
  views, 348
    Advanced tab, 366-371
    Basic tab, 362-363
    columns, 362
    field values, 349
    form formula, 373
    formulas, 350
    functions, 349
    Options tab, 363-364
    Security tab, 371-372
    Style tab, 364-366
    View selection, 372
  Web pages, 303-304
Properties command (Edit menu), 312, 378
Property Get statement, LotusScript subroutines, 524-525
Property InfoBox, opening, 138
Property Set statement, LotusScript subroutines, 524-525
proprietary, 12
Protocol field (Ports tab of Server document), 819
protocol-specific servers, 1135
protocols. *See also* **email; Internet; Web browsers; Web pages; Web sites; WWW (World Wide Web)**
  email, 17
  Extended SMTP, 924

PROTOCOLS

HTTP (Hypertext Transfer Protocol), 571, 1028
IIOP (Internet Inter-ORB Protocol), 21, 573-575, 753, 820
IMAP (Internet Message Access Protocol), 121, 1028
Internet, supporting, 28
IPSec (IP Security Protocol), 882
L2TP (Layer 2 Tunneling Protocol), 882
LDAP (Lightweight Directory Access Protocol), 153, 598, 750, 820, 824, 1028
LDAP V2 Protocol RFC1777, 121
LDAPv3 (Lightweight Directory Access Protocol), 1088
LDIF (LDAP Data Interchange Format), 1111-1113
MIME (Multipurpose Internet Mail Extensions), 121
mobile computing, 209-210
networks, Domino R5, 1074
NNTP (Network News Transfer Protocol), 122, 1028
non-Internet, 750
POP3 (Post Office Protocol Version 3), 122, 925, 1028
PPTP (Point to Point Tunneling Protocol), 881
SMTP (Simple Mail Transfer Protocol), 38, 748, 924
SOCKS, 876
SSL (Secure Sockets Layer), 820, 884
TCP/IP (Transmission Control Protocol/Internet Protocol), 232-237
x.500, 1119

Proxies subtab (Ports tab in Server document), 820-821

Proxy Server Configuration dialog box, 236

proxy servers, 821
add-ons, 877
application-level, 876-877
authentication, 877
circuit-level, 876
firewalls, 237, 876-879
networks, Domino R5, 1075
SOCKS protocol, 236, 876
socksified, 879
virus scanning, 878
Web, 236
Web caching, 877
Web page filtering, 877-878

proxy services for firewalls, 874

public access, views, 372

Public Address Book
ACLs updating, 424
changing, upgrading Domino servers and Notes clients from R4 to R5, 781
Domino Directory, Create privileges, 156
upgrading, 785-786, 792

Public Directory, 772
Domino Directory, managing email contacts, 164-165
Groups section, 81
location documents, 82
People section, 81
reviewing, 882
Server section, 82

Public identifiers, 498

public key encryption, 244, 861-862

Public Name and Address Book (NAB). *See* **Domino Directory**

Public scope, LotusScript Sub statement, 522

publishing
databases, 1132
to servers (Domino Design Component), 713-716

Pull command, 962-965

Pull-Only replication, 837, 949, 1128

Pull-Pull replication, 837, 949, 1128

Pull-Push replication, 837, 949-952

punctuation marks, changing question marks to exclamation points, 695

purging agent, data, Interfusion Energy (case study), 1175-1177

Push command, 962, 964-965

Push-Only replication, 837, 949, 1128

Push-Wait replication, 1128

pushpin icon, 248

Put statement, LotusScript, 537

pyramid of security, 847

Q

quality scale for passwords, 771
QueryAddToFolder event, 626
QueryClose event, 626
QueryClose routine, 673
QueryDragDrop event, 626
QueryOpen event, 626
QueryOpenDocument event, 626
QueryPaste event, 626
QueryRecalc event, 626
QuerySave routine, 673
question marks (?), 694-695
questions, students asking in Sametime, 199-200
QuickPlace Web site, 71
quiz boxes, 202
quizzes, Sametime, 201
quotas, databases, setting, 989-990
quotation marks, double (" "), 434, 550, 936

R

R5. *See* **Domino R5**
radio buttons, 329
random chart (eSuite), generated by JavaScript, 603
Random files (LotusScript), 535
rationales (upgrades), 1092-1093
Rawlings Web site, 725
RDBMS (relational database management systems), 730, 1158
Read public documents privilege (ACLs), 420
Reader access (ACLs), 429
Reader fields (ACL roles), 421
Reader level (ACLs), 414
readers, feedback to authors, 1180
readers field, 330
reading
calendars, delegating tasks, 171
documents, 146
email messages, 107-108

real-time collaboration, key terms, 191
real-time data, 1168-1169
real-time sharing of information, 191-192
real-time status of servers, 22
Realtime Activity, 1162
Recertify button, 915
Recertify Selected Servers command (Actions menu), 1031
recertifying Notes IDs, 915-916
recipients (email), adding, 118
recommendations for Domino domains, 762-763
records
　Composite Data, 667
　Compound Document, 667
　NotesRichTextStyle class, 668-669
　Person, 751
rectangles, drawing navigator object, 400
red exclamation points, 106
red lights (users names on buddy lists), 198
Redefine Styles button, 136
reference material
　Java, 462
　LotusScript, 462-464
reference parameters, 527
references, Domino Object Model classes, 1184-1185
refining ACL levels, 419-420
Refresh button, 54, 239
Refresh command (View menu), 109
Refresh Design command (Database menu), 277
refresh function (@Command functions), 1225
refreshing
　Domino database templates, 264
　Domino databases, 277
　views
　　default settings, 364
　　indexes, 367-368
　Web pages, 240
RegionDoubleClick event, 626
Register Organizational Unit Certifier dialog box, 771
Register Person dialog box, 905

Register Person-New Entry dialog box, 903
Register Servers dialog box, 773
registered users and servers (Domino Directory), 1012
registering
　Domino servers while installing, 774-775
　Notes users, 899-907
　servers, 773-774
　users from text files, 906-907
registration
　Microsoft Exchange, converting to Notes, 1109-1111
　Microsoft Mail, converting to Notes, 1107-1109
　Web registration database, downloading, 815
Registration Server button, 903
relational database management systems (RDBMS), 730, 1158
relational databases, 18
　Domino comparisons, 256-257
　Percussion Notrix, integrating data, 733
　Replic-Action, integrating data, 732
relational sources
　LEI (Lotus Enterprise Integrator), supporting, 739
　Sentinel, integrating data, 736
relational systems, SQL Pump, 734
relationships, 481-482
release 5 outlines (Domino databases), 257-258. *See also* Domino databases
　Action entries, 387
　creating, 384-385
　entries, 385-386
　hiding entries, 388-389
　Link entries, 387
　moving entries, 389
　Named Element entries, 387-388
　URL entries, 388
REM keyword (formulas), 439
Rem statement, 509
reminders on calendars, creating, 182
remote connections. *See* mobile computing
Remote Procedure Calls, 750
Remove from Trash button, 110

Remove Graphic Background command (Design menu), 400
Remove method, 644, 648
RemoveAll method, 643
removing. *See* deleting
Rename button, 908
Rename Selected User dialog box, 909
renaming Domino servers, 1032
reordering SmartIcons, 56
Repeat Interval field (Schedule tab of Connection document, Domino Directory), 837
Repeat Options dialog box, 173
repetition control flow, 512
　Do statement, 515
　End ForAll statement, 513-514
　For statement, 513
　ForAll statement, 513-514
　GoTo statement, 516
　labels, 516
　Next statement, 513
　Wend statement, 514-515
　While statement, 514-515
Replace Database Design dialog box, 278
replaceItemValue method (Java), 664
replacing
　Domino database templates, 264
　Domino databases, 278
Replic-Action, 732-733
replica copies of databases, 985-986
replica IDs, 223, 274
Replica task (Domino servers), 949, 1028
　access control, establishing, 952-953
　administration tools, 953
　objects, defining, 950-952
　server-to-server replication, 949
　workstation-to-server replication, 950
replicas. *See* replication
Replicate button, 964
Replicate command, 965
Replicate Databases of x Priority field (Routing and Replication tab of Connection document, Domino Directory), 836

REPLICATE FROM DIALOG BOX

Replicate from dialog box, 964
replication
    access control, establishing, 952-953
    ACLs, 426-429
    administration tools, 953
    of clusters, 1084
    commands, 965
    conflicts, *971-972*
    databases, 20, 948-949
        access control, establishing, 952-953
        administration tools, 953
        component selective replication, 954-956
        Connection documents, 958-960
        customizing, 961-962
        disabling replication, 963
        finding replicas, 85
        forcing replication, 964
        history, 951
        initiating, 957
        maintaining replicas, 968
        managing, 991
        monitoring, 968-972
        objects, defining, 950-952
        Pull-Only replication, 949
        Pull-Pull replication, 949
        Pull-Push replication, 949
        Push-Only replication, 949
        R4 format, 804
        refusing replication requests, 963
        replica IDs, 953
        Replica task, 949
        replicas, creating, 953-954
        Replicate command, 950-952
        replication direction, specifying, 962
        replication priorities, 963
        replication settings, 956-957
        replication time limits, 963
        scheduling, 957-961, 965
        scope of replication, 962
        server connections for replication, 958
        server-to-server replication, 949
        servers, 948
        setting up, 957
        testing, 967-968
        workstation-to-server replication, 950
        workstations, 948
    Domino Administrator, 953
    Domino databases, 266-267
    history, 951
    logs (Domino Administrator), viewing, 970
    mail, 1128
    mobile computing, 222-223
        initiating, 223-225
        modem connections, 225-226
    mobile computing locations, 217-218
    objects, defining, 950-952
    Pull-Only, 837, 949
    Pull-Pull, 837, 949
    Pull-Push, 837, 949
    Push-Only, 837, 949
    Replica task, 949-950
    Replicate command, 950-952
    schedules, in Location documents, 965-966
    servers, 948, 950-952
    troubleshooting, 1059
        clearing history, 1066-1067
        conflicts, 1065-1066
        document-level access lists, 1061
        documents disappear, 1062-1063
        documents not replicating, 1060
        problems between servers, 1063-1065
        Selective Replication formulas, 1061
        servers and ACL, 1060
        servers and Author access, 1060-1061
        time limits, 1062
        user types, 1062
    workstations, 948

Replication Activity, 1162

Replication command (File menu), 223, 804, 954, 957

Replication History dialog box, 951, 1067

Replication Monitor documents, creating, 970-971

Replication Settings (New Replica dialog box), 957

Replication Settings dialog box, 954, 1064
    Advanced page, 956
    Other page, 956
    Other tab, 963
    Space Savers page, 955

Replication tab
    Admin Client, monitoring servers, 1045-1046
    Domino Administrator, 899
    database replication monitoring, 968-969
    replication, 953

Replication Task field (Routing and Replication tab of Connection document, Domino Directory), 836

Replication Time Limit field (Routing and Replication tab of Connection document, Domino Directory), 837

replication topologies, 1129
    ACLs (Access Control Lists), 1133-1134
    controls, 1132-1133
    data flow, 1131-1132
    databases, 1129-1130
        implementing, 1130-1131
        publishing, 1132
    Domino Administrator topology, displaying, 969

Replication Type field (Routing and Replication tab of Connection document, Domino Directory), 836-837

Replication/Routing tab
    Connection document, 962-963
    Server Connection documents, 959

replicator function (@Command functions), 1225

Replicator icon, 61

Replicator page, 224-225
    Action Bar buttons, 967
    Notes desktop, 965-967

Reply button, 110

replying to email messages, 107, 110

ReplyToAll parameter, 658

Reporter task
    email routing, 939
    removing from NOTES.INI file, 784

request and approval process for network servers, 1118

Request Cross-certificate button, 854

Request Information button, 179

Request Move For Selected Entries dialog box, 910

requesting input (LotusScript), 469-472
requests, 1118
requirements (email), Domino IMAP server, 944
Reschedule dialog box, 180
rescheduling meetings, 180
Reservation command (Create menu), 186
Resource documents (Domino Directory Server Configuration documents), 842
Resource Reservations database, 186
resources
　Domino Designer, 294-295
　NotesPump/LEI, 1177-1178
　upgrading Domino R4 to R5, 805
　Web sites, building Web sites with Domino, 698-699
Resources twistie, 286-287
Respond button, 179
Respond with Comments button, 178-179
response documents, 350
　hierarchical, 364
　inheritance, 351-353
　response to response document comparisons, 353-354
response hierarchies
　Domino databases, 263
　removing, 802-803
response to response documents, 350, 353-354
Responses property, 650
Restrict Use button, 866
restricted agents, 817
restrictions (ACLS), group/users, 417
Restrictions tab
　Domino Directory Domain documents, 840
　Domino Domain document, 927
Results button, 971
Resume Next (On Error statement), 529
Retain View column sorting (user preference), 92
Return Receipt option, sending email, 107

Return statement (LotusScript), 530
returnType, Function statement (LotusScript), 523
reusing code (LotusScript), 538
　object code, 539-540
　source code, 538-539
reviewing
　agents, 817
　Public directory, 80-82
Revisions field (Domino databases), 263
Rexx, 452
RFC821 standard, 748
RFC822 standard, 748
rich text, 127-128
　attributes in rich text field, 668
　defining, 290
　fields, 330
　　Composite Data, 667
　　Compound Document, 667
　　file attachments, 141
　　graphics, 139-141
　　links, 136-137
　　tables, 138
　fonts, 128-130
　Highlighter, 130
　items, 666-669
　margins, setting, 133
　pagination, 131-133
　paragraph formatting, 130-131
　paragraphs, hiding, 133-134
　Permanent Pen, 129
　ruler bar, setting tabs, 132-133
　tabs, setting, 132-133
　text, hiding, 134
　Text Properties InfoBox, 127-128
　　collapsing, 128
　　fonts, 128-130
　　Highlighter, 130
　　links in fields, 136-137
　　margins, setting, 133
　　pagination, 131-133
　　paragraph formatting, 130-131
　　paragraphs, hiding, 133-134
　　Permanent Pen, 129
　　tabs, setting, 132
　　text styles, 135-136
　　text, hiding, 134
　text styles, 135-136
Rich Text Field (RTF), 1154
RichTextItem class (Java), 669-670
RichTextParagraphStyle class (Java), 670

RichTextStyle class (Java), 669-670
right double-click option (user preference), 91
Right function, 442
Right$ function, 522, 533
ring topology, 929, 958
RIP files, troubleshooting servers, 1057-1058
roles, 860
　ACLs, 421
　　assigning users, 422
　　creating, 421-422
　　of Domino Directory, 809
　Domino Directory, 1136
Roles page (Access Control List dialog box), 860
rolling out databases, 1000-1001
rollover buttons, creating, 717
Ronald MacDonald House of Detroit Web site, 720
Rosetta stone, 52
rounded rectangles, drawing navigator object, 400
Route at Once If field (Routing and Replication tab of Connection document, Domino Directory), 836
Router
　Domino Mail Server, 749-750
　shutting down, 790
router code (SMTP), 812
Router task (Domino servers), 1029
Router Type field (Routing and Replication tab of Connection document, Domino Directory), 836
Router/SMTP tab (Domino Administrator), 1019-1021
routines
　applets, 453
　ETHandler, 673
　get, 492-493
　QueryClose, 673
　QuerySave, 673
　scripts, 453
　set, 492-493
routing
　email, 927-929
　　alternate route selection configuration, 937
　　alternative route selection configuration, 936

between adjacent Domino domains, 932
between Domino Named Networks, 931
between non-adjacent Domino domains, 932
Collector task, 939
Connection documents, 932-933
disabling, 938
Domino Administrator Messaging tab, 939
Domino domains, 760
Event task, 939
forcing unscheduled routing, 936
foreign domain connections, 937-938
guidelines, 929
LOG.NSF file, 938-939
MAIL.BOX, 938
monitoring tools, 938-939
multithread configuration, 938
Non-adjacent Domino domains configuration, 933-935
Person document (Domino Directory), 928
priority levels, 935-936
Reporter task, 939
server connections, 930-932
Tell server command, 939
topologies, defining, 929
within Domino Named Networks, 931
SMTP, Server Configuration document, 793

Routing and Replication tab (Connection document, Domino Directory), 836-837

Routing Cost field (Routing and Replication tab of Connection document, Domino Directory), 836

routing problems, troubleshooting Passthru servers, 1052

Routing Task field (Routing and Replication tab of Connection document, Domino Directory), 836

Routing tasks field (Basics tab of Server document, Domino Directory), 811

Routing/Replication tab (Domino Connection document), 927

rows
$MediaTypes field, 320
Delete Special, 311
framesets, 390
Insert Special, 311
in tables
　adding, 310-311
　case-sensitive names, 320
　deleting, 311
views, 365-366

ROWS attributes (framesets), 390

RPC (Remote Procedure Calls), 750

RSA security, public and private keys, 244

rt.jar files, 572

RTrim$ function, 533

ruler bar, setting tabs, 132-133

rules
handling email, 119
　creating, 119
　specifying actions, 120-121
　specifying conditions, 119-120
horizontal, organizing data, 323

Rules view, 119

Run personal agents field (Security tab of Server document, Domino Directory), 817

Run restricted LotusScript/Java agents field (Security tab of Server document, Domino Directory), 817

Run unrestricted LotusScript/Java agents field (Security tab of Server document, Domino Directory), 817

run() method, 557-559

Runnable class, 561

running tasks for Domino servers, 1012

runNotes() method, 559

Runtime/Restart performance field (Transactional Logging tab of Server document, Domino Directory), 833

S

<S> tag (HTML), 308

S/MIME, 748

safe copying, ID files, 930-931

sales, online, 723-727

sales tax, calculating, 627-628

Sametime, 190
applications, sharing, 202-203
awareness button (red or green), 191
awareness information, 190
chat rooms, 199
client functionality, 191
collaborating, 191-193
documents, controlling, 192
drawing tools, 196-197
Follow tool, 203
H.323 standard, 190
IETF (Internet Engineering Task Force), 190
information, sharing in real-time, 191-192
instructors, drawing tools, 196
Java applets, 194
meetings, 203-204
navigation buttons, 194
participants, 198-199
Presentation Whiteboard, 195-197
quiz boxes, 202
quizzes, 201
servers, 191-192
shared viewing, 203-204
students, 197-201
synchronous collaboration, 191-192
T.120 International Telecommunications Union (ITU) standards, 190
technical components, 190-191
Viewer, 195-197
whiteboards, 195
　instructors preparing, 196
　instructors showing presentations, 196
　pencil icon, 198
　students' roles in presentations, 197
workbooks, 196
workspaces, 193

Save and Close button, 919

save conflicts, 971-972

Save method, 643, 647-648

Save Salami dialog box, 623

Save Set button, 57

SaveFileDialog method, 621-623

SaveOptions field, 320

SaveOptions:="0" statement, 321

SECURITY   1287

saving
Domino databases, 256
email memos, 105-106
forms, 274
views, DESKTOP.DSK file, 347

scalability
content/data growth, 1080
Domino R5, 1078-1082
Basic Scalability Model, 1079
clustering, 1083-1084
ICM (Internet Cluster Manager), 1084
SMP (symmetric multiprocessing), 1083
strategies, 1081-1083
enterprise/platform growth, 1080
servers, 746, 1085
strategies (Basic Scalability Model), 1081-1083
user requirement growth, 1081

scalar variables, LotusScript, 500

Scan for Unread (user preference), 89

scanners, 1153

scanning, 878, 1155

Schedule field (Domino Connection documents), 837

Schedule Meeting button, 160

Schedule tab
Domino Connection documents, 837, 927
Server Connection documents, 959

scheduled sessions, 193

Scheduler button, 176-177

schedules
Activities (NotesPump/LEI), 1162
appointments, 172-175
managing, 169
meetings, 160
Notes databases, 187-188
overview, 168-169
replication, 218, 960-961
software compatibility, 187
tasks, Domino servers, 1012
traveling, 185-186

scheduling control, replication topologies, 1132

scope
LotusScript, 496-498
Public, LotusScript Sub statement, 522
Static, LotusScript Sub statement, 521

SCORE (Supplier Cost Reduction Effort), Chrysler, 722-723

SCOS (single copy object stores), 863, 939-942, 1122

Screened Host firewalls, 875

Screened Subnet firewalls, 875-876

screens
Admin, 740
Calendar Preferences, 169-171
ezMerchant setup, 725
Internet Options, 242-247
New Rule, 119-120
Personal Web Navigator, 241

script libraries, 287, 297

Scripted Activity, 1162

ScriptHelper applets (eSuite), 601-603

scripting languages. *See* **LotusScript**

scripting software, 1145

scripts, 453
CGI, Internet security, 890
modems, 212
ZID, 735

Search Builder dialog box, 343-345

Search button, 54, 239

search features, upgrading Domino servers/Notes clients, 781

searching
names, mobile computing mail, 217
NotesView class (LotusScript), 639-640

secondary servers, 220, 247

Secret Encryption keys, 654

Section command (Create menu), 323, 338

section function, @Command functions, 1226

Section properties dialog box, 324

sections
data, organizing, 323-324
forms, 338-339

Secure Sockets Layers (SSLs), 274, 748, 820, 884, 907
certificates, 244-245
configuring, 244-245
mobile computing locations, 220

security. *See also* **IDs; passwords**
ACLs. *See* ACLs
administration certifiers, 859
administrator ID file, 848
application developers or managers, 858
applications, 848-849
authentication, 851-852
certificates, IDs, 850-851
certifier ID file, 848-851
cross-certification, 852-856
documents
digital signatures, 861-862
encryption, 652-655
fields, 864
mail encryption, 656-658
signing, 656
Domino applications, 848-849
Domino servers, 848
Don't overwrite free space, Domino R5, 1076
email, shared mail, 940
encryption keys (User ID dialog box), 865
fields, 332
files, 848-851
firewalls, 847, 872, 879-880
choosing type/configuration, 874
concept, 873
drawbacks, 876
Dual Homed, 873-874
ICSA (International Computer Security Association) Certification, 879
products, 879
proxy servers, 876-879
proxy services, 874
Screened Host, 875
Screened Subnet, 875-876
setting, 874
flat certificate exchange, 856-857
forms, access-controlled, 338-339
functions, 1219

SECURITY

ID files, 62-63, 799-800
  organization certifier ID files, 762
  organizational unit (OU) certifier ID file, 849-851
  user ID file, 848-850
Interfusion Energy (case study) Web site (self-service), 1168-1169
International encryption keys, 866
Internet, 883, 891
  authentication, 884
  CGI scripts, 890
  defense building, 888-889
  ECL (Execution Control List), 866-868
  email, 889-890
  encryption, 884
  granularity, 884
  Java applets, 868-869
  pitfalls, 889
  policies, 885-886
  problems, 885
  Security Risk Classification Model, 886-887
  Telnet, 890
  unwanted objects, networks, 889
  Web browsers, 869-870
Java applets, 96, 246-247
JavaScript, 97
LDAP, authentication on the Web, 852
local encryption, 848
mobile computing, 229
networks, 847-848
Notes
  cross-certification, 852-856
  Domino applications, 848-849
  Domino servers, 848
  encryption, 861-866
  flat certificate exchange, 856-857
  IDs, 849-851
  Internet, 866-870
  network security, 847-848
  overview, 846-847
  pyramid security, 847
  responsible people, 858-861
  server console passwords, 857-858
port encryption, Domino R5, 1075
RSA, public/private keys, 244
sending email, 107

servers
  access protection, 851
  administrators, 859
  authentication, 851
  certificates, 65
  consoles, 857-858
  IDs, 848-850, 870
  International encryption keys, 866
  responsible people, 858-861
  roles, 860-861
spoofing, 52
system administrators, 859-860
troubleshooting
  passwords, 1049-1050
  Web browser (HTTP) connections, 1050-1051
user preferences, 94-96
users, 858
VPNs (Virtual Private Networks), 880-883
Web Application Server, 753
Workstation, setting defaults, 798
workstations, 847

Security Options button, 94, 867

Security Risk Classification Model, 886-887

Security Settings fields (Domino Server document), 813-814

Security tab, 1015
fields, 813-817
view properties, 371-372

Seek statement, LotusScript, 536

segments, networks, 1074

Select Case statement, 511-512

SELECT keyword, formulas, 440

SELECT tag (HTML), 308

Select LDIF File dialog box, 1112

SelectDocument method, 627

selecting formulas, 433

selection flow control, 510-512

Selective Replication formulas, 1061

self-service Web site, Interfusion Energy (case study), 1167
AS/400, 1170-1176
audit trails, 1176

daily management, 1176-1177
data, 1175-1176
extending business, 1168
network configuration, 1169-1170
parsing agent, 1176-1177
performance, 1168-1169
purging agent, 1176-1177
security, 1168-1169
server configuration, 1169-1170

semicolon (;), 546, 906

Send & Receive button, 967

Send (Java applet), 194

Send and File button, 159

Send and Receive Mail button, 225

Send button, 105, 199

Send method, 656-657

sending
documents, 334
email, 103-104
  adding senders, 118
  options, 106-107
  priorities, 106-107
memos, 105-107
mobile computing, 217, 228-229
notifications, 1118
replication, 225

SendTo
command (File menu), 93
field, 657

Sent (email), 103

SentByAgent property, 657

Sentinel, 736-737

separators, 332

sequential flow control, 510

Server (Domino), mobile computing
connections, 227-228
Location document, 214-220
locations, selecting, 227
modems, 211-213
Passthru servers, 220-222
Personal Address Book, 213-214
ports, 208-211
protocols, 209-210
replication, 222-226
security, 229
sending mail, 228-229

SERVERS

Server Access fields (Domino Server document), 814-816
Server Administration (Admin Client), 1038-1048
Server command (Create menu), 1017, 1025, 1040
Server Configuration
   Configuration tab (Domino Administrator), 1013
   documents, 842, 1016
      configuring multiple servers, 1017
      creating, 1017-1022
      editing, 792-793
      External Domain Network Information document, 842
      Holiday document, 842
      NOTES.INI file modifications, 1023-1024
      Resource documents, 842
      server configuration settings updated, 1016-1017
      settings unspecified, 1022-1023
   SMTP routing, 793
Server Connection documents, 928, 959-960
Server documents, 810, 1012-1014
   Administration tab, 834
   Basics tab, 811-813, 1015
   Internet Protocols tab, 826-832, 1015
   Make this site accessible property, 696
   Miscellaneous tab, 832
   MTAs tab, 832, 1015
   Passthru servers, 221
   Ports tab, 818-820, 928, 1015
   Security tab, 813-818, 1015
   Server Tasks tab, 821-826, 1015
   Transactional Logging tab, 832-834, 1015
Server Groups, ACLs, 808
Server icon, 896
Server Location Information (Domino Server document), 812-813
Server name field (Domino Server document), 811
Server section (Public directory), 82

Server tab (Domino Administrator), 898, 964, 1038
Server Tasks tab (Domino Server document), 821-826, 1015
Server title field (Domino Server document), 811
Server Web Browser, 240
Server's phone number(s) field (Domino Server document), 812
server-document restrictions, troubleshooting, 1055
server-to-server replication, 949
ServerCreator role, 809, 860
ServerModifier role, 809, 860
servers
   access
      accessing DOM, 485-486
      authentication, 851
      protecting, 851
      troubleshooting, 1053
   administrators, security, 859
   ACLs, 417, 423-425, 428-429
   Additional Domino server (option), 767
   administration
      assigning, 1010
      clients, 38
      groups, 816
      upgrading, 787, 1097
   ADSL (Asymmetrical Digital Subscriber Line), 1125-1126
   agents, 817
   applications, upgrading, 800-801
   authentication, 851, 884, 1053
   authorization, 1055
   capacity planning, 1085-1089
   certificates, 65
   certification, 1053
   choosing, 747
   clustering, 1083-1084
   commands, 1008
   communications infrastructure, planning, 1124
   configuring, Interfusion Energy (case study), 1169-1170
   Connection documents, 958-960
   connections
      email routing, 930-932
      replication, 958
      tracing, 99, 234

CPUs, 1073
cross-certification, 852-856, 1054
databases
   Document table bitmap optimization property, 1076
   Don't maintain unread marks property, 1075
   performance, 1075
   planning, 1123
   replication, 957-958
DevPack (eSuite), installing, 604
DFC, loading, 715
disk drives, 1074
Domino, 13, 121-122, 746-747
   accessing, 706-707
   adding user IDs, 46
   administering, 1006-1012
   certification logs, 770-771
   configuring, 1012, 1016-1017
   cross-certifying, 930-931
   documents, 1013-1026
   domains, 1029-1031
   HTML documents, 695-696
   installing, 763-775
   moving, 1031
   networks, modifying, 1029
   new features, 37-40
   OU (organizational unit) certifiers, 771-772
   performance, analyzing, 1032-1034
   registering, 774-775
   renaming, 1032
   scalability, 746
   security, 848
   Server Configuration document, 1016-1024
   server infrastructure, 1009
   tasks, 1026-1029
   upgrading R4 to R5, 778-796
   Web browsers/Notes client comparison, 682
   Web sites, 681-682
Domino Administrator, 1137-1138
Domino Application Server, 751-754
Domino database templates, 263
Domino databases, 263, 267
Domino Design components, installing, 708-710

SERVERS

Domino Directory, 808-810, 1135
   ACL (Access Control List), 808-809
   Certifier documents, 842
   Configuration documents, 842
   Connection document, 834-835, 838-839
   Cross-Certifier documents, 842
   document groups, administering, 1136
   Domain documents, 839-841
   domains, 1135-1136
   forms, 809-810
   Mail-In Database documents, 843
   Program documents, 842
   roles, 1136
   Server Configuration documents, 842
   Server documents, 810-834
   User Setup Profile documents, 842
Domino email, 16
Domino Enterprise Server, 754-756
Domino Mail Server, 747
   email messages, addressing, 748-749
   Internet directory standards, 750
   Internet messaging standards, 747-748
   LDAP (Lightweight Directory Access Protocol), authentication, 750-751
   Router, 749-750
   routing, 927-938
Domino messaging server, 924
Domino R4, transferring MIME messages, 794
Domino R5
   Internet mail storage format, 796
   MIME messages, transferring, 794
   performance, 1073-1074
Domino SMTP R5, dial-up, 796
Don't overwrite free space property, 1076
Don't support specialized response hierarchy property, 1076
encryption, authentication, 863

end-to-end topology, 958
events, trapping, 1138
expired certificates, troubleshooting, 1053-1054
external, 1124
firewalls, 1075, 1124
First Domino server (option), 767
flat certification
   flat certificate exchange, 856-857
   troubleshooting, 1053
hierarchically certified, 1009
HTTP, CGI (common gateway interface), 1163
hub-and-spoke topology, 957
ICM (Internet Cluster Manager), 1084
IDs
   ciphers, 870
   files, 848-850
imaging, 1154
infrastructure, planning, 1122
Internet mail, 788-796
Internet messaging server, 924
ISDN (Integrated Services Digital Network), 1125
ISPs (Internet service providers), 1125
licenses, 746
Limit entries in $Revisions fields property, 1077
Limit entries in $UpdatedBy fields property, 1076
location security, 847
mail
   hop counts, 928
   planning, 1122-1123
   upgraded software systems, 1098
Mail Gateways, 1137
Maintain LastAccessed property, 1076
memory, 1074
mesh topology, 958
mobile computing locations, 215
modems, planning, 1124-1125
monitoring, 38, 1038-1046
MTA (Message Transfer Agent), 789
   file backups, 789
   NOTES.INI file upgrades, 796
   upgrading Administration Requests database, 793

networks, 1074
NNNs (Notes Named Networks), 818
NOTES.INI restrictions (port level), 1055-1056
Passthru, 816-817
   mobile computing configurations, 220-222
   planning, 1123
   troubleshooting, 1051-1053
performance, 1072, 1077-1078
platforms, 1073
policies (databases), 1077
port encryption, 1075
ports, settings, 709
problems, troubleshooting, 1063-1065
programs, automating administrative tasks, 1007
protocol-specific, 1135
proxy, 821
   add-ons, 877
   application-level, 876-877
   authentication, 877
   circuit-level, 876-877
   Domino R5, 1075
   firewalls, 237, 876-879
   SOCKS, 236, 876
   socksified, 879
   virus scanning, 878
   Web, 236
   Web page caching, 877
   Web page filtering, 877-878
publishing, 713-716
real-time status, 22
registering, 773-774, 1012
Replica task, 949-950
Replicate command, 950-952
replication, 948
   access control, establishing, 952-953
   customizing, 961-962
   direction, specifying, 962
   disabling replication, 963
   forcing replication, 964
   priorities, 963
   Pull-Only replication, 949
   Pull-Pull replication, 949
   Pull-Push replication, 949
   Push-Only replication, 949
   refusing replication requests, 963
   replication time limits, 963
   scheduling, 960-961, 965-966
   scope, 962
   troubleshooting, 1065-1066

ring topology, 958
Sametime server, 192
scalability, 1078
    *Basic Scalability Model,
       1079-1083*
    clustering, 1083-1084
    *ICM (Internet Cluster
       Manager), 1084-1085*
    *SMP (symmetric multiprocess-
       ing), 1083*
Secondary servers, 247
security, 851, 858-860, 865
server functionality, 191
server-document restrictions,
    troubleshooting, 1055
SMTP Gateway, 812
statistics, 39, 1042, 1138
task-specific, 1134
tasks
    calendaring, 187
    status, 1042
topologies, 929, 1126
    end-to-end, 958, 1126
    hub-and-spoke, 957, 1127
    mail routing, 1127-1129
    mesh, 958, 1127
    passthru, 1134-1135
    peer-to-peer, 1126
    replication, 1129-1134
    ring, 958
troubleshooting, 1056-1059
voice, components, 1144
WAN (wide area network),
    1126
Web Application Server,
    752-754

Servers tab (Domino Administrator), 1032

Server\Certificates view, 1011

Server\Clusters view, 1011

Server\Configurations view, 1011

Server\Connections view, 1011

Server\Deny Access Groups view, 1011

Server\Domains view, 1011

Server\External Domain Network Information view, 1011

Server\File Identification view, 1011

Server\Holidays view, 1012

Server\Licenses view, 1012

Server\Mail Users view, 1012

Server\Mail-In Databases and Resources view, 1012

Server\Networks view, 1012

Server\Programs view, 1012

Server\Servers view, 1012

Server\Setup Profiles view, 1012

Server\V3 Stats and Events view, 1012

Server\Web Configurations view, 1012

services, proxy (firewalls), 874
servlets, 453-454
    Java, 569-572
    multithreaded, 570
    single-threaded, 570

Session class, 492, 562-563, 610-613

Session methods (Java), 612

sessions
    scheduled, 193
    variables, accessing, 610

Set database quota to button, 990

Set ID File button, 771

Set Internet Address dialog box, 749

Set Internet Address tool, 908

Set keyword, 613, 615

Set Password button, 64

Set Password dialog box, 64

Set Path and Filenames button, 987

set routines, 492-493

Set statement, 505-506, 615

SetEnvironment function, 438

setting up
    Internet users, 907-908
    printers, 66-67

Settings by Character Set Groups tab (Domino Administrator), 1022

setup screens, ezMerchant, 725
shadowed identifiers, 497
shapes, navigators, 400

Share Frame window, 202

shared actions, 287, 374
shared copy object store
    (SCOS), 863
shared email
    administering, 939-940
    database management, 942
    messages, deleting, 942
    mobile users, 942
    security, 940
    setting up, 940-941
    user mail files, 941-942
shared fields, 286, 333

Shared Mail, 1122

shared nothing architecture,
    1083
shared objects (real-time collab-
    oration key term), 191
shared viewing, Sametime,
    203-204
shared views, 346-348
sharing Web pages, 250-251
Shift+Tab keyboard shortcut,
    108

Shockwave, 718

shortcuts. *See* keyboard short-
    cuts

Show Extended Accelerators (user preference), 94

Show Status button, 234

ShowHide function,
    @Command functions, 1226
showing Domino database tem-
    plates, 263
shutting down, 790
SiblingCount property, 640
Sign method, 656
Sign option, sending email, 107
signatures, 107, 111, 861-862
signing documents, 656

Simple Actions, 402-403, 454

Simple Mail Transfer Protocol.
    See **SMTP**

Single Category embedded
    views, 347, 379-380
single category views, 651
single copy object stores
    (SCOS), 939-942, 1122

Single data type, 498

SINGLE LOGON

single logon (Windows NT), 916

single-threaded servlets, 570

single-use fields, 333

Site Profile command (Create menu), 186

sites, Web. *See* Web sites

size, LotusScript limitations, 503-504

Size options page, 243

Size property, 649

sizing
Domino databases, 261-262
LotusScript databases, 633
view rows, 366
voice mail systems, 1143

slashes, forward (/), 548, 1025

SLIP/PPP protocol stacks, 228

small arrowheads, 145

small triangles, 144

SmartFilter Web site, 877

SmartIcons
adding, 56
bar, Domino Designer window, 284
context-sensitive set, 55
Create Table, 138
creating, 58-59
customizing, 55, 57
Cycle, 136
deleting, 56
dialog box, 56-58
Edit Document, 127, 146
editing, 57, 59
Formula dialog box, 58
function, @Command functions, 1226
navigator objects, 400
Print, 147
reordering, 56
settings, 55, 58
sets, naming, 56
ToolTips, 55
Universal set, 55
View Show/Hide Preview Pane, 103

SMP (symmetric multiprocessing), 1083

SMTP (Simple Mail Transfer Protocol), 38, 748
Extended SMTP, 924
Gateway, 812

listener, 811-812
mail, upgraded software systems, 1098
Message Transfer Agent (MTA), 121
router code, 812
routing, Server Configuration document, 793

SMTP/MIME MTA, 788-796

SMTP/MTA, 790-791

SNA, mobile computing, 209

snail mail, cross-certifying organizations, 856

SOCKS
Web site, 891
protocol, 876
servers, proxy, 236

socksified proxy server, 879

soft deletions, 348
Domino databases, 263
shared views, 347

software
access, 1145
auto attendant, 1145
call pursuit/find me, 1145
Domino R5, installing, 784, 792
fax client, 1151-1152
fax server, 1148-1150
growth expansion options, 1145
imaging technology integration, 1154-1155
integrating faxes, 1148
LCCOV (Lotus Calendar Connector for OfficeVision), 187
leaving messages, 1145
Lotus Organizer 97 GS, 187
message playback, 1145
Notes R5, installing, 798-799
scripting, 1145
support (fax/pager gateways), 1145
systems, upgrading, 1095-1099
telephone integration, 1145
time management, 187
voice mail, 1144-1145

sorting
documents, 354-356
groups (Personal Address Book), 153
mail, 92
Participant Status, 180

source code (LotusScript), 538-539

Source Domain field (Domino Connection document), 835

Source Server field (Domino Connection document), 835

sources, relational (Sentinel), 736

Space Savers page (Replication Settings dialog box), 955

Spacer icon, 56

spacing view rows, 366

spaghetti code, 510

spamming, 889-890

speaker, modem configurations, 212

Special command (Create menu), 113

special delivery, email memos, 106-107

special effects, tables, 317-318

Special menu command (Create menu), 113

speed
modems, troubleshooting, 1067
networks (Domino R5), 1074

spell checking
Check spelling, 585
email, 107
User Dictionary button, 89

Split Cells command (Table menu), 316

splitting
cells, tables, 316
domains, 1030-1031

spoofing, 52

Spreadsheet applets (eSuite), 584, 589-591
HTML code, 590
InfoCenter, 594

spreadsheets
AppletContainer applets, 605-607
eSuite, 605
HTML code, 591

SPX, mobile computing, 209

SQL Pump, 734

SQL statements, 256

SQL/Java Database Connectivity (JDBC) applets (eSuite), 599

square brackets [ ], 303, 434, 692, 1220

square icons, 70. *See also* bookmarks

squares, drawing navigator object, 401

SSLs (Secure Socket Layers), 274, 748, 820, 884, 907
    certificates, 244-245
    configuring, 244-245
    mobile computing locations, 220

stability, servers, 1057

Stack Replica Icons command (View menu), 954

StampAll method, 643

standalone applications
    Java applications, 567-569
    languages, 454

standard databases, 73

standards
    H.323, 190
    IETF (Internet Engineering Task Force), 190
    LDAPv3, 751
    messaging, email, 121-122
    networks, 1117
    RFC821, 748
    RFC822, 748
    T.120 International Telecommunications Union (ITU), 190

Start button, 967

Start New Task command, 1039

start() method, 557

starting Domino Designer, 282-283

state, hypertext links, 682

statements
    %include, 538
    Call, 656
    Class, 504
    Const, 499
    Const, 538-539
    Deftype, 503
    Delete, 506
    Dim, 500
    Do, 515
    End ForAll, 513-514
    End Function, 523
    End Property, 525
    End Sub, 522
    Erase, 501
    Exit For, 513
    Exit Property, 525
    For, 513
    ForAll, 513-514, 621
    Function, 522-524
    GoTo, 516
    grouping, syntax, 556
    If-Then-Else, 511
    Java, 552-553
    Let, 506
    Line Input, 536
    LotusScript, 509
        Get, 536
        GoSub, 530
        Input, 536
        On Error, 529
        Open, 535
        Print, 537
        Put, 537
        Return, 530
        Seek, 536
        Width, 537
        Write, 538
    Next, 513
    Option Base, 501
    Option Compare, 501
    Property Get, 524-525
    Property Set, 524-525
    Rem, 509
    SaveOptions:="0", 321
    Select Case, 511-512
    Set, 505-506, 615
    SQL, 256
    Sub, 521-522
    throw, syntax, 556
    try-catch, syntax, 556
    Type, 501
    Use, 539
    UseLSX, 539
    Wend, 514-515
    While, 514-515

Static keyword, 502

Static scope, LotusScript Sub statement, 521

static text, 125-126

static Web sites, 720

stationery, email, 103, 115, 117

statistics, servers, 1042, 1138

Statistics & Events database, 1134

Statistics Reporter task, stopping loading, 791

Statistics subtab (Server tab, Admin Client), 1044-1045

Statistics tab (Domino Administrator), 898

STATREP.NSF file, 1008

status, servers, 22, 1042

status bar, 59, 284

Status embedded tab (Servers tab, Domino Administrator), 1032

Status subtab (Server tab, Admin Client), 1038-1040

Status tab (Domino Administrator), 898

Stop button, 239, 1040

Stop Task command, 1039

storing
    binary codes, 545
    bookmarks, 61

Str$ function, 533

strategies
    Domino systems planning, 758
    scalability, 1081-1083

StrCompare function, 534

StrConv function, 534

string around a finger icon, 145

string handling functions, 1214

strings
    LotusScript, 530-534
    modems, 212

StrLeft function, 533

StrLeftBack function, 533

StrRight function, 533

StrRightBack function, 533

structured programming, 510-512

structures (Notes documents), 124

students
    applications, driving, 202-203
    drawing tools (Sametime), 197
    quiz boxes, 202
    Sametime, 199-201
    whiteboard presentations, 197

Style buttons, 315

Style tab, view properties, 364-366

styles, text, 135-136

Sub statement, LotusScript subroutines, 521-522

subforms, 337-338
  computed, 338
  Domino Designer, 286, 290-292

Submit button, 201

subobjects, 481

subprograms. *See* **subroutines**

subroutines, LotusScript
  calling, 525-526
  classes, 521
  coherence, 520-521
  event handlers, 525
  functions, 522-524
  GoSub statement, 530
  On Error statement, 529
  passing arguments, 526-528
  Property Get, 524-525
  Property Set, 524-525
  Return statement, 530
  strings
    LotusScript, 530-534
    modems, 212
  Sub statement, 521-522
  variables, 521

Subscription command (Create menu), 86

subscription databases, monitoring, 263

subscriptions, 86-89

subscripts, 500

Subset function, 443

Subtraction, 436

suffixes, variables, 498-499

summaries, Personal Web Navigator setups, 247-248

Sun Microsystems Java Web site, 548, 552

Supplier Cost Reduction Effort (SCORE), 722

Swing components (JFC), 546

Swing package (AWT), 461

switcher control, 75

switching windows, 60

symbols, (form fields), 291

symmetric multiprocessing (SMP), 1083

synchronizing directories, 916-917

synchronous collaboration, 191-192

synopsis, 286

syntax
  extended class (LotusScript), 663-664
  formulas, 433-434
  grouping statements, 556
  hierarchical names, 761
  HTML (Hypertext Markup Language), 306-307
  LotusScript, Domino Object Model classes, 1184
  NotesTimer object, creating, 671
  OpenFileDialog method, 621
  PickListCollection method, 623
  PickListStrings method, 623
  Print method, 626
  Prompt method, 624
  SaveFileDialog method, 622
  throw statement, 556
  try-catch statement, 556

system administrators
  anonymous users, 908
  authenticated users, 907
  certification, 920
  databases, managing, 976
  Domino Administrator, 896-900
  Domino Directory, 899
  groups, 917-919
  Internet addresses, 908
  Internet users, 907-908
  Notes IDs, 915-916
  Notes usernames, 908-913
  Notes users, registering, 899-907
  roles, 860
  security, 859
  user account administration, 916-917
  usernames
    deleting, 913-915
    managing, 908

system templates, customizing, 782

systems
  database integration, 1158-1164
  Domino
    administering, 22
    planning, 758
    strategy, 758
    teams, 758-759
  ERP (enterprise resource planning), 731
  file, Java applet access, 96
  information, 1165
  legacy, 730-732
  operating, database systems integration, 1159
  RDBMS (relational database management systems), 730
  relational, SQL Pump, 734
  software, 1095-1099
  topologies, scheduling database replication, 957-958
  transactional, 731
  voice mail, 1143-1145

T

T.120 International Telecommunications Union (ITU) standards, 190

Tabbed Table icon, 317

tabbed tables, 317

Table Border tab (Table properties dialog box), 313

Table command (Create menu), 138, 310

Table dialog box, 319

Table Layout tab (Table properties dialog box), 312, 316

Table Margins tab (Table properties dialog box), 313-314

Table menu commands
  Delete Selected Row(s), 311
  Merge Cells, 316
  Split Cells, 316
  Table Properties, 312

Table Programming tab (Table dialog box), 319

Table Properties command (Table menu), 312

Table properties dialog box, 312-317

Table Properties InfoBox, 138-139

Table Rows tab (Table properties dialog box), 317

Table/Cell Background tab (Table properties dialog box), 314

TableReader applets (eSuite), 599

TABS

tables, 137
    attributes, modifying, 138-139
    backgrounds, table/cell, 314-316
    borders, 312-313
    cells, 316
    collapsible, 317-318
    columns, 310-314
    creating, 309
    databases Interfusion Energy (case study), 1171
    Domino databases, 262
    hotspots, 320
    margins, 312-313
    nesting, 318
    programmatic control, 318-320
    properties, 312
    rich-text fields, 138
    rows, 310-311, 320
    SaveOptions field, 320
    SaveOptions:="0" statement, 321
    special effects, 317-318
    tabbed, 317
    timed, 318

tabs
    Administration, 834, 927, 1022
    administration client, 38
    Advanced, 317, 1022
    Analysis (Domino Administrator), 898
    Analysis embedded (Servers tab, Domino Administrator), 1033
    Analysis subtab (Server tab, Admin Client), 1040
    Background (Page properties dialog box), 304-305
    Basics, 106-107, 927, 932-933, 959, 1015-1018
        dial-up modems, 838
        fields, 810-813, 817, 835, 839
        LANs, 835
        Non-Adjacent Domain documents, 840
        Page properties dialog box, 303-304
        User ID dialog box, 65
    Border (Table properties dialog box), 312
    Calendar Information, 840-841, 927
    Cell Borders (Table properties dialog box), 312
    Certificates (User ID dialog box), 65

Colors (Table properties dialog box), 315
Comments, 927, 960
Configuration, 899, 925-927, 1007, 1017
    All Server Documents, 1015
    Configuration Documents, 1016-1024
    Current Server Document, 1013-1014
    document maintenance, 1012-1013
    replication, 953
    Server Configuration, 1013
    Server Connection documents, creating, 958
    Server Document tabs, 1014-1015
    servers, monitoring, 1048
Connections (Domino Administrator), 1024
Conversions Options (Domino Administrator), 1021
dial-up modems, 838
Domino Administrator Messaging, email routing, 939
Domino Connection document, 927
Domino Domain document, 927
Encryption (User ID dialog box), 65
Files, 898, 971, 976-977
    Database Action Bar, 981-982
    Folder Action Bar, 977, 979-981
    General Disk Information, 977
    servers, monitoring, 1045
Internet Protocols, 826-832, 1015
Java Applet Security (Location document), 868-869
LDAP (Domino Administrator), 1018-1019
Mail (Domino Administrator), 898
Mail Information tab (Domino Directory Domain documents), 840
Mail subtab (Messaging tab, Domino Administrator), 925
Messaging, 898-899, 925
    Mail subtab, 925-926
    Mail tab, 898

Tracking Center subtab, 925-926
Tracking Center tab, 899
servers, monitoring, 1046
MIME (Domino Administrator), 1021
Miscellaneous (Server document, Domino Directory), 832
Monitoring (Domino Administrator), 898
Monitoring subtab (Server tab, Admin Client), 1041-1044
More Options (User ID dialog box), 66
MTAs (Server Document), 832, 1015
NOTES.INI Settings (Domino Administrator), 1022
Other (Replication Settings), 963
People & Groups (Domino Administrator), 897, 1102
    certification, administering, 920
    groups, 917-919
    Internet addresses, 908
    Notes IDs, 915-916
    Notes users, registering, 899-907
    user account administration, 916-917
    usernames, 908-915
    users, 899-908
Ports, 818-821, 928, 1015
Printer, 148
Programs, 1024-1026
Replication, 899, 953, 968-969, 1045-1046
Replication/Routing, 959, 962-963
Restrictions, 840, 927
Router/SMTP (Domino Administrator), 1019-1021
Routing/Replication, 836-837, 927
Schedule, 837, 927, 959
Security, 813-817, 1015
Server, 898, 964, 1038
Server Document, 1014-1015
Server Tasks, 821-826, 1015
Servers (Domino Administrator), 1032-1033
setting
    ruler bar, 132-133
    Text Properties InfoBox, 132

Settings by Character Set Groups, 1022
Statistics (Domino Administrator), 898
Statistics subtab (Server tab, Admin Client), 1044-1045
Status (Domino Administrator), 898
Status embedded (Servers tab, Domino Administrator), 1032
Status subtab (Server tab, Admin Client), 1038-1040
Table Border (Table properties dialog box), 313
Table Layout (Table properties dialog box), 312, 316
Table Margins (Table properties dialog box), 313-314
Table Programming (Table dialog box), 319
Table Rows (Table properties dialog box), 317
Table/Cell Background (Table properties dialog box), 314
Tracking Center (Domino Administrator), 899
Tracking Center subtab (Messaging tab, Domino Administrator), 925-926
Transactional Logging, 832-834, 1015

tags, HTML. *See* **HTML, tags**

Tamura, Randall A., 1180

target frames, links, 397

task buttons, 60-61
Domino Designer window, 284
Xs, 61

Task command, 1040

task-specific servers, 1134

tasks
Collect, 940-942
Collector, email routing, 939
Domino servers, 1026-1029
Event, email routing, 939
Notes, 1025-1026
Replica, 949-953
Reporter, email routing, 939
servers
calendaring, 187
status, 1042

taxes, sales, 627-628

TCO (total cost of ownership), 582

TCP/IP (Transmission Control Protocol/Internet Protocol), 232
connections, 237
databases, 237
default timeout interval, 233
Location documents, 234-237
mobile computing, 209
Options button, 233
ports
defining, 232-234
drivers, verifying, 234
enabling, 233
servers, tracing connections, 234
setting up, 232

Team Room (5.0) template, 260

TeamFusion, 717

teams
Domino systems planning, 758-759
networks, sharing responsibility, 1117

technical components (Sametime), 190-191

technical planning, Domino systems deployment, 759

technology, imaging, 1152-1154

telephone integration software, 1145

telephones, cross-certifying organizations, 856

tell http restart command, 572

Tell Router Exit command, 938

Tell Router Quit command, 938

Tell server command, 939

Tell Task command, 1039

Telnet, 890

Template Server button, 770, 786

templates, 13
customizing, 782
Domino databases, 259-264
replication, 225

temporary variables, 434

testing
printing, 66-67
upgrades, 782, 1096-1097

text, 125
boxes, 400
concatenation, formulas, 437
editing/viewing comparison, 127
fields, 126-127, 329, 556
files, 906-907
functions, 442, 1226
indexes, 262, 277
hiding, 134
pop-ups, 405-406
rich text. *See* rich text
static/document-specific comparison, 125-126
values, formulas, 434

Text menu commands
Named Style, 135
Pass-Thru HTML, 301
Permanent Pen, 129
Text Properties, 301

Text Properties command (Text menu), 301

Text Properties InfoBox, 128
collapsing, 128
floating menu, 128
fonts, 128
Permanent Pen, 129
rich text, 127-137

TEXTAREA tag (HTML), 308

textured workspace (user preference), 91

Then clause, 511

third-party tools, integrating data, 732-737

Thread class, 557-559

threading, NotesThread class, 559

threads, multiple, 794

throw statement, 556

tilde (~), 496

time
formatting, 331-332, 360-361
functions, 443
mobile computing configurations, 208

time/date variables, 618-619

time limits, replication, 1062, 1133

time management
appointments, overview, 168-169
calendars, 185-188
anniversaries, creating, 181-182
appointments, scheduling, 172-175

*delegating reading or editing,
171*
elements, 169
entries, creating, 172
events, deleting, 182
group calendars, 184
meetings, 175-181
*preferences, setting up,
169-171*
reminders, creating, 182
Resource Reservations database, 186
To Do lists, managing, 182
viewing, 183-184
editing documents, 671-674
schedules, 169, 185-188
time values, formulas, 434
timed tables, 318
timeout interval, 233
timeout periods, password security, 846
titles, formulas, 433
To Do command (Create menu), 182
To Do lists, calendars, 182
To Do section (Calendar Preferences screen), 171
toggling
    Java applets, 193
    Permanent Pen, 129
toolbars, Domino Components, 710
Toolkit Without An Interesting Name (TWAIN), 1153
tools
    Admin, 1105
    administration, 953,
        1007-1011, 1099
    Agent Manager, 1008
    AgentRunner, 576-579
    applications, writing, 14
    authoring, 706, 710-714
    BeanBuilder, 717
    capacity planning, 1086-1087
    cc:Mail/Notes migration,
        1101-1104
    cluster analysis, 1034
    conversation (real-time collaboration key term), 191
    database
        analysis, 971
        replication, monitoring, 968
        *systems integration,
        1163-1164*

Decommission Server, 1034
DECS (Domino Enterprise Connection Services), 1163
Domino, programming, 21
Domino Administrator, 1007
Domino Connector Toolkit, 1164
Domino Designer, 19
Domino Upgrade Services, 1099
drawing (Sametime), 196-197
email, 118-119
end user (Domino Upgrade Services), 1099
Follow, 203
HTML (Hypertext Markup Language), 703-707
integrating data
    Lotus, 737-740
    Percussion Notrix, 733
    Replic-Action, 732-733
    Sentinel, 736-737
    SQL Pump, 734
    third-party tools, 732
    ZMERGE, 734-735
Internet Address, 794-796
JDBC (Java Database Connectivity), 1163
log analysis, Domino server performance, 1033
LOG.NSF file, 1008
Lotus Domino Connectors, 1163
Lotus Enterprise Integrator, 1164
Lotus eSuite, 717
LS:DO (LotusScript Data Object), 1163
migration (Notes), 1105-1106
monitoring email routing, 938-939
Notes, programming, 21
Organizer 97 GS migration, 1106-1107
People-Set Internet Address tool, 795
server commands, 1008
server programs, 1007
Set Internet Address, 908
Shockwave, 718
TeamFusion, 717
User, 1106
Web Administration, 1007
Tools button, 110, 169, 181, 1040

Tools command
    Actions menu, 77, 117, 169
        *Add Sender to Address Book,
            153, 156*
        *Add Sender to Personal
            Address Book, 118*
        Import Holidays, 181
        Out of Office, 118
        Visit Web Page, 161
    File menu, 63, 854
tools function, @Command functions, 1226-1227
Tools menu, 53
tools.jar files, 572
ToolTips, 55
topologies, 1126
    chain, 929
    email routing, 929
    end-to-end, 958, 1126
    hub-and-spoke, 929, 957, 1127
    mail routing, 1127-1129
    Mail Routing Topology map, 1047
    mesh, 929, 958, 1127
    passthru, 1134-1135
    peer-to-peer, 1126
    replication, 969, 1129-1134
    ring, 929, 958
    scheduling database replication, 957-958
    servers, 929
toString method, 665
total cost of ownership (TCO), 582
Trace button, 234
tracing server connections, 99, 234
tracking
    email, 1048
    meeting invitations, 178-179
Tracking Center (email), 1046-1048
Tracking Center subtab (Messaging tab, Domino Administrator), 925-926
Tracking Center tab (Domino Administrator), 899
transaction logging, 781
transaction processing monitor systems, 731
Transaction System Connectors, 1160

Transactional logging field, 832

Transactional Logging tab, 832-834, 1015

transactional systems, 731

transactions, logging, 262-263

transferring mail, mobile computing, 217

trapping events, 1138

trash
documents, 109
email, 103
soft deletions, 347

Trash view, 169

travel, location prompt (user preference), 89

Travel (Notes Direct Dialup) location, mobile computing, 214

Treat Document Contents as HTML view, 693

Treat page contents as HTML, 605

Treat View Contents as HTML view, 693

triangles, small, 144

Trim function, 442

Trim$ function, 533

troubleshooting
API programs, 1058
authorization, 1055
cross-certification, 1054
document-level access lists, 1061
documents, 1060-1063
Domino R5, 1077-1078
expired certificates, 1053-1054
flat certification, 1053
HTTP (Web browser connections), 1050-1051
modems, 1067-1068
NOTES.INI restrictions (port level), 1055-1056
Passthru parameters, 1052-1053
Passthru servers, 1051-1053
passwords, 1049-1050
replication, 1059-1067
security, 1049-1051
server-document restrictions, 1055

servers
access, 1053-1056
API programs, 1058
crashes, 1057-1058
not responding, 1056-1057
problems, 1063-1065
RIP files, 1057-1058
stability, 1057
start failures, 1057
UNIX core dumps, 1057-1058
visibility, 1058-1059

try-catch statements, 556

turning off
headline monitoring, 803
overwriting free space, 802

TWAIN (Toolkit Without An Interesting Name), 1153

twisties, 145
Resources, 286-287
views, 363

type scope, 497

Type statement, 501

type-ahead, mobile computing mail, 216

Typeahead (email), 104

U

<U> tag (HTML) tag, 308

UI (user interface), 616

<UL>tag (HTML), 308

Unary logical NOT operator, 436

Unary negative operator (change sign), 435

Unary positive operator, 435

uncontrolled mode (whiteboards), 197

undeleting Domino databases, 263

underscore (_), 509, 548, 795, 1025

Unicode, 94, 531

unified messaging, 1142

uniform resource locators. *See* URLs

uninitialized databases (Create method), 633

Universal set of SmartIcons, 55

UNIX core dumps, troubleshooting, 1057-1058

UnprocessedDocuments collection, 643

unread marks
Domino databases, 262, 277
maintenance, 802
viewing documents in Notes, 143
views, 368

Unread Marks command (Edit menu), 89, 108

unread rows, view colors, 365

unscheduled routing of email, forcing, 936

Until clause, 515

Updall task (Domino servers), 1029

Update task (Domino servers), 1029

Updated icon (HTML documents), 692-693

UpdatedBy field (Domino databases), 263

UpdateProcessedDoc method, 643

updating
ACL Administration server (Access Control Lists), 424
database designs, 1000
Domino databases
About documents, 270-271
Using documents, 271-272
Domino Directory, 570
full text indexes, 984-985
PATH environment variable, 577
servers, configuration settings, 1016-1017
view indexes, 367-368

upgrading, 1092
application servers, R4 to R5, 800-801
applications, R4 to R5, 778-780, 800
Business Partners, 1093
cc:Mail, 1104
MTA (message transfer agent), 1105
Notes migration tools, 1105-1106
Organizer 97 GS migration tool, 1106-1107
to Notes and Domino, 1101-1104
clients, R4 to R5, 797

databases
  performance improvements, 802-803
  R4 to R5, 800-804
Domino clusters, 797
Domino R4 to R5, resources, 805
Domino servers (R4-R5), 778-797
  Administration Requests database, 787-788
  administration server for Domino Directory, 787
  dial-up with Domino SMTP R5, 796
  Directory Assistance, 786-787
  Directory Catalog, 782
  domains, 781
  Domino clusters, 797
  Domino Directory, 785-786
  Domino R5 software installation, 784
  file backups, 784
  Internet mail servers from SMTP/MIME MTA to R5, 788-796
  leveraging, 783
  pilot upgrades, 782-783
  planning, 780-781
  process overview, 778-779
  production, 783
  Public Address Book, 785-786
  Public Address Book changes, 781
  Reporter task removal from NOTES.INI file, 784
  search features, 781
  system templates, 782
  testing, 782
  transaction logging, 781
Internet mail servers from SMTP/MIME MTA to R5, 788-796
issues, 1093-1095
messaging environments
  auditing, 1093
  converting, 1095
  planning, 1094
  preparing (Lotus Notes Domino), 1094-1095
Messaging Upgrade Program, 1093
Microsoft Exchange to Notes, 1109-1111
Microsoft Mail to Notes, 1107-1109

Notes clients (R4 to R5), 778-780, 797
  default Workstation security, 798
  Directory Catalog, 782
  domains, 781
  file backups, 798
  ID files security, 799-800
  Internet mail account documents, 799
  leveraging, 783
  Notes R5 software installation, 798-799
  passwords, 782
  Personal Address Book preferences, 799
  pilot upgrades, 782-783
  planning, 780-781
  process overview, 778-780
  production, 783
  Public Address Book changes, 781
  search features, 781
  system templates, 782
  testing, 782
  transaction logging, 781
Organizer 2x to Notes, 1106-1107
Public Address Book for Internet mail servers, 792
rationales, 1092-1093
software systems, 1095-1096
  administrative servers, 1097
  clients, 1099
  issues, 1096-1099
  mail servers, 1098
  SMTP mail, 1098
  testing, 1096-1097
  upgrade wizards, 1099
Upper Manhattan Empowerment Zone Web site, 883
UpperCase function, 442
Uptime Computer Solutions Web site, 724
URLs (uniform resource locators), 54, 239, 694
  Domino-generated, punctuation marks, 694
  entry outlines, 388
  hotspot links, 90
  Open URL icon, 54
  question marks, changing to exclamation points, 695
Usage Priority field (Basics tab of Connection document, Domino Directory), 835
Use all available space on log device field (Transactional Logging tab of Server document, Domino Directory), 833
Use Outline button, 396

Use statement, 539
Use the Port field (Basics tab of Connection document, Domino Directory), 835
Use Web Palette (user preference), 93
UseLSX statement, 539
user account administration, integrating with Windows NT, 916-917
user attribute functions, 1218
User Dictionary button, 89
User ID dialog box, 64, 854
  Basics tab, 65
  Certificates page, 855
  Certificates tab, 65
  encryption keys, 865
  Encryption tab, 65
  ID files, 64
  More Options tab, 66
user ID file, 848-850
user IDs
  ACLs (Access Control Lists), 414
  adding to Domino server, 46
  certifiers, 761
  creating, 761
user interaction functions, 1218
user interface (UI), 616
user interface functions, 443-444
user mail information (Domino Directory), 1012
User Migration
  Admin tool, 1105
  User tool, 1106
user preferences
  basic preferences, 89-94
  changing, 88
  international
    changing, 96-97
    mail and news, changing, 97-98
    ports, changing, 98-99
  Internet Options screen, 243-244
  security options for workstation, 94-96
User Preferences (Preferences command, File menu), 57, 121
User Preferences dialog box, 88, 210, 233, 243
  International icon, 96-97
  Mail and News icon, 97-98
  options, 88
  TCP/IP port, enabling, 233

User Registration Queue, 902
user requirement growth, scalability, 1081
User Setup Profile documents (Domino Directory), 842, 1012
User tool, 1106
user types of replication, troubleshooting, 1062
user-defined type variables (LotusScript), 501-502
UserAccess function, 444
UserCreator (Domino Directory ACL), 809
UserCreator role, 860
UserID function (@Command functions), 1227
UserModifier (Domino Directory ACL), 809
UserModifier role, 860
UserName function, 346
UserName property, 507, 613
usernames
    ACL levels, 414
    mobile users, change impact, 912-913
    parsing, 674-675
UserNamesList function, 444
UserRoles function, 444
users
    ACLs (Access Control Lists), 268, 416
        adding, 417-419
        assigning roles, 422
        roles, 421
        unspecified users, 427-428
    administering in Domino Directory, 899
    anonymous, setting up, 908
    authenticated, setting up and validating, 907-908
    calendar preferences, setting, 78-79
    cc:Mail, migration preparations, 1101-1102
    encryption, authentication, 863
    groups
        administering, 917
        creating, 918-919
        deleting, 919
        managing, 917-918
        modifying, 919
    Internet users, setting up, 907-908
    mail files, moving and unlinking, 941-942
    mail preferences, setting, 78
    mobile
        Replication Settings dialog box, Space Savers page, 955
        shared email, 942
    mobile computing locations, 220
    names on buddy lists (red or green lights), 198
    network users, naming, 1119-1122
    Notes IDs, recertifying, 915-916
    Notes usernames (changing)
        with Administration Process, 908, 910-913
        manually, 911
    Notes users
        naming (X.500 protocol), 1119
        registering, 899, 901-907
    registering
        with Domino Directory, 1012
        from text files, 906-907
    security, 858
    user account administration, integrating with Windows NT, 916-917
    usernames
        deleting, 913-915
        managing, 908
    Windows NT accounts, creating, 904-905
Users command, 1040
Using document (Domino databases), updating, 271-272
utilities, JavaDoc, 548
    Utility Applets (eSuite), 600, AppletContainer Applets, 605, 607
    InfoCenter applets, 600
    messaging, 604
    ScriptHelper applets, 601-603

V

VA (Visual Age), 575-576
validating Internet addresses, 908
value parameters, 527
values
    formulas, 432-435
    LotusScript, 506-507
variables, 498
    accessing in sessions, 610
    Amount, 471
    array, 500-501
    constants, 499-500
    data types, 498-499
    date and time, 618-619
    environment, 438-439
        CLASSPATH, 545-546
        PATH, updating, 577
    explicitly declaring, 503
    formulas, 434
    identifiers, 496
    implicitly declaring, 502-503
    item variable, 514
    lifetimes, 502
    list, 501
    LotusScript subroutines, 521
    LotusScript values, 506-507
    member variables, 479
    MyName$, 470
    naming, 507-508
    NotesSession, 506
    PersonType, 501-502
    Private, 498
    Public, 498
    scalar, 500
    scope, 496-498
    temporary, 434
    user-defined type, 501-502
    Variants, 499
Variant data type, 498
Variant type, arrays, 616
Variant variables, 499
VBA (Visual Basic for Applications), 452
Verifier property, 656
vertical bars (| |), 499
View Applets (Java), 687
View class (Java), 638
view columns, 144
view function (@Command functions), 1227-1228
View menu, 53, 364
View menu commands
    Design, 271
    Expand/Collapse, 145
    Refresh, 109
    Stack Replica Icons, 954
View Navigation pane, 384
view parameter, 445
View Participant Status, 180
view properties (ACL roles), 421
view selection functions, 1216-1217

VISUAL BASIC FOR APPLICATIONS 1301

View selection property, 372
View Show/Hide Preview Pane SmartIcon, 103
Viewer (Sametime), 196-197
  Presentation Whiteboard, 195-197
viewers, FarSite Viewer (Java applet), 194
viewing
  ACL changes, 423
  calendars, 183-184
  documents in Notes, 141-142
    categorized documents, 145-146
    copying documents, 146
    deleting documents, 143-144
    deselecting documents, 144
    elements of, 142
    icons, 144-145
    opening documents, 146
    pasting documents, 147
    printing documents, 147-149
    printing on alternate forms, 149
    selecting documents for batch processing, 144
    unread marks, 143
    view columns, 144
  ECL (Execution Control List), 867
  images, 1155
  replication logs (Domino Administrator), 970
  shared (Sametime), 203-204
  text versus editing, 127
views, 342, 346, 411. *See also* **columns**
  access lists, 371-372
  accessing (ODBC), 369
  ACL restrictions, 420
  actions, 373-374
  Administration Requests database, 1010
  aliases, 362
  browsers, 369-371
  Calendar, 168-169, 183-184, 362-363
  categories, 371
  color, 364-365
  column properties, 348-350
  columns
    creating, 350
    date formatting, 360-361
    deleting, 350
    fonts, 358-359
    HTML links, 361-362
    icons, 356-358
    naming, 361
    numeric formatting, 359-360
  comments, 362
  Contacts, 157
  Contacts By Category, 157
  corrupted in databases, repairing, 995-996
  creating, 342-343
  default settings, 363-364
  documents
    selecting for inclusion, 343-346
    sorting, 354-356
  Domino Designer, 286, 292
  email, 103
  embedded, 374-378
    Single Category, 379-380
  embedding, 409
  Generate HTML for all fields, 693
  Group Calendars, 184
  Groups, 162
  hiding, 362
  HTML (Hypertext Markup Language), 691-695
  indexes, 366-368, 371
  Meetings, 169
  Notes, 684
  NotesUIDatabase class, opening, 625
  opening, 343
  Personal Web Navigator, 241-242
  private, 346-348
    browsers, 347
  properties, 362
    Advanced tab, 366-371
    Basic tab, 362-363
    form formula, 373
    Options tab, 363-364
    Security tab, 371-372
    Style tab, 364-366
    View selection, 372
  Rules, 119
  saving (DESKTOP.DSK file), 347
  Server/Certificates, Certifier documents, 1011
  Server/Clusters, clusters, 1011
  Server/Configurations, Configuration Settings documents, 1011
  Server/Connections, Connection documents, 1011
  Server/Deny Access Groups, Deny List documents, 1011
  Server/Domains, Domain documents, 1011
  Server/External Domain Network Information, External Domain Network Information documents, 1011
  Server/File Identification, File Identification documents, 1011
  Server/Holidays, Holiday documents, 1012
  Server/Licenses, registered users and servers, 1012
  Server/Mail Users, user mail information, 1012
  Server/Programs, Program documents, 1012
  Server/Servers, Server documents, 1012
  Server/Setup Profiles, User Setup Profile documents, 1012
  Server/V3 Stats and Events, Monitor documents, 1012
  Server/Web Configurations, File Protection Settings documents, 1012
  Server\Mail-In Databases and Resources, Mail-In Database documents, 1012
  Server\Networks, Server documents, 1012
  shared, 346-348
  single category, 651
  Single Category embedded, 347
  Trash, 169
  Treat Document Contents as HTML, 693
  Treat View Contents as HTML, 693
  unread marks, 368
  View Participant Status, 180
Views design (Domino Designer), 343
VINES, Banyan, mobile computing, 209
virtual classrooms. *See* **collaborative learning**
Virtual Private Networks. *See* **VPNs**
viruses, scanning, 878
visibility of servers, troubleshooting, 1058-1059
Visit Web Page (Tools command, Actions menu), 161
Visual Basic for Applications (VBA), 452

Visual Workbench (Percussion Notrix), 734
voice cards, 1144
voice mail, 1143-1145
volume, modem configurations, 212
VPNs (Virtual Private Networks), 880-883
   IPSec (IP Security Protocol), 882
   L2TP (Layer 2 Tunneling Protocol), 882
   NAT (Network Address Translation), 883
   PPTP (Point to Point Tunneling Protocol), 881
   security, 880-881

W

WAN (wide area network), 1126
Web Administration, 1007
Web Ahead, 82
Web Ahead page, 242
Web Application Server, 752
   application design services, 752-753
   integration with IIS, 753-754
   server enhancements, 753
Web applications (common gateway interface), 1163
Web browsers, 17-18, 767. *See also* **email; Internet; protocols; Web pages; Web sites; WWW (World Wide Web)**
   ACLs, 427
   authentication, 884
   controls, 238-239
   cookies, 92
   documents, opening, 232
   Domino databases, 258, 369-371
   files, security, 869-870
   framesets, opening, 692
   HTML (Hypertext Markup Language), 306
   HTTP connections, troubleshooting, 1050-1051
   hypertext links, concepts of state or context, 682
   integrated, 237
   interfaces, 238-239
   InterNotes Web Browser, 237
   layout regions on forms, 337
   mobile computing locations, 217

Notes
   ActiveX or plugins, enabling, 92
   as default, 93
Notes client, 18
Notes databases
   accessing, 683-685
   R5 features, 687-691
   Web-oriented designs, 685-687
Notes view, 684
Personal Web Browser, 240
Personal Web Navigator, 239-240
   folders, 241-242
   Internet Options screen, 242-247
   Internet parameters, 244-247
   opening, 240
   screens, 241
   setup summary, 247-248
   views, 241-242
private views, 347
Server Web Browser, 240
servlets, invoking, 572
setting up on Location documents, 235
URLs (uniform resource locators), 239
versus Notes client, 682
workspace, comparing, 70
Web browsing, 17-18
Web pages, 14, 70, 239, 248, 300. *See also* **email; Internet; protocols; Web browsers; Web sites; WWW (World Wide Web)**
   browsing, 234
   caching, 82, 877
   Collaboration options, 243
   comparing with forms and documents, 325-326
   creating, 300, 303, 689
   customizing, 71-73
   data, organizing, 323-324
   default page, 70-71
   Domino Designer, 32-34
      agents, 286, 293-294
      design elements, 285-287
      fields, sharing, 296-297
      folders, 286, 292
      forms, 285
      forms and subforms, 290-292
      framesets, 285, 288
      image resources, 295
      Java applets, 295-296
      navigators, 286, 293
      outlines, 285-288
      pages, 285, 289-290
      resources, 294

      script libraries, 297
      starting, 282-283
      views, 286, 292
      window, 283-285
   email contacts, visiting, 161-162
   embedding elements, 409-410
   filtering, 877-878
   first page, creating, 689
   fonts, bitmapping, 290
   forms comparisons, 410-411
   framesets, creating, 690
   graphic backgrounds, 304-305
   graphic images, image resource library, 322-323
   Home pages, creating, 690
   hotspots, 290, 403-408
   Housekeeping, 243
   HTML (Hypertext Markup Language), 303-309
      syntax, 306-307
      tags, 307-309
      treating as, 303
   inserting in framesets, 397-398
   Internet Options screen, 242-243
   links, creating, 114, 251
   My News, 29
   Network preferences, 243
   offline browsing, 82
   opening, 232
      from desktop, 248
      from Personal Web Navigator, 248-250
   outlines, 395-397, 689-690
   Page Minder, 83, 242
   page properties, 303-304
   pictures, 321-322
   Presentation, 243
   previewing, 302
   refreshing, 240
   rich text, defining, 290
   sharing, 250-251
   Size options, 243
   tables
      backgrounds, 314-316
      borders, 312-313
      cells, 316
      collapsible, 317-318
      columns, 310-311
      columns, newspaper style, 313-314
      creating, 309
      hotspots, Click formulas, 320
      margins, 312-313
      nesting, 318

programmatic control, 318, 320
properties, 312
rows, $MediaTypes field, 320
rows, adding, 310-311
rows, case-sensitive names, 320
rows, deleting, 311
SaveOptions field, 320
SaveOptions:="0" statement, 321
special effects, 317-318
tabbed, 317
timed, 318
URLs (uniform resource locators), 239
hotspot links, 90
Web Ahead, 82, 242

Web palette (user preference), 93

Web Proxy field (Location document), 236

Web registration database, downloading, 815

Web Retriever (mobile computing locations), 220

Web Retriever Configuration, 245-246

Web Retriever subtab (Server Tasks tab in Server document), 825-826

Web Server Access fields (Security tab of Server document, Domino Directory), 814

Web server authentication field (Security tab of Server document, Domino Directory), 814

Web servers, proxy, 236

Web sites. *See also* **email; Internet; protocols; Web browsers; Web pages; WWW (World Wide Web)**
ADSL (Asymmetrical Digital Subscriber Line), 1126
background, 681-682
Binary Tree (ezMerchant), 724
brochureware, 720
Calendon WebTrans, 726
Casahl, 732
CGI scripts (security), 890
challenges, 697-698
Corporate Image, 724
creating, 20, 683
CyberCash, 726
DataMirror, 734
Ducat, 724
dynamic, 720-721

e-commerce, 720
Chrysler's SCORE (Supplier Cost Reduction Effort), 722-723
credit cards, 726
selling online, 723-727
EICentral, 740
Electro-Matic Products, 697
EntreVision, 724
ezMerchant, 724
framesets, creating, 690
Granite, 735
graphic images, 688
GraphWare Corporation, 1180
Group Computing Magazine, 722
Home pages, creating, 690
HTML (Hypertext Markup Language), 691-695
documents and Domino server, 695-696
documents and Notes databases, 697
IBM, 724, 1125
IBM Redbooks, 1177-1178
ICSA-certified firewalls, 891
IETF (Internet Engineering Task Force), 881-882
InternetWeek, 722
InterNoded, 724
IPSec (IP Security Protocol), 882
Ipswitch, 1075
Iris Today on Notes Net, 718
JavaWorld, 547
L2TP (Layer 2 Tunneling Protocol), 882
Lotus, 309, 722, 740, 805, 883, 1137
Lotus Developer, 702
Lotus Enterprise Integration, 1177
Lotus eSuite, 717
Lotus Notes Internet Cookbook, 228
Mayflower Software, 737
Microsoft, 706-707
Mindspring, 1125
navigating, 33
Netconnections, 805
Netcraft Web Server Survey, 702
NetObjects, 706
Nextgen, 724
Notes, 698, 815
Notes databases
accessed by Web browsers, 683-685
R5 features, 687-691
Web-oriented designs, 685-687

NotesBench, 1087
NotesBench Consortium, 1087
Offer Solutions, 724
Ohio State, 1119
outlines, creating, 689-690
Percussion Notrix, 733
pictures, 140
PPTP Specification, 881
products, 724-725
QuickPlace, 71
Rawlings, 725
resources, 698-699
Ronald MacDonald House of Detroit, 720
self-service, Interfusion Energy (case study), 1167-1177
SmartFilter, 877
SOCKS, 891
static, 720
Sun Microsystems Java, 548, 552
Upper Manhattan Empowerment Zone, 883
Uptime Computer Solutions, 724
Web browsers versus Notes client, 682
X.500 schema, 1119
Yahoo!, 726

Web subtab (Ports tab in Server document), 820

Web Tours, 240

welcome page (Notes client), 28-29

Welcome Page menu commands, Create New Page Style, 71

welcome pages. *See* **Web pages**

Wend statement, 514-515

While clause, 515

While statement, 514-515

whiteboards, 195
controlled mode, 197
controlling (pencil icon), 198
Presentation Whiteboard, 195-197
Sametime, drawing tools, 196-197
uncontrolled mode, 197

wide area network (WAN), 1126

width, embedded views, 378

Width statement (LotusScript), 537

WINDOW FUNCTION

window function (@Command functions), 1228
window title formulas, 441
Windows API (Application Programming Interface), 546
windows
    AppShare Content Window, sharing applications, 202
    Domino Designer, 283-285
        bookmarks, 284
        Design pane, 283, 285
        menu bar, 284
        Programmer pane, 292
        SmartIcon bar, 284
        status bar, 284
        task buttons, 284
        Work pane, 285
        Work pane, edit mode, 287
    multiple, opening, 60
    Notes, new features, 53
    right double-click option (user preference), 91
    Share Frame, 202
    switching, 60
Windows NT
    accounts, creating, 904-905
    directories, synchronizing with Notes, 916-917
    eSuite Workplace, 582
    Event Logger, redirecting Notes event logging, 917
    passwords, 63
    single logon, 916
    User Manager, registering Notes users, 907
Windows NT User Manager, deleting usernames, 914
wizards
    Mail Address Assistant, 155
    Notes Client Configuration, 49
    upgrade, 1099
Word Processor applet (eSuite), 584-586
Word Processor applets (eSuite), 591-593
Work Files applet, 584
Work pane (Domino Designer window), 285-287
workbooks, 196
workgroups on Internet, 240

Workplace (eSuite), 582
    applications, 583
    Calendar applet, 583
    desktop, 583
    SpreadSheet applet, 584
    Word Processor applet, 584-586
    Work Files applet, 584
workspace function (@Command functions), 1228
workspaces
    bookmarks, 84
    Sametime, 193
        Java applets, floating, 193
        navigation buttons, 194
        Viewer, 195-197
    textures (user preference), 91
    Web browser user interface, comparing, 70
Workstation Security dialog box, 94-95
workstation-to-server replication, 950
workstations
    cross-certification, troubleshooting, 1054
    locking, 96
    mobile computing configurations, 207-208
        connections, 227
        Internet connections, 227-228
        Location document, 214-220
        locations, selecting, 227
        modems, 211-213
        Passthru servers, 220-222
        Personal Address Book, 213-214
        ports, 208-211
        protocols, 209-210
        replication, 222-226
        security, 229
        sending mail, 228-229
    Replica task, workstation-to-server replication, 950
    replication, 948, 965
    security, 847
        security options, 94-96
        setting defaults, 798
World Wide Web. *See* WWW
Write Memo button, 158
Write public documents privilege (ACLs), 420
Write statement (LotusScript), 538

WWW (World Wide Web), 38, 702, 752. *See also* email; Internet; protocols; Web browsers; Web pages
    ICM (Internet Cluster Manager), 38
    LDAP authentication, 852
    Personal Web Navigator, 82-83
    sites. *See* Web sites
    Web Application Server, 752

X

X.25, mobile computing, 210
X.400 Domain documents (Domino Directory Domain documents), 841
X.400 MTAs, 938, 1137
X.500 protocol, 1119
X.500 schema Web site, 1119
XPC, mobile computing, 209
Xs near task buttons, 61

Y-Z

Yahoo! Web site, 726
ZID files, 734
ZID script, 735
ZIP files, 545, 554
Zisman, Mike, 680
ZMERGE, integrating data, 734-735

Turn to the *Authoritative* Encyclopedia of Computing

You'll find over 150 full text books online, hundreds of shareware/freeware applications, online computing classes and 10 computing resource centers full of expert advice from the editors and publishers of:

- Adobe Press
- BradyGAMES
- Cisco Press
- Hayden Books
- Lycos Press
- New Riders
- Que
- Que Education & Training
- Sams Publishing
- Waite Group Press
- Ziff-Davis Press

Get the best information and learn about latest developments in:

- Design
- Graphics and Multimedia
- Enterprise Computing and DBMS
- General Internet Information
- Operating Systems
- Networking and Hardware
- PC and Video Gaming
- Productivity Applications
- Programming
- Web Programming and Administration
- Web Publishing

When you're looking for computing information, consult the authority.
The Authoritative Encyclopedia of Computing at mcp.com.

What's on the CD-ROM?

This Special Edition Using Companion CD-ROM contains the text of this book in a Domino Database format. To access this database, use the following steps:

1. Open the Notes Client.
2. From the Menu, choose File, Database, Open.
3. Within the dialog box, choose the Browse button.
   Navigate to the CD-ROM Database.*
   (*Database folder=Root directory of CD-ROM)
4. Choose Select.
5. Choose Open.

Also on this CD-ROM you will find the Sample Databases and the Chapter Examples from *Special Edition Using Lotus Notes and Domino R5*.

To manually view and select the files you would like to use or view, click the Browse CD link from the CD-ROM interface or you may find these files organized by chapter in the root directory of the CD-ROM in the directory /SourceCode.

The CD-ROM also has a variety of other valuable components including:

- Over 30 different trial and shareware programs for use with Lotus Notes and Domino 5
- A collection of links to World Wide Web sites for information and news about Lotus Notes and Domino R5.
- Links to Que's web site for additional information and support for this Special Edition Using title.

Licensing Agreement

By opening this package, you are agreeing to be bound by the following agreement:

You may not copy or redistribute the entire CD-ROM as a whole. Copying and redistribution of individual software programs on the CD-ROM is governed by terms set by individual copyright holders.

The installer and code from the author(s) are copyrighted by the publisher and the author(s). Individual programs and other items on the CD-ROM are copyrighted or are under GNU license by their various authors or other copyright holders.

This software is sold as-is without warranty of any kind, either expressed or implied, including but not limited to the implied warranties of merchantability and fitness for a particular purpose. Neither the publisher nor its dealers or distributors assumes any liability for any alleged or actual damages arising from the use of this program. (Some states do not allow for the exclusion of implied warranties, so the exclusion may not apply to you.)

For some third-party software read this Important Note:

IMPORTANT NOTE: This software has a "time-out" feature so that it expires within thirty (30) days after you load the software on your system. The "time-out" feature may install hidden files on your system which, if not deleted, might remain on your computer after the software has been removed. The purpose of the "time-out" feature is to ensure that the software is not used beyond its intended use.

ADDITONAL NOTE: This CD-ROM uses long and mixed-case filenames requiring the use of a protected-mode CD-ROM Driver.